MICHIGAN BAR EXAM
ESSAY DECONSTRUCTION

MICHIGAN BAR EXAM ESSAY DECONSTRUCTION

HOLLY GLAZIER
Professor of Law
Thomas M. Cooley Law School

Wolters Kluwer
Law & Business

Published by Wolters Kluwer Law & Business in New York.

Wolters Kluwer Law & Business serves customers worldwide with CCH, Aspen Publishers, and Kluwer Law International products. (www.wolterskluwerlb.com)

To contact Customer Service, e-mail customer.service@wolterskluwer.com, call 1-800-234-1660, fax 1-800-901-9075, or mail correspondence to:

Wolters Kluwer Law & Business
Attn: Order Department
PO Box 990
Frederick, MD 21705

Printed in the United States of America.

2 3 4 5 6 7 8 9 0

ISBN 978-0-7355-0995-5

About Wolters Kluwer Law & Business

Wolters Kluwer Law & Business is a leading global provider of intelligent information and digital solutions for legal and business professionals in key specialty areas, and respected educational resources for professors and law students. Wolters Kluwer Law & Business connects legal and business professionals as well as those in the education market with timely, specialized authoritative content and information-enabled solutions to support success through productivity, accuracy and mobility.

Serving customers worldwide, Wolters Kluwer Law & Business products include those under the Aspen Publishers, CCH, Kluwer Law International, Loislaw, Best Case, ftwilliam.com and MediRegs family of products.

CCH products have been a trusted resource since 1913, and are highly regarded resources for legal, securities, antitrust and trade regulation, government contracting, banking, pension, payroll, employment and labor, and healthcare reimbursement and compliance professionals.

Aspen Publishers products provide essential information to attorneys, business professionals and law students. Written by preeminent authorities, the product line offers analytical and practical information in a range of specialty practice areas from securities law and intellectual property to mergers and acquisitions and pension/benefits. Aspen's trusted legal education resources provide professors and students with high-quality, up-to-date and effective resources for successful instruction and study in all areas of the law.

Kluwer Law International products provide the global business community with reliable international legal information in English. Legal practitioners, corporate counsel and business executives around the world rely on Kluwer Law journals, looseleafs, books, and electronic products for comprehensive information in many areas of international legal practice.

Loislaw is a comprehensive online legal research product providing legal content to law firm practitioners of various specializations. Loislaw provides attorneys with the ability to quickly and efficiently find the necessary legal information they need, when and where they need it, by facilitating access to primary law as well as state-specific law, records, forms and treatises.

Best Case Solutions is the leading bankruptcy software product to the bankruptcy industry. It provides software and workflow tools to flawlessly streamline petition preparation and the electronic filing process, while timely incorporating ever-changing court requirements.

ftwilliam.com offers employee benefits professionals the highest quality plan documents (retirement, welfare and non-qualified) and government forms (5500/PBGC, 1099 and IRS) software at highly competitive prices.

MediRegs products provide integrated health care compliance content and software solutions for professionals in healthcare, higher education and life sciences, including professionals in accounting, law and consulting.

Wolters Kluwer Law & Business, a division of Wolters Kluwer, is headquartered in New York. Wolters Kluwer is a market-leading global information services company focused on professionals.

I am honored to dedicate this book to Anne E. Gieschen, my incredibly intelligent, strong, and wise grandmother. "G'ma" as my family fondly called her, was so proud that this book was being published. I am deeply saddened that she passed before this book was published because she insisted she wanted to buy the first copy! But I am thankful that she was in my life for so many years. She was a woman of few words, but when they came, they were so very wise. She was always so accepting and supportive of our family for whatever path we each chose. She always saw my potential, even as a mouthy little kid when others were not quite so sure. She always seemed to see something in me that I never did, and I always left her feeling inspired to be better.

Thank you G'ma . . . I miss you.

CONTENTS

ACKNOWLEDGMENTS

There are so many people I would like to acknowledge who have helped contribute to this book along the way. It's been a work in progress for many years. First and foremost, I want to thank and acknowledge Carol Lycos, the most dedicated, conscientious, best secretary a person could ask for. The majority of Part II of this book is the result of her hard work. She spent countless hours rekeying previous bar exam questions, model answers, and student answers. She organized them, corrected them, and updated them twice each year and made sure everything was always in order for the benefit of the students. I'm not sure if she likes the term I use to describe her work ethic and abilities, but she is an underutilized "work horse" who probably does the work of three people. Carol, I cannot thank you enough for all you've done for this book and for me throughout the years. THANK YOU!

Next, I must thank my initial proofreader, Andy Draper. While he probably doesn't realize it, his intelligence continues to impress me. As one of his former teachers told him once, he has quite "the command of the English language," and I truly valued his assistance in the initial proofreading stages. Thanks, Andy!

But probably the people who contributed the most to this book are all the students who permitted me to use their bar exam "student answers" in this book. It truly is a gift from those who were in a very difficult and unfortunate position — only those who didn't pass the bar exam can obtain their bar exam answers. All of the student answers in this book were written by people who were initially unsuccessful in passing the bar exam. It just goes to show you that even those who are downtrodden want to help others. It also clearly demonstrates that you can prepare for some areas of the law, but if you cut corners, skip studying rarely tested subjects, or otherwise take short cuts in your bar preparation, it will cost you dearly. Many of the student answers in this book are very good, and the people who wrote them failed the bar exam because they gambled and didn't study all subjects. Still others may have not prepared enough for the MBE. Whatever the reason, I am very thankful for their generosity. As those who have used this book in the past know, the student answers are truly the most beneficial part of this book!

I would also like to thank my parents, Dr. William E. and Jenifer Whitehill for their unfailing support of me throughout my life. There have been a lot of ups and downs, but their support of me has never waivered. I would like to thank my mother for initially instilling in me the importance of good writing skills. She was always my proofreader when I was younger, and I was so impressed with how smart she was and still is. You taught me well, Mom! Thank you! And then there is my father . . . Pea Pod, you truly are my hero and someone I can only aspire to be. Thank you so much for all you have given me throughout the years and for teaching me so many life lessons. You are such a great role model for me, my children, and all the other lives you've touched along the way. You are the BEST!

Last, but certainly not least, I want to thank my two little inspirations that keep me going - Bailey and Chloe - my children. I am incredibly proud of them, and I realize more and more over time how truly blessed I am to have such bright, healthy, kind, and beautiful children. I love you two more than you will ever know!

MICHIGAN BAR EXAM
ESSAY DECONSTRUCTION

INTRODUCTION

WHAT IS THIS BOOK ALL ABOUT?

This book is designed to help individuals prepare for the essay portion of the Michigan Bar Exam[1] and is an excellent practice tool to help individuals earn more points on the essay portion of the exam. Part I of this book sets forth the fundamentals of the Michigan Bar Exam, including the format of the essay portion of the exam, an overview of how the subjects are tested and grouped, how the questions are drafted and graded, and other administrative information that is often not covered by commercial bar review courses. Part I also includes a section entitled "Essay Deconstruction," which breaks down the Michigan essays and provides essay writing guidelines and instructions tailored directly toward the Michigan Bar Exam. It presents a specific approach on how best to attack each essay to gain the most points. The section "How to Build a Great Essay—The 'RAC'" provides numerous practice examples to put the "essay attack" to work to build great essays. Although some substantive review of the law is covered based on past bar exam questions and model answers, this book does not provide a complete substantive outline of the law for each subject. Instead, this book is designed to supplement a commercial bar review course by giving additional help on the essay portion of the bar exam, which is often overlooked or not emphasized.

Part II of this book includes previous Michigan Bar Exam questions and model answers broken down by subject matter. A key component of this book is the actual student answers with the grade received for many of the essay questions. This feature is very valuable, as it provides samples of what the bar exam graders actually expect in an answer. Although the model answers certainly are valuable in terms of the specific law that is cited and tested, the model answers are often intimidating to those preparing for the bar exam who cannot possibly provide case citations or quotations to specific case law or rules. The student answers[2] are very valuable because they give you a better idea of what the graders actually expect and how they grade.

Please keep in mind that not all questions have student answers and others have more than one sample answer. Please pay close attention to the points received for the

1. This book does not address preparation for the Multistate Bar Exam (MBE). This book only supplements a full-service commercial bar review course by providing additional supplemental support, guidelines, and help on the essay portion of the Michigan Bar Exam.

2. Please note that the student responses are unedited.

student answer. Although most samples represent "good" answers (i.e., they received 8, 9, or 10 points), there are some samples that received 7 points (the minimum "passing" score for an essay), and a few that received very low scores to help you better understand the grading process.

WHO SHOULD USE THIS BOOK?

This book is intended for all first-time or repeat takers of the Michigan Bar Exam who want to substantially improve their performance on the essay portion of the exam.

WHY SHOULD YOU USE THIS BOOK?

All bar exam takers need a full-service bar review course to provide the updated substantive law that is tested on the Michigan Bar Exam, but this book provides additional supplemental information and guidance on the essay portion of the exam that is beyond what is provided by the bar review courses. The author of this book has worked extensively with the Michigan Bar Exam for over a decade and has helped thousands of students successfully pass the bar exam on their first shot. She also has an expertise in writing bar exam appeals and has successfully helped more than 100 Michigan bar exam takers pass the bar exam on appeal. As a result, she knows exactly what the graders are looking for in answers and has written this book in a manner to teach you the inside scoop on how to get the most points in your essays.

WHEN SHOULD YOU USE THIS BOOK?

Reviewing Part I of this book when you begin your initial bar exam preparation is a good idea to lay out the fundamentals of the Michigan Bar Exam itself. But to get the most benefit from this study tool, you should not even touch Part II of this book until *after* you have studied a subject thoroughly! Part II of this book is designed to assess your knowledge of the law after you have studied it by providing you with the tools to practice how the bar examiners test and grade your performance. For example, if Contracts is the first subject you have covered, then once you have completely studied the substantive outline on Contracts from your bar review materials, you should then test and practice your knowledge by working all of the Contracts questions that are grouped together in this book. Please read on to find out how to work the questions effectively!

HOW TO USE THIS BOOK EFFECTIVELY

To get the most benefit from this study tool, you should not use Part II of this book until after you have studied the subjects thoroughly! This book is designed to assess your knowledge of the law after you have studied it by providing you with the tools to practice how the bar examiners test and grade your performance.

The format of Part II breaks down past Michigan Bar Exam questions, model answers, and student answers (when available) by the subject matter tested according to the groups or "clusters" in which the subjects are typically tested. There are five board members on the Board of Law Examiners who are each typically assigned a subject matter "cluster" from which to draft three questions. Each of the five clusters contains a group of the 24 testable subjects from which the 15 bar exam essays are selected. The "clusters" are explained in detail in the section "Fundamentals of the Bar Exam."[3] To get the most out of this exercise, you should follow this study approach:

A. **Review the substantive subject matter** of a particular subject before answering any practice questions.
   1. Study the commercial outline on a particular subject and make your own flash cards, outline, flowchart, or whatever works for you to learn and retain the fundamental rules.
   2. The key is understanding the material and how it applies to factual situations, so be sure to record all examples. Please remember that every single bar exam question on both the MBE and essays are factual situations that apply the law. Therefore, this approach is the best way to learn it and truly understand how it applies.

B. Answer each essay question in the respective subject as follows ("Essay Attack"):
   1. **Read the call of the question first.**
   2. **Read the facts quickly but carefully** and highlight important words and phrases.
   3. **Reread the call of the question again carefully,** this time focusing on who you are and what the bar examiner is asking you to do.
   4. **Briefly *outline* your response,** structuring it around the call of the question and the issues spotted.
   5. **Write** out each response using the RAC method.[4]

C. **Compare and contrast your response with the model answer** and a student answer, if provided, to determine what you have done right, and what you have missed. Ask yourself these questions:
   - Did I miss an issue?
     Issue spotting is the most important part.
   - Did I not know the law?
     If so, take the time to go back and review that specific area of law.
   - Did I misread or misunderstand the question?

3. The "clusters" are described infra p. 9. The Essay Frequency Chart on p. 11 is broken down by the subject clusters. The bar examiners are not required to keep the same subjects within the clusters, and sometimes they do test subjects in different clusters. This is just a guide to help narrow your focus.

4. RAC stands for rule, application, and conclusion. You should apply this approach to each issue in a question. See infra page 28.

D. Incorporate relevant material into your substantive outline or flash cards or both.

- This is very important because if you don't do this, you will forget it later on. Essentially, you have to create a "tickler" type file for your brain to remember things. You can't retain everything as you go along, but the week or two before the bar exam when you have the time to go over things again, you want these things recorded to trigger your memory bank.

PART I MICHIGAN BAR EXAM OVERVIEW

FUNDAMENTALS OF THE MICHIGAN BAR EXAM

The Michigan Bar Exam is difficult because it consists of 15 essay questions that can be on any of 24 different subjects! At first blush, this seems to be an overwhelming task. However, through proper preparation, this task can be accomplished.

FORMAT OF THE MICHIGAN BAR EXAM ESSAY SECTION

The "state" essay portion of the Michigan Bar Exam is administered the day before the Multistate Bar Exam (MBE). It is a time-pressured exam that consists of 15 essay questions given over a period of 6.5 hours. This time frame essentially allows for 20 minutes per essay. However, no one is standing over you with a timer. As a result, you have to practice gauging your time to approximately 20 minutes per essay to be able to complete them all.

The bar examiners present the essays as follows:

- 9 questions are given in the morning (3 hours)
- 1.5-hour lunch break
- 6 questions in the afternoon (2 hours)

MICHIGAN SUBJECTS TESTED

- Real Property*
- Criminal Law*
- Partnerships
- Contracts*
- Civil Procedure*
- Sales*
- Secured Trans
- Negotiable Instruments
- Personal Property
- Criminal Procedure*
- Corporations*
- Professional Responsibility*
- Workers' Comp*
- Domestic Relations*
- Creditor's Rights
- Equity
- Wills/Trusts*
- Constitutional Law*
- Agency
- Evidence*
- Torts*
- No-Fault Insurance
- Conflict of Laws

---

* The 14 starred subjects are almost always tested as one (if not more) of the 15 essay questions. Although there is no guarantee, this "narrows" the field. Also, Michigan law is tested on the six MBE subjects on the essay portion, and majority rule or common law is tested on the MBE. Therefore, you must learn the distinctions.

DATE OF THE BAR EXAM

The Michigan Bar Exam, like most state exams, is administered two times per year, in February and July. It is always scheduled on the last Tuesday and Wednesday of February and July. The essay portion is on Tuesday, and the MBE is on Wednesday.

GRADING

The Michigan Bar Exam is graded by combining your essay score with your MBE score. Each section is weighted evenly (50/50) and averaged for a combined score that must be a 135 or higher to pass. This is an average score. Therefore, there is no minimum passing score for either the MBE or the essay. Because the MBE section is worth a total of 200 points (200 multiple choice questions valued at 1 point each), and the essay section is worth a total of 150 points (15 essays valued at 10 points each), to weigh the two scores evenly, a formula must be used. Historically, the bar examiners multiplied the total raw essay score by 4/3 or 1.3333 points to accomplish this conversion. However, starting with the February 2009 bar exam, the Michigan Board of Law Examiners changed this formula and began scaling the average Michigan essay scores on an exam administration to match the average national scaling of the MBE score to equate the level of difficulty over time. Essentially, each MBE administration, the National Conference of Bar Examiners (NCBE) performs a complex statistical analysis of performance on the MBE across the nation. A formula is then determined based on mean scores, standard deviations, and other statistical criteria to equate that exam to the level of difficulty of other MBE exams. This results in additional points being awarded, but it varies by exam. The Michigan Board of Law Examiners now applies that same equating formula to the raw essay scores. Therefore, this new formula not only converts the essay score to the 200-point scale, but it also results in additional points added due to this equating process. This is great news because, like the MBE, it amounts to additional "bonus" points! This is the current formula used:

$$\frac{\text{MBE Scaled Score} + \text{Scaled Essay Score}}{2} = \text{Combined Bar Exam Score}$$

If you haven't figured it out yet, this means that your essay scores are worth more than your MBE scores! This has proven to be very beneficial to those who are not good at multiple choice type testing. The following examples show how the formula works.

Example 1:

HISTORICAL FORMULA

MBE Score = 129; Raw Essay Score = 106; **4/3 (106) = 141**

NEW SCALING PROCESS

MBE Score = 129; Raw Essay Score = 106; **Scaled Essay Score = 148!**

OLD: $$\frac{129 + 141}{2} = \textbf{135 combined = PASS!}$$

NEW: $\frac{129 + 148}{2}$ = **139 combined = PASS!**

Under the new scaling process, only a raw score of a 101 is needed to pass (5 points less than the old formula)!

MBE Score = 129; Raw Essay Score = 101; **Scaled Essay Score** = 139

$\frac{129 + 139}{2}$ = 135 PASS!

Example 2:

HISTORICAL FORMULA

MBE Score = 133; Raw Essay Score = 98; **4/3 (98) = 130**

NEW SCALING PROCESS

MBE Score = 133; Raw Essay Score = 98; **Scaled Essay Score** = **137!**

OLD: $\frac{133 + 130}{2}$ = **131 combined = FAIL**

NEW: $\frac{133 + 137}{2}$ = **135 combined = PASS!**

HOW THE ESSAYS ARE GRADED

The highest obtainable score for each essay is 10 points. A score of 7 is considered "passing." Part II of this book is very helpful in terms of demonstrating how the essays are graded because actual student answers are provided for many of the questions.

Essentially, the graders issue a minimum passing score of 7 when you have identified all the main issues and demonstrate a basic knowledge and understanding of the law. However, it is not difficult to receive a 9 or a 10 on your responses, as the student answers in this book demonstrate. A complete response that identifies the issues, defines the relevant law, and provides a sound legal analysis (application of the facts to the law) will be given a 10. A Grading Guideline chart is presented on the next page that provides specific guidelines for what each point value represents.

There are typically 15 different graders for each question. For example, one grader will grade all of the answers for Question 1, another will grade the answers to Question 2, and so forth. As a result, you will have 15 separate individuals giving you a grade for each question. This is important to remember in terms of how you answer each question. If you spend 40 minutes on one question because you know it so well and earn 10 points, but you run out of time for the last question, a different grader will issue a 0 for the last response and will have no knowledge of how well you might have done on other questions. As a result, it is better to stay within the 20 minutes per essay time frame and maybe earn 8 points instead of 10 on that one question, and still have time to earn points on the last question.

Grading Guideline: Michigan Bar Exam Essays

Score	Defining Characteristics
10	Outstanding answer that is essentially "Perfect" as defined by the graders. This answer is well organized and tightly focused and specifically does exactly what the call of the question asks the examinee to do. This answer identifies all issues, defines all *relevant* rules (including exceptions, defenses, etc.), and provides a thorough application of the rules to all relevant facts contained in the question or by extrinsic information drawn from real-life experiences or common sense. Finally, it reaches the appropriate conclusion.
8–9	Excellent answer that is solidly above average but contains one or two minor flaw(s). This answer, however, clearly demonstrates the examinee's knowledge and understanding of all relevant issues, rules, and analytical ability (ability to apply the facts given to the rules). This answer is typically well organized, and identifies all issues. The following is a list of minor flaws that could cause a 1- or 2-point reduction from full credit: • Rule defined incompletely, or might be partially but not completely correct • Analysis might be missing some minor application of relevant facts • Answer contains all relevant components, but isn't well organized • Conclusion is different from model answer It's a fine line of distinction, but a 9 might have only one minor flaw, whereas an 8 might have two minor flaws.
7	Average answer and the minimum passing score on a question. A score of a 7 is considered a passing grade, although it would likely translate to a C in law school. This answer must at least identify all main issues, and demonstrate some knowledge of the applicable rules, with some application. This answer is typically not well organized and might have an incorrect statement of the law or incomplete analysis, but it essentially demonstrates to the grader that the examinee has a basic understanding of the relevant issues and rules.
5–6	Slightly below average, typically because answer completely missed one main issue, but did a fairly thorough job on other issues.

Score	Defining Characteristics
	These answers tend to be partially organized and complete on some issues, but there is one glaring error. Typically, it is missing an issue, or providing an incorrect statement of law. A 5 will likely have an additional minor flaw.
3–4	Below average and typically off-topic with only a sprinkle of relevant rules or application. These answers are typically unorganized and often discuss irrelevant issues and rules. These answers fail to examine an important issue or issues and neglect to bolster the analyses with specific facts contained in the question.
1–2	Far below average and typically nonresponsive to the call of the question, these answers display a fundamental inability to respond to the specific issues addressed in the questions. These answers are generally disorganized, unfocused, incoherent, and conclusory. They are typically very brief, leaving little for the grader to award points for.
0	A blank page, illegible essay, or one that doesn't respond at all to the question. A score of 0 is very rare, and should never occur without some sort of mistake.

CLUSTERS: HOW THE BAR EXAMINERS CHOOSE THE SUBJECTS TO TEST

Starting with the July 1998 Michigan Bar Exam, the Michigan Bar Exam Board members were given the option to draft their own questions. Prior to that, the questions were drafted by out-of-state professors. This means that practicing attorneys, not professors, are drafting most of the exam questions. This has often presented many "curve balls" on questions because lawyers are far removed from what is taught in law school. Many of the questions are based on Michigan cases, on areas of law you might not have covered in law school.

There are a total of 24 possible subjects that can be tested[1] among the 15 essay questions. Although there is no court rule stating that only one subject can be tested per question, generally most questions are limited to one subject.[2] There are five

1. Rule 3 of the Rules for The Board of Law Examiners.

2. There are exceptions. For example, No Fault Insurance has been tested with Workers' Compensation, Creditor's Rights has been tested with Real Property, and so on.

Michigan Bar Exam Board members who each draft a certain number of questions. The term *cluster* refers to how the subjects are divided among the board members. Historically, the subjects have been divided into five different clusters. Each board member is typically assigned a cluster from which three bar exam questions are drafted (see Michigan Essay Frequency Cluster Chart on page 11).

Please keep in mind that there is no specific rule that requires the bar examiners to use this procedure, but they have followed it (for the most part) for more than 20 years for administrative purposes, as it makes the grading process easier. When you sit for the exam, you are given five separate bluebooks in which to write your answers. The answers to the first three questions (from one cluster) are to be written in the first bluebook. The answers to Questions 4, 5, and 6 (from another cluster) are to be written in the second bluebook, and so on. In the end, the answers are distributed by bluebook to the board member who drafted those questions to be graded. Because this process clearly benefits the board members in terms of grading, it makes sense that it will continue. However, they can switch the subjects within the cluster, and they have done so on occasion. In fact, there have been some subject changes recently (i.e., Torts has shifted to the Civ Pro cluster, and Evidence seems to have shifted to the Contracts/PR cluster).

Knowing the clusters is beneficial for two reasons. First, it helps you narrow down what subjects are being tested. If you get into a situation where you don't know what subject is being tested by the question, you can narrow it down by looking at the other two questions tested in that group. Second, at lunch time, you know what clusters remain for the afternoon, which narrows down the field and your anxiety tremendously!

Review the Essay Frequency Cluster Chart on page 11 and note what subjects fall within each cluster. In addition to the preceding benefits, it also shows what subjects are tested the most frequently. One word of caution, however: Don't gamble! Many students try to take shortcuts and do not study all the subjects. The chart is a good guideline, but students fail each bar exam administration by gambling. For example, in July 2008, Secured Transactions was tested for the first time in eight years (16 bar exams!). Then, the very next bar exam (February 2009), it was tested again! Many students failed solely because they didn't bother to study Secured Transactions at all for either exam and completely bombed the question. If you want to gamble, go to Las Vegas, just please don't do it on the bar exam!

Following the cluster chart is a sample of the Michigan Bar results letter. After the letter are the Michigan Bar Exam Admission Policies and related information that you will receive from the Bar Examiners with your admission ticket about two weeks before the bar exam.

MICHIGAN ESSAY FREQUENCY "CLUSTER" CHART

Cluster	Subject	W 92	S 92	W 93	S 93	W 94	S 94	W 95	S 95	W 96	S 96	W 97	S 97	W 98	S 98	S 99
Prop/Wills Cluster	Real Prop.	15	9	7,9	4,6	15	7	4	7	11	10,11	13,15	1,2	5	13,14,15	13,14
	Personal Prop.				5			6	8		12			4		
	Wills	13	8	8		14	8		9	12		14	3	6		15
	Trusts	14	7			13	9	5		10						
	Creditor's Rights										15					
Con Law/ Crimes Cluster	Con. Law	11	13	13	13	9	1	2	5	7	7	1	9	2		1
	Crim. Law	12	14	14	14	7	2	1,3	4	8	8	2	7	3	3	2
	Conflicts															
	Crim. Pro.	10	15	15	15	8	3		6	9	9	3	8	1	1,2	3
Contracts/ PR Cluster	Evidence	3	2	11	11	5	11	8	11	5	5	11	10	13,15	4,5,6	5
	Partnership					3		15		14				12		
	Agency							15								
	Contracts	4	4	3				13	14	13	1,13	8	14		8,12	9
	Prof. Resp.	6	5	2	7	1	6	14	15	15	3	9	15	11	11	8
Civ Pro/Torts Cluster	Corporations	5	6	1	8		4		13		2	7	13	10	10	7
	State & Fed. Proc.	1,2	1,3	10,12	10,12	4,6	10,12	7,9	10,12	4,6	4,6	10,12	11,12	14		4,6
	Torts	11	5	1	12	14	10	1	2	14	4	4	7	7, 15	4	10
	No-Fault															
UCC/MI Cluster	Equity	15			6											
	Secured Trans.	8	12	4	3	10	13	11	2	1	15	5	6	9	9	12
	Negotiable Instruments															
	Sales	7	10	6	2,9	2,11	5,15	12	3	3		6	5	8	8	11
	Domestic Relations															
	Workers Comp															

Cluster	Subject	W 00	S 00	W 01	S 01	W 02	S 02	W 03	S03	W04	S04	W05	S05	W06	S06	W07	S07	W08	S08	W09	S09	W10	S10	W11
Prop/Wills Cluster	Real Prop.	13,14	5,6	2	8,9	4,6	5	11	8,9	12	7	8	6	5	10	8	12	11,12	7	11	15	11	7	7
	Personal Prop.			3		4	4	10	8	10	8	9	5	6			10			10	14	12	9	9
	Wills	15	4	1	7	5	6	10,12	7	11	9	7	4	4	12		11	10		12	13	10	3	
	Trusts															9			8					8
	Creditor's Rights									10	7		6		11	7					15			
Con Law/ Crimes Cluster	Con. Law	1		13	3		9	3	11	15		10	12	12	3	13	8	3	12	5	5	13	6	5
	Crim. Law	3	8	14	1	9	8	2	12	14	15	11	11	10	2	15		1	10	6	4	14	5	4
	Conflicts		9			7					14								9					
	Crim. Pro.	2	7	15	2	8	7	1	10	13	13	10, 12	10	11	1	14	7,9	2	11	4,5	6	15	4	6
Contracts/ PR Cluster	Evidence	12	15	8	13	15	13, 14	7,9	1	8	1	12, 14	13	2	9	6	15	14	2	1	1	5	14	15
	Partnership					3											6							
	Agency			4	6										15									
	Contracts	6	12	6	5	1	12	15	13	5	4	1	1	9	14	1	5	4	5	14	11	6	15	14
	Prof. Resp.	4	11	5	4	2	11	14	15	6	6	3	3	7	13	3	4	6	4	15	10	4	13	13
Civ Pro/Torts Cluster	Corporations	5	10	4			10	13	14	4	5	2	2	8		2		5	6	13	12	3	8	2
	State & Fed. Proc.	11	13,14	7,9	14	14	15	8	3	9	2	15	15	1	7	4	13	13	1	2	2	1	1	3
	Torts	8	2	10	10	12	3	4	5	1	12	6	7, 9	13	4	5	14	15	3	3	3	2	2	1
	No-Fault	8		12	12		2									5		15	3		3	2		1
UCC/MI Cluster	Equity			7														12						
	Secured Trans.	9																	13	8				
	Negotiable Instruments																					9		
	Sales	7	3	11	11	11	1, 4, 12	5	6	3,10	10	5		14	5,14	11	2	9			7		12	11
	Domestic Relations					10		6	4	2	11	4	8	15	6	10	1	8	14	7	9	8	11	12
	Workers Comp	10	1		10,12,15	13	2		2	7	3	13	14	3	8	12	3	7	15	9	8	7	10	10

Michigan Supreme Court
BOARD OF LAW EXAMINERS
Michigan Hall of Justice
P.O. Box 30104
Lansing, MI 48909

Phone: (517) 373-4453
Fax: (517) 373-5038
E-mail: ble-info@courts.mi.gov

May 19, 2011

Jane Doe
123 Kalamazoo St.
Lansing, MI 48901

Seat Number: -- PASSED

On the February 2011 examination, a combined score of 135 or above was necessary to pass the examination.

The combined score is calculated using the following formula:

$$\text{Combined score} = \frac{\text{Scaled Essay total + Multistate score}}{2}$$

Any fraction is discarded.

Your examination results reflect an MBE scaled score of 133.

Individual raw essay scores are as follows:

1	2	3	4	5	6	7	8	9	10	11	12	13	14	15	TOTAL
9	7	7	8	4	7	8	3	3	9	10	5	8	5	7	100

Your scaled essay score was 139.

Using the above calculations, you have PASSED the State Bar Examination with a combined score of 136.

THE BOARD OF LAW EXAMINERS OF MICHIGAN

MICHIGAN BAR EXAM
ADMISSION POLICIES
AND RELATED INFORMATION

TO THE APPLICANT:

The bar examination presents the types of stresses you will encounter in the real world. The stakes are high, time is short and the working conditions are not the best. We believe that how you adapt to those stresses is relevant to the determination of your character and fitness to practice law. If your reaction includes unwillingness to follow instructions and observe fairly simple rules, you may be referred to the Committee on Character and Fitness to demonstrate why such conduct should not disqualify you from entry into the profession.

Examination sessions are held in a very large room and you may expect all the usual irritations of sharing a large space with a large number of people. Although our experience with the heating and air conditioning at both venues has been good, you should dress in a manner which will allow you to adapt to unanticipated conditions of heat or cold. While we will make every effort to see that the space is comfortable and distraction-free, we will not be able to move you or adjust the temperature or other conditions in a manner which will suit everyone.

The Board of Law Examiners has implemented a policy regarding items that may be brought into the examination room and/or testing area. <u>See attached pink copy.</u>

Enclosed is an admission certificate. **<u>This certificate--no copy nor fax accepted--will admit you to the examination.</u>** At the beginning of each of the four sessions this certificate will be inspected along with your identification. ***<u>Keep the certificate with you at all times.</u>*** **<u>Since your test papers will only record your seat number, the certificate is your link to your results.</u>** We will collect the certificate from you at the beginning of the final session on Wednesday afternoon.

You are instructed to furnish your own Number 2 pencils for the Multistate examination. Equally important is a good eraser. Do not assume that the eraser furnished with the average pencil will erase as completely as you would like.

Beyond the usual examination instructions, you are advised of two additional important matters:

1) **Once the announcement is made that 15 minutes remain in an examination session, <u>no one</u> will be permitted to leave the examination room for <u>any</u> reason. You must remain in your seat until excused. Because the security of examination materials is at stake and because a problem in accounting for them might jeopardize the proper recording of <u>your</u> results, we expect you to put up with the inconvenience, or even discomfort, this might cause you.**

2) **<u>Note: No late-discovered writings will be accepted for grading. It is each applicant's responsibility to make sure the Board is in possession of your five bluebooks (Tuesday--essay day--three in the morning, two in the afternoon) and your answer sheets and Multistate booklets (Wednesday--MBE day--both a.m. and p.m. sessions) before the Board excuses the applicants from the examination room for each session.</u>**

The Board of Law Examiners

INSTRUCTIONS TO APPLICANTS
JULY 2011 BAR EXAMINATION
PLEASE READ CAREFULLY

1. The examination will be given on July 26 and 27 at the Breslin Center, on the campus of Michigan State University, corner of Shaw Lane and Harrison Road, East Lansing, Michigan. (See attached map.)

2. Enclosed is your admission certificate with your room location, name, address, and five-digit seat number, a/k/a applicant number (lower right-hand corner). Admittance to the examination room will require presentation of this certificate and some kind of photo identification. After entering the exam room, take the seat corresponding to the five-digit number. **Make note of your seat number (applicant number) for if you contact the Board in the future, you will need to know this number. (*Please note that this is not your State Bar applicant number.) This certificate will be turned in on the last day of the examination**.

3. Each day's session will start at 8:30 a.m. The essay exam on Tuesday the 26th will have a 3-hour morning session and a 2-hour afternoon session. The Multistate Bar Examination on Wednesday the 27th will be in two, 3-hour sessions.

4. If you wish to type the essay portion of the exam, notify this office **in writing** (no e-mails or faxes accepted) of that intent by **July 15, 2011** and include your name and seat number. You must supply the typewriter (a computer will not be allowed); paper will be supplied. The Board of Law Examiners does not assume responsibility for any power failure or equipment malfunction. Applicants using electric typewriters must be prepared to continue the examination by writing in the event of any power failure or equipment malfunction. No additional time or other consideration will be allowed for power failure or equipment malfunction. Typists should report to their assigned seats. You will be instructed where to go for typing at the appropriate time.

5. **BRING PENS** for the essay exam on the first day **and SHARPENED, soft lead (No. 2) PENCILS** (there will be no pencil sharpener available) for the Multistate exam on the second day. Bluebooks will be supplied.

6. Room and board are your responsibility. See attached copy of a listing of local motels and hotels.

7. **All applicants are required to take both portions of the exam except for those applicants who have made prior arrangements with the Board to transfer a Multistate bar examination score from another jurisdiction.** There are 150 possible points on the essay portion (15 questions with a possible 10 points per question) and 200 points on the MBE portion. A combined score of 135 or above is necessary to pass the exam using the following formula:

$$\text{Combined Score} = \frac{\text{Scaled essay total} + \text{MBE scaled score}}{2}$$

8. **ALL APPLICANTS WHO HAVE NOT FINISHED PRIOR TO THE FIFTEEN MINUTE WARNING WILL BE ASKED TO STAY IN THEIR SEAT AND WILL BE DISMISSED AFTER THE EXAMINATION HAS BEEN COMPLETED AND PAPERS HAVE BEEN PICKED UP BY THE BOARD OF LAW EXAMINERS.

9. **IF YOU FIND THAT YOU ARE UNABLE TO SIT FOR THIS EXAM, IMMEDIATELY NOTIFY THIS OFFICE OF THAT FACT AND RETURN YOUR CERTIFICATE, ALONG WITH A LETTER IN WRITING (NO FAXES OR E-MAILS ACCEPTED), TO THE ADDRESS LISTED BELOW.** Failure to so notify this office and the immediate return of your certificate may jeopardize your right to take a future exam.

10. Questions relating to administration of the exam should be directed to:

Board of Law Examiners
P.O. Box 30104 **Phone: (517) 373-4453**
Lansing, MI 48909

***NOTE:** **Unofficial results will be released to applicants who have not obtained character and fitness approval or have not passed the MPRE. However, no results will be released to those individuals for whom the Board has not received certification of the date of graduation with a J.D. degree from an ABA-approved law school.**

IF AN APPLICANT FAILS THE EXAM AND RECEIVES UNOFFICIAL RESULTS, THE APPLICANT WILL NOT BE ABLE TO REGISTER FOR A FUTURE BAR EXAMINATION UNTIL OFFICIAL RESULTS HAVE BEEN RELEASED TO THE APPLICANT.

The applicant will receive official results when the Board of Law Examiners office is in receipt of all of the following: (1) law school certification of date of graduation, (2) that the applicant has passed the MPRE with a score of 85 or above, and (3) character and fitness approval has been received and accepted by the Board of Law Examiners.

Michigan Board of Law Examiners Bar Examination Security Policy

Applicants are not permitted to bring any items into the examination room other than a clear plastic food storage type bag (maximum size one gallon), which may only contain:

Admission Certificate
Government Issued Photo I.D.
Wallet
Keys
Earplugs (not the big earphone/headphone type)
Pens, pencils, erasers
Medication and medical items
Facial tissue
Non-digital watch or timepiece
One clear plastic bottle of water/juice/soda per exam session

The following items are strictly prohibited and will not be permitted in the exam room or the testing area, which includes the examination room, rest rooms, and hallway:

Coats
Handbags
Purses
Hats, hoods or any other headgear (except items of religious apparel)
Backpacks
Duffle bags
Briefcases
Tote bags
Notes
Scratch paper
Books, magazines, newspapers or any other reading material
Bar review or other study material in any format or media
Electronic devices such as cell phones, calculators, pagers, cameras, radios, recording devices, hand-held computers, any type of personal digital assistant, wireless email devices, etc.
IPODs or similar devices
Headphones or headsets
Imaging devices
Any type of wireless communication device
Weapons of any kind, regardless of whether you have a permit to carry
Any other item not specifically allowed.

Be prepared to demonstrate that your clothing does not contain prohibited items.

It is best not to even bring the prohibited items to the examination site because they will not be permitted into the examination room and there is no place to store them. The Board will not be responsible for the loss or damage to personal property, so it is strongly recommended that any such items be left at home, in your hotel room, or in your car.

Possession of a prohibited device or item at the examination will be treated as a cheating incident and you may be immediately DISQUALIFIED AND EJECTED from the examination.

Michigan Board of Law Examiners Policy on Bar Examination Conduct

It is the policy of the Michigan Board of Law Examiners that the bar examination and related conduct of bar applicants be beyond reproach. Applicants are at all times to maintain a professional attitude toward other applicants, proctors, and other examination personnel. Conduct that results in a violation of security or disrupts the administration of the examination may result in immediate disqualification and ejection from the examination. Such conduct includes violation of the Board's Security Policy, cheating, failing to follow all rules and instructions governing the administration of the examination, or otherwise compromising the security or integrity of the bar examination.

BAR EXAM MENU / PRICING

Breakfast (Served 7:30 am - 9:00 am)

Bagel w/cream cheese	$1.50
Fruit	$1.00
Donut or Roll	$1.00

Lunch (Served 11:00 am - 1:30 pm)

Hot Dog	$2.50	Hot Dog Combo	$6.00
Bratwurst	$3.00	Bratwurst Combo	$6.50
Pizza	$3.00	Pizza Combo	$6.50
Chicken Caesar Wrap	$4.00	Chicken Caesar Wrap	$7.00
Chef Salad	$4.00	Nachos	$2.50

(Combos include Chips & 32 oz. Pop)

Snacks

Chips	$1.00	Caramel Corn	$2.50
Pretzel	$2.50	Extra Cheese	$1.00
Candy	$1.50		

Beverages

22 oz. Pop	$2.50	Coffee/Cappuccino	$1.00
32 oz. Pop	$3.00	Cocoa	$1.00
Milk	$1.00	Aquafina Bottled Water	$2.50
Juice	$1.50		

(Serve Pepsi Products)

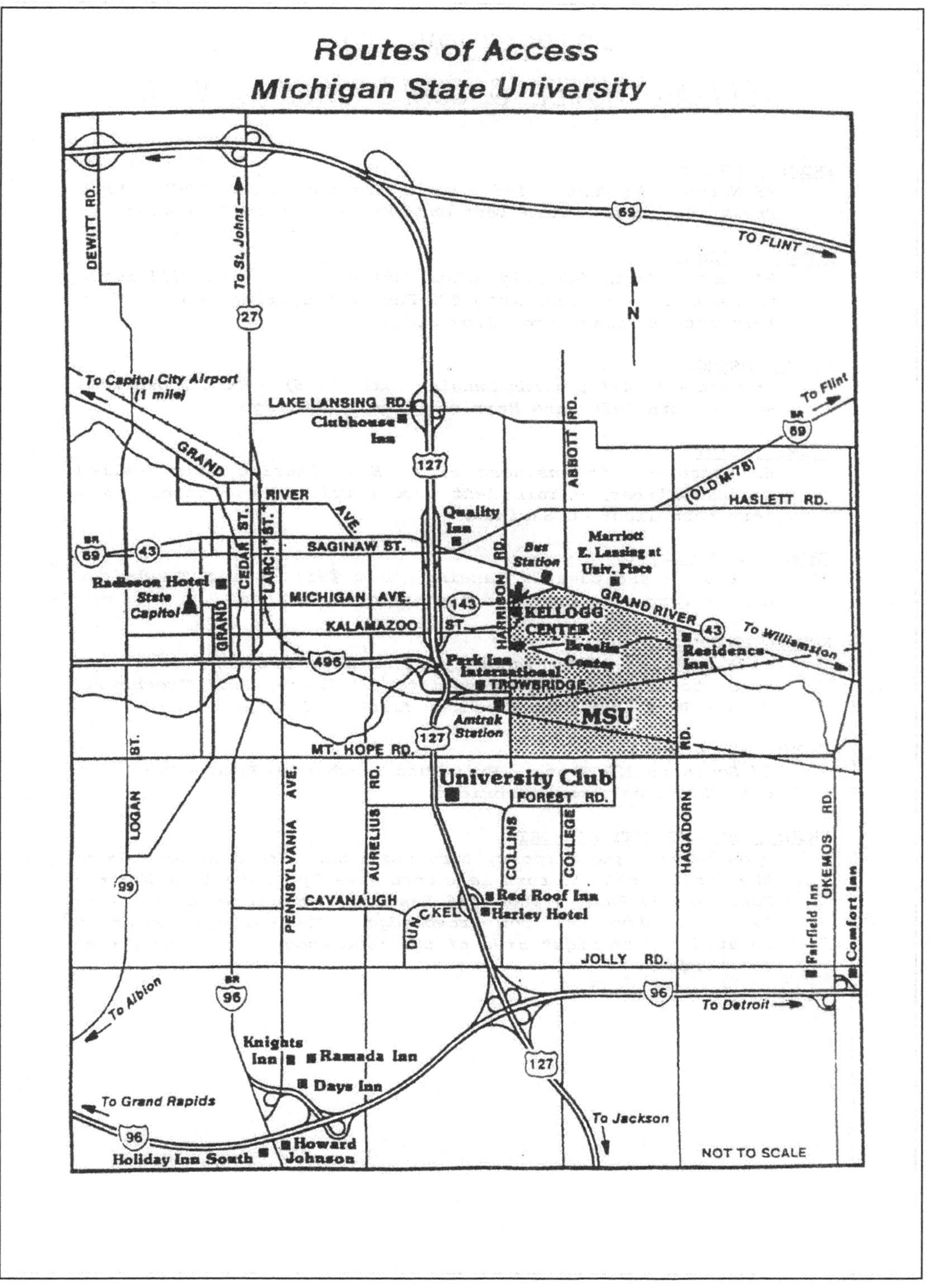
Routes of Access
Michigan State University
DEWITT RD.
To St. Johns
27
69
TO FLINT
N
To Capitol City Airport (1 mile)
LAKE LANSING RD.
Clubhouse Inn
127
ABBOTT RD.
To Flint
69
GRAND
(OLD M-78)
HASLETT RD.
RIVER
AVE.
Quality Inn
SAGINAW ST.
43
Marriott E. Lansing at Univ. Place
Bus Station
Radisson Hotel
State Capitol
CEDAR ST.
LARCH ST.
MICHIGAN AVE.
143
HARRISON RD.
GRAND RIVER
KELLOGG CENTER
KALAMAZOO ST.
43
To Williamston
GRAND
496
Breslin Center
Residence Inn
Park Inn International
TROWBRIDGE
MSU
Amtrak Station
127
MT. HOPE RD.
LOGAN ST.
PENNSYLVANIA AVE.
AURELIUS RD.
University Club
FOREST RD.
COLLINS RD.
COLLEGE
HAGADORN RD.
OKEMOS RD.
99
CAVANAUGH
DUNCKEL
Red Roof Inn
Harley Hotel
Fairfield Inn
Comfort Inn
JOLLY RD.
To Albion
96
96
To Detroit
Knights Inn
Ramada Inn
Days Inn
127
To Grand Rapids
To Jackson
96
Holiday Inn South
Howard Johnson
NOT TO SCALE

DIRECTIONS TO KELLOGG HOTEL & CONFERENCE CENTER

FROM: ANN ARBOR
23 North - 96 West - 496 towards Lansing (Exit #106) - Exit Trowbridge Road - Turn left onto Harrison from Trowbridge

FROM: CHICAGO
94 East - North (shortly after Battle Creek, sign will read: to Lansing) - 69 runs into 496 East - Trowbridge Road - Turn left onto Harrison from Trowbridge

FROM: DETROIT
96 West - To 496 towards Lansing (Exit #106) - Exit Trowbridge Road - Turn left onto Harrison from Trowbridge

FROM: FLINT
69 South - Exit Business 69 to East Lansing (also called Saginaw Street) - Turn left onto Harrison Road (there is a left turn light on Saginaw)

FROM: GRAND RAPIDS
96 East - 496 towards Lansing (Exit #95) - Exit Trowbridge Road - Turn left onto Harrison from Trowbridge

FROM: KALAMAZOO
94 East - 69 North (shortly after Battle Creek, sign will read: to Lansing) - 69 runs into 496 East - Exit Trowbridge Road - Turn left onto Harrison from Trowbridge

FROM: ST. JOHNS
27 South to 127 South - Exit onto Trowbridge Road - Turn left onto Harrison from Trowbridge

FROM: LANSING CITY AIRPORT
Upon leaving the airport, turn right onto Grand River - Go to the first light and turn left onto Waverly Road - Take Waverly Road to 496 East - Then 496 East to Trowbridge Road - Turn left onto Harrison from Trowbridge - The Kellogg Center is located on the right side of the road about four blocks from Trowbridge

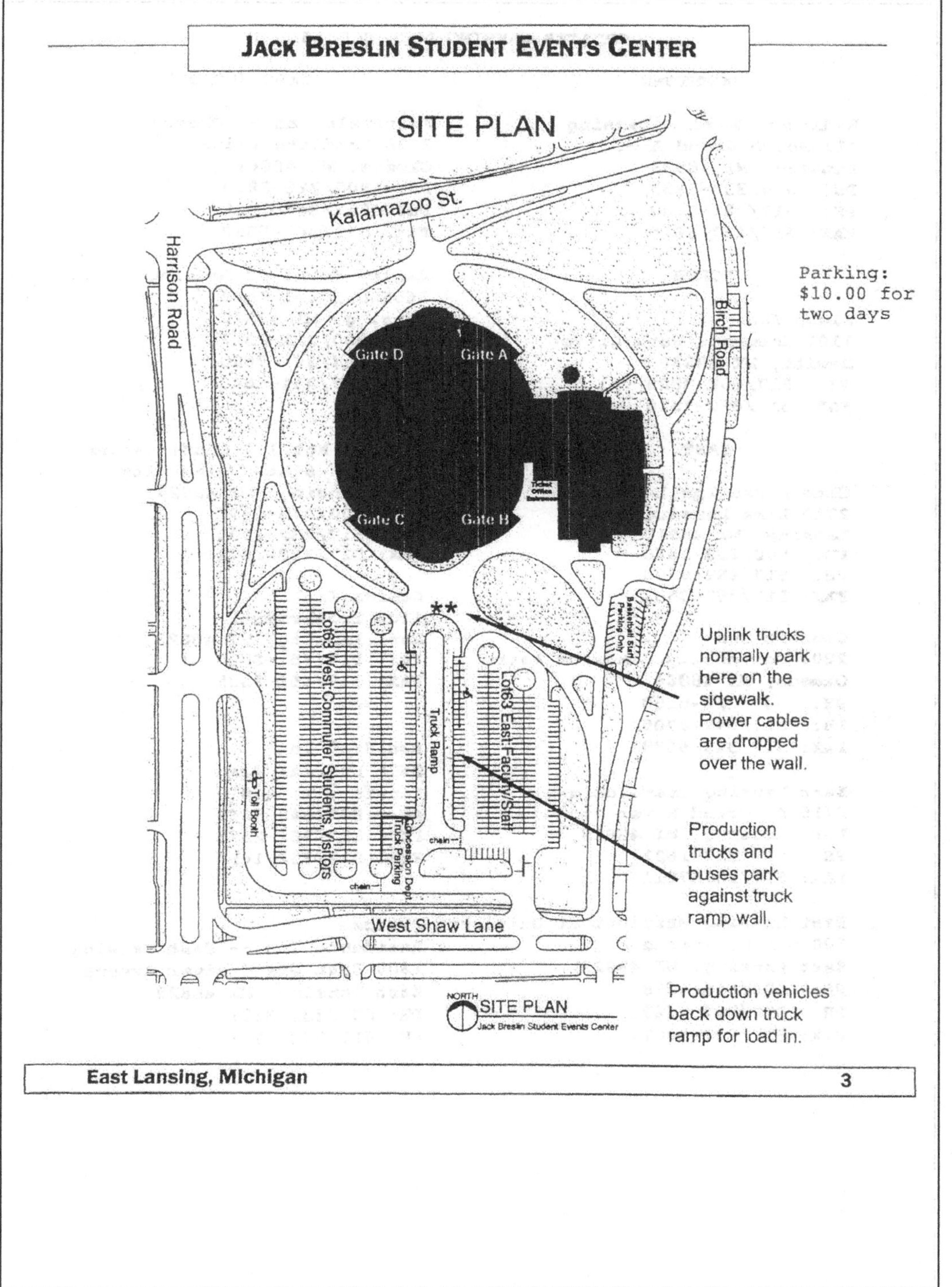
JACK BRESLIN STUDENT EVENTS CENTER
SITE PLAN
Kalamazoo St.
Harrison Road
Birch Road
Parking:
$10.00 for
two days
Gate D
Gate A
Gate C
Gate B
Lot63 West: Commuter Students, Visitors
Lot63 East: Faculty/Staff
Truck Ramp
Concession Dept. Truck Parking
Toll Booth
chain
Uplink trucks normally park here on the sidewalk. Power cables are dropped over the wall.
Production trucks and buses park against truck ramp wall.
West Shaw Lane
NORTH
SITE PLAN
Jack Breslin Student Events Center
Production vehicles back down truck ramp for load in.
East Lansing, Michigan
3

GREATER LANSING AREA HOTELS

DOWNTOWN

Radisson Hotel - Lansing
111 North Grand Ave.
Lansing, MI 48933
PH: 800/333-3333
PH: 517/482-0188
FAX: 517/487-6646

NORTH

Sleep Inn
1101 Commerce Park Drive
Dewitt, MI 48820
PH: 517/669-8823
FAX: 517/669-7816

EAST

Club House Inn Lansing
2710 Lake Lansing Road
Lansing, MI 48912
PH: 800/258-2466
PH: 517/482-0500
FAX: 517/482-0557

Comfort Inn
2209 University Commerce Park
Okemos, MI 48864
PH: 800/228-5150
PH: 517/349-8700
FAX: 517/349-5638

East Lansing Travelodge
2736 E. Grand River
East Lansing, MI 48823
PH: 517/337-1621
FAX: 517/337-7211

East Lansing Marriott at University Place
300 M.A.C. Avenue
East Lansing, MI 48823
PH: 800/646-4678
PH: 517/337-4440
FAX: 517/337-5001

EAST (CONT.)

Fairfield Inn -- Okemos
2335 Woodlake Drive
Okemos, MI 48864
PH: 800/228-2800
PH: 517/347-1000
FAX: 517/347-5092

Harley Hotel of Lansing
3600 Dunckel Road
Lansing, MI 48910
PH: 800/321-2323
PH: 517/351-7600
FAX: 517/351-4640

Kellogg Hotel & Conf. Center
Michigan State University
East Lansing, MI 48824
PH: 800/875-5090
PH: 517/432-4000
FAX: 517/353-1872

Ramada Inn
1100 Trowbridge
East Lansing, MI 48823
PH: 517/351-5500
FAX: 517/351-5509

Red Roof Inn
3615 Dunckel Road
Lansing, MI 48910
PH: 800/843-7663
PH: 517/332-2575
FAX: 517/332-1459

Residence Inn -- East Lansing
1600 East Grand River Avenue
East Lansing, MI 48823
PH: 800/331-3131
PH: 517/332-7711

University Quality Inn
3121 East Grand River Avenue
Lansing, MI 48912
PH: 800/228-5151
PH: 517/351-1440
FAX: 517/351-6220

SOUTH

Days Inn - South
6501 S. Pennsylvania Avenue
Lansing, MI 48911
PH: 800/547-7878
PH: 517/393-1650
FAX: 517/393-9633

Ramada Limited
6741 South Cedar Street
Lansing, MI 48911
PH: 517/694-0454
FAX: 517/694-7087

Holiday Inn South Convention Center
6820 South Cedar Street
Lansing, MI 48911
PH: 800/333-8123
PH: 517/694-8123
FAX: 517/699-3753

Econolodge
110 Ramada Drive
Lansing, MI 48911
PH: 517/394-7200
FAX: 517/394-0826

Regent Inn
6501 S. Cedar
Lansing, MI 48910
PH: 517/393-2030
FAX: 517/393-2542

Super 8 Motel
910 American Road
Lansing, MI 48911
PH: 800/800-8000
PH: 517/393-8008
FAX: 517/393-8009

WEST

Best Western Midway Hotel
7711 West Saginaw Highway
Lansing, MI 48917
PH: 800/528-1234
PH: 517/627-8471
FAX: 517/627-8597

Fairfield Inn -- West
810 Delta Commerce Drive
Lansing, MI 48917
PH: 800/228-2800
PH: 517/886-1066
FAX: same

Hampton Inn of Lansing
525 Canal Road
Lansing, MI 48917
PH: 800/426-7866
PH: 517/627-8381
FAX: 517/627-5502

Holiday Inn Conference Center
7501 W. Saginaw
Lansing, MI 48917
PH: 800/465-4329
PH: 517/627-3211
FAX: 517/627-5240

Quality Suites of Lansing
901 Delta Commerce Drive
Lansing, MI 48917
PH: 800/456-6431
PH: 517/886-0600
FAX: 517/886-0103

Red Roof Inn - West
7412 West Saginaw Highway
Lansing, MI 48917
PH: 800/843-7663
PH: 517/321-7246
FAX: 517/321-2831

WEST (CONT.)

Residence Inn - Lansing
922 Delta Commerce Drive
Lansing, MI 48917
PH: 800/331-3131
PH: 517-886-5030
FAX: Same

Sheraton Lansing Hotel
925 South Creyts Road
Lansing, MI 48917
PH: 800/325-3535
PH: 517/323-7100
FAX: 517/323-2180

ESSAY DECONSTRUCTION

Hopefully, one of the skills you learned in law school was writing your answers to exam questions according to what each individual professor wanted. The same applies to the bar exam. You need to write your answer according to what the bar exam graders are looking for. Please keep in mind that the graders are practicing attorneys, not professors. Therefore, their expectations are different. In all honesty, this is a good thing, because in most circumstances, they do not expect as much as many professors. They are mainly trying to determine if you can do what you have to do as an attorney: take a set of facts, identify the issues involved in the facts, provide the relevant fundamental rules of law, apply the rules to the facts given by providing an appropriate legal analysis, and reach an appropriate conclusion when asked.

For those of you who followed the traditional IRAC, CRAC, or a modified version of this approach, you are in luck. This essential approach applies to the Michigan Bar Exam. For those of you who didn't, start practicing! Before we get into how to build a great essay, though, it is important to first deconstruct the typical components of the Michigan essay questions. This will help you better understand how to build a great answer.

FUNDAMENTAL COMPONENTS OF THE ESSAY QUESTION

Most of the Michigan essay questions typically involve two fundamental parts: (1) the fact pattern, and (2) the call of the question or interrogatories.

The fact pattern typically includes a set of facts that vary in size, but typically take up about one page (although some questions might be only half a page and others might go onto two pages). You should consider every single fact given in an essay question as a clue to issues. The Michigan bar examiners rarely put in facts that are not relevant in some way. Therefore, make reading the facts a game. For every single fact, ask yourself, "Why did they give me this fact? What issue does it relate to?"

The fact pattern is then followed by a call of the question(s) at the end that directs you in terms of what role you are to play (judge, law clerk, defense attorney, prosecutor, etc.), and what you are being asked to do. This part of the question is crucial to an appropriate answer and is your guiding principle. Keep in mind that sometimes the Michigan bar examiners have two or three interrogatories at the end of the question, with each directing you to do a specific task. This is more common in the Evidence and Domestic Relations questions. In many ways, this multitiered approach makes the following task even easier.

ISSUE SPOTTING IS CRUCIAL

Issue spotting is probably the most important thing you have to do. Although it varies, and there is no set rule for the number of issues that can be tested on a question, the bar examiners are aware that only 20 minutes are allocated to answer each question. Therefore, typically there are only two or three main issues with perhaps a couple smaller ones. The reason issue spotting is so crucial is because it is precisely what you have to do as an attorney. When a client walks into an attorney's office, he or she has a set of facts. It is the attorney's responsibility to identify what area of law the facts pertain to and what specific legal issues are raised by the facts. This is precisely what you have to do for each of your 15 bar exam essay questions! In real life, if you miss a main issue, it's called malpractice. On the bar exam, if you miss a main issue, the grader cannot give you a passing score, even if you perform perfectly on the other issues. Therefore, at most, you start at a score of 6 and go down from there when you miss a main issue.

The good news is that the bar examiners often give excellent clues that help with issue spotting from the fact pattern and from the call of the question. Therefore, to improve your ability to issue spot follow these tips:

1. **Focus on the call of the question and determine what role you are playing.** Always start each essay question by reading the call of the question at the end of the facts first to determine what role you are playing. Are you the judge or law clerk? Are you the prosecutor or defense attorney? Plaintiff or defense attorney? The role you are assigned will help determine how you are going to do your legal analysis, which will guide what you are looking for from the facts. If you are a defense attorney, you will look for defenses and arguments from the facts as your main emphasis; however, you will also present the opposing side's position as well. If you are the judge or law clerk, you will look objectively at the facts to see what arguments each side will make and present the arguments and reach a likely conclusion.
2. **Focus on the call of the question and determine what task(s) they are asking you to do.** Are they asking for the defenses? Best arguments? Conclusions? This will direct you even more in terms of how to set up and start your answer, and what to look for from the facts.

CRUCIAL COMPONENTS OF YOUR ANSWER FOR EACH ISSUE TESTED

Once you spot the issues, the three fundamental components you need to put into your answer for each issue that is tested are (1) the rule(s) of law; (2) the analysis where you apply the facts to the rules; and (3) the conclusion, which is a natural consequence after providing the rule and analysis for each issue. All of this creates what I call the RAC. The R stands for the rule, the A stands for the analysis, and the C stands for the conclusion. Please read on, as this whole process is explained in the next task. We have finished deconstructing the parts to an essay; now it's time to learn how to "build" or "construct" a good essay!

HOW TO BUILD OR "CONSTRUCT" A GOOD ESSAY

It's now time to take all of the pieces of a typical Michigan essay that we just deconstructed and put them together to teach you how to build an excellent essay. Two approaches in terms of how to write the essays follow. Plan A is the approach you should use when you know what you are talking about and want to get every single point. Of course, this is optimal for all 15 essay responses, but unfortunately, it probably isn't realistic due to the nature of the Michigan Bar Exam. Typically, there is at least one question that is unusual and throws everyone. Therefore, another approach is presented—Plan B—which is how you want to approach an essay when you are not sure what to do. Before we get into either approach to actually writing your answer, however, there are several crucial steps you want to take before you even start to write your answer. The following sets forth a specific "Essay Attack" approach you want to take for handling each essay question.

ESSAY ATTACK

Read the Call of the Questions First—Always!

This helps identify the subject matter being tested, tells you what role you are playing (judge, law clerk, defense counsel, etc.), and tells you what to do. Use it to guide how you read the fact pattern to spot the issues.

Example:

Call of the question says: *"Were all the items properly admitted into evidence?"* This tells you up front this is an evidence question, which, after you have studied, should trigger the evidence checklist of what potential issues you want to look for when reading the facts:

- Relevance issue?
- Hearsay issue(s)?
- Hearsay exceptions issue(s)?
- Privileges issue(s)?

Read the Fact Pattern and Highlight Important Facts

A former member of the Board of Law Examiners has said that half of the mistakes made on the essays result from misreading the facts or call of the question. Therefore, as you read, circle, underline, or in some way highlight important facts that relate to the call of the question and make notes in the margins of potential issues next to the facts that support them.

Issue spotting is *extremely* important! Points are granted simply for spotting the issue, even if you reach the wrong conclusion. Therefore, as you read the fact pattern, note the issues in the margin next to the facts that support it so you don't forget to address them all.

Issue Spotting Tip: Dates, times, dollar amounts, quantities, and titles are almost always significant (e.g., UCC or not, Statute of Frauds triggered, etc.). Always highlight these terms.

Read the Call of the Question Again!

This time focus in on what the grader wants. Ask yourself, "Who am I and what do they want me to do?" Are they asking a yes or no answer up front? If so, then you want to start your answer with a conclusion! Simply restate the call of the question in a statement with an answer. Do they want you to state the different claims? Do they want you to present the arguments? What clues do you get from the call of the question? You want to use the call of the question to structure the outline of your answer, which is up next!

Outline Your Answer!

Before you start to write an answer, outline your response, even if it kills you! Set up your outline around what the call of the question is asking you to do because it organizes your response and provides a logical flow to your answer. It also provides a checklist to make sure you covered all issues.

How to Outline Your Answer

- Use the call of the question to guide you in how to outline your response.
- Briefly sketch out the issue or rule, and list the elements or requirements with all facts that support each element (both sides).
- Abbreviate and use your own shorthand system so it's fast! Only you need to understand it, so it can be ugly! This is for your use only, so don't waste time spelling everything out. This should only take maybe two or three minutes to do. If you know the rule, don't waste time writing it out in the outline, just abbreviate the name.

Use the following outline template as a guideline:

Outline Template

MAIN RULE/ISSUE
Element 1 → Facts (all facts that support or don't support)
Element 2 → Facts (all facts that support or don't support)
Element 3 → Facts (all facts that support or don't support)

EXCEPTION? DEFENSE? ISSUE #2? [WHATEVER THE QUESTION DICTATES]
Element 1 → Facts (all facts that support or don't support)
Element 2 → Facts (all facts that support or don't support)

This is a basic template. Of course, it will vary by rule or issue, number of elements, and so on, but it is an example of the basic outline format. By listing the base issue with a bulleted list of the elements or requirements, you are sketching out the rule. By placing the corresponding facts next to each element, you are sketching out the application part that supports each element, which will lead to the conclusion. This process essentially sets up your answer, one issue at a time, according to the RAC. If you do this, your answer will practically write itself when you simply apply the outline. If you practice doing this, you will get better and faster. Obviously, time is of the essence, so you can't waste precious time writing out full words and sentences in the outline. Therefore, follow these outlining shortcuts to get faster and then practice!

Outlining Shortcut Tips (Time Savers)

1. **Abbreviate like crazy.** Only you need to understand it, so use your own shorthand, and even just put the first letter of the element.
2. **Draw arrows to the facts instead of writing them out.** If there is room at the bottom of the essay question, use it to sketch out your outline on the same page. Then save time by simply drawing an arrow from the element to the facts supporting it in the question, instead of physically writing out the supporting facts.
3. **Remember to use the call of the question to guide your outline.** If the call of the question asks for arguments, then your list might be of arguments. Typically, these still require you to define a rule and list out the elements, but be sure to present your facts in the form of arguments on both sides.

Sample Outline of Statute of Frauds Issue:

TEMPLATE	*SAMPLE OUTLINE*
Main Rule	Statute of Frauds
Element 1 → Facts	1. Writing → purchase order
Element 2 → Facts	2. Signed by party to be charged → no!
Element 3 → Facts	3. Quantity → 500 bearings
Exception	Merchant Exception
Element 1 → Facts	1. Both merchants
Element 2 → Facts	2. Writing with quantity
Element 3 → Facts	3. No objection w/in reas. time

Write Your Answer

Essentially, it comes down to two choices: Plan A and Plan B. Plan A is what you want to use. This is when you know the answer and you want to knock it out of the park! Unfortunately, this won't happen on every question. Therefore, you must have a backup plan in place, for when you aren't really sure what the answer is. This is what I call Plan B. It's not our favorite plan, but the goal is to take a deep breath and rack up as many points as you can. First, though, let's start with Plan A.

PLAN A APPROACH: THE RAC

By now you should have heard of the IRAC (Issue, Rule, Application, Conclusion) approach, the CRAC (Conclusion, Rule Application, Conclusion) approach, or some modified version of it. Some people get all worked up about how to do this properly. Simply apply common sense. The part that truly counts is the RAC portion of it. For the Michigan Bar Exam, you want to give the rule (R), application or analysis (A), and conclusion (C) for each issue presented in the question. How you start your answer solely depends on what the call of the question asks you to do. If the question is in the format where it asks for a straight answer up front (the conclusion), then that's how you start it. If it asks you to identify the issues, then you start with the issues (I). It might say, "State the claims and defenses that are available." In this case, each "claim" would start with just that: "The first claim would be ___________." Then you would follow it with the rule, application, and conclusion (RAC) for each issue. If they wanted defenses, then you would start with just that: "The first defense would be ___________."

The following is an oversimplification and might need to be adjusted according to the question, but if you try to use these buzzwords for each portion of the RAC you should end up with a good, logical, organized answer:

RAC (Rule, Application, Conclusion):

Rule: *"Under Michigan . . ." OR*
"There are _____ requirements for a . . ."
Application: *"Here . . ." OR*
"In this case . . ."
Conclusion: *"Therefore . . ."*
"As a result . . ."

Again, how you start your response depends on the call of the question.

IRAC: Use this if you are asked to list the issue(s). Start with:

Issue: *"The issue in this case is . . ."*
"There are several issues in this case. The first issue is . . ."
Then, do the RAC!
Rule: *"Under Michigan . . ." OR*
"There are _____ requirements for a . . ."
Application: *"Here . . ." OR*
"In this case . . ."
Conclusion: *"Therefore . . ."*
"As a result . . ."

CRAC: Use this if you are asked to start with a conclusion. Start with:

Conclusion: *"Yes, the evidence should be admitted . . ." OR*
"_____ should recover for . . ."
Then, do the RAC!
Rule: *"Under Michigan . . ." OR*
"There are _____ requirements for a . . ."
Application: *"Here . . ." OR*
"In this case . . ."
Conclusion: *"Therefore . . ." OR*
"As a result . . ."

Tip: If you use CRAC, leave a couple of blank lines at the beginning of your answer and fill it in at the end, after you have done the analysis.

The following is a base template that can be used as a guideline to teach you how to write your essays according to the RAC method outlined in depth under the "Essay Attack" chapter. Of course, it must be modified to reflect the call of the question, but it is a good base structure to get accustomed to using the RAC approach for each issue in an essay. You might want to copy this to use as you initially practice writing other essays.

RAC Template

[1ST ISSUE]

R:
Under ____

____

____

____

____

____.

A: ***Here (or "In this case,")*** ____

____

____

____

____

____

____

____.

C: ***Therefore,*** ____

____.

[2ND ISSUE: Repeat process!]

R:
Under ____

____

____

____

____

____

____

____

____.

A: *Here (or "In this case,"),* ____

____

____

____

____

____

____

____

____.

C: *Therefore,* ____

____

____.

Sample Answer for Statute of Frauds Issue

C: *Marvelous Tools Corp. cannot avoid the contract based on the statute of frauds defense because the contract falls under the merchant exception to the statute of frauds.*

R: *Under the UCC in Michigan, generally the statute of frauds requires that a contract for the sale of goods for more than $1,000*[3] *must be in writing, provide the quantity, and be signed by the party to be charged. However, under the merchant exception, there does not need to be a signed writing if both parties are merchants, and there is no answer within 10 days from the person who gets a signed writing with a quantity term.*

A: *Here, the contract is for $4,000 and therefore falls under the statute of frauds. Although the purchase order is in writing and provides the quantity (500 bearings), it is not signed by Marvelous Tools Corp., which is the party to be charged. However, the merchant exception applies, which means no writing is required because both parties are merchants. Marvelous Tools received the signed acknowledgment from National Corp. and the invoice included the quantity term. Marvelous Tools also did not object within the 10 days. Instead, two weeks had gone by before Marvelous Tools raised the issue.*

C: *Therefore, Marvelous Tools cannot avoid the contract based on the statute of frauds because the contract falls under the merchant exception and Marvelous Tools failed to object within 10 days.*

3. Note that in Michigan, under the statute of frauds, the dollar amount for a sale of goods contract is $1,000. Under the UCC for the MBE, the dollar amount is $500. This is one example of a Michigan distinction in an MBE subject.

Notice that you know the issue tested, the question asked, and all of the facts of the question from this answer without ever reading the question![4] Also go back to the outline and see how it provides the base of the answer. This is precisely what you want to do on the bar exam to get all 10 points! It is not difficult to do when you know the issue and the rules being tested. When you do, follow this Plan A approach and knock it out of the park!

Putting it together: create canned answers

A great tool for prepping for the Michigan Bar Exam is to create canned answers for rules that are regularly tested, in your own words. As you study, begin to create these canned answers on flash cards, always using the RAC approach:

Example: Intentional Infliction of Emotional Distress—Canned Answer:

*One of the issues [**Issue**] in this case is whether the defendant can recover for Intentional Infliction of Emotional Distress. In Michigan [**Rule**], there are four requirements that must be satisfied for a successful claim. First, the defendant must act in a way that is extreme and outrageous. Second, the defendant must intend the conduct to be extreme and outrageous, or it's a result of recklessness. Third, the plaintiff must suffer extreme emotional distress. And fourth, the defendant's conduct must have caused the plaintiff's harm.*

*In this case, [**Application** - plug the facts given into the elements] . . . Therefore, [**Conclusion**] . . .*

Plan A is fantastic, and what you hope you can do on every single one of the 15 essay questions, but it isn't realistic. Typically, due to the fact that the exam is written by lawyers and judges, not professors, who are far removed from law school exams, there are usually at least one or two questions that throw everyone. This is when you have to take a deep breath and break out Plan B.

PLAN B APPROACH

The best thing to do is just accept and prepare for the fact that there will at least be one question where you either go completely blank or just aren't sure what the examiners want. This is where Plan B comes into play. What you need to do if you see a question where you are completely or at least partially "clueless" is follow these steps:

First: Don't freeze or panic! Instead, take a deep breath and say to yourself, "It's time to break out Plan B!" If you write nothing, you get nothing. Trust me, if you tap into your common sense and read the facts and call of the question carefully, you can pull out some points. The goal now is not to have a perfect answer; the goal is to get as many points as you can!

4. The actual question is not provided. This is an excerpt of one issue from a question that is being used to show that a well-written answer tells everything about the question without ever even reading it.

Second: Identify what subject you're in by looking to see what cluster you are in. Then start your answer with identifying the subject being tested: *"This is a property question."* Believe it or not, this alone will get you 1 point!

Third: Follow the same "Essay Attack" steps given earlier (i.e., read the call of the question, read the facts and make notes, etc.). The key now is to identify the issues as best you can and outline-dump the general principles you do know if you can. If you simply don't know the rules, then try to define the concept by using the facts presented. Present a thorough application or analysis of the facts and conclude with a "sort of" conclusion (i.e., *"Defendant will probably recover"*). Quite often, you can use the facts to define the rule if you know what the issue is, but you don't really know the elements or a good definition of the rule. The more you throw in, the more material you give them to award points for. My motto is "When in doubt, spell it out!"

> **Tip:** If you know the issue, but are not sure of the definition of the rule, make it up in very broad terms. Be confident about it, so the grader at least thinks you know what you are talking about. Trust me on this one! Keep in mind, the graders usually are not experts on the area of law that's being tested, and their knowledge is usually limited to the model answer. So if you sound like you know what you're talking about, even if you're wrong, you just might get the benefit of the doubt!

GRAMMAR, SPELLING, FORM, AND MORE

The truly important part of your answer is the content, not the grammar, spelling, and writing. With that said, good grammar and a well-written and organized answer certainly helps. In addition to the approaches already outlined, it will help make your answer more organized and easier to read. This, in turn, helps the grader give you more points (they like easy reading!):

1. **Headings:** Use headings where appropriate such as:
   - *Multiple Issues*: Treat each issue separately and separate with headings.

     EXAMPLE:

     "Negligence Claim:"
     "Strict Liability Claim:"
   - *Multiple Parties*: Deal with each person separately.

     EXAMPLE:

     "Paul's claim against Don:"
     "Paul's claim against third party:"
2. **Paragraphs:** Use paragraphs for each major rule, each issue or subissue, or any new thoughts. It is very difficult to read a page that is all in one paragraph.
3. **Sentences:** Use short, simple, declarative sentences. Avoid wordiness and long, complex, run-on sentences. Keep it short and simple. Also, separate the law or rules (R), the application of facts to the law (A), and the conclusion (C) into separate sentences. Because the graders are looking for all three, if you make it easy on them, you will be rewarded.

4. **Spacing:** Do not skip lines, but leave healthy margins. The goal is to make it easy for the grader to read. Use common sense.

   NOTE:

   Your answer will be photocopied and sent to the grader. If you don't leave margins on the sides and at the bottom, part of your text could get cut off!

5. **Handwriting:** Those of you who are computer users need to physically practice writing out essays even more. It's a different thought process. You also need to build up strength in your hand to be able to write for 3 hours! If you have bad handwriting, practice even more.
6. **One-sided pages:** Only write on one side of the page. Do not write on the back of the page because only the front of your page will be photocopied.
7. **Abbreviations:** Abbreviating is acceptable as long as it's understandable and you spell out what you are abbreviating first followed by the abbreviation in parentheses. Remember that there are 15 different graders for each essay. You want to make them happy and make grading your essay easy. If there are too many abbreviations, it gets confusing. So, if you intend to use the pi symbol (π) to refer to the plaintiff, then explain: "The plaintiff (π) . . ."
8. **Underlining:** When you are positive on certain concepts and buzzwords, it is acceptable to underline them to draw the grader's attention to your knowledge, but don't overdo it. If you are not sure, then don't underline anything!
9. **New answer, new page:** Always start an answer to a new question on a fresh page, and be sure to start by giving the question number. Never start a new answer on a page with part of the previous answer. Whoever copies your bluebook will likely not catch it and will make only one copy. Therefore, part of your answer will be missing for one of the questions.

FINAL WORDS OF WISDOM

- Read the call of the question, and give the examiners what they ask for.

  EXAMPLE:

  If the facts say the will is validly executed, don't discuss the requirements for a valid will.

- Don't be intimidated or discouraged.
  - You will receive credit for clear and well-reasoned legal arguments, even where you make an incomplete and incorrect statement of law.
- Hit every issue, even if you are not an expert (Plan B).
  - Points are given just for spotting the issue, even if your conclusion is wrong, and even if you don't give a complete definition of the rule.
- Pace yourself (20 minutes per question).
  - Once 20 minutes is up, skip a couple of pages and move on to the next question. Go back later if you have time.
- Practice correctly.
  - Master the law (study those outlines, make flash cards, and use mnemonics or whatever devices help you retain the elements and rules).
  - Physically write out the answers to as many practice essay questions as possible under the Essay Attack approach outlined earlier.

- Don't cheat. Write out all your answers under the approach.
- When time is short, at minimum, physically outline your answer before looking at the model answers.
- Study the model answers.
- Incorporate any substantive law learned into your outlines.
- Grade your answer and rewrite it correctly.

Now, it's time to put this essay approach to work and practice!

ESSAY "CONSTRUCTION" PROJECTS

The following are some essay writing exercises that are "building exercises" to teach you how to actually use the Essay Attack approach outlined previously. Complete them in order for the most effective way of learning how to write according to the Plan A and Plan B approaches provided.

Practice is the key to getting better at essay writing and earning more points on your bar exam essays, but few graduates actually do it. Many approach the bar exam with the ill-conceived notion that they know how to write essays because they've done it throughout law school. What they don't realize is that the Michigan Bar Exam essays are entirely different than law school essays. First, only 20 minutes is allocated for each. Very few law students, if any, have written 20-minute essays. Those who don't practice often run out of time because they write too much and never get to the last essay(s). Second, there are nine essays back to back in the morning, and six in the afternoon, each on a different subject. No law student has faced this much writing on different subjects. Third, many students now type law school exams, but you can't type the Michigan Bar Exam.[5] Writing by hand not only uses different muscles in the hand and wrist, but it is also a different thought process. You can't cut and paste, delete, and otherwise move text around as you process your thoughts. Instead, you have to write in cohesive, complete thoughts as you go along. You must practice this to develop fluid, well-written sentences.

The following practical essay building exercises are designed to apply the Essay Attack approach set forth previously to truly show you how it works and why it is successful. Going through these exercises after you read the previous material on the Essay Attack is probably one of the best things you can do to improve your essay performance.

STEPS TO BUILDING AN OUTSTANDING ESSAY

Step 1: Always Follow the "Essay Attack" for Each Essay[6]

1. Read the call of the question first, always!
2. Read the fact pattern and highlight important facts.
    - Issue spot by making notes in the margins next to the facts as your brain fires.
3. Reread the call of the question again.
    - This time focus on what the grader wants. Ask yourself, "Who am I and what do they want from me?"
4. Outline your answer.
    - Use the call of the question to guide you in how to outline your response.

5. On request and submission of the appropriate paperwork, the Michigan Bar Examiners do allow individuals to type the essays on an old-fashioned typewriter without memory that the examinee must supply. However, this method is not the same as typing on a computer, where you can cut and paste, delete, and otherwise move text around. Instead, it is much like writing the exam long hand.

6. Read earlier materials on the Essay Attack for details.

- Briefly sketch out the issue or rule, and list the elements or requirements, with facts supporting each.
- Abbreviate and use your own shorthand system so it's fast! Only you need to understand it, so it can be ugly!

5. Write your answer using the "RAC" (see supra p. 28).

Step 2: Practice Writing Out Essays!

Once you've studied a particular subject, practice writing out essays on that specific subject in this book by applying the Essay Attack method.

The following are some essay writing exercises (based on prior released Michigan bar exam essays) that are "building exercises" to teach you how to actually use the Essay Attack approach. Complete them in order for the most effective way of learning how to write according to the Plan A and Plan B approaches.

Exercise 1

In 1984, Bruce Barber owned one square block of real property in the City of Silver Springs. Bruce's property was between North Street and South Street, and First Avenue and Second Avenue. Four buildings of equal size took up the area. The front entrances to the buildings were on North and South streets. A very narrow alley ran parallel to North and South Streets, from First Avenue to Second Avenue. The alley provided very limited access to the rear entrances of the buildings. Bruce rarely used the rear entrance to his buildings. Bruce operated a carpentry business that specialized in the construction of custom poker tables in the building on the corner of North Street and Second Avenue. The other three buildings were vacant. In 1985, Alan Anderson purchased from Bruce the building on the corner of North Street and First Avenue. Bruce operated his carpentry shop from 7:00 a.m. to 3:00 p.m., Monday through Friday. Alan opened a nightclub in his building, which he operated from 4:00 p.m. to 2:00 a.m., seven days per week. The nightclub was a smashing success and became nationally known as the place to be seen in Michigan. In 1988, Alan made Bruce an offer to purchase the two vacant buildings on South Street, between First and Second Avenues. Alan indicated he wanted to demolish the buildings to provide surface parking for his nightclub. Bruce liked the idea of having a parking lot behind his building. Bruce accepted Alan's offer and provided Alan a warranty deed at the closing that made no express statement in the deed reserving to Bruce any rights in the property.

In 1989, Alan demolished the buildings and paved the area to create a surface parking lot. Alan also remodeled the nightclub to make the rear of the building the main entrance to the club. Prior to 1989, Bruce's employees and patrons accessed his shop through the North Street entrance. Also, Bruce accepted deliveries and sent shipments through the North Street entrance. However, commencing in 1989, Bruce created a rear entrance with a showroom to greet his cash-and-carry patrons and Bruce's advertisements and street signs informed Bruce's patrons to park behind the building and enter from the rear. Bruce also instructed his employees to park in the lot behind the building and enter his building through the back entrance. To ensure that his patrons, employees, and truckers had access to Bruce's rear loading dock and entryway, Bruce hired a contractor for guaranteed snow removal each day before 7:00 a.m. in the winter months and he hired a contractor to clean the parking lot on a daily basis of any debris left behind by nightclub patrons. Bruce never asked Alan for permission to use the parking lot. Bruce used Alan's parking lot without incident from 1989 until 2007. However, in 2007, as a result of the national poker boom, Bruce expanded his business hours and began to stay open until 10:00 p.m. As a result, some of Bruce's customers and many freight haulers calling on Bruce's business were partially blocking the entrance to Alan's nightclub during Alan's hours of operation.

Alan has come to you for advice on whether he can stop Bruce from using his parking lot. How would you advise Alan? Explain your answer.

[OUTLINE YOUR ANSWER TO THIS QUESTION BELOW]

How would you advise Alan?

Easement
↳ open & notorious
↳ over 7 years
↳ AP

SAMPLE OUTLINE TO EXERCISE 1

EBP [shorthand for Easement by Prescription]
- O [Open] → open to public and all to see, in ads
- C [Continuous] → used daily since 1989 (over 15 yrs)
- A [Adverse] → no permission & no express right to use reserved
- N [Notorious] → built loading dock, told employees & customers to park in Alan's lot, hired to clean lot & remove snow; acted as if he owned the lot
- NO E [only difference from adverse possession is no exclusive element]

Overburden/Excessive Use
- Use can't exceed scope or excessive use terminated not easement → recent use exceeded scope of prior use—extended hours, freight haulers blocked entrance

Exercise 1: RAC Building Exercise

[FILL IN THE BLANK SPACES BELOW]

I would advise Alan that he cannot stop Bruce from using his parking lot for the following reasons.

Easement by Prescription

[ISSUE]

The first issue is whether an easement by prescription was created.

[RULE]

Under common law, an easement is an interest in real property that gives a person the right to use another's land for a specific purpose. An easement can be created by express grant or by operation of law, such as an easement by necessity or an easement by prescription. An easement by prescription is similar to acquiring property by adverse possession and requires the following elements. The taking must be adverse or hostile (no permission or right to use the land). The use must be continuous and uninterrupted for at least 15 years, and it must be open or visible and notorious. This means the use is open to all and user acts as if property is his/her own.

[APPLICATION]

Here, Bruce did not ask for permission, & used the lot open & notoriously for over 15 years, plus he paid for snowremoval

[CONCLUSION]

Therefore, Bruce has an easement by prescription

Overburden of Excessive Use

[ISSUE]

The second issue is if there was an easement by prescription whether Bruce's change in use amounted to excessive use.

[RULE]

Under common law, where the easement is silent, the use of easement cannot exceed the scope of or overburden the easement or it amounts to excessive use. If it does, the remedy is to stop the excessive use but it does not terminate the easement.

[APPLICATION]

Here, the overlap in business hours may constitute an overbordenment on the issue.

[CONCLUSION]

Therefore, Bruce must stop the excessive use but may continue to use the parking lot.

Model Answer to Exercise 1

I would advise Alan that he cannot stop Bruce from using his parking lot because he has an easement by prescription, but he can stop the excessive use. Under common law, an easement is an interest in real property that gives a person the right to use another's land for a specific purpose. An easement can be created by express grant or by operation of law, such as an easement by necessity or an easement by prescription. An easement by prescription is similar to acquiring property by adverse possession and requires that the use be open and notorious, adverse (no permission or right to use the land), and continuous and uninterrupted for the statutory period of at least 15 years. Unlike adverse possession there is no requirement that the use be "exclusive."

Here, Bruce's use of Alan's land was open and notorious because he built a loading dock in plain sight to use Alan's property. He also told his employees and customers to park in Alan's lot. Finally, he hired a contractor to clean and do snow removal of Alan's lot. The use was also adverse because the facts state that there was no express right reserved in the deed allowing Bruce to use the land and the facts say that Bruce never asked Alan for permission to use the parking lot. The use was also continuous and uninterrupted since 1989, which exceeds the statutory 15-year period of time under Michigan law. Therefore, I would advise Alan that he cannot stop Bruce from using his lot because he has met all of the elements for an easement by prescription.

Although he can't stop him from using the parking lot, he can probably stop the excessive use that began in 2007. Under common law, where the easement is silent, the use of easement cannot exceed the scope of (overburden or excessive use) the easement. If it does, the remedy is to stop the excessive use but it does not terminate the easement. Here, Bruce's expanded use of the parking lot in 2007 exceeded the scope of the prior use. Bruce's prior use since 1989 took place without incident. However, in 2007, he extended his store hours, and freight haulers partially blocked Alan's entrance during Alan's hours of operation. Therefore, I will advise Alan that because Bruce has met the statutory time period for an easement by prescription, he can't stop him from using the parking lot, but he can at least stop the excessive use.

Exercise 2

Paula Passenger, a Michigan resident, was riding in an automobile driven by her boyfriend Mike Van Der Broek. As they were driving, they were discussing their relationship. When Paula broached the subject of marriage, Mike became extremely distracted. He lost control of the car and collided with a telephone pole. Mike escaped relatively unscathed, but Paula sustained severe injuries to her knees as a result of the crash.

The following are the undisputed facts regarding Paula's injury: She was hospitalized for a month and she missed a total of two months of work from her $6,000-per-month job as an engineer. After she was released from the hospital, she required six months of physical therapy. Before the accident, she enjoyed attending sporting events, dancing, and occasionally rock climbing. With physical therapy she has been able to continue participating in some of these activities, but she cannot participate as fully as she had before. Specifically, when attending sporting events, she must leave her seat and walk around every half-hour or she will experience pain. She can still dance, but she is no longer able to samba, which had been her favorite type of dance. Her doctor has opined that she might be able to samba again after more physical therapy. Finally, she can no longer go rock climbing per her doctor's orders. Paula is able to continue at her job as an engineer with no restrictions and she is able to perform all of her normal household chores. Her medical expenses have been paid.

Paula has asked for your advice. Assume Mike's negligence was a proximate cause of her injuries. Prepare a memorandum discussing what types of damages she can potentially recover in a suit against Mike and what she must show to recover. State and explain your conclusion about the merits of her claim for damages.

[OUTLINE YOUR ANSWER TO THIS QUESTION BELOW]

what kind of damages can Paula recover?
↳ 3P pain & suffering (threshold injury)
↳ wage loss

SAMPLE OUTLINE TO EXERCISE 2

NF Econ [shorthand for Economic Damages]
Priorities—
1. own—Paula
2. HH relative
3. owner/reg
4. driver—Mike
5. assigned claims
NF
—85% gross 1st 3 yrs not above $4929—above $6K so Mike resp. for difference
—medical—covered
—$20/day replacement 1st 3 yrs—none
Non—Econ
only if threshold met—
death—no
perm disfig—no
serious impair. bodily function—McCormick test
1. obj man impair (observable & perceivable actual symptoms)—legs impaired—obs—can't dance, etc.
2. imp bodily func—(value sign, conseq to injured)—impairs mobility—important
3. affects gen ability to lead normal life (capacity to live normally—no tempural req, can be brief)
—hospital stay 1 mo.
—missed 2 mos. work
—6 mos. PT
—no rock climbing or dancing samba
Mike will argue—not enough b/c
—can dance
—can work w/o restriction
—can go to sporting events

Exercise 2: RAC Building Exercise

[FILL IN THE BLANK SPACES BELOW][7]

Memorandum

To: Paula
From: Attorney

I believe you __may__ recover __economic__ damages under the no fault statute, and you can probably __also__ recover __economic__ damages from Mike for the following reasons.

[RAC#1: PRIORITIES]

[RULE]

In Michigan, damages for a person suffering an injury arising out of an automobile accident, regardless of fault, are governed by the Michigan No Fault system. Under the Michigan No Fault Statute, the injured party must first look __to their own policy__ for first-party no-fault economic benefits. If you don't have no-fault insurance, you would next look to the __policy of a resident relative__ ______________________.

If you have no such relative, then you would look to ~~the owner of the involved vehicle~~ ______________________, then to ______________________. If none of those parties is insured, then you would look to the __MACP__.

[APPLICATION]

Here, __Paula would look to her own policy__

____

____

____

____

____

____

____

7. Try to fill in the blank spaces under the "Rule" from memory. If you don't know, then look it up. If all else fails, you can "cheat" and look at the model answer, but it will help you retain it better by testing yourself and looking it up. The blanks are the buzzwords in the rules that really count and you want to know and remember.

____

____

____

____

____

____

____.

[CONCLUSION]

Therefore, ____

____

____.

[RAC#2: ECONOMIC DAMAGES]

[RULE]

Under the No Fault Statute, the first party economic benefits include _______% _______ wages for the first _______ years after the accident, but it cannot exceed the yearly statutory maximum amount of $___________; ______________; and ____________________________ expenses at a maximum of $_______/day for the first _______ years following the accident. The _______ party remains liable for any economic damages in excess of those reimbursed as first-party benefits.

[APPLICATION]

Here, ____

____

____

____

____

____

____

____

____

____

____

____

____

____

____.

[CONCLUSION]

Therefore, ____

____

____

____.

[RAC#3: NONECONOMIC DAMAGES]

[RULE]

In terms of noneconomic damages, under the No Fault Statute, you can only recover noneconomic damages from Mike if your injury meets the no-fault threshold injury of ______________, ______________, or ______________. The statute defines "serious impairment of body function" as "an ______________ manifested impairment of an ______________ body function that affects the person's ______________ ability to lead his or her ______________ life. The Michigan Supreme Court has recently overruled the former "Kreiner" test for determining whether a plaintiff has reached the threshold for noneconomic damages in the McCormick case. Under the McCormick test, the court should first determine whether there is a ______________ dispute regarding the ______________ and the ______________ of the person's injuries, and, if so, whether the dispute is ______________ to determining whether the serious impairment of body function threshold is met. If there is no factual dispute, or no material factual dispute, then whether the threshold is met is a question of law for the court. The court should next determine whether the serious impairment threshold has been crossed. There are three prongs that are necessary to establish a "serious impairment of body function": (1) an ______________ manifested impairment (______________ or ______________ from actual symptoms or conditions) (2) of an ______________ body function (a body function of ________, ______________, or ______________ to the injured person) that (3) affects the person's ________ ability to lead his or her ______________ life (influences some of the plaintiff's ______________ to live in his or her normal manner of living). Also, the serious impairment analysis is inherently fact- and circumstance-specific and must be conducted on a case-by-case basis. A brief impairment may be devastating whereas a near permanent impairment may have little effect. There is no _______________ rule or list of factors in making this determination, and there is also no "_______________" requirement as to how long an impairment must last, so it doesn't have to be permanent.

[APPLICATION]

Here, ____

____

____

____

____

____

____

____

____

____

____

____

____

____.

[CONCLUSION]

Therefore, ____

____

____

____.

Model Answer to Exercise 2
Updated with McCormick Test (February 2011)[8]

Memorandum

To: Paula
From: Attorney

I believe you can recover economic damages under the no fault statute, and you can probably also recover noneconomic damages from Mike for the following reasons. In Michigan, damages for a person suffering an injury arising out of an automobile accident, regardless of fault, are governed by the Michigan No Fault system. Under the Michigan No Fault Statute, the injured party must first look to his or her own insurer for first-party no-fault economic benefits.[9] If you don't have no-fault insurance, you would next look to the policy of an insured relative with whom you share a domicile. If you have no such relative, then you would look to the insurer of the owner or registrant of the vehicle, then to the driver's insurer.[10] If none of those parties is insured, then you would look to the assigned claims plan.[11] Here, Paula, you would first look to your own insurance company for first-party economic damages. If you don't have no-fault insurance, you would next look to the policy of an insured relative with whom you share a domicile. If you have no such relative, then you would look to the insurer of the owner or registrant of the vehicle, if it wasn't Mike's car, and then to Mike's insurer, as he is the driver.[12] If none of those parties is insured, then you would look to the assigned claims plan.[13]

Under the No Fault Statute, the first party economic benefits include 85% of gross wages for the first three years after the accident, but it cannot exceed the yearly statutory maximum amount of $4,929[14]; medical costs; and replacement/household service expenses at a maximum of $20/day for the first three years following the accident.[15] The at-fault party remains liable for any economic damages in excess of those reimbursed as first-party benefits.[16] Here, you lost two months of wages from

8. In July 2010, the Michigan Supreme Court overruled the original *Kreiner* test for determining whether the threshold for "Serious Impairment of a Bodily Function" based on *Kreiner v Fischer*, 471 Mich 109, 683 NW2d 611 (2004), and replaced it with a different test in *McCormick v Carrier*, 2010 WL 3063150 (Mich). The former *Kreiner* test has been repeatedly tested on the Michigan Bar Exam. Please note that when going through old essays from February 2010 and before, the model answers will be based on *Kreiner* and are no longer correct. You can still use the essays for practice, though; simply replace the "Rule" from the *Kreiner* test with the new *McCormick* test to determine if the threshold is met. Use this model answer as a "canned answer" and replace it with the old *Kreiner* test. This question was tested on the February 2007 Michigan Bar Exam. This model answer has been updated and applies the new *McCormick* test.

9. MCL 500.3114(1).

10. MCL 500.3114(4).

11. MCL 500.3172(1).

12. MCL 500.3114(4).

13. MCL 500.3172(1).

14. $4,929 per month is the maximum work-loss payment effective October 1, 2010 through September 30, 2011, but this figure typically increases each year.

15. MCL 500.3107(1)(b) and (c).

16. MCL 500.3135(3)(c).

a $6,000-per-month job. With the current maximum wage-loss benefit at $4,929 per month, it is less than 85% of your monthly salary. In other words, wage-loss benefits you receive from your insurer will not cover your total wage loss. Therefore, you may recover the remaining economic damages in an action against Mike. Because your medical expenses have been paid, and you were able to perform all your normal household chores, those benefits aren't recoverable.

In terms of noneconomic damages, under the No Fault Statute, you can only recover noneconomic damages from Mike if your injury meets the no-fault threshold injury of death, serious impairment of body function, or permanent serious disfigurement.[17] The statute defines "serious impairment of body function" as "an objectively manifested impairment of an important body function that affects the person's general ability to lead his or her normal life."[18] The Michigan Supreme Court has recently overruled the former *Kreiner* test for determining whether a plaintiff has reached the threshold for noneconomic damages in *McCormick v Carrier*.[19] Under the *McCormick* test, the court should first determine whether there is a factual dispute regarding the nature and the extent of the person's injuries, and, if so, whether the dispute is material to determining whether the serious impairment of body function threshold is met.[20] If there is no factual dispute, or no material factual dispute, then whether the threshold is met is a question of law for the court. The court should next determine whether the serious impairment threshold has been crossed. There are three prongs that are necessary to establish a "serious impairment of body function": (1) an objectively manifested impairment (observable or perceivable from actual symptoms or conditions) (2) of an important body function (a body function of value, significance, or consequence to the injured person) that (3) affects the person's general ability to lead his or her normal life (influences some of the plaintiff's capacity to live in his or her normal manner of living). Also, the serious impairment analysis is inherently fact- and circumstance-specific and must be conducted on a case-by-case basis. A brief impairment may be devastating, whereas a near permanent impairment may have little effect. There is no bright-line rule or list of factors in making this determination, and there is also no "temporal" requirement as to how long an impairment must last, so it doesn't have to be permanent.[21]

Here, the facts surrounding the nature of your injury were undisputed. Thus, the court may decide the issue as a matter of law. The court should next determine whether the serious impairment threshold has been crossed. The use of your legs has been impaired by the accident, and this impairment is observable from actual symptoms because you are unable to dance, rock climb, and perform other activities. Therefore, the first prong of an objectively manifested impairment is satisfied, allowing the court to proceed to the next step. The use of your legs is clearly an important body function as it affects the actual mobility of a person. Therefore, the second prong is satisfied. I will argue that the final step appears to also have been met because the injuries to your knees affect your general ability to lead your normal life. Your hospital stay was for one

17. MCL 500.3135(1).

18. MCL 300.3135(7).

19. 487 Mich 180, 215-216, 2010 WL 3063150, 14 (Mich. (Mich 2010) overruling *Kreiner v Fischer*, 471 Michigan 109, 131-134 (2004).

20. MCL 500.3135(2)(a)(i) and (ii).

21. *Id.*

month, and you missed a total of two months of work. This clearly influences your ability to live your normal life. In addition, you needed six months of physical therapy, which takes time and energy from your normal life. Furthermore, you are no longer able to rock climb or dance the samba, which was an activity you enjoyed prior to the accident. Mike's attorney will counter these arguments by arguing that you can do your job without restrictions and you are able to perform all of your normal household chores. You can also still attend sporting events, dance, and engage in most of your preinjury activities, and you may even be able to samba again with more physical therapy. Although you can no longer rock climb, there is no indication that rock climbing was a major part of the course of your life. Therefore, he will argue that your loss of the ability to participate in that activity does not entitle you to noneconomic damages.

Because the injury doesn't have to be permanent to recover noneconomic damages, I believe you have met the no-fault threshold injury. As stated, it seems you have satisfied the "serious impairment of a body function" under the *McCormick* test, and it appears you have a good claim for noneconomic damages, in addition to the economic damages set forth above.

Exercise 3

Darrell Smith is 22 years old and a Michigan resident. There is a history of mental illness in Darrell's family, and Darrell had a difficult childhood that included substance abuse by his father and protracted financial difficulties at home. While still living at home, Darrell procured his first full-time job as a computer programmer for a large Michigan bank that has significant real estate holdings. Darrell enjoyed his position at the bank and performed his job well for the first year.

Shortly thereafter, however, the decline in Michigan's real estate market led the bank to downsize by releasing a number of its employees. The downsizing caused an increased workload for those employees remaining. Darrell escaped the downsizing, but now found his job too demanding. After working for a couple weeks following the downsizing, Darrell told the bank he could no longer continue because the work was now too stressful.

Darrell did not report to work for the following three weeks upon advice of his family doctor. The bank accepted Darrell's inability to continue working in the more demanding environment and could not offer him a less stressful position in Michigan. The bank did, however, send Darrell a letter offering him a special position at the bank's North Carolina branch. The letter explained that there Darrell could provide financial advice to customers in a casual, relaxed atmosphere. The letter explained Darrell's salary there would only be slightly less than what he had earned in Michigan. The letter told Darrell to report there in a month.

Darrell does not want to relocate to North Carolina and he cannot return to work for the bank in Michigan. He seeks your legal advice on whether he has a viable claim for weekly wage-loss benefits for a mental disability under the Michigan workers' compensation statute and his chance of success with any such claim. What would you advise Darrell? Explain your answer.

[OUTLINE YOUR ANSWER TO THIS QUESTION BELOW]

SAMPLE OUTLINE TO EXERCISE 3

WC

Mental Disability—OK if arises out of actual events not unfounded perceptions & aggravates or accelerates in sign. manner (compare nonwork to work issues)

—stress due to downsizing & increased workload

—fine at work for yr b4 downsizing even w/ family history of mental illness

NC job

—can't refuse bona fide offer of reas. employment w/out good cause

—must be w/in reas. distance from home—NC NOT reas.

Exercise 3: RAC Building Exercise

[FILL IN THE BLANK SPACES BELOW][22]

[CONCLUSION]

I would advise Darrell that he ______________________________

______________________________.

Mental Disability

[RULE]

Under Michigan's Workers' Compensation Disability Act (WCDA), mental disabilities are recoverable when arising out of ____________ and not ____________. Also, the mental disability must have ____________, ____________, or ____________ by the employment in a ____________ manner. This is viewed by comparing ____________ related explanations for the problem to the ____________ related contribution.

[Application]

Here, ______________________________

____

____

____

____

22. Try to fill in the blank spaces under the "Rule" from memory. If you don't know, then look it up. If all else fails, you can "cheat" and look at the model answer, but it will help you retain it better by testing yourself and looking it up. The blanks are the buzzwords in the rules that really count and you want to know and remember.

____

____

____

____

____

____

____

____

____.

[Conclusion]

Therefore, ____

____.

NC Job Offer

[Rule]

Under WCDA, an employee is not entitled to weekly wage-loss benefits if he refuses a "________" offer of ____________ employment without ____________ or ____________ cause. However, to be a "____________" offer, it must be within a ____________ distance from the employee's residence.

[APPLICATION]

Here, ____

____

____

____

____

____

____

____

____

____

____.

[CONCLUSION]

Therefore, ____

____

____

____

____.

Model Answer to Exercise 3

I would advise Darrell that he has a good claim for weekly wage loss benefits for his mental disability and he does not have to accept the position in North Carolina for the following reasons.

Mental Disability[23]

Under Michigan's Workers' Compensation Disability Act (WCDA), mental disabilities are recoverable when arising out of actual events of employment, not unfounded perceptions of them. Also, the mental disability must have contributed to, aggravated, or been accelerated by the employment in a significant manner. This is viewed by comparing non-work-related explanations for the problem to the work-related contribution.[24]

Here, I would advise Darrell that the stress he encountered due to the company downsizing as well as his increased workload was clearly grounded in reality and not an unfounded perception of them. The main issue he needs to prove is that the stress contributed to, aggravated, or accelerated his existing mental illness in a significant manner. In comparing Darrell's family history of mental illness to the work-related stress, Darrell worked for a full year without incident and "performed his job well." His stress did not begin until the company downsized and his job grew more demanding to such a degree that his family doctor advised him not to return to work for three weeks. Therefore, I would advise Darrell that it seems he has a good claim for weekly wage-loss benefits because the job stress contributed to, aggravated, AND accelerated the mental disability in a significant manner.[25]

---

23. Where appropriate, it is often a good idea to use headings to separate different issues. This not only helps you stay focused on the specific issue individually, but also helps the grader find where you've hit the issues faster. This makes for a happy grader, and a happy grader is what we want!

24. MCL 418.301(2) - MCL 418.401(2)(b). See also *Robertson v DaimlerChrysler Corp*, 465 Mich 732 (2002).

25. The Michigan Bar Examiners noted in the model answer that some examinees discussed the definition of "disability" in their answers, which is defined by MCL 418.310(4). As noted, however, this specific question did not require a discussion of that specific issue. The "disability" issue is frequently tested on the Michigan Bar Exam, as you will see from the questions and model answers within this book, and the case cited is *Stokes v Chrysler LLC*, 481 Mich 266 (2008), which amplified this issue from *Sington v Chrysler Corp*, 467 Mich. 144 (2002).

NC Job Offer

Under WCDA, an employee is not entitled to weekly wage-loss benefits if he refuses a "bona-fide" offer of reasonable employment without good or reasonable cause. However, to be a "bona fide" offer, it must be within a reasonable distance from the employee's residence.[26]

Here, although Darrell has been offered a similar job in a less stressful atmosphere, it is in another state far away from Michigan. North Carolina is not within a reasonable distance from Darrell's residence in Michigan. Therefore, I would advise Darrell that he can refuse this job offer in NC because it is not reasonable.

26. MCL 418.301(5)(a) and MCL 418.301(9).

PART II MICHIGAN BAR EXAM QUESTIONS

This part of the book includes previous Michigan Bar Exam questions, model answers and some student answers beginning with the February 2001 Michigan bar exam. The material is presented one subject at a time in the order of the five clusters typically used by the Michigan bar examiners (see "Michigan Essay Frequency 'Cluster' Chart" on p. 11). Please remember that the bar examiners are not required to follow these clusters, and sometimes subjects are shifted into different clusters, which is reflected in this chart.

Please also keep in mind that not all questions have student answers and others have more than one sample answer. Also, please pay close attention to the points received for the student answer. Although most samples represent "good" answers, there are some samples that received 7 points (the minimum "passing" score for an essay), and a few that received very low scores to help you better understand the grading process.

To get the most benefit from this part of the book, you should not even start doing practice questions until after you have studied the subject thoroughly. This book is designed to assess your knowledge of the law *after* you have studied it. Therefore, be sure to follow the steps on "How to Use This Book Effectively" on pp. 2-4 as you approach each subject. Also, in order to practice writing outstanding answers according to what the bar exam graders are looking for, be sure to read and follow the instructions in the "Essay Deconstruction" and "How to Build or 'Construct' A Good Essay" on pp. 27-38 before you begin practicing.

CLUSTER ONE

REAL PROPERTY

Questions, Model Answers, and Student Answers

The following section includes prior Michigan Bar Exam questions and model answers for **Real Property**. Many of the questions also include actual student answers with the amount of points that were earned to give you a better idea of what the graders expect. The student answers are immediately following the model answer for each question. Please pay close attention to the points received on each question. Although most samples represent "good" answers (i.e., received 8, 9, or 10 points), there are some samples that received 7 points (the minimum "passing" score for an essay), and a few that received very low scores to help you better understand the grading process and what is expected.

February 2001—Question 2

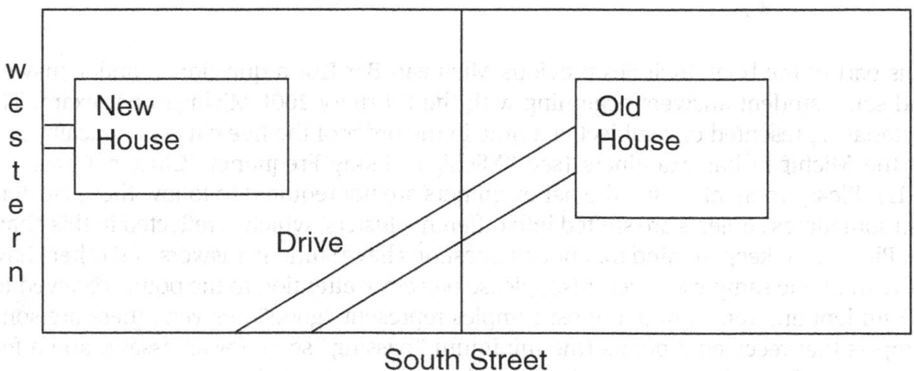

Five years ago, Able owned a tract of land situated north of South Street and east of Western Avenue. He lived in an old house on the site which had access to South Street over a drive. Able divided the tract into two parcels and sold the eastern lot with the old house to Baker. Able gave Baker a general warranty deed. The deed did not grant Baker any right to use the drive which now passed over the western lot retained by Able. Able, however, permitted Baker to use the drive.

About two years after Able sold the eastern lot to Baker, he decided to build a new house on the western lot he had retained. Before building, Able entered into a written contract with Baker in which each promised to the other that they would never permit their respective lots to be used for any purpose other than a single-family dwelling. The contract stated it was binding on the parties' heirs, successors, and assigns, and was promptly recorded in the Recorder of Deeds office. Able then built his new house which had access to Western Avenue over a short driveway.

Five months ago, Baker sold the eastern lot to Cox. Immediately after Cox took possession of the property, he began remodeling the old house to convert it into four apartment units. Able demanded that he stop but Cox refused.

Able has retained you. He wants to stop Cox from using the drive and converting the old house into apartments. Able can prove his new house will decline in value if Cox converts the old house into an apartment building.

What advice will you give Able? Can he stop Cox? Explain.

Model Answer to Question 2

Able probably cannot stop Cox from using the drive. A court would likely hold Cox enjoys an easement implied in law arising from Able's use of the drive before he divided the parcel. Able may, however, be entitled to an injunction which limits the use of the easement to a drive serving a single-family dwelling. As for the enforceability of the contract limiting the use of the lots, a court could enforce the restriction on use as an equitable servitude against Cox. Cox had record notice of the restriction and can be enjoined from violating its terms.

The Easement: The courts will imply the grant of an easement from a preexisting use, sometimes called a quasi-easement, where an owner of land subdivides and sells a portion of the property. The law presumes that the vendee of the subdivided parcel purchased his or her land with the understanding that he or she would be able to continue to use the quasi-easement. The Michigan Supreme Court states the doctrine as follows:

> "Where, during the unity of title, an apparently permanent and obvious servitude is imposed on one part of an estate in favor of another, which at the time of the severance is in use, and is reasonably necessary for the fair enjoyment of the other, then, upon a severance of such ownership, whether by voluntary alienation or by judicial proceedings, there arises by implication of law a grant or reservation of the right to continue such use. In such case, the law implies that with the grant of the one an easement is also granted or reserved, as the case may be, in the other, subjecting it to the burden of all such visible uses and incidents as are reasonably necessary to the enjoyment of the dominant heritage, in substantially the same condition in which it appeared and was used when the grant was made." *Rannels v Marx*, 357 Mich 453, 456 (1959).

In the problem, Able used the drive before he subdivided his land. The drive was reasonably necessary for Baker's use and enjoyment of the eastern lot. The lot had no other access to South Street. Under these circumstances, the courts are likely to imply a grant of an easement from Able to Baker arising from Able's preexisting use of the drive.

As the court made clear in *Rannels, supra*, the holder of an easement implied in law cannot increase the burden of the easement on the servient tenement. The use of the implied easement is limited to that which existed at the time the land was subdivided. "A principle which underlies the use of all easements is that the owner of an easement cannot materially increase the burden of it upon the servient estate or impose thereon a new and additional burden. *Delaney v Pond*, 350 Mich 685, 687 (1957).

Under this principle, a court could limit Baker's use of the easement to that of a drive serving a single-family dwelling. The burden of the easement on Able's land would increase if four apartment owners began using the drive. There would likely be more vehicles using the drive.

In the problem, Able and Baker clearly intended to bind their successors in interest to their mutual promises to restrict the use of their land to single families. The contract they executed and recorded was expressly made binding on their "heirs, successors, and assigns." Moreover, their promise "touched and concerned" the land as that phrase is understood in law. If a promise affects the use, value, or enjoyment of an interest in land, it is generally understood to meet the requirement that it "touch and concern" the land. *Greenspan v Rehberg*, 56 Mich App 310 (1974). Here, the promise was a restriction on use with evidence that it enhanced the value of Able's land. It is also clear that Cox had notice of the restriction. Able and Baker duly recorded their contract and the record imparts constructive notice of the restriction. *Cooke v Taube*, 372 Mich 132, 141 (1963). As a result, the restriction agreed to by Able and Baker would be enforceable against Cox as an equitable servitude. A court should, therefore, enjoin Cox's use of the old house as an apartment building.

Three Student Answers—February 2001

Question 2—Property—10 points

Advice to Able: The facts do not mention whether there is an alternative access to the main road after Able divided his one tract of land. If there is no other way out of the property Able divided and sold to Baker, then Baker will have an *implied easement* or *easement by necessity.* Able sold the house to Baker by general warranty deed which means Baker receives the benefit of all covenants, and easements of habitability which would include the driveway. Able also permitted Baker to use the driveway which would be rights granted under *easement by grant*—Easements by grant will run with land, and therefore, if it does exist, *Cox* will inherit the easement from Baker in perpetuity. If the easement was by necessity, the use will end once the necessity ends, which does not seem to be the case here. Able cannot stop Cox from using the driveway easement.

As to the ability of Able to stop Cox from building 4 apartment units, it appears that Able and Baker entered into an agreement in *writing* to restrict the use of the properties to single-family use. The writing stated it was binding on both parties and their heirs and successors. It was duly recorded, which gave Cox constructive notice of the restriction which will run with the land and bind subsequent land owners, including Cox. Able also has the right under *equitable servitude* to prevent Cox from building the 4 apartments—the *Statute of Frauds* has been satisfied with both the general warranty deed to Baker and with the recorded restrictions by Able and Baker. Able can stop Cox from building the apartments.

Question 2—Property—10 points

The Drive: In Michigan, easements can be granted or formed by prescription, necessity or contract.

Here, when Able split his parcel and sold the eastern lot to Baker, he allowed Baker to continue to use the drive to South Street. This was not done by necessity because Baker could have made a new drive directly to South Street. This was more of an implied agreement that allowed continued use of the driveway. It became a permissive easement.

Restrictions: Once Able built his new home, he and Baker entered into a written contract to restrict the lots to single-family dwellings. His restriction was binding on all heirs and successors. It also was recorded at the Recorder of Deeds Office.

When Baker sold to Cox, the restriction to single-family dwellings would run with the land. Cox would not be able to convert the house into multi-family housing. Also, with the easement for the driveway running from the servient lot, these continue to stay in place absent abandonment, agreement or merger of the dominant and servient lots (owned by one party again). But an easement cannot be expanded and increased usage is not allowed. Apartments would require several more vehicles traveling over the easement.

Therefore, Able can stop Cox from building or remodeling the house into apartments but cannot stop Cox from using the drive for personal use or the amount needed for a single-family dwelling.

Question 2—Property—9 points

Old House: Able and Baker entered into an equitable servitude. To have a valid equitable servitude, the writing must touch and concern the land, there must be intent on the part of the parties to bind successive heirs and assigns, and there must be notice. An equitable servitude is a restriction on one's use of land.

All these elements are met. There was intent on the part of both parties because they mutually entered into a contract. The new house added value to the land so the touch and concern requirement is met. And lastly there was notice. There are 3 kinds of notice—express (tell someone) implied (recording deed) and inquiry (go to the land and see). Cox had notice of the servitude because Able and Baker recorded the contract at the deeds office. Therefore, Able can stop Cox from building the apartment building. I would advise him to seek an injunction immediately. An injunction prevents or makes someone either do something or not do something. The injunction would force Cox to stop building.

The contract also satisfies the statute of frauds because it was in writing.

The Driveway: Able cannot stop Cox from using the driveway. The driveway is an implied easement. An implied easement exists when permission is given to use another's land. An implied easement also goes with the land regardless if it is mentioned in a subsequent deed. Able permitted Baker to use the driveway and as a subsequent owner, Cox also gets this easement because it followed the land. In an easement there are 2 parcels of land, the dominant and servient tracts, and the servient easement is burdened from the easement, which is why the easement passed to Cox—he has the servient estate.

Cox may be able to also argue an easement by necessity if the driveway was his only access to South Street because he would be land-locked.

July 2001—Question 8

The Lessor Realty Company ("Lessor") owned a number of downtown commercial buildings. The storefront in one of the buildings had been vacant for some time when Lessor agreed to lease it to Teresa Tenant ("Tenant"), a jeweler. Lessor agreed to defer the commencement of the lease term to allow Tenant time to remodel the storefront, rent free. In remodeling the space, Tenant installed several expensive, crystal chandeliers. Once Tenant completed the remodeling, Lessor and Tenant entered into a written lease agreement. The agreement established a monthly rental for a term of five years, beginning January 1, 1996, and ending December 31, 2000. The agreement had no special provisions for termination of the lease nor did it mention anything about the improvements Tenant had made.

Tenant opened her business on the first day of the lease term. Her business was successful. In 2000, however, she decided she would move her business to a suburban mall and would not seek to renew her lease with Lessor. Unfortunately, the space in the mall was not ready in the beginning of 2001. As a result, Tenant continued to do business downtown. Tenant remained in possession and paid Lessor rent for January, February, and March 2001. On March 15, Tenant hand delivered a written notice of termination to Lessor that purported to be effective on April 15. By April 15, Tenant had indeed vacated the store. On that date, she returned the keys to the landlord with fifteen days additional rent. When she moved out, Tenant removed the chandeliers.

Lessor has filed suit against Tenant. Lessor seeks rent for the entire year of 2001. Lessor also claims to own the chandeliers and seeks damages in conversion for their removal. Who shall prevail in this suit? Explain.

Model Answer to Question 8

This question raises issues concerning the termination of an estate for years and a tenant's right to remove trade fixtures. In the problem, the lease established an estate for years but the tenant held over. Under Michigan law, a holdover tenancy can be terminated on notice given in advance for the number of days equal to the rental period. There is no requirement, however, that the notice correspond to the beginning and ending date of the rental period. In the problem, Tenant seems to have given sufficient notice. She paid rent monthly and gave thirty days' notice to quit. Trade fixtures are items of personal property used by a tenant in a trade of business that have been affixed to the real estate in such a manner that the law would ordinarily treat them as personal property. Absent evidence that the parties had a contrary intention, a tenant is generally entitled to remove trade fixtures upon termination of a lease.

Termination of the Tenancy: An estate for years, or term of years, is created by lease with a defined term and with no provision for renewal. An estate for years ends on its stated termination date. 2 *Powell on Real Property* §16.03(1) (2000). Thus, in such a tenancy, there is no need for the tenant to give the landlord notice to quit. 2 *Powell on Real Property* §16.03(7)(a) (2000). If the tenant under a term of years holds over the stated term, a tenancy at sufferance or holdover tenancy is created. 2 *Powell on Real Property* §16.6(1) (2000). At common law, a landlord could elect to hold a tenant at sufferance to another term equal to the length of the original lease up to a maximum of one year. Michigan, however, has abrogated the common law by a statute that reads, in part, as follows:

> [A]n estate at will or by sufferance may be terminated by either party by 1 month's notice given to the other party. If the rent reserved in a lease is payable at periods of less than 3 months, the time of . . . notice is sufficient if it is equal to the interval between the time of payment. Notice is not void because it states a date for termination of the tenancy that does correspond to the conclusion or commencement of a rental period. MCL 554.131(1) (supp 2001).

Under this statute, Tenant gave Lessor sufficient notice to quit and would not be liable for rent beyond April 15. At the termination of the original term of the lease, Tenant became a tenant at sufferance. The statute authorizes a lessee to terminate a tenancy at sufferance on one month's notice. Because Tenant paid her rent monthly, the statute does not require her to quit at the end of a rental period. Her notice to Lessor on March 15 would thus be effective April 15. Accordingly she should have no further liability for rent.

Trade Fixtures: In the law of landlord and tenant, the term "trade fixtures" generally refers to items affixed to the real estate by the tenant for use in the tenant's trade or business. While fixtures are generally treated as real property, trade fixtures remain personalty and can generally be removed by a tenant before the expiration of the lease. 8 *Powell on Real Property* §57.06(2) (2000). Like most states, Michigan holds that the intent of the parties is the most important factor in determining whether an item is a trade fixture. *Id. see also, Biallas v March*, 305 Mich 401 (1943).

In the problem, the lease agreement had no provisions regarding fixtures. The facts of the problem give no other indication of the parties' intentions with regard to the chandeliers. Therefore, a court would likely hold Tenant could remove the chandeliers without liability to Lessor. It is unlikely the removal of the fixtures would cause a material injury to the real property. The chandeliers were installed in connection with preparing the space for Tenant's business as the parties had intended.

Two Student Answers—July 2001

Question 8—Real Property—9 points

-Tenancy by Years
 -year to year
-Month to Month tenancy
 -here monthly rental
-Require 30 days notice (given)
-Holdover Tenant - can evict or transfer to new month to month tenancy
 -she paid rent
-Fixtures
 -more or less permanent
 -here - probably permanent

The issues here are can Lessor compel tenant to pay for the entire year of 2001? And whether the chandeliers could be removed or not?

The first issue has to deal with whether this was a tenancy for years, where rent is paid yearly in a lump sum, or whether this was a month-to-month tenancy requiring rent on a month-to-month basis. Here, the terms of the lease agreement state that rent would be paid monthly for a term of five years. Rent was to be paid on a month-to-month basis so this is a month-to-month tenancy. To terminate a month-to-month tenancy, you must supply the lessor with 30 days written notice.

In this case, the tenant became a holdover tenant after the original lease expired in December of 2000 and tenant did not vacate the premises. When this happens, the landlord may either evict the tenant or the landlord/lessor may create a new lease based on the rental payments of the old lease—by method of payment (if there is an increase in rent, the holdover tenant will be subject to the increase). Here there was no rent increase so the tenant became subject to a new month-to-month lease at the current rent level. Tenant paid this rent for the months of January, February, and March 2001 as required by holdover tenants. And, as stated earlier, to break the lease, tenant gave written 30 days notice and vacated within that time. Therefore, the tenant did not violate the lease agreement and Lessor is not subject to a year's worth of rent.

As to the chandeliers, this is an issue of whether they are fixtures. Fixtures must be removed by tenant, if possible, prior to vacating the property. To determine if a fixture can be removed or if it becomes part of the lease property, you must look at the permanency of the fixture. If the fixture is permanent and would cause damage to remove it, it is the property of lessor. If not, then the tenant may remove the fixture. Here, the chandeliers are probably more permanent than an item like a shelf or washer or dryer. Considerable damage might occur removing the chandeliers. While tenant properly removed these items prior to vacating the property, he should not have and Lessor will most likely recover damages (in conversion) for their removal.

Comment: This example shows that credit will be awarded even though an examinee reaches a different conclusion. In this case, credit was given even though the examinee reached a different conclusion on the second issue, because he or she presented a sound argument based on the correct and relevant law.

Question 8—Real Property—8 points

Fixture - personal property permanently fixed to the land.
Intent at time of placement - how much damage to remove.
Tenancy for Years - year to year lease
Tenancy for sufferance - Holdover Tenant

The first issue is whether Tenant owes Lessor the rent for the entire year 2001. The rule is that when a *tenancy for years* ends and the tenant remains on the premises and continues to pay rent it becomes a *tenancy at sufferance* and the terms of the prior agreement would control. Since the *original agreement* called for *monthly payments* and tenant continued to pay monthly and lessor continued to accept, this would be the proper course. Tenant paid until the end of the month as would be required and gave 30 days notice. Lessor will not be able to recover for full year.

The next issue is whether Tenant could remove fixture (see definition).

The rule is that any *trade fixtures* are *always removable* if used in a trade or business. *Damage to property* is the *responsibility* of the *Tenant to repair.*

If these are deemed not trade fixtures then the *intent of the party* and *ease of removal* are factors assessed.

These *chandeliers were decorative but* used in a *business.* Either way due to the *price* the *intent* was probably not to leave and *removing* light fixtures *would not be destructive.* Tenant will not be liable for conversion but only pay to replace light fixture or repair.

July 2001—Question 9

In early April, Samuel and Stella Seller entered into a written contract to sell their farm to Victor Vendee with closing to be held on July 6, 2001. In the contract, Sellers agreed to convey "good and marketable title to our farm lying along the Big Sable River in Mason County, Michigan, consisting of 120 acres, more or less." The contract established the sales price and required Vendee pay an earnest money deposit for $25,000.

Vendee paid the deposit when he and the Sellers signed the contract but he now wants his money returned. A number of problems have arisen. First, Sellers postponed the closing schedule for July 6 to August 3. Second, Vendee discovered a judgment creditor of the Sellers had attached a lien to the farm three years ago. Finally, a surveyor hired by Vendee reported the farm is only 117 acres and that a portion of the farm is, in fact, located in Lake County, which adjoins Mason County.

Can Vendee rescind the contract of sale and recover his earnest money before the closing scheduled for next Friday, August 3, 2001? Why or why not? Be certain to discuss each of the issues raised by Vendee even if you believe one is determinative.

Model Answer to Question 9

Vendee probably cannot rescind and recover his earnest money prior to closing. The contract of sale entered by the parties is enforceable notwithstanding the minor errors in the property description. The delay in closing is not a material breach of the contract for sale which did not make time of the essence. The shortage in the acreage is probably not a material breach either. It appears the vendors were selling their farm as a whole, not a specified number of acres. Finally, while the judgment lien is an encumbrance, the contract to deliver marketable title is not breached until closing.

Enforceability of the Contract of Sale: Contracts of sale of land must conform with the Statute of Frauds. MCL 566.106(1) (Supp 2001). The essential terms of such an agreement must be in writing, signed by the person to be charged. *Zurcher v Herveat*, 238 Mich App 267 (1999). In the problem, the parties, the purchase price and a title standard were included in a signed writing. The writing, however, incorrectly described the property to be conveyed. Part of the tract described is located in an adjacent county and the total acreage stated is 2.5% short of the actual extent of the land measured by one survey. These discrepancies should not prevent the contract from being enforced. The purpose of the land description in a contract is to identify the property meant to be conveyed in the light of all the circumstances surrounding the negotiation of the contract. *Zurcher, supra*, at 294. Here, the contract described the land as the Seller's farm. It located the tract along a river and by using the phrase "more or less" indicated the stated acreage may not be exact. Under these circumstances, a court would likely conclude the contract was enforceable.

Materiality of Closing Date and Shortage of Acreage: Unless the parties to a land sales contract otherwise agree, time is not of the essence in its performance. *Walter v Lieberman*, 214 Mich 428 (1921). In the problem, there is no indication that the parties considered the time of the essence in the date of closing. A specified date for closing does not in itself make time of the essence in a real estate contract. *Range v Davison*, 242 Mich 73 (1928). Under the circumstances stated in the problem, a court would not likely hold a delay of one month to be material. Moreover, the parties may have agreed to the one month's extension and the rescheduled closing is only a week away.

When a contract for the sale of land is by the acre, a shortage can be material and warrant recision. On the other hand, if land is sold in gross, that is by tract or description, a small shortage is generally not deemed material. *Koch v Bird*, 140 NW 919 (Mich 1913). A designation that land is sold by stated acreage "more or less" does not allocate the risk of shortage. The phrase accounts for differences among surveys. The key question generally is whether the parties intended a sale of acreage or a sale in gross. *Detroit Edison Co v Malburg*, 149 F Supp 316, 363-364 (ED Mich 1957) (applying Michigan law).

It appears in the problem that the land was sold in gross. The parties referred to the tract as the Sellers' farm. The purchase price was unitary. The shortage was small, less than 3%, and may have been accounted for by the parties use of the "more or less." The shortage was revealed by a new survey. For these reasons, a court could hold the shortage was immaterial and did not support an action to rescind.

Breach of the Marketable Title Standard: The contract of sale at issue in the problem is marketable title. A judgment lien renders title unmarketable. *See, e.g., Madhaven v Sucher*, 105 Mich App 284 (1981). The duty to deliver a marketable title does not arise, however, until closing. A seller has the opportunity to clear title until the time set for performance. *Chappus v Lucke*, 246 Mich 272 (1929). Thus, in the problem, Sellers' obligation to deliver marketable title has not yet arisen. The contract will not be breached unless Sellers fail to clear the judgment lien by the time of closing which has been extended to August 3.

Two Student Answers—July 2001

Question 9—Real Property—9 points

The delay from rescheduling the closing from July 6 to August 3 is not material. Generally time is not of the essence unless it is specified in the contract. The facts do not indicate this so the change in the closing date is not a reason to rescind the contract.

The judgment lien on the property is a material item. The seller warranties good and marketable title. This is a title free from encumbrances. If the sellers use the proceeds from the sale to release the lien, then good and marketable title free from encumbrances may be obtained. If the sellers do not do this the title will not be free from encumbrances which could cause vendee to rescind the contract and recover his deposit of earnest money.

The property description is not completely accurate. If both parties have a meeting of the minds as to what exactly was included in the sale of the family farm then the description differences are not material. The fact that the farm was 117 acres instead of 120 is not material. Neither is the fact that part of the farm is in another county. The contract may be reformed to make changes from 120 to 117 and add the description adding Lake county as well as Mason county. The best vendee could hope for here is with the reformation of the contract to accurately describe the property, a price reduction could also be negotiated.

Therefore, the only way Vendee could rescind the contract and return his deposit is if the judgment lien on the property is not cleared either by the closing or with the proceeds of the closing. Then a valid title free from encumbrances could not be delivered and the warranty of good and marketable title cannot be delivered.

Question 9—Real Property—8 points

The 1st issue is whether Vendee (V) may rescind the sales K with Seller regarding the postponing of the closing scheduled for Aug 3 (which was set for July 6)? The rule is that unless there is an express "time of the essence clause," which may have been bargained for, the closing dates may be reasonably changed to later dates if not too distant in the future. On our facts, we have less than 1 month of additional time needed for closing. Several months (i.e. over 3 to 4+ would be clearly excessive) but under our facts, Vendee cannot rescind the sales K.

2nd, may Vendee rescind the sales K since it was determined a judgment creditor had a lien on the farm 3 years ago? The general rule is that the Seller may use the purchase sale price (or $25,000 to pay off the judgment lien creditor at the time of closing). Since Seller can still sell the property and use the proceeds of Vendee's 25k to satisfy judgment creditor, Vendee can't rescind the sales K on this prospective COA.

3rd, can Vendee rescind the sales K since the farm is only 117 acres and the farm is, in fact, located in Lake City, adjoining Mason City? The rule is that a buyer, or Vendee here, does not have to purchase land which may be reasonably subject to litigation in the future. However, the buyer is not entitled to perfect title. On our facts, it is arguable that there is not much variation between the initial grant of 120 acres in the contract versus the actual 117 reported by the surveyor. Probably not a good Vendee defense—sales K said sale consisting of "120 acres, *more or less.*" For Vendee's sake I would argue that there is a loss of material portions of land and therefore, the K is revocable. More importantly though, the land appears clearly subject to litigation since the title states the land is solely in Mason City, when in fact a portion is actually located in Lake City. Question: how much is located on the adjoining property? The effects of problems & litigation are unclear on the facts but litigation appears likely due to the contract sales description & variance between the actual grant. On this basis, & on this 3rd basis above, I would allow Vendee to rescind the land sales K & recover his earnest $ before the closing schedule for Aug 3, 2001.

I might add that if seller could remedy the variance in land grant (i.e. 120 v 117) & the litigation issue were taken care of prior to closing for the 3rd of Aug, the seller might be entitled to closing & be able to seek damages from Vendee, the prospective buyer. However, on the facts, it appears unlikely that the seller would be able to remedy the potential litigation issues discussed. Recission granted in Vendee's favor.

In this analysis, I would like to note importantly that this is a valid sales K for the purchase of land. This requires a *written* K, with adequate description of land to be conveyed, and a sales price is listed. Arguably, the terms of the sales agreement are not adequate (i.e. no financing requirement, total price, monthly installments) but as the K appears, it is valid as a sales K for land.

Unfortunately, for Seller's sake, the potential for future litigation is a reasonable assumption by buyer, Vendee, and the sales K is rescindable at Vendee's election.

February 2002—Question 4

Two years ago, Alex Able purchased a Victorian house near Grand Traverse Bay. Able planned to renovate and remodel the house as a bed and breakfast or inn. Able paid roughly half the purchase price of the house in cash from his own funds. He obtained the balance with the proceeds of a loan from his Aunt Betty Baxter. Able gave Baxter a mortgage on the house to secure the loan. Because Baxter expected to be repaid soon, she did not immediately record her mortgage. Able, however, immediately recorded the deed he obtained to the house at closing.

Able then began renovating the house. In connection with the renovation, he purchased three Austrian crystal chandeliers that illuminated the main entrance hall, dining room, and living room. Able also purchased four large Persian rugs which were laid in all the main public rooms of the house. The renovation of the house was completed with the wiring of the chandeliers and the laying of the rugs.

Shortly thereafter, an innkeeper, Donna Douglas, approached Able and asked whether he would be willing to sell the property. She admired the renovation and commented to Able that she was particularly taken with the chandeliers. Prior to making an offer, Douglas had a title search conducted which was dated March 15, 2001, disclosing Able as the titleholder and no mortgages. On March 30, Douglas made Able an offer on the house which Able agreed he would consider. Able then told his Aunt Betty to immediately record her mortgage. She did so. Neither Able nor Baxter informed Douglas of the mortgage.

After protracted negotiations, and on July 15, 2001, Able and Douglas entered into a standard contract for sale of real estate. Douglas tendered the agreed purchase price at closing and immediately recorded the deed to the property she received. When Douglas took possession of the property, however, she discovered the chandeliers and rugs had been removed. A week later she was served with notice of foreclosure action brought by Betty Baxter. Baxter's mortgage loan was in default.

Does Douglas have any defense to Baxter's foreclosure action? Explain. Can she recover the chandeliers and rugs from Able? Why or why not?

Model Answer to Question 4

Baxter will claim the protection of Michigan's recording act in her foreclosure action. Baxter's mortgage was recorded before Douglas acquired an interest in the property.

The law of fixtures governs Douglas' claim to the chandeliers and rugs. She would have a strong claim that the chandeliers were fixtures. They were firmly attached to the real property and her conversation with Able regarding the chandeliers would seem to indicate the parties intended to treat the items as fixtures. Douglas has a much weaker claim to the rugs as fixtures. They were probably not so firmly attached to the real property that the law would treat them as a part thereof.

The Foreclosure Action: Baxter should claim the protection of Michigan's recording act in the foreclosure action. Michigan has a "race-notice" recording statute that reads as follows:

> Every conveyance of real estate within the state hereafter made, which shall not be recorded as provided in this chapter, shall be void as against any subsequent purchaser in good faith and for a valuable consideration, of the same real estate or any portion thereof, whose conveyance shall be first duly recorded. MCL 565.29.

Under the statute, a good faith purchaser of real property will take free of any prior interest in the property unknown to the purchaser if the purchaser records before the holder of the prior interest records. In the problem, Baxter's mortgage was recorded before Douglas's deed. Therefore, Douglas had notice of the mortgage lien.

The Chandeliers: Douglas has a strong claim to the chandeliers under Michigan's law of fixtures.

A fixture is an item of personal property that has become so firmly affixed to real estate that the law treats it as real property. Michigan applies the three-part test used by most jurisdictions in order to determine whether goods have been fixtures. First, the Michigan courts examine the degree to which the goods have been annexed to the realty. Second, they look to the extent to which they have become adapted to the use of the real estate. Finally, they consider whether the parties intended to make the goods an accession to the real property. *E.g., Wayne County v Britton Trust*, 454 Mich 608, 610 (1997).

Applying the three-part test to the chandeliers, Douglas should argue that the chandeliers were affixed to the ceiling and connected to the electrical system of the house. The chandeliers were also adapted to the use of the real property. They illuminated major rooms of the house and undoubtedly provided an aura of elegance to the inn. Finally, Douglas' conversation with Able regarding the chandeliers would give her some evidence of an intention that the chandeliers would pass with the title to the real property.

If an item is a fixture, title to it passes with the conveyance of the real estate unless the vendor has reserved title to the item in the contract for sale. *E.g., Atlantic Die Casting Company v Whiting Tubular Products, Inc,* 337 Mich 414, 423-424 (1953). Therefore, Douglas should be able to claim ownership of the chandeliers passed with title to the house.

The Rugs: The Persian rugs present a considerably more difficult case for Douglas. A court is unlikely to hold they were fixtures under the three-part test. The rugs probably were not physically attached or annexed to the property in any permanent fashion. This was not wall-to-wall carpeting permanently tacked to the floor. Presumably, other carpet or floor covering would suit the use of the real property as an inn and there is no evidence the parties intended title to the rugs to pass with the house. Thus, absent other facts, such as evidence that the rugs were specially woven to conform to the shape of the rooms, Douglas would not have a particularly compelling case for recovery of the Persian carpets.

Student Answer—February 2002

Question 4—Real Property/Personal Property—8 points

A. Does Douglas have defense to Baxter's foreclosure action?

Yes. A bona fide purchaser who pays value in consideration for property w/out notice of a previous recording who then records after purchase has protection against other claims. Here, Douglas bought a house from Able. Douglas did a title search which only showed Able to be on the mortgage. Able did not inform Douglas that Baxter was on the mortgage but had not recorded it yet. Once Douglas purchased the house from Able, she recorded it immediately. A week later she was served w/ notice of foreclosure action brought by Baxter b/c her loan was in default. Under these facts, it is not Douglas's problem that Baxter's loan is in default. Her claim should be with Able. Able received the money from Douglas to pay the loan to Baxter. In addition, Douglas did not know of the agreement between Able and Baxter.

B. Can Douglas recover the chandeliers and rugs from Able?

1. Douglas should recover the 3 chandeliers.
   When a fixture becomes so annexed to a structure, it becomes part of the realty. Here, Able bought the chandeliers as part of the renovation & the renovation was not complete until the chandeliers were hung and wired. Chandeliers, especially ones of this size/type can be considered part of the realty by a perspective buyer. Especially when Douglas commented on them and considered them to be part of the style/renovation of the Inn. Removing them would probably cause damage to the house itself and a decrease in the value of the Inn as a whole.
2. Douglas should not recover the 4 rugs.
   Rugs are removable w/ ease and as such cannot be considered part of the realty. Removing the rugs would not affect the physical condition of the home.

February 2002—Question 6

Forty years ago, the Diamond Development Corporation ("Diamond") purchased thirty-five acres of farmland located on the outskirts of a metropolitan suburb. The farmland lay in between two county roads, Orchard Lane and County Road 109. Diamond dedicated part of the land for public streets and utility easements. It then had the county zoning authority rezone the site for residential rather than agricultural purposes. Diamond laid out the streets and subdivided the rest of the property into forty building lots. Diamond then offered these lots for sale through advertisements in the metropolitan newspaper that read:

> **Lots for Sale** - Prime residential lots suitable for building. Located minutes from the city in the area's most desirable suburb. Call Diamond Development Corp. today. [Phone Number Omitted]

Over the next eighteen months, Diamond sold 34 of the 40 lots. The deeds to these lots contained clauses in which the purchasers agreed to restrict their use of the lots to single-family dwellings. The deeds forbid any commercial use of the lots. All these restrictions were expressly made binding on the purchasers' "heirs, successors and assigns." None of the 34 deeds, however, restricted the property retained by Diamond. The company retained title to the six lots that fronted on Orchard Lane.

In the years that followed, the area around the Diamond subdivision grew considerably. The county widened Orchard Lane. It is now a major commercial road. A shopping mall opened on the property directly across Orchard Lane from the six lots in the subdivision Diamond had retained. Two years ago, the county rezoned the six lots. They are now zoned for commercial as well as residential uses. Shortly after the zoning change, Diamond sold all six lots to Vendee Shopping Center Company ("Vendee").

Vendee has recently announced plans to build a shopping center on the six lots. A number of homeowners who purchased lots in the subdivision over the years want to stop Vendee from building the center. The subdivision is still a residential neighborhood but three homeowners do use their properties for business purposes. One owner operates a day care center in her house. Two others have home offices. One is a certified public accountant and the other is an architect.

May the homeowners enjoin Vendee from building the shopping center? Explain.

Model Answer to Question 6

The homeowners in the subdivision will probably be able to enjoin Diamond from building the shopping center. The deeds to the lots sold to the homeowners or their predecessors did not restrict the six lots retained by Diamond Development Corporation ("Diamond"). A court, however, may imply such a restriction based upon the common development scheme Diamond established for the property. Such an implied servitude is called a "reciprocal negative easement" in Michigan law. It is binding on subsequent purchasers, like Vendee, if the residential character of the neighborhood is apparent.

Generally, the courts will not refuse to enforce subdivision restrictions that still serve their original purpose even though the area around the subdivision has changed, as this one did by becoming more commercial in character. Moreover, the isolated violations of the restriction mentioned in the problem, i.e., the day care center and home offices, are probably not substantial or pervasive enough to warrant a finding of waiver or abandonment of the restrictions.

Implied Reciprocal Servitudes: In *Sanborn v McLean*, 233 Mich 227 (1925), the Michigan Supreme Court held that a developer who sold lots in a subdivision restricted to residential uses impliedly restricted the land the developer retained. The court held an injunction should issue to enforce the restriction on the retained land if the plaintiff proved the developers had established a common development scheme for the lots sold and the lots retained:

> If the owner of two or more lots . . . (in a subdivision subject to a common plan) sells one with restrictions of benefit to the land retained, the servitude becomes mutual, and during the period of restraint, the owner of the lot or lots retained can do nothing forbidden to the owner of the lot sold. For want of a better descriptive term this is styled a reciprocal negative easement.
>
> *Id.*, 223 Mich at 229.

The court implied the reciprocal negative easement to protect the buyers in the subdivision. The common development plan established by the developer led the buyers to believe they were acquiring lots in a residential subdivision, and their expectation and reliance interests should be protected by the courts.

On the facts of the problem there is ample evidence that Diamond had established a common development scheme for all of the forty lots. They were laid out at the same time. They are connected by streets planned by Diamond. The lots were zoned, on Diamond's initiative, as residential properties. Diamond clearly marketed them as such.

In *Sanborn*, the court ruled that the reciprocal negative easement implied on the lots retained by the developer would be binding on subsequent purchasers to the same extent that the express restrictions on the lots sold were binding on assignees. *Id.*, 233 Mich at 232-33. The key question is whether the character of the development was apparent upon an inspection of the land. If the overall development is residential, a purchaser of an unrestricted lot in a subdivision can be charged with inquiry notice of the implied reciprocal restriction. *Id.*

Thus, if Vendee could observe the residential character of the subdivision upon a visual inspection of the property, the implied restriction will be binding on Vendee even though no document in the chain of title to the six lots purchased showed the restrictions. A title examination by Vendee would have revealed the six lots were once held in common with the restricted lots in the subdivision.

Changed Conditions: The Michigan courts recognize that conditions may change to such an extent that it would no longer be equitable to enforce subdivision restrictions on the use of land. However, substantial growth and zoning changes are insufficient standing alone to warrant the denial of injunctive relief under the changed conditions doctrine. The test is whether the essential purpose of the restrictions can no longer be served given the nature of the changed conditions. *See, e.g., Cooper v Kovan*, 349 Mich 520 (1957).

In the problem, the residential restrictions would seem to still serve their original purpose. They keep commercial development and traffic away from the homes in the subdivision. If Vendee's proposed development on the periphery of the subdivision goes forward, the noise, traffic, and other attendant effects will be brought that much closer to the homeowners.

Waiver or abandonment: Similarly, under Michigan law, isolated and insubstantial violations of residential restrictions do not bar enforcement of the restrictions when a more serious violation would occur. The courts are generally unwilling to find a waiver or abandonment of the restrictions unless violations have become so pervasive as to subvert the original scheme. *See, e.g., Jeffrey v Lathrup*, 363 Mich 15 (1961).

The existing violations mentioned in the problem should not prevent a court from enjoining Vendee's development of a shopping center. They are relatively isolated; three violations among 34 homes. Moreover, none of the existing violations destroy the residential character of the subdivision. Home offices and day care centers do not involve the traffic, noise and other effects that would fundamentally change the residential character of the subdivision if Vendee's construction of the shopping center proceeds.

Student Answer—February 2002

Question 6—Real Property—7 points

The homeowners can enjoin the building of the shopping center by enforcing the restrictive covenants in the deeds. The homeowners will need to show that when the suburb was created there was a common plan or scheme that intended for the neighborhood to be restricted to only residential use.

In this situation Diamond set up residential lots to be sold for residential uses. The facts show that all the other deeds have restrictive covenants, but do not tell us why the deeds that Diamond kept don't. It would be easier to show a common plan or scheme with these facts because all the property was acquired at once, and almost 90% of the neighborhood is restricted to residential use.

The intent of the developer was to restrict everyone in the suburb from running a business like a shopping mall in the suburb. The fact that several people run home businesses does not affect the outcome of enjoining the building of the shopping center. These small businesses do not add traffic, noise or other things that the restrictive covenants were designed to protect from. A shopping mall in this neighborhood would be outside of the common plan or scheme and therefore will be enjoined from building.

July 2002—Question 5

Acme Development Corporation ("Acme") purchased a large tract of land located next to a family farm owned by the Browns. Acme planned to subdivide the tract into building lots. By a written grant, signed by the Browns in 1978, Acme obtained the right to lay underground utility lines across the Browns' farm, which would provide "electricity, natural gas, and telephone service" to the planned development. Pursuant to the grant, Acme buried a gas line and underground cables across the Browns' farm in 1978. Acme, however, did not immediately record its written grant.

High interest rates delayed Acme's development of the planned subdivision until 1983. At that time, Acme recorded its grant, built and sold dozens of lots on the tract. In the meantime, however, the Browns had sold their farm to the Clarks in 1980. The Browns told the Clarks about Acme's utility lines. The general warranty deed from the Browns to the Clarks, however, made no mention of Acme's rights. The Clarks lived upon and operated the farm until 1998. At that time, they sold the farm to its current owner, Donna Davis, by means of a quit claim deed. That deed did not state anything of Acme's rights either, and Davis was unaware of the utility lines. The Clarks had forgotten what the Browns had told them about Acme's utility lines.

Last month, Davis received a letter from Acme informing her that Acme planned to lay a new, subterranean, fiber optic cable along the underground cables that crossed her land. The cable would provide high-speed data services to the homeowners in the subdivision. When Davis protested, Acme claimed it had the right to lay the new cable both by express grant and by prescription.

Davis has retained you. Please address the following questions:

1. **Does Davis have grounds to contest Acme's claim? Why or why not? Be certain to discuss all of the arguments you can make on Davis' behalf even if you think one or more are determinative.**
2. **Can Davis compel the Browns or the Clarks to defend her title if Acme's claim is lawful? Why or why not?**

Model Answer to Question 5

With regard to the first question raised in this problem, Davis has several promising defenses to Acme's claim of an easement to lay a fiber optic cable across her farm. First, Davis can claim the protection of the recording act. Second, Davis can contest Acme's claim that it acquired the easement by prescription by pointing out that Acme entered the farm with the permission of the Browns. Its entry was therefore not "hostile" or "adverse." Moreover, Davis can claim that because the cable and gas lines were buried, Acme's use of the easement was not "open and notorious" enough to ripen into an easement by prescription. As for the second question raised, Davis has a good claim against the Browns to defend her title as the Browns made a covenant of general warranty. The Clarks did not, however, and Davis would not likely have a claim against them on their quit claim deed.

The Utility Easement: Acme claims a right to lay the fiber optic cable on the basis of its acquisition of an easement through an express grant of the Browns. Davis purchased her farm with recorded notice that Acme had obtained the right to lay underground utility lines for "electricity, natural gas, and telephone service" to the planned development. Acme is impermissibly seeking to expand its easement.

Acme claims to have the right to lay a telephone cable by grant or prescription. Such a right arguably does not include the right to lay a fiber optic line for high speed data services. Generally, the holder of an easement may not increase the burden of the easement on the servient estate by expanding the scope of the easement. 14 Mich L & Practice 2d, Easements 31 (Transition Supp 2001). The courts have, however, permitted the holder of an easement to take advantage of technological advances without finding a new use to be a surcharge. *See, e.g., Glenn v Poole*, 423 NE2d 1030, 1033 (Mass App Ct 1981) ("The progression from . . . ox teams . . . to trucks is a normal development); *Henley v Continental Cablevision*, 692 SW2d 825 (MO Ct App 1985) (easement granted for electric, telephone, and telegraph service encompasses cable television).

Acme also claims the easement by prescription. Although the company has used the subterranean easement for more than twenty years, it cannot establish several of the elements Michigan courts require in order to establish an easement by prescription. Like most states, Michigan requires that a use of another's land must be "adverse" and "open" before it can ripen into a prescriptive easement. See generally,

14 Mich L & Practice 2d, Easements 11 and 12 (Transition Supp 2001). Here, Acme entered with permission of the owners, the Browns, and as such its entry would not be adverse. *Hopkins v Parker*, 296 Mich 375, 379 (1941). Moreover, because Acme buried its utility lines that crossed the farm, Acme's use would not be "plainly visible" upon an inspection of the property and thus not open or notorious enough to sustain a claim by prescription. *See Rose v Fuller*, 21 Mich App 172, 175 (1970).

The Title Covenants: Under Michigan law, as in most states, a general warranty deed includes a future covenant that the grantor will warrant and defend the grantee's title. Mich Comp Laws 565.151 (2001). This covenant runs with the land to remote grantees. It is breached if the warrantor refuses to defend the title from lawful claims. *See Wolfenden v Burke*, 69 Mich App 394 (1976); 10 Mich L & Practice 2d, Covenants 54 (2001). The grantor of a quit claim deed, however, covenants nothing.

In the problem, the Browns gave a general warranty deed and would breach their covenant to defend title if Acme's claim was lawful. The Clarks' quit claim deed would not warrant a defense against Acme's claim.

Student Answer—July 2002

Question 5—Real Property—7 points

The Issues

Can Acme prevail by either the express grant or by adverse possession? Does Donna have a valid right that will prevail?

Acme's Side: Acme will argue it should have a prescription easement (adverse possession) since its right to use the land for the utility lines was open (the original owner knew of it), exclusive, and continuous. Even without recording before the Browns sold to Clark, they have a good argument for a prescription easement. And by the time Donna purchased, she could have checked the record. Acme will also argue express grant, even though not recorded until 1983. It was clearly their right to lay utility lines, and a later purchaser was at least on inquiry notice that the lines were laid by the above-ground utility lines about them.

Donna's Side: Donna will argue that even though she only received a quit claim deed (and consequently only received the rights of the predecessor) she was a good faith purchaser, protected under the recording statute, as well as the Shelter Rule, i.e., she should get the same rights as the Clarks, from whom she purchased. And the Clarks were good-faith purchasers (they gave value, without notice of any problems) without notice of any record of the express grant.

Conclusion: Donna has a good argument that she was a good-faith purchaser who bought from another good-faith purchaser and should have the benefit of the Shelter Rule also. And she had no notice of the easement by Acme. However, even though Acme did not properly record until after the Browns sold to the Clarks. Yet the Browns told the Clarks about the lines and the lines were quite obviously there, so arguably even subsequent purchasers had notice. And by prescription, Acme can claim an easement by fulfilling the requirements for adverse possession. So Acme should prevail.

Davis cannot compel either former owners to defend her title, since she received a quit claim deed, which only transfers the rights of the previous owner. Even though the previous owner did receive a general warranty deed they themselves had notice (at least orally) of the utility easement. So here again, Donna probably cannot prevail.

February 2003—Question 11

Twenty years ago, Abigail Adams purchased a bungalow in a subdivision located next door to her best friend. At that time, Adams and her friend planted a hedge and installed a garden gate between their two lots. The hedge and gate did not lie, however, on the true boundary line between their two lots. Instead, the hedge encroached on Adams' lot by several feet. Shortly after the friends planted the hedge, Adams' neighbor discovered their mistake. She offered to pull up the hedge and replant it on the true boundary line, but Adams would not hear of it. She told her friend that the hedge was "fine where it was" and the two friends always treated the hedge line as the boundary between their lots.

Two years ago, Adams sold her lot to Bill Baxter by general warranty deed. The property description in the deed referred to the lot number noted on the recorded plat of the subdivision. The subdivision plat, of course, did not mark the boundary of the lot at the hedge line, but rather, at the line originally surveyed when the lots were laid out.

Soon thereafter, Baxter's employer, Corporation Finance Company ("Corporation") required him to relocate. To assist him in making the move, Corporation agreed to buy the lot from Baxter. The parties used a form contract for sale of real estate that included a promise that Baxter would deliver "marketable title" to the lot. The contract of sale also described the property by reference to the recorded plat. At closing on the property, Corporation accepted a quitclaim deed from Baxter as it usually did when it purchased property from its employees as part of a relocation. Soon thereafter, however, Baxter quit his job to join a competitor of Corporation, much to the dismay of his former employer.

Corporation tried to sell the bungalow, but found the house was too small for the current real estate market. It also discovered the house could not be enlarged under a local zoning ordinance because the lot was too narrow when measured by the hedge line. If the lot spanned to the original survey line as shown in the subdivision plat, however, Corporation could enlarge the house.

You have been retained by Corporation. Please address the following questions raised by your client:

1. **In a quiet title action, could Corporation obtain a ruling that it held title to the land between the hedge line and the original survey line as shown in the subdivision plat? Why or why not?**
2. **If Corporation would lose such a quiet title action, would it have a cause of action against Baxter for the misdescription of the property in the contract of sale? Discuss.**
3. **Again, assuming Corporation lost a quiet title action, would it have a cause of action against Adams? Discuss.**

Model Answer to Question 11

(1) Corporation is unlikely to succeed in an action to quiet title to the disputed boundary of the lot. Under the doctrine of acquiescence, a court would likely quiet title at the hedge line rather than the survey line. (2) A suit against Baxter under his promise to deliver marketable title would be subject to the defense of merger by deed. By accepting a quitclaim deed, Corporation may have lost any right to sue on promises with regard to title quality made in the contract of sale. (3) Corporation may have a cause of action against Adams, however. The covenant of general warranty contained

in her deed is a future covenant that runs to remote grantees. The covenant is breached if a grantee sustains a loss resulting from an assertion of superior title.

Quiet Title Action: Under Michigan Law, if adjoining property owners acquiesce to a boundary line for more than 15 years, the courts will treat that line as the legal boundary between the owners' lots. Unlike a claim based upon adverse possession, the doctrine of acquiescence does not require a showing that the possession of the land in dispute was "hostile" or without permission. *Killips v Mannisto*, 24 Mich App 256, 260 (2001); *Walters v Snyder*, 239 Mich App 453, 456 (2000).

In the problem, Adams helped plant the hedge that marked the boundary of the lots. She also permitted her neighbor to occupy the land between the hedge line and the survey line. Her neighbor's possession of this land was thus not hostile under the law of adverse possession because the neighbor occupied the strip of land with Adams' permission. Under the doctrine of acquiescence, however, Adams' grant of permission would be irrelevant. The doctrine of acquiescence would serve to quiet title at the hedge line. The two neighbors acquiesced in that line as the boundary between their lots for more than fifteen years. Under Michigan law, the courts would therefore treat the hedge as the legal boundary between the lots.

Action on the Contract of Sale: Ordinarily, a land vendor breaches a promise to deliver marketable title if the vendor cannot deliver a title reasonably free from doubt to the land described in the contract. *See, e.g., Madhaven v Sucher*, 105 Mich App 284, 288 (1981). A quitclaim deed, on the other hand, makes no promise with regard to title quality. It simply conveys whatever title the vendor had at the time it is tendered. 13 Mich L & Prac Encyclopedia, 2d Ed (Deeds) § 152 (2002). Generally, all promises in a contract to sell land which relate to title quality are held to merge into the deed that is accepted at closing on the sale. *Crane v Smith*, 243 Mich 447, 450 (1928). Thus, under the doctrine of merger by deed, a vendee who accepts a quitclaim deed at closing loses any right to sue on a promise to deliver marketable title set forth in the contract for sale.

In the problem, Baxter delivered a quitclaim deed to Corporation at closing which Corporation accepted. Baxter will undoubtedly claim that any suit on his promise to deliver marketable title merged into that deed and is now barred.

Action on the Warranty Deed: The covenant of general warranty in a deed warrants that the title conveyed is not subject to any lawful claim of superior title. *McCausey v Oliver*, 253 Mich App 703 (2002); *see also Simons v Diamond Match Company*, 159 Mich 241 (1909); MCL 565.151. The covenant of general warranty, like the related covenant of quiet enjoyment, is a future covenant, meaning it is breached at the time a paramount title is established. "[T]he covenant is prospective in character, and, until breach occurs, passes with the estate by descent or purchase." *Simons v Diamond Match Company, supra*, 248-249. In other words, the covenant runs with the land to benefit remote grantees of the warrantor. William B. Stoebuck & Dale A. Whitman, *The Law of Property*, § 11.13 p 911 (3rd ed 2000).

By giving Baxter a general warranty deed, Adams warranted that there were no lawful claims superior to the title she conveyed. This warranty would be breached if a quiet title action established that Adams' neighbor had superior title to the land described in the deed—the strip between the hedge line and the surveyed line marked on the plat of the subdivision. Adams' warranty would run to remote grantees, like Corporation. Thus, the covenant would be grounds for a suit by Corporation against Adams. Corporation should give Adams notice of the quiet title action to give her an opportunity to maintain the title she warranted. *See* 10 Mich L & Prac Encyclopedia, 2d Ed (Covenants) § 54 (2002).

Student Answer—February 2003
Question 11—Real Property—8 points

(1) This is a real property issue. This action would involve a dispute to whether "Corporation's" title is defective and in Breach of the Warranty to Deliver good and marketable title. A property owner may grant an easement or may determine with an adjacent property owner the rights to the property between themselves, and may by contract establish a boundary line to their properties by conduct, express or implied, oral or written and waive any future right to that part of the property. Here, Adams and Neighbor agreed after discovering a mistake as to the boundary that the hedge was good where it was placed.

Adam sold to Baxter by general warranty deed. The facts indicate that Adams did not disclose the boundary line change, but Baxter was on notice as to the true line because he had the plat description cited in his deed. Baxter accepted the property "as is" because he did not object to the defect in the title. Corporation accepts only what rights Baxter had at time of sale, because the sale was done by "quitclaim deed."

(2) No. The quitclaim deed does not have a description of the property as listed in the property records. However, a contract was signed with reference to the recorded plat which may give "Corporation" an action for "breach of contract."

(3) Corporation may have an action against Adams for breach of general warranty for the right to use of the land. However, Corporation cannot bring any other actions because they would have been extinguished when Corporation purchased the property.

July 2003—Question 8

Angela Antico collected and sold antiques. She also refinished furniture. On January 1, 2001, she took possession of a barn near Monroe, Michigan, under the terms of a written lease agreement. The owner of the barn, Lester Lessor, leased the structure and the surrounding land to Antico "for a term of one year, ending December 31, 2001, in return for rent of $200 per month due the first of each month."

Antico opened an antique store and furniture refinishing business in the barn. She remained in possession for an additional year past the term specified in the lease even though she and Lessor never discussed a renewal of her term. Antico continued to pay the monthly rent but her business never did particularly well. As a result, she notified Lessor on December 31, 2002, that she would be vacating the barn on January 31, 2003. When Lessor received Antico's notice, he told her that if she remained in possession past January 1, 2003, he would hold her to another year of the lease.

Antico ignored him. Instead, during January 2003, Antico sold everything she had in stock at the barn. Unfortunately, she also sold several items that did not belong to her. Oliver Owner left an antique desk with Antico and asked her to refinish the piece in December 2002. Antico instead sold the desk to one of her retail customers, Betty Buyer, in January 2003. Owner also left a sofa with Antico to be reupholstered. Antico sold the sofa to Second Hand City, Inc. along with all of her remaining inventory on January 30, 2003. Second Hand City carted the sofa away, along with the other remaining stock, in a moving van on January 31, 2003.

Lester Lessor found the barn vacant on February 1, 2003. He tried to re-let the premises but has been unable to find another tenant. Consequently, Lessor sued

Antico earlier this month seeking $1,200 representing the six months' rent due under the lease from January 1, 2003 to June 30, 2003. Meanwhile, Oliver Owner has sued Buyer and Second Hand City seeking to recover his desk and sofa.

Discuss the issues raised and the probable outcome of the suits filed by Lessor and Owner.

Model Answer to Question 8

Lessor will not be able to recover six months' rent from Antico. When the term of the original lease expired, Antico became a tenant from month to month. Her notice to quit was sufficient to terminate that tenancy. Lessor cannot recover any rent beyond that due from January 2003. Owner will probably be unable to recover the desk sold to Buyer, who would appear to have the rights of a buyer in the ordinary course of business. Second Hand City, on the other hand, would not have those rights as a buyer in bulk. Owner therefore should be able to recover his sofa.

Lessor's Suit for Rent: The original lease between Lessor and Antico created a term of years. The lease specified an ending date for the term with no provision for renewal. 20 Mich L & Prac 2d, Landlord and Tenant, § 51 (2003). When Antico remained in possession, without Lessor's objection, after her term expired, the parties did not renew their lease. Instead, under Michigan law, a new lease arose. Because the rent under the original lease was payable monthly, a tenancy from month to month commenced. Such a tenancy can be terminated on one month's notice. *Cox v McGregor*, 330 Mich 260 (1951); *Marks v Corliss' Estate*, 256 Mich 460 (1932); *see also* MCLA 554.134 (2003) (providing the same result for a holdover tenant). Thus, on December 31, 2002, Antico gave Lessor sufficient notice to terminate her lease at the end of January 2003. She would therefore be liable for rent due for the month but not for any longer period.

Oliver's Suit for Recover of the Desk and Sofa: When Owner left his desk and sofa with Antico a bailment was created with Owner as the bailor and Antico as the bailee. 4 Mich L & Prac 2d, Bailment, § 1 (2003) (defining a bailment as the "delivery of goods, without the passing of title, whereby the goods are to be returned when the purpose of the deliver has been fulfilled"). At common law, a bailee did not have title to bailed goods and could not convey title to a third person. *Ball-Barnhart-Putnum Co v Lane*, 135 Mich 275 (1903); see generally, 4 Mich L & Prac 2d, Bailment § 13 (2003).

The Uniform Commercial Code ("UCC"), however, created an exception to that rule. Under § 2403(2) of the UCC, a person who entrusts goods to a merchant who deals in goods of that kind empowers the merchant to transfer all the entrusters' rights to a buyer in the ordinary course of business. MCL 440.2403(2) (2003). A person who buys at retail from such a merchant will generally be held to be a buyer in the ordinary course if the person purchases the goods in good faith and without notice that the sale contravenes another's rights. MCL 440.1201(9) (2003) (defining the term "buyer in the ordinary course"). A person who buys in bulk, however, does not have the rights of a buyer in the ordinary course. *Id.*

Applying these principles to the problem, it would appear that Buyer is a buyer in the ordinary course. Antico sold used furniture like the desk. Buyer purchased the item in good faith at retail. She had no notice of Owner's right to the desk. As a buyer in the ordinary course under the UCC, Buyer would take the desk free of Owner's contrary claim of ownership. Second Hand City, however, purchased the sofa as part of a bulk sale. Moreover, the sale of all of Antico's remaining inventory was not an ordinary course transaction. As such, Second Hand City would not enjoy buyer in the ordinary course rights. The common rule would thus still govern Owner's claim to recover his sofa from Second Hand City. As a bailee, Antico did not have any title to convey to Second Hand City. Accordingly, Owner should be able to recover the sofa.

Two Student Answers—July 2003

Question 8—Real/Personal Property—10 points

Lessor suit for rent from Jan 1st to June 30th will probably be denied in part. He will be able to get the rent for January as the defendant used the premises until January 31st. So she is liable for January's rent. But she is a holdover lessee so she has to give a 30 day notice of when she will leave, and is liable for rent while staying there and can be treated as a tenancy by sufferance, so she could be treated as a trespasser. She notified him on December 31st that she would move out on January 31st, which is 30 days notice. He told her that she would be liable for a year's rent and hold her to another years leave if she didn't move out on or by January 1st. He could have treated her as a trespasser and had her stuff removed and take back the premises but chose not to. Defendant didn't agree to the new lease, so she is liable for January's rent and that's it with regards to lessor's suit.

Owner's suit against buyer and Second Hand City deals with two different types of purchasers. Buyer is an ordinary customer where Second Hand is in the business of selling. The buyer if she is a good-faith purchaser, then she keeps the desk, & owner will have to go after Antico for the value of the desk. But since Second Hand is in the business of selling he doesn't have the good faith purchaser defense so he must give back the sofa & go after Antico for the $ he paid for the sofa. So lessor can probably recover Jan. rent only & owner can probably get the sofa back.

Question 8—Real/Personal Property—7 points

In regards to the legal relationship between Antico and lessor, this is a commercial landlord-tenant relationship. After the first lease expired, tenant (Antico) was on a 30-day leave with either party able to cancel their contract with a 30-day notice. Antico had a right to leave the lease on January 31st, 2003, because she had given Lessor 30-days notice that she intended to do so. Lessor's attempt to hold her to an additional year lease upon her notice of termination will not be valid under the Statute of Frauds, a lease for a year or more must be in writing. Here there was not. However, Lessor will be able to sue for the $200—not paid during Antico's stay on the premises for the month of January 2003.

In regards to owner suing buyer & Second Hand City, owner will be successful in the tort of conversion. Though owner probably will not recover the desk & sofa, owner will be successful in receiving the fair market value of each at the time of the conversion.

July 2003—Question 9

You represent Beverly Byer. Ms. Byer is a real estate developer. At a wedding reception recently, she persuades Stephen Sellar to sell her his Detroit townhouse for a very attractive price. Sellar's wife had died a short time ago and he was contemplating moving. Byer urged him to undertake the move and she proposed a price for the townhouse. Sellar agreed to the price and Byer pulled a short memo pad from her purse. She wrote the following on a page of the pad: "Terms of Sale—1313 Collingwood Ave.—$150,000—Byer to pay all closing costs." Byer then handed the pad to Sellar and Sellar initialed the page just beneath the quoted terms.

Byer called you immediately after the reception. She asked you to do a quick title search on the property. You did the search and found that Sellar acquired the property from his father, apparently as a gift. The deed read, in part, "in consideration of their love and affection, I hereby grant to my son, Stephen Sellar, and his wife, Lois, all the real property known as 1313 Collingwood Avenue."

Sellar's father had acquired the property from the land company that had built the townhouse and developed the surrounding neighborhood about 100 years ago. The land company is still in business. The deed from the company to Sellar's father had an habendum clause that read "to the grantee and his heirs for so long as the property is used as a single-family residence only and for no commercial purposes whatsoever."

You did not find anything else significant in your title search. When you telephone Byer to tell her the results of your search, she tells you that she had recently physically inspected the property. She found out that Sellar, an accountant, has operated a tax service out of an office in the townhouse since the mid-1960s. Byer also tells you that Lois Sellar's will was just admitted to probate. The will left all Lois's personal property to Stephen Sellar and all Lois's real property to the couple's only child, Junior. Byer further tells you that Stephen Sellar has had second thoughts about moving and that he now wants to back out of the sale.

In your client's view, the property is a bargain at $150,000 and she wants to go forward with the sale if you think she will be able to clear the title in her name.

1. **Can Byer hold Sellar to the bargain struck at the reception? Explain.**
2. **Assuming she can, does she have a reasonable prospect of being able to clear the title of any competing claims? Describe those claims and assess whether Byer is likely to defeat them in a quiet title action.**

Model Answer to Question 9

Byer probably can hold Sellar to the contract for sale. The memorandum of agreement scribbled on the notepad would likely be held sufficient under the statute of frauds. Byer also had a fairly good prospect of clearing title in her name. There are two competing claims to the title: (1) the land company's claim that it holds a possibility of reverter in the property and (2) Junior's claim that his mother's interest as a tenant in common passed to him under her will. The land company's possibility of reverter became possessory four years ago. The company's failure to record or pursue it within the span of time makes in unenforceable. As for Junior's claim, his mother was a tenant by the entirety under Michigan law, not a tenant in common. Her interest in the townhouse therefore passed by right of survivorship to Stephen. Consequently, Junior did not acquire any interest in the property under the terms of Lois' will.

Statute of Frauds: Byer and Sellar entered a contract for the sale of the townhouse. Byer offered to purchase the townhouse and Sellar accepted the offer by agreeing to convey the property. The parties' mutual promises constitute sufficient consideration. The only obstacle to enforcement of the contract is the statute of frauds. Like most common law jurisdictions, Michigan requires contracts for the sale of land to be in writing signed by the person to be charged. MCL 566.108 (2003). To satisfy the statute, the writing must set forth the contract's essential terms. The writing must identify the parties, state the price and describe the property. See generally, 17 Mich L & Prac 2d, Statute of Frauds, § 72, at 478 (2003).

The writing prepared by Byer meets all these elements. The terms of the writing, including Sellar's initials, describe the parties in such a manner that they may be identified. See generally, 17 Mich L & Prac 2d, Statute of Frauds, § 73 at 478-79 (2003). Under Michigan's statue of frauds, the seller of the land or the seller's agent must sign the writing. MCL 566.108 (2003). No particular form of signature is required however. The seller's initials are sufficient if made by the seller with the present intention to authenticate the writing. *Archhold v Industrial Land Co*, 264 Mich 289 (1933). The memorandum prepared by Byer also describes the property by a Detroit street address which is generally sufficient under Michigan's statute of frauds. *See Wazniak v Kuzinski*, 352 Mich 431 (1958). Finally, the purchase price agreed to by the parties is stated in the memorandum from the notepad. The failure to state the time of payment or closing is not fatal. The law will imply that closing must occur within a reasonable time. *Duke v Miller*, 355 Mich 540 (1959). For these reasons, Byer has a good claim that the memorandum she prepared satisfies the statute of frauds and should permit judicial enforcement of her agreement with Sellar.

The Possibility of Reverter: The initial deed to the townhouse provided that Sellar's father would lose his right to possession of the property automatically if either he or his successors should ever use it for any commercial purpose. The deed thus granted Sellar's father a fee simple determinable. The land company that built the townhouse and prepared the deed retained a possibility of reverter. *See* Moynihan & Kurtz, Introduction to the Law of Real Property, 43-44 (2002).

Sellar began using the property for commercial purposes in the mid-1960s when he started operating a tax service. The determinable fee ended at that time and the land company holding the possibility of reverter then had an immediate right to possession. The land company never did anything to exercise or preserve that right in the ensuing years, however. Under Michigan law, an action to recover possession of real property must be brought within fifteen years. MCL 600.5821 (2003). The statute of limitations begins to run on the holder of a possibility of reverter as soon as the condition ending the determinable fee occurs. Moynihan & Kurtz, Introduction to the Law of Real Property, 138-139 (2002). Thus, any action brought by the land company to recover possession of the townhouse would appear to be time-barred.

Moreover, under Michigan law, the holder of a possibility of reverter must record a notice to preserve the future interest which lapses every thirty years unless rerecorded. MCL 554.65 (2003). The land company has never recorded any such notice and would thus lose its right to enforce its possibility of reverter. *See Ditmore v Michalik*, 244 Mich App 569 (2001).

Claim Under the Will: Sellar's father granted title to the townhouse to Stephen and Lois without clearly specifying the nature of the concurrent estate he conveyed. Junior will claim that it was a tenancy in common under the modern presumption for resolving such ambiguous grants of concurrent interests. *See* MCL 554.44 (2003). A tenant in common may devise his or her interest. Moynihan & Kurtz, Introduction to the Law of Real Property, 268 (2002). Junior could thus claim an interest in the townhouse under the terms of his mother's will which left him all her real property.

Two Student Answers—July 2003

Question 9—Real/Personal Property—9 points

Yes as long as there is an amount specified, the property can be identified with certainty and the instrument is signed by the charged party. In this instance we have a determined price. While it may be low the court will not look at the adequacy of the consideration as long as no fraud occurred. As for the description—an address is certainly sufficient to identify the property in question. And, because the seller, the charged party, signed the memo, the buyer can probably hold the seller to the deal struck at the reception.

The first question is who has actual title to the property? Because love and affection probably do not constitute valuable consideration there was probably not a valid conveyance of the land in question. So title may not properly be in seller's name.

The second problem came in when the property stopped being used solely as a residential property. Because this property is being used in violation for a covenant that runs with the land there is unmarketable title. Because this covenant runs with the land it is unlikely Byer can clear title unless she can show a change in circumstances. This would mean that either the property is no longer suitable for residential purposes or that all the surrounding property has changed and the covenant no longer has any meaning. Because there is nothing in the facts to suggest this it is unlikely Byer can clear title. However, if she was able to clear title she could make the deal happen. She could even get specific performance because land is always unique.

There is no problem with Lois leaving the property to Junior because in Michigan property owned by married people are awarded as tenant by the entirety. This means Seller cannot convey the property without the consent of his spouse. This would also mean that the memo to Byer from Seller by himself is invalid. So Byer cannot hold Seller to bargain struck at reception.

So no to both questions one and two.

Question 9—Real/Personal Property—8 points

In regards to Byer holding Seller to the bargain struck at the table the note on the memo suffices to satisfy the Statute of Frauds in that all necessary material information has been given including the initials acting as a signature of the one to be charged Stephen Seller. This validly agrees to contract all of Stephen's interest to Byer.

There are two competing claims to Byer's claim:

1) Lois & Stephen's son Junior has a claim in that he has an undeeded ½ interest in the home that was denied to him by his mother. Byer will not be able to defeat this unless the house was owned by Stephen & Lois in the entirety, which Michigan law does not recognize anyway. Therefore, she only owns the ½ interest sold to her. Plus the deed granted it to Stephen & Lois in fee simple, in fee common.
2) The land company also has a claim because it had a reversion any interest if the land was used for a commercial purpose it was being used for as a tax service office. Byer will stand a good chance of quieting title from the land company because of the changed circumstances of the neighborhood if they apply & for their implied compliance in the commercial use for decades.

February 2004—Question 12

You represent a real estate developer who is interested in purchasing two tracts of land. Your client has asked you to examine the title to each of the tracts and you have found the following:

Tract 1: The first tract is owned by Donny and Marie Tenance, a brother and sister, who acquired the tract pursuant to the terms of their uncle's will. The will left the tract to Donny and Marie "as joint tenants with rights of survivorship." Marie wishes to sell her interest.

Tract 2: Mark Anthony inherited this tract of land from his father seven years ago. The deed from his father's estate granted the land to "Anthony and his heirs." Anthony got married shortly after he inherited the tract and intended to build his family home on the site. The marriage did not work out. Anthony's wife, Cleo, left him shortly after the wedding ceremony. Although the couple has not formally divorced, Anthony has not seen Cleo since she left. Anthony would like to sell the tract, which only reminds him of the failed marriage.

Describe the various property interests your title examination has revealed for each of the tracts. Explain the nature of the title your client will be able to obtain from Marie Tenance and Mark Anthony.

Model Answer to Question 12

Under Michigan law, the grant of Tract 1 to Donny and Marie Tenance created a joint life tenancy with a remainder in the survivor. Thus, if the client purchased Marie's interest, the client would obtain a joint life estate which would ripen into a fee simple only if Marie survived Donny. If she did not, her interest in Tract 1 would come to an end, leaving the client with nothing.

Anthony's interest in Tract 2 would be subject to Cleo's right of dower. The client cannot acquire a clear title from Anthony without Cleo's release of dower.

Tract 1: In most American jurisdictions, a grant of property to two persons as "joint tenants with right of survivorship" creates a joint tenancy. *See* William B. Stoebuck & Dale A. Whitman, The Law of Property, 185-186 (3d ed 2000). As such, either of the joint tenants can sever the relationship by an *inter vivos* conveyance. Upon severance, the remaining tenant and the transferee would be treated as tenants in common. *Id.*, at 189. The Michigan courts, however, construe a grant to two persons as "joint tenant with right of survivorship" as a joint life estate with a remainder in the survivor. *See, e.g., Albro v Allen*, 434 Mich 271 (1990); *Butler v Butler*, 122 Mich App 361, 364 (1983). This construction preserves the survivorship feature of the conveyance. Neither of the joint owners can eliminate the other's remainder. *Albor, supra*, 434 Mich at 284-86; see generally, Byron D. Cooper, *Continuing Problems with Michigan's Joint Tenancy "with Right of Survivorship,"* 78 Mich Bar J 966 (Sept 1999).

In the problem, Donny and Marie Tenance would be treated as joint life tenants of Tract 1 with a remainder contingent upon surviving the other. Marie could transfer her life interest and contingent remainder to the client. The client, however, would only acquire an undivided half interest in the life estate, which would come to an end if Marie died before Donny. Thus, the client could only acquire a fee simple title if Donny died first or if Donny joined in the conveyance of Tract 1.

Tract 2: Michigan has codified the right of dower. A widow may claim a life estate in one third of any land in which her husband held an inheritable interest during marriage. MCL 558.1 (1988). Without his wife's consent, a husband cannot convey property free of dower. *See, e.g., Slater Management Corp v Nash*, 212 Mich App 30, 32 (1995) ("A husband may not bargain away his wife's dower interest.")

For the foregoing reasons, Mark Anthony cannot, without Cleo's release, grant a clear title to Tract 2. Anthony held the tract in fee simple, an inheritable estate. He stood seized of Tract 2 during his marriage, so dower attached. If the client purchased Anthony's interest in the tract and Cleo survived Anthony, she would have a right to one-third of the tract for the remainder of her life.

Student Answer—February 2004

Question 12—Real Property—9 points

In Michigan a conveyance that states "as joint tenants with rights of survivorship" (ASJTWFROS) is in severable. The conveyance gives each party indestructible life estates. However, any ambiguity in conveyance is treated as if the instrument conveyed a tenants in common which means each party has an undivided interest in the party.

Tract 1: Here, Donny and Marie acquired the property through a will which clearly stated AJTWFROS which means that each party has an indestructible life estate that cannot be severed without the other joint tenant. However, as counsel, the argument could be that a will is a proper conveyance of real property but it cannot determine how ownership is held therefore creating an ambiguity in the way title is held to tract 1—thus creating a tenant in common which Marie could sell. However there are problems with this conveyance because Marie would only be able to convey an undivided 50% interest in the property.

Conclusion—I would advise my client regardless how the courts will rule on the state of title, whether it is tenancy in common or ASJTWFROS. It would be in his best interest to not only get Donny to convey his interest w/ Marie but also get Donny's spouse to convey if Donny is married because of dower problems.

Tract 2: Here, the will conveyed title to Anthony and his heirs. Michigan courts have recognized that when a man owns real property in the state his spouse has a dower right in the property that cannot be terminated unless by deed, death, or otherwise. Here, Anthony married Cleo but never received a divorce and Cleo never signed off on the property therefore your client is taking the risk of buying Tract 2 subject to Cleo's interest. It would be in your best interest to advise your client to tell the seller (Anthony) to get an order quick title or get a divorce terminating the interest of Cleo.

Conclusion—Advise your client to obtain deeds from Marie, Donny, and his wife if married because although spousal rights do not attach to ownership of land held as joint tenancy with full rights of survivorship, the property could be construed to be held as tenants in common which dower rights do apply therefore to be on safe side, get a deed from all parties.

It is important to note if your client is able to obtain a Title Insurance Policy from a reputable insurer, your client may want to proceed with this safeguard.

July 2004—Question 7

Mike was the owner of certain real property located in Oakland County, Michigan. In 1999, Mike sold the property via land contract to Lucy and Larry, a married couple. In 2001, Lucy and Larry were divorced. Pursuant to the terms of the Judgment of Divorce, Larry retained possession of the property, while Lucy was given a judicial lien on the property for $20,000 and recorded it with the Register of Deeds. In 2003, Larry took out a mortgage with Friendly Bank in the amount of $200,000. Larry used the money to pay off the land contract, as Mike was his cousin. However, he did not pay off the lien held by Lucy. Larry then skipped town with the remainder of the money and is allegedly riding his motorcycle through Europe. As a result of his leaving the country, Larry has also failed to make the payments on the mortgage to Friendly Bank.

Friendly Bank has foreclosed on the mortgage, and is seeking to sell the home to recoup the money lost to Larry. Friendly Bank has filed an action seeking a declaratory judgment that the Bank's interest is superior to the lien of Lucy.

The case has been assigned to a partner in the firm you are working for, and she has asked you to determine the priority of the competing interest. Discuss which encumbrance would be given priority—the Friendly Bank mortgage or Lucy's lien—and why.

Model Answer to Question 7

A purchase money mortgage is one "which takes effect immediately, as part of the 'same transaction by which seisin was acquired by the mortgagor.'" *Graves v American Acceptance Mortgage Corp*, 469 Mich 608 (2204), quoting *Fecteau v Fries*, 253 Mich 51 (1931). A purchase money mortgage arises where the mortgagor purchases property and gives a mortgage for the purchase money as one transaction. *Graves, supra.* Thus, the issue in the question at hand is whether the use of the money from the mortgage to pay a land contract constitutes a purchase money mortgage.

The Supreme Court has held it is not. A land contract vests equitable title in the vendee (Larry), while legal time remains vested in the vendor (Mike). *Graves, supra.* Therefore, as Larry has equitable title to the property, he also has seisin, which is defined as "Possession of real property under claim of freehold estate . . . [p]ossession with an intent on the part of him who holds it to claim a freehold estate." *Graves, supra*, n 3, quoting Black's Law Dictionary (6th ed.) Thus, when the vendee (Larry) purchased the property on a land contract, he took equitable title which he may then sell, devise, or encumber, and has "in a real sense, purchased the relevant property." *Graves, supra*, p 616. Thus, the mortgage here is not a purchase money mortgage as the proceeds were not used to purchase the property, but rather to pay off a preexisting debt on the property which was owed to the vendor (Mike). Therefore, Lucy's lien would be given priority over the mortgage held by Friendly Bank.

Two Student Answers—July 2004

Question 7—Creditor's Rights—7 points

Michigan is a lien theory state for mortgage, not title theory state. It means that mortgagor retains the title of property and mortgagee (Bank) retains the lien on the property. Also, mortgagee has a right of foreclosure if mortgagor failed to pay. Also, among 2 competing mortgages, since Michigan adopted "race-notice" recording statute. It means Bone Fide Purchaser would prevail against prior (proceeding) purchaser unless Bona Fide Purchaser (BFP) records first than prior purchasers.

In this case, the property is located in MI and Larry resided in MI at the time he got the mortgage, therefore, Friendly Bank does have only the lien on its property, not title. Lucy also have the lien on the same property and Lucy recorded her lien w/ the register of Deed office, where is a proper place to record a lien in MI, and she recorded the lien before Larry got mortgage from the Bank.

Therefore, Lucy's lien has priority than the Friendly Bank's mortgage. Also, the Bank should have known that Lucy already had $20K lien (judicial lien) on the same property b/c she recorded with the proper office in MI.

(2) Foreclosure: Even if the Bank is a second lien holder, they insist "foreclosure" b/c of non-payment. However, Lucy's lien is prior to the Bank's mortgage, Lucy's lien is not disappeared/discharged.

It means Lucy has still valid lien on the foreclosed property and Larry is still liable for Lucy's lien amount $20K and any deficiency b/c the amount of foreclosure sale and the amount of mortgage $200K for the Friendly Bank.

(3) Conclusion: The Bank's argument, they are superior to the lien of Lucy, is wrong. And Lucy's lien has priority than the Bank's mortgage. And Larry is still liable for Lucy for $20K and any deficiency of sale for the Bank.

> **Comment:** This examinee received a passing score of 7. If he or she had used the buzzword "purchase money mortgage," it would likely be a 9. Notice the poor grammar, missing words, and so on. Although the graders typically do not take away points for it, good grammar and proper sentence structure could result in additional points.

Question 7—Creditor's Rights—2 points (Bad Answer)

Lucy's lien is superior and should be given priority. Her lien was a judicial lien, properly recorded in 2001. The Bank should have noticed the lien when it issued the mortgage in 2003 and required its payment before issuing the rest to Larry.

> **Comment:** This examinee got 2 points for three sentences. You should never limit a response to this. Even if you are unsure, outline dump some general principles. The graders look to give you points (obviously based on this example), not take them away.

February 2005—Question 8

Clyde is a single man who lives in a nice home on a small inland lake. He always got along well with his neighbors, the Turners, who had lived there since Clyde moved into his home in 1960. Both Clyde and the Turners are the original owners of their homes, both homes having been built in 1960. In 1970, the Turners erected a fence along what they believed to be the boundary line between the two pieces of property. While the true property line was actually ten feet closer to the Turners' home, neither party had a survey done nor did they discover the discrepancy.

After the Turners retired and moved to Florida in 2001, they sold their home to Geraldine, who was a recent millionaire after selling her internet company. Not working any longer, Geraldine liked to party into all hours of the night. The noise and traffic eventually forced Clyde to move, and he sold his home to Pat in 2002. Pat was also a recent millionaire, having sold her tuna casserole recipe to a large frozen food company.

Pat wanted to extend her home to build a giant indoor play area for her children and her cats. However, a survey revealed the fence between the two lots was not on the true property line. In order for Pat to build the playroom, she needs to move the fence towards Geraldine's house by ten feet, which would reflect the true boundary line. While Geraldine was out of town on vacation, Pat tore down the old fence and placed a new fence on the true property line ten feet closer to Geraldine's house. Upon her return, Geraldine immediately filed a lawsuit setting forth claims of adverse possession and acquiescence, alleging the disputed ten feet of property belonged to her, and not to Pat.

Discuss the elements of adverse possession and acquiescence and whether Geraldine will prevail on her claims.

Model Answer to Question 8

To prove a claim of adverse possession, Geraldine must show "proof of possession that is actual, visible, open, notorious, exclusive, continuous, and uninterrupted for the statutory period of 15 years, hostile, and under cover of a claim of right." *McQueen v Black*, 168 Mich App 641 (1988). The Michigan Supreme Court has held where "a landowner takes possession of land of an adjacent owner, with the intent to hold to the true line, the possession is not hostile and adverse possession cannot be established." *Warner v Noble*, 286 Mich 654 (1938), cited in *McQueen, supra*. Therefore, the claim for adverse possession must fail as the possession was not hostile.

To prove a claim of acquiescence, a plaintiff need only prove the parties (or their predecessors in interest) had agreed to a boundary line for the statutory period of 15 years. *Sackett v Atyeo*, 217 Mich App 676 (1996). The facts state that Clyde and the Turners both treated the fence as the true property line from 1970 until the time they moved. Geraldine can tack the time of the predecessors in interest, Clyde and the Turners, and satisfy the 15-year requirement. Therefore, Geraldine will prevail on her claim of acquiescence.

Two Student Answers—February 2005

Question 8—Real Property—10 points

The issue is whether Geraldine can prevail on her claim of adverse possession. The elements of adverse possession are:

1. Hostile
2. Exclusive
3. Length of time
4. Undisputed
5. Visible
6. Adverse

Geraldine did not take the 10 feet in a hostile manner. Even though she bought the property from Pat, Pat did not take the property in a hostile manner either so there can be no tacking. Pat gave the 10 feet with consent of Clyde.

The taking was exclusive to the Turners and now Geraldine. No other parties were involved.

In Michigan the time for adverse possession is 20 years; the time from 1970 to 2001 is 31 years. Therefore the time requirement has been fulfilled.

The landownership by adverse possession must be undisputed. Here, the land ownership is not undisputed. There is a dispute as to where the true property line belongs. Geraldine did not take by adverse possession undisputed land.

The taking must be visible. Geraldine and the Turners did visibly take the 10 feet in front of Clyde and Pat for more than 20 years.

The taking of the 10 feet was not adverse because Clyde consented to Turners in 1970.

Therefore, Geraldine will not succeed on her adverse possession claim because she has not met the requirements of hostile, undisputed, and adverse.

The next issue is whether Geraldine will prevail on her claim of acquiescence. Acquiescence is a claim made based on improvements made on the property. The facts are unclear on what, if any, improvements Geraldine made on the property.

> **Comment:** This is a classic example of how a grader made a mistake that benefited the examinee. This person missed the acquiescence issue entirely, and got the number of years wrong in the adverse possession but still got full credit. Please be aware that this answer should have earned 6 points, not 10 points—clearly an error benefiting the examinee.

Question 8—Real Property—9 points

Will Geraldine prevail on her claim of adverse possession and acquiescence against Pat?

Geraldine probably will prevail but not on the theory of adverse possession. To be adverse possession, the party (here it's Geraldine) in addition to the possession being open, notorious, exclusion, obvious, and continuous, it must also be adverse or in other words, hostile. Here Turner and Clyde acquiesce that the fence is, is where the property line would be. Turner and Clyde had horizontal privity to each other to enforce this upon future successors down the line regarding to those who they sell the land to. Therefore, Pat will not be able to claim the 10 feet of land that Geraldine is using.

Pat, however, may have a claim against Clyde for covenant of quiet enjoyment based upon a warranty deed if she received a warranty deed from Clyde. Clyde upon suit from Pat would probably be liable for damages based on the 10 feet that can't be given to Pat, i.e., a reduction in the contract price for the land but they would not be responsible for damages that it caused Pat because she can't put up a play-yard.

July 2005—Question 6

Jim was the owner of certain real property located in Grand Blanc, Michigan. In 1999, Jim sold the property via land contract to Scot and Kelly, a married couple. In 2001, Scot and Kelly were divorced. Pursuant to the terms of the Judgment of Divorce, Scot retained possession of the property, while Kelly was given a judicial lien on the property for $50,000 and recorded it with the Register of Deeds. In 2003, Scot took out a mortgage with Ourmoney Bank in the amount of $200,000. Scot used the money to pay off the land contract, since Jim was his good friend. However, he did not pay off the lien held by Kelly. Scot then skipped town with the remainder of the money and is allegedly living out his dream working as a carnival barker guessing weights and ages. As a result of his living on the road with the carnival, Scot has also failed to make the payments on the mortgage to Ourmoney Bank.

Ourmoney Bank has foreclosed on the mortgage and is seeking to sell the home to recoup the money lost to Scot. Ourmoney Bank has filed an action seeking a declaratory judgment that the Bank's interest is superior to the lien of Kelly.

The case has been assigned to a partner of the firm you are working for and she has asked you to determine the priority of the competing interests. Under what theory could the Bank claim that its mortgage be given priority and what would be the outcome? It must be assumed all transactions were recorded in the order of occurrence.

Model Answer to Question 6

A purchase money mortgage is one "which takes effect immediately, as part of the 'same transaction by which seisin was acquired by the mortgagor.'" *Graves v American Acceptance Mortgage Corp*, 469 Michigan 608 (2004), quoting *Fecteau v Fries*, 253 Michigan 51 (1931). A purchase money mortgage arises where the mortgagor purchases property and gives a mortgage for the purchase money as one transaction. *Graves, supra.* Thus the issue in the question at hand is whether the use of the money from the mortgage to pay a land contract constitutes a purchase money mortgage.

The Supreme Court has held it is not. A land contract vests equitable title in the vendee (Scot), while legal title remains vested in the vendor (Jim). *Graves, supra.* Therefore, as Scot had equitable title to the property, he also had seisin, which is defined as "Possession of real property under claim of freehold estate . . . Possession with an intent on the part of him who holds it to claim a freehold estate." *Graves, supra*, n 3, quoting Black's Law Dictionary (6th ed.). When the vendee (Scot) purchased the property on a land contract, he took equitable title, which he may then sell, devise, or encumber, and has "in a real sense, purchased the property." *Graves, supra*, p 834. Thus, the mortgage here is not a purchase money mortgage as the proceeds were not used to purchase the property, but rather to pay off a preexisting debt on the property that was owed to the vendor (Jim). Therefore, Kelly's lien would be given priority over the mortgage held by Ourmoney Bank.

Three Student Answers—July 2005

Question 6—Property/Creditor's Rights—10 points

The Bank will claim that its interest in the land is superior to Kelly because it has a Purchase Money Mortgage Security Interest (PMSI) in the land. The bank will claim that Kelly's interest is inferior to the Bank because she only holds a lien.

A Purchase Money Mortgage gives immediate priority in land and automatically attaches. This is money used to purchase land. It is usually superior to any other claim in the land.

On these facts, Scott did not use the money to purchase land. He used the money to pay off the debt to his friend Jim. Although it was used for the land contract deal, Scott already has possession of the property and the debt was an old debt. It—the money from the bank—was not used to *acquire* new property. Therefore the loan from the Bank is not seen as a purchase money mortgage to acquire new land. Therefore this would be a new debt or personal loan to Scott and would be inferior to Kelly's claim.

So in conclusion, the Bank would not have a superior claim to the land, it is not a purchase money mortgage with superior security interest because it was not used to acquire new land. But the money was used to pay a debt to a friend. So Kelly's interest in the land would have *priority* over the Bank's loan.

Question 6—Property/Creditor's Rights—10 points

The first issue is under what theory could the bank claim that its mortgage be given priority and what would be the outcome. The rule is that a Purchase Money Mortgage (PMM) has a Superior Security interest over other forms of interest. A Purchase Money Mortgage arises when a property owner borrows money from the lender and uses the money to buy the property. Any security interest given to the lender of such money has priority over other security interest in the property.

In this case, the property was purchased in 1999 via land contract. The money Scot took as a mortgage in 2003 was not used to buy the property although it was used to pay off the land contract. To qualify as a Purchase Money Mortgage, the money must be used to acquire the property. Since that is not the case, Our Money Bank does not have a superior mortgage over Kelly.

The next issue is the priority of Kelly's judicial lien. The rule is that any judicial lien is superior to any subsequent security interest if the interests are on the same property. In this case, Kelly obtained a judicial lien in 2001 upon divorce from Jim. Since the judicial lien came first in time before the Our Money Bank mortgage, the judicial lien has priority over the Bank, as the Bank was on notice of Kelly's judicial lien that was recorded. The outcome is that any proceed, which is any money realized from the sale will be used to pay Kelly's $50,000 first before the bank can have any money towards their mortgage.

> **Comment:** This is another excellent answer. Notice how the use of IRAC keeps the answer concise and well organized. Also note that this same issue was tested on a previous bar exam. Many students mistakenly assumed this was a Secured Transaction question. You learned creditor's rights in Secured Transaction in law school. However, the Michigan Bar Examiners test it separately in a different cluster.

Question 6—Property/Creditor's Rights—10 points

The issue is who has priority in the competing interests. The competing interests in question are the lien held by Kelly in the amount of $5,000 and the mortgage held by Our Money Bank in the amount of $200,000. Michigan is a race-notice jurisdiction, which means that the first to record who also has notice of all subsequent interests has priority. Here Kelly filed her lien with the Register of Deeds in 2001. Our Money Bank did not file the mortgage until 2003. If Our Money Bank did a title search they would have realized that Kelly had already recorded a lien on the property. If nothing else they had constructive notice because she did record the lien properly. Therefore, because Kelly filed first with notice, she has priority over Our Money Bank in the competing interests.

The next issue is under what theory could Bank claim that its mortgage be given priority. Bank could argue that their mortgage was a purchase money security interest

(PMSI) and therefore should be given superior priority over all claims. A PMSI is an interest given in money for an item. Scot used the money from the mortgage to pay off Jim. The court will probably not view the mortgage as a PMSI and therefore the mortgage will not be given superior priority over all competing interests.

The next issue is whether Bank can claim that they hold title to the property. This argument would fail because Michigan is a lien theory as opposed to a title theory jurisdiction. In lien theory jurisdiction, the mortgagor retains title the property.

The next issue is whether Scot is entitled to get his property back even though Our Money Bank wants to sell the home at a foreclosure sale. In Michigan, the owner of the property has a right to redeem his property for 6 months after the foreclosure sale. The owner only has to tender the amount due.

February 2006—Question 5

CAT LAKE	
The "sliver" HANK'S PROPERTY (deeded to Kenny in 2005)	
STEW'S PROPERTY	KENNY'S PROPERTY
OAKLAND STREET	

Stew and Kenny are neighbors, living peacefully on Oakland Street for the last 30 years. They both like the location, as Cat Lake is right behind their homes, separated by only a five-foot piece of property known as the "sliver." Cat Lake is a hot spot for fishing, and home to some of the biggest bass in Michigan. Both Stew and Kenny have used the vacant parcel of property behind their homes to access Cat Lake for the last 30 years. In fact, they often met there on their way to go fishing together.

However, the two longtime friends have gotten into a feud over who is the better fisherman. They no longer speak to each other, and try not to look at each other when crossing the property behind their homes on the way to the lake. Hoping to gain an advantage over Kenny, Stew decided to find Hank (the owner of the "sliver") and buy the property from him.

When Stew called Hank and made an offer for the property, Hank thought perhaps he could make some money from the hatred between the two neighbors. Hank called Kenny, who, of course, offered more than Stew. Hank then sold the property to Kenny. Within two days of buying the property, Kenny erected a fence on his new property that would prevent Stew from using the sliver to access Cat Lake.

When Stew saw the fence Kenny had erected, he immediately filed an action seeking a prescriptive easement over the sliver. The undisputed facts are that each person has used the property for access to the lake for the last 30 years until Kenny erected the fence to keep Stew off the property. Kenny has defended on the ground that Stew did not use the property every day, but only 2-3 times per week when he went fishing.

Discuss the elements of a prescriptive easement and the likelihood of success of Stew's claim against Kenny, as well as Kenny's defense to the claim.

Model Answer to Question 5

A prescriptive easement arises when the servient estate is used by someone other than the owner when the use is open, notorious, adverse, and continuous for 15 years. *Killips v Mannisto*, 244 Mich App 256 (2001). The prescriptive easement does not displace the true owner of the property, but rather grants the holder of the easement "qualified possession only to the extent necessary for enjoyment of the rights conferred by the easement." *Day v Molitor*, unpublished opinion per curiam of the Court of Appeals, decided December 27, 2005 (Docket No. 256489), citing *Schadewald v Brule*, 225 Mich App 26, 35 (1997).

The facts of this question are based on *Day, supra*. Therein, the plaintiff had used the sliver for parking and for egress and ingress to the road located behind the property of the parties. The Court of Appeals reversed the trial court, and found the plaintiff had met the requirements for a prescriptive easement. The Court of Appeals granted the plaintiff a prescriptive easement for ingress and egress, as even the defendants and their witnesses had testified to that use for the statutory period. The Court of Appeals relied not only on the testimony, but also upon the fact that the plaintiff had maintained a gated entrance to what was called the "stub parcel."

In this question, the appropriate response is that Stew would be entitled to a prescriptive easement for access to Cat Lake. Stew clearly had used the sliver for more than the statutory 15 years, and the use was open, notorious, and adverse to the interest of Hank. Kenny's defense is without merit insofar as the Michigan Supreme Court has held use need not be continuous, or daily, but only on an as-needed basis. Specifically, the Supreme Court held as follows:

> An omission to use when not needed does not disprove a continuity of use, shown by using it when needed, for it is not required that a person shall use the easement every day for the prescriptive period. It simply means that he shall exercise the right more or less frequently, according to the nature of the use to which its enjoyment may be applied. *Von Meding v Strahl*, 319 Mich 598, 613-614 (1948), quoting *St. Cecilia Society v Universal Car & Service Co.*, 213 Mich 569, 577 (1921).

Thus, the fact that Stew did not use the property on a daily basis will not be fatal to his claim of a prescriptive easement. His use on the days which he went fishing (admittedly 2-3 times per week) is sufficient to satisfy the continuity requirement and Stew's prescriptive easement will be granted.

Two Student Answers—February 2006

Question 5—Real Property—9 points

A prescriptive easement is much like adverse possession in that it is used openly and continuously for a period of years. Though the facts don't stipulate a time, no doubt Stew had over 30 years gained a prescriptive easement.

Kenny is arguing that Stan's use is not continuous because he didn't use the easement every day. This argument will fail because regular use suffices.

Stew is going to win because his use was open, Kenny knew about it. Also, he had been crossing the sliver for 30 years continuously and has now established an easement by prescription.

Since the easement touches and concerns the land and attached while Hank owned it and Kenny was on notice of it, Stew will prevail. Kenny will argue that he was not on notice but this argument will fail because his only purpose in building the fence 2 days after the purchase was to block Stew's easement and since Stew had not abandoned it, the easement is still valid.

Question 5—Real Property—9 points

Stew will be able to prove he had a prescriptive easement over the sliver.

The issue is whether Stew can prove his claim that he had a prescriptive easement over the "sliver".

A prescriptive easement is very similar to adverse possession. The elements are hostile (usage), open and notorious, and using the easement continuously for the statutory period.

The hostile element refers to the usage of the easement. In this case Stew used the easement to go fishing on a regular basis. Kenny knew he and Stew both utilized the easement, and he was aware of the frequency.

The open and notorious element can be proven by Stew. He can prove that he walked across the "sliver" to Cat Lake—and most of the time he utilized the easement. Kenny saw him because he met him on his property.

Using the easement continuously for the statutory period should not be a problem to prove. Although the facts don't state the statutory period for adverse possession, it's usually 10-15 years. In this case, Stew can prove (as Kenny knows), the easement has been in effect for the last 30 years.

Kenny is attempting to argue that Stew's usage was not continuous. Kenny is arguing that 2-3 times is not enough—that to be in adverse possession the easement should have been used more.

It will appear that Stew will be able to prove that 2-3 times a week is adequate to maintain the easement.

Kenny should be made to remove the fence, so that Stew can continue to utilize the easement.

July 2006—Question 10

After the development of the new addition to Metro Airport in Wayne County, Michigan, the county initiated actions to condemn parcels of land immediately south of the airport to construct a state-of-the-art business and technology park in the

1,300-acre area. All of the businesses within this "park" were to be owned and run by private-sector investors. The owners of at least 500 acres of those parcels refused to sell to the county and the county initiated condemnation proceedings. The owners of the parcels defended the action on various grounds, one of which was that this did not constitute a "public use" and therefore the property could not be condemned.

At trial, the county contended that the project would create thousands of jobs and tens of millions of dollars in tax revenue, while broadening the county's tax base from predominantly industrial to a mixture of industrial, service, and technology. According to expert testimony at trial, it was anticipated that the project would create thirty thousand jobs and add $350 million in tax revenue for the county.

Limiting your answer to the sole issue of whether the action of the county serves a "public use" and therefore would permit the condemnation, discuss and decide the issue.

Model Answer to Question 10

Const 1963, art 10 § 2 provides that "[p]rivate property shall not be taken for public use without just compensation being first made or secured in manner prescribed by law." While eminent domain is an attribute to sovereignty, "public use" is a limitation on the exercise of the power of eminent domain.

In Michigan, the "public use" requirement is not an absolute bar against the transfer of condemned property to private entities. However, the constitutional "public use" requirement does prohibit the state from transferring condemned property to private entities for a private use.

Condemnations in which private land is constitutionally transferred by condemning authority to a private entity are limited to those enterprises generating public benefits whose very existence depends on the use of land that can be assembled only by the coordination central government alone is capable of achieving.

The Michigan Supreme Court has also found that the transfer of condemned property to a private entity is consistent with the constitution's "public use" requirement when the private entity remains accountable to the public in its use of that property. In other words, the "public use" requirement is satisfied when the public retained a measure of control over the property.

Finally, condemned land may be transferred to a private entity when the selection of the land to be condemned is itself based on public concern. The property must be selected on the basis of "facts of independent public significance," meaning that the underlying purposes for resorting to condemnation, rather than the subsequent use of condemned land, must satisfy the Constitution's public use requirement. *Poletown Neighborhood Council v Detroit*, 410 Mich 616, 680 (1981) (Ryan, J., dissenting). An example of this type of situation would be in the condemnation of blighted housing and its subsequent resale of the properties to private persons.

In summary, the Supreme Court has approved condemnations on the basis on "public use" and subsequent transfer to private entities: (1) where "public necessity of the extreme sort" requires collective action; (2) where the property remains subject to public oversight after transfer to a private entity; and (3) where the property is selected because of the "facts of independent public significance," rather than the interests of the private entity to which the property is eventually transferred.

None of these three elements exist in this case. The business and technology park is certainly not an enterprise "whose very existence depends on the use of land that can be assembled only by the coordination central government alone is capable of achieving."

Second, the project is not subject to public oversight to ensure that the property continues to be used for the commonwealth owned and run by private sector investors. There is no mention in the facts of a formal mechanism planned to ensure that the businesses that would occupy what are now defendants' properties will continue to contribute to the health of the local economy.

Finally, there is nothing about the act of condemning defendants' properties that serves the public good in this case. The only public benefits cited by plaintiff arise after the lands are acquired by the government and put to private use. There are no facts of independent public significance (such as the need to promote health and safety) that might justify the condemnation of the defendants' lands.

In a case involving the same issue, the U.S. Supreme Court came to the opposite conclusion. In *Kelo v City of New London*, 125 S Ct 2655, 162 L Ed 2d 439 (2005), the U.S. Supreme Court held that the "public use" restriction was met in a development plan designed to revitalize the city's economy. The U.S. Supreme Court held that it has defined the term "public use" broadly and gives deference to legislative judgments as to what public needs justify the use of the taking of private property.

Wayne County v Hathcock, 471 Mich 445 (2004)

Student Answer—July 2006

Question 10—Real Property—9 points

This is a constitutional law question. The issue here is the condemnation of the property a taking or is it justified being for public use.

Firstly, the condemnation of the property by the county would be a taking of the parcels of lands and is thereby compensable to the owners. It would be a taking because the county is acquiring the property "after development of the new addition to Metro Airport." Also, the county would have the businesses placed upon the parcels to be "owned and run by private sector investors." Thus, it (the condemnation) would not be for "public use" but for private business.

Next, it could be argued that because the property would house the project that will create millions of dollars in revenue and create thousands of jobs that the condemnation is for "public use." However, this argument should fail because it will be private owners and operators of the businesses that will benefit from the taking of the parcels and also because the county will not be in control of the parcels for the greater good of the public. Therefore, the condemnation should not be permitted because the action of the county does not serve a "public use."

February 2007—Question 8

In 1985, Kate Woods moved to Ludington, Michigan, to live and work on Fred Farmer's farm. Fred's spouse had recently died and Fred needed help keeping up with the farm. In 2000, Bob Free, a resident of Ludington, began helping Fred and Kate with much of the heavy work on Fred's farm. Fred and Bob became good friends.

In 2003, Fred informed Bob that when Fred died, he wanted Bob to have his farm. Bob inquired why Fred would not give the farm to Kate. Fred indicated that while he cared greatly for Kate, he did not want Kate's son to have his farm after Kate died. Thereafter, Bob's involvement with Fred's affairs increased. Specifically, Bob became intricately involved in the operation of Fred's farm. Bob also began to manage all of Fred's personal and farm-related finances.

One year later, Fred again told Bob that upon his death, he wanted Bob to have his farm. Fred asked Bob to set up an appointment for him with an attorney. Bob contacted an attorney that he knew and set up an appointment for Fred. Bob drove Fred to the attorney's office and sat in on their meeting. Fred gave the attorney the deed to his farm and told the attorney that he wanted to do whatever was necessary to insure that Bob received Fred's farm upon his death. The attorney conducted an estate planning interview with Fred. The attorney determined that, other than personal and business bank accounts of insignificant value, the farm was Fred's only asset. Fred also indicated that while he cared greatly for Kate, he did not want to leave his farm to her because of her son. After satisfying himself that Fred fully understood what he was doing, the attorney prepared a new deed for Fred—a quitclaim deed that quit claimed the farm to Fred and Bob, "as joint owners with full rights of survivorship and not as tenants in common, subject to a life estate in Kate Woods for her natural life." The deed indicated it was executed "without payment of money, this transaction being a gift." Fred signed the deed.

On the way home from the attorney's office, Fred gave the deed to Bob and said, "I'm giving this to you so it won't get lost." Bob recorded the deed the next day. Upon returning from the meeting, Kate, who had become suspicious of Bob's motives, asked Fred where Fred and Bob had been. Fred told Kate he "went to an attorney to prepare a will" and that she ought not to worry because she was "taken care of in the will."

In January 2005, Fred told Bob that he intended to marry Kate and asked Bob to "give me the papers back." Fred told Bob "I want to make sure that Kate's granddaughter, Claire, has a roof over her head after Kate and I are gone." Bob declined to give Fred the recorded deed and told Fred he should talk to a lawyer. Fred died in June 2005, before marrying Kate. Kate was named personal representative of Fred's estate. Kate has come to you for legal advice.

Identify the legal claims that can be asserted against Bob that might permit a court to set aside the quitclaim deed. Discuss the arguments that can be made in support of and against these legal claims.

Model Answer to Question 8

There was no monetary consideration given for the deed. The deed states that it was executed "without payment of money, this transaction being a gift." Thus, Kate could claim that the conveyance must be set aside as an invalid *inter vivos* gift. A person who attacks the validity of a gift has the burden of proving that no gift was made. *Vander Honing v Taylor*, 344 Michigan 24, 29-30 (1955). For a gift to be valid, three elements must be satisfied: (1) the donor must possess the intent to transfer title gratuitously to the donee, (2) there must be actual or constructive delivery of the subject matter to the donee, unless it is already in the donee's possession, and

(3) the donee must accept the gift. *Davidson v Bugbee*, 227 Michigan App. 264, 268 (1997).

Acceptance is not an issue in this case, as it can be presumed because the gift is beneficial to Bob, the donee. *In re Handelsman*, 266 Michigan App. 433, 437-438 (2005), quoting *Davidson, supra.* Likewise, there can be little question about the intent of Fred to transfer title gratuitously to Bob. Fred repeatedly informed Bob of his intent, and Fred also discussed the matter with the attorney, who concluded that Fred fully understood the ramifications of this conduct and intended to give Bob his farm upon his death. Kate's best argument is that there was no actual or constructive delivery of the deed to Bob because Fred believed the document was a will, not a deed.

Whether a legal document is a deed or a will turns on whether it conveys a present interest in which case it is deemed a deed, or an interest on the death of the person who executed it, in which case it is a will. *Benton Harbor Federation of Women's Clubs v Nelson*, 301 Michigan 465, 470 (1942). That determination turns on the intent of the person who executed the document. However, for wills and deeds alike, the intent of the drafter is gleaned from the instrument itself, from the circumstances surrounding its creation, and from the manner in which the parties subsequently dealt with it. *Id.* at 471.

There is ample evidence to support the conclusion that Fred thought he had executed a will rather than a deed. Fred told Kate he had gone to the attorney to draft a will, when in fact the attorney drafted the quitclaim deed. Fred told Kate that she was taken care of in his will, when, in fact, Fred had no will. Fred had only the deed that granted Kate a life estate in Fred's farm. Further, the deed has some testamentary language, i.e., right of survivorship, that could have caused Fred to believe he was drafting a will rather than a deed. The deed was also drafted to address disposition of Fred's most valuable asset—his farm. Moreover, Fred did not give the deed to Bob with instructions that he record it. Rather, he gave the deed to Bob "so it won't get lost." This is the type of thing one would do with a will.

There is also evidence to support the conclusion that Fred did not intend to create a will. Fred brought his old deed to the attorney's office, and a new deed was drafted in accordance with Fred's wishes. The deed does not contain any language that would indicate it was a will, such as the words "will," "bequeath," or "death." Given this evidence, Fred may have understood that he was not executing a will at all, but instead a deed that operates as a will substitute.

Kate may also argue that the quitclaim deed is the product of undue influence. A presumption of undue influence exists upon a showing of: (1) the existence of a confidential or fiduciary relationship between the grantor and a fiduciary, (2) the fiduciary or an interest which he represents benefits from a transaction, and (3) the fiduciary had an opportunity to influence the grantor's decision in that transaction." *In re Estate of Karmey*, 468 Michigan 68, 73 (2003). A confidential relationship is one in which dominion may be exercised by one person over another. *Id.* To establish undue influence, it must be shown that the grantor was subjected to threats, misrepresentation, undue flattery, fraud, or physical or moral coercion sufficient to destroy free agency and impel the grantor to act against his inclination and free will. *Id.*

Kate can argue that there existed a fiduciary or confidential relationship between Bob and Fred sufficient to create a presumption of undue influence. Bob was "intricately involved" in the operation of Fred's farm. Moreover, Bob maintained all of Fred's finances. This supports the existence of a fiduciary relationship. Moreover, Bob selected Fred's attorney and sat in on the attorney-client meeting with Fred. This also supports the conclusion there existed a confidential or fiduciary relationship between Bob and Fred.

Bob will argue that he did not exercise undue influence over Fred. Rather, Bob merely facilitated Fred's inclination and free will. Bob was initially reluctant to take the farm and inquired why Fred did not want to give the farm to Kate. Bob did not again mention the issue. One year later, Fred again raised the issue by indicating he still wanted to give Bob the farm. Further, Bob only selected an attorney for Fred because Fred asked him to contact an attorney. In addition, the attorney who drafted the quitclaim deed inquired into Fred's desires and was satisfied that Fred fully understood the ramifications of his actions, which further dispels any suggestion of undue influence.

Student Answer—February 2007

Question 8—Property—8 points

This question deals with whether Fred made a valid inter vivos gift to Bob. A valid gift requires the gifter's intent to create a gift, valid delivery of the gift, and valid acceptance. A valid argument could be made that Fred never intended for a valid gift to Bob. The facts indicate that Fred told Bob "to give me the papers back."

On the other side, an argument could be made that Bob had a valid deed as a joint owner at rights of survivorship. However, the deed was given "without payment of money" or no consideration and therefore was not a valid real estate deal.

Further, a quitclaim deed makes absolutely no warranties of present or future title—so Bob may not have taken the farm as a joint owner.

A claim of undue influence by Bob could probably not be made as simple involvement at another's affairs and/or management of another's assets would not rise to the level of undue influence.

Question 8—Property—8 points

The issues here deal with intestate death and a valid gift.

The general rule is that if an individual dies intestate, without a will, his heirs would be entitled to testator's property by statutory law. They would only be able to collect property that has not been given away as a gift under the ademption rule.

The general rule for gifts is that there must be intent of the testator to give a gift to another individual without fraud, duress or misrepresentation. The gift must then be delivered and there must be an acceptance of the gift. Once there has been a valid acceptance, the gift is no longer subject to testator's/owner's revocation of the gift.

Here, the facts indicate that there was no fraud, duress or misrepresentation of any sort when Fred deeded his farm to Bob. An attorney was present to prove this. He had the intent element satisfied. There was delivery in the form of the deed, regardless that there was no money exchanged since it's a gift, and acceptance by Bob when he accepted the signed deed from Fred. Possession of the deed is enough to satisfy acceptance and is not mandatory to record the deed, although that would be a smarter decision in case Fred deeded the property to someone else before or after the conveyance of the gift of the farm.

An argument can be made that the deed held by an attorney would also be construed as a gift with symbolic delivery.

Now Kate has an argument that only personal and not real property can be gifted and might succeed if the laws support that finding.

Additionally, Kate can argue that the gift was revoked when Fred asked for the papers back since it was his intent to do so and that there was no proper delivery or acceptance when the attorney handed Bob the deed.

Bob can argue that this was a quitclaim deed and thus there was no power of reverter, thus Fred could not revoke the gift and also Bob had already accepted the gift, thus extinguishing Fred's power to revoke.

Even if Fred had made a valid will devising the farm to Claire, it was too late since Bob already had the farm under ademption and thus there is no farm for Claire to get.

Claire would get nothing under intestate and neither would Kate since Fred died before marrying her and this leaves no heirs to collect. Kate is not entitled to Dower or elective share and Claire would not be able to collect as an omitted child.

Bob has title to the farm and keeps it. If the gift is deemed improper since it was real property, Bob can argue that he received a deed and not a gift and thus had valid title.

July 2007—Question 12

In 1980, the Robert Jones subdivision was platted and provided for two very large lots on Lake Michigan. To the east of the lots was the Carl Spackler State Park. Lake Michigan was to the west of the lots. To the north of Lot One was Country Club Drive, a public road. To the south of Lot Two was the rear of the Robert Jones National Golf Course. The subdivision plat was originally recorded with a document entitled "Easements" that reflected the existence of two easements through Lot One to benefit Lot Two: (1) a center drive easement; and (2) a utility easement. The language granting the center drive easement provided "a twenty-foot wide drive easement running from Country Club Drive, through the center of Lot One, so as to provide access to Lot Two." The language granting the utility easement provided: "a ten-foot utility, water and sewer easement running along the eastern edge of Lot One from Country Club Drive to the northern edge of Lot Two, to be used to run any and all utility lines, water lines and sewer lines, from Country Club Drive to Lot Two. The plat was also recorded with a document entitled "restrictive Covenants" that provided, in relevant part, that "[n]o structure shall be constructed on any lot unless the structure has access to public utility lines, public water lines, and municipal sewer lines."

A copy of the original plat is provided below:

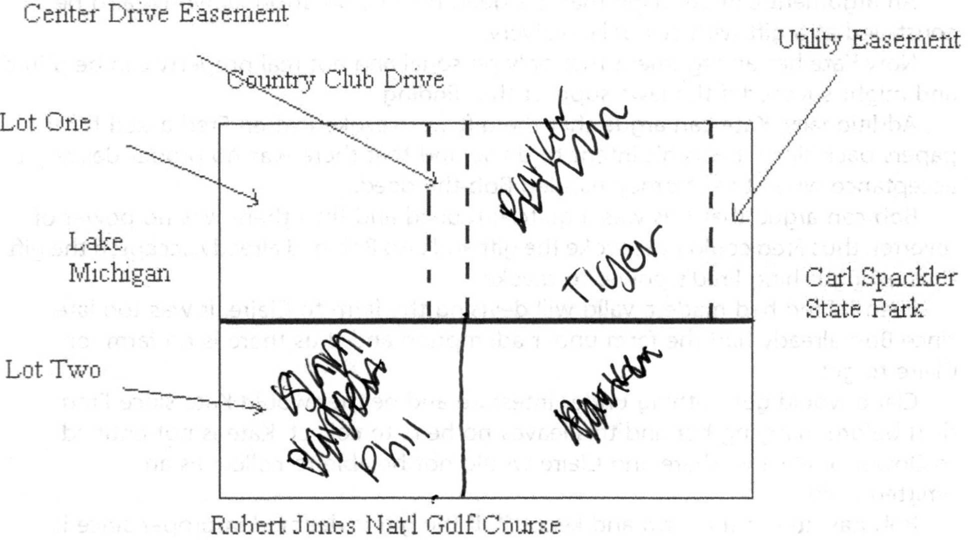

In 1990, the original purchaser of Lot Two, Sam Smee, divided his lot in two equal halves, through the middle of the center drive easement. Sam sold the eastern half of the lot to Arnie Parker, the original purchaser of Lot One. Sam kept the portion of Lot One that was on Lake Michigan. Neither Arnie nor Sam ever built anything on their lots.

Arnie sold his property to Tiger Forrest in 2005. Sam sold his lot to Phil Nickerson in 2006. Tiger immediately built a luxury home on his property. Phil informed Tiger that he intended to build a home on his lot. Tiger informed Phil that the land Phil purchased cannot be developed because it does not have access to any utility lines, public water lines, or municipal sewer lines. Moreover, Tiger indicated he would not grant Phil any easements to allow access to such services.

Phil filed suit in circuit court arguing that (1) he has a right to access utility and sewer services from the utility easement through Lot One, running along the eastern edge of the subdivision, (2) he has the right and ability to run sewer and utility lines underground or overland through the center drive easement, and (3) if all else fails, he is entitled to an easement by necessity.

Discuss Phil's arguments and Tiger's likely responses. Explain how the court is likely to rule and why.

Model Answer to Question 12

Phil claims a right to gain access to utility service through Tiger's property via any one of the three easements (utility easement, drive easement, and/or easement by necessity). An easement is an interest in real estate that gives one person the right to use another person's land for a specific purpose. An easement displaces the rights of the landowner only to the extent necessary to allow the holder of the easement to enjoy the rights conveyed under the easement. An easement is inherently limited and is generally confined to a specific purpose. Once created, easements pass with the land unless otherwise modified or extinguished.

The Utility Easement: When the subdivision was originally platted, the grantor provided for a utility, water, and sewer easement (the utility easement) through Lot One to benefit Lot Two. Phil can argue he has a right to access utilities by virtue of the existence of this easement in the chain of title. Tiger will argue that the utility easement no longer exists. Moreover, this easement never benefited the property owned by Phil. The court will rule in Tiger's favor on this issue.

An easement may be terminated when the titles to the dominant and servient estates are merged. *Von Meding v Strahl*, 319 Mich 598 (1948). A person cannot hold an easement over his or her own property. *Bricault v Cavanaugh*, 261 Mich 70 (1932). Thus, merger of title extinguished the utility easement that inured to the benefit of Lot Two when the portion of Lot Two to which the easement ran was sold to Arnie Parker, the owner of Lot One. Moreover, even if merger of the title did not extinguish the utility easement, it did not benefit the property purchased by Phil, since no portion of the easement reaches Phil's property. The utility easement cannot get to Phil's property without Tiger granting an extension of that easement through a portion of Tiger's property. Thus, at the time Phil purchased his property there existed no utility, water, or sewer easement that would allow Phil's property to gain access to such services. Contrary to Phil's claim, he has no right to access utility, water, and sewer lines through the utility easement documented in the original plat.

The Drive Easement: Phil also claims the right to run utility lines under and/or over ground through the drive easement. Phil will argue that such use of the land is not unduly burdensome of the land, since Phil already has a right to use this portion of the land for ingress and egress to his property. Moreover, if Phil places the utility lines above and below the ground, the burden on the land and property owner will be minimal as the need to enter the land will occur only infrequently for maintenance purposes. Tiger will argue that the drive easement should be strictly construed and limited to its stated purpose: to permit physical access to and from Lot Two. The court will rule that Phil has no right to expand his drive easement to include sewer, water, and utility lines.

Easements have traditionally been strictly construed in Michigan. "Once granted, an easement cannot be modified by either party or unilaterally. The owner of the easement cannot materially increase the burden of it on the servient estate or impose thereon a new and additional burden." *Schadewald v Brulé*, 225 Mich App 26, 36 (1997). Further, the Michigan Supreme Court recently rejected a party's attempt to expand the scope of an easement beyond the express language granting the easement. *DNR v Cardmody-Lahti Real Estate*, 472 Mich 359, 378-379 (2005). The language of the drive easement is clear—it is a drive easement; nothing more. The fact that the drive easement was not intended to operate as a utility easement is further established by the fact that the original grantor provided a utility and sewer easement elsewhere in the subdivision.

Easement by Necessity: Finding no relief through the merged and extinguished utility easement and the existing drive easement, Phil will argue he is entitled to an easement by necessity. Michigan law recognizes that an easement may be granted out of necessity where a landowner has subdivided his property and left one of the parcels landlocked. *Chapdelaie v Sochacki*, 247 Mich App 167, 172-173 (2001). Phil will argue he is denied the reasonable enjoyment of his land without the benefit of utilities. In order to develop his land he must have access to utilities; in order to gain access to utility services, Phil needs to use Tiger's land. Thus, an easement by necessity is appropriate.

Tiger will argue Phil is not entitled to an easement by necessity because Phil's land is not landlocked. Moreover, Phil is not denied reasonable enjoyment to his land. Phil may use his land for recreational activities. Significantly, at the time Phil purchased this land he knew or should have known he could not develop it. The restrictive covenant was recorded for all to see. It should have been equally clear to anyone looking at the record title of this property that there was no method of obtaining access to public utilities without obtaining an easement over Tiger's land. No easement over Tiger's property existed when Phil purchased his property. Phil purchased this property at his own risk, without any assurance he would be able to develop it.

The court will rule in favor of Phil and grant an easement by necessity. Michigan has joined a growing number of jurisdictions that recognize easements by necessity where the landowner is not physically landlocked from his property. *Tomacek v Bavas*, 276 Mich App 740 (2007). In *Tomacek, supra*, at 336, the Court of Appeals concluded that the common-law doctrine of easement by necessity includes a "right to access utilities for properties landlocked from utility services unless, consistent with the traditional principles of easement by necessity, the parties to the conveyance that left the property without such access 'clearly indicate[d] that they intended a contrary result'" quoting *Chapdelaine, supra*. As noted in the Restatement of Property 3d, § 2.15, comment D:

> [T]he increasing dependence in recent years on electricity and telephone service, delivered through overland cables, justify the conclusion that implied servitudes by necessity will be recognized for those purposes. Whether access for other utilities and services has also become necessary to reasonable enjoyment of property depends on the nature and location of the property and normal land uses in the community.

The intent of the original grantor who platted the land was that each lot have access to utilities, water and sewer lines, as evidenced by the utility easement. The intent of the restrictive covenant is not to keep the lots from being developed. To the contrary, the purpose behind the restrictive covenant is to insure that development is done properly with full access to public utility, water and sewer services. Moreover, nothing in the deed conveying the eastern half of Lot Two from Sam Smee to Arnie Parker supports the conclusion that the parties to that transaction intended to preclude the lakefront portion of Lot Two from being developed. An easement by necessity should be granted for the limited purpose of providing Phil access to utility and sewer services. Without such an easement, the court would conclude, Phil would be denied the reasonable enjoyment of his property.

Student Answer—July 2007

Question 12—Property—9 points

1. Whether Phil has a right to access utility and sewer services from the utility easement through Lot One and run it along the eastern edge of the subdivision. The user of the easement has no right to increase the burden: also called a surcharge on the original easement. Here this was an easement appurtenant

with Lot one as the dominant estate and Lot two as the servient estate. Moreover this lot was cut into two and then brought by Arnie, so the easement was extinguished by merger, when became part of lot one.

2. Whether Phil can run the sewer and utility lines underground? Here the user of an easement cannot increase the burden on the easement or expand the scope of an easement. Here this easement was for a road so that Lot two would have access to Country Club Drive. Therefore Phil cannot use this for utility lines, and the court could issue an injunction to prevent him under this argument.
3. Is Phil entitled to an easement by necessity? Probably would succeed under this argument. Easement by necessity would arise when the two parcels were split from lot number two. A purchaser of property would expect to have access to utility lines and sewer. Therefore when Sam divided his lot an easement by necessity arose as to the utility lines. Therefore Phil is likely to succeed.

Comment: Note that this answer is very brief, but cuts to the core substance and provides a brief analysis to the facts. Honestly, the grader probably was generous, but this is a situation where the examinee truly "nailed" the core issues and was rewarded.

February 2008—Question 11

John Smith recently purchased a three-unit residential property in East Lansing, Michigan. Each unit had one bedroom. At the time of the closing, two units were occupied. John immediately moved into the vacant unit. One tenant, Tammy Trump, was in the third month of a one-year lease. Tammy's lease requires payment of the rent on the first day of each month. Tammy's lease is silent regarding any recourse available to the landlord upon the failure to timely pay rent due. Tammy has a history of paying her rent late. In fact, Tammy was more than one month behind on her rent at the time of the closing on the property. Tammy is a single person with no dependents, but she has a cat. Tammy's lease expressly permits her to own one cat.

The second tenant is Sue Smart, who is a single woman with a six-month-old daughter born out of wedlock. Sue also has a cat. Sue always paid her rent timely, but she does not have a long-term lease. The rental agreement she executed with the prior owner runs from month to month, with both the tenant and landlord agreeing to provide the other with 30 days written notice prior to termination of the agreement. Rent is payable on the first of each month. Sue's month-to-month lease permits her to own one cat.

John wants to (1) implement as soon as possible a no-pet policy; (2) evict Tammy due to her habitual late payment history; and (3) evict Sue because she is unmarried and has a child born out of wedlock.

John has come to you for legal advice. Draft an opinion letter to John that addresses each of John's concerns. Limit your answer to the issues raised by John.

Model Answer to Question 11

When title in a leased property is conveyed to another, the transferee takes the property subject to the right held by tenants. Stated more simply, the new landlord stands in the shoes of the former landlord. All rights, duties, and obligations of the former landlord and tenants transfer to the new landlord and tenants. *Plaza Inv Co v Abel*, 8 Mich App 19 (1967). Thus, the lease of each tenant will govern John's relationship with them, until the term of each lease expires.

1. The No-Pet Policy: John is free to implement a no-pet policy immediately. Nothing in Michigan law precludes a landlord from discriminating among tenants on the basis of pet ownership. However, the policy cannot be immediately enforced as to either tenant. The policy can become effective as to Sue, who is in a month-to-month lease, upon 30 days' notice. In essence, by giving Sue 30 days' written notice of his intent to change the agreement, John is terminating the current 30-day lease and offering a new lease with a pet exclusion. Sue can accept the new lease by getting rid of her cat, or she can reject the lease and move out at the end of the 30-day period. By contrast, the no-pet policy is not enforceable as to Tammy until the end of her current one-year lease. At that time John can offer Tammy a new lease that expressly precludes pets. Like Sue, Tammy would be forced to get rid of her cat if she chooses to continue to live in her current residence.

2. Evict Tammy for Late Payment of Rent: Because Tammy's lease is silent as to the landlord's remedy for late payment of rent, John cannot terminate her tenancy merely because of her history of late payments. Such a basis for the termination of a tenancy must be expressly provided in the lease agreement. This does not mean, however, that John is without legal recourse that could result in the eviction of Tammy. MCL 600.5701, *et seq.*, summary proceedings to recover possession of premises, describes the steps necessary to file an action for eviction. Since Tammy is currently behind in her rent, John can serve upon her a seven-day written demand for nonpayment of rent, which requires payment of rent or possession of the premises within seven days after the date of delivery of the notice. After the expiration time on the service of the seven-day notice, if John has not received the past due rent and Tammy has not vacated the premises, he may file in the landlord tenant division of the district court a complaint for eviction. The seven-day notice and a copy of Tammy's lease must accompany the complaint. No earlier than seven days after the complaint has been filed, the court may set the matter for a hearing known as a summary proceeding, which should be limited to the issue of the tenant's nonpayment of rent. If Tammy appears at the hearing but she is unable to pay the past due rent, the court will issue a judgment for rent and possession. If Tammy appears at the hearing and expresses an unwillingness to pay the rent due to a problem with the premises, John should ask the court to require Tammy to pay the rent in an escrow account while the merit of Tammy's complaint is investigated. In either instance, a judgment requiring payment of the rent should issue. Tammy will then be afforded a ten-day appeal period during which time a Writ of Restitution may not issue. If Tammy pays her past due rent at any time during the court proceedings or within the ten-day period, John must accept the rent and cannot evict Tammy. However, if Tammy fails to pay her past due rent and does not evacuate the premises within the appeal period, John may obtain from the court a Writ of Restitution that will enable a court officer to physically remove Tammy and her belongings from the premises. If an appeal from the judgment is filed, John should move for an appeal bond and payment of the past due rent in an escrow account.

3. Evict Sue Because She Has a Child Out of Wedlock: John cannot evict Sue because she has a child out of wedlock. John desires to make a public housing determination on the basis of Sue's family and marital status. This is expressly precluded under the Michigan Civil Rights Act (CRA), MCL 37.2101 *et seq.*, which applies to real estate transactions, including residential landlord tenant transactions. Specifically, the CRA prohibits discrimination on the basis of religion, race, color, national origin, age, sex, height, weight, or marital or familial status. MCL 37.2101. The CRA carves out an exception to this rule as it relates to rental of owner-occupied residential property. MCL 37.2503(1)(a) provides, in pertinent part, that the CRA does not apply to the rental of "a housing accommodation in a building that contains housing accommodations for not more than 2 families living independently of each other if the owner or a member of the owner's immediate family resides in 1 of the housing accommodations". John may argue that since he resides in his rental property, he qualifies for this exception. However, this exception does not apply to John's rental property, which is limited to two family dwellings. Here, John's property has three units.

Student Answer—February 2008

Question 11—Real Property—9 points

Dear Mr. Smith,

This is an opinion letter, based on your property and landlord/tenant issues. The opinion I am rendering to you is based on Michigan law and the law as it stands as of today's date.

You stated that you would like to implement a no pet policy as soon as possible. Under Michigan law some of the agreements that are already in place may not be changed if they are considered to be benefits or burdens that run with the land. In your case you could argue that allowing a cat on the premises does not run with the land. Some examples are things like fences, driveways. Here you may be able to disallow pets. But one thing you should keep in mind is that, the previous owners of this property and the current tenants entered into valid lease agreements expressly allowing cats. They had what is called horizontal privy as to this matter. You and the previous owners are in vertical privy, therefore now you have to abide by the lease agreement signed by the former owner and the current tenants. When the lease runs out you are free to establish your own lease agreements with a no pet policy.

You may also want to know what to do with Tenant Tammy. You stated that she habitually pays her rent late and that before closing she was 1 month behind on rent. The lease is silent as to recourses as to late payments. If a lease is silent as to late payments your options under Michigan law include eviction. You can commence eviction proceedings against Tammy for violating terms in the lease requiring that rent be paid on the first day of the month. Please note that self-help is not an option. You have to go through the courts to commence eviction proceedings and you have to inform the tenant of your intentions. One problem you may run into is the privity issue. If the previous landlord allowed Tammy to pay rent late then Tammy could argue that paying rent late was allowed because to previous landlord never made an issue of it.

With regard to Sue, you cannot evict her because she is unmarried and has a child out of wedlock. You stated that Sue is a month to month tenant. According to the agreement you can require Sue to move out simply by giving her 30 days written notice. That is the agreement she made with the previous landlord and because of privity you can enforce the agreement.

I hope this letter answers your questions. If you have any further questions please do not hesitate to contact me.

Yours very truly,

Attorney

> **Comment:** This is an excellent response and directly answers the question asked. Incidentally, many students did not do well on this Property question mainly because they weren't prepared for it. Landlord/Tenant had not been tested on the Michigan Bar Exam in many years. This question reflects why you must be prepared for anything. Do not gamble!

February 2008—Question 12

In 1984, Bruce Barber owned one square block of real property in the City of Silver Springs. Bruce's property was between North Street and South Street, and First Avenue and Second Avenue. Four buildings of equal size took up the area. The front entrances to the buildings were on North and South streets. A very narrow alley ran parallel to North and South streets, from First Avenue to Second Avenue. The alley provided very limited access to the rear entrances of the buildings. Bruce rarely used the rear entrance to his buildings. Bruce operated a carpentry business that specialized in the construction of custom poker tables in the building on the corner of North Street and Second Avenue. The other three buildings were vacant. In 1985, Alan Anderson purchased from Bruce the building on the corner of North Street and First Avenue. Bruce operated his carpentry shop from 7:00 a.m. to 3:00 p.m., Monday through Friday. Alan opened a nightclub in his building, which he operated from 4:00 p.m. to 2:00 a.m., seven days per week. The nightclub was a smashing success and became nationally known as the place to be seen in Michigan. In 1988, Alan made Bruce an offer to purchase the two vacant buildings on South Street, between First and Second Avenues. Alan indicated he wanted to demolish the buildings to provide surface parking for his nightclub. Bruce liked the idea of having a parking lot behind his building. Bruce accepted Alan's offer and provided Alan a warranty deed at the closing that made no express statement in the deed reserving to Bruce any rights in the property.

In 1989, Alan demolished the buildings and paved the area to create a surface parking lot. Alan also remodeled the nightclub to make the rear of the building the main entrance to the club. Prior to 1989, Bruce's employees and patrons accessed his shop through the North Street entrance. Also, Bruce accepted deliveries and sent shipments through the North Street entrance. However, commencing in 1989, Bruce created a rear entrance with a showroom to greet his cash-and-carry patrons and Bruce's advertisements and street signs informed Bruce's patrons to park behind the building and enter from the rear. Bruce also instructed his employees to park in the lot behind the building and enter his building through the back entrance. To ensure that his patrons, employees, and truckers had access to Bruce's rear loading dock and entry way, Bruce hired a contractor for guaranteed snow removal each day before 7:00 a.m. in the winter months and he hired a contractor to clean the parking lot on a daily basis of any debris left behind by nightclub patrons. Bruce never asked Alan for permission to use the parking lot. Bruce used Alan's parking lot without incident from 1989 until 2005. However, in 2005, as a result of the national poker boom, Bruce expanded his business hours and began to stay open until 10:00 p.m. As a result, some of Bruce's customers and many freight haulers calling on Bruce's business were partially blocking the entrance to Alan's nightclub during Alan's hours of operation.

Alan has come to you for advice on whether he can stop Bruce from using his parking lot. How would you advise Alan? Explain your answer.

Model Answer to Question 12

There is no question that Bruce is using land that is rightfully titled to Alan. The issue is whether Alan, as a fee simple holder of the real property in question, can stop Bruce from using his land. The only way Bruce can rightfully use Alan's property is if Bruce can establish an easement right. An easement is an interest in real property that gives one person the right to use another's land for a specific purpose. *Eyde v State of Michigan*, 82 Mich App 531 (1978). Ownership is not at issue. An easement merely grants the right to use a piece of property but only to the extent necessary to enjoy the rights conferred by the easement.

An easement may be created by express grant or by operation of law. *Forge v Smith*, 458 Mich 198 (1998). An express easement must be very clear in its intent, *id.*, and it must be in writing. *Myers v Spencer*, 318 Mich 155 (1947). Here, there is no evidence of an express grant of an easement. The facts state that Bruce "provided Alan a warranty deed at the closing that made no express statement in the deed reserving to Bruce any rights in the property." Thus, Bruce can rightfully use the property only if he can show that he is entitled to an easement by operation of law.

An easement by necessity is one type of easement that may be created by operation of law. *Schmidt v Eger*, 94 Mich App 728 (1980); see also *Chapadelaine v Sochocki*, 247 Mich App 167 (2001). While older Michigan cases spoke of a requirement of strict or absolute necessity, see *Waubun Beach Ass'n v Wilson*, 274 Mich 598, 609 (1936), a "grant of an easement by necessity requires (in the least) a showing of reasonable necessity." *Tomecek v Bavas*, 276 Mich App 252, 256 (2007). "The scope of an easement by necessity is that which is reasonably necessary for proper enjoyment of the property, with minimum burden on the servient estate." *Schumacher v Dep't of Natural Resources*, 256 Mich App 103, 106 (2003). Here, there is no indication that Bruce cannot enjoy his property as he had before the addition of the rear parking lot. Thus, Bruce cannot sustain a claim for easement by necessity.

An easement will also be implied in law by prescription. A prescriptive easement is akin to fee title that passed by adverse possession. In order to claim a prescriptive easement, one must use without permission the land of another for a particular purpose and without interruption for a minimum period of fifteen years. MCL 600.5801 (4). Although case law presents several varying elements of an easement by prescription, Michigan courts have consistently identified that an easement by prescription requires elements similar to adverse possession except exclusivity. *Id.*, citing *Plymouth Canton Community Crier, Inc v Prose*, 242 Mich App 676, 679 (2000).

Thus, the following elements have been noted: actual use visible use, open use, notorious use, hostile use, use under cover of claim or right, and continuous use for fifteen years.

Recently, however, courts have only required that a prescriptive easement result from use of another's property that is open, notorious, adverse, and continuous for a period of 15 years. *See Higgins Lake Property Owners Ass'n v Gerrish Twp*, 255 Mich App 83, 118 (2003). (Citations omitted), citing *Plymouth Canton Community Crier, Inc, supra* at 676; *Goodall v Whitefish Hunting Club*, 208 Mich App 642, 645 (1995); MCL 600.5801 (4); *see also Marr v Hemenny*, 297 Mich 311 (1941); *Mumrow v Riddle*, 67 Mich App 693, 698 (1976); *Dyer v Thurston*, 32 Mich App 341, 343 (1971). The burden of proving the existence of a prescriptive easement rests on the party claiming the easement. *Stewart v Hunt*, 303 Mich 161 (1942).

Here, Bruce openly and notoriously used the easement for a period over 15 years. Bruce constructed a loading dock near Alan's property plainly to use the property. Bruce then, in plain sight, used the property for loading and unloading freight. Bruce also had his employees traverse the easement to enter his building and he directed his patrons by posting signs near the property to park on Alan's property and use the rear door to enter the building. Although Bruce's carpentry shop and Alan's club were not open for business during the same hours, there is little room for doubt that Bruce's use of Alan's property was open and notorious.

The term "hostile," as used in the law of adverse possession, is a term of art and does not imply ill will. *Plymouth Canton Community Crier, Inc, supra* at 681. Adverse or hostile use is use that is inconsistent with the right of the owner, without permission asked or given, that would entitle the owner to a cause of action against the intruder for trespassing. *Id.* Here, Bruce used the property for loading and unloading trucks without asking permission. Further, Alan did not offer permission yet Bruce treated this property as his own. He told his workers, and patrons, to park on Alan's property and enter his building by crossing Alan's property. Significantly, Bruce cared for the property as if it were his own, by cleaning it and insuring that it was free of snow and ice in the winter. Accordingly, Bruce's use of the property satisfies the hostile requirement.

In regard to continuous use, "a use is continuous when it is regular, even if not constant." *Dyer, supra*. Here, Bruce used the property to conduct regular business, from 1989 through the present. Bruce's use of the property included the use to facilitate shipments and deliveries, allowing access to patrons and employees through the rear entrance of the building, and maintaining the property. Thus, there is no credible argument that may be advanced that Bruce did not use the property continuously for more than 15 years. In sum, it appears Bruce may satisfy the central elements of a prescriptive easement.

However, Alan could persuasively argue that even if Bruce's prior use of the parking lot entitled Bruce to an easement by prescription, Bruce's current use is beyond the scope of the easement acquired and previously enjoyed. A prescriptive easement is generally limited in scope by the manner in which it was acquired and the previous enjoyment. *Heydon v MediaOne of Southeast Michigan, Inc*, 275 Mich App 267, 270-271 (2007), citing 25 Am Jur 2d, Easements and Licenses, § 81, p 579. "One who holds a prescriptive easement is allowed to do such acts as are necessary to make effective the enjoyment of the easement unless the burden on the servient estate is unreasonably increased; the scope of the privilege is determined largely by what is reasonable under the circumstances." *Id.* citing *Mumrow, supra* at 699-700. As mentioned, Bruce used the easement, for over 15 years without incident. Only when Bruce extended the store hours did a problem arise. Thus, Alan should file suit and argue that, to the extent Bruce can establish a prescriptive easement, the use of the easement during Bruce's newly extended store hours is an unwarranted expansion of the easement that places an unreasonable burden on Alan's estate.

A court could go either way on this issue. Full credit is awarded if the applicant recognizes the issue and cogently discusses the legal arguments.

Student Answer—February 2008

Question 12—Equity and Property—8 points

When Bruce sold the building to Alan in 1985 and in 1988, the two of them did not anticipate having to use Alan's parking lot. So, Bruce did not reserve use for himself and Alan did not reserve or restrict use either. The issue here is whether Bruce has a valid easement to use Alan's parking lot.

No, he does not. An easement is a right to use someone else's property by permission for a specific purpose. This right can be expressly given or passes with a deed. Here none of that is present in the facts. However, we could have an easement by prescription where the dominant estate, Bruce's property, adversely uses without permission openly, the servient property, Alan's property, for a specific purpose.

Here, Bruce used Alan's parking lot for deliveries, parking, rear entrance for customer, had hired snow removal and cleaning crew. This continued from 1988 to 2005 without incident and without objection from Alan. The required time for an easement by prescription under Michigan law is 15 years. From 1989 to 2004 would be 15 years so in 2005 would be over that required period so the easement by prescription would attach and it would touch and concern the land. So, Alan would have a hard time stopping Bruce from using the parking lot.

However, Alan can impose restrictions on the use of the parking lot by Bruce; because Bruce is trying to increase the use of the parking lot to more than he did before. This would be called burdening the easement with more and increased use than it was used for before during the time the easement was prescribed 1989-2005.

So, Alan can enjoin Bruce from the increase burdening of the easement by asking him to reduce his use back to the hours he used before and with less traffic. The increased traffic burden Alan's servient estate, overburdened the existing easement by prescription.

Comment: This is a well-written answer but it fails to break down the specific elements of easement by prescription (i.e., hostile, continuous, open, and notorious, but NOT exclusive like in adverse possession). If this student had done so, full credit would have been awarded.

July 2008—Question 7

The Water Wonderland subdivision was platted in 1990. The plat created 22 lots of equal size, in two rows of eleven. The row of lots to the West was on Lake Michigan. The row of lots was identified in the plat as the "Lake Front Row." The lots in this row were identified as Lakefront Lot 1 through Lakefront lot 11, running from the north to south.

The row of lots to the east of the Lake Front Row was identified in the plat as the "Nature Row." The lots in this row were identified in the plat as the Nature Lot 1 through Nature Lot 11, also running from north to south. The Nature Row was not on Lake Michigan. A notation on the plat map indicated that the Lot known as Lake Front Lot 6 was "dedicated to the joint use of all the owners of the Water Wonderland subdivision." In addition, there was a 10-foot-wide strip of land identified in the plat as a "drive" that ran from north to south, between the Lake Front Row and the Nature Row. The plat indicated that drive was "dedicated to the joint use of all the owners of the plat to provide access to all 22 lots in the subdivision." To the west of the drive was a 5-foot-wide strip of land that ran from north to south, parallel to the drive. The plat indicated the walk was "dedicated to the joint use of all the owners of the plat to provide access to Lake Michigan and Lake Front Lot 6."

All lots except Lake Front Lot 6 were developed by the platter of the subdivision. Each lot had built upon it a three-bedroom, two-bath, 1,500-square-foot home with a two-car attached garage. The subdivision sold out within one year. From its inception through 2006, the property was enjoyed by all 21 lot owners without incident. Between 1991 and 1999, the owners of the lots in the Lake Front Row constructed docks in front of their respective lots. Each dock could moor no more than two boats.

In 2006, the Midland Hunt Club, a nonprofit incorporated social club, purchased all eleven lots in Nature Row. Pursuant to the Hunt Club By-Laws, no more than 44 members could be on the property at any one time. Every weekend from May through October, 44 club members visited the property. Each Friday and Saturday night, club members would enjoy a fire maintained in a preexisting fire pit located on the beach-front of Lot 6. The club members would enjoy the beach and the fire in a peaceful manner until the very early hours of the morning. The owners in the Lake Front Row did not appreciate the Hunt Club. They felt there were too many members using the Lake Front Lot 6.

In the spring of 2008, the Hunt Club members arrived at the property with tools in hand and began to construct a six-foot-high wood fence along the border of Lake Front Lots 5 and 6, and 6 and 7 that stretched from the walk to the water. Additionally, the club began construction of a dock that was larger than any of the docks constructed by owners of the Lake Front Lots and was designed to hold as many as 11 boats.

The owners of Lake Front Lots 1-5 and 7-11 joined together to file suit against Midland Hunt Club. The plaintiffs asked the court for an injunction that would require the Hunt Club to: (1) cease construction and require removal of the dock and the wood fences; (2) limit to 22 the number of club members who can utilize Lake Front Lot 6 at any given time. No local zoning or land use ordinances apply.

How will the court rule? Explain your answer.

Model Answer to Question 7

The court will grant the plaintiff's motion as it relates to the construction of the fences and the dock. The court will deny the motion as it relates to the request to limit the number of Hunt Club members who use Lake Front Lot 6.

I. Removal of the Dock and the Fences: The right to construct a dock for the purposes of using and enjoying a lake is a well-recognized right of riparian owners. *McCardel v Smolen*, 404 Mich 89 (1978); *Blain v Craigie*, 294 Mich 545 (1940). If the Hunt Club is deemed to be a riparian owner and whether the Hunt Club possesses riparian rights is determined by the plat dedication. *Thies v Howland*, 424 Mich 282 (1985). "The intent of the plattors must be determined from the language they used and the surrounding circumstances." *Id.*, at 293. Here, the plat provides that Lake Front Lot 6 was "dedicated to the joint use of all owners of Water Wonderland subdivision." Additionally, a walk was put in place that was "dedicated to the joint use of all owners of the plat to provide access to Lake Michigan and Lake Front Lot 6." The term "joint use" suggests that the Hunt Club is not a riparian owner. In *Theis, supra*, the Michigan Supreme Court considered the right of back lot owners who were provided access by way of a walk that was dedicated in the plat. In *Thies*, the back lot owners in a waterfront subdivision constructed a dock at the end of their easement that granted lake access. The Supreme Court looked at the plat dedication, which dictated the walk to "joint use of all owners of the plat" and concluded that the use of the term "joint use" did not support the conclusion that a fee interest passed in the land that would afford the back lot owners riparian rights to construct a dock. *Thies* is distinguishable from the present case, however, because the plat did not dedicate a waterfront lot for the use of the subdivision owners.

In *Dobie v Morrison*, 227 Mich App 536, 537 (1998), the Michigan Court of Appeals held that the dedication of a waterfront lot in a plat to "the use of the owners of the lots in this plat which have no lake frontage" established an easement in favor of all back lot subdivision owners. However, the court held that the dedication did not create a passing of a fee interest that would include riparian rights. The dedication in the plat in *Dobie* was stronger for back lot owners than the dedication in the present case, since the *Dobie* dedication limited the use of the lake front lot to lot owners who did not have lake front property. By contract, here the plat dedicated Lake Front Lot 6 to all subdivision owners, regardless of whether the owner already had a lake front lot. Since the language of the dedication provides for joint use by all subdivision owners, the Hunt Club's interest in Lake Front Lot 6 is nothing more than an easement, which entitles them to reasonable use of the land, but does not permit them to construct a dock of any size. The court will order the Hunt Club to cease and order the removal of whatever structures had been constructed.

The same legal standard would apply to the construction of the fences. While the owners of Lake Front Lots 5 and 7 could construct a fence on their property line, the Hunt Club does not enjoy the same right. The Hunt Club simply does not own a fee interest in Lake Front Lot 6. In fact, the Hunt Club and the owners of the lake front lots possess identical rights to use Lake Front Lot 6. Nothing in the plat dedication would support the conclusion that the Hunt Club could construct and maintain fences on the property lines of Lake Front Lot 6. The court will enjoin the Hunt Club from doing so.

II. Limiting the Number of Hunt Club Members Who Utilize Lake Front Lot 6: The court will not reduce the number of Hunt Club members who can utilize Lake Front Lot 6 below 44, the maximum number of members who are permitted to use the property under the club's By-Laws. The permissible use of Lake Front Lot 6 will be determined by the intent of the plattors. *Thies, supra.* The intent of the plattors is determined by the language of the dedication and the surrounding circumstances. *Id.* Here, the platter created 22 lots, eleven of which did not sit on the lake. On each lot the platter contemplated there would be times when the 11 Nature Row lots would house at least 4 people each and that these people would use Lake Front Lot 6. Thus, the number of people emanating from the Nature Lots to use Lake Front Lot 6 is not per se unreasonable. Still, the Hunt Club merely holds an easement to use Lake Front Lot 6. Nonriparian land owners who are granted lake access through an easement may not unreasonably interfere with the riparian owners' use and enjoyment of the riparian property. *Park Trustee for Cass County v Wendt*, 361 Mich 247 (1960). Here, there is nothing provided in the facts that would suggest that the Hunt Club's use of Lake Front Lot 6 was unreasonable or otherwise interferes with the riparian rights of the lake front owners. Beach front fires are a common occurrence and a reasonable use of beach front property. While the Hunt Club members stayed on the beach until the "very early hours of the morning" they did so in a peaceful manner. There exists no basis for the court to interfere with the Hunt Club's use of Lake Front Lot 6 in this regard.

Two Student Answers—July 2008

Question 7—Real Property—9 points

The issues raised in the question are in regards to easements and equitable servitudes. On the issue of ceasing construction and requiring removal of the dock and wood fences, the court should issue the injunction.

Lot 6 is owned in joint tenancy by all the owners of the subdivision. This lot has been dedicated to the use of all owners in the subdivision. In addition there were two easements appurtenant created as "drives." Since the drives specifically state what they are for, they are limited to that use and no more. The Hunt Club cannot come along and decide to build a dock. They are on record notice of Lot 6 because it is noted in the plat map and they have actual notice because they can see by looking around that the use of the plot for years has not included construction of individual lots.

In Michigan equitable servitudes in Michigan Subdivisions are valid and enforceable. The Hunt Club must not use the land or easement for anything other than the intended uses. Even though they are not the original owners of the land, they are subsequent purchasers and are bound, regardless of privity, since it is not required. A restrictive covenant (equitable servitude) is a restriction on the use of land and is valid, so an injunction should be granted to enjoin them from building.

With regard to the second issue, limiting the number of club members who can utilize at any given time to 22 is not enforceable.

The covenant doesn't say that there is a limit to how many can be on land only that it is for all to enjoy.

However, a good argument would be that it is a residential subdivision and Hunt Club was on notice and shouldn't have been allowed to turn 11 lots into one social club. However, if the 44 members disturb the covenant of quiet enjoyment, the surrounding homeowners may have an action there. Landowners are allowed to use their land w/out unreasonable disruptions. Parties by the club members into the wee hours of the morning could be a nuisance and an injunction could be used to limit the disturbances. Nuisances are unreasonable interferences with landowners right and remedy of injunction will be enforced if court doesn't have to supervise. Even though today courts are more willing. This is not an issue because H would be a negative injunction to stop them from using it into wee hours of the morning.

In conclusion, the court will rule to enforce the injunction against the Hunt Club's construction of the docks and deny limiting the number to 22 unless plaintiffs show disturbance of covenant which touch and concern the land.

Question 7—Real Property—8 points

Conclusion: The owners will likely succeed in obtaining an injunction on count 1 to remove the fence and dock, but likely will not succeed on count 2, to limit the number of users of the communal lot.

Rule: To obtain an injunction, the moving party must prove there is no legal remedy available, they are likely to succeed, their injunction will burden less than the hardships not imposing one would create, that a bond is posted with the courts, and that enforcement will not burden the court.

Analysis—Issue #1: [sidebar] Because=B/C. B/C the decks and fence have not been completed, they will be easy to remove. The fence blocks access of landowners 5 and 7 to direct access to the communal lot and all the lake front owners to the walkway. The dock that club members are planning is considerably larger than that of other landowners, although it holds half as many boats as those that could be held by landowners in lots 1-5 + 7-12, it appears that it would harm the enjoyment of all to use lot 6, since that is where it is planned. It is unlikely that the landowners could get monetary damages, since what they want is to stop construction, no $, therefore, no legal remedy. The burden is on the club to take down the fence and dock does not harm very much—compared to the harm to the landowners to not have access to lot 6 and the walkway. Club members could always contract w/the lakefront owners to get dock space, rather than constructing a dock of their own. Enforcement will not hinder the court—they will quickly be able to determine if a fence is there or not (same w/the dock.)

Conclusion: Therefore, the injunction to remove the dock + fence will likely be granted.

Issue #2—Analysis: It will be considerably more difficult to get an injunction and limit the number of users on the shared lot. B/C there is no sort of money damages available for landowners based on a harm from a large number of others peacefully on the land and would be unlikely to succeed at such an action, an injunction may fail. Also, in balancing the hardships, the club members have a property interest being able to use the lot to gather; being annoyed, but otherwise unharmed, is far less than the harm the club members would have if the injunction were granted. Further, a court's ability to enforce such an injunction are [sic] extreme. Court officers cannot realistically be expected to count the # of people on a piece of land each weekend.

Conclusion: Therefore, the injunction to limit the number of people will NOT be granted.

> **Comment:** Note that neither student answer mentioned Riparian Water Rights or the Public Trust Doctrine. The reality is most examinees did not discuss these issues. As a result the graders ended up being very generous in scoring this question.

February 2009—Question 11

Joe and Trina Murphy purchased their house and lot, Lot 27 of Happy Land Subdivision, in 2001, and moved in immediately. Lot 27 was bounded on the north by Briggs Avenue. The other three sides of the lot were completely fenced in by a continuous chain link fence. Before they signed the purchase agreement, the Murphys walked the property with the seller, Dominico Brown, who told them that the lot included everything within the fence.

Brown had owned Lot 27 since 1973 and erected the fence in 1974. Since that time, he had maintained all of Lot 27 within the fence, planted a hedge along the fence on the east side of Lot 27, and installed a lawn sprinkler system that ran within six inches of the fence around the entire perimeter of the yard. When Brown erected the fence, he did so without any regard for where the actual surveyed boundary line was located. In 1984, Brown also built a large storage shed for his lawn tractor that literally hugged the fence on the east side of his property.

After the Murphys had purchased Lot 27 and lived there for seven years, their neighbor to the east, Alfred Zehnder, had a survey performed on his property, known as Lot 26, in connection with a refinancing of his home mortgage. The survey, which was accurate, showed that the Murphys' fence encroached on Zehnder's lot by about three feet, and that the Murphys' sprinkler system, hedge, and shed were located within that three-foot encroachment.

Zehnder's attorney wrote the Murphys a letter in October 2008, stating that they were trespassing on Lot 26 and demanding that they remove the fence, hedge, sprinkler system, and shed. The Murphys have sought your advice on this controversy.

Do not decide the case, but please advise them on their possible rights and potential liabilities in written memo.

Model Answer to Question 11

Mr. and Mrs. Murphy:

You have asked me to advise you regarding your rights with respect to the boundary line dispute between your neighbor, Mr. Zehnder, and you, with respect to Lots 26 and 27 of Happy Land Subdivision.

Trespass is an intentional and unauthorized invasion of another person's interest in the exclusive possession of his property. *Traver Lakes Community Maintenance Ass'n v Douglas Co*, 224 Mich App 335, 344 (1997); *Cloverleaf Car Co v Phillips Petroleum Co*, 213 Mich App 186, 195 (1995). So, at first blush, you are technically trespassing on Zehnder's property. However, that does not conclude the issue. You may have rights under the theories of adverse possession, prescriptive easement, or acquiescence.

Adverse Possession: A person who is a trespasser may be able to avoid being ousted from possession of another's land if the statute of limitations on trespass has run and certain other requirements are met. The theory is that if the record owner is barred from ousting you from land because of the 15-year statute of limitations, then nobody can oust you and, accordingly, you become the effective owner of the property. In order to secure title by adverse possession, the claimant must establish by clear and cogent proof that his or her possession is actual, visible, open, notorious, exclusive, continuous and uninterrupted for the statute period of 15 years, hostile and under cover of claim of right. *Burns v Foster*, 348 Mich 8, 14 (1957). You have been living on Lot 27 for only seven years.

Even though you have been living there for only seven years, you may be able to "tack" Mr. Brown's 27 or 28 years of possession onto your seven years in order to meet the 15-year requirement. Tacking is the ability to assume the adverse possession of one's predecessor. *Connelly v Buckingham*, 136 Mich App 462, 467-468 (1984). So, if

Mr. Brown's possession was adverse, you can add his 27 or 28 years to your seven years of possession to meet the 15-year possession requirement.

The existence of the fence for 34 years, the fact that the fence was built by Mr. Brown, the planting of the hedge in the disputed area, the construction of the shed in the disputed area, installation of the sprinkler in the disputed area, and the maintenance of that area by the owner of Lot 27 since 1973-1974 are evidence that your possession and your predecessor's was actual, visible, open, notorious, exclusive, continuous, and uninterrupted. Because Brown erected the fence without regard for the boundary line, the possession was hostile. *Werner v Noble*, 286 Mich 654 (1938), and *DeGroot v Barber*, 198 Mich App 48 (1993).

Acquiescence: There is an alternative theory, known as acquiescence, under which you might be able to acquire title to the property. The law of acquiescence applies the statute of limitations to cases of adjoining property owners who are mistaken about where the line between their property is. Adjoining property owners may treat a boundary line, typically a fence, as the property line. If the boundary line is not the recorded property line, this results in one property owner possessing what is actually the other property owner's land. Regardless of the innocent nature of this mistake, the property owner whose land is being possessed by another would have cause of action against the other property owner to recover possession of the land. After fifteen years, the period for bringing an action would expire. The result is that the property owner of record would no longer be able to enforce his title, and the other property owner would have title by virtue of his possession of the land. *See Jackson v Deemer*, 373 Mich 22, 26 (1964). This theory is based on an implied agreement between the adjoining property owners.

As discussed above, the fact that the fence between Lots 26 and 27 has been in existence since 1974 and that both owners treated it as their boundary shows an implied agreement that the fence was the practical boundary between the two lots. So, acquiescence is a viable theory in your case.

Prescriptive Easement: A prescriptive easement is similar to adverse possession. The difference is that if you are successful, you will not own the disputed area, but will have the right to use it. In order to obtain a prescriptive easement, you must show all of the same elements that are required for adverse possession except that the possession by the party claiming the easement does not have to be exclusive. *West Michigan Dock & Market Corp v Lakeland Investments*, 210 Mich App 505, 511 (1995). So, you could obtain a prescriptive easement even if the disputed area was used by the owners of both Lot 26 and 27, as long as you satisfy the other elements.

General: Adverse possession is not a favored theory. Therefore, you must have clear and convincing evidence to show adverse possession.

Student Answer—February 2009

Question 11—Real Property—8 points

To: Joe and Trina Murphy
From: Attorney
Re: Alfred Zehnder—Your neighbor on Lot 2

In looking at your case, as landowner of Lot 27, you do have right to the land.

Under the doctrine of adverse possession you are not trespassing on Alfred Zehnder. You own the right to that three feet because you have adversely possessed the land.

To have a successful claim under adverse possession you would have to show that you have possessed the land adversely, openly, hostile, and continuous for the statutory period which is 15 years in Michigan.

Even though you have been living on the lot for seven years, the prior owner's adverse possession period will tack onto your seven years. As you are well aware, Mr. Brown erected the fence in 1974, so counting from 1974 to 2009 gives you 35 years and as a result, you are not a trespasser. The three feet encroachment now becomes part of your lot and your neighbor cannot sue you for encroaching on his side of the property.

Another issue that may present itself is the boundary line dispute. There was no acquiescence between Mr. Brown and the neighbors and with that they might try to sue to enforce the boundary line.

I do not see any potential liabilities, your purchase agreement included everything within the fence and I do not believe the court is going to ask you to take down the fence. Therefore, your right to the land remains strong under the doctrine of Adverse Possession.

Good luck and all the best.

Attorney.

July 2009—Question 15

Mike and Kate went to MyBank in order to apply for a second mortgage on their home. On the loan application, Mike indicated that they were applying for a second mortgage and listed the name of their primary lender, Bank Zero. However, on some of the other relevant documents, Kate inadvertently forgot to disclose any information about their primary lender. During the application process, MyBank learned that Mike and Kate had just closed on their first mortgage during the preceding week, but that Bank Zero had not yet recorded its mortgage. Nevertheless, MyBank closed on their mortgage and recorded it on June 21, 2009. After firing about half of its staff and rehiring more competent employees, Bank Zero finally got around to recording its mortgage on June 23, 2009.

Although the extra cash flow from the second mortgage helped Mike and Kate stay afloat for a while, they began to sink further and further into debt. Eventually Mike and Kate defaulted on their mortgages to both MyBank and Bank Zero.

Discuss the relevant issues regarding the impending mortgage priority dispute between MyBank and Bank Zero, including your opinion on which bank has the superior lien. Explain your answer.

Model Answer to Question 15

"Michigan is a race-notice state, and owners of interests in land can protect their interests by properly recording those interests." *Richards v Tibaldi*, 272 Mich App 522 (2006), quoting *Lakeside Ass'n v Toski Sands*, 131 Mich App 292 (1983). A recorded instrument, such as a deed or mortgage, is considered "notice to all persons except the recorded landowner of the liens, rights, and interests acquired by or involved in the proceedings. All subsequent owners or encumbrances shall take subject to the perfected liens, rights, or interests." MCL 565.25(4). Pursuant to Michigan's recording statute, MCL 565.29, "the holder of a real estate interest who first records his interest generally has priority over subsequent purchasers." *Richards, supra* at 539.

It is clear from the facts above that although Bank Zero's mortgage was made first, MyBank' s mortgage was recorded first. Therefore, MyBank's mortgage takes priority if MyBank is a good-faith purchaser who paid valuable consideration. There is no dispute that MyBank is a purchaser who paid valuable consideration, so the only question is whether MyBank is a purchaser in good faith.

A bona fide purchaser is a party who acquires an interest in real estate for valuable consideration and in good faith, without notice of a third party's claimed interest. *Richards, supra* at 539. Notice can be actual or constructive. *Richards, supra.* Constructive notice exists [w]hen a person has knowledge of such facts as would lead any honest man, using ordinary caution, to make further inquiries concerning the possible rights of another in real estate, and fails to make such inquiries. *Kastle v Clemons*, 330 Mich 28, 31 (1951). The relevant issues are whether the facts were sufficient to give rise to the need to make further inquiry and, if so, whether due diligence was exercised in making the inquiry. *American Fed* S & *L Ass'n v Orenstein*, 81 Mich App 249, 252 (1978).

As the facts indicate, Mike clearly disclosed the name of the primary lender on his application. This could be considered actual notice to MyBank. In the very least, it should have lead MyBank to make further inquiries concerning the possibility of a superior lien. Therefore, before MyBank executed its mortgage, it had constructive, if not actual, notice that its mortgage was intended to be subordinate to the one issued by Bank Zero. As such, MyBank is not a good faith purchaser and Bank Zero's interests would be entitled to priority despite the fact that it did not record its mortgage first.

Student Answers—July 2009

Question 15—Property—8 points

Mortgage Priority

In this case we start with who had priority. In general the 1st to record has priority over the others—so even though Bank Zero had 1st mortgage they *never recorded* their interest. So normally other mortgagors/creditors would not have notice and could become a *BFP*—bona fide purchase. A BFP is one who purchases *for value* but has *no notice* of earlier encumbrances and in MI a BFP must record 1st because this is a *race-notice state.* But the facts show "MyBank" was not a BFP because though they gave value (as the mortgagee for consideration) MyBank had notice of Bank Zero's prior interest. MyBank could say it did not have *actual notice* because BankZero didn't record but MyBank had *inquiry and constructive notice* because of what M & K put on their loan application. So even though MyBank recorded 1st they are not the BFP.

Also it must be noted that since Bank Zero has *already closed* then all other junior mortgagors/liens and creditors' interest will get wiped out during foreclosure. So in my opinion Bank Zero has the superior lien because after foreclosure fees, attorney fees get paid off and after principal gets paid off then Bank Zero would be the first to get money. Since MI is a lien theory state, Bank Zero has a lien on M & K's property anyway. This means that once they foreclosed they now become the owner's of property and so once MyBank took the 2nd mortgage they took it with all the *encumbrances attached* to it. So MyBank has a mortgage already on this property since they took subject to the Bank Zero's first mortgage, so again MyBank does not have a superior lien.

February 2010—Question 11

In the spring of 2009, Peter Parker bought a Lake Michigan beachfront home from Debbie Drake. Drake advertised the property as: "A lovely cottage built in 1980; recently remodeled with new kitchen cabinets and fresh carpet and wall paneling throughout." Parker had an independent expert inspect the home and all accessible structural beams. The inspection report was favorable. A week prior to the closing date, Drake provided a Seller's Disclosure Act, indicating that, to her knowledge, there were no defects on the property. Specifically, Drake indicated that the home had no history of infestation. Drake subsequently executed a deed in Parker's favor, conveying Drake's fee simple interest to the property.

When summer arrived, Parker discovered that many people walked the beach in front of his home. Parker posted signs prohibiting trespassers on his beach. However, the beach walkers ignored the signs.

That same summer, Parker decided to remove wall paneling from the interior of the house and install drywall. When Parker removed the paneling from the lakeside exterior wall, he immediately noticed extensive termite damage to the wooden structural beams. Although the termites had since vacated the premises, the structural damage cost $20,000 to repair.

Discuss Parker's rights with respect to (a) preventing people from walking along his stretch of beach; (b) his recourse against Drake for denying any history of termite infestation in the home. Explain your answer.

Model Answer to Question 11

(a) Parker cannot prevent people from walking along land held in public trust by the state. The Great Lakes, as large navigable bodies of water, are natural resources and routes of commerce that are held in trust by the state for the benefit of the public. The state may convey "littoral" property (land abutting the Great Lakes) to private citizens, but only subject to the public trust. Pursuant to the public trust doctrine, the land between the "ordinary high water mark" and the water's edge is held in trust by the state for the use of all citizens. The "ordinary high water mark" is created by the changing water levels in the Great Lakes over time (not by the actions of tides as occurs for ocean-side property). That mark is described as the point where "the presence and action of the water is so continuous as to leave a distinct mark either by erosion, destruction of terrestrial vegetation, or other easily recognized characteristic." *Glass v Goeckel*, 473 Mich 667 (2005).

Parker has fee simple title to the water's edge. However, that fee simple overlaps with the public trust between the water's edge and the "ordinary high water mark."

Parker may prevent the public from trespassing onto his private property above the "ordinary high water mark," but has no recourse to prevent the public from walking the shore between the "ordinary high water mark" and the water's edge.

(b) Whether Parker has a claim against Drake for the incorrect statement on the Seller's Disclosure Statement depends on whether Drake had knowledge of the termites. Under the Seller Disclosure Act, MCL 565.950 *et seq.*, a party transferring property is required to provide a written disclosure statement to the purchaser. MCL 565.954(1). The statutory disclosure form requires the transferor to disclose any history of infestation, including termites. MCL 565.957(1). The party transferring the property is required to make each disclosure in "good faith," defined as "honesty in fact in the conduct of the transaction." MCL 565.960. However, the transferor is not liable for inaccuracies or errors in the disclosure statement in the information "was not within the personal knowledge of the transferor, or was based entirely on information provided by . . . [an expert], and ordinary care was exercised in transmitting the information." MCL 565.955(1). The transferor also cannot be held liable if the failure to disclose related to information "that could be obtained only through inspection or observation of inaccessible portions of real estate or could be discovered only" by an expert. MCL 565.955(1), (3).

Drake asserted that she had recently installed fresh wall paneling in the home. When that paneling was removed, the structural damage caused by the since-departed termite infestation was immediately visible. This evidence suggests that the damage and prior infestation by termites was within the personal knowledge of Drake and that she did not act honestly in failing to disclose that information in the Seller's Disclosure Statement.

Consistent with the Seller Disclosure Act, Parker can pursue a claim against Drake for fraudulent misrepresentation alleging that Drake (1) made a material representation; (2) that was false; (3) that Drake knew the representation was false at the time or recklessly made the statement as a positive assertion without knowledge; (4) Drake intended Parker to act on the statement; (5) Parker actually did act in reliance; (6) Parker was injured as a result. However, if Parker cannot prove that Drake actually knew about the prior termite infestation, Parker's claim will fail. The provisions of the Seller Disclosure Act preclude a claim for "innocent misrepresentation" because that claim does not require proof of knowledge. *Roberts v Saffell*, 280 Mich App 397 (2008), affd 483 Mich 1089 (2009).

Two Student Answers—February 2010

Question 11—Property—10 points

This is a property question. In regards to Parker's rights with respect to preventing people from walking along his stretch of beach he will find that he has very little rights in these regards. Michigan courts have held that an owner of property that fronts a beach on a public lake (not a private lake) such as Lake Michigan does not own the rights to the beach. He enjoys the lakes and this property belongs to the state. Therefore Parker's posted signs prohibiting trespassers on the beach are not legal and he must remove them from the beach. He can put these signs on his land that abuts the beach but not on the actual beach.

His recourse against Drake for denying any history of latent infestation would depend on a couple of factors. On the sellers disclosure statement, which is required to make buyers aware of known defects, it specifically stated that Drake said the home had no history of infestation. If Drake made this statement knowing there was then Parker should be able to recover the reasonable amount to repair the structure. The facts state that advertisement said new wall paneling throughout and this is the very same wall paneling that was taken down by Parker where he found the termite infestation. This would tend to show that indeed Drake did know of the infestation and lied on the disclosure statement. Therefore Parker should be able to recover damages.

Now Drake will argue that Parker had an independent expert say everything was fine but this does not mitigate the fact that Drake knew of the infestation. Drake may also try to argue that the infestation happened after the sale but based on the facts that the infection was found the same summer he bought it and the termites were gone, this is not a valid argument.

Question 11—Property—9 points

A) With respect to the beach in front of Parker's home, he has no right to prevent walkers from walking on the beach if it is public property or a public beach. Homeowners with beach front property don't typically own the beach fronting their home. To find out if the beach in front of P's home is private, he would need to get the land surveyed and find out the proper legal boundaries. If the beach does belong to him, he can continue to post signs that it is private property and those that violate the signs would be subject to a fine under relevant legal codes and prosecuted for trespassing.

B) The general rule in contracts dealing with the sale of real property is buyer beware (caveat emptor). Sellers have no duty to make premises safe for buyers. Buyers take property as is. The exception to this rule is significant defects know to seller that seller knows buyer is unlikely to discover. In other words seller must disclose latent defects. Seller must not take steps to actively conceal such defects. Here, D installed wood paneling along an area where below it had been extensive termite damage. Further D made no mention of the damage when selling the house to P and P didn't discover it until it was too late and D knew P would not have discovered the damage as it would have involved removing the paneling before buying it to discover it which was not going to happen.

In light of Debbie's active concealment (placing the paneling over the damage) Parker is entitled to rescission of the contract which is cancelling the contract.

July 2010—Question 7

Abel and Betty married in 1970, after which they purchased for cash a quaint farmhouse. The property was deeded to Abel and Betty, jointly as husband and wife. There was a cottage on the south end of the property, which Abel and Betty rented to tenants to supplement their income. Abel and Betty used a bimonthly lease agreement that allowed either party to terminate the lease with 60 days' notice.

In 2009, Betty discovered that Abel was having an affair with the current tenant, Lolita. Betty filed for divorce, but Abel died before the divorce became final. Following Abel's death, Betty demanded that Lolita vacate the cottage within 60 days. Lolita refused. Instead, Lolita showed Betty a quitclaim deed from Abel transferring the cottage to her in exchange for "love and affection."

Shortly thereafter, Carl sought repayment of a mortgage that Abel had executed on the cottage as security for a personal loan made by Carl to Abel. Abel had falsely informed Carl that he owned the cottage free and clear as his separate property.

Applying Michigan law, discuss Betty's (a) ownership interest in the cottage; (b) ability to eject Lolita; and (c) liability to Carl.

Model Answer to Question 7

(a) Betty is the sole owner of the cottage because she and Abel acquired the cottage as a tenancy in the entirety, and, upon Abel's death, joint ownership interest transferred to Betty alone under the right of survivorship. Under the common law, a tenancy in the entirety was created when a validly married couple took property as joint tenants and shared the unities of time, title, interest, and possession. *Budwit v Herr*, 339 Mich 265, 272 (1954). With the enactment of MCL 565.49, Michigan eliminated the unities of time and title. Under Michigan law, the deed of conveyance to a married couple must explicitly state if the parties intend to create a separate type of estate rather than a tenancy in the entirety. *DeYoung v Mesler*, 373 Mich 499, 502-504 (1964). The deed to Abel and Betty indicated only that the property was conveyed to them "jointly as husband and wife." Therefore, Abel and Betty clearly acquired a tenancy in the entirety. Under a tenancy in the entirety, each party has an indivisible interest in the whole property. *Rogers v Rogers*, 136 Mich App 125, 134 (1984). A tenancy in the entirety may only be terminated by (1) the death of a spouse, (2) divorce, (3) mutual assent, or (4) execution on a security lien by a joint creditor of both the husband and wife.

The judgment of divorce had not yet been entered when Abel died. Therefore, the tenancy in the entirety was not dissolved by divorce. However, the tenancy in the entirety *did* terminate when Abel died. At that time, Betty took sole title to the property through the right of survivorship. This right provides that in the event that one spouse dies during the course of the marriage, the surviving spouse automatically takes fee simple ownership in the entire property. The quitclaim deed to Lolita did not divest Betty of her ownership interest. As a tenant in the entirety, Abel did not have a separate or individual property interest that he could lawfully transfer to Lolita without Betty's assent. *Rogers, supra*, 136 Mich App at 134-135.

A quitclaim deed only passes "the estate which the grantor could lawfully convey by a deed of bargain and sale." MCL 565.3. As Abel could not lawfully transfer his interest in the tenancy in the entirety, the quitclaim deed transferred no property interest to Lolita.

(b) As Betty has the sole ownership interest in the cottage, she may eject Lolita consistent with the provisions of their lease agreement. The lease agreement allows either party to terminate the lease by giving 60 days' notice. This is consistent with MCL 554.134(1), which allows a party to terminate a periodic lease with at least one month notice. In the event that Lolita refuses to leave after 60 days, Betty will have to look to the court for relief; she will have to file summary proceedings to evict Lolita as a holdover tenant. MCL 600.5714(1)(c)(I).

(c) Carl may not execute the mortgage against the cottage. Betty did not sign the mortgage agreement in relation to the cottage, which is property held as a tenancy in the entirety. A tenant by the entirety may not unilaterally dispose of, or otherwise encumber the property; both tenants must act together to jointly encumber a tenancy by the entirety. *Berman v State Land Office Bd.*, 308 Mich 143, 144 (1944). Thus, Abel could not lawfully unilaterally encumber the property. Further, "land held by husband and wife as tenants by entirety is not subject to levy under execution on judgment rendered against either husband or wife alone." *Sanford v Bertrau*, 204 Mich 244, 247 (1918). Therefore, Carl has no action against Betty.

Two Student Answers—July 2010

Question 7—Real Property—10 points

The first issue is what ownership interest did Abel and Betty, and how Betty alone have in the cottage. The property was deeded to Abel and Betty jointly as husband and wife. Whenever property is deeded to both husband & wife the conveyed property is tenancy by the entirety. Each owner owns an undivided share and enjoys the rights of survivorship. Which means what if there is a surviving spouse at the time of death of the other spouse, the surviving spouse is entitled to the entire tenancy & full shares.

A tenancy by the entirety may be destroyed by divorce, however the divorce must be final. Here, although Betty filed for divorce, it was not final before Abel's death. Therefore Betty's rights of survivorship kick in and she is entitled to the undivided property.

As the sole owner of the property, Betty may order Lolita to leave the property. Betty however, must act in accordance with the terms of leasehold agreement b/t her & Lolita. Lolita has a bi-monthly lease agreement that allows either party to terminate the lease with 60 day notice.

Here Betty was within her rights to terminate the lease and provide Lolita with 60 days notice to vacate. Betty however can't eject Lolita until that time (the 60 days) have passed. Betty is entitled to rent during that time.

Lolita's quit claim from Abel will unfortunately not excuse her from her obligation to leave as Betty has requested. Abel's quit claim to Lolita was invalid b/c as previously stated, Abel and Betty had a joint tenancy by the entirety which requires both owners to act together when making a conveyance on the property, because Able acted alone in conveying the property to Lolita the conveyance was invalid and therefore not enforceable against Betty.

Question 7—Real Property—10 points

In regards to this real property and landlord tenant claim the main issue that arises are who has ownership, ability to eject tenant, and liability to a debtor.

Who has ownership is primarily easy if under modern view the husband and wife owned a joint tenancy with a right of survivorship. Absent the language, there is still jurisdictions that presume once a real property is purchased between married couples it is with the right of survivorship. Here Abel (A) and Betty (B) bought the house as joint tenants, when they got married and held as husband and wife. Therefore they are joint tenants with right of survivorship. Meaning the vesting of rights automatically occurs upon the death of another as long as the tenancy isn't terminated. A joint tenancy can only be terminated upon a showing of a few exceptions. Not unilaterally. The only way A and B could have terminated this tenancy was if either of them died before the other (which here A did) and the right of the surviving spouse would be fully vested into the ownership as sole owner. The other ways are through divorce which would then infer a tenancy in common, or if a party is a debtor in bankruptcy proceedings, or if BOTH parties dually sign off to changes. Here, of the remaining exceptions only divorce would have potentially been ok, however a filing of a divorce is not considered valid until judgment and since A died before then B got sole ownership of the home.

The next issue is the ability to eject Lolita, (a tenant). Although Lolita (L) will argue that she has interest because of the quitclaim deed the argument will fail because L's deed is not valid in many ways. First on a contractual basis, L's deed is invalid consideration for the interest. Courts do not allow love and affection to be consideration to a transfer of land interest (thus, no bona fide purchaser defense). Further L's quitclaim deed is invalid because A could have not given a unilateral interest to the cottage without B's signature. Therefore, L doesn't own the cottage B does, and L is only a tenant. Then we look to B's ability to be a landlord and properly evict L. Here there is a leased by terms (2 months) which is at will. Since either party can terminate for any cause B's ability to eject L was valid so long as sufficient notice was given. Here, Michigan Law requires a minimum of 30 days notice to evict a tenant unless unpaid rent then they can get the tenant out in 7 days. However, here B gave L 60 days notice of her demand to quit the premises which is valid both on the contract (bi-monthly lease) because it was with the time permitted. (Notice is to be at minimum the amount of the term of the lease, regardless to the time within the month the notice was given.) B's ability to terminate at will and having complete ownership of the home is sufficient to support her ejecting and evicting L out of the cottage.

The last issue is whether Carl has any chance of getting the money he loaned A from B or from interest in the real property and the answer is no. Carl's potential interest became void once A died. Obviously his lack of inquiry to determine who's cottage it was shows lack of due diligence, however, a joint tenant that survives the other tenant that dies does not have to forfeit interest into her land because of a past debt. Carl will argue that he should be entitled to some interest in the land but, without a judicial lien against A's property while he was alive is an empty interest and Carl can get noting from B or A's previous interest in the cottage.

Therefore, since Betty has been through so much trouble and pain from her deceased Abel, Bettey gets sole ownership of the cottage, without any interest of payments due to Carl and is able to evict the tenant L from the cottage.

PERSONAL PROPERTY

Questions, Model Answers, and Student Answers

The following section includes prior Michigan Bar Exam questions and model answers for **Personal Property**. Many of the questions also include actual student answers with the amount of points that were earned to give you a better idea of what the graders expect. The student answers are immediately following the model answer for each question. Please pay close attention to the points received on each question. Although most samples represent "good" answers (i.e., received 8, 9, or 10 points), there are some samples that received 7 points (the minimum "passing" score for an essay), and a few that received very low scores to help you better understand the grading process and what is expected.

February 2001—Question 3

Eight years ago, Paula Plaintiff purchased a print at a flea market. Both Plaintiff and the seller thought the print was a reproduction of a famous work. It was, however, a valuable original in excellent condition. Plaintiff showed her print to Don Dealer, another vendor at the flea market, who recognized it as an original. While Plaintiff was looking elsewhere, Dealer surreptitiously substituted a reproduction he had in stock for Plaintiff's original print. Plaintiff did not notice the switch and left.

Dealer immediately offered the print for sale at a reputable antiques auction house. David Defendant bought the print at auction. Neither he nor the auction house knew how Dealer had acquired the print. Defendant has displayed the print in his living room for the past eight years.

Earlier this year, Dealer was arrested for another crime. The police investigated every lucrative sale Dealer had made in the past ten years and uncovered Dealer's sale of Plaintiff's print. Upon questioning, Dealer confessed as to how he acquired and sold the print. The police informed Plaintiff, who demanded Defendant return the print. Defendant refused, and Plaintiff filed suit seeking recovery of the work.

Defendant claims he owns the print by purchase and that Plaintiff's claims are time barred. The statute of limitations on an action to recover personal property is six years.

If you were the judge assigned the action between Plaintiff and Defendant, how would you decide the case? Please prepare a brief opinion explaining your decision.

Model Answer to Question 3

Plaintiff's case against Defendant involves issues of good faith purchase and adverse possession of chattels.

Good Faith Purchase: Defendant appears to have been both a "good faith purchaser" and a "buyer in the ordinary course" of the print. Both these phrases are defined in the Uniform Commercial Code. UCC §§ 1-201 and 2-403, MCL 440.1201, 440.2403.

Defendant paid a fair price for goods from a person who deals in goods of that kind. UCC § 1-201(9). The Defendant appears to have acted honestly and thus in "good faith." UCC §1-102(19). He had no knowledge or actual or constructive notice that the sale of the print to him implicated Plaintiff's rights in any way. UCC §§ 1-201(9) and (25).

The Defendant's status as good faith purchaser or buyer in the ordinary course will not result in his acquiring title to the print, however. Both at common law and under the Uniform Commercial Code, a good faith purchaser cannot acquire good title from a thief. Only a person with voidable title can pass good title to a good faith purchase for value. UCC § 2-403(2). Thus, if the "entruster" is a thief, only a thief's rights are transferred by the merchant to a buyer in the ordinary course.

Similarly, under the Uniform Commercial Code, a person who entrusts goods to a merchant who deals in such goods empowers the merchant to transfer the entruster's rights to a buyer in the ordinary court of business. UCC § 2-403(2). Thus, if the "entruster" is a thief, only a thief's rights are transferred by the merchant to a buyer in the ordinary course.

In short, Defendant does not have a strong claim to the print as a result of his purchase at auction. Dealer stole the print and cannot pass good title to the item through any sale.

Adverse Possession of Chattels: Just as one can acquire title to real property through adverse possession, the common law recognized adverse possession of chattels as a source of title. The doctrine requires that one possess the chattel, adversely and openly, under a claim of right, continuously for the period dictated by the statute of limitations applicable to an action to recover personal property.

The stumbling block for most persons claiming adverse possession of personal property is the requirement that the possession be "open and notorious." That requirement is generally understood to mean that the possessor display the article in such a manner that the true owner can reasonably discover that it is being possessed adversely to his or her interests. *Vaut v Gatlin*, 31 OK 394, 397 (1912). In the problem, Defendant displayed the print privately, in his living room. As such, his possession of the print was probably not open and notorious enough to give him a claim to title by adverse possession.

In recent years, some jurisdictions have moved away from the doctrine of adverse possession of chattels as it was applied at common law. These courts instead employ tolling doctrines applicable to statutes of limitations in general in order to determine whether an action to recover a chattel is time barred. For example, in the leading case, *O'Keefe v Snyder*, 83 NJ 478, 492 (1980), the supreme court of New Jersey applied the discovery rule rather than the traditional elements of adverse possession in a replevin brought by an artist to recover one of her paintings. The court ruled the statute of limitations on the replevin action did not begin to run until after the artist could have discovered with due diligence who had possession of her painting. *Id.*

In the problem, the wrongdoer, Dealer, concealed his theft by substituting the reproduction for the original print. Plaintiff can claim the act of concealment tolled the statute of limitations running on her claim. *See McNaughten v Rockford State Bank*, 261 Mich 265, 268-269 (1933) (defining the tolling doctrine under Michigan law). See generally, Allen & Lamkin, Annot., *When Statute of Limitations Begins to Run Against Action for Conversion of Personal Property by Theft*, 79 ALR 3d 847 (2000).

Thus, while Defendant has a stronger claim to the print based on the expiration of the statute of limitations on Plaintiff's claim than he does as a good faith purchaser, Plaintiff probably should not be divested of title whether the court applies the doctrine of adverse possession or more generally applicable tolling principles involving discovery or concealment of a claim.

Two Student Answers—February 2001

Question 3—Personal Property—10 points

This is a question dealing with personal property. One can acquire title to personal property by adverse possession. In order to do so, the possession of the item must be open, notorious, hostile, and adverse to the owner's property rights. In this case, defendant displayed the print in his living room for 8 years. By displaying it in the living room he met all the requirements of adverse possession: open, notorious, adverse, and hostile. He held the picture out as his own to the general public; therefore, the defendant would probably own the picture by adverse possession. Furthermore, dealing with the issue of owning the picture from purchasing it: Defendant was a bona fide purchaser; that is, he gave value for the picture. He also did not have notice that the picture was stolen from the plaintiff. Thus he would probably take the picture as a purchaser. Plaintiff may want to find recovery via the dealer because the dealer broke the law by stealing the picture, which was an illegal act, and thus may avail some recovery for such actions.

Question 3—Personal Property—10 points

Statute of Limitations: The statute of limitations limits recovery to six years. But the facts state that Plaintiff just found out that she had once owned the original and she only knew of her claim within the past year. The time tolls (or begins) when a party to an action is injured or knows of the injury. Plaintiff may have had the actual painting switched eight years ago but there was no way to discover this until the dealer told the police. Therefore, Plaintiff's statute of limitations began upon her knowledge or discovery of the injury or harm. Her claim is not barred by the statute of limitations.

Defendant's Ownership of the Print: Defendant was a Bona fide Purchaser of the print. A Bona fide Purchaser who buys for value, in good faith and without knowledge of a claim or defense is allowed to keep his purchases. Here, Defendant bought the print from the auction house as a good faith purchaser. The facts claim the antiques auction was reputable, so there would be nothing to put Defendant on notice that the print may be stolen. Therefore, Defendant would keep the print as a Bona fide Purchaser.

Plaintiff's Recovery: Plaintiff may have a claim against the auction house and can certainly file a claim for recovery against the dealer.

February 2002—Question 4

Two years ago, Alex Able purchased a Victorian house near Grand Traverse Bay. Able planned to renovate and remodel the house as a bed and breakfast or inn. Able paid roughly half the purchase price of the house in cash from his own funds. He obtained the balance with the proceeds of a loan from his Aunt Betty Baxter. Able gave Baxter a mortgage on the house to secure the loan. Because Baxter expected to be repaid soon, she did not immediately record her mortgage. Able, however, immediately recorded the deed he obtained to the house at closing.

Able then began renovating the house. In connection with the renovation, he purchased three Austrian crystal chandeliers that illuminated the main entrance hall, dining room, and living room. Able also purchased four large Persian rugs that were laid in all the main public rooms of the house. The renovation of the house was completed with the wiring of the chandeliers and the laying of the rugs.

Shortly thereafter, an innkeeper, Donna Douglas, approached Able and asked whether he would be willing to sell property. She admired the renovation and commented to Able that she was particularly taken with the chandeliers. Prior to making an offer, Douglas had a title search conducted which was dated March 15, 2001, disclosing Able as the titleholder and no mortgages. On March 30, Douglas made Able an offer on the house which Able agreed he would consider. Able then told his Aunt Betty to immediately record her mortgage. She did so. Neither Able nor Baxter informed Douglas of the mortgage.

After protracted negotiations, and on July 15, 2001, Able and Douglas entered into a standard contract for sale of real estate. Douglas tendered the agreed purchase price at closing and immediately recorded the deed to the property she received. When Douglas took possession of the property, however, she discovered the chandeliers and rugs had been removed. A week later she was served with notice of the foreclosure action brought by Betty Baxter. Baxter's mortgage load was in default.

Does Douglas have any defense to Baxter's foreclosure action? Explain. Can she recover the chandeliers and rugs from Able? Why or why not?

Model Answer to Question 4

Baxter will claim the protection of Michigan's recording act in her foreclosure action. Baxter's mortgage was recorded before Douglas acquired an interest in the property.

The law of fixtures governs Douglas' claim to the chandeliers and rugs. She would have a strong claim that the chandeliers were fixtures. They were firmly attached to the real property and her conversation with Able regarding the chandeliers would seem to indicate the parties intended to treat the items as fixtures. Douglas has a much weaker claim to the rugs as fixtures. They were probably not so firmly attached to the real property that the law would treat them as a part thereof.

The Foreclosure Action: Baxter should claim the protection of Michigan's recording act in the foreclosure action. Michigan has a "race-notice" recording statute that reads as follows:

> Every conveyance of real estate within the state hereafter made, which shall not be recorded as provided in this chapter, shall be void as against any subsequent purchaser in good faith and for a valuable consideration, of the same real estate or any portion thereof, whose conveyance shall be first duly recorded. MCL 565.29.

Under the statute, a good faith purchaser of real property will take free of any prior interest in the property unknown to the purchaser if the purchaser records before the holder of the prior interest records. In the problem, Baxter's mortgage was recorded before Douglas' deed. Therefore, Douglas had notice of the mortgage lien.

The Chandeliers: Douglas has a strong claim to the chandeliers under Michigan's law of fixtures.

A fixture is an item of personal property that has become so firmly affixed to real estate that the law treats it as real property. Michigan applies the three-part test used by most jurisdictions in order to determine whether goods have been fixtures. First, the Michigan courts examine the degree to which the goods have been annexed to the realty. Second, they look to the extent to which they have become adapted to the use of the real estate. Finally, they consider whether the parties intended to make the goods an accession to the real property. *E.g., Wayne County v Britton Trust*, 454 Mich 608, 610 (1997).

Applying the three-part test to the chandeliers, Douglas should argue that the chandeliers were affixed to the ceiling and connected to the electrical system of the house. The chandeliers were also adapted to the use of the real property. They illuminated major rooms of the house and undoubtedly provided an aura of elegance to the inn. Finally, Douglas' conversation with Able regarding the chandeliers would give her some evidence of an intention that the chandeliers would pass with the title to the real property.

If an item is a fixture, title to it passes with the conveyance of the real estate unless the vendor has reserved title to the item in the contract for sale. *E.g., Atlantic Die Casting Company v Whiting Tubular Products, Inc*, 337 Mich 414 423-424 (1953). Therefore, Douglas should be able to claim ownership of the chandeliers passed with title to the house.

The Rugs: The Persian rugs present a considerably more difficult case for Douglas. A court is unlikely to hold they were fixtures under the three-part test. The rugs probably were not physically attached or annexed to the property in any permanent fashion. This was not wall-to-wall carpeting permanently tacked to the floor. Presumably, other carpet or floor covering would suit the use of the real property as an inn and there is no evidence the parties intended title to the rugs to pass with the house. Thus, absent other facts, such as evidence that the rugs were specially woven to conform to the shape of the rooms, Douglas would not have a particularly compelling case for recovery of the Persian carpets.

> **Comment:** Please note that this same question, model answer, and student answer are also provided under the Real Property section. Because the question combines the two subjects, it has been placed in both sections to ensure completion.

Student Answer—February 2002

Question 4—Real Property/Personal Property—8 points

A. Does Douglas have defense to Baxter's foreclosure action?

Yes. A bona fide purchaser who pays value in consideration for property w/ out notice of a previous recording who then records after purchase has protection against other claims. Here, Douglas bought a house from Able. Douglas did a title search which only showed Able to be on the mortgage. Able did not inform Douglas that Baxter was on the mortgage but had not recorded it yet. Once Douglas purchased the house from Able, she recorded it immediately. A week later she was served w/ notice of foreclosure action brought by Baxter b/c her loan was in default. Under these facts, it is not Douglas's problem that Baxter's loan is in default. Her claim should be with Able. Able received the money from Douglas to pay the loan to Baxter. In addition, Douglas did not know of the agreement between Able and Baxter.

B. Can Douglas recover the chandeliers and rugs from Able?

1. Douglas should recover the 3 chandeliers.

   When a fixture becomes so annexed to a structure, it becomes part of the realty. Here, Able bought the chandeliers as part of the renovation & the renovation was not complete until the chandeliers were hung and wired. Chandeliers, especially ones of this size/type can be considered part of the realty by a perspective buyer. Especially when Douglas commented on them and considered them to be part of the style/renovation of the Inn. Removing them would probably cause damage to the house itself and a decrease in the value of the Inn as a whole.

2. Douglas should not recover the 4 rugs.
   Rugs are removable w/ ease and as such cannot be considered part of the realty. Removing the rugs would not affect the physical condition of the home.

July 2002—Question 4

Alice Able owned an antique vase and pocket watch, which she wished to have appraised. She found the name of a downtown antiques dealer in the yellow pages and drove into the city to have the dealer appraise the items.

Able parked her car in a garage owned and operated by a downtown hotel. Entry to the garage was controlled by a mechanical gate. Upon entering the garage, the driver of a car presses a button on a machine that then dispenses a ticket and lifts the gate. The ticket notes the time and date. When a driver leaves the garage, he or she hands the ticket to an employee of the hotel who works at the exit booth. The employee charges the driver the appropriate fee based on the hours the driver's car was parked at the garage. From time to time, a security officer employed by the hotel patrols the garage. For the most part, however, the attendant at the exit booth is the only hotel employee working in the parking garage. A notice stating, "Remember to Lock your Car" appears on the tickets dispensed by the machine at the entrance of the garage and on several signs located throughout the interior of the garage.

Able received the ticket dispensed by the machine located at the garage entrance. She parked her car in the garage and locked her vehicle. She then carried the vase and pocket watch to the antiques dealer whose shop was located about two blocks from the parking garage. The dealer was impressed with both the vase and the watch. He told Able he wanted to do some more research on both items and asked her to return in a few hours, at which time he promised to have written appraisals ready for her. Able left to do some other shopping. She did not know the dealer was in financial straits.

About 20 minutes after Able left the antique store, the dealer sold her pocket watch to Bob Byer. Byer paid a fair price for the watch and knew nothing of how the dealer had acquired the item. Shortly thereafter, Carla Crash entered the antique shop. Fingering Able's vase, she dropped it and broke it to pieces. Crash apologized profusely and offered to pay damages for the vase. The dealer accepted $250 from her which the dealer used to pay a bankruptcy lawyer who filed a bankruptcy petition for the dealer that afternoon.

When Able returned to the shop for her appraisals, the antiques dealer was closed. Worse, her car was missing from the parking garage. The car has not been recovered although no one recalled seeing the vehicle leave the garage.

Able has retained you. She asks your advice on whether she can successfully sue the hotel for the value of her car and Crash for the value of the vase she left with the antiques dealer. Able also wants to know if she can recover the watch from Byer. What advice will you give Able? Explain.

Model Answer to Question 4

This question raises issues from the common law of bailments and the Uniform Commercial Code. First, the hotel that owned the parking garage will contest whether it had possession of Able's car and hence the duty of a bailee. Second, the woman that broke Able's vase, Crash, will raise her settlement with the antiques dealer as a defense in Able's action as bailor. Generally, a tortfeasor's settlement with a bailee bars a subsequent recovery by the bailor. Finally, the Uniform Commercial Code will make it difficult for Able to recover the watch from Byer. The antiques dealer seems to have been a merchant who dealt in antique goods like the watch. As such, he could transfer Able's title to a buyer in the ordinary course of business.

Liability of the Garage: A bailment is a relationship whereby one person, known as the bailor, gives to another, called the bailee, the temporary use and possession of property. The bailor retains title to the goods but the bailee has possession or temporary custody of them. *See, e.g., Goldman v Phantom Freight, Inc.*, 162 Mich App 472 (1987). 5 Mich L & Practice 2d, Bailments, § 1 (2000). A bailment does not arise unless the bailee has control over the goods. In parking garage cases, liability often turns on the owner of the garage. Generally, if a car and its keys are left with a parking lot attendant, the courts will find a bailment. On the other hand, if the car is parked and locked on a wholly unattended lot, the courts rarely find a bailment. See generally, Annotation, *Liability for Loss of Automobile Left at Parking Lot or Garage*, 13 ALR 4th, 362, 366-368 (1982). If a bailment has occurred, the owner of the parking lot or garage has undertaken the duties of a bailee and is generally held to be liable for a stolen car without a need for proving specific acts of negligence. *Id.* at 366-367. A Michigan statute largely codifies the foregoing principles of the common law. The statute presumes a garage owner for hire is liable for loss or damage to a car if "possession . . . care, custody or control" of the vehicle has been delivered to the garage owner or the owner's agent. MCL 256.541 (2001).

The hotel stands in something of a middle ground if one considers the bailment cases involving parking lots. Militating against a finding that the hotel has undertaken the duties of a bailee are the facts that Able parked her car herself and retained her keys. It's unlikely any employee of the hotel ever touched her car and the hotel gave her ample warning to lock her vehicle. On the other hand, the hotel garage was not wholly unattended. The hotel employee at the exit booth apparently let the car exit the garage, perhaps without a ticket. The hotel did provide some security in the garage and access to the facility was controlled. Under similar circumstances, courts in other jurisdictions have found bailments and hence liability on the part of the garage owner. *See, e.g., Allen v Hyatt Regency Nashville Hotel*, 668 SW 2d 286 (Tenn Sup Ct 1984). There is, however, ample authority for a contrary view. Annotation, *Liability for Loss of Automobile Left at Parking Lot or Garage, supra*, 13 ALR 4th at 404-416 (Collecting cases reaching both results). In short, Able should be advised she has a sound legal basis for suit but the hotel will undoubtedly challenge whether it had sufficient custody of her car so as to constitute a bailment.

Settlement with the Bailee: In contrast to the ample legal authority on bailments and parking lots, relatively few cases have addressed the preclusive effect of a tortfeasor's settlement with the bailee on any suit by the bailor for damage to bailed goods. The common law rule, first announced in a leading English case, compensated the bailee for such losses. *The Winkfield*, 1902 P42 (Ct App 1901). To the extent the tortfeasor has settled with the bailee in good faith for the value of the goods, the tortfeasor has a defense in any action by the bailor. See generally, C. E. Becraft, Annotation, *Bailment-Effect of Settlement by Bailee as a Bar in Action by Bailor*, 47 Mich L Rev 109 (1948). Thus, under the common law, Crash's settlement with the antique dealer would likely bar Able's suit against Crash for the value of the vase. Able should be advised that absent a showing that the settlement was inadequate or in bad faith, she will be unlikely to recover against Crash. She should file a proof or claim in the antique dealer's bankruptcy proceeding.

Sale of the Watch: At common law, a bailee was not considered to have any title to the bailed good and thus could not sell the goods to anyone. Under the Uniform Commercial Code, however, a person who entrusts goods to a merchant who deals in goods of the kind empowers the merchant to sell the entruster's title to a buyer in the ordinary course of business. MCL 440.2403(2). A buyer in the ordinary course of business is a person who buys the goods in good faith without notice that the sale contravenes the rights of others. MCL 440.1201(9). The sale of Able's watch to Byer appears to have been an ordinary course sale. The antiques dealer sells old watches. Byer paid a fair price in good faith. Able therefore is unlikely to be successful in a suit to recover the watch from Byer. Again, her remedy, if any, would be through a claim in the antique dealer's bankruptcy proceeding.

Two Student Answers—July 2002

Question 4—Personal Property (with sales issue)—10 points

This is a personal property question. Alice will mostly recover the value of her car from the hotel. Since the garage where her car was stolen was owned and operated by a downtown hotel, Alice was owed a higher duty of protection and the hotel will be liable for the loss of her vehicle because of the Innkeeper's heightened duty of care.

Here, they charged Alice for parking in their structure, had a security officer patrolling the garage and had a parking attendant to take the ticket exit booth. Alice even remembered to "lock her car." The hotel will be liable for the value of her car.

This is also a bailor-bailee situation where the hotel will be liable for lost, stolen, or damaged property left in its care.

Second, can Alice recover for the vase? Possibly, however, Crash did pay value for the broken vase to Antique dealer who fraudulently gave the $250 to his bankruptcy attorney. An owner of personal property that has been misappropriated will be able to collect the item's fair market value from the individual who misappropriated or converted the property to his own use. Able will have to go after Antique dealer, not Crash.

Finally, can A recover the watch from Byer? Probably. Antique dealer did not have title to the watch and sold it to Byer. Although, as an antiques dealer in the business of selling watches, Byer had no knowledge of the misappropriation and believed he was purchasing the watch from a legitimate seller, which may give Byer a defense.

Question 4—Personal Property (with sales issue)—8 points

The Issues: What recovery can Able get from the hotel? What from the Antiques dealer? The hotel was not a merchant but a bailee of Able's car: as a bailee, it has a duty that was limited to protect the car.

The Car: Able will argue the hotel was a secured creditor since it possessed the car; but probably this will not be found, as the hotel was not in the business of selling cars, but merely a bailee holding the car for the bailor, and as such, not liable for its theft. Able can seek damages for negligent caring for his property perhaps, but not for conversion.

The Vase and Watch: Since Able delivered his 2 other items to a dealer in the course of his normal business he can argue this was a secured transaction, since the dealer had possession of the property to recover the value of the property, but since dealer is bankrupt, the recovery won't be too much. He will get pennies on the dollar in value.

The Buyer: Buyer will be protected in his purchase, since he paid value for the watch without notice of any problem, and from a merchant in the ordinary course of business. He is such a "good faith purchaser," and will have priority over even Able. The dealer had voidable title to the watch, but can convey good title to a good faith purchaser.

February 2003—Question 10

Donna Decedent died recently. She left one living relative, her Uncle Harry, whom she never liked. Decedent never prepared a will, but she did plan for her death. She wanted her property to go to her closest friend, Amy Amicus, and her longstanding employee, Carl Clerk.

Decedent had developed a real estate business during her life. At the time of her death, she owned ten rental properties that produced a steady income from lease payments made by tenants under separate written leases. Using this income, decedent had invested in bearer bonds which she regularly placed in a safe deposit box at First Bank. She listed both herself and Amy Amicus as the owners of the safe deposit box. The card she signed when she first rented the box stated that she and Amicus were "joint tenants." At the time of Decedent's death, the bonds in the safe deposit box were worth a considerable sum of money.

Earlier this year, Decedent was diagnosed with a serious disease that required surgery. The day before the scheduled surgery, she called Carl Clerk into her office and handed him the ten written leases for each of her rental properties. She said to him, "Carl, I appreciate everything you've done for me. If things don't go well tomorrow, these are yours."

Decedent removed a sack of rare coins from her office safe. She handed the sack to Clerk and said, "Carl, you know my friend Amy Amicus. I want her to have these coins."

Sadly, Decedent's operation did not go well. She died shortly after the surgery. **Discuss who is entitled to the bearer bonds in the safe deposit box, the rental properties, and the sack of rare coins still held by Clerk.**

Model Answer to Question 10

Decedent's Uncle Harry has the strongest claim to all of the property mentioned in the problem. He would inherit the property as Decedent's next of kin. MCL 700.2103(1)(d). No legally effective gift was made of any of the property so as to remove it from the estate passing to Harry by intestacy.

The Bonds: The law requires a showing of three elements to establish a valid gift *inter vivos*. These are (1) the donor must intend to make the gift; (2) the gift must be actually or constructively delivered to the donee; and (3) the donee must accept it.

18 Mich L & Prac Encyclopedia, 2d Ed (Gifts) § 1 (2002). Ordinarily, the law will presume acceptance if the gift is beneficial to the donee. *See, e.g., Buell v Orion State Bank*, 327 Mich 43 (1950). Delivery, on the other hand, is not presumed. Generally, a donee must show that the donor parted with dominion and control of the given property. 18 Mich L & Prac Encyclopedia, 2d Ed (Gifts) § 4 (2002). It is usually ruled that a donor does not make a sufficient delivery of items left in a safe deposit box held jointly with the donee. *See, e.g., Taylor v Taylor*, 292 Mich 95 (1940). In such cases, the donor retains the ability to remove the items from the box and, therefore, has not fully parted with dominion and control. *Id.*

In the question, the bonds left in the safe deposit box remained under Decedent's control throughout her life. Harry will undoubtedly challenge whether these bonds were therefore ever "delivered" to Amicus so as to make a legally effective gift.

The Coins: Delivery may be accomplished through a third person. However, if the third person is an agent of the donor, the courts often hold the gift is not made until the property is actually delivered to the donee. The donor is deemed to retain control of the property so long as it remains in the agent's possession. As the principal, the donor has the power to recall the gift in the agent's hands. 18 Mich L & Prac Encyclopedia, 2d Ed (Gifts) § 5 (2002).

The problem states the sack of rare coins was still held by Carl Clerk at the time of Decedent's demise. Under the prevailing view, the coins therefore had not been effectively delivered to Amicus so as to complete the gift.

The Rental Properties: A gift *causa mortis* differs from a gift *inter vivos* in that it is made by the donor in contemplation of imminent death. 18 Mich L & Prac Encyclopedia, 2d Ed (Gifts) § 31 (2002). Real property cannot be the subject of a gift *causa mortis. See, e.g., In re Reh's Estate*, 196 Mich 210 (1917). Such gifts may be made of personal property only. 18 Mich L & Prac Encyclopedia, 2d Ed (Gifts) § 32 (2002). Under Michigan law, a lessor's interest under a lease has been held to be real property which could not be given *causa mortis. In re Reh's Estate, supra*, at 219-220.

It is, therefore, likely Harry would challenge the attempted gift to Clerk. It was clearly made in contemplation of death. Decedent was apprehensive about the surgery scheduled for the next day. She stated she was making the gift in case the surgery did not go well. Under prevailing Michigan authority, she attempted to convey an interest in real property, Decedent's interest under the leases. As such, the gift would fail. To survive, the gift would have to be characterized as personalty.

Student Answer—February 2003

Question 10—Personal Property—None Available

July 2003—Question 8

Angela Antico collected and sold antiques. She also refinished furniture. On January 1, 2001, she took possession of a barn near Monroe, Michigan, under the terms of a written lease agreement. The owner of the barn, Lester Lessor, leased the structure and the surrounding land to Antico "for a term of one year, ending December 31, 2001, in return for rent of $200 per month due the first of each month."

Antico opened an antique store and furniture refinishing business in the barn. She remained in possession for an additional year past the term specified in the lease even though she and Lessor never discussed a renewal of her term. Antico continued to pay the monthly rent but her business never did particularly well. As a result, she notified Lessor on December 31, 2002, that she would be vacating the barn on January 31, 2003. When Lessor received Antico's notice, he told her that if she remained in possession past January 1, 2003, he would hold her to another year of the lease.

Antico ignored him. Instead, during January 2003, Antico sold everything she had in stock at the barn. Unfortunately, she also sold several items that did not belong to her. Oliver Owner left an antique desk with Antico and asked her to refinish the piece in December 2002. Antico instead sold the desk to one of her retail customers, Betty Buyer, in January 2003. Owner also left a sofa with Antico to be reupholstered. Antico sold the sofa to Second Hand City, Inc. along with all of her remaining inventory on January 30, 2003. Second Hand City carted the sofa away, along with the other remaining stock, in a moving van on January 31, 2003.

Lester Lessor found the barn vacant on February 1, 2003. He tried to re-let the premises but has been unable to find another tenant. Consequently, Lessor sued Antico earlier this month seeking $1,200 representing the six months' rent due under the lease from January 1, 2003 to June 30, 2003. Meanwhile, Oliver Owner has sued Buyer and Second Hand City seeking to recover his desk and sofa.

Discuss the issues raised and the probable outcome of the suits filed by Lessor and Owner.

Model Answer to Question 8

Lessor will not be able to recover six months' rent from Antico. When the term of the original lease expired, Antico became a tenant from month to month. Her notice to quit was sufficient to terminate that tenancy. Lessor cannot recover any rent beyond that due from January 2003. Owner will probably be unable to recover the desk sold to Buyer who would appear to have the rights of a buyer in the ordinary course of business. Second Hand City, on the other hand, would not have those rights as a buyer in bulk. Owner therefore should be able to recover his sofa.

Lessor's Suit for Rent: The original lease between Lessor and Antico created a term of years. The lease specified an ending date for the term with no provision for renewal. 20 Mich L & Prac 2d, Landlord and Tenant, § 51 (2003). When Antico remained in possession, without Lessor's objection, after her term expired, the parties did not renew their lease. Instead, under Michigan law, a new lease arose. Because the rent under the original lease was payable monthly, a tenancy from month to month commenced. Such a tenancy can be terminated on one month's notice. *Cox v McGregor*, 330 Mich 260 (1951); *Marks v Corliss' Estate*, 256 Mich 460 (1932); *see also* MCLA 554.134 (2003) (providing the same result for a holdover tenant). Thus, on December 31, 2002, Antico gave Lessor sufficient notice to terminate her lease at the end of January 2003. She would therefore be liable for rent due for the month but not for any longer period.

Oliver's Suit for Recover of the Desk and Sofa: When Owner left his desk and sofa with Antico a bailment was created with Owner as the bailor and Antico as the bailee. 4 Mich L & Prac 2d, Bailment, § 1 (2003) (defining a bailment as the "delivery of goods, without the passing of title, whereby the goods are to be returned when the purpose of the delivery has been fulfilled"). At common law, a bailee did not have title to bailed goods and could not convey title to a third person. *Ball-Barnhart-Putnum Co v Lane*, 135 Mich 275 (1903); see generally, 4 Mich L & Prac 2d, Bailment § 13 (2003).

The Uniform Commercial Code (UCC), however, created an exception to that rule. Under § 2403(2) of the UCC, a person who entrusts goods to a merchant who deals in goods of that kind empowers the merchant to transfer all the entrusters' rights to a buyer in the ordinary course of business. MCL 440.2403(2) (2003). A person who buys at retail from such a merchant will generally be held to be a buyer in the ordinary course if the person purchases the goods in good faith and without notice that the sale contravenes another's rights. MCL 440.1201(9) (2003) (defining the term "buyer in the ordinary course"). A person who buys in bulk, however, does not have the rights of a buyer in the ordinary course. *Id.*

Applying these principles to the problem, it would appear that Buyer is a buyer in the ordinary course. Antico sold used furniture like the desk. Buyer purchased the item in good faith at retail. She had no notice of Owner's right to the desk. As a buyer in the ordinary course under the UCC, Buyer would take the desk free of Owner's contrary claim of ownership. Second Hand City, however, purchased the sofa as part of a bulk sale. Moreover, the sale of all of Antico's remaining inventory was not an ordinary course transaction. As such, Second Hand City would not enjoy buyer in the ordinary course rights. The common rule would thus still govern Owner's claim to recover his sofa from Second Hand City. As a bailee, Antico did not have any title to convey to Second Hand City. Accordingly, Owner should be able to recover the sofa.

Two Student Answers—July 2003

Question 8—Real/Personal Property—10 points

Lessor suit for rent from Jan 1st to June 30th will probably be denied in part. He will be able to get the rent for January as the defendant used the premises until January 31st. So she is liable for January's rent. But she is a holdover lessee so she has to give a 30 day notice of when she will leave, and is liable for rent while staying there and can be treated as a tenancy by sufferance, so she could be treated as a trespasser. She notified him on December 31st that she would move out on January 31st, which is 30 days notice. He told her that she would be liable for a year rent and hold her to another years leave if she didn't move out on or by January 1st. He could have treated her as a trespasser and had her stuff removed and take back the premises but chose not to. Defendant didn't agree to the new lease, so she is liable for January's rent and that's it with regards to lessor's suit.

Owner's suit against buyer and Second Hand City deals with two different types of purchasers. Buyer is an ordinary customer where Second Hand is in the business of selling. The buyer if she is a good-faith purchaser, then she keeps the desk, & owner will have to go after Antico for the value of the desk. But since Second Hand is in the business of selling he doesn't have the good faith purchaser defense so he must give back the sofa & go after Antico for the $ he paid for the sofa. So lessor can probably recover Jan. rent only & owner can probably get sofa back.

Question 8—Real/Personal Property—7 points

In regards to the legal relationship between Antico and lessor, this is a commercial landlord-tenant relationship. After the first lease expired, tenant (Antico) was on a 30-day leave with either party able to cancel their contract with a 30-day notice. Antico had a right to leave the lease on January 31st, 2003, because she had given Lessor 30-days notice that she intended to do so. Lessor's attempt to hold her to an additional year lease upon her notice of termination will not be valid under the Statute of Frauds, a lease for a year or more must be in writing. Here there was not. However, Lessor will be able to sue for the $200—not paid during Antico's stay on the premises for the month of January 2003.

In regards to owner suing buyer & Second Hand City, owner will be successful in the tort of conversion. Though owner probably will not recover the desk & sofa, owner will be successful in receiving the fair market value of each at the time of the conversion.

February 2004—Question 10

Acme Stereo and Television Company ("Acme") went out of business last week. Before its business failed, Acme sold audio and video equipment at retail. Acme offered home delivery for most of the items sold.

On its last day in business, Acme's delivery truck attempted to deliver a boxed stereo to Betty Baxter in unit 4B of a multiunit apartment building. Baxter did not answer her door bell, so the driver left the box in the building's rental office. No one was in the office at the time, but the door was open and the driver placed the box inside the open door. Now, no one who works in the office claims to have seen the stereo. It was never delivered to Baxter.

Later that same day, the driver attempted to deliver a television set to Cathy Carswell. When he arrived at her door, he saw a note Carswell had left there that requested the set be delivered to her neighbor, Deanna Davis. Carswell had asked Davis to accept delivery of the set earlier that morning. Davis had agreed to do so and she took delivery of the television from Acme's driver. Before Carswell picked up the television from her neighbor, however, a small fire in Davis' living room destroyed it. The fire was caused by a frayed electrical cord leading to an old table lamp Davis had meant to throw away long ago.

Finally, the driver attempted to deliver a radio to Ed Evergreen who had purchased the item the week before for use in his living room. Evergreen was not home so the driver returned the radio to Acme's warehouse where it is now claimed by Acme's creditors.

Assess the strengths and weaknesses of each of the following claims and explain who should prevail on each claim:

1. **A suit for the value of Baxter's lost stereo filed by Baxter against the owner of her building who runs the rental office;**
2. **A suit by Carswell against Davis for the damage to the television set; and**
3. **An action filed by Evergreen to recover the radio he ordered.**

Model Answer to Question 10

This question raises personal property issues from the law of bailments and sales. Generally, a bailee has a duty to use a proper degree of care in exercising custody over bailed goods. The duty does not arise, however, if there is no bailment. Ordinarily, a bailee must consent to a bailment. The owner of Baxter's apartment building did not. Baxter, therefore, has a weak claim for the lost stereo. Davis, on the other hand, did undertake the duties of a bailee by accepting custody of the television for Carswell. She appears, however, to be a gratuitous bailee and is only liable under traditional principles of law for gross negligence. Her carelessness in using the lamp with the frayed cord probably does not rise to that level. Finally, under the Uniform Commercial Code, a buyer of goods acquires a specifically enforceable right to the goods once they have been identified to the contract of sale. In Evergreen's case, that was done when the goods were marked for delivery to him and he should be able to recover his radio.

Baxter's Claim for the Stereo: In the problem, Baxter is suing the owner of her apartment building for the value of the stereo that Acme's delivery driver left in the rental office. It does not seem, however, that the owner of the building owed Baxter a duty to care for the stereo. The facts do not warrant a finding that the owner undertook the duties of a bailee. Ordinarily, a bailment cannot arise without the bailee's consent. The bailee generally must accept care and custody of the bailed goods. *See generally*, 5 Mich L & Prac 2d, Bailment § 4 (2000). No one in the rental office undertook that duty for the owner of the building. Thus, absent some agreement or practice of accepting deliveries for the tenants, the owner of the apartment building should not be liable to Baxter for the value of the lost stereo.

Carswell's Claim for the Damage to the Television: Davis, by contrast, did undertake the duties of a bailee. Carswell did ask Davis to accept delivery of the television set and Davis agreed to do so. Davis took physical possession of the set with an obligation to turn it over to Carswell, thus creating a bailment. *See, e.g., National Ben Franklin Ins Co v Bakhaus Contractors, Inc.*, 124 Mich App 510, 512, n2 (1983) ("The term bailment imports the delivery of personal property by one person to another . . . for a specific purpose, with a contract, express or implied, that . . . the property [be] returned or duly accounted for when the special purpose is accomplished or the bailor claims it.")

Bailments are generally classified as to whether the relation benefits the bailor, the bailee or both. *See generally*, 5 Mich L & Prac 2d, Bailment § 3 (2000). Traditionally, these classifications have been used to define the bailee's duty of care in exercising custody over the bailed goods. Thus, if a bailment was for the sole benefit of the bailee, the law required the bailee to use the highest degree of care in the custody of the goods. A benefit that was mutually beneficial, on the other hand, called for the exercise of ordinary care. A bailment for the sole benefit of the bailor, often called a "gratuitous bailment," entailed an even lower standard of care. *See generally*, 5 Mich L & Prac 2d, Bailment § 6 (2000). Under traditional principles, a gratuitous bailee was only liable for gross neglect if the bailed goods were damaged while in the bailee's possession. *Cadwell v Peninsular State Bank*, 1995 Mich 407 (1917). Recent commentators, however, have criticized the traditional classification scheme. They generally have proposed a single standard of care for all bailments, often stated as a duty of reasonable care under the circumstances. *See, e.g.*, Kurt Phillip Autor, *Bailment Liability: Toward a Standard of Reasonable Care*, 61 So Cal L Rev 2117 (1988).

Under either the traditional or modern approach, Carswell will have difficulty recovering from Davis. Davis accepted the duties of a bailee as a favor, without consideration. She did not treat the television any less carefully than she did her own things. Under the common law standard applied in Michigan for gratuitous bailees, she would not likely be found grossly negligent.

Evergreen's Claim to Recover the Radio: The Uniform Commercial Code expanded the right to a buyer of goods to specific performance of the contract of sale. Under § 2-716(3) of the Code a buyer of consumer goods has a specifically enforceable right to the goods as soon as they have been identified to the contract. UCC § 2-716(2), official comment 3 (2003). Goods are identified to a contract when they have been marked for shipment. UCC § 2-501(1)(b) (2003).

In the problem, Evergreen purchased the radio for his personal, household use. He would thus have a superficially enforceable right to the radio once it had been boxed for delivery to his house. He should therefore be able to recover the radio from Acme's creditors. It should be noted that even if one of those creditors had a security interest in Acme's inventory, Evergreen would take free of the interest as a buyer in the ordinary course of business. *See* UCC § 9-320(a) (2003).

Student Answer—February 2004

Question 10—Personal Property—None Available

July 2004—Question 8

Jose, a local attorney, is a very fashion-conscious individual. He takes great pride in the clothes and jewelry he wears, and has many of the items custom-made to his specifications. Among the items he owned was a set of diamond and gold cuff links that formed the letter "J." These cuff links had been stolen recently from his home. When he saw a similar pair being worn by James, another attorney, Jose complimented James on the cuff links and asked if he could look at the cuff links to see how they were made. James took one of the cuff links from his shirt cuff and handed it to Jose. Jose immediately recognized it as his by his initials, "JF" engraved on the back above the initials of his jeweler.

Jose asked James where he had purchased the cuff links. James indicated he had received them as a gift from his nephew Tyler. However, when pressed, James admitted he knew Tyler had stolen the cuff links, but thought no one else would ever know. Jose told James he believed the cuff links to be the ones that were stolen from his home. James refused to surrender the cuff links to Jose.

Jose has filed a statutory claim for conversion against James and Tyler, and seeks your advice on the likelihood of success. **Discuss Jose's likelihood of success against both James and Tyler insofar as Jose seeks the return of the cuff links and any other relief to which he may be entitled.**

Model Answer to Question 8

A statutory conversion claim may be brought pursuant to MCL 600.2919a. The statute allows recovery for a "person damaged as a result of another person's buying, receiving, or aiding in the concealment of any stolen, embezzled, or converted property when the person buying, receiving, or aiding in the concealment of any stolen, embezzled, or converted property knew that the property was stolen, embezzled, or converted." *Id.* The statute also allows the plaintiff to "recover three times the amount of actual damages, plus costs and reasonable attorney fees." *Id.*

Jose v James: Jose would succeed on this claim, as James admittedly knew the cuff links were stolen. Thus, James would not be ordered to return the cuff links, but would be liable to Jose for three times the value of the cuff links, plus reasonable attorney fees and costs.

Jose v Tyler: Jose would not prevail on his claim against Tyler, as Tyler is the person who actually stole the cuff links. The statute allows recovery only against a person who receives the property with knowledge the property has been stolen, embezzled, or converted. The express language of the statute does not allow recovery against the actual thief. *Campbell v Sullins*, 257 Mich App 179 (2003).

Student Answer—July 2004

Question 8—Personal Property—None Available

February 2005—Question 9

Larry worked as a chef in a popular restaurant in the metro Detroit area. He had been working as a chef for over twenty (20) years and even had a set of knives custom made with his name engraved on the side of the blades. The knives were recently discussed on a television show dedicated to fine chefs. It was disclosed the knives had a value of $10,000. When someone broke into the restaurant and stole the knives, Larry was very upset. A friend suggested he might find them on an Internet auction website, and he spent the next several weeks monitoring the popular sites.

Larry eventually found the knives on a popular auction site. The listing indicated the knives were being sold by a person in the Detroit area. Larry sent an e-mail to the person, stating he was a new chef who had always admired the great chef who had originally owned the knives. Larry stated he wanted to make sure the knives were original and not fakes. Kelly, who was selling the knives, responded to Larry's e-mail that the knives were in fact genuine and had been stolen by her friend Sheila from the great chef whose name appeared on the side.

Larry took this information to Rae, a lawyer friend who practiced tax law. Rae recalled a theory of recovery called "conversion" and had a clerk research the statutory basis for a conversion claim. Rae, as Larry's attorney, filed a claim for statutory conversion against Kelly and Sheila and sought any relief that was available under such a claim.

You currently work for the judge to whom the case has been assigned. She has asked you to determine what relief is available and may be granted against Kelly and Sheila pursuant to a statutory conversion claim. **Indicate what relief may be granted by her Honor against both Kelly and Sheila.**

Model Answer to Question 9

A statutory conversion claim may be brought pursuant to MCL 600.3929a. The statute allows recovery for a "person damaged as a result of another person's buying, receiving, or aiding in the concealment of any stolen, embezzled, or converted property when the person buying, receiving, or aiding in the concealment of any stolen, embezzled, or converted property knew that the property was stolen, embezzled, or converted." *Id.* The statute also allows the plaintiff to "recover three times the amount of actual damages, plus costs and reasonable attorney's fees." *Id.* However, there is no provision to compel the return of the stolen items. *Id.*

Kelly: Larry would succeed on this claim, as Kelly admittedly knew the knives were stolen. Kelly could be ordered to pay $30,000 (three times the value of the knives) but could not be ordered to return the knives under the statutory conversion claim. Kelly could also be ordered to pay reasonable attorney fees and costs incurred by Larry in having to bring the lawsuit.

Sheila: The court cannot order any relief against Sheila, even though she is the person who actually stole the knives. The statute allows recovery only against a person who receives the property with knowledge the property has been stolen, embezzled, or converted. Statutory conversion does not allow a claim against the individual who has actually stolen, embezzled, or converted the property. *Campbell v Sullins*, 257 Mich App 179 (2003). Therefore, the court may not grant any relief against Sheila based on statutory conversion.

Student Answer—February 2005

Question 9—Personal Property—8 points

Kelly and Sheila's Damages: According to Michigan's statute of conversion whenever a person aids, takes, knows goods are stolen, or takes property from another with intent to convert are liable under the statute.

Here, Sheila stole the knives and Kelly was selling the stolen knives, and both are liable under the statute.

Relief can be triple recovery of the value of the property, therefore Kelly and Sheila could be jointly and severely liable for the $30,000.

Side Issue: Larry could only receive 1 recovery for his knives.

July 2005—Question 5

Rae was quickly becoming addicted to shopping on E-Way, an Internet auction website. Her latest passion was antique luggage, which she was buying at a record pace. Matt, who owned an antique shop in Royal Oak, specialized in classic luggage, and had lost out on several items to Rae's last-minute bidding. Matt hired his friend Ben to steal the luggage from Rae's porch as the pieces were being delivered.

On his first trip to Rae's house, Ben found several packages sitting near the porch. He quickly loaded the packages into his truck and drove away. Ben gave the packages to Matt, who then offered the items for sale in his antique shop.

Rae, feeling a little depressed about not receiving the luggage she had purchased, decided to go shopping. As luck would have it, she walked into Matt's shop and immediately recognized the luggage as that which she had purchased on E-Way. Rae then filed a lawsuit against Matt and Ben, setting forth one claim of statutory conversion against both Matt and Ben. Discovery indicates the following facts that should be accepted as true:

1. Matt acknowledged the luggage was stolen and testified Ben stole the luggage at Matt's request.
2. Ben admitted to stealing the luggage.

You currently work for the judge to whom the case has been assigned. She has asked you to determine what relief may be granted against Matt and Ben pursuant to a statutory conversion claim, including whether the court may compel the return of the luggage, which is valued at $10,000.

Model Answer to Question 5

A statutory conversion claim may be brought pursuant to MCL 600.2919a. The statute allows recovery for a "person damaged as a result of another person's buying, receiving, or aiding in the concealment of any stolen, embezzled, or converted property when the person buying, receiving, or aiding in the concealment of any stolen, embezzled, or converted property knew that the property was stolen, embezzled or converted". *Id.* The statute also allows the plaintiff to "recover three times the amount of actual damages, plus costs and reasonable attorney's fees." *Id.* However, there is no provision to compel the return of the stolen items.

Matt: Rae would succeed on this claim, as Matt admittedly knew the luggage was stolen. Matt could be ordered to pay $30,000 (three times the value of the luggage), but could not be ordered to return the luggage under the statutory conversion claim. Matt could also be ordered to pay reasonable attorney fees and costs incurred by Rae in having to bring the lawsuit.

Ben: The court cannot order any relief against Ben, even though he is the person who actually stole the luggage. The statute allows recovery only against a person who receives the property with knowledge the property has been stolen, embezzled, or converted. Statutory conversion does not allow a claim against the individual who has actually stolen, embezzled, or converted the property. *Campbell v Sullins*, 257 Michigan App. 179 (2003). Therefore, the court may not grant any relief against Ben.

Two Student Answers—July 2005

Question 5—Personal Property—10 points

The relief pursuant to a statutory conversion claim against Matt will be a winning claim for Rae. The claim against Ben will *not* be a winning claim for Rae.

Under statutory conversion, when a retailer in the business of selling goods, such as to sell at his place of business he will be guilty under statutory conversion. Since Matt admitted to stealing the luggage through his agent in crime, Matt will be guilty of statutory conversion. Conversion is usually a crime, but because he is a seller in the business of selling antique goods and tried to resell stolen goods—courts will hold him liable under statutory conversion, especially since these are goods of value and antiques.

Ben will not be held liable under statutory conversion. The thief who directly steals the goods will not be held liable under statutory conversion. Maybe under conversion, but not statutory conversion under contracts. Only the seller is liable.

Matt will not be compelled by the court to return the luggage, since he will be liable for 3 times the amount of the value of the luggage. Therefore, he will and must pay Rae $30,000 in damages. Three times the amount of original value. He will not have to return the luggage since it is conversion (i.e., he gets to keep luggage).

These rules come from the law of personal property under Bailee/Bailor. Even though no agreement made under circumstances, we treat Matt as Bailor in order to punish severely (i.e., 3 times the value).

Question 5—Personal Property—10 points

The first issue is what relief may be granted against Matt and Ben pursuant to a statutory conversion claim. The rule is that a true owner recovers three times the value of the property against the person in possession of stolen property. The statutory conversion claim is directed at the person in possession and not the actual thief.

In this case, Matt hired his friend Ben to steal the luggage, and Ben gave the luggage to Matt. Also, Rae, who is the true owner found the luggage in Matt's shop. Since Matt was in possession of stolen property, Matt would be liable up to three times the value of the luggage, which is $10,000 × 3 = $30,000.

Another issue is the claim against Ben. As stated above, statutory conversion does not apply to the thief. In this case, Ben stole the luggage and gave it to Matt. Therefore, Ben is not liable.

Another issue is whether the court will compel the return of the luggage. The rule is that in a statutory conversion claim, the item is like a forced sale and the time will not be returned. The purpose of the statutory conversion is to penalize the holder of stolen property up to three times the value. It is doubtful if any true owner would desire the return of the property when the compensatory is three fold. However, the court will not compel the return of the luggage.

Comment: This is an outstanding answer. Notice the use of IRAC throughout. It should also be noted that the Michigan Bar Examiners tested this exact same issue (statutory conversion) three bar exams in a row. As a result, it pays to review all old bar exam questions and answers.

February 2006—Question 6

Scot and Kelly had recently gotten married. The couple had a beautiful honeymoon and returned just in time for Scot's annual golf outing with his friends. After an enjoyable afternoon on the links, Scot headed home to mow the lawn. When he went to take his wedding ring off right before working in the yard, he discovered he had lost it at the golf course. Knowing he could identify the ring based on the inscription inside the band, he offered a $5,000 reward for the ring. He was sure this would result in the return of the ring, since it was much more than the actual value of the gold band. He began to lose hope until he was telephoned by Rick.

Rick indicated that he had been golfing at the course where Scot had posted the reward flyer. After hitting his ball into the woods on the eighteenth hole, Rick wandered into the woods yet again to find his ball. When he finally found it, he discovered it had landed next to a gold wedding ring with an inscription inside. Rick put the ring in his pocket and continued his round of golf. When he reached the clubhouse, he saw the flyer offering the reward with Scot's telephone number. He called Scot and indicated he had found a ring that roughly matched the description in the flyer. The two agreed to meet the next day to determine if the ring was in fact the one Scot had lost.

When they met, Scot asked to inspect the ring. Rick, however, was afraid Scot would run away and not pay the reward, so Rick refused to allow Scot to actually see the ring. Scot has sued Rick for replevin and Rick has claimed he need not surrender the ring until he has been given the reward. Scot claims Rick waived his right to the reward by refusing to permit the inspection. **Discuss the claim of replevin, whether Rick must grant the inspection, and the validity of Rick's asserted lien.**

Model Answer to Question 6

Replevin has been codified in Michigan by MCL 600.2920, and is commonly referred to as a claim and delivery action. Such an action "may be brought to recover possession of any goods or chattels which have been unlawfully taken or unlawfully detained and to recover damages sustained by the unlawful taking or unlawful detention." MCL 600.2920(1). This is subject to four exceptions, only one of which may be an issue in the question presented. An action for replevin may not be brought by any person who "does not have a right to possession of the goods or chattels taken or detained."

Based upon Scot's refusal to pay the reward, his claim for replevin is inappropriate. The Michigan Supreme Court has held that one who finds lost property for which a reward has been offered may retain the property until such time as the reward is paid. *Wood v Pierson*, 45 Mich 313 (1881). As Scot does not have a right to possession, it should be argued his claim for replevin must be dismissed. Therefore, pursuant to statute, Scot's claim for replevin should be dismissed, as he does not have a right to possession of the ring until such time as the reward has been paid.

Finally, the assertion that failure to permit an inspection waived the right to the reward is also erroneous. The Supreme Court has held that failure to permit an inspection does not waive a claim to the reward. *Id.* Rather, it is incumbent upon the owner to prove ownership and at that time to pay the reward. If the finder (Rick) maintains the property due to a legitimate doubt as to the owner, it does not affect a waiver of the reward nor does it give rise to a conversion claim. *Id.*

Student Answer—February 2006

Question 6—Personal Property—8 points

The inspection should be allowed and if Scot makes proper identification of the ring, the reward should be given.

The issue is whether Rick must grant the inspection of the ring under the theory of replevin. Replevin is an action that is filed to force another party to turn over property that rightfully belongs to the owner. Typically when lost property is found, the finder must make reasonable measures to find the true owner. In this case, Scot made it easy for Rick to find him. Scot posted a flyer with his phone number.

A reasonable person would expect to be allowed to inspect the property that was found to ensure that it is in fact their lost property. In this case, Scot should be allowed to inspect the ring; an additional reason why inspection is proper is because he offered an award for the person who found the ring. The reward should be deemed as a condition precedent (a condition that must be met—returning the ring) prior to receiving the $5,000 reward.

A person can place a lien on property when they rightfully own the property or they are rightfully in possession of the property. Although Rick does have possession of the ring, he found the ring and he doesn't have the type of rightful possession that would grant him to place a lien on the personal property. Rick should be made to let

Scot inspect the ring, and upon inspection if the ring is Scot's, Scot should be made to uphold his offer and give Rick the $5,000 reward.

July 2007—Question 10

Bob Smith had a collection of Lladro figurines that he had amassed over several years. In 2006, Bob considered selling his Lladro collection after he lost his job. However, Bob remained reluctant to sell his collection, as several local collectors offered Bob only a fraction of the collection's true value.

Mary Moore suggested to Bob that he auction one or more of the pieces from his collection on eBay. Bob lacked the skill and confidence to participate in an Internet auction. Mary was proficient with computers and offered to assist Bob. Bob accepted Mary's invitation. Bob delivered a figurine to Mary, who took several digital photos of it, wrote a description of it, and posted it for the auction on the eBay website.

The figurine sold through eBay at a price nearly double what a local collector had offered Bob. Bob continued to sell figurines through eBay with Mary's help. Within no time Mary had sold for Bob a total of 20 figurines. After the 20th sale, Bob gave Mary four $100 bills with a personal note of thanks. Initially Mary declined the money, indicating she expected no money and wanted no money from Bob for her efforts in selling the figurines. However, Bob insisted that Mary take the money. Bob stated: "Please, take this money as my gift to you. You were kind enough to assist me when I needed help. Please accept this as a small token of my appreciation." Mary accepted the money.

Thereafter, Bob concocted a plan to put up for auction the remainder of his collection in a single sale—250 figurines in all. At Bob's request, Mary agreed to facilitate the sale on eBay. Mary spent over 200 hours on the auction project. Bob informed Mary: "I promise to give you 10% of the sale proceeds." Mary responded: "Thank you. That is very kind of you. However, as I told you previously, your money is unnecessary and not expected." The 250 figurines sold for $50,000.

Mary packaged and prepared for shipping the first 100 of the 250 figurines. Because Mary was short on time and extremely exhausted, she asked her neighbor, Betty, to package and prepare for shipping the remaining 150 figurines. Betty agreed. Mary knew Betty as a responsible person and Betty had expressed excitement and intrigue at the auction process.

The figurines packaged by Mary arrived safe and sound at the purchaser's business. However, all 150 figurines packaged by Betty were destroyed and rendered worthless. The shipping carrier concluded that the contents were not properly packaged. Bob does not know Betty. Bob holds Mary totally responsible for the misfortune. Bob has filed suit against Mary.

Discuss in detail the claims Bob may assert against Mary and the defenses Mary may have to the claims asserted by Bob.

Model Answer to Question 10

A bailment is made when personal property is delivered into the possession of another for a specific lawful purpose. Delivery of such goods is done with an express or implied contract that the goods will be properly cared for while out of the possession of the title owner. The title owner is the bailor and the party taking possession of the goods is the bailee. The parties to a bailment must agree that the personal property is to be returned or disposed of pursuant to the wishes of the bailor at the end of the bailment. There are three types of bailment recognized in the law: bailment for the sole benefit of the bailor; bailment for the sole benefit of the bailee; and bailment in which there is a mutual benefit to both parties.

A bailment for the sole benefit of the bailor exists when the bailor's goods are cared for by the bailee without a surcharge or fee and as a mere accommodation to the bailor. Under such bailment, the bailee is required only to act in good faith and is liable only for gross negligence. *Gerrish v Muskegon Savings Bank*, 138 Mich 46 (1904).

A bailment for the sole benefit of the bailee exists where goods are provided to the bailee on loan, at no cost. The bailee is required to use extraordinary care to protect the personal property of the bailor, and to insure that the goods are free from loss or damage. A bailee under this type of bailment is responsible for loss or damage that arises from even slight negligence. *Beller v Shultz*, 44 Mich 529 (1880).

A bailment for the mutual benefit of both parties exists when the bailor gives the bailee temporary possession of some personal property other than money, in which the bailee agrees to return the property to the bailor at some future time, and the bailor agrees to pay a fee or some form of compensation for the bailee's service. Under these bailments, the bailee is required to use ordinary care and ordinary diligence in conducting one's affairs. Bailments for hire exist where the bailee accepts the property with the understanding that the bailee is to perform a service that relates to the property. These bailments are also bailments for the mutual benefit of the parties.

Showing that the personal property in question was damaged or destroyed while in the possession of the bailee may make a prima facie case against a bailee. Thus, where it is established that the personal property that is the subject of the bailment has been damaged or lost, the bailee has the burden of rebutting the presumption that the loss is the fault of the bailee. The bailee may overcome the presumption by showing evidence that the loss is not the fault of the bailee—whatever level of fault may apply to him or her pursuant to the type of bailment.

Here, there exists no question that a bailment existed in this case. Bob provided Mary his Lladro figurines so that Mary could sell them for Bob through an eBay auction. Mary, the bailee, took possession of the figurines to sell them for Bob, the bailor, through eBay. There exists a factual issue in this case whether the bailment was for the sole benefit of Bob, the bailor, or for the mutual benefit of both parties.

Mary may persuasively argue that the bailment is a classic case of a bailment for the sole benefit of the bailor. Bob was in need of selling his assets. Bob did not know how to auction property on eBay. Mary, out of the kindness of her heart, volunteered to assist Bob in selling his property through eBay. This was an accommodation for Bob rather than a business opportunity for Mary. Mary did not contract for compensation or remuneration for her time. She knew her friend was in need and she graciously agreed to assist him. While Mary received $400 from Bob, Mary initially declined to accept the money and later only accepted the money because Bob presented it as a gift.

To constitute a gift: (1) the donor must possess the intent to transfer title gratuitously to the donee; (2) there must be actual or constructive delivery of the subject matter to the donee, unless it is already in the donee's possession; and (3) the donee must accept the gift. Acceptance is presumed if the gift is beneficial to the donee.

Comerica Bank v Goldman (In re Handelsman), 266 Mich App 433, 437-438 (2005), quoting *Davidson v Bugbee*, 227 Mich App 264, 268 (1997). The $400 came with a note of appreciation; not a receipt.

Even though Bob later told Mary he would compensate her some undefined percentage of the revenue generated from the eBay auction of the remainder of his collection, Mary responded to Bob that money was "unnecessary and not expected." For this reason, Mary will argue, she is in a bailment for the sole benefit of Bob, the bailor. As such, Mary will claim she should only be held to the requirement of acting in good faith and avoiding gross negligence. Mary will claim she did just that. She performed hundreds of hours of work for Bob gratuitously, and when she had no additional time available for him, she left the work in the able hands of Betty, who by all reasonable accounts appeared to be ready, willing and able to accomplish the tasks she agreed to perform for Bob. Mary ought not be found grossly negligent merely because Betty acted negligently.

Bob will claim that the bailment was for the mutual benefit of both parties. Bob will point out that he always compensated Mary for her time and effort, initially compensating her $400 for her time and effort in selling the first 20 figurines, and later by offering her a commission for executing and completing the mass sale of his collection. Bob will point out that Mary never rejected the money. When Bob offered Mary a commission ranging from 10% to 20% of the proceeds generated from his mass sale of the collection, Mary responded, "Thank you. That is very kind of you." Accordingly, Mary must be held to the standard of a bailee in a bailment for the mutual benefit of both parties.

Accordingly, Mary is responsible for her ordinary negligence and lack of diligence. Bob will argue that Mary negligently recruited Betty to package hundreds of valuable figurines that were extremely fragile. Mary failed to adequately train and supervise Betty. For that, Mary is negligent and liable for the value of the broken figurines.

Student Answer—July 2007

Question 10—Personal Property—None Available

February 2009—Question 10

Patrick Potter and Dorothy Devine became engaged in June 2008, after living together in Dorothy's home for several years. However, after Patrick's tenth high school reunion in September, he began having an affair with his married high school sweetheart, who became pregnant with his child. After Dorothy learned of the betrayal in January, she ended the engagement, the couple broke up, and Patrick moved out of Dorothy's home.

Patrick wants several items of property currently in Dorothy's possession. First, Patrick seeks Hammer, an English white retriever puppy that Dorothy presented to Patrick at his surprise birthday party in October. Second, Patrick seeks a pair of antique diamond cuff links that belonged to Dorothy's father. Dorothy showed Patrick a picture of her father wearing the cuff links in a family album and said that the cuff links were Patrick's, although they have remained in Dorothy's safe since her father's death several years ago. Third, Patrick wants returned to him the three-carat engagement ring that he gave Dorothy.

You are an attorney at the law firm of Cook, Adkins, and Tykoski. Patrick, your client, is contemplating bringing a lawsuit against Dorothy to compel the return of the items. Utilizing Michigan law, assess Patrick's likelihood of success on the merits. Explain your answer.

Model Answer to Question 10

Whether or not Patrick is entitled to each of three items depends upon whether a valid inter vivos was effectuated. In order for a gift to be valid, three elements must be satisfied: (1) the donor must possess the intent to transfer title gratuitously to the donee, (2) there must be actual or constructive delivery of the subject matter to the donee, unless it is already in the donee's possession, and (3) the donee must accept the gift.

It appears that Patrick will be able to compel the return of the dog. The facts indicate that Patrick was given the dog at his surprise birthday party in October, and the couple continued living together for the three months before their relationship ended. The facts indicate that Dorothy intended to give Patrick the dog, that it was actually delivered to Patrick, and that he accepted the dog at his birthday party.

Patrick will not be able to recover the cuff links. Although the facts indicate that Dorothy intended to transfer ownership of the cuff links, there has been no delivery of the cuff links to Patrick. In order to show delivery, there must be a showing that the donee possessed dominion and control over the gift. *Osius v Dingell*, 375 Mich 605 (1965). Here, Patrick never actually possessed the cuff links—he has only seen a picture of them. Moreover, the picture does not constitute constructive delivery. Constructive delivery occurs only where the gift is not capable of actual delivery because of the size or nature of the item, such as delivering the keys to a safe deposit box. Because Dorothy never delivered the cuff links to Patrick, a valid *inter vivos* gift was not created, and Dorothy can retain the cuff links.

Patrick will be able to compel the return of the engagement ring. An engagement ring is a conditional gift given in contemplation of marriage, and the gift does not become absolute until the marriage occurs. There are two lines of cases dealing with which party gets the gift when the condition is not fulfilled. Under a "fault"-based inquiry, the party responsible for the termination of the relationship loses the ring to the innocent party. Michigan, however, follows a "no-fault" inquiry. Because an engagement ring is a conditional gift, the donor is entitled to the return of the ring when the condition is not fulfilled without regard to fault. Thus, the fact that the engagement was broken due to Patrick's infidelity is irrelevant. *Meyer v Mitnick*, 244 Mich App 697 (2001).

Student Answer—February 2009

Question 10—Personal Property—8 points

1. Patrick will prevail at receiving the puppy. The puppy was a gift to Patrick for a birthday. Patrick had exclusive rights to the dog. A gift is valid if it is intended to be given, delivery of gift and acceptance of the gift. The gift was intentionally given to Patrick, title passed to him. Delivery was given, she presented him

with the dog and he accepted, which is clear because he wants the dog back. Bailor (Dorothy keeping dog). Bailee (the owner). Bailee wants back what is his.

2. Patrick will lose as to the cuff links. Dorothy may have intended to give the cuff links to Patrick but he never took delivery of them. They are small enough to take physical delivery of she has had them for "several" years and never gave them to him. Delivery element is not met so he will not get the cuff links under MI law for gifts.
3. Patrick may receive the return of ring. The ring was a gift/promise to Dorothy on the condition that they marry. Usually, under MI law, the cancellation of a wedding results in the return of the ring if the bride calls off the wedding. If the groom does then the ring doesn't have to be returned. In the case the groom cheated on the bride causing the bride to cancel the wedding. Since a condition of acceptance of the ring is to get married and they did not then the ring would be returned. If the Court determines Patrick's cheating as effectively breaching the contract/promise then Dorothy will be awarded the ring.

July 2009—Question 14

In early March 2009, Chris Cook hunted for deer without a hunting license on a 100-acre parcel of undeveloped property he owned in Kraft County, Michigan. After he shot and killed a doe, Cook noticed something beneath a tree with branches covering it arranged in a crisscross pattern. When Cook moved the branches, he found a small suitcase covered in spider webs.

After Cook returned home with the deer and the suitcase, he pried open the suitcase and discovered that the suitcase contained $125,000 in cash as well as a key to a safe deposit box from a local bank. The suitcase contained an inventory of the contents of the safe deposit box, indicating that the safe deposit box held a 4-carat diamond ring as well as several loose gemstones. The inventory was signed by "A.S.T." and was dated 2/27/2001.

You are the lawyer Chris Cook has consulted for legal advice. Utilizing Michigan law, discuss whether Chris Cook may claim an ownership interest in the deer, the cash, and the contents of the safe deposit box. Explain your answer.

Model Answer to Question 14

In Michigan, all wild animals (ferae naturae) "are the property of the people of the state." MCL 324.40105. Thus, "an individual may acquire only such limited or qualified property interest therein as the state chooses to permit." *People v Zimberg*, 321 Mich 655, 658 (1948). Here, the facts indicate that Chris did not have a hunting license; therefore, he did not have the state's permission to take the deer, and the deer remains the property of the state. It does not matter that Chris Cook hunted the deer on his own property. While the land might belong to Cook, the deer does not, and the state may restrict the taking and use of the deer as it sees fit. *People v Van Pelt*, 130 Mich 621, 624 (1902). In addition to facing misdemeanor criminal charges, MCL 324.40118(3). Chris Cook may also be required to reimburse the state $1,000 for the value of the deer. MCL 324.40119(1)(b).

Chris Cook may well be able to keep the $125,000. Under the Lost and Unclaimed Property Act, MCL 434.21 *et seq.*, Cook must either report the finding of the money or deliver the money to local law enforcement. If Cook wishes to receive the money in the event it goes unclaimed, Cook must provide his name and address to the law enforcement agency. If the owner of the money can be established, then the money is returned to the owner. The initials on the safe deposit box inventory, "A.S.T.," is the only potential clue regarding the owner of the money. If the legal owner of the money is not located within six months, MCL 434.24(7), then the $125,000 is to be returned to Chris Cook. MCL 434.26(1)(a). The statute, construed as a "finder's statute," applies whether the property was lost (accidentally misplaced) or mislaid (intentionally placed and subsequently forgotten). *Willsmore v Oceola Tp*, 106 Mich App 671 (1981), *superseded by statute* as stated in *People v $27,490*, unpublished opinion per curiam of the Court of Appeals, issued 11/26/1996 (Docket No. 173507).

As Cook only found the key to the safe deposit box, he could not claim any ownership interest in the *contents* of the safe deposit box under the Lost and Unclaimed Property Act. At most, he would be entitled to the property he found—the key. Under the Uniform Unclaimed Property Act, MCL 567.221 *et seq.*, all property held in a safe deposit box that goes unclaimed by the owner for more than 5 years after the lease period has expired is presumed abandoned. MCL 567.237. Abandoned property is turned over to the State and, if the owner does not claim the property within three years, the property is sold, MCL 567.243(1), and the proceeds revert to the general fund of the State. MCL 567.244.

Student Answer—July 2009

Question 14—Personal Property—8 points

Ownership of the Deer: Under Michigan law a person is permitted to hunt on his or her own property provided that such area is designated (zoned) as such, and provided that they have a valid hunting license. Under these facts, the deer would constitute personal property belonging to Chris. Chris was under a responsibility to obtain a proper license to hunt. The fact that he owns the property does not waive his requirement to get a hunting license. The public policy rationale is that authorities need to know what people are hunting and where these people are hunting. The obvious danger involved in hunting (shooting of rifles and guns) requires this.

Ownership of Cash: The Michigan law of finders requires that any property found be returned to the police if there are sufficient identifications to know who the rightful owner is. Under Michigan law the person who lost or misplaced the property is the "constructive owner" of the property, and is entitled to have this property returned to him or her.

Even though the suitcase was discovered on Chris's property he still needs to return the cash if he knows or reasonably should know who the property belongs to.

Under these facts, it is quite likely that it belongs to A.S.T. and if not, A.S.T. probably knows who the property belongs to.

If Chris makes an effort to return this to the police and the police to the "local bank" and the person cannot be located then the money will belong to him.

Contents of the Safe Deposit Box: These do not belong to Chris because he does not even have "custody" of the contents (rings, etc.). The law of finders applies to personal property. It does not apply to inventory lists. Here, the local bank has "lawful possession" of these contents. Mere possession of the key does not alter the fact that Chris does not have custody of these items.

February 2010—Question 12

Gregarious Greg's Self-Storage is a Michigan business that offers customers secured storage space for their personal property. On January 1, 2008, Biff signed a 2-year lease on a self-storage lot to store his collection of rare comic books, valued at $10,000. Under the terms of the lease, Biff is required to pay Greg $75 a month, payable at the beginning of each month.

Biff left Michigan for an extended vacation on November 15, 2009 and did not return until December 10, 2009. Before he left on his vacation, Biff forgot to pay his December 2009 rent payment for the storage facility, which was due to Greg on December 1. As a result of Biff's delinquency, Greg mailed Biff the following letter on December 2 by first-class mail:

> "Your self-storage rent in the amount of $75.00 is past due. If payment is not received by December 5, 2009, the contents of your storage space will be confiscated and sold."

On December 6, Greg posted the following classified advertisement on a popular Internet advertising site:

> "For sale. One-of-a-kind Comic Book Collection. Ten boxes, 1930s-50s, pristine condition! $3,000. Contact Greg at 517-555-5555."

As a result of this advertisement, Greg sold the comic book collection for $1,500 to Tammy, who responded to his advertisement, on December 8.

When Biff returned home on December 10, he discovered that the padlock to his storage space was cut and his comic books were missing. That afternoon, he confronted Greg about the empty storage space and discovered that Greg had sold his comic book collection to Tammy because he had failed to pay rent on the storage space.

Discuss whether or to what extent Michigan law allows Biff to recover (a) the comic book collection from Tammy; and (b) any monetary damages from Greg regarding the sale of his comic book collection. Explain your answer.

Model Answer to Question 12

(a) Biff will not be able to recover his comic book collection from Tammy: MCL 600.2920 codifies the common law action for replevin and allows a property owner to recover specific personal property that has been "unlawfully taken or unlawfully detained." Under the common law, even a good faith purchaser of property unlawfully taken or detained lacked title to that property as against the owner whose property has been converted. *Ward v Carey*, 200 Mich 217, 223 (1918). Thus, in the absence of any statute that precludes an action under MCL 600.2920, Biff can recover the comic book collection from Tammy if Greg unlawfully detained or took Biff's comic book collection.

However, the Self-Service Storage Facility Act, MCL 570.521 *et seq*, precludes Biff's recovery of the comic books. The Act creates a property right in "a purchase in good faith of the personal property sold" to enforce a lien created under the Act, "despite noncompliance by the owner with the [notice] requirements" of the Act. MCL 570.525(12). Thus, because the lien created under the Act applies to "all personal property . . . located at [a] self-service storage facility," MCL 570.523(1), if Tammy is a good faith purchaser of the comic books, she owns them free and clear of any claim by Biff. A good faith purchaser is one who is an "innocent purchaser of the property for value." *Bellows v Goodfellow*, 276 Mich 471, 475 (1936). There is nothing in the facts given to indicate that Tammy is not a good faith purchaser. However, if she had either actual or constructive knowledge that Greg's sale violated the Self-Service Storage Facility Act, she is not a good faith purchaser, and, therefore would not have a property interest in the comic books superior to Biff. In that event, MCL 600.2920 allows Biff to recover the comic books from Tammy as explained above.

(b) Biff will be able to recover monetary damages from Greg for the sale of his comic books: Under the common law, a lien is "a right or claim against some interest in property created by law as an incident of [a] contract." *Cheff v Haan*, 269 Mich 593, 598 (1934). An essential characteristic of a lien is the right of enforcement by sale of the encumbered property. *McClintic-Marshall Co v Ford Motor Co*, 254 Mich 305, 323 (1931). However, such sale only occurs when allowed by statute or approved by court order. *Aldine Manufacturing Co v Phillips*, 118 Mich 162, 164 (1898). Accordingly, under the common law, Greg would only have been able to detain Biff's property until the debt is paid. He is therefore without authority to sell Biff's property under the common law, absent a court order, and would be liable to Biff for conversion in the absence of statutory authority to sell the property.

The Self-Service Storage Facility Act, MCL 570.521 *et seq*, gives Greg the authority to sell Biff's property in certain circumstances. The Act gives a statutory lien to the owner of a self-storage facility on all personal property held at such facilities. MCL 570.525 provides a mechanism for enforcing the lien by sale and is the exclusive means of enforcing the statutory lien. MCL 570.525(1). However, the statute requires Greg to demand payment through "a written notice delivered in person or by certified mail," MCL 570.525(2)(c), and requires publication of an advertisement of the sale of Biff's property "once a week for 2 consecutive weeks in a newspaper of general circulation in the area where the self-storage facility . . . is located." MCL 570.525(5).

The Self-Service Storage Facility Act also provides Biff with a remedy for Greg's violation of the enforcement provisions of the Self-Service Storage Facility Act. MCL 570.526(1) allows Biff to "bring an action in a court of appropriate jurisdiction for the actual amount of the damages or $250.00, whichever is greater, together with reasonable attorney fees." He will be able to recover the full $10,000 value of his comic book collection (minus the $75.00 in rent owed Greg), plus reasonable attorney fees, if he can show that he would have paid the requested debt but for Greg's illegal sale in violation of the Self-Service Storage Facility Act's notice requirements. Given that he knew about the debt and sale immediately upon his return to Michigan on December 10, 4 days before the earliest payment deadline to which Biff is statutorily entitled, MCL 570.525(2)(b), he is likely to show such compliance. Moreover, even if Biff cannot show that he would have paid the requested debt prior to a lawful sale under the Self-Service Storage Facility Act, he is statutorily entitled to remaining proceeds of the sale after satisfying Greg's lien and any other "outstanding balances owed perfecting lienholders." MCL 570.525(13) and (14).

Two Student Answers—February 2010

Question 12—Personal Property—8 points

A bailment is a relationship between a bailor (owner of personal property) and a bailee (person with possession of owners property) in which the bailor entrusts his goods to bailee for a certain period of time usually agreed upon as stated in contract or custom and usage of bailment.

Here Greg's storage and Biff had a bailment relationship pertaining to Biff's comic books. In this case, this was a bailment for consideration as Biff was required to pay Greg $75 per month for the storage of his comics. In return, Greg was to store his comics in the allotted storage for the agreed upon time and using ordinary care (the standard of care largely required in bailments). In the event something happens to the bailed goods, while in bailee's possession, he is liable to the extent such ordinary care was breached.

Here, Biff had a duty to pay Greg his storage bill of $75 @ beginning of each month. B was late and G threatened to sell his comics if payment was not received by 5th of month, in which case payment was not received and B's comics were sold. The time in which G gave B to pay and the punishment attached was unreasonable.

There should have been a longer waiting period before such a punishment is attached. Usually 30 days. Further while goods are in bailee's possession he is not entitled to sell goods for profit or hold himself out as the owner, as he is only the possessor of the goods and retains no title to sell them.

A) As it relates to the comic books from Tammy's, Tammy was a bona fide purchaser (BFP) for value. She had no notice that the comics were really Biffs and BFPs have rights to all the world including the true owner. Replevin (retaking possession of goods) may not work here.

B) Biff could seek a conversion claim against Greg as G so seriously interfered with the rights and possession of Biff's comics that it resulted in converting it. In such case B would be entitled to the fair market value of the goods (10,000).

Question 12—Personal Property—8 points

This is a personal property question more specific a bailee-bailor situation because Greg had the property of Biff in a storage locker for which Biff paid for. In a bailee-bailor situation a bailor has a duty to keep the property in a manner to prevent harm from occurring.

In this case Biff will not be able to get his comic book collection back from Tammy because she purchased them without knowledge of them belonging to Biff. The advertisement made no mention that this being a sale of bulk items from a storage unit and as far as Tammy knew they belonged to Greg therefore she was a bona-fide purchaser for value.

Now Biff should be able to get money damages from Greg's unreasonable sale of his comic books when his payment was only 7 days late. Furthermore it was unreasonable for Greg to mail a letter on the 2nd day demanding payment on the 5th or else the contents would be sold. He did not give Biff enough time to respond before he put the items for sale. Basically Greg committed an improper conversion of Biff's property. Especially since all he owed was $75 and he sold the comic books for $1,500 and tried to sell them for $3,000.

It is my opinion that Biff should be able to recover the FMV of the comic books at the time of the conversion less the $75 he owed Greg.

July 2010—Question 9

Tammy's Taxidermy is located in a low-crime area in suburban Michigan. On July 1, Carolyn brought her deceased pet muskrat, Greggy, to Tammy's Taxidermy because she wanted to display Greggy in her home. After reviewing the details of the project, Tammy indicated that the muskrat would be ready on July 15. The next day, Jimbob brought in a muskrat for taxidermy work. Because Jimbob's muskrat, was smaller and the job slightly easier, Tammy told Jimbob that he could pick up the muskrat on July 13.

Tammy worked diligently and finished both muskrats early. On July 13, Jimbob returned to the store and paid for the taxidermy work. Tammy accidently gave Jimbob the wrong muskrat, giving him Carolyn's beloved Greggy. On July 14, an arsonist set fire to the business next door, and the fire spread to Tammy's store before either the fire department or Tammy's state-of-the-art sprinkler system could contain it. The muskrat that Jimbob brought to the store was completely consumed in the fire, with the exception of its tail, which had a distinctive white stripe on it. When Carolyn arrived at Tammy's store on July 15, Tammy presented Carolyn with the bad news and the charred remains. Carolyn immediately recognized that the muskrat was not the one she brought to the store and shrieked, "This isn't Greggy! Where's my Greggy?" Carolyn pulled out a picture she carried in her purse, noting Greggy's solid brown tail.

Carolyn has sued Tammy for negligence. She has also sued Jimbob to recover Greggy after Jimbob refused to return Greggy to her. Jimbob followed up with a suit of his own, asserting a claim against Tammy for negligence.

Assess (a) whether Carolyn can recover damages from Tammy; (b) whether Jimbob can recover damages from Tammy; and (c) whether Carolyn can recover Greggy from Jimbob.

Model Answer to Question 9

A bailment is created when the owner of personal property (the bailor) delivers his or her property to the possession of another (the bailee) in trust for a specific lawful purpose. *In re George L. Nadell & Co*, 294 Mich 150, 154 (1940). There were two separate bailment agreements here: between Carolyn and Tammy and between Jimbob and Tammy.

The obligations of a bailee depend on the nature of a particular bailment: whether the bailment is for the benefit of the bailee, for the benefit of the bailor, or for the mutual benefit of both parties. The nature of each bailment here was for the mutual benefit of both parties. The nature of each bailment here was for the mutual benefit of both parties, because Tammy agreed to return each muskrat to Carolyn and Jimbob at a future time, and Carolyn and Jimbob each agreed to pay Tammy for the taxidermy services. See *Godfrey v City of Flint*, 284 Mich 291 (1938). As the bailee in a bailment for the mutual benefit of both parties, Tammy is bound to exercise ordinary care of the subject matter of the bailment and is liable to Carolyn and Jimbob if she fails to do so. *Id.* at 297-298.

(a) Based on the facts, Tammy is likely negligent for mistakenly giving Greggy to Jimbob and is liable to Carolyn for damages. Tammy owed Carolyn a duty to exercise ordinary care, and the ordinary care of bailees includes surrendering bailed property only to the proper bailor. See *General Exchange Ins Co v Service Parking Grounds*, 254 Mich 1, 7 (1931). Accordingly, she is likely liable for the damages attendant to giving Greggy to Jimbob instead of Carolyn. If Carolyn is successful in recovering Greggy from Jimbob, however, her recovery will offset some or all of the damages she is entitled to from Tammy.

(b) Based on the facts, Tammy is likely not liable for damages to Jimbob's muskrat, which was damaged as a result of the arson next door. As with Carolyn, Tammy owes Jimbob a duty to exercise ordinary care. A showing that personal property was damaged or destroyed while in the possession of the bailee creates a rebuttable presumption of negligence. *Columbus Jack Corp v Swedish Crucible Steel Corp*, 393 Mich 478, 510-511 (1975). Here, this would require Tammy to "produce evidence of the actual circumstances of the fire . . . including the precautions taken to prevent the loss." *Id.* at 511. Under the facts presented, it is likely that Tammy can rebut the presumption of negligence because (1) her store is in a low-crime area, (2) the fire was not set as a result of her own negligence or the negligence of her employees, and (3) she has taken the precaution of a state-of-the art sprinkler system. See *Id.* at 511 n 3. Accordingly, she has likely exercised ordinary care in protecting Jimbob's personalty.

Tammy is, however, liable to Jimbob for monetary damages if Carolyn is successful in recovering Greggy from Jimbob (see part c, *infra*). As stated, Tammy owes Jimbob a duty to exercise ordinary care. Tammy's failure to exercise ordinary care in selling Carolyn's personal property to Jimbob is the only basis for Carolyn's recovery of Greggy from Jimbob. The amount of damages is Jimbob's actual loss, or "his bargain which he would have realized but for defendant's breach." *Demirjian v Kurtis*, 353 Mich 619, 622 (1958). Jimbob paid Tammy for Greggy, and, in the event of Carolyn's recovery of Greggy from Jimbob, he would have no stuffed muskrat to show for his payment to Tammy. Although Jimbob is not entitled to receive a muskrat from Tammy, because Tammy was not negligent as it relates to his personal property, neither was Tammy entitled to receive payment from Jimbob for a stuffed muskrat that did not belong to him. Therefore, Jimbob is entitled to recover his payment to Tammy in damages.

(c) Carolyn is likely able to recover Greggy from Jimbob. MCL 600.2920 codifies the common-law action for replevin and allows someone to recover specific personal property that has been "unlawfully taken or unlawfully detained," as long as the plaintiff has a right to possess the personalty taken or detained. MCL 600.2929(c). Carolyn remains the title owner of Greggy because a bailment does not change the title of personalty. See *Dunlap v Gleason*, 16 Mich 158 (1867). Under the common law, for the purposes of a replevin action, even a good faith recipient of property lacks title to that property as against the rightful owner. *Ward v Carey*, 200 Mich 217, 223 (1918).

Finally, the statutory exceptions to an action to recover property under MCL 600.2920 do not apply here. Carolyn is not trying to recover property "taken by virtue of a warrant for the collection of a tax, assessment, or fine," MCL 600.2920(1)(a), nor is she trying to recover property "seized by virtue of an execution or attachment." MCL 600.2920(1)(b).

Examinees discussing the application of the UCC to the facts will be awarded credit. Specifically, points will be awarded for addressing any of the following: (1) whether Tammy is a merchant; (2) whether as a taxidermist, Tammy deals in stuffed animals retail; (3) whether the taxidermy transaction can be characterized as sales; and (4) whether the sale to Jimbob will transfer good title to him thus making the muskrat not subject to Carolyn's attempt to replevy it.

Three Student Answers—July 2010

Question 9—Personal Property—10 points

A. Can Carolyn recover damages from Tammy? Tammy is held to be a bailor of goods. Michigan recognizes three types of bailment interest. 1) where bailment benefits the bailor, 2) where bailment benefits the bailee, and 3) where bailor and bailee are mutually benefitted. Under these facts, Tammy held on to Carolyn's muskrat while she did taxidermy work for Carolyn. Both Tammy and Carolyn benefitted from the service because Carolyn received a muskrat w/ taxidermy work performed on it and Tammy received payment for her work. Therefore because both bailor & bailee benefitted Tammy owed Carolyn a reasonable/standard duty of care. The facts assert that Tammy did not have the intent to give Jimbob the wrong muskrat and under ordinary care the mistake happened; therefore, Carolyn may probably not be able to recover form Tammy.

B. Can Jimbob recover damages from Tammy? As reasons stated (*supra*) Jimbob and Tammy mutually benefited from the bailment situation. Due to no fault of Tammy, an arsonist set her store on fire. From the facts, Tammy took reasonable steps to put in state-of-the-art sprinklers to prevent damage from a fire but the sprinklers did not work. Due to Tammy using prudent & ordinary care in having Jimbob's muskrat, Jimbob may probably not be able to recover from his damages. Unless, he can show that Tammy was grossly negligent and the facts do not show this assertion.

C. Can Carolyn recover Greggy from Jimbob? An individual may not hold claim to a possession that they don't have legal title to. In this case, Tammy gave Greggy to Jimbob. Tammy did not have legal title to Greggy in order to give that title to Jimbob. Although Jimbob may assert that he was a bonafide purchaser and Tammy is known for dealing with those specific goods, Jimbob will probably not succeed because he ultimately could not possess legal title into something that the seller never had legal title to give. Therefore, Carolyn may recover under specific performance for Jimbob to give her Greggy back because there is an inadequate other remedy at law. Carolyn has a property right and it is feasible for Carolyn to obtain Greggy.

Question 9—Personal Property—9 points

This is an equity matter and tort issue. (a) Carolyn may recover damages from Tammy if Carolyn can show that money damages will be an adequate remedy. Tammy negligently gave Jimbob Carolyn's property. The question is whether Tammy had a duty to Carolyn, and if she did, was there a breach, and what was the cause of the breach and damages.

Tammy was a bailor for the mutual benefit of both herself and Carolyn. She had a duty of ordinary care and breached this duty by giving Jimbob her property. But for this

Carolyn would have Greggy's tail at the minimum. The next question is whether the fire was a superseding cause. If it was then maybe Tammy's negligence would be negated. The actual cause of Carolyn's Greggy being missing is Tammy giving the muskrat to Jimbob by accident. The issues for damages are going to be hard to pinpoint because what value can be placed on a person's dead pet muskrat—how much is it worth. The court may require that Tammy pay Carolyn a little bit of money or a lot because people's pets are like family.

Carolyn will be successful in her negligence claim against Tammy unless the fire is a superseding cause and but for the fire Tammy could of gotten the muskrat back from Jimbob. This is unlikely because Tammy owned Carolyn an ordinary duty of care.

(b) Jimbob can also recover damages from Tammy. Tammy also owed Jimbob a duty of care and breached that duty when she gave him Carolyn's pet instead of his own. The cause of Jimbob's loss is really the fire and not Tammy's breach. He does not possess his pet muskrat. The only thing he may recover is its tail. The fire was a superseding cause and this may defect his ability to recover damages. Again it will be tough to put a monetary value on Jimbob's pet if he is able to recover.

(c) Carolyn can ask the court for specific performance or to recover her property from Jimbob because of the mistake by Tammy. The court will likely request that Carolyn be given her property back even though it was acquired by Jimbob innocently. The court will want to do what is fair and equitable under the circumstances. It would not be fair for Jimbob to possess her personal property. He obtained her property inadvertently and should be required to give it back to Carolyn if he still is in possession of it and has full knowledge that he is possessing property that does not belong to him. Carolyn should be able to recover her pet muskrat back from Jimbob.

Question 9—Personal Property—8 points

In Michigan, there are three different types of bailment situations: 1) for the sole benefit of the bailor (standard of care is reasonable); 2) for the sole benefit for the bailee (standard of care is extraordinary care, liable for slightest negligence); and 3) mutual benefit of both bailor & bailee, with standard of care as ordinary care, liable for negligence.

Here, we have a classic case of loss or damage done to personal property while it was in the care of a bailee. Here it's a bailment benefitting them both. The general rule for lost or damage to personal property while in the care of a bailee is that in the event of negligence, the bailee will be liable up to the fair market value if the item damaged or destroyed.

However, in Michigan, under the UCC, if the bailee is a merchant who regularly deals in those types of goods (Tammy Taxidermy deals regularly with dead animals) they are protected from negligent claims for loss of personal property because it is assured that when a person takes their good to a merchant bailee he or she can reasonably expect that the bailee will accidently convert the property to a good faith purchaser for (BPV) value. However, that is the case here—as we have a BPU buying Carolyn's "Greggy" for value and leaving with it. Jimbob is a BPV, takes Carolyn's Greggy by mistake, the next day the store is set on fire by an arsonist, which leaves Jimbob's muskrat charred, not Carolyn's Greggy.

Therefore, Carolyn can seek damages from Tammy Taxidermy for negligence in handling of her Greggy. However, Tammy can't compel Jimbob to give her Greggy back. (This would be an action of Replevin). Courts won't enforce it, may get monetary damages instead for conversion.

Jimbob can recover for damages from Tammy for causation from the fire. She is liable for ordinary negligence as the mutually benefited bailee.

WILLS/TRUSTS

Questions, Model Answers, and Student Answers

The following section includes prior Michigan Bar Exam questions and model answers for **Wills**. Many of the questions also include actual student answers with the amount of points that were earned to give you a better idea of what the graders expect. The student answers are immediately following the model answer for each question. Please pay close attention to the points received on each question. Although most samples represent "good" answers (i.e., received 8, 9, or 10 points), there are some samples that received 7 points (the minimum "passing" score for an essay), and a few that received very low scores to help you better understand the grading process and what is expected.

February 2001—Question 1

Douglas Decedent died earlier this year after a long and debilitating fight with cancer. Decedent owned three major assets shortly before he died. First, he owned a farm with his sister, Agnes. Douglas and Agnes had received the farm from their uncle who devised it to them as "joint tenants, with right of survivorship, and not as tenants in common." Second, Douglas held a sizable brokerage account in his own name. Finally, Douglas owned a valuable ring.

Shortly before he died, Douglas called a member of the clergy to his sickbed. He told the minister that he did not think he would live much longer. After praying with the minister, Douglas gave him the ring with instructions that the minister give it to Douglas' friend, Bill, who was serving with the military in the Balkans. The minister agreed to do so.

The next morning, Douglas asked the nurse who was attending to him to purchase two legal forms from a local stationary shop, a "Last Will and Testament" and a "Deed of Real Property." The nurse obtained the forms for Douglas and he filled them out in his own hand. In the form Deed, he filled in the blanks to give his interest in his farm to Bill. He signed and dated the Deed and had the nurse mail it to Bill.

Douglas then took the form Will and completed it. The form had a long blank space for listing specific items of property. In that space, Douglas wrote "I give all my property of whatever kind to the Cancer Society of America." He then signed and dated the form and gave it to the nurse to put with his personal effects.

When Bill received the Deed in the mail, he obtained a leave and flew home. Douglas died, however, just before Bill returned. Douglas's sole heir at law was his sister, Agnes. At Douglas' funeral the minister gave Bill the ring.

Who owns the ring, the farm and the brokerage account? Explain.

Model Answer to Question 1

For the following reasons: (1) Bill would have the strongest claim to the ring; (2) Agnes should be able to claim sole ownership of the farm; and (3) the Cancer Society should receive the stocks and bonds held in Decedent's brokerage account.

The Ring: Michigan recognizes that a person who contemplates an imminent death can make a valid gift *causa mortis* of personal property. In order to make a valid gift, the donor must intend to give the item to the donee. The donor must deliver the item to the donee and the donee must accept it. Acceptance is presumed if the item has value. *See generally, Brooks v Gillow*, 352 Mich 189, 197-198 (1958).

On the facts of the problem, it seems clear that Decedent intended to give the ring to Bill who also accepted it. The only issue concerning the validity of the gift is whether it was effectively delivered. Under Michigan law, if manual delivery of an item of personal property is impossible, the donor can make a valid gift of the item by giving irrevocable instructions to a third party to deliver the item to the donee. *See Lumberg v Commonwealth Bank*, 295 Mich 566, 568 (1940). Bill was overseas. Decedent gave the ring to the minister with clear instructions to deliver it, which the minister carried out. Under these circumstances, a court should hold Decedent made a valid gift of the ring.

Another issue involving the gift of the ring arises from the will that Decedent prepared after handing the item over to the minister. A gift *causa mortis* is distinct from a gift *inter vivos* in that it may be recalled by the donor prior to death. *See Brooks, supra*, at 197-198. However, a Will, executed by the donor subsequent to a gift does not in and of itself revoke it. *Lumberg, supra*, at 568; *Braidwood v Harmon*, 31 Mich App 49, 55-56 (1971). Here, the terms of Decedent's Will are not inconsistent with his prior gift. The silence of the Will with regard to the ring does not negate Bill's claim that there was a completed gift of the ring. Bill can claim that with this Will, Decedent was only attempting to dispose of his remaining property.

Bill, therefore, has the strongest claim to the ring. As the donee of a valid gift *causa mortis* he should prevail over the Cancer Society claiming under the Will or Agnes claiming the item under the laws of intestate succession.

The Farm: With regard to the farm, the principal issue is whether Decedent severed Agnes's right of survivorship when he conveyed the deed of his interest in the farm to Bill.

Under Michigan law, however, a long-standing line of cases construe language like that used by the uncle as creating something more than a mere joint tenancy. These cases reason that by specifically mentioning the right of survivorship a grantor, like the uncle, must have intended to preserve the survivorship right from unilateral termination by either tenant. As a result, the Michigan courts construe the language as a grant of joint life estates followed by a contingent remainder in the survivor, indestructible by the voluntary act of only one of the life tenants. *See, e.g., Ballard v Wilson*, 364 Mich 479, 481-84 (1961); *Ames v Cheyne*, 290 Mich 215, 218 (1939); *Jones v Green*, 126 Mich App 412, 414-16 (1983); *Albro v Allen*, 434 Mich 271 (1990).

Under Michigan law, therefore, the deed from Decedent to Bill would not sever Agnes' survivorship right. Upon Decedent's death, Agnes' remainder would become possessory free and clear of Bill's claim. Moreover, no interest in the farm would pass to the Cancer Society under the terms of Decedent's Will.

The Brokerage Account: If Decedent's Will is valid, the Brokerage account would belong to the beneficiary named in the instrument, the Cancer Society. If the Will is invalid, the account would pass under the law of intestate succession to Decedent's sole heir, Agnes.

The instrument prepared by Decedent does not meet the general requirements for a valid Will in that it lacks witnesses. It can, however, be admitted to probate as a holographic Will. When a testator signs and dates a document that purports to be his Will, it can be enforced without witnesses if the material portions of the instrument are in the testator's own handwriting. The fact that portions of a holographic Will are preprinted will not invalidate the instrument under Michigan law, which focuses on the testator's intent. MCL 700.2502(1), (2), and (3).

Under the facts of the problem, the words actually handwritten by Decedent on the form, Last Will and Testament, would be sufficient standing alone to make out a valid holographic Will. He signed and dated an instrument in which he wrote in his own hand that he intended to give all his property to the Cancer Society. That should be sufficient to make out the Cancer Society's claim to the brokerage account. Decedent's intent was clearly expressed in his own hand.

Student Answer—February 2001

Question 1—Wills—10 points

The first issue is whether Douglas Decedent (DD) devised the farm to Bill. On our facts, DD & Agnes owned the farm as Joint Tenants w/ rights of survivorship.
In Michigan, that means DD & A own the property together. Since DD died, Agnes would automatically take DD's share, due to the language rights of survivorship. On that basis, Agnes would take the farm.

As to the ring, DD was pending death or in a causa mortis situation. Here, he was in his sick bed and didn't think he would have much longer. The ring would be given to DD's friend, Bill since he had an intent to give the ring to Bill, who was in the Balkans. The delivery, which is sometimes problematic, was given to the Minister who agreed to give it to Bill. This is effective delivery (to take place when the minister saw Bill). And, acceptance is also effective because at Douglas's funeral, the minister gave it to Bill, which is assumed accepted unless express denial stated by donee.

As for the two legal forms, DD had an intent to give the farm to Bill. It appears that he created a holographic will since he "filled it out in his own hand," signed and dated the form. This would qualify as an effective holographic will. But, as stated, the land belongs to Agnes b/c she has JT [Joint tenancy] w/ rights of survivorship.

Finally, the brokerage account & who received this—Here, he again created a holographic will since major portions are in his writing, i.e. "All to Cancer Society of America," signed, and dated. So, we have an effective holographic will. In the will DD intended Cancer Society to get the brokerage acct. It is assumed the Cancer Society will accept, unless expressly denied. And delivery is effective too since the nurse was to put it with his personal effects as DD requested.

July 2001—Question 7

Several years ago, Alice obtained a form Last Will and Testament from the local printer. She completed the form Will and signed it in the presence of her next-door neighbor and her neighbor's 13-year-old son. Both the neighbor and her son subscribed their names as witnesses to the Will.

The form Will provided that all Alice's property "real, personal, and mixed" would pass to her husband, Bob. The Will further provided that in the event Bob predeceased Alice, all her property would pass to her adult daughter, Charlotte. Alice's major assets were stocks, bonds, and jewelry, which she had inherited and which she held in her own name.

Bob went into business sometime after Alice prepared her Will. The business did not succeed. As a result, Bob owes several creditors substantial sums of money. For this reason, when Alice decided to buy a new luxury car, she used her own funds and titled the car in her own name.

Shortly after Alice purchased the car, she died unexpectedly. Following the funeral, Bob drove the luxury car that had belonged to Alice to Alaska and back. Bob hoped the long drive would enable him to plan the rest of his life. During the trip, Bob decided that he would decline everything given him under Alice's Will. As a result, Alice's stocks, bonds, jewelry, and car would pass to Charlotte, leaving nothing for Bob's creditors to attach.

Bob filed Alice's Will for probate. He also filed a signed disclaimer of any property passing under the Will.

You represent one of Bob's creditors. Can your client reach any of the assets formerly owned by Alice? Explain why or why not. Note: Apply Michigan state law. Do not consider your client's remedies under the Bankruptcy Code or any other state or federal law.

Model Answer to Question 7

A creditor will have difficulty reaching any of the assets that belonged to the decedent, Alice, except, perhaps, the luxury automobile. Even though Alice's will was subscribed by only two witnesses, one of whom was a minor, the will would likely be admitted to probate. A thirteen-year-old would likely be found a competent witness under Michigan law. Furthermore, even if the will was defective, a creditor generally does not have standing to file a will contest. Therefore, a challenge to the will in order to reach the assets passing to Bob intestate will likely be unavailing. Bob also appears to have effectively disclaimed any interest in property passing under the will. Under Michigan law, a disclaimer is not a "transfer" of an interest in property which would allow a creditor to claim a fraudulent conveyance. One, however, cannot disclaim property one has already accepted. This may give the creditor a claim to the car. A court could rule Bob had accepted the car by driving it across the country and therefore could not later disclaim it.

Validity of the Will: Michigan requires two individuals to witness the signing of a will. MCL 700.2502(1)(c) (Supp 2001). Any witness who is generally competent to testify is deemed competent to witness a will. MCL 700.2502 (Supp 2001). A thirteen-year-old is generally able to understand the importance of testifying truthfully. A child of that age can appreciate the nature of a judicial proceeding and the child's testimony can be understood. Under Michigan law, it has been held as a general rule that a child of eleven is competent to testify. *Breneman v Breneman*, 92 Mich App 336 (1979); see also, MRE 601 (establishing a presumption that every person is competent to testify absent proof of a lack of mental capacity or other infirmity).

The problem gives no indication that the thirteen-year-old neighbor lacks capacity in any sense. He is old enough to understand the purpose of a will and the importance of formal execution of such a document. A court should permit him to testify that Alice had the requisite testamentary intention when she signed her will.

Standing to File a Will Contest: Even if the will in the problem was defective, a court would not likely permit a creditor to challenge probate. The courts have consistently held that it would open the door to too many will contests if general creditors of an heir, legatee, or devisee were permitted to challenge a will. The Michigan courts have generally restricted standing in will contests to the beneficiaries of a will and those to whom the law would cast property if the will is set aside. A creditor who must yet establish a claim and reduce it to judgment has an interest that is too contingent to support a will contest.

"[P]ersons without any interest cannot maintain an action to contest a will. Thus it has been held that a creditor of the testator has no such interest as will authorize him to maintain the action." *In re Vanden Bosch's Estate*, 207 Mich 80, 92 (1919), quoting Thompson on Wills § 518. Thus, in the problem, a challenge to Alice's will in an effort to reach Bob's intestate share would likely be unavailing. Even if the will was improperly executed, a creditor, like the client, lacks standing to file a contest.

Disclaimer: A creditor, like the client, may challenge a beneficiary's disclaimer of a bequest or devise. If the disclaimer is ineffective, property passing to the beneficiary can be reached by the creditor. In Michigan, a statute directs that a valid disclaimer is not a transfer by the beneficiary. In the words of the statute, "[t]he disclaimant is treated as never having received the disclaimed interest." MCL 700.2909(2) (Supp 2001). Under Michigan law, therefore, the question is whether Bob effectively disclaimed his interest to the property passing under Alice's will.

To be effective, a disclaimer must describe the interest disclaimed. The disclaimer must be a signed writing and it must be delivered. MCO 700.2903 (Supp 2001). By filing the disclaimer with the will, Bob effectively delivered the instrument. *See* MCL 700.2906(2) (Supp 2001). Thus, it seems Bob complied with the formal requisites for a valid disclaimer of his interest under the will. A court could rule, however, that Bob cannot disclaim the luxury car.

Under Michigan law, a beneficiary who knows of a bequest or devisee cannot disclaim an interest in the property bequeathed or devised if the beneficiary has already accepted it. MCL 700.2910(1)(c) (Supp 2001). Bob knew the contents of Alice's will when he drove her car to Alaska and back. As a result, a court could rule he had already accepted the car before he filed his disclaimer. If a court so holds, a creditor like the client could reach Bob's interest in the car.

Student Answer—July 2001

Question 7—Wills—8 points

Wills
- spousal exception—No
- Disclaimer—filed prior to probate of will

Valid will
- signed form
- 18 and competent
- signed by two witnesses in testator's presence
- regardless of age
- Charlotte becomes only determinable heir under the will—all assets determined pass to her upon disclaimer of husband, Bob

- If intestacy, then would go to Bob as spouse with first $50k and ½ remainder to Charlotte as descendent

The issue here is whether any of Bob's creditors can reach any of the assets formerly owned by his wife, Alice.

The first issue to address here is, is there a valid will? The will was signed, the form will, in front of two witnesses by the testator, Alice, who we must assume was over 18 years and had the requisite mental capacity to create a will. The will was also signed by two witnesses within the presence of the testator. The ages of the witnesses are irrelevant. Just because one of the witnesses was 13 does not invalidate the will. A witness can be a minor. As long as the will was signed within the presence of the testator or with testator's acknowledgment, the will complies with the requirements of Michigan's Estates and Protected Individual's Code (EPIC).

Here, therefore, we have a valid will. If it had been invalid Alice would have died intestate and the estate would have proceeded through intestate succession with the first $150,000 going to the spouse, Bob, and ½ of the remainder to the spouse and ½ of remainder to Alice and Bob's child, Charlotte. This would have made it easier for creditors to get assets belonging to Alice. However, here, we have a valid will. And, we also have a disclaimer by the spouse, the predetermined heir stated in the will. By disclaiming his rights to take under his wife's will prior to the probate of the will, he is effectively asking that he be treated as having predeceased his spouse. In that event, the will provides that all assets are to go to the daughter, Charlotte. Therefore, Charlotte now takes as sole beneficiary under the will and Bob's creditors cannot reach her as beneficiary of the assets of Alice.

February 2002—Question 5

You are a law clerk for a probate judge. The court has heard evidence for several days in adversary proceedings involving the estate of Arthur Ascot. The following account summarized that evidence:

At the time Ascot died, he owned a farm, known as Blackacre, in fee simple absolute. Blackacre's fair market value is approximately $1 million. Ascot also owned about $1.4 million in personal property consisting of stocks, bonds, and three rare diamonds. The diamonds are a rare color and have been appraised at $200,000. All of the parties to the probate proceeding stipulate to the validity of Ascot's will. The simple document was signed and property witnessed. It left all Ascot's real property to his daughter, Beverly, and all of his personal property to his son, Charles. Beverly and Charles are Ascot's only living relatives.

Ascot was dying and was bedridden at home during his last days. Shortly before he died, Ascot called his nurse into his sickroom. Ascot told his nurse that he was concerned he was not leaving his property in equal shares to his children. He, therefore, gave the nurse the three diamonds and asked her to give the stones to Beverly. The nurse agreed to do so. She put the stones in her purse and promised to give them to Beverly that evening. Ascot then wrote and posted a letter to Beverly that stated, "The three rare diamonds you have always admired are now yours." The letter arrived at Beverly's address two days later.

Tragically, Beverly never read the letter. She died in an automobile accident a few hours after Ascot had posted the letter. Ascot's nurse learned of the accident when she went to give Beverly the diamonds that same evening. The nurse immediately returned to Ascot's home. (She also lived there.) Before she could give Ascot the news of Beverly's death, however, he passed away, just five hours after his daughter's death. The nurse dutifully locked the diamonds in Ascot's home office safe, where Ascot kept them and where they have remained to this day.

Beverly left a valid will that devised "all of her property, real, personal and mixed," to her husband, David. By virtue of this will, David claims Blackacre and the diamonds from Ascot's estate. Charles contests David's claim to both the diamonds and Blackacre.

The probate judge has asked you to prepare a brief memo discussing the issues raised in the case and how they should be resolved. Summarize the legal basis of the claims to the diamonds raised by Charles and David. Explain how you would resolve these claims. Also, discuss who is entitled to Blackacre.

Model Answer to Question 5

Charles and David will each raise claims to the diamonds based on the law of gifts. Charles will claim that Ascot did not make a valid gift of the diamonds before he died. As a result, Charles will contend the diamonds should pass to him under the terms of his father's will. David, on the other hand, will claim Ascot completed a gift of the diamonds before he died with the posting of the letter to Beverly. David will argue that the diamonds consequently passed to him through Beverly's will.

As for Blackacre, because Beverly predeceased her father, she had no interest in the estate when she died. Consequently, David could not acquire any rights to the estate through Beverly's will, which spoke only from the moment of her death. When Ascot died, his will would not dispose of his real property. Because the stated beneficiary of Ascot's real property, Beverly, predeceased him, the devise lapsed. Ascot's real property would pass by intestate succession to his son, as his closest living relative.

The Claim to the Diamonds: Charles and David have raised claims to the diamonds that must be resolved under the law of gifts. A gift by a person in expectation of imminent death is called a gift *causa mortis* and is recognized by Michigan law. *See, e.g., Brooks v Gillow*, 352 Mich 189 (1958). There are three elements to a valid gift: (1) the donor must intend to pass title gratuitously to the donee; (2) the gift must be actually or constructively delivered to the donee; and (3) the donee must accept the gift. *See, e.g., Buell v Orion State Bank*, 327 Mich 43 (1950).

Charles will claim Ascot failed to complete a gift of the diamonds to Beverly. If Ascot failed to complete the gift, the diamonds would pass to Charles under Ascot's will. The will devised all Ascot's personal property to Charles.

Because there is strong evidence of Ascot's intention to make the gift, Charles will focus his challenge on the elements of delivery and acceptance. The law requires actual delivery of a gift or its equivalent to prevent fraud. The Michigan Supreme Court has cautioned that "the courts should not weaken the necessary element of delivery by permitting the substitution of convenient and easily proven devices." *Molenda v Simonson*, 307 Mich 139, 144 (1943). Charles should argue that the diamonds were capable of manual delivery but were not. They were in Ascot's possession at the time of his death. Charles has authority for the proposition that delivery to the nurse was insufficient. If the donor retains control over the subject of the gift, there has not been sufficient delivery. *See Loop v Des Autell*, 294 Mich 527 (1940). Because the nurse was Ascot's employee he could recall the gift any time prior to its acceptance by Beverly. Moreover, Charles will undoubtedly underscore the fact that Beverly died before she could accept the gift.

David, on the other hand, will claim the gift was complete. As such, the title to the diamonds passed to Beverly, who then had the power to devise them through her will to David. *See Braidwood v Harmon*, 31 Mich App 49 (1971). David will emphasize Ascot's clear intention to make the gift. He expressed his intention to the nurse. The gift was central to an understandable and reasonable estate plan to distribute his property equally between his two children, the natural objects of his bounty. Moreover, the letter Ascot posted to Beverly evinced an unequivocal intention to make the gift. David can cite authority finding a valid gift on "very slight evidence of delivery" when the donor's intention to make the gift was clear. *Cook v Frazier*, 298 Mich 374, 378 (1941). David can also argue that the letter constituted an instrument of gift. When Ascot posted the letter, he could no longer recall it. Michigan has long recognized the validity of gifts made by delivery of a written instrument. *See Ellis v Secor*, 31 Mich 185 (1875). David will also rely on the well-established presumption of acceptance when a gift has value to the donee. *See, e.g., Lumberq v Commonwealth Bank*, 295 Mich 566 (1941). David will claim this presumption became operative when Ascot posted the letter, the instrument of gift. Hence, he will assert the gift was complete at that time.
(The question asks each applicant to resolve the contest over the diamonds after summarizing the basis of each party's claim. Credit should be given for a thoughtful analysis in either party's favor. Scoring of the question should be based primarily on an applicant's ability to explain the legal basis of each party's claim.)

Two Student Answers—February 2002

Question 5—Wills—8 points

Ascot owned-Blackacre = 1 mil
Personal property = 1.4 mil
stocks, bonds, diamonds = 200,000
Valid will-Beverly = real property
Charles = personal property

The issues in this case are whether the diamonds which are personal property were effectively delivered to Beverly so as the diamonds go to her estate. And the other issue is whether David is entitled to Blackacre if Beverly predeceased her father?

The diamonds are personal property & was intended to be a gift causa mortis. Ascot was dying & was bed ridden. It was pretty certain he was going to die so he made a gift to his daughter. Now the issue becomes if the gift was effectively delivered to his daughter. Ascot gave the diamonds to his nurse to give to Beverly. Since Beverly was not aware of the gift & the letter giving her the gift had not reached her she did not have anything to represent the gift. The nurse was an agent of the donor (Ascot) so it should be construed that the agent is representing donor & no delivery will be made until the diamonds were given to Beverly. Additionally if the gift has not been delivered & the donee predeceases donor then the gift is not valid. David will claim that it was Ascot's intent for the diamonds to go to Beverly as evidenced by the letter Ascot wrote. If the letter was signed & dated it could be construed as a codicil to the will. But the letter was mailed to Beverly so it does not appear that Ascot intended it to be part of his will.

Since Beverly predeceased her father the gift was not a valid one & the diamonds are personal property which the will conveyed to Charles.

Blackacre was conveyed under Ascot's will to go to Beverly. However, if a beneficiary predeceases the testator the gift will lapse. Michigan has an antilapse statute but Beverly did not have any children. Under the antilapse statute the gift will go to the grandparents' descendants or step-children. Here Ascot did not have any descendants from Beverly so the gift lapses. David is not an heir of Beverly's so Charles will get the property unless the will provides an alternative if Beverly dies or has a residuary clause.

Question 5—Wills—8 points

First of all we need to decide whether there was a valid transfer of the stones to Beverly. If Ascot is bed ridden, an agent can act for him and transfer property if he had the intent to make the gift and there is a valid delivery and acceptance. There is an intent to gift, but there is no valid delivery & acceptance before her death. Since this gift would fail, it would pass back into Ascot estate (residuary clause).

The next issue is whether David has any claim to Blackacre. Since Beverly predeceased Ascot, her gift lapses and would pass back into Ascot's estate. The only thing that could save David (he gets Blackacre) is if there was an anti-lapse statute. Antilapse statutes apply only to family.

In this situation, since the diamonds were not validly transferred to Beverly, they would go to Charles under the will because they are personal property.

The title to Blackacre would also go back into the will because Beverly predeceased her father. A person must survive the testator for more than 120 hours to collect under the will or intestate succession. Since Bev died first, Blackacre would be distributed out of Ascot's will (in the residuary clause) and David would not get either diamonds or property.

July 2002—Question 6

David Decedent prepared and signed a will in the presence of three witnesses about ten years before he died. Decedent was a widower at the time and had two adult children, a son, Junior, and a daughter, Dottie. Decedent held two major assets at the time he prepared his Will, a stately house in Farmington Hills and a brokerage account held with a Detroit investment firm. The house and the account were of roughly equal value. The operative provisions of decedent's simple Will read, "I devise my house in Farmington Hills and the property on which it is situated to my son, Junior, and all the rest residue and remainder of my estate to my daughter, Dottie."

Three years ago, Junior died unexpectedly. Junior's Will read as follows:

> I give, devise, and bequeath all of my property, whether real, personal, tangible or intangible, of whatsoever kin and wheresoever situated including any property over which I may have a power of appointment at the time of my death, to my wife, Margaret, if she survives me, but if not, then to my lineal descendants, per stirpes.

Junior was survived by his wife, Margaret, and had no children or other lineal descendants.

Two years ago, David Decedent took ill. During the course of a long illness, he married the nurse who was caring for him, Clara Burton. Shortly after the marriage, Decedent sold a substantial number of the stocks and bonds he held in his brokerage account in order to purchase an annuity. The contract for the annuity, issued by the Fidelity Insurance Company, obligated Fidelity to pay a monthly income to David and Clara for the lifetime of the survivor of them.

Decedent died last week. His Will was duly admitted to probate.

Dottie, Clara, and Margaret intend to pursue all available claims to the assets Decedent held at his death. If they do so, how are these assets likely to be distributed? Explain with particular attention to the Farmington Hills house, the remaining assets in the brokerage account, and the annuity.

Model Answer to Question 6

The devise of the Farmington Hills house to Junior lapsed. Junior's will could not pass interest in the house to his wife. A will speaks only from the moment of death, and at the time of his death, Junior had no property interest in the house. Michigan's antilapse statute directs that when a named devisee predeceases the testator, that devise will descend to the devisee's lineal descendants. It will not pass the devisee's surviving spouse. Because Junior had no lineal descendants, the lapsed gift of the house would pass through David's estate. Dottie, as the beneficiary of the residuary clause in Decedent's will, would thus receive the house and brokerage account if Decedent's estate was distributed solely as directed in his will. Because the will does not provide for Decedents surviving spouse, however, Clara could elect to receive her statutory elective share. Thus, Dottie and Clara will ultimately share in the final distribution of the major assets of the estate, the Farmington Hills house and the brokerage account. Payments under the annuity contract are not within the estate and would continue to be paid to Clara outside probate. Under Michigan law, however, they might be considered in computing the amount of Clara's elective share.

Lapse: Generally, a devise of real property set forth in a will lapses if the named devisee predeceases the testator. *See generally*, 23 Mich L & Practice 2d, Wills 309 (1958). Like most states, however, Michigan has an antilapse statute. Mich Comp Laws 700.2604 (Supp Pamphlet 2002). Under the statute, the lineal descendants of the named devisee will take the devise. Mich Comp Laws 70.2603(1)(a) (Supp Pamphlet 2002). If the named devisee has no lineal descendants the property will pass through the residuary clause of the decedent's will. Mich Comp Laws 700.2604(1) (Supp Pamphlet 2002).

In the examination question, Junior predeceased the testator, Decedent. Junior had no descendants and hence the putative devise of the Farmington Hills house lapsed and the property became part of the residue of the estate. As such, it passed to Dottie through the residuary clause of Decedent's will.

Note that Junior's Will could not pass any interest in the Farmington Hills house to his wife, Margaret. A will speaks only from the moment of the testator's death. See generally, 23 Mich L & Practice 2d, Wills 176 (1958). At the time of his death, Junior had no interest in the house. He was merely the named devisee of Decedent's will. Decedent was free to revise the will and therefore, our law does not recognize an expected devise or inheritance as a property interest. The Farmington Hills house still belonged to Decedent when Junior died. When Decedent died, it became part of the residue of his estate as a lapsed devise.

Elective Share: Like most states, Michigan protects surviving spouses from disinheritance through the means of an elective share statute. Under Michigan law, a testator's surviving spouse may elect to take in lieu of the terms of the will, "one-half of the sum or share that would have passed to the spouse had the testator died intestate, reduced by one-half of the value of all property derived by the spouse from the decedent by any means other than testate or intestate succession upon the decedent's death." Mich Comp Laws 700.2202(2) (Supp Pamphlet 2002). (The spousal elective share was the same under the Revised Probate Code, repealed as of April 2000. Mich Comp Laws 700.282[1] [1995]).

In the examination question, Decedent's will left nothing to his widow, Clara. As a surviving spouse, Clara could thus elect to share the residue of the estate with Dottie. The residue would include both the Farmington Hills house and any remaining assets in the brokerage account. Decedent has property interests in both these assets at the time of his death and they would be included within his estate. *See* Mich Comp Laws 700.1104(b) (Supp Pamphlet 2002). His interest in the annuity, however, ended with his death. Clara would have the right to continue to receive monthly under the annuity according to its terms. As the problem states, the annuity provides for payments to Clara as Decedent's surviving spouse. It can be argued that under Michigan's elective share statute, Clara's share should be reduced by one-half the present value of these payments as "property derived by the spouse from the Decedent by any means other than testate or intestate succession upon the decedent's death." Mich Comp Laws 700.2202(2) (Supp Pamphlet 2002). There are no Michigan cases on this point, however. Even if the annuity payments reduce Clara's share, she will probably elect to take her elective share. She receives nothing, after all, under the terms of Decedent's Will.

Student Answer—July 2002

Question 6—Wills—9 points

Clara's Claim: When a testator dies and does not include his wife in the will, the wife still may take a share. If she and Testator did not have children together, as the case here, she may take only one-half of what she would take by intestate succession, minus any other property given *inter vivos* by Testator. Here, her intestate share would be ½ of 100,000 = 50,000, minus the value of the annuity.

Junior's Claim: Where a devisee predeceases Testator, his share "lapses" unless he has descendants protected by an anti-lapse statute. Here, Junior has no children in any case, and since he predeceased Testator, his wife cannot benefit from his will. A relative by affinity (marriage) has no rights under the marriage partner's rights. So Margaret, as wife of a predeceased devisee, takes nothing.

Dottie's Claim: Dottie comes out pretty well here. She takes all the property (real and personal) that doesn't go to Clara. So after Clara's rights are satisfied, Dottie takes all the rest.

Abatement: Clara's claim may be taken from any of the residue (first) and then, if necessary, from the house. So in order, the satisfaction of Clara's claim will come from (1) the brokerage account and then (2) the house. The annuity is Clara's, intended by Testator for her and a form of joint property. However, the value of it will still be deducted from Clara's intestate share.

February 2003—Question 10

Donna Decedent died recently. She left one living relative, her Uncle Harry, whom she never liked. Decedent never prepared a will, but she did plan for her death. She wanted her property to go to her closest friend, Amy Amicus, and her long-standing employee, Carl Clerk.

Decedent had developed a real estate business during her life. At the time of her death, she owned ten rental properties that produced a steady income from lease payments made by tenants under separate written leases. Using this income, decedent had invested in bearer bonds which she regularly placed in a safe deposit box at First Bank. She listed both herself and Amy Amicus as the owners of the safe deposit box. The card she signed when she first rented the box stated that she and Amicus were "joint tenants." At the time of Decedent's death, the bonds in the safe deposit box were worth a considerable sum of money.

Earlier this year, Decedent was diagnosed with a serious disease that required surgery. The day before the scheduled surgery, she called Carl Clerk into her office and handed him the ten written leases for each of her rental properties. She said to him, "Carl, I appreciate everything you've done for me. If things don't go well tomorrow, these are yours."

Decedent removed a sack of rare coins from her office safe. She handed the sack to Clerk and said, "Carl, you know my friend Amy Amicus. I want her to have these coins."

Sadly, Decedent's operation did not go well. She died shortly after the surgery. **Discuss who is entitled to the bearer bonds in the safe deposit box, the rental properties and the sack of rare coins still held by Clerk.**

Model Answer to Question 10

Decedent's Uncle Harry has the strongest claim to all of the property mentioned in the problem. He would inherit the property as Decedent's next of kin. MCL 700.2103(1)(d). No legally effective gift was made of any of the property so as to remove it from the estate passing to Harry by intestacy.

The Bonds: The law requires a showing of three elements to establish a valid gift *inter vivos*. These are (1) the donor must intend to make the gift; (2) the gift must be actually or constructively delivered to the donee; and (3) the donee must accept it. 18 Mich L & Prac Encyclopedia, 2d Ed (Gifts) § 1 (2002). Ordinarily, the law will presume acceptance if the gift is beneficial to the donee. *See, e.g., Buell v Orion State Bank*, 327 Mich 43 (1950). Delivery, on the other hand, is not presumed. Generally, a donee must show that the donor parted with dominion and control of the given property. 18 Mich L & Prac Encyclopedia, 2d Ed (Gifts) § 4 (2002). It is usually ruled that a donor does not make a sufficient delivery of items left in a safe deposit box held jointly with the donee. *See, e.g., Taylor v Taylor*, 292 Mich 95 (1940). In such cases, the donor retains the ability to remove the items from the box and, therefore, has not fully parted with dominion and control. *Id.*

In the question, the bonds left in the safe deposit box remained under Decedent's control throughout her life. Harry will undoubtedly challenge whether these bonds were therefore ever "delivered" to Amicus so as to make a legally effective gift.

The Coins: Delivery may be accomplished through a third person. However, if the third person is an agent of the donor, the courts often hold the gift is not made until the property is actually delivered to the donee. The donor is deemed to retain control of the property so long as it remains in the agent's possession. As the principal, the donor has the power to recall the gift in the agent's hands. 18 Mich L & Prac Encyclopedia, 2d Ed (Gifts) § 5 (2002).

The problem states the sack of rare coins was still held by Carl Clerk at the time of Decedent's demise. Under the prevailing view, the coins therefore had not been effectively delivered to Amicus so as to complete the gift.

The Rental Properties: A gift *causa mortis* differs from a gift *inter vivos* in that it is made by the donor in contemplation of imminent death. 18 Mich L & Prac Encyclopedia, 2d Ed (Gifts) § 31 (2002). Real property cannot be the subject of a gift *causa mortis. See, e.g., In re Reh's Estate*, 196 Mich 210 (1917). Such gifts may be made of personal property only. 18 Mich L & Prac Encyclopedia, 2d Ed (Gifts) § 32 (2002). Under Michigan law, a lessor's interest under a lease has been held to be real property which could not be given *causa mortis. In re Reh's Estate, supra*, at 219-220.

It is therefore likely that Harry would challenge the attempted gift to Clerk. It was clearly made in contemplation of death. Decedent was apprehensive about the surgery scheduled for the next day. She stated she was making the gift in case the surgery did not go well. Under prevailing Michigan authority, she attempted to convey an interest in real property, Decedent's interest under the leases. As such, the gift would fail. To survive, the gift would have to be characterized as personalty.

Comment: Please note that this same question, model answer, and student answer is also provided under the Personal Property section. Because the question combines the two subjects, it has been placed in both sections to ensure completion.

Student Answer—February 2003

Question 10—Wills—None Available

February 2003—Question 12

About 20 years ago, Alex Anderson read a magazine article entitled "Prepare Your Own Will." Using the forms in the article as a guide, Anderson typed the following document:

Last Will and Testament

September 3, 1982
Royal Oak, MI

I, Alex Anderson, being of sound mind declare this to be my last Will, I give my sailboat to my friends, Chuck and Deb Nabors. All the rest, residue and remainder of my estate I give to my wife, Betty, should she survive me, but if she should fail to survive me, then to my sons, Tom and Harry.

____
Alex Anderson

The foregoing instrument, consisting of a single typewritten page, was signed, sealed, published, and declared by Alex Anderson to be his last Will, in our presence, and we, at his request and in his presence and in the presence of each other, have hereunto subscribed our names as witnesses this third day of September, 1982.

Chuck Nabors
202 Maple Avenue
Royal Oak, MI

Deb Nabors
202 Maple Avenue
Royal Oak, MI

Anderson pulled the page from his typewriter and telephoned his neighbors, Chuck and Deb. They walked across the street and sat down with Anderson in his living room. Anderson signed the document where indicated and then each of the Nabors did the same.

Two years later, Betty Anderson gave birth to a third child, Richard, whom the Andersons called "Dick." At about the same time, Alex Anderson's brother died leaving a minor daughter, Annie. Soon thereafter, Alex Anderson took the document reproduced above from the drawer where he kept it. In his own hand, he wrote the words "and Dick and my niece, Annie" after the names of his sons, Tom and Harry. Anderson then returned the document to the drawer.

Alex and Betty Anderson never had a particularly happy marriage. They stayed together for the sake of the children but divorced soon after Dick entered college. Alex Anderson died earlier this year. He was survived by Betty, Tom, Dick, Harry, Annie and the Nabors. The document reproduced above was filed for probate.

How should Anderson's estate, including his sailboat, be distributed? Explain.

Model Answer to Question 12

This question raised issues involving (1) the validity of a will witnessed by interested persons; (2) the effect of divorce upon a will; (3) the proper procedure to amend a will; and (4) the rights of a child born after execution of a will.

Interested Witnesses: Michigan requires two individuals to witness the signing of a will. MCL 700.2502(1)(c). At common law an interested person was incompetent to witness a will. By statute, a number of jurisdictions, including Michigan, made an interested witness competent to testify to the validity of a will, but voided any bequest made to the witness. *See, e.g., In re Fay's Estate*, 353 Mich 83, 89 (1958). Today, under the Estates and Protected Individuals Code ("EPIC"), the "signing of a will by an interested witness does not invalidate the will or any provision of it." MCL 700.2505(2). Thus, interest no longer disqualifies a person as a witness nor invalidates any gift under a will. In the problem, the gift of the sailboat to the Nabors would not render them incompetent to witness Anderson's will. Moreover, current Michigan law would not require them to forfeit the bequest of the boat. Because the will is otherwise valid, the Nabors would receive the boat in the distribution of Anderson's estate.

Effect of Divorce: Under Michigan law, a divorce revokes any provision of a person's will that makes a gift to the person's former spouse. MCL 700.2807(1)(a). Consequently, the provision of Anderson's will leaving all his property to his former wife, Betty, would be deemed revoked. His estate, except for the specific bequest to the Nabors, would therefore pass under the residuary clause of his will.

Validity of the Amendment to the Residuary Clause: A codicil or amendment to a will must be executed with the same formality as the will itself. MCL 700.2502 and 700.1108(b). A handwritten codicil is valid as a holograph only if it is signed and dated by the testator. MCL 700.2502(1)(b) and (2), and 700.1108(b). An interlineation of the addition of words to a will, even if they are in the testator's hand, are generally deemed insufficient to amend a will. Such additions lack the testator's signature and proper attestation. *See, e.g., In re Houghten's Estate*, 310 Mich 613 (1945). Thus, Anderson's addition of handwritten words to his will is likely to be held ineffective as an amendment or codicil. Consequently, Anderson's niece, Annie, would not receive anything from his estate. Anderson's son, Dick, born after the execution of the will, would, however, have a claim to a share of the estate by statute.

Children Omitted from a Will: Michigan law provides relief to a child omitted from a parent's will who was born after the parent executed the instrument. MCL 700.2302. Unless a contrary intention appears, the after-born child is entitled to share in the property distributed under the will to the same extent as the children included in the instrument. MCL 700.2302(1)(b) and (2)(a). Any gift to the children included in the will is ratably abated to allow the omitted child to share in the estate. MCL 700.2302(1)(b)(iv).

In the facts of the problem, Anderson clearly intended Dick to share in his estate. His attempt to amend the instrument, although legally ineffective, manifests that intention. Dick therefore would be entitled to the same share in the estate as his siblings. Their shares would be abated accordingly.

Two Student Answers—February 2003

Question 12—Wills—10 points

The first issue is whether Anderson's will is valid. Michigan requires it to be signed by the testator and witnessed by 2 other people. It should also be dated, however, the courts can also overlook the date if it is the testator intent. Here we have no problems with assuming Anderson was of sound mind when it was drafted.

The Nabors are entitled to the sailboat as it was left pursuant to the will as drafted by Anderson. The fact that they witnessed the will should not create a conflict or prevent them from taking under the will, as long as the gift is not given because of fraud or duress. Here there is no problem Anderson drafted the will or if the Nabors even knew of the gift under the will.

The rest of the property is going to pass into the residue of the estate. Betty is not going to be able to claim anything because at the time of Anderson's death they were divorced. Therefore, we treat her as predeceasing him.

Anderson changed his will but did not initial or sign the change as required for a holographic will. Therefore the court can scratch out the part of the residue estate and ignore the handwritten change. Either way the remaining estate will be divided equally among the surviving children.

Question 12—Wills—9 points

The will appears to be valid it is dated, 2 witness' and signed by Alex. The witness signed in his presence, although that it not necessary. This will will go to probate.

The distribution of his estate is as follows. Betty gets nothing—the divorce severs this tie.

The modification to the Will was in Alex's handwriting. Common law would say that this revokes original Will and creates 2nd Will but Michigan will allow a change—this is a codicil and if there is a dispute the courts can use dispersing power (clear and concise evidence to show) Alex's intent. A codicil is a modification handwritten by decedent.

Alex's residual estate will be divided equally among his children, Tom, Dick, and Harry. Annie will likely get nothing since she is not mentioned in the original document. Tom and Harry have executory interest in the estate, but Dick is added because he is in the class of children.

The sailboat will go to his friends. Although not related, this appears to be a specific devise and the intent of Alex is clear.

Annie may also get nothing since she is too far removed down the lineal line and Alex has children. Alex did not mention any specific or demonstrative devise to his brother therefore there is nothing for Annie.

Michigan recognizes computer generated wills as long as they meet with formalities i.e. 2 witnesses dated, signed by testator which this does.

There may be an issue that the witnesses are also takers under the will, but not anymore. A witness can also take under the will as a beneficiary. Therefore they will get the sailboat.

RAP—no interest will vest, if at all from 21 years after the life in being at the time the interest was created. Michigan has a 90-year vesting rule. This is important because Tom and Harry were executory interests which are vested. Therefore this interest was valid and will vest.

July 2003—Question 7

When Teresa Testator prepared her will she held two major assets—her home in suburban Lansing, Michigan, and a brokerage account containing stocks, bonds and cash. Teresa's will, which was properly witnessed and notarized, directed her executor to convey the house "to the pastor of the Lansing New Life Church." The will's residuary clause left all Testator's remaining assets, including the brokerage account, to her "surviving grandchildren."

When Testator wrote the will, she had two grandchildren, Mary and Flo. One year after Testator signed the will, another granddaughter, Diana, was born, out of wedlock. Diana survived Testator. Mary, however, predeceased Testator, leaving no descendants. Mary's will left all her property to her husband, Barry. Flo also died before Testator. Flo was survived by her son, Little Stevie.

Neither Little Stevie nor Diana was named in the will which was found in Testator's safe deposit box following her death. Before she died, however, Testator did make some changes to the document. Testator became disenchanted with her church and pastor several months before her death. At that time, she removed the original of her will from the safe deposit box where she kept it. She took a red pen, lined out the phrase, "to the pastor of the Lansing New Life Church" and wrote above it in her own hand, "to Alma Mater College." Testator did not line out any other words from the rest of the printed sentence describing the devise of her Lansing suburban home. She signed and dated the document in the margin next to the interlineation and then returned the altered will to her safe deposit box where it was found.

Barry, Little Stevie, Diana, the pastor of the Lansing New Life Church, and Alma Mater College have all filed claims against Testator's estate. Describe how the brokerage account and the Lansing house should be distributed among these claimants. Be certain to discuss all the legal theories that would reasonably support any of the claims.

Model Answer to Question 7

Barry would have no claim to the estate. His wife, Mary, predeceased Testator. The bequest of the brokerage account to Mary lapsed. At the time Mary died, she had no right to any property described in Testator's will. Therefore, nothing could pass under Mary's will to Barry. The bequest to Flo also lapsed but her share would be preserved for Little Stevie under Michigan's antilapse statute. Diana would also be entitled to a share of the class gift of the brokerage account. She was Testator's grandchild and would share in the bequest even though she was born out of wedlock after the will was signed. Little Stevie and Diana will thus share the brokerage account.

As for the Lansing house, Alma Mater College would have a better claim than the pastor of the Lansing New Life Church. The interlineation made by Testator is probably enforceable as a holograph. Moreover, Michigan allows an alteration to take effect even if it fails to meet the formal requirements of a will if the testator's intention is clear.

The Brokerage Account: Testator made a bequest of her brokerage account to her "surviving grandchildren." She had three granddaughters but two, Mary and Flo, predeceased her. Mary left no descendants. The bequest to Mary, therefore, lapsed. Michigan's antilapse statute preserves a gift only for members of the class that leave descendants. MCL 700.2709(b) (2003).

Little Stevie would share the account with Diana. Under Michigan's Estate and Protected Individual Code, individuals born out of wedlock share in class gifts defined by a relationship to the decedent if they stand in that relationship. MCL 700.2707 (2003). Diana is Testator's granddaughter and she would therefore share in the gift of the brokerage account as a "surviving grandchild."

Barry would have no claim to the brokerage account under the terms of Flo's will. A will speaks only from the moment of death. 23 Mich L & Prac 2d, Wills § 176 (2003). At the time Flo died, she had no property interest in any of the assets that later passed through her mother's estate. Testator was alive at that time and still owned the assets.

The Suburban Lansing Home: Testator intended to change her will by giving her house to Alma Mater College rather than the pastor of her church. She did not, however, execute a codicil in accordance with the standard formal requirements required of a testamentary act. She made an interlineation to her will in her own hand, however. She also signed and dated the interlineations. Accordingly, her alteration of her will may be valid as a holograph. Michigan only requires the material portions of a holographic will or codicil to be in the testator's own handwriting. MCL 700.2502(2) (2003). Michigan also permits a court to consider printed language in addition to handwritten terms when the court is construing a holographic will. MCL 700.2502(3) (2003). Read with the printed portions of the will, Testator did sign and date a writing that clearly evinced her intention to give her suburban Lansing home to Alma Mater College. A court could thus treat her alteration of the will as a valid holograph.

Moreover, under Michigan law, a court can enforce an alteration made without the necessary formalities if the court finds the testator clearly intended to change her will. MCL 700.2503(c) (2003). There is substantial evidence Testator did intend to change her will. She had become disenchanted with her church. She altered her will, signed and dated the change, and returned the altered document to her safe deposit box. These acts all evince a serious intention to change the devisee of her house. Thus, even if Testator failed to make a valid holographic codicil, Alma Mater College would have good grounds to claim the suburban Lansing house over the pastor of the church.

Student Answer—July 2003

Question 7—Wills—10 points

House—! Pastor   Residuary to surviving grandchildren

Dispensing c/c evidence   antilapse

M + H—no F—L/S   D ok Pastor

For a will to be valid, the Testator must have testamentary intent and capacity. In this case the facts do not contradict the above assertions (Testamentary intent + capacity). Further, while the facts are silent, if Testator is at least 18 years old and signs the will and has 2 witnesses that witness the signature or Testator's acknowledgment of the signature, the will is valid. Thus, the will is a valid Legal Document for the Testamentary of Teresa.

Even though Mary's will left all her property to her husband, Bill, Bill will not take under the will. Mary only had an expectancy, which she did not satisfy—she predeceased her grandmother Teresa. The will to her husband does not change the result.

Little Stevie should be able to take under the will. While [h]is mother Flo, predeceased the Testator, Teresa, Little Stevie's interest would normally fail, but the anti-lapse statute will save it for Little Stevie. Little Stevie is a lineal descendant of the grandparent (not a grandparent or a stepchild which are also exception for anti lapse to work). Since Little Stevie is a lineal descendant of Testator, Teresa, anti-lapse will save Stevie's interest.

Diana has an interest because she is part of "surviving grandchildren."

Further the rule against perpetuities "surviving grandchildren" problem (if in fact there was one) is solved because the interest did vest within 90 years.

Testator Teresa can make changes in her will by deleting phrases if the dispensing power applies. The dispensing power will apply to cure procedural defects that would be fatal to the will (ex: only one signature as a witness). The dispensing power requires clear and convincing evidence to satisfy the change here in Teresa's will.

In this case, facts state Teresa signed the original will, which she retrieved from safe deposit box and further, Teresa signed the changes (which might also qualify as a holographic will (signed, dated unwitnessed, material portion in testator's handwriting—even though date, dispensing power may cure this also) and Teresa pointed out the change in the Margin. Under clear and convincing evidence, this may be sufficient for the dispensing power to cure the change in the will with the red pen by Testator Teresa.

Results: Barry loses, Pastor loses, and Little Stevie and Diana take ½ of the residuary while the house goes to Alma Mater College instead of Pastor.

February 2004—Question 11

Alice Adams, a widow, died not long ago. She and her deceased husband had three children, Betty, Charles, and David. David died six months before his mother. David left a will that devised all his property to his second wife, Eve. David's first marriage ended in divorce but David had two children with his first wife. Their names are Felix and Gert, and both survived David.

About a year before Alice died, Betty encountered a serious financial crisis. Consequently, Alice sent Betty a check for $30,000 with a handwritten note that read:

> Dear Betty:
>
> I've always wanted you and your brothers to share everything I own when my time comes. Because you need the money now, I am sending you a check for $30,000. I hope this sees you through your hard times.
>
> Love,
> Mom

When Alice died, she owned stocks, bonds, and other personal property worth approximately $60,000. All these assets were titled in Alice's name alone. Alice died intestate. Betty, Charles, Eve, Felix, and Gert all claim a share of the $60,000. Evaluate the strengths and weaknesses of each of these claims. Explain how the $60,000 should be distributed.

Model Answer to Question 11

Eve would have no claim to her mother-in-law's estate. She is not her mother-in-law's heir. Betty's claim would be subject to the defense that her mother gave her an advancement of $30,000. Accordingly, she would not be entitled to claim any part of the remaining $60,000. Charles would receive half of the remaining sum. The other $30,000 would be divided evenly between Felix and Gert, who would receive their father's share by representation.

Eve's Claim: The question calls for an evaluation of the strengths and weaknesses of each party's claim to the estate. Eve has the weakest claim. Under Michigan's law of intestate succession, Eve is not her mother-in-law's heir. MCL 700.2103 (2002). Thus, she could not claim an intestate share of her mother-in-law's estate. Eve also would not be able to succeed to the share of her deceased husband, David. As noted below, his share would pass to Felix and Gert. MCL 700.2103(a) (2002). Although David's will left all his property to Eve, David had no interest in his mother's estate at the time he died.

His mother, Alice, was still alive when David died and thus her assets were still hers alone. A will speaks only from the moment of death. *See, e.g., In re Hurd's Estate*, 303 Mich 504, 510 (1942). Therefore, David's will could not pass any interest in assets that still belonged to his mother.

Betty's Claim: Betty's claim to her mother's estate is weakened by the fact that she received $30,000 from her mother shortly before she died. Under Michigan's Estates and Protected Individuals Code, a lifetime gift made by an intestate to a putative heir is treated as an advancement if a writing made at the time of the gift indicates that was the decedent's intention. MCL 700.2109(2) (2002). The letter Alice wrote would seem to meet this standard. Alice's letter accompanied the $30,000 check. The letter stated it was Alice's wish that her children "share everything . . . when my time comes." This is a fairly clear indication of Alice's intention. Moreover, the check was written in an amount that was roughly one-third of the value of Alice's estate. Distribution of her estate in thirds makes sense as she had three children.

If the court finds a lifetime gift to be an advancement, the value of the gift is added to the probate estate. The estate is then divided among the heirs, with the lifetime gift deducted from the intestate share of the heir who received it. This process, sometimes called the "hotchpot" method, is not spelled out in the Michigan statute. It is the method used at common law, however, and is specified by the comment to Uniform Probate Code § 2-109, which served as a model for the Michigan statute. Uniform Probate Code § 2-109, comment (amended 2002), 8 ULA 27-28 (Supp 2003); *see generally*, William M. McGovern, Jr. & Sheldon F. Kurtz, Wills, Trusts and Estates, 65 (2d ed 2001). In the problem, the hotchpot method would create a total estate of $90,000. As noted below, Betty's share would be one-third or $30,000, which she received as an advancement. The balance of $60,000 would be divided among her surviving brother, Charles, and her brother David's children, Felix and Gert.

Charles, Felix and Gert: Under Michigan's statute of intestate succession an estate is divided among the children of a decedent if the decedent leaves no surviving spouse. MCL 700.2103(a) (2002). The estate is divided into shares equal to the number of descendants the decedent had in the first generation with a descendant who survived the decedent. Succeeding generations take by representation. MCL 700.2106 (2002). Thus, Charles would take one-third of his mother's estate, $30,000 from the hotchpot. Felix and Gert would split one third to take $15,000 each. Betty's entitlement to the remaining third is satisfied by the $30,000 advancement she received before her mother's death.

Two Student Answers—February 2004

Question 11—Wills—10 points

Alice died intestate with an estate valued at $60,000. The issue is how that estate should be distributed between her surviving descendants.

The first sub-issue is how to deal with the gift of $30,000 given to Betty a year before Alice died. There are 2 views on this:

1) This was a generous gift to help a daughter in difficult times. If this was only a "gift" with no intention of it being an early advancement on a later distribution of an estate, then Betty does not have to have this early share of the estate be held against her distribution share of the estate after Alice's death.

2) This $30,000 could be an advancement on the expected estate and could be considered part of the estate—and Betty will claim it as her distributed share.

The rule governing this issue requires that the donor must acknowledge her desire to have this be considered part of the estate, just distributed early and must be in writing, done contemporaneously with the gift. Here, Alice did write a letter, but only vaguely referred to the money and sharing with her brothers. The court may interpret this connection with "when my time comes" as specifically relating to her estate, but the note does not make this clear. It could be argued either way. If Betty had written a note acknowledging the gift as an early estate distribution it would also cover this issue and demonstrate it as part of the full estate.

Assuming the court did not believe this note made a complete acknowledgment of the decedent's desire for this $30,000 to be part of the estate, just distribution early, the estate would be distributed as follows:

$60,000 in stock, bonds and personal property (less any amounts for administrative expenses)
1/3 to Betty = 20K
1/3 to Charles = 20K
1/6 to Felix = 10K
1/6 to Gert = 10K who take due to anti-lapse statute in Michigan, allowing them to succeed to the deceased father's 1/3 share. The anti-lapse statute affects only lineal descendants.

If the court held the letter for $30,000 was valid as an advancement; estate total = $90,000 – Betty = 30K (already), now 0, Charles = $30K, Felix = $15K, Gert = $15K

Question 11—Wills—8 points

When a person dies without a will, their estate is distributed intestate. The Epic Rules govern distribution of an intestate estate. Michigan follows a Per Capita distribution which gives each surviving descendant an equal share depending on which generation the descendant is in list—kids, 2nd—grandkids, 3rd—great grandkids.

Betty: It is important to note that Betty is a direct descendant of Alice—the decedent and she will take her intestate share according to Per Capita distribution which would be a 1/3 (divided equally among kids at 1st generation), Betty, Charles and David. However, how do we treat the $30,000 payment to Betty at common law, a payment made before the decedent passed away was considered an advancement. Michigan Epic has modified this Rule by stating that in order for an advancement to be valid—there must be a contemporaneous writing by the decedent stating that payment is an advancement and there must be a writing of Betty—the one receiving the advancement acknowledging that the money is an advancement. Here, it can be argued that Alice's writing constituted a valid writing to fulfill the writing required under Epic. However, we have no acknowledgement by Betty therefore Epic requirements are not satisfied. Betty will receive a 1/3 distribution out of Alice's estate which equals $20,000.

Charles: Charles is entitled to his intestate share as well. In a Per Capita distribution system Charles will receive everything that his brothers and sisters receive. Here, Charles had a sister, Betty and a brother David which would make the 1st generation be divided by three. Each party would receive its 1/3 share. Charles would receive his 1/3 share of Alice's intestate estate $20,000.

Eve: Eve is the surviving spouse of one of the 1st generation descendants of Alice. Under common law—a surviving spouse is not entitled to intestate share of their spouse even if there is a will leaving everything to the spouse. Here, David would be entitled to his 1/3 share however he passed away before Alice, therefore his gift lapses. Eve receives nothing despite the will leaving David's share to her.

Under Michigan anti lapse statute if a gift lapses, the heir predeceases the decedent, and if the predeceased heir is a step child or descendant of grandparent then the lapsed gift will go to the surviving descents of that heir. Felix is the son of David and a descendant therefore he would get David's 1/3 share divvied equally with brother.

Gert: Under Per Capita distribution, Gert has to get an equal share as his brother because he is at the same generation therefore each child Felix and Gert receive $10 each.

July 2004—Question 9

Mary Peterson lived alone in her home until the time of her passing in 1995. Mary had two adult children, Paul Peterson and Sarah Peterson, neither of whom was married. Mary's will left her home (valued at $100,000) and her diamond jewelry (also valued at $100,000) to Paul and Sarah in equal parts. Rather than sell the jewelry and the home and split the proceeds, Paul and Sarah asked the probate court to approve Paul receiving the home and Sarah receiving the jewelry. The probate court approved this plan in 1996 without any protest from anyone. Paul immediately moved into the home with his girlfriend, Jane. The home was titled in Paul's name only, but he had orally promised Jane he would leave her the home in his will. However, Paul dies intestate in 2003.

Paul's sister Sarah opened an estate in the probate court, as the only living relative of Paul. Jane filed a statement and proof of claim alleging an interest in the home, in part based on her contributions toward the many improvements she and Paul made to the home and in part based on Paul's promise to leave her the home in his will (which he never executed, nor was a will ever drafted).

Jane was out of the state on a motorcycle tour across the country when the personal representative denied the claim and mailed notice to her home address. Now, ninety days after the claim was denied, Jane has returned and filed a lawsuit against the estate for what she asserts is her interest in the home. The personal representative has asked for dismissal of the lawsuit. You are the clerk for the judge assigned to the case and she has asked you to write a memo on how the motion to dismiss should be decided.

Discuss whether the lawsuit is timely and if the judge has discretion to allow the claim. Further, discuss the likelihood of Jane's success on the substantive merits of her claim.

Model Answer to Question 9

Jane has asserted a claim against the estate for her alleged interest in the home that she lived in for a number of years with Paul, the decedent. The personal representative has disallowed the claim, and Jane has only one option: She must file a lawsuit against the estate. Such a lawsuit must be filed within 63 days of notice of disallowance.

MCL 700.3806(2). However, an untimely claim may be allowed by the judge to "avoid injustice," in which case the court may grant an extension of time as long as the applicable statute of limitations has not expired. *Id.* The decision to grant an extension of time is within the discretion of the court. *In re Estate of Charles A. Weber*, 257 Mich App 558 (2003).

As for Jane's likelihood of success on the merits, the claim is without basis in the law. First, a promise to transfer an asset upon death is unenforceable absent a will or any other written document evidencing such intent on the part of the deceased. *Estate of Weber, supra*, citing *In re McKim Estate*, 238 Mich App 453 (1999). Further, the Court of Appeals has held Jane's claim based on her contribution toward the home is also without merit. *Estate of Weber, supra*, citing *In re Lewis Estate*, 168 Mich App 70 (1988). Therefore, Jane will not succeed on the merits even if the probate court allows her claim to proceed.

Student Answer—July 2004

Question 9—Wills—8 points

Whether the Lawsuit is Timely?

Motion to dismiss should be granted. The distribution of the estate would have taken place already. The suit is brought by a person that is not of any kin. A Judge can allow the claim to be heard, it is within his discretion. If Jane submits that she failed to receive notice because she was not within the state, at the time. She must show good cause.

Jane's success on the merits: Not Good. Jane, is only a girlfriend, Michigan abolished common law marriages in 1957. She claims she has an interest to the entire estate would fail however claiming she has made improvement if she has any evidence to show, receipts that her independent resources went to improve the property a court would likely allow her to have an interest, but her improvements would need to be substantial which increases the value of the property. She could claim that Sarah is unjustly enriched by her personal improvements. But unless she can show independent improvements her claim is not good. Sarah would argue that she was justly compensated by staying on the property, being given a place to stay.

The oral promise would not be enforced. A future promise is not enforceable in a court of law, because it can be revoked. (SOF) requires land agreements to be in writing. Future promises for land are not enforceable. Sarah could argue not having a will showed he had no intent to promise her anything.

February 2005—Question 7

Patrick and Joy lived here in the great state of Michigan. They had two children, Samantha and Joseph. Both Patrick and Joy had executed wills leaving everything to the other spouse. Each will contained a residual clause leaving everything to their children, who also served as witnesses to the will. However, they divorced shortly after Joseph, the youngest child, graduated from law school. On her way to the courthouse to watch Joseph in his first trial, Joy died as a result of a horrible car crash. Joy had not changed her will since the divorce and it has been admitted to probate.

Patrick has filed a claim for the estate, as have the children. The total value of the estate was $60,000.00.

You are currently employed by the probate judge where the will has been admitted. Discuss who should prevail in the claims for the estate. Specifically, address (1) whether the fact that the children served as witnesses to the will terminates their claims, and (2) whether Patrick will receive any interest in the estate.

Model Answer to Question 7

Michigan requires two witnesses to a will for the will to be valid. Under common law, any person who was to receive a gift under the terms of the will was unable to serve as a witness to the signing. However, if an interested person served as a witness to the will, the will was still valid but the specific bequest to the witness was void. *In Re Fay's Estate*, 353 Mich 83 (1958); MCL 617.63, 702.5, and 702.7, all repealed.

Currently, under the Estates and Protected Individuals Code ("EPIC") an interested person is permitted to serve as a witness. Specifically, EPIC states the "signing of a will by an interested witness does not invalidate the will or any provision of it." MCL 700.2505 (2). Therefore, the gift to the children will remain as valid as permitted by EPIC.

Regarding Patrick's claim to the estate, any devise or bequest to him was extinguished as a matter of law when the divorce was finalized. A divorce after the signing of a will operates to revoke any bequest to the former spouse. MCL 700.2807(1)(a). Therefore, Patrick would take nothing under the terms of the will and his claim will be denied.

In conclusion, Samantha and Joseph will each take thirty thousand dollars from the estate and Patrick will take nothing.

Three Student Answers—February 2005

Question 7—Wills—10 points

The fact that the children served as witnesses will not affect their claim to the will. While formerly in Michigan, an interested witness was precluded from taking under a will, Michigan has adopted a new probate code which allows witnesses to a will to take under the will.

Patrick will not prevail under the estate. Under the probate code, when parties divorce, the spouse who would have taken under the will is omitted and treated as if he or she has predeceased the testator. Patrick takes nothing.

Joy's estate will be split equally between Samantha and Joseph by way of the anti-lapse statute. Because Joy and Patrick are divorced, Joy's gift to Patrick lapses. Under the anti-lapse statute (which only applies when there is a will), to prevent a gift from lapsing, it goes to descendents of the testator's grandparents. Since Joseph and Samantha are descendents of the testator's grandparents, they will each inherit ½ of Joy's share to Patrick, in addition to everything they inherit from the residual clause of the will.

Question 7—Wills—10 points

1. Children's claims are not barred. At common law, parties interested in a will (i.e. would take under the will) could not act to witness the execution of the will. In Michigan, EPIC, the statute governing estates and wills, provides that interested parties may witness a will's execution and still take under the will.

Children acting as witness could trigger concern or allegations that they exerted undue influence on the testator so as to gain more benefit under the will than the testator really intended. However, no such allegations have been made here.

2. Patrick and Joy executed their wills while married and gave each other gifts in their wills. The question is, whether Joy and Patrick have to modify their wills after the divorce in order to avoid those gifts. Answer: No. The gifts are cancelled by operation of law. After the divorce happens, testamentor gifts made to the x-spouse and the x-spouse's family is voided automatically.
3. Patrick and Joy's children will each take ½ of the estate after allowances, taxes, expenses of estate, burial, last illness, creditors are satisfied.

Question 7—Wills—9 points

The children should prevail in the claims against the estate because Patrick's interest is terminated due to the divorce.

1. Can the children take under the will even though they were witnesses? Under former Michigan Law, a interested witness's claim under the will was terminated if they signed. However under the current Michigan law, it doesn't matter if the witnesses were interested or not. If an interested witness signs this does not terminate their right to take under the will.
2. Patrick, as the ex-husband, will not take anything under the will. A husband that is later removed from the life of the Testator (Joy) will also be removed from the will even if the will hasn't changed. Even if at the time the will was written, Joy had intent to give Patrick her estate, this intent terminates upon the termination of the marriage. The interest that Patrick had in the will becomes part of the residual estate.

Since the facts don't tell us otherwise, I'm going to assume that the will was validly executed. Therefore Patrick doesn't take as an ex-husband and his interest goes into the residual clause which then makes everything in the residual clause go to Joy's children in equal shares.

It should be noted that upon divorce from Patrick, if Joy had re-married prior to her death, Michigan law would allow her current husband to take under the omitted spouse statute and he would take ½ of his intestate share.

Here it would be ½ of $100,000 + ¾ balance (adjusted for inflation minus any gifts or insurance). Also this share would be given after all the homestead, family, and executor allowances have been paid.

July 2005—Question 4

Kelly and Scot lived in the great state of Michigan. They have two children, Tyler and Riley. Everything appeared to be wonderful until an outing to Traverse City to see the next big summer blockbuster being filmed. While watching the filming, Kelly and the star of the movie, Jude Lawyer, made eye contact and it was love at first sight. Shortly after falling for Jude, Kelly divorced Scot, and moved to Traverse City with her new husband, who had fallen in love with not only Kelly, but also the beautiful scenery of the area.

After the divorce, Scot died in a horrible car accident on his way to watch his sons play soccer for Central Michigan University. However, Scot had forgotten to update his will, which was made before the divorce. Scot's estate only consisted of personal property. The will left one-half of his estate to "Kelly, my lovely wife" and the other half to be divided between the two sons. The will was witnessed by the attorney who had drafted the will and Tyler, who was 19 at the time.

You are working as the law clerk to the probate court judge assigned to the estate. She has asked you to determine whether the will is valid due to Tyler's act of serving as a witness, and whether the provision of the will governs the distribution of the estate, and if not, how the estates should be distributed. Please discuss whether the will is still valid and how the estate should be divided.

Model Answer to Question 4

Regarding Kelly's claim to the estate, the bequest to her was extinguished as a matter of law when the divorce was finalized. A divorce, after the signing of a will, operates to revoke any bequest to the former spouse. MCL 700.2807(1)(a). Therefore, Kelly would take nothing under the terms of the will and her claim will be denied. Tyler and Riley would split the estate 50/50 as specified in the will.

Michigan requires two witnesses to a will for the will to be valid. Under common law, any person who was to receive a gift under the terms of the will was unable to serve as a witness to the signing. However, if an interested person served as a witness to the will, the will was still valid, but the specific bequest to the witness was void. *In Re Fay's Estate*, 353 Mich 83 (1958); MCL 617.63, 702.5, and 702.7 all repealed.

Currently, under the Estates and Protected Individuals Code ("EPIC") an interested person is permitted to serve as a witness. Specifically, EPIC states the "signing of a will by an interested witness does not invalidate the will or any provision of it." MCL 700.2502(20). Therefore, the gift to the children will remain as valid as permitted by EPIC and both sons will receive one-half of the estate.

Student Answer—July 2005

Question 4—Wills—9 points

The will is still valid in regards to the signature of Tyler serving as a witness. A valid will needs to be the intent of testator, testator must be 18, must sign or someone sign in his request and needs to be signed by two witnesses in presence or soon after.

In this case it shows two witnesses have signed, Attorney and son. Previous law stated an interested party of a will may not be a witness to the will. However, Michigan has changed this law and an interested party may be a witness to a will which he will benefit or receive something from. He is also 19, should have no problem with capacity—usually all people are competent at around 13 years, but court has discretion should be no problem here. It is valid in regards to Tyler's signature.

2nd issue—The provision of the will which states one-half of personal property will go to my wife will be struck and held as invalid. The rule is once a divorce occurs between two people married, the ex-spouses are entitled to nothing, 0 of everything.

In this case, Kelly divorced, facts don't indicate invalid, even if invalid she still would not get anything since she remarried and would be held to be guilty of a bigamy relationship. Since Scot died without revising the will and he is divorced from Kelly, Kelly will not receive anything.

The estate should be distributed to both sons, since they are the only heirs to Scot and it was his intent to give them his property from the will. Both sons will divide one-half of his personal property. Both seem to be adults as they both go to a university, so they will get the remains of his personal property.

> **Comment:** This answer would probably have received 10 points if it were better written. Take the time to formulate good sentences. This student got all of the law correct, but lost a point for poor writing.

February 2006—Question 4

Decedent, Stan Jones, died on April 1, 2005. Mary Jones was Stan's first wife, and she died five years before Stan. His surviving family consists of his surviving spouse, Nancy Jones, and four children from his marriage to Mary (Arnold, Bruce, Charles, and Dan) and four stepchildren (Wayne, Xavier, Yvon, and Zeke), who are Mary's children from a previous marriage. Stan had not adopted these stepchildren. When Stan died, his will read as follows:

> I hereby leave my entire estate to my wife, Mary Jones. In the event Mary Jones shall predecease me, I leave my entire estate to be divided equally between my four children and my four stepchildren.

Nancy has come to you seeking advice on how the will would be interpreted by the probate court. Nancy indicates the entire estate is worth $100,000. **Please discuss what share each person will receive and provide the reasoning behind your conclusion. For purposes of your answer, you may refer to the people involved as follows:**

Widow Nancy = NJ
Natural children = A-D
Stepchildren = W-Z

Model Answer to Question 4

The division of Stan's estate is governed by the Estates and Protected Individuals Code ("EPIC"), MCL 700.1101, *et seq.* The question addresses EPIC sections 2202 and 2301, including the recent amendment to section 700.2301, effective November 10, 2005. The essay question is also based on two Court of Appeals cases: *In Re Estate of Sprenkle-Hill*, 265 Mich App 254 (2005), *lv den* 474 Mich 998 (January 5, 2006), and *In Re Estate of Bennett*, 255 Mich App 545 (2003).

MCL 700.2202 is captioned "Election of surviving spouse," and MCL 700.2301 is captioned "Entitlement of spouse; premarital will." Under § 2202(2)(b), the surviving spouse of a decedent who dies testate may elect either to abide by the will or to receive a share of the decedent's estate, which is referred to as the spouse's "elective share." Specifically, the surviving spouse may elect to either (1) abide by the terms of the will, or (2) take one-half of the sum or share that would have passed to the surviving spouse if the decedent had died intestate, reduced by one-half of the value of all property derived by the spouse from the decedent by any means other than testate or intestate succession upon the decedent's death.

Under § 2301, a "pretermitted spouse," i.e., a surviving spouse who married the testator after the will was executed, is entitled to receive an intestate share of a specified portion of the state. The surviving spouse's share is calculated by deducting that which is granted to a child of the decedent, so long as the child is not also the child of the surviving spouse.

Sprenkle-Hill held that a surviving spouse who married the testator after the will was executed is not barred from claiming an elective share under the terms of § 2202, if that provision yields a larger amount and that the amount to which the surviving spouse was entitled under § 2301 will then be considered a part of the elective share. The court held that if the share available to a surviving spouse under § 2301 is greater than the elective share under § 2202, the surviving spouse will receive the full share under § 2301 by electing to abide by the terms of the will. The court found that the legislature's intent was to insulate all spouses from disinheritance while allowing the decedent's testamentary intent to be honored to the extent possible.

After *Sprenkle-Hill* was released, the Legislature added subsection (4) to MCL 700.2301. That subsection addresses the surviving spouse's right of election under § 2202. Specifically, the statute now provides: "A spouse who receives an intestate share under this section may also exercise the right of election under section 2202, but the intestate share received by the spouse under this section reduces the sum available to the spouse under section 2202(2)(b)."

Widow Nancy's Share: Under § 2202(2)(b), NJ would receive one-half of the sum or share that would have passed to her if Stan had died intestate. Her intestate share is calculated by reference to MCL 700.2102: "the first $100,000.00, plus ½ of any balance of the intestate estate if none of the decedent's surviving descendants are descendants of the surviving spouse." Because the estate is valued at $100,000, her intestate share would be $100,000. One-half of that amount is $50,000. Thus, her elective share is $50,000.

Under § 2301, NJ's share is calculated by determining NJ's intestate share ($100,000) and, per § 2301(a), deducting from it that which is granted to Stan's children. Stan's children were to receive one-half of the estate. Thus, $50,000 is deducted from the intestate share. Therefore, NJ's share under § 2301 is $50,000.

By operation of § 2301(4), NJ receives a total of $50,000.

The Children: Children A-D will take $12,500 each, as the natural children of Stan. They are entitled to the devise made to them under the will, as though Stan had not married Nancy. Thus, their 50% is divided equally between the four of them.

The Stepchildren: The stepchildren, W-Z, will receive nothing under the will because the devise to them is abated. Although the stepchildren may attempt to argue that Stan wanted them to have one-half of his estate, or to share equally with his natural children, this claim is without merit because of the size of the estate. Under § 2301(3), the surviving spouse takes her intestate share from the remainder of the estate after devises to children (not stepchildren) are subtracted. *In Re Estate of Bennett*, 255 Mich App 545 (2003). Because the share to NJ ($50,000) equals the amount of assets remaining, the devises to the stepchildren are reduced to zero. Had the estate been larger, the stepchildren might have received something. *Bennett* holds that stepchildren do not meet the statutory definition of "child."

Student Answer—February 2006

Question 4—Wills—8 points

This is a Wills question that asks who will take what share of Stan's $100,000 estate.

First, Mary Jones would not take anything under the will because she predeceased Stan. This would be true whether the will stated this or not. Next, Nancy is the current wife (widow) of Stan and they have 4 step children. However, the facts tell us that Stan has not adopted the step children and therefore, widow-2 would not be entitled to anything under the will.

Next there is the issue of Stan's widow (NJ) who was not included in the will. NJ and Stan had obviously already met and married NJ because he does include the step children in the will. Therefore, it would be a reasonable conclusion that NJ was purposefully left out of the will. However, the law has allowed a widow to take her elective share; this is to protect a widow who was intentionally left out of a will and would take nothing. But, here, the will specifically states that the estate shall be divided among his 4 children and 4 step children. Since, Mary and the step children are out, the battle comes between the 4 children and NJ.

Under the facts, it is more likely than not that the children (A-D) would take ¼ of Stan's estate. First, the distribution is provided in this manner in the will, which we have no reason to believe is anything but a legally valid and enforceable will. Next, although NJ would have an elective share option, because NJ and Stan have no children together, NJ would be entitled to $100,000 plus ½ the balance of the estate. Well, if this is so, that would entitle NJ to the entire $100k estate and she was intentionally left out of the will. Had the will been executed before Stan having met NJ, then she'd be an after married spouse and the law would provide her with a remedy because it wouldn't have been a purposeful omission. However, under these facts Mary, NJ, and the step children which were not adopted would not take and Stan's children (A-D) would take ¼ of Stan's $100,000 estate.

> **Comment:** The grader was very generous for this answer mainly because the correct rules are in the answer. The problem is in the improper application. Be sure to review the model answer and make flashcards for the rules.

July 2006—Question 12

George Harmon, a widower, executed his Last Will and Testament on July 1, 1990, and in it he included the following provision: "At my death I direct my personal representative to sell my cottage at Houghton Lake with the proceeds to be used for the benefit of the Good Faith Church of Lansing, Michigan. These proceeds are to be deposited in Capitol Bank and to be used solely for the purpose of building a new church. No part of the principal or interest is to be used for any other purpose." The residue of the estate was devised to the Foundation for Better Lansing to be used to fund other charitable bequests found in the will.

George died in 1997 and his cottage was sold for $150,000 with the proceeds deposited in Capitol Bank. By 2005, this account had grown to $225,000. The Good Faith Church determined that due to a slow membership increase and the increase in the cost of construction, it was not practicable to construct a new church. Good Faith then notified the Foundation that it wanted to use the funds to remodel the interior of the Church, air condition the building, and extend into the parking area to build a day care center for the use of members while attending church and church functions. The Foundation advised the Church that this was not a permitted use and both parties filed an action with the Probate Court, the Church to require release of the funds for the above purposes and the Foundation claiming that these funds should revert to the Foundation as residuary legatee.

Assume that the testimony established that a new church would never be built, and limiting your answer to the two competing claims, who will prevail in this action, and why?

Model Answer to Question 12

At common law, the Cy pres doctrine was used as a saving device when the specific purpose of the settlor could not be carried out then the charitable intention could be fulfilled as nearly as possible. The court adopted three requirements for application of Cy pres: (1) the court must determine whether a valid charitable trust has been created, (2) it must be shown that it is impossible or impracticable to carry out the specific purpose of the trust, and (3) the court must determine whether the testator had a general charitable intent. *In re Rood Estate*, 41 Mich App 405, 416-417 (1972); *In re Karp Estate*, 108 Mich App 129, 131-132 (1981).

In 1976, the Michigan Legislature adopted MCL 451.1201 *et seq.*, stating in the preamble that its purpose was "to establish guidelines for the management and use of investments held by eleemosynary institutions and funds," but this statute did not limit the application of the doctrine of Cy pres. While the statute used the term "obsolete, inappropriate or impracticable," the Court of Appeals has found that as a practical matter, there is no significant distinction between these terms and the language of Cy pres.

As a general rule, the trust fund will revert to a settlor's estate or heirs at law even in the absence of an express reservation clause if the settlor did not have a general charitable purpose, but instead contemplated one or more specific purposes that cannot be fulfilled because of impossibility or impracticability. In this case, the express language used limits to the use of this fund to build a new church and provided the fund is to be used for no other reason. Even though there is no time limit on when the church needed to be built, this does not affect the ultimate decision. An accumulation provision in a charitable trust is neither invalid nor inappropriate merely because its duration is indefinite or perpetual.

There are no facts to indicate that Mr. Harmon did not understand the effect of the language used in the will. The facts do not support any claim that a valid charitable trust was not created. Under the doctrine of Cy pres, the court could "save" this fund to be used for a charitable purpose. However, the court would have to find that there was a "general charitable intent" and the express language in the will does not support a general charitable intent.

Assuming that the purpose of this bequest cannot be met, the court would probably hold that there was no general charitable purpose but a specific purpose, and, under those circumstances, the foundation would prevail in this action.

Student Answers—July 2006

Question 12—Wills—8 points

In determining whether the proposed actions of church would be inside the scope of the testator's wishes the court must find that the proposed actions were within the testator's intent. Here Harmon said that the sole purpose of the gift was to construct a new church and the money was to be spent on nothing else. Because of this it would seem that doing anything to the contrary would be against the testator's intent. However, when a purpose behind a gift becomes frustrated the courts may inquire into a similar intent that the testator might have allowed here. Because Harmon stated very clearly in the will that the gift was intended only to build a new church, the court would probably find that remodeling of the current church was not w/in the scope of his intent. Remodeling the church could arguably be w/in the scope of Harmon's intent but the court would probably find that Harmon's intent was not to beautify the church but to strictly build another one probably because of space limitations. Also there are no facts in the case which state that the current church was in state of disrepair which could lead the court to determine that Harmon's gift was based on it. Also it could be argued that remodeling and building a day care could be almost as costly as building a new church. The day care would probably be definitely outside of the scope because Harmon said that the building of the church was the only thing the money should be used for. However some jurisdictions state that just because a gift states its to be used "solely for the purpose of" doesn't mean that a different use doesn't validate it however. I think here this would be beyond the scope of use Harmon's intended.

Question 12—Wills—8 points

The issue here presents a particular question regarding testator's intent and conditions within Wills.

Foremost, a valid will has been held to convey the last intentions of the devisee. In the absence of a will being invalidated for legal cause during probate, its devisement & distribution of the testator's assets will be upheld. Michigan's statutes under EPIC direct the courts to slightly amend a will if an ambiguity exists & attempt to rectify w/ the testator's intent as gained from the actual paragraphs in the document. Here, this is not the case; George's will specifically states how he wants his estate distributed. His clause, "proceeds . . . to be used solely for the purpose of building a new church" are explicitly clear. If the proceeds aren't used for the specific purpose as outlined, then evidently he intended the proceeds not be used. In effect, this gives the estate the right to take back the interest and re-distribute according to the residual clause providing for the Foundation for Better Housing. This most certainly would be the Foundation's argument.

The church on the other hand might want to have the will brought before the probate court to remedy this quandary on the basis that the testator's intent is being thwarted. It is extremely unlikely that the court would do so for the reasons outlined.

February 2007—Question 9

Ann and Bob Casey were two lawyers happily married to each other. The couple, fully engaged in their law practice, never had any children. As they enjoyed the fruits of their success in the prime of their careers, they realized that life is short and unpredictable and that it would be prudent to do some estate planning. Bob had two brothers, Donald and Eldridge, who died in a tragic boating accident. Bob's brothers were each survived by two daughters (Bob's four nieces). Ann had four sisters: Faye Jones, Georgia Smith, Hazel Brown and Irene Taylor. In 1985, Ann and Bob Casey, as husband and wife, executed a revocable trust that provided for Ann and Bob during their lifetimes. The revocable trust also contained a residuary clause that provided for the distribution of the remaining trust balance after the death of Ann and Bob. The residual clause provided:

> "The balance of the trust estate is to be divided equally and distributed to Faye Jones, Georgia Smith, Hazel Brown, Irene Taylor, with an equal share divided among the children of the deceased siblings of the settlers, Donald Casey and Eldridge Casey. In all cases, distribution is to be per stirpes."

Bob Casey died in 1996. Faye Jones died in 2005, leaving behind three sons (Ann's three nephews). Before Ann died, she informed her sister, Irene, that Ann and Bob always intended that a greater share of the remainder of their trust was to go to their surviving siblings. Irene claims Ann expressed an intent to change the trust to provide a greater share for Irene, Georgia and Hazel, and less for the children of Faye. Ann Casey died in 2006, without making any express attempt to change the trust. There remains a sizable amount in the trust.

A dispute has arisen over distribution of the remainder of the trust. Ann's three surviving sisters, Ann's three nephews, and Bob's four nieces are all claiming competing rights to the remainder of the trust. The trustee has filed a motion in the probate court seeking an order of distribution.

You are the probate judge. Write an opinion that divides the remainder of the trust. Provide the legal reasoning supporting your conclusions.

Model Answer to Question 9

Resolution of this case requires interpretation of the residual clause of the trust document. The primary goal in construing a testamentary instrument is to determine and give effect to the intent of the settlor. *In re Woodworth Trust*, 196 Mich App 326, 327 (1992). The first step in determining the intent of the settlor is to review the language of the testamentary document. "Where there is no ambiguity, that intention is to be gleaned from the four corners of the instrument." *Id.* Testamentary documents must also be interpreted in a way that gives affect to every word in the document. *Detroit Bank & Trust Co v Grout*, 95 Mich App 253, 268-269 (1980). Where the plain and ordinary meaning of the instrument gives rise to but one reasonable interpretation, the court must ignore extrinsic evidence of the drafter's intent and derive the intent of the drafter from the four corners of the instrument. *Woodworth, supra.* Where the instrument is ambiguous, a court can consider extrinsic evidence to determine the drafter's intent. However, "[t]he fact that the parties dispute the meaning of [a provision] . . . does not, in itself, establish an ambiguity." *Cole v Ladbroke Racing Michigan, Inc*, 241 Mich App 1, 14 (2000).

The residual clause of the trust created by Ann and Bob Casey is not ambiguous. Thus, the settlor's intent must be gleaned from the language of the trust. By using the precise phrase "with an equal share divided among the children of the following deceased siblings," the settlors explicitly provided that one share, equal to the shares provided for the siblings living when the trust was created, was to be divided among the children of the then-deceased siblings. Specifically, the "equal share" language identifies, by reference to the shares preceding the phrase, a division equivalent to that identified for "Faye Jones, Georgia Smith, Hazel Brown, [and] Irene Taylor." The term "divided" clearly indicates that the "equal share" so identified is then to be separated or dealt out to the persons thereafter identified.

The language, "[i]n all cases distribution is to be per stirpes" follows the directive that "an equal share [is to be] divided." Under MCL 700.2718(2):

> "If a governing instrument calls for property to be distributed 'per stirpes,' the property is divided into as many equal shares as there are surviving children of the designated ancestor and deceased children who left surviving descendants. Each surviving child, if any, is allocated 1 share. The share of each deceased child with surviving descendants is divided in the same manner, with subdivision repeating at each succeeding generation until the property is fully allocated among surviving descendants."

Used here, the "per stirpes" provision describes how the shares, once divided per the instruction of the trust, were to be subdivided.

Because the residual clause of the trust is unambiguous, extrinsic evidence regarding the intent of Ann and Bob in forming the trust is not pertinent or germane to the interpretation of the trust. Thus, evidence that Ann wanted her surviving sisters to have a greater share in the remainder of the trust than the share awarded to Faye's children would not provide a basis to reform the trust.

Accordingly, the remainder of the trust should be divided into five equal shares, with Georgia Smith, Hazel Brown and Irene Taylor each getting one share, or 1.5 of the remainder of the trust. The surviving children of Faye Jones (Ann's three nephews) should get one share that they would divide equally (1/15th each); that share being the share that would have gone to their mother had she not predeceased her parents. The final share would go to the four surviving children of Donald and Eldridge Casey (Bob's four nieces) to be divide equally among them (1/20th each); that share being the one share that the settlors expressly granted to the children of their siblings that had predeceased them at the time the trust was created.

Student Answer—February 2007

Question 9—Trusts—8 points

This is a trust question. The issue involves resolving the distribution of the trust. The trust made by Bob and Ann was revocable which means they could make modifications prior to their deaths. The trust was not irrevocable. No changes were made to the trust during their lifetime, therefore it should be admitted as written.

Bob and Ann are the settlers of the trust. The trust was made to provide for them in their lifetime and the *rest* was identifiable. The *residual clause* called for an equal distribution to all parties listed *per stirpes*. The language in the trust controls.

Although Ann may have expressed a desire to modify her revocable trust, she did not. There is nothing to indicate that she did not have the opportunity to make changes. As such, the individuals listed in the trust should take equally per stirpes as indicated by the document.

It is the desire of the court to maintain the intent of the settlors. In this fact pattern the intent appears to be that which was stipulated in the trust document absent a writing to the contrary with the required formalities.

July 2007—Question 11

Pierre LaPointe was born in Paris, France, in 1932. He was a young boy when American troops liberated France during World War II. Pierre greatly admired and respected the courage of the military troops who stormed the beaches of France. Pierre immigrated to the United States in 1960. Thereafter, he married, had three children and became a naturalized citizen of the United States. Pierre was a successful distributor of French wine. In 2001, Pierre visited the National World War II (WWII) museum in New Orleans. Pierre became good friends with the museum curator, Billy Weaver. In 2003, Pierre became a member of the museum's Board of Advisors.

In 2005, Pierre sold his business and purchased T-Bills with the proceeds. In December 2005, Pierre, without the assistance of a lawyer, executed in his own handwriting a document that was proclaimed to be a will. The document disposed of Pierre's property after his death by leaving 50% of his T-Bills to be divided equally amount his children. Pierre signed and dated it. It was also properly witnessed. Pierre sealed the document in an envelope, wrote "WILL" on the envelope and gave it to his wife.

In 2007, Pierre became terminally ill. At the time, Pierre's T-Bills were worth approximately $12 million. On June 6, 2007, Pierre was informed that his end was near. While still of sound mind, he signed and mailed to Billy Weaver the following note:

> June 6, 2007
> Billy,
> I intend to donate to the WWII museum two million dollars worth of Treasury Bills.
> Pierre LaPointe

Pierre died on June 9, 2007, without conveying any funds to the museum. While on his deathbed, Pierre told his wife and children that he had recently amended his will to give two million dollars worth of T-Bills to the WWII museum. Pierre told his family that there remained approximately ten million dollars for the family.

In July 2007, Billy Weaver contacted Pierre's wife and children to ask when the museum might receive the gift documented in the June 6 correspondence Pierre sent to Billy. The family acknowledged Pierre's fondness for the museum. The family also acknowledged that Pierre talked about making a sizable gift to the museum. However, the family concluded that Pierre's intentions were documented in a will he executed in December 2005. Because there was no mention of a gift to the museum in that will, the family was not inclined to honor any promise to make a future gift to the museum that may be referenced in the correspondence.

You represent the museum. Does the museum have a viable legal claim to the two million dollar gift mentioned in Pierre's June 6, 2007 correspondence? Explain your answer.

Model Answer to Question 11

The museum may assert a legally viable claim to the two million dollar gift referenced in the June 6 correspondence. The elements of a will are found in the Estates and Protected Individuals Code (EPIC), MCL 700.1101 *et seq*. A will is any testamentary instrument that, at a minimum, "excludes or limits the right of an individual or class to succeed to the decedent's property." MCL 700.1108(b). Any person of sound mind, 18 years of age or older may make a will. MCL 700.2501. Further, § 2502 of EPIC provides in pertinent part:

> (1) Except as provided in subsection (2) and in section § 2503 . . . a will is valid only if it is all of the following:
> (a) In writing.
> (b) Signed by the testator or in the testator's name by some other individual in the testator's conscious presence and by the testator's direction.
> (c) Signed by at least 2 individuals, each of whom signed within a reasonable time after he or she witnessed either the signing of the will as described in subdivision (b) or the testator's acknowledgment of that signature or acknowledgment of the will.
> (2) A will that does not comply with subsection (1) is valid as a holographic will, whether or not witnessed, if it is dated, and if the testator's signature and the document's material portions are in the testator's handwriting.
> (3) Intent that the document constitutes a testator's will can be established by extrinsic evidence, including, for a holographic will, portions of the document that are not in the testator's handwriting.

Here, the December 2005 instrument purports to dispose of Pierre's property after his death. Pierre wrote it when he was legally competent to dispose of his property and Pierre signed it, dated it, and the facts indicate the will was properly witnessed. Thus, the document satisfies all the requirements for a will under EPIC. The critical issue for the museum is whether the correspondence Pierre sent to Billy Weaver was a valid codicil to the December 2005 will.

Wills may be modified or altered by codicil. A codicil must satisfy all the requirements of a will under EPIC. The museum may persuasively argue that the June 6 correspondence from Pierre to Billy is a valid codicil to the will because Pierre created it, it makes a gift of two million dollars to the museum, and it is signed and dated by Pierre. However, on its face the correspondence is not testamentary, i.e., it is not written so as to take effect after the death of Pierre. Thus, the family could argue that the correspondence does not satisfy the requirements of MCL 700.1108. The family would claim that the phrase, "I intend to" does not reflect a testamentary intent, as it suggests that Pierre merely hoped to later amend his will. The family may also argue that Pierre's use of the word "donate" suggests the correspondence was not intended to be testamentary. Had Pierre intended the correspondence to be testamentary he would have used the word "leave," which strongly supports the conclusion that the gift was intended to take effect after his death. The family may support its argument by noting that Pierre had previously executed a valid will without a lawyer. It is clear from review of the 2005 will that if Pierre truly intended the correspondence to be a codicil to his 2005 will, he would have expressed his testamentary intent within the four corners of the correspondence.

While at one time the intent of a putative codicil had to be gleaned from the instrument itself, *see In re Henry's Estate*, 259 Mich 499 (1932) rev'd on other grounds, 324 Mich 568 (1949), it is very clear that under EPIC, the intent of the testator in the execution of a testamentary document may be ascertained from the extrinsic evidence. MCL 700.2502(3); *see also In re Smith, infra.*

The museum should assert that the letter satisfies all the requirements of a codicil to a will under EPIC. While nothing in the letter supports the conclusion that it is a testamentary instrument, the testamentary intent to Pierre in drafting the letter may be ascertained from extrinsic evidence. Pierre told his family that he recently amended his will to give the WWII museum two million dollars worth of T-Bills. Pierre further informed his family there remained approximately ten million dollars worth of T-Bills for the family. These facts support the conclusion that Pierre intended the correspondence to function as a testamentary instrument. All other form requirements under EPIC were satisfied. Pierre wrote the letter. Pierre signed and dated it. Thus, the requirements of MCL 700.2502(3) were met. Pierre, although near death, remained of sound mind. Thus, the requirements of MCL 700.2501 were satisfied.

The June 6, 2007 correspondence should be admitted into probate as a putative codicil to the December 2005 will. The probate court must make a threshold determination whether the codicil satisfies all the requirements under MCL 700.2502(2). If the probate court determines that the putative codicil fails to satisfy the requirements of § 2502, it may nonetheless be admitted into probate. However, the proponent of the codicil must establish by clear and convincing evidence that the decedent intended the writing to constitute a codicil to the will. MCL 700.2503. *See also In re Smith*, 252 Mich App 120 (2002).

The museum may also argue that if the June 6 note is not considered a valid codicil to the will under either § 2502 or § 2503, then Pierre gave the T-Bills to the museum as a gift *causa mortis*. A gift *causa mortis* is a gift of personal property made by the donor in view of his impending death from a present condition, accompanied by appropriate delivery under the circumstances. *In re Reh's Estate*, 196 Mich 210 (1917). The donor of a gift *causa mortis* must believe he is facing death from a condition, and he then predeceases the donee as a result of the condition. *In re Van Wormer's Estate*, 255 Mich 399 (1931).

The donor must possess the intent to gratuitously pass title to the donor. *Chamberlin v Eddy*, 154 Mich 593 (1908). Delivery, actual or constructive, must be made. *In re Van Wormer's Estate, supra*, and the donee must accept it. A donee is presumed to accept a gift that is beneficial to him. *Holmes v McDonald*, 119 Mich 563 (1899).

The family can argue that there was no delivery of the T-Bills and, therefore, there is no gift *causa mortis. Lumbers v Commonwealth Bank*, 295 Mich 566 (1940). Manual delivery is not required but can be accomplished constructively. The donor's motivation is irrelevant. *Jackman v Jackman*, 271 Mich 585 (1935). If delivery and acceptance are found, the fact the donor has the T-Bills is immaterial. *Id.*

Pierre was terminally ill when he mailed the note to Billy. Pierre died three days after mailing the note. Given Pierre's frail health, an argument can be advanced that the note amounts to constructive delivery of the T-Bills.

For these reasons, the museum has a viable claim to the two million dollar gift documented in the June 6 correspondence from Pierre.

Student Answer—July 2007

Question 11—Wills—9 points

Issue is whether Pierre validly changed his will to include the gift to the museum. Is the first will valid? A will is valid if in writing and witnessed by two people in the presence of the testator signing or shortly thereafter the testator acknowledges that the will is his and his signature. Or this could be a valid holographic will. A holographic will is in the testator's handwriting and contains the material portions, and is signed, and dated. Here this will by Pierre is a valid holographic will. But the will has no mention of the museum. The next issue is did Pierre make an effective change to his will. To have an effective change, the change must meet the will/codicil or holographic will requirements. The note that Pierre sent to the Museum probably would meet the holographic requirements. He signed and dated it, but a question is whether this note was in his handwriting. Whether the material portions giving of the gift in his writing the facts do not say. This would probably need to be decided by the court.

Also Michigan's dispensing power: the court can pass some of the requirements if not met, but only if there is a clear intent to donate. Here Museum would argue there was a clear intent to donate the money from the letter to Pierre's phone call to Museum talking to Pierre's family. The family would argue against this saying that Pierre made no legally valid change to his will. The court probably will find a clear intent on Pierre to donate, and can therefore under the dispensing power give the money to the museum.

Another argument is that Pierre made a gift causa mortis which is a gift of personal property made when someone is about to die. It requires that the person believes he is facing death, intent, delivery and acceptance. Also the person must die. Here, the note shows Pierre's intent to donate, he knew he was dying and he did die. The main issue is whether delivery occurred because acceptance is presumed. Constructive delivery is valid. Here, it can be argued that Pierre mailing the letter was constructive delivery.

February 2008—Question 10

Robert Bonds recently died, leaving behind Faith, his wife of 25 years. Robert and Faith had one child, James, who was an adult at the time of Robert's death. Robert and Faith owned a beautiful Oakland County, Michigan home that Robert's father conveyed by warranty deed to Robert and Faith as a gift to them on their fifth wedding anniversary. Robert was also the father of Barry French Bonds, a minor child, who Robert had with his longtime love interest, Tiffany French. Robert's paternity as to Barry is established and cannot be contested. James and Faith were not aware during Robert's lifetime that Robert had a long-running affair with Ms. French, nor were they aware that Robert was the father of Barry French Bonds. After Robert's death, Faith and James went to the local probate court and discovered that Robert had filed a will with the court. The will was drafted by Robert's attorney, properly executed and in legally proper form. The will was drafted before Barry was born. The will expressly stated, in relevant part, that:

> James is to receive nothing from the estate because James was a thoughtless and selfish son who cared nothing for me.

Faith is to receive nothing from the estate because she was a dreadful spouse who maintained the marriage only so she could inherit everything upon my death.

Tiffany French, the only woman to have provided me with true love and affection, shall receive 100% of my estate.

A review of records at the local office of the register of deeds also revealed that six months before his death, Robert granted to Tiffany a quitclaim deed for Robert's interest in the marital home.

How will the estate be divided between Faith, James, Tiffany and Barry? How will Robert's interest in the marital home be disposed? Explain your answer.

Model Answer to Question 10

I. The Division of the Estate: The division of the estate is governed by the Estates and Protected Individuals Code (EPIC), MCL 700.1101 *et seq.* Generally speaking, when a person dies testate, spouses and children who are not provided for in the deceased's will may still be entitled to a share of the estate. In limited instances, EPIC provides statutory rights to claim from an estate that may not be provided for in a will.

Where the testator expressly disinherits a child, that child receives nothing. See MCL 700.2302 (3) (entitling a child who is living at the time a will is executed but who is not provided for in the will a share of the estate only if the failure to provide for the child is "solely because the [testator] believes the child to be dead"). *See also Brown v Blesch*, 270 Mich 576 (1935) (reason for disinheriting an heir at law need not be disclosed in the will). Here, Robert expressly disinherited his son James. Thus, James shall receive nothing.

In regard to Barry, "a child born or conceived during a marriage but is not the issue of that marriage," EPIC recognizes him as Robert's child because Robert established paternity of Barry, MCL 700.2114(b)(iv). In contrast to James, Barry is not expressly disinherited in this will. Rather, Barry, who was born after the will was executed, is not mentioned in Robert's will.

MCL 700.2302(1) outlines the distribution due a child born after the execution of a will who is not provided for in the will. MCL 700.2302(1)(a) describes the share Barry would be due if Robert had no living children when he executed his will. Specifically, under this provision Barry would receive "a share of the estate equal in value to that which the child would have received had the testator died intestate, unless the will devised all or substantially all of the estate to the other parent of the omitted child". Since Robert had a living child at the time the will was executed (James), Barry's claim to the estate does not fall squarely within this provision. MCL 700.2302(1)(b) describes the share Barry would receive if Robert had "1 or more living children when he executed the will, and the will devised property or an interest in property, to one or more of the then living children. Under this provision, Barry would receive nothing, as MCL 700.2302(1)(b)(i)-(iv) essentially provide that Barry would take the same share as James. Since Robert did not devise property or an interest in property to James, Barry's claim does not fall squarely within this statutory provision either.

MCL 700.2302 is silent on the appropriate share to a child born after the execution of a will in which the child is not provided for under the facts presented here—where the testator has one or more children who were living at the time he executed his will but the testator expressly disinherited the then living children. While Barry may claim under MCL 700.1201 that Robert, by not expressly disinheriting him, intended that Barry receive a statutory share, it appears Barry will get nothing except, perhaps, a maintenance allowance pursuant to MCL 700.2403. Under MCL 700.2302(1)(b), Barry would get nothing because that would be equal to what James received.

An expression of disinheritance will not necessarily bar a spouse from taking from the estate. Pursuant to MCL 700.2202(2), a "surviving spouse of a decedent who is domiciled in this state and who dies testate may file with the court an election in writing that the spouse elects" to either "abide by the terms of the will," MCL 700.2202(2)(a), "take ½ of the share that would have passed to the spouse had the testator died intestate, reduced by ½ of the value of all property derived by the spouse from the decedent by any means other than testate or intestate succession upon the decedent's death," MCL 700.2202(2)(b), or "take her dower right" under statute, MCL 700.2202(c). MCL 700.2202(3) further provides that "unless the testator's will plainly shows a contrary intent; the surviving spouse electing under subsection (2) is limited to 1 choice." Here, Tiffany may argue that Robert's will plainly shows a contrary intent—Robert wanted Faith to take nothing. Faith may respond that a better reading of MCL 700.2202(3) is that a testator's express intent may allow a surviving spouse to take more, not less, than one option under MCL 700.2202. Tiffany will not prevail on this point. It has long been held that the right to take under the statutory election cannot be barred by a provision in the will. *In re Povey's Estate*, 271 Mich 627 (1935). Thus, Faith may claim under the will by making an election under the statute.

In addition, Faith can claim exempt property and allowances under MCL 700.2402 (Homestead allowance), MCL 700.2403 (Maintenance Exemption), and MCL 700.2404 (Household and Personal Effects Allowance). MCL 700.2402 states, "A homestead allowance is in addition to any share passing to the surviving spouse or minor or dependent child by the will of the decedent, unless otherwise provided, by intestate succession, or by elective share." Similar provisions in MCL 700.2403 and 700.2404 provide that these protections are in addition to anything the surviving spouse receives through the elective share provision under MCL 700.2202(2)(b). The balance of the estate would go to Tiffany, as expressed in Robert's will.

II. The Disposition of the Marital Home: Six months before his death, Robert executed a quitclaim deed to Tiffany. "A deed of quitclaim and release . . . shall be sufficient to pass all the estate which the grantor could lawfully convey by a deed of bargain and sale." MCL 565.3. A quitclaim deed does not carry any warranty of title with it. The disposition of the marital home turns on the question whether Robert could "lawfully convey" his interest in the marital home to Tiffany. When Robert and Faith were conveyed the home, they were married. "When a conveyance is made to two persons who are husband and wife, they presumptively become tenants by the entireties regardless of whether the grantor specifies it". Michigan Real Property Law, p 327 (ICLE 3rd ed 2005). Tenancy by the entireties is created by operation of common law rather than by the act of the parties through their deed. *Id.*, at 324. Neither a husband nor a wife may act alone to convey any part of real property that is held by both of them as tenants by the entireties. MCL 557.101-102; *Hearns v Hearns*, 333 Mich 423 (1952). Here, Robert attempted to convey to Tiffany his interest in his marital home. But since the home was held by Robert with Faith as tenant by the entireties, Robert lacked any legal power to encumber or in any way convey the marital property. Thus, the quitclaim deed from Robert to Tiffany conveyed nothing. Further, since a quitclaim deed comes with no warranty of title, Tiffany cannot seek redress against Robert's estate.

Student Answer—February 2008

Question 10—Wills—8 points

This is a Wills question.

Under Michigan law the contents of a validly and properly executed deed must be followed. It is presumed that a valid will contains the intent of the decedent because the decedent took the time to execute a valid will. Under Michigan law a wife that is not provided for in a will may still be entitled to her dower rights. There may be an argument to this if it is the clear and express intent of the decedent that the wife not receive anything. In Michigan a child born after the execution of the will may still be able to receive from assets of the decedent if that seems to be the intent of the decedent.

In this case Rob's will leaves nothing to his wife Faith. Despite Rob's clear intention that Faith receive nothing she may still be entitled to her dower rights. Additionally, the Michigan home may be given to Faith. The home was a gift to both Robert and Faith. Faith could argue that his gift constitutes a joint tenancy with rights of survivorship meaning that Robert can't unilaterally convey the property to someone else through a will. Alternatively, Faith could argue that this gift was a tenancy by the entirety given to a husband and wife, and here Robert also can't convey it by will or without the consent of Faith. So Faith will probably get the Michigan house despite the quit claim deed Rob gave to Tiffany.

James, Rob's adult son will receive nothing. James is not a child born after the execution of the will. Also, the will specifically excluded him from the will.

Barry will probably receive nothing either. Barry may be able to receive some of Rob's assets if it can be established that Barry was not included in will because he was born after it was executed. The facts are silent to this. AND also, if this is the case that intent must be shown. An argument for Barry would be that Rob may want to have included him because he was a son he had with Tiffany, the woman that he truly loved.

Tiffany, will be able to receive the rest of the Rob's estate excluding the Oakland County home. The quit claim deed may not be valid because of the reasons states above with regard to what Faith is entitled to.

Comment: This is a well-written answer, but it neglects to discuss the elective share. Technically, this omission should result in less than a passing score; however, the answer is so well written, the student received additional points.

July 2008—Question 8

Bruce, Sue and Sarah are siblings and beneficiaries of a trust created by their parents, Paul and Patti Parker. The trust was created in 1998 and provided that the two parcels of real estate (Parcel A and Parcel B that comprised the family farm) would be divided and distributed equally between the three siblings after the death of Paul and Patti. Parcels A and B were of equal size and value. The trust further provided:

> "We reserve the right to amend or revoke the Agreement, wholly or partly, and add assets to, or withdraw asset from, the Trust by a writing signed by us or on our behalf and delivered to the TRUSTEE during our lives."

After Paul died, Patti, being of sound mind and fully competent, amended the trust with the assistance of the lawyer who originally drafted the trust. Patti had discussed the proposed amendment with Sue and Sarah, but not Bruce. Pursuant to the amendment, Patti left Parcel A to Sue and Parcel B to Sarah. Additionally, Patti liked the idea of leaving Sarah a larger piece of property because Sarah took great care of Paul in his final days, while the conduct of Bruce and Sue during this time disappointed Patti.

After Patti died, Sue attempted without success to reach an agreement with Bruce to share Parcel A. Bruce felt that he was being short-changed and that he was entitled to ⅓ of Parcel A and B combined, not merely the ½ of Parcel A, as offered by Sue. Bruce brought an action in the probate court, asking the court to set aside the amendment to the trust executed by Patti after the death of Paul. Sarah answered Bruce's complaint, opposing the setting aside of the amendment.

Will Bruce prevail in his action to set aside the amendment to the trust? Explain your action.

Model Answer to Question 8

Bruce should argue that Patti lacked the authority to modify the trust after Paul's death. Generally, the court's sole objection in resolving a dispute over the meaning of a trust is to ascertain and give affect to the settlor's intent. *In re Nowels Estate*, 128 Mich App 174, 177 (1983). The first step in determining the intent of the settlor is to examine the language of the trust instrument. Whenever possible, a reviewing court should give each word in the trust instrument meaning. *In re Butterfield Estate*, 418 Mich 241, 259 (1983). Generally, if the language of a trust is not ambiguous, the settlor's intent must be gleaned from the four corners of the document. *In re Maloney Trust*, 423 Mich 632, 639 (1985). If the trust instrument evidences an ambiguity, a court may establish the settlor's intent by considering outside sources. *Id.*, quoting *In re Kremlick Estate*, 417 Mich 237, 240 (1983). Seemingly clear trust language may still evidence a latent ambiguity. A "latent ambiguity exists where the language and its meaning is [sic] clear, but some extrinsic fact creates the possibility of more than one meaning." *In re Woodward Trust*, 196 Mich App 326, 328 (1992). Thus, a court may consider facts extrinsic to the trust instrument for the purpose of considering the existence of a latent ambiguity. *In re McPeak Estate*, 210 Mich App 410, 412 (1995).

Bruce will argue the trust document is clear and unambiguous and requires that any amendment be executed by both settlors to the trust. Specifically, the statement indicating that "[w]e reserve the right to amend or revoke this Agreement . . . by a writing signed by us . . . and delivered to the TRUSTEE during our lives" clearly provided that any amendment to the trust required the approval of both Paul and Patti. Thus, after Paul dies, the power to amend the trust was extinguished. This interpretation of the agreement is consistent with Bogert, Trusts and Trustees (2d ed), § 993, pp 241-242, which states, "If the power to amend is reserved to two settlors, it must be exercised by both, and the survivor cannot use the power."

Bruce should also argue that no extrinsic facts detract the clear and unambiguous language of the trust. The fact that Patti decided to amend the trust after Paul died does not suggest the existence of more than one meaning to this trust. A settlor's attempt to exercise a power not provided for in the trust instrument does not indicate that the language of the trust contains more than one meaning. At best, it means that Patti subjectively misunderstood the unambiguous language at the time she attempted the amendment. 2 Restatement Trusts 3d, § 63, discusses a settlor's power to modify a trust, and provides:

> (1) The settlor of an inter vivos trust has the power to revoke or modify the trust to the extent the terms of the trust so provide.
> (2) If the settlor has failed expressly to provide whether the trust is subject to a retained power of revocation or amendment, the question is one of interpretation . . . .
> (3) Absent contrary provision in the term of the trust, the settlor's power to revoke or modify the trust can be exercised in any way that provides clear and convincing evidence of the settlor's intention to do so.

Under subparagraph (1), a settlor's power to modify a trust is determined by the terms of the trust. 2 Restatement Trusts 3d, § 4 states, "The phrase 'term of the trust' means 'the manifestation of intention of the settlor with respect to the trust provisions expressed in a manner that admits of its proof in judicial proceeding." There was no ambiguity in the trust instrument with respect to the settlor's power to modify it. The court's interpretation must be based on the four corners of the document. Thus, the settlor's power to modify the trust was restricted by the requirement that both sign the amendment during their joint lives.

Paragraph (2) of the restatement does not subject the matter to further interpretation because the settlor did not fail to provide whether the trust was subject to a retained power of amendment. The settlors expressly provided that the trust was subject to amendment, provided both settlors approved the amendment.

Paragraph (3) of the Restatement does not apply here because the condition set forth in paragraph (3)—"[a]bsent [a] contrary provision in the terms of the trust"—is not satisfied. The trust expressly provides a means for exercising the power to modify the trust, i.e., with a "writing signed by us or on our behalf and delivered to Trustee during our lives."

Student Answer—July 2008

Question 8—Trusts—7 points

The issue is whether Patti can validly amend her joint trust with Paul after Paul's death.

A trust is established for the benefit of another. The trustee holds the property for the beneficiaries. A trust is revocable unless agreed otherwise. A trust is amendable unless agreed otherwise.

Bruce will argue that Patti could not amend the joint trust after Paul's death. A joint trust becomes the survivor's trust after the death of a joint trustee. After Paul's death, Patti became the trust's only trustee. Bruce will point to the language of the trust most specifically "by a writing signed by us . . ." and argue that by "us" Patti and Paul meant both. This is a weak argument. There is no indication that Paul and Patti intended for the trust to be irrevocable or unamendable at the death of the other. The trust creator's intent controls. Had the couple intended otherwise, it would have been specifically stated in the trust.

Patti's reasons for amending the trust are irrelevant. Just because Patti wanted to leave Sarah a greater share because she took good care of Paul doesn't matter unless Sarah or Sue unduly influenced her into doing so. There is no indication of that here.

Sarah will argue that since the agreement of Sue to divide her parcel with Bruce wasn't in the amendment, Bruce isn't entitled to anything anyway. This is a valid argument. The court may find that since the trust was amended by Patti and didn't include Bruce, Sue wasn't legally obligated to half her parcel with him.

Bruce will probably not prevail in his action and the amendment will not be set aside.

February 2009—Question 12

You are a law clerk for a probate judge who has heard evidence for several days in adversary proceedings involving the estate of Jason Walker. The following summarizes the evidence:

Jason, a wealthy bachelor who lived a happy and healthy life, suffered a devastating stroke at 84 causing him to be partially paralyzed, unable to care for himself. Jason hated the idea of living in a nursing home and hired Carlee Caregiver, a registered nurse, to move into his home and provide 24-hour care. She was to assist Jason in continuing to live in his home, doing such things as managing his home health care, helping him with his personal needs, and domestic duties like housework. Carlee knew about Jason's wealth. He was by far her most lucrative client.

Soon after the stroke, Jason began to suffer from extreme depression over his loss of independence. His depression was so severe Carlee described it as his "black hole." In his "black hole," Jason would not talk for days, refused to see his family and friends, and made no effort to manage his personal affairs and finances.

Jason then worsened to his deepest depression. He refused to speak for weeks, was not compliant in his treatment, and generally hated the world. He was especially rude and nasty to his family for seemingly no reason at all.

One day, in the midst of this "black hole," Jason asked Carlee to take dictation as he often did when he wanted to write something but could not because of the paralysis. The letter, to his attorney, stated that he knew his family and had come to despise them. It stated further that he knew he was quite wealthy and he thought his wealth would be wasted on his family members. Finally, it asked the attorney to draft a codicil to his will changing the beneficiaries of his entire estate from his family to Carlee. Surprised by this, Carlee nevertheless dutifully drafted and mailed the letter.

Jason's attorney, also surprised by the letter, drafted the codicil as requested. Knowing Jason was homebound he met Jason at his home to execute the codicil. Carlee let him in and led him to Jason, then left them alone. The attorney showed the letter to Jason and described how he had implemented Jason's requests into the codicil. When he expressed concern about Jason disinheriting his family and leaving his entire estate to Carlee, Jason said "Screw my family and let me sign the damn thing."

The attorney gave Jason a pen and placed the codicil in front of him, but Jason could not sign his name without help because of the partial paralysis. Carlee often helped Jason sign his name when necessary, and the attorney had her come back into the room to help. As she usually did, Carlee put scrap paper in front of Jason, placed the pen in his hand, and gently helped him practice signing until he had a neat signature. She then put the codicil in front of Jason, placed the pen in his hand, and helped him sign the codicil. The attorney and Carlee signed the codicil as witnesses because they were the only people in the room.

Two months later Jason died of complications related to the stroke having never emerged from his deep depression. His family found out about the codicil shortly after his death and was shocked that they had been disinherited in favor of Jason's caregiver.

The probate judge has asked you to prepare a memo discussing the issues raised in the case and how they should be resolved.

Model Answer to Question 12

This question tests three of the most common types of will contest: lack of testamentary capacity, undue influence resulting in lack of free will, and the testator's failure to properly execute the will.

Testamentary Capacity: MCL 700.2501 states "An individual 18 years of age or older who is of sound mind may make a will." The case law has interpreted sound mind to consist of the individual must be able to (1) comprehend the nature and extent of his property; (2) recall the natural objects of his bounty; and (3) determine and understand the disposition of property which he wishes to make. *In re Sprenger's Estate*, 337 Mich 514 (1953); *In re Carmast's Estate*, 327 Mich 235 (1950); *In re Walker's Estate*, 270 Mich 33 (1935).

In this case, Jason Walker was 84 years old so he meets the threshold age requirement. The family will say that he suffered from a number of health problems including the effects of a stroke and deep depression all of which could affect his mental capacity. Carlee will counter that when Jason dictated the letter requesting the codicil he stated specifically that he (1) knew he was wealthy; (2) knew who his family was; and (3) felt that his wealth would be wasted with his family and directed a change in who was to be beneficiary of his will. The codicil was drafted to the specifics of the letter and attorney reviewed the letter with Jason when the codicil was executed. At the time of execution, having reviewed the letter that set forth the elements of testamentary capacity Jason executed the codicil without any indication that he was not of "sound mind" as defined by law. As such, the facts do not support a claim of lack of testamentary capacity.

Undue Influence: According to *Kar v Hogan*, 399 Mich 529, 537 (1976), a presumption of undue influence arises upon introduction of evidence which would establish (1) the existence of a confidential or fiduciary relationship between the grantor and a fiduciary, (2) the fiduciary or an interest that he represents benefits from a transaction, and (3) the fiduciary had an obligation to influence the grantor's decision in that transaction. In this case, the family will argue that Carlee was a fiduciary of Jason in that she was his employee and personal caregiver. She benefitted from the transaction because she will now inherit his wealth. Finally, she not only had opportunity to influence the grantor's decision, but she actively participated in it. She drafted the letter causing the codicil to be created, she placed the pen in his hand and helped him sign the codicil, and she witnessed the codicil. Thus, the presumption of undue influence has been met. *Kar v Hogan*, 399 Mich 529, 538 (1976). Furthermore, Jason was in a weak, paralyzed state and suffering from deep depression and the case law indicates that the lower the degree of the testatory's intellect or strength, the easier it is to infer that influence is undue. *In re Shepard's Estate*, 161 Mich 441 (1910); *Schneider v Vosburgh*, 143 Mich 476 (1906).

Carlee will counter that not all influence is undue influence and the burden of proof does not shift to her as a proponent of the codicil even though the presumption of undue influence has been met. Rather, only the burden of going forward with evidence the transaction was free of undue influence shifts to her. The burden of proof remains on the family throughout the case to show that the will was the product of undue influence and not the product of Jason's own free will. *Kar v Hogan*, 399 Mich 529 (1976). She will argue that Jason's letter to his attorney was a surprise to her and she drafted it exactly as he wanted by taking dictation as she usually did. She will also argue that even though she assisted Jason in signing the codicil, she acted only as was their usual practice in helping him sign something when he could not because of his paralysis. She will also argue that despite Jason's illness, he was of sound mind and capable of making his own decisions. Finally, she will argue that Jason obtained and consulted independent legal counsel regarding the codicil and he did so outside of her presence. Despite the presumption of undue influence having been met, the family has not met its burden in demonstrating that the codicil was the product of undue influence and not the product of Jason's own free will. Therefore, any presumption of undue influence has been rebutted.

Failure to Execute a Proper Will: A codicil to a will must be executed with the same requirements that a valid will must be executed. The family will argue that under the common law Carlee could not be a witness to a will that she was a beneficiary or interested person in. Carlee will counter that when EPIC took effect in 2000, the legislature modified the common law. EPIC 700.2505(1) states: "An individual generally competent to be a witness may act as a witness to a will." EPIC 700.2505(2) states further: "The signing of a will by an interested person, does not invalidate the will or any provision of it." Thus, EPIC has changed the common law and Carlee could properly witness the codicil despite being a beneficiary of the will. Therefore, the codicil was executed with the same requirements of a valid will.

Three Student Answers—February 2009

Question 12—Wills—9 points

Memorandum
To: Probate Judge
From: Law Clerk
Re: Jason's Codicil

This is a Wills Question. Jason has a will and he wants to change a provision in it. He wants Carlee his caregiver to get his estate not his family. He's wanting to do that in a codicil.

Under the Estates and Protected Individuals Code (EPIC) a person may have an attorney (or they could do it) draft a codicil. A codicil is where the testator wants to make changes to his/her will. In regard to formalities the codicil must be signed by testator and witnessed by two people. Here Jason has asked his attorney to draft a codicil to his will changing the beneficiaries of his entire estate. Here, Jason had Carlee write the letter as he often did—because of his paralysis. He instructed her to do the letter—she did.

With a codicil, the changes can't be such that it's so different from the will. Codicils will be enforced, but not likely whereas here, Jason has changed the beneficiaries in his will from his family to his caregiver. The codicil provisions would be completely different from the will. So in essence, this would be more of a revocation of the existing will to revoke former will, testator has to intend that that happen—he wants the codicil. There's likely to be problems down the road as the codicil has language completely different from the will, so it revokes the will. This would be revocation, though, testator's intent shows he wants caregivers to get estate, not his family, he's adamant about that. And he took action to change things—the codicil.

Here, the codicil was signed by Jason with the help of his caregiver. She often helps him sign his name—she put scrap paper in front of him and placed pen in his hand and gave him help to sign his name. She put codicil in from of him and helped him sign. Jason has paralysis, so he needs help. He wanted her help—its his intent that she help. The attorney and care giver each signed the codicil as witnesses. It doesn't matter that caregiver will take under the will—she can still be a witness. So, formation of codicil is met.

Jason's family will argue that codicil not valid. That caregiver influenced him, that she even signed the codicil. They'll try to prove under influence testator is no longer his and caregiver took over and that testator had no will of his own left. They'll claim she knew he was ill, he was wealthy, lives alone and that she took advantage of all of this. They also address Jason's lack of capacity—severe depression, etc.—but, testator still has capacity to create such documents for himself as long as he has lucid moments during his difficult times. It's clear what testator wanted. He wanted his family left out of his will and caregiver to take everything. He can change his beneficiaries if he wants. I don't believe that his family will be able to prove undue influence or be able to show he didn't have the capacity to change his existing will when he requested the codicil.

Jason asked for caregiver's help turned to her when he needed help, and relied on her. Codicil indicates what he wants—its his intent that caregiver get everything.

Question 12—Wills—9 points

To: Judge
Date: 2/24/09
From: Attorney
Re: Will Issues

Under MI law a Will is a device by which the testator disposes of other personal or real property or both. When determining if there is a will is valid. It must meet the following elements: must have 2 witnesses, must have testamentary intent, must be signed and although it does not need to be dated it should.

Testamentary Capacity Issue

Here there seems to be an issue with Jason's (J) testamentary intent. Intent may be is not the correct word, capacity. Facts state that J had a stroke was paralyzed (partially) and suffered from extreme depression over his loss of independence. As Curlee would describe it as a "Black hole" so there may be an issue as to whether J is competent even for his thoughts and nonetheless sign a will.

Curlee will argue that the letter she wrote to his lawyer is evidence enough of his capacity as he "knew he was quite wealthy and though his wealth would be wasted on his family."

Therefore capacity is not a strong argument for the family as this is to be a clear, convincing burden of proof.

Disinheritance of Family

Under MI law, disinheritance is allowed as long as it is expressly stated that is as long as the intent of the testator is known and there is no undue influence or fraud or duress then the testators intent will prevail in a situation like (i.e. he did not have a spouse-she could get elective share).

Further, one may make additions to or even change in their wills as long as the proper formalities are carried out.

Here J had a codicil made, therefore the codicil must be carried in the same manner as the first will was.

The facts are not absolute but it appears that this was Curlee who wrote a letter to an attorney. He drafted it. Came there and then they signed the will as witnesses. Note in MI this is ok. A lawyer as well as an interested party may sign the wills if no other parties are available.

J's family will certainly assert that J was unduly influenced through duress as Curlee was in complete control of his life at this point. 24 hour care, home care, health care, regularly drafted letters for him. Further they will assert that it is only after she came into his life that he disinherited them. That she knew how much he was worth. However Curlee will counter that she was just doing her job and never exerted any undue influence. And Curlee did what he wanted and intended to do.

Last argument family will make is that codicil is not valid because it was not properly signed.

However, this will most likely fail, as courts have recognized a simple (X) as a signature. As long as the testator intended it to be his signature it will be valid. Further the facts state this was not out of ordinary for (C) to do.

Question 12—Wills—9 points

To: Judge
From: Attorney
Re: Jason Walker Codicil

A codicil is an amendment to a will and must have the same elements as needed for a will. It must be signed by testator and witnessed by two witnesses. The fact that Carlee assisted Jason in signing the will is fine since this was customary and since this is what Jason wanted. The fact that Carlee was a witness to the codicil and also an interested party in the will is also appropriate under MI law. Prior to the lawyer executing the codicil he did express his concern about Jason disinheriting his family this inquiry was appropriate to determine if Jason is of sound mind. Jason passed this test my saying "screw my family and let me sign the damn thing." It is obvious that Jason had intent to have this codicil drafted and executed. Jason was not under duress or undue influence. His family will probably contest the will and argue that signature is not valid and that Nurse had undue influence on him she was frequently there caring for him. The court should rule that under the dispensing power statute there is clear evidence that Jason intended to have this codicil.

July 2009—Question 13

William Long passed away in early 2009 at the age of 89 leaving a probate estate worth one million dollars. William was never married and his only natural heirs are two adult sons named Carl and Joe. Carl and Joe have different mothers and were never able to get along when they were young. After his death, Carl and Joe searched all of William's personal effects in an attempt to find a formal will, but only found a handwritten letter, signed by William, and that was written when they were young. It states as follows:

> To whom it may concern:
>
> I have managed to save a little money and I want my children and the church to have it when I die. I intend for this letter to be treated as my Will and I know my family will honor it as such. I leave the contents of my home to my children to be split as equally as possible. I also leave my sons, Carl and Joe, $5,000.00 cash apiece. The rest of my estate I leave to Good Church in Flint, Michigan, to be used to help the poor of Flint.
>
> For personal reasons known to them, I know that my children do not get along. To avoid family conflict, it is my wish that any person who challenges this Will take nothing from my estate.
>
> Signed,
> William Long
> May 26, 1950
>
> I, Chad Ireland, hereby witness the signature of William Long on May 26, 1950.
>
> Signed,
> Chad Ireland
> May 26, 1950

Carl and Joe believe that the entire letter is in their father's handwriting although they do not remember the letter because it was written so long ago. They are both positive that the signature at the end of the letter is their father's signature. Carl and Joe remember Chad Ireland as one of their father's old drinking buddies and believe his signature is genuine. They found evidence, however, along with the letter that their bequest of $10,000 cash would have constituted nearly all of their father's estate in 1950.

You represent Good Church in Flint, Michigan, in the probate of William's estate and intend to have the letter admitted as William's Will. Carl and Joe have notified you that they intend to either challenge the validity of the Will or elect against the Will and take their share as though William died intestate. If they do so, how is the estate likely to be distributed under each scenario? Explain your answer.

Model Answer to Question 13

This question tests the effect of an "in terrorem" (no-contest) provision in a will, the elements of a valid will, and the ability of adult children of the decedent to elect against a will.

Effect of the "In Terrorem" (no-contest) Clause: The letter intended as a will states: "it is my wish that any person who challenges this will take nothing from my estate." Carl and Joe will have to overcome this restriction on contesting the will or they risk taking nothing from William's estate. Under the common law "in terrorem" (no-contest) clauses were strictly construed and enforceable. *Saier v Saier*, 366 Mich 515 (1962). Carl and Joe would argue that EPIC partially abrogated the common law in regards to "in terrorem" clauses by stating in MCL 700.2518: "A provision in a will purporting to penalize an interested person for contesting the will or instituting other proceedings relating to the estate is unenforceable if probable cause exists for instituting proceedings." So, the issue becomes whether or not probable cause exists to contest the will. The Restatement 3 of Property states: "Probable cause exists when, at the time of instituting the proceeding there was evidence that would lead a reasonable person, properly informed and advised, to conclude that there was a substantial likelihood that the challenge would be successful." 2 Restatement Property, 3d, Wills and Other Donative transfers, § 8.5, Comment c, p 195. Carl and Joe do not have probable cause under this test to challenge the will because there is not probable cause to object to this will in the given facts of this case. For example, the facts state Carl and Joe believe that the will is in their father's own handwriting even if they do not remember the letter. Further, even though it is not properly witnessed, the will is valid as a holographic will as is discussed below. Finally, even though one could speculate that leaving the bulk of the estate to the church may not have been William Long's intent, there are no facts presented indicating a reason to overturn the express provisions of the will making specific gifts of $5,000.00 apiece to Carl and Joe and the rest to Good Church.

Therefore, the "in terrorem" clause is valid and no probable cause exists to challenge the will. So, any person who challenges the will risks taking nothing from the estate of William Long. If Carl and Joe object, the entire estate is likely to be distributed to Good Church.

Elements of a Valid Will: Carl and Joe will argue that no formal will has been found and the letter dated May 26, 1950, is not a valid will. Thus, their father should be deemed to have died intestate and the assets passed via the laws of intestacy. Upon careful examination, their claim is without merit. MCL 700.2501 states: "An individual 18 years of age or older who is of sound mind may make a will." In this case William was about 30 years old when he drafted the will and no facts are presented that he was not of sound mind.

MCL 700.2502(1) states in pertinent part that a will must be witnessed by at least 2 individuals. Under this statute, the will is clearly deficient because it was witnessed by only one person.

However, MCL 700.2502(2) states: "A will that does not comply with subsection (1) is valid as a holographic will, whether or not witnessed, if it is dated, and if the testator's signature and the document's material portions are in the testator's own handwriting." In these facts the entire letter appears to be in William's own handwriting, it is signed, dated, and was clearly intended to be a will. As such, it is a valid holographic will whether or not it was properly witnessed. William will be deemed to have died testate, the will should be admitted to probate, and the assets distributed in accordance with the terms of the will.

Ability of Carl and Joe to Elect Against the Will: If a valid right to elect against the will were available to Carl or Joe, they could take advantage of it regardless of the enforceability of the "in terrorem" clause. However, unlike a surviving spouse, adult children have no right to elect against a valid will and take their partial intestate share. They must challenge the validity of the will and be successful in that challenge as discussed above. It is plausible that an answer might discuss the "omitted children" statute or the stand exemptions and allowances that minor dependent children could receive against the terms of a valid will under EPIC. This analysis is fine, if included, as long as the answer correctly determines that Carl and Joe are not entitled to any exemptions or allowances under EPIC because they are adult children and they were not omitted from the will under the "omitted child" statute, MCL 700.2302.

Student Answer—July 2009

Question 13—Wills—8 points

Issue: Can the sons of William elect to take the intestate share of the will. Under Michigan which follows EPIC, the rule is that only the spouse can take an elective share under intestacy. Therefore the sons would take nothing.

How will the estate be distributed under a valid will scenario. The rule is to give clear effect to the words as written. Here, it is clearly stated in the will if any person challenges under the will, will take nothing; this is an in terrorem clause and will be upheld in Michigan. If Carl and Joe challenge the validity of the will, then they will take nothing. The gifts would lapse and would not be saved by the anti-lapse statute. The church would take the entire estate which is in the residue.

In the event they are allowed to take under intestacy Michigan follows per capita at each generation and would each take 500,000 dollars leaving the church with nothing. Under intestacy the church would not have a claim to the estate.

This is a valid Holographic will. This is the testator's own writing, signed and dated.

February 2010—Question 10

Dennis Dwayne, age 51, was a successful race car driver living in Michigan. He was married to Barbie and had twin 5-year-old boys, Ronnie and Paulie, and a 12-year-old stepdaughter named Kathleen.

In May 2009, Dennis was diagnosed with an inoperable brain tumor and given a year to live. Wanting to get his affairs in order, Dennis drafted his will on his personal computer. After printing his will, he signed and dated the document in the presence of his mother, Jean, who signed the document as a witness.

In October 2009, Barbie went to the fertility clinic, where she and Dennis had sought treatment previously, and had an embryo implanted without Dennis's knowledge. The frozen embryos had been stored since the twins' birth. Before Dennis received his diagnosis, the couple planned to have more children. Barbie believed that an infant would give Dennis a reason to continue fighting the disease, and planned to surprise Dennis with the news of her pregnancy as a Christmas gift.

Unfortunately, Dennis lost his battle with cancer and died in early December 2009, before Barbie told him about her pregnancy. Locating the will, Barbie was shocked to learn that the terms of the will split Dennis's wealth evenly between Marcel, Dennis's auto mechanic, and Dennis's mother, Jean.

Barbie contested Dennis's will, claiming that the will was invalid. Barbie seeks to recover Dennis's estate for the benefit of herself, Ronnie, Paulie, Kathleen, and the unborn baby boy, whom she plans to name Dale. Jean, on the other hand, sought to uphold the validity of the will.

Applying the Michigan law, discuss the arguments most likely to be advanced by Barbie and Jean, and the likelihood of Barbie, Ronnie, Paulie, Kathleen, the unborn baby, and Jean being able to take a share of Dennis Dwayne's estate. Explain your answer.

Model Answer to Question 10

Pursuant to Michigan law, MCL 700.2502(1), a will is only valid if it is (1) in writing; (2) signed by the testator; and (3) signed by at least 2 individuals who witnessed the testator's signature. Here, Dennis Dwayne's will was in writing, and signed by Dwayne, but it was only witnessed by one witness, Jean. Because the will was only signed by one witness, the document does not qualify as a valid will.

While a holographic will does not need to be witnessed, MCL 700.2502(2), it must be dated, signed by the testator, and the material portions of the will must be in the testator's handwriting. Here, the facts indicate that the will was created and printed on a computer. Because the material portions of the will were not in the testator's handwriting, the document fails as a holographic will.

It is irrelevant that Jean, an interested party, witnessed the will. The signing of a will by an interested witness does not invalidate the will. MCL 700.2505(2).

Jean will argue the validity of the will despite its noncompliance with the precise requirements of MCL 700.2502 because MCL 700.2503 provides that a testamentary document will be treated as if it is in compliance with the law if the proponent of the will (in this case, Jean) establishes by clear and convincing evidence that the decedent intended the document to constitute his will. If Jean's argument is successful, the will of Dennis Dwayne will be upheld as valid, and Jean will take 50% of Dennis' estate.

However, Michigan has an elective share statute, designed to protect spouses against disinheritance. Under MCL 700.2202(2), Barbie may choose to (1) abide by the terms of the will; (2) take her dower right of a ⅓ life estate in all land owned by Dennis at any time during the marriage, MCL 588.1; or (3) take ½ of the amount she would have received had Dennis died intestate (discussed below), reduced by ½ of the value of all property Barbie received from Dennis by any means other than testate or intestate succession. This includes jointly held bank accounts, life insurance proceeds, and large transfers made within 2 years before the decedent's death. MCL 700.2202(7).

In addition to the elective share statute, Barbie is entitled to a homestead allowance of at least $15,000, MCL 700.2402, an exempt property allowance of at least $10,000, MCL 700.2404, and a reasonable family allowance, MCL 700.2403. The family allowance may be paid as a lump sum of $18,000, MCL 700.2405(2). All of the allowances are adjusted annually for inflation, MCL 700.1210, and have priority over all claims against the estate except for administration costs and reasonable funeral and burial expenses. § 2402; § 2403(2); and § 2404(2). Thus, Jean's 50% share of Dennis's estate is reduced by Barbie's elective share, as well as the statutory allowances.

Barbie will argue that Dennis' will is invalid because it neither qualifies as a will nor a holographic will, for the reasons discussed above. Further, Barbie will argue that Jean failed to prove by clear and convincing evidence that Dennis intended the document to constitute his will.

In the event that Barbie's arguments are successful, then Dennis will have died intestate. As a surviving spouse with shared descendants, Barbie will take the first $150,000, plus ½ of the remainder of the estate. MCL 700.2102. The minimum amount is adjusted annually for inflation. MCL 700.1210.

The remainder of Dennis' estate goes to his descendants by representation. MCL 700.2103(a). Ronnie and Paulie, as children of Dennis, will clearly take a portion of the estate. Kathleen, as a stepchild, will be unable to take a portion of Dennis' estate because a stepchild is specifically excluded as a child entitled to take by intestate succession. MCL 700.1103(f).

Lastly, the unborn baby (Dale) will most likely take a portion of Dennis' estate. A child conceived by a married woman with the consent of her husband using reproductive technology is considered to be the couple's child for the purposes of intestate succession. While Dennis was unaware that Barbie had a frozen embryo implanted in October 2009, his consent to the child's conception is presumed unless the contrary is shown by clear and convincing evidence. MCL 700.2114(1)(a). Here, the facts indicate that the couple planned to have more children before Dennis received his diagnosis. However, a contrary argument could be made that Dennis could not have consented to the conception of the child where he was unaware of the implantation procedure that occurred in October.

While baby Dale was not alive at the time his father died, he is treated as though he were living for the purposes of intestate succession if Dale survives for 120 hours (5 days) after his birth. MCL 700.2108.

Three Student Answers—February 2010

Question 10—Wills—8 points

This is a wills question. To have a valid will, the will must be in writing and signed by two witnesses and dated. Even if a will does not meet these qualifications, it can still be held valid as a holographic will.

The will in this case was only signed by one witness therefore. It is not a valid will but nevertheless it still valid as a holographic will as done as long as it is the intent of Dennis to have it be his last will & testament. An argument can be made that since it was done on a computer and not in Dennis own handwriting that it is invalid holographic will because the important parts of the will were not done in Dennis's own handwriting. This decision however will be left up to the court but in looking at it, the court will look at the intent of the party and it would seem his intent was a valid will. I suppose an argument could also be made that because he was dying from a brain tumor that the tumor caused him to lose the capacity to write his will but based on the facts that argument would probably fail.

If the writing was to be found to be a valid will, this does not mean Barbie will recover nothing because according to MI law she still has her dower rights in the property which means she will get a life estate in ⅓ of all her husbands' property until she dies. Additionally she will be allowed a family allowance; homestead allowance because she is caring for Dennis children.

The family allowance is a set amount but their homestead allowance can vary and the court has held that $10,000 is not an excessive family allowance. These allowances are allowed because Barbie need to care for the children of Dennis and should not be allowed no money to do so.

Now if she chooses her dower rights she loses all the rights that maybe allowed. In Michigan if a valid will is found, the surviving spouse has the right to

1. Take share according to will
2. take ½ interest share of the estate
3. dower rights ⅓ in a life estate of her husband

Since she is getting nothing from the will she will have to choose from 2 or 3 whichever gives her more. She will still be entitled to the homestead allowance and family allowance as well also $10,000 in personal property.

If the will is invalid and Dennis died intestate, Barbie will be able to take $201,000 & ½ estate since she has children with Dennis and the rest will pass through succession.

If she were not to have had children with Dennis then his mother Jean would have a right to ¼ of his property after Barbie took $201,000 and ¾ of the estate.

Therefore Jean, his mother will argue the will is valid therefore she must choose between his dower rights or ½ of $201,000 and ½ of estate. She would have received interstate. She will then argue that after the necessary expenses are paid the will will be divided accordingly to his intent.

1. Admin Expense—these are expenses that come off the top
2. Burial Expenses
3. Family allowance
4. Homestead allowance
5. Federal taxes
6. 10,000 personal property
7. State tax
8. Medical expenses
9. Other creditors

Barbie will argue she is the surviving spouse entitled to the right explained earlier & she will win because she is his spouse and must take care of his children will or no will she has rights as a surviving spouse.

Question 10—Wills—8 points

The question is whether Barbie the wife of Dennis who has passed can prove her husband's will invalid and who takes.

The first question is whether there is a valid will in Michigan in order to have a valid will there must be a competent person intending to will, a written will, and two witnesses who sign the will in testators and either watching sign or having testator acknowledge his signature. The will must also be signed (Michigan does not require a signature at the end.)

Here we have a will and competent testator as far as we can tell from the facts who intended to make a valid will. (to be competent a testator must know who the intended beneficiaries are) However, we only have one signature. This would make the will invalid, but the probate court can determine by clear and convincing evidence that the will was made valid.

It is also possible for this will to be looked at as a holographic will, which MI does allow. A holographic will is where the material portions of the will are handwritten and it is signed and dated at the bottom of the will. Here the will is signed and dated, but the will is not hand written and so a holographic will would fail. The probates court's decision to the validity of the will is based on if there was intent to omit Barbie and her children. If the court does find intent to omit Barbie and her children then Barbie's only recourse is to ask for her elective share. Barbie's elective share would be one half her intesto share minus any gifts of personal property within the last two years and any property she has rights by survivorship and any insurance k and rights she can redeem. The rest of the property would go to Marcel and Mother Jean.

If the court finds that the will is valid. In this scenario the unborn child would get his interstate rights as an after omitted beneficiary.

(Dower a ⅓ in all property of husband is not in MI)

It is possible the court will find that Jean was an influence or caused duress to her son. If they find this the will also be void.

If the probate court finds the will void then Barbie will take her interstate share of the first $150,000 plus ½ the remaining interest and her children Ronnie and Paulie and adopted child Kathleen will take with unborn child the remaining on half.

The four will split the one half share.

No one else will take—not mom, Jean, or Dennis.

Wife is not an omitted spouse after the will originally.

If the will is found valid by the probate court mom and Dennis will take unless mom takes elective share.

Question 10—Wills—8 points

Under Michigan law, a valid will must meet 3 requirements: it must be signed by the testator, it must be signed by 2 witnesses, and the witnesses must sign the will after a reasonable time in witnessing the testator's signature on in his presence.

Under Michigan law, a holographic will is valid if it is written in the testator's handwriting, is signed, & dated.

In this case, Barbie will argue that Dennis' will is not a valid will b/c it doesn't meet the requirements of a valid will. Dennis did sign the will, but he only had one witness, Jean signs it. He must have two witnesses sign it for it to be valid.

This will also cannot be considered to be a holographic will, b/c the material portions of the will are not in Dennis' handwriting. Instead, he drafted it using his computer.

Barbie may also argue that Jean cannot sign the will as a witness b/c she is an interested party due to the fact that Dennis left a portion of his wealth to her. But that is no longer the case in MI, a witness may be an interested party.

Jean will argue that the will is valid b/c Dennis signed and dated it. But that does not meet the requirements of a valid will.

Jean may also argue that it was Dennis' intent to deliberately leave Barbie and his children out of the will.

Barbie does have options. Under MI law, a widow can elect to take an elective share, a testate share, or her dower right. Since the will is not valid, Barbie cannot take a testate share, which would leave her w/nothing anyway. Barbie should select an elective share, which is the first $150,000 plus ½ the balance of the estate b/c she has children (Ronnie & Paulie) from Dennis. The $150,000 is now adjusted for inflation.

Barbie is also entitled to the homestead allowance ($15,000); the exemption of personal property ($10,000) and the family allowance ($18,000) all of these numbers have also been adjusted for inflation.

The unborn baby will be considered an after born child and will take the same amount as Ronnie and Paulie under Barbie. But Kathleen is Dennis' step-daughter & is not entitled to anything.

Barbie should not elect the dower right b/c that is only $\frac{1}{3}$ of the estate. Therefore, Barbie is better off in taking her elective share.

July 2010—Question 3

After a lucrative medical career as an anesthesiologist, Bradford died from natural causes in 2010. Bradford's wife, as well as his only child, David, predeceased him. David's twin daughters, Erin and Morgan, survived Bradford. Upon Bradford's death the following will was found:

> "I, Bradford, intend this document to be my final will and testament. I hereby provide for the following dispositions of property upon my death:
>
> "(1) I leave my beloved 1965 Aston Martin DB5 sports car to my dear childhood friend, Greg.
>
> "(2) ~~I leave $200,000 to my alma mater, State College~~. (*I no longer leave anything to the college /s/Bradford, 12/8/2004*)
>
> "(3) I leave one half of the remaining final value of my estate to my fellow members of the Caravaggio Club, who are equally as dedicated as I to the preservation of classical art, to be divided equally among them.
>
> "(4) I leave the second half of the remaining final value of my estate to my son, David.
>
> "/s/ Bradford 1/1/1999
>
> "Witness 1/s/Caleb 1/1/1999 Witness 2/s/Michael 1/1/1999"

David's death in 2009 occurred as the result of a car crash while borrowing his father's Aston Martin. The crash wrecked the car completely. Bradford's insurance company paid $195,000 to Bradford pursuant to his casualty policy. He did not replace the car.

After the death of Bradford in 2010, the following information is properly entered into evidence at probate:

- Bradford's estate is worth $2.0 million.
- The Aston Martin, specifically bequeathed to Greg, originally sold for $10,000 in 1965, was worth $100,000 at the time the will was made, and had a fair market value at the time of Bradford's death of $200,000.
- The later-written note on item #2 on the will has been authenticated as Bradford's handwriting and signature.
- At the time the will was signed, the Caravaggio Club had three members (none of whom were related to Bradford). However, upon Bradford's death, only one elderly member, Courtney, remained alive, although the other members left descendants.

- Both of David's daughters, Erin and Morgan, are currently alive (several months after Bradford's death).

Assuming that Bradford's will is valid and applying Michigan law, account specifically for the four bequests that Bradford made in the will and determine how the estate should be distributed. Explain your answer.

Model Answer to Question 3

This wills question tests the knowledge of several factual complications that may arise when probating a valid will. The correct disposition of Bradford's estate is:

1. Greg is entitled to a $200,000 payment from the estate as the fair market value of the Aston Martin: This raises an issue of *ademption:* that is, there is specifically bequeathed property in the will that is *no longer a part of the estate at the testator's death.* In Michigan, there is a *presumption of non-ademption*, MCL 700.2606(1)(f), which is a change from the prior rule in Michigan where ademption would operate to cause the gift to fail entirely. *Hankey v French,* 281 Mich 454, 462-463 (1937). Where another statutory provision does not compensate the beneficiary for the value or replacement of specifically bequeathed property, the devisee is entitled to the value of the property unless the facts and circumstances show that the ademption was intended by the testator or within the testator's manifested plan of distribution. MCL 700.2606(1)(f). Notably, a beneficiary potentially has a right to any insurance proceeds for injury to the specifically devised property unpaid at the death of the testator, MCL 700.2606(1)(c), or property procured by the testator as a replacement for the specifically devised property. MCL 700.2606(1)(e).

Here, Bradford bequeathed his Aston Martin to Greg, but the car was destroyed in an automobile accident prior to Bradford's death, and therefore cannot be given to Greg per the terms of the will. The presumption of nonademption operates in favor of Greg: Because the facts and evidence demonstrate that the ademption was *not* intended—the car was accidentally destroyed in the year prior to Bradford's death—Greg should be entitled to the cash equivalent of the Aston Martin. (Note that although Bradford received insurance proceeds from the destruction of the Aston Martin, Greg does *not* have an interest in these proceeds [$195,000] because the proceeds were fully paid *prior* to the testator's death. Note also that because Bradford never replaced the Aston Martin, Greg can have no interest in any replacement property.) Thus, the cash legacy should be equal to the value for the vehicle at the time of the disposition, which would likely be an amount similar to its fair market value of $200,000.

2. State College receives nothing: The primary goal in the construction of wills is to determine the testator's intent. *In re Edgar Estate*, 425 Mich 364, 378 (1986). Changes to the face of a will shall be enforced pursuant to the statutory dispensing power if there is clear and convincing evidence that the testator intended the change by the addition or alteration. MCL 700.2503(c). Here, there is likely clear and convincing evidence that Bradford intended to change his will and thus remove the bequest to State College. On the face of the will, the bequest is crossed out, followed by specific words of disinheritance in the testator's handwriting that are signed and dated by the testator. This demonstrates an intent to remove entirely the original gift from the will by clear and convincing evidence, and the probate court should honor this intent by awarding nothing to the college.

3. One half of the remaining value of the state ($900,000) goes to Courtney, the sole remaining member of the Caravaggio Club. (Any heirs of prior deceased members of the club receive nothing.): A testator may properly make a gift to a class of people, i.e., persons who are members of a common group where the intent of the testator is to create a class, however, only members of the class who survive the testator take their share of the gift. MCL 700.2104, MCL 700.2604(1), Michigan Law & Practice 2d Wills, §§ 213-214. The Rule of Convenience provides that the class closes when the testator dies; subject to exceptions not applicable here, any person who is not a member of the class at that time will not take. Here, although the Caravaggio Club had three other members (in addition to Bradford) at the time Bradford made his will, only Courtney survived Bradford's death. Because the class closed upon Bradford's death, the two members who predeceased do not take their shares of the gift. (Note that because they were not related to Bradford, the Anti-Lapse Statute cannot prevent their gifts from lapsing.) Accordingly, their estates/descendants have no valid claim to their shares, which are distributed proportionately to the remaining class member(s). Thus, Courtney takes the entire interest (one half of the remaining value of the estate, $900,000).

4. Erin and Morgan, the twin daughters of David, receive one half of the remaining estate ($900,000), pursuant to Michigan's Anti-Lapse Statute, to be divided equally: The general rule in Michigan provides that if a beneficiary predeceases the testator, then the gift lapses; a will cannot distribute property to a deceased person. See MCL 700.2104, MCL 700.2604(1). However, Michigan has modified this general rule through the enactment of an Anti-Lapse Statute. MCL 700.2603(1). The statute provides that if the predeceasing beneficiary is a grandparent or descendant of a grandparent or a stepchild of the testator, and the descendants are alive after 120 hours of the testator's death, then the gift will pass to the descendants of the beneficiary. Here, because David predeceased the testator, his gift would normally lapse, but for Michigan's Anti-Lapse Statute. Because David, as Bradford's son, is a descendant of Bradford's grandparents, the Anti-Lapse Statute operates to save the gift that would have been dispensed to David. This gift will instead pass to David's descendants, his daughters Erin and Morgan, and will be divided equally between them. MCL 700.2718.

Student Answer—July 2010

Question 3—Wills—8 points

Gift to Greg: The gift to Greg, Bradford's friend, can no longer happen as the testator, Bradford, wishes because it was amended in 2009. In Michigan when a car is wrecked and the insurance proceeds are paid out and the car was intended for a gift in a will, the rule gives the fair market value of the item will replace the Aston Martin gift to Greg. Therefore, Greg shall get the sum of $200,000 which is the fair market price.

Gifts to Caravagio Club: Since Courtney is the only living member of this club, she will seek to gain the gift as the only representative of the club as the testator wished in his will. In Michigan, the will terms effective at the time the testator died and since she is the only member alive, she will get the gift of half of the remaining value of Bradford's estate. She will get $400,000 of Bradford's estate.

Gift to State College: In Michigan, a valid revocation can express physical or by a subsequent instrument. Here, Bradford left out the gift to his Alma Mater, State

College and specifically stated he did not intend for them to get anything under his will. This is a valid revocation; they get nothing.

Gift to David: In Michigan, if an intended beneficiary predeceases the testator, the gift lapses unless there are descendants alive to take at the time of the death of the testator. Here, David preceded his father, Bradford, but left his twin daughters, Erin and Megan.

Erin and Megan are the Testator's living descendants and will take under Michigan's Anti-lapse statute. They seek to take $900,000 of their grandfather's estate.

CREDITOR'S RIGHTS

Questions, Model Answers, and Student Answers

The following section includes prior Michigan Bar Exam questions and model answers for **Creditor's Rights**. Many of the questions also include actual student answers with the amount of points that were earned to give you a better idea of what the graders expect. The student answers are immediately following the model answer for each question. Please pay close attention to the points received on each question. Although most samples represent "good" answers (i.e., received 8, 9, or 10 points), there are some samples that received 7 points (the minimum "passing" score for an essay), and a few that received very low scores to help you better understand the grading process and what is expected.

February 2004—Question 10

Acme Stereo and Television Company ("Acme") went out of business last week. Before its business failed, Acme sold audio and video equipment at retail. Acme offered home delivery for most of the items sold.

On its last day in business, Acme's delivery truck attempted to deliver a boxed stereo to Betty Baxter in unit 4B of a multiunit apartment building. Baxter did not answer her doorbell, so the driver left the box in the building's rental office. No one was in the office at the time, but the door was open and the driver placed the box inside the open door. Now, no one who works in the office claims to have seen the stereo. It was never delivered to Baxter.

Later that same day, the driver attempted to deliver a television set to Cathy Carswell. When he arrived at her door, he saw a note Carswell had left there that requested the set be delivered to her neighbor, Deanna Davis. Carswell had asked Davis to accept delivery of the set earlier that morning. Davis had agreed to do so and she took delivery of the television from Acme's driver. Before Carswell picked up the television from her neighbor, however, a small fire in Davis' living room destroyed it. The fire was caused by a frayed electrical cord leading to an old table lamp Davis had meant to throw away long ago.

Finally, the driver attempted to deliver a radio to Ed Evergreen who had purchased the item the week before for use in his living room. Evergreen was not home so the driver returned the radio to Acme's warehouse where it is now claimed by Acme's creditors.

Assess the strengths and weaknesses of each of the following claims and explain who should prevail on each claim:

1. **A suit for the value of Baxter's lost stereo filed by Baxter against the owner of her building who runs the rental office;**
2. **A suit by Carswell against Davis for the damage to the television set; and**
3. **An action filed by Evergreen to recover the radio he ordered.**

Model Answer to Question 10

This question raises personal property issues from the law of bailments and sales. Generally, a bailee has a duty to use a proper degree of care in exercising custody over bailed goods. The duty does not arise, however, if there is no bailment. Ordinarily, a bailee must consent to a bailment. The owner of Baxter's apartment building did not. Baxter, therefore, has a weak claim for the lost stereo. Davis, on the other hand, did undertake the duties of a bailee by accepting custody of the television for Carswell. She appears, however, to be a gratuitous bailee and is only liable under traditional principles of law for gross negligence. Her carelessness in using the lamp with the frayed cord probably does not rise to that level. Finally, under the Uniform Commercial Code, a buyer of goods acquires a specifically enforceable right to the goods once they have been identified to the contract of sale. In Evergreen's case, that was done when the goods were marked for delivery to him and he should be able to recover his radio.

Baxter's Claim for the Stereo: In the problem, Baxter is suing the owner of her apartment building for the value of the stereo that Acme's delivery driver left in the rental office. It does not seem, however, that the owner of the building owed Baxter a duty to care for the stereo. The facts do not warrant a finding that the owner undertook the duties of a bailee. Ordinarily, a bailment cannot arise without the bailee's consent. The bailee generally must accept care and custody of the bailed goods. *See generally,* 5 Mich L & Prac 2d, Bailment § 4 (2000). No one in the rental office undertook that duty for the owner of the building. Thus, absent some agreement or practice of accepting deliveries for the tenants, the owner of the apartment building should not be liable to Baxter for the value of the lost stereo.

Carswell's Claim for the Damage to the Television: Davis, by contrast, did undertake the duties of a bailee. Carswell did ask Davis to accept delivery of the television set and Davis agreed to do so. Davis took physical possession of the set with an obligation to turn it over to Carswell, thus creating a bailment. *See, e.g., National Ben Franklin Ins Co v Bakhaus Contractors, Inc,* 124 Mich App 510, 512, n2 (1983) ("The term bailment imports the delivery of personal property by one person to another . . . for a specific purpose, with a contract, express or implied, that . . . the property [be] returned or duly accounted for when the special purpose is accomplished or the bailor claims it.")

Bailments are generally classified as to whether the relationship benefits the bailor, the bailee or both. *See generally,* 5 Mich L & Prac 2d, Bailment § 3 (2000). Traditionally, these classifications have been used to define the bailee's duty of care in exercising custody over the bailed goods. Thus, if a bailment was for the sole benefit of the bailee, the law required the bailee to use the highest degree of care in the custody of the goods. A benefit that was mutually beneficial, on the other hand, called for the exercise of ordinary care. A bailment for the sole benefit of the bailor, often called a "gratuitous bailment," entailed an even lower standard of care. *See generally*, 5 Mich L & Prac 2d, Bailment § 6 (2000). Under traditional principles, a gratuitous bailee was only liable for gross neglect if the bailed goods were damaged while in the bailee's possession. *Cadwell v Peninsular State Bank*, 1995 Mich 407 (1917). Recent commentators, however, have criticized the traditional classification scheme. They generally have proposed a single standard of care for all bailments, often stated as a duty of reasonable care under the circumstances. *See, e.g., Kurt Phillip Autor, Bailment Liability: Toward a Standard of Reasonable Care*, 61 So Cal L Rev 2117 (1988).

Under either the traditional or modern approach, Carswell will have difficulty recovering from Davis. Davis accepted the duties of a bailee as a favor, without consideration. She did not treat the television any less carefully than she did her own things. Under the common law standard applied in Michigan for gratuitous bailees, she would not likely be found grossly negligent.

Evergreen's Claim to Recover the Radio: The Uniform Commercial Code expanded the right to a buyer of goods to specific performance of the contract of sale. Under § 2-716(3) of the Code a buyer of consumer goods has a specifically enforceable right to the goods as soon as they have been identified to the contract. UCC § 2-716(2), official comment 3 (2003). Goods are identified to a contract when they have been marked for shipment. UCC § 2-501(1)(b) (2003).

In the problem, Evergreen purchased the radio for his personal, household use. He would thus have a superficially enforceable right to the radio once it had been boxed for delivery to his house. He should therefore be able to recover the radio from Acme's creditors. It should be noted that even if one of those creditors had a security interest in Acme's inventory, Evergreen would take free of the interest as a buyer in the ordinary course of business. *See* UCC § 9-320(a) (2003).

Student Answer—February 2004

Question 10—Creditor's Rights—None Available

July 2004—Question 7

Mike was the owner of certain real property located in Oakland County, Michigan. In 1999, Mike sold the property via land contract to Lucy and Larry, a married couple. In 2001, Lucy and Larry were divorced. Pursuant to the terms of the Judgment of Divorce, Larry retained possession of the property, while Lucy was given a judicial lien on the property for $20,000 and recorded it with the Register of Deeds. In 2003, Larry took out a mortgage with Friendly Bank in the amount of $200,000. Larry used the money to pay off the land contract, as Mike was his cousin. However, he did not pay off the lien held by Lucy. Larry then skipped town with the remainder of the money and is allegedly riding his motorcycle through Europe. As a result of his leaving the country, Larry has also failed to make the payments on the mortgage to Friendly Bank.

Friendly Bank has foreclosed on the mortgage, and is seeking to sell the home to recoup the money lost to Larry. Friendly Bank has filed an action seeking a declaratory judgment that the Bank's interest is superior to the lien of Lucy.

The case has been assigned to a partner in the firm you are working for, and she has asked you to determine the priority of the competing interest. Discuss which

encumbrance would be given priority—the Friendly Bank mortgage or Lucy's lien—and why.

Model Answer to Question 7

A purchase money mortgage is one "which takes effect immediately, as part of the 'same transaction by which seisin was acquired by the mortgagor.'" *Graves v American Acceptance Mortgage Corp*, 469 Mich 608 (2204), quoting *Fecteau v Fries*, 253 Mich 51 (1931). A purchase money mortgage arises where the mortgagor purchases property and gives a mortgage for the purchase money as one transaction. *Graves, supra.* Thus, the issue in the question at hand is whether the use of the money from the mortgage to pay a land contract constitutes a purchase money mortgage.

The Supreme Court has held it is not. A land contract vests equitable title in the vendee (Larry), while legal time remains vested in the vendor (Mike). *Graves, supra.* Therefore, as Larry has equitable title to the property, he also has seisin, which is defined as "Possession of real property under claim of freehold estate . . . Possession with an intent on the part of him who holds it to claim a freehold estate." *Graves, supra*, n3, quoting Black's Law Dictionary (6th ed.) Thus, when the vendee (Larry) purchased the property on a land contract, he took equitable title which he may then sell, devise, or encumber, and has "in a real sense, purchased the relevant property." *Graves, supra*, p616. Thus, the mortgage here is not a purchase money mortgage as the proceeds were not used to purchase the property, but rather to pay off a preexisting debt on the property which was owed to the vendor (Mike). Therefore, Lucy's lien would be given priority over the mortgage held by Friendly Bank.

Two Student Answers—July 2004

Question 7—Creditor's Rights—7 points

Michigan is a lien theory state for mortgage, not title theory state. It means that mortgagor retains the title of property and mortgagee (Bank) retains the lien on the property.

Also, mortgagee has a right of foreclosure if mortgagor failed to pay. Also, among 2 competing mortgages, since Michigan adopted "race-notice" recording statute. It means Bone fide Purchaser would prevail against prior (proceeding) purchaser unless Bona fide Purchaser (BFP) records first than prior purchasers.

In this case, the property is located in MI and Larry resided in MI at the time he got the mortgage, therefore, Friendly Bank does have only the lien on its property, not title. Lucy also has the lien on the same property and Lucy recorded her lien w/ the register of Deed office, where is a proper place to record a lien in MI, and she recorded the lien before Larry got mortgage from the Bank.

Therefore, Lucy's lien has priority over the Friendly Bank's mortgage. Also, the Bank should have known that Lucy already had $20K lien (judicial lien) on the same property b/c she recorded with/ the proper office in MI.

(2) <u>Foreclosure</u>: Even if the Bank is a second lien holder, they insist "foreclosure" b/c of non-payment. However, Lucy's lien is prior to the Bank's mortgage, Lucy's lien is not disappeared/discharged.

It means Lucy has still valid lien on the foreclosed property and Larry is still liable for Lucy's lien amount $20K and any deficiency b/c the amount of foreclosure sale and the amount of mortgage $200K for the Friendly Bank.

(3) Conclusion: The Bank's argument, they are superior to the lien of Lucy, is wrong. And Lucy's lien has priority than the Bank's mortgage. And Larry is still liable for Lucy for $20K and any deficiency of sale for the Bank.

Comment: This examinee received a passing score of 7. If he or she had used the buzzword "purchase money mortgage," it would likely be a 9. Notice the poor grammar, missing words, and so on. Although the graders typically do not take away points for it, good grammar and proper sentence structure could result in additional points.

Question 7—Creditor's Rights—2 points (Bad Answer)

Lucy's lien is superior and should be given priority. Her lien was a judicial lien, properly recorded in 2001. The Bank should have noticed the lien when it issued the mortgage in 2003 and required its payment before issuing the rest to Larry.

Comment: This examinee got 2 points for three sentences. You should never limit a response to this. Even if you are unsure, outline dump some general principles. The graders look to give you points (obviously based on this example), not take them away.

July 2005—Question 6

Jim was the owner of certain real property located in Grand Blanc, Michigan. In 1999, Jim sold the property via land contract to Scot and Kelly, a married couple. In 2001, Scot and Kelly were divorced. Pursuant to the terms of the Judgment of Divorce, Scot retained possession of the property, while Kelly was given a judicial lien on the property for $50,000 and recorded it with the Register of Deeds. In 2003, Scot took out a mortgage with Ourmoney Bank in the amount of $200,000. Scot used the money to pay off the land contract, since Jim was his good friend. However, he did not pay off the lien held by Kelly. Scot then skipped town with the remainder of the money and is allegedly living out his dream working as a carnival barker guessing weights and ages. As a result of his living on the road with the carnival, Scot has also failed to make the payments on the mortgage to Ourmoney Bank.

Ourmoney Bank has foreclosed on the mortgage, and is seeking to sell the home to recoup the money lost to Scot. Ourmoney Bank has filed an action seeking a declaratory judgment that the Bank's interest is superior to the lien of Kelly.

The case has been assigned to a partner of the firm you are working for and she has asked you to determine the priority of the competing interests. Under what theory could the Bank claim that its mortgage be given priority and what would be the outcome? It must be assumed all transactions were recorded in the order of occurrence.

Model Answer to Question 6

A purchase money mortgage is one "which takes effect immediately, as part of the 'same transaction by which seisin was acquired by the mortgagor.'" *Graves v American Acceptance Mortgage Corp*, 469 Michigan 608 (2004), quoting *Fecteau v Fries*, 253

Michigan 51 (1931). A purchase money mortgage arises where the mortgagor purchases property and gives a mortgage for the purchase money as one transaction. *Graves, supra.* Thus the issue in the question at hand is whether the use of the money from the mortgage to pay a land contract constitutes a purchase money mortgage.

The Supreme Court has held it is not. A land contract vests equitable title in the vendee (Scot), while legal title remains vested in the vendor (Jim). *Graves, supra.* Therefore, as Scot had equitable title to the property, he also had seisin, which is defined as "Possession of real property under claim of freehold estate . . . Possession with an intent on the part of him who holds it to claim a freehold estate." *Graves, supra,* n 3, quoting Black's Law Dictionary (6th ed.). When the vendee (Scot) purchased the property on a land contract, he took equitable title, which he may then sell, devise, or encumber, and has "in a real sense, purchased the property." *Graves, supra,* p 834. Thus, the mortgage here is not a purchase money mortgage as the proceeds were not used to purchase the property, but rather to pay off a preexisting debt on the property which was owed to the vendor (Jim). Therefore, Kelly's lien would be given priority over the mortgage held by Ourmoney Bank.

Three Student Answers—July 2005

Question 6—Property/Creditor's Rights—10 points

The Bank will claim that its interest in the land is superior to Kelly because it has a Purchase Money Mortgage Security Interest (PMSI) in the land. The bank will claim that Kelly's interest is inferior to the Bank because she only holds a lien.

A Purchase Money Mortgage gives immediate priority in land and automatically attaches. This is money used to purchase land. It is usually superior to any other claim in the land.

On these facts, Scott did not use the money to purchase land. He used the money to pay off the debt to his friend Jim. Although it was used for the land contract deal, Scott already has possession of the property and the debt was an old debt. It—the money from the bank—was not used to *acquire* new property. Therefore the loan from the Bank is not seen as a purchase money mortgage to acquire new land. Therefore this would be a new debt or personal loan to Scott and would be inferior to Kelly's claim.

So in conclusion, the Bank would not have a superior claim to the land, it is not a purchase money mortgage with superior security interest because it was not used to acquire new land. But the money was used to pay a debt to a friend. So Kelly's interest in the land would have *priority* over the Bank's loan.

Question 6—Property/Creditor's Rights—10 points

The first issue is under what theory could the bank claim that its mortgage be given priority and what would be the outcome. The rule is that a Purchase Money Mortgage (PMM) has a Superior Security interest over other forms of interest. A Purchase Money Mortgage arises when a property owner borrows money from the lender and uses the money to buy the property. Any security interest given to the lender of such money has priority over other security interest in the property.

In this case, the property was purchased in 1999 via land contract. The money Scot took as a mortgage in 2003 was not used to buy the property although it was used to pay off the land contract. To qualify as a Purchase Money Mortgage, the money must be used to acquire the property. Since that is not the case, Our Money Bank does not have a superior mortgage over Kelly.

The next issue is the priority of Kelly's judicial lien. The rule is that any judicial lien is superior to any subsequent security interest if the interests are on the same property. In this case, Kelly obtained a judicial lien in 2001 upon divorce from Jim. Since the judicial lien came first in time before the Our Money Bank mortgage, the judicial lien has priority over the Bank, as the Bank was on notice of Kelly's judicial lien that was recorded. The outcome is that any proceed, which is any money realized from the sale will be used to pay Kelly's $50,000 first before the bank can have any money towards their mortgage.

Comment: This is another excellent answer. Notice how the use of IRAC keeps the answer concise and well organized. Also note that this same issue was tested on a previous bar exam. Many students mistakenly assumed this was a Secured Transaction question. You learned creditor's rights in Secured Transaction in law school. However, the Michigan Bar Examiners test it separately in a different cluster.

Question 6—Property/Creditor's Rights—10 points

The issue is who has priority in the competing interests. The competing interests in question are the lien held by Kelly in the amount of $5,000 and the mortgage held by Our Money Bank in the amount of $200,000. Michigan is a race-notice jurisdiction, which means that the first to record who also has notice of all subsequent interests has priority. Here Kelly filed her lien with the Register of Deeds in 2001. Our Money Bank did not file the mortgage until 2003. If Our Money Bank did a title search they would have realized that Kelly had already recorded a lien on the property. If nothing else they had constructive notice because she did record the lien properly. Therefore, because Kelly filed first with notice, she has priority over Our Money Bank in the competing interests.

The next issue is under what theory could Bank claim that its mortgage be given priority. Bank could argue that their mortgage was a purchase money security interest (PMSI) and therefore should be given superior priority over all claims. A PMSI is an interest given in money for an item. Scot used the money from the mortgage to pay off Jim. The court will probably not view the mortgage as a PMSI and therefore the mortgage will not be given superior priority over all competing interests.

The next issue is whether Bank can claim that they hold title to the property. This argument would fail because Michigan is a lien theory as opposed to a title theory jurisdiction. In lien theory jurisdiction, the mortgagor retains title the property.

The next issue is whether Scot is entitled to get his property back even though Our Money Bank wants to sell the home at a foreclosure sale. In Michigan, the owner of the property has a right to redeem his property for 6 months after the foreclosure sale. The owner only has to tender the amount due.

July 2006—Question 11

Acme Bank was in the process of making a construction loan to Better Built Homes, which was involved in the construction of a residential development of approximately 100 homes. Prior to making the loan, Acme had a title search performed and there were no liens of record. Better Built, being an aggressive developer, had a subcontractor begin grading the property that morning of June 1, 2004, based on the assurance of Acme that the loan was approved and that the closing was scheduled for the next day. The closing was held on June 2, 2004, at 1:30 p.m. At that time, the total amount of the loan was disbursed to Better Built. Immediately following the closing, Acme took the mortgage to the Register of Deeds and had its mortgage recorded at 2:15 p.m. on June 2, 2004.

The grading subcontractor, Roll'em Flat, completed its work by June 30, 2004 and was paid in full by Better Built. As the project continued, Better Built began to experience delays in construction, which substantially delayed completion of the project and all home sales. In the meantime, True Line Carpenters had framed in a number of homes but was not being paid per its contract with Better Built. True Line filed a contractor's lien on September 1, 2004, claiming that the first day of performing work on the project was August 3, 2004. Due to delays in construction and the inability to start the home sales, Better Built was unable to pay their bills as they fell due and defaulted on the loan to Acme Bank. Other subcontractors were not paid and also filed liens. No lien was filed prior to the recording of the mortgage, and no subcontractor, other than Roll'em Flat, performed any work prior to the mortgage being recorded.

Acme started foreclosure on the mortgage and claimed to have a first lien interest on the real estate by virtue of the mortgage recorded on June 2. True Line and all other subcontractors who had been paid filed an action in the circuit court claiming that the Acme mortgage interest was subordinate to all properly perfected mechanic's liens.

Assuming that all of the mechanic's liens were properly perfected, who would have the prior lien interest—Acme or the mechanic's lien holders, and why?

Model Answer to Question 11

In this case, the mortgage was recorded before the lien was filed. However, under the Construction Lien Act, all liens date back to the date of the first improvement on the property. Specifically, MCL 570.1119 provides:

"(3) A construction lien arising under this act shall take priority over all other interests, liens, or encumbrances which may attach to the building, structure, or improvement, or upon the real property on which the building, structure, or improvement is erected when the other interests, liens, or encumbrances are recorded subsequent to the first actual physical improvement."

In this case, the "first actual physical improvement" was made before any advance was given on the mortgage. The facts do not disclose that the Bank received a contractor's statement or any waiver of lien. Once any lien has priority over a mortgage, then all subsequent liens enjoy that priority. An actual physical improvement, as defined under the act, generally requires that grading of the property would certainly be a visible on-site improvement. The Michigan Supreme Court has held "We believe MCL 570.1119(3) continues to reflect the longstanding tradition of affording priority in the payment of those laborers, contractors, and suppliers who provide the building blocks and whose physical efforts go into a construction project. The underlying intent and purpose of the act is to protect the right of lien claimants to payment for wages or materials when others have been provided with notice that there may be outstanding liens against the property because construction work is in progress." *Williams v Works, Inc v Springfield*, 408 Mich 732, 742 (1980).

Even though Roll'em Flat was paid in full, that does not change the fact that the first visible improvement to the real estate occurred before the mortgage was filed. As stated previously, other lien claimants date the effective date of their lien to the first date of improvement regardless of when they file their own lien.

There is a recognized risk to institutional lenders. MCL 570.119 (4) does provide for some protection, as it provides that advances made by mortgage lenders after the first actual physical improvement is made may still enjoy priority over construction liens under MCL 570.1119 (4), if the mortgagee has received a sworn statement from the contractor pursuant to MCL 570.1110, has made disbursements pursuant to the contractor's sworn statement, and has received waivers of lien from the contractor and all subcontractors, laborers, and suppliers who have provided notices.

Student Answer—July 2006

Question 11—Creditor's Rights—None Available

February 2007—Question 7

Henry Homeowner owned a home in Grand Rapids, Michigan. The balance owed on the home was secured by two mortgages: a first mortgage and a future advance mortgage, i.e., a home equity line of credit. The limit on the line of credit was $150,000. The first mortgage was duly recorded on April 1, 1990. The future advance mortgage was recorded by the mortgagee, Stone Financial Bank, on June 15, 2002.

Henry sought to refinance his home loans. City National Bank agreed to refinance the loans. City National Bank paid off the first mortgage, which was discharged. City National Bank sent correspondence to Stone Financial Bank indicating City National Bank would be refinancing Henry Homeowner's property. City National Bank requested a payoff amount for the advance future mortgage. Stone Financial Bank sent a mortgage payoff statement to City National Bank. The mortgage payoff statement identified the mortgagor and the property, and included a conspicuous statement warning "[a]ny amount received by Stone Financial Bank will be credited toward the home equity line of credit and will not terminate Henry Homeowner's home equity line of credit without Henry Homeowner's signature directing and authorizing the discharge of the mortgage and closure of the line of credit." The mortgage payoff statement provided a signature line where Henry Homeowner could sign to have the line of credit terminated and the mortgage discharged.

City National Bank mailed a check to Stone Financial Bank for the full amount owed on the line of credit. The check was sent with a cover letter and a copy of the mortgage payoff statement. The mortgage payoff statement did not contain any signature from Henry Homeowner. The cover letter, signed by a City National Bank loan officer, stated "[e]nclosed is a copy of your mortgage payoff statement and a check to pay off the above-referenced future advance mortgage. Please discharge the mortgage and close the mortgagor's line of credit." Stone Financial Bank posted the payment to Henry Homeowner's line of credit account, but did not close the account or discharge the mortgage. On December 30, 2005, City National Bank recorded its mortgage. After City

National Bank had recorded its mortgage, Henry Homeowner used the entire $150,000 line of credit from Stone Financial Bank and defaulted on both loans. The banks foreclosed on the property. City National Bank filed an action in the circuit court seeking to quiet title and a determination that its lien takes priority over the lien held by Stone Financial Bank. The litigants filed cross motions for summary disposition.

Discuss the arguments each litigant will advance and the likely ruling on the cross motions for summary disposition.

Model Answer to Question 7

An action to quiet title is an action in equity, MCL 600.2932(5). City National Bank will argue it is inequitable to elevate the lien of Stone Financial Bank over the lien of City National Bank because Stone Financial Bank knew that City National Bank intended to have its mortgage take priority over all other recorded interests. City National Bank twice informed Stone Financial Bank of its intent to refinance Henry Homeowner's property, pay off the advance future mortgage, and become the primary lien holder on Henry Homeowner's property. The first notice was given to Stone Financial Bank when City National Bank requested a loan payoff amount. The second notice was given to Stone Financial Bank when City National Bank paid off the advance future mortgage, returned Stone Financial Bank's mortgage payoff statement and instructed Stone Financial Bank to discharge the mortgage and close the mortgagor's line of credit.

Moreover, pursuant to the loan payoff statement, Stone Financial Bank agreed to discharge its mortgage upon receipt of the payoff amount and instruction from the mortgagor that the line-of-credit account be closed. Here, there was a payoff of the indebtedness to Stone Financial Bank and a request that the mortgage be discharged and the line of credit closed. While this request came from a mortgagee seeking priority over Stone Financial Bank rather than from the mortgagor, Henry Homeowner, the failure of Henry Homeowner to expressly ask for the discharge of mortgage and the closing of his line of credit ought not form a basis to allow Stone Financial Bank to ignore its actual knowledge that City National Bank and Henry Homeowner intended to make City National Bank the first priority lien holder by closing the line of credit issued by Stone Financial Bank and refinancing Henry's home loans. There exists no equitable basis to give Stone Financial Bank priority over city National Bank, especially since its claims arise from money advanced after Stone Financial Bank had actual notice of the actions of City National Bank.

Stone Financial Bank will argue that this action is governed by Michigan's recording statutes. Once a mortgagee records its mortgage, "[a]ll subsequent owners or encumbrances shall take subject to the perfected liens, rights, or interests." MCL 565.25(4). Here, Stone Financial Bank was first (as between the parties) to record its mortgage (June 15, 2002) and nothing done by Henry Homeowner or City National Bank extinguished Stone Financial Bank's first recorded lien. Payment of the outstanding balance did not deprive Stone Financial Bank of its priority ahead of later recorded encumbrances because Stone Financial Bank held a future advance mortgage. A future advance mortgage reserves priority for later advanced loans "as if the future advance was made at the time the future advance was recorded." MCL 565.902. Thus, payment of an outstanding balance, without simultaneously terminating the line of credit, will not deprive the future advance mortgagee of lien priority.

City National Bank's cover letter requesting that Stone Financial Bank "discharge the mortgage and close the mortgagor's line of credit" is inconsequential. Stone Financial Bank indicated that such action would not be taken without Henry Homeowner's signature directing and authorizing the discharge of the mortgage and closure of the line of credit. When a financial institution creates a contractual relationship with a client, an unauthorized third party cannot modify or direct that the contract be altered. Here, Stone Financial Bank made it very clear that the mortgage would not be discharged and the line of credit closed without the express written consent of the mortgagor, and City National Bank presented no evidence that it acted with the consent and authority of the mortgagor, Henry Homeowner.

The circuit court will grant summary disposition in favor of Stone Financial Bank. Actions to quiet title brought under the Revised Judicature Act are "equitable in nature." MCL 600.2932 (5). However, a court may not use its equity powers to avoid the application of a statute. *Stokes v Millen Roofing Co*, 466 Michigan 660, 671 (2002). Moreover, equity follows the law. Here, Stone Financial Bank was first to record its lien. Because it was first in time, it is first in right over City National Bank. Nothing done by Henry Homeowner or City National Bank required Stone Financial Bank to extinguish its lien. As such, Stone Financial Bank's lien takes priority over the lien of City National Bank.

Student Answer—February 2007

Question 7—Creditor's Rights—7 points

The cross motions for summary disposition will not be granted.

The issue is whether City National Bank (CNB) has priority over the lien held by Stone Financial Bank.

A purchase money mortgage enjoys super priority over previously properly recorded security interest in real property if the money obtained was used to secure or satisfy a mortgage. Priority is established based upon the value provided and the act of recordation.

Here, Stone Financial properly recorded its interest as a future advance mortgage in June 2002. When CNB approached Stone Financial regarding pay-off, CNB was provided a conspicuous statement requiring the signature of homeowner and what would result if any amount was received. Stone Financial would argue that the statement adequately placed CNB on notice of how the amount would be applied absent the signature of the owner. Stone Financial would further assert that they complied with the notification/correspondence that they provided to CNB. Stone Financial would conclude that their interest is superior to CNB because they in fact are not a purchase money mortgage and as such do not enjoy a super priority to them.

CNB would argue that because they paid off the first mortgage that they stand in the shoes of the first mortgage and that as such a substitute that they do enjoy a super priority and that their interest is superior to Stone Financial.

CNB would assert that the cover letter that accompanied the pay-off amount was a substitute to the requested signature and had greater force and authority than the statement Stone provided. CNB would offer Stone's action of cashing the check as agreement with the letter and acknowledgment of its effects.

Therefore, the likely ruling is that CNB would have a superior interest because they were able to step into the shoes of the first mortgage as a purchase money mortgage interest.

July 2009—Question 15

Mike and Kate went to MyBank in order to apply for a second mortgage on their home. On the loan application, Mike indicated that they were applying for a second mortgage and listed the name of their primary lender, Bank Zero. However, on some of the other relevant documents, Kate inadvertently forgot to disclose any information about their primary lender. During the application process, MyBank learned that Mike and Kate had just closed on their first mortgage during the preceding week, but that Bank Zero had not yet recorded its mortgage. Nevertheless, MyBank closed on their mortgage and recorded it on June 21, 2009. After firing about half of its staff and rehiring more competent employees, Bank Zero finally got around to recording its mortgage on June 23, 2009.

Although the extra cash flow from the second mortgage helped Mike and Kate stay afloat for a while, they began to sink further and further into debt. Eventually Mike and Kate defaulted on their mortgages to both MyBank and Bank Zero.

Discuss the relevant issues regarding the impending mortgage priority dispute between MyBank and Bank Zero, including your opinion on which bank has the superior lien. Explain your answer.

Model Answer to Question 15

"Michigan is a race-notice state, and owners of interests in land can protect their interests by properly recording those interests." *Richards v Tibaldi*, 272 Mich App 522 (2006), quoting *Lakeside Ass'n v Toski Sands*, 131 Mich App 292 (1983). A recorded instrument, such as a deed or mortgage, is considered "notice to all persons except the recorded landowner of the liens, rights, and interests acquired by or involved in the proceedings. All subsequent owners or encumbrances shall take subject to the perfected liens, rights, or interests." MCL 565.25(4). Pursuant to Michigan's recording statute, MCL 565.29, "the holder of a real estate interest who first records his interest generally has priority over subsequent purchasers." *Richards, supra* at 539.

It is clear from the facts above that although Bank Zero's mortgage was made first, MyBank's mortgage was recorded first. Therefore, MyBank's mortgage takes priority if MyBank is a good-faith purchaser who paid valuable consideration. There is no dispute that MyBank is a purchaser who paid valuable consideration, so the only question is whether MyBank is a purchaser in good faith.

A bona fide purchaser is a party who acquires an interest in real estate for valuable consideration and in good faith, without notice of a third party's claimed interest. *Richards, supra* at 539. Notice can be actual or constructive. *Richards, supra.* Constructive notice exists [w]hen a person has knowledge of such facts as would lead any honest man, using ordinary caution, to make further inquiries concerning the possible rights of another in real estate, and fails to make such inquiries. *Kastle v Clemons*, 330 Mich 28, 31 (1951). The relevant issues are whether the facts were sufficient to give rise to the need to make further inquiry and, if so, whether due diligence was exercised in making the inquiry. *American Fed S & L Ass'n v Orenstein*, 81 Mich App 249, 252 (1978).

As the facts indicate, Mike clearly disclosed the name of the primary lender on his application. This could be considered actual notice to MyBank. In the very least, it should have caused MyBank to make further inquiries concerning the possibility of a superior lien. Therefore, before MyBank executed its mortgage, it had constructive, if not actual, notice that its mortgage was intended to be subordinate to the one issued by Bank Zero. As such, MyBank is not a good-faith purchaser and Bank Zero's interests would be entitled to priority despite the fact that it did not record its mortgage first. ✓

Student Answer—July 2009

Question 15—Creditor's Rights—8 points

Mortgage Priority

In this case we start with who had priority. In general the 1st to record has priority over the others—so even though Bank Zero had 1st mortgage they *never recorded* their interest. So normally other mortgagors/creditors would not have notice and could become a *BFP*—bona fide purchaser. A BFP is ones who purchases *for value* but has *no notice* of earlier encumbrances and in MI a BFP must record 1st because this is a *race-notice state.* But the facts show "MyBank" was not a BFP because though they gave value (as the mortgagee for consideration) MyBank had notice of Bank Zero's prior interest. MyBank could say it did not have *actual notice* because Bank Zero didn't record but MyBank had *inquiry and constructive notice* because of what M & K put on their loan application. So even though MyBank recorded 1st they are not the BFP.

Also it must be noted that since BankZero has *already closed* then all other junior mortagors/liens and creditors' interest will get wiped out during foreclosure. So in my opinion Bank Zero has the superior lien because after foreclosure fees, attorney fees get paid off and after principal gets paid off then Bank Zero would be the first to get money. Since MI is a lien theory state, Bank Zero has a lien on M & K's property anyway. This means that once they foreclosed they now become the owners of property and so once MyBank took the 2nd mortgage they took it with all the *encumbrances attached* to it. So MyBank has a mortgage already on this property since they took subject to the Bank Zero's first mortgage, so again MyBank does not have a superior lien.

CLUSTER TWO

CONSTITUTIONAL LAW

Questions, Model Answers, and Student Answers

The following section includes prior Michigan Bar Exam questions and model answers for **Constitutional Law**. Many of the questions also include actual student answers with the amount of points that were earned to give you a better idea of what the graders expect. The student answers are immediately following the model answer for each question. Please pay close attention to the points received on each question. Although most samples represent "good" answers (i.e., received 8, 9, or 10 points), there are some samples that received 7 points (the minimum "passing" score for an essay), and a few that received very low scores to help you better understand the grading process and what is expected.

February 2001—Question 13

The City of Pleasantville had an ordinance that provided: "It shall be unlawful for a person to disturb the public peace and quiet by shouting, whistling, loud or vulgar conduct, or the playing of musical instruments, radios or other means of amplification, at any time or place so as to unreasonably annoy or disturb the quiet comfort and repose of persons in the vicinity."

It was a hot summer day, and Harry Stern, dressed in a t-shirt, cut-off shorts, and sandals, was walking on the sidewalk near a public park, reading a newspaper when he stepped in a large pile of dog manure. This diverted his attention from the comic section he was reading and he began a tirade at the "stupid *#*#* that let their dog *#*#* on the sidewalk" and that if he found the person who did this, he was going to "take their dog and *#*#*. They ought to have their *#*#* head examined."

While Harry wasn't yelling this loud enough so that everyone in the park heard him, Mary and Ruth Harris, two elderly sisters who were sitting on the park bench nearest Harry heard this outburst and reported Harry to the police. While Harry was busy washing his foot in the park fountain, he was approached by the officer who took the report from the sisters, and Harry was placed under arrest for violation of this ordinance.

Harry presents himself in your office and retains you to defend him on the charge of violating this ordinance. **Assuming for the purposes of this question that all of these facts can be proven and that Harry's language would be characterized as vulgar and offensive, what are the issues involved and the probable result?**

Model Answer to Question 13

The issue is whether this ordinance is unconstitutionally vague or overbroad and significantly compromises freedom of speech as found in the First Amendment, as applied to the states through the Fourteenth Amendment. Rules governing the construction of statutes apply with equal force to the interpretation of municipal ordinances. Perhaps the saving language of this ordinance is found in the phrase "to reasonably annoy or disturb," as this language has been interpreted as creating the reasonable personal standard. An ordinance is unconstitutional if it does not provide fair notice of the type of conduct prohibited, encourages subjective and discriminatory application by delegating to those empowered to enforce the ordinance the unfettered discretion to determine the ordinance has been violated.

The reasonable person standard that is found within this ordinance assures that a person of ordinary intelligence has a reasonable opportunity to know what is prohibited and serves to prevent any discriminatory or subjective application by police officers, judges, or juries. Certainly an argument could be made that the ordinance, by using the word "annoy" or "disturb" is overbroad, vague, and not subject to the reasonable person standard. What may annoy or disturb one person, does not necessarily annoy or disturb another; but the courts have held that the term "annoy" when coupled with the reasonable person standard is not unconstitutionally overbroad.

When considering this issue, the court should consider the realistic potential of the ordinance to chill constitutionally protected speech. Again, the insertion of the reasonable person standard saves the ordinance from this challenge. This standard precludes the application of the ordinance to speech, although vulgar and offensive, that is protected by the First and Fourteenth Amendments. An ordinance is presumed to be constitutional and will be construed as constitutional unless the parties challenging it clearly establish its unconstitutionality. This ordinance was designed to serve a legitimate and significant governmental interest of preserving the peace and quiet of the municipality and therefore is not unconstitutionally overbroad.

People of Plymouth Township v Hancock, 236 Mich App 197 (1999).

Student Answer—February 2001

Question 13—Con Law—8 points

Very similar to the famous MI case regarding a gentleman who was swearing in a canoe. Harry's case of being arrested for violation of the ordinance prohibiting a person from "disturbing" the public peace and quiet by shouting, whistling, loud or vulgar conduct, etc., presents the primary issue of one's constitutional right to free speech pursuant to the First Amendment. The First Amendment of the U.S. Constitution is applied to the states via the Due Process Clause of the 14th Amendment. Free speech is for the most part protected under the First Amendment; however, there are particular types of speech that receive greater or lesser protection from others. Being that the words used by Harry were &#, etc., we can assume they were swear words and probably quite vulgar in nature. Harmful and offensive language is not protected by the First Amendment.

Harmful and offensive varies and being that it was two elderly sisters who overheard Harry's words, harmful and offensive might be more broad than average. However, the court's use of reasonableness standard, what would be more broad than average. However, the courts use a reasonableness standard: what would be harmful or offensive to the reasonable person of ordinary providence, not one of the Harris' grandmas or a small child. The fact pattern states that Harry's words were not spoken loud enough to be heard by everyone in the park. However, the outburst/shouting of words was heard by the Harris sisters.

One can reasonably assume by the # of vulgar and offensive words used by Harry stepping in the dog manure that he meant to or intended to say the words as well. The issues involved center around free speech and the fact that Harry was in a traditional public forum, that being a public park, and that the laws of the constitution toddle down to even the local level making this ordinance applicable to Harry. This sort of activity would undergo the highest level of scrutiny, strict scrutiny, which may be difficult for the municipality to meet all prongs. The probable result is that Harry will not be convicted under this ordinance.

July 2001—Question 3

Jerry Slickcraft was a longtime Michigan state senator and was unable to run for office due to term limits. Many of his buddies were still in the legislature and Jerry formed a small, minimally capitalized, new company that used a combination of recycled tires, paper, and aluminum cans to make asphalt for highways. His was the only company in the country that manufactured asphalt with this composition. His friends in the legislature, at his request, passed a bill that imposed a 10% excise tax on all new asphalt to be applied to highways located in Michigan and excluded from this tax any asphalt manufactured using the combination of recycled tires, paper, and aluminum. Several manufacturers of asphalt fought the imposition of this tax as being unconstitutional but were unsuccessful in their efforts.

The state was prepared to award Jerry a large contract as the low bidder on a major interstate highway reconstruction project when CDE Asphalt, a large, multibillion-dollar, out-of-state corporation that provides asphalt throughout the United States, filed suit seeking an injunction and seeking to have the court determine that the tax was unconstitutional.

Directing your answer solely to the claim that the tax is unconstitutional, what is the constitutional issue that should be raised, and what do you anticipate the results of this complaint to be?

Model Answer to Question 3

The issue involved is whether the tax and its exemption violates the commerce clause found in US Const, Art 1, §8, Cl. 3. The commerce clause provides that "Congress shall have the power . . . to regulate commerce with foreign nations and among the several states." This provision has been interpreted as prohibiting the states from discriminating against interstate commerce (the dormant commerce clause). The Supreme Court has stated a cardinal rule of commerce clause jurisprudence is that "[no state, consistent with the commerce clause may, 'impose a tax which discriminates against interstate commerce . . . by providing a direct commercial advantage to local businesses.'" *Bacchus Imports, LTD v Dias*, 468 US 263, 268 (1984).

In this case, the statute is intended to, and does, provide a direct commercial advantage to local business, even though Slickcraft Asphalt is a small, newly formed corporation and may not pose a competitive threat to the large, multibillion-dollar, out-of-state corporation. The discrepancy of the size of the corporation does not save the tax from constitutional challenge. The Supreme Court held, "We need not know how unequal the tax is before concluding it is unconstitutionally discriminatory." *Bacchus, supra*, at 269, quoting *Maryland v Louisiana*, 451 US 725.

Student Answer—July 2001

Question 3—Constitutional Law—None Available

July 2002—Question 9

John Lewis was celebrating his 21st birthday by having a party at his second-story apartment. John had consumed an overabundance of alcohol and was undeniably intoxicated. John went out onto his balcony for a breath of fresh air and placed his hands on the top of the wood railing to take a deep breath. As he was exhaling, the railing collapsed due to rotten wood and poor installation. John fell off his balcony and landed on top of the railing, which landed on the concrete parking lot. John suffered fairly significant personal injuries. At the hospital where he was treated, blood was drawn and as a portion of the blood workup, his blood alcohol count was tested which registered at .23.

No one disputes the accuracy of this reading, the admissibility of this reading, or the fact that John was intoxicated. Nor is there any claim that John's intoxication was a proximate cause of the balcony railing failure or his fall.

John sued the owner of the apartment building whose sole defense was a statute that provided that anyone who was intoxicated, i.e., blood alcohol count of .10 or higher, who was injured at the time of intoxication, could not recover any monetary damages, regardless of liability as to how the injuries occurred. The defendant filed a Motion for Summary Disposition based on the statute, and John's attorney responded by claiming that this statute was unconstitutional.

What is the constitutional question that is involved? What argument will the parties present?

Model Answer to Question 9

The issues presented deal with equal protection and due process. US Const, Am XIV; MI const 1963, art 1, §2. The equal protection provision of the federal and state constitutions are co-extensive and the Michigan courts review due process claims similar to that of equal protection claims. There are three methods of review when the constitutionality of a statute is challenged for equal protection or due process, i.e., strict scrutiny, the traditional or rational basis test, or the intermediate scrutiny/ substantial relationship test.

This statute does not create a classification based upon suspect factors such as race or national origin where the court applies a high standard of review or strict scrutiny. This statute would probably be examined under the traditional or rational basis test as the statute is arguably related to a legitimate government purpose and/or socio-economic legislation. Under this test, the party claiming the statute to be unconstitutional must show that it is arbitrary and capricious and unrelated to a legitimate government purpose.

It would be argued by the plaintiff that this statute places all responsibility on intoxicated plaintiffs and relieves a tortfeasor from any liability to anyone deemed intoxicated. There is no sharing of fault or apportionment of liability. There is no rational relationship between the intoxication and the injury when the intoxication plays no role whatsoever in causing the injury. A person who is drinking but not intoxicated would potentially have a claim for injuries, even if he was partly at fault. To totally eliminate a claim because of intoxication would, as plaintiff would argue, deny him compensation without due process of law. Plaintiff would further argue a denial of equal protection as he is being treated differently than sober plaintiffs or plaintiffs who have been drinking even though there is no relationship between the drinking and the injury.

Plaintiff would claim that he cannot be deprived of compensation for his injuries without due process of law. There is no rational objective basis to deny compensation based upon a level of intoxication to one totally without fault who is injured by the negligence of another.

On the other hand, the defendant would argue that statutes are presumed to be constitutional and under the rational basis test, the courts will uphold the statutory classification where it is related to a legitimate government purpose. In Michigan, a plaintiff does not have a fundamental interest or substantial right in existing remedies, and is therefore not denied due process by this statute. Intoxicated persons do not meet the classification requirements for a strict scrutiny test and they are not of a protected class. Under the rational basis test, the statute is reasonably related to a legitimate government interest of increasing the responsibility of intoxicated individuals and discouraging such intoxication. Intoxication is recognized as a health and safety problem and a statute which discourages intoxication promotes the general health and welfare and is therefore rationally related to a legitimate government purpose.

The legislature can, for socioeconomic reasons and in the government interest, place full responsibility on any conduct of an intoxicated individual. There is a rational basis to bar intoxicated plaintiffs from recovery and require that all persons become personally responsible for the extent of their drinking. This purpose would serve a legitimate state interest and serve to defeat the argument that this statute is arbitrary and capricious.

Even though the statute does not bar recovery to injured plaintiffs who have been drinking a rationally based classification need not be precise in its classification nor is it void because it results in some unfairness. While the precision with which the line is drawn may appear somewhat arbitrary, if it is reasonably related to a legitimate government interest, it is not violative of equal protection. *See, Wysocki v Felt*, 248 Mich App 346 (2001).

Student Answer—July 2002

Question 9—Constitutional Law—7 points

John would want to argue that the statute violates his equal protection and substantive due process rights made applicable to the states via the 14th Amendment were violated.

The statute bars individuals, who have been injured due to their intoxication, from recovery of any monetary damages, regardless of liability. It leaves John with no adequate remedy for his injuries, nor does it provide any process for which John can turn to for recovery.

I would also argue that the statute is vague and overbroad and does not further any legitimate government interest.

> **Comment:** Although very brief, this answer nails the two issues tested, and therefore earned a passing score of 7 points. It demonstrates how important issue spotting is.

February 2003—Question 3

In 1997, after a nonjury trial, James Chick was convicted of a misdemeanor OUIL. Mr. Chick, who was indigent, represented himself at the trial, and after being convicted, his license was suspended and he was fined $350.00. In January 2001, Mr. Chick was charged and convicted in circuit court of felony drug charges. Appointed counsel represented Mr. Chick at all times in the circuit court case. When he was sentenced, the circuit judge added 24 months to the sentence on the basis of the misdemeanor conviction of OUIL. Mr. Chick's attorney objected to the addition of the 24 months to his sentence, claiming that the court could not consider the OUIL conviction for sentencing because an attorney did not represent Mr. Chick at the misdemeanor trial. **What is the Constitutional issue that is involved, what are the arguments for and against the use of the misdemeanor conviction to enhance the sentence, and what will be the probable decision?**

Model Answer to Question 3

The Sixth Amendment to the Constitution provides for the right to an attorney and has been applied to the states through the Fourteenth Amendment. Mr. Chick would argue that he is being imprisoned for a period of 24 months for a conviction that took place when he was not represented by counsel. He will argue that the imprisonment for this time period is a direct result of his conviction when unrepresented and that no person may be imprisoned for any offense unless he was represented by counsel at the trial. While not stated in the facts, an individual can waive his right to an attorney and if that occurs, there is no violation of the right to counsel. The facts are silent on whether there was a waiver. In this case, since the facts disclosed that there was no jail time imposed in the misdemeanor case, the courts have held that there was no right to an attorney in that case. Whether there was a waiver or not is immaterial based on the facts of this question.

The People will argue that due to the sentence in the misdemeanor offense, his constitutional right to an attorney was not violated. The Sixth Amendment only requires an attorney for a charge where incarceration results from a conviction. Although the circuit judge may not consider a defendant's prior misdemeanor conviction that was obtained without benefit of counsel or a valid waiver of the right to counsel, he may consider the conviction where there was no right to counsel because there was no incarceration. In the present case, Mr. Chick did have counsel in the felony trial and the sentence was for this conviction and the additional 24 months was simply an enhancement of the punishment for this conviction. The U.S. Supreme Court has upheld this type of sentencing enhancement in the case of *Nichols v United States*, 511 US 738 (1994).

Argersinger v Hamlin, 407 US 25 (1972) and *Alabama v Shelton*, 535 US 654 (2002).

Student Answer—February 2003

Question 3—Constitutional Law/Criminal Procedures—8 points

Issue

Was James entitled to an attorney in 1997?

Rule

An individual has a constitutional right to an attorney if the sentence that could potentially be imposed could place the individual in prison. Furthermore, an individual an indigent has a right to an attorney because they cannot afford one and this right will be imposed if the individual has a jury trial. You have a right to a jury trial if more than 6 months in prison.

Here, James may have been entitled to an attorney because he was indigent, however, he had a non-jury trial and he only had his license suspended and was fined $350. James served no time in jail for his misdemeanor OUIL.

In conclusion, in 1997 James would not have been entitled to an attorney.

Issue

What are the arguments for and against the use of the misdemeanor conviction to enhance the sentence?

Rule

A judge may enhance a sentence if they determine by preponderance of the evidence that there was a prior, similar charge that would constitute such an enhancement. Here, the misdemeanor conviction was for an OUIL, a drunk driving, and four years later an unrelated charge of felony drugs. Even though enhancing a sentence may be allowed, in this situation it seems evident that a judge will probably not legitimately be able to find a connection between the two convictions in order for an enhancement to be constitutional. To add an additional 2 years because of a drunk driving 4 years prior does not seem rationally related and most likely unconstitutional. In conclusion, the probable decision will be that in this situation the judge cannot enhance a sentence against James due to his previous misdemeanor OUIL.

July 2003—Question 11

Harold Bines had a very stormy marriage and even more turbulent divorce. During the divorce proceedings, the circuit court issued a civil personal protection order that prohibited Bines from coming onto the property where his wife lived, and from threatening or assaulting her. Several weeks after being served with this order, Bines came into her home, yelled at her that he was going to kill her, hit her with his fist, shoved her down the basement stairs and beat her head on the concrete floor until she was unconscious.

This resulted in a charge being issued by the court for criminal contempt and a two-day nonjury trial was conducted. At the trial, Mrs. Bines was required to prove that her husband knew of the civil protection order and that beyond a reasonable doubt he had committed an assault as defined by the state criminal code. At the trial, his divorce attorney represented Mr. Bines and Mr. Bines testified and admitted that he knew of the order but denied assaulting his wife, claiming she must have just fallen down the steps. The court found that beyond a reasonable doubt a criminal assault had occurred and sentenced Mr. Bines to the maximum penalty of one year in jail.

Shortly after this trial and conviction, the county prosecuting attorney filed charges against Mr. Bines of assault with intent to murder. These charges arose out of the same incident from which Mr. Bines had been convicted and sentenced. The maximum penalty for a conviction of this offense was life, or any term of years. MCL 750.83.

Mr. Bines retained a different attorney to represent him on these new charges. His attorney advised him not to worry since this charge was going to have to be dismissed because to try him on this charge would violate his constitutional rights.

What right is Mr. Bines' attorney referring to, where is it found in the U.S. Constitution, and is the attorney correct in this analysis? Discuss and decide.

Model Answer to Question 11

Mr. Bines's attorney is referring to the double jeopardy provision of the U.S. Constitution. This provision is found in the Fifth Amendment and is applied to the states via the Fourteenth Amendment. The protection afforded by the Double Jeopardy Clause provides that no "person shall be subject for the same offense to be twice put in jeopardy of life or limb." This clause protects against the successive punishments and successive prosecutions for the same criminal offense. Criminal contempt that is enforced through non-summary proceedings is considered a crime in the ordinary sense and the Double Jeopardy Clause applies to such proceedings.

The test to determine if the two charges can survive a double jeopardy challenge is the "same element" test. This test looks at whether each offense contains an element not contained in the other, and if not, they are the same offense within the meaning of the Double Jeopardy Clause. Even though the same conduct is the subject of the charge, the U.S. Supreme Court has overruled the "same conduct" test as a consideration in deciding double jeopardy issues.

In this case there are different elements in the two charges. In the assault with intent to kill, the element of intent is present and it is not present in the criminal contempt charge. Likewise, in the criminal contempt charge, an element of that charge was that Mr. Bines had knowledge of the personal protection order and that is not an element in the subsequent charge.

The lawyer for Mr. Bines correctly identified the issue, but is wrong in the analysis of the issue.

United States v Dixon, 509 US 688.

Two Student Answers—July 2003

Question 11—Constitutional Law—7 points

Mr. Bine's Attorney is referring to the Constitutional Right of Double Jeopardy. This right prohibits the government for trying a Defendant twice for the same crime, which was only committed once. The Double Jeopardy clause is applicable to the states via the 14th amendment of the constitution.

In this case, Bines was tried for "assault as defined by the state criminal code". He was also convicted of this crime. The Prosecutor now wants to charge Mr. Bine's w/ Assault with intent to Murder. Under The Federal Constitution, this would be permissible because even though the crimes are similar, there is an additional Element of intent to Murder. This means that assault and assault with intent to murder are not the same crime and thus, Double Jeopardy would not attach under the Federal Constitution.

However, in Michigan, there is a narrower construction of Double Jeopardy. The prosecutor must charge the Defendant with all the possible crimes the first time or otherwise Double Jeopardy attaches to the crimes that were charged. In this case, the prosecution could have charged Bines with "assault with Intent to commit murder". However, the Prosecutor in the facts did not do this. The Prosecutor only charged Bines with the lesser included offense of Assault. Prosecutor could have charged Both Assault and Assault with intent to commit murder because they are 2 separate crimes, assault w/intent to murder has the specific intent of intending to murder the victim, which must be proven by the Prosecutor beyond a reasonable doubt. Moreover, the Prosecutor had the facts in the problem to back up the higher charge—defy personal protection order and throwing victim down the stairs—those two facts could have maintained a conviction of Assault w/intent to Murder.

Conclusion. Under Fed law, there is not Double Jeopardy, and Bines could be charged w/assault with intent to commit murder.

However, this was a Michigan Court Trial, and since Prosecutor did not charge Bines w/assault with intent to murder the first time, Double Jeopardy bars the prosecution of Bines because of Double Jeopardy, which is narrower in construction under the laws of Michigan than the Federal government.

Question 11—Constitutional Law—7 points

The right Mr. Bine's attorney is referring to is the right against double jeopardy which is found in the 6th amendment to the U.S. Constitution and is applicable to the states via the 14th Amendment. The right against double jeopardy states that defendant cannot be convicted or held twice in jeopardy for the same crime.

In determining whether two crimes are different we use the Blockburger test. This test states that if one offense requires an element to be proven that the other offense does not, then they are different crimes and can be separately prosecuted. On these facts, Bines was first convicted of criminal assault. The second set of charges filed against Bines was for assault with the intent to commit murder. State will argue that these are two separate offenses because the second charge required the prosecution to prove that Bines had the specific intent to commit murder in addition to the elements of assault. Therefore, they should be able to prosecute him for the second charge. Bines on the other hand, will argue that these two offenses are the same because the second charge had arisen out of the same incident from which he was first charged and convicted. Furthermore, there was a final conviction on the merits.

Comment: This is a good answer, but the student incorrectly stated that the Double Jeopardy Clause was in the 6th Amendment instead of the 5th Amendment.

February 2004—Question 15

In 1999, William Varius had been married to Helen Varius for over five years. William had a "spotty" employment record and supplemented his income by robbing 7-11 stores. William became so successful at this that he became known as the "7 come 11 bandit". The police had few clues and instituted a public campaign for someone to come forward with information on the bandit. Helen became suspicious over time concerning the amount of money William had to spend when he never held a steady job. Finally, in June 1999, she confronted William with the source of these funds and he told her "You have been reading about me for months." William went on to relate to his wife how he surveyed the stores for weeks at a time to determine when they would have the fewest customers and how he would change his appearance for each robbery.

Helen was disenchanted with her life with William and this was the final blow. She filed for divorce and it was granted in April 2000. In October 2000, the legislature amended the statute that provided "a married person or a person that has been married previously shall not be examined as to any communication made between that person and his or her spouse or former spouse during the marriage." The amended statute provided that the decision whether to testify about marital communications lies with the person testifying.

The police had been suspicious of William for some time, but could never obtain any concrete evidence. After the divorce, in early 2001, they approached Helen concerning any information that she may have. She proved to be a willing witness and with her testimony and other circumstantial evidence, William was charged with a series of the 7-11 robberies.

At the time of trial, William's attorney objected to Helen testifying about any statements William made to Helen during their marriage. It is contended that this change in the law violates the prohibition of *ex post facto* law.

Where is the prohibition of *ex post facto* laws found? What is an *ex post facto* law? What would be the argument for and against this statute constituting an *ex post facto* law? What do you believe would be the ultimate decision of the courts?

Model Answer to Question 15

The prohibition of *ex post facto* laws is found in the US Constitution, Art 1, §10, cl 1 and the Michigan Constitution, Art 1, §10. An *ex post facto* law has been defined as "Every law that makes an action done before the passing of the law, and which was innocent when done, criminal; and punishes such action. Every law that aggravates a crime, or makes it greater than it was, when committed. Every law that changes the punishment, and inflicts a greater punishment, than the law annexed to the crime, when committed. Every law that alters the legal rules of evidence, and receives less, or different, testimony, than the law required at the time of the commission of the offense (sic) in order to convict the offender." *Carnell v Texas*, 529 US 513; 146 L Ed 2d 577; 120 S Ct 1620 (2000), citing *Calder v Bull*, 3 US 386, 390.

The argument for the defendant would be that this law changes the rule of evidence and permits different testimony for the conviction which testimony was not admissible at the time the offense was committed. A law that reduces the quantum of evidence required to convict is *ex post facto*. A law that retroactively eliminates an element of the offense, increases the punishment for an existing offense, or lowers the burden of proof is an *ex post facto* law.

In this case, all the statute does is to permit the admission of evidence that was not admissible at the time of the offense. This does not alter or lower the burden of proof or reduce the quantum evidence necessary to convict. The statute only removes an existing restriction upon the competency of certain persons as witnesses. This relates to procedure rather than substance and the state can regulate the procedure at its pleasure.

For these reasons this law would be found not to be violative of the prohibition against *ex post facto* laws. *See People v Dolp-Hostettler, Lawyers Weekly* 07-48860.

Student Answer—July 2004

Question 15—Constitutional Law—None Available

February 2005—Question 10

Defendant James Lawless broke into the home of Michael Ford armed with a gun and threatened to shoot and kill Mr. Ford if he didn't lead him to his safe in the basement and give him the contents. Mr. Ford led Lawless into the basement, opened the safe, and gave Lawless $3,500 located in the safe as well as a great deal of valuable jewelry. Lawless was ultimately arrested and tried on multiple criminal counts. Lawless was convicted of armed robbery and safe robbery and was sentenced to 15 to 40 years imprisonment for the armed robbery conviction and 7½ years to 40 years on the safe robbery conviction.

For the purposes of this question, the pertinent language of the armed robbery statute provides that: "a person who in the course of committing a larceny of any money or other property and in the course of engaging in that conduct, possesses a dangerous weapon is guilty of a felony punishable by imprisonment for life or for any term of years."

For the purposes of this question, the pertinent language of the bank, safe, and vault robbery statute provides: "Any person who, with intent to commit the crime of larceny, or any felony shall threaten to kill or shall put in fear any person for the purpose of stealing from any . . . safe or other depository of money or other valuables shall be guilty of a felony punishable by imprisonment in the state prison for life or any term of years."

On appeal, Lawless claims that the conviction and sentences for both armed robbery and safe robbery violated his constitutional rights. **What constitutional right is Lawless referring to, and is he correct in this assertion? Why or why not?**

Model Answer to Question 10

The issue that should be raised is whether the convictions and sentences for armed robbery and safe robbery violate provisions of the Federal or Michigan constitutions prohibiting multiple punishment for the same offense.

The Double Jeopardy Clause of the United States Constitution is found in the Fifth Amendment and applies to the states through the Fourteenth Amendment. The Michigan Constitution has essentially the same prohibition at Art 1, §15.

The purposes of double jeopardy protections against successive prosecutions for the same offense are to preserve the finality of judgments in criminal prosecutions and to protect the defendant from prosecutorial overreaching. The purpose of the double jeopardy protection against multiple punishments for the same offense is to protect the defendant from having more punishment imposed than the legislature intended.

In this case, since there was a single trial the issue would be whether the two convictions involve the same offense and violate the prohibition against multiple punishments for the same offense. The statute dealing with the robbery of a safe is intended to protect structures intentionally constructed to protect valuables while the armed robbery statute is intended to protect persons from assaultive taking by means of a dangerous weapon.

The statute dealing with larceny from a safe requires for its violation the intent to access a safe. It does not require that the offender be armed with a weapon. The focus of the armed robbery is on the person being assaulted with a weapon.

The two statutes each contain elements not contained in the other. The armed robbery statute does not contain an element of intent to steal property from a safe. These were two separate and distinct offenses. When the defendant threatened to kill Michael if he didn't go and open the safe, the violation of the "safe" statute was complete. The violation of the armed robbery statute was not completed until Michael, after threats of death by shooting, opened the safe, and defendant took the money and jewelry.

These were separate offenses and sentencing the defendant on both of these convictions did not violate the double jeopardy rights of the defendant. *People v Ford*, 262 Mich App 443 (2004).

Credit can be given to the applicant if there is a discussion of the "social norms" test as discussed in *People v Robideau*, 419 Mich 458 (1984). This test requires the court to identify the type of harm the legislature was intending to prevent and where two statutes prohibit violations of the same social norm generally the legislature did not intend separate punishments. While these statutes do not appear to be of this type, extra credit should be given for a discussion of this issue.

Student Answer—February 2005

Question 10—Constitutional Law—8 points

The Constitutional Right that Lawless is referring to is the Double Jeopardy Clause of the U.S. Constitution. This clause is implied to the States via the Fourteenth Amendment of the U.S. Constitution.

Double Jeopardy is the right of an accused not to be tried twice for the same crime. The reason for this clause/right is to protect the defendant from undo harassment, unnecessary expenses, inconvenience, embarrassment, etc. In order for the crime to apply the defendant must have been through a conviction or an acquittal and is being tried again. There are exceptions to the double jeopardy clause when 1) two states try the defendant, 2) the state + federal government, 3) mistrial due to the defendant's reasons, etc.

None of these exceptions apply here. However, the test used to apply the double jeopardy doctrine is of the same crime and the elements test is used to see if it is the same crime.

Here, the defendant James is charged for armed robbery and safe robbery. We need to check the elements of each crime to determine if both charges contain the same elements and therefore the double jeopardy clause will apply. Here, although two robbery charges one for armed and one for safe they have different elements. The robbery elements are larceny elements such as the trespassory taking of the personal property of another with the intent to permanently deprive the owner of his/her property, plus for robbery the taking from the person or the person's presence with force or an apprehension of force or bodily injury. For armed robbery we need an additional element that the force must be by a dangerous weapon. The safe requires under the statute to be larceny from a safe or deposition of money.

Both crimes[s] have the same elements of larceny however, not both require to have dangerous or deadly weapons. Therefore, the armed robbery is a different crime from the crime of safe robbery because the crimes require different elements.

Also, here Lawless may be charged for burglary. Finally, under Michigan law when a statute specifically makes a crime that requires a separate sentencing must be respected. Here, the legislation has created the bank, safe, + vault robbery statute that make this larceny type of a crime as a separate + different crime, the safe crime. Therefore, since the two crimes do not require the same elements Lawless was not tried twice for the same crime. Therefore, the double jeopardy clause of the U.S. Constitution does not apply. Both convictions will stand.

July 2005—Question 12

The state of Michigan has a statute that provides that a district judge, in order to preserve the public peace, could, after a hearing, require a person to post a bond to conserve the peace as required by the laws of the state. The statute provided that the court could require security for up to two years, incarcerate an individual for the period for failure to provide the ordered security or for violation of the provisions of the bond. Provisions were made for a hearing to determine if the individual could afford to post security and provided various criteria for the court to follow concerning this issue. The statute further provided that upon receipt of a complaint under oath that a person has threatened to commit an offense against the person or property of another, the court was to examine the complainant under oath and any witnesses before ordering any bond be posted.

John Jones filed a written complaint under oath against his next door neighbor William Strange, concerning a long-standing dispute the two were involved in concerning a joint driveway. Jones' complaint alleged that Strange told him that if Jones left his car in the driveway again, Jones "would never park that car in the driveway again." Jones claimed that this was a threat to both himself and his car, and asked the court to require Strange to post security to insure that nothing was done to injure his car or himself. Strange appeared at the hearing and did not deny making the statement, did not contest his ability to pay for a bond, but stated he did not violate any statute, and argued the court had no authority to require any bond under these circumstances. The court was not impressed with the Strange argument and ordered that he post a bond of $25,000 to be in effect for two years in order to preserve the public peace. Failure to post the bond would result in Strange being incarcerated for up to two years or until the bond was posted.

Strange consulted you concerning an immediate appeal. What constitutional issues do you believe should be raised, and why? What do you believe will be the probable result?

Model Answer to Question 12

An issue that should be presented is whether the statute is unconstitutionally vague and in violation of the Due Process Clause of the 14th Amendment. Statutes are presumed constitutional, and "courts have a duty to construe a statute as constitutional unless unconstitutionality is clearly apparent. A statute may be unconstitutionally vague if: (1) it does not provide fair notice of the conduct proscribed; (2) it confers on the trier of fact unstructured and unlimited discretion to determine whether an offense has been committed; and (3) its coverage is overly broad and impinges on First Amendment freedoms." Vagueness challenges not involving First Amendment freedoms are analyzed in light of the facts of the particular case. *In re Gosnell*, 234 Mich App 326 (1999).

From the language provided in this question, it could be argued that the phrase "conserve the peace" fails to provide fair notice regarding the prohibited conduct. There was no definition or description within the language of the statute of conduct that constituted a breach of the peace. The Michigan Court of Appeals has held that the second portion of the statute that provides "to commit an offense against the person or property of another" gives adequate notice of the prohibited conduct. This was interpreted to involve some threat of personal violence and that a person of ordinary intelligence is provided a reasonable opportunity to know what is prohibited. The statue itself is not void for vagueness.

Another issue that is present is whether the statute violates due process by allowing the district judge to impose a sentence in excess of one year, which is the district courts' jurisdictional limit. The Michigan Court of Appeals has approved such a sentence on the basis that the duty to keep the peace is separate and distinct from the performance of ordinary judicial functions. The Michigan Constitution provides and requires such judges to be conservators of the peace and, based upon this authority, the court can sentence under such a statute beyond the one-year period.

It is not necessary for the applicant to address the above issue to obtain a passing grade, but if this issue is addressed, extra credit should be given. Likewise, since the question specifically is limited to constitutional issues, no credit should be given for any discussion of the burden of proof and whether the court was factually correct in its decision.

Student Answer—July 2005

Question 12—Constitutional Law—7 points

The issue is what constitutional issue has been violated.

Strange will argue that his *due process rights* have been violated. There is a due process violation when a person's life, liberty, or property rights have been taken away/ violated. Strange will argue that his *procedural due process* rights were violated. The statute provided that the court was to examine the complaint and any witnesses before ordering any bond be posted. Here, Strange appeared at the hearing but the court did not listen to his arguments and immediately ordered bond in the amount of $25,000. Strange will argue that he did not receive his fair day in court. Strange will also argue that the court did not determine whether he could post the bond. It was simply post the bond or be incarcerated for up to 2 years.

Based on these facts, Strange will probably win his argument that he did not receive his fair day in court and therefore his procedural due process rights were violated.

Strange will also likely argue that there was no rational basis for this statute. Requiring someone to post bond or be incarcerated does not serve a rational relationship to preserving the public peace.

The state will argue that there is a rational relationship between the statute and preserving the peace. They will argue that if people know the repercussions, they will be less likely to breach the peace. Strange will also argue that this statute is *vague* and overbroad. A statute which is vague and overbroad on its face is per se unconstitutional.

Strange will probably win this argument because it is very vague on many levels. It does not name any certain offenses, only says commits an offense, it also does not list the criteria that the court must follow.

It is most likely that the Court of Appeals will find that this statute is vague and overbroad and therefore per se unconstitutional. Therefore, Strange should not be required to post a bond of $25,000 or be incarcerated for up to 2 years.

February 2006—Question 12

Carl Petterson was a close friend of Joseph Deer. Joseph had been arrested by City Police Department and during the arrest, Joseph was beaten quite badly. The criminal charge against Joseph was dismissed in motion, and Joseph then sued City on a variety of claims.

At a motion in the civil case, Carl showed up in court to show his support of his friend Joseph. Carl wore a tee shirt and on the front there was large lettering that stated "Kourts, Kops = Krooks and Injustice." Presiding Judge Battle took one look at the tee shirt and told Carl to remove the shirt, cover it up, or leave the courtroom. Carl politely declined and told Judge Battle he was exercising his constitutional rights. Judge Battle again told Carl to remove the shirt and this time told him if he refused to remove the shirt or himself from the court, he would be held in contempt. Carl again stated he was only exercising his constitutional rights and refused to remove the shirt or leave the courtroom. Judge Battle ordered Carl arrested for contempt and placed in jail for 10 days.

Carl spent the 10 days in jail and subsequently filed an appeal seeking to have the finding of contempt reversed. **Without regard to whether this appeal is moot, what constitutional rights and issues are involved, and was the trial court correct in its decision? Explain why.**

Model Answer to Question 12

The First Amendment of the United States Constitution provides, "Congress shall make no law . . . abridging the freedom of speech." US Const, Am I. The analogous provision in the Michigan constitution provides that "[e]very person may freely speak, write, express, and publish his views on all subjects, being responsible for the abuse of such right; and no law shall be enacted to restrain or abridge the liberty of speech or of the press." Const 1963, art I, §5.

Speech or expression that is restricted because of the content of the message it conveys is subject to the most exacting scrutiny. The content of speech in a courtroom may only be restricted if it constitutes an imminent threat to the administration of justice. The danger must not be remote or even probable; it must immediately imperil the administration of justice.

Even though the message on the shirt criticized the integrity of the court and one of the parties involved, the shirt was being worn during a motion and did not affect any party's right to a fair trial. Carl was not disturbing the proceedings and there was no jury present that would be influenced by the shirt. Therefore, there was no serious or imminent threat to the administration of justice and no compelling state interest was served by requiring appellant to remove his shirt or leave the courtroom. The shirt and the statement it made or the refusal to remove it or leave the courtroom did not constitute criminal contempt. *In re Contempt of Dudzinski*, 257 Mich App 96 (2003).

Student Answer—February 2006

Question 12—Constitutional Law—None Available

July 2006—Question 3

Andrea Molson is a Michigan Court of Appeals judge who, at 69 years old, is healthy, both physically and mentally. Judge Molson is considering a run for reelection to the Court of Appeals. She will turn 70 years old two weeks before the election. The Michigan Constitution contains a provision that "no person shall be elected or appointed to a judicial office after reaching the age of 70 years." This provision would prevent Judge Molson from being reelected.

You are the law clerk for Judge Molson. Draft a memorandum to her addressing the merits of a challenge to the state constitutional provision.

Model Answer to Question 3

This question addresses the Equal Protection Clause. Under the Fourteenth Amendment, no state shall "deny to any person . . . the equal protection of the law." The state constitutional provision at issue, Mich Const, art 6, section 19, is similar to a mandatory retirement provision that the United States Supreme Court held did not violate the Equal Protection Clause in *Gregory v Ashcroft*, 501 US 453; 111 S Ct 2395; 115 L Ed 2d 410 (1991). The Gregory case addressed a provision of the Missouri Constitution that states that "all judges other than municipal judges shall retire at the age of 70 years."

1. The provision makes a classification based on age, which the United States Supreme Court has repeatedly held is not a suspect classification under the Equal Protection Clause. Therefore, the appropriate standard of review is the "rational basis test." *Id.*

2. In cases where the classification burdens neither the suspect class nor a fundamental interest, courts are reluctant to overturn government action on the grounds that it denies equal protection of the laws. In this case, the government action is a constitutional provision—reflecting the judgment of the state legislature that proposed it as well as that of the Michigan citizens who voted for it.
3. Under the rational basis test, the provision will not be overturned "unless the varying treatment of different groups or persons is so unrelated to the achievement of legitimate purposes that we can only conclude that the [people's] actions were irrational." *Id.* In *Gregory*, the Supreme Court found that the state of Missouri had a legitimate—compelling—interest in maintaining a judiciary capable of performing the demanding tasks that judges must perform. The court found the mandatory retirement provision to be rationally related to the interest, noting that physical and mental capacity can diminish with age.
4. The fact that Judge Molson herself is physically and mentally fit is not sufficient to nullify the provision. A state does not violate the Equal Protection Clause merely because the classifications made by its laws are flawed.

The person challenging the provision must show that the facts on which the classification is based could not reasonably be construed as legitimate by the decision maker.

Two Student Answers—July 2006

Question 3—Constitutional Law—9 points

Standing
In order to bring a claim the plaintiff must have standing to bring the claim. Standing means that there is an actual or threat of impending harm, causation means there is a casual connection between the harm to the person who is acting and the government and redressibliliy, meaning if the plaintiff receives what they ask for the harm will cease. Also the law suit must be ripe meaning there is an actual harm or immediate threat of harm. In this case Molson has standing because she wanted to run for re-election. However she will not be able to under present statute because she will be seventy. She would be suing on the unconstitutionality of the statute and if it was repealed she would be able to run.

Equal Protection
The equal protection clause of the 14th Amendment as applied to the states protects people from laws that are discriminatory against certain people. There are three levels of scrutiny. Strict scrutiny which involves state discrimination of aliens, race/origin which the government must prove a substantial & compelling interest for the law to be valid. Intermediate scrutiny which is gender discrimination & legitimacy where government must show that the act of law is reasonably related to a legitimate governmental interest. Rational basis which applies to everything else. Here plaintiff must show that the law is not rationally related to an impartial government interest. Molson would have the burden of proving that the law discriminating on age was not rationally related to an impartial government interest. Because rational basis scrutiny is the lowest level of scrutiny it will be hard for her to prove this. As long

as the government has some sort of important interest the law will be upheld. Some potential government interests are having to elect new judges during the term due to death because of old age. The court will have to decide this; however, the law will probably be upheld.

Question 3—Constitutional Law—8 points

TO: Judge
FROM: Law Clerk

Age Discrimination

Judge, under the 14th Amend, the statutes that discriminate against certain classes of people are judged under various degrees of scrutiny. There is strict scrutiny if the state statute discriminates against race, & fundamental right. Intermediate if the discrimination is based on gender & illegitimacy. Finally there is rational basis if the discrimination is based on a non suspect class, such as age. In rational basis, the plaintiff must prove the statute is not rationally related to a legitimate state interest.

Here, the statute prohibits any person from reaching the age of 70 from being elected or appointed to a judicial office. So, since the statutes involves age—non suspect class. We must find a non rationally related reason. This will be difficult because the state will say that as people get older their mental facilities start to fail. Judges must always be alert. And even though there may be a few judges who can function of 70 years old, the few individual harm does not outweigh the state's interest in ensuring that the judiciary is in good physical & mental health. Therefore, judge, you will not be able to overcome the burden of proving that the statute is not rationally related to a legitimate state interest.

February 2007—Question 13

From 2000-2003, several Fortune 500 companies opened offices in Michigan, which attracted many individuals who were seeking work to move to Michigan from other states. Established Michigan residents feared that the new arrivals could influence elections and impose their preferences on all Michigan citizens.

In January 2004, the Michigan Legislature enacted the Michigan Well-Informed Voter Act. The Act provides: "An individual may not vote in a Michigan state election until the individual has resided in the state for more than one year." According to the Michigan Legislature, this provision will help to insure that only "well-informed voters" cast ballots.

After the Legislature adopted the Michigan Well-Informed Voter Act in 2004, a number of new Michigan residents organized a picket line to protest its enactment. A peaceful protest occurred in Lansing, on February 2, 2004. Protesters formed a picket line on a Lansing public sidewalk that was located about 100 yards from the State of Michigan Capitol Building. The protesters were arrested for violating Lansing Municipal Ordinance 605. The ordinance prohibits "all organized demonstrations within 500 yards of the state capitol, except for peaceful labor picketing."

1. **Analyze and discuss whether the Michigan Well-Informed Voter Act violates the United States Constitution.**

2. Analyze and discuss whether Lansing Municipal Ordinance 605 violates the United States Constitution.

Model Answer to Question 13

(1)(A) Right to Vote: This question addresses the Equal Protection Clause. Under the Fourteenth Amendment no state shall "deny to any person . . . the equal protection of the law." Applied to the states, the Fourteenth Amendment is the "vehicle" for extending constitutional safeguards.

The Equal Protection Clause is implicated when the state decides to treat people differently. For most types of regulation—economic, business and general regulatory—differences are tested under the rational basis test, requiring "any rational reason" from the state. Under the rational basis test, the petitioner must prove that the law lacks a rational basis and is unrelated to any legitimate objective.

For fundamental rights and protections the state is subject to a higher burden to justify any regulations. This burden is known as "strict scrutiny" and requires regulation to be narrowly tailored and necessary for a compelling government interest. The government must prove that the law is necessary to achieve a compelling interest.

The state of Michigan has acted in a way to implicate the Fourteenth Amendment by creating a residency rule requiring one-year residency before voting in state elections. The interest it cites is a valid one, insuring that only "well-informed" voters vote. However, residency rules concerned with the fundamental right of voting for this purpose are subject to review under the strict scrutiny standard. While the interest may be "compelling," the Michigan Well-Informed Voter Act is not narrowly tailored. Indeed, the act does not guarantee that any voter who has resided in Michigan for more than one year will be "well-informed." The mere act of living in a place for a period does not guarantee that the resident will be a "well-informed voter." The act is not narrowly tailored and necessary to meet its stated objective. In fact, the act is premised on the fear of Michigan long time residents that new residents could "influence elections." The Constitution and courts seek to protect the right to vote, that is, the right to "influence elections." In short, the act is unconstitutional.

(B) Right to travel: Besides the right to vote, the act may have the effect of hindering the right of Michigan's citizens to travel (and live and work) across state lines. Individuals have the right to move from one state to another, and state laws that have the effect of hindering this right will require a strong government justification.

(2)(A) Free Speech—Public Forum: The First Amendment (and Fourteenth Amendment applied to the states) restricts most forms of "content control" for speech. Unless speech is "less protected" because it is commercial (intermediate) or unprotected (fighting words, incitement to violence), content controls are presumed invalid.

Even in public forums though, time, place and manner (TPM) restrictions are allowed, as long as they are content and viewpoint neutral, leave alternative opportunities for the speech to take place, and are narrowly tailored to serve a significant state interest. If the sidewalk near the Capitol is a public forum, then the Lansing ordinance is unconstitutional. Public forums are those public areas traditionally set aside for exercise of First Amendment rights.

As a public forum, no content or viewpoint restrictions are allowed. The subject ordinance allows "peaceful labor picketing" within 500 yards, but no other groups. The ordinance in effect grants one group privileges over other groups.

Even as a TPM regulation, this law is questionable. It can be argued that 500 yards from the Capitol is a great distance, and that protestors from more than 500 yards away might not be noticed. While restrictions on noise may be reasonable, the 500-yard distance is questionable under the TPM reasonable restriction test.

(B) Free Speech—Nonpublic forum: Nonpublic forums may regulate by content, but not viewpoint. Although this ordinance does not provide explicitly that some groups may not protest, that is what is implied. Thus, even as a nonpublic forum, this law is questionable under the TPM reasonableness test because it is not viewpoint neutral. It can be argued that Lansing's ordinance violates the Constitution.

Student Answer—February 2007

Question 13—Con Law—8 points

1. The Due Process clause of the 5th Amendment to the U.S. Constitution as applied to the States through the due process clause of the 14th Amendment provides that no citizen shall be deprived "due process of law." "Due process" has evolved into specific fundamental rights of citizens subject to a strict scrutiny level of review where the state gov't bears the burden of proof that the statute affecting the fundamental right is necessary to achieve a compelling state interest. One specific fundamental right is the right to interstate travel. This right includes the right to be treated the same as all other citizens of a state—regardless of whether a person's recently relocate to the state or not. The fundamental right to interstate travel is therefore evoked when a state imposes certain durational, residency requirement to receive "benefits" from the state. Certain *limited* durational residency requirements may e OK to acclimate a new state citizen to a state's rules and requirements.

The statute in these facts is unconstitutional because of its "more than one year" durational residency requirement. The state will be unable to prove that this statute is *necessary* for a compelling interest as the only interest advanced is to favor the political views of those "long-term" Michigan residents. On the other hand, a "30-day" statute may have been ok.

2. The Lansing ordinance is also unconstitutional as it violates an individual's First Amendment free speech rights. Any regulation affecting "speech" in a public forum must be content-neutral, narrowly tailored to a substantial interest, and leave open alternative channels of communication. Additionally, regulations may be unconstitutional because they're vague or overbroad, by either not giving a citizen adequate notice of what conduct is prohibited or by restricting constitutionally protected speech.

Under the facts, a sidewalk—public sidewalk—is a public forum subject to the above rules. The ordinance is not narrowly tailored as it likely restricts constitutionally protected speech by prohibiting "all organized demonstrations." The regulation is also content-based—as an exception is made for *labor picketing*—but no other kind of picketing.

July 2007—Question 8

In 2002, the SuperHealthAddsMagic Mineral (SHAM) was discovered. SHAM erases fine lines and wrinkles, removes middle-aged spread and stray hairs, and has been scientifically proven to add 10 years to a user's life. In those states where SHAM is plentiful, companies began manufacturing processed SHAM and making it available to consumers through direct shipping from the plant via telephone or Internet orders placed by the consumer.

In 2003, SHAM was found in the soil around the Detroit River. Scot and Kelly Zug saw an opportunity to profit from the SHAM market, so they formed a processing plant and a distribution company in Michigan to sell SHAM. They packaged and sold their processed SHAM product as "REAL SHAM" ("RS").

Scot and Kelly convinced the Michigan Legislature to enact a law prohibiting the import of SHAM products into the state. The purpose of the law was to encourage Michigan consumers to buy Michigan products.

Marilyn Mature ("MM") decided to order some SHAM products via the Internet. She found Scot and Kelly's RS product online, but after researching all of the SHAM websites, found one in Alabama with discounted prices on its own SHAM product. MM placed her order online with the Alabama company, called AlabamaShama ("AS"), only to be told that Michigan state law precludes direct shipment of out-of-state SHAM.

Marilyn Mature and AlabamaShama contact you, a licensed Michigan attorney, to find out if there is any way to challenge the Michigan law. What would you advise? Discuss all issues that are presented.

Model Answer to Question 8

Standing is found when: (1) the plaintiff suffers an injury in fact, that is concrete and specific to the plaintiff, (2) the harm is "fairly traceable" to the government's action, and (3) the court has redress to remedy the injury.

Marilyn Mature is a Michigan resident who seeks to purchase the banned product. MM suffers an injury in fact—the inability to buy the product she wants to buy—and the harm is traceable to Michigan's law barring SHAM imports. M has standing. AlabamaShama is a corporation wishing to sell its SHAM product in Michigan but suffers an injury in fact—AS is prohibited from selling its product due to the Michigan law. AS likewise has standing.

The Commerce Clause precludes any state from imposing laws that pose an undue burden on interstate commerce or prevents the free flow of interstate commerce. In *Granholm v Heald*, 544 US 460, 472 (2005), the Court stated:

> Time and again this Court has held that, in all but the narrowest circumstances, state laws violate the Commerce Clause if they mandate 'differential treatment of in-state and out-of-state economic interests that benefits the former and burdens the latter.' *Oregon Waste Systems, Inc v Department of Environmental Quality of Ore*, 511 US 93, 99 (1994). See also *New Energy Co of Ind v Limbach*, 486 US 269, 274 (1988) . . . The mere fact of nonresidence should not foreclose a producer in one State from access to markets in other States. *HP Hood & Sons Inc v Du Mond*, 336 US 525, 539 (1949).

"State laws that discriminate against interstate commerce face 'a virtually *per se* rule of invalidity.'" *Heald*, p 47, quoting *Philadelphia v New Jersey*, 437 US 617, 624 (1978). *Heald*, p 489, also stated "we still must consider whether either State regime 'advances a legitimate local purpose that cannot be adequately served by reasonable nondiscriminatory alternatives.'" The burden is on the state:

> Our Commerce Clause cases demand more than mere speculation to support discrimination against out-of-state goods. The burden is on the State to show that "the *discrimination* is demonstrably justified,"' *Chemical Waste Management, Inc v Hunt*, 504 US 334, 344 (1992) (emphasis in original). The Court has upheld state regulations that discriminate against interstate commerce only after finding, based on concrete record evidence, that a State's nondiscriminatory alternatives will prove workable. *See, e.g., Maine v Taylor*, 477 US 131, 141-144 (1986). *Heald*, p 492

Michigan's prohibition of SHAM products from other states discriminates against interstate commerce. Accordingly, the State of Michigan must show that it is utilizing the prohibition because it is necessary to achieve a legitimate local purpose, and has no alternative means of doing so.

Here, Scot and Kelly convinced the Michigan Legislature to enact the law to encourage Michigan consumers to buy Michigan products. While the purpose is arguably legitimate, this blanket prohibition is not the only means that would achieve that purpose and is not the least restrictive means available. The law creates a monopoly for RS in view of the fact that there are similar products offered out of state.

Additionally, the law violates the Equal Protection Clause in its treatment of state versus out-of-state suppliers. AS is an out-of-state SHAM supplier who suffered discrimination because the Michigan supplier is allowed to be the sole provider in Michigan.

Student Answer—July 2007

Question 8—Constitutional Law—9 points

The issue is whether there is any constitutional challenges which may be raised against this law.

1. The *commerce clause* of the constitution gives congress the power to regulate commerce & instrumentalities of commerce between the several states.
   In areas where congress has not acted, which has to do with interstate commerce, is called the *negative* or *dormant commerce clause.* States can legislate as long as it does not *discriminate against or place an undue* burden on interstate commerce.
   In this case, the state enacted legislation in an area where congress had not yet acted. This law prohibits the import of Sham products into the state. This legislation *stops the free flow of commerce* at its borders. It discriminates against all states but Michigan & protects the Sham manufacturers in Michigan. Thus, the legislation violates the Commerce Clause & would be found unconstitutional.
2. The *equal protection* clause prohibits the gov't from discriminating based on certain classes of people. Marilyn & Alabama Sham may argue that the statute discriminates based on if you live inside or outside the state of MI. But because residency is not a suspect class, the court would apply rational basis scrutiny. This test leaves the burden of proof on the P to show that there is no legitimate reason for the law & the law is not rationally related to this purpose. Thus, the crt could find that even the slightest reason would be good enough to pass this test. I believe the legislation would be found constitutional under this test.

In conclusion, the best way to challenge this statute would be the Commerce Clause.

February 2008—Question 3

Defendant Terry O. Rist is charged with violation of the Michigan Anti-Terrorism Act. The charge against Terry O. Rist is based on electronic chat room conversations he engaged in, using the screen name "skin-head-sadistic." His primary topics in the communications were his feelings of hate and his plans for the infliction of death and terror upon his own family members and other individuals he perceived as deserving of the fate he chose for them.

The Anti-Terrorism Act criminalizes communicating to any other person a serious expression of intent to commit an act of terrorism. Particularly, the Act criminalizes communicating to any other person a serious expression of an intent to commit a "willful and deliberate act" constituting "a violent felony" under Michigan law, which the communicator "has reason to know is dangerous to human life," and is "intended to intimidate or coerce a civilian population or influence or affect the conduct of government."

1. **Did Terry O. Rist violate the Act?**
2. **Is the Act constitutional?**

Model Answer to Question 3

This question is based on *People v Osantowski*, 274 Mich App 593 (2007), in which the Court of Appeals held that the Anti-Terrorism Act was constitutional as against free speech objections and vagueness objections.

1. In *Osantowski*, the defendant communicated his plans for the inflection of death and terror on his family and other individuals. The defendant argued that the statute was vague and failed to provide fair notice of proscribed conduct.

   The court opined that true threats need not include an intent for direct intimidation of a specific victim, finding that fear of violence to others can engender disruption similar to the disruption engendered by fear of violence to oneself. The court held that true threats of violence fall outside First Amendment protections even in the absence of direct victim intimidation. As in this instance, even those threats not intended to be conveyed to the potential victim can be criminalized because of the state's overwhelming interest in preventing the disruption that can result from such threats. The court found that there was a violation of the Act.
2. Regarding the constitutionality of the Act, issues addressed by the *Osantowski* court included: (1) whether the Act's proscribed conduct was indefinite/vague/overboard for purposes of the First Amendment, and (2) whether the Act provided fair notice of the proscribed conduct for the purposes of the Due Process Clause.

   Regarding the First Amendment, statements alone can be without First Amendment protection. Although the right to free speech entitles an individual to advocate certain ideas regardless of their popularity, it does not extend to the threatening of terror, inciting of riots, or placing another's life or property in danger.

The *Osantowski* court held that the conduct proscribed, threatening to commit a "violent felony," was clearly without constitutional protection under the First Amendment. The court found that the Act prohibits only "true threats," as it encompasses the communication of a serious expression of intent to commit an act of unlawful violence to a particular individual or group of individuals. Further, the court found that because the Act requires the existence of an intent to "intimidate or coerce," it extends beyond the type of speech or expressive conduct afforded protection by the First Amendment. The Act by its terms does not sweep within its ambit other activities that in ordinary circumstances constitute an exercise of freedom of speech.

Regarding notice requirements afforded under the due process clause, to afford proper notice of the conduct proscribed, a statute must provide a person of ordinary intelligence a reasonable opportunity to know what is prohibited. A statute cannot use terms that require persons of ordinary intelligence to speculate regarding its meaning and differ about its application. For a statute to be sufficiently definite, its meaning must be fairly ascertainable by reference to judicial interpretations, the common law, dictionaries, treatises, or the commonly accepted meaning of words.

The *Osantowski* court held that the Anti-Terrorism Act was constitutional: the Act did not violate the right to due process of law. The court held that the meaning of the Act is readily ascertainable. Specifically, the Act criminalizes communicating a serious expression of an intent to commit a "willful and deliberate act" constituting "a serious felony" under Michigan law, which the communicator "has reason to know is dangerous to human life," and is "intended to intimidate or coerce a civilian population or influence or affect the government." The *Osantowski* court found that based on this language and the definitions of terms used, the Act provides a person of ordinary intelligence a reasonable opportunity to know what behavior or conduct is prohibited.

Student Answer—February 2008

Question 3—Constitutional Law—7 points

1. Terry did violate the act.

Under the Anti-Terrorism Act, one who communicates to any other person a serious express of intent to commit an act of terrorism, or a serious expression of an intent to commit a willful and deliberate act constituting a violent felony, and has reason to know is dangerous to human life, and is intended to intimidate or coerces . . . is guilty under this act.

Here, risk is communicating via the internet with potentially thousands of other people about his feelings of hate and his plans for an infliction of death and terror on his family members and other individuals he perceived as deserving of whatever fate he chose for them. These are all serious expressions with intent to commit a willful act. Infliction of death and terror is a felony. Thus Risk has violated the act.

2. The Act is constitutional.

Under the 1st Amendment as applied to the states via the 14th Amendment, no state can control the content of speech because of the message it conveys, unless it is unprotected speech.

In this case, speech amounting to hate crime would fall under unprotected speech and thus is not constitutionally protected. Therefore the Act is constitutional.

> **Comment:** This answer received a minimum passing score of 7 points and is a great example to demonstrate what a 7 really means. If you compare this answer to the model answer you will see the student correctly identified the issues and reached the correct conclusion, but details in the rules and analysis were missing. This is especially true in the second issue where the student failed to define and discuss vagueness and notice.

July 2008—Question 12

In their effort to "clean up Homer County," the Board of Commissioners recently passed an ordinance, providing as follows:

(1) A Review Panel is hereby established to review all sexually graphic material before sale by any person or entity in Homer County.

(2) Subject to subsection (3), no person or entity in Homer County may sell any sexually graphic material.

(3) A person or entity in Homer County may sell an item of sexually graphic material if (a) the person or entity first submits the item to the Review Panel and (b) the Review Panel, in the exercise of its sole discretion, determines that the item is not pornographic.

(4) Any person or entity in Homer County that fails to comply with subsections (2) or (3) is guilty of a misdemeanor, and is punishable by incarceration in jail for one year and/or by imposition of a fine.

VideoPlay, Inc., a local video store, has brought an action claiming that the ordinance violates the First Amendment to the United States Constitution.

Discuss the arguments VideoPlay, Inc. can make in support of its claim.

Model Answer to Question 12

The First Amendment, applicable to the states through the Fourteenth Amendment, provides that no government shall interfere with the right to free speech.

I. Facial Attacks

(A) Prior Restraint

Under the First Amendment, speech cannot be enjoined before it occurs. Here, the Homer County ordinance mandates that sexual material may only be sold if it is first submitted to the Review Panel and the Panel, in its sole discretion, determines the item is not pornographic.

The ordinance does not provide any standards that the Panel should use to evaluate requests. Without procedural safeguards—no sole discretion, articulate standards, and appellate review—the ordinance's authorization scheme is an invalid prior restraint.

(B) Overbroad
The ordinance prohibits "sexually graphic material." This would prohibit not only obscene material (which is unprotected and can constitutionally be prohibited—see below), but also material that can be viewed in numerous PG-13 and R-rated movies that are released. Accordingly, it can be argued that the ordinance is unconstitutionally overbroad.

(C) Vagueness
The Homer County ordinance is vague because it provides no standards/factors/definitions that enable anyone to determine what exactly is prohibited. Since material is not clearly "sexually graphic" until the Panel decides that it is, the ordinance does not enable individuals to recognize their own culpability. The ordinance is likely to be found unconstitutionally vague.

II. Regulation of Speech

(A) Content-Based Regulation
Content-neutral time, place, and manner restrictions need only pass intermediate scrutiny to be constitutional. However, *content-based* restrictions must pass strict scrutiny. The Homer County ordinance is content-based because it restricts material according to what it depicts—sexually graphic material. Therefore it must pass strict scrutiny.

(B) Obscenity/Profane and Indecent Speech
Obscenity is a form of unprotected speech. It can be regulated, based on content, without meeting strict scrutiny.
Here, the Homer County ordinance may regulate obscenity without meeting the strict scrutiny test. The provision prohibiting the sale of "sexually graphic material" may be valid if "sexually graphic material" is defined as limited to obscene material.

(C) Compelling State Interest
Generally, when "sexually graphic material" is involved, the interest is in protecting children from such materials and in protecting the City's tourism industry. Therefore, it most likely qualifies as a compelling state interest. It will have to show that the ordinance is necessary to achieving those interests.

(D) Necessary and Least Restrictive Means
A law is necessary when it provides the only way to achieve the compelling state interest. Homer County will not be able to show that its ordinance is the least restrictive means of protecting its interest. Protection could be accomplished by the use of content-neutral time, place, and manner restrictions, such as requiring people to keep such materials off the streets, and for sale only during normal business hours. Because less restrictive alternatives are available, the ordinance will fail strict scrutiny, and is therefore an unconstitutional violation of the First Amendment.

Three Student Answers—July 2008

Question 12—Constitutional Law—9 points

Q: What is Video Plays best argument for a First Amendment claim?

The right to freedom of speech is a fundamental right under the First Amendment. The government cannot infringe upon an individual fundamental right without a compelling government interest and it can only use means that are narrowly tailored. This restriction applies to state and local governments through the 14th Amendment.

The First Amendment right to freedom of speech is not absolute. The government can place valid time, place and manner restrictions as long as the restrictions are content neutral. This would not be applicable here as the ordinance attempts to restrict "sexually graphic material" and not when, how, or where such material may be distributed.

In arguing against the ordinance Video Play should first address the validity of the statute on its face. By prohibiting "any sexually graphic material" the statute may be found not to describe with sufficiency what is prohibited. Instead a review panel is given authority to proscribe or determine what is sexually graphic without putting its citizens on notice. Next Video Play, Inc. may try to argue that the statute was not created for a compelling government issue. The purpose of "cleaning up Homer County" may be found to be a moral standard then compelling interest.

Therefore, Video Plays best arguments are that the statute is void on its face and infringes upon a fundamental right.

Question 12—Constitutional Law—8 points

This is a Constitutional Law Question. The preliminary issue is "whether the statute" is invalid based on 1st Amendment "Right to Free Speech."

1st Amendment right to free speech is applicable to the states through the 14th Amendment Due Process of Law Clause.

Under the 1st Amendment, free right to speech cannot be constrained absent a number of exceptions.

A statute prohibits "speech" or "regulates" certain conduct will be invalid if on the face speech gives "unfettered" discretion, "prior restraint", vague or overbroad.

The statute at issue is content specific, the statute specifically regulates the "conduct" or "expression" in which the speech is aimed.

Certain speech is "unprotected" speech that creates "clear and present" danger, defamation, fighting words, or "obscenity."

The current statute gives the review panel board unfettered discretion; "exercise of its sole discretion," to determine that the "item is not pornographic."

Further, unfettered discretion is that the review board "review ALL sexually graphic material before sale by any person or entity in Homer County."

This falls under a prior restraint, Content-Specific Speech, in this case "sexually graphic material" that is regulated by a statute is constitutionally invalid if on its face is a prior restraint or gives unfettered discretion.

This "statute" meets both of the "above requirements," however absent a protected right that inflict a certain level of strict scrutiny, commercial/content neutral intermediate scrutiny or rational basis scrutiny, the speech fails under unprotected speech.

If the speech that is being regulated in the statute is obscenity it falls under "unprotected" speech and statute/regulation is valid absent the above reasoning.

Obscenity is defined as the sexual depiction of sexual acts that (national standard) appeal to the most prurient in taste and lacks all scientific, political, literary, and esthetic value based on community standard.

Video Play would argue they have standing, to bring such a suit because they have a "personal stake" in the outcome of the litigation, injury in fact at every stage because the statute prevents them from selling such material in their video store without . . .

Video Play will argue the statute is invalid on its face because it is content-specific and given "unfettered discretion" prior restraint in violation of 1st Amendment to the "review panel board."

Review Panel Board will argue speech fails under "unprotected speech"; obscenity and fits well within the definition and therefore can be "regulated" such argument will fail because of unfettered discretion and prior restraints of making it a misdemeanor.

Question 12—Constitutional Law—8 points

VideoPlay can make the following argument in support of its claim that the ordinance violates the First Amendment.

Under the 1st Amendment, as applied to the states, generally the gov. may not regulate protected speech based on its content. However, the gov. may regulate less protected or unprotected speech such as obscenity, providing it lacks scientific, literary, artistic and political social value, and appeals to the prurient interest based on community standards.

Moreover, 1st Amendment rights are subject to strict scrutiny standard. The gov. has to prove there is a compelling gov. interest for the law and that the means are narrowly tailored.

Here, the gov. is attempting to regulate speech by requiring review, per the ordinance, of "all" sexually graphic material before sale by any person or entity in the county.

While the gov. may have a compelling interest to protect the health, safety and welfare of its citizens by curtailing the sale of obscene material, this Ordinance clearly encompasses all sexually graphic material and does not narrowly define what is sexually graphic and what is not sexually graphic. It leaves it up to the Review Panel to determine this.

Additionally, the ordinance can be challenged based on it being overbroad and vague.

The language in the ordinance must be written in such a way as to give notice to a reasonable person of reasonable intelligence as to what conduct is proscribed.

Here, again the same facts apply. The ordinance does not define what sexually graphic material is and it includes all sexually graphic material to be reviewed, and it leaves it up to the discretion of a Review Panel to determine this.

February 2009—Question 5

Vickie Victim owned a duplex in Hillsdale, Michigan, in which she lived in one unit and rented the other unit to Peter Perp. In the early morning hours of July 1, 2008, Peter found himself craving crack cocaine, but he had no money with which to purchase the drug. Peter broke into Vickie's unit to search for cash. Vickie confronted Peter. Peter overpowered Vickie and eventually strangled her to death. Peter took $500 from Vickie's bedroom and purchased drugs with the money. The next day Peter was arrested and charged with first-degree premeditated murder. Peter was declared indigent and the court appointed trial counsel to represent Peter in the circuit court. After waiving a preliminary examination in the district court and being arraigned on the information in the circuit court, Peter, overtaken with guilt, announced to the circuit court and his lawyer that he did not want or need the assistance of trial counsel and he demanded that the court accept his plea of guilty as charged. The circuit court accommodated Peter and accepted his guilty plea. Peter was sentenced to life in prison with no possibility of parole and the trial court entered the judgment of conviction and sentence. The following day, Peter arrived at prison and had a change of heart. Peter immediately wrote a letter to the trial court and the clerk of the circuit court in which Peter expressed his desire to exercise his right to an appeal. Peter also asked for the appointment of counsel to represent him on appeal. The clerk of the court and the trial court received the correspondence a few days after the trial court entered Peter's judgment of conviction and sentence, and filed the correspondence in the official court file.

1. **Describe and discuss defendant's right to appellate review in the state court. Limit your answer to a discussion of appellate review in state court. Do not discuss possible claims that defendant may assert on appeal.**
2. **Discuss whether the trial court is obligated to honor Peter's request for the appointment of appellate counsel.**

Model Answer to Question 5

Describe and discuss defendant's right to appellate review in the state court: At one time there existed a right to appeal to the Michigan Court of Appeals all criminal convictions, even convictions that were the product of a guilty plea or a nolo contendere plea. However, in 1994, the people of Michigan amended the Michigan Constitution to eliminate the right to appeal criminal convictions that result from nolo contendere and guilty pleas. See Mich Const 1963, Art 1, 520. Here, defendant's conviction is the result of a plea of guilty. Therefore, Peter has no right to an appeal.

Art 1, § 20 of the Michigan Constitution provides, however, that "an appeal by an accused who pleads guilty or nolo contendere shall be by leave of the court." Peter's appellate remedies are therefore limited to the filing of an application for leave to appeal. Unlike an appeal by right, where the Michigan Court of Appeals must provide plenary review of the merits of every timely filed claim of appeal, the determination of whether to grant plenary review of the merits of claims asserted in an application for leave to appeal is left to the discretion of the Court of Appeals.

MCR 7.205(A) describes the time requirements for filing an application for leave to appeal in the Michigan Court of Appeals: "An application for leave to appeal must be filed within 21 days after entry of the judgment or order to be appealed from or within other time as allowed by law or rule." Thus, Peter has the opportunity to timely file an application for leave to appeal in the Michigan Court of Appeals.

Further, MCR 7.205(F) permits the filing of delayed applications for leave to appeal. An appellant bringing a delayed application for leave to appeal must not only provide the court with a statement of appellant's allegations of error and the relief sought, the appellant must also explain the delay for failing to timely file an application for leave to appeal. MCR 7.205(F)(l). The Court of Appeals may consider the reason for the delay in filing when assessing whether to grant or deny the application. Like a timely application for leave to appeal, whether to grant plenary review of the delayed application for leave to appeal is left to the discretion of the Court of Appeals.

Should Peter be denied leave to appeal in the Court of Appeals, he may seek leave to appeal in the Michigan Supreme Court. MCR 7.302. Such applications are rarely granted. The decision whether to grant an application for leave to appeal is left to the discretion of the Supreme Court. *Id.*

Discuss whether the trial court is obligated to honor Peter's request for the appointment of appellate counsel: The Sixth Amendment to the United States Constitution provides that "[I]n all criminal prosecutions, the accused shall enjoy the right * * * to have the assistance of counsel for his defense." In *Gideon v Wainwright*, 372 US 335 (1963), the United States Supreme Court held that the Sixth Amendment right to counsel was a fundamental right and that the Fourteenth Amendment required states to provide indigent criminal defendants with appointed counsel at state expense to assist at trial. In *Douglas v California*, 372 US 353 (1963), the Supreme Court of the United States concluded that the Fourteenth Amendment extends the right to appointed counsel for indigent defendants to first appeals as of right, following a criminal conviction. And in *Ross v Moffitt*, 417 US 600 (1974), the Supreme Court of the United States concluded that the United States Constitution does not require states to appoint counsel to aid an indigent convict to assist in discretionary appeals to the state's highest court or to the United States Supreme Court.

In *Halbert v Michigan*, 545 US 605 (2005), the Supreme Court of the United States determined that in regard to the appointment of counsel, Michigan's constitutionally mandated review system for plea-based convictions is governed by *Douglas, supra.* Therefore, Michigan must appoint counsel to indigent defendants who plead guilty or nolo contendere to assist in obtaining first leave discretionary review before the Michigan Court of Appeals. The U.S. Supreme Court based its holding in *Halbert* on two aspects of Michigan's criminal appellate process. First, in disposing of applications for leave to appeal, the Michigan Court of Appeals looks to the merits of the claims asserted by the defendant. *Id.* at 617. Accordingly, the Court of Appeals' ruling is the first and likely to be the only direct review of the merits of defendant's conviction and sentence. Second, indigent defendants seeking review before the Court of Appeals are ill equipped to represent themselves. *Id.* Persons unskilled in the law will not be able to assist the appellate court in assessing the legal merits of their claims.

The Michigan Court Rules were amended to reflect the United States Supreme Court's holding in *Halbert.* MCR 6.425(G)(1)(c) gives indigent defendants 42 days to request appellate counsel. The trial court must grant a timely filed request for the appointment of appellate counsel. *Id.* Here, defendant sent to the trial court and the clerk of the court correspondence that requested the appointment of appellate counsel. This correspondence was filed and made part of the court record within 42 days of Peter's judgment of conviction and sentence. Pursuant to MCR 6.425, *Halbert v Michigan, supra*, and the Fourteenth Amendment to the United States Constitution, the trial court must appoint appellate counsel to assist Peter in his pursuit of appellate review before the Michigan Court of Appeals of his plea-based conviction.

Student Answer—February 2009

Question 5—Constitutional Law—None Available

July 2009—Question 5

Chris Cop, a Michigan State Police trooper stationed in Marquette, Michigan, vacationed in Las Vegas. While there, Chris rented a car. Chris was driving back to his hotel after a night of hitting the Las Vegas club scene when he observed on the roadside several police cars with lights flashing. Traffic slowed immediately and Chris observed police officers in the road, between the lanes of traffic. The officers approached every car. Within one minute, an officer approached Chris's car. The officer informed Chris that the stop was a sobriety checkpoint to investigate the possibility that he might be too intoxicated to drive. The officer asked Chris to blow into a portable breath-testing device. Chris, who never consumes alcohol, complied with the request and passed the test. The officer released Chris.

Chris recognized that this procedure would greatly enhance the public safety, as it would result in the arrest of many drunk drivers and produce a deterrent effect over the long term. When Chris returned to Michigan, he persuaded his supervisor to implement a roadside sobriety checkpoint on a Sunday morning from 1:00 a.m. to 3:00 a.m., one-half mile down the road from the busiest pub in Marquette. The supervisor at the Marquette State Police post issued a press release announcing her intent to conduct a roadside sobriety checkpoint. The press release provided the date, time, and location at which the checkpoint would be implemented and noted that police records show a high incidence of drunk driving arrests in that place and time frame. The press release indicated that every car on the designated roadway would be stopped during the checkpoint and that warning lights and signs would clearly be visible as drivers approach the checkpoint area. The press release indicated that a portable breath tester would be used and that the length of the stop would be minimal. The ACLU vowed to challenge these sobriety checkpoints as being in violation of the federal and state constitutions.

Discuss whether the implementation of sobriety checkpoints violates the Michigan Constitution. Discuss whether implementation of sobriety checkpoints violates the United States Constitution. Explain your answer.

Model Answer to Question 5

A. Sobriety Checkpoints Under the Michigan Constitution: The discussion whether sobriety checkpoints are constitutionally permissible under the Michigan Constitution does not end with the determination that such conduct does not violate the Fourth Amendment to the United States Constitution. The Michigan Constitution of 1963 contains a provision prohibiting unreasonable searches and seizures. Specifically, Const 1963, art 1, § 11, provides in pertinent part:

> The person, houses, papers and possessions of every person shall be secure from unreasonable searches and seizures. No warrant to search any place or to seize any person or things shall issue without describing them, nor without probable cause, supported by oath or affirmation.

While the above-quoted provision is similar to the Fourth Amendment of the United States Constitution, it is not identical to it. Michigan courts are obligated to interpret the Michigan Constitution independent of the rights and protections afforded under the United States Constitution. "When there is a clash of competing rights under the state and federal constitutions, the Supremacy Clause, art VI, cl 2, [of the United States Constitution] dictates that the federal right prevails." *Sitz v Dept of State Police*, 443 Mich 744, 760 (1993) *(Sitz II)*. However, where a right is given under the United States Constitution, it does not necessarily follow that a state constitution must be interpreted as providing the identical right. *Id.* "[B]ecause these texts were written at different times by different people, the protections afforded [under each document] may be greater, lesser, or the same." *Id.* at 762 (citations omitted). Michigan "courts are not obligated to accept what [is] deemed to be a major contradiction of citizen protections under [the Michigan Constitution] simply because the United States Supreme Court has chosen to do so" [in its interpretation of the United States Constitution]. *Id.* at 763.

In *People v Collins*, 438 Mich 8, 25 (1991), the Michigan Supreme Court held that the prohibition against unreasonable searches and seizures found in Const 1963, art 1, § ll, should "be construed to provide the same protection as that secured by the Fourth Amendment, absent 'compelling reason' to impose a different interpretation." A compelling reason exists where there is a "principled basis in this history of [Michigan] jurisprudence for the creation of new rights." *Sitz II, supra* at 763.

In *Sitz II, supra,* the Michigan Supreme Court specifically considered the constitutionality of sobriety checkpoints and concluded there existed compelling reason to interpret Const 1963, art 1, § 11, to provide greater protection than the protection afforded under the Fourth Amendment to the United States Constitution. Specifically, the Michigan Supreme Court observed that the Michigan Constitution has historically been interpreted to provide the people traveling on public roadways the fullest protection available under the law. *Id.*, at 775, citing *Pinkerton v Verberg*, 78 Mich 573, 584 (1889). Further, the Michigan Constitution has historically been interpreted to distinguish between searches and seizures made for administrative or regulatory purposes from searches and seizures involving criminal investigations. The Michigan Supreme Court noted that "seizures with the primary goal of enforcing criminal law have generally required some level of suspicion." *Id.*, at 778 (citation omitted). The Michigan Supreme Court also cited several cases in which it discussed and reaffirmed the notion that reasonable cause is required to stop or search cars operated on Michigan's public roadways. *E.g., People ex rel Attorney General v Lansing Municipal Judge*, 327 Mich 410 (1950) (striking down as unconstitutional a statute that permitted certain searches, including some involving automobiles, without a warrant); *People v Stein*, 265 Mich 610 (1933) (observing that "[i]f conditions demand a special rule of search on highways, the remedy is by amendment of the [Michigan] Constitution"); *People v Roache*, 237 Mich 215, 222 (1927) (stating "[n]o one will contend that an officer may promiscuously stop automobiles upon the public highway and demand the driver's license merely as a subterfuge to invade the constitutional right of the traveler to be secure against unreasonable search and seizure."); *People v Kamhout*, 227 Mich 172, 187-188 (1924) (stating that police officers "have no right to stop and search an automobile * * * for the purpose of ascertaining whether it is being used [to further illegal activity] unless they have * * * reasonable grounds of suspicion * * * as would induce in any prudent man, an honest belief that the law is being violated").

The Michigan Supreme Court concluded that the jurisprudence and constitutional history of Michigan provided a compelling reason to interpret the prohibition against unreasonable searches and seizures found in the Michigan Constitution more expansively than the protection afforded under the Fourth Amendment to the United States Constitution. Thus, the Michigan Supreme Court held that sobriety checkpoints violate Const 1963, art 1, § 11. *Spitz II, supra* at 778. For these reasons, the ACLU likely will prevail in its claim that the Michigan Constitution bars the implementation of sobriety checkpoints on Michigan roadways.

B. Sobriety Checkpoints Under the United States Constitution: The Fourth Amendment to the United States Constitution protects against unreasonable searches and seizures absent a warrant issued upon a showing of probable cause. An exception to the warrant requirement allows searches or seizures of automobiles when there is probable cause to believe that evidence of a crime will be found in a lawfully stopped vehicle or that the vehicle contains or is contraband. *Florida v White*, 526 US 559, 563-565 (1999). The Fourteenth Amendment to the United States Constitution imposes upon the various states the protections provided under the Fourth Amendment. Here, the Michigan State Police plan to stop every vehicle at a designated time and place in order to investigate whether the driver is intoxicated and operating the vehicle in violation of Michigan law. These stops, regardless of duration, constitute seizures within the meaning of the Fourth Amendment. *United States v Martinez-Fuerte*, 428 US 543, 556 (1976) (holding a Fourth Amendment "seizure" occurs when a vehicle is stopped at an illegal alien checkpoint). No warrant was issued authorizing these seizures and no probable cause existed to justify the police action. Thus the dispositive issue regarding the constitutionality of the proposed sobriety checkpoint under the Fourth Amendment is whether the warrantless activity proposed by police is reasonable. *Michigan State Police v Sitz*, 496 US 444, 450 (1990).

When determining the reasonableness under the Fourth Amendment of a warrantless seizure, courts employ a three-part balancing test derived from *Brown v Texas*, 443 US 47 (1979). Applying the *Brown* factors in the context of the facts presented here, a reviewing court should consider the following three factors: (1) the interest of the state in preventing accidents caused by drunk drivers; (2) the level of intrusion and delay imposed on motorists passing through the checkpoint; and (3) the effectiveness of sobriety checkpoints in achieving the state's goal. In *Sitz, supra*, the Supreme Court of the United States applied these three factors to determine that roadside sobriety testing does not offend the Fourth Amendment to the United States Constitution.

The Supreme Court observed that states have a "grave and legitimate" interest in curbing drunk driving. Statistical evidence supports the conclusion that thousands of highway deaths are caused by intoxicated drivers. *Sitz, supra* at 451.

The Supreme Court also concluded that the level of intrusion and delay imposed upon motorists passing through the checkpoint was reasonable—less than one minute. The Supreme Court emphasized "the circumstances surrounding a checkpoint stop and search are far less intrusive than those attending a roving patrol stop. Roving patrols often operate at night on seldom-traveled roads, and their approach may frighten motorists. At traffic checkpoints, the motorist can see that other vehicles are being stopped, he can see visible signs of the officers' authority, and he is much less likely to be frightened or annoyed by the intrusion." *Sitz, supra* at 453, quoting *People v Ortiz*, 422 US 891, 894-895 (1975).

The Supreme Court also concluded that sobriety checkpoints are an effective method of advancing the interests of the state to diminish drunk driving. The question whether sobriety checkpoints are effective is distinct from the issue whether they are the best method of deterring drunk driving. The Supreme Court noted that deference must be given to local "governmental officials who have a unique understanding of, and a responsibility for, limited public resources, including a finite number of police officers." *Sitz, supra* at 454.

For these reasons, the ACLU will not likely prevail in its attempt to prevent sobriety checkpoints as being violative of the United States Constitution.

Student Answer—July 2009

Question 5—Constitutional Law—7 points

This is a constitutional law question.

The implementation of sobriety checkpoints does not violate the U.S. Constitution. The argument would be made that a random check point violates an individuals right to privacy. An individual's right to privacy (RTP) is protected by the constitution.

The overreaching reason for sobriety checkpoints is to ensure the health; safety; and welfare of citizens. The U.S. Constitution allows states to interpret any laws not regulated by the U.S. Constitution states are given this thru the 14th amendment. Because the 14th amendment gives freedom to the states to protect the welfare of its citizens, a sobriety checkpoint does not violate the U.S. Constitution.

In Michigan, on the other hand, sobriety checkpoints have been deemed to violate the Michigan Constitution and the RTP of Michigan citizens. A random checkpoint does not involve probable cause which is what the Michigan Supreme Court says an officer needs to search a car under the automobile exception to search a person or their breath.

The MI law interprets a citizen's right to privacy to include their breath as they are driving. An officer may pull a car over with probable cause and then they may use a breathalyzer if they have probable cause to think the occupant driver was intoxicated. Some signs would be slurred speech, dilated eyes, smell of alcohol on the breath or in the car, plain view/smell of any contraband and/or the general actions of the driver (including how the driver acts and how well his driving skills were)

Michigan does not authorize random (or every car) breathalyzers. MI does not feel the overreaching benefit of "Public welfare" is greater that an individuals RTP.

On the other hand, the U.S. constitution permits states to determine their own levels of public welfare in relation to their citizens RTP. Per the U.S. Constitution a sobriety checkpoint which is noticed as to time, place, and how cars will be checked (every one, every third, etc.) would be valid.

Comment: Examinees bombed this question because they didn't know the slight difference between the MI Constitution and the U.S. Constitution and didn't know the *Sitz* case. Generally speaking, the grader was very generous in grading this question, mainly because most were clueless. This answer received a minimum passing score of 7 points even though she or he didn't even mention the Fourth Amendment by name. However, this is an outstanding example of "Plan B." The examinee fell back on common sense in terms of automobile searches, recognized there were no sobriety tests in Michigan, but there were in other states, and did an excellent job of providing confident sounding educated BS!

February 2010—Question 13

The City of South Pointe is an affluent community located on Lake Michigan. At one time, every home in South Pointe was valued in excess of $1,000,000. Traditionally, South Pointe homes were sold by word of mouth. A property owner would inform neighbors of the intent to sell and several prospective buyers would submit offers. For many years, this marketing method produced rapid and lucrative sales. "For Sale" signs, although not precluded by ordinance, were never posted in front of the homes and were considered socially acceptable.

When the economy soured, many residents lost their homes to foreclosure. Banks that owned the foreclosed properties began posting "For Sale" signs in front of the homes. Property sales slowed to 20-year low. Home values dropped by 30 percent in 2008. The sight of all the "For Sale" signs caused concern for many residents. Residents, worried about the value of their homes, put their homes up for sale. Virtually every home offered for sale displayed a "For Sale" sign contributed to falling property values. Home values continued to drop in 2009.

Fearful that the declining property values will adversely impact the City tax base and would further cause existing residents to leave their community, on October 1, 2009, the South Pointe City Council enacted the following Sign Ordinance:

> It shall be unlawful for a homeowner to post in front of his or her home any sign that indicates the home is for sale. Persons who violate this ordinance shall be fined $1,000. This ordinance shall take effect on December 1, 2009.

On December 15, 2009, Jack Jones decided to sell his home. He posted a "For Sale" sign on his front lawn and was issued a citation for violating the Sign Ordinance. **What is the best argument Jack can advance to contest the citation and ordinance? Explain your answer.**

Model Answer to Question 13

Jack's best argument is to challenge the constitutionality of the ordinance as a violation of the free speech guarantee of the First Amendment to the United States Constitution. Applicable to state and local governments through the Fourteenth Amendment, the First Amendment provides that government shall make no law abridging the freedom of speech. Here, the City of South Pointe has implemented an ordinance that bars the placement of "For Sale" signs on residential property. Such signs are a form of commercial speech. *Linmark Assoc, Inc v Township of Willingboro*, 431 US 85 (1977).

Commercial speech is not entitled to the same scope of protection as political speech or expressive speech. *Rochester Hills v Schultz*, 459 Mich 486, 489 (1999). Nonetheless, commercial speech is constitutionally protected from unwarranted governmental regulation. *Id.* A determination whether commercial speech has been unconstitutionally regulated turns on consideration of four factors. A reviewing court must consider whether: (1) the speech concerns lawful activity and is not misleading; (2) the government's restriction is justified by a substantial governmental interest; (3) the regulation directly advances the asserted governmental interest; (4) the regulation is more extensive than necessary to serve the governmental interest. *Id.* citing *Central Hudson Gas & Electric Corp v Public Service Comm of New York*, 447 US 557, 561 (1980).

Here, the speech subject to restriction concerns the sale of real property, a lawful activity. No reasonable argument may be advanced that "For Sale" signs are misleading. This factor weighs in favor of striking down the ordinance.

The government interests that caused the City Council to enact the ordinance were substantial. A local government has a substantial interest in the value of property within the community. This is particularly true in Michigan, where the ability of a local government has a substantial interest in encouraging people to maintain residence within the community. *Linmark Assoc, supra* at 96. Thus, the second factor weighs in favor of upholding the ordinance.

However, the ban on "For Sale" signs does not directly advance these vital government interests. The mere fact that homes display "For Sale" signs, will not cause the value of other homes within a community to decrease. The precipitous fall in real estate values is the product of a bad economy and an excess in the supply of homes offered for sale, regardless of whether the offer to sell is advertised by the placement of a sign in front of the home. Thus, the third factor weighs in favor of striking down the ordinance.

Finally, to make the extent it may be argued that the ordinance serves one or more of the above described governmental interest, the regulation of speech contained in the ordinance is far more extensive than necessary. The regulation bans the dissemination of truthful information that promotes and facilitates the exchange of residential property. The exchange of residential property relates to one of the most important decisions a person can make: where to live and raise a family. *Id.* Additionally, the ordinance is premised on the notion that residents of South Pointe who are provided this information will act contrary to their best interests and the best interest of the City by selling their property and moving out of South Pointe. However, the protection afforded speech by the First Amendment to the United States Constitution is based on the notion that "people will perceive their own best interests if only they are well informed, and that the best means to that end is to open the channels of communication rather than to close them. *Id.* at 97, quoting *Virginia Pharmacy Bd v Virginia Citizens Consumer Council*, 425 US 748, 770 (1976).

Considering the four factors described above, it is likely that a reviewing court would strike down the ordinance because it is an unwarranted restriction on truthful and legitimate commercial speech, contrary to the First Amendment to the United States Constitution.

Student Answers—February 2010

Question 13—Constitutional Law—None Available

July 2010—Question 6

In 2006, the United States Congress passed the Shrimp Industry Relief Act (SIRA), which the President signed into law. This act provided in part:

> The shrimp industry having been crippled by Hurricane Katrina, the United States shall subsidize this industry at a rate of fifty million dollars annually for up to 10 years. Congress shall annually appropriate the funds for such subsidy only to the extent needed. These funds shall be made available to entities engaged in the harvesting of shrimp from the Gulf of Mexico. Distribution of funds shall be administered through the Office of the Secretary of Agriculture.

Congress appropriated fifty million dollars pursuant to the act each year thereafter. The day after the 2010 appropriation became law, the President declared that the gulf coast shrimp industry was fully recovered from the effects of Hurricane Katrina. Consequently, the President signed the following Executive Order:

The shrimp industry in the Gulf of Mexico having fully recovered from the devastation of Hurricane Katrina, the Agriculture Secretary shall cease allocating subsidies available under the Shrimp Industry Relief Act. In order to promote the consumption of healthier food, the Agriculture Secretary shall hereafter use the funds made available under said act to subsidize businesses engaged in the harvesting and sale of organic vegetables.

The Shrimp Association filed suit against the Agriculture Secretary, demanding that the funds allocated under the SIRA continue to benefit its members.

Assume the plaintiff has standing and the doctrine of sovereign immunity does not bar this suit.

Describe and discuss the legal arguments relating to the President's authority to order the Agriculture Secretary to cease allocating subsidies available under the SIRA.

Describe and discuss the legal arguments relating to the President's authority to order that funds appropriated under the SIRA be used to subsidize the organic vegetable industry.

Model Answer to Question 6

The issue presented here relates to the extent, if any, the President may exercise power to modify, alter or otherwise impede the SIRA.

The President's authority to act "must stem either from an act of Congress or from the Constitution itself." *Youngstown Co v Sawyer*, 343 US 579, 585 (1952). Article II of the Constitution vests without reservation or qualification executive power in the office of the President. In comparison, Article I delegates to Congress the legislative powers "herein granted." These distinctions in grants of authority support the notion that the President has certain inherent powers beyond those expressly stated in the Constitution.

In *Medellin v Texas*, 552 US 491, 524-525 (2008), the Supreme Court of the United States recognized as the "accepted framework" Justice Jackson's tripartite scheme for judicial review of presidential authority. *Youngstown Co*, 343 US at 587 (Jackson, J. concurring). First, "[w]hen the President acts pursuant to an express or implied authorization of Congress, his authority is at its maximum, for it includes all that he possesses in his own right plus all that Congress can delegate." 343 US at 635. Second, "[w]hen the President acts in absence of either a congressional grant or denial of authority, he can only rely upon his own independent powers, but there is a zone of twilight in which he and Congress may have concurrent authority, or in which distribution is uncertain." *Id.*, at 637. In such a circumstance, presidential authority can derive support from "congressional inertia, indifference or quiescence." *Ibid.* Finally, "[w]hen the President takes measures incompatible with the expressed or implied will of Congress, his power is at its lowest ebb," and a court will sustain his actions "only by disabling the Congress from acting upon the subject." *Id.* at 637-638.

Here, the President's Executive Order directs the Agriculture Secretary to take two actions. First, it directs that the Agriculture Secretary "cease allocating subsidies available under the [SIRA]." Second, it directs the Agriculture Secretary to "use the funds made available under said act to subsidize businesses engaged in the harvesting and sale of organic vegetables."

I. The President's Authority to Order the Agriculture Secretary to Cease Allocating Subsidies Available Under the SIRA: The Agriculture Secretary may argue that the

President is granted authority under the SIRA to cease the distribution of subsidies. This power in the President is implied from the fact that the act calls upon the executive branch, through the Agriculture Secretary, to administer the subsidy program. Further, the act provides that subsidies are to be funded "only to the extent needed." Thus, the Agriculture Secretary will argue, the executive branch is in the superior position to determine what funds are needed to administer the program. Here, the President declared that the "shrimp industry in the Gulf of Mexico [had] fully recovered from the devastation of Hurricane Katrina." Thus, the Agriculture Secretary will argue, the President's order falls under the first prong of Justice Jackson's tripartite inquiry and, as such, a reviewing court should give great deference to the authority of the President.

The Shrimp Association will argue, however, that while subsidies to its members are not perpetual and, as stated by Congress, should only be funded to the extent needed, Congress reserved to itself the determination whether continuation of the subsidy was necessary. The act provides that "Congress shall annually appropriate the funds for such subsidy only to the extent needed." Here, Congress appropriated in 2010 funding for the subsidy, thereby indicating that the continuation of the subsidy was necessary. Nothing expressly stated in the act supports the conclusion that the President was granted the power to determine the continued necessity of the Congressional grant of the subsidy or that the President could cease funding of the subsidy once the funds were appropriated. Thus, the Shrimp Association will argue, the President's exercise of authority falls under the third prong of Justice Jackson's tripartite inquiry because the President's action is inconsistent with the action taken by Congress. Thus the President's authority is at its weakest and the President's action should be deemed unauthorized.

Moreover, the Shrimp Association may argue the President is under an affirmative constitutional duty to see that the will of Congress is done. US Const Art 2 § 3 provides that the President "shall take Care that the Laws be faithfully executed." Here, Congress determined in its wisdom to authorize a subsidy to assist a sector of the economy that was "crippled" by a natural disaster. While the President may declare that the industry is recovered, it is for Congress and not the President to undue the subsidy once appropriated. In the absence of legislation repealing or otherwise ending the appropriation, the Association may argue the President is constitutionally required to implement the SIRA in the manner provided by Congress.

II. The President's Authority to Order that Funds Appropriated Under the SIRA Be Used to Subsidize the Organic Vegetable Industry: Review of the President's authority to order that the funds be used to subsidize the organic vegetable industry may arguably fall under the second prong of Justice Jackson's three-part inquiry, as Congress was silent in regard to subsidizing the organic vegetable industry. However, a stronger argument may also be advanced that this aspect of the President's order falls under the third prong of Justice Jackson's three-part test because funds used to implement the President's order are diverted away from a program specifically authorized by Congress.

This said, there is little doubt that the President is encroaching on the power constitutionally vested in the Congress when he orders the funds be used to subsidize the organic vegetable industry. The foundation of our federal constitution rests on the principle of separation of powers. Congress, in executing its policymaking authority under Article I of the Constitution, had the authority to assist through a government subsidy an industry that was adversely impacted by a natural disaster. US Const Art I § 1; Art I § 8 cl 18. By contrast, "[t]he Constitution limits [the President's] functions in the lawmaking process to the recommending of laws he thinks wise and the vetoing of laws he thinks bad." *Youngstown*, 343 US at 587.

The President's Executive Order usurps from Congress the power to legislate. The President can ask Congress to enact laws to promote the consumption of healthier foods and to subsidize the organic vegetable industry, but he cannot direct that a presidential policy be executed in a manner prescribed by the President. *Youngstown*, 343 US at 587. This is particularly true where the Congress has authorized and appropriated funds to implement legislation enacted by Congress and the President is directing a member of his cabinet to refrain from doing that which is specifically directed by Congress and instead to use the appropriated funds to effectuate a different policy. *Id.*

The Agriculture Secretary may argue the President possesses residual emergency powers not expressly enumerated in the Constitution and that these powers permit him to order the Secretary to divert the funds earmarked for the gulf coast shrimp industry to the organic vegetable industry. *US v Bishop*, 555 F2d 771 (CA 10, 1977). Here, the claimed emergency would emanate from poor dietary habits of Americans. However, in the instances where emergency powers are recognized, the emergency is much more exigent than dietary concerns. See CJS, War Powers of the President, § 54. A reviewing court is likely to conclude the President exceeded his presidential authority and thus the Agriculture Secretary cannot use funds in the manner described in the Executive Order.

Student Answer—July 2010

Question 6—Constitutional Law—None Available

CRIMINAL LAW

Questions, Model Answers, and Student Answers

The following section includes prior Michigan Bar Exam questions and model answers for **Criminal Law**. Many of the questions also include actual student answers with the amount of points that were earned to give you a better idea of what the graders expect. The student answers are immediately following the model answer for each question. Please pay close attention to the points received on each question. Although most samples represent "good" answers (i.e., received 8, 9, or 10 points), there are some samples that received 7 points (the minimum "passing" score for an essay), and a few that received very low scores to help you better understand the grading process and what is expected.

February 2001—Question 14

Mark Williams drove a truck for a company that supplied Twinkies for vending machines. While making a delivery to Butch's Truck Stop, Mark was walking from his truck to the shop carrying a box of Twinkies when he was approached by Harry Sweetooth. Harry was wearing a long trench coat, had his left hand in the coat pocket, and his right hand was covered with a blue scarf. Harry then asked Mark if he could have some of those Twinkies, and Mark replied, "I can't do that, or I would lose my job." To this Harry responded, "What is more important, your job or your life?" Mark reconsidered his job security, placed a case of Twinkies on the sidewalk and walked back to the truck.

Mark drove the truck away from this location and called the police on his cellular phone. Within several minutes, the police were in the area and observed a man (who matched the description of Harry) walking down the street eating a Twinkie. At the time the officer stopped him, Harry was wearing a blue scarf around his neck and a long trench coat. With his consent, Harry was searched and no weapons or any other personal objects were found on his person. Harry voluntarily told the police that he never intended to scare Mark, he never intended to threaten Mark, and what he said was simply a joke based upon a movie he had seen on television the night before. The box of Twinkies was found on the sidewalk where Mark left them, and there were no Twinkies missing. Mark told the officer that while he did not see any weapon, since his life was threatened, he assumed that Harry had a weapon in either his coat pocket or under the scarf.

Harry was arrested. You are the Assistant Prosecuting Attorney and the arresting officer comes to you seeking a complaint and warrant.

Limited to the following potential charges, which ones could be sustained by the facts of this case, which ones could not be sustained, and why?

1. **Armed robbery,**
2. **Unarmed robbery,**
3. **Assault with intent to rob and steal being unarmed.**

Model Answer to Question 14

Under the facts of this case, a charge of armed robbery, MCL 750.529, would not be sustained. The statute on armed robbery requires that the robber be armed with a dangerous weapon, or any article used or fashioned in a manner to lead the person so assaulted to reasonably believe it to be a dangerous weapon. There must be some article or object that the assailant possesses and it is used in a manner to induce the reasonable belief that this article is a dangerous weapon. The facts in this case establish that Mark never saw a weapon, was never told a weapon existed, there was no gesture made indicating the presence of a weapon, nor was he threatened in a manner that would give rise to the belief that any certain weapon existed, i.e., "I will shoot you"; "I will cut your throat", etc. Words or threats alone can never be dangerous weapons, and the facts must show that the assailant possessed some article, not just that the victim thought he was armed.

A charge of unarmed robbery would probably not be sustained under the facts of this case because the statute provides that "any person who *** by putting in fear, feloniously robs or takes from the person of another *** any property which may be the subject of the larceny." From the facts, it does not appear that Harry actually took anything from Mark, including the Twinkies. Credit can be given if the applicant argues that when Mark placed the Twinkies on the ground, this was sufficient to constitute a taking and therefore the unarmed robbery charge would be appropriate.

Harry could be charged and convicted of "assault with intent to rob while unarmed." This offense requires an assault, which has been defined for the purpose of this statute as containing a mental element where the actor engages in some form of threatening conduct designed to put another in apprehension of an immediate battery. It is not a requirement that the accused possess the actual ability to carry out the threat. For the purpose of this statute, the lack of ability to carry out the threatened harm is irrelevant as long as the victim reasonably apprehends an imminent battery. It is not the secret intent to the assaulting party nor the undisclosed fact of his ability or inability to commit a battery that is material, but whether the acts cause the victim to reasonably believe that the assailant will do what is threatened. *See People v Banks*, 454 Mich 469 (1997); *People v Reeves*, 458 Mich 236 (1998).

Student Answer—February 2001

Question 14—Criminal Law—9 points

Armed robbery is the same as larceny + force. Someone must take something (property) with the intent to permanently deprive the owner of it. In the present case, the box of twinkies was found on the sidewalk where Mark had left them and there were no twinkies missing. Therefore there was no moving of the twinkies; moreover, when the police found Harry he stated he never intended to steal the twinkies (no specific intent) and he wasn't found with a weapon on him, therefore due to lack of evidence to prove the elements of the case of armed robbery this charge would probably not be sustained by the facts. Furthermore the unarmed robbery would fail to be sustained for the same reason armed robbery fails to be sustained, in that the twinkies were never moved from the spot where Mark put them and Harry said he had no intention of stealing the twinkies due to robbery being a specific intent crime. On the other hand, assault with intent to rob and steal being unarmed may be sustained if it is found that Mark had an eminent fear of danger when Harry responded with the words "what is more important, your job or your life?" I believe this could constitute an assault; however, Harry may not have the requisite specific intent to rob and steal. Probably sustained but would be a matter of fact to be decided by the jury.

July 2001—Question 1

Thomas Casey was a renowned trial lawyer who was out celebrating a very large personal injury verdict. The celebration continued into the early morning hours and consisted of drinking a large quantity of intoxicating beverages. It is undisputed that Mr. Casey was intoxicated when he left the party to drive home.

While driving home, Mr. Casey, who was traveling within the speed limit, struck a bicyclist who rode out in front of the Casey vehicle contrary to a stop sign at a side street. The street was not illuminated by any exterior lighting. The bicyclist did not have a light on the bicycle, was wearing dark clothing and was himself found to be intoxicated. The bicyclist was killed in this accident.

Mr. Casey was charged with a violation of MCL 257.625(4), which provides "a person, whether licensed or not, who operates a motor vehicle upon a highway or other place open to the general public or generally accessible to motor vehicles, including an area designated for the parking of vehicles within this state, while under the influence of intoxicating liquor or while this person's ability is visibly impaired because of intoxicating liquor and by the operation of the motor vehicle causes the death of another person, is guilty of a felony."

Mr. Casey retains you to represent him on this felony charge. He wants you to advise him of the strengths and weaknesses of his case, and what would be the issues at trial. What do you tell him and why?

Model Answer to Question 1

The issue in this case is whether the legislature, in enacting the statute, intended to require fault as a predicate to a finding of guilt. An analysis of the statute requires a determination as to whether this statute creates a strict-liability crime that does not require any proof of any fault other than the act of driving while intoxicated. The argument for a strict-liability statute would essentially be that the crime is proven by establishing that defendant was operating a vehicle, while intoxicated, and the vehicle caused the death of another. Motive or intent is not an issue as this is not a part of the statute. Contrary to this statute, many strict-liability statutes are found in regulatory measures of the police power where the emphasis of the statute is designed to achieve a social betterment rather than a punishment of a crime.

The statute in question that provides the defendant is guilty of a felony is actually designed to punish drivers when their drunken driving caused another's death. The Michigan Supreme Court has determined that it would be absurd to impose a felony conviction by virtue of interpreting the statute as divorcing the defendant's fault from the resulting injury. It is the burden of the prosecutor to prove causation, i.e., the people must establish that the intoxication produced a change in the driver's operation of the vehicle that caused the death of the victim. This, of course, would be a question for the trier of fact, but based upon the facts presented in this question, it would appear that Mr. Casey would have a reasonable defense to the felony charge. *People v Lardie*, 452 Mich 231 (1996).

Student Answer—July 2001

Question 1—Criminal Law—9 points

Crim Law
Pros:

- Celebration—large quantity of alcohol
- Undisputed Intoxication
- Was statute designed to protect people like the victim? Yes
- Was this the type of accident statute was designed to protect against? Yes

Defenses:

- Not illuminated street
- No light on bicycle
- Dark clothing
- Intoxicated
- No known defenses
- Intoxication only defense in specific intent crime
- This is general intent

The issue here is whether or not Mr. Casey can be convicted of the felony charge.

The law here is a general intent crime because it does not state that you have to specifically intend to drive while intoxicated in the designated areas listed by statute. In this particular case, Mr. Casey was ingesting a "large quantity of alcohol" at the celebration. It is undisputed that he was intoxicated. The statute under which he is charged was designed to protect people like the victim, bicyclist. This accident was also of the type the statute was designed to protect against. The language of the statute indicates that it is designed to prevent intoxicated persons from operating a motor vehicle in specific public areas. The purpose here, no doubt was to prevent this type of behavior as well as prevent any drunk driving related injuries that might result from such conduct. The statute provided that if a person is visibly impaired and under the influence of intoxicating liquor, they can be guilty of a felony if they cause the death of another person.

Here, Mr. Casey might argue that the victim contributed to his own death through his negligence. The victim ran a stop sign, he did not have a light on the bicycle, he was wearing dark clothing, and he himself was intoxicated. Under the statute, however, the defendant, Mr. Casey, cannot argue contributory negligence because the statute imposes a strict liability for its violation. Mr. Casey violated the statute according to its terms—the victim was the type of person, any person who was supposed to be protected by the statute and the accident was the type the statute was supposed to prevent. Mr. Casey cannot argue that victim violated the statute because the statute only applies to motor vehicles, not bicycles. Intoxication is also not a defense for Mr. Casey because even though Mr. Casey was intoxicated, voluntary intoxication is not a defense to a general intent crime, only specific intent crimes.

Therefore, I would advise Mr. Casey that we should seek some sort of plea bargain with the prosecutor's office because he is most likely guilty of violating this statute, MCL 257.265(4).

Comment: Notice that this answer reaches a different conclusion than the model answer but only 1 point is deducted. This example demonstrates the importance of knowing the law and making "logical" analysis, regardless of the conclusion, is what is important.

February 2002—Question 9

Bruce had a girlfriend by the name of Gloria and they had been "dating" on and off for several years. Their relationship could best be described as "tumultuous" with frequent arguments that never resulted in any physical abuse. After their final, final breakup, Gloria began dating Bruce's brother Mike. One evening while driving her car, Gloria saw Bruce standing near his favorite party store. She drove the car next to the curb, rolled down the passenger side window, and yelled out to Bruce, "Your brother is a lot more man than you ever were." Bruce, taking offense to this remark, pulled out a knife from his pocket and said, "When I finish with you no one is going to want to look at you." Bruce was approximately 10 feet from the passenger side door when he made this statement. Before moving from his position, Gloria, who had suddenly realized she might have gone too far, became fearful of Bruce and immediately drove her car away. Gloria reported this incident to the police who found witnesses that confirmed her statement. Bruce was then charged with felonious assault.

Bruce comes into your office and discusses retaining you to represent him on this charge. He wants to know the elements of this offense; what, if any, are his defenses; what lesser charges, if any, could he be convicted of; and what you expect the prosecutor to argue concerning the charge of felonious assault. What do you tell him?

Model Answer to Question 9

The offense of felonious assault is defined as (1) simple assault, (2) aggravated by the use of a weapon, and (3) including the element of present ability or apparent present ability to commit a battery. Included in the definition of an assault is an act that places another in reasonable apprehension of receiving an immediate battery. There is no question from these facts that Gloria experienced reasonable apprehension of receiving an immediate battery. The issue is whether, considering the distance between the two, Bruce had the apparent or present ability to commit a battery. You emphasize to Bruce that he was approximately 10 feet away, it does not appear that he stepped forward, and Gloria was on the driver's side of the car talking to him through the passenger window. From these facts, it could be successfully argued that Bruce did not have the apparent or present ability to commit a battery. The prosecutor would argue that until Gloria drove away there was nothing to stop Bruce from completing the battery or for that matter throwing the knife at Gloria.

While it may be difficult for the Prosecutor to prevail on the charge of felonious assault, Bruce would probably be convicted of simple assault, which would be a lesser-included offense of the felonious assault charge. *People v Sanford*, 402 Mich 460, 479 (1978); *People v Johnson*, 407 Mich 196, 210 (1979); *People v Grant*, 211 MA 200 (1995).

Student Answer—February 2002

Question 9—Criminal Law—7 points

A felonious assault is the specific intent of a person to commit a battery, which is a harmful or offensive touching. Felonious assault also adds the element of committing an assault with a weapon. For a specific intent crime as we have here we do need the (1) intent to commit the crime *and* (2) the close proximity. Future threats are not enough. Here we do have a weapon, Bruce's knife, which fulfills the "felonious" element. Now to the assault. Even if Bruce had the intent to harm Gloria w/his knife by saying "When I finish w/you no one is going to want to look at you," he was only making a future threat and therefore not imminent & in close proximity. Gloria (Prosecutor) may argue that she did not see this as a future threat b/c under close proximity, Bruce was only 10 feet from the passenger side door when he made the statement. If this future threat does not amount to an assault, then Bruce may even be charged w/no crime b/c it negates the intent & that negated the weapon.

I would advise my client that b/c of the future threat he lacked the specific intent to commit the crime, but his past relationship w/Gloria may be highly considered b/c of their frequent arguments. However, there was never any physical abuse & that will benefit Bruce & negate the fact that Gloria was scared & that he went too far b/c he never did in the past!

July 2002—Question 8

Billy Bob Johnson and his buddy John (Big Dog) Smith were driving Billy Bob's pickup truck from south Alabama to northern Michigan for the annual smelt run. They had heard on their CB radio that at mile marker 375 in the Upper Peninsula of Michigan on northbound I-75 the police were conducting a roadside stop of vehicles to check for drunk drivers. As they were approaching mile marker 375, they saw flashing lights and a sign indicating that all cars were to pull off on the shoulder and stop. Billy Bob and Big Dog had never heard of such silliness and decided the smelt were running and so were they. They simply stayed in their lane of travel and continued down the road. Shortly thereafter they were pulled over by two sheriff cars. Both Billy Bob and Big Dog exited the pickup when asked to do so. The truck was searched and nothing illegal was found. Both Billy Bob and Big Dog were stone cold sober. They were both placed under arrest and charged with fleeing and eluding.

The statute, in pertinent part, provides that "a driver of a motor vehicle who is given by hand or light a visible signal by a police officer, acting in the lawful performance of his or her duty, directing the driver to bring his or her vehicle to a stop, shall not willfully fail to obey that direction and attempt to flee or elude the police officer."

Over one year before this occurrence, the Michigan Supreme Court had unanimously ruled that all stops to check for drunk drivers were unconstitutional. The Sheriff's Department involved in this case did not believe the Court meant what it said and in any event did not feel that the decision applied to the Upper Peninsula.

You are appointed to represent the driver of the truck, Billy Bob Johnson. You enter a plea of not guilty and demand a jury trial. Confining your answer to the pending charge, what is your defense, or defenses, how is this issue decided, and what will be the probable outcome?

Model Answer to Question 8

The first issue that is presented is whether the sheriffs were acting in the lawful performance of their duty. Based upon the facts of this case, it appears that there was no legal justification for the stop since these particular stops had been determined by the highest court to be unconstitutional. The Court of Appeals has concluded that the necessary element of a lawful arrest that exists on a charge of resisting arrest also applies to a charge of fleeing and eluding. An essential element of the fleeing and eluding is that the attempted stop must have been lawful and to be a lawful stop, the officers must demonstrate that they had probable cause for the stop. *People v Grayer*, 235 Mich App 737 (1999).

Without probable cause, an essential element of the crime does not exist. Whether the facts would support a conviction of the charge by a jury is not the issue that needs to be determined. The issue is whether probable cause existed for the stop or attempted stop of the truck out on the roadway. The existence of probable cause is a legal question to be decided by the trial court as compared to a jury.

There are no facts in this case that would support a finding of probable cause for stopping the truck. The Michigan Supreme Court had struck down the statute that formed the basis for the attempted stop and based upon the facts there was no probable cause for the sheriff's department stopping the defendants' vehicle. The charges in this case should be dismissed on a motion of the defendant.

Student Answer—July 2002

Question 8—Criminal Law—10 points

Billy Bob & John are liable under valid Michigan law while traveling through the state. The question here is whether they are criminally liable under the statute, which the Michigan Supreme Court held unconstitutional prior to this incident.

A person can lawfully resist an unlawful arrest. Here, the statute, as unconstitutional, does not hold Billy liable for fleeing & eluding. Police only stopped the truck because it failed to obey their sign to pull over. No other probable cause. Police would have a valid basis to continue this procedure if they had not known of the court's decision and reasonably relied on the statute. Statutes are presumed to be constitutional until held otherwise. Here, the police completely disregarded the Ct's decision. Billy should ask that charges be dismissed. The court will probably dismiss.

February 2003—Question 2

James Daley was a longtime drug dealer and his ex-girlfriend, Wanda Corley, was one of his best sellers. James and Wanda broke up when James accused Wanda of selling drugs at a higher price than what she reported to him and keeping this extra for herself. The more James thought about this, the angrier he became. Finally, he decided to go to Wanda's apartment and told his new roommate, Billy Snitch, he was going to "even things out." James knew Wanda generally had weapons in her apartment and that she favored a large bolo knife as her weapon of choice.

James was accompanied to Wanda's by Billy Snitch, who provided the following testimony that was uncontradicted:

> James went to Wanda's home and brought with him his trusty six-shooter. Without bothering to knock or ring, he opened the screen door of the home and said, "I've come to right a wrong." Wanda, who was standing about 15 feet away from him, picked up her knife and replied, "I'm finally going to get a chance to fix that ugly face of yours." Wanda took one step toward James, and he took one step back into the open doorway and pulled out his gun and shot and killed Wanda.

James was convicted of second-degree murder. At trial, he requested the trial court instruct the jury on self-defense and imperfect self-defense. The trial court refused to instruct the jury on any theory of self-defense, stating that James was not entitled to this defense as a matter of law.

You are the clerk for the Court of Appeals judge assigned to write the opinion on the appeal. **What are the elements of second-degree murder and was James entitled to any instruction on self-defense? Why or why not?**

Model Answer to Question 2

Second-degree murder requires that the defendant caused the death of the victim and that the killing was done with malice and without justification. Malice is the intent to kill, the intent to do great bodily harm, or the intent to create a high risk of death or great bodily harm with knowledge that death or great bodily harm will be the probable result. Malice may be inferred from the facts and circumstances of the killing. *People v Harris*, 190 Mich App 652 (1991).

The primary issue deals with James' intent and that is not necessarily clear from the facts provided. Self-defense is not available when the defendant is the aggressor, unless he withdraws from any further encounter with the victim and communicates that withdrawal to the victim.

It appears from the uncontested facts that James was the aggressor and while he took a step backward, there is no indication that he was intending to withdraw from any encounter, nor did he communicate this intent to Wanda.

Imperfect self-defense is a qualified defense that can mitigate second-degree murder to voluntary manslaughter. It negates the element of malice. The determination as to whether this defense is permitted is based upon the intent with which the accused brought on the quarrel or difficulty. Malice may be inferred and in this case, it would be reasonable to infer that James has created the situation intending to either take a life or inflict grievous bodily harm. This intent is sufficient to deny James the availability of imperfect self-defense.

An argument can and should be made concerning the possible uncertainty of James' intent. The statement to "even things out" or to "right a wrong," taken alone does not necessarily support a finding that he intended to kill or commit grievous bodily harm. However, when taken in conjunction with the loaded gun and the entry into the house without permission, the trial court would be correct in its decision to deny James's request for any instruction on self-defense.

Finally, there is a significant question as to whether James, under any circumstances, was entitled to use deadly force. From the facts of this case, it appears that James was at the threshold of walking out the door from a person who was approximately 15 feet away carrying a knife. While James is certainly going to contend that he was entitled to defend himself from a risk of death or great bodily harm, the fact is that he could have apparently left and he gave Wanda no notice of his intention to use deadly force. His actions as set forth in these facts would be sufficient to deny any basis for an instruction on self-defense.

People v Kemp, 202 Mich App 318 (1993).

Student Answer—February 2003

Question 2—Criminal Law—8 points

Second-Degree Murder

Issue: Whether James can be found guilty of second degree murder.

Rule: In every crime there are 3 things that must all come together in order to complete the crime.

1. *Mens rea:* this is the degree of guilt one (the defendant) has in their mind.
2. *Actus rea:* this is the actual conduct that the defendant does making him or her guilty.
3. *Causation:* The defendant is the actual cause of the criminal outcome.

With second degree murder, the mens rea isn't as high as first degree which requires intent to kill. Second degree murder requires the defendant to intend to cause serious bodily injury likely to cause death, willful or wanton conduct that the defendant should know is likely to cause death or felony-murder killing where a death occurs in the commission of an inherently dangerous felony.

It should be noted that Michigan requires the prosecution to show malice. In addition, the prosecution is required to show *all* elements beyond ALL reasonable doubt.

Application: Here we're told that the more James "thought about this", he became angrier. This means that he had an angry mind when he went over to Wanda's house. The prosecution can use this to set the stage for a showing of a willful or wanton mind.

In addition, the prosecution can say that James, by going to the house with the weapon knowing Wanda had weapons were facts that James should've known were likely to lead to serious bodily injury.

Conclusion: Thus, I think the prosecution can show that he is guilty of 2nd degree murder beyond a reasonable doubt.

Self Defense

Issue: Can James use self defense to mitigate the murder down to manslaughter?

Rule: In Michigan, we recognize imperfect defense as a way to mitigate second degree murder. This occurs when the defendant is claiming self defense and the facts show that he acted unreasonably.

Self defense is where the defendant is acting in such a way that he is protecting himself from harm. The defendant can only use deadly force when such force is used against him.

Application: James force here was clearly unreasonable. First, he had a duty to retreat when reasonably available. Here, he could have walked out the door which he did.

In addition, he could be viewed as the initial aggressor since he's the one who first came to the house. This imperfect defense is what the defense must prove by a preponderance of the evidence.

Conclusion: The court should allow James the chance to present this defense to the fact finders. They then can decide whether this defense mitigates 2nd degree murder.

July 2003—Question 12

Charles Benson went to the local hardware store looking for a hatchet to use on some tree branches at his home. He was quite surprised at the high price for a good hatchet ($125) and felt that this was a rip-off. Charles decided that what was good for the store was good for him and walked out of the store with the hatchet under his camouflaged jacket. Unfortunately, Charles was seen placing the hatchet under his jacket and leaving the store without paying for it. Carla Brown, the employee who saw the incident, went into the parking lot and confronted Charles as he was getting into his pickup. Carla told Charles that she saw what he had done and he was to return to the store with her. Charles stepped out of the pickup and said that if she didn't immediately shut up and go back to the store, his hatchet would start being used on her instead of his tree branches. Carla did go directly back into the store, but not until she memorized Charles' license plate number. Charles was arrested about an hour later at his home in the process of trimming one of his trees.

Charles was charged with various criminal offenses including armed robbery as set forth in the Michigan statute. MCL 750.529. Charles, after making bail, comes into your office and explains everything that happened and asks you to represent him. You agree to represent Charles, and after confirming his story, you decide to file a motion to dismiss the armed robbery charge. **What will be the basis for your motion and what will be your chance of success?**

Model Answer to Question 12

Based on a recent decision of the Michigan Court of Appeals, you should be successful in your motion. The relevant language of the armed robbery statute is "any person who shall assault another and shall feloniously rob, steal and take from his person, or in his presence . . . property which may be the subject of a larceny, such robber being armed with a dangerous weapon or any article used or fashioned in a manner to lead the person so assaulted to reasonably believe it to be . . . shall be guilty of a felony."

The critical issue in regard to the armed robbery charge is whether the threat with the hatchet was a continuation of the theft of the hatchet from the store that will turn the larceny into an armed robbery. The "transaction approach" that has found some favor in the law looks at the robbery as not being complete until the robber has escaped with the stolen merchandise. Under this approach, the robber can turn a larceny into an armed or unarmed robbery if he employs the requisite degree of force to effect his escape or retain the property. The missing element in this case, and the missing element in the transactional approach, is that there is no taking from the person. Charles stole from the store, he did not take anything from Carla. The Michigan Court of Appeals in the decision of *People v Scruggs* has not determined that the armed robbery and unarmed robbery statute require a taking from the person accompanied by contemporaneous application or threat of force or violence. If the force and/or threat is used later to retain the property, no armed or unarmed robbery has occurred.

People v Scruggs, 256 Mich App 303 (2003).

Two Student Answers—July 2003

Question 12—Criminal Law—10 points

We would argue that all the elements needed for an armed robbery are not present. To have an armed robbery you need a larceny with force. A larceny consists of the taking or carrying away with person property with intent to permanently deprive. We can say that we have this because Mr. Benson is taking personal property that is not his and he is going to keep it. However because it is a robbery it needs to be from a person. Since Mr. Benson took the hatchet from the store not from and individual there is no robbery. If he had taken the hatchet out of another's hands or off another person—threatened them with force—then the elements of armed robbery would have been met. Under these circumstances no actual force is necessary; the threat of force is enough to satisfy that element. Since the prosecution cannot show or prove that Mr. Benson took the property from a person by force or threat of force the elements of the crime are not satisfied. Therefore the motion to dismiss should be granted as to an armed robbery charge.

We may also argue that when he went to the store he did not intend to steal the property. He went to the store intending to purchase the hatchet but when he thought he was being ripped off only then did he decide to not pay for the property.

Again, one of the elements would be missing so the charge would have to be dismissed.

Question 12—Criminal Law—8 points

Robbery—The taking, carrying away the personal property of another with intent to steal with force or in presence. The basis will be that he can't be charged with armed robbery because then the stealing of a hatchet—which could be considered as the "arm" in armed robbery creates the armed robbery just by stealing the hatchet. It would not be successful because if he just stole the hatchet it would be larceny but since he used force or threats of immediate bodily injury to Carla to steal it and get away then it is armed robbery. He could also try to argue that Carla doesn't own the hatchet, she is just an employee at the store, but Carla is an agent of store, (example robbing bank teller), so it is not a good argument. He took the hatchet, and carried it out of the store & was personal property of another, & he had intent to steal & stole it with force in presence. He could also argue that it is not a person or closely associated with a person: example—snatching purse if no struggle then a larceny, but if a struggle then robbery. Here the worker tried to stop him & he threatened her with a weapon & a threat of immediate bodily harm so it is armed robbery.

February 2004—Question 14

Dave Billings was a twenty-one-year-old who had left home to see the US. He had some money from work in his hometown and was able to supplement his income with odd jobs in a variety of towns while he hitchhiked around the country. One evening while hitchhiking, an older male who gave his name as Jesse picked him up. After driving for approximately one hour, Jesse told him he needed to stop and get some fuel. Jesse pulled the car into an all-night gas station, and Dave agreed to pay for the gas. As Dave was fueling the car, the tank being on the driver's side, Jesse went into the station. Upon returning to the car, Jesse told Dave that the attendant was alone and that this was the perfect setup to make some money. Jesse opened the trunk and retrieved a large pearl-handled pistol. Jesse told Dave the pistol was his withdrawal card and told Dave to stay outside the car and keep a lookout and honk the horn if anyone was coming.

Jesse was never found and never charged with any crime. Unfortunately for Dave, there was both a video and sound recording at the gas pumps and everything that was said and done was on tape. Dave's attorney at first tried to suppress the tape, but was unsuccessful. Dave testified at his preliminary examination and stated that he didn't know Jesse; he really didn't know what Jesse was going to do when he went in the station, that he was only standing outside the car to stretch his legs and was just starting to walk to the passenger's side when Jesse ran out of the station. At the conclusion of the preliminary examination, Dave's attorney moved to dismiss the charges, claiming that as a matter of law, the charge of aiding and abetting a felony murder could not be sustained.

Assume that the necessary elements are present for felony murder and, confining your answer solely to the motion concerning this charge, what are the arguments for and against this motion and what will be the probable result?

Model Answer to Question 14

Dave's attorney would probably argue that a defendant cannot be convicted of aiding and abetting if the guilt of the principal has not been shown. There has not even been any charge issued against the "principal" and it is not known who this person is. While the guilt of the principal needs to be established, the principal does not have to be convicted in order for a defendant to be charged and convicted of aiding and abetting. The Michigan courts have also held that the identity of the principal is not necessary to convict as long as there is sufficient evidence of the guilt of the principal. *People v Wilson*, 196 Mich App 604 (1992); *People v Brown*, 120 Mich App 765 (1982).

The elements necessary to support a finding of aiding and abetting a felony murder are:

1. Felony murder was committed by the defendant or some other person;
2. The defendant performed acts or gave encouragement that assisted the commission of felony murder;
3. The defendant intended the commission of felony murder or had knowledge that the principal intended its commission at the time he gave aid and encouragement. *People v Carines*, 460 Mich 750 (1999).

The key questions center on Dave's knowledge and intent. This can be shown by circumstantial evidence. Dave certainly had reason to believe that an armed robbery was about to occur. Dave never verbally assisted or encouraged Jesse to commit a criminal act. From the facts it could be argued that Jesse was going to do this whether Dave acted as a lookout or not. On the other hand, by standing at the driver's side of the car where he could reach the horn, and not objecting to the statement made by Jesse before Jesse reentered the station, could support a finding that he did aid and/or encourage Jesse in the commission of this felony.

Based upon the facts of this case, it would be probable that the motion to dismiss would be denied and Dave would be required to stand trial.

Student Answer—February 2004

Question 14—Criminal Law—10 points

This issue deals with whether Dave is guilty of aiding and abetting? In MI, aiding and abetting, under the accomplice liability theory is where the prosecutor must prove that the aider and abetter or accomplice was 1) Present; 2) had actual knowledge that the Principal would commit a crime and 3) aided, abetted, encouraged, assisted the Principal in the furtherance of the crime.

Here, Dave was 1) *Present* (although Dave's attorney could argue that initially Dave as a hitchhiker and not knowing what Jesse was up to when he picked Dave up). 2) However the prosecutor will successfully argue that although Dave did not initially know Jesse's intentions, he soon came to learn of his intention b/c Jesse told Dave "this was a perfect time to make some money." Later, Jesse showed Dave his gun, so Dave "knew" that Jesse was going to commit a crime. Dave had actual knowledge that Jesse would commit a crime. 3) Prosecution will successfully argue that Dave therefore aided and abetted Jesse by "staying in the car and keeping a look out" and honk the horn if he saw anyone. Here prosecutor will argue that Dave had an opportunity to run or *"withdraw"* meaning he had time to contact the police before

Jesse committed the crime. In MI, a party must withdraw and let other accomplices know his intention to give them sufficient time to withdraw. Here Dave did neither. Rather, he remained there in the car as a look out. He was not threatened by Jesse whereby he could not leave. Therefore, the prosecutor will be successful in proving that Dave acted as an aider and abetter and encouraged and assisted the principals in the furtherance of the crime.

In MI, the aider and abetter can still be found guilty as an aider and abetter even though the principal is found not guilty. Therefore, although Jesse was never found or charged w/the crime, Dave can still be convicted as an aider and abetter. Here, Dave's attorney will *not* prevail in dismissing the charge of aiding and abetting. In addition, in MI, the prosecutor must prove malice for all murder convictions. If prosecutor proves malice in a felony murder conviction, the defendant will be guilty of 1st degree murder. The underlying felony charge will be bumped up to 1st degree murder.

July 2004—Question 15

Maxine Larson, a 45-year-old female, was of marginal intelligence, and through a variety of physical complaints, managed to receive social security disability. In addition to the limited social security benefits she was receiving, she was able to obtain living accommodations in a subsidized senior citizen apartment. Everyone living in the building was required to be able to provide for themselves, but a large number were quite elderly with a multitude of physical disabilities and illnesses.

Maxine was a problem from her first day of living there, arguing with other residents and refusing to follow any of the rules of the apartment. The landlord advised her that he was going to give her a seven-day notice to quit and she would have to find other housing. Maxine became enraged at this and told the landlord that he better change his mind or he would be sorry. She continued to brood on the unfairness of it all and decided that if she wasn't going to be able to live in her apartment, no one was going to live there. The next evening she waited until 9:00 p.m. and poured lighter fluid on her bed and lit it with a match. When the fire started, she left the apartment and walked outside. Martha Sands lived two doors down from Maxine and smelled the smoke. Martha had a severe heart condition but was able to call 911 and walk outside the building before the fire trucks arrived.

All of the residents were able to exit the building safely, but the building ultimately burned to the ground. While outside in her nightgown watching the fire, Martha suffered a fatal heart attack. During the attempts to put out the fire, and before Martha collapsed, Maxine commented to two other residents, "I'm glad no one was hurt and I guess this will show him."

An investigation was conducted and it was determined that the source of the fire was Maxine's bedroom and that an accelerant had been used. Coupled with the statement she made to the landlord and the two residents, Maxine was charged with first-degree felony murder. At trial, the testimony of both the landlord and the residents was admitted, and the conclusion that the fire was deliberately set was unopposed by any evidence of the defendant. The medical examiner testified that in his opinion,

Martha's fatal heart attack was a result of the stress and excitement caused by the fire. On cross exam, he admitted that Martha could have died at any time from heart failure and, in fact, in view of the condition of her heart, he was surprised she lived as long as she did. At the conclusion of the prosecutor's proofs, Maxine made a motion for a directed verdict of not guilty of felony murder. The trial court denied the motion and Maxine was then convicted of the charge.

On appeal Maxine argues that under these facts she cannot be convicted of first-degree felony murder. She claims there is insufficient evidence to convict her of arson, that there is no evidence that she intended to kill anyone as evidenced by her statement while standing outside and before Martha died, and that there is insufficient evidence to support a finding that the fire, if it was arson, was the proximate cause of Martha's death.

Discuss and decide these issues.

Model Answer to Question 15

Arson is an offense included in the felony murder statute. MCL 750.316. Arson is defined as the willful or malicious burning of any dwelling house, either occupied or unoccupied. From the facts of this case, there is evidence that a rational trier of fact could find that Maxine committed the crime of arson. This evidence includes the statement made to the landlord, the statements made during the fire to other residents, and the findings as a result of the arson investigation. For those reasons, the appellate court would not reverse the conviction on the basis that arson had not been proven.

The intent to commit the underlying felony, standing alone, is not sufficient to establish the necessary mens rea for murder. Even if taken at face value, the statement that she was glad that no one was injured does not preclude a conviction of felony murder. First-degree felony murder does not require a specific intent to kill. First-degree felony murder requires a showing of malice. Malice is defined as the intention to kill, the intent to do great bodily harm, or the wanton and willful disregard of the likelihood that the natural tendency of defendant's behavior is to cause death or great bodily harm. Even if Maxine did not intend to kill anyone, the setting on fire of her bed at 9:00 p.m. in an apartment house occupied by the elderly is sufficient for the trier of fact to find that there was a wanton and willful disregard of the likelihood that her actions would cause death or great bodily harm.

Maxine's claim that due to the health of the deceased, the death was not a foreseeable consequence of Maxine's acts, would also not be sufficient to require the court to reverse the conviction. A criminal defendant takes the victim as found. By starting the fire, Maxine set into motion a series of events that adversely affected the residents of the apartment complex. The tenants were forced to flee their apartments and became victims of Maxine's intentional act. It did not matter that the other residents were able to survive the consequences of her action; Martha was not. Maxine found a victim who had severe heart problems and is required by law to take the victim as she finds her. There was sufficient evidence presented where the trier of fact could find that the death was both foreseeable and proximately caused by the fire.

The Court of Appeals would not reverse the jury conviction of first-degree felony murder. *See People v McKenzie*, 206 Mich App 425 (1994); *Matter of Robinson*, 180 Mich App 454 (1989).

Two Student Answers—July 2004

Question 15—Criminal Law—9 points

Maxine Larson, a 45 year old female was charged with 1st degree felony murder. A felony murder is the result of a serious felony and a death results. Robbery, arson, burglary, rape, is the types of felony that would be considered for felony murder.

Arson is a type of felony that would include felony murder. Although Maxine did not intend to kill anyone, intent to is not required only intent to commit the arson.

If Maxine is convicted of the felony arson she could then be convicted of felony murder.

In this case the medical examiner testified that in his opinion Martha's fatal heart attack was a result of the stress and excitement caused by the fire. Since the medical examiner would be an expert and if he satisfied the court as to his expertise the jury then could consider his opinion as to the cause of Martha's death or the jury may disregard his opinion.

After all on cross examination he stated he was surprised Martha lived this long. The investigator concluded the fire started in Maxine's bedroom and that an accelerant had been used.

Coupled with the statement Maxine made to landlord "he better change his mind or he would be sorry" and the statement she made to two other residents "I'm glad no one was hurt and I guess this will show him" a jury could find Maxine responsible for setting the fire and therefore guilty of 1st degree felony murder.

Moreover Maxine should have known even with marginal intelligence that starting a fire in a senior citizen apartment may result in serious injury or death.

Question 15—Criminal Law—9 points

Arson

The crime of arson consists of the intentional burning of a dwelling house of another. Here, the intentional setting fire to an apt in an apartment house, with the use of an accelerant, in her bedroom would be enough to find Maxine (M) guilty of arson. It is reasonably foreseeable that the "dwelling houses of another" would burn in the course of intentionally starting a fire in one of the apartments. Therefore, M is guilty of arson. In addition to this, there were statements made as threats to the landlord whom would be injured if he lied in the apt. house also. This should all be enough to convict M of arson.

Felony Murder 1st

To be convicted of felony murder the death must have occurred as the result of or in the commission of the felony. Here, even though there is no malice by M to want to cause harm to anyone it is foreseeable that a death could occur in setting a fire to an apt. house. It could be argued that by M fighting and arguing with the other residents that she had malice towards all of them, in addition to burning all of their homes down.

In addition, a defendant takes the victim as they find them, so Martha's heart failure could not be considered because it could be argued that if not for the fire, she may have lived longer. Therefore, M's conduct, setting the fire, proximately caused Martha's death by exasperating her heart condition.

Therefore, because M did not oppose the evidence that the fire was deliberately set at trial, in light of the evidence that it started in M's bedroom and but for the fire Martha may have lived longer than that night, M's conviction should stand as is.

February 2005—Question 11

John James and Harry Carr went to a Quality Dairy convenience store at approximately 10:30 at night with the intent of robbing the store. Harry walked in the store alone to see if there were any customers. There was no one present except the clerk and Harry went back out to the car and told John that the clerk was alone. They both walked back in the store and as they approached the clerk, John pulled a pistol from under his coat. John pointed the gun at the clerk and Harry walked around the counter to the cash register. Harry told the clerk to open the cash drawer and the clerk told Harry that it was locked and could not be opened. Harry then told John to shoot the clerk, claiming he was lying. Harry then tried to open the register and found it was locked. Harry then took the clerk's wallet and watch and began walking toward the door and again told John to shoot the clerk. John just followed Harry out the door without shooting anyone.

John and Harry were caught within five minutes of leaving the store when the clerk called in their car's license number. Harry was charged and convicted of armed robbery and violation of the felony firearm statute under a theory of aiding and abetting. The felony firearm statute provides: "A person who carries or has in his or her possession a firearm when he or she commits or attempts to commit a felony." The aiding and abetting statute provides: "Every person concerned in the commission of an offense, whether he directly commits the act constituting the offense or procures, counsels, aids, or abets in its commission may hereafter be prosecuted, indicted, tried and on conviction shall be punished as if he had directly committed such offense."

You are appointed to represent Harry on appeal, and at Harry's instruction, you are told to only appeal the felony firearm conviction. **What will your arguments be concerning the felony firearm conviction and what will the probable result be?**

Model Answer to Question 11

The purpose of the aiding and abetting statute is to permit conviction of a defendant of the principal offense whether he directly commits the act constituting the offense or procures, counsels, aids, or abets in its commission. Aiding and abetting means to assist the perpetrator of a crime. An aider and abettor is one who is present at the crime scene and by word or deed gives active encouragement to the perpetrator of the crime, or by his conduct makes clear that he is ready to assist the perpetrator if such assistance is needed.

The standard for establishing felony-firearm under an aiding and abetting theory is whether the defendant's words or deeds procured, counseled, aided, or abetted another to carry or have in his possession a firearm during the commission or attempted commission of a felony-firearm offense.

Under the facts of this case you would argue that while Harry aided and abetted in the commission of the armed robbery, there are no facts that demonstrate that he did anything to aid or abet the possession of the firearm. At one point in Michigan, it was necessary for such a conviction to establish that the defendant procured, counseled, aided or abetted the principal in obtaining or retaining possession of the firearm. The Michigan Supreme Court has recently decided that what is required to be proven is that defendant aided and abetted another in carrying or having in his possession a firearm while that other commits or attempts to commit a felony. It is still necessary to establish that the defendant performed acts or gave encouragement that assisted in the commission of the felony-firearm violation. The amount of advice, aid, or encouragement is not material if it had the effect of inducing the commission of the felony. Harry would be found to have aided or abetted the possessing of the gun just as though he aided or abetted John in acquiring or retaining possession of the gun.

Based on the foregoing, you would not be successful in basing your appeal solely on this issue. *See People v Harris, People v Moore*, 470 Mich 56 (2004).

Student Answer—February 2005

Question 11—Criminal Law—9 points

The issue is whether Harry's conviction will stand on appeal.

Elements of Statute for Felony Firearm

1. a person who carries a firearm, or
2. a person who has possession of a firearm where he or she commits or attempts to commit a felony

Here Lawless has a good chance to win on appeal because the prosecution cannot prove the elements of the crime of Felony Firearm Statute because Lawless did not carry or possess the gun.

Probable Result

Lawless may however, be charged the *Aiding and Abetting Statute* regardless if John James is convicted or not because Harry did all he could to encourage the crime. 1) He cased out the store, 2) went out and told John the clerk was alone, 3) they both walked back into the store, 4) Harry demanded the clerk open the cash drawer, 5) Harry told John to shoot clerk, 6) Harry took watch and wallet from clerk and told John again to shoot clerk. More then enough to meet the statutory requirement of Aiding and Abetting.

July 2005—Question 11

Joan Hoover was pumping gas into her car at an all-night gas station located on a busy street in Lansing, Michigan. George Davis approached her from the street side of the gas station with a knife in his hand. He put the knife up to her face and told her to give him her purse and step away from the car. She did this and he jumped in the car and drove away.

The gas station attendant saw what had occurred and called the police. Joan was able to provide both the description of the car and license number. George had driven approximately two miles when he was pulled over by three patrol cars. Joan's purse was not in the car, but upon being searched, three fifty dollar bills, one twenty and three ones were found in George's pocket. This was the exact number and type of bills that Joan had informed police were in her purse.

George was charged and tried for armed robbery. At trial, he testified that he took the car, but never pulled a knife, nor in any way did he threaten Joan. He claimed he jumped in the car as he was being pursued by a gang who were intent on killing him. He further claimed that the money was his and he never saw any purse.

At the conclusion of trial, George's attorney requested that the court instruct the jury on the crime of "Unlawfully Driving Away an Automobile" (UDAA). It was the defendant's claim that this offense was a cognate lesser included offense and that he was entitled to such an instruction.

The trial court refused the instruction and George was convicted of armed robbery. George now appeals raising the sole issue that it was reversible error not to instruct on UDAA since he had requested the instruction. **Discuss the issues and provide your opinion as to the probable outcome of this appeal.**

Model Answer to Question 11

This question requires the applicant to know the distinction between necessarily lesser included offenses and cognate lesser included offenses. Necessarily included lesser offenses encompass situations in which it is impossible to commit the greater offense without first having committed the lesser. "Cognate" lesser included offenses are those that share some common elements, and are of the same class or category as the greater offense, but have some additional elements not found in the greater offense.

MCL 768.32 governs inferior-offense instructions. It provides that a jury may convict a defendant of an offense inferior to that charged in the indictment or an attempt to commit that offense. In *People v Cornell*, 466 Mich 335 (2002), the Supreme Court concluded that the statute only permitted consideration of necessarily included lesser offenses. Under *Cornell*, a lesser included offense instruction is only proper where the charged greater offense requires the jury to find a disputed factual element that is not required for a conviction of the lesser included offense. *Cornell* further provides that the inferior-offense instruction is only appropriate where a "rational view of the evidence" would support such an instruction. Prior to *Cornell*, a jury could also be instructed on cognate offenses if the greater offense and the lesser offense were of the same class or category, and if the evidence adduced at trial would support a conviction of the lesser offense.

Conviction of UDAA clearly does not require proof of several elements of the greater offense of armed robbery, such as an assault, the perpetrator being armed with either a dangerous weapon or an article that the victim reasonably believes to be a dangerous weapon, taking property from the person or presence of the victim by the use or threat of violence, and intent to take the property permanently. Thus, UDAA is not a necessarily lesser included offense of armed robbery.

The trial court properly refused to give the instruction and the conviction should be affirmed. *People v Cornell*, 466 Mich 335 (2002). *People v Mendoza*, 468 Mich 527 (2003).

Student Answer—July 2005

Question 11—Criminal Law—None Available

February 2006—Question 10

Ray Brown was involved in an ongoing dispute with Charles Wilson over the nonpayment of a gambling debt. At one point, this dispute turned physical with Wilson, the much larger man, beating Brown quite severely. Even after this beating, the dispute continued with Wilson publicly stating that "he was going to get satisfaction." Brown was known to carry a .45 caliber pistol and was the owner of a shotgun. One day Wilson showed up at Brown's apartment and found the front door open with Brown in plain view sitting in a chair. On the wall of the apartment approximately 10 feet from the doorway where Wilson was standing, was Brown's shotgun. Brown claimed that Wilson saw the shotgun and said "This is my lucky day" and began to walk toward the shotgun. Brown shot Wilson with the .45 that he had concealed in the chair, killing Wilson immediately. Wilson fell backward into the hallway with his feet even with the doorway.

Brown was charged with second-degree murder. Brown, through his attorney, claimed the shooting was in self-defense. Brown testified to the above facts at the preliminary examination, but was bound over for trial.

Discuss the elements of self-defense, how they would apply in this case, the burden of proof, and the facts you believe the parties would rely upon to support their positions.

Model Answer to Question 10

Once evidence of self-defense is introduced, the prosecutor bears the burden of disproving it beyond a reasonable doubt.

A killing in self-defense "is justifiable homicide if the defendant honestly and reasonably believes that his life is in imminent danger or that there is a threat of serious bodily harm." When a defendant uses deadly force, the test for determining whether he acted in lawful self-defense has three parts: (1) defendant honestly and reasonably believed that he was in danger, (2) the danger which he feared was serious bodily harm or death, and (3) the action taken by the defendant appeared at the time to be immediately necessary, i.e., defendant is only entitled to use the amount of force necessary to defend himself.

Self-defense normally requires that the actor try to avoid the use of deadly force if he can safely and reasonably do so, for example, by applying nondeadly force or by utilizing an obvious and safe avenue of retreat. However, a defendant is not "required to retreat from a sudden, fierce, and violent attack" or "from an attacker who he reasonably believes is about to use a deadly weapon." Under such circumstances, as long as the defendant honestly and reasonably believes that it is necessary to exercise deadly force in self-defense, "he may stand his ground and meet force with force."

Regardless of the circumstances, if the defendant is attacked in his own home, he "is never required to retreat where it is otherwise necessary to exercise deadly force in self-defense."

In this case, Brown claimed that he shot Wilson after Wilson appeared at the doorway of his apartment and made a statement regarding the shotgun and began to walk toward the shotgun. There is no evidence that there was anywhere Brown could retreat and with the history between the two, there was a basis to believe that Brown feared serious bodily harm or death.

A fact that shows this was not self-defense was the location of Wilson's body. The facts state that Wilson was killed immediately and his feet were in the doorway and his body in the hall, not the apartment. The physical evidence would tend to disprove the claim of self-defense. Another fact is that it appears Brown began firing as soon as Wilson began to walk toward the shotgun without first brandishing the .45 and ordering him to stop. Whether these facts would be sufficient to disprove the defense "beyond a reasonable doubt" would be for the trier of fact to determine. *People v Brown*, COA #250582, January 27, 2005. *People v Riddle*, 467 Mich 115 (2002).

Student Answer—February 2006

Question 10—Criminal Law—8 points

Brown's claim of self defense would usually require an effort by him to retreat to safety. However, in Michigan no retreat is necessary if you are in your own home. Here, Brown alleges that Wilson entered his home, walked toward him with a shotgun, and verbally threatened his life. In utilizing self defense, the person asserting it may not be the initial aggressor and nothing in the facts state that Brown was threatening Wilson. Also, Brown is only entitled to use enough force to protect himself but it would appear from the facts given that deadly force would be justified. It is arguable that because Wilson's feet were even with the doorway, that he was not close enough to the shotgun to be a real threat. Given the fact that Brown had the pistol on his person, Brown bears the burden of proof to assert self defense.

Comment: This is not a very good answer and is an example of an examinee "getting lucky" to get an 8. Given the fact that the examinee did not actually state the burden of proof ("beyond a reasonable doubt") as requested, and assigned it to the wrong party, this person should have received a 6.

July 2006—Question 2

Tom and Rich are walking down the street when they happen across Jim. Tom asks Jim if he knows how to get to the nearest store to buy some cigarettes. Jim tells Rich and Tom to keep going until they reach the corner, and then make a right. Tom says, "Thanks," and as they start to walk away, Tom asks Jim if he could get a cigarette from Jim. Jim, being the nice guy that he is, says, "Sure," and reaches into his pocket to give Tom a cigarette.

As Jim pulls out the pack of cigarettes, Rich pulls out a pistol and tells Jim to turn over his wallet. Tom is shocked by this turn of events, and begins to back up away from the robbery. Tom says nothing and does nothing about the robbery. Once Jim has turned over his wallet, Tom and Rich begin to walk away. Jim also continues to walk away and sees a police officer on the next block. Jim tells the officer what had just happened, and the officer finds only Tom on the next block. Rich cannot be found and Tom refuses to give the officer Rich's name.

Tom is charged with armed robbery under an aiding and abetting theory. Discuss the elements of armed robbery as well as the elements which must be shown to prove the aiding and abetting theory. Finally, indicate whether you believe the charge will result in a valid conviction against Tom, and why.

Model Answer to Question 2

Elements of Armed Robbery: The elements of armed robbery are: (1) an assault, (2) a felonious taking of property from the victim's presence or person, (3) while the defendant is armed with a dangerous weapon. *People v Carines*, 460 Mich 750, 757-758 (1990).

Elements of Aiding and Abetting: To support a finding that the defendant aided and abetted a crime, the prosecution must show: (1) the crime charged was committed by the defendant or some other person, (2) the defendant performed acts or gave encouragement that assisted the commission of the crime, and (3) the defendant intended the commission of the crime or had knowledge that the principal intended its commission at the time the defendant gave aid and encouragement. *Id.* "An aider and abettor's state of mind may be inferred from all the facts and circumstances. Factors that may be considered include a close association between the defendant and the principal, the defendant's participation in the planning or execution of the crime, and evidence of flight after crime." *Id.* It does not matter how much help, advice, or encouragement that the defendant actually gave, although mere presence is sufficient.

Success of the Charges: Nothing in the facts above indicates Tom gave any encouragement to Rich during the commission of the crime. Further, nothing presented indicated Tom had any prior knowledge of Rich's intention to rob Jim. Thus, it is unlikely the prosecution against Tom will be successful on the armed robbery charge under an aiding and abetting theory. However, some answers may rely upon the fact that Tom and Rich were together and that Tom failed to identify Rich when arrested; thus, some answers may suggest that the charges will be successful against Tom, although Tom was not charged with being an accessory after the fact.

Two Student Answers—July 2006

Question 2—Criminal Law—8 points

Tom will not be convicted of aiding and abetting Rich in this criminal law question.

To prove armed robbery, the state has the burden of persuasion to a jury that all the elements must be met. They are: (1) the trespassory taking, and (2) carrying away, (3) the property of another, (4) with the intent to permanently deprive; this is otherwise known as committing a larceny. However, when in conjunction of a larceny the victim is put in apparent imminent harm by virtue of a deadly weapon such as a pistol, armed robbery exists. Here, it was Rich who pulled a pistol on Jim with the intention to threaten Jim into giving Rich his wallet with the presumed intent to permanently deprive and walk away. Consequently, all the elements of Armed Robbery have been met.

However, the underlying issue here, is whether Tom can be convicted for assisting as an aidor and abettor of Rich's plan. The short answer is no. To constitute "aiding & abetting," the courts have held that a premeditated plan even if moments before the undertaking were conspired to assist and further the illegal act of the principal. Here, Tom asked Rich for a cigarette and Rich accepted as a common courtesy, the facts do not state if there was an underlying agenda or conspiracy. A conspiracy is defined as an agreement between two people (minimum) whereby all that is required is an act in furtherance of the plan. Additionally, the facts state Tom was "shocked" by Rich's conduct and attempted to back away. Even though Tom didn't have a duty to assist a stranger for events he didn't contribute to, he also can't be held liable for Rich's unforeseeable criminal activity. Therefore, in my opinion as previously reasoned, Tom should not be convicted for the aiding & abetting charge whereas Rich ought to be convicted for the Armed Robbery.

Question 2—Criminal Law—8 points

Robbery is the trespassory taking and carrying away of the property of another with intent to permanently deprive plus the use of force or the threat of force of property taken from the plaintiffs person and in their presence. Rich's actions constitute a robbery. Rich took Jim's wallet with the intent to permanently deprive and he actually carried it away which meets all the requirements for larceny. In order for Rich to be found guilty of robbery he must have done it with force or threat of force. Here, Rich's use of the gun meets this element. Also he must take the item from the victim's person and in their presence. Arguably Rich took the wallet from Jim's person because the wallet was probably in his pocket but every jury would find it wasn't from his person the taking would be found to have been done in his presence so Rich is guilty of robbery.

Tom will not be found guilty of aiding & abetting. In order for a person to be found guilty the person must encourage with specific intent that the crime would come about. Here the facts say that Tom was shocked when the robbery happened and the facts also say that he did nothing, in Michigan presence alone and has met make someone guilty of aiding and abetting. So Tom will not be guilty. Also Tom's backing away from the crime shows that he had no intent to be a part of the crime.

February 2007—Question 15

There was a string of home invasions in southern Tyler County, Michigan. A number of items were stolen, including several firearms from the homes. The police were unable to crack the case until they received a tip regarding a car that was seen in the area of one of the homes the night the home was burglarized. After checking the license plate number given to them by the tipster, the police discovered the car belonged to Timmy Turner, who lived in Riley County, Michigan.

The police officers went to Timmy's home to ask him a few questions. Upon arrival, Timmy let the officers into his home and agreed to answer some questions. He showed them his secret hiding spot where he had kept the stolen guns. Timmy confessed to breaking into the homes in Tyler County and was prosecuted for those crimes. The statute setting forth the offense of Home Invasion—Second Degree, MCL 750.110a(3), provides:

> A person who breaks and enters a dwelling with intent to commit a felony, larceny, or assault in the dwelling, a person who enters a dwelling without

permission with intent to commit a felony, larceny, or assault in the dwelling, or a person who breaks and enters a dwelling or enters a dwelling without permission and, at any time while he or she is entering, present in, or exiting the dwelling, commits a felony, larceny, or assault is guilty of home invasion in the second degree.

Timmy entered a guilty plea to the home invasion charges in the Tyler Circuit Court, and was sentenced to a minimum term of three years with the Michigan Department of Corrections. However, the prosecuting attorney in Riley County was unsatisfied, and decided to charge Timmy with receiving and concealing a stolen firearm, contrary to MCL 750.535b(2), which provides:

> A person who receives, conceals, stores, barters, sells, disposes of, pledges or accepts as security for a loan a stolen firearm or ammunition, knowing that the firearm or ammunition was stolen, is guilty of a felony, punishable by imprisonment for not more than 10 years or by a fine of not more than $5,000.00, or both.

Thus, a warrant was issued for Timmy's arrest charging him with receiving and concealing a stolen firearm. Timmy was brought from his cell at the State Prison of Southern Michigan and arraigned on the new charge.

After he was bound over to the Riley Circuit Court, Timmy's counsel filed a motion to dismiss the charge. His counsel argues the charge violates Michigan's Double Jeopardy Clause, Const 1963, art 1, § 15.

You have been asked by the judge to whom the case is assigned to provide a memorandum discussing the merit or lack of merit in the motion. Discuss whether the new charge of receiving and concealing a stolen firearm violates the Double Jeopardy Clause of the Michigan Constitution. Discuss the three types of protections afforded by the Double Jeopardy Clause, and discuss which are applicable to the facts above.

Model Answer to Question 15

The fact pattern is based upon *People v Nutt*, 469 Michigan 565 (2004). The Supreme Court held the second charge of receiving and concealing a stolen firearm did not violate the Michigan Constitution's Double Jeopardy Clause. The Court stated the Michigan Constitution protects a person against being placed in jeopardy twice for the same offense. This prohibition protects against three specific types of jeopardy: First, one may not be prosecuted a second time for the same offense after an acquittal. Second, one may not be prosecuted a second time for the same offense. Third, one may not be punished more than once for the same offense. *Nutt, supra*, p 575, citing *People v Torres*, 452 Michigan 43 (1996). The second form of protection is at issue in the instant question.

Michigan applies the *Blockberger* test to determine if the subsequent offense has the same elements as the first conviction. *Nutt, supra*, p 588. The *Blockberger* test originated in *Blockberger v United States*, 284 US 299 (1932). The test is whether the two charges require proof of the same elements. In Michigan, the two statutes set forth above in the fact pattern clearly do not share any of the same elements. Thus, the Michigan Supreme Court found the subsequent prosecution for receiving and concealing a stolen firearm after the initial prosecution for home invasion—second degree, did not violate the Michigan Constitution's Double Jeopardy Clause.

Two Student Answers—February 2007

Question 15—Criminal Law—9 points

Double jeopardy attaches when the jury commenced, a plea is entered, or an adjudication has been entered, or jury deliberations have begun. In this situation, Timmy was charged with home invasion. He confessed, voluntarily, knowingly, and intelligently to breaking into the homes. The prosecutor subsequently charged Timmy with receiving and concealing a stolen firearm.

Double jeopardy attaches if the two offenses have separate elements and are not a lesser included offense. A cognate included offense can be tried separately. The two charges have separate elements. As such, he can be convicted and tried on both counts. The legislature intended for the offenses to have separate punishments. This second case is the functional equivalent of a count 2 on the charge sheet/ indictment. There is no violation of the Michigan Constitution in charging Timmy with receiving and concealing a stolen firearm above and beyond the initial home invasion charge.

Double jeopardy seeks to prevent multiple convictions of the same crime and multiple punishments. In this situation, the crimes are distinctly different.

Question 15—Criminal Law—8 points

The issue is whether the second charge of receiving and concealing a stolen firearm violates the double jeopardy clause of the MI constitution. The double jeopardy clause protects persons charged with a crime from being charged twice with the same crime, convicted twice and being charged in dual sovereigns. Double jeopardy attaches once a defendant has been charged.

Here, Timmy would want to keep from being charged twice with the same crime. In Michigan to avoid being charged twice for the same crime the second offense must contain an element not included in the first offense. Here, Timmy was first charged with Home invasion, neither of these contain the same elements so the double jeopardy clause is not violated here.

However, Timmy may argue that since he was already tried and sentenced in one county, Tyler County, that he may not be then later charged in Riley County. However, MI will allow two separate sovereigns to charge a defendant twice. Here, the charges are completely unrelated and do not contain the same elements; they are punishable by different years in prison and the second one can be punishable by prison or fine.

His sentences can be served consecutively and one does not have any bearing on the other. The dual sovereign approach only applies where there are two states charging the defendant; here it is two separate counties.

Therefore, it does not look as though the charge of receiving and concealing a stolen firearm violates the double jeopardy clause of the MI Constitution.

February 2008—Question 1

Defendant Robby Larson stole a car stereo from a department store. He was subsequently involved in a physical altercation and struggle with the store's loss prevention officer and other employees outside of the store after he was confronted about the unpaid merchandise. Defendant argues that there is insufficient evidence to show that he used force and violence during the robbery as contemplated by MCL 750.530. Defendant contends that the evidence presented showed that he was merely trying to evade capture by wrestling himself free, and not that he was directing any force or violence at any person outside of that context.

MCL 750.530 provides:

> (1) A person who, in the course of committing a larceny of any money or other property that may be the subject of larceny, uses force or violence against any person who is present, or who assaults or puts the person in fear, is guilty of a felony punishable by imprisonment for not more than 15 years.
>
> (2) As used in this section, "in the course of committing a larceny" includes acts that occur in an attempt to commit the larceny, or during commission of the larceny, or in flight or attempted flight after the commission of the larceny, or in an attempt to retain possession of the property.

Discuss the merits of defendant's argument in view of the statute.

Model Answer to Question 1

In *People v Passage*, 277 Mich App 175 (2007), the Court of Appeals found that this argument lacked merit, holding that the statute's clear and unambiguous language punishes a defendant for using force or violence, committing an assault, or placing a person in fear during flight or attempted flight after the larceny was committed. The statute makes no distinction between using force to evade capture as part of a physical struggle against pursuers in an effort to break free from their grasp or attempts at restraint and force used affirmatively and not within that context. Rather, the use of force used against a person during the course of committing a larceny, which includes the period of flight, is sufficient under the statute. "Force" is nothing more than the exertion of strength and physical power. *Random House Webster's College Dictionary* (2001). Exerting strength and physical power to free oneself from another's grasp constitutes "force" under MCL 750.530.

In *Passage*, there was evidence that the defendant engaged in the use of force during flight, or attempted flight, by physically struggling with the department store's personnel and attempting to kick them. Therefore, there was sufficient evidence to support the robbery conviction, given that there was no dispute that the defendant committed a larceny.

Three Student Answers—February 2008

Question 1—Criminal Law—10 points

Robby has been charged under MCL 750.530. This is a criminal law question. Under Michigan Law larceny is the wrongful taking of another's property with the intent to permanently deprive another person of that property.

Here robbery is subject to larceny charges under MCL 750.530. Robby argues that there is not enough evidence to charge him under the statute because force or violence was not used during the robbery. The statute describes that a person is guilty under the statute if force or violence is used in the course of committing a larceny.

Here Robby was involved in a physical altercation and struggle with the store's loss prevention officer and other employees. The physical altercation and struggle will probably meet the element in the statute because the altercation and struggle can be construed as "force or violence" or under "putting a person in fear." The Loss Prevention officer and other employees are people that this statute would protect.

Robby claims that he was just trying to get away and not be captured by wrestling himself free, and not using force or violence outside of that context.

The statute is very clear in defining "in the course." Looking at the facts and applying the statute, Robby's actions would probably meet it as he was "in flight or attempted flight after commission of the larceny." Robby even himself admits he was trying to evade capture. This could be construed as trying to complete the larceny or retaining possession of the property. Even though Robby says he was trying to wrestle himself free, he probably put employees and the LP officer in fear.

The fact that Robby was already out of the store will not help him either because the statute clearly says "in the course," and could also be attached to "after the commission of the larceny."

In conclusion, Robby's arguments have very little merit.

Question 1—Criminal Law—10 points

This is a criminal law question. The issue is whether the defendant should be charged for robbery pursuant to MCL 750.530. Specifically, whether he used force to constitute a robbery.

A robbery is the taking and dispossession of an item; with the intent to permanently deprive by the use of force. Accordingly, to the statute, robbery, larceny includes the use of force that happens at 5 stages. (1) acts that occur in an attempt to commit the larceny, (2) during the commission of the larceny, (3) or in flight, (4) or attempted flight after the commission of the larceny, (5) an attempt to retain possession of the property.

In this fact pattern Robby Larson used the amount of force that is described in the statute at stage 3, 4, and 5.

The facts indicated that Robby did have an intent to permanently deprive the store of the radio, and had took and displaced the radio into a different location when he took the radio outside the store. The force that Robby partook in happened after the larceny was completed. In traditional robbery, the force must be used in order to gain possession of the intended item. Accordingly, in this statute force can be used after the robbery took place. While outside the store, Robby was in flight—in that he had possession of the goods outside of the store in which the goods were rightfully stored. Steps outside of the store can constitute flight.

Secondly, he used force during this flight- which constitutes robbery according to the statute. If he is not found on stage 3, then his attempted flight after the commission of the larceny counts. He is apprehended by the loss prevention officers and other employees while in flight. A physical altercation occurred and this is sufficient to constitute force, this is contemplated by the statute. It is attempted flight, because he was apprehended by employees. The struggle constitutes force.

If he is not found guilty in stage 4 then he will be found guilty in stage 5, "in an attempt to regain possession of the property." When Robby tried to wrestle himself free, this act could be characterized as an attempt to regain property. The facts do not state that he returned the property to the employees. And Robby's own statement that he was trying to evade capture shows that he was in flight or attempting to flee. This statute is different from common law robbery in that force can take place at any stage of the robbery including after the completed act. Defendant cannot claim that he did not use force, according to the statute. Even evading capture, without intending to use force to gain possession of the property is considered robbery under the statute.

Question 1—Criminal Law—9 points

The Defendant's argument will fail as to the Michigan Statute. However this statute may be in conflict with the defendant's procedural rights.

Here the Defendant by his own contention states that there was evidence presented that there was at least some contact with another to evade capture by wresting himself free. According to the statute while attempting flight after the commission of the larceny he used force, (commits a battery) which would be an unlawful touching of another. Defendant admits to wrestling to free himself. The defendant does not have to intend to use force or violence to be guilty of a battery.

Here another element of the statute deals with the larceny. Larceny is when a person unlawfully deprives another of property with the intent to permanently deprive them of that property. The facts don't tend to dispute any of these elements. The Defendant is arguing the increase of the punishment due to the force/violence issue.

His argument as to during the mere robbery will fail because the mere fact that the robbery, removal of the property, has already occurred does not end the total action. The commission of the crime is not terminated until the Defendant has returned to a place of safety. Therefore, in the course of would include evading capture, where the wrestling occurred.

This would not be enough to prove that defendant should not have the enhance punishment.

July 2008—Question 10

Danny was walking his dog at the park when he saw a metal object that appeared to be a gun lying in the grass. To make sure a child did not find it and hurt someone, Danny picked it up and placed it in his pocket. He noticed the pistol was missing several pieces, but he was not sure it was operable or beyond repair. Unfortunately, Danny forgot he had put the pistol in his jacket pocket and mistakenly wore the jacket while driving to the store later that afternoon. On the way to the store, Danny's car was struck by a drunk driver, and Danny was slightly injured.

While the emergency workers attended to Danny's injuries, the police officer that had responded to the scene noticed a bulge in the jacket pocket. The officer, through his years of experience, recognized the outline of a handgun, and asked Danny to remove the pistol from his pocket. Danny, who had forgotten about the pistol, apologized and handed the pieces to the officer and explained that he had found the pieces in the park. The officer recognized the handgun was missing several pieces, including the firing pin, magazine, and some springs, thus rendering it inoperable.

The officer asked Danny if he had any prior record, and Danny candidly admitted he had been convicted of felony embezzlement ten years ago. He had successfully completed his probation, and was discharged from probation more than five years ago. The officer arrested Danny, who is now charged with being a felon in possession of a firearm, contrary to MCL 750.224f(1) and possession of a firearm in the commission of a felony, contrary to MCL 750.227b.

The statute defines a firearm as "a weapon from which a dangerous projectile may be propelled by an explosion, or by gas or air." MCL 750.222(d).

Danny's attorney has filed a motion to dismiss. In the motion, his attorney raises only one issue. Counsel contends the gun was admittedly inoperable and thus did not fit the definition of "firearm" under the statute.

You are the clerk to the trial court judge to whom the case is assigned. The Judge has asked you for a memorandum addressing the issue raised by defense counsel. Please address whether the pieces Danny had in his possession satisfy the statutory definition of a "firearm." Explain your answer.

Model Answer to Question 10

The Michigan Supreme Court addressed this issue in *People v Peals*, 476 Mich 636 (2006). The defendant therein was charges with the offenses as in the fact pattern above. In *Peals*, the Supreme Court held the pieces fit the definition and affirmed the defendant's conviction. The court focused on the term "may" as found in the definition of "firearm." *Id.*, pp 641-642. The Court also noted the legislation failed to use the terms "operable" or "inoperable." *Id.*, p 642. To hold that pieces of a firearm, or that a firearm which is missing a piece, does not meet the statutory definition of "firearm" would be to permit a felon to avoid prosecution merely by hiding a minor piece. *Id.*, p 643.

The Court determined that operability is not a requirement, and thus as the firearm was missing pieces which made it inoperable, it remained a firearm. *Id.*, p 653. The Supreme Court noted the Court of Appeals had held operability was not a factor in felony firearm cases, the purpose of the statute being to protect the public. As the Supreme Court quoted with approval, "The victim is no less frightened if the gun (most likely unknown to him) just happens to be inoperable." *Id.*, quoting *People v Pierce*, 119 Mich App 780, 783 (1982). Thus, the correct answer is that the trial court should deny the motion as operability is not an element within the statutory definition of "firearm." The key to the issue is the statute's use of the term "may," which permits even an inoperable gun to fall within the definition. The Court noted that it was possible that a firearm could be substantially redesigned or altered that it would cease to be a firearm under the statutory definition. Operability would still not be the test. The question would be whether the weapon was so substantially redesigned or altered that it would no longer fall within the category of weapons described in MCL 750.222(d). The Court gave an example of a cannon plugged with cement and displayed in a park.

Three Student Answers—July 2008

Question 10—Criminal Law—10 points

MEMO

To: Judge
From: Clerk
RE: Statutory Firearm Statute

The issue before us is whether or not the object that Danny had in his possession fits the statutory definition of a "firearm" pursuant to MCL 750.222(d).

MCL750.222(d) defines a firearm as "a weapon from which a dangerous projectile may be propelled by an explosive, or by gas or air."

The "gun" Danny had was missing several pieces, including the firing pin, magazine, and some springs. Therefore, in its present state, the "gun" was rendered inoperable.

Danny's attorney's motion to dismiss is based only on the issue that the object Danny has does not fit MCL 750.222(d) definition of a firearm *simply* because it is inoperable.

In applying the statute to the case at hand, it is unlikely that Danny's attorney will succeed in his motion/to dismiss by asserting it is not a gun simply because it is inoperable.

The statute does *not* state that the weapon has to be presently operable. Rather, it simply defines it as a *weapon from which dangerous projectile may be propelled.*

In strictly applying the statute, Danny's "object" was a firearm. It *was a weapon* in which *dangerous projectile may be propelled by an explosive.* Therefore, the gun Danny had seems to fit the statutory definition of a firearm. The statute, again, does *not* define a *firearm* as being *"presently"* able to propel an explosive. Therefore, it would be deemed that any weapon that has the *"potential"* for *dangerous projectile* to be propelled by an *explosive* is a firearm.

As a result, Defense Counsel's motion will likely be *denied* because the *one issue* that it raises would likely *fail to exclude* the weapon Danny had as a firearm.

For purposes of this statute, Danny's *"object"* in possession is a *"firearm"* pursuant to MCL 750.222(d).

Note: [The other parts of the gun could be "readily accessible", therefore, it is a matter of safety to enforce this statute as it stands.]

Question 10—Criminal Law—9 points

Defense counsel is arguing that the pieces Danny had in his pocket did not meet the definition of "firearm" as provided in MCL 750.222(d).

Defense counsel will argue that the pistol was missing several pieces, including the firing pin, magazine, and springs, which rendered the pistol inoperable. The statute requires that the "firearm" be able to propel a dangerous projectile. Since the pistol is inoperable, it is unable to satisfy the definition of firearm.

The prosecution will probably argue that, at the time Danny picked up the pistol, he didn't know it was inoperable. The statute also doesn't address whether the weapon needs to have the present ability to propel a dangerous projectile or if it is merely capable of doing so. If the pistol was in full working order, it would have the ability to propel a dangerous projectile. Danny could easily take the pistol, get it repaired, and use it. The use of the words "may" support the argument that the weapon needs to be capable of propelling a dangerous projectile, not having the present capability.

The motion to dismiss should be denied because the pistol is probably a "firearm" under the statute.

Question 10—Criminal Law—9 points

The statutory definition of a firearm under MCL 750.222(d) is "a weapon from which a dangerous projectile may be propelled by an explosive, or by gas or air." When Danny first saw the shining object lying on the ground he noticed that it was a pistol, but unsure if it was operable. In the MCL definition of a firearm it does not say that the gun must be operable. It only sates that: it must be a weapon, which a pistol is; from which a dangerous projectile *may be propelled*, which depending on what is done with the weapon even in its "inoperable" state a projectile could be propelled from the barrel of the gun by an explosive, or by gas or by air.

Since the statute doesn't require it be operable, the fact it was missing several pieces (firing pin, springs) doesn't render it unable to propel a dangerous projectile. Therefore, the pistol in Danny's possession is a firearm according to the statutory definition.

February 2009—Question 6

Late one night, Dan Defendant was enjoying a beer at his neighborhood pub, when Andy Aggressor entered the bar and accused Dan of having an affair with Andy's spouse. Andy punched Dan several times in the head and face. Then, Andy pulled a hunting knife out of his coat and told Dan he intended to slit Dan's throat. Dan ran out of the pub and Andy followed. Andy got into his car and drove toward Dan at a high rate of speed. Dan ran behind the bar, into an alley, and jumped over a fence and into his neighbor's yard. Dan went into his home, where he lived with his brother Dave. Dan possessed two unregistered handguns that were hidden in his home. Dan loaded the guns and went into his garage where he placed one gun underneath the driver seat and one gun underneath the passenger seat of Dave's car. Dan then went back into his home to inform Dave that they had to leave their home immediately because Andy Aggressor had beat him, pulled a knife on him, and threatened to kill him. Dan informed Dave that an enraged Andy would be coming to their home at any moment to carry out his threat to kill Dan.

Dan had placed the two loaded guns in Dave's car so that both Dan and Dave would have a weapon with which to defend themselves should Andy confront them. However, Dan did not tell Dave that he had placed the guns in his car because Dan knew that Dave, who was on probation at the time, would not allow Dan to possess any weapon in his car. Neither Dan nor Dave had a permit to carry a concealed weapon. Dave started his car and, with Dan in the passenger seat, drove at an excessively high speed out of his garage and down his residential street. Within seconds, a car parked on the street turned on its headlights and pulled out behind Dave. Dan, fearful that Andy was operating the car following them, reached under the passenger seat, pulled out his gun and told Dave, "I hope we won't need to use this." The car trailing Dave turned out to be a police car. Almost immediately after Dan pulled his gun out from under his seat, the police car activated its overhead flashers and pulled Dave over. Dan stuffed his gun back underneath his seat as Dave pulled to the side of the road. Upon checking Dave's identification, the officer making the stop discovered that Dave had an outstanding arrest warrant issued for Dave's failure to appear in court on a traffic violation. The officer then checked Dan's identification and discovered that Dan had an outstanding arrest warrant arising from Dan's failure to pay child support. Upon arresting both Dan and Dave, the officer conducted a lawful search of Dave's car incidental to the arrest of its occupants and the two guns were discovered and seized. Dan and Dave were each charged with carrying a concealed weapon.

Discuss the charges and any defenses each defendant may assert.

Model Answer to Question 6

Dan and Dave Defendant are charged with carrying a concealed weapon. When a defendant is charged with carrying a concealed weapon in a vehicle, the prosecution must provide each of the following elements beyond a reasonable doubt:

1. That the instrument or item was indeed a dangerous weapon, in this case a gun.
2. That the dangerous weapon was in a vehicle that defendant was in.
3. That the defendant knew the instrument was in the vehicle.
4. That the defendant took part in carrying or keeping the dangerous weapon in the vehicle. CJI2d, 11.2.

1. The Charges Asserted Against Dave: Dave may argue that the prosecutor cannot present evidence to establish the third and fourth elements of this offense. At the time Dave began to drive his car, he was wholly unaware that there were any guns in his car. Dan placed the guns in the car. The facts indicate that "Dan did not tell Dave that he had placed the guns in his car because Dan knew that Dave, who was on probation at the time, would not allow Dan to possess any weapon in his car." The prosecution may argue that because the guns were found in Dave's car he should be found to have constructive knowledge that they were there. *See People v Gould*, 225 Mich App 79, 87 (1997). Moreover, there is no question that Dave knew Dan had at least one gun in the car as the facts indicate that shortly after Dave drove away from their home, Dan pulled out a gun and told Dave, "I hope we won't need to use this."

Dave may also argue that even if the prosecution successfully establishes that he knew that at least one gun was in his car, the prosecution will have a very difficult time establishing the fourth element of this offense—that "defendant took part in carrying or keeping the dangerous weapon in the vehicle." Dan placed the guns in the car without notice to Dave and Dave did not become aware of the presence of even one gun in his car until just before the police stopped his car. The undisputed facts also show that while Dan placed the gun in the car for possible use by Dave, Dave was never aware of the gun under the driver seat of his car until the police discovered it in a search of the car. Dan's intent cannot be transferred to Dave. Dave may argue that these facts are simply not enough to establish that he took part in carrying or keeping the dangerous weapon in his car. The prosecution will argue, however, that even momentary innocent possession of a concealed weapon is not a defense to a charge of carrying a concealed weapon. *People v Hernandez-Garcia*, 477 Mich 1039 (2007). The jury will have to determine whether Dave, who was trying to assist his brother to avoid a lethal and possibly fatal confrontation with a criminal aggressor and who was wholly unaware of Dan's activities until, just moments before the police stopped his vehicle, can be found to have taken part in his brother's scheme to carry and keep dangerous weapons in Dave's car.

2. The Charges Asserted Against Dan: By contrast, Dan will have a much more difficult time establishing a defense. The facts clearly establish that Dan knowingly possessed a gun in the car and that Dan was the primary and sole person responsible for placing, carrying, and keeping a gun in Dave's car. Dan may argue the defense of necessity. This defense is available where a defendant violates a criminal law in order to avoid a greater harm to himself or others. *See People v Luther*, 53 Mich App 648 (1974).

In order to benefit from this defense, Dan must establish he acted under threat of present, imminent, and impending danger. *People v Hubbard*, 115 Mich App 73 (1983). A future threat is insufficient to support a necessity defense. *Id.*

The prosecutor has sufficient evidence to establish a prima facie case against Dan. Dan may have a difficult time establishing necessity as the threat from Andy was not imminent and impending once Dan was within his home. The facts suggest that Dan was motivated by his very legitimate concern for his safety, as Andy Aggressor had threatened his life and had taken steps toward carrying out this threat. While self-defense is often a legal defense available to criminal acts, self-defense is not a defense to the charge of carrying a concealed weapon. *People v Townsel*, 13 Mich App 600 (1968).

Student Answer—February 2009

Question 6—Criminal Procedure—None Available

Comment: Examinees did not do well on this question. Many were thrown by the charge of "carrying a concealed weapon" because they had not been exposed to the elements of that crime and panicked. If presented with this situation, the Plan B approach is to look at the name of the charge itself and break it down using common sense. For example: "Carrying" speaks for itself. Dave never "carried" the gun, so that element isn't met. "Concealed weapon" also speaks for itself. The point is, don't panic! Use common sense and Plan B it!

July 2009—Question 4

In June of this year, Debbie Defendant walked into her local police department and offered to confess to murder. After being apprised of all of her constitutional rights, including her right to counsel, and her right against self-incrimination, and after making a full, complete, voluntary, and knowing waiver of all of her constitutional rights, Debbie confessed to murdering her 82-year-old father in September 1992. Debbie claimed that she became tired of caring for her father, who resided with her. Debbie stated that after careful consideration of her situation, she decided to poison her father. She confessed to stealing a lethal drug from a pharmacy at which she worked in 1992. Then one evening in September 1992, she mixed the lethal drug into some warm milk that was consumed by her father. Her father died in his sleep shortly after drinking the milk. The county coroner arrived at Debbie's home the morning following her father's death. The death certificate prepared in conjunction with her father's death indicated that death was the product of natural causes. No autopsy was performed and no photographs of the crime scene were taken. Debbie arranged for her father's body to be cremated.

Realizing that incarceration will not be pleasant, Debbie stopped talking to police. Thereafter, police obtained a valid warrant to search Debbie's home. The search of Debbie's home did not reveal the presence of any lethal drugs. The pharmacy at which Debbie worked closed in 1995, and no records remain from the pharmacy. Further, while the pharmacist who owned and operated the pharmacy recalled Debbie

Defendant having worked for him, he had no record or recollection of any drugs that were not accounted for during Debbie's employment.

The local prosecutor charged Debbie with first-degree premeditated murder.

Discuss the charge asserted against Debbie Defendant. Will the prosecutor be successful in the prosecution of Debbie Defendant? Explain your answer.

Model Answer to Question 4

A. Discuss the Charge Asserted Against Debbie Defendant: The prosecutor has charged Debbie Defendant with first-degree premeditated murder. The elements of this offense are:

1. Defendant caused the death of the deceased;
2. Defendant intended to kill the deceased;
3. The intent to kill was premeditated;
4. The killing was deliberate; and
5. The killing was not justified or excused under the law. CJI2d 16.1; MCL 750.316(1)(a).

Here, Debbie's confession provides evidence as to every element of the crime of first-degree premeditated murder. Simply stated, Debbie confessed to the intentional, deliberate, and premeditated murder of her father. Murder perpetrated by means of poison is premeditated murder. MCL 750.316(1)(a). Nothing in the fact pattern supports the conclusion that this murder was justified or excused under the law. Thus, Debbie Defendant's confession provides evidence of every element of the charge of first-degree premeditated murder. This said, the prosecution will likely fail in this prosecution.

B. Will the Prosecutor Be Successful in the Prosecution of Debbie Defendant? In Michigan, a prosecutor may not introduce in evidence the inculpatory statements of an accused without proof of the corpus delicti. *People v McMahan*, 451 Mich 543, 548 (1996). The corpus delicti rule guards against erroneous convictions for criminal homicides that never occurred. The rule also minimizes the weight accorded to confessions by requiring collateral evidence to support a conviction. *Id.* at 548-549 (internal quotations and citations omitted); see also *People v Konrad*, 449 Mich 263, 269 (1995).

The corpus delicti rule "provides that a defendant's confession may not be admitted unless there is direct or circumstantial evidence independent of the confession establishing (1) the occurrence of the specific injury (for example, death in cases of homicide) and (2) some criminal agency as the source of the injury." *Konrad, supra*, at 269-270, citing *People v Cotton*, 191 Mich App 377, 394 (1991); *see also McMahan, supra*, at 548-549. It is not necessary to prove all elements of the charged crime before the confession is admissible. *People v Ish*, 252 Mich App 115, 117 (2001). Further, evidence of the above elements need not be proved beyond a reasonable doubt. It is sufficient if the trial court determines that these elements are established by a preponderance of the evidence. *People v King*, 271 Mich App 235, 241-242 (2006). In so doing, courts may draw reasonable inferences and weigh the probabilities. *People v Mumford*, 171 Mich App 514, 517 (1988).

Here, the death of Debbie Defendant's father is not disputed. The only issue is whether a preponderance of the evidence showed that the death of the deceased was caused by a criminal agency. Nothing presented in the facts of this case, other than Debbie Defendant's confession, establishes that the death of the deceased was caused by a criminal agency. The death certificate of the deceased indicates he died of natural causes. There was no evidence preserved from the crime scene that can be reviewed and reassessed in light of Debbie's confession. No photos were taken and no autopsy was performed. There is no body to exhume to search for evidence of a poison. The home of Debbie Defendant was searched and no evidence turned up establishing that Debbie possessed a lethal poison. The records of Debbie's former employer, the place where she claimed to have taken the poison, no longer exist, and her former employer cannot attest to any drugs missing during Debbie's tenure.

The prosecution will not be able to satisfy the corpus delicti rule. Without independent proof that the death of Debbie Defendant's father was caused by some criminal agency, Debbie's confession cannot be admitted against her and the prosecutor will not be able to convict Debbie as charged.

Student Answer—July 2009

Question 4—Criminal Law—8 points

Issue 1
Was Debbie's confession voluntarily given and constitutional? Could the confession be used?

Rule
A defendant must make a knowing and voluntary waiver of Miranda rights. Here Debbie made a knowing and voluntary waiver and her confession would be admissible in a court of law.

Issue 2
Will the prosecutor be able to convict Debbie of first degree murder?

Rule
First degree murder is premeditated and deliberate killing of another individual, acting with a depraved heart, meaning a reckless indifference toward human life, or murder during the commission of a felony. Here, the facts indicate that Debbie's confession demonstrates first degree murder because she was pre-meditated in planning the commission of the murder by mixing the position in the milk of her father. If the confession is written and signed or the police testimony is very strong, this would likely give the prosecutor a good chance of convicting Debbie of first degree murder.

However, there are many holes in the prosecutor's case. First, the death certificate shows the father died of natural causes; this would be admissible evidence as a public record. Second, no autopsy was performed and the body was cremated, so there is not ability to prove her father was murdered. Under the Corpus Delicti doctrine there must be a dead body and proof of criminal means and criminal means cannot be proven with the body cremated.

Third, the search warrant of Debbie's home revealed no evidence of the crime. Fourth there are no records from the pharmacy to prove the substance was removed. Fifth, the owner has no recollection of Debbie or anyone else taking drugs being unaccounted for.

All of these instances make a conviction for first degree murder unlikely because of a lack of corroborating evidence, unless the confession was written or recorded. Even then the prosecutor would face great difficulty in getting a first degree murder conviction.

February 2010—Question 14

Betty and Bob Burns were deeply in debt and experiencing financial hardship. Betty called her neighbor, Hanna Hand, to discuss her financial troubles. Betty's home was well insured. Betty expressed the intent to burn down her own home to collect insurance proceeds. Betty asked Hanna to set the fire for her and again Hanna declined, stating, "I want no part of your crime." Betty then asked Hanna whether Hanna kept gasoline for her lawn equipment in her garage. Hanna indicated she had two full containers of gasoline in her garage. Betty asked Hanna to keep her garage door unlocked that evening, so Betty could take Hanna's gasoline. Hanna confirmed that she would leave her garage door unlocked. Betty thanked Hanna and took the gasoline from Hanna's garage. The following day, while Bob was away, Betty poured the gasoline throughout her home. When Bob returned, he smelled gasoline and traced it to the rear of the home. There he found Betty distributing the gasoline. Bob was shocked to see Betty distribute the last few ounces of gasoline and ignite the fire. Bob grabbed Betty by the arm and escorted her out of harm's way. Neither Bob nor Betty made any attempt to call the fire department or extinguish the fire. The couple stood outside and watched as their home was engulfed in flames.

Discuss the facts and law that would support the imposition of criminal liability, if any, on Betty, Hanna, and Bob. Explain your answer.

Model Answer to Question 14

The Criminal Liability of Betty: The crime of arson is statutorily defined in Michigan. MCL 750.71 through 750.80. In regard to the facts presented here, the Michigan Legislature has imposed criminal liability on persons who willfully or maliciously burn a dwelling house, MCL 750.75 (a 20-year felony), or insured property, MCL 750.75 (a 10-year felony). In order to be guilty of arson of a dwelling, there must be proof beyond a reasonable doubt that a home or a building within the cartilage of the home was intentionally set on fire. MCL 750.72. The home need not be occupied. *Id.* In order to be convicted of arson of an insured property, there must be proof beyond a reasonable doubt that an insured property was intentionally set on fire for the purpose of making a claim of insurance with the insurer. MCL 750.75. Here, Betty can be charged with violating both of the above-referenced statutory provisions. The facts establish that she intentionally set fire to her home, an insured property, so that she could make an insurance claim.

Convictions for arson of a dwelling house and for arson of insured property do not violate state and federal constitution guarantees against double jeopardy. *People v Ayers*, 213 Mich App 708 (1995). These two arson statutes protect against different harms, and impose different and escalating penalties. One protects those endangered by dwelling fires and requires proof of the burning within the cartilage of a home and the other protects insurers and requires proof that the perpetrator of the act intended to defraud the insurer. *Id.*

The Criminal Liability of Hanna: Hanna did not burn anything. Nonetheless, Hanna may be guilty of arson of a dwelling, MCL 750.72, and arson of an insured property, MCL 750.75, as an aider and abettor of Betty. MCL 769.39. Aiding and abetting is not a separate offense. Rather, it is a statutorily defined theory of prosecution that imposes vicarious criminal liability. *Id. People v Robinson*, 475 Mich 1, 6 (2006). One who procures, counsels, aids, or abets in the commission of an offense may be convicted and punished as if she directly committed the offense. *Id.* To support a finding that a defendant aided and abetted a crime, the prosecutor must show that: (1) the crime charged was committed by the defendant or some other person; (2) the defendant performed acts or gave encouragement that assisted the commission of the crime; and (3) the defendant intended the commission of the crime or had knowledge that the principal intended its commission at the time he gave aid and encouragement. *People v Moore*, 470 Mich 56, 67-68 cert den sub nom *Harris v Mich*, 543 US 947 (2004).

Here, the facts indicate that Betty committed the crimes of arson of a dwelling and arson of insured property. Hanna, notwithstanding her protestations, assisted the commission of these crimes by allowing Betty to use Hanna's gasoline to commit the arson. At the time Hanna aided Betty, Hanna knew that Betty intended to commit these crimes. Accordingly, Hanna may be convicted of MCL 750.71 and MCL 750.75 as an aider an abettor.

The Criminal Liability of Bob: Bob did not burn his home and he did not aid in the commission of the arson committed by Betty. The facts tell us Bob was shocked to see Betty distribute the last few ounces of gasoline and ignite the fire. Bob grabbed Betty by the arm and escorted her out of harm's way. While Bob came upon Betty in the course of the commission of her crime and he did nothing to stop her from completing the crime, Bob cannot be guilty of arson as an aider and abettor.
A defendant's mere presence at a crime, even with knowledge that the offense is about to be committed, is not enough to make him an aider and abettor. *People v Norris*, 236 Mich App 411, 419-420 (1999). Some advice, aid, or encouragement is required. Here, nothing provided in these facts supports the conclusion that Bob aided Betty in the commission of the arson. Accordingly, Bob is not guilty of any criminal conduct.

Student Answer—February 2010

Question 14—Criminal Law—9 points

This is a criminal law problem dealing with arson.

Under Michigan law, in order to have arson, we need at least a charring or complete burning down of ones dwelling home. At common law it had to be a dwelling but under modern law it can apply to any building or vehicle.

In this case when Betty poured the gasoline and left the house on fire a valid crime of arson was committed. Arson is a general intent crime and all that matters is the actus reas which is the act of burning the house.

Betty can have criminal liability imposed on her for arson. Although Betty solicited Hanna to burn down her house Hanna refused. Solicitation is the procuring of ones services to commit a crime. Under the law solicitation occurs immediately when the person asks the other to commit the crime on her behalf. Here this would fail because Hanna refused.

Conspiracy would be another charge that could be levied upon Betty. Here Betty planned to burn down her house with Hanna. Under common law in order to have a valid conspiracy plurality was required which meant two people were required at least. Here this would fail because Hanna did not willingly partake and agree to be a part of their crime. However under modern law, plurality is no longer required and Betty can be the sole participant to the conspiracy.

Betty can be charged for conspiracy and for Arson because they are two separate crimes.

Hanna on the other hand can be charged with aiding and abetting. This requires that the person has knowledge of the crime, lends assistance or encouraged the act to occur. Here Hanna, although she refused to participate, did assist when Betty asked her if she had gasoline and to leave her garage open. Hanna knew what Betty intended to do and let her do it by assisting her by keeping her garage open and telling her there was gasoline inside. Thus Hanna can be charged as an aider and abettor.

Bob on the other hand is not subject to any criminal liability. The only thing he could be found is guilty of negligence but that is a tort, not a crime. Here Bob was shocked to see Betty pour the gasoline and light it on fire. He just pulled her to safety. He did fail to call the fire department or the police or extinguish the flames, but that was more negligence.

Thus Betty can be charged with conspiracy and arson and Hanna can be charged as aider and abettor.

July 2010—Question 5

Patti Police was working undercover at "The Bar," a lounge known for illegal drug activity. Dan Defendant encountered Patti at The Bar. Patti indicated she enjoyed smoking crack cocaine. Dan, eager to impress Patti, informed her that he would bring some crack cocaine for her the following evening. In fact, Dan knew nothing about crack cocaine.

Later that night, Dan informed his friend, Sam Salt, of his encounter with Patti. Sam had just purchased a 2001 BMW from a used car dealer. Sam indicated he was shocked when he discovered a bag filled with a substance Sam believed to be crack cocaine in the glove box of his BMW. Sam indicated the crack was in a brown bag inside his garage. Sam refused to give Dan any of the substance because he feared doing so would subject him to criminal liability. Sam intended to throw the substance out the next time trash was to be collected from his neighborhood.

Dan immediately went to Sam's home to take some crack from Sam's garage. The garage was attached to Sam's home. Sam and his girlfriend were inside Sam's home at the time. Dan pried open the locked garage door, and found the brown paper bag containing the substance in the corner of the garage. Dan placed in an envelope a small portion of a white rocky substance.

The next evening, Dan arrived at The Bar and handed Patti the envelope that contained the substance. Patti took possession of the envelope and Dan was immediately placed under arrest. When the substance was sent to a police lab for analysis, it was discovered that it was not crack cocaine at all, but rather rock salt, which the previous owner of the BMW apparently kept in the car for snow and ice emergencies.

Discuss the charges, if any, which may be brought against Dan in relation to: (1) Dan's conduct at Sam's home; and (2) Dan's conduct at The Bar. Explain your answer.

Model Answer to Question 5

Dan committed two acts that may expose him to criminal liability. First, he entered Sam's garage by prying open a locked door. Second, Dan attempted to give Patti a substance he believed to be a controlled substance. Each act is addressed separately.

I. Dan's Conduct at Sam's House: Dan can be charged with common law burglary or first-degree home invasion in violation of MCL 750.110a(2). Dan can also be charged with misdemeanor larceny, for stealing the rock salt from Sam's garage.

The elements of first-degree home invasion are: (1) the defendant broke and entered a dwelling or entered the dwelling without permission; (2) when the defendant did so, he intended to commit a felony, larceny, or assault, or he actually committed a felony, larceny, or assault while entering, being present in, or exiting the dwelling; and (3) another person was lawfully present in the dwelling or the defendant was armed with a dangerous weapon. *People v Sands*, 261 Mich App 158, 162 (2004), MCL 750.110a(2). The elements of common law burglary are similar to first-degree home invasion except that common law burglary must be committed under cover of night and there is no requirement that a person legally be within the dwelling or that defendant be armed with a dangerous weapon. See *People v Saxton*, 118 Mich App 681, 690 (1982), citing LaFave and Scott, Handbook of Criminal Law, § 96, p 708.

The term "dwelling" is statutorily defined as "a structure or shelter that is used permanently or temporarily as a place of abode, *including an appurtenant structure attached to that structure* or shelter." (Emphasis added.) MCL 750.110a(1)(a). At common law, the term dwelling included any structure within the curtilage of the home. Applied under either setting, there can be little doubt that when Dan pried open the locked door to a "garage attached to Sam's home" he broke into a dwelling.

At the time Dan broke into Sam's garage, Dan intended to commit a felony; the possession of crack cocaine, a controlled substance. Further, at the time Dan entered Sam's garage it was his intent to commit a larceny. In fact, Dan completed the larceny when he took the rock salt from Sam's garage. The crime of larceny is described by statute as "stealing [money, goods, or chattels] of another person." MCL 750.356(1)(a). If the value of the goods stolen is less than $200, the crime is a misdemeanor. MCL 750.356(5). Nonetheless, the act remains a larceny for purposes of home invasion in the first degree.

Finally, because Sam and his girlfriend were in his home at the time Dan entered Sam's garage, the final element of first-degree home invasion is satisfied. The applicant need not discuss both common law burglary and home invasion to receive full credit in this portion of the question. A thoughtful analysis of either charge would suffice.

II. Dan's Conduct at The Bar: Whether Dan is exposed to criminal liability for distributing rock salt to Patti while under the mistaken belief that he was providing her crack cocaine is a closer question. In *People v Thousand*, 465 Mich 149, 158-159 (2001), the Michigan Supreme Court observed that "the concept of pure legal impossibility applies when an actor engages in conduct that he believes is criminal, but is not actually prohibited by law: 'There can be no conviction of criminal attempt based upon D's erroneous notion that he was committing a crime.' *Perkins & Boyce, supra, p 634.*"

Notwithstanding the Court's discussion of the impossibility defense to criminal liability, the Court rejected the notion that the impossibility defense is rooted in the common law. *Thousand* at 163. The Supreme Court focused on the specific language of Michigan's attempt statute, MCL 750.92. The Court was "unable to discern from the words of the attempt statute any legislative intent that the concept of 'impossibility' provide any impediment to charging a defendant with, or convicting him of, an attempted crime." *Id.* at 165.

Here, it may be argued that Michigan's attempt statute has no application because the attempt is subsumed under the crime of delivery itself. *People v Alexander*, 188 Mich App 96 (1991). Thus, whether Dan is exposed to criminal liability for his attempt to deliver cocaine to Patti will turn on the language of Michigan's controlled substance statute. MCL 333.7401 provides, in pertinent part that "a person shall not . . . deliver or possess with intent to deliver a controlled substance." The above-cited statutory language makes the intent to deliver equivalent to actual delivery. Thus, the attempt is equivalent to the principal charge of delivery.

Further, the delivery statute requires the possession of a controlled substance. This is also supported by Michigan's criminal standard jury instructions, which sets forth five elements for the unlawful possession of a controlled substance with the intent to deliver. The first three of these elements are pertinent to this issue:

> First, that the defendant knowingly possessed a controlled substance.
>
> Second, that the defendant intended to deliver this substance to someone else.
>
> Third, that the substance possessed was a controlled substance and defendant knew it.

Applied to the facts presented in this case, it may be argued that Dan cannot be convicted of possession with intent to deliver a controlled substance because he never possessed a controlled substance. The fact that he believed what he was doing was illegal does not transpose his otherwise legal activity into criminal conduct.

Conversely, it may be argued that, under Michigan's attempt statute, a defendant may be charged with an attempt to commit a crime where there is evidence of (1) an attempt to commit a crime; and (2) any act towards the commission of the intended offense. *Thousand*, at 164. Here, when Dan gave Patti rock salt believing it to be crack cocaine, he attempted to commit a crime—the delivery of a controlled substance. However, it is arguable whether Dan committed "any act" towards the commission of the intended offense of possession with the intent to deliver a controlled substance. The defendant will argue that no aspect of Dan's possession and delivery of rock salt, a legal substance, amounted to an act toward the commission of the offense. By contrast, the prosecution may argue that the home invasion perpetrated by Dan was committed with the intent to steal crack cocaine for the purpose of delivering it to Patti. This action constituted an act undertaken to perpetrate the crime of delivery of a controlled substance. Just as in *People v Thousand*, where the impossibility defense was found inapplicable to the charge of attempted distribution of obscene material to a minor where defendant was in fact distributing the material to an adult undercover police officer, defendant here may be charged with an attempt to distribute crack cocaine even though what he in fact distributed to Patti was a legal substance.

Dan may also be charged with possession with intent to deliver an imitation controlled substance in violation of MCL 333.7341(3), a felony punishable by imprisonment of not more than two years. MCL 333.7341(8). This statute defines "imitation controlled substance" as "a substance that is not a controlled substance . . . [which] by representation . . . would lead a reasonable person to believe that the substance is a controlled substance." Defense counsel may argue that no reasonable person looking at rock salt would conclude that it is crack cocaine. The prosecution will respond that both Sam and Dan believed it to be crack cocaine and both represented the salt to be crack cocaine. This evidence is sufficient to present the question to the jury. In response, defense counsel may also argue that a person actually believing the substance to be a controlled substance may not be charged with this crime, as they lack the intent to distribute an imitation. The prosecutor may respond, however, nothing in the statute supports the conclusion that the distributor must in fact be aware of the imitation status of the substance.

Student Answer—July 2010

Question 5—Criminal Law—8 points.

Dan will likely be charged with burglary. Burglary is the breaking and entering of a dwelling, of another at nighttime with the intent to steal.

The facts indicate that Dan pried open Sam's garage door. A garage is normally not considered a dwelling, however when its attached to a residence, it falls within the curtilage of the home. Dan entered Sam's garage w/o permission with intent to steal the "crack" that was in Sam's BMW. The facts also indicate that it was night time so it is likely that the elements of burglary were met because Dan broke into Sam's garage, at nighttime to steal. The only factor really at issue would be whether the garage is considered part of Sam's home.

Dan will also likely be charged with larceny. Larceny is the tresspassory taking, of property of another, with the intent to steal. Here Dan intended to go the Sam's garage and steal the "crack". He entered Sam's garage without permission for the purpose taking the "crack". There are no facts indicating that Dan intended to give the "crack" back to Sam after showing it to Patti. Therefore, Dan will likely successful be charged with larceny.

As to conduct at the bar, Dan will likely argue that Patti entrapped him into committing a crime and had it not been for her suggestion and his desire to please her, we would not have stolen the "crack" from Sam.

However, Dan may also be charged with possession of an illegal narcotic with intent to distribute and also conspiracy to distribute an illegal narcotic. Dan's lack of knowledge about crack or his mistaken belief that the rock salt was crack won't be a defense to burglary. But may be a defense to other chargeable crimes if they are considered specific intent.

CONFLICTS OF LAW

Questions, Model Answers, and Student Answers

The following section includes prior Michigan Bar Exam questions and model answers for **Conflicts of Law**. Many of the questions also include actual student answers with the amount of points that were earned to give you a better idea of what the graders expect. The student answers are immediately following the model answer for each question. Please pay close attention to the points received on each question. Although most samples represent "good" answers (i.e., received 8, 9, or 10 points), there are some samples that received 7 points (the minimum "passing" score for an essay), and a few that received very low scores to help you better understand the grading process and what is expected.

February 2002—Question 7

Big Time Corporation was incorporated in Delaware, and had their world headquarters in Detroit, Michigan. Big Time entered into a contract with Handyman Corporation to renovate one of Big Time's plants located in Illinois. Handyman was a Michigan corporation and the contract was signed at Big Time's world headquarters. The contract had a provision that required Handyman to indemnify and hold Big Time harmless from any lawsuit alleging a personal injury for work being performed at the plant in Illinois. Due to an oversight, the contract did not contain any statement as to what state law would be applied in the event of any dispute between the parties.

Handyman hired Harry Jones as an independent contractor to remove rust from some of the presses that were located in the Illinois plant of Big Time. In performing his work, one of the presses being cleaned was mistakenly started by a Handyman employee, causing a severe injury to the hand of Mr. Jones. Jones sued both Big Time for inadequate protection devices at the press start button, and Handyman for the action of their employee. The suit was filed in Wayne circuit court. Illinois had a statute that provided that indemnification clauses such as found in the contract were void under Illinois law. Under Michigan law, identical indemnification provisions as found in the contract were found to be valid. Big Time filed a declaratory judgment action in Wayne circuit court seeking to enforce the indemnification provision, which would require Handyman to defend the Jones suit and pay any damage award. Handyman filed a motion to dismiss the complaint for declaratory judgment.

Directing your answer solely to the issue of the conflicting statutes, what arguments would be advanced by Handyman, what arguments would be advanced by Big Time, and how would you expect the Court to rule and why?

Model Answer to Question 7

States such as Michigan have held that the place where the contract is entered into is the law to be applied. The national trend, and now Michigan, has moved beyond this rigid approach and now the general rule is that the law of the place having the most significant relation with the matter in dispute will be the law that is applied.

There are a number of factors that are applied to resolve this issue and some of those are (a) the place of contracting, (b) the place of negotiation of the contract, (c) the place of performance, (d) the location of the subject matter of the contract, (e) the domicile, residence, nationality, place of incorporation, and place of business of the parties.

In the present case, Handyman would contend that the contract was to be performed in Illinois, the subject matter of the contract was in Illinois, and therefore Illinois law should be applied. Since the contract was being performed in Illinois, that state would have "the more significant interest in enforcing a statute designed to regulate or deter specific business practices." *Chrysler Corp v Skyline Industries*, 448 Mich 113 (1995).

Big Time would argue, and probably successfully, that the contract was formed in Michigan, the parties to the contract are Michigan corporations, and most importantly the parties negotiated and agreed to the indemnification clause. It would make little sense to apply Illinois law and invalidate a provision of the contract that the parties expressly agreed upon. "Prime objectives of contract law are to protect the justified expectations of the parties and to make it possible for them to foretell with accuracy what will be their rights and liabilities under the contract." *Chrysler Corp, supra.*

Based on the foregoing, the decision in this case would probably be in favor of Big Time.

Student Answer—February 2002

Question 7—Conflicts of Law—8 points

Big time-corp Delaware, headqtr Detroit, MI
Handyman-MI corp
K Signed-MI
Plant- FL
Suit-MI

Illinois statute indemnification clauses void
MI statute indemnification clauses void

The issue is whether the Wayne Circuit Court should look at Michigan law or whether the court should look to Illinois law.

Traditionally Michigan applied the law of the place where the injury occurred. However, Michigan has since adopted the restatement to apply lex loci delicti (the law of the forum).

Handyman would argue that the law of Illinois should be applied because then the indemnification clause would be void & Big Time would have to share in the liability. If Jones is from Illinois then Handyman could argue the plaintiff is from Illinois & that is where the injury occurred so the law of Illinois should apply.

Big Time will argue that Michigan law should apply & therefore the indemnification should apply & therefore the indemnification clause is valid. Big Time will argue that Michigan should apply its own law because the act may have occurred in Illinois but all the other contacts are Michigan related.

The Michigan court will then look at the interests behind each of the statutes & assess the contacts of the parties. If one state has a substantially greater interest than Michigan, Michigan will apply that states law. Michigan will also decide if by choosing one states law over another due process & full faith & credit would be violated.

In this case the Illinois statute has interests of making sure the plaintiff gets full recovery so Illinois wants the plaintiff to be able to sue all the people responsible. In this case, Handyman is a smaller corporation & may not have the resources that Big Time has.

The Michigan statute is seeking to protect contracts between businesses & not allow Handyman to run away from liability. Michigan wants the proper people to pay for damages & there may be an element of protecting corporations.

The contacts to Michigan are significant Handyman is incorporated here, Big Time has world headquarters here the contract was entered into here. Michigan also applies lex loci contractus (law of the places of contract). Since Michigan seeks to apply the law of the forum & the law of the place of the contract Michigan will apply its own law. The indemnification clause is valid.

This decision would not violate due process or full faith & credit. There will be no unfair surprise to Handyman because he is incorporated in Michigan & he should also be aware of the contract law in the state where he is from.

July 2004—Question 14

Susan Archer was employed by Kendall Corporation, an Ohio corporation. She was riding as a passenger in a car rented at the Hertz Dealership in Monroe, Michigan. This vehicle was registered in Michigan. The driver, Ann Smith, was also an employee of Kendall Corporation and the two were on a business trip driving to Grand Rapids, Michigan to see a customer of Kendall. Just outside of Lansing, Michigan, on I-96, they were involved in an accident caused solely by John Dawson, a Michigan resident. Susan filed a lawsuit in Michigan against John Dawson and included in the lawsuit was a claim against Interstate Insurance Company for underinsurance benefits. Underinsurance benefits are payable when the tortfeasor's insurance coverage is not adequate to compensate the injured party for their injuries.

Susan was able to settle her case against John Dawson and continued her claim against Interstate. Interstate was an Ohio corporation, licensed to do business in both Michigan and Ohio. Interstate issued a policy of insurance to Kendall that provided an endorsement for underinsurance coverage to all of Kendall's employees involved in an auto accident while in the course of their employment. The endorsement had an exclusion that required that the vehicle in which the employee was riding be a vehicle registered in the state of Ohio. There was an Ohio Supreme Court decision that had considered this exclusionary language and held that such language was against Ohio's public policy and would not be enforced. Both the Michigan Insurance Code and the Michigan Supreme Court had considered the exact exclusionary language as contained within the Interstate policy and upheld this exclusion.

Susan and Interstate stipulated to the facts and agreed that the entire claim was dependent on which state's law was to be applied to the exclusionary language found in the insurance policy. Both sides moved for summary disposition.

You are employed as a law clerk for the judge who is assigned this case. You are directed by your employer to write a memorandum setting forth the applicable

law and come to a conclusion as to which state's law should be applied. What are the factors to be considered? What will your conclusion be, and why?

Model Answer to Question 14

Michigan no longer follows the rule that a contract dispute is to be resolved by the law of the state in which the contract was entered into. Michigan now favors a more "policy" centered approach "where the rights and duties of the parties with respect to an issue in contract are determined by the local law of the sate, with respect to that issue, has the most significant relationship to the transaction and to the parties." There are several factors that can be considered: (1) The place of contract, (2) the place of negotiation of the contract, (3) the place of performance, (4) the location of the subject matter of the contract, and (5) the domicile, residence, nationality, place of incorporation, and the place of business of the parties.

Kendall does business in more than one state and has employees working and driving vehicles in more than one state. The contract was to cover the employees no matter where they were working at the time of the accident. The facts of this case do not state where the contract was negotiated but since both corporations are Ohio corporations, it could be assumed the contract was negotiated and signed in Ohio. The facts do not indicate that the contract contains any language as to what state law is to be used in the interpretation of the contract. The contract does not cover employees of an Ohio corporation who are in the course of business for that company when the claim would accrue. Finally, the plaintiff is a resident of Ohio.

Michigan has very little involvement in this dispute. The accident occurred in Michigan and John Dawson is a Michigan resident. Mr. Dawson is neither interested nor involved in this claim. The only parties who are interested in this dispute are either Ohio residents or Ohio corporations.

It is reasonable for an Ohio resident to look to Ohio law to interpret a contract between her employer, and another Ohio corporation. The insurance company that issued the policy obviously intended it to cover the employees of the Kendall Corporation. By contracting with an Ohio company to provide insurance coverage to employees of the company, Interstate should reasonably have contemplated that it would be bound by Ohio law. There is no public policy argument that would require Michigan courts to enforce Michigan law in interpreting a contract between Ohio corporations involving an Ohio resident.

Ohio law should be the law applied and the exclusion would not be enforceable. *See Mitchell v Travelers* (unpublished Court of Appeals #234941) decided 12/13/02.

Student Answer—July 2004

Question 14—Conflicts of Law—None Available

July 2008—Question 9

Brenda Business, a resident of Michigan, is the sole proprietor and operator of five very successful golf training facilities located in Michigan that specialize in servicing the needs of women golfers. In addition to having a first-rate practice facility with many accomplished women teaching professionals, each location features a full-service spa and a pro shop that limits its inventory to golf equipment designed for women.

Brenda decided it was time to expand her business to other states. Brenda purchased a 40-acre parcel of property in Akron, Ohio, very near the Firestone Country Club. Carl Contractor, a resident of Indiana, constructed each one of Brenda's five Michigan locations. Brenda and Carl met at one of Brenda's golf facilities to discuss Brenda's Akron, Ohio project. Brenda and Carl agreed that Carl would construct the Ohio facility and that they would adopt the terms and conditions that governed the construction of each of Brenda's other facilities. Brenda indicated that she would have her Michigan attorney draft a contract and forward it to Carl in Indiana for his review. Consistent with all prior contracts, the draft sent to Carl by Brenda's attorney provided that the project would be done on a "cost plus basis." Carl would be paid the cost of constructing the facility plus a profit of $100,000. The contract was silent on the law that would govern any disputes that might arise from the construction project. The contract was also silent with regard to the law under which the contract would be interpreted. Carl, Brenda, and their attorneys met for lunch in Wayne County, Michigan, at which time Brenda and Carl signed their contract.

After the contract was signed and Carl had ordered and had shipped to Akron the raw materials needed to start the job, Brenda and Carl went to Akron to review the site. Brenda and Carl arrived in Akron one day early, so that they could play golf at the Firestone Country Club before getting to business the next day. Brenda set up a golf game with two prominent members of the Firestone Country Club.

On the last hole, Brenda was in the process of striking a three-foot putt that, if sunk, would have won her the match. Carl inadvertently drove his golf cart into a tree, making a loud noise. The noise distracted Brenda, causing her to miss the putt. Brenda was so angry, she threw her putter at Carl, striking him in the head and causing serious injuries. As the ambulance took Carl away, Brenda yelled out, "Go home. You are fired. You will never work for me again."

Carl brought a breach of contract action and a negligence action against Brenda in the Wayne, County Circuit Court. Believing that Ohio enacted tort reform that may substantially limit Carl's damages, Carl's counsel filed a retrial motion to have Michigan law govern both causes of action. Brenda opposed the motion.

How will the court rule? Explain your answer.

Model Answer to Question 9

In *Sutherland v Kennington Truck Service, Ltd*, 454 Mich 274 (1997), the Michigan Supreme Court addressed Michigan's conflict of law rules:

> Michigan courts apply Michigan law unless a "rational reason" to do otherwise exists. In determining whether a rational reason to displace Michigan law exists, we undertake a two-step analysis. First, we must determine if any foreign state does have an interest in having its law applies. If no state has such an interest, the presumption that Michigan law will apply cannot be overcome. If a foreign state does have an interest in having its law applied, we must then determine if Michigan's interest mandate that Michigan law be applied, despite the foreign interests.

First, it must be determined if any foreign state has an interest in having its law applied. The only states that can be said to have an interest in the litigation are Michigan, Ohio, and Indiana. In regard to Indiana, the only interest is Carl's Indiana residency. Under a "Michigan choice-of-law analysis, a plaintiff's residency is determined as of the date of the injury." *Hall v General Motors Corp*, 229 Mich App 580 (1998). Thus, Indiana must be considered Carl's residence. Even though Indiana has an interest in the case through Carl's residency, "plaintiff's residence, with nothing more, is insufficient to support the choice of a state's law." *Home Ins Co v Dick*, 281 US 397, 408; 50 S Ct 338, 74 L Ed 926 (1930). Thus, the only remaining states that can be said to have an interest in the litigation are Michigan and Ohio.

We must determine if Ohio has an interest in having its law applied. At one time, "[t]he predominant view in Michigan [was] that a contract is to be construed according to the law of the place where the contract is to be entered into." *Chrysler Corp v Skyline Indus Services, Inc*, 448 Mich 113, 223 (1995). However, in *Chrysler*, the Court held that "the rigid 'law of the place of contracting' approach has become outmoded in resolving contract conflicts." Rather, the Michigan Supreme Court noted that sections 187 and 188 of the Restatement (Second) Conflicts of Law, "with their emphasis on examining the relevant contracts and policies of the interested states, provide a sound basis for moving beyond formalism to an approach more in line with modern-day contracting realties." *Id.* at 124. Section 188 of the Restatement of the Law 2d, Conflict of Law (1971), suggests several interests to consider as factors relevant to determining the applicable law in a contract case: "(a) the place of contracting; (b) the place of negotiations of the contract; (c) the place of performance; (d) the location of the subject matter of the contract, and (e) the domicile, residency, nationality, place of incorporation, and place of business of parties."

Brenda would argue that Ohio has the greatest interest because the contract services were to be performed there and the subject matter of the action is located there. Carl, on the other hand, would emphasize that the parties negotiated and entered the contract in Michigan and that Brenda resides in Michigan and her business is largely operated in Michigan.

In regard to the contract claim, the trial would likely apply Michigan law. The "[p]rime objectives of contract law are to protect the justified expectations of the parties and to make it possible for them to foretell with accuracy what will be their rights and liabilities under the contract." *Chrysler, supra* at 126 citing comments to § 187 of the Restatement (Second) Conflicts of Law. However, "[f]ulfillment of the parties' expectations is not the only value in contract law; regard must also be had for state interests and for state regulation." *Id.* The parties' expectations are best reflected by the negotiation and execution of the contract, which occurred in Michigan. In addition, given the parties' history of similar construction contracts within Michigan, the trial court could readily conclude that the parties were justified in expecting Michigan law to apply to every aspect of the contract claim. Although Brenda would argue that Ohio has a substantial interest in regulating the performance of the contract, the parties had not yet begun the actual construction of the project. Thus, Ohio's interest in having its law applied is not significant and Michigan law would apply.

In regard to a tort action for personal injury, section 146 of the Restatement of the Law 2d, Conflict of Laws (1971), suggests several interests to consider as contracts relevant to determining the applicable law in a tort case: "(a) the place where the injury occurred, (b) the place where the conduct causing the injury occurred, (c) the domicile, residence, nationality, place of incorporation, and place of business of the parties, and (d) the place where the relationship, if any, between the parties is centered."

Brenda would argue that Ohio has the greatest interest because the conduct causing the injury and the injury causing event occurred in Ohio. Carl, on the other hand, would emphasize that Brenda resides in Michigan and their business relationship is largely centered in Michigan.

In regard to the tort claim, though a closer call, the trial court would likely apply Michigan law. Although Ohio, the state where the injury occurred, has an interest in conduct within its borders, the interest in the litigation is minimal when one of the parties is an Ohio resident. *Olmstead v Anderson*, 428 Mich 1, 28 (1987). "This rationale holds true whether the parties are from the same state . . . or, as here from different states. The operative fact is that neither party is a citizen of the state in which the wrong occurred." *Id.* Moreover, although "[t]he injury state always has an interest in conduct within its borders, whether or not its citizens are involved . . . the issue in the case does not involve conduct, but, instead, damages or limitation thereof." Further, Brenda is a Michigan resident and it is not unfair or unexpected that Michigan law be applied to the tort claim. Thus, the trial court will likely apply Michigan law in both claims.

Student Answer—July 2008

Question 9—Conflicts of Law—9 points

Conclusion: In this question of conflicts, a Michigan court is unlikely to have any interest in the matter, and will likely find that the law of Ohio governs the contracts issue, and law of Indiana governs the tort issue.

Issue # 1—Breach of Contract

Rule: Where there is a conflict of law instance in a contracts action, Michigan courts will likely look to see which state has the most "substantial" contact.

Analysis: Generally speaking, a contract's "most substantial contact" is with the state where it will be performed. The contract at issue here is going to be performed in Ohio, and it appears as if it was formed in Michigan. However, the actions leading to the breach and its repudiation occurred in Ohio. B/C the restatement generally states that one must look to the place w/the most significant contacts, Ohio law will prevail in the breach of contract action.

Conclusion: Therefore b/c the most significant contacts in the contract action are in the state of Ohio, its laws will apply in the breach of contract.

Issue #2—Torts Claim

Rule: MI has specifically repudiated the Restatement 1st rule, and now applies a "government interest" test to determine which jurisdiction has a stronger need to see the law upheld.

Analysis: Under *Sutherland*, MI courts look to see which state has a greater interest in seeing its laws upheld. In this particular case, it could be Ohio, Indiana, or Michigan.

Ohio: Place of harm: ordinarily this will have a strong interest in having its laws upheld. However, b/c the party injured lives elsewhere and will likely not use many state resources in the long term it will not likely have a strong interest in having its laws upheld.

Michigan: Place of claim, where D lives. Michigan has perhaps the least interest in having its laws upheld—the harm occurred elsewhere, and to a person living in a 3d jurisdiction. The only connection is that they appear to have a more plaintiff-friendly laws and the D lives in MI. B/C the injured party is not a MI resident and the harm did not occur there, they will have little interest in upholding its law.

Indiana: Place where P lives. B/C the P lives here, uses its resources if he is unable to work—or needs health care, its needs will be the strongest, and they will likely want Indiana law to apply for the tort claim.

Conclusion: B/C Ohio's interests are weak, Michigan's are non-existent, and Indiana's are strong, therefore, Indiana law will prevail in the tort action.

Comment: Note that this answer received 9 points even though the conclusions were wrong! This is mainly due to the correct detailed definition of the rule and analysis.

CRIMINAL PROCEDURE

Questions, Model Answers, and Student Answers

The following section includes prior Michigan Bar Exam questions and model answers for **Criminal Procedure**. Many of the questions also include actual student answers with the amount of points that were earned to give you a better idea of what the graders expect. The student answers are immediately following the model answer for each question. Please pay close attention to the points received on each question. Although most samples represent "good" answers (i.e., received 8, 9, or 10 points), there are some samples that received 7 points (the minimum "passing" score for an essay), and a few that received very low scores to help you better understand the grading process and what is expected.

February 2001—Question 15

John Young was bowling, and while getting a beer, became involved in an argument with Harold Todd and William Easley. The argument proceeded outside, when suddenly Todd pulled a gun and shot Young, once in the shoulder and once in the neck. Young was able to get into his car and attempted to drive to the hospital. Approximately one-half mile down the road, he pulled into a gas station, where he stopped the car and fell out onto the pavement. The operator of the gas station called the police who arrived at the scene in less than three minutes. Young was still conscious and when questioned by the officers, managed to tell them where he was shot and described his assailants. Young described Todd as a white male approximately 6 feet tall, weighing approximately 250 pounds and wearing a Detroit Lions jacket and Detroit Tigers hat. Easley was described as a black male, 5 feet 5 inches tall, weighing 125 pounds, and wearing an orange hunting vest and Caterpillar tractor hat.

The officers immediately returned to the bowling alley and when they didn't see anyone in the parking lot, entered the bowling alley and saw two males matching the description of Todd and Easley, each wearing the hats described by Mr. Young. Upon approaching the two, the officers saw on the bench where they were bowling, jackets as described by Mr. Young. The two suspects were taken into custody and driven to the gas station where Mr. Young was just being loaded into an ambulance. Todd and Easley denied owning the jackets and refused to put them on, although they still had their hats on. Mr. Young identified them as his assailants.

Todd is tried and convicted of assault with intent to commit murder and retains you to handle his appeal. As Todd's attorney you determine that the only basis for an appeal would be to challenge the on-scene identification.

What is the basis for your appeal, and what do you anticipate the issues to be argued?

Model Answer to Question 15

The issue to be raised is whether the on-scene identification denied Todd's right to counsel as set forth in *People v Anderson*, 389 Mich 1565 (1973). There are several decisions in Michigan on this issue. The U.S. Supreme Court has concluded that the right to counsel only attaches to corporeal identifications conducted "at or after the initiation of adversary judicial criminal proceedings." *Kirby v Illinois*, 406 US 682 (1972). The Michigan Supreme Court in the *Anderson* decision did not follow the *Kirby* case and held that the right to counsel pertains to all pretrial procedures. *People v Dixon*, 85 Mich App 271 (1978), has held that if the police have more than a mere suspicion that the suspect is wanted for the crime, the officer cannot return the suspect for an at-the-scene identification. Subsequently, *People v Turner*, 120 Mich App 23 (1982), determined that at-the-scene identification without counsel is permissible unless the police have "very strong evidence" that the person stopped is the offender. The most recent decision has held that a prompt on-the-scene identification regardless of the degree of suspicion or evidence, is permitted. *People v Winters*, 225 Mich App 718 (1997).

The answer must identify and discuss the issue of the right to counsel, when this right commences, the promptness of the identification in this case, and the issue concerning the strength of the evidence available when the identification is made. While not included in the facts, additional points should be given to a discussion on whether any subsequent identification is made by a lineup, or in Court and how that affects the at-the-scene identification.

Student Answer—February 2001

Question 15—Criminal Procedure—8 points

On Scene ID

An on the scene ID is generally valid—if the ID is made relatively soon after the events in public.

Here, although the victim's description of his assailants is broad, generic, & could apply to a great number of men, it can still be valid. The officer immediately spotted Todd at the place the shooting occurred—minutes after it occurred & were taken into custody—before the booking, the victim positively ID'd Todd.

All facts considered, the I.D. may or may not be upheld. A defendant does not have a right to an attorney when victim is viewing photos or in a public place.

However, the ID took place here in public, after defendant was in custody, but before 6th Amendment Right to counsel attached.

**Right to counsel* attaches at *arraignment* for crime of poss. Punishment of 6 months or more incarceration.

The identification was too *suggestive*. Any competent attorney would object to a lineup like this—if actual procedures in a police station were followed.

*Note that counsel should be present at a line-up w/procedures to object to overly suggestive line-ups.

This identification, I would say, was overly suggestive.

July 2001—Question 2

James Johnson was charged with criminal sexual conduct, first degree. His defense was that this was a consensual encounter after which the complainant, a married woman, began to feel remorseful.

After the encounter, James went to the nearest police station and told the police he was worried this woman may claim she had been raped. The police were well aware of James and had heard this same story on two prior occasions. Both of these occasions resulted in a charge of "criminal sexual conduct, first degree" and an acquittal.

Prior to commencing the jury trial, the judge excluded from evidence the two prior charges, but indicated he would allow the other two women to testify. The prosecutor was unable to locate these women and the judge denied the prosecutor's motion for an adjournment.

As the jury trial in this case progressed, it became apparent that there was little chance of a conviction. Mr. Johnson, who testified in his own behalf, was a compelling witness. After repeating the story of why he went to the police, the prosecutor, on cross-examination, asked him "That is exactly the same story you told after you raped those two other women, isn't it?" As the defense counsel rose and stated, "I move for a mistrial because ***", the court, without waiting to hear more, stated: "Granted," and declared a mistrial. A couple days later, the prosecutor found the two women who were both willing to testify. The prosecutor refiled the charges and the defense counsel moved to dismiss.

What would be the basis for the motion to dismiss and what would the arguments be, both for and against this motion?

Model Answer to Question 2

The motion would be based on the provision found in both the Michigan and Federal Constitutions that provides no person shall twice be put in jeopardy for the same offense. Michigan Constitution 1963, Art 1 § 15; US Constitution, Amendment 5.

Generally speaking, the double jeopardy clause does not bar a retrial where the prosecution or the judge made an innocent error or where the cause prompting the mistrial was outside of their control and/or the result of the defense counsel's misconduct. It is important in considering the motion to balance society's interest in affording the prosecution one full and fair opportunity to present evidence to the jury with the accused's interest in limiting the state to have one attempt at obtaining a conviction. The prosecutor knew that the prior charges were inadmissible, but asked this highly prejudicial question. When innocent conduct of the prosecution or judge forms the basis of the motion by the defense counsel, a retrial is generally allowed. However, it appears in this case that the defendant's motion for mistrial was prompted by intentional prosecutorial conduct.

The prosecutor could argue that it was defense counsel who moved for mistrial and therefore defendant waived the double jeopardy argument. The defendant does not waive the double jeopardy protection by moving for a mistrial under these circumstances. The court has the authority to discharge a jury when, in taking all of the circumstances into consideration, there is a manifest necessity for the act, or the ends of public justice would be otherwise defeated. Even if defense counsel had not made this motion and even though the basis for the motion had not been completed, the Court may on its own, order a mistrial when there is a manifest necessity for the act, or the ends of public justice would be otherwise defeated.

It is reasonable to infer from the facts of this case that the prosecution was aware of the negligible chances of a conviction and asked this question to prompt a mistrial in order to give the prosecution a second shot at convicting the defendant. Under these circumstances, protection under the double jeopardy provision of the Constitution would be properly invoked, even though the motion for mistrial was made by defense counsel. *People v Dawson*, 431 Mich 234 (1988).

Student Answer—July 2001

Question 2—Criminal Procedure—None Available

February 2002—Question 8

Mad Max Mayhem had a long history of criminal assaults and violence. He was well-known to all the police officers of Pleasantville. His wife, Mary, finally had had enough of the assaults, criminal charges, and bizarre behavior and filed for divorce, obtaining a personal protection order. Shortly after Max was served with the divorce papers, he followed Mary to the Meijer store where she normally shopped. As Mary was getting out of the car, Max rapidly approached her, pulled a gun, told her to get in the front seat and drive away, mentioning that "if he couldn't have her, no one was going to." Max sat in the back seat, giving Mary the opportunity to leave the front seat with Max in the back and run into the parking lot looking for assistance. Max finally extricated himself from the back seat and was last seen by Mary running into the Meijer store with the gun in his hand.

Mary called the local police on her cell phone and within minutes two officers, Johns and Crist, arrived outside the Meijer store and found Mary. She told them Max had run into the store with the gun and that was the last she saw of him. Both officers entered the store and found Max shopping in the women's lingerie section, with no sign of the gun present. The officers approached Max with their guns drawn, told him to freeze, and advised him he was under arrest. Officer Johns then asked Max "Where did you put the gun?", and Max pointed to a pile of empty cardboard boxes and said, "It's in the box labeled 'water pistols.'" Officer Johns searched the pile of boxes and found the loaded revolver in the box labeled "water pistols." Officer Crist, who had remained with Max, saw the gun being retrieved, and then advised Max of his Miranda rights. Max immediately told Officer Crist he did not want to talk to them and he wanted a lawyer.

Max was charged with a variety of criminal offenses, including assault with a dangerous weapon. MCL 750.82. Max's attorney filed a timely motion to suppress

Max's statement and the revolver from being received into evidence. **What is the basis for this motion? What should be the prosecution's response? What will be the result of this motion?**

Model Answer to Question 8

Max's attorney's motion would request to suppress the initial statement as to the location of the gun and the gun. Defendant would contend that a statement regarding the whereabouts of the gun was made before he was advised of his Miranda rights. This violated the Miranda rule, and that the gun was the fruit of the poisonous tree and should be excluded from evidence.

The prosecutor would respond that the Miranda rule does not apply to situations involving police questions reasonably prompted by a concern for public safety. The presence of the hidden gun somewhere in the store obviously posed a danger to the general public. The questions the police directed to Max were only those questions necessary to secure the gun in order to protect the public and were not a part of the investigatory process of the alleged crime itself.

Based upon the facts of this case, the police officers' knowledge that Max was a potentially dangerous person who shortly before had a revolver and in all probability had secreted the revolver somewhere in the store, would be sufficient facts to support the public safety exception to Miranda and would result in the denial of the motion of defense counsel. *People v Attebury*, 463 Mich 662 (2001); *New York v Quarles*, 467 US 649 (1984).

Student Answer—February 2002

Question 8—Criminal Procedure—8 points

Max's attorney is filing a motion to suppress the statement based on the 5th Amendment Miranda rights and the revolver for being the fruit of the poisonous tree in violation of Wong Son.

When a defendant is in custody, the police cannot illicit a statement w/out first obtaining a voluntary and intelligent waiver from the defendant in order to interrogate a defendant, the defendant must first be given Miranda warnings appraising him of his right to remain silent under the 5th Amendment. The 5th Amendment is applicable to the states via the 4th Amendment through incorporation.

The purpose of Miranda warnings is to prevent the police from unfairly eliciting a statement from a defendant who is in a custodial interrogation situation.

In this case the officers failed to give Max his Miranda warnings before they asked for his gun to be located. Max was under arrest and gave a statement. Max's attorney therefore will argue that the police violated his 5th Amendment rights and that any evidence obtained should be suppressed.

July 2002—Question 7

As a new lawyer, you are assigned the defense of Ralph ("The Nut") Swanson. Ralph was involved in a fight at a local restaurant and after he had hit his adversary in the head with a beer bottle knocking him unconscious, Ralph continued to kick and stomp on this unfortunate soul causing permanent paralysis. The incident was viewed by at least six patrons, two waiters, and the maitre d', all of whom willingly testified at Ralph's trial on a charge of assault with intent to commit murder.

Even though this was your first trial, you decided to make a number of objections to try to break the continuity of the prosecutor's proofs. After the second day, you concluded all you were doing was really causing both the judge and jury to become quite angry with you and your client. You then decided to take a passive role for the remainder of the case. The prosecutor, in his closing argument, urged the jury to convict Ralph, stating that every member of the jury had a civic duty to find the defendant guilty and to remove people like him from the public. The prosecutor further stated that Ralph should be put away for the rest of his life because if they didn't he was obviously so nuts that he would ultimately kill someone, and it could be one of them or a member of their family.

While listening to this argument, you felt the prosecutor was probably making an improper argument, but you were concerned with making another objection, and possibly having his objection overruled, so you did nothing. Finally, the prosecutor told the jury that Ralph's nickname was obviously well-earned based upon his previous assaults. No prior assaults were ever introduced into the record and you stood up and made the appropriate objection. The trial court sustained your objection and instructed the jury that the prosecutor's argument was not evidence and they were to disregard that statement.

The jury returned a guilty verdict on the original charge in record time and without even waiting for the lunch break. Ralph consulted an experienced criminal defense attorney who took one look at the transcript and determined that he would gladly handle the appeal.

Disregarding any possible issue concerning the criminal charge, what issues should the defendant raise on appeal? What are the arguments that both the prosecution and defense will make? What is the probable result and why?

Model Answer to Question 7

The defendant's appeal will be based upon the improper argument concerning the civic duty of the jurors, that portion of the argument where the prosecutor argued facts not in evidence that were highly prejudicial to the defendant, and the failure of the defense counsel to timely object, denying the defendant effective assistance of counsel.

Failure to Object: The prosecutor in this case would argue that even if there was improper argument, a cautionary instruction would not have changed the outcome, as Ralph's guilt was clear and established beyond a reasonable doubt. It is true that the prosecution's appeal to the civic duty or social fears of the jurors could constitute error, requiring reversal. *People v Biondo*, 76 Mich App 155. The failure to object generally precludes appellate review of the prejudicial remarks unless the prejudice was so great that it could not have been cured by a timely cautionary instruction. The prosecutor would claim that the failure to object precludes the appellate court from deciding this issue. Even if the court considered this issue, the guilt of defendant was so clear that these statements had no effect on the verdict.

The defendant, on the other hand, will argue that there was no basis for such statements and they were made solely to inflame the jury and to have the jury decide the guilt or innocence based on their fears rather than the facts. Defendant would claim that this argument has been condemned by the courts and is so prejudicial that a cautionary instruction would have been useless, and therefore the lack of an objection does not affect his appeal and/or right to a new trial.

Objection With Instructions: The prosecution's statement concerning past assaults was objected to and the issue becomes whether the cautionary instruction was sufficient to cure the error. The objection in this case was timely and the instruction was proper and this issue standing alone would not form a basis for a new trial. However, the defendant would argue that coupled with the other improper argument, he was denied a fair trial. *People v Lasenby*, 107 Mich App 462 (1981).

Ineffective Assistance of Counsel: Finally, to establish ineffective assistance of counsel, the defendant must show:

(1) counsel's performance was below an objective standard of reasonableness under prevailing professional norms; and
(2) there is a reasonable probability that but for the counsel's error the results of the proceedings would have been different.

Counsel's assistance is presumed effective and the defendant bears the burden of proving otherwise. In this case, objections should have been made which were not. Defendant, on appeal, would contend that even though this may have been a part of the trial strategy, the statements of the prosecutor were so out of line that an objection was necessary. The appellate court would probably rule that the prejudicial effect could have been cured by a timely instruction had an objection been made. The appellate court, however, would probably look to the facts of this case and conclude that the defense counsel's failure to object cannot be said to have denied the defendant a fair trial that would have resulted in the defendant's acquittal. *See People v Toma*, 462 Mich 281 (2000).

Student Answer—July 2002

Question 7—Criminal Procedure—8 points

The Crime Itself

Was Defendant guilty of attempted murder? Prosecution must carry the burden of proof of beyond a reasonable doubt to show 1) specific intent to murder, 2) make a substantial step toward murder, 3) murder being killed another human with malice or recklessness, or awareness of high probability of death or great bodily injury. Here, probably those elements are present, on the facts given.

Objections

The defense attorney must properly object if evidence is admitted that shouldn't be admitted, or to prosecutorial misconduct. Here, Prosecution improperly introduced prior bad acts of Defendant in his closing remarks, plus calling Defendant insane. Neither of those remarks were based on admitted evidence in the case, and were improper and highly prejudicial to Defendant. At this point, defense counsel should have moved for a mistrial due to prosecutorial misconduct.

Competent Counsel and the Judge

To preserve an issue for appeal, counsel must object or an issue is waived for purpose of appeal. The judge was correct in sustaining defense counsel's objection over Prosecution's closing remarks, preserving the issue for appeal.

The Appeal

Appellate counsel will argue the judge abused his discretion by not declaring a mistrial, which is probably reversible error. Also counsel can argue Defendant was incompetently represented. However, this argument on its own is unlikely to prevail, since the original defense counsel (while too timid to object, perhaps) did object concerning the improper remarks.

Conclusion

Defendant is likely to be able to get new trial on appeal.

February 2003—Question 1

John Cotter was a 15-year veteran of the Plainview Police Department and for years had suspected Eddie Smith of selling quantities of marijuana out of his house located at 24127 Rockdale in Plainview. Finally, acting on a tip of a recognized police informant, John obtained from a magistrate a search warrant that permitted the police to search:

"The premises commonly referred to as 24127 Rockdale, Plainview, Lost County, Michigan. The premise is a single family home, green in color with white trim located at the North West corner of Rockdale and Sunnyvale Streets. Also to be searched is any and all rooms, closets, storage space, cupboards, furniture and appurtenant structures located on the premises. The property to be searched for is any form of marijuana, cocaine and/or controlled substance."

The warrant accurately described the appearance and location of Eddie Smith's house which was the house that Officer Cotter intended to search.

Officer Cotter led the search party and presented the warrant to Eddie Smith, who opened the door and let the officers in for the search. A complete and thorough search of the house failed to turn up any controlled substance or, for that matter, any item that was not legal to possess.

As the officers were preparing to leave, one of them observed a van in the driveway for the home underneath the basketball hoop. When asked, Mr. Smith acknowledged the van was his, and when asked if they could search the van, he told them "not without a warrant to search the vehicle." Officer Cotter referred to the warrant that had been presented to Mr. Smith, told Mr. Smith that the warrant was sufficient, and went outside to search the van. The windows were darkened and observations of the interior of the van were not possible. The door to the van was then opened through the use of a crowbar. Upon entering the van, Officer Cotter discovered approximately five pounds of marijuana located inside a large gym bag.

Eddie Smith was charged with the felony of possession with intent to deliver marijuana. You are appointed to defend Eddie on this charge. **Assuming that the warrant was validly issued, and accurately described the house of Eddie Smith, what is the basis for the motion, what would be the prosecutor's response, and what would be the expected result?**

Model Answer to Question 1

A motion to suppress should be filed by defense counsel. A motion to suppress can be used to challenge the validity of a search conducted pursuant to a warrant.

A search warrant is required to designate and describe the house, building, location or place to be searched and the property to be seized. MCL 780.654. Generally speaking, it has been held that the description in a search warrant is sufficient to satisfy the particularity requirement if the description is such that the officers can, with reasonable effort, ascertain and identify the place intended to be searched. *People v Hampton*, 237 Mich App 143 (1999).

In this case, the warrant does sufficiently identify the premises to be searched, the question is whether the definition of premise can be extended to include a vehicle on the property. It could be argued that the term "premise" denotes the buildings and appurtenant structures located on a tract of land. A car is not a building or appurtenant structure and can be readily identified and listed in any search warrant. The failure to list the car results in the failure to accurately describe and define the location to be searched and the search of the car is therefore illegal.

However, a search of the "premises" has been held to include permission to search the entire area where the object of the search may be found including closets, furniture, drawers, and containers whether specified in the warrant or not. *United States v Ross*, 456 US 798 (1982). The appellate courts have increasingly held that a car found on the premises should be viewed in the same way as any other personal effects. It is considered as no less fixed than a purse or container found on the premises. Based upon the current status of the law, the search of the car pursuant to this warrant would be upheld. *See People v Jones*, 249 Mich App 131 (2002).

Student Answer—February 2002

Question 1—Criminal Procedure—None Available

July 2003—Question 10

Joe Butler was 20 years old when he was arrested without a warrant while driving an orange Hummer with a dented left fender. A vehicle fitting this description was seen leaving the scene of a reported and confirmed double homicide. Officer David Price made the stop and arrest at approximately 11:30 p.m. Officer Price gave Butler the appropriate Miranda warnings and drove him to the police station where he was placed in a holding cell. After receiving the Miranda warning, Officer Price told Butler that he was arrested because he was driving a vehicle leaving the area of a double homicide and they believed that he had information on this crime or that he was involved. Butler told Officer Price that a friend of his, William Owens, had called him and asked him to drive the vehicle over to his girlfriend's residence and that he, Butler, knew nothing about any homicide. He claimed he met Owens on the street about a block from where the homicides occurred.

Before Officer Price could investigate Butler's story, he was called out of town on a family emergency and Butler's case was referred to Officer Woods. Before Officer Woods had an opportunity to investigate or speak with Butler, a hostage situation arose which required all on-duty officers. After the hostage situation was resolved, Officer Woods attempted to find Mr. Owens, or any witness, that could validate Butler's statement, and was unable to do so.

Officer Woods then went to the jail holding cell where he met with Butler and told him the reasons for the delay, and that he was yet to be able to confirm Butler's story. Butler had been in the holding cell for approximately 40 hours at this point, and had been allowed food, water, and the opportunity to sleep. Prior to Officer Woods questioning Butler, he began to read Butler his Miranda rights.

At this point Butler interrupted Officer Woods and stated that he knew his rights, that he had time to think about this, and that it would just be a matter of time before they found out that both he and Owens were in the house where the homicides had occurred. Butler said that while he was holding a gun on the two deceased, it was Owens who shot both of the people and that he, Butler, had nothing to do with the actual shootings. Butler signed a statement as to his involvement in the killings and one hour later Butler was taken before a magistrate where he was arraigned on felony charges all related to the murders.

Assume that probable cause exists for the arrest and limit your answer to the statement made by Butler to Office Woods concerning the shooting and the written statement. What are the issues involved concerning these statements?

Model Answer to Question 10

By statute in Michigan, a person arrested without a warrant must be brought before a magistrate for arraignment without unnecessary delay. MCL 764.13, 764.26. The question presented provides that there was probable cause for the arrest so the issue is whether the statements made by Butler should be suppressed as they were given prior to his arraignment and during a period of time that could be an "unreasonable delay." There is an argument to be made that any statement made during a period of unreasonable delay should be automatically excluded from evidence. That is no longer the law in Michigan.

The statute providing for the prompt arraignment is not a constitutional right. The facts in this case support a finding that the statement was voluntary but that alone does not end the inquiry.

The United States Supreme Court in *Riveside Co v McLaughlin*, 500 US 44, 56-57 (1991), has indicated that the arraignment must take place no later than 48 hours after the arrest, and beyond that time period the delay is presumptively unreasonable and violative of the Fourth Amendment. In this case, the delay did not reach the 48-hour period and therefore is not presumptively unreasonable.

In Michigan, unnecessary delay in arraignment is only one of the factors that is to be considered in evaluating the voluntariness of a confession. The test to determine if it is voluntary or not is "in considering the totality of all the surrounding circumstances, the confession is the product of essentially free and unconstrained choice by its maker, or whether the accused's will has been overborne and his capacity for self-determination critically impaired."

There are a number of factors that are to be considered in making this decision. In this case it does not appear that the police intended to cause the delay that did occur so they could obtain a statement. There is no indication that Mr. Butler requested an attorney. Some additional factors to be considered are his age, education, previous experience with the police, length of questioning, the physical and mental condition of the accused, if the accused was deprived of food or sleep, or whether he was abused in any way. The focus on reaching a determination is not necessarily the length of the delay, but what occurred during the delay. *People v Ciprian*, 431 Mich 315 1988).

A possible issue is whether Officer Woods should have continued with the Miranda warnings after he was interrupted, or whether the interruption constituted a waiver. While this is not the principal issue involved, a chief discussion on this should be credited to the writer's score.

Student Answer—July 2003

Question 10—Criminal Procedure—8 points

In Custody + Interrogation

Confessions by a Defendant must be voluntary + knowingly made by the Defendant. Miranda Rights—right to remain silent, anything you say can be used against you- Right to an Attorney—if you cannot afford one, the attorney will be appointed by the Court. Mirand[a] Rights are required when a potential Defendant is in Custody and there is an interrogation—(Police know that questions are likely to elicit an incriminating Response). In this case Butler was in Custody because he was arrested upon probable cause and put in a jail holding cell. There was also an interrogation—and Butlers First statement about the homicides is Admissible. It satisfied both the in custody and interrogation requirement. Miranda was given and waived and the Defendant told his story.

Situation #2, after the emergency hostage situation, requires further analysis. It appears that statement #2 (after the 40 hour lapse in time from the first Miranda warnings) was a confession. The facts also indicate that it was knowing and voluntary Butler interrupted the officer as he was going to read Butler his rights (Miranda) again. Butler was in-custody; Butler was still in the holding cell. And further, there was going to be an interrogation of Butler again, but Butler cut off the reading of Butler's rights by Officer Woods. It may be argued that since Butler was not read his rights a second time, the statement is inadmissible. However this will probably not work for Butler's benefit.

Butler re-engaged the officer and waived the regarding of his rights. Officer Woods was not putting any pressure upon Butler to talk—in fact, this is when Butler re-engaged the officer Woods and confessed to his (Butler's) involvement in the crime. Butler's statement #2 the confession admitting his (Butler's) involvement in the Crime was knowing and voluntary and spoken to Woods after Butler waived his Miranda Rights.

The statements of Butler both #1 (initial arrest) and #2 (statement after 40 hours delay and waive of Miranda) will be permitted to be used against the Defendant.

Further, there is no problem with the 40 hour wait. Woods was out checking out Butler's #1 story and looking for witnesses. Since the Government has 48 hours to charge a person with a crime, which was not exceeded here, there were no due process violations.

Both of Butler's statements are admissible under this fact pattern.

February 2004—Question 13

Charles Jones was charged with first-degree criminal sexual conduct. This charge arose out of actions by Mr. Jones at a party held at his home when the victim was encouraged to drink excessively and then was subsequently assaulted by Mr. Jones.

Two witnesses also present at the party were listed by the prosecutor as witnesses. Both of these witnesses were friends of the victim who had been present at the party and who witnessed the various actions of Mr. Jones both before and after the sexual assault. Mary Smith, the prosecuting attorney, interviewed both witnesses prior to any charges being filed. Mary Smith took copious notes concerning the interview and maintained these notes in her trial file. The names and addresses of both witnesses were provided to the defense counsel in a timely and appropriate manner.

Prior to trial, defense counsel made a timely demand for all statements made by witnesses whom the prosecutor intended to call at trial. MCR 6.201(A)(2). No documents were produced, nor was any mention made of the notes taken by Mary Smith concerning her interviews. Two days prior to the trial, Mary Smith met with both witnesses and, using her notes, she questioned the witnesses concerning their observations and, from time to time, would remind them what they had said at their previous interview. During the course of the trial, upon cross-examination by the defense attorney, the first witness, in order to support her testimony, volunteered that her testimony was the same as what she already told Ms. Smith who had a written record of it. Out of the presence of the jury, both witnesses were then questioned and testified as to the interviews with Mary Smith and to the fact that Ms. Smith took a large number of written notes at the first interview. Ms. Smith admitted to the court the existence of her written notes, but argued that these were not required to be produced.

You are serving as the clerk for the trial court who took a recess for you to research the issue and advise her what decision should be reached. What do you tell the judge and why?

Model Answer to Question 13

Based upon the facts, these interview notes could not be considered a substantially verbatim recital of an oral statement by the witnesses that were contemporaneously recorded. There is no indication in these facts that the witnesses were given the interview notes to read, review, and assign. The Michigan Court Rules define a statement as being "a written statement signed or otherwise adopted or approved by the person making it or a stenographic, mechanical, electrical or other recording or transcription of a statement." None of these circumstances exist in this case. While an argument could be made that these notes were used to refresh the memory of the witnesses and therefore under MRE 612(b) these notes would be admissible, in this case there is no showing the notes were given to the witnesses for their review or to refresh their memories. The facts merely state that the prosecutor, from time to time, would use the notes to remind the witnesses of what they said earlier.

A further reason why these notes would probably not be considered admissible is that they would be considered part of the work product as defined by MCR 6.210(C). There is no indication that defense counsel was unable to obtain any statement from these witnesses. The name and address of each witness was provided and there was nothing to prohibit defense counsel from interviewing these witnesses prior to trial and obtaining their version of the events. Typically, interview notes constitute paraphrasing of statements, and highlights of the witnesses' comments that are filtered through the attorney's own subjective impressions of the witnesses. These notes likely contain a mental impression, conclusion and opinion of the attorney and as such constitute work products, and are protected from discovery.

People v Holtzman, 234 Mich App 166 (1999).

Student Answer—February 2004

Question 13—Criminal Procedure—None Available

July 2004—Question 13

Daniel Miller was convicted of second-degree murder in 1984. The trial was highly publicized in the state. The conviction involved the death of Susan Lash, an acquaintance of Miller's. She was found with a crushed skull in the woods in Branch County, Michigan near Miller's farm. Miller was convicted primarily based on circumstantial evidence. He was the last person seen with Susan when they left a bar together the night before her body was found. They had argued on and off during the night, and when confronted by investigating officers, Miller made a number of inconsistent statements and had scratches on his face. The autopsy found skin under the fingernails of Ms. Lash, which was matched by blood test to Miller. Miller claimed they had an argument after they left the bar, that she had scratched him, and that he had left her off on the highway approximately five miles from where she was found.

Miller exhausted his appeals and remained confined to the state prison. In 1999, John Teaver was arrested in the state of Florida for the murder of a young woman. The evidence against Mr. Teaver was not very strong. The police suspected that he had committed a large number of murders in Florida, but they didn't have any solid evidence of this. He told the investigators that he would confess to a number of Florida murders and one he committed in Michigan if there could be an agreement that he would be sentenced in Michigan and serve all his time for any murders he committed in that state. This would permit him to avoid the death penalty for any murders that took place in Florida. After obtaining the agreement of the authorities in Florida, Mr. Teaver claimed to be the party who had murdered Susan Lash. Mr. Teaver volunteered to take a polygraph and did so. When asked, Mr. Teaver admitted to the murder but his answer was read to be "equivocal." While he was able to provide some of the details concerning Susan's murder, these "details" had all been reported in the papers. It was established that at the time of the murder Mr. Teaver was staying in Michigan and within a hundred miles of the murder site. Mr. Teavor was unable to take the detectives to the murder site because, "It was too long ago." When asked if the victim was dressed or undressed or had other injuries, he indicated that it was too long ago to remember. While the polygraph did not demonstrate any confirmed falsehoods, very few statements had any direct relationship with the murder of Susan Lash.

Daniel Miller filed a motion for a new trial based on newly discovered evidence and further seeks to admit the polygraph administered to Teavor in Florida.

The trial court denied the motion for new trial.

What factors must exist for a new trial to be granted on newly discovered evidence? Is the polygraph admissible and, if so, what must be established for its admissibility? Would you expect the trial court's decision to be upheld on appeal? Why or why not?

Model Answer to Question 13

In seeking a new trial for newly discovered evidence, the defendant must show that (1) the evidence itself, not merely its materiality, is newly discovered; (2) the evidence is not merely cumulative; (3) the evidence would render a different result probable on retrial; and (4) the defendant could not with reasonable diligence have produced it at trial. The court in its discretion may consider the result of a polygraph exam in a postconviction hearing on a motion for new trial based on newly discovered evidence if: (1) it is offered on behalf of the defendant; (2) the test was taken voluntarily; (3) the professional qualifications and the quality of the polygraph equipment meet with the approval of the court; (4) either the prosecutor or the court is able to obtain an independent examination of the subject or of the test result by an operator of the court's choice, and (5) the result is considered only with regard to the general credibility of the subject.

The decision to grant a new trial is within the trial court's discretion. In this case it is unlikely Mr. Miller would be successful in obtaining a new trial. While the "new evidence" meets three of the four criteria, it is unlikely to render a different result probable on retrial. There is nothing in the facts to indicate that the polygraph does not comply with the standards for its admissibility except (5) dealing with credibility. There is nothing contained in the statement of Mr. Teaver that could not have been obtained through the media. The polygraph is largely irrelevant and demonstrated a lack of critical information. This, coupled with the clear motive of Teaver to confess to the Michigan crime and avoid charges in Florida, creates serious question of Mr. Teaver's credibility. The determination of credibility is within the trial court's discretion. A confession that does not coincide with established facts does not warrant a new trial. Under these circumstances the trial court's decision to deny the motion for new trial would be upheld. *See People v Cress*, 468 Mich 678 (2003).

Student Answer—July 2004

Question 13—Criminal Procedure—None Available

February 2005—Question 10

Defendant James Lawless broke into the home of Michael Ford armed with a gun and threatened to shoot and kill Mr. Ford if he didn't lead him to his safe in the basement and give him the contents. Mr. Ford led Lawless into the basement, opened the safe and gave Lawless $3,500 located in the safe as well as a great deal of valuable jewelry. Lawless was ultimately arrested and tried on multiple criminal counts. Lawless was convicted of armed robbery and safe robbery and was sentenced to 15 to 40 years imprisonment for the armed robbery conviction and 7½ years to 40 years on the safe robbery conviction.

For the purposes of this question, the pertinent language of the armed robbery statute provides that: "a person who in the course of committing a larceny of any money or other property and in the course of engaging in that conduct, possesses a dangerous weapon is guilty of a felony punishable by imprisonment for life or for any term of years."

For the purposes of this question, the pertinent language of the bank, safe and vault robbery statute provides: "Any person who, with intent to commit the crime of larceny, or any felony shall threaten to kill or shall put in fear any person for the purpose of stealing from any . . . safe or other depository of money or other valuables shall be guilty of a felony punishable by imprisonment in the state prison for life or any term of years."

On appeal, Lawless claims that the conviction and sentences for both armed robbery and safe robbery violated his constitutional rights. **What constitutional right is Lawless referring to, and is he correct in this assertion? Why or why not?**

Model Answer to Question 10

The issue that should be raised is whether the convictions and sentences for armed robbery and safe robbery violate provisions of the Federal or Michigan constitutions prohibiting multiple punishment for the same offense.

The Double Jeopardy Clause of the United States Constitution is found in the Fifth Amendment and applies to the states through the Fourteenth Amendment. The Michigan Constitution has essentially the same prohibition at Art 1, § 15.

The purposes of double jeopardy protections against successive prosecutions for the same offense are to preserve the finality of judgments in criminal prosecutions and to protect the defendant from prosecutorial overreaching. The purpose of the double jeopardy protection against multiple punishments for the same offense is to protect the defendant from having more punishment imposed than the legislature intended.

In this case, since there was a single trial the issue would be whether the two convictions involve the same offense and violate the prohibition against multiple punishments for the same offense. The statute dealing with the robbery of a safe is intended to protect structures intentionally constructed to protect valuables while the armed robbery statute is intended to protect persons from assaultive taking by means of a dangerous weapon.

The statute dealing with larceny from a safe requires for its violation the intent to access a safe. It does not require that the offender be armed with a weapon. The focus of the armed robbery is on the person being assaulted with a weapon.

The two statutes each contain elements not contained in the other. The armed robbery statute does not contain an element of intent to steal property from a safe. These were two separate and distinct offenses. When the defendant threatened to kill Michael if he didn't go and open the safe, the violation of the "safe" statute was complete. The violation of the armed robbery statute was not completed until Michael, after threats of death by shooting, opened the safe, and defendant took the money and jewelry.

These were separate offenses and sentencing the defendant on both of these convictions did not violate the double jeopardy rights of the defendant. *People v Ford*, 262 Mich App 443 (2004).

Credit can be given the applicant if there is a discussion of the "social norms" test as discussed in *People v Robideau*, 419 Mich 458 (1984). This test requires the court to identify the type of harm the legislature was intending to prevent and where two statutes prohibit violations of the same social norm generally the legislature did not intend separate punishments. While these statutes do not appear to be of this type, extra credit should be given for a discussion of this issue.

Student Answer—February 2005

Question 10—Constitutional Law—8 points

The Constitutional Right that Lawless is referring to is the Double Jeopardy Clause of the U.S. Constitution. This clause is implied to the States via the Fourteenth Amendment of the U.S. Constitution.

Double Jeopardy is the right of an accused not to be tried twice for the same crime. The reason for this clause/right is to protect the defendant from undo harassment, unnecessary expenses, inconvenience, embarrassment, etc. In order for the crime to apply the defendant must have been through a conviction or an acquittal and is being tried again. There are exceptions to the double jeopardy clause when 1) two states try the defendant, 2) the state + federal government, 3) mistrial due to the defendant's reasons, etc.

None of these exceptions apply here. However, the test used to apply the double jeopardy doctrine is of the same crime and the elements test is used to see if it is the same crime.

Here, the defendant James is charged for armed robbery and safe robbery. We need to check the elements of each crime to determine if both charges contain the same elements and therefore the double jeopardy clause will apply. Here, although two robbery charges one for armed and one for safe they have different elements. The robbery elements are larceny elements such as the trespassory taking of the personal property of another with the intent to permanently deprive the owner of his/her property, plus for robbery the taking from the person or the person's presence with force or an apprehension of force or bodily injury. For armed robbery we need an additional element that the force must be by a dangerous weapon. The safe requires under the statute to be larceny from a safe or deposition of money.

Both crimes[s] have the same elements of larceny however, not both require to have dangerous or deadly weapons. Therefore, the armed robbery is a different crime from the crime of safe robbery because the crimes require different elements.

Also, here Lawless may be charged for burglary. Finally, under Michigan law when a statute specifically makes a crime that requires a separate sentencing must be respected. Here, the legislation has created the bank, safe, + vault robbery statute that make this larceny type of a crime as a separate + different crime, the safe crime. Therefore, since the two crimes do not require the same elements Lawless was not tried twice for the same crime. Therefore, the double jeopardy clause of the U.S. Constitution does not apply. Both convictions will stand.

February 2005—Question 12

William Strong was charged with the rape of a 14-year-old girl. The young girl named Kathy had made statements to the investigators and a juvenile court officer and a community mental health counselor. She testified at the time of the preliminary examination, and her testimony was consistent with what she had told the police. After the preliminary examination, the defendant's attorney made a motion to view the records of both the juvenile court officer and mental health counselor. The basis for the motion was that there may be some inconsistencies in what she told these two counselors and that the defendant should have an opportunity to review these records so he could properly confront witnesses and conduct an effective cross-examination. The trial court denied this request, citing the statutes that made this information confidential.

During the trial, the prosecutor called William's brother, John, to the stand and asked him if William told him that he had sex with a young girl by the name of Kathy. John denied ever being told this by William. John was then asked if he made this very statement to the investigating officer and John again denied ever telling anyone that William had made such a statement. The prosecutor then called the investigating officer to testify, and over defense counsel's objection, the office testified that John did tell him that William had stated that he had sex with a young girl by the name of Kathy.

During the closing argument, the prosecutor told the jury that Kathy has always been consistent in her testimony. "What she testified at trial is the same that she told police, the same that she testified to at the preliminary exam, the same that she told the counselors that she had treated with and the same that she has told me." Defense counsel objected to this statement, but the trial court overruled the objection.

On appeal, Strong's attorney raised two issues. The first issue was improper conduct by the prosecutor in the closing argument, and the second issue dealt with the alleged improper testimony of the investigating officer as to the statement allegedly made to him by John Strong.

Confining your answer to these two issues, what do you believe the outcome of the appeal will be and why?

Model Answer to Question 12

William Strong will likely win this appeal.

In the closing argument, the prosecutor created the inference that he had seen the counseling records and they were consistent with Kathy's trial testimony. A prosecutor may not argue the effect of testimony that was not entered into evidence at trial. If the counseling records were inadmissible because of the statutory privilege, it is error for the prosecutor to argue to the jury what was allegedly in these records. A prosecutor also cannot vouch for the credibility of facts and evidence not in the case. There was no evidence of what Kathy told the counselors and there was no evidence of what she had allegedly told to the prosecutor. An objection to this argument was made but overruled by the court. Without a curative instruction this argument is an error and would, standing alone, probably result in a reversal of the conviction.

The second issue raised on appeal should assure that the conviction would be overturned. Again, there was a timely objection made to the testimony of the investigating officer and again, the objection was overruled. While prior inconsistent statements may be used to impeach credibility, this was improper impeachment. Even though John was the prosecutor's witness, that wouldn't prevent the prosecutor in attacking his credibility if done correctly. MRE 607. What occurred here is that the statement purportedly used to impeach the credibility of the witness went to the central issue of the case. This testimony went to prove the truth of the matter asserted. The alleged admission could have been introduced through the testimony of John but once he denied such admission being made, it was impermissible hearsay to allow the officer to testify to such a statement allegedly made to John. This is not harmless error. This statement was essentially a confession of the crime being charged being placed before the jury by hearsay testimony.

Based on the two issues raised on appeal, the conviction in this case should be reversed. *See People v Stanaway*, 446 Mich 643 (1994).

Student Answer—February 2005

Question 12—Evidence—9 points

As to the alleged improper testimony of the investigating officer, Strong's attorney will argue that the statement is inadmissible hearsay. Hearsay is an out of court statement offered for the truth of the matter being asserted. Strong's attorney will argue that the statement is being offered to show that William did commit the crime he is being accused of. Testimony of this nature is improper if used for this purpose.

However, the prosecutor will argue that the statement is being used to impeach John's statement and show that John's statement to the officer was a prior, inconsistent statement. Under this theory, a prior inconsistent statement is an exception to the hearsay rule. Alternatively, the prosecutor may argue that the statement is part of a regularly kept record by the investigating officer as part of his investigation. However, there is no indication in the facts that the officer referred to a police report. It appears he is relying on a communication that was merely spoken to him. If he is relying on the information as part of a police report, then the regularly kept records exception to the hearsay rule would apply. Since no police report is mentioned in the facts, it is not likely that the objection was overruled on this basis.

Additionally, there is the danger of unfair prejudice in this statement being allowed to come in. The jury may interpret it as being true because it was being stated by a police officer.

Therefore, since the regularly kept business record exception does not apply, and even if the prior inconsistent statement exception did apply, the potential for prejudice to the jury and use of the statement to show defendant's propensity to commit the crime he is charged with, the appeals court would probably rule that the defendant should receive a new trial. This is reversible error, rather than harmless error which is how the court will weigh the issue. In order to find harmless error, that would mean there is a likelihood of defendant being convicted regardless of the error. It does not seem to me that a determination such as that could be made barring the officer's statement. William will prevail on this issue.

As to the statement made by the prosecutor, this was definitely improper. By stating to the jury that the victim's testimony has been consistent with what she told everyone, including the prosecutor. The prosecutor is, in essence, vouching for the credibility of the victim. Once again this holds the potential for unfair prejudice to the defendant. The prosecutor may be viewed by some members of the jury as being in a position of authority. If the prosecutor is vouching for the credibility of the witness, some members of the jury might assume that the prosecutor is stating unequivocally, that Kathy is telling the truth.

It is against the Rules of Professional Conduct for the prosecutor to suggest to the jury that Kathy is telling the truth just because she stated it to the prosecutor. Therefore, on this issue, the court of appeals would also find reversible error. It is the jury's job to decide if Kathy is being truthful based on the evidence presented, rather than on the prosecutor vouching for her.

July 2005—Question 10

Jessie Davis was a well-known drug dealer in the Lansing, Michigan area. The police had finally placed an undercover informant within Jessie's close circle of dealers. On June 2, at the request of Jessie, the informant obtained and delivered one pound of marijuana to Jessie at his home on Wealthy Street in Lansing. Jessie allegedly had a buyer for this who was coming to his home on June 3. Jessie and the informant were supposed to split the proceeds of this sale. The informant, doing what he does best, informed the police of the presence of this large amount of marijuana in the home as well as the potential sale.

As the informant was leaving the home on June 2, the home was placed under surveillance and a search warrant obtained for the premises. All proper procedures were followed and a search warrant for Jessie's home was issued. At approximately 3:00 a.m., on June 2, the police went to the home to execute the warrant. They knocked on the door twice with their battering ram, announced their presence, and then immediately knocked the door in. Between the knock and the fall of the door, a period of approximately five (5) seconds elapsed.

Jessie was found in bed asleep. He was shown the warrant and the search commenced. Finally, after three hours of searching, the police found a concealed panel, and in it they found the marijuana that had been delivered by the informant the day before.

Michigan has a statute that provides:

> The officer to whom a warrant is directed, or any person assisting him, may break any outer or inner door or window of a house or building, or anything therein, in order to execute the warrant, if, after notice of his authority and purpose, he is refused admittance, or when necessary to liberate himself or any person assisting him in execution of the warrant.

A motion to suppress has been filed by Jessie's attorney based on a violation of the above-cited statute. Confining your answer to the search and seizure, assume the warrant was validly issued and the marijuana seized was clearly the marijuana delivered by the informant. What issues are presented and what is the probable result?

Model Answer to Question 10

The Michigan statute that is set forth in the question is called the "knock and announce" statute. As the attorney for Jessie, you would contend that the statute was not complied with as the police forcibly entered the premises without providing Jessie with sufficient time to respond to the knock and announcement that they were the police. You would argue that the knock and announce statute has its basis in the Fourth Amendment and, if the statute is violated, evidence seized as a result would be properly excluded.

Based upon the facts and the brief period of time between the knock and the entry, it would be probable that the statue was not complied with. Jessie did not have time to refuse entry, assuming that he would. One of the purposes of the statute is to allow the occupants the "brief opportunity" to order their personal affairs before the officers enter. However, it also has been stated that the purpose of the statute is not meant to allow the occupant the time to destroy evidence.

Assuming that there is a violation of the statute, that does not necessarily require a finding that the evidence should be suppressed. The knock and announce statute does not control the execution of a valid warrant, it merely delays entry. There is some disagreement among federal courts on the use of the "inevitable discovery" doctrine. However, the Michigan Supreme Court has approved of the application of this doctrine in knock and announce cases. In considering this doctrine, the Michigan Supreme Court has approved the following statement: "it is hard to understand how the discovery of evidence inside a house could be anything but 'inevitable' once the police arrive with a warrant." The occupant or defendant would not be allowed to contend that, had the officers announced their presence and waited longer to enter, he would have had time to destroy the evidence.

There are no facts in this situation that disclose that the police executed on this warrant in an illegal fashion. Even though it took them some time to find the marijuana, that does not invalidate the search and seizure. Although there is a probable violation of the knock and announce statute in Michigan, under these circumstances it will not result in the suppression of this evidence. *People v Jackson*, (Unpublished opinions per curiam of the Court of Appeals, issued April 1, 2003 [Docket No. 2362541]). *People v Stephens*, 460 Mich 626 (1999).

Student Answer—July 2005

Question 10—Criminal Procedure—8 points

In Jessie's motion to suppress, his attorney will likely raise the issue of whether the police officers' entry was in violation of the statute. Whether the police officers exceeded the scope of their warrant by searching for 3 hours and entering a concealed panel.

Under the fruit of the poisonous tree doctrine, any evidence that was produced as the result of an unlawful search must be suppressed and excluded from evidence. Here, Jessie is seeking suppression of the marijuana found in his home based on the argument that the police officer's entry was unlawful and therefore all evidence procured from that unlawful entry is tainted and must be suppressed. The statute allows an officer to break down an outer or inner door if "after notice of his authority and purpose, he is refused admittance."

Jessie's attorney will argue that he did not refuse admittance and therefore, the officers had no authority to knock down his door, because he was asleep when the officers arrived at his home. He will further argue that the authority to knock down the door is triggered only when the person therein refuses the officers' admittance. And because Jessie did not refuse admittance, the officers' breaking of the door and subsequent admittance was unlawful and because the officers' presence was a violation of his 4th Amendment expectation of privacy in his home, all evidence procured as a result of this violation must be suppressed as to avoid injustice. Jessie's attorney may also make the argument that even if Jessie had not been asleep when the officers arrived at his home, only 5 seconds elapsed between the officer's knocking on the door and tearing it down. He will argue that 5 seconds is not enough time for a person to allow admittance to their home (to walk over to the door, unlock an open it); meaning, as shown by the very short period of time between the knocking and tearing the door down, the police had no intent to affect a lawful entry, as required by statute. And because the officers did not and had no intent on affecting a lawful entry onto the premises, all evidence procured as a result of that entry should be suppressed.

Although compelling and creative arguments, the court will likely find that the officers' entry was lawful under the statute. The purpose of the knock and announce requirement is to respect the defendant's expectation of privacy in the home, give him notice of police presence and intent to enter and afford him a reasonable opportunity to open his door, as opposed to it being torn down.

However, in the interest of preserving evidence that may be destroyed and protecting officer lives and well-being, defendants are given only a short time period to respond to the knock and announce before breaking down the door.

According to the facts, the police knocked on the door twice with a battering ram and announced their presence before breaking down the door. This provided Jessie with ample notice of police presence and intent to enter and their breaking down of the door was not in violation of the statute; therefore, the marijuana is admissible.

Jessie's attorney may also argue that the officers exceeded the scope of the search warrant by remaining on the premises for 3 hours and by searching in a concealed panel. The court will likely find that the officers did not exceed the scope of the warrant because, under the statute, the officers are allowed to break anything within the building or home to be searched in execution of warrant which; here, is searching for marijuana. Furthermore, there is no time limitation for a lawful search so long as the time spent was necessary to perform the necessary search under the warrant.

Because the officers were lawfully on the premises and did not exceed the scope of the warrant the marijuana will likely be admissible at trial.

Comment: This is another question that troubled many students. Most correctly determined that the knock and announce statute was violated, but very few discussed the fact that the evidence would come in under inevitable discovery doctrine. This example did not address it and even incorrectly concluded that the knock and announce statute wasn't violated, yet still received 8 points. It represents the generosity often extended in grading and the fact that a thorough analysis racks up the points!

February 2006—Question 11

John Tinning was charged with first-degree criminal sexual conduct. The victim was a 14-year-old girl who was examined in the emergency room of General Hospital. Dr. Jose Cruz was one of the two examining physicians, and Mary Jones was one of the nurses on duty and present at the time of the exam. On the information, the prosecutor listed as *res gestae* witnesses both examining doctors and all three of the nurses that were in the examining room at the time. One month prior to the trial, Dr. Cruz returned to his home in the Philippines to set up his practice of medicine. The prosecutor was unaware of this move until five weeks before the trial when it issued the subpoenas. The subpoena for Nurse Jones was served four weeks before the start of trial.

Thirty days prior to trial, the prosecutor listed the witnesses it intended to call. Dr. Cruz was omitted from this list and Nurse Jones was included. One copy of this list was properly served upon defense counsel. Nothing further was done concerning these witnesses until after the prosecution rested without calling either Dr. Cruz or Nurse Jones, who failed to appear and honor the subpoena.

The other doctor who examined the victim in the emergency room was listed and called as a witness, as were the other nurses who were also present at the time of the examination.

At the conclusion of proofs, defense counsel requested the court to instruct the jury pursuant to CJI2d 5.12, which provides: "________________ is a missing witness whose appearance was the responsibility of the prosecution. You may infer that this witness' testimony would have been unfavorable to the prosecution's case."

The trial court refused to give this instruction and defendant was convicted. One of the issues raised by the defendant on appeal was the failure of the trial court to give the requested instruction concerning these *res gestae* witnesses.

What do you believe the decision of the Court of Appeals will be, and why?

Model Answer to Question 11

In 1986, the statute requiring the prosecutor to list and produce at trial all *res gestae* witnesses was amended. When the prosecutor did not satisfy this statutory obligation, the missing witness instruction was available to address the situation. As amended, the pertinent portion of the statute now states:

> (1) The prosecuting attorney shall attach to the filed information a list of all witnesses known to the prosecuting attorney who might be called at trial and all *res gestae* witnesses known to the prosecuting attorney or investigating law enforcement officers.
>
> * * *
>
> (3) Not less than 30 days before trial, the prosecuting attorney shall send to the defendant or his or her attorney a list of the witnesses the prosecuting attorney intends to produce at trial.
>
> (4) The prosecuting attorney may add or delete from the list of witnesses he or she intends to call at trial any time upon leave of the court and for good cause shown or by stipulation of the parties.
>
> (5) The prosecuting attorney or investigative law enforcement agency shall provide to the defendant, or defense counsel, upon request, reasonable assistance, including investigative assistance, as may be necessary to locate and serve process upon a witness. The request for assistance shall be made in writing by defendant or defense counsel not less than 10 days before the trial of the case or at such other time as the court directs.

In this case, Dr. Cruz was not listed as a witness who would be produced at trial. Defense counsel who was served with this list did not seek the assistance of the prosecutor or the court in any attempt to secure Dr. Cruz as a witness or to adjourn the trial due to Dr. Cruz's absence. It could also be argued that Dr. Cruz' testimony would be cumulative as the other examining doctor was produced as a witness. According to these facts, there is nothing to show how the prosecutor or the court could force Dr. Cruz to return from a foreign country to testify, nor are there any facts that would show that his testimony would be at all helpful to the defendant.

Nurse Jones was listed as a witness who would testify at trial. The People discharged their duty when they subpoenaed Nurse Jones. Under the amended statute, this is all the prosecutor is required to do. The defendant may rely on the appearance of a witness on the prosecutor's witness list without further need to subpoena that witness himself. However, the statute imposes no particular penalty on the prosecutor for a witness' failure to honor a subpoena. There is no justification for an instruction that Nurse Jones as a missing witness would have testified favorably to the defendant. Such a rule would make as much sense as instructing the jury that a witness subpoenaed by the defendant who fails to appear would have testified favorably to the prosecutor. Finally, as in the case of Dr. Cruz, the other nurses who were present at the time of the exam were present and testified. There are no facts to show that Nurse Jones would have testified in any respect different than the nurses who did appear and testify.

The Court of Appeals would affirm the trial court. *People v Perez*, 255 Mich App 703 (2003), rev'd in part, *People v Perez*, 469 Mich 415 (2003).

Student Answer—February 2006

Question 11—Criminal Procedure—None Available

July 2006—Question 1

Shelia was driving her 1979 Ford Econoline van to the Grateful Dead tribute concert with her friend Andrea. In her rush to get to the show on time, Shelia was driving twenty miles per hour over the posted speed limit of 65 mph. Officer Jones stopped Shelia for speeding. After he approached the vehicle and asked Shelia for her license and registration, Officer Jones recognized the smell of marijuana coming from inside the van. Officer Jones asked Shelia if he could search the vehicle, and Shelia gave permission for the search. The officer then asked Shelia and Andrea to exit the vehicle, and he then looked under the front seats for the marijuana he had smelled.

Office Jones found nothing under Shelia's seat, but found 10 marijuana cigarettes under Andrea's seat. Andrea was arrested and charged with possession with the intent to distribute marijuana. Andrea's counsel has filed a motion challenging the search on two grounds. First, he asserts because Andrea did not consent to the search, the search was invalid. Second, her counsel argues the search is invalid as the officer did not obtain a search warrant prior to looking under the seats.

Discuss the merits of both arguments and the likely ruling on the defendant's motion to suppress the marijuana.

Model Answer to Question 1

Alleged Lack of Consent to the Search: Because Shelia is the driver and owner of the vehicle, her consent is sufficient to permit a valid search of the van. *Florida v Jimeno*, 500 US 248 (1991); *People v Dagwan*, 269 Mich App 338 (2005). This consent to search the van extended to any containers found therein. *Dagwan, supra.* Thus, the claimed lack of consent on the part of Andrea is without merit and does not affect the validity of the search of the van. The motion will be denied.

Lack of Search Warrant: As indicated above, the consent by Shelia is sufficient to permit the full search of the vehicle and any containers found therein. *Id.* Also, the prosecution will rely upon the "plain smell exception" to search warrant requirement. *People v Kazmierczak*, 461 Mich 411 (2000). The Michigan Supreme Court held that the smell of marijuana by a person qualified to recognize the smell as contraband is sufficient to justify the search of a motor vehicle without the need for a search warrant. *Id.* The Supreme Court also stated that the smell of marijuana alone by a person qualified to know the odor is sufficient in and of itself to justify a warrantless search of a motor vehicle and there need be no other probable cause. *Id.* Therefore, Andrea's motion will be denied.

Likely Ruling on the Motion to Suppress: The motion will be denied. The owner of the van gave permission for the search, which is a recognized exception to the search warrant requirement. Further, the recognition of the smell by Officer Jones is sufficient to provide probable cause for the warrantless search of the van. Thus, the motion will be denied.

Two Student Answers—July 2006

Question 1—Criminal Procedure—10 points

This is a criminal procedure question. Firstly, the counsel challenges the search of the vehicle on the grounds that Andrea did not consent to the search and therefore the search is invalid. This argument is likely to fail based on the fact that it is Shelia's 1979 Ford Econoline van. And since Shelia "gave permission to search the van, it was a valid search pursuant to her consent.

In addition, the fact that the officer, Jones, had smelled the "marijuana coming from the van" gave him probable cause enough to search the immediate area of the van without Shelia's consent. Therefore, Andrea's counsel's argument should fail for the search of the van was invalid.

Secondly, Andrea's counsel raises the argument that the search was invalid because Officer Jones did not obtain a search warrant prior to looking under the seats. This argument is also likely to fail as stated above that since it was Sheila's van and she consented to the search and the fact that the seats are within the immediate area, arm's reach, that the Officer would be entitled to search under the seats where Sheila and Andrea were sitting.

Therefore, based on the two arguments as presented by Andrea's counsel, the court is not likely to grant the defendant's motion to suppress the marijuana.

In addition, the fact that Sheila was speeding at a rate of 20 mph over the speed limit also gives Officer Jones enough probable cause to ask to search the van in which Sheila gives her consent. Therefore, once again, the search was valid.

Question 1—Criminal Procedure—9 points

Automobile Exception: Generally for a search to be valid there must be a search warrant that pleads with particularity the items to be seized, the location and must be issued by a neutral and detached magistrate. However, a warrantless search will be deemed valid if it fits within one of the exceptions.

In this case a (automobile exception) police officer with reasonable suspicion, an anticipatable fact that he be suspicious of a crime may pull a car over and look in the car at items which are in plain view. If the police then has probable cause he may search the car. In this case the police officer had probable cause because Sheila was breaking the speed limit so he had a right to pull her over. The officer also had probable cause because he smelled the marijuana. He had probable cause to then search any area within the plaintiff's living space which would arguably include under Andrea's seat which is where he found the marijuana.

Consent: Consent is an exception to having a valid search warrant if it is given knowingly and willfully. It appears here that this was the case, there is no evidence to the contrary. The defense will argue that since Andrea didn't consent the search was invalid. This argument will fail because Andrea lacks standing because this isn't her vehicle. Also police officers don't have to tell defendants that they don't have to give consent. Therefore the search was valid so the marijuana will come in.

In possession with intent to distribute marijuana—the defendant must knowingly possess the marijuana with an intent to distribute it in order to be found guilty. Here the feds only show possession. There is no evidence that Andrea had the predisposition to sell. Just that they were under the seat. The state will try to argue that the possession shows intent. This argument will fail because there is no evidence of her intent to sell. So the charge of intent will be lost but she could get charged with possession if the state can prove she actually had possession and control of the substance. Here the state will need to prove that the marijuana belonged to her.

February 2007—Question 14

Pat and Brian were sitting in Brian's backyard listening to a baseball game on the radio, when an argument and altercation ensued between the two. Brian was killed by a gunshot.

Pat originally claimed to the police that Brian began to threaten him and Brian drew a gun. Pat claimed he and Brian began struggling over the gun, and it accidentally discharged, killing Brian. However, Pat's story began to change during the course of several interviews and the prosecuting attorney charged him with murder. Pat was charged with open murder pursuant to Michigan Compiled Law 750.318, which states as follows:

> The jury before whom any person indicted for murder shall be tried shall, if they find such person guilty thereof, ascertain in their verdict, whether it be murder of the first or second degree; but, if such person shall be convicted by confession, the court shall proceed by examination of witnesses to determine the degree of the crime, and shall render judgment accordingly.

Pat entered a guilty plea to the charge of murder, and the judge then conducted the hearing in accordance with the statute set forth above. After listening to several witnesses, the judge turned to Pat and asked him to step forward. The judge administered the witness oath to Pat, and then proceeded to ask several questions. Pat's attorney failed to object to any questions or answers, and also failed to assert Pat's Fifth Amendment right to remain silent.

The judge asked several questions, and Pat began to change his story yet again from any of the versions he had previously given the police. Pat admitted he had started the argument with Brian with the intention of escalating it in hopes of getting Brian angry enough to draw a weapon. When Brian did in fact produce his gun, Pat took that as his chance and shot Brian. The judge found Pat guilty of first-degree murder and sentenced him to life without parole, as required by statute.

Pat has now appealed, alleging only that the trial court erred in calling Pat as a witness. Thus, Pat claims his right against compelled self-incrimination was violated and he should have a new trial. The prosecution contends Pat waived that right by failing to object to the questioning and/or failing to assert the privilege at the time of trial.

Ignoring any other issues that may arise from the facts presented above, discuss the merits of Pat's appeal and the prosecution's arguments in response to the appeal.

Model Answer to Question 14

The issue is whether a defendant may be compelled to answer questions during the hearing to determine the degree of murder pursuant to statute. The Michigan Supreme Court addressed a case very similar to the one in question in *People v Watkins*, 468 Michigan 233 (2003). There, the defendant failed to assert his right and the Court found the Fifth Amendment privilege is "not self-executing." The defendant's failure to object and assert his privilege was fatal to a subsequent assertion that his right had been violated.

Further, the Court found that while the Fifth Amendment right extends to sentence hearings, it did not extend to the degree hearing. The hearing held by the court to determine the degree of the murder is considered part of the guilty plea, and not the sentence phase of the proceeding. The Court indicated the trial court is obligated to examine the defendant to find factual support for the guilty plea being offered by the defendant. Thus, the Court concluded the questioning of the defendant during the degree hearing was simply an extension of the guilty plea and examination of the defendant was proper. Therefore, the Michigan Supreme Court rejected the subsequent assertion of the defendant's Fifth Amendment privilege and affirmed the trial court's decision.

Student Answer—February 2007

Question 14—Criminal Procedure—10 points

The first issue is whether the trial court erred in calling Pat as a witness. The statute clearly states that if a person is convicted by confession, the court shall proceed by examination of witness to determine degree of the crime and shall render judgment accordingly. Here, Pat entered a guilty plea to the charge of murder therefore the judge had a right and followed the statute to call him as a witness.

Therefore, the issue becomes was Pat's 5th Amendment right against self-incrimination violated. The witness *defendant is the holder* of this *privilege and it can only be invoked by the witness defendant.* Here, Pat proceeded to the stand because the judge called him into question, however, the facts do not indicate that Pat invoked his fifth Amendment privilege. It was not the job of Pat's attorney to object to him testifying and his attorney should only have to object if there is reason to. It is not necessarily malpractice if an attorney does not object to a line of questions that the attorney deems proper.

Further, the statute only compels testimony after there is a confession. Here, Pat is pleading guilty—there is no need to protect his self-incrimination. Pat not only waived his privilege, but he also committed perjury because the judge placed him under oath and he lied about his encounter with Brian. Pat's chance of success on appeal is very slim.

Therefore, the prosecutor was correct; Pat waived his privilege and the conviction should stand.

July 2007—Question 7

Stan had received a bike for his birthday. After riding the bike all day, he left it sitting in the front yard while he went inside to get a drink of water. When Stan returned five minutes later, his bike was missing. He told his parents, who then filed a police report with Officer Cartman. On his way back to the police station, Officer Cartman saw Butters riding a bike that matched the description of Stan's missing bike. Officer Cartman stopped Butters, and discovered the bike was indeed Stan's missing bike. Butters was arrested and taken to the police station to be processed. Officer Cartman alleges Butters admitted to stealing the bike because he felt Stan picked on him at school. Defense counsel for Butters requested an evidentiary hearing to determine the admissibility of the statement pursuant to *People v Walker*, 374 Mich 331 (1965).

At the evidentiary hearing, Officer Cartman testified Butters was not under the influence of drugs or alcohol during the interview. He also testified Butters understood the questions and responded appropriately. Officer Cartman testified he offered Butters some food and water, and that Butters did not appear to be tired. The prosecution rested after the testimony of Officer Cartman, and Butters took the witness stand to testify regarding the interview. However, much to everyone's surprise, Butters testified he never made a statement to Officer Cartman. Butters denied even talking to Officer Cartman. The defense then rested.

You are the clerk for the trial court judge to who this case is assigned. She has asked you for a memorandum on how to dispose of this situation. Explain your answer.

Model Answer to Question 7

Where a defendant challenges the admissibility of a statement, the admissibility is to be determined by the court prior to trial, as a matter of law. *People v Walker*, 374 Mich 331 (1965). However, where law enforcement alleges a defendant has made an incriminating statement, and the defendant denies having made the statement, the defendant is not entitled to an evidentiary hearing. *People v Weatherspoon*, 171 Mich App 549 (1988). The Court of Appeals has since held a defendant may be entitled to a *Walker* hearing where the defendant claims he signed a fabricated statement under duress. *People v Neal,* 182 Mich App 368 (1990). In *Neal,* the Court of Appeals held:

> At the hearing the trial court must determine, assuming the defendant made the statement, whether he did so voluntarily. If it is found that the defendant voluntarily made the statement, the defendant is free to argue to the jury that the police fabricated it. However, if the trial court at the hearing finds the statement was involuntarily made, the statement is inadmissible, regardless of the defendant's claim that he never actually made it. *Neal, supra,* p 372.

This has been clarified by the Court of Appeals in *People v Bell,* unpublished opinion per curiam of the Court of Appeals, issued August 5, 1997 (Docket No. 187997). In *Bell,* the Court of Appeals held once a defendant denies making a statement, he is no longer entitled to an evidentiary hearing challenging the admissibility of the statement. This is an issue for the jury to determine. Logically, this is the only conclusion since if the defendant denies making a statement: he cannot assert he made the statement involuntarily, under coercion, or unknowingly. Therefore, the appropriate course of action would be to terminate the evidentiary hearing without rendering a decision on the admissibility of Butters's alleged statement.

Applicants may also be awarded points if they discuss the appropriate factors. When a defendant challenges a confession, the burden rests squarely on the prosecution to demonstrate the admissibility by a preponderance of the evidence. *People v Daoud,* 462 Mich 621 (2000). In determining the admissibility of a confession, the court must review the totality of the circumstances surrounding the making of the statement. *People v Ciprian,* 431 Mich 315 (1988). The factors to be considered include the defendant's age, education or intelligence level, prior experience with police officers, length of delay between the arrest and the interrogation, whether the defendant was informed of his rights, and whether the defendant was under the influence of drugs or alcohol. *Id.* The court must also consider whether the defendant was threatened with abuse, or deprived of medication, sleep, food, or drink. *Id.* Here, the court need not address the factors for the reasons set forth above, but the applicants may be awarded points for discussion of the factors demonstrating knowledge in this area of the law.

Student Answer—July 2007

Question 7—Criminal Procedure—None Available

> **Comment:** This is an example of the bar examiners testing very specific Michigan law. Examinees did not do well on this question because most were not familiar with a "Walker hearing." It demonstrates how important it is to learn the Michigan distinctions of the MBE subjects, particularly in Criminal Law.

July 2007—Question 9

Officer Jones was dispatched to the scene of a potential breaking and entering of a garage, involving a person wearing blue jeans and white t-shirt. Upon arrival, Officer Jones found Randy wearing blue jeans and a white t-shirt, and holding a hammer and a crowbar. Officer Jones asked Randy to place the objects on the ground, and Randy complied. Officer Jones then proceeded to perform a pat-down search to determine if Randy was carrying any weapons. During the pat-down, Officer Jones felt something which he described as a hard, narrow, cylindrical object approximately three inches in length. He felt the ends of the object to determine if there was a point, like a blade or a hobby knife, and the ends were flat. Based upon his experience, the officer indicated he believed the object to be a pipe used for smoking crack cocaine, and he removed the pipe from Randy's pocket.

The pipe contained a small amount of cocaine residue, and Randy has been charged with possession of cocaine. Randy has challenged the seizure of the item from his pocket, alleging the officer was not permitted to remove it once he determined it was not a weapon. The prosecution has responded that the officer recognized the item as illegal contraband and was legally permitted to remove the object from Randy's pocket without a search warrant.

Defense counsel has filed a motion to suppress the pipe from evidence, claiming the warrantless removal from Randy's pocket was improper. **Discuss whether the officer was permitted to remove the item from Randy's pocket. Note the attorneys have stipulated that the officer was permitted to perform a pat-down search based upon the facts and circumstances surrounding the event in question.**

Model Answer to Question 9

This question addresses the "plain feel" exception to the search warrant requirement, which was set forth by the United States Supreme Court in *Minnesota v Dickerson*, 508 US 366 (1993). The Michigan Supreme Court adopted this exception in *People v Champion*, 452 Mich 92 (1996).

Pursuant to *Champion*, an object felt during an authorized pat-down search may be seized without a warrant if the item's incriminating character is immediately apparent, that is, if the officer develops probable cause to believe that the item felt is contraband before going beyond the legitimate scope of the pat-down search.

The *Champion* court articulated the degree of certainty required that an object felt during a pat-down search is contraband before a police officer may remove the object from the person being searched. The court held that the "immediately apparent" qualification in *Dickerson* does not require a higher degree of certainty. Rather, the degree of certainty required for plain feel seizures is probable cause. The *Champion* court "emphasize[d] that courts applying the plain feel exception must appreciate the totality of the circumstances in the given case." *Champion*, p 112.

In this case, the seizure would be upheld as the incriminating nature of the crack pipe was immediately apparent during a valid pat-down search. Thus, the search is valid and the pipe should not be excluded from evidence.

Student Answer—July 2007

Question 9—Criminal Procedure—9 points

The issue is whether the police officer was permitted to remove the item from the pocket.

Since the officer was permitted to perform a pat-down search for his safety, the officer may feel for any weapons to remove that weapon if it is in a pocket. Also, under the *plain feel doctrine* an officer may remove an item from an inner pocket if the officer has probable cause to believe that the item is contraband. For the officer to have the p.c. is based on the officer's own experience and training. Therefore, since the officer had the right to pat-down and p.c. to believe that the item was contraband, which the facts state he based on his experience, the officer was permitted to remove the item. Subsequently, the pipe may be introduced into evidence.

Comment: Although brief, this answer covers all bases and limits the response to what the question specifically asked for.

February 2008—Question 2

Bill had just purchased a new Mercedes and was taking his friend Josh for a ride. Unbeknownst to Bill, Josh had skipped his court date two weeks ago, and a bench warrant had been issued for his arrest. Josh was well known to the local law enforcement officers, especially Officer Pernick, who had arrested Josh on several occasions including the most recent one for which the bench warrant had been issued. Officer Pernick was on routine traffic patrol when he saw a new Mercedes passing him on the road at a high rate of speed. As he looked and admired the shiny new vehicle, Officer Pernick recognized Josh as the passenger. Knowing the court had recently issued a bench warrant for Josh's arrest, Officer Pernick decided to stop the vehicle for speeding and arrest Josh on the bench warrant.

Officer Pernick activated his lights, and Bill stopped his car. Josh was arrested without incident. Officer Pernick performed a search of the car after arresting Josh, and found a bag of marijuana under Bill's seat. Bill has been charged with possession of marijuana, and has filed a motion challenging the search which led to the discovery of the marijuana.

Assume the facts set forth above accurately reflect the testimony of Officer Pernick and Bill as given during an evidentiary hearing. Also assume that the stop of the vehicle was proper and is not being challenged by Bill or his counsel. You are the clerk for the judge to whom the matter is assigned. The judge has asked you for a memorandum giving your recommendation on how to rule on the motion. Explain the basis for your recommendation.

Model Answer to Question 2

This question requires the application of *New York v Belton*, 453 US 454 (1981), *People v Catanzarite*, 211 Mich App 573 (1995), and *People v Mungo*, 277 Mich App 577 (2008). In *Belton*, the United States Supreme Court held that where a police officer makes a valid arrest of a passenger in a vehicle, the officer is permitted to search the interior of the vehicle as well as any containers located therein. The holding in *Belton* was applied to Michigan by the Court of Appeals in *Catanzarite*.

In *Catanzarite*, the defendant's vehicle was stopped as he was towing a trailer which did not have a license plate. The officer asked the defendant and his passenger for identification, and ran computer checks on each person. A computer check showed the passenger had an outstanding arrest warrant for disorderly person, and the passenger was arrested on the warrant. After the arrest, the officer searched the vehicle and found cocaine in a small bag being held by the defendant. The defendant challenged the search of the bag and the subsequent seizure of the cocaine. The Court of Appeals, relying upon *Belton*, held the search was proper. The Court of Appeals held law enforcement officers may search the interior of the vehicle after arresting a passenger.

In *Mungo*, a traffic stop was made of the defendant's vehicle. A computer check of defendant's passenger revealed outstanding warrants and he was arrested. Defendant's vehicle was searched and a handgun was found under the defendant's seat. Defendant was then arrested and charged with carrying a concealed weapon. Defendant moved to suppress evidence of the gun. The Court of Appeals held under *Belton* that the search was permissible, noting that a full search of the vehicle was allowable even though the passenger had already been removed from the vehicle, handcuffed, and placed in a secure area.

Thus, the search in the instant fact pattern would be upheld, and the motion to suppress the marijuana would be denied.

Student Answer—February 2008

Question 2—Criminal Procedure—9 points

MEMO
TO: JUDGE
FROM: CLERK
RE: Motion to Suppress for Illegal Search

The ISSUE here is whether the search of a vehicle was lawful pursuant to arresting the passenger for a bench warrant.

The Fourth Amendment guarantees the right against unlawful searches and seizures. There are, however, lawful searches within the law. First, if a warrant is obtained, officers may perform the search. Here, however, the officer did not have a warrant. Since that is the case, we have to look to at warrant exceptions. First, if the officer saw the contraband in plain view it may be seized. Here, this is unlikely because the bag of marijuana was under Bill's (the driver) seat. Another exception is the Automobile exception. An officer may search a car if there is probable cause. Here the officer saw Josh in the car, and knew who Josh was and he was arrested by him and failed to appear in court. That fact alone, coupled with the fact that the automobile was Bill's, should not be enough to give rise to probable cause to search the automobile.

Next, another exception to a warrant is search incident to an arrest, which gives rise to a cursory (wing-span) search of the inside of the automobile. Under the driver's seat would still be presumed to be in the wing-span of a passenger. Therefore, pursuant to a lawful arrest, the officer would be entitled to search the interior of car.

Another exception would be an inventory search when the vehicle is impounded. Here, it is unlikely that the vehicle will be impounded since it was driven by Bill. Bill was not arrested.

Therefore, if the search of the auto is valid pursuant to the arrest of the passenger, it is a valid search and the discovery of the marijuana would be lawful. However, the facts tell us that Josh was arrested without incident. That is unlikely to disqualify the search incident to arrest because Josh was in fact arrested.

Comment: This is a well-written answer. The reason full credit was not given is the student did not mention the rule that police can search a vehicle based on an arrest of a passenger. The student's knowledge of this rule, however, is apparent based on the analysis given. This is why only one point was deducted.

July 2008—Question 11

Scot Lynch is charged with controlled substance violations arising out of the search of his residence in Royal Oak, Oakland County, Michigan. The search was conducted pursuant to a search warrant issued by a judge of the Royal Oak District Court. The affidavit in support of the warrant contains allegations arising from the use of a confidential informant. Specifically, the affidavit indicates the informant conducted two controlled purchases of cocaine from the residence, both within thirty days before the affidavit, and one within forty-eight hours of the affidavit being presented in support of the search warrant. The controlled purchases were made with prerecorded funds, which had been given to the informant by the officer. Upon execution of the warrant, some of the prerecorded funds were found in the home. Scot now seeks to suppress the evidence found in the home, alleging the warrant was not based on appropriate probable cause.

Scot contends the affidavit fails to establish the credibility of the confidential informant and fails to provide a substantial basis to determine that contraband would be found in the home. Addressing the credibility of the confidential informant, the affidavit states in pertinent part as follows:

> (F) That the Affiant believes the confidential informant to be reliable and/or credible for the following reasons:
>
> (1) The CI was cooperating voluntarily.
>
> (2) The CI followed all instructions given by Affiant during the controlled purchase.
>
> (3) That Affiant believes the CI was/is telling the truth based on his own observations.
>
> (4) That the CI's forthcoming statements indicating prior involvement in illegal narcotics purchases are against his/her penal interest.

You are the assigned staff attorney for the judge to whom the case is assigned. **Please write a brief memorandum addressing the issues presented, relevant authority, and make a recommendation regarding whether the motion to suppress the evidence should be granted or denied.**

Model Answer to Question 11

The Michigan Supreme Court has held a trial court must review the affidavit and search warrant "in a common-sense and realistic manner." *People v Russo*, 439 Mich 584, 604 (1992). An affidavit must demonstrate probable cause to search the premises, which is defined as "only the probability, and not a prima facie showing, of criminal activity." *Id.* Such probable cause is found to exist "when acts and circumstances warrant a reasonably prudent person to believe that a crime has been committed and that the evidence sought will be found in a stated place." *People v Brzenzinski*, 243 Mich App 431, 433 (2000). In reviewing the affidavit in the case at bar, the court would find sufficient probable cause. The affiant indicates not only one controlled purchase of cocaine by the confidential informant, but two such purchases. The most recent of the purchases occurred within forty-eight hours of the affidavit being presented in support of the search warrant. Further, Scot Lynch has not presented anything to call the credibility of the confidential informant into question. He simply states the affidavit does not contain sufficient information upon which to form an opinion of the informant's credibility. This is not enough, as the court would find there is sufficient information, including that the informant identified Scot Lynch as the person from whom he purchased the cocaine on both occasions. Therefore, the court would find the affidavit contains sufficient information regarding the credibility of the confidential informant and sufficient probable cause to believe the contraband would be found in the locations to be searched. As such, the motion should be denied.

Three Student Answers—July 2008

Question 11—Criminal Procedure—8 points

This is a *4th Amendment* issue regarding the admissibility of evidence obtained in Scott's *home* pursuant to a *search warrant.*

A person is protected by the *4th Amendment* against *unreasonable searches and seizures.* This reasonable expectation of privacy is applicable to the *states* through the *14th Amendment.*

It is fundamental that a search warrant be grounded upon *probable cause.* It is also necessary that it be authorized under *oath or affirmation* by a *neutral and detached magistrate.*

Police are allowed to use information by a confidential informant to obtain a warrant. Such information can be regarded as giving probable cause so long as the informant is *credible* and the officer believes it *veracity* in good faith.

Additionally, controlled buys are allowed to assist in strengthening a case and building probable cause. The police officer had probable cause to believe that since the informant made a purchase at the residence within 48 hours that contraband would be found at the home as well as the pre-recorded funds given to the informant for the controlled buy. The relevance of the purchase closer to 30 days out is not weighed as heavily, but it does show a pattern of dealings of purchasing cocaine from the house. However, all three buys and pre-recorded funds, coupled with the officer's dealing with the informant support a finding of *probable cause.*

The motion to suppress should be *denied.* The search was conducted with a valid warrant. The evidence was seized pursuant to an execution of a valid warrant.

Question 11—Criminal Procedure—8 points

The issue is whether the affidavit established the credibility of the confidential informant (CI) and if the affidavit provided a substantial basis to determine contraband was in the home.

An affidavit in support of a search warrant must contain information that the police officer believes to be true and be sufficient probable cause for the search. The police officer must believe the CI is credible. If the search turns up nothing or the statement in the affidavit ultimately are not true, as long as the officer did not know of the falsity at the time of the affidavit the search is still valid and any evidence that is found is admissible.

Officer had reason to believe the CI was credible and telling the truth. The CI's accounts of previous transactions were very detailed and were based on recent events. He cooperated fully with officer and followed instructions. He was forthcoming in his involvement in narcotics purchases. Although the officer from the facts had never received information from this CI before, that doesn't per se indicate the CI isn't credible. Had officer and the CI been in contact on other instances that turned out successful, that would be a good reason to believe the CI was credible.

Additionally, the pre-recorded funds given to CI by officer were found in Lynch's home. Although this does not help the probable cause for the affidavit, this does mean that CI is credible; he had done business with Lynch, so he was telling the truth about the transactions.

In order to have probable cause, the officer must reasonably believe a crime is afoot. From the statement of the CI, the officer could conclude that Lynch is involved in narcotics activity.

The motion to suppress should be denied. The CI was credible and there was probable cause for the warrant.

Question 11—Criminal Procedure—8 points

To: Judge
From: Staff Attorney
RE: Motion to Suppress Evidence obtained by use of confidential informant granted/denied.

The first issue is whether the affidavit failed to establish the credibility of the confidential informant.

Generally police may use confidential informants as long as they are credible, and reliable. Factors the court will look at include whether the informant has been involved in previous cases, and given credible information in the past, as well as if he gives information willingly and voluntarily.

Here, the affidavit states the CI cooperated voluntarily, he followed all instructions given by Affiant, the Affiant believed him to be credible and that the CI statements indicating prior involvement in illegal narcotics purchases are against his/her penal interest.

Thus, it appears the affidavit does establish the required credibility of the CI.

The next issue is whether the affidavit failed to provide substantial basis to determine contraband would be found in the home.

For a warrant to issue, the officer must have probable cause, and state with particularity what the warrant is for, location of items to be found, etc. and must be issued by an impartial magistrate.

Here, the warrant was issued by a judge in Royal Oak District Court. The affidavit contained allegations arising from the use of the CI. The affidavit indicated the CI conducted two controlled purchase of cocaine from the residence, both within 30 days before the affidavit, and one within 48 hours of the affidavit. The controlled purchases were made with pre-recorded funds given to the CI by the officer. Upon execution of warrant, some of the pre-recorded funds were found in the home.

Because the warrant was stated with particularity and there was probable cause, the motion to suppress the evidence should be denied.

February 2009—Question 4

Police Officers Smith and Jones were investigating drug trafficking among a gang of teenagers who were suspected of manufacturing methamphetamine and distributing it in local high schools. The police officers suspected that the gang was manufacturing the drugs in the home in which Paul Pusher lived with his parents. However, at this stage of their investigation they did not have enough evidence to obtain a warrant to search the home. One day, while Officer Smith was attending to paperwork at the station, Officer Jones observed a group of teenagers enter through the front door of the home of Paul Pusher. One of the teenagers appeared to be carrying a small propane tank. After approximately 30 minutes, Officer Jones knocked on the front door of the Pusher home to inquire about the contents of the tank. Officer Jones did not observe that the boys, accompanied by Paul Pusher, had left the home through the rear door shortly after their arrival.

When nobody answered the front door, Officer Jones went to the rear of the house and knocked on the rear door. Nobody answered. Officer Jones looked into a basement window located next to the rear door of the home. He observed a Bunsen burner with an extraordinarily high flame burning under a petri dish filled with liquid and solid substances. Based on his experience, Officer Jones believed this was a lab constructed for the manufacture of methamphetamine. Officer Jones knew that such labs often result in explosions that expose the public to hazardous chemicals. Officer Jones feared that the apparently unattended and excessively large flame burning under substances he suspected to be dangerous chemicals could result in an explosion. He again knocked loudly on the rear door, but nobody responded. Believing that the residents in neighboring homes were in peril and recognizing that evidence of a crime could be destroyed in an explosion, Officer Jones forced his way into the home and extinguished the flame. Once in the basement, Officer Jones observed a large quantity of suspected methamphetamine located under the table on which the Bunsen burner was placed.

Officer Jones then extensively searched through the entire premises and found several guns and $25,000 in cash in the attic of the home. Officer Jones seized the lab paraphernalia, the drugs, the guns, and the cash and called Officer Smith to inform him of his find.

Officer Smith indicated that he was in the process of talking to Paul's parents, Bob and Alice Pusher. The Pushers appeared at the police station to express concern over the gang of teenagers with whom their son Paul was associating. They feared that Paul was engaged in illegal drug activity. After learning of Officer Jones' discovery, Officer Smith informed the Pushers that the officer with whom he was speaking on the telephone observed through a basement window of the Pusher home activity that is consistent with the illegal manufacture of methamphetamine. Officer Smith then asked the Pushers, "May the police have permission to search your home?" The Pushers freely and voluntarily consented to a search of their home.

Paul Pusher, age 18, was charged with the manufacture and distribution of methamphetamine and possession of a firearm during the commission of a felony. His lawyer has filed a motion to suppress the guns, cash, drugs, and paraphernalia found in the home.

Discuss the legal arguments that may be advanced for and against Paul's motion and how the trial court is likely to rule.

Model Answer to Question 4

The Fourth Amendment to the United States Constitution guarantees the people the right to be free from unreasonable searches and seizures. Likewise, the Michigan Constitution also guarantees against unreasonable searches and seizures. Mich Const. 1963, Art 1, § 11. The protection afforded under the Michigan Constitution is equivalent to the protection provided under the federal constitution. *People v Faucett*, 442 Mich 153, 158 (1993). As a general matter, where evidence has been seized in violation of the right to be free from unreasonable searches and seizures, the court will suppress the illegally seized evidence and preclude it from being admitted in the related criminal prosecution. This is known as the exclusionary rule. E.g., *Mapp v Ohio*, 367 US 643 (1961) (exclusionary rule applicable to states).

Generally, in the criminal context, a search or seizure conducted without a warrant is unreasonable unless there exists both probable cause and a circumstance establishing an exception to the warrant requirement. *People v Tierney*, 266 Mich App 687, 704 (2005). Several exceptions to the warrant requirement have evolved in the law. One such exception is known as the exigent circumstance warrant exception. Under this exception, evidence that is seized from a dwelling without a warrant may be admitted in a criminal prosecution if at the time the law enforcement officers entered the dwelling they had probable cause to believe that: (1) a crime was recently committed on the premises; (2) the dwelling contained evidence of illegal activity or the perpetrators of the suspected crime. Additionally, the prosecution must present specific and objective factual evidence that establishes the existence of an actual emergency whereby immediate action is necessary to either: (1) prevent the eminent destruction of evidence; (2) protect law enforcement officers or others from harm; or, (3) prevent the escape of a suspected perpetrator. *People v Cartwright*, 454 Mich 550 (1997), citing *In re Forfeiture of § 176,598*, 443 Mich 261, 266 (1993).

The validity of an entry into a dwelling in which exigent circumstances are claimed must be based on the facts as perceived by law enforcement at the time of the entry. *People v Olajos*, 397 Mich 629, 634 (1976). The entire premises may be examined as long as it relates to the purpose of addressing the exigent circumstances that justified the entry. *Mincey v Arizona*, 437 US 385 (1978). Further, law enforcement officers are free to seize evidence in plain view. *Id.* However, searches into specific areas outside the scope of the emergency are not warranted under this exception. *Id.*

Another is the consent exception to the warrant requirement, which allows search and seizure when consent is unequivocal and specific, and freely and intelligently given. *People v Galloway*, 259 Mich App 634, 648 (2003). Although consent to a search must ordinarily be given by the person affected, a third party may consent to the search when the consenting person has equal right of possession or control of the premises. *People v Brown*, 279 Mich App 116, 131 (2008).

Further, even if evidence is unconstitutionally seized, evidence is not to be excluded if law enforcement would have inevitably discovered the evidence regardless of the unconstitutional conduct. *People v Stevens* (*After Remand*), 460 Mich 626, 637 (1999). Under this exception, evidence illegally seized in violation of the Fourth Amendment may nonetheless be admitted in a criminal prosecution if the prosecution establishes by a preponderance of the evidence that the evidence inevitably would have been discovered by lawful means. *Nix v Williams*, 467 US 431 (1984). The prosecution is not required to prove the absence bad faith under this rule. *Id.*

Under the facts presented in this case, Officer Jones clearly entered the curtilage of the Pusher home without a warrant when he proceeded to the rear door of the home. However, in *Hardesty v Hamburg Twp*, 461 F3d 646 (CA 6, 2006), the court recognized that police officers are permitted to enter private property and approach and knock on the front door of a home in order to ask questions of persons inside the home. Where there is no response at the front door of a home, an investigating officer may also proceed around the house and knock on a rear door of the home in order to initiate a conversation with persons believed to be in the house. *Id.* Therefore, the officer's entry into the curtilage to effectuate the knock and talk investigative technique did not violate Paul Pusher's Fourth Amendment rights.

Once at the rear door, the facts indicate that Officer Jones "looked into a basement window located to the rear door of the home." Looking through a window of a home does not violate Paul Pusher's Fourth Amendment rights, since Officer Jones was legitimately at the rear of the home. *People v Custer*, 248 Mich App 552, 561-563 (2001). After Officer Jones looked through the window, he forcibly entered the Pusher home without a warrant. Thus, absent an exception to the warrant requirement, the evidence will be suppressed under the exclusionary rule.

The prosecution will have an excellent argument that entry into the Pusher's home was authorized due to exigent circumstances. Upon peering into the basement window of the Pusher's home, Officer Jones observed what he believed to be a laboratory designed to manufacture illegal drugs. Thus, he had reason to believe that a crime was recently committed on the premises and that the premises contained evidence of illegal activity. Additionally, Officer Jones observed "an extraordinarily high flame burning under a petri dish filled with liquid and solid substances." The facts tell us that Officer Jones believed this was a lab constructed for the manufacture of methamphetamine. Officer Jones knew that "such labs often result in explosions that expose the public to hazardous chemicals." Thus, based on the perceptions of the officer, the prosecutor will be able to present specific and objective factual evidence that established the existence of an actual emergency such that immediate action was necessary to prevent the imminent destruction of evidence and protect Officer Jones and the persons residing in nearby homes.

However, the establishment of exigent circumstances will justify only the seizure of the drugs and paraphernalia found in the basement that was in the vicinity of the Bunsen burner. The cash and weapons found in the Pusher's attic do not in any way relate to the exigent circumstances that justified the entry. In *United States v Buchanan*, 904 F2d 349, 357 (CA 6, 1990), the court held that "police who believe they have probable cause to search cannot enter a home without a warrant merely because they plan subsequently to get one." Any other view would tend in actual practice to emasculate the search warrant requirement of the Fourth Amendment. Thus, to justify the admission of this evidence, the prosecution will rely on the inevitable discovery rule to justify admission of the cash and guns.

Specifically, the prosecution will argue that the Pushers were at the police station reporting their concerns of suspected criminal activity that possibly involved their son at the time Officer Jones was searching the attic. In the course of reporting their concerns to law enforcement, Officer Smith requested and received permission from the Pushers to search their home. While Paul Pusher may have an expectation of privacy in the private room in which he resided in his parents' home, *see People v Flowers*, 23 Mich App 523 (1970), the attic cannot be considered Paul's private area. Paul's parents "freely and voluntarily" consented to a search of their home. Thus, the prosecution will argue, discovery of the evidence in the attic was inevitable.

Paul's defense counsel may advance an argument that because consent to search was obtained only after Officer Jones had illegally seized the cash and guns from the attic, this evidence remains subject to exclusion under the exclusionary rule. Regardless, however, given the parents' consent, the prosecution can nonetheless show that tainted evidence would ultimately have been obtained in a constitutionally accepted manner. *People v Kroll*, 179 Mich App 423, 429 (1989). In other words, the prosecution can show that Officer Smith would have searched the attic pursuant to a valid consent and discovered the cash and guns irrespective of Officer Jones' conduct. *See United States v Kelly*, 913 F2d 261 (CA 6, 1990) (holding consent to search may be obtained after an unlawful search).

Student Answer—February 2009

Question 4—Criminal Procedure—8 points

Pursuant to Michigan Rules of Criminal Procedure, the defendant's motion will be denied because even though the search was not incident to a valid search warrant there, were exigent circumstances. The officer viewed with his own eyes the liquid burning in a petri dish from an open window. The plain view exception applies here. Suspected gang members entered the house with a propane tank and the cop only knocked, he did not enter. He saw through a window the burning and with his experience he believed it was a lab. This combination will give rise to probable cause to get a warrant. But an exception to the warrant requirement existed—exigent circumstance—because officer has a duty to protect others from danger. Labs are known to explode and harm people also. Evidence may be destroyed so he entered. When he found the meth he began to "sweep" the house for assailants. He did see gang members enter so his sweep of anywhere a person can hide, such as the "attic" is reasonable Michigan courts have held. This is where he found the further evidence. The search was pursuant to probable cause an exigent circumstance. Based on totality of circumstances.

If the court finds the initial view of window behind house is within the curtilage, defendant may say evidence found is fruit of poisonous tree and the exclusionary rule will apply. This will also meet an exception. Later independent means to find evidence. The parents were at precinct giving consent to search their home. Which would have found the meth lab and the guns, cash, drugs and paraphernalia. So even if the initial search was invalid, the evidence can still come in under later independent means like the case, the Christian Burial case, where police got the location from defendant of a dead girl was found illegally but the evidence was still allowed because the location of the body would have been found eventually by the search party of the little girl.

Here, even though consent was obtained after the search, the parents were there to ask for help and would have given consent to search. They were not aware of the search yet and had no reason to feel coerced into saying yes. Consent was voluntary.

Comment: This answer is a bit unorganized, but it does address all issues in the model answer. Also, notice that the examinee couldn't recall the name "inevitable discovery," so instead defined it as "Later independent means to find evidence." Excellent Plan B strategy to get credit!

July 2009—Question 6

Wendy Witness observed an assault and robbery committed against an elderly woman, Sarah Smith, who was walking in her neighborhood. Wendy was approximately 30 feet away from the scene of the crime, which was committed at noon on a sunny day. Wendy's view of the crime was unobstructed. Sarah could not describe her assailant, stating only that the assailant took her purse, which contained one credit card. Wendy described the assailant as a clean-shaven Caucasian male, approximately 20 to 22 years old, 5 feet 8 inches tall, and 150 pounds. Wendy indicated the assailant had short black hair and wore blue jeans, white running shoes, and a white sweatshirt. Later that day, Peter Perpetrator, a clean-shaven 24-year-old Caucasian male with short black hair, 5 feet 10 inches in height, and weighing 160 pounds, was arrested on an outstanding warrant unrelated to the crime against Sarah Smith. When police inventoried Peter's personal items, they discovered that Peter had a credit card issued to Sarah Smith. Police believed Peter committed the crime against Sarah. The next morning, police placed Peter in a lineup with five other Caucasian males. During the lineup and at the time of his arrest, Peter wore blue jeans, white running shoes, and a white t-shirt. All participants in the lineup were clean shaven, had short hair, and wore blue jeans and white running shoes. Additionally, the persons in the lineup other than Peter are described as follows:

Age	Height	Weight	Hair	Shirt
18	6'0"	170	brown	black t-shirt
25	6'2"	190	black	blue sweatshirt
19	5'11"	170	brown	beige t-shirt
22	5'11"	180	brown	black sweatshirt
23	6'0"	175	black	white button shirt

No lawyer assigned to protect Peter's interests was present during the lineup. Before Wendy viewed the lineup, she was told by police that a suspect was in custody and would be in the lineup. Within seconds of Wendy viewing the lineup and without any prompting from police, Wendy identified Peter Perpetrator as the assailant. Wendy stated, "I am certain he is the assailant." Peter was charged with assault and unarmed robbery.

Discuss the law and procedure Peter's defense counsel will use to support a motion to suppress Wendy Witness' identification of Peter Perpetrator. How will the trial court rule on such a motion? Explain your answer.

Model Answer to Question 6

Peter's counsel may file a motion to suppress Wendy Witness' identification of Peter and request the trial court conduct a pretrial evidentiary hearing to determine whether the lineup procedures employed in Wendy's identification of Peter violated Peter's due process rights. *United States v Wade*, 388 US 218 (1967). It is unlikely that Wendy Witness' identification of Peter will be suppressed.

A lineup may be found to be so suggestive and susceptible to misidentification that it denies a criminal defendant due process of law. *Stovall v Denno*, 388 US 293, 301-302 (1967); *People v Hickman*, 470 Mich 602, 607 (2004); *People v Lee*, 391 Mich 618 (1974). To challenge an identification on the basis of lack of due process, "a defendant must show that the pretrial identification procedure was so suggestive in light of the totality of the circumstances that it led to a substantial likelihood of misidentification." *People v Kurylczyk*, 443 Mich 289, 302 (1993); *People v Williams*, 244 Mich App 533, 540 (2001). Where a defendant raises a credible argument that the lineup procedure is constitutionally suspect, a trial court should conduct an evidentiary hearing to decide the matter.

Here, there are many facts Peter's counsel can cite to support his argument that the lineup was unduly suggestive. First, the persons used to participate in the lineup featured many physical characteristics that varied greatly from the physical characteristics initially cited by Wendy to describe the assailant to the police. Wendy described the assailant as having short black hair, wearing a white sweatshirt, 5′8″ tall, 150 pounds, and between 20 and 22 years of age. No person in the lineup wore a white sweatshirt and no person, other than Peter, was less than 5′11″ tall. The persons participating in the lineup other than Peter, who weighed 160 pounds, weighed between 170 and 180 pounds—substantially more than the 150-pound description Wendy initially offered to police. Three of the lineup participants had brown hair rather than black hair, as described by Wendy. And all but one of the lineup participants fell outside the age range cited by Wendy to describe the assailant.

Further, the participants in the lineup featured many physical characteristics that varied from the physical characteristics of Peter. Peter was the shortest person in the lineup at 5 feet 10 inches tall. Peter was also the lightest person in the lineup, weighing 160 pounds. These facts are arguably significant because Wendy described the assailant as being only 5 feet 8 inches tall and 150 pounds. Thus, counsel may argue, the witness may have concluded that the shortest and lightest person in the lineup (Peter) must be the assailant. Counsel should also point out that Peter was the only person in the lineup wearing a white t-shirt—clothing very similar to a white sweatshirt Wendy indicated the assailant was wearing during the commission of the crime. Finally, only one of the lineup participants was older than Peter, and two of the lineup participants were substantially younger than Peter (5 and 6 years younger).

The fairness of an identification procedure is evaluated in light of the total circumstances. *Kurylczyk, supra* at 311-312, 318; *People v Murphy* (On Remand), 282 Mich App 571, 584 (2009). Discrepancies between the physical characteristics of an accused, the description of the assailant provided police by the witness, and the persons who participated in the lineup do not necessarily render the lineup procedure defective. *Id.* at 289, 312, 318; *People v Hornsby*, 251 Mich App 462, 466 (2002). There is no requirement that the lineup participants approximate the description of the assailant that the witness provided to police. All that is required is that the lineup participants approximate the culprit's description. *Id.* at 312; *People v Holmes*, 132 Mich App 730, 746 (1984). Differences in the appearances of lineup participants generally pertain to the weight of an identification and not to its admissibility. *Hornsby, supra*, at 466. Differences are significant only to the extent that they are apparent to the identifying witness and substantially distinguish the defendant from the other lineup participants. *Kurylczyk, supra* at 312; *Hornsby, supra* at 466.

Here, nothing in the differences cited by defense counsel would make it apparent to Wendy Witness that Peter Perpetrator was the assailant. Although not all the lineup participants had black hair, all of them had short dark hair. Thus, this subtle distinction in hair color will not render the lineup invalid. Also, Michigan courts have held that minor variations in height will not render a lineup unduly suggestive. *People v Rivera*, 61 Mich App 427 (1975) (concluding difference in height of up to 4 inches is legally insignificant). Here, there was only a 2-inch difference in height between Peter Perpetrator and the other lineup participants. Similarly, differences in the clothing worn by lineup participants generally will not render the lineup procedure defective. Here, Peter was presented in the lineup wearing the same clothing he was wearing at the time of his arrest. This was permissible. *People v Gunter*, 76 Mich App 483 (1977).

A court reviewing the fairness of a lineup will also consider the opportunity of the witness to view the culprit at the time of the crime, the witness's degree of attention, the accuracy of the witness' prior description of the culprit, the level of certainty demonstrated by the witness at the identification, and the length of time between the crime and the identification. *Neil v Biggers*, 409 US 188, 199 (1972); *People v Solomon*, 391 Mich 767 (1974). Applying these factors to the facts presented in this case, there is little doubt that the court would conclude the lineup did not violate Peter's constitutional rights. Wendy observed the crime without obstruction from 30 feet away, at noon on a sunny day. While there are some variations between the description of the assailant that Wendy provided to police and the physical appearance of Peter Perpetrator, these variations are minor. Peter has short black hair, as described by Wendy. In addition, Wendy described an assailant that featured the approximate age and weight of Peter. While Peter is 5′10″ tall and Wendy described the assailant as being 5′8″ tall, given all the other similarities between Peter and Wendy's description of the assailant, this minor difference in weight will not taint the identification. Further, the length of time that passed between the crime and the lineup was very short—the lineup was held only one day after the crime. Significantly, Wendy proclaimed certainty in her identification. These factors weigh strongly in favor of concluding the lineup procedures withstand constitutional challenge.

Peter's counsel may argue that the lineup is unduly suggestive because police informed Wendy that "a suspect was in custody and would be in the lineup." However, the fact that the complainant was told that the culprit would be in the lineup is not unduly suggestive as a matter of law. *People v McElhaney*, 215 Mich App 269, 287 (1996).

Additionally, counsel may argue that the absence of defense counsel during the lineup process creates an inference that the process was unduly suggestive.

However, an accused is not entitled to be represented by counsel at identification procedures conducted before the initiation of adversarial judicial criminal proceedings. *Hickman, supra* at 609. Given the analysis provided above, the prosecutor will have little problem meeting its burden.

Two Student Answers—July 2009

Question 6—Criminal Procedure—8 points

This is a criminal procedure question. This question includes first, the right to counsel. An arrestee has the right to an attorney, as provided by the 6th amendment and that right attaches upon arraignment.

> **Comment:** Wrong! RTC attaches at the initiation of adversarial proceedings.

This question also deals with W's identifier of the defendant. Defendant on scene identification is permitted in Michigan. MI allows and MI courts have held on-scene immediate identification (or shortly after the crime) does not violate the MI constitution or the rights of a defendant.

Here, the question that arises is the Bias of the lineup. In W's description of assailant, she described him as being 5'8" tall. All the other persons in the lineup aside from PP were over 5'11". PP was the shortest in the lineup and several inches shorter than the next shortest person in the lineup. It is true all persons in the lineup were Caucasian males with dark hair. But, all other men in the lineup were also much heavier built men than PP.

WW had described her assailant as being about 150 lbs. The other men in the lineup were all over 170 lbs—some even a good 40 lbs heavier than her description. PP was the smallest coupled with the fact PP was shortest; the fact that he was toughest built may be bias.

Additionally W remembered the assailant had a white "sweatshirt" on. In the lineup only 2 men (one being the PP) had fully visible white shirts and the others had colored shirts. This may be another bias in the lineup.

A defendants 5th/6th amendment rights to counsel do not include having a lawyer present at a line up unless it's a lineup after arraignment.

The witness identification of PP is likely going to stand. All in all, the men in the lineup were fairly similar looking. Additionally, although the lineup was after the assault by a few hours (later that day) it was within a reasonable time period that the crime was still fresh in WW's mind.

Also, WW stated, "I am certain he is the assailant," when she identified him. The totality of the circumstances will likely lead the court to deny the defense counsel's request to suppress the identification. Wendy needed no prompting from police and was easily able to quickly identify PP with apparent certainty.

> **Comment:** Although this examinee incorrectly stated when the Sixth Amendent Right to Counsel attaches, he or she did a fantastic analysis of the lineup being overly suggestive. This example shows how important it is to work with the facts!

Question 6—Criminal Procedure—8 points

Issue 1
Is the credit card issued to Sarah Smith admissible to prove assault and robbery against Peter?

Rule
Probable cause must exist for a valid search or a search can be legally conducted contemporaneous with an arrest.

Here, the facts indicate that Peter was arrested on an outstanding warrant unrelated to the crime against Sarah Smith. Although, the crime was unrelated, a search would be lawful with a contemporaneous arrest. However, the credit card, was obtained when police inventoried Peter's personal items in the arrest. Since it's not Peter's personal property it is admissible.

Issue 2
Can Peter's defense suppress Wendy's identification of Peter?

Rule
A defendant does not have a right to counsel present at identification lineups. Police officers also may not lead a witness or tell the witness that the alleged person is in the lineup. Here, the facts indicate that the assailant had short black hair, blue jeans, white running shoes, and a white sweatshirt. Peter entered the lineup wearing all those items, while the other men had blue jeans and white running shoe from a white sweatshirt. Peter being the only one wearing the assailant's clothes created a preference to the witness. This unfairly prejudices Peter, and the evidence of the photo lineup should be excluded.

Secondly, Peter was put in the lineup with other men that were all taller than him. The witness believing the suspect was 5′8″ and seeing a man shorter than all the other men creates a subtle message that Peter is guilty since he is shorter than all the other men and wearing the assailants clothing. This should also exclude the lineup.

Thirdly, Sarah was coached into the fact the assailant was in the lineup, when police told her the suspect was in custody and in the lineup. Peter wearing almost exactly the same clothes as the assailant (white t-shirt instead of white sweatshirt) being the shortest man in the lineup, and weighing considerably less than all the other men, and Sarah being told the suspect was in the lineup, all unfairly prejudiced Peter in the identification. Under the totality of the circumstances, this identification must be ruled inadmissible because it unfairly prejudices Peter.

Also, as defense counsel, the charge of assault should be withdrawn because of the merger doctrine. Assault merges into robbery and Peter should only be charged with robbery. The trial court should exclude evidence of the photo lineup since 4 different factors resulted in unfair prejudice to Peter's, but different shirts than the assailant. The other men in the lineup had blue, beige or black shirts. One man had a white button down shirt, much different.

February 2010—Question 15

Bob Smith is a lifelong Michigan resident who is married with two children. He has been employed as a sales representative for the same employer for 15 years. Bob's children participate in the local youth soccer association. In 2007, Bob was elected treasurer of the soccer association. In the spring of 2009, the prosecutor charged Bob with misappropriation of the soccer association's funds, in violation of MCL 750.279. The maximum sentence imposed for this felony is 4 years. MCL 777.16o. Bob was arrested and released after he posted a $25,000 cash bond.

Bob retained a lawyer and trial was scheduled for December 21, 2009. On the trial date, Bob fired his lawyer in open court. Bob stated, "I want to represent myself. I have been preparing my defense since my arrest. I am aware of all my rights, and I know I have the right to represent myself. I simply do not believe that any lawyer will be able to represent me as effectively as I will be able to represent myself. I want to represent myself and I want to start the trial today." The trial court responded, "Is anyone making you say this, you are charged with a felony?" Bob said, "No one is making me say this and I know I am charged with a felony." The trial court then said, "Very well, Mr. Smith. You have the absolute right to represent yourself. You appear ready, willing, and able to proceed. Your request for self-representation is granted."

The prosecutor presented properly admitted evidence that established beyond a reasonable doubt each element of misappropriation of funds. The trial court admitted all evidence Bob introduced in his defense. Nonetheless, Bob did a miserable job of representing himself. The jury convicted Bob as charged. Upon receiving the jury verdict, the trial court revoked Bob's bond and remanded him to the county jail where he awaits his sentencing. Bob immediately retained new counsel to represent him in the trial court through his sentencing. Bob has asked his new trial counsel to do whatever he could to obtain Bob's release from incarceration.

What action may Bob's new counsel take prior to imposition of Bob's sentence that could result in Bob's release from incarceration? Describe and explain the best arguments that may be advanced to support this action and any expected counterarguments the prosecutor may make.

Model Answer to Question 15

Bob has sought the assistance of trial counsel after his jury conviction but before imposition of his sentence. Bob's newly retained counsel should immediately file a motion for a new trial pursuant to MCR 6.431 and MCL 770.1. A motion for new trial in a criminal proceeding may be made at any time before the filing of a claim of appeal. MCR 6.431(A). Here, because the new time for filing a claim of appeal has not passed, a motion for new trial would be timely.

The trial court may grant a motion for new trial "on any ground that would support appellate reversal of the conviction or because it believes that the verdict has resulted in a miscarriage of justice." MCR 6.431(B). MCL 770.1 similarly provides that a judge "may grant a new trial to the defendant, for any cause for which by law a new trial may be granted, or when it appears to the court that justice has not been done."

Bob has a significant appellate issue relating to his self-representation.

The right to self-representation is implied in the Sixth Amendment to the United States Constitution and expressly guaranteed by Michigan statute, MCL 763.1, and the Michigan Constitution, Const 1963, art 1, §13. However, the right to self-representation must be measured against the right to counsel. Thus, before allowing a defendant to represent himself the trial court must comply with the waiver of counsel procedures set forth by the Michigan Supreme Court in *People v Anderson*, 398 Mich 361, 367-368 (1976). Specifically, a trial court must: (1) make sure the waiver request is unequivocal; (2) make sure the waiver is knowingly, intelligently, and voluntarily made; and (3) be satisfied that the defendant will not disrupt, unduly inconvenience, and burden the court or the administration of court business.

Further, the trial court must comply with MCR 6.005 (D), which requires the trial court to inform a would be pro per criminal defendant of charges, the potential maximum prison sentence and any mandatory minimum sentence required by law; to advise him of the risks inherent in self-representation; and to afford him the opportunity to consult with counsel before deciding to proceed without counsel. Strict compliance with the requirements of the court rule and case law is not required. *People v Russell*, 471 Mich 182 191 (2004). However, to substantially comply with the requirements of the court rule and case law, "the court [must] disclose the substance of both *Anderson* and MCR 6.005 (D) in a short colloquy with the defendant, and make an express finding that the defendant fully understands, recognizes, and agrees to abide by the waiver of counsel procedures." *Id.* at 191.

Here, the colloquy between the defendant and the trial court fell far short of the minimum requirements of Michigan law. While the prosecutor will point out the trial court asked defendant one question to see if the request was voluntary, "Is anyone making you say this?" the judge did not follow up or ask any questions to determine if the request was knowingly or intelligently made. The trial court failed to test whether defendant's declaration of his right to represent himself was without equivocation. The trial court should have inquired of the defendant the reason supporting his conclusion that he would be more effective in presenting his defense than would "any lawyer." The court failed to inform the defendant of the dangers of self-representation. The trial court should have informed defendant that the trial is governed by rules of procedure and evidence and that at trial it is exceedingly difficult for a person untrained in the law to comply with these procedural requirements. In failing to discuss these procedural aspects of the trial, the court also lacked any basis to support a conclusion that defendant would "not disrupt, unduly inconvenience, and burden the court of the administration of court business." *Anderson* at 368. The court also failed to inquire whether defendant had a grasp of the substantive aspects of the charges asserted against him or the potential defense that may be available to him. While the prosecutor will point out that the court reminded defendant he was charged with a felony, the court made no mention of whether defendant understood the ramifications of a felony conviction. There was no discussion of the specific charge asserted against defendant nor the maximum or potential penalty defendant could face upon conviction. Defendant was not afforded an opportunity to discuss his decision with his lawyer before the trial court accepted his waiver of the right to counsel and his assertion of his right to self-representation. While defendant stated that he knew his rights, defendant is not a lawyer. Thus, absent inquiry by the court, it would be impossible to determine whether defendant actually was aware of his many rights and intelligently waived those rights when defendant stated, "I am aware of my rights." Simply put, the exchange between defendant and the trial court does not establish that defendant made a knowing and intelligent waiver of his rights to counsel and his assertion of his rights to self-representation.

Because there exist strong appellate grounds to support reversal of Bob's conviction, the motion for new trial should be granted. Upon the granting of the motion for new trial, Bob's new counsel should move for reinstatement of his release bond. The court should grant such a motion, as a criminal defendant not charged with murder or treason is generally entitled to have a reasonable release bond established pending trial. Const 1963, art 1 §§15, 16; MCL §§765.5, 765.6.

Student Answer—February 2010

Question 15—Criminal Procedure—None Available

July 2010—Question 4

Debbie Defendant is charged with one count of assault with intent to do great bodily harm less than murder (GBH), a 10-year felony. At the arraignment on the information, the prosecutor informed Debbie and her counsel there would be no reduced plea offers extended in this case. Consequently, Debbie's counsel asked the trial judge whether she would offer any insight into how Debbie might be sentenced should she plead guilty to the GBH charge. The trial judge stated on the record that based on her limited knowledge of the case, she would consider sentencing Debbie to six months in the county jail should Debbie plead guilty to the GBH charge.

The prosecutor objected and indicated that Debbie's criminal history required that she be sentenced to the maximum term of incarceration permitted under law. Debbie stated on the record that she was pleased with the court's sentencing proposal and given the court's assessment, she would agree to plead guilty to the GBH charge. The trial court accepted the plea, referred Debbie to the probation department for preparation of a presentence investigation report (PSIR), and set a sentencing date. The prosecutor, disgruntled over the trial court's sentencing proposal, immediately filed a motion to set aside the plea and assign the case to another judge due to improper participation by the court in the sentence negotiation process. The prosecutor's motion was set to be heard on the sentencing date.

On the date set for sentencing, the trial judge, relying on information contained in the PSIR, refused to sentence Debbie to six months in the county jail. The judge stated she would, however, impose a sentence of 24 to 120 months imprisonment to be served in the state prison, such sentence falling within the low end of the applicable sentencing guideline range. The prosecutor continued to demand imposition of a tougher sentence and asked the court to rule on his motion.

How should the court rule on the prosecutor's motion? Explain your answer.

Describe and discuss Debbie's remedies, if any, to the trial court's refusal to sentence her to six months in the county jail.

Model Answer to Question 4

I. How Should the Court Rule on the Prosecutor's Motion? The trial court should deny the prosecutor's motion to set aside the plea and assign the matter to a different judge. As a general principle, judicial involvement in the bargaining of a sentence should be limited. *People v Killebrew*, 419 Mich 189 (1982). A limit on judicial intervention is necessary "to minimize the potential coercive effect on the defendant, to retain the function of the judge as a neutral arbiter, and to preserve the public perception of the judge as an impartial dispenser of justice." *Id.* at 202. However, judicial involvement in preconviction negotiation of a sentence is not precluded as a matter of law. This is because the Legislature has vested sentencing authority and discretion with the court and the court "may not abdicate this function by allowing sentence agreements to control the sentencing process." *People v Cobbs*, 443 Mich 276, 281 (1993).

In *Cobbs*, the Michigan Supreme Court discussed the propriety of a trial court disclosing the court's thoughts on sentencing prior to the acceptance of a plea. The Supreme Court stated, "At the request of a party, and not on the judge's own initiative, a judge may state *on the record* the length of sentence that, on the basis of the information then available to the judge, appears to be appropriate for the charged offense." *Cobbs*, 443 Mich at 283 (emphasis in original, footnote omitted). The Supreme Court noted that the coercive position of the court is minimized where the court is not initiating the sentencing discussion but is merely responding to an inquiry regarding sentencing. Further, the court must take care to avoid express or implied alternative sentencing possibilities, such as sentencing variations that may arise from the exercise of the right to trial by jury. This is also necessary to avoid the potential of coercion. *Id.* The Supreme Court concluded that "[t]he judge's neutral and impartial role is enhanced when a judge provides a clear statement of information that is helpful to the parties." *Id.* at 284.

The Supreme Court also addressed the concerns that are at the root of the prosecutor's motion to set aside the plea. The Court stated, "Where a defendant pleads guilty or nolo contendere to the charged offense, there can be no infringement of the prosecutor's charging authority. Neither does this procedure limit the prosecutor's right to introduce additional facts at appropriate points during the remaining pendency of the case, such as during allocution at sentencing." *Cobbs*, 443 Mich at 284 (footnote omitted). The prosecutor has wide latitude in the discretion to charge, but once a decision to charge is made, the prosecutor has no right to dictate the sentence. That right and duty vests exclusively with the court and the prosecutor's role in sentencing is limited to informing the court. Here, the court did nothing improper. It is clear from the facts presented that the trial court did not initiate the discussion regarding sentencing. The court merely responded to defense counsel's inquiry. The judge further indicated that the sentence was based on the "limited knowledge of the case" then available to her. The court did not impose upon the prosecutor any obligation to reduce the charge or in any way impact or influence the discretion of the prosecutor. The prosecutor's motion to set aside the plea should be denied. After ruling on this motion, the trial court should refrain from sentencing defendant or taking any further action in this matter until after there has been a de novo review of the motion to reassign the case to a different judge. The motion is, in essence, a motion to disqualify the judge because of bias. Such motions are subject to de novo review by the chief judge of the circuit of a judge assigned by the State Court Administrator's Office. MCR 2.003(D)(3)(a).

II. Describe and Discuss Debbie's Remedies, If Any, to the Trial Court's Refusal to Sentence Her to Six Months in the County Jail. Although Debbie pled guilty with the expectation that she would be sentenced to six months incarceration in the county jail, she has no right to force the trial court to impose such a sentence. *Cobbs*, 443 Mich at 283, made it very clear that "[t]he judge's preliminary evaluation of the case does not bind the judge's sentencing discretion." As the case proceeds it is likely that additional facts will become known to the court that impact sentencing determinations. *Id.* When the sentencing court expresses the inability to follow the preliminary sentence evaluation, a defendant who relied upon such evaluation to enter a plea of guilty has the "absolute right to withdraw the plea."

Additionally, to the extent the defendant wishes to withdraw a plea so offered and proceed to trial, the judge who has expressed opinions relating to sentencing remains subject to the disqualification rules under MCR 2.003. Debbie may conclude that the revised sentence offer shows an inability for the court to preside over her case as an impartial arbiter. However, a decision not to sentence a defendant consistent with a preliminary sentencing evaluation is not a per se basis for recusal. "A judge's candid statement of how a case appears at an early stage of the proceedings does not prevent the judge from deciding the case in a fair and evenhanded manner later, when additional facts become known." *Id.*

Here, Debbie stated on the record that she was "pleased with the court's sentencing proposal and given the court's assessment, she would agree to plead guilty to the GBH charge." Thus it may fairly be said that Debbie relied upon the court's preliminary sentencing evaluation when she entered her plea. Accordingly, Debbie has two options: proceed with the sentence and accept the imposition of a 24- to 120-month sentence to be served in prison, or withdraw her plea. To the extent she wishes to withdraw her plea, she may also seek disqualification of the judge, although unless Debbie waives her right to a jury such that the court is also the trier of fact, it is unlikely that disqualification would be granted. As a practical matter, Debbie would be well advised to remain with this judge and keep her plea of guilty. It is clear the prosecutor is seeking a penalty greater than that which the judge is now offering. Further, the facts indicate that the court's latest proposed sentence is at "the low end of the applicable sentencing guideline range." Thus, absent a finding she is not guilty, Debbie is not likely to achieve a better sentencing result.

Student Answer—July 2010

Question 4—Criminal Procedure—None Available

CLUSTER THREE

EVIDENCE

Questions, Model Answers, and Student Answers

The following section includes prior Michigan Bar Exam questions and model answers for **Evidence**. Many of the questions also include actual student answers with the amount of points that were earned to give you a better idea of what the graders expect. The student answers are immediately following the model answer for each question. Please pay close attention to the points received on each question. Although most samples represent "good" answers (i.e., received 8, 9, or 10 points), there are some samples that received 7 points (the minimum "passing" score for an essay), and a few that received very low scores to help you better understand the grading process and what is expected.

February 2001—Question 8

Douglas Dalton was charged with three counts of first-degree criminal sexual conduct involving his eight-year-old granddaughter, Victoria, for whom he would occasionally provide overnight care while Victoria's mother was working. Victoria told her mother, and later a counselor and a police officer, that Dalton would digitally and orally penetrate her whenever he bathed her before bedtime. The penetration would occur during a "game" invented by Dalton called "This Little Piggy," in which Dalton would kiss and tickle Victoria from her feet to her head. At trial, Victoria testified that she remembered this happening three times during the fall of 1999, twice during the week of Halloween and again on Thanksgiving Day. Victoria's mother confirmed that Victoria had stayed overnight at Dalton's home during these time periods. Victoria additionally testified that Dalton told her after each game of "This Little Piggy" that the game was their secret, and that Victoria's grandmother and mother would be very angry at Victoria if they found out about it.

Before trial, the prosecution notified the defense that it intended to introduce evidence that Dalton had committed similar acts of sexual misconduct against another one of his granddaughters. The prosecution explained that this evidence was relevant to show a scheme, plan, or system, and absence of accident. At trial, over the objection of the defense, the prosecution was permitted to present the testimony of Victoria's 13-year-old cousin, Cathy. Cathy testified that, starting when she was about seven years old and continuing until she was ten, Dalton would sometimes touch the inside of her genitals while playing this game. Cathy did not tell anyone about what happened until recently because Dalton had told her that the game was a special secret between them and that Cathy's mother and father would be very upset and angry with her if they ever found out.

The jury convicted Dalton of three counts of first-degree criminal sexual conduct. On appeal, Dalton argues that the trial court committed reversible error in admitting Cathy's testimony. Dalton contends that the testimony was improperly admitted to show his character and propensity to commit acts of sexual misconduct.

You are the assistant prosecuting attorney assigned to this appeal. What will you argue to the Court of Appeals with respect to this issue?

Model Answer to Question 8

The trial court's decision whether other acts evidence is admissible is within the trial court's discretion and will be reversed only where there has been a clear abuse of discretion. *People v Crawford*, 458 Mich 376, 383; 582 NW2d 785 (1998).

MRE 404(b)(1) provides that "[e]vidence of other crimes, wrongs, or acts is not admissible to prove the character of a person in order to show action in conformity therewith." The rule further provides that such evidence may be admissible for other purposes, "such as proof of motive, opportunity, intent, preparation, scheme, plan, or system in doing an act, knowledge, identity, or absence of mistake or accident when the same is material."

Accordingly, in order to admit evidence of other acts, the prosecutor must first offer the evidence under something other than a character or propensity theory. MRE 404(b)(1). *See People v Sabin (After Remand)*, 463 Mich 43, 55-56; 614 NW2d 888 (2000); *People v VanderVliet*, 444 Mich 52, 75; 508 NW2d 114 (1993).

Second, the evidence must be relevant to an issue of fact of consequence at trial. MRE 401; MRE 402. Relevant evidence is defined by MRE 401 as "evidence having any tendency to make the existence of any fact that is of consequence to the determination of the action more probable or less probable than it would be without the evidence." Relevant evidence is therefore evidence that is both "material" (related to any fact that is of consequence to the action) and "probative" (tending to make the existence of a fact of consequence more or less probable than it would be without the evidence). *See Savin, supra* at 56-57; *People v Mills*, 450 Mich 61, 66-68; 537 NW2d 909 (1995).

Third, the trial court may exclude the admissible evidence of other acts "if its probative value is substantially outweighed by the danger of unfair prejudice, confusion of the issues, or misleading the jury, or by considerations of undue delay, waste of time, or needless presentation of cumulative evidence." MRE 403. *See Savin, supra* at 57-58; *VanderVliet, supra* at 74-75.

Finally, upon request, the trial court may provide a limiting instruction under MRE 105. *Sabin, supra* at 56; *VanderVliet, supra* at 75.

The assistant prosecuting attorney should argue that the other act's evidence was admissible to show Dalton's plan, scheme, or system in doing an act. Evidence of similar misconduct is logically relevant to show that the charged act took place "where the uncharged misconduct and the charged offense are sufficiently similar to support an inference that they are manifestations of a common plan, scheme, or system." *Sabin, supra* at 63. While general similarity between the charged and uncharged acts does not by itself establish a plan, scheme, or system, the existence of common features between the charged and uncharged acts contained common features beyond mere commission of acts of sexual abuse. Dalton had a grandfather-granddaughter relationship with both Victoria and Cathy. Both granddaughters were of similar age at the time of the alleged abuse. Both granddaughters described a "game" called "This Little Piggy," which involved kissing and tickling while the girls were undressed. Furthermore, both girls testified that Dalton encouraged their silence by characterizing the game as a "secret" and by telling them that other family members would be angry with them if they found out. The trial court did not abuse its discretion in determining that the charged and uncharged acts contained sufficient common features to infer the existence of a common system used by Dalton in committing the acts against Victoria and Cathy, and that Cathy's testimony was therefore relevant to prove that Dalton committed criminal sexual conduct against Victoria. *See Sabin, supra* at 61-67.

The assistant prosecuting attorney should argue further that the trial court did not abuse its discretion in declining to exclude Cathy's testimony under MRE 403. The other acts evidence was relevant to show the *actus reus* of the offense. Although there is always the potential for prejudice when other acts evidence is admitted, the trial court did not err in determining that this danger did not "substantially" outweigh the probative value of the evidence.

In addition to arguing that Cathy's testimony was properly admitted, the assistant prosecuting attorney should argue that the error, if any, was harmless. Reversal of a conviction on the basis of a preserved, nonconstitutional claim of error is precluded unless the defendant demonstrates that, "upon an examination of the entire cause," it affirmatively appears that the error asserted undermined the reliability of the verdict, thereby making the error "outcome determinative." *People v Snyder*, 462 Mich 38, 45 (2000); *People v Lukity*, 460 Mich 484, 495-96 (1999). The assistant prosecuting attorney should argue that, in the context of the untainted evidence—including Victoria's testimony—Dalton had failed to demonstrate that it is more probable than not that the outcome would have been different without the alleged evidentiary error.

Two Student Answers—February 2001

Question 8—Evidence—9 points

Evidence of prior bad acts committed by defendant may always be admissible to show motive, intent, common plan or scheme, & bias. However, such evidence (unless it goes towards a character trait for honesty) is discretionary. The court may allow the evidence in. In deciding whether to allow the evidence, the court will conduct a "balancing test," to see if the evidence is more probative than prejudicial.

In this case, the extrinsic evidence of a common plan is the testimony of a 13 year old child who says defendant used to commit CSC against her also. Defendant was never charged or convicted of the accusation. The evidence is prima facie prejudicial against defendant. But it also tends to substantiate the victim's testimony and shows a common plan. Tough call!

Here, the trial court allowed the testimony. Unless there is evidence that clearly does not substantiate the trial judge's discretion, the ruling will not be overturned. The standard of review at the COA level is clear & convincing evidence. Here, it is not so clear that the overall weight of evidence is so one-sided against the judge's discretion.

Note that the evidence may still come in during impeachment of any of the witnesses and/or the defendant by simply asking "were you aware that the defendant engaged in CSC against any other family members?"

Question 8—Evidence—8 points

As assistant prosecuting attorney assigned to this case, I would argue to the Court of Appeals that this appeal was brought here properly in that Defendant preserved his right to appeal by having his counsel properly object to the introduction of similar acts of sexual misconduct against another granddaughter, the same being relevant to show a scheme, a plan, or absence of accident. Such objective as noted on the record entitled Defendant to be before this court as such objective was not granted.

The issue we are dealing with regards the admission of evidence relating to prior bad acts in relation to character evidence under named circumstances and in most instances evidence of prior bad acts is not admissible as its value is more prejudicial to the Defendant than probative. However, in the case at hand we are dealing with children rendering this matter very serious and sensitive and to make matters worse, family. We don't have an issue of hearsay here, presented in court to prove the bulk of the matter asserted, as 13 year old Cathy is not or did not testify as to something she or anyone else really said or spoke, but rather as to an event that occurred.

It's the opinion of the state that the evidence of the prior misconduct should have been allowed so as to show this is not the first time this has occurred; it has occurred before and Defendant had gotten away with it and now—not saying Defendant is a bad person with many habits of legendary criminal record—this can be introduced because it relates to and directly deals with the crime Defendant is accused of.

Though the allowance of Cathy's testimony may seem prejudiced to Defendant, it would appear that the state's case against Defendant was already strong enough with the arrest and conviction on the charges still could have been obtained.

It is my argument that no reversible error occurred.

July 2001—Question 13

Dudley Dopefiend was driving down Michigan Avenue in Ingham County, Michigan, when he was stopped for speeding. Officer Mike McDonald became suspicious when he noticed the smell of burnt marijuana. Officer McDonald asked Dopefiend if he had any drugs in the car. Dopefiend responded that he did not, and told Officer McDonald that he was free to "look around." During the course of the search, Officer McDonald found a dufflebag stuffed under the front passenger seat. When he asked Dopefiend whether he could look inside, Dopefiend responded, "whatever." Inside the dufflebag was 650 grams of cocaine in a plastic bag. Despite his protestations that the dufflebag was not his, Dopefiend was arrested and charged in state court with the crime of possession with intent to deliver more than 650 grams of cocaine.

At trial, Dopefiend's defense was that he was "set up." He testified that the cocaine was not his, and that he had never even seen cocaine before. In support of his defense, Dopefiend presented the testimony of William Winston. Winston testified that Dopefiend was a childhood friend and that he knew from personal experience that Dopefiend was an honest, hardworking person who would never become involved with drugs.

In an attempt to impeach Winston's testimony, the prosecutor presented as a rebuttal witness Winston's ex-girlfriend, Rhonda Riley. Over Dopefiend's objection, Riley testified that Winston has a reputation of being a liar. Riley further testified, again over objection, that Winston is not worthy of belief because she once saw him falsify an application for a concealed weapons permit.

The jury convicted Dopefiend as charged. Dopefiend has filed an appeal arguing that the trial court erred in allowing Riley to testify about Winston's claimed reputation for untruthfulness and about seeing him put false information on a concealed weapons permit application.

You are a law clerk in the Court of Appeals. Advise your judge on the merits of the issues raised in Dopefiend's appeal.

Model Answer to Question 13

Dopefiend has a valid argument with respect to one of his two claims of error.

As an initial matter, Riley was properly permitted to testify about Winston's reputation for truthfulness. MRE 608(a) provides that:

> [t]he credibility of a witness may be attacked or supported by evidence in the form of opinion or reputation, but subject to these limitations: (1) the evidence may refer only to character for truthfulness or untruthfulness, and (2) evidence of truthful character is admissible only after the character of the witness for truthfulness has been attacked by opinion or reputation evidence or otherwise.

Because Riley's testimony was admitted for the purpose of attacking Winston's credibility, and because the testimony concerned only Winston's character for untruthfulness, it was properly admitted pursuant to MRE 608(a).

However, Riley should not have been permitted to testify that she saw Winston falsify an application for a concealed weapons permit. MRE 608(b) provides that:

> [s]pecific instances of the conduct of a witness, for the purpose of attacking or supporting the witness' credibility, other than conviction of crime as provided in Rule 609, may not be proved by extrinsic evidence. They may, however, in the discretion of the court, if probative of truthfulness or untruthfulness, be inquired into on cross-examination of the witness (1) concerning the witness' character for truthfulness or untruthfulness, or (2) concerning the character for truthfulness of untruthfulness of another witness as to which character the witness being cross-examined has testified.

Riley's testimony constituted "extrinsic evidence" concerning a specific instance of Winston's conduct. Although MRE 609, which permits the admission of evidence concerning certain crimes for impeachment purposes, might have provided a basis for the admission of Riley's testimony had Winston been convicted of a crime in connection with his alleged falsification of the concealed weapons permit application, Riley did not testify that Winston was ever convicted of any crime. Accordingly, the trial court should have sustained Dopefiend's objection to that portion of Riley's testimony. The prosecution could have asked the trial court, in its discretion, to allow it to ask Winston on cross-examination whether he had ever lied on an application for a concealed weapons permit. Such deceptive conduct would certainly be probative of truthfulness. However, the prosecution could not, consistent with MRE 608(b), introduce extrinsic evidence of this conduct.

Two Student Answers—July 2001

Question 13—Evidence—9 points

Evidence—character of witness
608—Reputation and opinion by lay person as to reputation of liar permissible
608 & 609—False info on CCW permit—prior bad acts to attack witnesses character as to truthfulness—609 for any convictions—none here
no extrinsic evidence
only permissible to attack credibility for truthfulness on cross—or as rebuttal witness
607—anyone can be impeached

The issue here is what are the merits of the issues raised in Dopefiend's appeal?

Dopefiend raises two issues in his appeal regarding character evidence of a witness, used by the prosecutor's witness, to impeach the witness of the defendant, Dopefiend. Firstly, the defendant objects to the testimony of Riley, a rebuttal witness called by the prosecutor, against a character witness of the defendant, Winston. Defendant objects to statements by Riley that Winston had a reputation for untruthfulness. Under Michigan Rules of Evidence 608, reputation and opinion testimony can be used to rebut and impeach the testimony of another witness. Such testimony can come from a lay witness, however biased, and is permissible.

Secondly, Defendant has an objection to testimony by Riley that she saw Winston put false information on a concealed weapons permit application. Under Michigan Rules of Evidence (MRE) such testimony of prior bad acts by the witness must relate to the witness' character for truthfulness and must only be permitted on cross-examination or rebuttal. No extrinsic evidence is permitted. If such conduct resulted in a felony conviction, then MRE 609 would apply and regardless of punishment, under MRE 609(a)(2), such crimes of untruthfulness would be relevant. However, in this case the facts do not show that the witness was convicted of such actions.

The defendant might argue that such conduct by Winston was hearsay because it was conduct, out of court, being offered in court for its truth regarding Winston's character. The prosecution can argue that it is not being offered as true but as evidence of impeachment and therefore not hearsay at all.

Consequently, under 608, since both statements regarding the merit of the defendant's claim concern the truthfulness of a character witness used in criminal proceeding where character is not at issue—the appeal should be denied. The lower court correctly allowed the rebuttal testimony of Riley to impeach the character of a witness. (Under MRE 607, anyone (witness) can be impeached).

Question 13—Evidence—9 points

The first issue is whether defendant, Dopefiend, may testify on behalf of his own criminal trial. The U.S. Constitution allows this personal testimony & it is relevant to the fact finder as to the guilt or non-guilt of a defendant regarding the offense (MRE 401). Dopefiend can testify on his behalf claiming he was "set up" even if he knows he is lying.

Dopefiend may also call a witness in his defense to substantiate defendant's claim that Dopefiend was an "honest, hard-working person" who would never become involved with drugs. This witness testimony is based on personal opinion of the witness, based on his own perception of the defendant, from past life time experiences.

On our facts, it appears that defendant, Dopefiend, "opened the door" to be impeached regarding Winston's testimony. The rule is that the prosecutor may either question the defendant's witness about his opinion or knowledge of defendant—which the prosecutor chose not to—or present a rebuttal witness.

On our facts, the prosecutor may call a rebuttal witness to testify as to Winston's truthfulness. Opinion or reputation evidence is allowed to impeach the witness. Winston's girlfriend likely has personal knowledge of Winston's reputation as she was intimately in contact with him & may have even associated with Winston's friends. This impeachment evidence would be allowed. On the other hand the specific act of putting false info on a concealed weapons permit would not. There is no felony conviction nor misdemeanor, & the specific act is therefore not allowed.

As to advising my judge, the trial ct did not err in allowing Riley to testify about Winston's claimed reputation but did err in allowing testimony about seeing him put false info on a concealed weapons permit application.

February 2002—Question 15

Prudence Patterson was shopping in downtown Whoville. As she entered the Acme Anvil Shop, she tripped over a piece of weatherstripping on the threshold of the door, fell, and fractured her hip.

Dennis DeFang, owner and proprietor of the Acme Anvil Shop, ran to help her as she lay on the floor of the store. He called to one of his employees to call for an ambulance. Prudence protested that she didn't have health insurance and couldn't afford an ambulance. Dennis assured Prudence not to "worry about it." He stated that he would "take care of the bills."

Six months later, Prudence filed suit against the Acme Anvil Shop, seeking $500,000 for damages relating to the injury. DeFang initially offered to settle the case, but withdrew the offer when Prudence refused to settle for less than $200,000. DeFang balked at that amount of money, stating that he merely leased the property, did not own it and was not responsible for the condition of the weatherstripping.

Through the course of discovery, Prudence's attorney learned that the Acme Anvil Shop was covered by a $1,000,000 liability policy. He also learned that, after Prudence was injured, Dennis DeFang replaced the weatherstripping with a narrower type that was not as likely to pose a trip hazard.

The Acme Anvil Shop has filed a motion to dismiss the case, claiming that there is no evidence showing that Acme Anvil Shop was responsible for the weatherstripping or was negligent. In response, Prudence's attorney points to DeFang's offer to "take care of the bills," his offer to settle the case, the insurance policy, and DeFang's replacement of the weatherstripping after Prudence's fall.

You are the judge deciding the motion. Discuss the propriety of the evidence proffered by the plaintiff in opposing the motion to dismiss.

Model Answer to Question 15

Under MRE 409, statements offering or promising to pay medical expenses are not admissible to prove liability for an injury. The underlying policy of the rule is to encourage assistance to an injured person. (*Wade & Strom*, Michigan Courtroom Evidence, p 165.) However, the evidence is admissible to prove other matters, such as control over the instrumentality that caused the injury. In this case, the evidence of DeFang's statements would not be admissible to establish liability but would be admissible to show control over the weatherstripping.

Similarly, evidence of a settlement offer is not admissible to prove liability under MRE 408. The rule also prohibits the admission of any statements made during compromise negotiations. However, evidence that is otherwise discoverable is not excluded merely because it is presented or raised during settlement negotiations. In this case, DeFang's offer to settle would not be admissible to establish the Anvil Shop's liability.

Under MRE 411, evidence of the presence or absence of liability insurance is not admissible to establish negligence or wrongdoing. However, evidence of liability insurance may be admissible for other purposes, such as proof of agency, to show bias or prejudice, or to prove ownership or control, if controverted. In Prudence's case, evidence of the insurance policy is not admissible to show the Anvil Shop's negligence. However, it would be admissible to prove DeFang's control over the premises.

DeFang's replacement of the weatherstripping would be governed by MRE 407. When remedial measures are taken after an event which, if taken previously, would have made the event less likely to occur, evidence of the subsequent remedial measures is not admissible to prove negligence or wrongdoing. However, this evidence is admissible when offered for other purposes, such as impeachment, ownership, control, or to show the feasibility of precautionary measures, if controverted. In this case, evidence that DeFang replaced the weatherstripping after Prudence's fall would not be admissible to establish negligence, but would be admissible to prove that DeFang was in control of the weatherstripping.

Two Student Answers—February 2002

Question 15—Evidence—10 points

The statement to take care of the bills cannot be used to show culpability on the part of Dennis. The rules of evidence exclude statements such as these because they are usually made by a good Samaritan who speaks only to calm down a hurt person. This situation is a little different because Dennis offered to take care of the bills after finding out about Prudences $ situation. Either way, evidence about taking care of bills will not stop a motion to dismiss. The offer to settle the case and anything else said in contemplation of settling is also inadmissible under the rules. This would also not stop a motion for dismissal.

The insurance policy of Dennis cannot be used to show liability but can be used to show ownership & control. In this case, ownership of the store is an issue because Dennis is claiming that he only leases and is therefore not liable. Since this is an issue in the case, evidence of liability insurance can be used to show ownership and control. The replacement of the weather stripping is inadmissable to show liability but like the insurance policy can be used to show ownership and control. This is called a subsequent remedial measure.

Both the insurance policy and subsequent remedial measure can be used to oppose the motion of dismissal.

Question 15—Evidence—10 points

Issue

Acme's motion to dismiss—is there enough evidence or are the Plaintiff's proofs enough?

Plaintiff's proofs are enough to proceed with the case based on the evidence.

(1) Offer to take care of the bills

Normally offers to pay medical expenses by a defendant can not be used to prove liability. Here, Prudence was covered about the $ b/c she had no insurance + defendant made the statement in order to get an ambulance there. Thus, they may be admissible for the purpose of showing the plaintiff's state of mind and that the events occurred at the defendant's store. Plus, if defendant is claiming non responsibility, this fact could show defendant was in fact an authority/responsible person for the store to give such an act.

(2) Offer to settle the case

Normally settlement offers are not allowed to prove liability or into evidence in general. However, if defendant is going to claim that they merely leased the property then it may be used to show ownership (authority to settle) or for impeachment purposes.

(3) Insurance policy

Defendant wouldn't be covered for that much w/out being more than a leasee. Can go to show ownership.

(4) Replacement of weatherstrip

Normally subsequent remedial measures by defendant are not allowed for public policy reasons but here they could be used to show ownership + control over the premises.

Overall, the plaintiff has enough evidence to proceed with the claim. Especially when viewed in favor of the non-moving party. In addition, if defendant is claiming non-ownership/resp, these may be issues of fact for jury to decide (as is the duty of defendant to its business invitees when they are injured on the premises).

July 2002—Question 13

Kosmo Kranmer and his portly friend, Neeman, discovered that they could earn extra cash by giving sausage making demonstrations and selling kielbasa at county fairs around the country. While on a tour stop at the Bay County Hog Festival. Kranmer suffered a severe eye injury when the Sausage Queen meat-rolling machine he was operating malfunctioned and began shooting out pellets of pork at speeds nearing 100 miles per hour.

In the ambulance on his way to the hospital, Kranmer phoned his attorney, Jackson Child, to determine whether he had a cause of action for his injuries. Child exclaimed that he was familiar with the Sausage Queen—known in plaintiff's bar circles as the Tasty Death Trap—and its manufacturer, Vandelay Industries. After agreeing to represent Kranmer in a products liability action against Vandelay. Child enthusiastically boarded a plane bound for Michigan and began interviewing eye witnesses that afternoon.

In preparation for trial, Child hired several engineers and meat industry specialists to examine the Sausage Queen and prepare reports. Child ultimately retained only Abe Groman, the "sausage king of Chicago," to testify at trial.

A year later, Kranmer filed his product liability action against Vandelay. Vandelay defended on the basis that Kranmer and Neeman had altered the Sausage Queen, rendering it unstable and unfit for use. Counsel for Vandelay filed a discovery request seeking (1) Child's notes regarding witnesses' statements on the day of the accident; (2) responses to interrogatories concerning the identity and findings of all experts hired in preparation for trial; and (3) any documents reflecting Child's impressions and theories of the case. Vandelay explained that the statements of the eyewitnesses were crucial to its defense because the witnesses' memories had faded by the time Kranmer initiated litigation and because no other contemporaneous evidence existed. Vandelay also explained that it wished to compare its experts' conclusions with those of Kranmer's experts. Vandelay additionally issued a subpoena duces tecum to the keeper of the records of Karamazov Fairs, Inc., the organizer of the Hog Festival, seeking production of a videotape believed to include footage of Neeman taking apart and reassembling the Sausage Queen prior to the demonstration.

Child refused to turn over the requested materials, contending that they were all privileged work product. Bay Circuit Judge Dabu Dhatt ordered disclosure of all of the requested materials. Judge Dhatt additionally denied a motion to quash the subpoena issued to Karamazov and ordered that the videotape be produced for inspection. Child decried the ruling as outrageous, egregious, and preposterous, and immediately filed an interlocutory appeal, which was granted.

You are a law clerk to one of the judges on the Court of Appeals panel that will decide this appeal. Advise your judge concerning the merits of Kranmer's appeal, focusing specifically on whether the four categories of requested items are discoverable under the Michigan Court Rules.

Model Answer to Question 13

MCR 2.302(b)(1) provides that parties may obtain discovery "regarding any matter, not privileged, which is relevant to the subject matter involved in the pending action, whether it relates to the claim or defense of the party seeking discovery or to the claim or defense of another party, including the existence, description, nature, custody, condition, and location of books, documents, or other tangible things and the identity and location of persons having knowledge of a discoverable matter." The information sought need only be "reasonably calculated" to lead to the discovery of admissible evidence.

However, MCR 2.302(b)(3)(a) provides further that a party may obtain discovery of documents and tangible things prepared in anticipation of litigation or for trial by or for another party or another party's representative "only on a showing that the party seeking discovery has substantial need of the materials in the preparation of the case and it's unable without undue hardship to obtain the substantial equivalent of the materials by other means."

(1) Child's Notes Regarding Eyewitnesses' Statements: These notes were probably subject to disclosure. The trial court might properly have determined that, because the witnesses' statements were taken shortly after the accident and because Vandelay was unable to begin its investigation of the accident until several months later, Vandelay had demonstrated that it had a substantial need for the notes and would not be able to obtain the substantial equivalent of the materials due to the witnesses' declining memories. *See Lynd v Chocolay Twp*, 153 Mich App 188 (1986).

(2) Interrogatories of Hired Experts: The trial court properly ordered Kranmer to answer interrogatories to the extent they applied to Abe Groman's anticipated testimony. Pursuant to MCR 2.302(b)(4)(a)(i), "where an expert is expected to testify at trial," facts known and opinions held by the expert acquired or developed in anticipation of litigation or for trial are obtainable through interrogatories directed at a party. Under this Rule, a party is required to identify each person he expects to call as an expert witness at trial, to state the subject matter about which the expert is expected to testify, and to state the substance of the facts and opinions to which the expert is expected to testify and a summary of the grounds for each opinion.

However, the trial court erred in ordering interrogatories concerning the identity and findings of any other hired experts because they were not expected to testify at trial. Under MCR 2.302(b)(4)(b), a party generally may not discover the identity of and facts known or opinions held by an expert who has been retained or specially employed by another party in anticipation of litigation or preparation for trial and who is not expected to be called as a witness at trial unless the requesting party shows "exceptional circumstances under which it is impracticable for the party seeking discovery to obtain facts or opinions on the same subject by other means." Where counsel simply wished to compare the findings of Kranmer's experts with those of Vandelay's own experts, no showing of exceptional circumstances was established.

(3) Child's Impressions and Theories: The trial court erred in ordering disclosure of the requested documents containing Child's impressions and legal theories. Pursuant to MCR 2.302(b)(3)(a), "the court shall protect against disclosure of the mental impressions, conclusions, opinions or legal theories of an attorney or other representative of a party concerning the litigation."

(4) Karamazov Videotape: Pursuant to MCR 2.305, a party may issue a subpoena to a nonparty to compel production or inspection of designated items. The videotape is not protected from disclosure as privileged trial preparation material under MCR 2.302 because (1) it was not prepared in anticipation of litigation and (2) it was not prepared by a party or a party's representative. MCR 2.302(3)(a); *see also In re Subpeona Duces Tecum to Wayne Co Prosecutor*, 191 Mich App 90 (1991). Because the videotape contents may be relevant to Vandelay's defense or may lead to the discovery of admissible evidence, the trial court did not err in ordering its production.

Two Student Answers—July 2002

Question 13—Evidence—9 points

1. Child's notes regarding witness statements the day of the accident—work product. An attorney's notes, thoughts, impressions, legal theories are privileged work product. Opposing may only request if they show it would cause undue

hardship & there is no other way to get the information. Vandelay falls short here. He may go out and interview the witnesses on his own. As for the witness memory fading—make the argument to a jury. (See #3)

2. Responses to interrogatories concerning the identity & findings of all experts hired in preparation for trial. Childs will only need to produce Abe Groman, the specialist retained for trial, not the others. Vandelay is free to seek its own specialists, experts, interview them, etc. The only expert report that is discoverable is the one actually used for trial.
3. Any documents reflecting Child's impressions & theories of the case—clearly work product. These do not even include witness statements as in #1 above. The witness statements could be discoverable, but not the attorney's notes and certainly not his thoughts & impressions.
4. Subpoena duces tecum regarding the video tape—discoverable. It goes directly to Vandelay's defense that Neeman altered the machine. Any evidence that tends to be relevant should be admissible. This video tape does not fall within the attorney work-product privilege as Child asserted.

Question 13—Evidence—9 points

Attorney's Work Product Rule: Child will want to protect his own work he has done in preparation for trial. Under the work product rule, he may not be compelled to produce his opinions and mental impressions for the other side. However, if the other side argues they will not be otherwise able to get the information they need to defend, the court may look at privileged material "in camera" and cover the parts related to the attorney's work product (mental impressions) and leave the rest to assist the other side.

However, if the other side could adequately find out information otherwise, without undue hardship, this request will be denied. An attorney cannot seek the other side's work product if the attorney is being lazy. One year after the incident does not mean Defendant is unable to find out enough information to defend, as witnesses and evidence are still recent and fresh. Child will argue that his notes of the witnesses apos; statements and his mental impressions are privileged work product and should not be subpoenaed by the other side.

Defendant's Side: Defendant will argue it has been one year since the incident and it would be a hardship to get discovery without reference to Child's materials, even work product materials. And the video tape is objective materials, not produced in anticipation of litigation, so is not privileged in any way. The identification of experts, plus their findings, is not privileged in any way either, so cannot be resisted by Child.

Conclusion: The court is likely to order (properly) that the identification of experts (here just 1 expert), his findings, and the video tape are all properly discoverable by Defendant, as Child must allow them to be discoverable as required by rules of discovery. However, Child's work product (impressions) cannot—without a showing of hardship—be compelled by Defendant. The witnesses' statement are also work product, but if Defendant cannot obtain and interview the witnesses after 1 year, the court may view them in camera, and blocking out any mental impressions by Child, allow (for hardship purposes) Defendant to obtain them.

July 2002—Question 14

Damian Draconian has been charged with open murder in the death of his mother, Vonda Draconian. According to police reports, Mrs. Draconian was found dead in her bathtub on January 16, 2002. According to the coroner, the cause of death was drowning. Draconian pleaded not guilty, stating that he was attending a Star Trek convention at the time of his mother's death.

At his trial, the prosecutor calls Nancy Nurse to the stand. Nancy worked as a private duty nurse for Gladys Goodfellow, Vonda's sister. Nancy testified that Gladys died on January 3, 2002 after a long illness. Nancy further testified that, on December 28th, Gladys woke up after taking a nap and made the following statement to Nancy: "Listen, I don't have much longer to live, and I have to let somebody know this before I die, just in case. Yesterday, Damian visited me and told me that he was very angry with his mother and wanted to kill her and would make it look like an accident."

Defense counsel immediately objected, stating that this unanticipated testimony was inadmissible as hearsay.

You are the trial court judge. How do you rule on defense counsel's objection? Explain your decision.

Model Answer to Question 14

Nancy Nurse's testimony is hearsay. Hearsay is an out-of-court statement, offered to prove the truth of the matter asserted. MRE 801(c). Hearsay is not admissible unless it falls within one of the exceptions contained in the Michigan Court Rules. MRE 802.

In this case, there are two out-of-court statements contained within Nancy's testimony—Draconian's statement to his Aunt Gladys, and Gladys' statement to Nancy Nurse. As such, Nancy's testimony is hearsay within hearsay, which is not admissible unless each part of the combined statements fall within one of the hearsay exceptions. MRE 805.

Draconian's statement to Gladys is admissible as a party admission under MRE 801(d)(2)(a). A statement is a party admission when the statement is offered against a party and is the party's own statement, either in an individual or representative capacity.

Gladys' statement to Nancy Nurse is not admissible as a statement under belief of impending death under MRE 804(b)(2). To qualify under 804, the declarant must be unavailable. To qualify under MRE 804(b)(2), the statement must be offered in a homicide prosecution or civil action, it must be made by a declarant when the declarant believes his or her death to be imminent, and the statement must concern the cause or circumstances of the declarant's impending death.

In this case, the statement is being used in a homicide investigation, and was made when Gladys believed her death to be imminent. However, the statement does not concern the cause or circumstances of Gladys' death. Therefore, it is not admissible under that exception.

The statement is also not admissible as an excited utterance, MRE 803(2). Under that exception a statement is admissible if it relates to a startling event or condition and if it is made while the declarant remains under the stress of the startling event. Here, assuming that the statement made by Draconian to Gladys was a startling event, nothing in the fact pattern suggests that Gladys was still under the stress of the startling event when she made the statement to Nancy Nurse.

The statement is also not admissible under the catch-all hearsay exceptions for an unavailable witness, 804(b)(6). Pursuant to 804(b)(7), a hearsay statement is admissible if it is not specifically covered by the other enumerated hearsay exceptions and has equivalent circumstantial guarantees of trustworthiness. The judge must make a determination that the statement is evidence of a material fact, that the evidence is more probative than any other evidence that can be procured through reasonable efforts, and that the purpose of the rules and the interest of justice will best be served by admission of the statement into evidence.

This hearsay exception, MRE 804(b)(7), also contains a notice requirement. The proponent of the statement must advise the opposing party of its intention to offer the statement. The notice must provide the details of the statement, including the name and address of the declarant. The notice must be provided in advance of the trial or hearing, allowing sufficient time for the adverse party to prepare for the evidence. If the notice requirement is not satisfied, the statement *may not* be admitted.

In this case, the fact pattern indicates that the testimony was unanticipated; therefore, defense counsel did not have notice of the statement. Even if the statement met all of the other requirements of 804(b)(6), it cannot be admitted into evidence.

Defense counsel's objection should be sustained.

Student Answer—July 2002

Question 14—Evidence—10 points

Gladys' Statement

Was Gladys' statement hearsay? And if so, was there an exception to allow it in?

Hearsay is an out-of-court statement offered in evidence to prove the truth of the matter asserted. Here, Gladys was speaking out of court and the statement—if offered to prove Damian did the crime—would be to show Damian's crime. So on its face, it is hearsay.

Is there any exception to hearsay to allow the statement in for another purpose? A dying declaration of someone (Declarant) believing death is imminent may be allowed in to show plan or motive (proper non-hearsay purpose), but here Gladys was not dying and didn't indicate she believed she was dying. She just knew she would die soon. So probably this statement will not be allowed in.

Any other exception to get the Hearsay in?

Another exception to the Hearsay rule is a party admission. Here Gladys told Nancy Damian planned to kill his mother, and how he would do it. An exception to hearsay is a party admission (of guilt). Here Damian told another person he planned to kill his mother and how he would do it; this makes his statement, even though hearsay, a party admission.

The Conclusion

The problem here is, Damian did not make the admission to Nancy; he made it to Gladys, who told it to Nancy, so it's hearsay within hearsay. Each level of the hearsay must be a proper exception, which is not met here. The likely result is that the statement is not admissible, since (although in itself a party admission) it was not spoken to Nancy, but to a third person. There is no exception related to Nancy herself, so the statement is not likely to be admissible. It is "hearsay within hearsay."

February 2003—Question 7

Sideshow Dobb, a small-time crook with a somewhat below average IQ, was charged with the February 2003 attempted murder of Vart Vimpson in Springphield, Michigan. At trial, Judge Snider allowed the prosecutor, over defense counsel's objections, to cross-examine Dobb concerning four of his numerous prior convictions:

(1) a 2001 felony conviction for the attempted murder of his wife, Velma, for which he was imprisoned from February 2001 to February 2003;

(2) a 2000 misdemeanor conviction for false personation of a public officer following an incident in which Dobb donned the police chief's uniform, stole his police car, and issued a traffic citation to Fred Flanders, resulting in Dobb's imprisonment in the Springphield jail for the statutory maximum of one year;

(3) a 1998 felony conviction for armed robbery stemming from another unfortunate impersonation incident in which Dobb dressed up as a beloved children's television character and held up the local QuickieCart convenience store, resulting in Dobb's imprisonment from 1998 to 2000; and

(4) a 1992 felony conviction for false pretenses with intent to defraud for using Monopoly money to pay Phat Tony for a one-half interest in his Legitimate Businessman's Social Club, for which Dobb was imprisoned from February 1992 to February 1998.

Dobb denied that he was convicted of any of the above crimes. Judge Snider then allowed, over defense counsel's objection, the admission into evidence of public records establishing that Dobb was convicted of each of these offenses. Judge Snider did not indicate his reasons for allowing admission of the evidence.

Dobb has appealed from his conviction for the attempted murder of Vimpson. **You are a law clerk at the Michigan Court of Appeals. Advise your judge whether there is any merit to appellate counsel's argument that Judge Snider erred in allowing the prosecutor to impeach Dobb with evidence of his four prior convictions.**

Model Answer to Question 7

Background: Pursuant to MRE 609(a), for the purpose of attacking the credibility of a witness, evidence that the witness has been convicted of a crime is admissible if the evidence has been elicited from the witness or established by public record during cross-examination, and (1) the crime contained an element of dishonesty or false statement, or (2) the crime contained an element of theft, and (A) the crime was punishable by imprisonment in excess of one year or death under the law under which the witness was convicted, and (B) the court determines that the evidence has significant probative value on the issue of credibility and, if the witness is the defendant in a criminal trial, the court further determines that the probative value of the evidence outweighs its prejudicial effect. Under

MRE 609(b), for purposes of determining probative value under MRE 609(a)(2)(B), the court may consider only the age of the conviction and the degree to which a conviction of the crime is indicative of veracity; additionally, for purposes of determining prejudicial effect, the court shall consider only the conviction's similarity to the charged offense and the possible effects on the decisional process if admitting the evidence causes the defendant to elect not to testify. Under MRE 609(c), evidence of a conviction under the rule is not admissible if a period of more than ten years has elapsed since the date of the conviction or of the release of the witness from the confinement imposed for that conviction, whichever is the later date.

Pursuant to MRE 608(b), specific instances of the conduct of a witness for the purpose of attacking or supporting his credibility may not be proved by extrinsic evidence except as provided under MRE 609. Such specific instances of a witness's conduct may, in the discretion of the court, if probative of truthfulness or untruthfulness, be inquired into on cross-examination of the witness concerning the witness's character for truthfulness or untruthfulness.

1. 2001 Attempted Murder Conviction: The trial court erred in allowing the prosecutor to present evidence of Dobb's attempted murder conviction for purposes of impeachment. The conviction does not contain an element of dishonesty, false statement, or theft and was therefore not admissible under MRE 609(a). Furthermore, evidence of a conviction of attempted murder is not probative of Dobb's veracity and therefore was not admissible under MRE 608(b); moreover, extrinsic evidence is not admissible under MRE 608(b).

2. 2000 False Personation: The trial court properly allowed the prosecutor to present evidence of Dobb's misdemeanor conviction for false personation of a public officer. Under MRE 609(a)(1), use of extrinsic proof of a conviction of a crime containing an element of dishonesty or false statement is proper. Furthermore, there is no requirement under MRE 609(a)(1) that such a crime be punishable by imprisonment in excess of one year or death. Because false personation of an officer includes an element of dishonesty or false statement, the public record of this conviction was admissible.

3. 1998 Armed Robbery Conviction: This evidence would presumably have been admissible pursuant to MRE 609(a)(2), which permits the admission of extrinsic evidence to establish a conviction of a crime containing an element of theft where the crime was punishable by imprisonment in excess of one year or death and where the court determines that the evidence has significant probative value on the issue of credibility and that the probative value of the evidence outweighs its prejudicial effect. However, under MRE 609(b), Judge Snider was required to articulate, on the record, his analysis of the probative value and prejudicial effect of the evidence. Judge Snider erred in allowing the prosecutor to present evidence of the conviction without performing this analysis on the record.

4. 1992 False Pretenses Conviction: The trial court properly permitted the prosecutor to present extrinsic evidence of Dobb's false pretenses conviction under MRE 609(a)(1). Although the conviction itself was more than ten years old, pursuant to MRE 609(c), such a conviction is admissible as long as a period of more than ten years has not elapsed since the release of the witness from the confinement imposed for that conviction. Because Dobb was not released from confinement until 1998, extrinsic evidence of the conviction was properly admitted.

Student Answer—February 2003

Question 7—Evidence—8 points

Issue

Whether the prosecution can use the 4 prior convictions to impeach Dobb's testimony.

Rule

As a general rule, character evidence is inadmissible to prove character. The exception is where it is used to impeach testimony of a witness.

Prosecution may ask the witness about prior convictions, but may not introduce extrinsic evidence to prove it.

In addition, crimes older than ten years (if conviction of the crime was more than 10 years from the date of current testimony) cannot be used.

Furthermore, felonies may all be inquired into. However, misdemeanors may only be inquired into if they are crimes involving truth or honesty.

Application

1992—Here, the 1992 crime is over ten years since the conviction. Thus the prosecution won't be allowed to ask Dobb about it.

1998—This is not older then 10 years and it's an armed robbery which is a felony, thus this one will be allowed in.

2000—This crime isn't older than ten years. Also it's a crime involving honesty so it'll come in.

2001—This conviction is probably the best one (along with the false personation crime) to attack Dobb's creditability. Here, it's the prosecution's goal to try to poke holes in Dobb's testimony (through impeachment) so the jury won't buy his testimony.

Issue

Whether the judge committed reversible error?

Rule

If the judge abuses his discretion in such a way as to cause a plain error in the outcome of a trial, than this is reversible error.

Application

Here, there doesn't appear to be a plain error. Allowing the 1992 conviction in was likely harmless error. Dobb already has another 2 felonies and a conviction for impersonation of an office.

It's not likely that simply allowing the 1992 conviction to be inquired into will be considered plain error.

February 2003—Question 9

After billionaire tycoon Franklin Fatcat died intestate, Paul Parity comes to your law office for a consultation. He claims that he is Fatcat's illegitimate child and the rightful heir to the Fatcat fortune. In addition to being willing to submit to scientific testing, Parity offers the following documentation to establish that Fatcat is his father:

1. A 1971 newspaper clipping of Parity's birth announcement, wherein Fatcat is named as the father.
2. Three birthday cards sent to Parity as a child, allegedly sent by Fatcat and signed, "Your father, Franklin Fatcat."
3. A photocopy of a notarized copy of Franklin Fatcat's advanced medical directives, listing Parity as next of kin.

You have decided to take Paul Parity's case. Aside from hearsay issues, discuss any other potential obstacles that you will need to consider in order to have this evidence admitted in court.

Model Answer to Question 9

As a "condition precedent to admissibility," evidence such as documents, signatures and voice recordings must be authenticated. MRE 901. This requirement is satisfied by evidence of authenticity sufficient to support a finding that the evidence is what the proponent claims it to be. While some documents are self-authenticating, MRE 902, other documents require extrinsic evidence to establish authentication.

The 1971 birth announcement is self-authenticating. MRE 902(6). No extrinsic evidence of authenticity is required.

The three signed birthday cards require authentication. The genuineness of the signature could be established by non-expert opinion, if the non-expert was familiar with Fatcat's signature and did not acquire his or her familiarity for the purposes of the litigation. MRE 901(b)(2). The genuineness of the signature could also be established by an expert witness or the trier of fact, if the questioned signature is compared to a known signature. MRE 901(b)(3).

Acknowledged documents, such as Franklin Fatcat's notarized advanced medical directives, are self-authenticating. MRE 902(8). However, Parity possesses a photocopy, not the original document. Generally, the original is required, except as otherwise provided in the rules or by statute. MRE 1002.

There are a few exceptions to the general rule requiring the original document. The original document is *not required* if it is lost or destroyed, cannot be obtained by judicial process or legal procedure, or the original document is in the possession of the adverse party, who does not produce it at the hearing. MRE 1004. Under those circumstances, a duplicate is admissible to the same extent as the original document, unless a genuine question is raised regarding the authenticity of the original *or* it would be unfair to admit the duplicate in lieu of the original. MRE 1003.

Student Answer—February 2003

Question 9—Evidence—9 points

Issue

Aside from hearsay issues, potential obstacles that will be needed to be considered?

Rule

We must look into the authentication of the documents. Authentication can be done through witness verification or it can be self verified. We must also look at impeachment problems. Furthermore, we may have an issue with the Best Evidence Rule. In a civil case, character evidence may come into play because with child custody issues we may use opinion, reputation, and specific acts to prove child custody.

Here, with Statement #1 it is self authenticating because it is a newspaper and newspapers are self authenticating. The birthday cards are probably not self authenticating because we really don't know who wrote it until we have a: (1) witness verify the handwriting (2) expert compare handwriting or (3) jury compare handwriting. The photocopy will probably be self authenticating because it was notarized and notarizations are usually self authenticating. Next, impeachment problems may come up because these statements may be impeached by prior inconsistent statement or prior statement made under oath, deposition, or trial. The Best Evidence Rule may come up with statement #3, the photocopy because the original is the best evidence unless it can be shown that there is valid reason why the original can't be obtained. Next, character evidence may play a role since this is a civil case involving child custody. To determine paternity we use DNA in Michigan. Here, in character evidence we can use opinion, reputation, or specific acts to verify the child's paternity and if he truly is the son of Fatcat. In conclusion, we may have some problems, especially with the birthday card, unless a witness verifies handwriting and the photocopy of medical directives will play a problem with the Best Evidence Rule, but will probably come in because notarized.

July 2003—Question 1

Darwin Dilmore, age 49, was arrested and charged with first-degree criminal sexual conduct involving his then four-year-old niece, Valerie. According to the complaint, Dilmore digitally penetrated Valerie while in the swimming pool at a family picnic. While Dilmore admits attending the family picnic and swimming in the pool, he denies that any sexual contact took place.

Prior to the commencement of the trial, the prosecution provides notice that it intends to call Walter Wilson as a witness. Wilson plans to testify that four years ago, when Wilson was thirteen years old, Dilmore offered Wilson beer and cigarettes if Wilson would pose nude and permit Dilmore to take pictures. The prosecution maintains that the evidence is relevant to establish a scheme, plan or system of molestation.

Defense counsel makes a motion to exclude the evidence, arguing that the evidence is irrelevant and highly prejudicial.

You are the state judge assigned to this case. Based on current Michigan case law rules of evidence, how will you decide the motion and why?

Model Answer to Question 1

The judge should exclude the evidence. MRE 404(b) is the evidentiary rule that governs the admissibility of the evidence. Generally, evidence of other crimes or acts is not admissible to prove the character of a person in order to show that the person acted in conformity with that character. However, evidence of other crimes or acts can be admissible *for other purposes*. The rule provides:

(1) Evidence of other crimes, wrongs, or acts is not admissible to prove the character of a person in order to show action in conformity therewith. It may, however, be admissible for other purposes such as proof of motive, opportunity, intent, preparation, scheme, plan, or system in doing an act, knowledge, identity, or absence of mistake or accident when the same is material, whether such other crimes, wrongs, or acts are contemporaneous with, or prior or subsequent to the conduct at issue in the case.

(2) The prosecution in a criminal case shall provide reasonable notice in advance of trial, or during trial if the court excuses pretrial notice on good cause shown, of the general nature of any such evidence it intends to introduce at trial and the rationale, whether or not mentioned in subparagraph (B)(1), for admitting the evidence. If necessary to a determination of the admissibility of the evidence under this rule, the defendant shall be required to state the theory or theories of defense, limited only by the defendant's privilege against self-incrimination.

In order to be admissible under MRE 404(b): (1) the evidence must be offered for a proper purpose; (2) the evidence must be relevant; and the probative value of the evidence must not be substantially outweighed by unfair prejudice. *People v VanderVliet*, 444 Mich 52 (1993). In addition, the trial court may, upon request, provide a limiting jury instruction.

The issue in this case is whether the evidence is being offered for a proper purpose under MRE 404(b). The theory of logical relevance proffered by the prosecutor is one of scheme, plan, or system. In *People v Sabin*, 463 Mich 43 (2000), the Michigan Supreme Court clarified this theory of logical relevance. Scheme or plan can happen in one of two circumstances—where the charged and uncharged acts are each a piece of a larger plan, OR where a scheme is used repeatedly to perpetuate separate but similar crimes.

Generally similarity is insufficient to establish a plan, scheme or system. There must be a "concurrence of common features." The common features must indicate the existence of a plan rather than a series of spontaneous acts, but the plan need not be distinctive or unusual.

In this case, there are not discernable common features between the charged and uncharged acts. The differences in age, gender, familial status do not indicate any common features. In addition, the circumstances of the charged and uncharged acts are markedly different. The charged act involves a penetration in a family swimming pool, while the uncharged act involves an offer to take nude pictures (no touching or penetration) in exchange for beer and cigarettes. Because there are no common features between the charged and uncharged acts, the evidence is not properly admissible to show a scheme, plan or system.

Two Student Answers—July 2003

Question 1—Evidence—9 points

This is a case where the prosecutor is trying to bring in a specific incident or act. The prosecutor also argues that it is a scheme, plan, or system of molestation but in fact its not the same scheme, plan or system. The witness will testify that 4 years ago the defendant offered beer & cigarettes for him to pose nude, which is a different crime than CSC 1st degree. So it's not the same scheme. I, the judge, should look to see if the probative value is greater than the prejudice. The testimony would be extremely prejudicial & under our laws prior crimes are not admitted as it is highly prejudicial and would create a bias in the trier of fact to convict the defendant based on the past criminal act. Past criminal acts only come in if it is a felony or crime involving dishonesty and within the past 10 years and only for impeachment of a witness. The defendant is not a witness so it is not for impeachment but for its substance. It is too prejudicial, it is not part of the "same scheme, plan or system", and it's not for impeachment purpose so therefore I will grant defense attorney motion and exclude the evidence. The two victims had different ages, the crime in this case involves sexual penetration of a minor, while the witness will testify to trying to get witness to pose nude & offering alcohol + cigarettes to a minor. Two misdemeanors & one felony but the felony is too prejudicial to come in. It is relevant to a degree but . . . [Student ran out of time.]

Question 1—Evidence—9 points

I would grant the motion. Under Michigan law including sex offenses a defendant's prior sexual act will not be admitted. The only time previous acts of sex will be admissible is when there is a defense of consent or where the parties will lose due process rights by not allowing into evidence the previous acts. According to the facts the prosecution is trying to admit this evidence under a common scheme or plan. The facts do not indicate this type of plan. There is nothing here to suggest that the defendant is using the same plan of modus operandi to molest these children. In one case the defendant was at a pool while attending a picnic. In the other instance the defendant was offering an underage child beer and cigs to pose nude. There is no common scheme or plan nor are the results or circumstances even close to being similar. One instance involves penetration while the other includes nude pics. Allowing this information into evidence would be more prejudicial than probative However this is not a prior conviction so there is less problem with this being considered admission of a prior bad act. While this information may be relevant it is probably more prejudicial then probative. Any information is relevant if it tends to help a jury understand what is going on. While most relevant information is allowable there are some exceptions, one being the facts we have here. Since the information does not show a common scheme or plan it is more prejudicial than probative.

February 2004—Question 8

Derrick Dartman is approached by Seth Seller, who is carrying a baggie labeled "Fat Jerky." Seller explains that Dartman can have the svelte body he's always dreamed of if he starts immediately on a Fat Jerky regimen. Seller states that Fat Jerky is an all-natural, completely legal laxative. Dartman, who is planning to audition to perform his German dance on Star Search, decides that he could stand to lose a couple pounds before becoming rich and famous. Dartman's friends, Lyle and Sam, warn Dartman that the "Fat Jerky" is really an illegal controlled substance, but Dartman waves them off, saying, "Screw you guys. I'm going home." Dartman then purchases the baggie of Fat Jerky. Officer Barlady, who has observed the transaction from behind a mail box, arrests Dartman and Seller. Dartman is charged with possession of methamphetamine. Seller is released in exchange for his testimony against Dartman.

The trial court rules against Dartman with respect to several evidentiary matters.

1. At trial, Seller is called to the stand by the prosecution and testifies that he told Dartman before the sale that Fat Jerky was really crystal meth. Seller then dies on the stand before defense counsel has an opportunity to cross-examine him concerning that testimony. Defense counsel seeks admission of Seller's former testimony given at Dartman's preliminary examination, that Seller told Dartman that the Fat Jerky was legal. The trial court refuses to admit the preliminary examination testimony.
2. The trial court refuses, on hearsay grounds, to allow defense counsel to call Lyle and Sam to the stand to testify that they heard Seller tell Dartman that Fat Jerky was legal.
3. Officer Barlady testifies that the packet of Fat Jerky was tested by Officer Ann Hash in the North Park Crime Laboratory and that Hash's lab report indicated that the Fat Jerky contained methamphetamine. Barlady explained that although he personally had no knowledge of the accuracy of the report, and that he in fact wasn't familiar with this "methwhatchamacallit," Hash was a well-respected police chemist who had never once misidentified a diet pill masquerading as crystal meth. Sadly, Hash had recently been abducted by aliens and was unavailable to testify. Over defense counsel's objection, the trial court holds that a sufficient foundation exists for admission, as a public record or business report, of Hash's report identifying the substance as methamphetamine.

Dartman is convicted as charged.

You are a law clerk for Dartman's hired appellate counsel. Is there ground for error in the trial court's evidentiary rulings with respect to (1) Seller's preliminary examination testimony, (2) the proposed testimony of Lyle and Sam, and (3) Hash's lab report?

Model Answer to Question 8

1. First, Seller's preliminary examination testimony was not inadmissible hearsay. Under MRE 804(b)(1), former testimony given as a witness at another hearing of the same or different proceeding is not excluded by the hearsay rule where the declarant is unavailable if the party against whom the testimony was offered had an opportunity and similar motive to develop the testimony by direct, cross, or redirect examination. Moreover, Seller's statement was not hearsay in any event because it was not being offered to prove the truth of the matter asserted (i.e., that the Fat Jerky was not an illegal substance). Rather, it was being offered to prove Dartman's state of mind (i.e., his belief that the Fat Jerky was or was not an illegal substance).

Additionally, under MRE 613(b), extrinsic evidence of a prior inconsistent statement by a witness is generally not admissible unless the witness is afforded an opportunity to explain or deny the evidence and the opposite party is afforded an opportunity to interrogate the witness thereon. However, Rule 613(b) also provides that such evidence may be admitted if "the interests of justice otherwise require." Here, Seller died on the witness stand before the defense had an opportunity to cross-examine him regarding his testimony that he told Dartman that the Fat Jerky was crystal meth. Therefore, even though Seller was unavailable to explain or deny the prior statement or to be examined by the prosecution regarding the statement, the statement was arguably admissible, in the interest of justice, to impeach his testimony.

2. A similar analysis applies to the proffered testimony of Lyle and Sam. First, the testimony was not hearsay because it was not offered to prove the truth of the matter asserted, but to prove that the statement was made and was the basis for Dartman's state of mind. Second, this extrinsic evidence of Seller's prior inconsistent statement was arguably admissible "in the interests of justice" under MRE 613(b).

3. The trial court reversibly erred in admitting Officer Hash's lab report. Under MRE 803(8), the hearsay rule does not exclude records setting forth (a) the activities of a public office or agency or (b) matters observed pursuant to duty imposed by law as to which matters there was a duty to report, "excluding, however, in criminal cases matters observed by police officers and other law enforcement personnel." The lab report at issue, prepared by Officer Hash, was adversarial. It was specifically prepared to establish the identity of the substance as methamphetamine. Because the report helped to establish an element of the crime by use of hearsay observations made by Officer Hash, the report cannot be admitted. *People v McDaniel*, 469 Mich 409 (2003). Nor was the report admissible under 803(6), which provides that records kept in the course of a regularly conducted business activity are not excluded by the hearsay rule "unless the source of information or the method or circumstances of preparation indicate lack of trustworthiness." The lab report was prepared in anticipation of litigation. Thus, it was inadmissible hearsay because the circumstances of its preparation indicated lack of truth worthiness. *McDaniel, supra.*

Student Answer—February 2004

Question 8—Evidence—None Available

Comment: Students did not perform well on this Evidence question. Therefore, there is no example of a "good" student answer. This question is a good example of how the Michigan Bar Examiners test Evidence. Notice that you not only need to know the specific rules of Evidence, but it is imperative that you know how to apply them to specific circumstances. The more examples you have that demonstrate how each rule works, the better. This model answer provides an excellent source from which to develop flash cards.

July 2004—Question 1

Peter Pabst spends a warm evening in July 2004 downing mass quantities of cheap beer at the corner bar. He then gets into his car and pulls into traffic. Almost immediately he is involved in a collision with a Dandy Sausage Company delivery truck driven by Dudley Dawg. Officers arrive at the scene and arrest Pabst, who is passed out in a heap of frozen bratwurst, for driving while intoxicated. Pabst, who was convicted in 2002 of operating a vehicle while under the influence of intoxicating liquor (OUIL), pleads guilty to a felony charge of OUIL, second offense; however, he is later permitted to withdraw the plea. Pabst ultimately pleads *nolo contendere* to a reduced misdemeanor charge of operating a vehicle while visibly impaired (OVI) and is sentenced to the maximum term of imprisonment (93 days).

Pabst subsequently brings a civil action against Dawg and Dandy Sausage Company, seeking compensation for damages to his car. Dandy defends on the basis that it did not own the delivery truck at the time of the accident. Dandy and Dawg additionally defend on the basis that Pabst was driving while intoxicated at the time of the accident and was 100 percent comparatively negligent in causing the accident.

On appeal from judgment awarding Pabst damages, Dandy and Dawg claim error concerning only the following evidentiary rulings of the trial court:

1. The trial court allowed Pabst to present a certificate of automobile insurance issued to Dandy, valid March through August 2004, listing the delivery truck as an insured vehicle.
2. The trial court refused to allow the defense to impeach Pabst's testimony with evidence of his 2002 OUIL conviction.
3. The trial court refused to admit evidence that Pabst had pleaded guilty of OUIL, second offense, following the accident.
4. The trial court refused to admit evidence of Pabst's conviction of OVI stemming from the accident.

You are a law clerk for the Court of Appeals. Draft a memo for your judge addressing whether error occurred in any of the cited evidentiary rulings.

Model Answer to Question 1

1. The trial court did not err in allowing the certificate of automobile insurance into evidence. Under MRE 411, evidence that a person was or was not insured against liability is not admissible upon the issue whether the person acted negligently or otherwise wrongfully. However, MRE 411 "does not require the exclusion of evidence of insurance against liability when offered for another purpose, such as proof of agency, ownership, or control, if controverted." Dandy claimed that it did not own the delivery truck at the time of the accident. The certificate of insurance issued to Dandy, listing the truck as an insured vehicle, was properly admitted to refute Dandy's asserted lack of ownership.

2. The trial court properly refused to allow the defense to impeach Pabst's testimony with evidence of his 2002 conviction of OUIL. Pursuant to MRE 609(a), for the purpose of attacking the credibility of a witness, evidence that the witness has been convicted of a crime is admissible if the evidence has been elicited from the witness or established by public record during cross-examination, and (1) the crime contained an element of dishonesty or false statement, or (2) the crime contained an element of theft, and (a) the crime was punishable by imprisonment in excess of one year or death under the law under which the witness was convicted, and (b) the court determines that the evidence has significant probative value on the issue of credibility and, if the witness is the defendant in a criminal trial, the court further determines that the probative value of the evidence outweighs its prejudicial effect. The crime of OUIL contains neither an element of dishonesty or false statement nor an element of theft; thus, evidence of conviction was inadmissible under MRE 609(a).

3. The trial court properly refused to admit evidence of Pabst's guilty plea. According to MRE 410(1), evidence of a plea of guilty which was later withdrawn is not admissible, in either civil or criminal proceedings, against the defendant who made the plea.

4. The trial court properly refused to admit evidence of Pabst's OVI conviction. Under MRE 410(2), evidence of a plea of *nolo contendere* is generally inadmissible, in either civil or criminal proceedings, against the defendant who made the plea. However, MRE 410(2) further provides that a plea of *nolo contender* is admissible in a civil proceeding, to the extent that evidence of a guilty plea would be admissible, to support a defense against a claim asserted by the person who entered the plea. Dandy and Dawg defended on the basis that Pabst was 100-percent responsible for causing the accident due to his intoxication. Thus, if evidence of a guilty plea of OVI would have been admissible, the *nolo* plea would also have been admissible to support the comparative negligence defense raised by Dandy and Dawg. Under MRE 803(22), evidence of a final judgment of conviction entered upon a plea of guilty (or upon a plea of *nolo contendere* if evidence of the plea is not excluded by MRE 410) is not excluded by the hearsay rule, but only if the crime is "punishable by death or imprisonment in excess of one year." The OVI conviction was a misdemeanor, punishable by no more than 93 days' imprisonment. Thus, evidence of the judgment of conviction of OVI was properly excluded on the ground that it constituted inadmissible hearsay.

Three Student Answers—July 2004

Question 1—Evidence—10 points

(1) **Certificate of Automobile Insurance:** First we must address the issue whether the certificate would be relevant. MRC401 defines relevant evidence as evidence that has a tendency to make any fact that is of consequence to the determination of the action more probable or less probable than without it.

Here, the Certificate of Insurance is relevant evidence to the action. MRE will not allow proof of insurance to show that a defendant was negligent but it can be admissible to show ownership of the vehicle. Therefore, if the certificate was to show ownership, it wasn't an error of the trial court.

(2) **Refused to allow defense to impeach Pabst testimony of 2002 OUIL conviction:** This is a civil case, and Pabst's 2002 OUIL conviction cannot be used to impeach him. Past acts, are not permitted under the MRE for impeachment purposes. (MRE 403) states that although evidence is relevant if its probative value is "substantially" outweighed by the prejudicial effect, it will not be admissible. Here the court was correct in determining it inadmissible.

(3) **Refused to admit evidence of Pabst guilty plea:** According to MRE, Pabst's guilty plea was withdrawn, and he later pled nolo contendere. Nolo contendere pleas in Michigan Courts are not admissible in a civil or criminal case.

(4) **Pabst conviction of OUI:** Here Pabst pled nolo contendere so as to receive a reduced sentence. As earlier stated the Michigan Courts will not allow evidence to be admitted of a nolo contender plea in a civil case or criminal case. The Court can use its balancing tool under MRE 403, finding it to be too prejudicial to Pabst therefore not allowing the plea to be admitted. The Trial Court did not err on this evidentiary ruling.

Question 1—Evidence—10 points

Issue is whether there is error in any of these evidentiary rulings.

1. This is allowed into evidence. Generally, proof of insurance is not allowed to show wrong doing or negligence, but it is allowed to show ownership, control, or for impeachment. Here Dandy claims they did not own delivery vehicle at time of accident. Certificate of Auto Insurance would show ownership. Therefore, it is allowed into evidence.
2. This would be correct. In Michigan, a conviction is allowed to impeach any witness on cross exam. However, if the conviction is a felony it must be theft (in Michigan) and Judge must explain on record why probative value outweighs undue prejudice. Here, felony was not for theft, it was OUIL. Therefore, court properly refused to allow evidence of OUIL conviction. Also, conviction must be less than 10 years old from date of release from jail or conviction date.
3. Court was correct here. Plea was withdrawn and is not conviction. Michigan courts do not allow this into evidence. Therefore, Pabst's guilty plea of OUIL 2nd offense not admitted.
4. The Court is correct here. OUI is a misdemeanor. This is not conviction for dishonesty or false statement. Therefore it does not come in. Michigan allows right to counsel for imprisonment over 92 days, here 93 days, therefore, has right to counsel.

Question 1—Evidence—9 points

On appeal from a judgment awarding Pabst damages, Defendants Dandy and Dawg claim error concerning 4 evidentiary rulings of the trial court. In reviewing decisions made by the trial court, the Court of Appeals generally will not substitute its own discretion for that of the trial court. The Court of Appeals will reverse if there is abuse of discretion.

The 1st issue is whether the trial court erred by allowing Pabst to present a certificate of automobile insurance issued to Defendant #2, Dandy, which provided it was valid March through August 2004, using the delivery truck as an insured vehicle. The admission of the certificate was proper under the Michigan Rule of Evidence (MRE) to show ownership. Admission of insurance or proof of insurance would be improper if the Plaintiff, Pabst was offering it to show the Defendant (or in this case Defendants) were capable of paying for the damages. As applied, the Defendant Dandy's defense was that it did not own the delivery truck at the time of the accident. Plaintiff is allowed to then provide evidence contrary to the defense, in this case that the vehicle was in fact owned (and subsequently insured) by Dandy.

The 2nd issue is whether the trial court erred by refusing to allow the defense to impeach Pabst's testimony with evidence of his 2002 OUIL conviction. Under Federal Rules of Evidence, as well as the MRE, evidence of specific instances of a party's past conduct is improper to show action in conformity therewith. In other words, it's generally improper to move for admission of evidence of past conduct to demonstrate that the party (usually the Defendant) behaved this way before so he's done it again. However, use of a party's or witnesses' conviction is proper if it involved dishonesty or false statement, regardless of how long the person was incarcerated for, with the additional limitation that it not be older than 10 years (looking at the date of incarceration or date of release, whichever is later). The conviction must also be relevant under 401 (MRE) and the probative value must outweigh the prejudicial effect of admission. Here, the trial court does not appear to have erred by not allowing the Defendant to impeach the Plaintiff with evidence of the 2002 OUIL conviction. The conviction does not involve dishonesty/false statement. The conviction also does not satisfy the requirement that the conviction be one that has a minimum sentence of 1 year, when not involving dishonesty or false statement. Pabst ultimately pled no contest to the reduced misdemeanor charge of OVI and was sentenced to the maximum term of only 93 days.

The 3rd issue of whether the trial court erred by refusing admission that Pabst pled guilty of OUIL second offense, following the accident was proper, because he was subsequently allowed to withdraw the plea.

The 4th issue of whether the trial court erred by refusing to admit evidence of Pabst's conviction of OUI stemming from the accident was improper. The Defendants 2nd defense was that Pabst was driving while intoxicated at the time of the accident and was 100% comparatively negligent in causing the accident. Under MI No Fault (Insurance) laws, comparative negligence is a factor in whether the Plaintiff can recover damages. If Pabst was in fact at least 51% at fault, he should not be allowed to recover. The Defendants are allowed under MRE to present evidence of the conviction to establish and support their defense

February 2005—Question 12

William Strong was charged with the rape of a 14-year-old girl. The young girl named Kathy had made statements to the investigators and a juvenile court officer and a community mental health counselor. She testified at the time of the preliminary examination, and her testimony was consistent with what she had told the police. After the preliminary examination, the defendant's attorney made a motion to view the records of both the juvenile court officer and mental health counselor. The basis for the motion was that there may be some inconsistencies in what she told these two counselors and that the defendant should have an opportunity to review these records so he could properly confront witnesses and conduct an effective cross examination. The trial court denied this request, citing the statutes that made this information confidential.

During the trial, the prosecutor called William's brother, John, to the stand and asked him if William told him that he had sex with a young girl by the name of Kathy. John denied ever being told this by William. John was then asked if he made this very statement to the investigating officer and John again denied ever telling anyone that William had made such a statement. The prosecutor then called the investigating officer to testify, and over defense counsel's objection, the officer testified that John did tell him that William had stated that he had sex with a young girl by the name of Kathy.

During the closing argument, the prosecutor told the jury that Kathy has always been consistent in her testimony. "What she testified at trial is the same that she told police, the same that she testified to at the preliminary exam, the same that she told the counselors that she had treated with and the same that she has told me." Defense counsel objected to this statement, but the trial court overruled the objection.

On appeal, Strong's attorney raised two issues. The first issue was improper conduct by the prosecutor in the closing argument, and the second issue dealt with the alleged improper testimony of the investigating officer as to the statement allegedly made to him by John Strong.

Confining your answer to these two issues, what do you believe the outcome of the appeal will be and why?

Model Answer to Question 12

William Strong will likely win this appeal.

In the closing argument, the prosecutor created the inference that he had seen the counseling records and they were consistent with Kathy's trial testimony. A prosecutor may not argue the effect of testimony that was not entered into evidence at trial. If the counseling records were inadmissible because of the statutory privilege, it is error for the prosecutor to argue to the jury what was allegedly in these records. A prosecutor also cannot vouch for the credibility of facts and evidence not in the case. There was no evidence of what Kathy told the counselors and there was no evidence of what she had allegedly told to the prosecutor. An objection to this argument was made but overruled by the court. Without a curative instruction this argument is error and, standing alone, would probably result in a reversal of the conviction.

The second issue raised on appeal should assure that the conviction would be overturned. Again, there was a timely objection made to the testimony of the investigating officer and again, the objection was overruled. While prior inconsistent statements may be used to impeach credibility this was improper impeachment. Even though John was the prosecutor's witness, that wouldn't prevent the prosecutor from attacking his credibility if done correctly. MRE 607. What occurred here is that the statement purportedly used to impeach the credibility of the witness went to the central issue of the case. This testimony went to prove the truth of the matter asserted. The alleged admission could have been introduced through the testimony of John but once he denied such admission being made, it was impermissible hearsay to allow the officer to testify to such a statement allegedly made to John. This is not harmless error. This statement was essentially a confession of the crime being charged being placed before the jury by hearsay testimony.

Based on the two issues raised on appeal, the conviction in this case should be reversed. *See People v Stanaway*, 446 Mich 643 (1994).

Student Answer—February 2005

Question 12—Evidence—9 points

As to the alleged improper testimony of the investigating officer, Strong's attorney will argue that the statement is inadmissible hearsay. Hearsay is an out of court statement offered for the truth of the matter being asserted. Strong's attorney will argue that the statement is being offered to show that William did commit the crime he is being accused of. Testimony of this nature is improper if used for this purpose.

However, the prosecutor will argue that the statement is being used to impeach John's statement and show that John's statement to the officer was a prior, inconsistent statement. Under this theory, a prior inconsistent statement is an exception to the hearsay rule. Alternatively, the prosecutor may argue that the statement is part of a regularly kept record by the investigating officer as part of his investigation. However, there is no indication in the facts that the officer referred to a police report. It appears he is relying on a communication that was merely spoken to him. If he is relying on the information as part of a police report, then the regularly kept records exception to the hearsay rule would apply. Since no police report is mentioned in the facts, it is not likely that the objection was overruled on this basis.

Additionally, there is the danger of unfair prejudice in this statement being allowed to come in. The jury may interpret it as being true because it was being stated by a police officer.

Therefore, since the regularly kept business record exception does not apply, and even if the prior inconsistent statement exception did apply, the potential for prejudice to the jury and use of the statement to show defendant's propensity to commit the crime he is charged with, the appeals court would probably rule that the defendant should receive a new trial. This is reversible error rather than harmless error which is how the court will weigh the issue. In order to find harmless error, that would mean there is a likelihood of defendant being convicted regardless of the error. It does not seem to me that a determination such as that could be made barring the officer's statement. William will prevail on this issue.

As to the statement made by the prosecutor, this was definitely improper. By stating to the jury that the victim's testimony has been consistent with what she told everyone, including the prosecutor. The prosecutor is, in essence, vouching for the credibility of the victim. Once again this holds the potential for unfair prejudice to the defendant. The prosecutor may be viewed by some members of the jury as being in a position of authority. If the prosecutor is vouching for the credibility of the witness, some members of the jury might assume that the prosecutor is stating unequivocally that Kathy is telling the truth.

It is against the Rules of Professional Conduct for the prosecutor to suggest to the jury that Kathy is telling the truth just because she stated it to the prosecutor. Therefore, on this issue, the court of appeals would also find reversible error. It is the jury's job to decide if Kathy is being truthful based on the evidence presented, rather than on the prosecutor vouching for her.

February 2005—Question 14

You are trying your first case as an assistant district attorney for the Washtenaw County prosecutor's office, *People v Dooley*. Duncan Dooley is charged with the murder of his girlfriend, Velma Victor.

Your theory is that Dooley was a jealous and controlling boyfriend. On March 27, 2004, he happened to see Velma having lunch with her work colleague, Wally Wallace. That evening, he drove to Velma's apartment. After bursting through the door, he accused her of having a sexual relationship with Wally and slapped her repeatedly when she denied it. Finally, infuriated by Velma's denials, he pulled out a handgun and fired two shots at Velma, killing her. In an attempt to cover up his crime, he ransacked the apartment, taking her television, her stereo, and several pieces of jewelry. These items were never recovered.

Dooley claims that he had nothing to do with the crime. He maintains that he spent the entire afternoon and evening watching college basketball with his friend, Lester Leeds. The defense plans to call Leeds, who will testify consistent with Dooley's claim.

The district attorney thinks it is critical that you undermine Leeds's credibility. To this end, she asks you to call (1) Albert Ames, an LSAT proctor, who will testify that he caught Leeds cheating on the 2002 LSAT exam; (2) Betty Bridges, Leeds' twelfth grade English teacher, who will testify that Leeds was widely thought to be a cheater by the high school faculty when he was a student in the mid-1990's; and (3) Casey Cook, Leeds' probation officer, who will testify that Leeds was convicted of malicious destruction of private property in 2003.

Write a short memo assessing the likelihood that the court will admit the described testimony from Ames, Bridges, and Cook.

Model Answer to Question 14

The testimony of Albert Ames is inadmissible under MRE 608(b). This rule bars extrinsic evidence of "[s]pecific instances of the conduct of a witness, for the purpose of attacking or supporting the witness' credibility." Because Ames' direct testimony would be extrinsic evidence of Leeds' cheating on the 2002 LSAT, it is inadmissible. (A top-notch answer would note, however, that the prosecution may, subject to the court's discretion, inquire into the LSAT incident while cross-examining Leeds.)

The testimony of Betty Bridges is likely to be admissible. MRE 608(a) states: "The credibility of a witness may be attacked or supported by evidence in the form of opinion or reputation" if the evidence relates to the witness' character for truthfulness or untruthfulness. Because Bridges would be testifying about Leeds' reputation for truthfulness among his high school faculty, this testimony is likely to be admissible under MRE 608(a). Credit should be given if the applicant argues the testimony is irrelevant because it is not pertinent to the question of Leeds' current reputation.

Finally, the testimony of Casey Cook is inadmissible under MRE 609(a). Evidence of a prior conviction is admissible only if *inter alia,* the crime contains an element of dishonesty, theft, or a false statement. Malicious destruction of private property is not a crime that involves dishonesty, theft, or a false statement. Accordingly, evidence of this conviction is barred by MRE 609(a).

Student Answer—February 2005

Question 14—Evidence—9 points

In attempting to impeach the credibility of a witness, specific acts of conduct are not admissible. The witness can only be impeached by reputation or opinion evidence. Additionally, evidence that a witness was arrested or convicted of a crime is also inadmissible. Therefore, in these facts, Albert Ames' testimony that he caught Leeds cheating on the LSAT is inadmissible because it refers to a specific act of conduct.

Betty Bridge's testimony that Leeds had a reputation for being a cheater is admissible because reputation or opinion testimony of a witness is allowed under the Federal Rules of Evidence.

Casey Cook's testimony that Leeds had a prior conviction for malicious destruction of property is not admissible because evidence of a prior conviction to impeach a witness is not allowed under the Federal Rules of Evidence.

The testimony of the specific act of conduct and the conviction are excluded under the exclusionary rule. Although the prosecutor is allowed to use reputation or opinion evidence to impeach the witness, he or she may not do so in their case in chief. The prosecutor can only use this evidence to rebut the witness's testimony, which in this case referred to the defendant having an alibi.

In conclusion, the court will admit Bridge's testimony, but will not admit Ames's or Cook's testimonies.

July 2005—Question 13

Peter Pinto was an employee at Dahlia's Dog Grooming Boutique. Last winter, Dahlia fired Peter, citing Peter's frequent "sick" days as the reason. However, Peter believed that the reason given by Dahlia was a pretext and that, in fact, he had been fired because of his Ruitanian heritage. Informed by his lawyer that it was a violation of Michigan's Civil Rights Act for an employer to terminate an employee because of his national origin, Peter filed suit against Dahlia in the Newaygo circuit court.

You are a law clerk for Judge Jones, who is presiding over the trial of *Pinto v Dahlia's Dog Grooming Boutique*. During the damages phase of the trial, Peter intends to introduce the expert testimony of Edwina Eggers, a professor of vertebrate biology at Newaygo County Community College. According to her deposition testimony, Professor Eggers intends to present the following theory:

> Peter was so distraught after losing his job at Dahlia's that he began a daily habit of binge eating junk food to ease his pain. As a result, Peter gained 175 pounds since his last day of employment at Dahlia's, putting a great deal of extra strain on his already overtaxed heart. Accordingly, Peter's likely life span was significantly reduced as a result of Dahlia's discrimination. Indeed, according to Professor Eggers, Peter will die of a massive heart attack by the age of 45.

Based on this expert testimony, plaintiff intends to seek $225 million in damages for the reduction in Peter's life expectancy caused by Dahlia's discrimination.

Before trial, defense counsel filed a motion to exclude the entirety of Professor Egger's testimony under MRE 702 and sought a hearing on that issue.

You are Judge Jones' clerk. Write a brief memo for Judge Jones addressing (1) whether she should grant the motion for a hearing on the admissibility of Eggers' testimony under MRE 702 and (2) whether Eggers' expert testimony is admissible under the Michigan Rule of Evidence.

Model Answer to Question 13

TO: Judge Jones
FROM: Law Clerk
RE: Admissibility of Eggers' Expert Testimony

I recommend that you grant defendant's motion for a hearing. MRE 702 provides that expert testimony is admissible only if the trial court initially finds that "scientific, technical, or other specialized knowledge will assist the trier of fact to understand the evidence or to determine a fact in issue." MRE 702. See also MRE 104(a) (providing that preliminary issues of qualification shall be determined by the court). The Michigan Supreme Court held in *Gilbert v Daimler Chrysler*, 470 Mich 749, 782 (2004), that this rule imposes a duty on the trial court to act as a gatekeeper during all stages of expert testimony. Therefore, as a precondition to admitting Professor Eggers' testimony, you are required to determine that the expert testimony will assist the trier of fact and meet the additional conditions noted below. Neither MRE 702 nor *Gilbert* specially require a hearing, but, given the nature of Professor Eggers' testimony and the clear requirement that trial court vet proffered expert testimony before allowing a jury to hear it, a hearing is the most prudent course of action.

Plaintiff bears the burden of proving that Professor Eggers' testimony is admissible under MRE 702. *Gilbert, supra*, at 781. It is unlikely that plaintiff will carry this burden.

The testimony of an individual expert is admissible only if the subject matter of the testimony will "assist" the trier of fact, and the expert witness is "qualified as an expert by knowledge, skill, experience, training, or education." MRE 702. Therefore, you ensure both that Professor Eggers' testimony will assist the jury to understand some issue in the case and that she is "qualified" as defined in MRE 702 to speak on the subject of her testimony.

On the question of Eggers' qualifications, Professor Eggers is a vertebrate biologist who purports to offer psychological and medical testimony—viz., that employment discrimination led to a psychological condition which will, in turn, lead to medical complications resulting in plaintiff's untimely death. It is unlikely that Eggers has the training or education required to give expert testimony on this issue. Moreover, given the apparent discrepancy between Eggers' training and the subject of her testimony, it is unlikely that her testimony on damages will truly assist the trier of fact. *Gilbert, supra*, at 789 ("An expert who lacks 'knowledge' in the field at issue cannot 'assist the trier of fact.'") At the very least, plaintiff should be required to demonstrate to your satisfaction that Eggers' training is fundamentally related to the subject matter of her proposed testimony.

Student Answer—July 2005

Question 13—Evidence—4 points (Bad answer)

1) The judge should grant the motion for the hearing regarding whether the Professor's testimony should be admissible. The judge should determine whether she can be qualified as an expert. She can be qualified if she is practicing in the area in which she intends to testify and based on her knowledge in the area and custom in the practice. Here, she is a professor of vertebrae biology and wants to give an opinion on Peter's emotional distress over losing his job. I think the judge should grant defense counsel's motion to exclude the testimony of Professor as an expert.

2) The Professor's testimony would be admissible as an opinion on how his life has changed if she has personal knowledge of his life now versus his life before he was fired. But her expert testimony would be denied. She wouldn't be able to discuss that he might die of a heart attack or his life span, only that he began to eat junk food.

Comment: This is a well-written *bad* answer because it is substantively incorrect. It is very important to read the call of the question carefully. In the first part of this question, students are merely asked whether the judge should grant the motion for a hearing to *consider* the issue of admitting the expert testimony. It isn't until the second part of the question that students are asked whether the testimony would be admissible.

February 2006—Question 2

John Smith was at a large electronics store. As he exited the store, the security alarms sounded. He walked quickly toward his vehicle with a security guard in hot pursuit. As John was loading expensive electronic equipment into his vehicle, the guard confronted him. The guard brought John back inside the store for questioning. After over an hour of questioning, the security guard released John because John had his receipt and proved that he had purchased the equipment. John has sued the store and the security guard for false imprisonment.

The defense attorney has filed a motion *in limine* to preclude the introduction of the following evidence presented by John:

1. *The deposition of Ed Employee.* Ed, an employee of the store, testified at a deposition that the equipment John had in his possession was clearly marked with a "paid" sticker. The attorney representing both the store and security guard was present, but did not cross-examine Ed at the deposition. Unfortunately, Ed has since passed away. John's attorney wants to read Ed's deposition testimony into evidence.
2. *The written statement of Carl Customer given to John's attorney several days after the incident.* Carl, feeling very guilty, told John's attorney (and subsequently made a written statement) that he stole a satellite radio from the electronics store at the same time John did. Carl was not detained by security. Carl showed John's attorney the satellite radio still in its original packaging. Carl has since disappeared and John's attorney has been unable to locate him, although John's attorney has used all reasonable means to locate Carl and secure his presence.
3. *Evidence that the security guard assaulted a customer in the parking lot in a dispute over a parking space.*

You are a clerk for the judge hearing the defense motion. Prepare a memorandum addressing the arguments for and against admitting the evidence.

Model Answer to Question 2

1. The testimony qualifies as hearsay because it is an out-of-court statement offered to prove the truth of the matter asserted. However, MRE 804(b)(5) allows for deposition testimony to be admitted when the declarant is unavailable and the person whom it is admitted against had an opportunity to cross-examine the witness with a similar motive to develop testimony. That the defense counsel chose not to cross-examine Ed is not a disqualifying factor so long as he had the opportunity to do so. Under MRE 804(a)(4), a witness is unavailable if he or she cannot testify because of death. In this case, the prior testimony of Ed Employee should be admitted.

2. This statement is also hearsay. However, the statement is admissible under MRE 804(b)(3), which permits the admission of statements against penal interest. A statement is "against penal interest" when, at the time of its making, it subjects the declarant to criminal liability such that a reasonable person would not have made the statement unless he believed it to be true.

Additionally, where the statement exposes the declarant to criminal liability and is offered to exculpate the accused, the statement is not admissible unless corroborating circumstances clearly indicate the trustworthiness of the statement. In this case, the evidence would not be offered to exculpate the accused, as this is a civil claim for false imprisonment rather than a criminal case. However, Carl showing the radio to John's attorney in its original packaging would provide sufficient corroboration. An applicant noting this distinction should be given credit.

The witness is "unavailable" under MRE 804(a)(5) because John's attorney has used all reasonable means to obtain the presence of Carl Customer. Therefore, the statement should be admissible.

3. As a general proposition, character evidence, including prior bad acts, is inadmissible to prove conformity with that character. MRE 404(b). However, prior bad acts evidence is admissible to prove motive, opportunity, plan, etc. MRE 404(b)(1). The Michigan Supreme Court has established factors for the admissibility of prior bad acts evidence. *People v Vandervliet*, 444 Mich 52, 74-75 (1993). The proponent of the evidence must show that the evidence is offered for something other than propensity, that the evidence is relevant under MRE 402, and that the unfair prejudice does not outweigh the probative value. *People v Knox*, 469 Mich 502, 509 (2004). This evidence does not appear to be offered for a proper purpose. The prior bad act is not "sufficiently similar" to the subject matter of the instant lawsuit to show any proper purpose. *People v Sabin*, 463 Mich 43, 63 (2003). Besides the location, the assault does not involve a purported theft or any other relationship to the incident giving rise to this lawsuit. Therefore, the evidence should be excluded.

Student Answer—February 2006

Question 2—Evidence—10 Points

Memorandum
To: Judge
From: Law Clerk
Date: 2/21/06
Re: John Smith

> **Comment:** Always use a "memo" heading when asked to draft a memorandum.

The first issue is what is a motion in limine? A motion in limine is a motion by an attorney that states "this evidence is way too prejudicial that given its admission, it will automatically improperly influence the jury." With this in mind, the first issue is whether the statement of Ed Employee can be admitted. The facts state that he testified that the equipment had a "paid sticker". Hearsay is a statement by a defendant that's out of court in order to prove the truth of the matter asserted. Here, the defendant is unavailable so it would come in under the hearsay exception. Former testimony is when defendant is unavailable and subject to cross. Here, the defendant wasn't subject to cross, so it's going to come in under the hearsay exception of former testimony. Next, a statement against interest may be the exception. A statement against interest is a statement made in anticipation of abridgment of penal interest. Here, it could be argued that the statement was a disposition against his interest. This is subject to debate. The employee had nothing to lose. He wasn't being sued for false imprisonment, so it wasn't against his interest. Therefore, the testimony should not be read into evidence because it's hearsay.

The next issue is whether Carl customer made a statement against his interest. The facts state that Carl "felt guilty" meaning he could be subject to penal penalties. The rule is that: 1) against some penal or some legal interest and 2) is unavailable. Here, the facts state that Carl has since disappeared and he made the statement that he was "guilty". Given these facts, the defendant might fall into the exception of as statement against interest and this could be admitted.

The evidence of a security guard assaulting someone else could be considered a specific instance of conduct. Specific instances of conduct are only allowed for motive, intent absence of mistake, identity, or common plan/scheme or to impeach the testimony (only for cross examination). Otherwise, it is inadmissible character evidence. Assault and false imprisonment are two different things, so this probably will not be admissible unless the security guard testifies. Even then an assault has nothing to do with false imprisonment or a motive to lie. So I would deny this evidence.

Given the above facts, admit the statement from Carl as statement against interest, but deny Ed and security guards conduct as hearsay and inadmissible character evidence.

July 2006—Question 9

Paul Plaintiff purchased an automobile on credit, providing a security interest in the automobile to the dealership, Don's Automotive. Paul made his first few payments on time, but soon after purchasing the car, suffered severe financial difficulty. After providing the required contractual notice, Don's Automotive repossessed Paul's car. Paul claims that during the repossession, his garage door and several items in the garage were destroyed. Don's Automotive claims that it towed the car from the street and had no contact with the garage. Paul brought an action against Don's Automotive for damage to his property. Don's Automotive answered and filed a motion *in limine* to exclude the following evidence:

1. One week after Don's Automotive repossessed Paul's car, it implemented a new policy forbidding any employee from entering a garage to repossess collateral.
2. Don's Automotive's insurance policy which covers property damage occurring in the course of repossessions.
3. The statement of Bud Smith, a former employee of Don's automotive. Bud was one of the employees who repossessed Paul's car. In his statement to Paul's attorney, Bud admitted that another employee of Don's Automotive damaged Paul's property. Bud made the statement after he was fired from Don's Automotive.

4. Evidence of other repossessions where employees of Don's Automotive entered the garage of delinquent debtors to repossess collateral.

You are the law clerk for the judge hearing Don's Automotive's motion *in limine*. Prepare a memorandum discussing the arguments for and against admitting the four pieces of disputed evidence.

Model Answer to Question 9

1. Under MRE 407, subsequent remedial measures are inadmissible to prove culpable conduct. In this case, the new policy would make it less likely that the alleged conduct would occur again. Thus, the new policy is a remedial measure, and it is inadmissible unless it is offered for a proper purpose, such as to prove ownership, control, or feasibility of the remedial measure. Because none of those things appear to be at issue under the facts, the policy is inadmissible. However, the new policy may be used for impeachment if the need arises during trial.
2. Under MRE 411, evidence that a person is or is not insured is inadmissible for proof that the person acted wrongfully. However, the proof of insurance is admissible for other purposes, such as to prove agency, ownership, or control, or to establish bias of a witness. Because agency, ownership, and control are not at issue, the evidence is inadmissible. However, if appropriate, the policy may be admitted to show witness bias.
3. Bud's statement is inadmissible. It is hearsay because it does not meet any exception to MRE 802. The closest exception is MRE 801(d)(2)(D). Under that exception, statements made by agents or servants that relate to their agency or employment are not hearsay. However, the statement must be made during the course of the agency relationship. In this case, the facts clearly state that Bud made the statement after the relationship ended. No other exceptions apply.
4. The evidence is admissible. MRE 406 allows for evidence of the routine practice of an organization to prove action in conformity with that routine practice.

Two Student Answers—July 2006

Question 9—Evidence—9 points

This is an evidence question.
The issues presented in Don's motion in limine are as follows:

(1) The fact that Don's changed its policy against any employee from entering a garage to repossess collateral should not be allowed to be used in evidence against Don's as it is a subsequent remedial remedy designed to protect those who have collateral that is going to be repossessed. As it is a measure that would protect Paul from a harm it should not be used against Don's and therefore should be excluded.

(2) The fact that Don's has an insurance policy which covers property damage in the course of repossessions should also be excluded because it is irrelevant to the issue of whether or not Don's is responsible for the damage to P's property.

(3) The statement of Bud Smith should be excluded as hearsay but falls within an exception of a statement against a party opponent but should only be admitted if he is unavailable to testify at trial. Bud's statement could be

biased since he was fired from Don's and therefore he should be required to testify under oath if he available. If he unavailable his statement could provide evidence that Don's employees have been in P's garage and is in fact responsible for P's loss.

(4) The fact that D's employees have entered the garages of delinquent debtors to repossess collateral should be allowed for the purpose of showing course of conduct by Don's employees when they are repossessing collateral. However, it could be excluded as not a proper way to show how Don's employees acted in this specific instance of P's damaged property. But, if this is typical conduct by Don's employees at the time of P's collateral being repossessed then it should be allowed and thereby not excluded.

Question 9—Evidence—8 points

(1) Don's new policy is valid and non-admissible as a public policy measure under MRE 407, Subsequent Remedial Measures (SRM). SRM are inadmissible b/c we want the public to correct deficiencies w/o a potential of assuming liability.

(2) D's insurance policy coverage for repossession is also inadmissible to prove action in conformity to liability coverage. However, plaintiff can argue that the mere fact he has coverage may be admissible for identification purpose it is admissible as a collateral matter.

(3) Bud Smith's statement ought to be excluded as inadmissible hearsay. Hearsay under MRE 801 is statement/association by an out of court declarant meant for the truth of the matter asserted. Here, since Bud is no longer an employee when he made his statement, he was speaking in his role of agent under a vicarious liability argument. Consequently, Bud's statements don't fall within MRE 801(2) as an admission of a party opponent. On the other hand, plaintiff can argue that Bud's statement falls w/in a state of mind exception. The state of mind exception, 803(3), will allow inadmissible hearsay statements if the statement reflects his state of mind during the event complained of. More likely this argument will fail & the statement will be excluded.

(4) This evidence ought to be held inadmissible if the court reasons that under a MRE 403 analysis, the prejudicial effect will outweigh the probative value of its admission. While the evidence is relevant to plaintiff's argument, as defined by MRE401, any evidence that makes a fact of consequence more probable than not.

February 2007—Question 6

Peter Pedalist was riding his bicycle down Sunnybrook Lane when Darren Daredevil struck Peter with his motor scooter, causing serious injuries. Peter filed a lawsuit against Darren seeking compensation for his injuries.

Peter plans to have Wally Witness testify on his behalf. Wally is a retired social studies teacher who lives on Sunnybrook Lane and witnessed the incident. Wally plans to provide the following points of testimony. First, Wally plans to testify that, in his opinion, Darren's motor scooter was traveling at approximately 40 miles per hour at the time of the incident. Second, Wally plans to testify that he heard Gertrude Goner, an elderly neighbor who is now deceased, say that Darren should not have consumed all that alcohol before riding the motor scooter. Gertrude made her statement approximately two weeks after the incident. Third, Wally plans to testify that he heard Darren offer to pay Peter's medical expenses after the incident. Lastly, Wally plans to testify that Peter would have sustained the same injuries even if he had been wearing his bicycle helmet.

You are an associate in the law firm representing Darren Daredevil. Prepare a memorandum analyzing the admissibility of Wally's proffered testimony.

Model Answer to Question 6

Wally's proposed testimony regarding Darren's speed is admissible. Under MRE 701, a layperson can provide opinion testimony if the opinion is within the general competence of a layperson, is rationally based on the perception of the witness, and if the testimony is helpful to the determination of a fact in issue. As Wally witnessed the incident, and Darren's fault is at issue, he will be able to give opinion testimony that Darren was traveling at approximately 40 miles per hour at the time of the incident, provided the proper foundation is laid establishing that Wally is competent to estimate vehicle speed. If Wally is an experienced driver, and has experience estimating car speed, this should be sufficient to qualify Wally to give this lay opinion testimony. *See People v Oliver*, 170 Michigan App 38 (1988).

Wally's proposed testimony regarding Gertrude Goner is not admissible. Gertrude's statement is hearsay under MRE 801, as it is an out-of-court statement offered for the truth of the matter asserted. Gertrude's death renders her unavailable to testify under MRE 804(a)(4). Because nothing in the facts suggests that Gertrude's statement falls under any of the hearsay exceptions contained in MRE 803 or 804, Wally will not be able to testify regarding Gertrude's statement.

Wally's testimony regarding Darren's offer to pay Peter's medical expenses is also not admissible. While Darren's statement is an out-of-court statement offered for the truth of the matter asserted, Darren's statement is not hearsay under MRE 801(d)(2)(A). Although Darren's statement is a party admission because it is Darren's own statement and is being used against him, MRE 409 provides that evidence of an offer to pay medical expenses is not admissible to prove liability for the injury. Therefore, while Darren's statement is not hearsay, it is not admissible.

Lastly, Wally will not be able to testify that Peter would have sustained the same injuries even if he had been wearing his bicycle helmet. Whether Peter would have sustained the same injuries if he had been wearing his bicycle helmet is not within the knowledge of a lay person, and requires expert testimony. Under MRE 702, a witness may be qualified as an expert by virtue of "knowledge, skill, experience, training, or education." The facts indicate that Wally Witness is a retired social studies teacher, and does not indicate that he has any knowledge or education that would permit him to provide expert opinion testimony regarding Peter's injuries.

In conclusion, only one portion of Wally's testimony is admissible.

Two Student Answers—February 2007

Question 6—Evidence—9 points

The first issue is whether Wally can testify as to his opinion of the speed of the bicycle. A layperson/witness may testify as to the speed of a car or something related to a vehicle by opinion evidence only. Here, Wally plans to testify that the motor scooter was traveling approximately 40 miles per hour; this is proper and this evidence may be admissible.

The second issue is whether the testimony about what the deceased Gertrude's comment is admissible or hearsay. Hearsay is any out of court statement offered for the truth of the matter asserted. Here, Gertrude's comment is hearsay. However, hearsay may be admitted when it meets on the hearsay exceptions. Here, the declarant Gertrude is unavailable; when a declarant is unavailable the proffered testimony may still come in if it is present sense impression, former testimony, or impeachment. Here, none of these apply because although Gertrude can give opinions about someone being intoxicated, here, it was that Darren was intoxicated before riding the motor scooter, it may not be present sense impression because she made the statement two weeks later and present sense impression must be made contemporaneous with perceiving the event. Here was not and this testimony should be excluded.

The third issue is whether Wally's testimony of Darren's offer to pay medical bills is admissible. Offers to pay medical bills are not admissible to prove liability or guilt. Here, the offer was made by Darren to Peter and was overheard by Wally. However, it is not admissible to prove guilt or liability, only control, motive, intent, absence of mistake, common plan or scheme. Further it is hearsay not within any exception. This testimony is not admissible and should be excluded.

Finally, the issue is whether Wally can offer this evidence of Peter's injuries even though he is not an expert. A lay witness cannot testify as to causes of injuries, only expert witness with the proper skill, expertise, education could testify to this. Wally's testimony about how Peter sustained his injuries is inadmissible lay testimony and should be excluded.

Question 6—Evidence—9 points

Dear Reader,

Wally Witness is a prospective witness who has personal knowledge of the accident. He can testify for the following:

1. In his opinion Darren's scooter was traveling 40 mph. A lay person's opinion testimony is admissible if it's not based on scientific facts. Wally is a lay person giving testimony about what he observed; this should be allowed in.
2. Wally's testimony about what Gertrude said is hearsay. Hearsay is an out-of-court statement offered to prove the truth of the matter. Here, the matter is Darren's negligence in striking Peter, this is an issue and Gertrude's statement is hearsay. Gertrude is now deceased and is unavailable; however, she made the statement two weeks after the incident. This does not fall within any of the exceptions. It is not present sense impression or excited utterance. It will not come in.
3. Darren's offer to pay Peter's medical expenses cannot come in. Generally, offers to pay medical expenses are not admissible to prove liability.
4. Wally's statement about Peter wearing his safety belt is not hearsay but it calls for speculation. Speculation not based on relevant facts is not admissible. Wally is not an expert, therefore this statement is out.

July 2007—Question 15

Patty Pontoon filed a lawsuit against Darlene Deville, seeking damages for an alleged assault that occurred at the Tuscola County Fair. In addition to Patty's testimony, plaintiff's counsel plans to call three eyewitnesses to testify regarding the occurrence and details of the assault: Brenda Bean, Eve Ebb, and Nancy Nubs.

You are the attorney representing Darlene Deville, who denies that an assault occurred. While preparing for trial, you have gathered the following evidence. First, a week after the incident occurred, Brenda Bean told her neighbor, Myrna Mitchell, that Darlene did not assault Patty. Second, Clara Clementine is prepared to testify that Eve Ebb has a reputation in the neighborhood for being a notorious liar. Third, Nancy Nubs served three years in prison after being convicted of subornation of perjury in 1996.

Using the Michigan Rules of Evidence, evaluate each piece of evidence. In the event that the trial judge does not share your assessment of the admissibility of the evidence, what further steps must be taken under the Michigan rules to preserve your position on the evidentiary issue?

Model Answer to Question 15

Brenda Bean's statement to Myrna Mitchell that defendant did not assault plaintiff is hearsay under MRE 801(c) because it is an out-of-court statement which would be offered by the defense to prove the truth of the matter asserted—that the assault never occurred. Thus, under MRE 802, the statement is not substantively admissible unless it falls into one of the hearsay exceptions. The facts do not indicate that any of the hearsay exceptions are applicable. While a prior inconsistent statement of a testifying witness is not considered hearsay under MRE 801(d)(1), this rule applies *only if* the prior statement was given under oath subject to the penalty of perjury. Here, there is no indication that Brenda's statement to Myrna was given under oath, so MRE 801(d)(1) does not apply.

However, while Brenda's statement is not substantively admissible, it is admissible as impeachment evidence under MRE 613. MRE 613(a) provides that Brenda's prior statement need not be in writing, so her verbal statement satisfies MRE 613(a). The contents of Brenda's statement need not be disclosed to her at the time defense counsel questions her unless opposing counsel requests disclosure. Moreover, provided that Brenda is first given an opportunity to explain or deny her inconsistent statement to Myrna and plaintiff's counsel is given an opportunity to question Brenda, Myrna may testify and provide extrinsic evidence on the conflicting statement. Stated otherwise, under these circumstances, MRE 613(b) permits Myrna to testify about Brenda's prior inconsistent statement to her concerning the assault incident.

Clara Clementine may testify that Eve Ebb has a reputation for untruthfulness under MRE 608(a) in order to attack Eve's credibility. However, as a foundational matter, Clara must have personal knowledge of Eve's reputation in the neighborhood in order to testify. MRE 602.

Nancy Nubs' credibility may be impeached by her 1996 perjury conviction. Under MRE 609(a), the evidence is admissible if the evidence is either elicited from Nancy or established by public record during cross-examination of Nancy. Moreover, because subornation of perjury is a crime containing an element of dishonesty or false statement under MRE 609(a)(1), it is admissible without regard to considering its probative value, as is required for criminal convictions containing an element of theft under MRE 609(a)(2). While Nancy's perjury conviction is eleven years old, the ten-year time limit contained in MRE 609(c) applies to either the date of the conviction *or* the date the witness was released from the confinement imposed for the conviction, whichever is the *later* date. Because Nancy served a three-year prison sentence, only eight years have lapsed since Nancy was released from prison and the conviction is not time barred.

If the trial court excludes defendant's evidence, defense counsel is required to make an offer of proof in order to preserve the ruling for appeal. MRE 103(a)(2). In order to make an offer of proof, an attorney must make the substance of the evidence known to the court and put it on the record. Failure to make such an offer of proof generally precludes appellate review of the trial court's evidentiary ruling. See MRE 103(a); *People v Hackett*, 421 Mich 338 (1984).

Two Student Answers—July 2007

Question 15—Evidence—9 points

This is an evidence question and is asking about the relevancy and admissibility of each piece of evidence.

Brenda Bear (BB)

The first piece of Evidence we would like to introduce is that BB told her neighbor Myrna that Darlene (D) did not assault Patty (P). The issue with this statement is that it is hearsay. It is an out of court statement to prove the truth of the matter asserted. Generally hearsay is not admitted unless it can come in under an exception. In this particular situation there are no hearsay exceptions to allow this statement to come in. The only way it could be used is for impeachment purposes of BB.

Clara Clementine (CC)

We would then like to put CC on the stand to testify that Eve Ebb (EE) has a reputation in the neighborhood for being a liar. In this situation a witness's testimony can be attacked—if on the stand—by using only opinion or reputation evidence. CC is looking to use reputation evidence (although not a specific event) that EE has a reputation in the neighborhood as being a liar. This evidence will be permitted.

Nancy Nubs (NN)

Plaintiff is looking to have NN testify on her behalf. However, we would like to introduce evidence of her conviction of perjury (lying on the stand) to show her lack of truthfulness. She spent 3 years in prison & was released in 1999. B/C there is a 10 year back limitation this conviction, although it began in 1996, the last date in which activity was in 1999. This falls within the time limit and may be used. We are looking to bring this conviction in to show she has lied in the past & will likely lie again & therefore her testimony cannot be trusted. This method of impeachment is permissible.

The judge will likely admit the 2 & 3 points of evidence we are trying to prove. The first piece of evidence might be held inadmissible due to a lack of hearsay exception. However to preserve this issue it is important that we attempt to get the stmt in & get it on the record. If an appeal is ever put into place, it has a possibility, although slight, of being reviewed & overturned. Any evidence that is not placed into the record in the first trial has no chance of ever being appealed or preserved.

Question 15—Evidence—9 points

First, Brenda Bean's statement to Myrna was a statement which was out of court & to prove the truth of the matter asserted—so it is hearsay. There are no hearsay exceptions to get this statement in substantively. However, it can be used to impeach Brenda when and if she testifies that there was an assault on Patty by Darlene. If she denied making this statement to Myrna there can be no further extrinsic evidence to prove she did say it.

Second, Clara's testimony regarding Eve's reputation in the community cannot come in substantively, but it can to impeach. The testimony cannot come in because it is a civil trial and it is regarding the witness's reputation. However, it can come in to impeach because it places her truth in issue—and is thereafter extrinsic evidence and can come in to this testimony.

Third, Nancy's perjury conviction could be used to impeach and proven extrinsically because she was released from prison within 10 years (released in 1999). Since the crime was for perjury and she was released less than 10 years ago, it may be used to impeach her once she takes the stand and may be proved by extrinsic evidence if she denies it.

In order to use any of these witnesses you would have to notify opposing counsel of your intent to use them and what type of witnesses they would be (e.g.: impeach, reputation, etc.).

February 2008—Question 14

Petunia Potter went to her weekly hair appointment at Harriet's Hair Hive. When she arrived, her walker caught on a rubber door mat located just inside the front door of the salon. As a result, Petunia tripped, fell, and fractured her hip.

After Petunia fell, Rita Receptionist rushed over to assist Petunia. Crying and upset, Rita apologized. As Petunia was being placed into the ambulance, Harriet arrived at the salon. Harriet also apologized, and promised to pay all of Petunia's medical expenses.

Petunia spent several weeks in the hospital, followed by several months of rehabilitation. While Petunia was in the hospital, Harriet's Hair Hive was completely remodeled, and the rubber mat was removed from the front door.

Petunia filed a negligence suit against Harriet's Hair Hive. While the suit was pending, Harriet offered to settle the case for $20,000, stating she knew that it was only a matter of time before someone hurt themselves on the mat. Petunia refused the settlement offer because she knew Harriet was "loaded."

In support of the negligence claims, Petunia's attorney plans to offer the following evidence: (1) Rita's apology to Petunia; (2) Harriet's promise to pay Petunia's medical bills; (3) the emergency room report, in which Petunia told the treating physician that she fell due to "Harriet's absolute negligence," (4) the fact that the mat was removed after Petunia's fall; (5) Harriet's settlement offer and inculpatory statement made during settlement negotiations; and (6) a copy of the salon's one million dollar liability insurance policy.

You are the attorney representing Harriet's Hair Hive. Evaluate the admissibility of each piece of evidence under the Michigan Rules of Evidence. Explain your answer.

Model Answer to Question 14

Rita's apology to Petunia: As an out-of-court statement, Rita's statement is hearsay. Under MRE 801(c), hearsay is an out-of-court statement offered to prove the truth of the matter asserted. Because the fact pattern indicates that Rita was crying and upset and made the statement right after Petunia fell, the statement is most easily admissible as an excited utterance under MRE 803(2). Hearsay is admissible under MRE 803(2) where the statement relates to a startling event, and is made while the declarant was under the stress of the event. Petunia's fall was a startling event, and Rita's demeanor and tears indicate that she was still under the stress of the event.

However, even if admissible under MRE 803(2), the statement is likely to be excluded as irrelevant. Under MRE 801, "relevant evidence" is evidence that has any tendency to make a consequential fact more or less probable than it would be without the evidence. Rita's tearful apology has no bearing on whether Harriet's Hair Hive acted negligently toward Petunia.

Harriet's statement to Petunia: Under MRE 409, Harriet's offer to pay for Petunia's medical expense is not admissible to prove liability.

The emergency room report: Petunia's out-of-court statement to the treating physician is hearsay. Under MRE 803(4), statements made for the purposes of medical treatment or medical diagnosis are admissible. Statements regarding the cause or the source of an injury are also admissible, but only "insofar as reasonably necessary" to diagnosis and treatment. Because there is no basis to conclude that attributing the fall to Harriet's absolute negligence" is reasonably necessary to Petunia's diagnosis or treatment, the statement will fail under that hearsay exception and the statement will be inadmissible.

Mat was removed after Petunia's fall: Evidence of a subsequent remedial measure is inadmissible to prove negligence or culpability under MRE 407.

Harriet's settlement offer: Under MRE 408, Harriet's settlement offer, as well as any statements made during the course of settlement negotiations, are not admissible to establish liability.

Harriet's liability insurance policy: Under MRE 411, evidence that Harriet had a liability insurance policy is not admissible to show negligence or culpability. Evidence of liability insurance is admissible when offered for another purpose, such as proof of agency, ownership, or control, but those purposes are not at issue under the fact pattern presented.

Three Student Answers—February 2008

Question 14—Evidence—10 points

This is an evidence question.

1. Admissibility of Evidence:

Rita's apology → statement

Rita's apology is a hearsay statement under MRE 801. Her statement is being offered for the truth of the matter asserted and is an out of court statement made by declarant (Rita). Hearsay statements are inadmissible unless they meet an exclusion or an exception.

Rita's statement might be able to be introduced under an exclusion to hearsay, specifically admission by a party opponent. Rita is the receptionist and not owner of the salon but she worked for Harriet and may be construed as an agent. If Petunia is trying to introduce this she may be met with the hurdle of double hearsay. Each layer of hearsay has to fall under an exclusion or an exception.

2. Harriet promised to pay Petunia's medical bills: Evidence of a promise to pay medical bills may not be used to show liability. This evidence can only be introduced to show ownership or control if those issues are in question. Harriet's offer to pay medical bills is something the kind of evidence the courts does not want introduced for public policy purposes. They don't want someone's offer to pay to be used against them later. Statements of liability coupled with agreement to pay medical bills may be used. Here Petunia will try to get Harriet's apology statement in.

3. The emergency room report was hearsay and does not fall under any hearsay exclusion or exceptions: Petunia would argue that it is allowed under hearsay exception of medical reports for purposes of diagnosis. Petunia's statement was not made for that purpose, it was made to prove that Harriet was negligent. This evidence is inadmissible.

4. Removal of mat after Petunia's fall is also inadmissible: Subsequent remedial measure cannot be introduced to show liability only to show ownership or control if it is an issue. This kind of evidence is not allowed for public policy purposes. Don't want to punish someone for fixing an unsafe condition.

5. Settlement offer inadmissible to show liability: Courts prefer the parties settle and if statements made in settlement negotiations are admissible it would remove the incentive for parties to settle.

6. Liability insurance evidence only allowed to show ownership or control not allowed to be introduced to show liability or ability to pay.

Question 14—Evidence—10 points

1. Rita's apology to Petunia may be admissible as a present sense impression. It is hearsay, an out of court stated for the truth of the matter asserted, but it is admissible under the present sense impression exception. Rita ran right over, and said I am sorry when the patron tripped. It may also be a party admission. It may also be brought in for impeachment purposes.
2. Harriet's promise to pay medical bills is inadmissible. It is contrary to public policy. Hence, Not admissible to show admission.
3. The ER report may be allowed under a business records exception to hearsay. However the statement "Harriet's absolute negligence" will be deemed inadmissible because it is an out of court statement offered for the truth of the matter asserted.
4. The fact that the mat was removed after the fall will not be brought in because it is a subsequent remedial measure. We want to encourage people to repair hazards. Therefore, it is not admissible to show ownership or control, but it may be admissible to show ownership or control of the premises.
5. An offer to settle is not admitted because we want to encourage people to settle their disputes. Therefore, as a matter of public policy, the settlement offer may not be brought in. However, her statement claiming the reason is because Harriet was "loaded" may be brought in.
6. A copy of the salon's one million dollar liability insurance policy may only be brought in to show ownership/control of the property. A "copy" is just as good as the original for the purposes of the "best evidence rule."

Question 14—Evidence—10 points

Petunia Potter vs. Harriet Hair Hine
Issues of admissibility of the following evidence:

1. Rita's apology to Petunia = this apology would be hearsay as an out of court statement introduced for the truth of the matter asserted. The issue is whether there is an exception. This would probably be admissible as an excited utterance exception because Rita made it right during the injury, or it can be admitted if a receptionist is considered Harriet's agent.
2. Harriet's promise to pay medical bills = is inadmissible as an offer to pay medical bills.
3. Emergency Room Report = is inadmissible hearsay not falling under an exception, they would try to admit it as a statement made for diagnosis but comments about who's fault it was isn't necessary for medical treatment.
4. The Removal of the Mat = Is inadmissible because subsequent remedial measures are inadmissible as against public policy because it would prevent businesses from making repairs to avoid admitting liability.
5. Harriet's Settlement Offer and Statement = This would be inadmissible because offers of settlement and statements made during settlement negotiations are inadmissible as against public policy because admissibility of statements would prevent a settlement.
6. Copy of Salon's Liability Insurance = Is inadmissible because proof of insurance is inadmissible because it isn't relevant to fault or a material issue in the case.

July 2008—Question 2

David Dawkins was arrested and charged with domestic violence against his live-in girlfriend, Velma Valliant. According to the complaint, David repeatedly punched and kicked Velma while the two attended David's high school reunion. David claims that he was acting in self-defense and that Velma attacked him after enjoying too much champagne.

Several weeks prior to the commencement of the trial, the prosecution provided notice that it intends to call Andrea Aims and Betty Bark as witnesses. Andrea will testify that she was David's girlfriend three years ago and that David physically abused her by slapping, punching and kicking her. Betty will testify that she was David's girlfriend eleven years ago and suffered very similar physical abuse. The prosecution maintains that their testimony is relevant because it tends to show that David acted in conformity with his past behavior on the day of his assault against Velma.

In addition to the testimony of Andrea Aims and Betty Bark, the prosecutor plans to call all 87 people who attended the high school reunion, who will testify that they saw David punching and kicking Velma, and that Velma was not the aggressor.

Defense counsel made a motion to exclude the evidence, arguing that this evidence was inadmissible, irrelevant, and highly prejudicial. Additionally, defense counsel plans to call Tom Tinker as a defense witness. Tom plans to testify about several past instances where he witnessed Velma's aggressiveness at social gatherings.

You are the judge assigned to the case of *People of the State of Michigan v David Dawkins.* Based on current Michigan law and rules of evidence, decide whether the testimony of Andrea Aims, Betty Bark, the reunion attendees, and Tom Tinker will be admissible. Explain your answer.

Model Answer to Question 2

A. Andrea Aims & Betty Bank: Generally, under MRE 404(b), evidence of other crimes or acts is not admissible to prove the character of a person in order to show that the person acted in conformity with the character. However, evidence of other crimes or acts can be admissible for other purposes. The rule provides:

> (1) Evidence of other crimes, wrongs, or acts is not admissible to prove the character of a person in order to show action in conformity therewith. It may, however, be admissible for other purposes, such as proof of motion motive, opportunity, intent, preparation, scheme, plan, or system in doing an act, knowledge, identity, or absence of mistake or accident when the same is material, whether such others crimes wrongs, or acts are contemporaneous with, or prior or subsequent to the conduct at issue in the case.

To be admissible under MRE 404(b): (1) the evidence must be offered for a proper purpose; (2) the evidence must be relevant; and (3) the probative value of the evidence must not be substantially outweighed by unfair prejudice. *People v VanderVliet*, 444 Mich 52 (1993). In addition, the trial court may, upon request, provide a limiting jury instruction. The purpose offered by the prosecutor is that the evidence shows that David acted in conformity with his past behavior. Because that is not a proper purpose under MRE 404(b), the testimony is not admissible under the evidentiary rule.

However, in 2006 the Michigan Legislature enacted MCL 768.27b, which permits the admission into evidence a defendant's other acts of domestic violence "for any purpose for which it is relevant." Thus is contract to the general evidentiary rule of MRE 404(b), prior acts of domestic violence are admissible in a domestic violence prosecution for propensity purposes under MCL 7658.24b. The statute specifically provides, however, that acts occurring more than 10 years before the charged offense are inadmissible unless the admission of the evidence "is in the interest of justice." MCL 768.27b(4). Because Betty Bark had a relationship with David eleven years ago, and because her testimony would be largely duplicative of the testimony provided by Andrea Aims, Betty's testimony would be excluded. Andrea's testimony, however, is admissible under MCL 768.27b.

B. The Reunion Attendees: Under MRE 401, evidence is relevant if it tends to make a consequential fact more probable or less probable than it would be without the evidence. The testimony of the reunion attendees, providing an eyewitness account of the assault and refuting defendants' self-defense claim, is certainly relevant evidence. However, under MRE 403 even relevant evidence may nevertheless be excluded if its probative value is substantially outweighed by considerations of needless presentation of cumulative evidence. In this case, the testimony of the 87 attendees is likely to be cumulative. Therefore, while some of the attendees will be permitted to testify, all 87 will not.

C. Tom Tinker: Tom Tinker will not be allowed to testify. Under MRE 404(a) evidence of a person's character is not admissible for the purpose of providing that a person acted in conformity with their character on a particular occasion. While MRE 404(a) provides several exceptions to this rule, none of those exceptions are applicable to Velma Valliant—she is not the accused (MRE 404(a)(1), she is not the alleged victim of homicide (MRE 404(a)(2)). While Velma may be impeached with the evidence of her character for aggressiveness (MRE 404(1)(4)), specific instances of her prior aggressive conduct may not be proved by extrinsic evidence under MRE 608(b). Thus, while Velma's credibility may be attacked by questioning her about the specific instances of aggressive conduct, the defense attorney will be limited to the responses Velma provides during cross-examination, and cannot attack her credibility through the extrinsic evidence of Tom's testimony.

Student Answer—July 2008

Question 2—Evidence—9 points

All evidence is admissible unless it is not allowed!!
Factors that determine this are:

1) Relevancy and if hearsay can only come in if there is an exception
2) Prejudicial effect

Hearsay is a statement that is being offered for the truth of the matter asserted. Relevancy has to do with making a material fact more probable or less probable. If it makes a material fact one of these then it will help the jury and the information will be let in. Of course, if the prejudicial effect outweighs the probative value then it will NOT be allowed in. The judge is the one that ultimately determines this b/c evidence although very important is not supposed to confuse or overwhelm the jury and prejudice the defendant.

Character evidence is generally not allowed to show that D acted in conformity. It is too prejudicial and will generally persuade the jury to convict even b/4 the evidence has been completed. Therefore, the rules of evidence do not usually allow character evidence in. However, if the D "opens the door" either by getting on the stand and saying how wonderful and non-violet he is then the prosecution can bring in witnesses to dispute the D's fairytale. However this testimony is limited to opinion and reputation of the D.

<u>Andrea Aims and Betty Bank testimony</u>

As stated above if this is used as character evidence then it can only be used after the D calls his character into question. If D does then Betty and Andrea's testimony will be limited to opinion and reputation they will not be able to testify to specific acts as indicated by saying they were abused when d slapped punched and kicked Andrea. However they both, Betty and Andrea could testify that D is violent.

Also, this testimony could come in under prior bad acts. Usually prior bad acts are *not* admissible and cannot be used to impeach to show that the D acted in conformity. However, if the bad act is to show motive, intent, mistake (lack there of), identity or common plan or scheme it will be allowed in.

The fact that D punched and kicked Velma just as he did Andrea and Betty could show the commonalities of the actions of D.

87 people who attended the high school reunion

Although their testimony is relevant and permissible because it was what they witnessed, and would be present sense impression or state of mind exceptions to hearsay rule. All 87 people will not be permitted to testify b/c the testimony would be too long and too confusing to the jury. You only need one to state what happened at the incident.

Tom Tinker

As to Tom's testimony the character rules of the victim are an issue. However, Tom's testimony will be allowed against Velma but he too cannot speak of specific acts he can only give reputation or opinion about Velma and once he does this it opens the door to *his*, Tom's reputation and the prosecutor can now bolster Velma's reputation.

As a side note: Tom has every right to bring a self defense claim as an issue in this case.

February 2009—Question 1

The Acme Party store in Suburb City was recently burglarized. When police investigated, they discovered that the floor of the store was littered with Wally's Wintergreen chewing gum wrappers and that a case of beer was missing. The perpetrator left behind a note in very distinctive handwriting that said, "I admit that I did this, but I only did it because I needed beer." After conducting a thorough investigation, the police arrested Dennis Dwayne, the leader of a small religious sect that worships Sasquatch and strictly forbids the consumption of alcohol. Dwayne plans to testify that he was out of town at the time of this incident.

The prosecutor plans to offer four pieces of evidence against Dennis Dwayne. First, the prosecutor plans to offer the testimony of Gladys Gage, Dwayne's housekeeper of three years, who will testify that, whenever she cleans Dwayne's home, the floors of his home are routinely covered in Wally's Wintergreen chewing gum wrappers. Second, the prosecutor plans to offer the testimony of Carolyn Clark, Dwayne's administrative assistant at the Sasquatch Temple, who will identify the distinctive handwriting on the note left in the store as being Dwayne's. Third, the prosecutor plans to admit only the first portion of the note—"I admit that I did this." Lastly, the prosecutor plans to offer the testimony of Dr. Hubert Hubris, a theologian who will testify that Dwayne's testimony is not credible because of his unusual doctrinal beliefs in the divinity of a fictional beast.

You are the defense attorney in the case of the *People of the State of Michigan v Dennis Dwayne*. Using the Michigan Rules of Evidence, assess the admissibility of the evidence against Dwayne. Explain your answer.

Model Answer to Question 1

The testimony of Gladys Gage is admissible. Under MRE 406, evidence of a person's habit is admissible to prove that a person's conduct on a particular occasion was in conformity with their habit. Under this evidentiary rule, evidence of the habit need not be corroborated. *Id.* Thus, Gladys can testify that Dwayne has a habit of leaving Wally's Wintergreen chewing gum wrappers on the floor.

The testimony of Carolyn Clark is also admissible. MRE 901(1), evidence must be authenticated or identified as a condition precedent to its admissibility. In order to properly authenticate or identify the author of the note left at the crime scene, Carolyn's non-expert opinion regarding the handwriting must be based on familiarity that was not acquired for the purposes of the litigation. MRE 901(b)(2). Here, Carolyn's familiarity with Dennis Dwayne's handwriting was premised upon her relationship with him as his administrative assistant, and was not acquired for the purposes of the criminal trial.

The letter itself is admissible as a party admission under MRE 801(d)(2)(A). The statement is allegedly Dwayne's statement, and it is being offered against him. While the rule contains an exception for statements made in connection with a guilty plea to a misdemeanor motor vehicle violation or motor vehicle civil infraction, those exceptions are not implicated here.

While the letter is admissible as a party admission, the defense attorney can seek the admission of the *entire* letter under MRE 106. Under this rule, otherwise known as the "rule of completeness," if a portion of a writing or recording is introduced by a party, then the adverse party can seek to have introduced any other parts of the writing or recording "which ought in fairness to be considered contemporaneously." In this case, admission of the second portion of the statement is favorable to Dwayne because it makes it less likely that Dwayne was the culprit because it indicates that motive for the crime was to obtain beer, while Dennis Dwayne maintains that religious beliefs preclude him from consuming alcohol.

Lastly, the testimony of Dr. Hubert Hubris is not admissible. Under MRE 610, evidence regarding a witness's beliefs on matters of religion is not admissible to show that the witness' credibility is impaired. Thus, Hubris will not be able to opine that Dwayne's credibility is suspect because of his unorthodox religious beliefs.

Three Student Answers—February 2009

Question 1—Evidence—10 points

1. Gladys Gage testimony: testimony may be admissible if it demonstrates a habit of conducting certain habits. Although it's a hearsay, out of court statement offered to prove the truth of matter asserted, it falls under the hearsay exception rule.
2. Carolyn Clark: lay person opinion testimony on identifying handwriting is admissible if the witness has personal knowledge of defendant's handwriting. Here, being as Dwayne's administrative assistant, surely she's exposed to and is familiar with Dwayne's penmanship.
3. The letter is admissible because it is a party admission being offered against the defendant. Note: under rule 106, if a portion of evidence is being admitted to the Court, the entire evidence should also be admitted in to avoid unfair prejudice to the defendant. As such, the defense can argue that prosecutor's intention of introducing in the self-incriminating portion of the note.
4. Dr. Hubris: even though Dr. Hubris might be qualified as an expert witness, he cannot attack on one's religious belief, which is protected by the First Amendment of U.S. Constitution

Comment: Note that full credit was awarded even though Gladys Gage's testimony in part 1 was incorrectly characterized as hearsay. It isn't. It is character evidence being offered to show character in conformity, which is generally inadmissible. However, habit is one exception that applies here. The grader missed this.

Question 1—Evidence—9 points

The issue is whether the prosecutor's various forms of evidence will be admissible against Dwayne.

To be admissible, evidence must be relevant. Relevant evidence is evidence that makes any fact more or less probable in the outcome, determination of the case. The evidence may be admissible for one purpose and not another.

Hearsay is an out of court statement, made by a declarant, offered to prove the truth of the matter asserted. There are exclusions and exceptions to this rule.

All evidence is subject to a balancing test. The rule weighs the probative (beneficial) value of the evidence against the prejudicial value of the defendant. If the prejudicial value outweighs its benefit, it is excluded.

Gladys-Gum Wrappers

Character evidence is inadmissible to show that someone acted in conformity with that character. Habit evidence is admissible to show that a person always done something in a given circumstance.

Gladys seeks to testify that Dwayne leaves the same kind of Gum wrappers found at the crime scene in his home. She will state that he does this "routinely."

"Routinely" is an indication of habit and would be admissible as habit evidence.

Defendant should argue that numerous people may have that habit and that it should be excluded as inadmissible character evidence. He should also argue its exclusion as highly prejudicial per rule 403.

Carolyn-Handwriting

A person familiar with another's handwriting may give their opinion in court as to whether certain handwriting matches that of someone whose handwriting she is familiar with. It does not have to be an expert.

The sample must be authenticated to be admissible-show that it is the one from the crime scene, chain of evidence, etc.

Here, Carolyn is Dwayne's administrative assistant and is therefore, probably very familiar with his handwriting. If so, she would be permitted to giver her opinion as to whether it is Dwayne's writing.

Dwayne should argue that she isn't familiar.

Note

Next is the issue regarding the Note. Since it is an original document, it can come into evidence per the best evidence rule. But the note must come in in its entirety. Part of a piece of evidence cannot come in if defendant chooses. It is up to defendant's counsel to demand the entire note be brought in.

And admission by a party opponent though hearsay is admissible under an exception to the rule.

Doctor's opinion

This testimony is inadmissible. Evidence of a person's character is inadmissible as discussed. The doctor could testify as to defendant's reputation in the community regarding truthfulness if defendant had testified but the facts are silent on that. The doctor testifying about a defendant's crazy beliefs would also be very prejudicial to defendant.

Question 1—Evidence—9 points

Evidence is subject to Michigan Rules of Evidence

1) Testimony by housekeeper-her testimony is not hearsay and is admissible as to testimony as to habit. Housekeeper of 3 years is familiar with their employee habits. Here housekeeper witnessed "routinely" that his house was covered with wrappers. She was an employee or agent of Dwayne's and was testifying as to her own visual observations as to Dwayne's habits. Testimony is not to show truth of the matter asserted but to show tendency for a particular habit. She is not testifying as to the wrappers at the store are his but that he at his home routinely discards wrappers on floor.
2) Testimony of Assistant-Admissible because expert witness is not needed to show handwriting analysis of a person. Only need a person who has specific knowledge of person's writing who can identify it. Here, a secretary has specific knowledge of her employer's hand writing. She deals with it daily and can actually tell if it is his particular handwriting.
3) Prosecutor admitting portion of Note: Admissible if the prosecutor can lay a proper foundation for the note. Also, if Defense so wishes the full entirety of note can be presented because the defendant is entitled to have all evidence produced against him so he can have a complete defense. Only showing part of evidence may seem unfair like they are being manipulated. Defendant is also entitled to present evidence explaining or not acknowledging that he wrote the note. This evidence is original found at scene of crime. If a chain of custody for the writing is established will be admissible.
4) Expert Testimony by Theologian: inadmissible: expert testimony is relevant if the expert has specific knowledge in the area and the testimony will explain a fact to the jury. The expert testimony is to assist the trier of fact with an issue. This particular expert is not doing any such thing. He is using evidence of religious belief to show uncredibility which will not be allowed in a court o law. The expert may be classified an expert in other situation not this case though. His beliefs are not at issue. His religion didn't play a part in this crime only it may have been an issue for motive. Particular religion cannot show uncredibility of defendant.

All this evidence is subject to judges discretion because in a criminal case evidence must be more probative then prejudicial effect.

July 2009—Question 1

Dan Dechini is on trial for the murder of Cameron Cole, Dechini's arch nemesis and primary sales competitor to Dechini's narcotics empire. According to the prosecutor's theory, Dechini opened fire on Cole as he left a local pizzeria on a Tuesday evening in

September. Dechini plans to present an alibi defense to the jury, claiming that he was tango dancing at a club with his longtime girlfriend, Kelli Kolada.

The trial prosecutor, Amber Starr, wants to present several pieces of evidence in the trial against Dechini. First, during preliminary plea discussions with the prosecution, Dechini offered to turn over the murder weapon in exchange for a reduced charge. Second, the prosecutor plans to call Miguel Morales, a third-grade special education student who speaks no English, to testify that he saw Dechini's vehicle leaving the pizzeria parking lot at a high rate of speed the evening of the murder. The prosecutor plans to use Miguel's mother, Carolina, to interpret during Miguel's testimony. Third, the prosecutor plans to call Circuit Judge York, who overheard Dechini coaching Kelli Kolada in the courthouse corridor regarding his alibi defense concerning their evening of tango dancing.

Utilizing the Michigan Rules of Evidence, assess the admissibility of the prosecutor's evidence. Explain your answer.

Model Answer to Question 1

1. Dechini's Statement: Normally, Dechini's statement would be substantively admissible against him under MRE 801(d)(2)(A) as the admission of a party-opponent. To be admissible under that rule, the statement must be (1) the party's own statement, and it must be (2) offered against the party. However, because Dechini's inculpatory statements occurred during the course of plea negotiations with the prosecutor, MRE 410(4) precludes the admission of the statement against Dechini. MRE 410(4) states that any statement made during plea discussions with the prosecutor that do not result in a guilty plea or result in a withdrawn guilty plea, are not admissible against the defendant. Note that Dechini's statement *can* be used in a perjury trial if the statement was made by the defendant under oath, on the record and in the presence of counsel. However, in the context of the murder trial, Dechini's statement is not admissible against him.

2. Testimony of Miguel Morales: Although Miguel is young and a special education student, MRE 601 provides that every person is presumed competent to be a witness unless the court determines, after questioning the witness, that the witness does not have sufficient physical or mental capacity or sense of obligation to testify truthfully. Thus, Miguel's testimony against Dechini, placing his car at the scene of the crime, is presumptively admissible, but he may be subject to challenge before he is allowed to testify. The defense must challenge Miguel's competency to trigger the court's obligation to assess the child's competency. Moreover, under MRE 604, Miguel's interpreter is subject to the expert qualification rules, and must make an oath or affirmation to make a true translation. The prosecutor is not prohibited from selecting its own expert. MRE 706(d). The court must determine that Carolina's specialized knowledge will assist the jury to understand the evidence and that she is qualified by knowledge, skill, experience, training, or education to interpret for Miguel. MRE 702. Because Miguel does not speak any English, an interpreter is required. Thus, Carolina will be permitted to interpret if the court is satisfied that she is qualified to do so accurately.

3. Testimony of Judge York: Whether Judge York's testimony is admissible depends on whether the judge is presiding over Dechini's trial. Under MRE 605, a judge presiding over a trial may not testify in that trial as a witness, and the defendant need not make an objection in order to preserve the issue on appeal. However, if Judge York is not presiding over Dechini's trial, then there should be no impediment to the admissibility of the testimony, which is relevant to rebut Dechini's alibi defense.

Three Student Answers—July 2009

Question 1—Evidence—9 points

This is an evidence question. First we look at the admissibility of the murder weapon. The general rule is that plea negotiations are not admissible as against a defendant as a matter of public policy. Plea discussions are encouraged to help keep the court docket free and are excluded from being admitted as a matter of public policy. Also, open communications are encouraged to get defendants to take pleas in order to expedite the court docket and save taxpayers time and money.

Next, we must look at whether Miguel can testify. The facts state that Miguel is in the third grade. A witness is deemed qualified to testify if they are of sound mind, know the difference between right and wrong, and know the difference between truth and a lie. It has been held in Michigan that just because a child is a minor, they are not disqualified from testifying because they are young, so long as the child understands truth and a lie. A child in the third grade (ages 8 or 9 years of age) should have the capacity to know what is the truth and should be allowed to testify as to what he saw.

Additionally, because Miguel's natural language is not English, this will not bar him from testifying. It is permitted by the court rules to have a translator interpret the testimony of a witness.

The question here is whether Miguel's mother may act as an interpreter. The interpreter is typically provided by the court and must be an unbiased third party. While the facts don't show Miguel's mother is affiliated with either side of this case-she may not be permitted to interpret. This will be up to the court to decide. Also the court can contact the 1-800 number to obtain a translator.

The last issue deals with the possible testimony of a judge. It is the general rule that a judge is not permitted to testify in any adversarial proceeding he/she is presiding over. It is unclear if he is presiding over this case.

Also, the issue become whether KK's discussion with her client is deemed privileged. Typically privilege is given to attorney/client communications, but those communications are severed (do not remain confidential) if a third party hears it.

The issue here is whether the judge in passing by the conversation in the courthouse corridor was intruding on a confidential attorney/client conversation that is privileged. If the corridor is typically a place attorneys prep their clients in lieu of their office the conversation may still be deemed confidential. Additionally, it is not improper for an attorney to coach a witness on how to answer questions (such as stick to the shortest and concise answers, don't elaborate, and respond with "yes" or "no", etc.) and there may be nothing improper for the judge to testify to, so long as the attorney was not coaching the witness to lie.

Comment: Notice the notation "KK's discussion" used in the second to last paragraph. Who is KK? The grader probably had to go back to the question to figure it out. Remember, using abbreviations is fine as long as it is clear. This examinee should have written "the witness, Kellie Kolada (KK)" to let the grader know who he or she was referring to.

Question 1—Evidence—8 points

First, the facts state that Dechini plans to present an alibi defense but they do not state that he was tango dancing when the purported murder happened. So his alibi will only be relevant if he was dancing when the murder occurred. Second, Dechini's offer of the murder weapon is not admissible as substantive evidence. The general rule is that preliminary hearings are conducted to review the evidence as the actual trial. Preliminary hearings are conducted to review the evidence, hear motions but they are not strictly governed by the rules of evidence.

Also, offers made in preliminary hearings (offers to settle, or retracted offers to settle) are not admissible at trial. The public policy rationale is that we want people to settle their cases without the fear that the statements will hurt them during the trial.

On the other hand, this may not be an offer to settle because there are no statements being made by the defendant: he is simply offering the gun in exchange for a reduced charge. On balance, the offer will not come into trial because of the public policy rationale discussed earlier.

Next, the issue is can Miguel testify at trial as to what he saw. The general rule is that anyone can be a witness (i.e. is competent to be a witness) as long as two requirements are satisfied: 1) the person has personal knowledge and 2) the person understands the significance of telling the truth. Whether someone is competent to testify is the judge's decision. Here, assuming that Miguel is a three year old can meet these two requirements he will be able to testify. However, the issue may be the relevancy of his testimony. According to the facts, Miguel saw Dechini speeding away from the pizza place, on the night of the murder. This may be relevant because it places the defendant at the crime scene and casts a doubt that he was tango dancing.

On balance, the testimony of Miguel comes in despite his age and any deficiencies in learning.

Next, Miguel's mother will not be able to act as an interpreter. The general rule is that interpreters must be expert witnesses. That is they must be proficient and have an expertise as an interpreter.

Lastly, the judge's testimony may be admissible as a party admission. Judges are not permitted to testify in cases they are presiding over. Here the facts do not state that the judge is the presiding judge in this case. If the judge is presiding over this matter than he would not be able to testify because he would lose his ability to be unbiased and fair.

Lastly, the fact that the defendant is "coaching" on how his girlfriend should testify is not permissible and a violation of the Model rules. If this can be proven the defendant may be subject to court contempt order or possibly other criminal charges. However, the issue is bringing the statement into trial. The prosecutor can use this to impeach Kelli's credibility while she is on the witness stand by asking her about the coaching.

Question 1—Evidence—8 points

This is an evidence question. The prosecutor wants to present several pieces of evidence in the trial against Dechini.

1. Murder Weapon/Preliminary Plea Discussions: The evidence is inadmissible. Preliminary plea discussions are not admissible nor is the information obtained during the plea discussions. Dechini during the plea discussion.

Dechini offered, during plea negations to talk about the murder weapons in exchange for a reduced charge. Evidence from/during plea negations is not going to be admitted because courts wants to encourage parties to resolve matters. This evidence is inadmissible.

2. Miguel Morles' Testimony: A person can testify as a witness as long as he/she is competent to do so. Age can be an issue-too young if a person doesn't understand the nature of what he is doing, or doesn't understand what it is that is being asked of him. Here, Morales is a third grade special education student who speaks no English. That is ok, as his mother would be in court to interpret. During Miguel's testimony the defense will argue that Moralez is not competent to testify-his special education student and he does not speak English. Miguel's testimony is admissible-he can testify to what he saw-Dechinis vehicle leaving his pizzeria parking lot at a high rate of speed the evening of the murder. Just because Miguel is a special education student doesn't mean he can't think for himself, that the court can testify to what he saw. There are varying degrees of special education students, and no facts to show he is not competent to testify. Miguel can give his opinion as to what he saw that day, and use his mother as an interpreter. Defense may argue that his mother shouldn't interpret for her son because of a conflict of interest, and that another interpreter should be brought in. But she knows her son, he trusts her and she can interpret for son. Thus Miguel will be able to testify as to what he saw as admissible.
3. Circuit Judge York: This would be an out of court statement offered to prove the truth of the matter asserted-hearsay. Also, this is a circuit court judge-facts don't state whether he is presiding over the case. If he is, he can't testify. If he is not presiding over the case, and the prosecutor wants to call him, prosecutor would argue that this information is pertinent to the case. Dechini was coaching Kelli in the courthouse regarding his alibi defense concerning their evening together. Judge could testify to what he observed and his observations. But it would be discreet out of court statements. This information could be used regarding admission by a party opponent. Defendant's saying he has an alibi. Then coaching someone about it. Still, if Judge is presiding over the case, he can not testify.

Thus plea negations will not come in, Miguel's testimony will come in, Miguel's testimony will come in, and judges' observations may come in, if he is not the presiding judge in the case.

February 2010—Question 5

John Jones has owned Sunshine Bakery for many years. In November, he had a "Grand Re-Opening" to celebrate his new redesigned store. Many people, including local media, were on hand for the event. Ms. Grandy, an 85-year-old woman, attended the event. After purchasing a few items, she went to exit the building. Seeing a golden opportunity, Jones held the door open for Ms. Grandy as she started down the steps while a local news photographer clicked away. Suddenly, Ms. Grandy fell from the top step. After her fall, Jones helped Ms. Grandy to her feet, and an off-duty nurse provided some bandages for Ms. Grandy's scraped knees. After about

30 minutes, and as Ms. Grandy was about to leave, Jones said "I'm sorry about this, and even though it was not my fault, would you accept $100 and a month's worth of pie if we can forget about this unfortunate event?" Ms. Grandy refused, stating "It sure was your fault, and I'll see you in court." As she left the scene she heard Jones exclaim, "I knew I should have had that step repaired."

A week later, Ms. Grandy received in the mail a photograph of her at the time she started to fall. On her way to thank the news photographer, Ms. Grandy passed the bakery, where she saw to her amazement that the steps had been completely replaced. Angered, she went to see a lawyer, who filed a premises liability suit entitled *Grandy v John Jones and Sunshine Bakery*. At trial, Ms. Grandy's attorney sought to have his client testify on direct examination to the following:

1. That upon leaving the scene she heard Jones state, "I knew I should have had that step repaired."
2. That Jones knew he was negligent because he offered her $100 and a month's worth of pie.
3. That within a week the faulty steps were replaced with new ones.

Finally, her lawyer also sought to have the photograph admitted through Ms. Grandy.

Defense counsel objected to the testimony, as well as to the attempt to admit the photograph.

Discuss whether the testimony and exhibit should be admitted. Explain your answer.

Model Answer to Question 5

The first issue is whether Ms. Grandy can testify to what Jones said after she fell. Since this raises a hearsay issue, the applicant should first set out the appropriate definitions. Hearsay "is a statement, other than the one made by the declarant while testifying at the trial or hearing, offered in evidence to prove the truth of the matter asserted." MRE 801(c). Hearsay is not admissible unless it comes within an exception. MRE 802. All out-of-court statements offered to prove the truth of the matter asserted are not inadmissible hearsay. In particular, a statement is not hearsay if it is offered against a party and it is the party's own statement. MRE 801(d)(2)(A).

For several reasons, Ms. Grandy should be allowed to testify to what Jones stated. First, the statement is not hearsay because it is a statement made by a party opponent. Clearly Jones was the declarant, and he is a defendant in the case. Thus, it is admissible. It could also be argued that it is not hearsay because it is not being offered for the truth of the matter asserted; i.e., that Jones should have fixed the stairs, but to instead prove that as the owner, Jones was on notice that the stairs were defective. See *Clark v Kmart*, 465 Mich 416, 419 (2001). (Notice of dangerous condition is relevant in premises liability cases.) Either way, it is not hearsay and is admissible.

Points should be awarded if the applicant determines that the evidence is relevant, MRE 401, and the probative value is not substantially outweighed by unfair prejudice. MRE 403. Finally, this is not a declaration against interest, as Jones is available to testify. MRE 804(b)(3); MRE 804(a)(4), *Sackett v Atyeo*, 217 Mich App 676, 684 (1996). It is also not admissible as a present sense impression, MRE 803(1), or as an excited utterance, MRE 803(2), as the facts reveal that Jones made the statement at least 30 minutes after the fall, and there is nothing to suggest that he was under any stress of excitement from seeing Ms. Grandy fall. *See Johnson v White*, 430 Mich 47, 57-58 (1988) and *Hewitt v Grand Truck WR Co*, 123 Mich App 309, 320-322 (1983).

The second issue is whether Ms. Grandy can testify to Jones' offer to settle her potential claim. Initially, it should be noted that, for the reasons outlined above, the statement is not hearsay because it is an admission of a party opponent. MRE 801(d)(2)(A). However, under MRE 408 evidence of an offer to furnish consideration to compromise a claim that is disputed as to either amount or validity is inadmissible.

The third issue is whether Ms. Grandy can testify about the replaced stairs she saw a week after the accident. MRE 407 precludes evidence of subsequent remedial measures that if made previously would have made the event less likely to have occurred. Ms. Grandy's testimony is clearly prohibited. No facts have been provided to suggest that it was offered to show ownership, control, or feasibility of the measure, and its only possible use would be to prove that Jones and the bakery were negligent.

As to the final issue, "[t]o lay a proper foundation for the admission of photographs, a person familiar with the scene depicted in the photograph must testify, on the basis of personal knowledge, that the photograph is an accurate representation." *Knight v Gulf & Western Properties, Inc*, 196 Mich App 119, 133 (1992). The original photograph is normally required for admission, MRE 1002, but a duplicate would be admissible in the absence of doubt as to the duplicate's authenticity. MRE 1003. Here Ms. Grandy can testify to the accuracy of the scene depicted in the photograph, as she was there when it occurred. There is also nothing to suggest that the photo was not the original. Additionally, neither the fact that she did not take the photo, *Ferguson v Delaware International Speedway*, 164 Mich App 283, 291 (1987), nor the fact the scene has partially changed since the photo was taken, *Knight, supra* at 133, precludes her from establishing its foundation for admission.

Four Student Answers—February 2010

Question 5—Evidence—10 points

This is an evidence issue:

1) Although this statement seems like it would be hearsay because it is being offered to prove that Jones should have had the step fixed, it will treated as a party admission because Jones is a party and he said it, thus the court will allow it in as evidence.
2) Settlement officers are never allowed in to prove that the other party was negligent because courts like to encourage settlement; however this was not a settlement offer because at the time that Mr. Jones gave that statement, Grandy made no mention that she was going to bring suit. This statement would be allowed in.
3) This is a subsequent remedial measure. This type of evidence is never allowed in to prove that someone is at fault. Courts want to encourage repair as a public policy reason. Make repairs when necessary and if subsequent repairs were allowed to be used as evidence against a party, nobody would make repairs. The only time a subsequent remedial measure would be admissible is if it was being used to show something like the party owned the thing in which you

were injured by. Here, this is not the case, because facts clearly indicate that Jones was the owner. The subsequent remedial measure will not be allowed into evidence.

4) A photo can admitted into evidence if it is relevant and if it is authenticated. Authenticated can be shown by a person testifying that the picture is a fair and accurate description of the place that is being described and that nothing has subsequently changed from that picture. It does have to be authenticated by the person who took that picture. It can be authenticated by anyone with knowledge and familiarity of the scene and situation. Here Grand will be able to authenticate it. It is of her falling from the step in which this cause of action statement from. The picture is admissible.

It is important to remember that when using all evidence it must be relevant. It has to have a tendency to prove that something is more or less probable to have occurred by using this evidence. The probative value of the evidence cannot be substantially outweighed by its prejudicial value. If all of the above evidence is deemed to be relevant then my answers to each issue above stands.

Question 5—Evidence—9 points

This is an evidence question.

Evidence will be relevant if it has any tendency, however, slight to make a material fact of the case more probable or less probable then the case would be without the evidence. Also, all evidence is admissible unless; a) it is excluded by an evidentiary rule or b) in the discretion of the court, the judge as referee finds that the evidence should be substantially more prejudicial than pragmatic. Additionally, an out of court statement asserted by an out of court declarant is considered hearsay if it is offered to prove the truth of the mattered asserted.

The statement "I knew I should have had that step repaired," is hearsay, however, the judge may allow the statement in as a party admission. The judge would likely find that this statement's prejudicial value substantially outweighs any pragmatic concerns. This goes to the ultimate issue of the case and if admitted would certainly make the jury believe John was negligent in repairing the step. Thus, this statement would not be admissible testimony.

Next, the statement that Jones knew he was negligent b/c he offered her $100 per month and a month's worth of pie will not be permitted as testimony. Under MRE, Statements entered on behalf of settlement negotiations will not be permitted as testimony. The testimony is a statement of settlement negotiations b/c Jones was trying to offer pie in lieu of Grandy forgetting the incident. Thus, the testimony would not be admissible.

Next, testimony relating to the faulty stairs being repaired will not be permitted b/c it is evidence of subsequent remedial measure. Subsequent remedial measures will not be permitted in as testimony. For public policy reasons courts do not want to prevent individuals/corporations to be prevented from making repairs after an injury has occurred on the premises. Thus, the court will not allow this statement to come in as evidence of subsequent remedial measures.

The Photograph

The photograph will be admissible. Under MRE, a photograph can be authenticated by an individual who can testify that the photograph is familiar to them and that is an authentic picture displaying what it purports to represent. The lawyer for Grandy can admit the picture through her familiarity with the situation.

Question 5—Evidence—8 points

This is an Evidence question.

Testimony 1- "I knew I should have had that step repaired": Admissible. This is being offered by prosecution as an out of court statement to prove the truth of the matter asserted and is typically hearsay. However there are statements considered non-hearsay and one is party admissions. Party admissions are statements made by a party and they are admissible. It is possible it could also come in as an excited utterance exception to hearsay because Jones exclaimed the remark in the excitement of the event.

Testimony 2- Offer to pay $100 and a months worth of pie: Admissible. Statements made when offering to pay for injuries when there is not yet a controversy and thus damages or injury not in question are admissible. But not admissible to prove negligence.

Testimony 3- testimony that faulty steps were replaced: Admissible

Subsequent remedial measures are not admissible to show culpability or negligence but is admissible to prove ownership or control or feasibility of safer condition.

Exhibit- Photograph: Admissible. Photographs can be introduced as exhibits if they are relevant and can be authenticated if a witness can testify that what is depicted in the photograph is what they saw an is an accurate depiction of people, actions or places at the time is was taken.

Question 5—Evidence—8 points

A issue of fact is admissible unless such would be more prejudicial than dispositive.

1) I knew I should have had the step repaired: That statement will be admitted to show the defendant did have prior knowledge of the issue. Thus because showing prior knowledge not based on the matter asserted and would not be hearsay, and thus admitted.
2) $100 + Month Pie: offers of settlement are inadmissible to prove fault in the ultimate matter. Thus this statement would be excluded.
3) Fixed steps: Subsequent remedial repairs are not allowed to show the person is at fault. We want society to take steps to ensure accidents don't happen again. The repairs would be allowed if offered to show ownership, insurance or that an alternative feasible design was available, so this issue ultimately rests on what is the statement being offered for.
4) Photograph: The photo would be admitted if the proper foundation was laid. Just because Grandy did not take the photo does not mean that Grandy can't authenticate it. Grandy had first hand knowledge of the events and would be able to testify that the picture is a fair and accurate representation of events that day, thus authenticating the photo.

July 2010—Question 14

Dirk, a one-time karate instructor who has worked only sporadically in recent years, has gained a reputation as a "tough guy" in his Michigan hometown. A large, bearded man, Dirk is often seen hanging out at various bars and street corners in his omnipresent Detroit Tigers cap. Dirk has been suspected, but never charged, in several incidents in which individuals who were behind in their payments to Lloyd, a local loan shark, received anonymous telephone calls threatening them with bodily harm. Now, however, Dirk is charged with felonious assault in the beating of Victor, who was surprised from behind in his own back yard and beaten unconscious with a flurry of punches to the chest, jaw and neck. Victor never saw his attacker and could offer no information to identify him. Asked if he knew who might have a motive to harm him, Victor admitted that he owed money to Lloyd and had recently received a call warning him to pay up or he would get hurt. Dirk denies the charge and claims he was home alone playing solitaire at the time of the attack. It appears Dirk will also defend on the basis that he and Victor are drinking buddies and he would have no reason to hurt Victor.

Victor's initial shout of surprise and the sound of punches and groans attracted the attention of his next door neighbors, Harry and Wilma. Harry looked out the upstairs window and became agitated. He shouted to Wilma: "Someone is beating up our neighbor Victor! It's a big guy with a beard and a baseball cap! He's hitting him in the head . . . and the chest . . . and again . . . and again! It looks like that no-good Dirk!" At the time, Wilma was across the room talking on a wall phone to their daughter Donna. Wilma also became very excited; she breathlessly repeated to Donna exactly what Harry was telling her he saw, but she did not cross the room. This continued for approximately thirty seconds until Harry said the attack was over and Wilma ended her call with Donna.

A few weeks later, Harry and Wilma's car was hit by a drunk driver. Harry was killed and Wilma received injuries that wiped out portions of her memory, including any recollection of the beating incident. The prosecutor intends to have Donna testify about what Wilma told her on the phone the day of the incident to establish that Dirk was the attacker.

The prosecutor also wants to introduce the testimony of John, another borrower who was late in repaying Lloyd, and who came forward to volunteer information. Two weeks before the incident involving Victor, John was attacked by someone who jumped him from behind in his apartment entryway and tried to stun him with a blow to the head. But John was more fortunate. He used his three years of karate training to dodge the attacker and parry the blows aimed at his head and chest. John recognized the attacker as his former karate instructor, Dirk, who turned and ran. Although at first John did not report this experience because he feared something worse might happen to him, John is now prepared to testify about it at Dirk's trial.

Evaluate the probable admissibility of the above evidence. What issues and outcomes do you see? Explain your answer.

Model Answer to Question 14

The question whether Donna can testify to what Wilma told her Harry was saying raises several connected hearsay issues. Hearsay "is a statement, other than the one made by the declarant while testifying at the trial or hearing, offered in evidence to prove the truth of the matter asserted." MRE 801(c). Hearsay is not admissible unless it comes with an exception. MRE 802. MRE 803 enumerates a variety of circumstances in which statements or documents are not excluded by the hearsay rule, regardless of whether the declarant is available as a witness. MRE 804 states additional exceptions that may apply when the declarant is unavailable.

The purpose of Donna's proposed testimony is to place before the jury Harry's contemporaneous tentative identification of Dirk as Victor's attacker. Because Donna did not hear this directly from Harry but only heard Wilma's statement about what Harry was saying, this is an instance of "hearsay within hearsay." To be admissible, each level of hearsay must fall within an exception to the hearsay rule. MRE 805; *Merrow v Bofferding*, 458 Mich 617 (1998).

Wilma's statement to Donna is admissible under MRE 803(2) as an excited utterance: a "statement relating to a startling event or condition made while the declarant was under the stress of excitement caused by the event or condition." Having her husband shouting that their neighbor was being severely beaten is certainly a "startling event or condition," and Donna can testify that her mother, Wilma, was excited and under stress at the time she made her statement. Harry's statement within Wilma's statement must also be admissible for Wilma's statement to have any value, and it is. Harry's simultaneous description of what he saw happening next door is admissible both under MRE 803(2) as an excited utterance and under MRE 803(1) as a statement of present sense impression—a description of an event or condition made while the declarant, Harry, was perceiving the event.

Note: Some examinees may raise the issue of whether the statements of Harry and Wilma, who are not testifying at the trial, should be excluded under the Sixth Amendment confrontation clause analysis of *Crawford v Washington* because Dirk did not have a prior opportunity to cross-examine them. This question does not present such an issue because the statements of Harry and Wilma are not "testimonial statements," *e.g.* statements given at a prior trial or hearing or during a police interrogation.

The purpose of introducing John Jones' testimony about a completely different incident is to show that Dirk attempted a similar assault on another "customer" of Lloyd's, and it is thus more probable that Dirk committed the assault on Victor. The obstacle to introducing John's testimony is MRE 404(b)(1); "evidence of other crimes, wrongs, or acts is not admissible to prove the character of a person in order to show action in conformity therewith." But such "other acts evidence" may be admissible for other purposes, such as "proof of motive [or] scheme, plan or system (surprising the victim from behind and disabling him with a flurry of blows).

If the proponent of "other acts" evidence articulates a reason for its introduction beyond just showing a party's propensity for certain conduct (which is not enough), the court conducts a further analysis to determine its admissibility. *People v Vandervliet*, 444 Mich 52 (1993). The evidence must be relevant and its probative value cannot be substantially outweighed by the danger of undue prejudice, in light of other means of proof for the proposition in question. (The court may also take into account whether a limiting instruction would be effective in cushioning the unfairly prejudicial impact of the evidence.) Here, the evidence tends to establish Dirk's identity as Victor's attacker, but one can argue about how strongly it does this. The court will probably find that the evidence fails the balancing test. The method used in the two assaults is similar, but it is not strikingly unique. Because John will give eyewitness testimony that Dirk recently committed an assault other than the one with which he is charged, there is a strong risk that the jury will in effect convict him of that offense rather than the charged offense. It is doubtful that a limiting instruction can sufficiently cure this risk. [This is the recommended analysis, but it is possible to argue the other side of any of the factors in this paragraph, and appropriate credit should be given for any logically framed position that balances relevance and unfair prejudice.]

Student Answer—July 2010

Question 14—Evidence—None Available

PARTNERSHIP/AGENCY

Questions, Model Answers, and Student Answers

The following section includes prior Michigan Bar Exam questions and model answers for **Partnership and Agency**. Many of the questions also include actual student answers with the amount of points that were earned to give you a better idea of what the graders expect. The student answers are immediately following the model answer for each question. Please pay close attention to the points received on each question. Although most samples represent "good" answers (i.e., received 8, 9, or 10 points), there are some samples that received 7 points (the minimum "passing" score for an essay), and a few that received very low scores to help you better understand the grading process and what is expected.

July 2001—Question 6

Joseph Myers was employed by Community Mortgage Company. Joseph occupied a small office in a shopping mall and was authorized to process mortgage applications. Joseph reported to the principal office located several miles away.

June Smith came into Joseph's office seeking financing to purchase a vacant lot where she hoped to build a home. June had recently inherited $25,000 in cash, but prior to this windfall had a horrible credit rating and had been turned down by a number of mortgage companies. Joseph took the information and submitted the application to Community Mortgage, which was summarily rejected. He advised her of this rejection and then told June that if she wanted, he would help her out and obtain the financing and purchase the property in his name, using her down payment. After the transaction was closed, Joseph was to place June's name on the title, and she was to make monthly payments to him in the same amount he owed for the mortgage payments. The agreement to convey the title back to June was written on a blank note pad. Joseph obtained the financing and purchased the property in his name. After closing, June approached Joseph about placing the property in both their names, and Joseph continually stalled.

Subsequently, June discovered that Joseph had sold the property to a third party at a significant profit. This profit did not last long as Joseph was a heavy investor in tech stock and was caught in the stock market crash, losing everything. June consults an attorney who determines it is useless to sue Joseph for damages, but decides to sue Community Mortgage and Real Estate Company for the actions of Joseph while an employee of that company.

What are June's attorney's legal theories on this matter, and what will be the defense?

Model Answer to Question 6

Plaintiff's Claim: The legal theory that June would proceed under would be Respondeat Superior and failure to survive. June would claim that she believed she was dealing with Community Mortgage through its employee; that she came to the office of Community Mortgage, which office was simply staffed by its employee, Joseph Myers; that Community Mortgage has an obligation to its customers to be responsible for the acts of its employees.

June would continue to claim that Mr. Myers was obviously authorized to process mortgage applications and that is, in fact, what he did for her. Whether Mr. Myers had this authority to personally finance the purchase of the property is immaterial, since his conduct was within the apparent scope of his authority.

Defendant's Response: The defendant would contend that while Joseph Myers was an employee, he acted clearly outside the scope of his employment when he engaged in this private transaction with June. June was advised that her application with the mortgage company was denied and it is reasonable to assume that at that point she knew she was no longer dealing with Mr. Myers as an employee of the mortgage company, but as an individual. The mortgage company was not financing the purchase and there is no showing from the facts of this case that the mortgage company received any benefit from this transaction.

A reasonable person in the exercise of reasonable prudence would not believe that Mr. Myers, who was having the title to the property placed in his name, was acting on behalf of Community Mortgage.

Generally speaking, determination of whether the employee is acting outside of his authority is a question of fact; but summary disposition is available where it is apparent from the facts that the employee is attempting to accomplish a purpose of his own.

The employer's duty to supervise is also related to the employee's performance of work within the scope of his employment. If it is found that the employee is acting outside of the scope of employment, there is generally no responsibility of the employer, unless it can be established that his is a pattern of conduct known and approved by the employer. There are no facts available that would support a claim that this was a common act or an act approved on prior occasions by the employer. The plaintiff's case would rise or fall on the Respondeat Superior claim. *Smith v Merrill Lynch*, 155 Mich App 230 (1986). Central Wholesale Co v Sefa, 351 Mich 17 (1957). *Norris v State Farm Ins*, 229 Mich App 231 (1998).

Student Answer—July 2001

Question 6—Agency—None Available

February 2002—Question 3

Ellen Ready was the owner of a small building and a liquor license that was being held in escrow. John Gladhander, who was unemployed, was dating Ellen and ultimately began living with her. John had plans for the operation of a sports bar and talked Ellen into activating the license and opening a bar in her building.

John worked at the bar as bartender/short-order cook and was in charge of hiring and firing. Ellen handled the books, the payroll, and all the ordering. From time to time when they were "flush," Ellen would give John cash in different amounts. The bar became a success, much more so than Ellen and John's living arrangement. After approximately three years, Ellen and John separated and when John showed up for work, he was advised by a new bartender/bouncer that he was not needed and to hit the road. John hit the road and went directly to his lawyer's office. He claimed that he was Ellen's partner and wanted the partnership dissolved and his fair share of the partnership profits and equity. John acknowledged there was no written partnership agreement but claimed that Ellen often told him that he was the best partner she ever had.

John's lawyer files suit on his behalf seeking ownership rights as a partner or alternatively dissolution of the partnership and his fair share of the equity of the partnership as an equal partner with Ellen.

Directing your attention solely to the partnership issue, what arguments can be presented for John and Ellen, and what would you anticipate the ultimate court decision to be?

Model Answer to Question 3

Generally, the determination of whether a partnership exists is a question of fact since it is the intention of the parties that is of prime importance. The elements of partnership include a voluntary association of two or more people with the legal capacity to carry on a business for profit.

John would argue that the bar was originally his idea and he was equally responsible for the success of this business and acted in a capacity typical of an owner rather than employee. John would also argue that the payments made to him were not regular as a salary would be and were his share of the profits and that is prima facie evidence that he is a partner.

On the other hand, Ellen would point out that she owned the property and the liquor license and never placed John on the title to either. John, she would point out, never made a capital contribution and did not perform any work that an employee would not perform. Furthermore, she would claim the payments made to John were really wages for his work performed rather than a sharing of the profits. Ellen would emphasize that the living arrangement is not helpful to support John's claim of a partnership. *Tyranski v Piggins*, 44 Mich App 570 (1973); *Carnes v Sheldon*, 109 Mich App 294 (1981). Finally, Ellen would point out that there was no partnership agreement, there was never a certificate of co-partnership filed or even drawn up, and while she would admit calling John the best partner she ever had, it had nothing to do with the operation of the bar.

The burden of proof is on the party alleging the existence of the partnership. The limited facts presented create a close question and the ultimate decision is not critical, although John would probably lose. As long as the appropriate arguments are recognized and the issue of burden of proof is recognized, a passing grade is appropriate.

Miller v City Bank, 82 Mich App 120 (1978).

Student Answer—February 2002
Question 3—Partnership—10 points

ISSUE: Can John gain partnership status of the sports bar notwithstanding Ellen's objection?

John's argument that ownership rights as a partner should be granted: Even though there was no written partnership agreement, Ellen had often told John that he was "the best partner she ever had." John was led to believe by Ellen that they were partners. John acted as though he was a partner. From the very beginning it was John's idea to open a sports bar. Once it was opened, he worked at the bar for three years. He did a variety of things from the bartender-cook-hiring & firing. These activities show a high level of overall responsibility to the bar as well as authority. John & Ellen lived together & it was only when John & Ellen's relationship failed that John was not allowed to be a part of the bar anymore. Ellen did not even give him notice that he may not work there or offered any compensation for his time, work, and dedication to the sports bar.

Ellen's argument that ownership rights as a partner should not be granted: Ellen never agreed to a partnership arrangement verbally or in a writing. No ownership or title changes were made. Ellen owned the building and the license. John paid no consideration for the use of and put up no assurances of financial backing if the sports bar business was a flop. Ellen was on the hook herself. She should be able to profit by her ownership of such. John's statement that Ellen said he was the "best partner she ever had" could be taken under a different context than what John is trying to use it for. Because John and Ellen lived together, the partner comment could mean to signify their personal relationship/their living arrangements. John did work at the store but he was also paid by Ellen and Ellen was in charge of running the sports bar financially. John gave no substantial input to the business other than what an employee could do.

Anticipation of the ultimate court decision: Without other facts being presented, the court would probably deny John's request to be given partnership status in the sports bar.

July 2006—Question 15

John Jones was injured in an automobile accident and was taken by ambulance to the emergency room of Municipal Hospital. The emergency room doctor, Dr. Smith, took one look at the x-rays of Mr. Jones' back and told him that he should be seen by Dr. O. Mr. Jones' wife made a call to Dr. O's office and was advised that Dr. O was currently at Universal Hospital making rounds and could be seen there.

Mr. Jones was then transported by his family to Universal Hospital and, upon arriving at "reception," asked to see Dr. O. Dr. O was able to see Mr. Jones in less than one hour in the Universal Hospital emergency room. After reviewing the x-rays from Municipal Hospital, Dr. O advised both Mr. Jones and his family that surgery was necessary. Mr. Jones was admitted to Universal Hospital and later that night Dr. O operated on Mr. Jones. The operation was less than a success and Mr. Jones lost the use of both legs.

Mr. Jones consulted an attorney who had the matter reviewed by an expert. The expert concluded that the only reason that Mr. Jones had lost the use of his legs was because of the malpractice committed by Dr. O.

Mr. Jones and his lawyer found out that Dr. O was a private practitioner who had a very small office, and while he was an orthopedic surgeon, he had a very limited practice. Mr. Jones' attorney filed a lawsuit naming Municipal Hospital, Dr. Smith, Universal Hospital and Dr. O as defendants. Universal Hospital has filed a motion for summary disposition on the grounds that Dr. O was an independent contractor and the hospital, therefore, was not liable for his actions. Mr. Jones is contesting the motion on the basis that Dr. O was an agent of Universal Hospital and, as such, the hospital was responsible for his malpractice.

Limiting your answer to the issue of agency between Dr. O and Universal Hospital, discuss the principles involved. What will be the outcome of this motion, and why?

Model Answer to Question 15

In general, a hospital is not vicariously liable for the negligence of a physician who is an independent contractor and simply uses the hospital's facilities to provide treatment to his own patients. However, if the patient looked to the hospital to provide medical treatment, and the hospital made a representation that medical treatment would be afforded by physicians working at the hospital, an agency by estoppel may be found.

An agency is ostensible when the principal intentionally, or by want of ordinary care, causes a third person to believe him to be the principal's agent when he is not actually employed by the principal. There are three elements necessary to establish the creation of an ostensible agency: (1) the person dealing with the agent must do so with belief in the agent's authority and this belief must be a reasonable one, (2) the belief must be generated by some act of neglect on the part of the principal sought to be charged, and (3) the person relying on the agents authority must not himself be guilty of negligence. Here, Universal Hospital, as the putative principal, must have done something that would create in the patient's mind the reasonable belief that Doctor O was acting on behalf of Universal Hospital. The most critical question is whether the patient "looked to" the hospital treatment.

The fact that a doctor used a hospital's facilities to treat a patient is not sufficient to give the patient a reasonable belief that the doctor was an agent of the hospital. Also, the fact that a doctor has staff privileges at a hospital, by itself, is insufficient to establish an agency relationship.

In this case, there are no facts that would support a conclusion that the hospital did anything to cause a belief that Dr. O was an employee of the hospital. Mr. Jones was not referred to Universal Hospital for treatment; he was referred to Dr. O. The fact that Mr. Jones found Dr. O at Universal Hospital and was treated there does not create an agency relationship between the hospital and Dr. O. Mr. Jones did not look to the hospital for treatment, he was looking to Dr. O. Based upon the facts of this case, there is no agency, and Universal Hospital's motion for summary disposition should be granted.

Student Answer—July 2006

Question 15—Agency—6 points given on exam, 3 more earned on appeal; total of 9 points

If DR. O is an agent of Universal Hospital, then Universal Hospital can have liability for DR. O's malpractice. Agency can be express or implied. Here, since the hospital says he was an independent contractor they are saying he was no expressly an agent of the hospital. But under implied agency theory, the fact that Jones saw patients in the hospital and performed surgery there implies or infers that he worked there and that the hospital had knowledge of it. To all appearances to Jones, DR. O was an agent of the hospital. Even the fact that the other DR. told Jones to find DR. O at the Universal Hospital leads to the conclusion that Dr. O was an agent of the hospital. Clearly the hospital allowed Dr. O to operate in the hospital—they had knowledge. Jones was admitted to the hospital, under DR. O's care that took place at the hospital. The hospital provided the tools, the operating room, etc. These things point more toward agency than an independent contractor status. The argument of independent contractor would have more merit if upon arrival at the hospital; Jones was told he must see DR. O off-site at his own office. This would have clued Jones in that there may be some separation between DR. O and the hospital. But this is not in our facts and to all appearances Dr. O worked for university hospital with their knowledge. As a result of Dr. O's limited practice—the hospital should have been aware of the potential of malpractice due to his inexperience. If Jones's lawyer found this out, certainly the hospital could have too. Therefore, based on implied agency theory, the court should dismiss or rule against the summary disposition by hospital and allow Jones to proceed in his malpractice case.

July 2007—Question 6

Sid and Beth were business persons in Ann Arbor, Michigan, who met on a red-eye flight into Detroit Metro from Los Angeles. Sid was returning from a convention of real estate agents and Beth was returning from her annual continuing education course in accounting. Both were energized and eager to put what they had learned to good use. As they sat discussing what they had each learned, they contemplated going into business together. Sid told Beth about a business he was considering forming that would buy real estate and obtain leases for income. He had already prepared a business plan, but asked Beth to be his partner. They would each make equal contributions of capital and share the profits and losses of the enterprise. Sid would use his skills in the real estate market to find "good buys" on property—like a hot parcel Sid had heard about on Empire Road. Beth would use her contacts to arrange financing and do the books.

Beth said she would meet with her banker-friend, Dave, in the morning about some financing arrangements Dave had been telling Beth about the week before. Sid indicated that he would call his attorney in the morning to set up an appointment to discuss how much it would cost to draft a partnership agreement. Sid, knowing from the last time he formed a partnership that his attorney required a $1,000.00 retainer to formalize the agreement and file any necessary documents, asked Beth for $500.00 in cash as they got off the plane.

The next day, Sid met with his attorney. He paid the $1,000.00 retainer with the money Beth had given him and $500.00 of his own money. At the same time across town, Beth met with Dave about financing the purchase of some real estate for her and Sid. During the course of their discussion, Beth and Dave decided they would form a partnership instead of the Sid and Beth arrangement. Beth and Dave then purchased the Empire Road property, found a tenant, and have been collecting rents. Beth never returned Sid's many phone calls. Sid's attorney writes Beth a letter alleging that a partnership existed between Sid and Beth, and that Beth owed a fiduciary duty to Sid, which she breached.

Beth comes to you for advice and assistance. Analyze Sid's claim and apprise Beth of her chance of success if Sid sues Beth alleging a partnership and a breach of fiduciary duty.

Model Answer to Question 6

A partnership exists where the parties agree and intend to enter into a relation "in which the elements of partnership may be found." *Miller v City Bank & Trust Co*, 82 Mich App 120, 124 (1978). The elements of a partnership are generally considered to include: "A voluntary association of two or more people with legal capacity in order to carry on, via co-ownership, a business for profit. Co-ownership of the business requires more than merely joint ownership of the property and is usually evidenced by joint control and the sharing of profits and losses." *Id.*

The Michigan Uniform Partnership Act, MCL 449.1 *et seq.*, defines a partnership as an association of two or more persons to carry on as co-owners a business for profit. MCL 449.6(1).

It has also been held in Michigan that absent an express agreement, the test to be applied in determining whether a partnership existed is to examine the acts, declarations and conduct of the parties in relation to the business and from the nature and scope of the business in which the acts are committed. *Western Shoe Co v Neumeister*, 258 Mich 662, 667 (1932). See also, *Van Stee v Ransford*, 346 Mich 116 (1956).

The Michigan Supreme Court recently held that the question of intent to form a partnership is not solely determinative of whether a partnership actually existed. *Byker v Mannes*, 465 Mich 637, 653 (2002). "Pursuant to MCL 449.6(1), in ascertaining the existence of a partnership, the proper focus is on whether the parties intended to, and in fact did, 'carry on as co-owners a business for profit' and not whether the parties subjectively intended to form a partnership" *Id.* The court further stated that it is unimportant whether the parties would have labeled themselves as "partners," as partners need not be aware of their status as "partners" in order to have a legal partnership. *Id.* "The gist of the partnership relation is mutual agency and joint liability." *Lobato v Paulino*, 304 Mich 668, 675 (1943). It has also been held that important indicia of a partnership include the filing of certificate of partnership, common authority in the administration and control of the business, a common interest in the capital employed and sharing in the profits and losses of the business. *Barnes v Barnes*, 355 Mich 458, 462 (1959).

The party alleging the partnership has the burden of proving that it exists. *Grosberg v Michigan Nat'l Bank Oakland*, 113 Mich App 610, 614 (1982), aff'd 420 Mich 707 (1984).

In Michigan, a fiduciary relationship arises from "the reposing of faith, confidence, and trust and the reliance of one upon the judgment and advice of another." *First Pub Corp v Parfet*, 246 Mich App 182, 189 (2001); citing *Vicencio v Jaime Ramirez, MD, PC*, 211 Mich App 501, 508 (1995). Partners stand in a fiduciary relationship to one another, and are charged with the duty of honesty, good faith, and full and frank disclosure of all relevant information. *Van Stee, supra* at 133; See also, *Johnson v Ironside*, 249 Mich 35 (1929).

Further, MCL 449.21(1) provides that:

> Every partner must account to the partnership for any benefit, and hold as trustee for it any profits derived by him without the consent of the other partners from any transaction connected with the formation, conduct, or liquidation of the partnership or from any use by him of its property.

If Sid can establish that he and Beth formed a partnership, he has a good claim for breach of fiduciary duty against Beth, and thus he would be entitled to a share of the profits generated by the Empire Road property.

In *Harper v Warju*, unpublished opinion per curiam of the Court of Appeals, issued December 17, 1999 (Docket No. 211650); 1999 Mich App LEXIS 2204, the Court of Appeals found a partnership did exist where both parties contributed a portion of a down payment on a residence purchasing the property together, with the agreement to split expenses equally with the goal of building quick equity.

Here, the parties never took any steps to formalize a partnership, such as filing a certificate of partnership, as required by MCL 449.101, or signing a partnership agreement. The fact that they each paid half of a retainer for an attorney to draft formal documents does not appear to rise to the level of establishing a partnership, as they never carried on any business.

An argument can be made that a fiduciary duty arises under MCL 449.21(1) "from any transaction connected with the formation . . . of the partnership"; however, no partnership was ever formalized, so it is unlikely that a court would extend this statute to cover the conduct of Beth.

Student Answer—July 2007

Question 6—Business Organizations—9 points

The first issue is whether the discussion on the plane between Sid (S) and Beth (B) constituted a partnership. In Michigan, a valid partnership is an agreement between two people to go into business with one another, for profit. Here, it seems that they both had the intent, however nothing was in writing. Usually, partnerships could be perpetual and thus would need to be in writing to satisfy the statute of frauds. Here, the facts do not state whether or not S and B wanted to enter the partnership for a certain amount of time or not. Therefore, a court could find that no actual partnership really existed between B and S from their conversation.

However, Sid will argue that in fact a partnership was formed because B gave S $500.00 to split the attorney fee to draft a p-ship agreement and all the necessary documents. S will argue that he detrimentally relied on B's promise to enter a p-ship together. S does have strong evidence that both parties intended to form a p-ship and that S created one for them.

The next issue is what are B's chances of success in defending a claim by S for breach of a fiduciary duty. First, assuming that a p-ship did exist, S would most likely succeed in this claim. Partners owe a fiduciary duty to the p-ship and each other. They must treat each other with loyalty, honesty, and good faith. Here, S disclosed info about the empire road property in hopes that it could be acquired for the p-ship. B took this information and used it for her own personal gain. This was done in bad faith and would most likely be held a breach of her fiduciary duty, which she could be held liable for damages.

Overall, it seems that S would have a fairly strong case against B.

CONTRACTS

Questions, Model Answers, and Student Answers

The following section includes prior Michigan Bar Exam questions and model answers for **Contracts**. Many of the questions also include actual student answers with the amount of points that were earned to give you a better idea of what the graders expect. The student answers are immediately following the model answer for each question. Please pay close attention to the points received on each question. Although most samples represent "good" answers (i.e., received 8, 9, or 10 points), there are some samples that received 7 points (the minimum "passing" score for an essay), and a few that received very low scores to help you better understand the grading process and what is expected.

February 2001—Question 6

Harvey Letsgo writes travel books for twenty-somethings who want to travel through Europe on the cheap. Last year he was contacted by Tina Brown, the president and chief editor for Foodors Publishing. Tina asked him to write a tour guide for Portugal. Tina and Harvey met at Tina's office in Detroit. Tina told Harvey, "If you'll forgo an advance, I'll promise to reimburse you your expenses and guaranty that you'll receive at least $100,000 in royalties. Are you interested?" Harvey said, "You bet!!" Without reading it, Harvey then signed a document that read as follows:

> Contract
>
> The undersigned, Harvey Letsgo, and Foodors Publishing Company hereby agree that Letsgo will prepare a tour guide for Portugal. Letsgo agrees that Foodors shall have exclusive rights to publish and market any manuscript prepared by Letsgo pursuant to this Agreement. Foodors shall have the right to review the manuscript, and determine, in its sole discretion, whether the book is acceptable for publication. If the book is acceptable for publication, and is produced Foodors shall pay Letsgo a royalty of $1.00 per book. Foodors retains complete discretion as to the price and number of books printed.
>
> Signed,
> Harvey Letsgo
> Foodors Publishing

Harvey then spent six weeks traveling through Portugal and three months preparing the manuscript. During that time, Harvey did not work on any other book projects, and indeed, declined an offer from Bob Baedecker to work on a tour book about Norway saying, "Foodors has offered me way too much money not to complete this book on Portugal in a timely fashion."

When the manuscript was complete, Harvey delivered it to Tina. Tina reviewed it, but has not yet told Harvey whether Foodors will publish it. Since he had an extra copy of the manuscript, Harvey also showed it to Baedecker. Baedecker has offered to purchase the manuscript for $150,000 cash plus reimbursement for any documented expenses ($30,000, in this case). Harvey just read the contract with Foodors and noticed to his great shock and dismay that it said nothing about the guaranteed royalty of $100,000 or reimbursement of expenses. Harvey has come to you for advice. He tells you that typically his books sell 40 to 50,000 copies, so that unless Foodors has something up its sleeve, there is no way that he'll make $100,000 under this contract.

Harvey has asked you the following questions:

1. **Does Harvey have an enforceable contract with Foodors that will prevent him from selling the book to Baedecker?**
2. **Assuming that Harvey's contract with Foodors is enforceable, does it include a guaranty of $100,000 in royalties plus expenses? Advise him.**

Model Answer to Question 6

Contract Formation: There's no real issue of formation here. A contract is a mutual manifestation of intention to be bound, and here there is a written agreement bearing the signature of both parties.

Contract Enforceability—Consideration: The first major issue here is whether the contract is supported by consideration. Restatement (Second) of Contracts, §70. While Letsgo has granted Foodors an exclusive license to publish his book, it is unclear whether Foodors has actually given anything in return. Under the contract, as written, Foodors has no obligation to do anything at all. They can accept the book for publication if they feel like it. They can price the book any way they like, and they can print and sell as many or as few books as they see fit. As such, this may fall into the category of an "illusory promise," and may fail for lack of consideration. Restatement §77.

Most students should be familiar with the case of *Wood v Lucy, Lady Duff Gordon*, in which Justice Cardozo finds that an exclusive distributorship agreement, much like the one involved here, was nonetheless enforceable because Wood (in this problem Foodors) was subject to an implied duty of good faith. Restatement §205. Therefore, Brown would be under an obligation to review the book and accept it if it was indeed acceptable, and reject it only for a good faith reason. Similarly, Foodors would be under an obligation to use good faith efforts to market the book. Thus students should conclude that the requirement of consideration is met, and that Letsgo can't sell the book to Baedecker without being liable to Foodors for damages.

Obviously, if the agreement contains the $100,000 guaranty, it is supported by consideration.

Contract Enforceability—Promissory Estoppel: Letsgo might argue that he relied on the contract when he spent his own money to finance his trip to Portugal. However, at this stage of the analysis, this doesn't help, because he's only trying to get out of the contract so he can sign up with Baekdecker. (It will be helpful to him when he tries to argue that the $100,000 guaranty *is* part of the agreement.)

Parole Evidence: Whether the $100,000 guaranty is part of the contract will turn on an application of the parole evidence rule. The parole evidence rule governs when and whether extrinsic evidence will be admitted to establish the existence of a prior agreement not contained in a writing. The rule is stated in Restatement §213:

> (1) a binding integrated agreement discharges prior agreements to the extent that it is inconsistent with them.
>
> (2) a binding completely integrated agreement discharges prior agreements to the extent that they are within its scope.

Parole Evidence—Full vs. Partial Integration: If the agreement is a partial integration, it is intended to be final as to the terms contained in the agreement, but can be supplemented by additional consistent terms. Restatement §216. Here, there is no question that the contract is an integration (i.e., final), at least as to the terms that it contains. If it is a full or complete integration, then it may not be supplemented at all. Here, there is no integration clause, or language stating that this is the "complete agreement of the parties," or language saying that all "prior agreements merge into this final agreement." Therefore, it is likely that a court would find this to be a partial integration (i.e., an agreement that is final only as to the terms that are contained in the document itself). Indeed, under Restatement §214(b), Harvey might be able to present evidence of the prior agreement for the very purpose of establishing that the "agreement . . . is . . . partially (rather than completely) integrated."

Parole Evidence (Partial Integration)—Additional vs. Inconsistent Terms: Where an agreement is a partial integration, courts will allow the plaintiff to present extrinsic evidence of additional consistent terms, but will exclude extrinsic evidence of terms that contradict the terms contained in the writing. Restatement §216. The guaranty of $100,000 plus reimbursement might be viewed as an "additional" term, in that the "$1/book" royalty does not say anything one way or the other about a guaranteed minimum. On the other hand, one might argue that the $1/book royalty establishes the level of compensation, and that adding in a guaranteed minimum plus reimbursements contradicts the written term. This could go either way.

But there is a deeper problem. The guaranteed minimum was a very important term in the contract to Harvey. A court is likely to view its omission from the written contract as strong evidence that it was not part of the original bargain. This point is made (in reverse) by Restatement §216(2), which states: "An agreement is not completely integrated if the writing omits a consistent additional agreed term which is *** such a term as in the circumstances might naturally be omitted from the writing." This is not the sort of term which would "naturally have been omitted." Thus, on balance, it is likely that, even though this agreement was a partial integration, the parol evidence rule would likely exclude evidence of the guaranteed minimum.

Parole Evidence—Promissory Estoppel: One possible counter argument lies in the fact that Letsgo relied on the oral promise to his detriment by fronting the price of writing the book. According to the problem, Letsgo's expenses total $30,000. This was a large expenditure, for a $1/book royalty, if Letsgo's books usually sell on the order of 50,000 copies. Restatement §90 would allow a court to enforce the oral guaranteed minimum if Brown should reasonably have expected the promise of a $100,000 minimum to induce action, and such reliance occurs. However, the absence of the guaranteed minimum from the written contract undercuts Letsgo's argument that reliance was reasonable.

Unconscionability: Some students might argue that the contract is unconscionable in the absence of the guaranteed minimum. Most courts require both a procedural and substantive element before finding a contract unconscionable. Procedural unconscionability turns on sharp bargaining practices or deception, while substantive unconscionability looks to the terms themselves. Here, both elements are present, and there's an argument, though it's not a clear winner. On the procedural side, one could argue that the oral guaranteed minimum was used in order to trick Letsgo into signing a one-sided contract, and on the substantive side, Letsgo is not getting very much in return for fronting $30,000 in expenses. Still, Letsgo appears to be a relatively sophisticated party, and he would certainly have recognized the problems if he'd read the agreement.

Student Answer—February 2001

Question 6—Contracts—None Available

Comment: This was a very difficult question and students did not do well. Therefore, there are no student answers for this question.

July 2001—Question 5

James and Mary Jones owned a parcel of land on Blue Moon Lake. The Joneses considered developing the land and had the appropriate municipal authorities test the property to determine if a septic system could be installed. The report that they received stated that the ground was solid clay and a septic system could be constructed to pump sewage across and down the road to an existing sewer system. Rather than go to this expense, the Joneses decided to list the property for sale. In their listing it was specifically stated that the property was being sold "as is" and that a septic system could not be installed on the property and the sewage would have to be pumped to the sewer system. Harry Goodluck decided to buy the property anyway and purchased it on a land contract for $50,000. Similar lakefront property on Blue Moon Lake that could use a septic system sold from $100,000 to $125,000. After purchasing the property, Harry began excavation to start construction and found a large sand deposit on one corner of his lot. He had the same inspector come to the lot and upon seeing this sand deposit, the inspector concluded that a septic system could be installed in this location and issued Harry a permit to do so. Upon hearing of Harry's good fortune, the Joneses filed suit against Harry asking for the property back and/or the difference in value of what Harry paid and what the property was worth if the septic system could be installed.

What is the legal theory for this complaint, what will you expect Harry's response to be and what will be the result of this case?

Model Answer to Question 5

The complaint in this case would seek rescission or modification of the contract based on mutual mistake. Rescission of a contract is an equitable remedy to be granted only in the sound discretion of the trial court. Rescission is appropriate where the mistaken belief relates to a basic assumption of the parties upon which the contract is made, and which materially affects the agreed performances of the parties. Rescission is not available to relieve a party who has assumed the risk of loss in connection with the mistake. The erroneous assumption in this case does not materially affect the agreed performance of the parties. Harry purchased the property with the intent of building a home and bearing the expense of pumping sewage. Plaintiffs also could have built their home with the expense of pumping the sewage. In this case, both parties were innocent but the "as is" clause in the listing agreement demonstrates that Harry would bear both the risk and benefits of the present condition of the property. Likewise, the court would not reform the contract. Reformation is available when there is clear and convincing evidence that the contract should be reformed in order to carry out the true agreement of the parties. To reform a written instrument, the mutual mistake must be common to both parties and common to the instrument. There is no mistake as to the instrument actually entered into. The mutual mistake is of an extrinsic fact and the instrument is not capable of reformation. *Dingeman v Reffit*, 152 Mich App 350 (1986).

Student Answer—July 2001

Question 5—Contracts—None Available

February 2002—Question 1

Marsha Cummings was involved in a serious automobile accident in Wayne County, Michigan on July 4, 1996. At the time of the accident, Marsha was 21 years of age but living at home with her parents. The accident was caused when the other driver turned in front of Marsha's vehicle at an open intersection. The other driver claimed Marsha was going too fast, but all witnesses supported Marsha's claim that she was not speeding and was the victim of this accident.

Denial Insurance, the insurance carrier for the other driver, did not think much of their insured's claim, and met with Marsha and her father on a number of occasions. On each occasion, both the local agent and claims manager told them that once Marsha had substantially recovered from her injuries they would offer a "full and equitable" settlement. Marsha agreed with this procedure and did not hire an attorney nor take any action to enforce her claim.

Marsha had a number of operations covering several years, and in September of 2000, when no more surgery was contemplated and she had recovered as best as possible, she contacted Denial Insurance to discuss settlement. Denial, true to their name, told her for the first time that she was speeding and did not have any claim. Marsha promptly filed suit and Denial defended on the basis that their insured was not liable for the accident and that the three-year statute of limitations had expired on

Marsha's claim. Defendant then filed a motion for summary disposition based on the statute of limitations defense.

Without discussing any claim of fraud, what would be the basis for the Plaintiff's answer to the motion, and the Defendant's response?

Model Answer to Question 1

The Plaintiff should claim that the Defendant's use of the statute of limitations is barred by the doctrine of promissory estoppel. The doctrine of promissory estoppel is dependent on the existence of contract or contract principles. This is a claim where under contract law a promise which the promisor should reasonably expect to induce forbearance by the promisee or a third person and which does induce forbearance, is binding if injustice can be avoided only by enforcement of the promise. The promise must be clear, definite and not a prediction of future events. *First Sec. Savings Bank v Aitken*, 226 Mich App 291 (1997).

There was no duty of Denial to pay or to promise to pay a fair settlement. If there was such an obligation, it was the result of a promise made by Denial. The facts state that the promise was made on several occasions by both the agent and the claims manager so there should be no question but that Denial could be bound by these promises. There is no question from the facts that Marsha relied on the promises and withheld taking any action until her condition had stabilized. This also benefited Denial in saving it attorney fees and court costs.

The Michigan Supreme Court in a case similar to this, *Huhtala v Travelers Ins*, 401 Mich 118 (1977), determined that since this claim was based on contract principles, it was a suit against the insurance carrier, not the driver at fault, the six-year statute of limitations for contract actions would apply and would not bar this action.

While the Michigan Supreme Court determined that these facts created promissory estoppel and not equitable estoppel, the concurring opinion held that an issue of equitable estoppel was presented which if established at trial would prohibit the imposition of the statute of limitations as a defense. Equitable estoppel under these circumstances could be found to exist if the insurance carrier instead of making an express promise continually asked for more information and continued to imply that this is a case that they would like to see settled. Once the negotiations continued past the limitations period the carrier then advised that since the statute had expired they could not do anything for the Plaintiff.

The Defendant would contend that the promise itself is not definite in amount and only speaks of "fair and reasonable" and cannot rise to the level of an enforceable promise. The Defendant would also argue that this is in the form of a prediction of a future event and therefore cannot rise to the level required for promissory estoppel. The Plaintiff would respond that it was not indefinite in that the damages would be the value of the claim, up to the insurance limits, that would have been available in a tort action against the at-fault driver. Plaintiff would also argue that the promise was not a prediction of a future event, but of a definite promise to pay a determinable sum in the future.

While the Supreme Court has held that such a promise would result in a denial of the motion for summary disposition motion, the conclusion is not critical to a passing grade as long as adequate discussions are presented for both sides of the issue.

Student Answer—February 2002

Question 1—Contracts—None Available

Comment: Students did very poorly on this question and there were no good answers. This is a difficult, unrealistic question because it simply would not happen in Michigan due to no-fault insurance. As a result, many students confused this as a no-fault question. This is a perfect example for demonstrating how knowing the clusters can help. The following two questions on this exam were clearly professional responsibility and partnership. By narrowing down the remaining subjects in this cluster, it is clear that this must be a contracts question.

July 2002—Question 12

Bill Jones owned a large tract of land that had more white birch on it than any other property in the Western United States. Exclusive Furniture Company specialized in white birch furniture and entered into a written five-year contract with Bill who was to furnish 50,000 linear feet of white birch each year, for a total of 250,000 linear feet for the five-year term of the contract. For the first two years of the contract, Bill was to be paid $7 per linear foot and for the last three years he was to be paid $8.50 per foot. The contract also provided that in the event Bill could not, or did not, supply the required quantity in any one year, Exclusive could terminate the contract and seek other suppliers. Bill would be responsible for any extra cost that Exclusive would have to pay to fulfill the contract.

In the first year of the contract, Bill was a little slow in getting started and was only able to supply Exclusive with 35,000 linear feet of wood. Exclusive did not terminate the contract or purchase the difference from another supplier. In the second year, Bill supplied Exclusive with 45,000 linear feet. Exclusive was about to declare the contract terminated and seek another supplier but knew that the price of white birch was now $10 a linear foot and rising. Bill and Exclusive agreed in writing that Bill would provide 40,000 linear feet for the remaining three-year period at $9 per linear foot. Bill only supplied 25,000 linear feet for the third full year and Exclusive notified Bill that the contract was terminated. Exclusive then found a new supplier at the then best available price of $12 a linear foot. Exclusive sued Bill claiming damages for the difference between $12 a linear foot and $7 a linear foot for the shortages for the first three years and for the balance of the 100,000 linear feet for the remaining two years.

Discuss the issues presented and the arguments of each party.

Model Answer to Question 12

The principal issue presented deals with the effect of a modification of a contract. While under the facts of this case there exists consideration for the modification, that is not a necessary element for the modification to be enforceable under Michigan law when the modification is in writing. MCL 566.1. The modification did not address the contingency present in the original contract of Bill not being able to perform or how damages were to be calculated. Furthermore, the modification did not address the shortages that occurred in the first two years of the contract.

Generally speaking, absent an intent to the contrary, a modification agreement will normally supersede prior agreements covering the same subject matter. When the subsequent agreement only covers a portion of the subject matter covered by the earlier agreement, Michigan courts have held that there has been no merger and that portion of the earlier agreement that has not been modified remains in effect. *Joseph v Rottschafer*, 2348 Mich 606 (1929).

The contract itself was for a total of 250,000 linear feet. It did not anticipate being completed until the end of five years. It did, however, anticipate the possibility of shortages each year and provided for a method of calculating damages for this nonperformance.

Since the modification did not release Bill from the shortages occurring in the first two years, he could be held responsible for the increase in the cost of the lumber as per the agreement. The facts of this case do not state if there was an increase in the cost of the birch during the first two years of the existence of the contract and if there was an increase, how much it was.

Exclusive has a duty to mitigate its damages and could not sit back and do nothing as the price rose. Bill would argue that he should not be held responsible for the difference between the $12 and $7 a foot since the shortages could have been made up at the end of the second year at the $10 per linear foot cost and perhaps less.

Bill would also claim that the modification raised the price to $9 a linear foot and that this expressly changes the linear foot price and therefore changed the difference that he could be charged for a shortage from $7 to $9. According to the contract terms, Bill was to be responsible for any extra that Exclusive would have to pay to fulfill the contract, so beginning the third year, the difference would be between the $9 and $12 a linear foot figure, not the $8.50 a linear foot and not the $7 per linear foot.

Exclusive would contend that Bill could not take advantage of the $9 linear foot price since he never fully performed under the modification at that price. Exclusive would contend that, at best, Bill would be responsible for the difference between the $8.50 linear foot price and the $12 price. The court would have to determine if Bill substantially performed under the modified agreement before Bill would be allowed to obtain the benefit of this agreement. Based on the facts presented, it would appear unlikely that a court would determine that Bill substantially performed under the modified agreement where the price would be $9 per linear foot. *See Pulpwood Co v Perry*, 158 Mich 272 (1909).

Student Answer—July 2002

Question 12—Contracts—7 points

The contract between Bill Jones (Jones) & Exclusive Furniture Company (EFC) is within the statute of frauds and appears to be valid. Within the contract is a termination clause and a clause regarding remedy for any breach—liquidated damages.

A modification of a contract must be written if the original (& modification) are subject to the statute of frauds. Here the parties put the modification in writing as required. The modified contract allows for Jones to get $9 per linear foot, not $7.

Jones will argue he should only have to pay the difference between 12/9 not 12/7 & that EFC waived its right to recover the first 3 years because they continued to do business even after Jones' breach. To impose liability for the first 3 years is a penalty—not liquidated damages.

EFC will argue to hold Jones to the original contract & the modification only applied to the quantity and price—not the damages clause.

> **Comment:** This is another example of an answer that is not very good, but earns a minimum passing score of 7 points because it correctly identifies the issues and gives a basic definition in a conclusory fashion. Be sure to do a thorough application of the facts to the rules to earn additional points.

February 2003—Question 15

On March 1, 2002, Harvey and Jennifer Jones, husband and wife, entered into a written purchase agreement with the Slippery Slide Development Corporation to purchase a lot designated as #13 on a preliminary plat of Serenity Acres. The agreement provided for a down payment of $2,000 to be credited to the $25,000 purchase price. The contract provided that it was subject to acceptable soil borings and final plat approval.

Slippery Slide submitted an amended plat on March 15, 2002, which changed some of the configuration of the streets and green space area, but did not affect lot #13. Mr. and Mrs. Jones had no problem with the proposed changes. While the municipality was considering the plat, Slippery received an offer for the entire unplatted parcel of land for three times what it had paid for it. Deciding to go for the quick buck, Slippery, on April 30, 2002, sold the entire parcel to Smith Development. On that same date, Slippery sent a letter to Mr. and Mrs. Jones stating that it was discontinuing its efforts to plat the property and tendered the $2,000 down payment to them. Smith, using the same proposed plat that Slippery had submitted, obtained final plat approval on May 15th and sold lot #13 to Mark and Mary Conway for $65,000 on May 16, 2002.

Upon receiving the tender of the $2,000, Mr. and Mrs. Jones made an appointment with a lawyer. They met with the lawyer on June 1, 2002, and decided to reject the tender and sue for breach of contract damages and/or specific performance of the contract.

Slippery filed an answer to the complaint denying any liability, claiming that the contingencies in the contract were never met, the contract was too indefinite as to performance, and alternatively that the damages could not exceed the $25,000 sale price.

Discuss and decide the relative merits of the complaint and defense.

Model Answer to Question 15

There was a valid enforceable contract, which was breached by Slippery Slide. Even though there were conditions precedent, the fact that they were not performed does not defeat Plaintiffs' claim. When a contract is subject to the occurrence of a future event, there is an implied agreement that the promisor will place no obstacle in the way of the happening of such event. The failure to obtain final plat approval was the result of the actions of Slippery Slide and no one else. The Defendant cannot take advantage of its failure to continue the plat process and defeat the Plaintiffs' claim. The condition of acceptable soil borings was for the benefit of the Joneses and there would have been no need to obtain these until there was plat approval. Although there was no definite time set for performance, that alone does not render the contract unenforceable. The courts would determine that the Defendant was required to obtain the plat approval within a reasonable period of time. From the facts it appears that this would have been accomplished by Slippery Slide within a reasonable time had they not sold the property.

There can be no specific performance since the property has been sold and lot #13 conveyed to a good faith purchaser.

Plaintiffs should be able to collect damages in the amount of $40,000. Plaintiffs are entitled to the benefit of the bargain. Damages are measured by the difference between the agreed price and the value at the time of breach. The contract was for a platted lot. In order to give the Plaintiffs the benefit of the bargain, the value of the property should be determined when platted. To determine damages in this fashion would place Plaintiffs in as good a position as they would have been in had Defendant not breached the contract.

Stanton v Dachille, 186 Mich App 247 (1990).

Student Answer—February 2003

Question 15—Contracts—9 points

Jones and Slide had a valid contract. There was nothing indefinite about it. It was in writing to satisfy the statute of fraud as required, since it was an interest in land. The parties were identified and the price mentioned in the contract. Also in the contract were two conditions: that it was subject to acceptable soil borings and final plat approval. The changes did not affect #13, which was the subject of the contract, and Mr. & Mrs. Jones had no problem with it.

Slippery cannot get out of this contract because it is valid and enforceable and held together by the $2,000 that Mr. & Ms. Jones paid as consideration. All of the requirements for a land sale contract were in place; a writing, offer and acceptance, parties paid valuable consideration of $2,000, parties were identified, and purchase price noted.

Slippery cannot reject the tender because the offer to purchase was already accepted. They can sue in equity for specific performance, where the court would force them to convey the property, but here, the property has already been conveyed to the Conways.

Slippery would have to give the Joneses their expectation under the contract and pay them the difference between what they would've bought the property for and what they will have to pay for a similar property.

Since land is unique, and that is why specific performance is often granted in breach of contract for the sale of real property, I don't see how the Jones could get specific performance here, because the land was already sold to the Conways.

The breach was in bad faith and it was done to try to get more money and the court should recognize that and award the Jones more than the contract price of $25,000. They should be given their expectation under the contract and they should recover the difference between the contract price and the fair market value of a similar price of land. That would put them in the same position they would have been in if the contract had been performed.

July 2003—Question 13

Plaintiff Harry Kelly entered into a written contract with Daylite Corporation whereby Harry would act as an independent contractor selling auto parts manufactured by Daylite to retail stores throughout the United States. Harry was to be paid a 3% commission on all sales unless otherwise agreed in writing. The contract was for a three-year period and provided that the contract could only be modified in writing.

One month prior to the end of the three-year period, Daylite was having some financial difficulty, but had developed a new product that it felt was going to increase its sales dramatically. Daylite allegedly approached Harry and proposed extending the commission contract, but due to the expected huge increase in sales, stated that the commission rate would be 2.5% for the first full year, 2% for the second full year and 1.75% for the third full year.

No written agreement was signed, but after the initial three-year period had expired, Harry began selling the new product and received and cashed the commission checks based on the sliding scale. Harry sold the new product for the next three-year period and at the end of this period Harry demanded that Daylite pay him the difference between the 3% commission that was in the written contract and the amount that he received for the last three years. Daylite refused to pay and Harry sued.

Harry claimed he never agreed to accept anything less than the 3% commission, that Daylite's claim of the sliding scale was barred by the statute of frauds and that by its express written terms, the contract could not be modified except by another writing. Harry also claimed that he knew the commission checks were not based on the 3% figure, but that he was willing to accept this as a partial payment to help Daylite launch this new product and minimize its initial start-up cost.

Harry's attorney filed a motion to strike the affirmative defense of the statute of frauds. What are the arguments for and against this motion, and what is the probable result?

Model Answer to Question 13

Harry would contend that the general rule is that where an original contract was required to be made in writing, under the statute of frauds, any modification of the agreement should also be in writing. The statute generally provides that an agreement, contract, or promise is void unless that agreement, contract, or promise or a note or memorandum of the agreement, contract, or promise is in writing and signed with an authorized signature by the party to be charged with the agreement, contract, or promise which from its terms is not to be performed within 1 year from the making of the agreement.

There are several defenses available to Daylite. If the statute of frauds did apply, an argument can be made that the commission checks sent to Harry with the reduced commission amount constituted a sufficient writing to comply with the statute of frauds. While there are no published Michigan cases on this issue, there is a federal decision *Adell Broadcasting Corp v Cablevision Industries*, 854 F Supp 1280 (ED Mich, 1994), that concluded that under Michigan law an endorsed check was a sufficient writing to satisfy the statute of frauds.

Daylite could also argue that Harry is equitably estopped from raising the statute of frauds. The recent decision of *Kelly-Stehney & Associates, Inc. v MacDonald's Industrial Products, Inc.*, 254 Mich App 608 (2002), reluctantly recognized that this doctrine has been used by the Supreme Court as an exception to the statute of frauds. *See Opdyke Investment Co v Norris Grain Co*, 413 Mich 354, 365 (1982). Equitable estoppel may arise where (1) a party, by representations, admissions, or silence intentionally or negligently induces another party to believe facts, (2) the other party justifiably relies and acts on that belief, and (3) the other party is prejudiced if the first party is allowed to deny the existence of those facts. Daylite can claim that Harry knew of the difference in the commission checks and never objected to them. Harry can argue that a question of fact exists as to whether he induced Daylite to believe that he had assented to this change on the basis that he did so only to aid Daylite in the early development of this product. However, there is no indication that Harry ever objected to the receipt of these checks or ever placed in writing the alleged reason he continued to accept them. "A party's failure to object to the terms of a modification of an agreement within a reasonable time is an indication that the parties agreed to the modification." *Evans v FJ Boutell Driveway Co, Inc*, 48 Mich App 411, 421 (1973).

Finally, if Daylite was required to pay the higher commission, it would be prejudiced. Had Harry timely objected to the lower commission, Daylite would have had the opportunity to find another sales representative at the lower commission rate.

Harry would claim that any reliance by Daylite on this alleged oral agreement was not reasonable because any modification to the contract was required to be in writing. However, the courts have concluded that a clause in a contract stating that it cannot be orally modified is not necessarily binding. Parties to a contract are free to mutually waive or modify their contract notwithstanding a written modification or anti-waiver clause. A waiver of this provision in the contract is proven through clear and convincing evidence of a written agreement, oral agreement or affirmative conduct establishing mutual agreement to modify or waive the provisions in the original contract. A party may not unilaterally alter the original contract. To establish a waiver, mere silence is not enough and the party claiming the waiver must produce clear and convincing evidence that the parties mutually agreed to modify or waive their contract.

Based on the foregoing, it would appear that Harry would not be successful. While Harry remained silent, his actions would probably be sufficient to sustain the claim that the contract itself was modified. He sold a new product and was paid and accepted a different commission. Even though there was no written modification, there was affirmative conduct that would appear to establish a mutual agreement to modify the original contract. Finally, from the facts it would appear that the court could apply the doctrine of equitable estoppel which would leave Harry without the statute of frauds as a defense.

Quality Products & Concepts Co v Nagel Precision, Inc, 469 Mich (2003).

Student Answer—July 2003
Question 13—Contracts—7 points

Since Harry is an independent contractor, and Daylite Corp could be considered a merchant, the UCC statute of frauds will not be applied; thus, common law statute of frauds principles will control the disposition of this question.

Here, we have an oral contract that Harry will sell goods (auto parts manufactured by Daylite) to retail stores in the United States. There was a sliding scale of payment based upon sales. However, the oral contract came after a written contract that stated that all modifications must be in writing.

The initial contract the (first 3-year K) had to be in writing to satisfy the statute of frauds—It was a contract that could not be performed within one year's time. Thus there is no problem for the written K.

However, the problem is the oral contract, which was a modification of the written contract. A modification that is within the statute of frauds must be made in writing.

The motion should be denied for Harry because the modification was within the statute of frauds (was not in writing), thus the statute of frauds will prevent Harry from winning the motion.

Harry could also argue promissory estoppel—that he relied to his detriment in cashing the checks.

February 2004—Question 5

Harold Smith owned a farm implement repair business called Smith Implement Repair Service, and had three locations in Ingham County. John Green, Inc. was a national farm implement manufacturer and entered into negotiations to purchase the business of Harold Smith. A purchase agreement was signed on May 1, 2002, whereby Harold was to sell his buildings, equipment and good will to John Green, Inc., for $1,000,000. The agreement further provided that Harold Smith agreed he would not open or operate any competitive business in the mid-Michigan area for a period of three years from the date the purchase agreement was signed. The contract defined the mid-Michigan area as including, but not limited to, the counties of Clinton, Eaton, Ingham, Jackson, Livingston and Shiawassee. These counties are contiguous to Ingham County, and, in some instances, include areas over 75 miles from the nearest location of Smith Implement Repair Service. After pocketing the cash, Harold moved to a beautiful home on Coldwater Lake in Gratiot County (the county just north of Clinton).

John Green, Inc. had intended to open a number of repair facilities in the counties listed in the non-competition agreement. Due to economic conditions, John Green, Inc. decided to withhold entering these counties until its economic picture improved. The locations acquired from Mr. Smith were operated by John Green, Inc. and were very successful. After six months of enjoying his retirement, Harold decided it was time to go back to work and opened two new farm implement repair shops. The first was located in Gratiot County, two miles from the county line of Clinton and Gratiot, and the second shop was in southeast Livingston County, approximately 70 miles from his closest establishment in Ingham County. These shops were named Harold Smith Farm Implement Repair Service and opened for business January 15, 2003.

John Green, Inc., upon discovering Harold's new business ventures, felt that Harold violated the terms of the non-competition agreement. On February 1, 2003, John Green, Inc. filed suit to enjoin the operations of Harold Smith Farm Implement Repair Service. In this suit John Green, Inc. was able to produce evidence that it had broken ground on March 1, 2003 for two new repair centers, one in Clinton County approximately 25 miles from Harold's new location in Gratiot County. Construction was expected to be completed by May 15, 2003. The second center was to be located in Eaton County at least 50 miles from either of Harold's new locations.

How do you believe this will be resolved? Why?

Model Answer to Question 5

The common law of Michigan upheld non-competition agreements under what has been referred to as the rule of reason. This was defined in various ways but originally it was said that "if, considered with reference to the situation, business and objects of the parties, and in the light of all the surrounding circumstances with reference to which the contract was made, the restraint contracted for appears to have been for a just and honest purpose, for the protection of the legitimate interests of the party in whose favor it is imposed, reasonable as between them and not specifically injurious to the public, the restraint will be held valid."

There have been several changes in the common law, the first being a statute prohibiting non-competition agreements, irrespective of their reasonableness and declaring such agreements to be against public policy, illegal and void. This statute is no longer in force and currently Michigan permits reasonable non-competition agreements between employer and employees. The statute further states that to the extent the agreement is found to be unreasonable, a court may limit the agreement to render it reasonable in light of the circumstances in which it was made.

An agreement can be made that the current statute only permits non-competition agreements between employer and employee, thereby invalidating other non-competition agreements. Such agreements are again to be considered void and illegal. The Court of Appeals in Michigan has rejected this argument and has essentially returned to the common law rule of reasonable approach to non-competition agreements that fall outside of the employment arena. The court, by statute, is authorized to limit the agreement to render it reasonable in light of the circumstances in which it was made. Even though this is not a non-competition employment agreement, the court would likely follow the statute and enforce the agreement in accordance with its reasonable interpretation.

In the instant case, the agreement would be subject to challenge for a number of reasons. First of all, the agreement provides for non-competition for a three-year period. While there is no definitive period of time that a non-competition agreement can remain in effect, it is possible that a three-year period would be invalidated. The courts have upheld one-year periods as being reasonable. *Robert Half International, Inc v Van Steenis*, 784 F Supp 1263 (1991). In the present case, there was no violation of the agreement until the new repair shops were opened for business in January 15, 2003. This would fall within a period of one year and should the court adopt such a time period, it would then look to the reasonableness of the geographic prohibition.

The geographic area covered by the prohibition would also be subject to challenge. The area included, even with the defined counties, would cover several hundred miles in various directions and involve a number of smaller cities. The use of the phrase "mid-Michigan area including but not limited to the counties of Clinton, Eaton, Ingham, Jackson, Livingston and Shiawassee" would probably, at best, be interpreted as being limited to the geographic area specifically listed in the agreement. A radius of 100 miles from the closest location could be upheld by the court. Anything beyond this distance would be questionable. A distance of 50 miles was held to be unreasonable in the case of *Robert Half International* but the reasonableness of both the time and distance is dependent on the facts of each case.

The opening of Harold's location in Livingston County is within the time prohibition, even if the court reduced it to one year. The location also violates the terms of the agreement in that it is located in Livingston County which was a specifically designated county in the agreement. If the court did not look beyond the defined counties and required a certain distance from the nearest facility, i.e., 50 miles, then John Green, Inc. would prevail concerning this particular location. However, if the court limited the non-competition agreement to a one-year period, Harold Smith could then recommence operations after the year had expired.

Again, looking at the Livingston County store, both the time and distance is prohibited by the agreement and the agreement's prohibition would probably be enforced by the court. The location in Gratiot county is outside of the specific counties listed and even though within the time period, it would probably be found to be outside of the agreed area and permissible. This would hold true even though John Green, Inc. was starting to construct a facility within 25 miles of Harold's Gratiot County facility. This facility was not expected to be completed until May 15, 2003, and if the court used one year as a reasonable period of time, this would fall outside of the prohibited time period. If the court is determining one year to be reasonable, the first facility to be opened by John Green, Inc. does not assist John Green, Inc. in arguing that the new facilities of Harold Smith violated the terms of the non-compete agreement.

Student Answer—February 2004

Question 5—Contracts—None Available

July 2004—Question 4

John and Mary Smith were interested in purchasing a home located at 711 Verdale Avenue. Their son-in-law, who was a real estate broker, was representing them in the purchase of the home. The seller of the property advised John and Mary that there had been a problem with the IRS and a lien had been placed on the property five years previously. Both the seller and John and Mary's son-in-law advised them that these liens were only good for four years and there was nothing to worry about. John and Mary contacted Stacy Title Company to do a title search and to provide title insurance. They did not advise Stacy Title that the seller told them there was an IRS lien on the property. A commitment to issue title insurance from Stacy Title Company was obtained and the recorded IRS lien was not discovered. A title policy was then issued and it failed to include any mention of the tax lien. John and Mary purchased the home and lived in it for five years before they decided to sell and buy a bigger house.

Bill and Kathy Jones made an offer to purchase the property from the Smiths and the tax lien was discovered. It was also discovered that John and Mary's son-in-law and the prior seller were wrong, that the lien was still valid and should have been included in the title policy issued by Stacy Title Company. In order to sell the house, John and Mary paid off the lien and then sued the title company claiming that when the policy of title insurance was issued, it required the company to pay for the lien that it missed.

The title commitment specifically required the insured "to notify the Company and any and all possible liens or encumbrances and the failure to do so renders the commitment and any policy issued pursuant to the commitment null and void as to such lien.'

The title policy that was issued subsequent to the commitment only required notice to be given of any unrecorded liens and contained an "integration clause" that provided that the policy represents the entire contract between the insured and the Company. Stacy Title Company defended the claim on the basis that the requirement to notify them of the lien was a condition precedent to the issuance of the policy, and since the lien was known to the Smiths, the policy was void. Alternatively, it was the claim of Stacy Title that even if the policy was not void, there was no coverage for the lien that was not disclosed.

Discuss and decide.

Model Answer to Question 4

A condition precedent is a condition that must be met by one party before the other party is obligated to perform. A condition subsequent is a condition that, if not met by one party, abrogates the other party's obligation to perform. A title commitment is an offer by a title company to issue a policy of a title insurance upon performance of conditions set forth in the document. In this case the language in the title commitment did not state that a title policy would not be issued, or any policy issued would be void, if the proposed insured did not disclose all known liens. It did state that the policy would be void as to any undisclosed known lien. This language is more in the form of a condition subsequent than a condition precedent. If the condition is not met the policy would still be effective when and if it was issued, but the lien would be excepted from coverage.

In this case, the policy was issued and the provision in the policy concerning liens only required disclosure of recorded liens. This provision would not apply to the IRS lien because it was recorded. Even though the commitment would except from coverage the IRS lien, the policy as issued contained an integration clause that stated that the policy constituted the entire contract between the parties. Parties are free to execute a substituted agreement, which supersedes the terms of the original agreement. That is what occurred in this instance. The policy states that it is the entire contract between the parties and the Smiths were entitled to rely on this statement. Based on the language of the title policy it superseded the commitment and there is coverage for the IRS lien.

See Archambo v Lawyers Title Insurance, 466 Mich 402 (2002).

Student Answer—July 2004

Question 4—Contracts—3 points (Bad answer)

1) Whether Title Company's "Notice Provision" Is Valid: Contract is a mutual assent and if parties understand "offer" and "acceptance," and "considerations."

Contract would be valid. Here the Smiths presumed to read the provision and made contract w/Title Company regarding title search. Therefore, probably, that provision would be valid.

2) Whether the Smiths' Mistake Affect to Enforceability or Validity of the Contract b/n the Smiths and Title Company: This situation would be unilateral mistake b/c title company did NOT make any mistake and the Smiths mistakenly believed that IRS's lien was no longer effective, in fact, it was effective. Under unilateral mistake, generally the contract would not be entitled any rescission on reformation or modification because other party was already relied on the contract and performed their contractual duties. However, if a mistake is very minor and not related materially to the subject matter of contract, such as, simple miscalculation, Contract may be entitled to modification. In addition to, if other party knew a mistake, there might be likely given some equitable remedy. Here the Smiths made mistake and that mistake was material b/c IRS's lien was so affected to the title quality; and title company did not know that mistake. Therefore, Title Company might prevail.

However, a subsequent purchaser, Bill and Kathy Jones, easily found and discovered the IRS's tax lien on the Smiths property. It means that the tax lien was very obvious b/c it was recorded and it would not be justifiable for title company's work quality. Title Company would made gross negligent to conduct title search diligently. Therefore, even if, "Notice provision" existed, the Smiths would have a cause of action against Title Company.

Depending on the Ct's determination, the policy would be valid or would be void as discussed above.

> **Comment:** There were no "good" answers to this contract question, but this is an example of a bad answer that earned 3 points even though the examinee missed the main issue of condition precedent. Notice the missing words, poor sentence structure, and grammar errors.

February 2005—Question 1

James Lord had owned a small manufacturing business, which he decided to close. Among the many issues that were involved was a dispute he had with Ace Insurance Company. Ace provided workers' compensation insurance for the company and there was a question as to how much was still owed on premiums for the balance of the time that the company continued to do business.

After numerous letters and phone calls, James decided to end the debate once and for all. He sent the company a check for $1,253.33 and marked on the check "paid in full." He also sent a brief letter with the check that showed the manner in which he calculated the amount due and concluded with a statement, "here is a check for what is owed. This is full and final payment. Nothing else is owed to you."

Ace cashed the check and sent a letter in return mail stating that "James knew that these calculations were wrong and that they did not agree that the debt was paid in full." Ace then started suit claiming that there remained due and owing the sum of $1,250.00 for unpaid premiums. James hired an attorney who filed an answer to the complaint claiming that nothing further was owed to Ace.

What is the basis for this defense? What do you believe the outcome of this case will be and why?

Model Answer to Question 1

The answer will claim that there was an accord and satisfaction. James will assert that when Ace cashed the check with the notation "paid in full" this constituted an accord and satisfaction. James will further claim that the letter that accompanied the check clearly indicated that this was tendered to settle this issue.

An accord and satisfaction can be used to discharge a contract. It has been held that an "accord" is an agreement, which is substituted for the underlying contract, and that "satisfaction" is the execution or performance of such new agreement. For there to be an accord and satisfaction, the tender must be accompanied by an explicit and clear condition indicating that, if the money is accepted, it is accepted in discharge of the whole claim. If the creditor is fully informed of the condition accompanying acceptance, the creditor cannot sever from the acceptance the condition and claim the acceptance is not in full satisfaction of the debt.

The question that arises is whether the condition was "clear and unequivocal." The law requires the tender must be clear, full and explicit. Placing on the check the statement "paid in full" does not, standing alone, affect an accord and satisfaction. The letter did not contain language to the effect that if the check was cashed the claim was settled. The letter could be interpreted as merely setting forth what James was willing to admit that he owed. The burden of proving that there was an accord and satisfaction is on defendant James, and the failure to make this tender in clear and explicit language will probably defeat the claim of accord and satisfaction.

Nationwide Mutual Ins Co v Quality Builders, Inc, 192 Mich App 643 (1992). *Fuller v Integrated Metal Technology, Inc*, 154 Mich App 601 (1986). *Faith Reformed Church of Traverse City v Thompson*, 248 Mich App 487 (2001).

Student Answer—February 2005

Question 2—Contract—9 points

Here James had sent a check to the insurance company stating that the check was payment in full satisfaction of the amount owed.

The issue is what the basis for this defense is based upon. The fact that James wrote paid in full is based on the satisfaction of the debt.

However, to be "paid in full" it must be done in good faith without an intent to fraudulently pay less. In order for a "paid in full" check to be valid it must be written in a conspicuous place for the payee to see. It can't be written in small print where no one would see it.

The outcome of this case will depend on if the insurance company cashed the check. If they cashed the check then the case will be dismissed because once you cash, it is determined that you agree to accept the payment as full satisfaction of the debt owed. Simply cashing the check and sending a letter disputing the claim is not enough to be able to raise a claim for the amount the insurance company feels is unpaid.

The insurance company should have retained a lawyer prior to cashing the check because James will most likely win because the insurance company cashed the check.

Comment: Notice that this examinee didn't use the buzzword "accord and satisfaction" but still got almost full credit for the answer.

July 2005—Question 1

Plaintiff, Better Beer Company, on June 29, 1998, entered into a contract with Flying Pigeons, Inc., a Michigan corporation. Flying Pigeons, Inc. owned and operated a hockey team called the Flying Pigeons. Better Beer had an exclusive right to furnish all the beer for events at the arena owned by the Flying Pigeons. The original contract was for a period of five years, beginning September 1998 and continuing through the end of the 2002 season, i.e., March 2003. Payments were at the rate of $15,000 a year.

The beer flowed for the first four years and Better Beer could not have been happier. During the fifth year, Better Beer began negotiations with Flying Pigeons, Inc. to extend the contract. Due to the success of Better Beer, there were a number of competitors seeking the contract after the expiration of the 5-year term. Better Beer, knowing a good thing when it saw it, agreed to pay a $100,000 "renewal fee" plus pay a yearly amount of $22,000. This agreement was reached on February 1, 2003.

Everything went just fine until the National Hockey League went on strike in the summer of 2003 and did not commence its hockey season in September 2003. The Flying Pigeons were a minor league team of the Skating Fools, a National Hockey League team. The Skating Fools notified the Flying Pigeons that it would not subsidize the Flying Pigeons and the Pigeon hockey team folded their wings and disbanded.

To fill the void in the use of the arena, Flying Pigeons, Inc. entered into a contract with a newly formed cricket league. This league would play as many home games as the Flying Pigeons, but the attendance was anticipated to be about a tenth as that of the Pigeons' hockey games. Better Beer asked for a refund of their $100,000 renewal fee and rescission of the contract. Flying Pigeons, Inc. refused saying that Better Beer still had the exclusive right to sell beer at the arena during cricket games over the same period of time and for the same number of games.

Better Beer filed a lawsuit in circuit court seeking refund of the renewal fee and rescission of the contract. You are the law clerk for the judge assigned to this case. You are instructed to draft a memo concerning the issues involved and to provide a recommendation as to the validity of this claim.

Model Answer to Question 1

Under these facts, issues are presented of supervening impossibility/impracticability and/or frustration of purpose. The doctrines of frustration of purpose and supervening impossibility/impracticability are related excuses for nonperformance of contractual obligations and are governed by similar principles.

To date, the Michigan Supreme Court has not ruled on the issue of whether frustration of purpose is grounds for rescinding a contract. There is case law to the effect that the frustration of purpose doctrine does not apply to errors in prediction as to future occurrences or non-occurrence. However, Michigan courts have shown a willingness to apply this doctrine under certain circumstances. To apply this doctrine there must be a change in circumstances that makes one party's performance virtually worthless to the other, frustrating his purpose in making the contract. Furthermore, the event that occurred must not have been reasonably foreseeable at the time of the contract, must not be the fault of the frustrated party, and the parties in the contract have not allocated the risk involved in the frustrating event.

Under the facts set forth in this question, it does not appear that there was any reason to anticipate the hockey strike and there was no provision in the contract that dealt with the possibility that there would be no hockey team let alone no hockey season.

On the other hand, the contract is not impossible to perform if it is read in the context of simply being the exclusive supplier of beer for this arena. It appears that the contract will not be as profitable, but from the facts, it does not appear that there was any requirement as to a minimum number of beer sales during an event or during the season.

The fact that a significant payment was made which was based on the past performance of beer sales at hockey games, may well be the deciding factor. Obviously, the $100,000 would not have been paid with knowledge of the significantly lower sales. Better Beer was not necessarily predicting the volume of beer sales, it was predicting and relying upon the existence of a hockey team and a hockey season.

Based upon the facts provided, a recommendation that the contract be rescinded and the $100,000 repaid would be logical and supported by the law. However, if the answer identifies the issues and argues that rescission should not be permitted, a passing grad should be given.

Tri-State Rubber & Equipment, Inc v Central States Southeast & Southwest Areas Pension Fund, 677 F Supp 516 (ED Michigan, 1987). *Liggett Restaurant Group v City of Pontiac*, 260 Michigan App 127 (2003). *Jabero v Harajli*, Unpublished opinion per curiam of the Courts of Appeals, issued June 15, 2004 (Docket Nos. 243494, 246737). *Lone Star Steakhouse & Saloon v Hammond*, Unpublished opinion of the Court of Appeals, issued April 13, 2004 (Docket No. 245002).

Two Student Answers—July 2005

Question 1—Contracts—9 points

This question involves a written, 5-year contract (K) between Better Beer Company (Better) and Flying Pigeons, Inc (Flying). This is essentially a requirements K—that is, Better promises to furnish *all* beer for events at the arena, owned by Flying. Such Ks are valid & enforceable. The original K was valid.

The issue in this case is whether Better can 1) seek refund of the renewal fee and 2) seek rescission of the new K, the Feb 1, 2003 agreement. Here, the K doesn't specify that Better will furnish beer at Flying Pigeons hockey games only—to the contrary, the K specifically applies that Better supply beer at the *arena.* Flying would therefore argue that Better shouldn't be able to rescind its Feb 1 agreement.

Better would argue that this change in attendance—1/10th the attendance at the hockey games—drastically changes the amount of beer it can sell (i.e., selling much less beer). It is implied that drastic changes in requirement/output Ks *may* excuse a party from performance. That is the case here—Better should be able to rescind (cancel) its K with Flying based on the fact that the central purpose of the K ("supplying beer") has failed considering it will lose significant sales if forced to supply beer for the cricket games. Therefore, Better should rescind its K.

As for the renewal fee, Better should be able to get it back from Flying based on the previous arguments. Neither party took the risk of loss in its K—& it wasn't foreseeable that the hockey team would disband. On that basis, Better will be excused on the basis of impossibility.

Comment: Many students analyzed this as a sales question under the UCC dealing with commercial impracticability. Because the facts state in one part the contract is an exclusive dealings contract to "furnish" all beer, and later it says "exclusive right to sell beer" there is an ambiguity. "Furnish" would indicate a service and common law would apply. "Sell" invokes the UCC. Credit was given on appeal for the UCC analysis as well.

Question 1—Contracts—8 points

From: 00234
To: Judge Matter
Re: Claims of Rescission
Date: July 26, 2005

The issue is whether Better Beer has a claim of rescission and the refund of the renewal fee. Rescission is the cancellation of a contract and operates as if the contract never took place. The rule is that the court will not grant rescission unless there is fraud, mutual mistakes that goes to the material essence of the contract, duress, etc.

In this case, Better Beer entered into contract with Flying Pigeons to furnish all beer for events at the arena owned by the Flying Pigeons. And in its renewed contract, it paid $100,000 as renewal fee. Here, there is no fraud; the parties are not mistaken as to the terms of the contract. However, there is a changed circumstance as a result of the National Hockey League strike. The strike resulted in disbandment of Pigeon hockey team. The void created by the team was filled with a cricket league, which resulted in less attendance.

The fact that there is a changed circumstance does not make the contract impracticable or impossible. Better Beer contracted for exclusive right to furnish bear is not affected. Therefore, there is no result in rescission. A bad deal does not result in rescission. Better Beer must stick to the contract.

Comment: This student identified the issue correctly, but did not define "contract impracticable or impossible," or provide an application. Had he or she done so, this answer would likely be a 10.

February 2006—Question 9

Joseph Smith was 50 years old and lost his job as an accountant at Nice Manufacturing when Nice when out of business. He applied for a job as an accountant with Grant Excavating. On the application for employment, there was a provision stating that employment with Grant was "at will" employment and a statement that "I agree that any action or suit against the firm arising out of my employment or termination of employment, including, but not limited to, claims arising under state or federal civil rights statutes, must be brought within 180 days of the event giving rise to the claim or be forever barred." Joseph objected to that provision, but was told he had to use that form to apply.

Joseph signed and submitted the application and was hired on June 1, 2004. He worked as an accountant until just before his six-month review was conducted, and was terminated on November 15, 2004. Joseph claimed his termination was the result of age discrimination, but the company placed in his personnel file that he was terminated for unsatisfactory performance.

Joseph consulted an attorney in February 2005, and after obtaining his personnel file, an age discrimination lawsuit was filed on May 25, 2005. Grant filed a motion to dismiss based on the failure to comply with the time requirements to bring such a suit. Mr. Smith's attorney, in response, argued that the statute of limitations for bringing such a claim in Michigan is three years and the provision in the employment application was not part of the contract; and, if it was, it was unreasonable and unenforceable as an adhesion contract.

Discuss the issues and provide your opinion as to the probable outcome.

Model Answer to Question 9

It can be argued that the application for employment does not impose any obligation upon the defendant and therefore it is not binding on the parties. However, the enforceability of a contract depends on consideration and not mutuality of obligation. In Michigan, the terms of an employment application have been recognized as being a part of the employment contract between employer and employee and the fact this was found in the application for employment would not be a basis to avoid the application of the statute of limitations provision.

The Supreme Court has recently dealt with the definition and application of law of an adhesive contract. The term "adhesion contract" may be used to describe a contract for goods or services offered on a take-it-or-leave-it basis. But it may not be used as a justification for creating any adverse presumptions or for failing to enforce a contract as written.

The court stated it is of no legal relevance that a contract is or is not described as "adhesive." In either case, the contract is to be enforced according to its plain language. Regardless of whether a contract is adhesive, a court may not revise or void the unambiguous language of the agreement to achieve a result that it views as more fair or more reasonable. There is no evidence that plaintiff did not have any realistic alternative to employment with defendant. While plaintiff's bargaining power may have been unequal to that of defendant, he was free to accept or decline the job.

Even before the Supreme Court limited the impact of a contract of adhesion, it had determined that a shortened statute of limitations to 180 days by agreement was not inherently unreasonable. There are no facts in this case that demonstrate that this shortened time period did not give the plaintiff an adequate opportunity to investigate and determine whether he has a claim or not. It has always been the law that the courts would not invalidate contracts as adhesion contracts where the challenged provision is not unreasonable.

Rory v Continental Ins, 473 Mich 457 (2005).

Three Student Answers—February 2006

Question 9—Contracts—10 points

This is a contracts question.

Joseph Smith will be time barred from bringing his claim for waiting past 180 days.

The issue is whether the statute of limitations provision—180 days listed in the contract is valid to prevent the case from being adjudicated.

Mutual assent in a contract is derived when both parties agree/stipulate to the written words in the contract. Generally, a court will uphold the terms in the contract if it appears to be fair and reasonable with respect to the individual—if a business developed the contract.

In this case, the employer Grant Excavating drafted the employment contract that each applicant must sign. The application included the agreement with the statute of limitations. Although Joseph objected to the provision, he still signed it, thus stipulating to it.

The provision, if deemed reasonable, will be upheld, as previous case law has proven.

In this case, Joseph had 6 months to give rise to the claim. However, Joseph elected to wait eight months before consulting an attorney. Further, almost four months passed before filing the claim.

Based on the facts it appears that the company was both fair and reasonable.

Per the defense cited by Mr. Smith's attorney, Michigan has a 3 year statute of limitations; the defense will not be upheld. As the courts have held in the past, if the parties contract to different terms, and the terms are fair and reasonable—the terms of the contract will be enforced.

In this case Grant Excavating contract application will be upheld, and Joseph's claim will be barred for waiting too long to file a claim.

Question 9—Contracts—10 points

An employment contract is a contract for services and must be in writing to satisfy the statute of frauds. Joseph read, understood, and signed the agreement. Therefore the clause is enforceable.

It would be difficult to prove age discrimination on the facts given because the company hired him knowing how old he was.

The "at will" clause also allows the company to terminate the agreement without cause and is effective because Joseph could have also terminated at will.

The statute of limitations can be shortened by agreement therefore arguing that his statute of limitation is inconsistent with the contract will not be persuasive.

A Michigan court will find the 180 days reasonable and anything more than 3 years unreasonable (the state SOL of 3 years is intended to be a limitation).

A signature on a job application indicates that everything above it is true. Many companies state the terms of employment on the application or use statements made on the applications to terminate employment later on, so the argument that the application is separate from the employment contract will not prevail because the Michigan court will apply custom and usage to find that his signing the employment application constituted an acceptance of the terms of employment.

A contract of adhesion is a "take it or leave it" proposition. There is nothing in the facts indicating that Mr. Jensen was being pressured to accept the terms of employment therefore, this argument will also fail.

Mr. Jensen will probably lose this suit.

Question 9—Contracts—8 points

Age discrimination is not a suspect class and so the burden of proof is on the plaintiff bringing the suit. Thus the burden here is on Smith to prove that he was terminated because of his age and his personnel file stated that it was due to poor performance. The facts do not give any additional information and it is unlikely based upon the information that he could meet his burden of proof.

Also, the contract provisions are usually upheld and his employment required all suits to be brought within 180 days, which Smith did not do. However, Michigan has enacted a statute providing the timeframe during which such actions may be brought which could arguably override the contract provision. However, the employment agreement was an "at will" agreement in which either side may terminate employment for any or no reason. Under these circumstances, it is unlikely that Smith would prevail in his suit. In addition, the provision in the application requiring the suit to be filed within 180 days would not likely be held unreasonable. Such clauses have been enforced even when they were in fine print on the back of cruise ship tickets.

July 2006—Question 14

On May 3, 2003, George Harding, of Harding Fabrics, went from Michigan to New York to negotiate with Harold Tranter, of Fabrics Unlimited, for an order of fabric. The parties had done business on prior occasions without any difficulty. Mr. Harding told Mr. Tranter of the immediate need to acquire 10,000 yards of a specific fabric which had been provided before by Fabrics Unlimited. On that occasion, the price was set at $75 per yard, based on the "Apex Index," a nationally recognized index, which set the price of fabric at the date of delivery. Here, the parties reached a written agreement that the shipment was required to be delivered by June 1, 2003, and that the Index would again be used to establish the price as of the date of delivery.

George returned to Michigan from his buying trip on May 31, 2003, only to find that the party who wanted this particular fabric had cancelled their order. The day following the cancellation of the fabric, i.e., June 1, 2003, and before George could reach Fabrics Unlimited, the fabric was delivered with an invoice showing the nature and quantity of fabric with the price to be set as of June 1, 2003, according to the Apex Index. Unknown to both of the parties, the Apex Index had been permanently closed for two weeks due to financial difficulty.

George, on June 1, 2003, notified Harold at Fabrics Unlimited that he didn't want or need the fabric and would be shipping it back. Harold told George that the fabric was his and Harding Fabrics owed Fabrics Unlimited $750,000. George countered that no price had ever been agreed upon nor could it be, as the Apex Index was no longer in existence. The fabric was refused and shipped back as there was no other use of this particular type of fabric. Fabrics Unlimited then sued Harding Fabrics for breach of contract.

Limiting your answer to the issue of whether there is and can be a contract without an agreed-upon price, please discuss and decide whether Fabrics Unlimited will prevail in this action.

Model Answer to Question 14

This question calls into play the UCC as it applies to contracts. The failure to fix a price at the conclusion of the negotiations does not automatically render the contract unenforceable

MCL 440.2305 provides in pertinent part:

> (1) The parties if they so intend can conclude a contract for sale even though the price is not settled. In such a case the price is a reasonable price at the time for delivery if (a) nothing is said as to price; or (b) the price is left to be agreed by the parties and they fail to agree; or (c) the price is to be fixed in terms of some agreed market or other standard as set or recorded by a third person or agency and it is not so set or recorded.
>
> (2) A price to be fixed by the seller or by the buyer means a price for him to fix in good faith.
>
> (3) When a price left to be fixed otherwise than by agreement of the parties fails to be fixed through fault of one party the other may at his option treat the contract as cancelled or himself fix a reasonable price.
>
> (4) Where, however, the parties intend not to be bound unless the price be fixed or agreed and it is not fixed or agreed there is no contract. In such a case the buyer must return any goods already received or if unable so to do must pay their reasonable value at the time of delivery and the seller must return any portion of the price paid on account.

In this case, the parties had dealt with one another on other occasions and had dealt with this same fabric. The method of setting the price was agreed upon, i.e., the use of the Apex Index. The inability to use the Apex Index due to its closing does not render this agreement unenforceable, but calls into place MCL 440.2305 (1)(c), which would require that the price be set at a "reasonable price."

While the facts do not show how long ago the price for this material was set at $75 per yard, that may be indicative of a reasonable price. If there were similar Indexes in existence at the time, those could also be used as evidence of a "reasonable price." It would be possible for Fabrics Unlimited to compare their cost to produce the fabric now as compared to when the fabric was shipped and priced at $75 a yard. There could also be experts on this fabric and its reasonable price, or various methods to determine what would be reasonable.

The answer should recognize that the absence of an agreed-upon price does not render the contract unenforceable, that a reasonable price can be fixed, and some methods as to how this price could be fixed.

Two Student Answers—July 2006

Question 14—Contracts—8 points

This is a contracts question.

The first issue is there a contract (K) between the parties and the answer is yes. There is because the parties agreed upon all terms and the (K) was formed.

The next issue is there a (K) without an agreed upon price. The answer is yes because it was to be determined. As in the previous instance of the parties dealings by the "Apex Index." Simply because the Index is closed the (K) should not fail because there is alternate ways to determine price such as FMV (Fair Market Value) and also because the parties have had previous dealings with the same material, another option would be to charge the same price.

The fact that George no longer needs the material due to the party canceling its order is of no consequence to the Fabric (K). It should not fail as a (K) because of the above arguments and Fabrics Unlimited should prevail.

Question 14—Contracts—8 points

Agreed-Upon Price

Under the Michigan laws governing the sale of goods, a contract will not fail because there is no price term. Instead a reasonable price will be the price. Here, there was a contract for fabric. Fabric is a good; so the UCC applies. There was a contract, but it did not specify a price term. Harding now says there is no contract, because of the absence of the price term. The contract says they will use the Apex Index. However, the Apex Index is closed. Well, a missing price term will not invalidate—void a contract. The court will place in a reasonable price. Therefore Fabrics Unlimited will prevail; because a reasonable price will be place in for the price.

February 2007—Question 1

Skyway Limited ("Skyway") leased commercial space to Kasper Systems, Inc. ("Kasper"), with a lease term through December 2002. In June 2001, Kasper determined that it needed more space and found that Kasper intended to leave the premises in December 2001, and that Skyway should begin to look for new tenants. Kasper referred two prospective tenants to Skyway during the balance of 2001, but no lease was ever agreed upon. Kasper moved out in December 2001, but continued to pay rent to Skyway through March 2002. At this point, Kasper discovered that Skyway had begun to renovate the premises leased to Kasper. Kasper then sent a check to Skyway for two additional months of rent with a letter that stated this check was being sent "in full and final payment of any and all lease obligations Kasper might have to Skyway." Kasper further informed Skyway that Skyway had failed to mitigate its damages, wrongfully refused to lease the premises to companies that were willing to lease the same premises and in the same condition as Skyway, and that the renovation of their space terminated the lease agreement. The check was deposited into Skyway's account and Skyway sent Kasper a letter stating that Skyway did not accept the "full and final payment" condition contained within the letter.

Two months later, Skyway sued for the balance due under the lease through December 2002. Kasper defended on the same basis as set forth in the letter to Skyway and claimed there was an accord and satisfaction.

Discuss and decide the issue of whether an accord and satisfaction exists under these facts.

Model Answer to Question 1

This case is governed by *Hoerstman Gen Contracting v Hahn*, 474 Michigan 66 (2006). There the Court held that MCL 440.3311, not the common law, applies to an accord and satisfaction involving a negotiable instrument such as a check. Since a check was used here, the statute applies. *Hoerstman*, p 71, cited Black's Law Dictionary (7th ed.) for a definition of accord and satisfaction:

> An agreement to substitute for an existing debt some alternative form of discharging that debt, coupled with the actual discharge of the debt by the substituted performance. The new agreement is called the *accord*, and the discharge is called the *satisfaction*. (Emphasis in original.)

Under MCL 440.3311(1), to prove the existence of an accord and satisfaction, a defendant must show (1) a good faith tender to the claimant as full satisfaction of the claim (good faith means honesty in fact and the observation of reasonable commercial standards of fair dealing, MCL 440.3103[1][d]); (2) the claim was unliquidated or subject to a bona fide dispute (an unliquidated claim is one in which the liability of the party or the amount of the claim is in dispute); (3) the claimant obtained payment of the instrument.

Where the defendant satisfies these elements, the issue is whether the claim was discharged. This can be done in two ways. The first is under MCL 440.3311(2), if the instrument or an accompanying written communication contained a conspicuous statement to the effect that the instrument was tendered as full satisfaction of the claim. "Conspicuous" is defined by MCL 440.1201(10) as:

> A term or clause is conspicuous when it is so written that a reasonable person against whom it is to operate ought to have noticed it. A printed heading in capitals (as: non-negotiable bill of lading) is conspicuous. Language in the body of a form is "conspicuous" if it is in larger or other contrasting type or color. But in a telegram any stated term is "conspicuous." Whether a term or clause is "conspicuous" or not is for decision by the court.

The second is under MCL 440.3311(4), if the claimant knew the instrument was tendered in full satisfaction of the claim. Here, defendant's letter to plaintiff established the good-faith nature of the dispute regarding the rent defendant owed plaintiff. Defendant made clear that it disputed whether plaintiff had acted in good faith in its efforts to obtain replacement tenants or mitigate damages, and also disputed whether it owed rent on the premises after plaintiff began its renovation activities.

On the issue of liquidated damages, the claim is "unliquidated" and could be the subject of an accord and satisfaction because it was subject to a bona fide dispute.

The third element is satisfied because Skyway obtained payment of the check by depositing it into its account. The fact Skyway sent a letter that explicitly stated that it did not accept the condition does not defeat the defense of accord and satisfaction. No such action is recognized by MCL 440.3311.

With respect to discharge, the facts state an accompanying letter stated the check was being sent in full and final payment. This arguably was conspicuous under MCL 440.1201(10). Therefore, a discharge would occur under MCL 440.3311(2). There are no facts stated that would support application of one of the exceptions found in MCL 440.3311(3); for example, there is no evidence Skyway tendered repayment. Discharge is also probable under (4) because the letter from Skyway acknowledges the full and final payment condition stated in Kasper's letter. This arguably shows Skyway knew within a reasonable time before collection of the instrument was initiated, that Kasper tendered the instrument in full satisfaction of the claim.

It is for these reasons that an accord and satisfaction did exist and defendant will prevail in this matter.

Student Answer—February 2007

Question 1—Contracts—8 points

An accord and satisfaction is a concept under contracts law. An accord is when a party to an enforceable contract agrees to accept substituted performance not originally bargained for under the enforceable contract for future performance due from the other party. A satisfaction accompanies an accord and is the actual execution of the substituted performance. Kasper, as a commercial lessee, owed money to Skyway through the entire term ending in December 2002. Therefore, the focus must be on whether the facts indicate that Skyway agreed, expressly or impliedly, to accept substituted performance from Kasper not bargained for under the Contract. Although there is no express agreement to accept substituted performance from Kasper, Skyway began to renovate Kasper's leased premises. This may be strong evidence that Skyway impliedly or constructively agreed to accept some other kind of performance from Kasper—yet at the same time Skyway never agreed to a new lease term with any other tenant to cover the remainder of Kasper's lease obligation. At the same time though, Skyway did accept a check from Kasper in full and final payment of all Kasper's lease. The facts do not indicate that Skyway and Kasper disagreed about the amount due under the lease and Skyway went as far as depositing the check into his own account. So it also may be argued that payment by Kasper of a check marked "full and final payment" that was deposited in Skyway's account that was due was acceptance of substitute performance by Kasper in lieu of the original lease terms.

July 2007—Question 5

Tweety Equipment and Leasing Co. owns several gravel trucks and associated equipment which it rents out to local businesses. On May 1, 2005, Tweety entered into a Lease Agreement with Squid-Ro Trucking for trucks and equipment to be used in Squid-Ro's operations. The lease was for a term of one year, ending April 30, 2006, with lease payments to be paid by Squid-Ro to Tweety in the amount of $4,400.00 per month, payable on the first day of the month. The lease contained the following provision:

> **Liquidated Damages:** Because of the difficulties and inconvenience in attempting to establish the loss, for every day after the expiration of the term of this lease that Squid-Ro retains possession of the trucks and equipment, Squid-Ro shall pay to Tweety as liquidated damages, and not as a penalty, the sum of $1,000.00 for each day that Squid-Ro remains in possession.

Squid-Ro used the trucks and equipment on a job site until July 31, 2006, at which time it returned the equipment to Tweety. Squid-Ro continued to pay Tweety $4,400.00 per month from May 2006 through July 2006, which payments were accepted by Tweety. On August 1, 2006, Tweety demanded $1,000.00 per day from Squid-Ro under the Liquidated Damages provision of the contract, for each day past May 1, 2006 that Squid-Ro had possession of the trucks and equipment. After Squid-Ro refused to pay, Tweety filed suit for breach of contract, requesting $92,000.00 in damages.

Assume you represent Squid-Ro and you are about to file an Answer, raising, among other things, the affirmative defenses that (1) the acceptance by Tweety of the rent payments of $4,400.00 for May, June and July 2006, constituted a waiver under Michigan law, and (2) the demanded increased daily rent for May, June and July 2006, constituted an impermissible penalty and not liquidated damages under Michigan law.

Discuss the strengths and weaknesses of your defense as it relates to waiver and liquidated damages, and discuss any other defense that may apply.

Model Answer to Question 5

As Squid-Ro's attorney, your best arguments are (1) that by accepting the monthly rent for May, June and July 2006, Tweety waived any right to come back and enforce the liquidated damages provision; and (2) that the $1,000.00 daily rent increase is an impermissible penalty and not liquidated damages.

1. Waiver: Squid-Ro's best argument is that Tweety, with knowledge of the payment terms and liquidated damages provision, waived the terms of the agreement by affirmatively accepting the rent checks for May, June and July 2006.

In Michigan, a party to a contract may waive the other party's breach thereof. A waiver is voluntary and intentional abandonment of a known right. *Roberts v Mecosta Co Hosp*, 466 Mich 57, 64 n 4 (2002). It has long been held that "a waiver implies an intention to overlook a deficiency, or to forego a right to have the effect remedied or to have compensation therefore, and necessarily implies knowledge of the defect that is waived, or acquiescence under circumstances reasonably implying unconditional acceptance of the work as full performance." *Eaton v Bladwell*, 108 Mich 678, 680-681 (1896). However, a party may not unilaterally modify a contract by waiver. "This principle follows from the contract formation requirement that is elementary to the exercise of one's freedom to contract: mutual assent." *Quality Products and Concepts Co v Nagel Precision, Inc.*, Mich 362, 372 (2003). The mutuality requirement may be met by affirmative conduct establishing mutual agreement to waive the terms of the original contact. *Quality Products, supra* at 374.

2. Liquidated Damages: Squid-Ro's best argument is the $1,000.00 per day increase bears no relationship to actual damage to Tweety, as under the agreement the increase is disproportionate to the monthly rental amount involved in the original transaction.

Concerning liquidated damages, a court would begin by reviewing the contract, looking to the language used in its plan and ordinary meaning, avoiding constrained and technical interpretations. *UAW-GM Human Resources Ct v KSL Recreation Corp*, 228 Mich App 486, 491-492 (1998). Generally, parties to a contract may agree to the amount of damages that will be owed in the event of a breach. A contractual provision for liquidated damages is nothing more than agreement by the parties fixing the amount of damages. *Papo v Aglo Restaurants of Sane Jose, Inc*, 149 Mich App 285, 294 (1986). "The distinction between a valid liquidated damages clause and an illegal penalty depends on the relationship between the amount stipulated to in the liquidated damages clause and the subject matter of the cause of action." *Papo, supra* at 294. Further, courts are to sustain a provision for liquidated damages if the amount is reasonable in relation to the potential injury suffered and not unconscionable or excessive. *UAWGM, supra* at 508. Parties are not permitted to stipulate unreasonable sums as damages. *Moore v St. Clair Co*, 120 Mich App 335, 340 (1982). The fact that they used the term "liquidated damages" as the title of the provision, and that the provision stated the payment was not a penalty, does not establish that the provision was valid. *Id.*

Additionally, the defense that the contract term was extended by the parties also may apply under these facts.

See *Kmart of Michigan, Inc v 250 Martin Investments, LLC, et al*, unpublished opinion per curiam of the Court of Appeals, issued April 14, 2005 (Docket No. 251378).

Student Answer—July 2007

Question 5—Contracts—10 points

The first issue to discuss is whether Tweety (T) waived an action for breach against Squid-Ro (SR) by accepting the late payments for the 3 months (SR) went over the lease. The facts state that SR and T entered into a 1 year lease that consisted of payment at the beginning of each month for $4,400. The lease end date was determined at the formation to be April 30, 2006. SR used the equip. and truck until the last day of the lease (July 31, 2006) and returned everything. SR did hold-over the lease term and seemed to continue on a month-to-month lease with Tweety. Tweety accepted the payments when they could have informed SR that they had terminated the lease they contracted to and would need to sign a new agreement in order to keep providing its equipment. SR would argue that it would be unequitable for Tweety to be able to continue accepting payments without thinking a new lease (or continued lease) was agreed on. It seems that Tweety did waive a cause of action for a breach by SR.

Next, is the issue of liquidated damages. A liquidated damages agreement is something that parties enter while contracting when in the event of a breach; the damages amount seems to be uncertain. In order for a liquidated damages clause to be valid it must be reasonable under the circumstances and terms of the contract. Here, SR was paying $4,400.00 a month according to the lease agreement. The liquidated amount that Tweety is alleging is for $92,000.00 which seems completely unreasonable—$1,000, a day everyday SR is in "wrongful" possession of the equipment. It seems that this would be grossly unproportional and would be held void.

Therefore, it seems that SR has a good chance in defending against Tweety as to its waiver and invalid liquidated damages clause of the lease.

February 2008—Question 4

Don Developer was the owner of a vacant parcel of lake front property on Lake Huron, on which he hoped to develop a condominium project. The property's shoreline is swampy, full of weeds and generally not usable for sunbathing or other recreational purposes. As part of the planned condominium project, and to help maximize his profit, Don sought to obtain permits from the appropriate governing agencies to haul in sand for a beach and to construct a boat dock for condo owners. However, Don was repeatedly denied permits as the land was protected breeding grounds for an endangered shorebird. After another denial, deciding to cut his losses, Don listed the property for sale, describing it as follows:

> Prime Lake Huron frontage. Breeding grounds for rare shorebird. Permits not obtainable for sand fill and/or dock construction—property being sold "as is, where is" for $100,000.

Betty Buyer saw the listing and became interested in purchasing the property. One week after Betty contacted Don about the property, they executed a land contract, whereby Betty purchased the property "as is, where is" for $100,000. Unbeknownst to Don, two weeks before the land contract was executed, the stringent habitat protection standards for the shorebird were removed.

A few months after the land contract was executed, Betty reads in the local newspaper about the removal of the shorebird protection standards. She then contacts the pertinent governing agencies and finds out that she can obtain permits to haul in sand for a beach and to construct a dock. Betty obtains the appropriate permits and is prepared to start construction of a condominium development on the site.

Don learns that Betty successfully obtained the permits and she is about to start construction. Knowing the property with the permits is worth twice as much as the purchase price, Don comes to see you for legal advice about getting his land back or reforming the land contract to get more money from Betty.

What advice would you give Don? Explain your answer.

Model Answer to Question 4

To get his land back, Don would need to make a case for rescission of the land contract based upon a mutual mistake of fact—that the permits were unattainable when he and Betty entered into the land contract. You should advise Don that he would lose any action for rescission of the land contract.

In Michigan, a contract may be rescinded because of a mutual mistake between the parties. However, rescission is only granted in the sound discretion of the trial court. In determining whether rescission is appropriate, a court should ask: (1) was there a mistaken belief entertained by one or both of the parties to a contract, and, (2) if so, what is the legal significance of the mistaken belief?

A contractual mistake, under Michigan law, has been defined as "a belief that is not in accord with the facts. The erroneous belief of one or both of the parties must relate to a fact in existence at the time the contract is executed. That is to say, the belief that is found to be the error may not be, in substance, a prediction as to a future occurrence or non-occurrence." *Dingeman v Reffitt*, 152 Mich App 350, 355 (1986); *citing Lenawee Co Bd of Health v Messerly*, 417 Mich 17, 26 (1982).

Rescission is appropriate where the mistaken belief relates to a basic assumption of the parties on which the contract is made, and that materially affects the agreed performances of the parties. However, rescission is not available to a party who has assumed the risk of loss, and when cases of mistake involve two innocent parties, courts are required to determine which blameless party should assume the loss resulting from the mistake they shared.

Here, when the parties entered into the land contract, they were mistaken in the belief that the permits were unattainable. Betty will argue that Don assumed the risk of loss because he sold the property "as is, where is." This is similar to the facts in *Dingeman*. There, the Michigan Court of Appeals stated: "The 'as is' clause incorporated into the contract is persuasive indication that the parties intended the [seller] would bear both the risks and the benefits of the present condition of the property." Here, a court would find in Betty's favor on the issue of rescission.

In the alternative, Don would like to reform the land contract to get more money from Betty. Reformation of the contract is also not obtainable for Don under Michigan law. The burden of proof would be on Don to present clear and convincing evidence that the land contract should be reformed to carry out the true agreement of the parties. In order to obtain reformation of a written agreement on the ground of mistake, the mistake must be mutual and common to both parties to the instrument. *Dingeman*, at 358; *citing Stevenson v Aalto*, 333 Mich 582, 589 (1952). "If the asserted mutual mistake is with respect to an extrinsic fact, reformation is not allowed, even though the fact is one that would have caused the parties to make a different contract, because courts cannot make a new contract for the parties." *Id., citing E R Brenner Co v Brooker Engineering Co*, 301 Mich 719, 724 (1942). Here, like *Dingeman*, the mistaken fact was not as to an intrinsic fact concerning the land contract entered into, but rather an extrinsic fact, and, therefore, the land contract cannot be reformed.

Student Answer—February 2008

Question 4—Contracts—9 points

The Issue is whether Don can Rescind or Reform the contract pursuant to a Mistake.

A mistake will generally allow a contract to be rescinded or reformed if there is a mutual mistake (by both parties) of a material inconsistent term in the written contract. Parol evidence would by then used to see if the additional term may be brought in. The mistake, if made by the seller and the buyer was unaware of it; will render the buyer able to make a decision whether to rescind, reform, or simply enforced. However, if the buyer knows of the mistake, and simply keeps quiet the contract may possibly be rescinded. The mistake must be to an issue material to the contact.

Here, however, there is not a mistake. Don's intent was to sell the property, and Betty's intent was to purchase the property. Betty did not know that the protection standards were removed, nor was that her basis for contracting to purchase the land. Here Betty was ultimately benefited. However, she was not aware of the mistake, therefore, she can enforce the contract. Also performance was already complete when the land contract was executed. Betty now has an Equitable Right of Redemption and may use, sell, or subdivide the land as she pleases.

The fact that Don was unaware is not relevant since his intent was clearly to sell the land, and he did so when Betty bought it.

My Advice to Don would be to argue that the mistake was mutual and that "as is where is" and "permits not obtainable for sand fill and/or dock construction" is an express condition of the contract that serves as a contingency. The Land Contract was the contract to certain conditions. Therefore, Don will likely be unsuccessful in his attempt to Reform or Rescind the Land Contract.

Comment: This is a well-written answer using the IRAC approach. It probably would have received full credit if it had said "mistake in value" is not considered a material mistake and that Don assumed the risk of the error by using the term "as is where is."

July 2008—Question 5

The Stroes decided that it was time to retire, so they offered for sale their family run party store, along with fixtures and a liquor license. The Koors offered to purchase the liquor license and fixtures, not the store, for $55,000. The Stroes accepted the offer, but with the condition (accepted by the Koors) that the Stroes' attorney approve the contract. The agreement specifically stated: "This purchase agreement is subject to review and approval by our attorney on or before October 28, 2008." The Stroes submitted the agreement to their attorney, but she was on vacation and not available to immediately review the agreement.

After dropping the Koors' agreement off at their attorney's office, the Stroes received another offer, this time from the Smiths. The Smiths offered to purchase the store, fixtures and liquor license for $250,000. The Stoes accepted this offer as well, with the Smiths agreeing to the same condition, i.e., that the Stroes' attorney must review and approve the agreement.

Upon her return from vacation, the Stroes' attorney reviewed both agreements. She approved the Smiths' agreement, and rejected the Koors' agreement because the Smiths offered to buy everything and at a much better price. Naturally, the Koors were unhappy, for not only are there only a few liquor licenses available in town, but they felt the Stroes unfairly submitted another competing agreement before theirs was reviewed by the Stroes' attorney.

The Koors now come to you, the top litigator in town, to obtain specific performance of the agreement. **Can the Koors' agreement be enforced against the Stroes? Explain your answer.**

Model Answer to Question 5

The issues presented in this question are whether the attorney acceptance clause is a condition precedent, if it is, what power did it give the attorney, and did the Stroes' submission of the Smith agreement at the same time as the Koors' agreement place an obstacle to acceptance of the Koors' agreement. The question is based on *Harbor Park Market v Gronda*, 277 Mich App 126 (2007), lv den 481 Mich 851 (2008).

The attorney approval clause in both agreements is a condition precedent. A condition precedent is "a fact or event that the parties intend must take place before there is a right of performance." *Mikonczyk v Detroit Newspapers*, 238 Mich App 347, 350 (1999). If the condition is not satisfied, then there is no cause of action for failure to perform. *Berkel & Co v Christman Co*, 210 Mich App 416, 420 (1995).

It is also true that implied within the condition precedent is an agreement "that the promisor will place no obstacle in the way of the happening of such event." *Mehling v Evening News Ass'n*, 374 Mich 349, 352 (1965). Such an obstacle usually must take the form of an affirmative act, or refusing to do something required by the agreement. If the party does prevent the occurrence of the condition, the condition is excused or discharged. *Id.* at 352.

Here, the attorney approval clause is a condition precedent. The clause clearly provides that the agreements are "subject to" the approval of the attorney, and thus without the attorney's approval, no agreement would be enforceable.

There is also a question as to the extent of power given to the attorney under the clause. This can easily be answered by reference to Michigan law that provides that courts are to apply the plain and unambiguous language contained in contracts. Courts cannot place, by implication or otherwise, terms into a contract where none exist. Instead, courts must hold parties to the agreement plainly expressed in writing. The clause here is very plain, and contains no ambiguity. There are no limitations to the attorney's power of review, so she could decide to approve or disapprove a contract for any and all reasons. Here, she approved the Smith agreement for business rather than legal reasons, but again there was no limitation to the scope of review granted by the clause. Courts are not permitted to place restrictive language in a contract when the parties themselves have failed to do so. Thus, the Koors have no valid argument on that basis.

Finally, the most difficult question is whether submission of the two agreements at the same time violated the laws of condition precedents stated above. It did not. Again, looking to the terms of the attorney approval clause, there was no limitation as to the number of agreements that could be submitted to the attorney. The parties could have supplied such language, but they did not. Bad faith on the part of the Stroes cannot be found when the only acts they took in regard to the Koors' agreement were allowed by, or at least not precluded by, the agreement. There is also no suggestion in the facts that the Stroes instructed their attorney, once they had received the Smith agreement, to reject the Koors' agreement. Instead, the facts only show that the Stroes made two agreements that both required their attorney review and approve as a contract. The Stoes acted pursuant to these terms, and cannot be found to have actively interfered with the happening of the condition precedent.

Two Student Answers—July 2008

Question 5—Contracts—10 points

1. The first issue is whether the Koors' agreement can be enforced against Stroes.

The elements of a valid contract in Michigan are (1) legal subject matter, (2) legal capacity to contract of each party, (3) an offer, (4) acceptance, (5) and consideration.

Here we have all 5 so we can infer a valid contract.

2. The existence of a Condition Precedent.

Conditions precedent are those conditions that must be satisfied before the other party has a duty to perform. The non-occurrence of a condition precedent will discharge the other party's duty to perform.

Here, the approval of the Stroes' attorney was a condition precedent to the Stroes' duty to execute the sale to the Koors. Because both parties understood that the attorney would need to approve the sale, when she didn't, there was no contract.

3. Stroes lack of good faith

Parties to a contract in MI are presumed and expected to act in good faith. When the Stroes's contacted the Smiths about buying their store they were not acting in bad faith, necessarily. The Koors did not provide any consideration to the Stroes to have the offer open only to themselves. Absent such consideration, it was not a breach of good faith for the Stroes' attorney to approve the better sale for Stroes. After all, the Stroes' attorney is obligated to work for the best interests of her clients, the Stroes.

4. Specific Performance

In MI, the equitable remedy of Specific Performance is only available in extraordinary circumstances where land (Real Property) or unique chattels are in issue, and there is no adequate remedy at law.

Here, it is likely that some liquor store fixtures and a liquor license are not unique enough to warrant Specific Performance.

Although, it may be initially difficult, the Koors will be able to secure other fixtures and a liquor license.

This claim will fail.

Question 5—Contracts—10 points

Conclusion: Specific performance of the agreement will not be an appropriate remedy where approval is conditioned on meeting a condition precedent, which is not met.

Rule: Specific performance is an adequate remedy where monetary damages are inappropriate or difficult to determine, particularly in the sale of unique chattels or real property. A condition precedent is where a stated event, which may or may not happen, whose occurrence will excuse the condition, must be met before performance will commence.

Analysis: Nothing in the agreements excluded the Stroes from receiving, and having their attorney evaluating other offers for the sale of the business. The condition precedent, getting attorney approval, MUST be met first. B/C the Koors' offer was not approved, the condition fails. Once the condition fails, the other side's performance is excused. The "performance" here is the sale of the business—without attorney approval, it will not be allowed. One cannot be forced to sell their property to the first bidder, esp. where the condition depends on another's approval.

Conclusion: Therefore, the specific performance will be an entirely inappropriate remedy b/c the sellers have the option of taking multiple, higher bids in selling real property and the business, when a condition precedent fails.

February 2009—Question 14

In late 2007, Mighty Machines, a manufacturer of industrial machinery, and Plush Resorts, an exclusive resort chain, signed a contract in which Mighty Machines reserved all of the rooms and connected venues (spa and golf facilities, etc.) at Plush Resorts' Traverse City, Michigan conference center for its annual executive strategic planning retreat during the last week of February 2009. Mighty Machines budgeted $1,000,000 for the retreat. The contract called for the prepayment of a non-refundable deposit of $100,000 on signing (which was paid), an additional $400,000 payment on February 1, 2009, and $500,000 at the conclusion of the event. It also included a sentence stating that the parties' execution of the contract constituted "a merger of all previous proposals, negotiations and representations with reference to the reservation described in this contract." The contract further stated that any disputes would be resolved by applying Michigan contract law.

Mighty Machines had a policy of holding executive retreats at locations that had received a four-star rating from the Mobil Travel Guide. In the late 2007 discussions, Mighty Machines told Plush Resorts that the four-star rating was a condition of its willingness to book and hold the event at its facility. Plush Resorts assured Mighty Machines: "This resort has consistently had Mobil four-star ratings for the past twenty years. [This was true.] You don't need to worry about that." Relying on this statement, Mighty Machines did not ask to put language in the contract to provide that it could cancel without penalty if Plush Resorts lost its four-star rating.

Both companies had a tough year in 2008. The rating of Plush Resorts' Traverse City conference center was dropped from four to three stars, effective August 1, 2008. Also, the national economy entered a severe slowdown in 2008. Because of steep sales declines, Mighty Machines started its strategic planning in August 2008 (it could not wait for the 2009 retreat) and slashed many forms of discretionary spending, including executive retreats. On September 1, 2008, it sent Plush Resorts a letter announcing it was canceling the contract because (1) Plush Resorts no longer had the four-star rating that it had promised; (2) Mighty Machines no longer had a business need for a February 2009 strategic planning session since this work was already complete; and (3) "other current conditions" made it "financially infeasible" to hold the retreat. Mighty Machines did not offer to pay Plush Resorts anything on account of the cancellation.

Plush Resorts comes to you on October 1, 2008, alarmed by this news and concerned that new reservations are drying up because of the economic slowdown. You are told that despite diligent efforts (calls to convention brokers, ads in travel magazines and the *Wall Street Journal*, etc.), Plush Resorts has been unable to find another taker for the week Mighty Machines had reserved, and doubts it will be able to. Plush Resorts wants to discourage other corporate customers from canceling. At this point, it is well known that Mighty Machines is having a negative cash flow because of declining sales; however, there is no suggestion that it is in danger of running out of cash or filing for bankruptcy.

Plush Resorts requests your advice on the following: (1) can it file suit against Mighty Machines immediately or must it wait until February 2009; (2) will Mighty Machines have valid defenses if Plush Resorts sues for breach of contract; and (3) what damages can Plush Resorts expect to recover if it is successful. What advice do you give? Explain your answer.

Model Answer to Question 14

For the following reasons, I would advise Plush Resorts ("PR") that it would be likely to succeed in a breach of contract suit against Mighty Machines ("MM"), which could be brought immediately.

1. PR does not have to wait until after MM's performance under the contract is due (February 2009) to sue. MM repudiated the contract (also called an anticipatory

breach) on September 1, 2008. If a party to a contract unequivocally declares its intention not to perform its obligations before they are due, the nonbreaching party may immediately bring an action for damages. *Stanton v Dachille*, 186 Mich App 247, 252 (1990).

2. The fact that PR no longer holds a four-star rating is not an adequate excuse for MM to breach the contract even though the rating was discussed during the parties' negotiations. The contract does not make it a condition of MM's performance that PR have the four-star rating; in fact, the contract includes an express merger or integration clause providing that the parties' complete agreement with respect to the reservation is stated in the contract. While MM may argue that parol (also called extrinsic) evidence of these discussions can be admitted to show that PR's maintaining a four-star rating was part of the parties' agreement, that argument should not succeed.

In general, parol evidence of prior or contemporaneous agreements or negotiations is not admissible to vary or contradict the terms of an unambiguous written contract. The chief exceptions to the parol evidence rule allow parol evidence to be admitted to show that (1) the parties did not intend the document to be a complete and final expression of their agreement (a "fully integrated" agreement), or (2) the agreement was only partially integrated because essential elements were not reduced to writing, or (3) the contract has no legal effect because of fraud, illegality, or mistake. *NAG Enterprises, Inc v Allstate Industries, Inc*, 407 Mich 407, 410-411 (1979). But exceptions (1) and (2) cannot apply because Michigan law does not allow extrinsic evidence on the threshold question of whether the contract is integrated when the parties include an express merger clause declaring that the written contract is the entire agreement. *UAWGM Recreation Center v KSL Recreation Corp*, 228 Mich App 486, 493-497 (1998). This is consistent with the general principle, strongly emphasized by Michigan courts, of respecting unambiguous agreements that the parties have written for themselves and not making new contracts for them. Nor does exception (3) apply. What PR told MM was not a misstatement of an existing fact, so MM has no basis to argue that it was fraudulently induced to make the contract or made it under a mistake of fact (which, in any case, would have to be mutual). At most, the statement about the four-star rating was a promise about a future state of affairs, but that promise is not part of the parties' agreement because of the merger clause.

Comment: The drafter believes that full credit should be given for all answers that spot a potential parol evidence issue and recognize that the merger clause is fatal to parol evidence arguments. "Extra" credit can be given to those who identify circumstances where parol evidence may be admitted while recognizing that under Michigan law the merger clause controls. Some credit can be given if the applicant fails to recognize the merger clause as conclusive, but rationally argues that testimony about the rating discussion may be admissible under one or more of the above-stated exceptions to the parol evidence rule.

3. The next question is whether MM can successfully defend on the ground that other changes in conditions occurring after the contract was signed, and not caused by either party, have made it "impracticable" for MM to perform the contract or "frustrated the purpose" of the contract. The essence of the modern defense of impracticability (formerly called "impossibility") of performance because of changed

circumstances is that since the contract was executed the promised performance has become impracticable because it now involves some extreme or unforeseeable difficulty, expense, injury or loss. Mere increased difficulty or financial strain are not enough to invoke this defense. While MM is more financially pinched in September 2008 than it was one year earlier, the cost of renting the facility is the same cost it agreed to and it is capable of making the required payments.

The defense of frustration of purpose is a closer question, but also unlikely to prevail. The conditions to applying frustration of purpose are: (1) the contract must be at least partially executory (here this is true); (2) the frustrated party's purpose in making the contract must have been known to both parties at the time the contract was made (this is also true); (3) this purpose must have been thoroughly frustrated by an event not reasonably foreseeable at the time the contract was made, which event is not due to the fault of the frustrated party and the risk of which he did not assume (MM can make a non-frivolous argument that this is also true). *Liggett v City of Pontiac*, 260 Mich App 127, 134-35 (2003). MM could argue that the extent of the economic slowdown and the resulting need for it to rush its strategic planning has made the meeting unnecessary, that this urgency was not its doing and was unforeseeable when the contract was made, and that it did not assume this risk. However, the comments to the Restatement (Second) of Contracts, 5265, suggest a high standard for finding frustration: "The object must be so completely the basis of the contract that, as both parties understand, without it the transaction would make little sense," and "the non-occurrence of the frustrating event must have been a basic assumption on which the contract was made." It is doubtful that MM can meet that standard. When the contract was made, the parties assumed that there would be recreation as well as strategic planning going on (MM reserved other amenities besides meeting rooms). Furthermore, accelerating strategic planning was MM's decision, and some useful business meetings at the resort could still take place.

Comment: This is a more extended discussion of the frustration doctrine than an applicant can be expected to provide. Full credit on this point should be given if an applicant recognizes and correctly labels the possibility of a "frustration" defense being raised, and further recognizes that frustration is not to be found too easily in order to preserve the stability of commercial relationships.

4. The logical approach to damages would be to seek the most common measure of contract damages, PR's "expectation interest." Sometimes called "benefit of the bargain damages," this measure is intended to place a party in the same position it would be in if the breaching party had fully performed its contract obligations. Here, the starting point for measuring PR's expectation interest is the unpaid balance of the contract price: $900,000. PR could add to that any other reasonably foreseeable loss caused by the breach Restatement (Second) of Contracts, §347(b), such as advertising to find a replacement. The unpaid price must be reduced for any expenses that PR avoids by not having to perform. *Id.*, §347(c). Thus, if during litigation MM develops evidence that PR saved on wages or other expenses (buying food, providing limos, etc.) that it would have paid as part of providing the promised accommodations to MM, that evidence will reduce PR's $900,000 expectation interest. And PR must also keep up reasonable efforts to mitigate its damages by finding a replacement for MM.

Comment: The concepts of (1) adding in incidental and consequential losses and (2) keeping an eye on mitigation are nonessential to full credit.

Student Answer—February 2009

Question 14—Contracts—8 points

1. Mighty Machines' cancellation on September 1, 2008 operated as an anticipatory repudiation. Plush has the option to file a suit against mighty immediately. It is a bilateral contract while the nonperformance of one party cannot trigger the performance of the other party, Mighty is in breach to Plush.
2. Mighty will say the condition for them to decide to hold executive retreat at Plush was that Plush had to receive a four-star rating from the mobile travel guide. However, under the parole evidence rule, the language in the contract appeared to be final and integrated, "a merger of all previous proposals negotiations and representation with reference to the reservation described in this contract." Any previous or contemporaries oral agreement that contradicted to the contract will be kept out. Further, Mighty will argue there is a frustration of purpose/impracticability. Due to the slowdown in business, mighty cannot afford a retreat. However, as the fact indicated that there is no suggestion that Mighty is in danger of running out of cash or filing for bankruptcy. Mighty has a duty to perform according to the contract in good faith a best effort.
3. Plush had tried to mitigate the damage in good faith though to no avail. If Plush is successful in suing Mighty for breach of contract. Plush is entitled to its lost profits, consequential damage and incidental damage, though Plush will not get the remaining $900,000.oo originally contracted.

July 2009—Question 11

Best Brakes contracts to be exclusive sales representative for Allied Aftermarket Products, a Michigan corporation that manufactures brake parts and oil/engine filters. Best Brakes' contract is to sell Allied's brake products line throughout Michigan from January 1, 2007 through December 31, 2008. The contract also provides that only an Allied vice president has authority to modify any contract provision and that any and all modifications must be mutually agreed upon and in writing. The Best Brakes' contract does not cover sales of Allied's filter products because another sales representative, Fab Filters, has a similar contract to sell that product line throughout Michigan.

In June 2007, one of Best Brakes' largest customers, Excellent Auto Repairs, expressed dissatisfaction to Best Brakes with the service Fab Filters was providing. Excellent Auto asked Best Brakes to take over Allied's filter sales to Excellent Auto, promising that it would mean a significant increase in filter business.

Allied's Vice President of Operations, Paul Processes, also heard from Excellent Auto of its desire to switch its filter business to Best Brakes. Wanting to please the customer, Processes called Best Brakes and confided that Allied wanted it to handle the filter sales for Excellent Auto. Best Brakes agreed and asked Processes to confirm the agreement in writing. Processes, not wanting to put anything in writing at least until Fab Filters' contract expired, responded that his word was binding on Allied and was all that was needed, and that Allied would pay Best Brakes commissions on all sales—brake parts and filters—starting immediately. Processes also promised that any renewal agreement would include both brake parts and filters.

Satisfied, Best Brakes began handling filter sales to Excellent Auto. However, when Best Brakes received its quarterly commission payment, Allied included no payment for the filter sales. Best Brakes promptly called Processes, who explained that Best Brakes' contract only covered brake products and that, since there had been no written modification as required by the contract, there would be no commissions on filter sales.

Best Brakes would like to sue Allied to collect the commissions on filter sales that it believes it has earned, and should continue to earn at least through the end of its contract term. What advice do you give Best Brakes? Explain your answer.

Model Answer to Question 11

For the following reasons, I would advise Best Brakes that it has a cause of action for breach of contract because the original contract was modified, despite the absence of a written modification.

1. Despite the written modification and anti-waiver clauses of the contract, Best Brakes and Allied retain the power to mutually modify the contract or waive certain of its terms. Because the parties retain their freedom to contract, notwithstanding such clauses, it is settled that a written contract may be varied by a subsequent parol agreement even where the original contract provided that it could not be changed except by written agreement. *Reid v Bradstreet Co*, 256 Mich 282, 286 (1931).
2. The freedom to contract does not permit a party to unilaterally modify an existing bilateral contract, but it does allow Best Brakes to establish a waiver and/or modification by clear and convincing evidence that the parties mutually intended to modify or waive provisions of the original contract. Processes was an Allied Vice President who was vested with authority under the contract to modify it. Processes evidenced his assent to the modification by promising Best Brakes that commissions on all filter sales would commence immediately despite the absence of a written modification. Best Brakes evidenced its mutual assent by then pursuing and obtaining sales of filter products. This evidence, if proven, is sufficient to establish a mutual agreement necessary to give effect to the modification. [NOTE: This can be characterized as either a mutual agreement to modify the existing contract or a mutual agreement to enter into a new contract covering the same subject matter as the original contract.] *Quality Products v Nagel Precision*, 469 Mich 362, 369-372 (2003); *Klas v Pearce Hardware & Furniture Co*, 202 Mich 334, 339-340 (1918).
3. Because Processes made an affirmative statement, albeit oral, assenting to the modification, there was also a waiver, i.e., a voluntary and intentional abandonment of a known right. Vice President Processes' affirmative direction to proceed forthwith with filter sales in exchange for commissions demonstrated a voluntary and intentional abandonment of Allied's rights at issue under the contract.

4. As to any rights upon renewal, Best Brakes' efforts to attempt to enforce the oral modification upon any renewal 18 months hence would be subject to challenge under the statute of frauds. Without a writing to support a promise to include a term some 18 months hence, the statute of frauds would probably *prohibit* any attempt to enforce such alleged rights. *Kelly-Stehney v McDonald's (on remand)*, 265 Mich App 105, 110-116 (2005).
5. This *is* not a case where alternative relief can be sought under *quantum meruit.* Under *quantum meruit*, the law will imply a contract in order to prevent unjust enrichment when one party unfairly receives and keeps a benefit from another. The facts here seem to fit in this framework, except for the well-established rule that an implied contract cannot exist if there *is* an express contract between the same parties covering the same subject matter. *Morris Pumps v Centerline Piping*, 273 Mich App 187, 194 (2006).

Student Answer—July 2009

Question 11—Contracts—None Available

February 2010—Question 6

Mall management contracted with Landscape Design to develop a landscape design for a new shopping mall. Mall management told Landscape Design that it envisioned an "upscale" mall with designer boutiques, while acknowledging Michigan's tough economic circumstances. On April 2, 2008, Mall Management and Landscape Design entered a contract, which included this provision:

> Mall Management agrees to pay Landscape Design for landscape design services, including master planning, budgeting, grading and drainage, irrigation and lighting, a fee equal to 8% of the cost of implementing the design, except that and in addition to the foregoing, preliminary work shall be paid at the hourly rate of $150. Prior to submission of any design plan, Landscape Design must comply with cost limitations, if any, imposed by Mall Management.

During the preliminary design phase, Landscape Design and Mall Management met to discuss design concepts. No cost limitation on the plan was discussed, although Mall Management mentioned it was having problems attracting upscale retailers. On September 10, 2008, Landscape Design presented its preliminary plan to Mall Management, with an invoice for 458 hours worked, reflecting a balance due of $68,700.

After paying the invoice, Mall Management asked Landscape Design to budget the cost of plan implementation. On September 28, 2008, Landscape Design presented a cost estimate of $1,152,600 with an additional invoice for 32 hours worked, or $4,800, compiling the estimate.

On October 15, 2008, Mall Management notified Landscape Design that the economy required scaling back the plan and that any future plan must comply with a $700,000 cost limitation.

On December 10, 2008, Landscape Design presented its revised plan with an estimate of $865,600, explaining that it could make no further cuts without jeopardizing the project's integrity.

Mall Management demanded that Landscape Design further revise the plan to satisfy the cost limitation. Landscape Design repeated it could not do so. Mall Management then forwarded the plan to another design firm, which indicated the current plan could not be reduced and that design planning would have to start from scratch. Mall Management refused to pay any additional sums to Landscape Design, demanded that Landscape Design refund sums already paid, and hired the other firm, which submitted a plan within the cost limitation.

Landscape Design has contacted you for advice on whether it can recover any additional amount from Mall Management or whether it must refund any money it already received. What advice do you give? Explain your answer.

Model Answer to Question 6

For the following reasons, I would advise Landscape Design that it may safely retain the amount it already collected for the preliminary design, but that, because it breached the contract by submitting a noncompliant revised plan, the most it can recover in addition is the amount owed under the second invoice covering the budget estimate it prepared on the preliminary design.

1. In the contract, Landscape Design agreed that it had to comply with cost limitations, if any, imposed on it by Mall Management. Because there was no cost limitation at the time Landscape Design supplied its preliminary design, Landscape Design was contractually entitled to keep the payment at the $150 hourly rate that it received for this work. *Zannoth v Booth Radio Stations*, 333 Mich 233, 242-243 (1952).
2. Landscape Design also was contractually entitled to payment at the $150 hourly rate for providing the estimated cost of the preliminary design, in light of the fact budgeting was within the scope of the contract and Mall Management's request related to the preliminary design. *Id.* Therefore, Landscape Design should recover on the second invoice in the amount of $4,800.
3. Once Mall Management imposed the cost limitation as a condition precedent, however, Landscape Design was required to present only designs that complied with the cost limitation. Any design that did not comply was a breach of contract by Landscape Design, relieving Mall Management of its duty to perform. In addition, Mall Management afforded Landscape Design with an opportunity to cure (which Mall Management was not required to do), which Landscape Design refused to do. *Id.* 333 Mich at 246; *Able Demolition v City of Pontiac*, 275 Mich App 577, 583-584 (2007).
4. An issue also may be raised as to whether Landscape Design's breach was a substantial breach, because only a substantial breach would be sufficient to relieve Mall Management of its obligation to perform. The question under these circumstances is whether, despite the breach, Mall Management obtained the benefit it reasonably expected to receive. Because in this case, Mall Management reasonably expected to receive a final design plan that could be implemented within its cost limitation, it did not receive the benefit it reasonably

expected, and the breach was substantial. *Able Demolition*, 275 Mich App at 584-585; *Michaels v Amway Corp*, 206 Mich App 644, 650 (1994).

5. Nor is the amount for the revised plan available under a theory of quantum meruit, which would require that Mall Management have unfairly received and retained a benefit from Landscape Design. The revised plan was unusable, and therefore of no benefit to Mall Management, which had to hire and pay for another landscape design firm to start from scratch. *Zannoth*, 333 Mich at 243; *Morris Pumps v Centerline Piping*, 273 Mich App 187, 194 (2006).
6. This also is not a situation that is amenable to a frustration of purpose of performance or impossibility defense, although this writer recommends that a test taker who raises the issue be provided one point for recognizing it as a potential issue. To the extent the frustration of purpose defense is recognized in Michigan, it requires that the frustrating event be one that was not reasonably foreseeable at the time the contract was made and was not a risk that was assumed by the breaching party. While Landscape Design concluded that it was unable to modify its existing design to abide by the cost limitations could be imposed and, once imposed, were a condition precedent to performance. Both parties were also aware of an unfavorable economic climate at the time the contract was entered. Under these circumstances, the imposition of a cost limitation was foreseeable and was a risk that Landscape Design assumed. *Rooyakker v Plante & Moran*, 276 Mich App 146, 159-160 (2007).

Student Answer—February 2010

Question 6—Contracts—None Available

July 2010—Question 15

Joe is a former major league baseball player who made millions of dollars during his career, and who was now toiling in the minors as manager of the Hens, a minor league team in Montana. Joe dreamed of managing a major league team, but as a cigarette smoker, he was very concerned about major league baseball's unwritten policy of no smoking on the field or in the dugouts, even though all dugouts are open-air dugouts. In 2009, Joe was asked to meet with Al (a wealthy businessman who made his fortune in hot dog franchises), owner of the Roosters, a major league baseball team in Michigan. At the meeting, Al asked Joe if he would manage the Roosters, to which Joe instantly agreed. However, much to Al's surprise, Joe did not want to be paid. Instead, he asked that Al give a free hot dog franchise to his brother Steve. Additionally, and not knowing that Michigan law required employers to permit employees to smoke in any open air area, Joe also asked that Al agree to allow him to smoke in the dugout and when on the field. Al quickly agreed, thinking he had struck the bargain of a lifetime. Al then wrote out on a napkin "manage Roosters for 2 years, free franchise for brother Steve and Joe freely smokes in dugout/field", signed his name to it, and left. After Al signed the napkin, Joe put it in his pocket and left.

Joe's first year as manager was a disaster. Al was furious about his hiring decision. After a 15-0 loss, Al confronted Joe in the dugout and angrily stated, "I never should have hired you, and our 'napkin agreement' is as worthless as the paper it was written on. You never signed the agreement, and I didn't give you anything you did not already have. You're done! And, by the way, from now on your brother will have to pay for his franchise."

Can Joe and/or his brother successfully enforce the contract against Al? Explain your answer.

Model Answer to Question 15

This question raises issues of (1) consideration, (2) statute of frauds, and (3) standing to sue as a third party beneficiary.

With respect to consideration, the applicant should point out that every valid contract requires some form of consideration. *Detroit Trust Co v Struggles*, 289 Mich 595, 599 (1939). Courts do not inquire into the sufficiency of consideration, *Gen Motors Corp v Dep't of Treasury*, 466 Mich 231, 239 (2002). Consideration requires a bargained for exchange, i.e. a benefit on one side, or a detriment suffered, or service done on the other. *Id.* As to Al's implied charge that there was no consideration for the contract ("I didn't give you anything you did not already have"), two issues arise. The first issue to be addressed is the impact Michigan's smoking law has on Al's promise to allow Joe to smoke in the dugout and on the field. The performance of a preexisting legal duty is not sufficient consideration for a new promise, *46th Circuit Trial Court v Crawford County*, 476 Mich 131, 158 (2006), because "doing what one is legally bound to do is not consideration for a new promise." *Yerkovich v AAA*, 461 Mich 732, 741 (2000). Here, Al had a preexisting legal duty to allow Joe to smoke in all open air spaces, which would include the dugout and field. Hence, the duty Al undertook in the managerial contract with Joe was the same as he was required to do under state law, so performance of the preexisting duty did not provide legal consideration for the contract between Joe and Al. *Alar v Mercy Mem Hosp*, 208 Mich App 518, 525 (1995).

Second, it can still be argued that there is consideration supporting the managerial contract, as consideration for a contract can be in the form of a benefit extended to third parties, *Plastray Corp v Cole*, 324 Mich 433, 440 (1949). Thus, Joe's brother receiving a free hot dog franchise is consideration to support the contract, as it was a benefit conferred on a third party by Al at Joe's request. Additionally, if one of the forms of consideration fails, but another survives, that surviving consideration will normally support the contract. *Nichols v Seaks*, 296 Mich 154, 160 (1941). Consequently, there is consideration supporting the managerial contract.

The next issue is Al's assertion that the contract is invalid because it was written on a napkin and Joe did not sign it. The statute of frauds requires that any contract that is not to be performed within a year of making the agreement must be in writing and signed by the person against whom performance is sought. MCL 566.132(1) (a). Joe's two-year employment contract cannot be performed within a year, so it must comply with the statute. *Marrero v McDonnell Douglas Capital Corp*, 200 Mich App 438, 441 (1993). To do so, the written document must contain the essential terms of the agreement. *Opdyke Investment Co v Norris Grain Co*, 413 Mich 354, 369 (1982). Here, the essential terms of the contract—the job, its length, and the consideration—were all contained on the napkin. Additionally, Joe would be seeking to enforce the agreement against Al, who signed the napkin. Hence, the statute of frauds is satisfied.

The final issue is Joe's brother's ability to sue Al to enforce the promise of a free hot dog franchise. In order to sue Al as a third party beneficiary, Joe must have been an intended third party beneficiary of the managerial contract. MCL 600.1405. "A person is a third-party beneficiary of a contract only when that contract establishes that a promissor has undertaken a promise *directly* to or for that person." *Schmalfeldt v North Pointe Ins Co*, 469 Mich 422, 428 (2003). This third party is not a signatory to the contract, but is the beneficiary of the contract between the promissor and promisee. *Jt Admin Comm v Washington Group Int'l, Inc*, 568 F3d 626, 631 (CA 6, 2009), citing Williston on Contracts, §37:23 (4th Ed, 1990). In deciding whether the parties intended to make someone a third party beneficiary, a court must determine from the form and meaning of the contract itself whether they objectively intended that person as a third party beneficiary. *Kammer v Asphalt Paving Co v East China Twp Schools*, 443 Mich 176, 189-190 (1993).

Joe's brother is a third party beneficiary of the managerial contract. The contract specifically identified him as the recipient of a free franchise, establishing the objective intent of the parties. Al knew that he was undertaking an obligation specifically to Joe's brother, undertook that obligation for at least a year, and the contract is otherwise enforceable.

Student Answer—July 2010

Question 15—Contracts—8 points

Joe and his brother can successfully enforce the K against Al. The facts indicate a clear "meeting of the minds," a valid offer and acceptance and consideration. B/c the K was for a term longer than 2 years, the statute of frauds requires that it be in writing, provided enough facts of the contract include the terms of the K and be signed by the party against it is to be enforced.

Here Joe and Al entered into K where Joe's brother was the intended beneficiary. The K was in writing, it doesn't matter that it was on a napkin, the writing is sufficient. It also sets forth the terms of the agreement, what each party will get what. As the consideration, the courts don't look into the adequacy of consideration as long as each party got what it bargained for.

The K is enforceable against Al, although Joe didn't sign it. As an intended beneficiary Joe's brother has rights against Al as if he stepped in Joe's shoes. And given that Joe's brother has been running the franchise for at lest a year, there is significant reliance and his rights in the K have vested.

Therefore, Joe & his brother can sue Al for damages they're suffered due to Al's breach and any foreseeable consequential damages.

PROFESSIONAL RESPONSIBILITY

Questions, Model Answers, and Student Answers

The following section includes prior Michigan Bar Exam questions and model answers for **Professional Responsibility**. Many of the questions also include actual student answers with the amount of points that were earned to give you a better idea of what the graders expect. The student answers are immediately following the model answer for each question. Please pay close attention to the points received on each question. Although most samples represent "good" answers (i.e., received 8, 9, or

10 points), there are some samples that received 7 points (the minimum "passing" score for an essay), and a few that received very low scores to help you better understand the grading process and what is expected.

February 2001—Question 5

Lawyer A has been handling a client's case for over a year. Lawyer B calls Lawyer A and state the client wishes to hire Lawyer B and discharge Lawyer A. Lawyer B asks Lawyer A to send over the file.

What are Lawyer A's ethical obligations?

Model Answer to Question 5

Lawyer A should first verify with the client that the client in fact wants to discharge Lawyer A. Lawyer A should counsel client on the implications of changing counsel, whether there may be an increase in fees or costs to the client, whether there will be any delay while successor counsel becomes acquainted with the matter, etc. MRPC 1.4(b).

If the client in fact wants to discharge the lawyer, Lawyer A should also give the client an accounting, and a report on the status of the case. MRPC 1.16(d), 1.15(b). If the matter is before a tribunal, the client should be advised that the judge may deny any motion to withdraw, and that until the motion is granted, Lawyer A remains responsible for client's representation.

Lawyer A should not send the representation file unless the client directs it to be shared with successor counsel.

Student Answer—February 2001

Question 5—Professional Responsibility—10 points

Lawyer A's ethical obligations are to inform his client that he has received notice that client wishes to discharge A and hire Lawyer B via written correspondence. Lawyer A should state in such correspondence that if client wishes his file to be transferred to B, he must execute a valid authorization for A to do so. A could go as far as to include such authorization for client's execution.

If client executes the authorization for the file to be transferred, Lawyer A must explain that the attorney/client relationship ceases to exist because the second legal representation on whatever matter(s) will no longer be provided. Lawyer A may be obligated to file a Motion to Withdraw as counsel with the court adding client's choice as the reason for which such representation is ceasing. If the valid authorization is signed, Lawyer A must cease all work with such file so as to not obtain any additional charges to client. Lawyer A has the right to collect any unpaid or outstanding balance owed by client to him for services rendered prior to termination of attorney/client relationship.

With respect to sending over the file, Lawyer A should thoroughly make photocopies of his client's file for his own records and safe-keeping, especially for malpractice insurance purposes. Lawyer A would return any original documents to client (deeds, certificates, etc.) and written permission to forward the same to the new attorney. Otherwise bearing authorization and all, Lawyer A should send the file to Lawyer B.

Other miscellaneous issues to consider: whether Lawyer A is ethically obligated to maintain client confidences gained or discussed throughout the one year of representation and he is unless authorized in writing by the client to do otherwise. Lawyer A cannot take (ethically) the word of Lawyer B throughout this whole process and must consistently consult with his client.

Lastly, if any retainer was given, any unused portion must ethically be returned by Lawyer A to client. If any funds of the client were being held by Lawyer A in an escrow, trust, or IOLTA account, they must also be returned to and acknowledged in writing by the client.

July 2001—Question 4

Five research professors made a medical discovery and jointly sought a patent. One professor worked for Michigan State University, and the other four worked for Harvard University. Pursuant to employment agreements at each university, the professors signed over their patent rights to their respective universities. Two Harvard professors subsequently retired and left the school.

A dispute has arisen between the schools concerning patent royalties, and a lawsuit was filed in the federal court in Michigan. Law Firm M represents Michigan State University and Law Firm H represents Harvard University. The professors frequently talk to one another about the case, and relay information they learn back to their respective university counsel. Law Firm M has hired an investigator to collect information in Massachusetts. The investigator has been in contact with the retired professors.

Law Firm H has filed a motion to disqualify Law Firm M alleging that the contacts between professors and between the investigator and the professors are unethical. What is Law Firm M's defense and how should the judge rule?

Model Answer to Question 4

Contacts are governed by MRPC 4.2, which prohibits contacts between an attorney and a party represented by counsel about the subject matter of the representation unless the party's counsel consents. There is no question that Law Firm H has not consented to the contacts.

Although Law Firm M has not made the contacts directly, MRPC 8.4 prohibits a lawyer from doing through another what the lawyer cannot do directly. MRPC 5.3 requires the law firm to have in place procedures to ensure that agents under the lawyers' direction and control comport their conduct to the ethics rules.

The investigators hired by Law Firm M are under the law firm's control, and their actions are governed by ethics rules. If it is improper for the law firm to directly contact the professors, it is also improper for the investigators to do so. *Upjohn v Aetna*, 1991 WL 490026 (WD Mich).

When dealing with an organizational "party," the rule applies to the organization and any constituents (a) who are managers or supervisors, (b) whose statements may constitute admissions of the entity, or (c) whose actions may be imputed to the entity.

This is so because the information held by the lower level employees of an entity may be necessary for the entity to implement the lawyer's recommendations. Communications between entity counsel and entity constituents are held under the entity's client-attorney privilege. *Upjohn Co v United States*, 449 US 383 (1981).

The professors still employed at Harvard are key witnesses in a dispute about the patent and the patent agreement. Their statements may constitute admissions and their actions may be imputed to the entity, since whatever rights the professors assigned to the universities can be no more than the professors originally held. Any contacts between the investigators and the currently employed Harvard professors would be improper.

There is a split of authority on whether former constituents of an entity party may be contacted. Since the lawsuit was filed in Michigan, Michigan law applies. In *Valassis v Samelson*, 143 FRD 118 (ED Mich 1992), the court held that former constituents, even high level constituents, can never be "parties" under Rule 4.2, and may be contacted without consent of entity counsel. ABA Op 91-359 also reasons that the rule was never intended to address contact with former employees and not prohibit those contacts. The contacts between the investigators and the retired professors are not improper.

The professors, however, are not "agents" of the lawyer. The currently employed professors are not constituents of the client entity. The ethics rule does not govern the conduct of parties and their constituents, and nothing prevents the parties from speaking to each other directly. ABA Op 92-362 explicitly permits a lawyer to advise a client that the lawyer may not contact the opposing party directly, but that the client may. Law Firm M is not guilty of misconduct by virtue of the professors' contacts among themselves.

Disqualification is a severe sanction and should not be granted if another lesser sanction is available, such as excluding the evidence obtained from the currently employed Harvard professors. In this case, Law Firm M would be responsible for the conduct of the investigators, which as shown above did not violate the contact rule, and would not be responsible for the conduct of the professors. Michigan State University should not be deprived of its choice of counsel by disqualification, and Law Firm M should not be removed from the case. Law Firm M would still be subject to attorney disciplinary proceedings if the investigators made contact with currently employed Harvard professors.

Student Answer—July 2001

Question 4—Professional Responsibility—None Available

February 2002—Question 2

Simka and Raphael became friends in high school and stayed in touch throughout college and professional school. Simka became a lawyer, and Raphael took over the family's profitable business. Simka has been representing the family business and Raphael personally for several years.

Raphael's business has been going so well that he asked Simka to identify some investment opportunities for him. Simka suggested that Raphael invest $500,000 in some timeshare condos in Puerto Vallarta, but did not mention that Simka already had a 30% interest in the condos. Simka negotiated on Raphael's behalf with the 70% interest owners, but they could not come to an agreement because the 70% owners wanted a minimum of $700,000 for their interest. Instead, Simka sold Raphael half of Simka's own 30% interest for $500,000. The paperwork was drafted by Simka, and Raphael and Simka signed it.

Raphael subsequently found out that he overpaid for the 15% interest he purchased, and demanded that Simka either arrange for conveyance of the 70% interest Raphael thought he was purchasing, or that Simka agree to rescind the deal.

Has Simka engaged in unethical conduct?

Model Answer to Question 2

Since Simka represented Raphael's business and Raphael personally, the condo deal is a "business transaction with a client" and governed by MRPC 1.8(a). That rule prohibits such transactions unless (1) the transaction and terms are fair and reasonable to the client and fully disclosed in writing to the client in a manner that can be understood by the client, (2) the client is given a reasonable opportunity to seek advice of independent counsel, and (3) the client consents in writing.

Although Raphael has signed the papers Simka prepared, the other components of the rule have not been met. Simka charged Raphael $500,000 for a 15% interest arguably only worth $150,000 (if $700,000 for 70% interest was a fair price). Simka did not tell Raphael he was a part owner of the property he recommended. Simka did not give Raphael an opportunity to seek advice from independent counsel.

Raphael would argue that he considered Simka to be his lawyer in the matter. Simka was his lawyer in personal and business matters, and had been for a period of time. Simka knew Raphael did not use other counsel. Simka negotiated with the 70% interest owners as Raphael's representative. Simka drafted the paperwork that closed the transaction. At no time did Simka tell Raphael she had an interest in the condos. Simka also breached MRPC 1.7(b) by attempting to represent Raphael in the transaction while at the same time looking out for Simka's own interests. There is no way Simka could exercise independent professional judgment for Raphael in determining a fair price for the condo interest, while at the same time trying to maximize Simka's own sales price.

Simka would argue that she was never Raphael's investment advisor, and did only business legal work for Raphael. As friends, Raphael and Simka would frequently discuss things that did not involve their professional relationship. Simka was not acting as a lawyer when she identified an investment opportunity, and Simka did no more than convey Raphael's offer to the 70% owners.

Since Simka represented Raphael in business matters, MRPC 1.8(a) is triggered and has been violated. It does not matter whether Simka was Raphael's lawyer in the particular transaction. Since Simka's personal interest was involved in the transaction, and the transaction is adverse to Simka's own client, Simka could not act as Raphael's representative under MRPC 1.7(b).

Student Answer—February 2002

Question 2—Professional Responsibility—9 points

ISSUE

Has Simka engaged in unethical conduct?

EVENT

Buying timeshare condos in Puerto Vallarta by Simka for Raphael.

Unethical Conduct Issues

1) Self dealing: An attorney is not allowed to benefit from his/her client's business involvements or information for the purpose of monetary gain/financial benefit. Here, Simka represented Raphael as an attorney. Raphael asked for advice on investment opportunities to benefit his business. Simka suggested he invest in timeshare condos in Puerto Vallarta. Simka had 30% interest in the condos, but he did not disclose this to Raphael. Relying on his attorney's advice, he invested in the timeshare ($500,000). Because Simka would stand to benefit monetary gains from his client's investment he is not allowed to do so under professional conduct rules. Simka participated in self-dealing activities when he recommended (& that was the *only* rec. he made) to his business client that he invest in a company he had also invested in, especially when he did not disclose the fact that he was an investor to his client.

2) Conflict of Interest: An attorney may not proceed in an action that would create a conflict of interest between two separate clients or between a client and himself. Here, the latter applies. Simka represented Raphael personally & in a business capacity representing Raphael's family business. Raphael inquired of Simka of how to invest money from the business. Raphael was recommended to invest his business $ in a timeshare already invested in by Simka. Raphael was going to purchase a 70% interest, with Simka already owning 30%. In essence, the two would be partners. However, as Raphael's attorney, Simka would be responsible for Raphael's investment while obviously being concerned about his own. As an attorney, Simka could not do both while being able to maintain the proper considerations of what is in the best interest of the client and their financial affairs.

3) Consent: An attorney must gain consent from a client throughout the relationship. Here, Simka told Raphael that he would purchase 70% of the timeshare for Raphael for 500,000. However, he could not make this happen, so he bought 15% for 500,000 for Raphael. Raphael did not know, wasn't given a choice, and did not consent to the deal. Simka acted unethically in making significant decisions for his client without their consent.

CONCLUSION

Simka has engaged in unethical conduct in handling his clients business affairs.

July 2002—Question 11

After an auto accident, the injured passenger filed suit against Tire Mfg. and Car Manufacturer. In preparing a defense for Tire Mfg., Lawyer Carroll discusses with the client the need to test the tires to determine what happened in the accident. Tire Mfg. owner suggests that its in-house laboratory test the tires, and if the results are favorable to Tire Mfg. to have the tests duplicated in an independent lab. Carroll seeks a court order allowing him to send the tires for evidentiary analysis, which is granted on condition that the tires are not "tampered with, changed, or destroyed."

Carroll arranges for the tires to be sent to Tire Mfg. for in-house testing by Janine, Tire Mfg.'s Director of Testing. Janine's test results are favorable for Tire Mfg.'s defense. The tires are then sent by Tire Mfg. to Acme independent testing facility. Acme is unable to duplicate Janine's test results. Carroll interviews Janine and Acme's tester to determine why the results differ. Janine says that when she received the tires, one had a "bubble" that separated the tire from the rim. Janine says that she performed no tests that would be affected by the presence or absence of the bubble. Acme says the tires they received had no bubble, and that bubbles could indicate the presence of foreign material, a tire weakness, or other indicator that they would have tested.

What are the ethical considerations of Carroll presenting Janine as an expert to testify at trial regarding her test results?

Model Answer to Question 11

Carroll should evaluate his duties of diligence and loyalty to his client, and his duties of candor to the tribunal and fairness to opposing parties.

The first key element is that the tires are not in the same condition after the testing as they were before the testing. When received by Janine, one tire had a bubble. When received by Acme, there was no bubble. The court order granted access to the tires for testing only on condition that the tests did not alter the evidence. Carroll has no conclusive information revealing how the altered evidence occurred, and does not know that it occurred because of testing. Carroll may not present evidence that Carroll knows has been altered, MRPC 3.3(a)(1), and may not obstruct the opposing party's access to evidence. MRPC 3.4(1). The lawyer may not silently assert that the condition of the evidence has not changed since the time of the incident, and may not fail to inform the court or counsel as to the true nature of the evidence. MRPC 8.4(b) prohibits a lawyer from engaging in deceitful conduct. If Carroll is going to present evidence about the tire tests, Carroll must disclose to the opposing party and the tribunal that the tires were altered during testing.

Although Janine is not an "independent" expert, Janine is now the only person who has tested the actual unaltered tires. The value of Janine's testimony is diminished by the fact that no other lab was able to duplicate her results, and since the tires are altered, no other lab can exactly duplicate her tests. There is conflicting opinion among Tire Mfg.'s own experts regarding the effect any "bubble" would have on the test results, the test accuracy, or the accident. MRPC 3.3(a)(1) prevents a lawyer from making false statements of material facts. Janine cannot testify without disclosure that the current tires are different from the tires Janine examined.

MRPC 3.3(a)(2) requires a lawyer to disclose material facts when disclosure is necessary to avoid assisting in a client's fraudulent act. Although it could be argued that the tire tampering had to have occurred when the tires were in Tire Mfg.'s custody, Carroll has no knowledge of any acts committed by Tire Mfg. that are criminal or fraudulent to bring the matter within the mandatory disclosure of MRPC 3.3(a)(2). Mere inconsistent opinion among the experts, or even suspicions of the lawyer, are not sufficient.

After disclosure that the condition of the tires has changed, Carroll is not prevented from using Janine as a witness, as long as she testifies truthfully.

Student Answer—July 2002

Question 11—Professional Responsibility—None Available

February 2003—Question 14

Harvey and Helen Parker, a married couple, developed financial problems and worried about losing their 200-acre homestead. They transferred the real estate title to their son to avoid creditors. Two years later, Harvey and Helen decided to sell their homestead, but wanted to do so quietly without drawing creditor attention to themselves. They hired lawyer Travers to act as their agent for the sale, and instructed him not to reveal their identities. Development Company became interested in purchasing the property for a new shopping mall. The sale terms were negotiated by Travers and Development Company's lawyer, Dumont.

At no time was any action filed by creditors against Harvey and Helen Parker.

Development Company held itself out as experienced in building shopping malls for rural environments. It would incorporate duck ponds, nature preserves, and dirt paths among the stores, in order to maintain the rural feeling. Development Company was very interested in any environmental problems connected to the site, and was also attempting to get tax incentives from the local municipality. Dumont conducted his own due diligence on these issues, but did ask Travers whether the Parkers had ever been contacted by any government or regulatory agency regarding the property. Travers answered that he was unaware of any such contacts.

Three days before the scheduled closing, Travers learned that the Parkers' son was the registered owner of the property. When he questioned the Parkers about the matter, they told him that they had been making payments through the son for two years, in order to hold off creditors. They also mentioned that they were selling the property because they believed that the northeast portion had been used as a dump site without their knowledge or consent. They again told Travers not to reveal their identity to the purchaser and not to do anything that may delay the closing.

What are Travers' obligations to Development Company and Dumont?

Model Answer to Question 14

MRPC 4.1 prohibits a lawyer from knowingly making a false statement of material fact to another person.

Travers was not aware of any environmental problems at the homestead when he answered Dumont's questions, therefore, his initial answer did not violate his ethics duty. Travers has a duty to correct his answer, however, when the Parkers inform him of the possible dump site. The environmental issues are material to the sale. Also, Travers has a duty to correct his previous answer. To remain silent would be equivalent to making a false statement, and could expose Travers to liability under MPRC 8.4(b), conduct involving dishonesty, fraud, deceit, or misrepresentation. Although disclosure would be adverse to the Parkers' interest and contrary to their instructions not to do anything that would delay the sale, diligent representation of the Parkers does not include lying to Dumont.

Dumont never asked Travers who had title to the homestead, and therefore Travers has no statement to correct under MRPC 4.1. Travers has no duty to perform Dumont's due diligence regarding the matter, or to volunteer answers to questions Dumont should have asked. The Comment to MRPC 4.1 addresses undisclosed principals, indicating that such is not improper *as long as nondisclosure does not constitute fraud.*

In this instance, the Parkers transferred title to their son, and are therefore not the title holders of record. Under MRPC1.2(c) Travers may not allow his services to be used to assist the Parkers in fraud. On the one hand, the transfer of the title to the son may have been fraudulent in avoidance of creditors. On the other hand, the Parkers held themselves out as the true sellers of the property, and Travers assisted them in the sale transaction. Travers has a duty under MRPC 1.4(b) to provide the Parkers with all information necessary to make an informed decision about the sale and the disclosures. Part of that information and counseling includes telling the Parkers that under MRPC 1.6(c)(3), Travers has discretion, although not a duty, to disclose confidences and secrets to rectify the consequences of a client's illegal or fraudulent act, in furtherance of which the lawyer's services have been used.

If the Parkers cannot be persuaded to allow Travers to make the appropriate disclosures, Travers must withdraw from representation. MRPC 1.16(a).

Student Answer—February 2003

Question 14—Professional Responsibility—9 points

Travers's obligations to Development Company and Attorney: Now that Travers has learned of the dumpsite on the property, know that Development Company is concerned with this; Travers is under a duty to notify them of this dump site before closing. He owes the same duty to the company's attorney. Travers must also reveal the son as the owner of the property since he holds true title.

The issue of defrauding creditors and misrepresenting themselves to the buyer: Since Travers just learned of the Parkers past 2-year attempt to evade creditors he must keep this secret because it's a past crime and he owes the Parkers the duty of confidentiality. This applies when an attorney client privilege exists, when the client has sought out an attorney (as here) for legal advice and expects that all communications between them remain confidential. However, Travers does not and cannot allow a crime to continue; he must tell the Parkers of his disapproval and ask them to reveal themselves as the true owners of the property and cease defrauding creditors. If they persist in their actions he may withdraw from representing them. This is all according to the rules of Professional Responsibility of an Attorney.

Travers is under a duty to disclose future crimes and to disclose any defects in the property known to him at the time of closing. He cannot misrepresent his client falsely to Dumont either.

July 2003—Question 15

Newgate Construction submitted a bid to City for the opportunity to rebuild the main street bridge. The current bridge accommodated two lanes of traffic. Newgate's proposal included widening the bridge to create parking spaces on the bridge. When the bid was awarded to Carpetworks, Newgate hired lawyer O'Hara, a former mayor of City, to protest the bid award.

O'Hara arranged a lunch meeting with Ginny, the City clerk, who received all bids. O'Hara had originally hired Ginny when he was mayor, and had served as her political mentor when she ran for the Clerk's office. Without telling Ginny that he had been hired by Newgate, O'Hara asked Ginny if the City officials believed that a new bridge would do good things for the local economy and bring more business to the downtown area. Ginny sarcastically said "some" City officials apparently believed that, because one of them was resurfacing an abandoned lot for extra parking. Ginny told O'Hara that Carpetworks was the contractor on the resurface job, and that the word around the office was that Carpetworks did the job for a "deep discount." The City official who owns the lot also voted on the contract bids. O'Hara warns Ginny that she should not be discussing these matters with anyone else, if she is to have a successful political future.

O'Hara reported the conversation to Newgate, pointing out that parking on the bridge would compete with parking in the official's lot. Newgate now wants O'Hara to contact City's lawyer and offer to refrain from reporting the bidding bias and irregularity to law enforcement authorities, if City will agree to award the contract to Newgate. Newgate also wants O'Hara to give Ginny $2,500 in anticipation of her testifying in the bid protest proceeding.

How should O'Hara proceed?

Model Answer to Question 15

Although Ginny is an official of the City, no action has been filed and the City and its constituent officials are not "represented by counsel in the matter." The prohibition in MRPC 4.2 against contacting persons represented by counsel does not apply.

Ginny, as City Clerk, is "unrepresented," and O'Hara was required to comply with MRPC 4.3. O'Hara could not appear "disinterested" and should not give any advice other than advice for Ginny to seek legal counsel. Instead, O'Hara appears to have played upon his personal relationship with Ginny to get her talking, never admitted his interest on behalf of Newgate, and "advised" her regarding not to tell anyone else what she told him.

Threat: It is illegal for public officials to receive favors from City vendors or to accept personal favors in exchange for City contracts. If Ginny's information is true, then the lot owner is culpable. The question is whether raising the lot owner's misconduct is improperly using threats of criminal charges in exchange for settling a civil matter. The Michigan Rules of Professional Conduct do not have a specific rule that addresses criminal threats, but several existing rules may apply in a particular case. Michigan Ethics Opinion R1-78 notes that omission, and states in part:

> No specific ethical rule prohibits a lawyer, when acting in good faith and without purpose of harassment, to call to the attention of an opposing party the possible applicability of a penal statute or make reference to specific criminal sanctions, or to warn of the possibility of criminal prosecution, even if done in order to assist in the enforcement of a valid right or legitimate claim of a client.

Whether O'Hara violates the underlying concept greatly depends upon how O'Hara raises the matter with the City attorney. If withholding criminal charges is discussed as a means of avoiding City embarrassment and increasing confidence in City government, mentioning it in the context of resolving Newgate's matter would not be improper. If the matter is raised to coerce or intimidate City officials, it would be improper.

Witness Compensation: MRPC 3.4(f) prohibits O'Hara from requesting that Ginny not voluntarily provide information to another party. Ginny is not a constituent of Newgate or a relative of the client. MRPC 3.4(b) prohibits a lawyer from offering an improper inducement for testimony. Offering Ginny $2,500 in anticipation of testimony, when there is no proceeding pending where testimony would be taken, smacks of improper inducement.

O'Hara's best course of action would be to file the bid protest. In the course of negotiations with City counsel after the protest is filed, O'Hara may find an opportunity to inform the City attorney of possible improper conduct in the awarding of the bid to Carpetworks, as discussed above.

Student Answer—July 2003

Question 15—Professional Responsibility—None Available

Febuary 2004—Question 6

Developer owns 100 prime acres near the outskirts of city. Developer has been working with Builder and Engineer for two years on a variety of development options, including expanding an existing office building into office suites and building condominiums. The existing office building is occupied by the Mika family business and they are interested in buying the office building and the surrounding property.

The Mikas retain Lawyer Logan to represent their interests. Logan's fee agreement includes the following language:

> Lawyer agrees to handle client's case and charges client a $15,000.00 retainer under the following terms: The retainer funds will remain in our client trust account for the duration of our representation, then shall be applied to the final billing statement. If the total legal fees and expenses incurred are less than the retainer amount, the balance will be refunded at the conclusion of our representation.

Logan bills monthly, but the Mikas neither forward a retainer nor make payments. Logan incurs fees totaling $8,200.00 while negotiating with Developer's Lawyer Devon for a lease with option to buy. The purchase agreement provides that the Mikas place $85,000.00 in a non-interest bearing escrow for the closing. The money is paid to Logan, who deposits it in a non-interest bearing trust account. Logan pays himself $8,200.00 from the escrow funds.

Before closing, the relationship between the Mikas and Developer breaks down. Devon files suit on behalf of Developer, seeking the escrow monies and damages. Logan counterclaims on behalf of the Mikas, alleging environmental and structural problems. The Mikas demand that Logan return the closing escrow funds to them. Developer discusses the counterclaims with Engineer and Builder, and the three agree to contribute $25,000.00 each to a "settlement fund" to be held by Devon. Developer and Builder send their checks to Devon, which are deposited into an interest-bearing trust account. Engineer promises to wire the money to the account within ten (10) days. On the fourth day, the Mikas agree to settle the entire dispute if they receive one-half the amount of the closing escrow, and if the settlement offer is accepted within 24 hours. Developer, Engineer and Builder all timely agree to settle, but monies from Engineer have not been received.

Devon has incurred fees of $21,000.00 in filing the lawsuit, responding to the counterclaim and negotiating the settlement. Logan has incurred an additional $17,000.00 in responding to the lawsuit, filing the counterclaim and negotiating the settlement.

Analyze whether the lawyers have ethically handled the escrow funds, and how the remaining escrow funds should now be handled.

Model Answer to Question 6

The applicable ethics rule is MRPC 1.15, safekeeping of property. Logan has custody of $85,000.00 in escrow, and Devon has custody of $50,000.00 in escrow. The settlement of "all claims" is payment of $42,500.00 to the Mikas.

The escrow money the Mikas gave to Logan for the closing was for a specific purpose, and put into Logan's custody for safekeeping for that specific purpose. Logan was required to preserve the asset for that purpose, and may not take his fees from that money. The engagement language that allows Logan a retainer does not specifically say the retainer may be taken from the closing escrow. Logan's use of the closing escrow for his own purposes is misappropriation.

Logan cannot deposit the escrow into a non-interest bearing account, even if the parties so stipulate. MRPC 1.15(d) requires all funds held by a lawyer to be placed into interest-bearing accounts. The parties may not overrule a Supreme Court mandate. If the parties want the account to be non-interest bearing, then a lawyer may not be the escrow agent.

When agreeing to hold the closing escrow, Logan takes on fiduciary duties to Developer in addition to lawyer-client duties to the Mikas. Logan may not unilaterally distribute the escrow funds to either party when he knows the funds are in dispute. MRPC 1.15(c). At the settlement of the lawsuit, Logan must disburse half the closing escrow to the Mikas and half to the Developer. Logan should then bill for his outstanding fees.

Devon may hold the settlement escrow even though only Developer is Devon's client, but Devon undertakes fiduciary duties to Engineer and Builder when agreeing to hold the money for all three. MRPC 1.15(a). Since Devon has consent from Developer, Builder, and Engineer to settle the case, Devon has sufficient authority to settle even though Engineer has not sent his money. MRPC 1.8(g).

Although Engineer has not contributed funds to the settlement escrow, all funds in the escrow were intended to pay settlement, and Devon has a duty to promptly disburse once the settlement has been accepted. MRPC 1.15(b). Since the litigation was settled for one-half of the closing escrow, the settlement escrow and any accrued interests should be divided and returned to Builder and Developer who deposited the funds. Devon should then bill Developer for his legal fees, and cannot take them from the escrow.

Student Answer—February 2004

Question 6—Professional Responsibility—8 points

Attorney Logan established a clear retainer agreement with Mikas. They were to pay him $15,000 to handle the case, with any left over to be returned. This was a standard, acceptable agreement.

The Mikas agreed, signed, and never paid. Logan sent monthly statements. No money was received until a deal was established and the Mikas sent $85,000 to be used for an escrow account for the purchase closing. These funds were clearly designated for that purpose and not meant to be used for attorney fees or case expense. At the time of the payment the Mikas owed Logan $8,200—a reasonable fee—but they did not pay him for that. Logan should not have taken the $8,200 out of that account to pay himself, even though he had a valid claim and contract with the Mikas.

By the end of the settlement the Mikas wanted half of their escrow returned, $42,500, and they owed Logan an additional $17,000, so a total of $25,200. The escrow account could be held up in "contract negotiations," releasing the $42,500 to Mikas and holding the remainder in escrow until Mikas straightened out their bills with Logan, or until he takes them to court to get his payment correctly. He should not have paid himself out of the escrow account.

Attorney Devon has incurred $21,000 in fees owed to him. The $50,000 settlement account would cover this, but the fund is still "unpaid" by the engineer. It would be unfair to the other 2 parties to pay Devon $21,000 and then have the Developer and Builder split any remainder. They should wait until all $75,000 is gathered in the settlement account and then pay off Devon.

July 2004—Question 6

Under the contingent fee agreement, Partner Session and Associate Anis represent a class of 125 plaintiffs alleging fraudulent billing practices by Phone Company, the local telephone company.

Phone Company is represented by inside counsel Ferris and outside counsel Multistate. Phone Company does not believe its charges are improper, but does not want to engage in lengthy litigation which damages its reputation in the highly competitive local phone market. Also, Phone Company does not want to defend "copy cat" suits in other parts of the country, and does not want to litigate again against Partner and Associate.

At a meeting to see if settlement is possible, Ferris proposes a "package" with two terms:

(1) $1,500,000 to be paid by Phone Company to the plaintiffs, and
(2) promises from Session and Anis never to represent clients on any billing or rate claims against Phone Company or any of its affiliates.

Anis tells Session that she believes the term (2) is contrary to ethics rules. Session then suggests that Phone Company hire Session's firm for future consulting services, instead of term (2). Ferris agrees, as long as the cost of the consulting agreement is part of the $1,500,000 of term (1). Ferris and Session eventually agree to a consulting agreement valued at $250,000, and the ultimate settlement amount for term (1) is finalized at $1,750,000. Multistate drafts the settlement agreement and all counsel and Phone Company execute it. Session sets up a series of meetings with each individual plaintiff to offer the settlement and get their written consent.

Discuss any ethical considerations and whether the four lawyers have acted properly.

Model Answer to Question 6

The terms of the settlement are governed in this case by MRPC 5.6(b). The rule does not allow a lawyer to "offer or make" an agreement "restricting the lawyer's right to practice" as a condition of settlement. Anis was correct that Ferris' first suggestion of term (2), that Session agree not to take cases against Phone Company, would violate the rule.

The whole purpose of making Session a "consultant" is to make Session the lawyer for Phone Company, and thereby prevent Session from taking future cases against Phone Company. This arrangement also violates MRPC 5.6(b), because it is a settlement restricting the plaintiff's counsel from taking certain kinds of cases in the future. In addition, when this term is made part of the settlement for plaintiffs, Session's own interest in getting the consulting arrangement is in conflict with Session's duties to the plaintiffs, triggering MRPC 1.7(b). Session could not possibly be exercising independent professional judgment on behalf of plaintiffs while also trying to make his own "deal" with Phone Company. For these reasons, the consulting arrangement is improper under MRPC 5.6(b) and 1.7(b).

In addition, the consulting fee is "blended" into the settlement amount. The actual amount available to the plaintiffs is only $1,500,000, since only Session is entitled to the consulting amount. The consulting amount is apparently in addition to whatever legal fees Session and Anis are otherwise entitled to. The consulting arrangement must be disclosed to the plaintiffs before they consider agreeing to the settlement. MRPC 1.4.

If the terms of the settlement agreement violate MRPC 5.6, and the rule also prohibits "offering or making," then all of the lawyers have violated MRPC 5.6 by signing the agreement. In addition, Multistate drafted the agreement with the tainted terms, Ferris proposed it, and Session negotiated it. Only Anis has lesser liability, since she raised the ethics problem. MRPC 5.2(b) permits a subordinate lawyer to follow a supervisory lawyer's decision regarding an arguable question of professional ethics.

MRPC 8.3 requires reporting when the lawyer (a) has knowledge (b) of another lawyer's significant ethics violation, (c) that raises substantial questions about honesty, trustworthiness, or fitness. The rule is not triggered, however, when the information is protected by MRPC 1.6. MRPC 1.6 protects confidences and secrets. "Confidences" refer to information protected by the attorney-client privilege. Here, since the settlement terms were negotiated with opposing counsel, they cannot be privileged. "Secrets," however, include anything related to the representation that would be embarrassing or detrimental to the client or that the client has requested be protected. Settlement agreements with potentially invalid terms could be held void, which would be detrimental to the clients. Without client permission, the lawyers have no duty to report.

Student Answer—July 2004

Question 6—Professional Responsibility—3 points (Bad answer)

Session: When Session suggested the Phone Company hire their firm for future consulting services, this is a conflict of interest. He cannot nor can his firm do this; he is supposed to be representing his plaintiffs of the class action suit. Instead he's negotiating for future business. This violates the duty he owes to every plaintiff that he is supposed to represent them due diligently.

Ferris: Ferris agreeing to hire Session's firm, as a consulting services is violating the MRP because a client must 1st agree that his firm or attorney may consult with another attorney, otherwise this breaks clients right to keep his information a secret and privileged. This cannot be agreed on prior to client's approval unless they do not disclose any information, which is not what is intended here.

Anis: By representing Plaintiffs and by working and being present among this conversation for negotiating consulting fees, she is violating MRP if she fails to disclose and report Session and Ferris for their misconduct. Not reporting such conduct makes Anis in violation of the Rules as well.

Multistate: Is violating the MPR by drafting such a settlement. He too is in violation because, by participating he should decline.

By substituting (2) provision do not compete clause is unethical on its face; this is violating the rules because you can't prohibit the practice of law.

> **Comment:** Although this is not a good answer, based on how the graders typically grade, this examinee should have received at least 4 if not 5 points for this response. Remember, there are typically 15 different graders for each question. If this examinee were within 1 or 2 points of passing, this is an example of something that would be appealable.

February 2005—Question 3

Cassandra has decided to form a law firm with two other lawyers, Hemi and Tandy. Cassandra tells Hemi and Tandy that she will get her former law school professor, Vellux, to set up a professional corporation in which they will be equal shareholders. Vellux meets with Cassandra, drafts incorporation papers and a shareholder agreement, and mails them to each of the lawyers. The lawyers and Vellux have a conference call during which Vellux answers the lawyers' questions.

After the call is concluded, the lawyers execute and file the papers establishing Ingham County Lawyers, P.C. Almost immediately, however, the lawyers have disagreements about the style of firm management and the direction of the firm's business, including establishing bank accounts, compensation draws, hiring staff, and business development activities. After the papers are filed, Hemi calls Vellux objecting to the condescending way Cassandra treats staff. Tandy calls Vellux complaining about Hemi spending firm money on a new computer system. Cassandra calls Vellux to help persuade the other shareholders to host a reception for prospective clients currently being represented by other firms.

Ultimately Cassandra asks Vellux to dissolve the firm so that her relationship with Hemi and Tandy is terminated, but she wants the right to continue to use the firm name and she wants sole ownership of the client lists.

1. **What arguments would Hemi and Tandy make in objection to Vellux representing Cassandra?**
2. **What arguments would Vellux make in support of his representation of Cassandra?**

Model Answer to Question 3

This question involves identification of "who is the client" for purposes of Vellux's ethics duties, and what was the scope of his representation. A common situation for business lawyers when setting up a corporation is whether the lawyer represents the entity, all the organizers, or just some of the organizers. It is the lawyer's responsibility to clarify who is the client. MRPC 1.2(c), 1.4(b), 1.13(d).

Hemi's and Tandy's Arguments: Hemi and Tandy will argue that Vellux may not represent Cassandra in dissolving the corporation and advocating Cassandra's personal interests in dissolution, because Vellux represents the corporate entity and also represented them personally.

Although Cassandra made contact with Vellux for the drafting of the incorporation papers and bylaws, the legal work was clearly for the corporation, not for Cassandra personally. The documents established a separate legal entity, not a personal business for Cassandra. Vellux sent copies of what he drafted to all the shareholders, not just Cassandra. He also talked to all of the shareholders together about the content of the documents. Under MRPC 1.13(a), Vellux therefore represented the entity, not the individual shareholders. It was based upon this conduct that the shareholders believed they could properly rely upon Vellux to assist them in dealing with problems within the corporation. Although each of the shareholders had different concerns, all of their questions dealt with the success of the entity, not with their personal interests. Under MRPC 1.13(d), Vellux had a duty to clarify who was the client when the shareholders called him about their complaints. Vellux never did so.

In the alternative, Hemi and Tandy may argue that Vellux was their lawyer and owed duties to them personally. Vellux undertook a joint representation of all three shareholders in setting up the entity. At the time, there was no conflict under MRPC 1.7(a) or (b) because all the shareholders agreed to the incorporation and organization. Representing one of the clients to dissolve what Vellux himself put together for the clients jointly would be a violation of MRPC 1.9(a), as the subject matter of the new representation is substantially related to the prior representation of the three clients.

As a lawyer for the entity, Vellux may not represent Cassandra personally without the consent of the remaining shareholders. MRPC 1.13(e). Further, since Cassandra wishes to dissolve the entity, her representation is adverse to the entity and to the other shareholders. Under MRPC 1.7(a) and (b) the conflict is not waivable.

Vellux's Arguments: Vellux will argue that he had a prior relationship only with Cassandra, that he was contacted to do the legal work by Cassandra, and that he drafted the incorporation papers on the basis of input only from Cassandra. Therefore he was acting only as Cassandra's lawyer. When he explained the papers to the other shareholders, they were "unrepresented," and he merely answered questions based on the content of the papers as drafted for Cassandra. The shareholders independently decided to file the papers he drafted, and he did not file them on behalf of the corporation.

Vellux will argue that when the shareholders called him with complaints about the other shareholders, he was not acting as their lawyer, but merely as a sounding board. Treatment of staff, spending money, and holding receptions are not legal decisions, but rather are business decisions of the corporation. When Cassandra asked Vellux to dissolve the firm, Vellux had no conflict of interest that would prevent him from assisting Cassandra, because he never had an attorney-client relationship with the other shareholders or with the corporation.

Two Student Answers—February 2005

Question 3—Professional Responsibility—9 points

1. The first argument that Hemi and Tandy should make is conflict of interest. The issue is whether there is a conflict of interest in Vellux representing Cassandra. The MRPC states that when an attorney has represented a client or clients he cannot litigate against them as a result of confidential information gained during the representation unless there has been *consent.* Here Vellux represented and consulted with all three: Cassandra, Tandy, and Hemi in a professional and legal capacity. He has gained confidential information on Hemi and Tandy. According to the MRPC he cannot represent Cassandra against Hemi and Tandy without their consent. They are deemed to be former clients of Vellux. He can potentially use information that can be used against them.

2. Vellux can argue that Hemi or Tandy were not clients and there was no legal representation. He did not meet them; he only spoke to them through a conference call. He can argue that Cassandra was a client since he helped draft the documents with her and there is no conflict of interest. Finally, he can argue that since he didn't represent Tandy or Hemi he has gained no confidential information that can be used against them.

> **Comment:** This is a pretty good answer, but the examinee missed the argument that Vellux was representing the corporate entity, not them ("who is the client" issue). Even missing this issue resulted in only losing one point.

Question 3—Professional Responsibility—9 points

1. Hemi and Tandy will object to Vellux representing Cassandra since it appears Vellux has held himself out as the firm's lawyer and not Cassandra's personal lawyer.

This brings about an important issue in that Vellux had no business by dual representation of all 3 partners when he prepared the corporation. He is giving mixed signals.

On one hand, Vellux appears to have been principle (lawyer) of sort setting up this firm and on the other hand he appears to have been Cassandra's personal lawyer, representing her interest. None the less, now Vellux has conflicts to deal with and should not represent any of the three, Cassandra, Tandy, or Hemi when they dissolve this PC.

In conclusion, Vellux has kept confidences and secrets of Hemi and Tandy and would have a conflict representing only Cassandra now. Vellux should not represent any of them in this action—too many conflicts.

2. Vellux will argue that Cassandra was his client to begin with and never represented Hemi or Tandy. Vellux will say he should be allowed to continue to represent Cassandra because as lawyers Tandy and Hemi knew this and waived any conflict. Vellux will lose his argument though—this all has the appearance of impropriety and he needs to be disqualified for representing the three. Conflict of interest and potential disclosure of secrets and confidences are there. Tandy and Hemi both disclosed information to Vellux that could be seen as attorney-client (since they are officers of PC) that it appears he represented.

Conclusion: Vellux should not represent Cassandra. Too many conflicts, adverse issues and violation of Rules of Professional Conduct and appearance of impropriety.

Even if Vellux didn't represent the PC, it appears his actions with Tandy and Hemi would still be a conflict. Also, if his argument is he represented Cassandra all along, he wasn't acting the most appropriate when he took calls from Tandy and Hemi about Cassandra.

Conflicts and Breaches of Confidences.

July 2005—Question 3

The application for admission to the bar asks the following questions:

> Have you ever been a party to any civil litigation? If so, provide the complete case caption and a description of the underlying circumstances.
>
> Have you ever (a) entered a guilty plea or a no contest plea to a criminal offense which was taken under advisement or otherwise did not result in conviction, or (b) had a criminal conviction expunged or set aside? If so, provide the complete case caption and a description of the underlying circumstances.

Bar applicant Vanessa has received a notice to appear for a character and fitness interview relating to Vanessa's experiences while in undergraduate school. One of the instances that will be discussed is a wild campus party during which Vanessa engaged in underage drinking and a fist fight with an older male student, Kenny. Vanessa and Kenny were subsequently arrested and their statements were taken by local police. They each pled no contest, and each was sentenced to one year probation and 100 hours community service, upon successful completion of which their records were expunged. Vanessa kept complete records of the incident, and hired Lawyer Sullivan to represent her at the character and fitness interview.

Kenny failed the bar examination and has contacted Lawyer Sullivan for assistance regarding appealing his score. Because of his representation of Vanessa, Sullivan knows Kenny was involved in the undergraduate incident and, out of curiosity, reviews Kenny's application materials. Sullivan discovers that Kenny never disclosed the incident.

What are Sullivan's obligations?

Model Answer to Question 3

This question highlights the lawyer's obligation to protect confidences and secrets.

Because Sullivan has a complete set of records from Vanessa, he knows that Kenny has violated MRPC 8.1(a)(1) by knowingly making a false statement of material fact in his bar application. Sullivan was hired only to appeal Kenny's test score, and thus the scope of his representation is limited under MRPC 1.2(b), but Sullivan chose to review Kenny's application materials and now knows he did not disclose. Therefore, Sullivan is arguably representing Kenny "in connection with a bar admission application" as contemplated by MRPC 8.1(a)(2), and has an affirmative duty "to disclose a fact necessary to correct a misapprehension known by the person to have arisen in the matter."

The only exception to Sullivan's affirmative disclosure is if the information is protected by Rule 1.6. MRPC 1.6 protects confidences (privileged communications) and secrets (other information gained in the relationship that would be embarrassing or detrimental to the client). The fact that Kenny did not disclose the undergraduate arrest is, at minimum, "detrimental" information gained in representing Kenny, and protected by MRPC 1.6.

MRPC 1.6(c) permits disclosure of confidences and secrets (1) with consent of the client after full disclosure, (2) when permitted or required by the rules, (3) to rectify a client fraud in which the lawyer's services were used, (4) to prevent a crime, and (5) to collect a fee. Discretionary options (4) and (5) clearly do not apply. Option (3) does not apply because Sullivan did not assist Kenny in failing to disclose, and appealing the test scores does not impact any determination on Kenny's character or fitness. This is especially true in Michigan, where test score appeals are handled by the Board of Law Examiners and character and fitness is initially handled by the State Bar, separate and independent entities.

As to option (1), although Kenny's nondisclosure was learned when representing Kenny, Sullivan cannot counsel Kenny about the matter without somehow revealing information gained from Vanessa. The undergraduate incident and Kenny's role in it were learned from representing Vanessa and are only proven through Vanessa's records. Similarly, Sullivan cannot seek consent from Vanessa without revealing that Kenny failed to disclose. Vanessa and Kenny might not even know the other is a bar applicant. Duties of confidentiality to each client seem to prevent Sullivan from providing the "full disclosure" necessary to fall within option (1).

Sullivan could attempt to obtain the undergraduate incident records from the police and the courts, in order not to use Vanessa's records, but they may not be available due to the expungement. Vanessa's character and fitness interview is confidential, and her file materials will never become "generally known" to fall outside the protection of her confidences and secrets.

Option (2) requires cross reference to MRPC 3.3(a) (2), "a lawyer shall not knowingly . . . fail to disclose a material fact to a tribunal when disclosure is necessary to avoid assisting a criminal or fraudulent act by the client." As noted above in discussing option (3), Sullivan had no part in Kenny's initial nondisclosure and had not been hired with respect to Kenny's character and fitness investigation. Sullivan's assistance in connection with test scores does not assist Kenny in his nondisclosure. Thus there does not appear to be any rule or law that requires or permits disclosure to all within option (2).

Thus none of the exceptions to MRPC 1.6 permit Sullivan to reveal Kenny's nondisclosure. Sullivan should advise Kenny in a general way that under MRPC 8.1(b)(2), Kenny has a continuing obligation to update the bar application, but cannot mention the specific incident which Sullivan only knows about through Vanessa. Sullivan does not violate any duties by continuing to represent Kenny in his test score appeal. MRPC 1.16 would only require withdrawal if Sullivan's continued representation would be in violation of a rule.

Two Student Answers—July 2005

Question 3—Professional Responsibility—8 points

The issue is what legal obligations a lawyer has to disclose information about a client or potential client.

More importantly it must be resolved whether Sullivan can even represent Kenny in this matter. Sullivan is representing Vanessa in her character and fitness interview. He is not actually doing any legal work for her. He has an obligation to represent her fully and fairly and competently.

Kenny wants to hire Sullivan to prepare his appeal for the bar exam. Even though Vanessa and Kenny were involved in a matter before, their current issues have no significance on the past. However, Sullivan should still get consent from both Vanessa and Kenny to be able to represent both of them at the same time. Sullivan must explain that representing one of them will have no effect on the representation of the other. If they both consent and understand what Sullivan has explained, he is free to represent both parties. The issue becomes whether Sullivan has an obligation to report Kenny's failure to report his omissions form his bar application regarding his undergraduate incident. A lawyer has an obligation to report all violations of other lawyers and judges. Lawyer also has an obligation to report possible future crimes of their current clients. Based on the relationship between Sullivan and Kenny, Kenny would argue that because of the attorney client privilege, Sullivan cannot reveal what he knows because it happened in the past in this case, Sullivan has an obligation to Kenny to discuss with him the ramifications of not telling the truth on his bar application. Sullivan should explain that lawyers have a duty to be honest and forthcoming. Bar applicants also have a duty to be honest on their application. Sullivan should advise Kenny to now correct his mistake with the State bar. Bar applicants have a duty to update information.

Sullivan does not have a legal obligation to turn Kenny in for this violation but should strongly advise Kenny to turn himself in. To uphold the integrity of the legal profession, it would probably be the best to report Kenny because all current lawyers and future lawyers are held to a higher standard when it comes to telling the truth.

Comment: This was a complex PR question, and most students did a poor job on it. Read the model answer for a substantive review of the rules and to learn the interplay of them with this fact pattern. The next example shows a "bad answer" that only earned 3 points.

Question 3—Professional Responsibility—3 points (Bad answer)

The issue in this question is what are Lawyer Sullivan's obligations involving Vanessa and Kenny.

Vanessa: The facts state that Vanessa is going through a character and fitness interview. The issue at hand is the fight she was involved in with Kenny. Although her charge was expunged, and the facts indicate that Vanessa completed probation and 100 hours of community service, SHE *must* disclose this information. All bar applicants *must* disclose all information as required by the Michigan Bar. If the applicant does *not* properly disclose something OR claims a 5th Amendment/14th Am. Privilege, the Michigan Bar *may* reject the person's admission.

Kenny: As for Kenny, there is a potential conflict of interests. Kenny is representing Vanessa & Kenny in *different* settings. Vanessa—character and fitness interview, while Kenny is appealing his bar examination. This issue becomes the topic of disclosing Kenny did *NOT* disclose he got in a fight/was charged for fighting Vanessa.

I think it *is* proper for Sullivan to take Kenny's appeal. The Professional Responsibility rules indicate that a lawyer does *NOT* need to disclose *past* fraud. In this case, Kenny *already* passed Character & Fitness to take the Bar exam. Therefore, Sullivan/Lawyer does *not* have to disclose the criminal offense.

Therefore, Sullivan may take Kenny's appeal.

> **Comment:** This is an example of a bad answer that only earned 3 points. Compare this with the model answer to identify all the missed issues.

February 2006—Question 7

At Large Law Firm a lawyer desiring to take on a matter must: (a) submit names of parties and counsel to the firm's Conflict Coordinator who runs a computer check against all matters and parties in the firm's conflict database; and (b) resolve all conflicts of interest reported by the Conflict Coordinator, draft an engagement letter, and submit the information to the Accounting Department so the matter may be opened. The parties and the conflicts are rechecked by Accounting before opening the file.

Real Estate Company has been negotiating with its shopping center tenants for a number of months but has made little headway. Negotiations are suspended for the holidays. Real Estate Company asks Conway, a member of Large Law Firm, to take over the negotiations for Real Estate Company, and to prepare to institute litigation if the negotiations fail. Conway submits information to the firm's Conflict Coordinator, including the fact that certain tenants are represented by the Mercer Law Firm. The conflict check comes back clean, with no adverse matches.

On December 28, Large Law Firm performs a conflict check on lawyer candidate Helene and her current employer, Mercer Law Firm. The conflict check shows that the firm has no adverse matters with Helene or Mercer Law Firm. Large Law Firm extends an offer to Helene, which she accepts and begins work as an associate on January 5.

On January 15, Real Estate Company contacts Conway to write letters to get negotiations restarted. Conway drafts an engagement letter and submits all required information to Accounting to open the matter. The matter is returned to Conway for conflict resolution when it is determined that Helene worked on the same negotiations for the tenants while she was employed at Mercer Law Firm.

Discuss whether Conway and Large Law Firm may represent Real Estate Company.

Model Answer to Question 7

This question tests knowledge of the unique provisions of the Michigan Rules of Professional Conduct regarding lawyer mobility in private practice.

Under the general rule for imputed disqualification, if one lawyer in the firm is disqualified from representing a client in a matter, all other members of the firm are also disqualified. Rule 1.10(a). Therefore, if Helene cannot represent Real Estate Company's interests, then no one at Law Firm may do so.

In this instance, Helene not only worked for Mercer Law Firm, she worked for Mercer Law Firm for the tenants and against the interests of Real Estate Company. Helene therefore falls within MRPC 1.9(a), because she formerly represented a client in the same matter; she may not represent Real Estate Company's interests without her former clients' consent.

Helene also falls within MRPC 1.9(b), because by working on the negotiations for the tenants, she had to have "acquired" protected information.

Under Michigan Rule 1.10(b), a law firm may avoid imputed disqualification in some instances when a lawyer joins the firm, by screening the transferring lawyer from the matter and the fee, and by giving written notice to the appropriate tribunal. However, MRPC 1.10(b) would permit Law Firm to avoid imputed disqualification only for Helene's MRPC 1.9(b) disqualification. It does not permit Law Firm to represent a client when Helene is disqualified under MRPC 1.9(a).

Law Firm may not represent Real Estate Company without waivers from the tenants represented by Helene when she was at Mercer Law Firm.

Since Helene is disqualified under MRPC 1.9(a), the timing of the conflict checks, the opening of the Real Estate Company matter, and the hiring of Helene makes no difference. If Helene had not personally worked on the Real Estate Company tenant matters, and only learned information because of her presence at Mercer Law Firm, then Large Law Firm could argue that screening Helene would avoid imputed disqualification. The question would then be whether establishing screening on January 15, when Helene had been working at Large Law Firm since January 5, was adequate.

Student Answer—February 2006

Question 7—Professional Responsibility—10 points

This is a professional responsibility and ethics question specifically dealing with whether Conway and Large Law Firm may represent Real Estate Company. The issue presented is whether Conway can represent Real Estate Company if an attorney hired after Large Law Firm (LLF) was hired, but before they restarted negotiations, has previously represented the opposing party.

Generally, the rules of professional conduct are designed to ensure the utmost protection to clients. They ensure the client gets honest, competent counsel and that the client's rights are handled fairly. The situation involves a potential conflict of interest because a lawyer recently hired by Large Law Firm previously represented the opposing parties (tenants).

First and foremost, it is not Helene who is actually handling the negotiations, it is Conway. However, Helene now works for the law firm on the opposite side of the matter that she was previously on. Next, after looking at the dates, you can see the facts state Conway was hired by Real Estate Co. on December 15. However, negotiations had ceased for the holidays. Conway did the required conflicts check and found no conflict. On December 28, Helene was extended an offer of employment by Large Law Firm after no conflicts were found between Helene nor Helene's firm and Large Law Firm. Helene began working on January 5 and on January 15, Conway submits the matter to the conflicts department to be checked and Helene pops up as a conflict.

LLF, to make sure it complies with all rules of professional conduct and ethics, should notify the opposing side of the potential conflict. Note that tenant's counsel should be notified because tenants are represented and you may not have direct contract with an adverse represented party unless attorneys agree. Once the tenants are notified, if they agree to the representation of LLF, then there is no conflict. Consent by the parties adversely affected by the conflict will make representation OK. This notice is required to be fair to those affected parties. We, as attorneys, want to provide honest, competent, unbiased legal representation to our clients and this requires complete and full disclosures of any conflicts of interests.

Lastly, LLF would not need to withdraw as counsel so long as the parties involved consent to the representation. The only issue would be that the information be completely and honesty given so that the adverse parties can give an informed and intelligent consent.

July 2006—Question 13

Riley and Co. sought bids to build a socket assembly machine. Gruenwald Mfg. presented the lowest bid, while Swavee Corp. submitted the second lowest bid. Riley awarded the contract to Gruenwald, paying $50,000 upon signing the contract, and agreeing to pay an additional $350,000 when the machine was installed and operational. The machine had to be installed and operational within eight months or Riley would not be able to deliver parts to its customers under contracts worth $4 million to meet its contract delivery obligations with its customers. After six months, the socket assembly machine was not operating correctly and it appeared to Riley that Gruenwald would not be able to complete the contract. Riley told Gruenwald that the contract was terminated, and he contracted with Swavee Corp., Gruenwald's main competitor, to build the machine. Riley also hired Lawyer Benson to sue Gruenwald for anticipatory breach on the contract.

Benson knows that the outcome of the case will largely depend upon the testimonial and documentary evidence introduced at trial. Benson comes to you, as the law firm's ethics lawyer, asking whether the following actions are appropriate:

1. **Benson received a call from someone called Ollie, who says he has possession of "evidence" that Gruenwald falsified its bid in order to get the contract. Ollie says he will turn that evidence over to Benson for $5000. Benson wants to pay the money to see the evidence.**
2. **Benson reviewed the discovery documents received from Gruenwald, including 15,000 emails between employees at Riley and employees at Gruenwald. After searching the emails with the electronic software, Benson identified three emails between Cornwall, Riley's project manager, and Gruenwald's director of manufacturing which indicate an ambiguity in the machine specifications provided by Riley. Benson wants to tell Cornwall not to speak with anyone at Gruenwald or with Gruenwald's counsel or investigators, not say anything about these emails, and to generally make himself "unavailable."**

3. Matilda, Gruenwald's project manager on the Riley contract, resigned from Gruenwald and now works for Swavee. Benson wants to interview Matilda as a fact witness, and wonders whether he can offer to pay her for her time in meeting with him, attending her deposition and attending trial.

Model Answer to Question 13

This question focuses upon the lawyer's duties when identifying witnesses.

1. MRPC 3.4(b) prohibits a lawyer from "offering an inducement to a witness that is prohibited by law," and MRPC 8.4(c) prohibits a lawyer from engaging in conduct prejudicial to the administration of justice. The Comment to MRPC 3.4 explains that:

> It is not improper to pay a witness' expense or to compensate an expert witness on terms permitted by law. It is improper to pay an occurrence witness any fee for testifying beyond that authorized by law, and it is improper to pay an expert witness a contingent fee.

Whether Ollie would be a witness is not clear, but where it is likely that if Ollie's evidence is useful to Riley's case, Benson authenticity, truthfulness or some other foundation. Under the common law of most jurisdictions, a fact witness may be paid for time and expenses incurred as a witness, as long as the payment is not an inducement to testify in a particular way. The proposed payment is not connected with any time or expense of Ollie being a witness.

Ethics rules do not prohibit the payment on the facts provided. MRPC 1.4 requires that a client be provided sufficient information to make informed decisions, and MRPC 1.3 requires the lawyer to provide diligent representation. Benson should present Ollie's offer to Riley and let Riley decide how to proceed. Benson cannot directly pay Ollie's demand, because MRPC 1.8(e) only permits a lawyer to advance costs and expenses of litigation for which the client remains responsible.

2. Since Cornwall is Riley's employee, MPRC 3.4(f)(1) permits Benson to request that Cornwall not volunteer information to Gruenwald. However, MRPC 3.4(a) does not permit Benson to ask Cornwall not to be "available," since that would "unlawfully obstruct another party's access to evidence."

3. Unless Benson has consent from Gruenwald's counsel, Benson is prohibited by MRPC 4.2 and its Comment from contracting Gruenwald managers and supervisors whose statements may constitute admissions or whose acts may be imputed to Gruenwald. Matilda is a former manager of Gruenwald, and there is a split of authority among the states as to whether the prohibition applies to former managers. Both ABA Opinion 91-359 and *Valassis v Samelson*, 143 FRD 118 (ED Mich 1992), conclude that former managers are not covered by the prohibition, and Benson may contact Matilda without consent from opposing counsel.

MRPC 3.4(b) permits Benson to offer to pay Matilda's reasonable expenses for being a witness. American Bar Association Opinion 96-402 notes that the rule does not prohibit paying a fact witness for expenses or for loss of time due to the testimony or preparation for testifying, including research. The key is that the witness compensation not be related to the substance of testimony, i.e., a witness should not be paid for telling the truth, that the compensation be "reasonable" to avoid tainting the testimony, and that the compensation not be a secret arrangement.

Student Answer—July 2006

Question 13—Professional Responsibility—None Available

February 2007—Question 3

Wonder Lawyers PLLC is a general practice law firm. When its lawyers agree to handle plaintiff personal injury litigation, the firm advances the costs and expenses of the litigation, and pays them out of the case recovery. When its lawyers agree to handle real estate matters, the firm advances the costs and expenses for environmental studies, inspections and government compliance, which are paid at the closing.

Many of the personal injury and real estate matters are not begun and concluded in a single fiscal year, but are begun in one year and carry over to subsequent years. Wonder Lawyers PLLC has found it difficult to budget for potential advances of costs and expenses, and does not want to deny a client effective representation because of lack of funds. The firm is considering adopting one or both of the following proposals, if they can be ethically implemented:

1. In personal injury matters, the firm would seek a bank loan as a fund to cover potential costs and expenses. The bank will be repaid from the case recoveries, and the interest charged on the loan will be passed on to the clients at the conclusion of representation. The firm would provide the names of clients and sufficient details about the cases to allow the bank to evaluate the cases as collateral.
2. In real estate matters, the firm would require the client to pay an advance retainer to cover the costs, and expenses will be paid from the retainer. When the retainer is depleted, the client must replenish it to its original level until the transaction either closes or is abandoned. Any remaining balance at the close of the representation would be refunded to the client.

Discuss the ethical propriety of these options for Wonder Lawyers PLLC.

Model Answer to Question 3

1. Lawyers are not required to advance costs and expenses of a representation matter. When the matter is litigation, MRPC 1.8(e) applies. Unlike the ABA model rule, which permits the lawyer to forego collection of costs and expenses from the client if the litigation is unsuccessful, the Michigan rule requires that the client remain ultimately responsible for payment of the costs and expenses. If Wonder Lawyers PLLC is going to continue to advance litigation costs and expense, it needs to find a reliable source of funding. One solution is a loan from a bank. However, the firm should note the limits on any disclosure it makes to the bank lender. MRPC 1.6 prohibits the disclosure of confidences or secrets unless the client consents—none of the disclosure exceptions apply to the bank loan. Although the identity of the clients is not always privileged, i.e., "confidences" under the ethics rule, it can be a "secret," i.e., "information gained in the professional relationship that the client has requested be held inviolate or the disclosure of which would be embarrassing or would likely to be detrimental to the client." MRPC 1.6(a). Also, MRPC 1.6(b)(3) prohibits using a

confidence or secret for the advantage of the lawyer unless the client consents after full disclosure. Finally, since plaintiff personal injury engagements must be in writing, the engagement agreement is a convenient place to make the disclosure to the client about the interest charge and providing information to the bank. If these precautions are taken, there is nothing improper about the law firm obtaining a loan.

2. Prior to the 2005 amendments to MRPC 1.15, the rule only required advance fees to be deposited into a trust account. With the amendment, however, MRPC 1.15(d) states: "A lawyer shall hold property of clients or third persons in connection with a representation separate from the lawyer's own property. All client or third person funds shall be deposited in an IOLTA or non-IOLTA account." Since the proposed retainer is for costs and expenses that have not been incurred, it is still the client's money and must be deposited into the law firm's trust account. There is nothing unethical about requiring the client to replenish a retainer when it is depleted, as long as the client has been told about and understands the obligation. MRPC 1.4 requires that the client be provided all information necessary to make informed decisions about the representation. One way to satisfy this requirement is for the law firm to place the cost/expense retainer balance on the client's billing statements (if billing statements are regularly sent), so the client will have advance warning of when replenishment is required. If these precautions are taken, there is nothing improper about the law firm requesting a replenishing retainer to cover costs.

Student Answer—February 2007

Question 3—Professional Responsibility—8 points

This is a professional responsibility issue.

A lawyer is to serve his or her client diligently under the Michigan rules of Professional Responsibility—Rule 1.1.

Now the issue here is whether Wonder Lawyers PLLC "Wonder Lawyer" can implement two proposals to help represent their clients in the future. Based on the wording of the two proposals, they would be in violation of ethical behavior of an attorney.

In the first proposal, a law firm might seek a loan to help cover expenses, however this gives rise to an independent party seeking to pay a client's costs and expenses. It sounds unorthodox, but if the attorneys from Wonder Lawyer give their informed consent that the lawyers can obtain the loan, it would not be a problem. However, the law firm must make sure that the Bank in no way acts on the process of the lawsuit or control the ways the lawsuit is handled.

Additionally, the providing the names of the clients and sufficient details about the cases should not be implemented since it would violate the confidentiality of the information between attorney and client. Now an attorney can reveal confidential information if he has received informed consent, in writing is better, from his client. However, the client's information could be easily released outside the bank, and that is not what the client wants even if it is not considered confidential under Rule 1.6. Thus, to ensure the confidentiality of the information between client and attorney, even if it's for the benefit of the client, this part of the provision must not be implemented.

In the second proposal, attorneys can require clients to pay a retainer to cover costs and expenses, the retainer must be held in a separate account and [not mingled] with other accounts, especially attorneys or law firm accounts. Here, Wonder Lawyers would be placing retainer fees in its business account, thus violating the rule of commingling accounts. Wonder Lawyers can place the retainer in a bank account, escrow, or non escrow, and allow it to collect interest too. Wonder Lawyers should not implement the provision of placing retainer of clients in its business account, but in a bank account, separate from other clients' accounts and especially separate from lawyers' accounts.

Additionally, the provision dealing with replenishing retainer agreements is unethical. The general rule is you ask for a reasonable amount for a retainer and once it is depleted, you add the further costs and expenses to the client's bill. You cannot ask for a retainer agreement to be repaid unless it deals with a different legal issue and is not the same issue being litigated. Here, Wonder Lawyers cannot ask for a retainer to be replenished once it has been depleted. Wonder Lawyers can continue to charge the client the costs and expenses onto the bill and get it repaid through repayment of the lawsuit at the end of the case when it has ended. As for the remaining balance, they can deduct it from the final bill to the client or return it or keep for future representation of the client. It would be up to the client to decide.

Thus, if those provisions have not been changed, proposal two would be unethical if approved.

July 2007—Question 4

The Big Corporation, a multinational corporation whose U.S. subsidiary is based in Michigan, manufactures a world-famous set of Acme Knives, which are well known for their usefulness at cutting meat for barbecues. In 2005, Big began to receive reports that several of its Acme Knives have proven defective, with the blade flying off the handle in the middle of cutting, causing injuries. This information is leaked to the press in connection with a story about a young mother named Sally Smith, who lost three fingers as a result of this type of accident. Smith is in a hospital in Michigan.

Arthur Intrepid of the law firm Intrepid & Thrifty, a well-known class-action firm based in Michigan, reads the Big story and asks you for a memo answering the following questions under the Michigan ethics rules:

1. **May I go to visit Smith in the hospital and ask her to be the named plaintiff in a class action against Big? [Assume a named plaintiff in a class-action case is treated the same as any other client.] I won't pressure her; I'll just identify myself, give her my card, tell her what I do and ask her to call me.**
2. **I just got a list of those who bought Acme Knives in Michigan from a public source. May I send each of those people an e-mail, explaining that I learned they could potentially be a plaintiff in a lawsuit against Big, telling them what the potential upside is for them, and ask them to call me for more information?**
3. **Can I have one of my office staff members stand on a street corner and hand out a flyer, saying "You could be owed millions! If you have bought an Acme Knife in the last six months, call up the class-action lawyers at Intrepid and**

Thrifty and see if you can be part of a nationwide class-action lawsuit we are organizing." The flyer contains a telephone number to call, but no law firm name or address.

Model Answer to Question 4

A hospital visit is in-person solicitation, which is prohibited under Michigan Rule 7.3 and under *Shapero v Kentucky Bar Assoc*, 486 US 466 (1988), since Intrepid has no family or prior professional relationship with Sally.

Intrepid obtained the list from a public source, which means his possession of the list is not improperly obtained. An e-mail communication could be considered akin to direct-mail letter-writing, or akin to a phone call, since it is sent in real time. ABA Model Rule 7.3 takes the position that "real-time electronic contact" amounts to forbidden solicitation. Michigan has no specific rule on e-mail communication, but Michigan Ethics Opinion RI-276 concludes that e-mail directed to a specific addressee or group of addresses is permitted as direct-mail solicitation. The Ethics Opinion clarifies that interactive e-mail communication is governed by rules on in-person solicitation. More and more businesses are using e-mail in the regular course of business as a substitute for US Mail, i.e., as letter substitutes. In this instance, the Michigan people who bought knives could be considered persons "so situated that they might in general find such services useful," and thus would fall into the solicitation exception for prohibited mail solicitation. If the communication content would clearly show it is from a lawyer, and leaves it up to the prospective client to respond if interested, the communication by e-mail would probably not be considered a violation of the Michigan rule.

Michigan rules do not require the name of a lawyer in an ad nor an "advertising" label. The issue is whether a preprinted notice handed out to strangers is mere "advertising," restricted only by requirements of MRPC 7.1 that it not be false, fraudulent, deceptive or misleading, or whether it is improper in-person "solicitation" to persons not known to need the legal services being offered. Given the pitch used by the person handing out the flyers, the situation taken as a whole is more solicitation than advertising, and the hand-out would not be proper. In some circumstances merely handing out a flyer, without any verbal communication, could be considered permissible advertising. In this instance, the hand-out without verbal communication would still be improper as deceptive by omission, since it does not reveal that the phone number is a law office.

Student Answer—July 2007

Question 4—Professional Responsibility—8 points

1. The issue in the question is if the solicitation is valid. Under the Ethics Rules solicitation of a client by person to person (or face to face) or by telephone in real time is prohibited. That is so to protect the clients and to keep attorneys from advertising for self reason or motivated by money. This situation would be prohibited by the rules. Even if you're not pressuring her, the attorney is still there in person while the patient is in peril. She may feel pressure; even if the attorney is not expressly stating he will represent her he is impliedly doing it. By just identifying himself, giving her his card and telling her to call him he is

seeking to represent her. Therefore, it will be a violation of the rules, especially since he received the news by the press and is personally going to see her.

2. As long as the attorney received the list of names from a public source, that's okay. With that the attorney can send an email to the individuals to give them notice. An email is not like a live, in person contact where the person may feel pressured to act. Here the person can delete the email and disregard it if they wish to do so.
3. Again, the staff member can stand and hand out flyers for the class action as long as they aren't individually approaching someone they know is affected by the action. But the flyer must comply with the advertising of ethical rules. The flyer cannot be false or misleading. It appears by the language of the flyer it is not misleading or not false; it is only to inform possible class action members. But the flyer must also have on it the law firm's name and attorney responsible for the ad, which this does not contain. It only contains the phone number. This would be a violation of the rules.

Comment: This is a fairly good answer. The main missing component that prevented it a perfect score was the failure to discuss the comments the staff member was shouting under the third issue. Always read the facts carefully and assume every fact is important and should be discussed in your answer.

February 2008—Question 6

Mingo Corp. has two separately incorporated subsidiaries, Alpine Inc., a manufacturing company, and Vesper Inc., a distributor. The Mingo Corp. inside lawyer has the title "general counsel" and reports to the Mingo Corp. board of directors. The Alpine Inc. inside lawyer has the title "compliance counsel" and reports to the president of Alpine Inc. The Vesper Inc. inside lawyer has the title "employment counsel" and reports to the Vesper Human Relations director. The corporations are located in one massive industrial complex, having adjacent addresses. Financial and technology service staffs are centralized in Mingo office space.

In 2005, the law firm Griffey and Shula, P.C. defended Alpine Inc. in a contract dispute against its suppliers. The 2005 settlement established a five-year price schedule for raw materials, and its Notice provision listed the Alpine compliance counsel and a Griffey and Shula P.C. lawyer as contacts for the parties.

In 2008, Griffey and Shula P.C. began representing 13 plaintiffs allegedly wrongfully terminated by Vesper Inc. Mingo Corp. and Vesper Inc. were named as defendant. Mingo Corp. has moved to disqualify Griffey and Shula P.C.

1. **What factors should be used to determine whether a conflict exists? Explain your answer.**
2. **Should Mingo Corp. prevail? Explain your answer.**

Model Answer to Question 6

A conflict analysis should begin with "who is the client." Many current-client conflict cases involve disagreements about whether the lawyer representing one member of a corporate family also represents other affiliates of the corporation so as to make it improper for the lawyer to handle unrelated adverse matters.

If Alpine is the Only Client: In this case, the law firm represented Alpine, and is listed as a contact on the settlement agreement that covered future prices for five years through 2010.

If Alpine is considered a former client, because the litigation is concluded, then the MRPC 1.9 conflict test is whether the prospective matter is materially adverse to the former client and "the same or substantially related" to the former matter. Because the employee termination at Vesper is not "substantially related" to the supplier contracts at Alpine, under this analysis there would be no conflict requiring the law firm's disqualification.

Alpine may be considered a current client, because the settlement agreement set prices for five years, the law firm was listed as a contact on the agreement, and thus the law firm has continuing duties to Alpine. In *Jones v Rabanco Ltd.*, 2006 U.S. Dist LEXIS 53766 (WD Wash, 2006), the court found that since the law firm took no affirmative steps to terminate its responsibilities under a similar settlement provision, the law firm should be deemed to have a current client-lawyer relationship. If Alpine is a current client, the conflict test under MRPC 1.7(a) does not apply, because employment litigation is not "directly adverse" to Alpine, i.e. Alpine is not named in the suit. The conflict test under MRPC 1.7(b) is whether the duties to Alpine would "materially limit" the representation of the employment plaintiffs. If so, then the law firm must reasonably believe the employment representation will not be adversely affected (MRPC 1.7(a)(1)) and get consent from the plaintiff clients.

Does the Alpine Relationship Impute to the Corporate Family: American Bar Association Ethics Opinion 95-390, applying a rule identical to Michigan's rule, addresses conflicts of interest that may arise in the corporate family context. The opinion observes that there is a split of authority, with some courts requiring disqualification and other courts denying disqualification when counsel for a corporate party files suit against a corporate affiliate. In determining whether representation is permitted, the ABA opinion suggests consideration of the following factors:

1. whether legal work for one entity if intended to benefit all affiliates or entails collecting confidential information from all of them, such as stock issues or financing;
2. whether counsel was engaged by or reports to officers of the other affiliates;
3. whether the affiliate shared protected information with the lawyer with the expectation that the lawyer would use it in representing the affiliate, or for the purpose of furthering the representation;
4. whether one affiliate is the alter ego of the other.

Restatement Lawyers (2000) §121 Comment d, indicates that for conflict of interest purposes, the client is the corporation that retains the lawyer, not other companies in which the corporation has an ownership interest or that hold an ownership interest in the corporation. The comment advises, however, that the lawyer's obligations extend to an affiliated entity where financial loss or benefit to the nonclient entity will have a direct, adverse impact on the client. Also, the comment says that a client's significant control of an entity may suffice to require the lawyer to treat the affiliated entity as a client for the purpose of determining whether a lawyer's representation of another client with interests adverse to the affiliated entity entails a conflict of interest.

In this instance, although Mingo is the parent company, there are no facts suggesting that the law firm was in contact with Mingo or Vesper during the Alpine representation. The Alpine corporations are adjacent and share financial and IT services, they appear to have separate management. It is not apparent how any costs, expenses, or judgment in the employment suit would impact Alpine, except indirectly through its parent.

Under the facts provided, any conflict with Alpine should not impute to the other corporate family members in the employment matter. Mingo should not prevail.

Student Answer—February 2008

Question 4—Professional Responsibility—None Available

July 2008—Question 4

When Sarah accepted a position as associate with Big Law Firm, she signed an agreement that included the following:

> You acknowledged that Big Law Firm expects you to devote all your effort to Big Law Firm clients and business, and that you will comply with all policies and rules of Big Law Firm for as long as you work here. If you decide to leave Big Law Firm for private practice elsewhere, you agree that you will not contact any clients of Big Law Firm to obtain work. Further, if any of your future employers undertake matters relating to clients of Big Law Firm, you agree to immediately notify Big Law Firm.

For five years, Sarah works under the supervision of partner Sheldon in answering requests coming in on the firm's employment hot line. Human Resources managers employed by clients of the firm would call the hot line with questions about compliance with employment laws, leave, or termination questions. The hot line questions Sarah answers rarely last more than five minutes. If Sarah does not know the answers or the answers are more complex than could be answered in five minutes, Sarah refers the caller to Sheldon, and works with him on those matters.

Sarah has interviewed for a position with Small Law Firm. Before extending an offer, Small Law Firm asks Sarah to confirm that she is not working on any matters where Small Law Firm is opposing counsel, and to give some estimate of how much business and which clients Sarah thinks she could bring to Small Law Firm.

Sarah intends to poll the Human Resources managers when they use Big Law Firm hotline, tell them she is thinking of a new position, and ask whether they would consider giving her work if she changed firms. Sarah also intends to contact Big Law Firm conflicts of interest person, and ask for a client list of all cases where Small Law Firm appears as opposing counsel. **If Sarah does this and gives the information to Small Law Firm, does she violate any of her ethical duties?**

Model Answer to Question 4

Practice Restrictions: Both Michigan Rule of Professional Conduct 5.6 and ABA Model Rule 5.6 prohibit "employment agreements" that "restrict[s] the right of a lawyer to practice after termination of the [employment] relationship" unless the restriction is limited to retirement benefits. In this case, the employment agreement Big Law Firm presents to Sarah prohibits Sarah from contracting any Big Law Firm clients. The restriction is not limited to conduct while Sarah is still employed by Big Law Firm, but extends, apparently without limit, after Sarah leaves Big Law Firm. A limitation on solicitation of clients is considered a "restriction on right to practice," and that portion of the employment agreement is improper. Michigan Ethics Opinion RI-86 (1991).

It should be noted that although MCL 445.774a allows covenants not to compete provided they are "reasonable as to its duration, geographical area, and the type of employment or line of business," the Supreme Court's adoption of MRPC 5.6 post-dates the statute and is promulgated in furtherance of the Court's supervisory power over the bar. Non-compete agreements are not permitted for lawyers.

Solicitation: Sarah intends to poll HR callers about moving their business. MRPC 7.3 permits phone contacts if the lawyer has a "prior professional relationship" with the prospective client. It could be argued that hotline contacts with HR managers lasting five minutes or less are not sufficient to create "professional relationships" within the rule. Hotline calls that have merely been referred to Sheldon do not create a "professional relationship" with Sarah. The burden is upon Sarah to show that she had sufficient prior contact to polling HR callers.

On the other hand, Sarah is not placing the calls, but merely seizing the opportunity to sound out the HR managers when they use the hotline. In fact, Sarah has a duty under MRPC 1.4 to provide clients with all information necessary to make an informed decision about their representation, and one of those decisions is who will be their counsel. Further, the hotline clearly creates a "professional relationship" between Big Law Firm and the callers, and Sarah is still part of Big Law Firm. It is most likely that the act of phone polling the HR managers does not violate MRPC 7.3.

Content: Sarah may "announce" her plans to leave Big Law Firm as long as her announcement does not amount to solicitation (discussed above) or otherwise violate MRPC 7.1. Contacts permitted under MRPC 7.1 must be truthful and non-deceptive. When Sarah tells the HR managers of her proposed move without first telling Big Law Firm, her contact is deceptive and prohibited under MRPC 8.4(c) ["It is professional misconduct for a lawyer to (b) engage in conduct involving dishonesty, fraud, deceit, misrepresentation, or violation of criminal law, where such conduct reflects adversely on the lawyer's honesty, trustworthiness, or fitness as a lawyer."]

Further, MRPC 7.1 provides that "A communication shall not: (a) contain a material misrepresentation of fact or law, or omit a fact necessary to make the statement considered as a whole not materially misleading; . . . (c) compare the lawyer's services with other lawyers' services, unless comparison can be factually substantiated." It is unlikely that Sarah could speak to the HR managers about the possibility of moving their law business without inviting and discussing some sort of comparison with Big Law Firm services. Such comparisons cannot yet be factually substantiated by Sarah, because she does not yet know enough about Small Law Firm.

Conflict Check: MRPC 1.9 and 1.10 address lateral moves between law firms. If a lateral lawyer is adequately screened by the new employer, the new employer can avoid imputed disqualification caused by the participation of the lateral lawyer at the former law firm. A screen is not adequate unless it is established promptly, so Small Law Firm has a valid interest in knowing whether a screen will be necessary.

Sarah's request for a list of all cases where Small Law Firm appears as opposing counsel, prior to her advising Big Law Firm of her intention to leave, is deceptive under MRPC 8.4(c), following the same reasoning as above. In addition, MRPC 1.6 requires a lawyer to maintain confidences and secrets of clients, and under certain circumstances the mere identity of a client may be protected. The facts that there is an opposing counsel, and that therefore there is some matter in dispute, does not mean the matter is public, and that information about the representation may be disclosed. Further, most conflict lists have more information than just client names and opposing counsel: conflict lists could contain addresses, witnesses, information about payment of fees, account numbers, timekeepers working on the file, etc. This proprietary information of Big Law Firm cannot be disclosed by Sarah without permission of Big Law Firm, and in some cases, the clients. Finally, Small Law Firm should be able to check its own conflict database to determine whether Big Law Firm is opposing counsel in any of its matters.

Sarah should not request the conflict check for her personal interests without the permission of Big Law Firm.

Two Student Answers—July 2008

Question 4—Professional Responsibility—8 points

Sarah has a duty to avoid conflicts of interest. In addition, she has a duty to keep and preserve atty/client confidentiality.

First, the "poll" Sarah intends to conduct is unethical. She may not use the "poll" to solicit business for another firm during her employment with Big Law Firm. Generally, hot lines do *not* create a conflict if they are used as intended. However, once you gain identity and privileged info, the conflict may attach. It is merely impossible to keep a file of every hotline caller for conflict purposes. Here, however, the hotline indicated that the people calling are employees of Big Law Firm's clients. That means that the duty of conflict would extend to the hot line callers since they are "agents" of the firm clients.

Therefore, Sarah would be violating PR ethical rules by trying to solicit the firm's clients for another firm. (Duty of loyalty)

In addition, Sarah is breaching her duty of confidentiality by giving Small Law Firm a list of all cases from Big Law Firm where they appear as opposing counsel. Sarah will have a duty to go to the conflicts of interest person at Small Law Firm (not Big Law Firm) once she is employed there and has a client who could possibly have been a former client of Big Law Firm.

In addition, Sarah signed an agreement to *not* contact any clients of Big Law Firm to obtain work. A contract restricting an attorney's right to practice is *not* permitted. In addition, Sarah does *not* have to notify Big Law Firm regarding matters in which Small Law Firm represents Big Law Firms former clients.

Her duty would be to notify Small Law Firm of that possible conflict. Then it may either be imparted to the firm, or Sarah would simply be screened in that matter to prevent her duty of conflict of interest if she gained privileged info during her employment at Big Law Firm. An argument may also be made that hotline calls generally are not enough to establish privileged info for purposes of conflict.

Question 4—Professional Responsibility—8 points

Sarah (S) would violate ethical principles based on agreed upon response to contact.

Under the ethics rule, an attorney cannot agree to any constraint upon the ability to practice. Here Big Law Firm (B) is asking S to agree not to contact any of their clients. If S is no longer employed at B she is free to contact clients if she honors any confidence matters. In MI, there is not a non-compete clause that is upheld under the law. Therefore while S owes a duty during employment, it does not go beyond that and honorary confidential information.

Notification of Clients Being Taken

The issue here relates to confidential information. Under the law, an attorney working in opposition to former clients must obtain consent from all parties. Here B's asking if future employers take matters related to S's clients under B that they be informed. They are within their rights to protect clients and S should follow this. *S confirming* not *working* in opposition to Small Firm (SF) the issue here is also regarding confidential information.

Under the ethics rules attorneys owe a duty of confidential support to clients and no conflicts of interest. Here S would need to disclose to SF if she worked in opposition to them in any matters. The facts note that she answered the employment hotline and may not have knowledge of some matters, but even when she referred she worked with a colleague (Sheldon) on matters. A conflict check is appropriate. Issues about compliance, employment law and termination are likely to come up at SF and these make clients w/ conflicts.

Can S give estimate on which clients and how much business. The issue here is confidential matters. Under the ethics rules S owes a duty to clients. Here SF is asking for specific clients that S could bring. This is against the policy of S's working for B because she continues to be an agent of B as principle while she is employed. Under the law an agent cannot benefit from the expertise of a principle without the consent of the principle.

Here S continues to represent B on the hotline, and as the calls come in, the facts note she plans to poll clients for business when she goes to SF. She cannot avoid the matter of conflict and disloyalty to the principle (B) by saying to callers she is "thinking" of a new position. Therefore she cannot answer SF's question regarding clients she will bring, nor can she poll callers to see if they will follow her to SF. These are both in transgression of ethical behavior, according to the Michigan Code of Ethics in Court Rules (MCR).

> **Comment:** There were a lot of confusing abbreviations used in this answer. Using abbreviations is OK, but be sure to spell out the word first and follow it with the abbreviation you intend to use in parentheses. And do not overuse abbreviations so your answer becomes hard to understand. Remember, a happy grader is your friend!

February 2009—Question 15

Caroline, an associate in Jackson Law Firm, is defending Sharik in an auto negligence matter brought by Max, who was a passenger in the car Sharik was driving when the accident occurred. Caroline hears that Max may not be as injured as he has claimed. Max lives in Caroline's neighborhood, and when she scouts his house she sees Max engaged in activity that he would not be able to perform if he had the injuries he claims. Caroline gives this information to Parker, an investigator hired by Sharik's insurance company, but because Max is a neighbor, Caroline tells Parker she does not want to be identified in his investigative report. Parker includes the information in his investigative report as from "an anonymous source." Parker does not, independent of Caroline's report, verify this information.

During discovery, Max's counsel seeks a copy of Parker's investigative file and to depose Parker. At Parker's deposition, which Caroline is defending, Parker testifies that the information about Max's capacity came from a third-party source, but Caroline asserts that he cannot reveal the name of the "informant" because it is covered by the attorney-client privilege. After the deposition, and in anticipation of Max's challenge to the claim of privilege, Caroline and Parker decide they will have Parker's son Matt sign a sworn statement that Matt was the "anonymous source" who discovered Max's condition.

In a regular review of the status of cases in the office, Caroline's boss, Jackson, discovers what Caroline has done. **Under the Michigan Rules of Professional Conduct, what ethical issues are raised by Caroline's conduct, and what corrective steps, if any, should Jackson take?**

Model Answer to Question 15

There is nothing ethically improper about Caroline directly investigating the facts of the case, or her cruising Max's neighborhood to see what can be seen from the public road. There is no indication that Caroline had any contact or communication with Max during those trips, and thus MRPC 4.2, Communication with a Person Represented by Counsel, is not triggered. Caroline should have known, however, that her direct investigation could make her a witness in the case in which she is counsel of record. MRPC 3.7, Lawyer as Witness, forbids a lawyer from being an advocate at trial in a matter in which the lawyer is also a necessary witness on contested facts. The extent of Max's injuries will clearly be contested, and if Caroline was the only one who observed Max, her testimony would be "necessary." Therefore Caroline has created a situation where she cannot be advocate at trial. Since Caroline's testimony would be consistent with the interests of her client, however, Caroline's firm is not disqualified under MRPC 3.7(b). Jackson should rectify this matter by reassigning the case to someone else in the firm.

The improper actions of Caroline and Parker are (a) falsely representing in the investigative report that the source was "anonymous," (b) claiming attorney-client privilege at deposition when the source of the information was requested, and (c) having Matt execute a false statement that he was the source of the information. The applicable ethics violations are MRPC 3.4, Fairness to Opposing Party and Counsel (obstructing another party's access to evidence, concealing evidence, failing to comply with a reasonable discovery request, and requesting a person other than a client to refrain from voluntarily giving relevant information to another party), MRPC 4.1, Truthfulness in Statements to Others (making a false statement of material fact or law to a third person), and MRPC 8.4, Misconduct, (violating the Rules, inducing another to violate the Rules, engaging in dishonesty and deceit, and engaging in conduct prejudicial to the administration of justice). Caroline did not just withhold her identity as the source of the information about Max; she compounded the problem by arranging for Matt to lie. She allowed her personal interest in avoiding disclosure to interfere with her judgment on behalf of her client, in violation of MRPC 1.7(b), Conflict of Interest: General Rule. These are substantial violations that go to the core of the justice system. Jackson's duty to report Caroline to the Attorney Grievance Commission, pursuant to MRPC 8.3, Reporting Professional Misconduct, has been triggered.

In addition, Jackson and the counsel replacing Caroline should determine whether they have disclosure duties under MRPC 3.3, Candor Toward the Tribunal. Michigan Ethics Opinions establish that discovery proceedings and depositions are "before the court" and trigger duties under MRPC 3.3. MRPC 3.3(a)(1) has not been violated, because no false statement of material fact has yet been made—Matt's sworn statement has not been presented. MRPC 3.3(a)(2) has not been violated, because there has been no criminal or fraudulent act by Caroline's client. MRPC 3.3(a)(3) does not apply, because it addresses controlling legal authority. MRPC 3.3(a)(4) is not violated, because Matt's false affidavit has not yet been presented. MRPC 3.3(a) duties continue to "the conclusion of the proceeding." It is unclear whether the "proceeding" in this instance is Parker's deposition, or the entire discovery period, but in any event if the claim of privilege is challenged Parker's deposition is still open. It does not appear that Jackson has any affirmative duty to make any disclosure to the court. Caroline's conduct is not protected by MRPC 1.6, Confidentiality of Information, since it does not involve any communication between Caroline and her client. Further, it is in the interests of the client for Caroline's information to be disclosed in the matter. Jackson should reveal Caroline as the source of the information about Max's condition.

Student Answer—February 2009

Question 15—Professional Responsibility—8 points

An attorney cannot participate in fraud. By having Parker's son sign a sworn statement that Matt was the "anonymous source" when in fact it was Caroline is fraud. The attorney-client privilege protects information obtained as a result of the client attorney relationship such as preparation for trial, confidences and secrets between client and attorney. An attorney must not do anything that is adverse to its client's interest by having Parker lie about the anonymous source is not helping her client's case and subjecting Caroline and her boss to sanctions.

Jackson, Caroline's boss can be sanctioned also since he is her boss and also aware of Caroline's inappropriate conduct. He must tell her to correct this situation by contacting the opposing party and tell them the truth and Jackson must report Caroline's misconduct to the attorney grievance committee.

An attorney should not be a witness on client's case so this must be why Caroline does not want to be known as anonymous source.

July 2009—Question 10

While a member of Carpet & Wall, P.C., Tim represented Manuel in personal affairs and on matters involving Manuel's business ventures. One of the matters involved the formation of a business entity ICON, where Manuel became one of three managing members who found investors to invest in the ownership of an office building. No one else at Carpet & Wall participated in any of the Manuel matters. After five years with Carpet & Wall, Tim moved his practice to Law Enterprise, LLC. At Manuel's request, Carpet & Wall transferred Manuel's files to Tim at Law Enterprise, LLC.

Carpet & Wall currently represents the non-managing investors in the office building in a business dispute that does not involve Manuel. In addition, disputes have now arisen between the non-managing investors and the managers of ICON, including Manuel. The claims include fraud and misrepresentation concerning the nature of the investment and other representations made at the time of the investment. Tim still represents Manuel.

May Carpet & Wall, P.C. represent those interests adverse to Manuel? Explain your answer.

Model Answer to Question 10

This is a straight-forward conflict question addressing imputed conflicts.

If Tim were still a member of Carpet & Wall, P.C., MRPC 1.9(a) would apply. Under that rule, the firm would not be able to represent interests materially adverse to Manuel, where the former matter is substantially related to the prospective matter. Since Tim was at Carpet & Wall when he assisted Manuel in setting up the business whose operations would now be challenged, no one at Carpet & Wall would be able to represent the non-managing investors against Manuel without Manuel's consent. Tim's representation would impute to the rest of the firm under MRPC 1.10(a).

There is a special rule, however, when lawyers change firms. MRPC 1.10(c) says Carpet & Wall is disqualified only if both the following criteria exist: (1) the prospective representation is substantially related to the former representation, and (2) lawyers remaining in the firm have information protected by MRPC 1.6 (privilege or confidences and secrets) that is material to the matter. The facts indicate that only Tim worked on matters for Manuel while Tim was at Carpet & Wall, and that the Manuel files were transferred when Tim left the firm. As long as Carpet & Wall has no protected information about Manuel (including paper or electronic archives) that is material to the prospective matter, the ethics rules do not prohibit representation of the nonmanaging investors. It does not matter whether Tim represents Manuel on the prospective dispute.

Student Answer—July 2009

Question 10—Professional Responsibility—8 points

Yes, Carpet & Wall P.C. (C & W) will be able to represent those interests adverse to Manuals.

The general rule is that once a attorney is disqualified from representing a firm the entire firm is disqualified. Here since Tim represented Manual while he was a member of C & W there is a chance that another attorney learned confidential information that may prejudice Manual against him in the representation of the clients currently adverse to Manual.

But, there is an exception called the "revolving door" where lawyers once prosecuted people moved to private practice. The exception also covers situations such as this where one lawyer changes law firms.

Under this exception, as long as any C & W attorney who has obtained confidential information from Tim's prior representation of Manual is "shielded" from participating in the current litigation, C & W may represent the clients adverse to Manual. These lawyers will also not be permitted to share any of the fees that C & W collects in representing the clients that are adverse to Manual. This shield principle is absolute with respect to those disputes that do not involve Manual. The claims of fraud and misrepresentation however are a direct conflict because Manual is an adverse party will be permissible as long as the attorneys at C & W do not have confidential information they can use against Manual. To prevent this, they must be shielded from the representation and will not be able to share in any of the fees from that representation.

February 2010—Question 4

Brenda purchased the assets of Baker, Inc. and was subsequently sued by creditors of Baker on a theory of successor liability. Brenda retained Charles, a partner at Webster Law Firm, to defend her in the litigation.

Plaintiffs served interrogatories through Charles. Charles forwarded the interrogatories to Brenda, but did not discuss with Brenda any aspect of how to properly respond to them. Charles did not file any responses or objections to the interrogatories. Plaintiffs filed a motion to compel discovery. Charles did not file any responses or objection to the interrogatories. Plaintiffs filed a motion to compel discovery. Charles failed to respond to the motion in any way. The motion was granted. Charles took no action to comply with the court order compelling Brenda to answer the interrogatories. A second motion to compel was filed and granted after Charles again failed to respond in any way to the second motion to compel. Charles took no action to comply with the second court order requiring Brenda to answer the interrogatories. Plaintiffs' counsel filed a motion for entry of default as a discovery sanction for Brenda's failure to comply with two court orders requiring her to answer the interrogatories. Charles failed to respond in any way to the motion for entry of default and the court granted the motion and entered a default against Brenda.

Upon receiving the order entering the default against Brenda, but before the court heard plaintiffs' motion for entry of a default judgment, Charles asked firm associate Marcus to take whatever steps are necessary to set aside the default and protect Brenda's interests. Marcus learned that Charles timely sent to Brenda copies of each order to compel discovery as well as the order granting entry of the default. However, there was no evidence that Charles otherwise communicated with Brenda. Concerned about the manner in which Charles handled the file, Marcus decided to discuss Brenda's case with Daniel, the managing partner of the Webster Law Firm.

Discuss the Webster Law Firm's ethical obligations. Is the firm required to report Charles to the Attorney Grievance Commission or can it still take steps to resolve the client's complaint quietly within the firm? Explain your answer.

Model Answer to Question 4

The legal profession is a self-governing profession. MRCP 8.3 requires lawyers to report certain lawyer misconduct to the Michigan Attorney Grievance Commission.

> A lawyer having knowledge that another lawyer has committed a significant violation of the Rules of Professional Conduct that raises a substantial question as to that lawyer's honesty, trustworthiness, or fitness as a lawyer shall inform the Attorney Grievance Commission.

Rule 8.3 has three thresholds that must be met before reporting is required: (1) knowledge; (2) significant violation(s) of the rules; (3) substantial questions as to another lawyer's honesty, trustworthiness, or fitness.

Rule 8.3 does not require a lawyer to report every violation of a Rule of Professional Conduct; it is meant to be limited to violations which go to the heart of the profession. Thus, a lawyer who is contemplating whether he or she is under an obligation to report suspected misconduct must make reasonable value judgments about the significance of the lawyer's misconduct and whether it is required to be reported.

Knowledge: Both Daniel and Marcus have knowledge of Charles' conduct. Marcus was asked to clean up the mess, and thus had to review the case file and research the legal support for setting aside the default. Daniel, the managing partner of the firm, was put on notice of Charles' conduct by Marcus, who was concerned about the manner in which the file was handled by Charles.

Significant Violation: Charles has violated MRPC 1.1:

> A lawyer shall provide competent representation to a client. A lawyer shall not:
>
> (a) handle a legal matter which the lawyer knows or should know that the lawyer is not competent to handle, without associating with a lawyer who is competent to handle it.
>
> (b) handle a legal matter without preparation adequate in the circumstances; or
>
> (c) neglect a legal matter instructed to the lawyer.

The stated facts do not raise any issue involving subpart (a), but they do show violations of subparts (b) and (c). Charles did not adequately prepare to respond (or object) to the interrogatories in compliance with applicable discovery deadlines; indeed, he did not prepare at all. His multiple failures to respond and to appear in court also evidence neglect of the matter entrusted to him. Neglect involves indifference and a lawyer's consistent failure to carry out the obligations assumed to the client or a conscious disregard for the responsibility to the client. (ABA Informal Ethics Opinion 1273 [1973].) Appearance for a hearing is required by court rule, and a violation is arguably within MRPC 8.4(c), conduct prejudicial to the administration of justice. Failure to appear may also be a violation of MRPC 1.3, requiring a lawyer to act with reasonable diligence in representing a client.

Substantial Question of Honesty, Trustworthiness or Fitness: There is no indication that Charles lied, withheld information from the client, or tried to cover up what had occurred. However, any lawyer knows that ignoring interrogatories is potentially prejudicial to a client, and that failure to show up at a court hearing is an egregious error. Charles failed to do this on three occasions, plus he did not tell the firm of a problem or seek support on the case from others in the firm before the court hearings were missed and the problem had been exacerbated. Even then, instead of informing the firm management, he assigned to an associate the responsibility of fixing the problem. It does not appear that Charles discussed with the client the nature of discovery obligations or gave advance notice of his intent not to appear for the hearings. Taken together, these failures show a glaring lack of appreciation for his duties to the client and to his firm. Charles' conduct also inconvenienced the opposing party and the opposing counsel, who had to prepare for and attend hearings that otherwise would not have been required.

The Comment to MRPC 8.3 defines "substantial" as follows:

> This rule limits the reporting obligation to those offenses that a self-regulating profession must vigorously endeavor to prevent. A measure of judgment is, therefore, required in complying with the provisions of this rule. The term "substantial" refers to the seriousness of the possible offense and not to the quantum of evidence of which the lawyer is aware.

Charles' conduct was "serious"—a default was entered against Brenda because of his repeated neglect to take action and appear for hearings. Whether it raises a substantial question as to his "honesty, trustworthiness or fitness" to practice can be debated, but on these facts doubts should be resolved in favor of reporting such flagrant indifference to a lawyer's professional obligations to client and firm. No mitigating reasons for the conduct have been offered, and Charles' failure to inform the firm in a timely fashion is an exacerbating circumstance that reflects poorly on his trustworthiness.

Daniel and the firm should also take immediate action to remedy the consequence of Charles' neglectful conduct. MRPC 5.1(c)(2) provides in pertinent part that a:

> lawyer shall be responsible for another lawyer's violation of the rules of professional conduct if . . . the lawyer is a partner in the law firm in which the other lawyer practices . . . and knows of the conduct at a time when its consequences can be avoided or mitigated but fails to take responsible remedial action.

The facts indicate that a default was entered against Brenda, but at the time the firm became aware of Charles' conduct a default judgment had not yet entered. The firm must take swift action to remove Charles from the file; fully inform Brenda regarding the status of her case; and move to set aside the default that was entered against Brenda due to Charles' neglect. Additionally, the firm should investigate whether Charles' conduct in Brenda's case represents an isolated instance or a pattern of neglect and indifference. The firm should, at a minimum, establish internal procedures to monitor Charles' calendar and prevent recurrences.

Student Answer—February 2010

Question 4—Professional Responsibility—None Available

July 2010—Question 13

Larry is engaged in the general practice of law. Larry has just had a conversation with a new potential client, Camilla, who wants to divorce her husband Dennis.

Larry represented Dennis several years ago in an action brought by creditors of Dennis's closely held corporation. The creditors sued Dennis in his personal capacity and attempted to reach his personal assets. Larry successfully defended Dennis against claims that the corporation fraudulently conveyed assets to him and that the corporate entity should be disregarded (piercing the corporate veil). Larry's representation of Dennis included handling extensive discovery regarding Dennis's personal assets and negotiations regarding possible satisfaction of corporate debts by Dennis's personal assets.

Larry would like to enter into a fee agreement in which Camilla agrees to pay, in addition to Larry's usual reasonable hourly rate, an additional sum based upon the amount involved, results obtained by Larry, and value added to the representation by Larry's expertise, reputation and ability. Larry ordinarily enters into oral fee agreements.

Camilla has told Larry that she is not sure how Dennis will react to the news that she wants a divorce. He may retain counsel and fight. But, there is a chance that he may be cooperative, amicably divide up their assets, and negotiate in good faith regarding Camilla's requests for spousal and child support. Camilla can afford a lawyer and is willing to pay to get what she is entitled to. However, she is also cost conscious and does not want to pay more than is necessary. She has asked Larry if he can just work "as needed" on the case, and in the background, at least initially. Specifically, Camilla asked whether Larry could simply draft the complaint for divorce, a motion and brief for a temporary restraining order regarding the transfer of assets, and related documents, without putting his name on the pleadings or filing an appearance.

May Larry represent Camilla? Is the proposed fee arrangement permissible? May Larry agree to draft various papers for Camilla to file with the court with only her signature on them? Explain your answers.

Model Answer to Question 13

On these facts, Larry may not represent Camilla absent consent by Dennis after consultation with Larry. Also, even if Larry could represent Camilla, he would have a duty not to use confidences and secrets obtained from Dennis unless Dennis consented after consultation with Larry.

MRPC 1.9(a) provides that "A lawyer who has formerly represented a client in a matter shall not thereafter represent another person in the same or a substantially related matter in which that person's interests are materially adverse to the interests of the former client unless the former client consents after consultation." Here, the divorce and the previous matter handled for the husband are not the same matter. However, they are substantially related.

"A subsequent representation is substantially related to a former representation if (a) the subject matter of the representation is the same, (b) the factual or legal issues overlap, or (c) there is likelihood that confidential information obtained in the former representation will have relevance to the subsequent representation." State Bar of Michigan Committee on Professional Ethics Opinion RI-282, citing RI-46, RI-95. *See also Alpha Capital Management, Inc v Rentenbach*, Mich App (2010), Mich App LEXIS 548 (March 23, 2010) (matter substantially related when former client might have disclosed confidences which could be relevant or detrimental to him or her in the current litigation; the lawyer "might have acquired" such information if the facts should have been discussed or if it would not have been unusual for them to have been discussed). *Trustees v Premier Plumbing & Heating Inc*, 2008 US Dist LEXIS 55867 (July 23, 2008). Here, the assets held by Dennis will be relevant in the divorce matter. Dennis need not prove that Larry actually possesses confidential information. *Trustees, supra*, compare, Model Rule, cmt [3]. Given the legal and factual issues in Larry's prior representation of Dennis, and the likelihood (indeed, virtual certainty in light of the facts set forth in the question) that Larry learned confidential information regarding Dennis's financial situation, the matter Larry handled for Dennis is substantially related to Camilla's matter.

Even though the terms "materially adverse" may not be well defined in the law, there can be no reasonable argument that the interests of divorcing parties are not materially adverse. This is so even if the parties are relatively cooperative; their interests are still adverse.

Because the interests of Camilla and Dennis are materially adverse, and their matters are substantially related, Larry is prohibited from representing Camilla under MRPC 1.9(a) unless Dennis consents to Larry's representation after consultation. Additionally, Larry is prohibited from revealing to Camilla confidences or secrets gained in his professional relationship with Dennis, MRPC 1.6(b)(1). He is also prohibited from using confidences or secrets, or, indeed, "any information relating to the representation," to the disadvantage of Dennis (unless Dennis consents after consultation). MRPC 1.6(b)(2); MRPC 1.8(b); MRPC 1.9(c).

It is not clear whether Larry's proposed fee arrangement is permissible under the Rules of Professional Conduct.

A Michigan lawyer shall not enter into an agreement for, charge or collect an illegal or clearly excessive (unreasonable) fee. When a lawyer has not regularly represented a client, the lawyer has a duty to communicate the basis or rate of the fee to the client, preferably in writing, before or within a reasonable time after commencing representation. MRPC 1.5(b). Although Larry's agreement recites several factors that are appropriate in determining reasonableness under MRPC 1.5(a), some courts and ethics committees have held or opined that using these factors to enhance a fee otherwise subject to straightforward computation may convert the arrangement into a contingent fee.

Contingent fees are generally allowed subject to certain exceptions. MRPC 1.5(a)(8); MRPC 1.5(c). One such exception is for "domestic relations" matters. MRPC 1.5(d) ("A lawyer shall not enter into an arrangement for, charge, or collect a contingent fee in a domestic relations matter"). A clause similar to the one Larry proposed was recently found by the State Bar of Michigan's Committee on Professional Ethics to be a contingent fee and therefore impermissible in a divorce case. RI-346. But *see Alexander v Inman*, 974 SW2d 689, 693 (Tenn, 1998) ("under the terms of the agreement between Inman and the attorneys, there is no question that they would be paid regardless of the outcome of the case. Payment itself is certain; only the exact amount of payment is uncertain").

Contingent fees must be in writing and must "state the method by which the fee is to be determined." MRPC 1.5(c). Although it is always advisable to memorialize a fee arrangement in writing, the fee dependent on results obtained and other factors recited in the question need not be reduced to writing unless it amounts to a contingent fee, and if it is such, it would be impermissible in a domestic relations matter.

Again, Larry's path is not clear with regard to Camilla's proposed limited scope of representation and ghostwriting project. Camilla is asking Larry to "unbundle" the legal services he would ordinarily deliver in a divorce representation. A lawyer may limit the objectives of the representation if the client consents after consultation, so long as the representation is in accordance with the Rules of Professional Conduct and other law. MRPC 1.2(b) and comment. A lawyer may not make a false statement to a court or fail to disclose client fraud on a tribunal. MRPC 3.3(a)(1) and (2). Nor may a lawyer engage in conduct involving dishonesty, fraud, deceit, or misrepresentation. MRPC 8.4(b).

There are two possible conclusions that can be drawn. The first is that unless a rule of professional conduct or of civil procedure requires client or lawyer to disclose drafting assistance to a court, there is no misrepresentation by either the client or the lawyer. Thus, the lawyer has not violated MRPC 3.3(a)(1) or MRPC 8.4(b) by making a false statement to the court. Nor has the lawyer assisted in client fraud in violation of MRPC 1.2(c), 3.3(a)(2), or 8.4(b). The State Bar Committee on Professional Ethics recently found that, assuming compliance with the Michigan Rules of Professional Conduct and other law, a lawyer may, without appearing or otherwise disclosing his or her assistance, assist a pro se litigant by giving advice on the content of documents to be filed in court, including pleadings, by drafting those documents and giving advice about what to do in court. RI-347. *See ABA Formal opinion 07-446* (May 5, 2007) (no violation of rules similar to MRPC 1.2[c], 3.3[a] (2), or 8.4(b) requiring disclosure of client fraud upon tribunal and proscribing dishonest lawyer conduct); *Arizona Ethics Opinion 05-06* (July 2005) (no violation of rules similar to MRPC 3.3(a)(1) or 8.4(b)).

The second conclusion is that because a court assumes that a party who files a pleading under his or her own name is actually unrepresented, a lawyer who ghostwrites a pleading is helping a client mislead a court. Courts tend to hold the pleadings of unrepresented litigants to less stringent standards. *Kircher v Ypsilanti Twp*, 2007 US Dist LEXIS 93690 (Dec 21, 2007). Thus, a benefit is being unjustly obtained when a lawyer assists a client by drafting a pleading without disclosing it to the court. See also *Grievance Administrator v Miller*, 06-125-Rd (HP, 2/7/2009) (suspending for 180 days an attorney who prepared bankruptcy petitions for filing by clients *in propria persona* to avoid the requirement that attorneys, but not parties representing themselves, file bankruptcy pleadings electronically).

Student Answer—July 2010

Question 13—Professional Responsibility—8 points

Larry Rep Camilla.

Can an attorney represent a client whose interest are directly adverse to the lawyers former client. Unless both clients consent after consultation and this conflict is imputed to the firm. A lawyer may not represent a client whose interest are directly adverse, in the same or substantially related matter to the lawyers former client unless both clients consent. Here the facts tell us that Larry gained protected information while representing Dennis several years ago, in a suit brought by creditors. Although a divorce action is not the same or substantially related matter to the action by the corporation, Larry has gained information about Dennis, i.e. his personal assets, that could be used to Camilla's advantage, and Dennis is a former client of Larry's thus Larry should seek the consent of both before undertaking the representation.

Furthermore, Larry should not use any information that he gained while representing Dennis to his disadvantage without first seeking his consent after consult here Larry should not use Dennis's information gained during Larry representing of him to his disadvantage without consent.

Proposed Fee,

Can a contingent fee be taken in a divorce case? A contingent fee must be in writing must set forth the manner in which it will be calculated. Furthermore, a contingent fee can never be taken in a divorce case. Moreover a fee must be reasonable, based on the lawyers skill the difficulty of the case, the opportunities foregone. Here the facts tell us that Camilla is seeking Larry's services for divorce and Larry want to make the fee based on results obtained which is contingent, because we have a divorce case and a contingent fee agreement the fee agreement is not permissible.

Larry owes a duty to the tribunal and cannot place Camilla's name on any document not signed by him. All pleadings must be signed by the lawyer and that indicate that the lawyer has read then and they are based on fact, well grounded fact, and the pleading are not brought for an improper purpose. He can't place her name on the pleadings without this.

CLUSTER FOUR

CORPORATIONS

Questions, Model Answers, and Student Answers

The following section includes prior Michigan Bar Exam questions and model answers for **Corporations**. Many of the questions also include actual student answers with the amount of points that were earned to give you a better idea of what the graders expect. The student answers are immediately following the model answer for each question. Please pay close attention to the points received on each question. Although most samples represent "good" answers (i.e., received 8, 9, or 10 points), there are some samples that received 7 points (the minimum "passing" score for an essay), and a few that received very low scores to help you better understand the grading process and what is expected.

February 2001—Question 4

Harry Reiff was employed by Big Time Trucking Company as a customer service representative. His written contract of employment did not have a non-compete clause. In his capacity as a customer service representative, which involved scheduling of shipments and preparing the trailers for shipment, Harry was on good terms with a number of large clients and became such a valuable employee he was given the title of Vice President of Operations.

After he became vice president, Harry was approached by a potential new customer (West Coast Perishable Food Products) who needed to ship its products in refrigerated trailers. Big Time Trucking was involved primarily in the shipping of automotive parts and out of its 1,800 trailers, only 10 were refrigerated. West Coast needed at least 100 trailers for its shipping needs and Harry approached the President and CEO of Big Time, Joe Pesci, and told him of this prospective customer and of other customers he had heard of, all of whom needed refrigerated trailers. Mr. Pesci displayed a lack of interest and told Harry refrigerated trailers were much more expensive to purchase and maintain, and that they were doing just fine shipping automotive parts.

Harry, sensing a great opportunity, told West Coast that he would obtain the necessary trailers within 60 days, and gave Big Time and Joe his 30-day notice of termination. Harry knew that several of Big Time's customers were interested in shipping some of their products, other than automotive parts, in refrigerated trailers. While still employed with Big Time, Harry was contacted by various refrigerated trucking companies who were interested in dealing with Harry with refrigerated trailers. Harry told these companies that he would talk to them about this once he was no longer employed with Big Time.

The contract with West Coast was signed two days before the expiration of Harry's 30-day notice period, and called for Harry to receive commissions of $30,000 per year for the three years of the contract. Two weeks after his termination of employment with Big Time, Harry concluded negotiations with three other shippers for refrigerated trailers, each contract paying Harry $25,000 per year for the term of the contract, each of which was three years. These three shippers were customers of Big Time and continued to ship automotive parts with Big Time.

Harry's business became wildly successful and in his first year of operations in providing shippers with refrigerated trailers, Harry earned over $500,000 in commissions. Joe, upon learning of Harry's contracts and his success, becomes furious and sues Harry in circuit court.

What is the basis for Big Time's lawsuit, and what damages can be claimed? What is Harry's defense? What is the probable outcome?

Model Answer to Question 4

Big Time would claim that Harry, as a corporate officer, is under a fiduciary obligation not to divert a corporation business opportunity for his personal gain. By acquiring the pecuniary benefit for himself from these third parties through his fiduciary relationship, Harry would be accountable for the profit made.

Except with the full knowledge and consent of his principal, an agent cannot take advantage of the knowledge acquired of his principal's business to make a profit for himself at his principal's expense. The question is unclear as to whether Harry informed Mr. Pesci of his contacts with West Coast. While the facts indicate that Mr. Pesci rejected this business opportunity, the fact that this contract clearly was negotiated while Harry was a corporate officer would probably result in Harry being liable to Big Time for the profits realized from his contract with West Coast.

Harry would argue that he did not breach his fiduciary duty because he offered the opportunity to provide refrigerated trailers and this opportunity was rejected. Based upon the facts, Harry did not negotiate any other contracts until after he was no longer an employee. Absent the non-compete agreement, once Harry's employment terminated, he could use his skill, experience, and general knowledge to set up this company, which did not compete with the business of Big Time. Even if there was a non-compete clause, the fact that Harry's new business dealt solely with refrigerated shipping, it would be reasonable to conclude that Harry's business was not competing with Big Time.

Based upon the facts as presented, Harry would probably be responsible for the profits earned from the contract with West Coast, but would not be responsible in damages for the balance of his business operations.

Central Cartage Co v Fewless, 232 Mich App 517 (1998).

Student Answer—February 2001

Question 4—Corporations—8 points

Harry is an officer of Big Time and owes a duty of loyalty to the company. As such, he must disclose any business opportunities presented to him which would conflict with his duties as an officer of Big Time. When approached by West, Harry fulfilled that duty by reporting to the CEO, Joe. Joe expressed no interest and Harry then fulfilled his duty of loyalty.

Harry decided to pursue this opportunity, resigned from Big Time, and gave 30 day notice. However, Harry still had a loyalty duty to Big Time for those 30 days and thus he properly refrained from dealing with shippers until his employment ended. He concluded his negotiations with the three other shippers two weeks after termination.

The basis of the lawsuit against Harry is one of breach of duty of loyalty and thus a lost business opportunity for Big Time, self-dealing.

While Big Time can claim loss of business for West and the three companies that contacted Harry during his employment, the facts do not support that argument very well. Harry promptly disclosed the West deal and the three others were delayed until after termination.

The contract with West was signed two days before expiration of the 30 day notice and thus Big Time may have some basis to claim the $30,000 for three years. However, this may be offset by Harry's disclosure to Joe and his lack of a non-compete clause. A court could find Harry had some liability here and award damages.

Another argument in Big Time's favor is that Harry did not disclose contact by the three other companies to Joe. Given that information, Joe's response may have been different. It appears that Harry may have some liability to these three contracts as well.

In a worst case scenario, Big Time could recapture the value of these lost contracts—some $315,000.

The probable outcome is very speculative in my mind—I would likely award some damages to Big Time, but significantly less than $315,000 because for the most part Harry fulfilled his duty of loyalty. He disclosed to West, resigned, did talk to three others but held them off until after his termination—he is minimally liable, if at all.

July 2002—Question 10

John Burnes, III was the president and sole shareholder of the investment firm, Burnum and Burryem, Inc. The corporation had been in business several years and over those years had accumulated retained earnings of approximately $50,000. Mr. Burnes was told by the corporate public accountant that he could keep at least this much in the account without it being taxed, and if it was distributed during the corporation's existence it would be regular income, or if distributed at the time the corporation dissolved, it would be treated as a capital gain.

The investment strategy of Burnum and Burryem dealt largely with heavy investments of the "dot com" section, and business slowly deteriorated so that very little money was being earned. A customer of the business, Harry Whiplash, tripped over his cane when leaving the office and filed suit for personal injuries. The business had, at that time, minimum liability coverage of $50,000; and John was assured in writing by corporate counsel, who was also defending the claim, that the claim was frivolous and should be fully covered by insurance.

While the claim was pending, John decided there was no sense in continuing the failing business and dissolved the corporation. All current debts were paid and John, as president and sole shareholder, drew as a final distribution the $50,000 in retained earnings. Approximately one year after the corporation was dissolved and the distribution to John was made, a runaway jury awarded Harry the sum of $100,000 for his injuries. Harry now looks to John for the payment of the excess over the insurance limits, contending that John had no right upon dissolution to take the retained earning and not to make appropriate arrangements for this potential liability.

Discuss and decide the issues that would be involved in this matter.

Model Answer to Question 10

In Michigan, a director is liable to the creditors of the corporation where a distribution is made to shareholders before or during the dissolution of the corporation when there are no provisions made for liabilities anticipated to arise after the effective date of dissolution. MCL 450.1855(a). However, a director or officer is not liable if he or she discharges their duties in good faith with the care of an ordinary prudent person in a like position and in a manner he or she reasonably believes to be in the best interest of the corporation. MCL 450.1541(a). In the discharge of duties, a director or officer is entitled to rely upon opinions, reports or statements of legal counsel and public accountants.

In this case, John was told by the accountant that he was free to take these retained earnings at the time of dissolution of the corporation. While John had a duty to make provisions for anticipated liabilities after dissolution, he was also entitled to rely on the advice of legal counsel. John has relied upon the written opinion of his legal counsel that the case was without merit, and insurance was in place that would cover any judgment.

Based on the facts of this case, John acted in good faith. He made provisions to pay existing creditors and relied upon the advice of the accountant that he was free to make this distribution, and relied in good faith upon the corporate attorney that the contingent liability had little or no value. *Reed v Burton*, 344 Mich 126 (1955).

Based on the facts of this case, it is probable that a judgment of no cause for action will enter in favor of John.

Student Answer—July 2002

Question 10—Corporations—7 points

Assuming that all relevant documents (Art of Inc,) were properly filed & the corporation is in good standing, John, as the president & shareholder, has a duty of care & loyalty to the Corp. John must do what a reasonably prudent business person in a like situation would do with regard to business decisions.

Here, John consulted and relied on advice from the corp. CPA and attorney: retaining the $50,000 in the account; & believing the tort claim would be covered by insurance. John, in reliance on the advice, decided in his best judgment to dissolve a failing business.

The question becomes whether Harry can recover from John personally for his injuries. Generally, corporations are liable to the extent of its assets and corp. officers & shareholders are insulated from liability. However, courts may pierce the corp. veil if the status is merely a guise for officers, directors (incorporators) to attempt to hide behind. Additionally, courts are more likely to pierce the corp. veil for tort/personal injuries.

Again, you need to look at how John conducted business—was it a true corp.? Did he make sound, prudent business decisions? If so, he's probably protected from liability.

February 2003—Question 13

Fast Pace Corporation is a closely held corporation owned by four shareholders, each of whom own 250 shares of the total 1000 common shares of stock issued. Each of the shareholders—Matthew, Mark, Luke and John—are also officers and directors. John, as the President, was earning $150,000 per year, which far exceeded the salaries of the other three. John was experiencing continued hostility from the other three shareholders/directors over whether the corporation should expand and if so, to what extent. John wanted to wait on any expansion until the company developed a new product line. Matthew, Mark and Luke finally decided to depose John as both President and director.

The corporate by-laws provided that a special meeting of the Board of Directors and shareholders could be called either by the President or by two directors, not including the President, upon giving the remaining shareholders/directors 24 hours' notice. The notice was to state the date, time, place and purpose of the meeting. The by-laws further provided that a director and officer could only be removed on the affirmative vote of the majority of shareholders present and voting. The by-laws did not provide for cumulative voting.

On July 1st, written notices were given by Matthew and Mark to all of the directors and shareholders that a special meeting would be held on July 3rd for the purpose of reducing the number of directors from four to three and removing John as a director. On July 2nd, everyone was present at the country club, and after a "two martini" lunch, all four individuals stayed to discuss the situation of the corporation. It became apparent that no amicable resolution was going to be reached so Matthew, Mark and Luke decided they might as well vote then and there on reducing the directors from 4 to 3 and eliminating John as director. Matthew, Mark and Luke all voted in favor and John objected to the proceeding but voted against the proposal. Declaring that the vote passed 3-1, Matthew then made a motion to remove John as President. Matthew, Mark and Luke voted in favor of the motion, but John refused to vote saying that this was not proper procedure and left the room.

John now brings an action in the appropriate court challenging the actions of the Board and seeking to have the votes declared illegal and void. Confine your answer solely to the validity of the votes. What will be the result of this lawsuit and why?

Model Answer to Question 13

Actions of a closely-held corporation create special problems for a minority shareholder and are closely scrutinized by the courts. The facts eliminate any issue of cumulative voting and a discussion of this should not provide for any extra credit. The sole issue in this case deals with the notice and the voting that occurred prior to the time and place set forth in the notice of special meeting.

The notice complies with the statute and by-laws in that it provides the date, time, place and stated purpose for the meeting. The notice, however, did not provide any

mention of the proposal to remove John as president. Courts have held the time notice requirement is to permit the shareholders the opportunity to attend the meeting. Another purpose of the time notice is to allow the shareholder the opportunity to prepare and to study the proposal. If there is a deficiency in the time notice requirement, but the shareholder attends the meeting, he has not been harmed by inadequate notice of the time of the meeting. Also, because of the purpose of the meeting, John should not need much time to study the issue.
A director of a corporation is not to be trapped into the attendance of a meeting against his will. Generally speaking, a Board of Directors cannot meet except at a regular consensual meeting. In this case, all members of the Board were present and on the vote reducing the number of directors, everyone voted. By voting on this issue, it could be effectively argued that John waived any objection to the proceedings in which he participated.

As to the vote to remove John as president, he has a valid objection. The by-laws require that the notice specify the purpose of the meeting. The removal of John as president was not included in the notice. Even though he attended the meeting, he refused to participate in this vote and thereby did not waive his objection to this issue. While this may be a moot point since a new meeting can be called, this would at least give John an opportunity to seek counsel and perhaps seek to enjoin his removal and/or protect his salary.

Darvin v Belmont Industries, Inc., 40 Mich App 672 (1972).

Student Answer—February 2003

Question 13—Business Organization—None Available

July 2003—Question 14

Janice Corporation was a small profitable corporation selling a select line of women's clothing. John Stroud, the original founder, was the President, director and owned 35% of the stock. His son William was the Vice President, Treasurer, a director and owned another 14%. Carl Young owned 12% of the stock, was also a director and was often at odds with the Strouds as to how the corporation was being run and the salaries being paid. William Stroud had formed his own company named "Williams" of which he was a 55% shareholder. His company was involved in the production and sale of cosmetics and men's and women's shoes.

Janice Corporation sent to all its shareholders a written proposal wherein Janice proposed a merger with Williams and a sale of all its shares to Williams at $9 a share. At the time of this proposal, the shares of Janice were valued at $7.50. A proxy was sent to all the shareholders, and of the shares voting, 80% approved the merger and sale.

Mr. Young was incensed with this transaction and filed suit to set it aside. He claimed that he knew of two other companies who had been willing to offer approximately $9.50 a share and approximately $9.60 a share respectively. He claimed that the Strouds knew of these other companies' interest and failed to pursue them due to their conflict of interest. While there were two other companies that had expressed some interest in acquiring the Janice stock, there was nothing in writing to substantiate this and how serious the companies were. Neither the Strouds nor Young disclosed or informed the other shareholders of the alleged interest of these companies. Young alleged that the Strouds breached their fiduciary duty by failing to obtain maximum value for the stock and that their actions were detrimental to the interest of the corporation and its shareholders.

It was discovered that Mr. Young had not voted his proxies either for or against the sale, claiming that he intended to do so but just got too busy looking for and obtaining a commitment from alternative purchasers. His response was that his lack of voting did not make any difference since the Strouds essentially controlled the corporation and all that was needed to approve the sale was their vote.

Discuss the issues that will be presented at trial and the probable result.

Model Answer to Question 14

The assent of a shareholder to a corporate transaction generally means that the shareholder can not later challenge the validity of the transaction in court. This rule does not apply if the non-dissenting shareholder can prove that any complaint or objection to the transaction would have been futile. A court would probably hold that the lack of a vote against the proposal would have the same effect as an affirmative vote. Beyond that is the fact that his claim that a negative vote would have been futile is pure speculation. There is no proof or facts that suggest that had he raised this issue and presented the other prospective purchasers that the remaining shareholders would have approved the transaction. Moreover, there are no facts to establish that the other companies were ever going to make an offer or if they did what the offer price was.

Mr. Young's contention that the corporation did not obtain the "maximum" value for the shares would also not sustain his cause of action. The test is not whether the price of the stock was at the maximum value but whether it was fair to the corporation. If the transaction was fair to the corporation when entered into, the material facts of the transaction and the directors' interest were disclosed to the board and to the shareholders entitled to vote, and they ratified the transaction, then the courts will not set aside the transaction. In this case, there is no claim that the interest of the Strouds was not made known to the directors or the shareholders. There is no showing that the purchase price was not a fair price particularly since it exceeded the market price by $1.50 per share and there were not other offers made to either the corporation or through Mr. Young.

Under the circumstances presented, Mr. Young would not prevail in this litigation. *Camden v Kaufman*, 240 Mich App 389 (2000).

Student Answer—July 2003

Question 14—Corporation—7 points

The first issue that will be presented at trial is that because Mr. Young was too busy and did not vote against the merger, he will be deemed to have accepted the Janice Corporation's proposal. The rule is that if a director dissents a proposal by the corporation, he must dissent at the meeting or give his dissent in writing to the corporate secretary at the end of the meeting. On these facts, Mr. Young did not do this, so his input on the proposal will not be recognized. All that is needed to pass a vote is quorum, which is a majority of disinterested directors present at the meeting and a majority of those disinterested directors or shares must vote for the proposal to pass it. Here, 80% of the shares voting approved the merger and therefore it passed. Therefore, Mr. Young will lose on the voting issue because he failed to be present at the meeting and dissent the proposal and a majority of disinterested shares approved it.

The next issue presented will be whether the Strouds breached their fiduciary duty of loyalty to the corporation by failing to maintain the maximum value for its stock. The directors of a corporation have a duty of loyalty to act in good faith and do what is in the corporation's best interests. However, a court will not second guess a director's decision if it believes the decision was made in the best interests of the corporation. This is called the business judgment rule. Young may have a valid argument that what the Strouds did was not in the best interests of the corporation because the Strouds knew of the other companies' interest and failed to pursue them. However, the court would probably say that the Strouds' decision will not be second-guessed because they made this decision to not pursue the other companies' stock because of a conflict of interest. Therefore, Young will probably lose on his duty of loyalty argument.

February 2004—Question 4

The Youngston Corporation was a private Michigan corporation engaged in the development of small shopping centers within the state of Michigan. The company had 15 shareholders who held between 100 and 5,000 shares of its 50,000 shares of outstanding stock. John Phillips owned 100 shares of the company evidenced by a single stock certificate. In March 2002, the Board of Directors was approached by Big Time Corporation that was involved in the development of shopping centers throughout the Midwest. Big Time instigated discussions concerning the proposed acquisition of Youngston in order to gain a presence in Michigan and to take over some of the ongoing projects of Youngston.

Both the articles of incorporation and by-laws of Youngston provided in such an instance that the shareholders, such as John, were entitled to vote on any merger or sale and had the right to dissent as provided by Michigan law. The Board of Directors sent to all the shareholders all required information concerning this proposed sale, the required information concerning their right to dissent, and their recommendation that the sale be approved. John, at this point, thought he would wait to see what happened at the shareholders meeting before he made any final decision, so he did nothing.

A meeting of the shareholders was held on June 25, 2002, and the required numbers of votes were cast in favor of the sale and authorizing the Board to negotiate and fix the compensation to be paid to Youngston for its stock. John did not vote his shares. The negotiations were successfully concluded and the sale was scheduled to occur on September 1, 2002. On July 1, 2002, the corporation again sent to the shareholders appropriate notices which included, among other information, a statement that the negotiations had been completed, that the sale was to occur on September 1, 2002, and that the "fair value" of the shareholders stock was set at $25.00 per share which was the price Big Time offered to pay.

John had purchased his stock for $5.00 a share when Youngston was first incorporated in January 2000. After he received the statement from Big Time that the stock was being valued at $25.00 per share, he heard that the value of Big Time stock was going to greatly appreciate because of this acquisition. He then decided it was time to see how much more he could get for his shares if he dissented. On August 10, 2002, John sent to Youngston a notice that objected to the determination of the fair value of the stock at $25.00 per share and claimed that true fair value was $45.00 per share based on the expected increased value of the stock once the sale was completed. Big Time ultimately replied to John's letter by sending him a check in the amount of $2,500.00 representing payment of $25.00 per share for his 100 shares.

John comes into your office and relates the facts as set forth above. **What do you advise John are his remedies?**

Model Answer to Question 4

The best advice that you can give John is to cash the check.

The sale that occurred is outside of the course of business and would give rise to dissenters' rights even if this were not provided for in the articles and corporate by-laws. However, in order to properly exercise his dissenter's rights, he needs to follow the requirements found in the statute. MSA 450.1761 *et seq.* The statement of facts states that the Company provided John the appropriate notices, therefore this is not an issue. Once John received the notice of the proposed action he was required to provide to the Company, before the vote of shareholders, written notice of his demand for payment for his shares. If he had done this and then the vote of the shareholders approved the sale, the Company would have been required to send John a notice no later than 10 days thereafter advising him of the action of the Corporation and advising him where the demand for payment must be sent and where his shares must be deposited. John would then be required to demand payment and deposit his shares where directed. John would also be required to provide the corporation with this estimate of the fair value of the shares.

John did not provide the first notice required demanding payment for his shares. At this point, the corporation was not required to give John further notices, but it did. According to the facts, after the vote the corporation again provided the appropriate notices and John still failed to perform as required. John was required to deposit his stock certificate and provide his written demand for payment within 30 days after he received the notice from the Company that the sale had been approved and the Corporation was prepared to purchase his shares for $25.00 per share. John failed to do any of this and therefore waived any right he may have retained to pursue a different price.

Finally, John's claim that the price was not fair because the stock should be valued based on the anticipated increase in the value because of the sale is not an appropriate method to determine "fair value." Fair value is determined immediately before the effectuation of the corporate action.

Student Answer—February 2004

Question 4—Corporations—3 points (Bad Answer)

John was provided appropriate notice of all meetings and chose to do nothing.

The $25 per share John was offered is more than the $15 per share he paid so he is not taking a loss.

John also cannot prove that the stock will indeed appreciate. John's remedies are to accept the $2,500 check, return the check and keep his shares, or ask for a determination of how the $25 fair market value was arrived at.

Comment: Students did very poorly on this question. The above example is given to represent the type of response that is worth 3 points. Corporations is tested quite often and many students struggle with it. It is very important that you study the material, but also review all old corporation questions to see how it is tested.

July 2004—Question 5

Able Machine Company was a Michigan corporation, solely owned by John McCoy, his brother William McCoy, James Hatfield, and his brother George Hatfield. The McCoys' father started the business, and the four men all worked in the business making it a very successful machine repair business. Over the years, stock was issued, and by 1995 John and William owned 60% of the stock and James and George owned 40%.

Over the last four years of their relationship, the Hatfields, by agreement of all of the parties, were primarily engaged in attempting to start up Builders Co., another Michigan corporation that would manufacture small motors, and the McCoys continued running Able Company. The McCoys came to the Hatfields in 2000 and informed them Able Company's business was slowing down and that they did not know how much longer it could continue to pay the salary and benefits they had all been receiving. The McCoy's offered to buy out the Hatfield's stock in Able for one million dollars and convey to the Hatfields the stock the McCoys held in Builders Co.

James and George reviewed the financial records and noticed that Able Company was not making the money that it had in the past. James and George decided that Builders was going to be a success and that the million dollars would be a good deal and help them with continuing to develop this company. They sold their stock to the McCoys and all went well for one year. At the end of one year, the McCoys sold Able Company to Big Time Machine Repair for $15,000,000. The Hatfields were able to discover that there were some preliminary discussions between Big Time and the McCoys approximately a half-year before the Hatfields sold out to the McCoys.

The Hatfields consult with you and hire you to represent them against the McCoys and/or Able Company. What action do you take on behalf of the Hatfields?

Model Answer to Question 5

A tender should first be made to the McCoys of the $1 million paid to purchase the Hatfields' stock. A suit to rescind the agreement purchasing the stock could then be commenced based upon allegations of fraud, breach of fiduciary duty, or innocent or negligent misrepresentation. Without making the tender, the Hatfields will be unable to prevail in this action.

The Hatfields would not be able to file a shareholders' derivative action seeking damages for fraud, breach of fiduciary duty, innocent or negligent misrepresentation, as they are not current shareholders of Able Machine Company.

The Michigan Business Corporation Act provides that a shareholder derivative action requires that (a) the shareholder was a shareholder of the corporation at the time of the act or omission complained of, (b) the shareholder fairly and adequately represents the interest of the corporation in enforcing the right of the corporation, and (c) the shareholder continues to be a shareholder until the time of judgment, unless the failure to continue to be a shareholder is the result of corporate action in which the former shareholder did not acquiesce. Since the Hatfields are not current shareholders they would no longer have standing to commence a shareholder derivative action.

Further, the Hatfields voluntarily sold their stock to the McCoys. While a claim could be made that their consent to this sale was obtained through fraud, breach of fiduciary duty, or innocent or negligent misrepresentation, without first making the tender, such action could not be maintained.

A suit for damages in their individual capacity under the Michigan Business Corporation Act would also be unavailing. While MCL 450.1489 provides that a direct or individual cause of action may also be brought against a corporation for illegal or fraudulent acts to the shareholder, the statute still requires that the action be brought by a current shareholder.

See *McCarth v Miller*, unpublished opinion Court of Appeals No. 231829, 02/21/03. Leave denied, 469 Mich 976 (2003).

Student Answer—July 2004

Question 5—Corporations—5 points (Failing Answer)

Proper action, file a suit claiming that the McCoys breached their duty of loyalty, and the fiduciary duty they owed to the Hatfields.

Under these facts, Able Company is a closely held corporation and the McCoys holding 60% of stock and Hatfields holding 40%.

In a closely held corporation, each SH, can also be a Director, depending on how their Articles and By Laws are stated. In 2000, when the McCoys informed the Hatfields how slow the business was, they failed to disclose to Hatfields that they were in preliminary discussions with Big Time. Although such negotiation may have been in the best interest of the corporation, this cannot be done without full disclosure.

The Hatfields, if they are in a directors position; there would need to be full discussion among all directors on such a matter. The Hatfields could bring a derivative suit as share holders because although they did sell out, they owned stock in Able Company at the time of the incident giving rise to the action.

This would require an appraisal to determine actual damage under these facts, but the Hatfields do have a case for the McCoys breaching their fiduciary duty owed to each and all of the 4 men.

Comment: There were no "good" answers to this question, but this is an example of a 5. This examinee earned 5 points even though he or she missed the main issue of standing. Most examinees missed the standing issue because recent graduates are not used to seeing "standing" in other subjects. Standing is an issue in any civil case, regardless of the topic. Please keep that in mind.

February 2005—Question 2

John Majors developed a company called Major Tool and Die. He was the sole stockholder until his son Ned graduated from college. At that point, John hired his son as Vice President and gave him 1,000 shares of the company stock. John and Ned were the sole shareholders with John holding 3,000 shares and Ned the 1,000 shares. John was the President and the Articles of Incorporation provided that by a majority vote of the shareholders the Board membership could be changed. John and Ned were the only members of the Board of Directors when Ned was first hired. John had indicated to his son that after an undetermined period of time, he would sell some of his stock to Ned so they would own an equal number of shares and that John would always share in the profits of the company.

After five years, Ned became more assertive in the manner that the business was conducted, claiming they should change suppliers and that the salaries paid to other employees were too high. At this point, John was earning over $150,000 in salary and every year the company declared a $50,000 bonus to both John and Ned. The two began to engage in frequent arguments. Finally, John called a special meeting, and at the meeting declared that Ned was fired and was dismissed from the Board of Directors. John then named his daughter as the other Board member. At that time, John was still the President and the owner of 3,000 shares of stock and Ned the owner of 1,000 shares of stock.

Ned consulted an attorney and it was decided that they would file a lawsuit and rely solely on MCL 450.1489. The pertinent portions of this statute provide:

> A shareholder may bring an action . . . to establish that the acts of the directors or those in control of the corporation are illegal, fraudulent, or willfully unfair and oppressive to the corporation or to the shareholder.
>
> The statute further defined that:
>
> "willfully unfair and oppressive conduct" means a continuing course of conduct or a significant action or series of actions that substantially interferes with the interests of the shareholder as a shareholder.

Discuss the strengths and weaknesses of Ned's case as they relate solely to the claim that was filed. What in your opinion is the probable outcome, and why?

Model Answer to Question 2

In Michigan, this case will be decided based on the language of the statute. The Michigan statute specifically provides that minority shareholders can bring suit for oppression "only for conduct that substantially interferes with the interest of the shareholder as a shareholder."

Ned would claim that his employment with the company and his position on the Board of Directors were "shareholder interests" that were unlawfully taken from him by the majority shareholder. He would argue that in close corporations, shareholders often work for the corporation and dividends are often paid in the form of salary. Generally, shareholders in closely held corporations are also in a management position. Finally, Ned could argue that the term "oppression" as found in the statute should be interpreted as "conduct that defeats the 'reasonable expectations' of a shareholder."

Employment and board membership are not generally listed among rights and automatically accrue to shareholders. Some states have enacted statutes that specifically protect the interest of minority shareholders in their capacities as employees and directors, and some states without such statutes have protected these interests through court decisions.

The statute in this case specifically addresses this very issue and is clear in its terms that a suit for oppression of a shareholder's interest can only be sustained for conduct that substantially interferes with the interest of the shareholder as a shareholder. The harm that was suffered in this case was in his capacity as an employee and director, not a shareholder.

While some states have also adopted a "reasonable expectations test" as a guide to defining "oppression," no state has done so without some reference to this in the statute.

The arguments made by Ned have support in some jurisdictions, but the Michigan statute is unambiguous, and since the alleged damage was not to his interest as a shareholder, Ned would not be successful in this particular suit.

Franchino v Franchino, 263 Mich App 172 (2004).

Student Answer—February 2005

Question 2—Corporation—8 points

Ned will lose.

Ned will have to establish that his father's conduct was willfully unfair and oppressive to the shareholder. According to the statute, this means that John's conduct was "a significant action" that interferes with Ned's interest as a shareholder.

Ned's first task will be to show that his dismissal as a board member and employee harmed his interests as a shareholder.

In Ned's favor, John, the majority shareholder, dismissed Ned summarily. John had no hope of overcoming his father's position at the meeting, in which the two could have been acting as both shareholders and board members. It is not clear that John was given any opportunity to state his case or defend his position on the board or as an employee.

Also in Ned's favor is the fact that the corporation was declaring bonuses to Ned and John, but not dividends. Therefore, Ned will suffer a financial loss as a result of John's action.

Finally, John's promise to sell some of his shares to Ned, to make Ned an equal # of shares, and that Ned would always share in the profits of the company are compromised by John's summary dismissal of Ned. Although the promises were without consideration it is possible that Ned reasonably, foreseeably relied on them to his detriment. If so, John has willfully damaged Ned's shareholder rights by denying him the ability to acquire additional shares and coupled with the lack of dividends, this suggests that Ned's ability to share in the profits of the corporation as a shareholder has been damaged.

To the detriment of Ned's case, John called a special meeting—again Ned and John could have been acting as both shareholders and board members at the meeting. Such a special meeting is within the rights of a shareholder. Presumably proper notice was given of the meeting, or at least Ned waived notice by attending the meeting and not objecting to lack of notice.

Shareholders have the right, according to the Articles, to change the board by a majority vote of the shareholders. Michigan law permits incorporators or shareholders and the board to provide for removal of board members in the Articles. Those provisions then become the governing rule for corporate conduct. John, as majority shareholder, would also have the majority of votes, assuming 1 vote per share, as is usually the case.

So, John followed proper procedure to remove a director and, his removal of Ned was for a proper business purpose. Ned's philosophy fundamentally differed from John's and would, in John's view adversely impact the corporation if left unchecked.

Ned's ability to exercise shareholder rights has not been diminished, he may still vote, collect dividends, etc.

Comment: This question could have been answered without any knowledge of corporation law. The examiners simply asked to apply the statute. This is common on the bar exam and in practice but law students are not used to it. If you are given a statute, apply it and focus on every word.

July 2005—Question 2

The Asbestos Are Us Corporation manufactured and installed asbestos in every conceivable type of commercial and multiple residential building located in the state of Michigan. When the company became aware of the health risk associated with asbestos and the multiple and significant claims that could be filed against the company, it decided that it had to dissolve. The company ceased active business operations and filed a Certificate of Dissolution as required by statute. The Certificate of Dissolution was stamped as filed on April 1, 2003. The company also provided notice of dissolution by publication and notified all parties who had sent a notice of a claim for damages due to the asbestos. The company then proceeded to distribute all of its assets in accord with Michigan law. The company had insurance coverage for liability claims through Acme Insurance Company. The limit of the insurance coverage was $10,000,000.

Some parties had made claims and dealt directly with the insurance carrier and received settlements. As of April 1, 2004, all claims that had been presented had been settled. The payments totaled $4,500,000.

On or about December 1, 2004, Johnny C. Lately discovered through a chest x-ray that the cough he had been experiencing for the last three months was caused by damage to his lung that was progressive and would ultimately result in his premature death. There was no dispute that his condition was a direct result of breathing asbestos. Johnny had worked for a company that had installed asbestos as a subcontractor of Asbestos Are Us. Johnny filed suit against Asbestos Are Us.

Disregard any proximate cause argument and assume that the corporation was dissolved in accord with the statue. Limiting your answer to the status of the corporation at the time this suit was filed, what are the issues that are presented, and what, in your opinion, will be the results?

Model Answer to Question 2

There are several issues that should be raised. The first issue deals with the limitation period to file the claim. MCL 450.1842a(3) provides that all claims against a dissolved corporation are barred unless the claimant commences a proceeding to enforce the claim against the dissolved corporation within one year after the publication date. The courts have determined that this is not a statute of limitation, but a "corporate survival statute." Credit should not be deducted for calling this a statute of limitation issue.

The question clearly states the date of publication, the date the suit was filed, and that the dissolution followed the statute. Unless there is some way to avoid the effect of the statute, the claim would be barred.

This one-year time period may be extended by the courts upon a showing of good cause and as long as the corporation has not made a complete distribution of its assets. It could be argued that "good cause" exists since Johnny did not discover the existence of this disease until after the one-year period had expired. The argument would continue that the company has not distributed all of its assets since it still has $5,500,000 left on its insurance limits.

These issues have been decided in this state. The purpose of the "survival statue" is to allow claims under certain conditions to be filed after the effective date of dissolution. It was the decision of the court that the legislation created a process whereby a dissolved corporation can bar future claims, thus cutting off the possibility that the corporation's potential liability could never be completely resolved. The issue of the discovery of the disease does not affect this time period. The claim has to be presented within this time period or it is barred. If the claim is barred, there is no liability of the insurance carrier to pay any further claims and therefore the policy has no further value. There is nothing to be distributed, as this is not an asset of the corporation.

A passing score should recognize that there is a time period after the dissolution to file a claim, that this time period can be extended for good cause, and discuss whether the insurance policy is an asset of the company.

Gilliam v Hi-Temp Products, Inc., 260 Michigan App 98 (2003).

Student Answer—July 2005

Question 2—Corporation—9 points

The issue at hand is what should the liabilities of the corporation be, and is Johnny likely to be able to sustain a suit. The facts have stated that dissolution was properly executed, so this is not a factor. The issue regarding the dissolution is the responsibility of the corporation at dissolution. According to MBCA, the corporation is responsible to first pay debt and obligations, then to pay out shareholders. The corp. is required also by MBCA to provide enough funds to wind up and to pay all creditors (in this case, possible asbestos claimants in one event that only one successful in suit). Here, in the facts, at winding up, the corp. had $10 M insurance coverage to pay for asbestos claimants. Also in the facts, one year after the corp. dissolved, total claims had only totaled $4,500,000. Because the insurance company covered up to $10 M and there was only $4,500,000 of total asbestos claim, it can be deferred that the corp. maintained enough to cover such claims, thus the corp. is in compliance with MBCA.

The second issue at hand is should Johnny be barred in bringing suit against the corp. In other words, would Johnny be barred by a statute of limitations (S of L) or by MBCA for bringing a claim. According to MBCA, claims can be brought against the corp. for up to a year after dissolution. Here, in the facts Johnny brought his claim 1 year and 8 months after the corp had dissolved. As a matter of public policy, the corp. can't be indefinitely held to liabilities. Because the claim was brought after the one year deadline, the corp. would be protected from such claims and Johnny would be barred from bringing suit against the corp.

The subissue may be can Johnny bring a tort claim against the directors/officers of the corp. The General rule of MBCA is that the directors and officers are shielded from personal liability unless they have engaged in contact (i.e. co-mingled funds, used corp. prop. for personal use, etc.) that would allow for the piercing of the corp. veil. Here, in the facts, the corp. hasn't done anything that may subject the directors/officers to personal liability, thus Johnny also would be able to bring a tort suit against the individual officers/director, even though Michigan's tort statute of limitation is 2 years.

In conclusion, the corp. has acted in accordance with MBCA and has not breached duty of care/loyalty owed. Furthermore, the corp. gave the notice that they were required to give. If the court holds that Johnny should have acted within the 1 year after dissolution then Johnny can't bring suit. However, if Johnny's time to bring suit didn't begin to toll until he was aware of the illness (12/04/04) then he would have still had 2 months to bring suit and he wouldn't be barred from bring suit. So, the corp. didn't act improperly and can't pierce corp. veil, but depending on how it is determined regarding when the time began to toll, Johnny may/may not be barred in bringing suit against the corp. (no personal liability for director/officer).

Comment: Most students bombed this question because they missed the statute of limitations issue. This is an example of an unusual question that would be immediately apparent to practitioners but not recent graduates. Whenever an extended time period is given before filing a claim, always consider the statute of limitations.

February 2006—Question 8

Harold Jensen was a retired banker who had more time on his hands than he knew what to do with. He acquired stock in a relatively new corporation called Easy Slide Corporation. Ever since he became a minority shareholder in Easy Slide Corporation, Harold had a continuing battle with the management. He disapproved of nearly every action taken by the corporation even though the value of his shares had continued to rise and the company achieved a profit for the four years that it was in operation. Harold just knew that the company should have been doing better than it was and he was convinced that the officers of the company were somehow pocketing large sums of unreported cash. Harold voiced his concerns at every meeting of shareholders but was unable to garner any support from the other shareholders of the company.

Harold decided that it was time for him to take more aggressive steps. On April 1, 2005, Harold sent to the company a letter that stated, "As a minority shareholder, I demand to see all of the financial records of the corporation including all contracts, all invoices, copies of all bank records, including checks and deposits made in the last four years. I also demand copies of the individual income tax returns of all officers of the corporation."

On April 4, 2005, the corporation sent Harold a response stating that its attorneys were reviewing the matter and would be in touch. Harold was now convinced that the company was hiding information and that his suspicions about fraud and mismanagement were true.

Harold filed a lawsuit in Ingham Circuit Court claiming that by not permitting the inspection of the records as requested, the corporation violated the Business Corporation Act. Harold requested that the court order the records produced and award him costs and attorneys' fees.

You are the law clerk for the circuit judge. Prepare a memorandum on whether Harold should prevail on his complaint, and why.

Model Answer to Question 8

In Michigan a shareholder's right to inspect corporate records is set forth at MCL 450.1487, which provides in pertinent part:

> (2) Any shareholder of record . . . shall have the right during the usual hours of business to inspect for any proper purpose the corporation's stock ledger, a list of its shareholders, and its other books and records, if the shareholder gives the corporation written demand describing with reasonable particularity his or her purpose and the records he or she desires to inspect, and the records sought are directly connected with the purpose. A proper purpose shall mean a purpose reasonably related to such person's interest as a shareholder.
>
> (3) If the corporation does not permit an inspection within 5 business days after a demand has been received in compliance with subsection (2), or imposes unreasonable conditions upon the inspection, the shareholder may apply to the circuit court of the county in which the principal place of business or registered office of the corporation is located for an order to compel the inspection. If the shareholder seeks to inspect the corporation's books and records other than its stock ledger or list of shareholders, he or she shall first establish that he or she has complied with this section respecting the form and manner of making demand for inspection of the documents, that the inspection he or she seeks is for a proper purpose, and that the documents sought are directly connected with the purpose. If the shareholder seeks to inspect the corporation's stock ledger or list of shareholders and has established compliance with this section respecting the form and manner of making demand for the inspection of the documents, the burden of proof shall be upon the corporation to establish that the inspection that is sought is for an improper purpose or that the records sought are not directly connected with the person's purpose.

In this case, Harold did not give any reason in support of his request nor did the company respond to Harold within the five-day period. A "proper purpose" is one that is reasonably related to the person's interest as a shareholder. Under the common law, a shareholder stated a proper purpose for an inspection by raising doubts whether corporate affairs had been properly conducted by the directors or management. The courts have held that idle curiosity or mere speculation of mismanagement is insufficient to justify an inspection, but the legislature did not intend to erect a formidable obstacle for shareholders. Under the statute, a proper purpose for inspection is one that in good faith seeks information bearing upon protection of the shareholder's interest and that of other shareholders in the corporation, and is not contrary to the corporation's interests. There is nothing in these facts other than speculation that support the request. The courts do appear to favor such requests so if this was made in the proper form and if Harold could support the request with some factual allegations, the court would probably order the records produced.

By statute, the corporation must either approve or reject the request within the five-day period. In this case, the corporation did neither. Had Harold's request complied with the statute, the corporation was required to respond timely. Lacking a request that complied with the statute, the corporation's response, or lack therefore, does not give a basis for the relief requested.

The request for the officers' income tax returns is not contemplated by statute and would not be permitted. Once Harold made a proper request and obtained the records, it is possible that the individuals could be named as defendants and discovery of their personal records allowed.

North Oakland County Board of Realtors v Realcomp, Inc, 226 Mich App 54 (1997).

Two Student Answers—February 2006

Question 8—Corporations—8 points

Memorandum
To: Judge
RE: Jensen v Easy Slide Corp.

Under the Business Corporation Act (BCA) a shareholder has the right to review the financial records of the corp. upon showing good cause. The BCA also requires 90 days written notice to the Board of Directors (Board) requesting the corp. to stop its actions prior to the shareholder filing suit unless such request would prove ineffective. The facts here indicate that Easy Slide was increasing in value and was continuously making a profit. As a result, there is no legitimate reason for Jensen to request review of the corporation's financial records. Additionally, he has no legal right to inspect contracts or invoices, bank records, or the personal tax records of the officers. There is also no indication of oppressive conduct or that his letter requesting access to company records was ineffective so his filing suit was premature. Also, if the company stock is publicly traded, Jensen has the option of selling his shares and so he is unlikely to prevail in his complaint.

Question 8—Corporations—8 points

Issue 1: Whether Harold should prevail on his complaint.

Generally, officers of a corporation has a duty of loyalty to the company. That is, the officer must act in good faith and make knowledgeable decisions that help make the company a profit. A breach of duty of loyalty can come up when the officers are taking excessive compensation from the company. The Business Judgment Rule is a rebuttable presumption that the officers are running the corp. with good faith and making knowledgeable decisions in the best interest of the company. To prevail on the claim of breach, the plaintiff must first rebut the presumption with evidence.

Here, Harold began making money with the company almost immediately. His shares rose and the corporation profited every year it was in operation. The only evidence Harold has that the officers were committing fraud and mismanagement is that they did not respond to his request promptly. Harold asked for an assortment of accounting items that can't be gotten immediately because Harold wanted an extensive list and the corporation should be given a reasonable amount of time to respond. Because of the reasoning above, Harold will not prevail on his complaint.

February 2007—Question 2

Jack Phillips was a real estate agent and had formed several different corporations in connection with his business. One of his companies was Phillips Equity Real Estate Inc., a Michigan corporation. This company leased office space by virtue of a seven-year written lease from Land Owners, Inc. All of the real estate agents who conducted business from the leased premises were agents of another company of Mr. Phillips, Phillips Real Estate, Inc., and were licensed under this company. All the sales that were closed at these premises were credited to an account of Phillips Real Estate, Inc., and Phillips Real Estate, Inc. would receive all the income from the sales, pay all expenses and make all the disbursements. Jack Phillips was the sole stockholder and president of both corporations.

Phillips Equity Real Estate, Inc. filed its annual reports and was in good standing with the State of Michigan. The lease payments were timely made for three years with an electronic transfer of funds from an account under the name of Jack Phillips d/b/a Phillips Real Estate. After a full three years, Phillips Equity Real Estate advised Land Owners that it could no longer afford the lease payments and the office was closed. Land Owners did everything necessary to mitigate its damages, but in the end sued for the loss of 1½ years of rent payments. Phillips Equity Real Estate, Inc. had ceased doing any business and had no assets. Suit was brought against Jack Phillips individually, and Jack Phillips d/b/a Phillips Real Estate, Inc.

Defendants moved for summary disposition on the basis that Phillips Equity Real Estate, Inc. was a Michigan corporation in good standing and that the contract was between this corporation and plaintiff. Plaintiff's complaint did not contain any allegations of fraud, and defendants have asserted that without allegations of fraud, the only liability could be that of Phillips Equity Real Estate, Inc.

You represent plaintiff. Do you have a cause of action against Jack Phillips? Explain your answer.

Model Answer to Question 2

The law treats a corporation as an entirely separate entity from its stockholders, even where one person owns all of the corporation's stock. The traditional basis for piercing the corporate veil has been to protect a corporation's creditors where there is a unity of interest of the stockholders and the corporation, and where the stockholders have used the corporate structure in an attempt to avoid legal obligations.

There is no single rule for when the corporate entity may be disregarded. The courts consider all relevant facts in light of the corporation's economic justification to determine if the corporate form has been abused. The Michigan Court of Appeals has used the following standard for piercing the corporate veil: (1) the corporate entity is merely an agent or instrumentality of its shareholders or another entity; (2) the corporate entity was used to commit a fraud or wrong; and (3) the plaintiff suffered an unjust loss or injury. *SCD Chemical Distributors, Inc. v Medley*, 203 Michigan App 374, 381 (1994).

There is now a question as to whether fraud needs to be proven in order to pierce the corporate veil. In a recent decision of the Court of Appeals, the trial court was reversed when it required plaintiff to prove fraud to pierce the corporate veil. Instead, the court held that plaintiff could pierce the corporate veil if it showed that the corporate defendant was "defendants' 'agent,' 'mere instrumentality,' or device to avoid legal obligations."

In the present case, there is no evidence of fraud in the creation of Phillips Equity Real Estate Company. However, it is clear that this corporation was a mere agent or instrumentality of which was also its only liability. It shared the same stockholder and president and did not share in any of the profits generated in the real estate business.

If to pierce the corporate veil a showing of fraud is not required, then in this instance the corporate veil will be pierced. A final decision may depend on what panel is drawn in the Court of Appeals.

See L & R Homes Inc. v Jack Cristenson Rochester, Inc, 475 Michigan 853 (2006) and *Foodland Distributing v Al-Naimi*, 220 Michigan App 453 (1996).

Student Answer—February 2007

Question 2—Corporations—10 points

Under the Doctrine of Joint and Several liability, a plaintiff with a cause of action can sue an individual jointly or severally. Here Jack Phillips was the sole stockholder and the Corp Phillips Equity no longer exists. Therefore Landowner can sue Jack Philips, individually.

Also, under the Agency Theory, where a person holds himself out as an Agent of the Principal, and a 3rd party believes that he is an agent, an Agency exists. The agent can also Bind the principal in a K. Here, Phillips Equity Real Estate held themselves out as agents of Jack Phillips. Thus, Landowners can now sue Jack Phillips b/c of the contract entered into with Phillips Real Estate.

Also, under the Doctrine of Piercing the Corp Veil a plaintiff can go through the corp. up to the stockholder and hold the stockholder liable. Gen. there must be a co-mingling of funds, and shareholder does not treat the corp. as the actor ego.

Here, all sales closed at the premises credited to the acct of Phillips Real Estate, Phillips R.E. received all income from sales, pay all expenses and make all distributions. So there is co-mingling of funds with all the real estate agents who conducted business from the premises. Also, Jack Phillips is the sole stockholder.

Therefore, the court is in a position to pierce the corp. veil and hold the stockholder (Jack Phillips) liable.

February 2008—Question 5

Concrete Additive Inc. ("Company") is a Michigan corporation. Its shareholders are Al, Bonnie and Chris, each of whom owns the same number of shares of Company's common stock. Al, Bonnie and Chris have served on Company's board of directors since its formation. Al, a chemical engineer with an MBA in finance, is Company's President and Director of Research, and Bonnie, an accountant, is its Secretary/ Treasurer and Chief Financial Officer.

Company's products consist of concrete additives, including a product called Concrete Filler. In addition, Al recently developed Fiberlight, a fiber substance, that when mixed with concrete yields lighter and stronger concrete. Fiberlight has been approved by the State Concrete Testing Agency ("SCTA") for poured concrete uses and, to date, that has been Fiberlight's only use. However, Al believes Fiberlight will work in all concrete applications and has told that to his fellow directors on numerous occasions.

Outdoor Decorations Inc. ("ODI") manufactures outdoor concrete decorations by injecting concrete into molds. Three weeks ago, Al received a call from a representative of ODI to purchase 500 bags of Concrete Filler, a product that ODI usually uses in its injection process. ODI is not a regular customer of Company and contacted Company in hopes of finding a new supplier for Concrete Filler.

Al told ODI's purchasing agent about Fiberlight and suggested that ODI purchase Fiberlight instead of Concrete Filler. After being assured by Al that Fiberlight would work in the concrete injection process, ODI's purchasing agent agreed to purchase Fiberlight. When ODI received a truckload of Fiberlight, its production manager called Al because the Fiberlight was not as fine of a consistency as Concrete Filler. The production manager was concerned that the Fiberlight would cause undue resistance in the injection process. Al assured ODI's production manager that the Fiberlight would work. Satisfied with Al's assurances, ODI's production manager indicated ODI would accept the Fiberlight and process a payment to Company.

One week ago, ODI started an injection run using Fiberlight. Two molds blew out damaging ODI's equipment and causing severe injury to several visitors who were on a tour of ODI's plant. ODI's president immediately called Al and advised Al as follows: (i) that he had checked with the SCTA and learned that Fiberlight had not been approved for injection use, (ii) that the remaining Fiberlight is useless to ODI, (iii) that ODI would be turning the matter over to legal counsel to recover for the damage to its equipment, (iv) that Company should expect to hear from the SCTA who had told ODI that it would be imposing a $50,000 fine on Company, and (v) that Company would likely be sued by the injured visitors. Al kept this information to himself and did not report it to anyone else at Company.

Two days ago, at a meeting of Company's board, Al failed to report the call from ODI's president. Al, fearing the ODI incident would ruin company financially and prevent Al from getting further funds from Company, moved to declare a $25,000 dividend to each shareholder. Bonnie, unaware of the impending legal difficulties and fine from the SCTA, reported that, based on information provided to her by Company's accounting department, Company was operating profitably, had good cash flow, was current with all creditors, and had cash reserves of $150,000. The board unanimously approved and declared the dividend, and Bonnie issued checks that day.

Yesterday, Al and Bonnie received notice of the $50,000 fine from the SCTA and were served with a complaint filed by counsel for one of the injured visitors. Bonnie immediately advised the other directors and shareholders that Company is self-insured up to $500,000 and that, given the fine, the lawsuit, the related legal fees to be incurred by Company, and the recent dividend, Company would not be able to pay its debts as they come due.

Could Company successfully sue any or all of the members of the board of directors to recover the dividend that was distributed? Explain your answer.

Model Answer to Question 5

Company would be successful in a suit filed against Al to recover the dividend that was improperly made by the directors, but would be unsuccessful in recovering the dividend from Bonnie or Chris.

The board of directors may authorize and a corporation may make distributions, unless the articles of incorporation otherwise restrict this authority. MCL 450.1345. "Distributions" are transfers of money or other property to or for the benefit of its shareholders which would include a cash dividend. MCL 450.1106(4). Generally, then, unless Company's articles of incorporation provide otherwise, its board would be permitted, subject to certain statutory limitations, to make a distribution in the form of a cash dividend.

The Michigan Business Corporation Act, as amended (The "MBCA"), imposes restrictions on the payment of distributions. MCL 450.1345(3) provides:

A distribution shall not be made if, after giving effect thereto:

> (1) the corporation would not be able to pay its debts as they become due in the usual course of business; or
>
> (2) the corporation's total assets would be less than the sum of its total liabilities plus (unless the articles of incorporation permit otherwise) the amount that would be needed, if the corporation were to be dissolved at the time as of the distribution, to satisfy the preferential rights upon dissolution of shareholders whose preferential rights upon dissolution of shareholders whose preferential rights are superior to those receiving the distribution.

The two basic limitations on the ability to make distributions are often referred to as the "equity insolvency test" (paragraph 1 above) and the "balance sheet test" (paragraph 2 above). The facts do not provide sufficient information to make a definitive determination under the balance sheet test; however, it appears clear that the equity insolvency test has been violated.

The equity insolvency test provides that a corporation may not legally make a distribution if, after giving effect thereto, the corporation would be unable to pay its debts as they become due in the usual course of its business. Bonnie has advised the directors and shareholder, that, given the SCTA fine, the fact that Company is self-insured and facing a lawsuit and has made a cash distribution to its shareholders, Company will not be able to pay its debts as they come due. If the directors had been advised by Al of the call from ODI's president, they would have known prior to voting for the dividend that the $50,000 fine would be coming, and that Company would be facing lawsuits from both ODI and the injured visitors. Applying the equity insolvency test, then the dividend should not have been declared or paid.

Once it is determined that the dividend was improper, one must address the liability of the board members who voted for the dividend to repay it back to the corporation. Section 551 of the MCBA imposes joint and several liability upon directors who vote for, or concur in, the declaration of a distribution to shareholders contrary to the MCBA or to restrictions in a corporation's articles of incorporation. MCL 450.1511(1)(a). However, a director who otherwise faces liability under §551(1), is afforded protection if he or she complied with §541a of the MBCA, which imposes duties of good faith and due care, and demands a reasonable belief that actions taken are in the best interests of the corporation. Thus, Company's directors will have joint and several liability for the dividend unless they can find shelter under §541a of the MCBA.

Under §541a of the MCBA, a director must discharge the duties of his or her position in good faith, with the care of an ordinarily prudent person in like position would exercise under similar circumstances, and in a manner reasonably believed to be in the best interests of the corporation. MCL 450.1541a(1). In discharging his or her duties as a director, a director may rely upon information presented by directors, officers or employees who are reasonably believed to be reliable and competent in the matters presented, by legal counsel, accountants, engineers or other persons as to matters reasonably believed to be within the person's professional or expert competence, or by a committee of the board which is reasonably believed to merit confidence. MCL 450.1541a(2). Reliance, however, is not permitted if the director or officer has knowledge that would make reliance unwarranted. MCL 450.1541a(3).

Under the business judgment rule, absent any evidence of fraud, bad faith or self-dealing (in the usual sense of personal profit or betterment), there is a presumption that the directors of a corporation acted in good faith and in the honest belief that the action taken was in the best interest of the corporation. In each case, a director's claim of good faith reliance will be measured by reasonable belief in the completeness and accuracy of information, the reliability and competency of the individual, or the committee's performance within its designated authority and in a way that the director believes merits confidence. Accordingly, if a director reasonably believes that the information the director has received from a reliable source and is accurate, the director may make his or her decision based upon that information.

In the case of Company, the directors can be segregated based upon their knowledge of the ODI situation or lack thereof. On one hand, Al was fully aware of the ODI situation and the fact that a fine and lawsuits were likely. Al also believed that the ODI related claims would have a significant impact on the Company. Nevertheless, Al intentionally withheld this information from his fellow board members and moved for the declaration of the dividend. On the other hand, Bonnie and Chris believed that Company was solvent, were unaware of any claims related to the ODI incident and reasonably believed when they voted for the dividend that it would not impact the Company or its ability to pay debts as they came due.

Al cannot avail himself of the protection provided by §541a of the MBCA. He intentionally withheld material information from the board, which, if disclosed, would have resulted in a different decision by the board. In withholding the information, Al breached his fiduciary duty to Company. Thus, under §551(1)(a) of the MCBA, Company should be able to recover the dividend from Al.

However, Bonnie and Chris should be protected by §541a of the MBCA as they appear to have acted reasonably and in good faith. They had no reason to know of the ODI related claims. Accordingly, Company should not be able to recover the dividend from Bonnie and Chris.

Finally, Al should not be able to look to Bonnie or Chris for contribution.

Three Student Answers—February 2008

Question 5—Corporations—10 points

The company can sue the board of directors to recover the dividends.

Here Al as a board of director has two duties toward the corporation:

1) Duty of Care: this duty is that Al must act as a prudent reasonable person (director) would act under the similar circumstances. Usually directors are not liable for the corporation, but can be liable if they breach the duty of care to the corporation.

What is the duty of care? Here Al as a director must act prudently meaning he must do appropriate homework and must investigate, check on his acts, make informed decisions, he can't just abandon his duties.

The business judgment rule applies here to the director, if it is not met, the director is held liable. The director has his duty of care and must act what is in his business judgment would confer benefits on the corporation -> he must do his homework, must investigate, make informed decision.

Here the SCTA approved Fiber light to be used for poured concrete. Al erroneously believed that that fiber light will work in all concrete application and he told this to his fellow directors.

Al turned out to be mistaken here. The Fiber light doesn't work in the injection use. He turned out to be wrong. The business judgment rule is met and satisfied, because Al doesn't have to be right as long as he believes and does investigate and does his homework.

Al should not be held liable for breaching duty of care because he acted on a belief that Fiber Light would be OK. Therefore, Al should not be liable, and the corporation can't sue him for breach of loyalty.

For breach of care we need to show causation -> here have causation -> loss and lawsuit.

However Al breached the duty of loyalty. Duty of loyalty in Al upon a reasonable belief must act in the best interest of the corporation. There must be a "conflict of interest" here between the director and the company. Al did breach this duty because he wants to get dividends and then gave dividend to all shareholders even though he knew the company would be ruined. He should be held liable to the corporation, if he or the corporation is hurt or damaged by his (Act) causation.

The company is damaged this way because it might get insolvent to carry out its debts, -> The company will not be able to pay its debts as it comes due.

Therefore Al breached his duty of loyalty to the corporation—he acted against the interest of the corporation and left the corporation in debt.

Therefore, the company can successfully sue only Al for his breach of duty of loyalty but not on his duty of care. Causation element is met, because there is harm to the corporation that was the rest of Al's conduct.

Comment: This is an example of a poorly written, unorganized answer that still got the job done! It reflects the fact that even if you are not the best writer, if you know the law and do legal analysis, you will be rewarded.

Question 5—Corporations—9 points

Concrete Additive Inc., Company is Michigan corporation, so Michigan Law would apply to it.

An officer of a corporation owes a fiduciary duty to the corporation, which mean that he or she has a duty to act on the best interest of the corporation. Also, an officer of a corporation must report truthfully events to other shareholders and to the board of directors that may have a significant effect on the corporation.

Al is Company's President, thus an officer of the corporation, owing the duties mentioned above.

During his negotiations with ODI he made certain assertions and made decisions that apparently affected the Company. The effects on the company were all item (i)-(v) communicated to Al by ODI's president. These items were very serious and should have been mentioned to the Company's shareholders and BOD (board of directors). Especially the fact that SCTA would impose a fine of $50,000 to Company, the impeding lawsuits, and recover of damages of their equipment.

These would be events that would seriously affect Company's financial future. Al had at least two opportunities to report these events, but he did not because he was afraid by doing so the Company would be ruined financially and he personally would not get more funds. The two opportunities were (1) when he first learned of the information and (2) at the meeting of Company's Board. Thus Al failed to act based on his fiduciary duty owed to Company.

Further, Al declared a dividend of $25,000 to be paid to each shareholder of Company. This violated his fiduciary duty further, because declaring a dividend when as president and officer of Company knew of the impending fines and litigation, he acted out of self-serving purpose, i.e. to pay himself and other shareholders out of fear that he might not receive any more funds, thus not serving the best interest of Company.

Also, his violation continues when he approves that payment of a $75,000 total in dividends (3 x $25,000) after the accountant Bonnie advised that there were enough cash reserves to pay the dividend. Ordinarily, dividends would not be paid in a corporation if there is impending litigation, or specific fines imposes + due to paid or other contingencies. Obviously, Al's decisions were wrong.

Violating his fiduciary duty to Company and causing the Company to go bankrupt since Bonnie announced it would not be able to pay its debts after all these events were discovered.

Company should be able to successfully sue to recover the dividend distributed through a derivative lawsuit brought by any of the other shareholders as long as they were shareholders when the events occurred + when the lawsuit is filed. Here it seems this would be the case.

Question 5—Corporations—9 points

This is a Corporations question.

Yes as to Al. Al breached his fiduciary duties to the company. First he has a duty to the company to do what is best for the company. As President he has the actual authority to attempt to increase business by selling their products to new companies, however he also had a duty to report any and all possible negative implication to the company. Here he did not. He was worried about not receiving funding and poor financial stmts. Then when discussing the companies financial situation and approved the dividends disbursement he did not disclose the possible future consequences. Therefore breaching his Duty of Loyalty and Care. He knew or at least was warned of the neg. outcome and had a duty to inform the others. So as to do what was in the best interest of the company.

The others however b/c they were unaware of the possible financial difficulties did not know that the financial information could be reasonable relied upon and would not be held accountable.

B/c this is a corporation each individual can not be personally sued unless there is a breach of Fiduciary Duty. Corporations formed properly are liable for all assets and liabilities of the corporation not individually.

It could be suggested that Al by talking ODI into using a "new" product not designed for that purpose had gone outside of the scope of the business for personal gain, and also breached a Warranty of Merchantability b/c ODI relied on his assurance for a particular purpose.

Therefore, it could be possible to recover the dividends disbursed to Al, but for the remaining they would not be required to return them. Unless they were improperly disbursed due to insolvency b/c there can be no dividends if the company cannot pay it's debts and there are no profits. Here Bonnie as secretary determined that the insurance money would not cover all of the added costs and maintain paying it's regular debts therefore the dividends must be returned.

July 2008—Question 6

Troubled Company Inc. ("Company"), is a Michigan Corporation which is owned by five shareholders: Bob, Charlene, Denise, Ed, and Frank. Bob owns 60% of Company's shares and Charlene, Denise, Ed, and Frank each own 10% of company's shares. All shareholders have the same rights, preferences and obligations, including voting rights (one per share). Company's board of directors consists of three members: Bob, Charlene, and Denise. Bob is president of Company. Company has historically paid generous dividends to its shareholders. Bob has received a combined salary and bonus of $1 million per year for the last several years.

Company, once a highly successful manufacturing enterprise, has struggled recently, suffering substantial losses and diminished cash flow in the last couple of years. Although the near-term outlook for its core business is not bright, its research and development department is in the final stages of developing a new product which is based on propriety technology and which could be of substantial value to Company in the future. To bring the new product to market, however, requires additional testing, various governmental approvals and substantial legal and infrastructure expenditures. The best estimate of Company's management is that it is likely that the product will ultimately be developed and will receive all approvals, but that the process could take as long as 12 to 18 months, possibly longer, and will require substantial additional capital. Management believes that if the new product comes to market, it will be enormously successful and not only return the Company profitability, but substantially increase Company's value.

Company's lender, Subprime R Us Bank ("Bank"), has a long-term lending relationship with Company. Company currently is indebted to Bank under a term loan which is currently scheduled to mature in five years. Company is generally able to make payroll and other payments to its vendors, but as a result of Company's poor recent performance and diminished cash flow, it recently ceased paying out dividends and is unlikely to meet its upcoming quarterly principal and interest installment payment to Bank. This non-payment will constitute a default under Company's loan agreement with Bank and will give Bank the right to accelerate all of Company's indebtedness. Company does not have sufficient cash on hand to repay the indebtedness and will need to either negotiate a refinancing with Bank or obtain new financing, sufficient not only to repay Bank, but to further develop its existing new product. Company's management believes that the current fair market value of Company (if it were sold quickly), is probably slightly greater than the amount owed to Bank and Company's other creditors, not that its fair market value, it and when the new product comes to market, will be substantially greater than its current fair market value.

Company has advised Bank that it may be unable to meet its upcoming payment and had asked Bank to restructure its obligations. Bank adamantly refused to even discuss restructuring, and Bank and its counsel have strongly urged Company's management to sell Company now, in order for Company to obtain sufficient funds to repay Bank and its other creditors. Bank has another customer that would purchase Company for an amount which is at best slightly above the amount owed to its creditors, leaving very little, if any, proceeds available for return to its shareholders and leaving Bob out of a job. Bank has also told Bob that he should reduce his $1 million per year compensation in light of Company's troubles. Charlene and Denise are also concerned that Bob continues to receive substantial compensation at a time when Company's liquidity crunch has resulted in a cessation of dividend payments to its shareholders and an inability to make its bank payments. Charlene is concerned that if the new product cannot be brought to market, Company will fail and there will be even less funds available to pay Bank (and nothing for the shareholders) and that the directors have exposure to Ed, Frank, and Bank, or all of them, for not deciding to sell Company now. Bob wants to continue operating in the current manner.

Bob had invited you (Company counsel) to attend a Company board meeting scheduled for this afternoon to advise the board on its duties in this situation. How do you advise? Explain your answer.

Model Answer to Question 6

A corporation's directors owe fiduciary duties to the corporation and its shareholders. These fiduciary duties include the duties of care and loyalty. The duty of care requires that directors exercise the same care that another reasonable person on the same board would exercise under similar circumstances. The duty of loyalty prohibits self-dealing. This situation appears to involve the duty of care more than the duty of loyalty.

The standard for judicial review as to whether a board exercised due care is the "business judgment rule." This rule presumes that business decisions are made by disinterested and independent directors on an informed basis and with good faith belief that their decision will serve the best interest of the corporation and its shareholders. If the directors are sued with respect to a decision they have made, a court will first examine the decision only to the extent necessary to reach a conclusion as to whether the plaintiff has proven facts that overcome the business judgment rules' presumption that the decision in question was made by disinterested and independent directors on an informed basis and with good faith belief that the decision serves the best interest of the corporation and its shareholders. If the presumption cannot be overcome by the plaintiff, the business judgment rule precludes the court from further examining the merits of the underlying business decision. In other words, where the directors have acted in an appropriate fashion, the business judgment made immunizes them from liability for their decision irrespective of the outcome of the decision (i.e., no "20/20 hindsight").

Generally, the corporation's decision as to what it does with its assets falls within the business judgment rule and the decision as to whether to sell, retain or expend Company's assets would normally not be subject to second-guessing if the directors have met the business judgment rule standard. Strictly speaking, therefore, in the normal course, no shareholder can compel a board to sell Company, even if it later turns out that a sale would have been the wisest decision at the time. As a result, the board should not be concerned about the exposure to outside shareholders if it comports itself in a manner which is sufficient to meet the business judgment rule standards; a thoughtful analysis of the new products' potential and viability by the board (with the help of an independent advisor, if practicable) would create a helpful record.

In this situation, the question also arises as to whether the director's traditional duties to Company's shareholders have somehow shifted to Company's creditors because Company is insolvent.

Generally, directors do not owe a fiduciary duty to a corporation's creditors. In fact, directors could face liability for favoring creditors over shareholders. Courts have typically concluded that debt instruments and similar instruments of credit create contractual obligations on the behalf of the corporation and contractual entitlement to performance by the corporation, as opposed to come equitable interest in the corporation which would provide the creditor some additional rights. In other words, the creditor has negotiated, whether in a loan instrument, purchase agreement or other contract or course of conduct, specific tights and remedies upon non-payment and does not requires any additional protection from the corporation's board.

However, when the corporation becomes insolvent it becomes less clear as to whether the directors' duty is to the corporation's shareholders or creditors. This situation, often referred to as the "zone of insolvency," has resulted in a substantial amount of case law and controversy in the past few years. Generally, courts look at which of the two types of insolvency the corporation is facing—whether it is unable to pay its debts as they become due or whether the actual value of the corporation is less than the amount that it owes to creditors. The two are quite distinct—inability to pay debts as they come due could come from temporary cash shortages or lack o adequate capitalization, whereas, value is the ongoing value of a enterprise. For example, a company may be undercapitalized, but have a strong product, franchise or propriety rights or other asset possible of substantial which creates unrealized value beyond what is owed to the creditors. Such a corporation is technically insolvent under one standard (unable to pay its debts as they become due), but not under the other (its value is greater than amounts owed to the creditors). A court should distinguish between the two situations: if the insolvency arises from an inability to pay debts as they become due, but where there is potential value beyond the amounts owed to the creditors, the directors should continue to be to the shareholders (i.e., to protect shareholder value), but if the value of the enterprise if demonstrably below amounts owed to creditors, depending upon the circumstances.

In this case, Company management believes in good faith that its difficulties are temporary and that there is reasonable (not certain) chance that its new product will come to market, and will substantially increase the value of Company. As a result, counsel can recommend to the board that it continues to owe a fiduciary duty to its shareholders. This duty does not require an immediate sale of Company and could include directing management to take actions necessary to forestall collection action by Bank and otherwise seeking to stall Bank's efforts while Company attempts to obtain additional financing.

Of course, if circumstances later change (i.e., the new product appears unmarketable, Company is unable to raise the necessary funds to operate, etc.), the board may have to revisit its decision. Reports from outside consultants, e.g., financial advisors, can help the board establish a record as to the appropriateness of its process and deliberation.

An interesting variable here is that the board is comprised of only three of Company's shareholder; had it been comprised of all five shareholders, one could have argued that at least on the surface there appears to be some conflict in the shareholders making the decision to factor themselves over creditors; however, even then if their actions as directors fall within the business judgment rule they should be protected, irrespective of whether they are shareholders.

The other issue to be raised at the board meeting is Bob's compensation. Although one could argue that Bob's decision to stay the course unduly benefits him at the expense of Company, its shareholders and creditors, his compensation should not affect the application of the business judgment rule. Unless bank has some contractual right to require Bob to reduce his compensation, Bob's compensation should remain within the board's authority. Charles and Denise could outvote Bob on this issue or require him to accept a reduced salary or to accrue salary until Company can afford to pay it.

Student Answer—July 2008

Question 6—Corporations—8 points

I would advise the board that its duties include a review of all available information to make a sound decision in the best interest of the corporation.

The issue presented is whether or not the Company should sell, reduce Bob's compensation in light of the Company's troubles, or forego the plans to bring the new product to market if it cannot be accomplished timely.

The decisions the company has to make are guided by the duties of the board to act in the best interest of the company. In this situation, the duties include loyalty, prudent decisions based upon sound analytical data reasonable in light of the circumstances. The business judgment rule allows the board not to be personally responsible for mistakes provided they acted in the best interest of the corporation. The board is allowed to rely on the assessment of accountant and other relevant third parties in carrying out their duties. Although the board may find themselves in a difficult situation, as long as the members are not competing with the corporation for their own personal pecuniary gain, or conflictly representing two sides or trying to usurp the corporation then the recommendations of the board can be fully considered.

Here a challenge lies with Bob's interest. His compensation may be overcome because all of the voting members had to agree to it. Otherwise, Charlene's concern regarding their inability to pay may need to be further explored if another company in the same situation would sell or not. To sell or not would best be determined based upon a careful review of the information and analysis available.

Therefore, my advice would be to serve prudently based upon your best judgment considering the circumstances.

February 2009—Question 13

Sandy Smith established a charter fishing company to pursue his lifelong dream of being a fishing guide. Sandy purchased a boat, and then created and filed the articles of incorporation for his new Michigan corporation, "Fish-On Charters, Inc."

In order to have complete control over the company, Sandy decided that Fish-On's board of directors would consist of himself, his wife Betty, his mother-in-law Barbara, and his stepson Bobby. Each had an equal vote on the board, and each was granted one share in the corporation. Sandy believed that since he was the only fisherman of the four, the others would defer to him and that he would basically run the business on his own. Betty, Barbara and Bobby attended the annual board meetings at Sandy and Betty's house, and at the first meeting they approved the purchase of liability insurance for the directors of the company. Sandy was the only corporate employee and the only one to receive a salary. Sandy and Betty also convinced Barbara and Bobby to allow Sandy to have complete control over the financial books, including the checking account, for convenience sake.

The first few years of business were profitable for Fish-On, and Sandy received the total net profits—$75,000.00—as his salary. This salary was approved by the board, as was the decision to not invest any money back into the company. This same pattern was repeated for each of the next four years. Record keeping was not a priority for anyone involved, so only corporate tax returns were filed each year. Additionally, to save a few dollars, Sandy decided after the second year, and without the knowledge of the other directors, to cancel the corporate and director liability insurance. By the fifth year, however, the customer base had dwindled, and the boat was worn, outdated, and leaky. Sandy, however, chose not to make repairs, and unilaterally decided to start pocketing the revenue from every third guided trip, hoping to lift his salary back up to the $75,000.00 range. Sandy also began to put the boat to personal use.

A customer, Jane Doe, sued Fish-On Charters, Inc. and its shareholders/directors for a personal injury she suffered as a result of falling on the wet floor of the dilapidated boat. However, Jane also discovered that, because of decisions made over the years, Fish-On Charters had no insurance and no assets except the old worn-out boat worth a paltry $5,000. Jane, therefore, also seeks to hold Sandy, Betty, Barbara and Bobby liable individually for her damages. All defendants filed motions for summary disposition, arguing that Jane's efforts to hold the four shareholders individually liable should be rejected.

You are the law clerk to the local circuit judge. Prepare a bench memorandum on the issues raised, and discuss their proper resolution.

Model Answer to Question 13

This question raises the issue of piercing the corporate veil and holding the shareholders liable for any judgment. With respect to this issue, the examinee should discuss whether the corporate veil of Fish-On Charters, Inc. could be pierced so as to establish personal liability against the shareholders for any personal injury judgment.

Because the shareholders of Fish-On Charters, Inc. participate in the management of the corporation, and family members control the majority of stock, it is considered a closely held corporation under Michigan law. *Estes v Idea Engineering and Fabricating, Inc*, 250 Mich App 270, 281 (2002).

As a general matter, the law treats a corporation as an entity separate from its shareholders, even where one individual owns all the corporate stock. *Kline v Kline*, 104 Mich App 700, 702 (1981). In some limited circumstances, courts will disregard the corporate form and hold a director personally liable for corporate debt. To do so is called "piercing the corporate veil," and though not a cause of action, it is a doctrine that fastens liability on an individual who uses the corporation as an instrumentality to conduct his own personal business with individual liability arising when a fraud or injustice is committed on third parties dealing with the corporation. *In re RCS Engineered Products Co., Inc*, 102 F3d 223, 226 (CA 6, 1996). Although there is no one rule or test for deciding when it is appropriate to pierce the corporate veil, Michigan courts have generally said that to pierce the corporate veil, the corporate entity must be found to be a mere instrumentality of another individual or entity. *Foodland Distributors v Al-Naimi*, 220 Mich App 453, 456 (1996). The court must also find that the corporate entity was used to commit an injustice, wrong or fraud, and there must have been an unjust injury or loss to the plaintiff. *Rymal v Baergen*, 262 Mich App 274, 293-294 (2004). All facts and circumstances surrounding the corporation, its economic justification and its operation, must be considered to determine if the corporate structure has been abused. *Klager v Robert Meyer Co*, 415 Mich 402, 411-412 (1982).

Because we are dealing with a motion for summary disposition, the question is whether there are sufficient facts to allow the case to go to the jury. MCR 2.116(C)(1). Here, in order for Doe to recover from these individual defendants personally, she must pierce the corporate veil. She clearly will not succeed as to Betty, Barbara and Bobby, but might have enough evidence as to Sandy. Although Betty, Barbara and Bobby participated in a couple of poor decisions (not reinvesting and allowing Sandy complete control over the bank account), and allowed the corporation to be run very informally and without much supervision, none of them utilized the corporate entity or property for their own personal use. Thus, there is no genuine issue of material fact that none of the three used Fish-On Charters as an instrumentality to commit a wrong or fraud. They should not be held personally liable. The better argument is against Sandy.

The facts show that Sandy exercised complete dominion and control over Fish-On Charters, and disregarded corporate formalities to benefit himself. For example, Sandy unilaterally decided to discontinue all liability insurance held by the company, and to pocket corporate revenues for his own use, in order to maintain his salary level despite reduced revenues. Sandy sought out directors who he believed would give him full authority over the company, and convinced them to cede control over the bank account. Sandy also used the boat for his personal use, helping to eliminate the line between personal and corporate property. Fish-On Charters was essentially the "alter ego" of Sandy. Thus, sufficient facts support the argument that Sandy used Fish-On Charters as an instrumentality of his own.

The next question is whether Sandy used the corporate entity to commit a wrong or fraud. The evidence on this point is that Sandy must have used the corporate entity to discontinue the liability insurance. Arguably Sandy misused or disregarded the corporate form by not repairing the boat (which led to Doe's injury) for the sake of his own pecuniary gain, ignoring any real corporate formalities, and purposefully nominating shareholders whom he could control. Also, Doe can argue that she suffered an unjust loss in that she will likely recover a judgment against the company, but cannot recoup the monies because Sandy had operated the company recklessly with the sole purpose of lining his own pocket, rather than reinvesting into the company.

The motion as it pertains to Sandy should be denied. The motion should be granted as to personal liability against Betty, Barbara and Bobby, and denied as to Sandy.

Student Answer—February 2009

Question 13—Corporations—8 points

To: Local Circuit Judge
From: Law Clerk
Regarding: Jane Doe v Fish on Charters, Inc.

This is a close corp. where stock is not publicly traded. In a corporation it is an entity separate from its owners who are the shareholders. This affords the shareholders protection from having their personal assets attacked when the corporation is sued. The issue here is whether Sandy, Betty, Barbara and Bobby can be held personally liable because they are share holders of Fish on Charters, Inc.?

Shareholders of a corporation can be held personally liable when the corporate veil is pierced. This can occur when the corporation is not really acting as a separate entity from the owners. Here this is occurring. Record keeping was not occurring, Sandy was pocketing money from the corp and using the boat for personal use. This appears as if the corporation was just an alter ego of Sandy.

July 2009—Question 12

In 2000, Roger Smith purchased 500 shares of stock in Big Loans Are Us (BLAU), a publicly traded Michigan corporation. The purchase price was $10 a share. As residential real estate loans became more readily available through the 2000's, BLAU revenues dramatically increased, as did its stock value. Indeed, by January 2008, the value had skyrocketed to $50 a share, and there seemed to be no end in sight to the good fortunes of BLAU and its stockholders. Because the number of loan applications more than quadrupled during this same time frame, BLAU increased the number of entry-level employees and management-level employees. By the end of 2007, BLAU had 250 management-level employees.

At the start of 2008, new loan and refinance requests started to decline. Nevertheless, to reward the hard work of its management-level employees, and in recognition of the financial success of recent years, the BLAU board of directors decided to grant each management-level employee 1,000 shares of BLAU stock. Thus, the board approved the issuance of 250,000 new shares, which doubled the number of outstanding shares.

Meanwhile, in the next few months, loan and refinance applications continued to decline. Layoffs ensued. Within five months of the decision and issuance of the shares, BLAU's stock price spiraled downward, reaching $20 by June 1, 2008. Roger Smith was furious, as he had planned on selling his 500 shares at $50 a share and paying for part of his granddaughter's college education. As a retired CPA for a Fortune 500 company, Smith believed that the decision to issue so many new shares diluted the value of all outstanding shares, and was done at a time when the overall economy and BLAU's business was on a clear downturn. He was so upset with the decision that he sent a letter to the board on June 15, 2008, asking that the Board reverse its decision to grant the stock.

Not having heard back from the board, and after dropping off his granddaughter at college, on September 30, 2008, Smith sued the board of directors for breach of the duty of loyalty and good faith, while also naming BLAU as a defendant. Smith sought to recover the lost stock value he suffered, to set aside the stock issuance, and for other damages against the board. The case proceeded through some limited discovery, including Smith's deposition. During the deposition Smith became so frustrated with BLAU, that he sold his stock the next day, November 15, 2008, for $8 a share.

Defendants have now filed a motion to dismiss, which only addresses Smith's ability to bring these claims. It does not address the merits of the claims. You are the clerk to the local circuit court judge. Prepare a memo describing whether Smith can sue in any capacity. Explain your answer.

Model Answer to Question 12

This question raises the ability of Smith to successfully maintain a suit against the individual directors and BLAU. The successful applicant should first acknowledge that Smith may bring this in both an individual and derivative basis, and then proceed to discuss (1) whether the statutory requirements for bringing a derivative suit have been met, and (2) whether there are grounds for Smith to maintain these claims on an individual basis. The proper conclusions are that plaintiff does not meet all the statutory requirements for bringing a derivative claim and that he is alleging an injury that is also an injury to the corporation, and so he cannot maintain this case in his individual capacity. His case should be dismissed.

General Principles: Initially, the applicant should receive points for noting that the motion challenges Smith's standing to sue and who is the real party in interest. *Michigan National Bank v Mudgett*, 178 Mich App 677, 679 (1989). *See also Leite v Dow Chemical Co*, 439 Mich 920 (1992). Credit should also be given if the applicant recognizes that the shareholder and corporation are separate entities, *Belle Isle Grill Corp v Detroit*, 256 Mich App 463, 473-474 (2003).

Derivative Claims: In general, "a suit to enforce corporate rights or to redress or prevent injury to the corporation, whether arising out of contract or tort, must be brought in the name of the corporation and not that of a stockholder, officer or employee." *Belle Isle, supra* at 473-474. The normal practice is for a derivative suit to be brought by one or more shareholders suing in a representative capacity. In particular, a shareholder can maintain a suit for injuries to a corporation by meeting the statutory requirements set forth in MCL 450.1492a, which states:

> A shareholder may not commence or maintain a derivative proceeding unless the shareholder meets all of the following criteria:
> (a) The shareholder was a shareholder of the corporation at the time of the act or omission complained of or became a shareholder through transfer by operation of law from one who was a shareholder at the time.
> (b) The shareholder fairly and adequately represents interests of the corporation in enforcing the right of corporation.
> (c) The shareholder continues to be a shareholder until the time of judgment, unless the failure to continue to be a shareholder is the result of corporate action in which the former shareholder did not acquiesce and the derivative proceeding was commenced prior to the termination of the former shareholder's status as a shareholder.

A shareholder also may not commence a derivative suit unless he has made a written demand upon the corporation to take suitable action and either 90 days have elapsed since the demand, a rejection is received from the corporation, or irreparable injury would result to the corporation by waiting the 90 days. MCL 450.1493a. A plaintiff who does not satisfy all of these criteria cannot maintain a derivative claim on behalf of the company.

Additionally, because the suit is brought for the benefit of the corporation, "[a]ny recovery runs in favor of the corporation," *Futernick v Statler Builders, Inc.*, 365 Mich 378, 386 (1961), quoting *Dean v Kellogg*, 294 Mich 200, 207-208 (1940), and the corporation is usually brought into the case as a defendant. *Id.* Also, generally a shareholder who acquiesces or participates in a decision cannot later challenge it in court.

Here, Smith made a written demand on the corporation, and waited 90 days to file suit, satisfying MCL 450.1493a. He also was a shareholder at the time he filed suit, and there is nothing to suggest that he could not fairly and adequately represent the interest of the corporation in the lawsuit. In fact, given his business experience and training, an argument could be made that he does. Smith also properly sued BLAU as a defendant to make it a party. There is also no suggestion that Smith or any other shareholders had any input in this decision. However, Smith fails to satisfy the requirement that he remains a shareholder through the time of judgment, as he sold his 500 shares of stock during the pendency of the litigation. His divesting of the shares also did not result from corporate activity, but from his own voluntary sale of the publicly traded stock. Thus, he cannot maintain this derivative suit.

Individual Claims: A claim can be brought in the name of the individual if the shareholder "can show a violation of a duty owed directly to the individual that is independent of the corporation." *Belle Isle Grill, supra* at 474. Thus, Smith may be able to pursue these claims in his own right if he can show "a violation of a duty owed directly to him" *Michigan National Bank, supra.* However, this "exception does not arise merely because the alleged violation resulted in injury to both the corporation and the individual; rather, it is limited to cases in which there is a breach of duty that is owed to the individual personally." *Belle Isle Grill, supra* at 474. The allegations in Smith's case do not show that a duty owed separately to Smith was violated.

Although Smith personally lost value in his stock allegedly due to the corporate acts at issue, the corporation also suffered the same injury due to the decreased value of its shares/assets. *Gaff v Federal Deposit Ins Corp*, 814 F2d 311, 315 (CA 6, 1987). This is also the same injury suffered by other shareholders. Hence, Smith cannot maintain this individual claim, the motion should be granted and the case dismissed.

Student Answer—July 2009

Question 12—Corporations—None Available

February 2010—Question 3

Acme Anvil, Inc. ("Acme") is a Michigan corporation. Its primary shareholders are Amber and Greg, who together own 46% of the company's common stock. Nine other family members own the remainder of the common stock, each possessing 6%. This stock distribution has remained the same since the company's formation in 2001. Both Amber and Greg have served on Acme's Board of Directors since 2001. Greg is the President and Chief Executive officer of Acme, while Amber serves as the Vice President and Chief Financial Officer.

In 2007, Acme entered into a 5-year contract with the Ironic Iron Company, agreeing to purchase iron ore from Ironic at prices significantly above the market value. Amber entered into the contract on Acme's behalf after her psychic told her that iron prices would triple over the next few years.

Unhappy with the company's performance over the past two years, Uncle Bob, one of the shareholders, discovered that the reason for Acme's dismal performance was its contract with Ironic Iron. Uncle Bob demanded a meeting of the shareholders in order to elect new directors. In anticipation of a shareholder's meeting, Uncle Bob drafted a confidential agreement, signed by each of the nine minority shareholders, agreeing to vote for cousins Chris and Tammy as corporate directors in lieu of Greg and Amber.

Amber and Greg refused to hold a shareholders' meeting, claiming that the corporate by-laws did not require an annual shareholder meeting. Additionally, Aunt Faye, one of the minority shareholders who had signed Uncle Bob's agreement, indicated that she changed her mind and would not vote to oust Amber and Greg, as she simply could not be "mean" to her niece and nephew.

Discuss whether Uncle Bob can compel a shareholders' meeting, the probability of ousting Greg and Amber, and any possible legal recourse against Amber. Explain your answer.

Model Answer to Question 3

Recourse Against Amber: As officers and directors of Acme Anvil, Amber and Greg are required to discharge their fiduciary duties to the corporation (1) in good faith; (2) with the care that an ordinarily prudent person in a like position would exercise under similar circumstances; and (3) in a manner he or she reasonably believes to be in the best interest of the corporation. MCL 450.1541a(1)(a)-(c). Certainly, Amber would argue that she acted in good faith by entering into the contract because she believed that the price of iron ore would skyrocket, and that a long-term contract fixing the price would benefit the company. In exercising her business judgment, Amber is entitled to rely on information provided by consultants or experts as to matters Amber "reasonably believes are within the person's professional or expert competence." MCL 450.154a(2)(b). In this case, Amber's psychic has no professional or expert competence regarding iron ore speculation, so it is unlikely that her reliance on the psychic's predictions will be deemed reasonable. Pursuant to MCL 450.154a(4), an action can be filed against Amber for breach for fiduciary duty within three years after the cause of action accrued. Here, the cause of action is timely.

However, a suit to redress injury caused to the corporation must generally be brought in the name of the corporation rather than an individual stockholder. *Michigan Nat Bank v Mudgett*, 178 Mich App 677 (1989). Therefore, Uncle Bob will have to file a derivative action on behalf of Acme in order to seek damages for Amber's breach of fiduciary duty. Because Uncle Bob was a shareholder at the time the 2007 contract was signed, continues to be a shareholder, and "fairly and adequately represents the interests of the corporation," he is eligible to file a derivative action. MCL 450.1492a. Pursuant to MCL 450.1493a, Uncle Bob cannot commence a derivate action until he makes a written demand upon Acme Corporation to take action against Amber, and has either waited ninety days from the date the demand was made or received notice that the demand has been rejected by the corporation.

Shareholder's Meeting: Even if the corporation by-laws do not provide for an annual meeting of the shareholders, Uncle Bob can compel a meeting of the shareholders by filing an application with the circuit court of the county in which Acme Anvil's registered office is located, provided that no date for an annual meeting has been designated for 15 months after the organization of the corporation. MCL 450.1402.

The Probability of Ousting Greg and Amber: Because the nine minority stockholders collectively control 54% of the Acme Anvil stock, each minority shareholder will have to vote in favor of ousting Greg and Amber in order to install Tammy and Chris as directors. While Aunt Faye subsequently changed her mind about removing Greg and Amber, she signed a voting agreement expressly agreeing to vote for Tammy and Chris. Pursuant to MCL 450.1461, the voting agreement is "specifically enforceable." Uncle Bob and the rest of the minority shareholders will be able to specifically enforce the voting agreement, and will be able to remove Greg and Amber as directors.

Two Student Answers—February 2010
Question 3—Corporations—8 points

This question is a Michigan Business Corporation question.

Can Bob Compel a Shareholders Meeting?

No. Bob will be unable to hold a valid shareholders meeting. Under MI law, a valid shareholders meeting can be called only by reasonable notice by the board of directors. Further, the bylaws can dictate who can call a shareholders meeting. In this case, the bylaws will control the time and manner as to when and how the shareholders meeting will occur. Further, the bylaws do not require an annual shareholder meeting. Thus, Bob is unable to call a meeting of the shareholders by himself.

Probability of Ousting Amber and Greg

When the bylaws are silent with regards to how many votes each shareholder can have, the MI Business Rules will fill the gaps. Under MI law, we can presume that each shareholder no matter how large the company has one vote. At a valid shareholders meeting the shareholders can vote out on who they want as officer/directors of the company. If there is an urgent need to have the director removed the shareholders could petition the court for an ex parte injunction. In this case, there are 11 shareholders. The majority does not want to remove Amber and Greg, however, this needs to be done in compliance with the rules for a valid shareholder meeting coupled w/a proper shareholder's vote. A secret confidential agreement will not be a proper means to oust Amber and Greg. Thus, the probability of removing them in this way will fail.

Legal Recourse Against Amber

The business judgment rule presumes that a decision made by a director of the corporation is in the best interest of the company. The standard of care owed to the company by the director is one of a reasonable prudent person acting in a like situation. Further, the presumption is that the director did the necessary background work, evaluated the pros and cons of the business decision, and that the decision was based on the sound principles of economic sense. In order to rebut the presumption under the business judgment rule a shareholder will need to show that the decision grossly deviated from that of an ordinary director in the same position. Further, the lawsuit is based on an injury to the corporation. Since corporations are entities treated similar to people, the action in law and any recovery from it will go to the corporation.

In this case, Amber entered into a 5 yr contract w/Acme to purchase iron significantly above market value. Further, her decision was not based on sound principles of market activity or reasonable economic principles. Conversely, her decision was based on her advice from a psychic. Assuming, the company is not speculating in the derivates or commodities market, her decision would be far from those of an ordinary prudent director in her position. Thus, a court likely would find that Amber's decision did violate the principles of the business judgment rule.

Recourse against Amber would be limited to the possibility of having her removed from her position by the shareholders. It is not likely she would be personally liable for damages to the corporation.

Question 3—Corporation—2 points (Bad answer)

This is a business organization question dealing with corporations.

> **Comment:** Two out of 10 points were given just for this! Word to the wise: Write more!

July 2010—Question 8

The W.E.C. Supergenius Company (WECS) is a Michigan corporation located in Bedbug County, Michigan. WECS produces dynamite-based explosives.

Dennis is an employee of the Acme Explosive Company. He also owns three percent of WECS stock. He made a proper written demand in February 2010 for a list of WECS's major accounts. Dennis claimed that the purpose for the request to inspect was to ensure that WECS was maximizing profitability.

Ed, through his attorney, made a proper written demand in April 2010 to inspect a list of the WECS shareholders. Ed, owner of a single share of WECS stock, indicated that the purpose for demanding the list of shareholders was to get himself placed on the board of directors.

WECS refused to comply with either request. WECS claimed that Dennis had no right to review corporate documents because he was employed by WECS's competitor, and that Ed had no right to the documents because he only owned one share of stock, and because he made his demand through an attorney.

Subsequently, both Ed and Dennis filed suit in Bedbug County circuit court, demanding the corporate records sought as well as attorney fees.

Applying Michigan law, discuss Dennis and Ed's likelihood of obtaining the corporate documents, as well as obtaining the other relief sought. Explain your answer.

Model Answer to Question 8

Under MCL 450.1487(2), "[a]ny shareholder of record, in person or by attorney or other agent, shall have the *right*" to inspect "for any proper purpose the corporation's stock ledger, a list of its shareholders, and its other books and records."

Under the statute, a shareholder is required to give the corporation a written demand, "describing with reasonable particularity" the shareholder's purpose, the records sought, and that "the records sought are directly connected with the purpose." A "proper purpose" under the statute is defined as a purpose reasonably related to the person's interest as a shareholder.

The statute also requires that the written demand be delivered to the corporation "at its registered office in this state or at its principal place of business." The statute also specifically contemplates that a demand is permissible through "an attorney or other agent" so long as the demand is accompanied by documentation which authorizes the "agent to act on behalf of the shareholder."

If the corporation does not permit an inspection within 5 business days after a proper demand has been received, or if the corporation imposes unreasonable conditions upon the inspection, the shareholder may apply to the county circuit court in which the principal place of business or registered office of the corporation is located to seek a court order to compel the inspection. MCL 450.1487(3).

The burden of proof depends upon the type of document sought. If the shareholder seeks to inspect the stock ledger or list of shareholders (and has otherwise complied with the written demand requirements), the burden of proof is on the *corporation* to show that the demand was made for an improper purpose or that the records sought are not directly connected with the shareholder's stated purpose.

If the shareholder seeks records *other than* the stock ledger or list of shareholders (and has otherwise complied with the written demand requirements), the burden is on the shareholder to establish that the inspection is for a proper purpose and that the documents are directly connected with the stated purpose.

The court has the discretion to permit the shareholder to inspect corporate books and records "on conditions and with limitations as the court may prescribe and may award other or further relief as the court may consider just and proper." Additionally, if the court orders shareholder inspection of corporate records, then the court "shall also order the corporation to pay the shareholder's . . . costs, including reasonable attorney fees, incurred to obtain the order unless the corporation proves that it failed to permit the inspection in good faith because it had a reasonable basis to doubt the right of the shareholder . . . to inspect the records demanded."

Because WECS refused to comply with Dennis and Ed's written demands within 5 days after the demands were received, both Dennis and Ed can file actions in Bedbug County Circuit Court.

Because the statute allows "any shareholder of record" the right to inspect corporate records, the fact that Ed only owns one share of stock is irrelevant. The statute contains no minimum requirement. Additionally, the fact that he made his demand through an attorney is irrelevant, as the statute specifically contemplates making a demand through an attorney. Ed has demanded a list of shareholders, and has complied with the statute concerning the form and manner of the demand. The burden is on the corporation to show that the demand was made for an improper purpose. Seeking a shareholder list to get elected to the board of directors is a proper purpose pursuant to *George v International Breweries, Inc*, 1 Mich App 129 (1965).

Dennis has demanded a list of WECS's major accounts. Because the document sought is neither a stock ledger nor a list of shareholders, the burden is on Dennis to establish that the inspection is for a proper purpose and that the documents are directly connected with the stated purpose. Assuming that ensuring maximum profitability is a proper shareholder purpose, his claim should fail because a list of the major accounts is not "directly connected" with maximizing profitability. This is particularly true considering that Dennis is employed by WECS's competitor, and the information could be used by Acme to the detriment of WECS. If the demand is not sought in good faith for the protection of the interests of the corporation or the stockholders, a stockholder is not entitled to an order compelling the inspection of corporate documents. *See Slay v Polonia Pub Co*, 249 Mich 609, 616 (1930).

Assuming that Ed's claim prevails, he is entitled to "costs, including reasonable attorney fees." Even if Dennis prevails on his claim, he would not be entitled to attorney's fees if WECS can show that it had a good faith reasonable basis to doubt Dennis's right to inspect the list of major accounts. MCL 450.1487(5).

Student Answer—July 2010

Question 8—Corporation—8 points

Issue can Dennis demand an accounting on the corporation? Can Ed get a list of shareholders from the corporation?

Law: When a shareholder demands that a corporation produce documents concerning profitability is termed obtaining an accounting of the corporation. Shareholders must describe the particular purpose for the accounting and must be made by written demand on the board of directors. The board of directors are in charge of managing the corporation and appointing officers. It is within the board's discretion to make available the accounting. A shareholder may demand the list of other shareholders as long as the demand is in writing and the amount of shares held by the shareholder is unimportant. This list of shareholders can be used to create voting agreements which are valid in MI. If the demand for accounting or for the shareholder list is rejected by the board a shareholder would be allowed to bring a derivative suit in circuit court, but only after the demand has been rejected by the board.

Analysis: Dennis's demand for accounting would likely not be granted b/c the purpose is tenuous at best, it looks like his true intentions is to get Wels accounts list. Ed will likely prevail and the corporation would likely need to give him a list of shareholders because it is within his rights and as long as proper written demand & purpose was giving. Ed should get the document.

Conclusion: Dennis will likely not get the accounting demand b/c it is basically a request for major accounts and Ed will likely get the list of shareholders if proper demand and purpose.

CIVIL PROCEDURE

Questions, Model Answers, and Student Answers

The following section includes prior Michigan Bar Exam questions and model answers for **Civil Procedure (State and Federal Procedure)**. Many of the questions also include actual student answers with the amount of points that were earned to give you a better idea of what the graders expect. The student answers are immediately following the model answer for each question. Please pay close attention to the points received on each question. Although most samples represent "good" answers (i.e., received 8, 9, or 10 points), there are some samples that received 7 points (the minimum "passing" score for an essay), and a few that received very low scores to help you better understand the grading process and what is expected.

February 2001—Question 7

Carlos Estes is an anti-abortion protestor who demonstrated on public property in front of Michigan Bank Source (MBS) for over four months. Carlos began his protest when MBS posted signs in the front of its building advocating certain political candidates that Carlos considered to be "pro-choice." In response to the signs posted by MBS, Carlos would stand on the sidewalk at the customer entrance of MBS's building, display large signs containing various anti-abortion slogans and graphic photographs, and attempt to deliver his anti-abortion message to MBS's customers and employees.

After four months of Carlos' sidewalk demonstrations, MBS had its attorney file an action for tortious interference with contractual and business relations, alleging that Carlos' protesting had caused it to lose business. MBS's attorney also requested preliminary injunctive relief to prevent Carlos from protesting outside MBS's building on the next weekend, because MBS was promoting a weekend of special low-interest mortgage financing. Additionally, MBS requested the trial court to grant it permanent injunctive relief to bring a halt to Carlos' protests outside MBS's building.

At the hearing on MBS's motion for preliminary injunctive relief, MBS's president and other witnesses generally claimed that Carlos' protests had driven away several potential customers from the bank. However, MBS was unable to affix a dollar value to the amount of business that had been lost. The trial court entered the preliminary injunction, which provided, in pertinent part:

> Defendant *** is preliminarily enjoined from in any way intimidating any people, at or in front of plaintiff's building *** or from interfering with any business

conducted at the location or from trespassing on plaintiff's property, and from displaying any signs, messages, or communications at or in front of MBS's premises.

Carlos has appealed, challenging only the issuance of the preliminary injection.

You are a law clerk in the Court of Appeals. Advise your judge on whether it was procedurally proper for the trial court to grant MBS's request for preliminary injunctive relief.

Model Answer to Question 7

The object of a preliminary injunction is to preserve the status quo, so that upon the final hearing the rights of the parties may be determined without injury to either. *Gates v Detroit & M R Co*, 151 Mich 548, 551 (1908). Preliminary injunctions are authorized under MCR 3.310. In determining whether a preliminary injunction should issue, there are four factors to consider: (1) the likelihood that the party seeking the injunction will prevail on the merits; (2) the danger that the party seeking the injunction will suffer irreparable injury if the injunction is not issued; (3) the risk that the party seeking the injunction would be harmed more by the absence of an injunction than the opposing party would be by the granting of the relief; and (4) the harm to the public interest if the injunction issued. *Fruehauf Trailer Corp v Hagelthorn*, 208 Mich App 447, 449 (1995). The party seeking a preliminary injunction has the burden of establishing that the relief should be granted. MCR 3.310(A)(4); *Campau v McGrath*, 185 Mich App 724, 727-728 (1990). The Court of Appeals reviews the trial court's decision for an abuse of discretion. *Fruehauf Trailer Corp, supra* at 449.

MBS failed to establish that it would suffer irreparable harm in the absence of a preliminary injunction. MBS presented testimony suggesting that it had experienced and faced the threat of further loss of potential business as a result of Carlos's activities. However, MBS provided no evidence of any specific earnings that had been or would be lost. In any event, economic injuries do not constitute irreparable harm because they can be remedied by damages at law. *International Union, United Automobile, Aerospace and Agricultural Implement Workers of America, UAW, Local 6000 v Michigan*, 194 Mich App 482, 507 (1992).

MBS also failed to establish the likelihood of its success on the merits of its claim for tortious business interference. In order to prove its claim of tortious interference with a contractual or business relationship, MBS must, in part, establish "the intentional doing of a per se wrongful act or the doing of a lawful act with malice and unjustified in law for the purpose of invading the contractual rights or business relationship of another." *Feldman v Green*, 138 Mich App 360, 378 (1984). It is clear that a boycott, at least to the extent that it is supported by speeches and nonviolent picketing, is lawful activity entitled to constitutional protections. *NAACP v Claiborne Hardware Co*, 458 US 886, 907; 102 S Ct 3409; 73 L Ed 2d 1215 (1982). This is so even if the purpose of the picketing is to induce customers not to patronize the business. *Id.* at 909.

Regarding the risks to the parties in granting the preliminary injunction, Carlos would probably be harmed more by an injunction than MBS would be by the absence of one because of the risk of potential constitutional violations to Carlos. He conducted peaceful and lawful demonstrations. Likewise, there could be potential harm to the public interest if the injunction is issued because of the severe ramifications resulting from a restraint on the exercise of individual constitutional rights. The harm to MBS appears to be purely economic, which can be remedied by damages at law.

In sum, MBS failed to meet its burden of establishing that a preliminary injunction should be issued under MCR 3.310(A). The Court of Appeals should hold that the trial court abused its discretion in granting the preliminary injunction, and, thus, vacate the trial court's preliminary injunctive order.

Grading comment: Although some knowledge of the substantive law of tortious interference with contractual and business relations and first amendment law is assumed, these are not the primary focus of the question. The primary issues are the likelihood of success on the merits and the balancing of the relative harms. Additional points may be given for correct articulation of the substantive law in these areas.

Two Student Answers—February 2001

Question 7—State & Federal Practice (Civil Procedure)—10 points

In considering whether a preliminary injunction should be granted a court must consider: (1) whether $ damages would be enough, (2) plaintiff's likelihood of success on the merits, (3) harm to Plaintiff if injunction is not granted, (4) harm to Defendant if injunction is granted, as well as (5) public consideration. Since it would be impossible to know how much business is driven away or will be driven away in the future, $ damages probably aren't enough. The harm to Plaintiff could be substantial, but to grant the injunction infringes on the Defendant's right to free speech. Because the Defendant is on public property and exercising free speech, the Plaintiff won't likely be successful on the merits at trial and therefore the preliminary injunction should not have been granted.

Question 7—State & Federal Practice (Civil Procedure)/Equity—8 points

First Amendment Rights & Preliminary Injunctive Relief—Generally speaking, the gov't must have a necessary measure that furthers a compelling gov't interest to interfere with the fundamental right of free speech in a public forum. The forum is public here—a sidewalk. The speech that is enjoined is protected. However, the actor seeking relief is not a government (federal or state).

Therefore, we must go to equity principles. An injunction may be granted by the court in situations where the harm is immediate and mere money damages, i.e., remedies at law are inadequate. Here, it is inadequate to merely assert a tort claim against Carlos, b/c it will not/may not stop him from protesting & scaring away customers. Therefore, remedies at law for Bank are inadequate.

Yes; considering Bank is a private, not a public entity, the preliminary injunction is proper. However, immediate harm must be shown. At this Bank is worried about the upcoming week of business—actual harm has not yet been proven. On this basis, the bank needs more evidence of immediate actual harm.

February 2001—Question 9

Paul Parker, president of Paulco, Inc., a Michigan corporation, was planning a business trip to Los Angeles. He was meeting the following Tuesday morning,

November 14, with executives of a company that was interested in purchasing the rights to manufacture his new exercise machine, the Paulco Ab-Pounder. Paul called the Dealtime Travel Agency to arrange a flight to Los Angeles. The Dealtime agent, David Dickerson, told Paul that his flight on Sunny Day Airlines would be leaving at 5:00 p.m. on Monday, and that he should pick up his nonrefundable round-trip ticket at the airport.

When Paul arrived at the airport on Monday afternoon, a Sunny Day Airlines representative told him that Sunny Day had no record of him. Although he eventually made it to Los Angeles the next day, Paul missed his morning meeting. To make matters worse, the company that was interested in Paul's Ab-Pounder decided that it no longer wanted to do business with him. Paul subsequently filed a breach of contract suit against Dealtime.

Dealtime has filed a motion for summary disposition under MCR 2.11(C)(10) on the ground that Paul was mistaken about the date for which he purchased his plane ticket. In support of its motion, Dealtime offers an affidavit from Dealtime's president, Duke Donley. In the affidavit, Donley avers that David Dickerson, the agent that spoke with Paul (who no longer works for Dealtime and cannot be located), told Donley that Paul had requested a ticket for Monday, November 20, not November 13.

In his response, Paul argues that Dealtime's motion should be denied. In support of his position, Paul has submitted to the court his deposition in which he testified that David Dickerson verbally confirmed Paul's reservation for November 13, not November 20. Paul also argues that Dealtime's motion is not properly supported. For the latter reason, Paul also seeks sanctions.

You are the judge assigned to the case of *Paul Parker v Dealtime Travel Agency.* How do you rule on Dealtime's motion for summary disposition and Paul's request for sanctions?

Model Answer to Question 9

A motion filed under MCR 2.116(C)(10) tests the factual support of a plaintiff's claim. *Smith v Globe Life Ins Co,* 460 Mich 446 (1999). In reviewing such a motion, the court considers the pleadings, affidavits and other documentary evidence filed in the action or submitted by the parties in the light most favorable to the nonmoving party. The motion is properly granted if the evidence presented shows that there is no genuine issue of material fact and the moving party is entitled to judgment as a matter of law. *Harts v Farmers Ins Exchange,* 461 Mich 1, 5 (1999).

There are two reasons why Dealtime's motion for summary disposition should be denied. First, Paul correctly argues that Donley's affidavit is improper. MCR 2.119(B)(1) provides that an affidavit filed in support of a motion must "(a) be made on personal knowledge; (b) state with particularity facts admissible as evidence establishing or denying the grounds stated in the motion; and (c) show affirmatively that the affiant, if sworn as a witness, can testify competently to the facts stated in the affidavit." Only documents whose content or substance is admissible in evidence may be considered in determining whether to grant or deny a motion for summary disposition. MCR 2.11(G)(6). *Maiden v Rozwood,* 461 Mich 109, 121-123 (1999). Donley's affidavit cannot be considered in support of Dealtime's motion because its content would not be admissible in evidence. Although David Dickerson would be competent to testify about the conversation he had with Paul, *see* MRE 801(D)(2) (statement made by a party-opponent), Dickerson's statement to Donley is hearsay. Accordingly, because Dealtime has offered no evidence to support its claim that Paul requested a ticket for November 20 rather than November 13, Dealtime's motion for summary disposition should be denied.

Second, even if Dealtime had offered an affidavit from Dickerson, Dealtime's motion should still be denied. Because Paul offered his own deposition testimony supporting his claim that Dickerson confirmed Paul's reservation for November 13, not November 20, there is a genuine issue of material fact upon which reasonable minds could differ. Therefore, summary disposition would be inappropriate in any event. *See Vicencio v Ramirez, MD, PC*, 211 Mich App 501, 508-09 (1995).

Concerning Paul's request for sanctions, MCR 2.114(D), which applies to motions, provides that the signature of any attorney or party constitutes a certification that "(1) he or she has read the document; (2) to the best of his or her knowledge, information, and belief formed after reasonable inquiry, the document is well grounded in fact and warranted by existing law or a good-faith argument for the extension, modification, or reversal of existing law; and (3) the document is not interposed for any improper purpose, such as to harass or to cause unnecessary delay or needless increase in the cost of litigation." A trial court "shall impose" an appropriate sanction for a violation of this rule. MCR 2.114(E).

Here, Dealtime's motion clearly was not supported by a proper affidavit. However, there is nothing to indicate that the motion was filed for any improper purpose. Therefore, Paul's request for sanctions probably should be denied.

Student Answer—February 2001

Question 9—Civil Procedure—7 points

A motion for summary disposition is a motion that dismisses a case because there is no material issue of fact in controversy. That doesn't seem to be the case in the present situation. Dealtime offers an affidavit from Dealtime's president which states that the agent who spoke with Paul told him Paul requested a ticket for Monday, November 20, not November 13. However, Paul has rebutted that statement by offering a court deposition that was under oath that David Dickerson verbally confirmed Paul's reservation for November 13. This would be a conflicting issue, thus the motion for summary disposition should not be given. Paul's request for sanctions also should not be given because even though the court may give sanction within its discretion, sanctions usually are given due to bad faith of a party. There don't seem to be any facts that suggest this is the case. By Paul arguing Dealtime motion not being properly supported and requesting sanctions shouldn't be given because if Dealtime reasonably believed there was no material issue of fact, which seems to be the case due to the president not being able to reach the Dealtime agent, thus having to give an affidavit stating what the agent told him. Sanctions should not be given because the motion was brought without bad faith and not brought to delay or hinder the proceedings. Further the deposition comes in because it is not hearsay; it was a prior consistent statement in a legal proceeding. Also, the affidavit comes in because Paul cannot be located.

July 2001—Question 14

Pierre Tottery, age 56, has been employed at the Acme Anvil Company for twenty-seven years as an anvil engineer. Pierre applied and was interviewed for an executive position with the company. After several interviews of Pierre and other applicants, the job was awarded to Wesley Whipple, a 30-year-old man who had been with the company two years. Pierre, convinced that he had been denied the promotion on the basis of his age, filed an age discrimination suit against the Acme Anvil Company.

Acme filed a motion for summary disposition under MCR 2.116(C)(10), claiming that there was no evidence that Pierre's age was a factor in selecting Wesley for the position.

In his answer, Pierre argues that the motion should be denied. In support of that position, Pierre submitted two affidavits. The first affidavit was from Agnes Busybody, who works in the accounting department of Acme. In the affidavit, Agnes avers that she was told by an executive secretary (who has since retired and moved to Florida) that Pierre was deemed "too old" to implement the innovative changes that the company envisioned. The second affidavit was from Miles McCarty, Wesley's neighbor. Miles avers that Wesley Whipple is a lazy slob who talks to himself and doesn't cut his grass.

In response, Acme contends that the proffered evidence is insufficient to create a genuine issue of material fact under the Michigan Court Rules.

You are the law clerk assigned to the case of *Tottery v Acme Anvil Company*. What advice will you give your judge on how she should rule on Acme's motion for summary disposition?

Model Answer to Question 14

A motion under MCR 2.116(C)(10) tests the factual sufficiency of the complaint. In evaluating a motion for summary disposition brought under this subsection, a trial court considers affidavits, pleadings, depositions, admissions, and other evidence submitted by the parties in the light most favorable to the party opposing the motion. Where the proffered evidence fails to establish a genuine issue regarding any material fact, the party making the motion is entitled to judgment as a matter of law. MCR 2.116(C)(10), (g)(4). *Quinto v Cross & Peters Co*, 451 Mich 358 (1996).

The reviewing court should evaluate a motion for summary disposition under MCR 2.116(c)(10) by considering the substantively admissible evidence actually proffered in opposition to the motion. MCR 2.116(C)(6); *Maiden v Rozwood*, 461 Mich 109, 121-123 (1999).

The Acme Anvil Company is entitled to summary disposition as a matter of law. The first affidavit by Agnes is based on a statement given to her by a third party. As hearsay, it is not substantively admissible evidence and may not be used to establish a genuine issue of material fact.

The second affidavit by Miles McCarty should not be considered in evaluating the summary disposition motion because it is not relevant to any issue in the case. Under MRE 401, relevant evidence is that having any tendency to make the existence of any consequential fact more or less probable than it would be without the evidence. Because the evidence is irrelevant, it is inadmissible. MRE 402.

The affidavits submitted in response to the motion should not be considered. Because Tottery has failed to create a genuine issue of material fact, the Acme Anvil Company should prevail in its motions for summary disposition.

Student Answer—July 2001

Question 14—Civil Procedure—10 points

The motion for summary disposition should be granted when there is no genuine issue of material fact viewing the evidence most favorable to the moving party.

To decide if there is an issue, we must examine the 2 affidavits submitted.

First - the affidavit of Agnes. Is the information relevant? Yes, the statement Pierre was too old is directly relevant and probative to the age discrimination case. However, the statement by Agnes that she was told by an executive secretary is hearsay, an out of court statement made by someone other than the declarant while testifying at trial to prove the truth of the matter asserted. The question is whether the statement falls into any exception to the hearsay rules. The only exceptions that may apply here are the state of mind exception or the declaration against interest exception.

The state of mind exception may apply to the state of mind of the Acme Company at the time the statement was made that he was too old to implement the changes.

To have the declaration against interest apply, the person making the statement must be unavailable. The executive secretary has retired and moved to Florida and she is unavailable. The declaration against interest would be based on the interest of the company. Another problem of the first affidavit is that it is double hearsay. We would have to have exceptions to both parts of the hearsay rules which we do not have.

Both state of mind and declaration of interest arguments are very weak and Agnes's affidavit would not be an exception to the hearsay rule.

The second affidavit from Whipples (W) neighbor that he does not cut his lawn is not relevant. It does not provide any tendency to any fact that W was not qualified for the promotion he received.

The judge should grant the motion for summary disposition since the information in the affidavit #1 is hearsay not subject to any exception, #2 evidence is not relevant. There is no genuine issue of material fact to be resolved based on the information presented.

February 2002—Question 14

Assume that you are an Assistant City Attorney for the City of Menominee, Michigan. On February 15, 2002, City Attorney Liz Tomdi forwarded you a case for handling, which Assistant City Attorney Judd Kibby had previously handled.

On Tuesday, February 1, 2002, Perdoo Corporation, a highway construction firm registered in the state, filed a complaint in Menominee Circuit Court and served process on the City, seeking monetary damages in the amount of $20,000 against the City for an alleged breach of contract. The contract includes the following clause:

> The City and Perdoo Corporation have entered into an agreement with BABS Dispute Services, Inc., to arbitrate and resolve any and all disputes between the City and Perdoo Corporation pertaining to this Contract.

Immediately upon your initial review of the file, you notice that Perdoo Corporation served process on Mary, the City's cleaning lady. In addition, a copy of the complaint did not accompany the summons.

Before this matter was transferred to you, Assistant City Attorney Kibby did not file a responsive pleading. However, he did make a motion for summary disposition solely based on insufficient service of process. That motion was denied.

Today is February 16, 2002. Discuss any potential dispositive issues that could have been raised by Kibby, whether you may still raise them, and, if so, under what limitations.

Model Answer to Question 14

The fact pattern presents several bases for motion for summary disposition that could theoretically be made by the City. MCR 2.116. (Evaluators should note that applicants may refer to the motion as a motion for summary judgment, the term used by the Federal Rule of Civil Procedure 56.) However, the question also includes timing issues that may limit the success of those potential motions.

The first potential ground for summary disposition is a lack of subject matter jurisdiction, MCR 2.116(C)(1), based on the fact that Perdoo has made a claim against the City for $20,000. The circuit court has exclusive subject matter jurisdiction over actions where the amount in controversy is $25,000 or more. Accordingly, the circuit court does not have subject matter jurisdiction. A motion for summary disposition based on subject matter jurisdiction "may be raised at any time." MCR 2.116(D)(23). Therefore, neither the time line nor the fact that Kibby previously filed a summary disposition motion serves as a bar to the availability of this motion by the City.

The second ground for the granting of a motion for summary disposition pertains to an affirmative defense, the agreement to arbitrate, MCR 2.116(C)(7). The contractual clause included in the fact pattern is clearly an arbitration clause. Accordingly, a motion for summary disposition on the basis of the arbitration agreement would be properly granted if timely made. *Rembert v Ryan's Family Steak Houses, Inc*, 235 Mich App 118 (1999). While a motion for summary disposition based on a plaintiff's claim being barred because of an affirmative defense, like an agreement to arbitrate, may be raised in a motion prior to the responsive pleading, if it is not, it must be raised in the responsive pleading. MCR 2.116(D)(2). In this case, a responsive pleading is due within 21 days after service of the pleading. MCR 2.108(A)(1). Accordingly, the City has five days to file a responsive pleading including the affirmative defense based on the agreement to arbitrate.

Third, from the fact pattern, it appears that there are clearly problems with both the process and the service of process. The service of process on Mary, the City's cleaning lady, is insufficient under the court rule governing the appropriate persons that can receive process for a governmental entity. MCR 2.105(G). As to the sufficiency of the process itself, a plaintiff must serve a summons and a copy of the complaint. MCR 2.105(G). Assistant City Attorney Kibby filed a motion based on the sufficiency of the service of process, but not the sufficiency of the process itself. However, as to a motion for summary disposition based on insufficiency of process, such a claim has to be raised in the City's first motion or in the responsive pleading, whichever is filed first, or else it is waived. MCR 2.116(D)(1). Since Kibby filed a motion for summary disposition as to the insufficiency of the service of process, without claiming insufficiency of the process, the City has waived the ability to move for dismissal on that basis.

Student Answer—February 2002

Question 14—Civil Procedure—10 points

Michigan Circuit Courts are courts of general jurisdiction & they are allowed to take most cases. They have jurisdiction over all subject matter with 2 exceptions: if the claim is for $25,000 or less it must be filed in the district court & the other exception applies to federal law. In this case Perdoo is seeking $20,000 in damages, so the company should have filed their claim in the district court. Dismiss for lack of subject matter jurisdiction.

Additionally Michigan is a fact pleading state. This should be done with specificity so the person against whom the claim is brought can reasonably anticipate why they are being hauled into court. Perdoo served the summons but not the complaint. Without a copy of the complaint the city has no notice of what to plead in a responsive pleading. Also a summary disposition motion would be filed because Perdoo did not arbitrate as they had agreed with the city.

In Michigan there is a 21 day period for the respondent to file a responsive pleading or an answer. The city's cleaning lady was served on February 1 & it was only February 16. So there are 6 days left to file. Must file before the 21 days expires unless waive service of process then 28 days to respond. When responding the response should be pled with specificity. Additionally it will be important to get proper service of process.

July 2002—Question 15

You are an associate of a law firm that represents Lane Harring, an avid fan of the Arenac Appleseeds, a minor league baseball team. Lane was injured when Sam Salami, the third baseman for the visiting Boston Biscuits, angrily threw his baseball glove at Lane while he sat in the bleachers, causing a loss of hearing in Lane's left ear. A partner at your law firm has filed a complaint on behalf of Lane alleging battery and negligent infliction of emotional distress against both the Boston Biscuits and Salami in Arenac Circuit Court. Defense attorney Daniel Moore is representing both Salami and the Boston Biscuits and has filed an answer to the complaint denying liability. The partner has now assigned you to manage the file.

The trial judge, on his own initiative, has referred the matter to case evaluation. Neither your firm nor Moore have agreed to any form of case evaluation, nor did either file a motion requesting that the trial judge consider case evaluation. However, your partner thinks that Lane's potential for success is greater with a trial on the negligent infliction of emotional distress issue, but that case evaluation might be a better avenue for the battery claim. Accordingly, your partner suggests the following alternative strategies: (1) object to case evaluation altogether by questioning the trial judge's authority to order case evaluation without the parties' consent or request, or (2) allow the case evaluation to proceed on both claims, but plan to only accept the decision as to the battery claim and take the emotional distress claim to trial.

Finally, your partner has asked you to outline for the client the case evaluation process should the evaluation panel issue a unanimous evaluation.

Discuss the likelihood of prevailing under these strategies and provide the client outline requested.

Model Answer to Question 15

This case presents an opportunity for a bar candidate to express a basic understanding of our court rules on case evaluation. In 2000, the Michigan Supreme Court adopted new rules regarding case evaluation that revolutionized alternative dispute resolution in Michigan's trial courts.

Strategy 1: A trial judge may order case evaluation on his own initiative. MCR 2.403(b)(1) provides:

> The judge to whom an action is assigned or the chief judge may select it for case evaluation by written order no earlier than 91 days after the filing of the answer
>
> (a) on written stipulation by the parties,
> (b) on written motion by a party, or
> (c) on the judge's own initiative.

Accordingly, the fact that neither party requested case evaluation is irrelevant and not a basis for validly objecting to the trial judge's action.

Second, case evaluation of tort cases filed in circuit court is *mandatory*. MCR 2.403(a)(2). An outstanding candidate may note that "the court may except an action from case evaluation on motion for good cause shown if it finds that case evaluation of that action would be inappropriate." MCR 2.403(a)(2). However, strategy preferences would not amount to "good cause."

Accordingly, it is unlikely that Lane can prevail via objecting to the trial judge's authority to order case evaluation on his initiative.

Strategy 2: A party must accept or reject evaluation in its entirety. MCR 2.403(L)(1). Accepting a case evaluation means accepting all claims in the action. *Cam Constr v Lake Edgewood Condo Ass'n*, 465 Mich 549 (2002). Accordingly, strategy 2 also is not a good strategy for Lane.

Case Evaluation Process for Client: If all the parties accept the panel's evaluation, judgment is entered in accordance with the evaluation. MCR 2.403(m). If the evaluation is rejected, the Action proceeds to trial in the normal fashion. MCR 2.403(n)(1). However, depending on the outcome of the trial, the rejecting party may be liable for costs in the event of a unanimous decision of the evaluation panel. MCR 2.403(O)(1) provides:

> If a party has rejected an evaluation and the action proceeds to verdict, that party must pay the opposing party's actual costs unless the verdict is more favorable to the rejecting party than the case evaluation. However, if the opposing party has also rejected the evaluation, a party is entitled to costs only if the verdict is more favorable to that party than the case evaluation.

The rules also define what is more favorable:

> For the purposes of subrule (O)(1), a verdict must be adjusted by adding to it assessable costs and interest on the amount of the verdict from the filing of the

complaint to the date of the case evaluation, and, if applicable, by making the adjustment of future damages as provided by MCL 600.6306. After this adjustment, the verdict is considered more favorable to a defendant if it is more than 10 percent below the evaluation, and is considered more favorable to the plaintiff if it is more than 10 percent above the evaluation. If the evaluation was zero, a verdict finding that a defendant is not liable to the plaintiff shall be deemed more favorable to the defendant.

MCR 2.403(O)(3).

Accordingly, a candidate should recognize that when a case evaluation panel issues a unanimous evaluation, he must advise his client of the consequences surrounding a decision regarding whether to accept the evaluation or not.

Two Student Answers—July 2002

Question 15—Civil Procedure—9 points

(1) Object to case evaluation altogether

The trial court can (and often does) order case evaluation (mediation) in civil suits. This is proper & to question the judge would not likely get a desirable result: the judge would continue the order & possibly hold the firm/attorney in contempt.

(2) Allow the case evaluation & plan to only accept a decision as to the battery claim

Probably the better choice. The parties are not bound by mediators decision. It only gives an idea of what a case may be worth, if anything. Settlement is encouraged by the courts, but if parties cannot agree, even after case evaluation, then they may still proceed to court. (Mediators are usually 3 attorneys familiar with certain types of cases that can evaluate the issues & attempt to get parties to reach an agreement). A consequence of not following the recommended mediation is that if plaintiff loses or a jury comes back with an award less than what the case was evaluated at, they are liable to the prevailing party for attorney fees and costs.

The best approach would be to go in with an open mind on all issues to see if a settlement can be reached. Ultimately, the best interest of the client should prevail—once the client is informed of all possibilities, the client should decided how he wants to proceed.

Question 15—Civil Procedure—9 points

Alternate Dispute Resolution: Courts regularly employ case evaluation (a form of alternate dispute resolution) to reduce litigation expenses and for purposes of judicial economy. Even though parties may not move to seek case evaluation, a judge may on his own motion suggest it. A judge may allow a "summary trial," an abbreviated trial, so that parties may test their evidence with a jury that will be non-binding.

In Michigan, a case evaluation panel of several attorneys is utilized to evaluate each lawsuit and test its strength and each side's probability of success on the merits. An attorney may accept or refuse the case evaluation but if an attorney refuses to settle or proceeds to trial after the case evaluation committee finds he does not have a good case, he is more limited in the damages he can seek if he loses.

Good Faith: Here, attorneys for Plaintiff are required to deal in good faith with the court. By "planning" to object to the case evaluation, they are trying to act in other than good faith with the court. The motion is not proper. They could only validly do this in good faith, not the case here.

Accept Some, Reject Some: The court may on its own motion require the attorneys to submit to case evaluation. If the case evaluation committee is unanimous, the Plaintiff's attorney should accept it and settle or face limitation of damages if they proceed to trial. If just one cause of action is approved for trial, they should follow the recommendation of the case evaluation committee.

Conclusion: Plaintiff's attorneys will show bad faith if they in bad faith object to case evaluation. And if the committee is unanimous, they should settle with Defendant or proceed to trial on one or both of the causes of action.

February 2003—Question 8

You are an associate attorney at a large law firm that is representing Pete Pollard, a 20-year-old college student at Western Michigan University in Kalamazoo, Michigan (Kalamazoo County). During spring break, Pollard went skiing at the High Danger Ski Resort in Boyne City, Michigan (Charlevoix County). While skiing, Pollard was injured when he fell into a barbed-wire fence located in the middle of the ski slope. Pollard resides throughout the entire calendar year in Kalamazoo, traveling to his parents' home in Lapeer County only for holidays. The High Danger Ski Resort is owned and operated by Dangerous Retreats, Inc., a Michigan corporation with its registered office in Traverse City, Michigan (Grand Traverse County) and its principal headquarters in Green Bay, Wisconsin. In addition to the High Danger Ski Resort, Dangerous Retreats, Inc. also owns and operates the Danger Ski Resort in Kalkaska, Michigan (Kalkaska County) and the Extremely High Danger Ski Resort in Petoskey, Michigan (Emmet County). Pollard wishes to file a tort action under state law against Dangerous Retreats, Inc. for his injuries at the High Danger Ski Resort, alleging $100,000 in damages.

A senior partner at your law firm has discussed the case with you and has asked you to start "working up the complaint." As a matter of strategy, he indicates that he would like the case filed in state court, not federal court, if possible.

Discuss (1) what type of Michigan state trial court, if any, has subject matter jurisdiction over the lawsuit and (2) what county or counties have proper venue to hear the case if subject matter jurisdiction does exist. In addition, if you determine that the case can be brought in a Michigan state court, discuss whether an attempt by the defendant to remove the case to federal court will be successful.

Model Answer to Question 8

State Court Subject Matter Jurisdiction: In the aggregate, the Michigan court system is one of general jurisdiction. This means that absent a specific federal law preserving exclusive federal jurisdiction over a claim, any action can be brought in *some* Michigan court. Because general state tort law is not reserved exclusively for federal courts by federal jurisdiction law, there is a Michigan state trial court in which to file Pollard's tort action. The relevant inquiry is which one.

The Michigan court system offers several types of trial courts: district, circuit court, probate court and the court of claims. Michigan *circuit courts* have general original jurisdiction in cases involving more than $25,000. MCL 600.8301. As a tort matter, the probate court does not have subject matter jurisdiction. Because the amount involved exceeds $25,000, the district court (or any municipal court) does not have subject matter jurisdiction. Further, because defendant Dangerous Retreats, Inc. is a private entity, not the state, the court of claims does not have subject matter jurisdiction.

For these reasons, a Michigan state circuit court is the state court with subject matter jurisdiction over plaintiff's tort action.

Venue: The general Michigan venue statute provides that an action may be brought in the "county in which a defendant resides, has a place of business, or conducts business, or in which the registered office of a defendant corporation is located." MCL 600.1621(a). If defendant does not meet the criteria of 1621(a), the proper county is one in which plaintiff meets the same criteria of (a). MCL 600.1621(b). Accordingly, if the general venue statute was applicable, the following circuit courts would be proper venues to hear Pollard's lawsuit because of defendant's business activities in those counties: Charlevoix County, Grand Traverse County, Kalkaska County and Emmet County.

However, this general venue statute is subject to several exceptions, one of which pertains to tort actions. MCL 600.1629 provides in pertinent part that in an action based in tort, proper venue is:

> (a) The county **in which the original injury occurred *and* in which either** of the following applies is a county in which to file and try the action:
>
> (i) The defendant resides, has a place of business, or conducts business in that county.
>
> (ii) The corporate registered office of a defendant is located in that county.
>
> (b) If a county does not satisfy the criteria under subdivision (a), the county in which the original injury occurred and in which either of the following applies is a county in which to file and try the action:
>
> (i) The plaintiff resides, has a place of business, or conducts business in that county.
>
> (ii) The corporate registered office of a plaintiff is located in that county.
>
> (c) If a county does not satisfy the criteria under subdivision (a) or (b), a county in which both of the following apply is a county in which to file and try the action:
>
> (i) The plaintiff resides, has a place of business, or conducts business in that county, or has its corporate registered office located in that county.
>
> (ii) The defendant resides, has a place of business, or conducts business in that county, or has its corporate registered office located in that county.

Under the facts of the hypothetical, the injury at issue occurred in Charlevoix County. Further, defendant "has a place of business," and/or "conducts business" in Charlevoix County because of the location of the High Danger Ski Resort (Charlevoix County). Under the venue statutes, one meets the "conducting business" element where there is "some real presence such as might be shown by systematic or continuous business dealings inside the county." *Coleman v Gurwin*, 443 Michigan 59, 62

(1993). Accordingly, pursuant to MCL 600.1629, the proper venue for Pollard's tort action is the Charlevoix County Circuit Court.

Removal to Federal Court: A case can only be removed from a state court to a federal court if the case could have been originally filed in a federal court. 28 USC 1441(a). Under these facts, subject matter jurisdiction does not lie with a federal court so the case could not have been filed in federal court. Accordingly, any effort by defendant to remove the case will be unsuccessful.

The primary theories of federal subject matter jurisdiction are diversity jurisdiction and federal question jurisdiction. Diversity jurisdiction and federal question jurisdiction exists where a plaintiff and defendant are domiciled in two different states and the amount at issue is greater than $75,000. Because plaintiff Pollard and defendant Dangerous Retreats, Inc. are from the same state (Michigan), and although the amount in controversy exceeds $75,000, the requirements for federal diversity jurisdiction are not met. The fact that defendant is also headquartered in Green Bay, Wisconsin is insufficient to establish diversity. For diversity jurisdiction purposes, a corporation is considered a citizen both of the state in which it is incorporated (Michigan) and of the state in which it has its principal place of business (Wisconsin). Because Pollard is a resident of Michigan, no diversity is present.

The fact that Dangerous Retreats, Inc. is a citizen of Michigan provides an additional rationale prohibiting diversity removal. Where the basis of removal is diversity and one of the defendants is a citizen of the state in which the state action was brought, the action is not removable.

Further, Pollard's cause of action lies in tort, which is clearly governed by state law (as stated in the hypothetical). Accordingly, federal question jurisdiction is not appropriate.

Student Answer—February 2003

Question 8—Civil Procedure—10 points

The type of state court that has subject matter jurisdiction is the Circuit Court, which hears cases and controversies in excess of $25,000. The defendant has alleged damages in the amount of $100,000.

The counties that would have proper venue to hear the case would include Charlevoix County because that is where the accident occurred. The plaintiff could also file in either Kalkaska or Emmet counties based upon the principal place of business of the defendant corporation, Dangerous Retreats, Inc. Finally the plaintiff could file in Grand Traverse County because that's the location of the Dangerous Retreats registered office.

Removal to Federal Court because there is neither complete diversity of parties, nor a Federal question involved, an attempt by the defendant to remove the case to federal court will not be successful.

> **Comment:** This is an example of the graders being very generous. This answer is brief but nails all the issues. Normally this type of response would earn a 7 or 8 because there is not a great deal of analysis.

July 2003—Question 3

Dweezil Dappa, a resident of Toledo, Ohio, was traveling with his family to their summer cottage in Sandusky, Ohio for the Independence Day weekend. Dappa stopped at a store in Toledo just outside the Michigan border and purchased a package of That's Going to Leave a Mark Fireworks. At the insistence of his eight-year-old son, Dappa performed a "sneak preview" fireworks display in the store parking lot. The display proceeded without incident until Dappa lit a Master Blaster 2000, which took off like a rocket and landed in Patrick Pluggs' backyard in Temperance, Michigan, where Pluggs was relaxing pool side. The resulting explosion and fire rendered Pluggs permanently hairless from the armpits up.

Pluggs has filed a personal injury action against Dappa in the federal district court in the Eastern District of Michigan. Dappa, who was served process while he was on a business trip in Wisconsin, moves for summary judgment on the ground that the court lacks personal jurisdiction over him. Pluggs opposes summary judgment and presents evidence that Dappa owns Tattoos For You, Inc., a Toledo tattoo parlor that advertises extensively in Michigan, performs 60% of its tattoos on teenagers from Temperance, and obtains all of its needles from a Detroit supplier.

You are a law clerk for the federal district court judge hearing Pluggs' case. Advise your judge whether the court has personal jurisdiction over Dappa.

Model Answer to Question 3

The court has personal jurisdiction over Dappa in Pluggs' personal injury action.

Pursuant to Federal Rule of Procedure 4(k)(1), each federal court shall analyze personal jurisdiction as if it were a court of the state in which it is located. Accordingly, whether the court has personal jurisdiction over Dappa is dependent upon Michigan's long arm statutes.

Additionally, a personal jurisdiction analysis is a two-fold inquiry: (1) do the defendant's acts fall within the applicable long arm statute, and (2) does the exercise of jurisdiction over the defendant comport with due process? *Starbrite Distributing, Inc v Excelda Mfg Co*, 454 Mich 302 (1997).

There are generally two types of long arm statutes: unlimited statutes, which give courts the maximum jurisdiction permissible under the Due Process Clause, and limited long arm statutes, which specify in detail when courts may exercise jurisdiction.

Michigan's general long arm statutes, MCL 600.701, 600.722, 600.721, and 600.731, permit a court to hear any action against a defendant (1) who is present in Michigan at the time process is served, (2) who is domiciled in Michigan at the time process is served, (3) who consents to the exercise of personal jurisdiction, (4) which is a corporation, partnership, or association that is incorporated or formed under Michigan law, or (5) which is a corporation, partnership, or association that carries on a "continuous and systematic part of its general business" within Michigan.

Michigan's limited long arm statutes, MCL 600.705, 600.715, 600.725, and 600.735, permit a court to hear an action against a defendant arising out of (1) the transaction of any business within Michigan; (2) the doing or causing an act to be done, or consequences to occur, in Michigan resulting in an action for tort; (3) the ownership, use, or possession of real or tangible personal property situated within Michigan; (4) a contract to insure a person, property, or risk located within Michigan; (5) a contract for services to be rendered or for materials to be furnished in Michigan by the defendant; (6) the defendant's service as an officer of a corporation incorporated under the laws of Michigan or having its principal place of business within Michigan; or (7) the maintenance of a domicile in Michigan while subject to a marital or family relationship that is the basis of a claim for divorce, alimony, separate maintenance, property settlement, child support, or child custody.

Dappa is not subject to the general jurisdiction of the court because he was served in Wisconsin, is domiciled in Ohio, and did not consent. Although Dappa owns a business that arguably carries on a "continuous and systematic part of its general business" in Michigan by actively soliciting Michigan customers and obtaining supplies from a Michigan supplier, Tattoo You, Inc., is not the defendant in Pluggs' lawsuit. Thus, the provisions of the general jurisdiction statute that pertain to corporations are inapplicable.

However, Dappa is subject to the limited jurisdiction of the court under MCL 600.705(2), which provides that a court may render a judgment arising out of "[t]he doing or causing an act to be done, or consequences to occur, in the state resulting in an action for tort." Although Dappa's tortious act occurred in Ohio, the conduct caused consequences to occur in Michigan, and the court has personal jurisdiction over Dappa and may render judgment against him in Pluggs's tort action.

It may also be noted that MCL 600.705(1), regarding "the transaction of any business within the state," is inapplicable because Pluggs' tort action does not arise out of such transaction of business.

Finally, Dappa has sufficient minimum contacts with Michigan to satisfy due process concerns. Pursuant to *International Shoe Co v Washington*, 326 US 310, 316; 66 S Ct 154; 90 L Ed 95, "due process requires only that in order to subject a defendant to a judgment in personam, if he be not present within the territory of the forum, he has certain minimum contacts with it such that the maintenance of the suit does not offend 'traditional notions fair play and substantial justice.'" Because Pluggs' injuries, which occurred in Michigan, were the foreseeable and conceivable result of Dappa's tortuous conduct, sufficient minimum contacts exist to assert personal jurisdiction. *See James v Hrp, Inc*, 852 F Supp 620, 625 (W D Mich, 1994); *Cole v Doe*, 77 Mich App 138, 143 (1977).

Three Student Answers—July 2003

Question 3—Civil Procedure—9 points

For a Michigan Court to have personal jurisdiction under a long-arm statute there must be a statute giving personal jurisdiction and it must be constitutional. Personal jurisdiction can be given by consent, express or implied, presence or long-arm statute. The Michigan long-arm statute provides that defendant's act must be substantially related to state such as business transactions, marriages, insurance contract, etc. The defendant must avail himself of Michigan benefits. Further, he must expect to be hauled into Michigan courts because minimum contacts such as business transactions are ok. Here, Dappa would expect to be hauled into court for any action based on his business practice because he certainly has availed himself and would expect to be hauled into court for his business practices, but plaintiff's attorney would not be able to use this to sue Dappa for a personal injury action that arose outside the scope of business.

For jurisdiction to exist in federal court there must be a federal question and complete diversity of citizenship and matter in controversy must exceed 75K. Here, there is complete diversity and 75K but no Federal question. In Michigan there is jurisdiction for tort cases, like this one, where plaintiff and substantial events of cause of action occurred as here. There court could find personal jurisdiction here.

Defendant could argue that the acts in Michigan were not within the jurisdiction because the defendant was in Ohio and defendant would not expect to be hauled into court because he is not a citizen of the state. This would not be the case here because defendant was at the state line and could reasonably expect his acts to extend to Michigan.

Question 3—Civil Procedure—10 points

State court have general jurisdiction. A fed court has limited jurisdiction. For a fed crt to have personal jurisdiction over a defendant they must either (1) have a question of fed law or constitutional matter. In these facts the plaintiff does not meet this req. (2) Diversity issue: must have plaintiff and defendant from separate states and case and controversy exceeding $75000.00.

Here, Dappa is a resident of Ohio, and Patrick is a resident of Michigan. Even though Dappa has a business in Ohio, the corporation is not being sued, so we look to defendant's domicile: the place where he resides with intent to stay.

The facts do not discuss if they meet the $75,000 requirement.

Michigan will have personal jurisdiction over the defendant in a tort action if the tort happened in that state.

The problem we have in this matter is that defendant did not avail himself to Michigan laws as he was in Ohio, but we could argue that defendant has availed himself to Michigan with minimum contacts. Defendant had a business in Michigan. It also could be argued that dangerous activity of fireworks on the border of Ohio-Michigan made it foreseeable that a tort could happen in Michigan and the defendant would have to defend a claim.

Question 3—Civil Procedure—8 points

Personal jurisdiction (PJ) is defined as the court's power over the person who is the subject of the lawsuit. There are three ways in which the court can obtain personal jurisdiction over a defendant. The first method is through express or implied consent. On these facts, it is clear that Dappa neither expressly nor impliedly consented to PJ because he filed a motion for summary judgment on the basis that the federal district court lack PJ over him. Therefore, there can be no PJ over Dappa through consent.

The second way to get personal jurisdiction over Dappa would be through presence. Plugg may have a good argument here in opposing the motion for summary judgment. There are three ways to get PJ through presence. They are actual presence, domicile, or through the defendant doing ongoing, continuous and systematic business in the state where the cause of action occurred. The last method of obtaining presence, continuous business in the forum state, would be Plugg's best argument for obtaining PJ over Dappa her. On these facts, Dappa owns a tattoo parlor in Toledo, but the parlor's clients, 60% of them, come from Michigan, the parlor advertises in Michigan and obtains all of its needs from Detroit. Therefore, I would advise my judge that a presence argument through continuous business in Michigan, where Pluggs' accident occurred, would be successful to deny Dappa's motion of summary judgment.

Another way the court could get PJ over Dappa would be by way of Michigan's long-arm statute. For Michigan's long-arm statute to apply there must be a specific connection between the defendant and the cause of action such that the defendant purposely availed itself of the benefits in Michigan and reasonably anticipated being hailed into a Michigan court. Injuries in tort are one way of getting PJ over the defendant through the long-arm statute. On these facts, Pluggs is bringing a personal injury action against Dappa and it is pretty obvious that Dappa has purposefully availed himself of Michigan's benefits by taking Michigan clients, advertising in Michigan and getting supplies from Michigan where Pluggs' cause of action occurred.

Therefore, I would advise my judge that Pluggs would be successful more than likely in obtaining PJ over Dappa by way of Michigan's long-arm statute for the reasons stated above. Dappa's motion for summary judgment should again be denied.

February 2004—Question 9

Your first appointment of the day is with Manfred Mullet, who has asked for a few minutes of your time in order to discuss a grievance he has against the rock band Screed. Manfred enters your office wearing a well-worn Screed t-shirt and sits down to explain his problem. He relates that as soon as he learned that his favorite rock band, Screed, would be playing the State Theater in Detroit last December, he started to save his earnings from his paper route to buy a ticket. He camped out overnight in front of the box office, although no one else lined up to buy tickets. Manfred purchased a ticket for $95 and, on December 12, 2003, he arrived at the State ready to rock.

But Screed was a huge disappointment. The lead singer, Steve Stoop, seemed to be extremely intoxicated. He stumbled around the stage, slurring the lyrics he managed to remember, and yelled obscenities at the audience between songs. In all, Screed played four songs and gave a 25-minute show before Stoop passed out on stage. When the curtain closed and the other band members walked off stage, Manfred concluded that he had spent $95 for nothing. Most of the 125 members of the audience shrugged and went home. Manfred, however, was so distraught that he sat in the front seat of his Geo Prism and sobbed miserably for three or four hours before heading home.

Manfred explains to you that he should be the lead plaintiff in a class action against Screed. He thinks that he is entitled to the cost of his ticket, plus $250,000 damages for the emotional distress he suffered from the huge letdown of seeing his favorite band perform so terribly. He asks you if his complaint has the makings of a class action.

What factors must you consider in determining whether Manfred's complaint should be brought as a class action, and how would you weigh each factor? What procedural steps must you take to establish a class action?

Model Answer to Question 9

In determining whether Manfred has any basis for a class action, his lawyer must consider the factors listed in MCR 3.501. Manfred has a possible class action only if:

(a) the class is so numerous that joinder of all members is impracticable;
(b) there are questions of law or fact common to the members of the class that predominate over questions affecting only individual members;
(c) the claims or defenses of the representative parties are typical of the claims or defenses of the class;
(d) the representative parties will fairly and adequately assert and protect the interests of the class; and
(e) the maintenance of the action as a class action will be superior to other available methods of adjudication in promoting the convenient administration of justice.

Therefore, Manfred's lawyer must consider numerosity, commonality, typicality, and superiority.

In determining whether class action is superior to other methods of adjudication, a court considers the factors listed in MCR 3.501(2):

(a) whether the prosecution of separate actions by or against individual members of the class would create a risk of
 (i) inconsistent or varying adjudications with respect to individual members of the class that would confront the party opposing the class with incompatible standards of conduct; or
 (ii) adjudications with respect to individual members of the class that would as a practical matter be dispositive of the interests of other members not parties to the adjudications or substantially impair or impede their ability to protect their interests;
(b) whether final equitable or declaratory relief might be appropriate with respect to the class;
(c) whether the action will be manageable as a class action;
(d) whether in view of the complexity of the issues or the expense of litigation the separate claims of individual class members are insufficient in amount to support separate actions;
(e) whether it is probable that the amount which may be recovered by individual class members will be large enough in relation to the expense and effort of administering the action to justify a class action; and
(f) whether members of the class have a significant interest in controlling the prosecution or defense of separate actions.

It is more important that the applicant recognize these factors as governing the certification of a class than that the applicants weigh the factors for or against a class action.

When these factors are applied, it is evident that Manfred does not have a strong basis for a class action. On the one hand, there are 125 potential plaintiffs. Therefore, it may prove to be impractical to join each individual party (and more practical to bring a class action). But the remaining factors weigh against bringing a class action. Manfred is obviously a devoted Screed fan, as he was the only person in line to buy tickets and even wore his Screed t-shirt to meet with his lawyer. There is a serious question, then as to whether Manfred's claims are representative of the other putative class members. And the fact that he's seeking emotional distress damages indicates that personal issues might predominate over common issues. Thus, the "commonality" and "typicality" factors weigh against bringing a class action.

The final factor, "superiority," also weighs against a class action. Given the prominence of Manfred's individual issues—his emotional distress, his extreme grief and anguish over the Screed's lousy performance—his lawyer should suspect that his personal claims overlap only marginally with his fellow class members. Therefore, there is little reason to believe that judicial efficiency will be served if Manfred is the lead plaintiff in a class action. Also, the small amount that other putative class members are likely to recover—at best, the $95.00 ticket price—may be trumped by the cost of initiating and maintaining a class action.

To establish a class action, a plaintiff must move to have a class certified within 91 days after filing a complaint. After certification, plaintiff must provide "reasonable" notice to putative class members as directed by the trial court. Notice must describe the nature of the action, possible "financial consequences for the class," and any possible counterclaims. Notice should also explain that putative class members can affirmatively opt-out of the class by following a particular procedure, that the outcome of the class action will be binding on all putative class members, and that any class member may intervene in the action. Ordinarily, plaintiff must cover the expense of notification.

Student Answer—February 2004

Question 9—Civil Procedure—9 points

This case involves a class action suit. To bring a class action suit, one has to be part of a class. The factors to look for are 1) a common class of people and 2) sharing same interests. The first thing is anyone who purchased a ticket to the concert would be eligible/qualify for a class. In our case, all people who attended the Screen concert would be eligible. Manfred qualifies as he paid for the ticket—anyone could join this class action. They all have the same interest in that everyone was a Screed fan.

Manfred would have to get a group of the fellow concert attendees to sign on to his class action suit—he could place an advertisement as the attorney can also do since this is a class action suit. Since most people left, it will be hard for Manfred to find people to join him.

Ultimately, even if Manfred could bring his class action suit, the very most he could recover is his $95 ticket. The $250,000 damages for emotional distress are not recoverable. In order to recover, Manfred would have to bring a separate individual action against Screed. Further, he would have to make an emotional distress case proving all elements, including some type of injury. Since this probably wouldn't be "extreme or outrageous" conduct for a rock concert, Manfred will probably lose.

Also, you need to show a multiplicity of potential actions. Instead of having a number of suits based on the same action, group all together.

July 2004—Question 2

You are an attorney with the in-house legal department of the Detroit Devils, a semi-professional lacrosse team, and have just received a copy of a complaint filed by

Paula Proode, the club's former massage therapist. She alleges that she was constructively discharged from her position with the Devils because the players told dirty jokes, routinely made suggestive statements and hung pictures of scantily clad supermodels in their locker room. Proode alleges that she reported these problems to management on a number of occasions, and her supervisors simply shrugged off those complaints. She now seeks damages for sexual harassment under the Michigan Civil Rights Act. In addition, Proode claims that the Devils breached her employment contract by failing to deal with the sexual harassment after she gave them notice.

As you are reviewing Proode's complaint, lead counsel Carl Cobb enters your office and closes the door. He explains that the Devils have just discovered that Proode deliberately uploaded a virus onto the club's computers before resigning. Cobb tells you that he wants you to file a counterclaim under the Michigan Virus Prevention Act of 1998 (MVPA) in order to recover the $60,000 in damages caused by Proode's virus.

He adds that there is another claim that the Devils might raise. Proode's employment contract prohibited her from working as a massage therapist for any other lacrosse team during her employment with the Devils. The Devils have learned that Proode was working as a massage therapist for the Grand Rapids Geese, another semi-professional lacrosse team, during her tenure with the Devils.

Cobb asks whether (in addition to the MVPA claim), the Devils should file a counterclaim for breach of contract. He mentions that he typically practices in federal court and is unfamiliar with the Michigan court rules governing counterclaims.

Draft a memo that addresses (1) whether the Devils should file a breach of contract counterclaim and (2) any differences between the Federal Rules of Civil Procedure and Michigan Court Rules that might affect the decision whether to file a breach of contract counterclaim.

Model Answer to Question 2

(1) We should file a breach of contract counterclaim. If a party files a pleading that states a claim against an opposing party, the court rule governing compulsory joinder comes into play. According to MCR 2.203(A), a pleading that states a claim must include all other claims arising out of the transaction or occurrence that is the subject matter of the action, assuming that those additional claims do not require the presence of parties over whom the court cannot acquire jurisdiction. *Id.* Because our answer to Proode's complaint will include a counterclaim under the MVPA (and is therefore a "pleading that states a claim"), MCR 2.203(A) requires that we join any claim arising out of the transaction or occurrence underlying Proode's suit or our counterclaim. Our breach of contract claim arises out of the same contract that is the basis for Proode's contract claim. If we fail to raise the breach of contract claim along with our MVPA claim, we may be barred from litigating the breach of contract claim in the future under the principles of claim preclusion and compulsory joinder. In order to avoid waiving our breach of contract claim, we should raise it as a counterclaim to Proode's lawsuit.

(2) Michigan's rule of compulsory joinder differs from the federal rules. Fed R Civ P 13(a) states that "a pleading shall state as a counterclaim any claim which at the time of serving the pleading the pleader has against any opposing party, if it arises out of the transaction or occurrence that is the subject matter of the opposing party's claim."

Thus, compulsory joinder applies under the federal rules regardless of whether a responsive pleading "states a claim." If the federal rules applied, we would be required to raise our breach of contract claim in a responsive pleading regardless of whether we also filed a claim under the MVPA. Under the Michigan rules, however, we are required to file a breach of contract claim only because we are also raising a claim under the MVPA and are therefore filing a "Pleading that states a claim."

Two Student Answers—July 2004

Question 2—Civil Procedure—8 points

1. Whether the Devils should file a counter claim?

Under Michigan Court Rule a party can bring any and all actions against another. In the Proode vs Devils action, plaintiff is claiming that 1) she was sexually harassed and 2) there was a breach of employment contract.

The Devils have a valid counter claim as to Proode's 2nd claim. She had an exclusive contract with the Devils and she breached it when she performed messages for the Grand Rapids Geese. As to the sexual harassment, this is a separate claim with distinct evidentiary rites and must be proven or disproved accordingly.

2. Differences between Federal and Michigan Rules that might affect the decision to file the counter claim.

Under a Federal System, a counter claim arising under the same transaction or occurrence must be brought by the party or it is lost and it can be brought if an independent subject matter jurisdiction is brought.

Also, under a federal court, a compulsory counter claim is said to have supplemental jurisdiction and the court can hear it.

Under this case, in the sexual harassment claim Proode is alleging that Devils also breached the employment contract—therefore the same transaction that gave rise to the sexual harassment is give rise to the breach of employment contract and it is compulsory in nature and thus any counter claims Devils might have must be brought together or lose it.

Michigan does recognize the compulsory counter claim and therefore if the case is filed in Michigan the claim need not be brought in as a counter claim.

If a case is filed in Federal court, since they are limited jurisdiction courts, plaintiff must show complete diversity; i.e. no plaintiff is of the same state as any of the defendants and a good faith allegation that damages exceeds 75,000.

As to the counter claim under the Michigan Virus Protection, if brought separately it will not meet the minimum amount, so must bring it in as compulsory counter claim arising under same transaction or occurrence.

Question 2—Civil Procedure—8 points

I. Breach of Contract—counter-claim

In Michigan courts all counter claims are permissive counter-claims, unlike at the federal level where they allow compulsory counter-claims. Permissive counter-claims are those that do not necessarily arise out of the same transaction or occurrence as the original claims filed. Here, in our case Ms. Proode has filed her complaint alleging breach of contract from her employment contract. Our firm's claim of breach of contract for Ms. Proode working as a massage therapist for another team arises out of the same transaction or occurrence as Ms. Proode's employment contract, therefore it meets the standard of a permissive counterclaim which we may file now but would not be barred from filing at a later date.

II. Michigan and Federal Differences

In federal court counter-claims that are compulsory arising out of the same transaction or occurrence must be brought or they are lost. Here the claim, if filed in federal court (facts do not indicate) the claim regarding breach of contract would be barred from being filed at a later date. However, the claim for loading the computer virus would not be under the Federal Rules or in Michigan as it does not tend to have a sameness of transaction or occurrence. Therefore, if the matter were filed in federal court, the breach of contract counter-claim would also have to be filed or it would be lost.

III. Service and Where File

Furthermore, in Michigan service of process is different than at the federal level. The facts do not indicate how the complaint was received, but Michigan requires 21 days to file an answer if personal service and 28 days to answer if mail service. Also, if personal jurisdiction, venue or improper service is not raised in the first responsive pleading then it is waived, unlike subject-matter jurisdiction.

In the federal courts, you have 10 days to file an answer which can be increased to 60 days if you request a waiver.

Additionally, depending on where Ms. Proode filed her claim she will have to meet personal jurisdiction and subject-matter jurisdiction. In Michigan the amount alleged by the defendant is irrelevant in computing the required amount in controversy for filing in Circuit or District court which require more than 25,000 and 25,000 or less respectively.

February 2005—Question 15

Paul Patient, an 85-year-old resident of Shady Acres Nursing Home, had been complaining of a sore throat. Phil's Phlebotomy, an independent contractor hired to perform laboratory services for Shady Acres, sent technician Dudley Drawer to draw Patient's blood. Several days after having his blood drawn, Patient was discovered dead in his bed.

Patient's daughter, Patrice Posey, brought a wrongful death action against Drawer, theorizing that Patient died of a blood clot that was caused when Drawer negligently drew his blood.

Drawer moved for summary disposition under MCL 2.116(C)(10), arguing that Posey had failed to present evidence demonstrating the existence of a genuine issue of material fact with respect to Drawer's negligence. In support of his motion, Drawer submits the affidavits of two county medical examiners stating that there was no indication that Patient had died of a blood clot or of any cause traceable to the phlebotomy and that, instead, Patient had likely died of a stroke.

In opposition to the summary disposition motion, Posey submits (1) her own affidavit, in which she stated that she would be able to present at trial the testimony of a pathologist that Patient's death was proximately caused by a blood clot induced by a negligently performed blood draw, (2) an excerpt from a Shady Acres report indicating that another Shady Acres resident had previously stated to a nurse that

Drawer did not seem to know what he was doing, and (3) the affidavit of a physician stating, in its entirety, "It is my belief, based on my medical knowledge and experience, that Dudley Drawer was negligent in drawing Paul Patient's blood."

The trial court granted Drawer's motion for summary disposition.

On appeal, Posey argues that the trial court erred in granting summary disposition in favor of Drawer. In her appellate brief, Posey cites an excerpt from a textbook, *Principles of Hematology*, stating that strokes were often caused by improperly performed blood draws.

You are a law clerk at the Court of Appeals. Advise your judge regarding whether summary disposition was properly granted to Drawer. Limit your answer to the issues raised and evidence proffered by the parties as analyzed under the Michigan Court Rules.

Model Answer to Question 15

The trial court properly granted summary disposition in favor of Drawer under MCR 2.116(C)(10).

A motion under MCR 2.116(C)(1) tests the factual sufficiency of the complaint. In evaluating a motion for summary disposition brought under (C)(10), a trial court must consider the affidavits, pleadings, depositions, admissions, and other evidence submitted by the parties, in the light most favorable to the party opposing the motion. MCR 2.116(G)(5); *Maiden v Rozwood*, 461 Mich 109, 119-120 (1999). If the proffered evidence fails to establish a genuine issue regarding any material fact, the movant is entitled to judgment as a matter of law. MCR 2.116(C)(10); MCR 2.116(G)(4); *Maiden, supra* at 120. Only substantively admissible evidence that is actually proffered in opposition to the motion may be considered. *Maiden, supra* at 121.

Posey failed to demonstrate the existence of a genuine issue of fact for trial. First, her affidavit, stating that she would be able to present evidence at trial to support her claim, was insufficient to overcome the (C)(10) motion. "A litigant's mere pledge to establish an issue of fact at trial cannot survive summary disposition under MCR 2.116(C)(10)." *Maiden, supra* at 120.

Second, the excerpt from the Shady Acres report was not substantively admissible and thus could not be considered by the trial court. Although the report itself was presumably admissible as a business record, MRE 803(6), the reference in the report to the statement of another Shady Acres resident was inadmissible hearsay. "When the document to be admitted contains a second level of hearsay, it also must qualify under an exception to the hearsay rule." *Maiden, supra* at 124; see also *Merrow v Bofferding*, 458 Mich 617 (1998).

Third, the physician's affidavit did not create a question of fact. The affidavit stated merely that it appeared to the affiant that Drawer was negligent. This is a legal conclusion that does not create a question of fact regarding Drawer's negligence. *Maiden, supra* at 129, n 11; see also *Downie v Kent Products*, 420 Mich 197, 205 (1984).

Finally, the Court of Appeals may not, in reviewing the trial court's grant of summary disposition, consider the excerpt from the *Principles of Hematology* textbook. In reviewing the propriety of a grant of summary disposition, the appellate court is governed only by the evidence that was before the trial court at the time the motion was granted. *Maiden, supra* at 126; see also *Quinto v Cross & Peters*, 451 Mich 358, 366 (1996). The textbook evidence was submitted for the first time on appeal, and it is irrelevant to the Court of Appeals' analysis.

Two Student Answers—February 2005

Question 15—Civil Procedure—10 points

Under Michigan Court rules summary disposition is brought under MCR 2.116(C)(10). We look at the facts in the light most favorable to the non-moving party and would only grant summary if no material facts were in dispute upon which reasonable minds could differ.

This is a medical malpractice action which requires affidavits to show that there was a breach of the standard of care to submit a claim. This, however, is a causation problem. Defendant presents two affidavits that blood clot was cause of death of phlebotomist. Posey's affidavit promise is not enough—it is mere speculation. The other two proofs (1) Shady Acres report is inadmissible hearsay at trial and cannot be considered and (2) who was physician what was his experience, knowledge, and basis for opinion.

The text book of Principles of Hematology is a learned treatise which only an expert would testify to in trial.

I do not believe that the judge's ruling to grant summary disposition was improper. Plaintiff merely offers evidence of hearsay, conjecture and speculation. Defendant offers facts, backed up by appropriate expert's affidavits.

Plaintiff, even viewing in her best light has not sufficiently shown that she will be able to prove causation or negligence. Reasonable minds on a jury will not differ that 2 medical examiner offerings overcome an old lady, an unnamed physician with unspecified qualifications and a non-admissible affidavit by the attorney which is improper and does not fulfill court rules.

TRIAL COURT WILL PROPERLY GRANT SUMMARY DISPOSITION UNDER 2.116(C)(10)

Yes, there is a dispute but proof to sustain a case is insufficient on plaintiff's part. More like a 2.116(C)(8) case for summary disposition. As a side note but not relevant to change my answer strokes can be caused from blood clots—so what caused the stroke?

Question 15—Civil Procedure—9 points

Properly granted—P establishes issues of legal conclusions, but not of fact.

An MCL 2.116(C)(10) motion must be supported by documentary evidence that there is no genuine issue of fact. D fulfilled this requirement with the L affidavits.

P may overcome the motion by proffering documentary evidence that establishes a genuine issue. P has not fulfilled this burden.

The rule provides that P may use affidavits to establish a fact issue and that is exactly what she used. The credibility of the evidence is for a jury—not a judge—to decide, so the fact that document evidence has been proffered and that evidence goes to the primary issue of D's negligence is enough to defeat a 2.116(C)(10) motion.

But: The proffered evidence is problematic—text book—it is too late to bring this evidence on appeal—even if it was helpful to overcome the motion (which it isn't) a text book isn't admissible unless an expert witness testifies that the book is authoritative treatise—which didn't happen here.

Physician's affidavit and the promised testimony and the pathologist; both testimonies are conclusory—they state conclusions of law, not statements of fact—and would not be permissible in court. P must present documentary evidence of fact not testimony of witnesses that merely state legal conclusions.

The resident's statement is also a problem—she states her conclusion that D was incompetent but there is no factual evidence to support the conclusion.

The evidence would be admissible if a business document (probably), but again—the statement only states a conclusion—not a fact about D's skill or methodology besides, resident isn't an expert qualified to offer her opinion as to D's competence.

P established that there is a legal question, but has not provided evidence of any fact that is at issue.

July 2005—Question 15

Looking for more excitement, David, a Flint stockbroker, decided to open his own private hedge fund: Brookwood Investments. Paula, a mathematics lecturer at the local university, was frustrated with her mediocre investment returns and decided to invest in Brookwood Investments. In June 1995, Paula and David entered into a written "Hedge Fund Investment Agreement" under which Paula gave David $500,000 to invest and agreed not to withdraw her money for two years. The agreement further provided that David was entitled to 20% of the profits per year as a management fee. The remainder of the profits, as well as Paula's initial $500,000 investment, would be returned to her at the end of the two-year lock-up period. Paula assumed all downside risk, including the loss of her initial investment.

Recognizing the exponential growth in hedge funds in the state and the unlikely litigation related to hedge funds that would ensue, in January 1995, the Michigan Legislation enacted, and the Governor signed, the Private Hedge Fund Litigation Act (PHFLA). Section 201 of the PHFLA provides:

> The Michigan Securities Commission shall have original and exclusive jurisdiction in all disputes arising out of hedge fund investment agreements * * * A party may appeal a Commission order to the Michigan Court of Appeals within twenty-eight days from entry of the Commission's order * * *.

David's hedge fund performed phenomenally well. At the end of the two-year period, David made $5 million in profits for Paula over and above the amount deducted for his management fees. Thrilled with David's performance, Paul did not even notice that David neglected to return the initial $500,000 she invested when he delivered her a check for $5 million in June 1997. However, over the next several years, Paula spent the entire $5 million spoiling her grandchildren and was completely broke. In July 2005, she filed suit in Genesee circuit court claiming that David breached the "Hedge Fund Investment Agreement" they signed and still owed her $500,000.

In answering the following question, assume that federal securities laws do not apply and that there are no federal preemption issues:

You are David's attorney. What are David's defenses? When must they be raised? Who will prevail?

Model Answer to Question 15

David has two defenses to be raised under MCR 2.116(C)—one based on the circuit court's lack of subject matter jurisdiction and one based on the statute of limitations for contracts. David would likely prevail on both motions.

Subject Matter Jurisdiction—MCR 2.116(C)(4): Subject matter jurisdiction is the authority of "the court to exercise judicial power over that class of case . . . of the kind or character of the one pending." *Joy v Two-Bit Corp*, 287 Mich 244, 253 (1938). The Michigan Constitution provides that the "circuit court shall have original jurisdiction in all matters not prohibited by law." Const 1963, art 6, §13.

David would file a motion for summary disposition under MCR 2.116(C)(4), arguing that the Genesee County circuit court lacks subject matter jurisdiction over Paula's lawsuit. Although the circuit court would normally possess jurisdiction over this breach of contract case, §201 of the Private Hedge Fund Litigation Act (PHFLA) specifically divests the circuit court of subject matter jurisdiction by providing that "the Michigan Securities Commission shall have original and exclusive jurisdiction in all disputes arising out of the hedge fund investment agreements." Thus, §201 of the PHFLA and Const 1963, art 6, §13, in tandem, effectively strip the circuit court of subject matter jurisdiction. If Paul wants to sue David for breach of contract, she must bring her action in the Michigan Securities Commission.

A party's assertion that a court lacks subject matter jurisdiction "may be raised at any time." MCR 2.116(d)(3); *Nat'l Wildlife Fed'n v Cleveland Cliffs Iron Co*, 471 Mich 608, 630 (2004). As such, David may file his (C)(4) motion at any time during the lawsuit, even on appeal.

Statute of Limitations—MCR 2.116(C)(7): There is a six-year statute of limitations for breach of contract actions in Michigan. MCL 600.5807(8). In this case, the breach of the "Hedge Fund Investment Agreement" occurred in June 1997, when David did not return the initial $500,000 that Paula invested. However, Paula did not file suit until July 2005. Accordingly, she missed the June 2003 deadline by over two years. Arguing that Paula's lawsuit is time barred under the six-year limitations period provided by MCL 600.5807(8), David would file a motion for summary disposition under MCR 2.116(C)(7).

Unlike a (C)(4) motion, which may be made at any time during the proceedings, a (C)(7) motion "must be raised in a party's responsive pleading." MCR 2.116(D)(2). If David does not file a (C)(7) motion in his responsive pleading, his (C)(7) defense will be deemed waived. *See Huntington Woods v Ajax Paving Industries Inc.*, 179 Mich App 600 (1989).

Three Student Answers—July 2005

Question 15—Civil Procedure—10 points

1. The Genesee Circuit Court does not have jurisdiction over this matter. Circuit courts have jurisdiction over amounts in controversy over $25K. However, the MI statute says that the MI Securities Commission has original, exclusive jurisdiction arising out of hedge fund investment agreements. Paula brought suit in the wrong court. This defense must be raised in answer to complaint. No Jurisdiction.
2. David can also raise potential statute of limitations defenses 1997-2005. This must also be raised in 1st response.
3. David can also raise as a defense that this is an ex post facto law as applied to their contract because contract was entered into on June 1995 and law was passed January 1995. This law would have to be applied retroactively to this contract and that is generally not allowed.

4. David can also argue that no law may be passed that changes rights of contracts. This law changes the parties' rights under their contract and that would be unconstitutional as applied to this contract.

Ultimately David wins at least as the case is currently filed in circuit ct = no jurisdiction.

David may lose if it gets to Commission and Statute of Limitations has not run.

Question 15—Civil Procedure—10 points

The Genesee Circuit Court has jurisdiction that is original & general. General jurisdiction is jurisdiction that isn't specifically provided to another court. Here, we have a Michigan statute that gives the Michigan Securities commission exclusive jurisdiction in all hedge fund investment agreements. Therefore, Genesee Circuit Court does not have jurisdiction over this claim filed by Paula.

So, David is going to file a motion to dismiss (motion for summary disposition in Michigan) on his first responsive pleading (which will be the motion rather than answer to the complaint) & state that there is no subject matter jurisdiction on this hedge fund agreement because the statute gives the Michigan Securities Commission exclusive jurisdiction. He would file this motion with the Genesee County Circuit Court with 21 days if served personally or within 28 days if served by certified mail.

Also, in the same motion to dismiss (or motion for summary disposition) David can

Question 15—Civil Procedure—10 points

In Michigan, circuit courts have original and exclusive jurisdiction over all civil cases unless expressly stated or exempted from and a specific jurisdiction is stated, and if the damages are less then $25,000 then district court has jurisdiction.

Since we have a statute erected by the legislature of Michigan and approved by the Governor which states the Michigan Securities Commission shall have original and exclusive jurisdiction in all disputes arising out of hedge fund investment agreements, the circuit court does not have jurisdiction, that is, it does not have subject matter jurisdiction over these cases. Therefore, David has a defense that will be granted if raised.

This may be raised (SMT) at anytime during trial. Only personal jurisdiction, service of process that is invalid and statute of limitations must be raised in first reply.

Venue is not a defense, since Michigan is where David lives (Genesee is county for Flint)—not a great defense can be raised at any time.

Another defense David has is statute of limitations. Paula is bringing this suit almost 8 years later! I have not heard of any statute of limitation to last this long, at least not for this situation. I believe she would 3 years to bring claim under tort or even up to 6 years if by contract, since they did have a contract. However 8 years is past even the 6 yrs exception. Statute of limitation defense should be brought in first reply.

Final outcome—case will not be heard by the Circuit Court of Genesee so long as David brings statute of limitations or SMT defense. If he doesn't bring the statute of limitations in first reply it is waived! SMT can be brought as defense at any time.

Just in case, PJ—personal jurisdiction which is jurisdiction a court has over a person or his property is not a big issue—they both reside in Michigan—general PJ look at domicile—where they intend to live forever until they change it.

February 2006—Question 1

In June 2004, Paul Plaintiff, a professional bodybuilder, and David Defendant, a wealthy businessman, contracted to endorse David's cutting-edge vitamin supplements. The contract included the requirement that Paul maintain a weight of no more than 165 pounds. Paul and David subsequently got into a shouting match at their local gym over whose turn it was to use the Preacher Curl machine. At one point, David shouted in the midst of the crowd of onlookers, "Well, I think everyone knows how you got to look the way you do!" and lunged towards Paul. Several patrons restrained David before a physical altercation could ensue.

Humiliated by the incident, Paul could not bring himself to return to the gym for several months. His dedicated workouts all but ceased, and he replaced his meticulous diet with steady portions of ice cream and pork rinds. Paul tacked on an additional 150 pounds to his once sculpted physique. He survived solely on the income he received from his endorsement contract with David.

Paul consulted an attorney and sued David for defamation. After a bench trial, the judge entered a judgment in Paul's favor.

David was furious that Paul had sued him. Immediately following the trial, David refused to honor the remainder of the endorsement contract and withheld money owed to Paul.

In January 2006, Paul filed a breach of contract claim against David and added an assault claim stemming from the gym altercation. David answered by simply denying each claim. During discovery, David testified that he had not intended to place Paul in apprehension of imminent harm and that Paul's weight gain of 150 pounds breached their contract.

Following the conclusion of discovery, David brought a motion for summary disposition under MCR 2.116 (C)(7), (8) and (10).

Utilizing the differing procedural standards the trial court must consider when evaluating summary disposition under MCR 2.116 (C)(7), (8) and (10), assess the most probable arguments for David's motion for summary disposition under the three asserted bases, and the likelihood of success under each.

Model Answer to Question 1

MCR 2.116 (C)(7): Based on the facts presented, David's (C)(7) motion could raise one of the enumerated (C)(7) defenses; ***res judicata.*** *Res judicata* is an affirmative defense. *E & G Finance Co v Simms*, 362 Mich 592, 596-97 (1961).

In order for *res judicata* to apply to Paul's second action, (1) the first action must have been decided on the merits, (2) the matter contested in the second action must have been (or could have been) resolved in the first action, and (3) both actions involve the same parties or their privies. *Sewell v Clean Cut Management*, 463 Mich 569, 575 (2001). Michigan courts apply *res judicata* broadly to bar not only claims already litigated, but every claim arising from the same transaction that the parties, exercising reasonable diligence, could have raised but did not. *Id.*

Thus, on the merits, Paul's assault claim is barred by *res judicata.* First, the assault claim could have been brought in the first defamation action, since both claims arose out of the same transaction or occurrence. Second, the first action was clearly decided on the merits. Finally, both actions involved the same parties, Paul and David. By contrast, the breach of contract action is not barred by *res judicata* or any other basis listed in MCR 2.116(C)(7). It could not have been brought with the defamation claim because David did not withhold payments under the contract until after the first action concluded.

However, David's (C)(7) *res judicata* motion concerning the assault claim will also fail because of his apparent procedural error in responding to Paul's complaint. Pursuant to MCR 2.111(F)(2)(a) and MCR 2.116(D)(2), an affirmative defense must be pled no later than the party's first responsive pleading. This can be accomplished by motion or the assertion of the affirmative defense in the answer as the first responsive pleading. MCR 2.116(D)(2). Failure to assert an affirmative defense in one of these two ways results in a waiver of that defense. Because it appears that David answered the complaint by simply denying the merits of the assault claim while failing to raise *res judicata* as an affirmative defense, he waived the affirmative defense he could have raised under (C)(7). Notwithstanding that David has meritorious *res judicata* defense to the assault claim, he will be forced to defend it on the merits.

MCR 2.116(C)(8): When deciding a motion under (C)(8), which can be raised at any time, the trial court must determine whether the opposing party has failed to state a claim on which relief can be granted. In doing so, the trial court may only consider the pleadings. MCR 2.116(G)(5). To that end, David can prevail only if he is able to show that Paul's complaint failed to state a claim. Considering the brief facts given in the question, Paul's complaint likely sets forth a prima facie case of assault and breach of contract. David's (C)(8) motion would therefore fail.

MCR 2.116(C)(10): When judging a motion under MCR 2.116(C)(10), which also can be raised at any time, the trial court tests the factual sufficiency of the complaint by considering the affidavits, depositions, admissions, and other documentary evidence (including all inferences that can be drawn from that evidence) in light most favorable to the non-moving party. MCR 2.116(G)(5); *Maiden v Rozwood*, 461 Mich 109, 119-120 (1999). If the evidence fails to establish a genuine issue of material fact, then the moving party is entitled to judgment as a matter of law. MCR 2.116(G)(4). The evidence offered in support must be admissible to support a genuine issue of material fact in favor of the non-moving party. MCR 2.116(G)(6).

Based on the evidence gathered in discovery, David's (C)(10) motion should fail, and Paul's suit should survive. David contested Paul's allegation that he breached the contract by testifying that Paul breached the endorsement contract because of his significant weight gain. Moreover, David denied that he intended to assault Paul. Construing this evidence in the light most favorable to the non-moving party (Paul), there appears to be a genuine issue of material fact as to both claims. A jury must resolve these fact disputes between the parties as to which one breached the contract and whether David committed an assault.

Two Student Answers—February 2006

Question 1—Civil Procedure—10 points

Issue #1: Whether David will be granted the summary disposition motion under 2.116 (c)10?

A summary disposition motion under 2.116 (c)10 tests whether there is any genuine issue of material fact from which reasonable minds could not differ. This motion looks at evidence obtained during discovery in a light most favorable to the non moving party. The judge does not weigh the evidence, but looks at it on its face.

Here, regarding the assault claim, David testified in his disposition that he had no intention of putting Paul in apprehension of fear. Paul still claims from his complaint that he was in fear.

Since there is a factual dispute regarding David's intent during the gym altercation, there remains a genuine issue of material fact that must be decided by the jury. Regarding the breach of contract claim, the original contract stipulated that Paul maintain a weight of no more than 165 pounds. After the gym incident, Paul clearly gained an additional 150 pounds, breaching the contract. Since Paul's weight cannot be disputed, there is no genuine issue of material fact regarding the breach of contract claim and reasonable minds could not differ that Paul breached the contract so summary disposition of this claim is probably proper under 2.116 (c)10.

Issue #2: Whether David should be granted summary disposition as to 2.116 (c)8?

Summary dispositions under 2.116 (c)8 are basically the same as (c)10 by which they use the pleadings to see if there is a genuine fact issue in the case. Here, since Paul claimed both breach of contract and assault in his complaint and David denied the allegations in the answer, there are genuine issues at dispute in this case to be determined by the fact finder. Therefore, summary disposition should be denied for both claims under 2.116 (c)8.

Issue #3: Whether David should be granted summary disposition under 2.116 (c)7?

A summary disposition under 2.116 (c)7 just bars a claim when it had the opportunity to be used in a previous cause of action. Here, Paul filed an assault charge which arose out of the same transaction as the defamation claim and should have been brought then. Because the assault was connected to the events that lead to the defamation charge, Paul cannot bring it in this action.

Question 1—Civil Procedure—8 points

This question deals with civil procedure. Specifically, the question asks what the most likely arguments David could logically make utilizing MCR 2.116 (c)7, 8 and 10.

The first issue involves that of the lawsuit filed. Paul sued David for defamation and the judge entered judgment in Paul's favor. Paul subsequently sued David for breach of contract in January of 2006. This breach of contract suit is valid and not barred by the statute of limitations because a contract claim has a two year statute of limitations. However, the suit filed by Paul raises questions of claim preclusion (Res Judicata). Paul sued David in defamation based on the gym altercation that took place. His subsequent lawsuit against David for assault stemmed from the gym altercation. This is a claim that should have been brought with the original claim because it arose from the same transaction or occurrence.

Next, there is the issue of summary disposition argued by David. MCR 2.116 (c)7, 8 and 10 are the Michigan court rules which allow a party to ask the court for a verdict in its favor because there is either no matter in controversy for which the court adequately can give relief or there is no genuine issue of material fact therefore no logical jury could reasonably hold for the plaintiff. Should this case be barred under Res Judicata or alternatively issue preclusion (Collateral Estoppel) then the judge would need to make a ruling as to the weight of the evidence presented to determine how to rule.

In this case, Paul filed a breach of contract claim when David refused to honor his contact with Paul. The facts further state that David, following the verdict for Paul, refused to honor the remainder of the endorsement contract. Paul asserted an assault claim. However, David replied under oath that he never intended to place Paul in apprehension of imminent harm and that Paul's weight gain breached their contract.

Under these facts, the judge would more than likely deny the MCR (c)7, 8 and 10 motions filed by David. There is sufficient evidence to allow this matter to go to the fact finder—Paul asserts assault; David denies the elements needed for assault; Paul asserts breach of contract; David assets Paul breached by gaining so much weight.

Therefore, there is a genuine issue of material fact for a jury to determine and further, there is an adequate relief that the court can provide to Paul by compelling David to perform under the terms of the contract and money damages for the assault. The motions are likely to be denied.

July 2006—Question 7

In January 2005, Donald's Widget Emporium (Donald), a widget refurbishing company incorporated in Michigan with its principal place of business in California, agreed to supply Peter, a resident of Wayne County in Michigan, with 10,000 widgets valued at $10 a piece. However, Donald refused to ship the widgets to Peter. Peter properly served Donald and properly filed a complaint in Wayne Circuit Court alleging breach of contract.

You are an associate in the law firm representing Donald. The senior partner seeks your advice given the three scenarios presented below.

Draft a concise memorandum addressing the issues presented in each scenario.

1. **For the purposes of the above scenario only, Donald wants to remove the case to a U.S. District Court in California. Can Donald remove the case and, if so, where? Explain your answer.**
2. **For the purposes of this second scenario only, assume that Peter brought a second claim alleging a violation of the Widget Protection Act of 2000, a federal statute that entitles purchasers of widgets to treble damages in the event widget suppliers breach their widget contract. Donald wants to remove the case to a U.S. District Court in California. Can Donald remove the case, and, if so, where? Explain your answer.**
3. **For the purposes of the third scenario only, assume that Donald did not attempt to remove this case to federal court. Donald believes that there is a lack of personal jurisdiction. Advise how Donald must raise this argument and advise whether Donald will succeed with this argument on the merits. Explain your answer.**

Model Answer to Question 7

(1) Donald cannot remove the case to any federal court. Federal courts are courts of limited jurisdiction. Pursuant to 28 USC 1441(a), a defendant may remove any action brought in a state court of which the district courts of the United States have original jurisdiction. The federal court does not have original jurisdiction in this case because there is neither federal question nor diversity.

1. *Federal Question*: A state common law breach of contract claim does not arise under the Constitution, laws or treaties of the United States. 28 USC 1331. Therefore, no federal question is raised.
2. *Diversity Jurisdiction*: Diversity jurisdiction is unavailable because, although the $75,000 jurisdictional amount is satisfied, the parties lack complete diversity since Donald and Peter are both citizens of Michigan. Where a federal question is not present, an action is removable only if none of the parties in interest properly joined and served as defendants is a citizen of the state in which the action is brought. 28 USC 1441(b). A corporation is deemed a citizen both of the state where it is incorporated and the state where it has its principal place of business. 28 USC 1332(c)(1). Accordingly, Donald is a citizen of both Michigan and California.

(2) Donald can remove the case to federal court, but not to a federal court in California. The federal court now has original jurisdiction in the form of a federal question because Peter brought a claim arising under a federal statute, the Widget Protection Act of 2000. 28 USC 1331. Donald is entitled to remove to federal court.

Although Donald can remove the case, the appropriate venue is limited by statute. Under 28 USC 1441(a), it is appropriate to remove only to a district court "embracing the place where such action is pending." In this case, the state action is not pending in California. It is pending in Wayne Circuit Court in Michigan. Were Donald to remove the case, he could do so to a federal district court in Michigan, the Eastern District of Michigan.

(3) Donald must file a motion for summary disposition pursuant to MCR 2.116(C)(1), alleging that the court lacks jurisdiction over Donald. This motion must be raised in Donald's first motion or first responsive pleading, or it will be waived. MCR 2.116(D)(1).

Donald likely will not prevail on its claim that the Wayne Circuit Court lacks jurisdiction over Donald. In Michigan, a state court has jurisdiction over a person if two prongs are satisfied: (1) Michigan's long arm statutes and (2) federal constitutional due process. By statute, Michigan has general personal jurisdiction over a corporation incorporated under Michigan law. MCL 600.711. Michigan also has limited personal jurisdiction over a corporation that, among other things, transacts business within the state or enters into a contract for materials to be furnished in the state by the defendant. MCL 600.715. Donald is incorporated under the laws of Michigan and contracted to furnish materials (widgets) to Peter, so there appears to be no personal jurisdiction problem under the Michigan long-arm statutes.

Turning to the due process prong, Donald must show a lack of minimum contacts with the forum state, Michigan, or that it has received insufficient notice of the suit. Donald cannot successfully claim there is a lack of minimum contacts. Donald established minimum contacts with Michigan by domiciling itself in Michigan by incorporating in this state. *See Milliken v Meyer*, 311 US 457 (1940). In addition, Donald intentionally directed its activities toward the forum state by contracting with a Michigan resident and purposefully availed itself of the benefits and protections of Michigan law. Regarding the notice requirement, the facts concede that Donald was properly served, so it has proper notice of the lawsuit.

Two Student Answers—July 2006

Question 7—Civil Procedure—9 points

1. Removal of a case can be done by a defendant if he was to remove a case to fed court as long as there is all the defendants agreed there is subject matter jurisdiction. This applies when there is an issue of a fed question or when there is diversity i.e. the plaintiff resides in the same place as the def the suit is for over $75000. In cases of removal the claim will be denied if the def is from the same state as the forum state. Here there is no fed question so the case cannot be removed on that ground. In terms of diversity. Although the amt in controversy exceeds $75000, Donald is incorporated in the state of Michigan which is where the case was filed so no removal.

2. This case would be able to be removed because it involves federal law i.e. subject matter jurisdiction applies this case would be able to be removed to the county where defendants substantial place of business is in California or where the matter arose.

3. Personal jurisdiction is the power of the court over the person or property. Personal jurisdiction lies where the defendant is domiciled, has its principal place of business, substantial contacts, & is incorporated. In this case the State of Michigan would have personal jurisdiction over Donald because his business was incorporated in Michigan. Also personal jurisdiction is constitutional in Michigan because Donald had substantial contact w/the forum state i.e. MI, because of his incorporation there.

Question 7—Civil Procedure—8 points

This is a civil procedure question.

(1) This is an issue of subject matter jurisdiction (SMJ). The U.S. District Court in Calif. is a federal court which can only hear cases based on diversity or case or controversy arising under federal law. Because Donald (D) is incorporated in the state of MI it may also be sued there by Peter (P). Therefore there is not true diversity and thus the U.S. District Court in Calif. lacks SMJ. The cause of action is a breach of contract theory and Peter has an interest in having the state of MI's law based on his cause of action in the place where it is located and does business. Therefore D should not be allowed to remove the case because his place of incorporation is in MI in addition to his business dealings within the state, it should be reasonably foreseeable to D that he could be sued in MI.

(2) This issue also raised a violation of a federal statute which would give SMJ to the federal courts. However, it is still unreasonable for P to travel to Calif. for his claims against D because he is still bringing a breach of contract claim and there is still his interest in having MI state law applied to that claim. Therefore if D still seeks to remove the case it could be removed to U.S. District court in MI as it would have SMJ based on the federal statute claim.

(3) This is an issue of personal jurisdiction (PJ) of D. If a party wishes to challenge PJ he must raise the issue in his first response to P's claims or else he is said to have accepted PJ over him. D will not be likely to succeed with a lack of PJ claim because one, he has MI as his place of incorporation, two, he does business within the state and therefore it is foreseeable that he could be sued within the state by his current conduct. Therefore, a claim of lack of PJ will not succeed.

February 2007—Question 4

Your client, Andy's Bicycle Helmets, Inc., ("Andy") has recently been sued by Paulie Patron in a premises liability action after Paulie slipped and fell in the store's public restroom. Paulie sustained fairly serious back injuries. You conferred with your client, which indicated it was willing to settle Paulie's claim for $10,000. You have also kept in touch with Paulie's attorney, who informs you that Paulie is willing to settle for no less than $150,000. The trial court submits the claim to case evaluation and the panel unanimously evaluates the claim at $100,000. Andy, outraged by the case evaluation award, now wants to go to trial. Your client is unaware of Michigan's rules regarding case evaluation and it is your obligation as its attorney to inform Andy about the risks of accepting or rejecting the case evaluation award.

Write a memorandum explaining these rules to your client and advising it how the rules apply to this case.

Model Answer to Question 4

MCR 2.403 sets forth the rules governing case evaluation. In general, case evaluation is intended to force parties to make a serious evaluation of the merits of their respective cases and parties are aided in this assessment by a panel of independent lawyer/evaluators selected pursuant to MCR 2.404. The case evaluation rule imposes substantial sanctions for a party's improvident rejection of a case evaluation award.

Both Parties Accept the Case Evaluation: A party may accept a case evaluation award. If the other party also accepts the case evaluation award, then a judgment will enter in accordance with the evaluation and the judgment will be deemed to dispose of all claims in the action. MCR 2.403(M)(1). If Andy and Paulie both accept the $100,000 case evaluation award, a judgment will enter in accordance with that evaluation, and "upon the parties' acceptance of a case evaluation all claims in the action [are] disposed." *CAM Constr v Lk Edgewood Condo Ass'n*, 465 Michigan 549, 555 (2002).

One Party Accepts and the Other Party Rejects the Case Evaluation: On the other hand, if one party rejects a case evaluation award and the opposing party accepts the award, the rejecting party may be required to pay the opposing party's "actual costs." Actual costs are (1) costs taxable in any civil action, and (2) a reasonable attorney fee based on reasonable hourly or daily rate as determined by the trial judge for services necessitated by the rejection of the case evaluation. MCR 2.403(O)(6).

If one party has rejected the case evaluation award, and the action proceeds to a verdict, that party must pay the opposing party's actual costs "unless the verdict is more favorable to the rejecting party than the case evaluation." MCR 2.403(O)(1). The "verdict" is the jury verdict, the judgment of the court after a non-jury trial, or a judgment entered as a result of ruling on a motion after rejection of the case evaluation. MCR 2.403(O)(2). The verdict must be adjusted by adding assessable costs and interest on the amount of the verdict from the filing of the complaint to the date of the case evaluation, and, if applicable, by making an adjustment for future damages. MCR 2.403(O)(3).

Whether a verdict after adjustment is favorable is determined by comparing the verdict to the case evaluation award. A verdict is more favorable to the defendant if it is more than 10 percent below the evaluation, and it is more favorable to the plaintiff if it is more than 10 percent above the evaluation. *Id.* If the evaluation was zero, a verdict finding that a defendant is not liable to the plaintiff is deemed more favorable to the defendant. *Id.*

If Andy is the only party that rejects the case evaluation award, a party is entitled to costs only if the verdict is more favorable to that party than the case evaluation award. MCR 2.403 (O)(1). The same definition of "verdict" and the same determination of favorability apply where both parties reject the case evaluation.

If both Andy and Paulie reject the $100,000 case evaluation award, the verdict must be more favorable to either rejecting party for that party to be entitled to actual costs. That means that the verdict must be more than 10 percent above the $100,000 case evaluation award—in excess of $110,000—for plaintiff Paulie to receive actual costs. For defendant Andy, the verdict must be more than 10 percent below $100,000—less than $90,000—for Andy to receive actual costs. If the verdict falls within those amounts—$90,000 to $110,000—neither party is entitled to actual costs.

Andy must be advised of the pitfalls of accepting and rejecting the case evaluation award. See MRCP 1.2(a), 1.4(a), (b). Although he may be convinced that Paulie's claim is not worth more than $10,000, he must take into consideration that he might be required to pay not only the verdict, but also Paulie's taxable costs and reasonable attorney fees. Paulie's legal fees incurred following case evaluation through trial could be quite considerable. Given the enormous disparity between the value that Andy attached to Paulie's claim and the value that Paulie attached to his claim and the fact that the case evaluation award is ten times greater than his valuation of Paulie's claim, you might advise Andy to reconsider his decision to go to trial in light of the greater exposure he faces because of case evaluation sanctions.

Student Answer—February 2007

Question 4—Civil Procedure—8 points

To: Client
From: Attorney
Date: Feb 27, 2007
RE: Case Evaluation

In Michigan case evaluation is used to try to settle cases before they go to court. There is usually a panel at about 3 lawyers and they evaluate the case and come up with award they think is suitable for the type of action being pursued. It is up to the client to pursue case evaluation or it can be court ordered. Here, you requested that the case be settled for $150,000 therefore, it was not court ordered. Also the panel does not have to decide the award amount based on what either side submits.

Further there are some risks in accepting and rejecting an award. Here, if Andy accepts the award, the other side may have to pay more than what they initially wanted to settle for which $100,000. Further, for a premises liability action, there are a number of damages a jury could confer upon the other side which might exceed $100,000. If Andy decides to take the case to court, the jury could award more than what the case evaluators recommended. Also, just because the panel unanimously reached this claim amount does not mean that Andy has to take the evaluation award but he may impose some consequences if he refuses. First, he may receive lower than $150,000 he anticipated and the $100,000 the case evaluators decided on.

Further, he may have to pay both sides court cost and attorneys fees for refusing to take the evaluator's award, if the court finds that he acted in bad faith by bringing the case to trial instead of accepting the evaluator award.

Therefore, Andy maybe taking more of a risk by taking the case to trial since the evaluator award might be more than what he would receive at trial and is only $50,000 less than what Andy initially anticipated.

July 2007—Question 13

Perry visited Dwayne's home one Saturday afternoon. While Perry leaned on a wooden railing that enclosed the veranda where the two were talking, the railing collapsed. Perry fell backwards onto the front lawn, landing on his back.

Although Perry denied that he was injured immediately after he fell, he later filed a premises liability suit against Dwayne seeking to recover damages for his injured back. During discovery, Dwayne desired to have Perry examined by a physician chosen by Dwayne to determine the extent of Perry's alleged back injuries. Perry agreed to be examined and arranged a meeting with Dwayne's physician, Dr. Strangelove. Perry's attorney, Yost, accompanied Perry to Strangelove's office to observe the examination. Uncomfortable with Yost's hulking presence, Dr. Strangelove refused to examine Perry. Perry has refused Dwayne's subsequent attempts to schedule another physical examination.

Incensed by the wasted time and expanse, Perry has moved for sanctions against Dwayne seeking, in addition to costs for the bringing of the motion, a court order that his back injury was now established for purposes of this action.

You are Dwayne's attorney and are analyzing the merits of the discovery sanction motion filed by Perry and considering what advice to give to your client. **First, explain whether Perry will prevail on his motion for sanctions. Second, advise your client whether you can secure Perry's physical examination. Explain your answer.**

Model Answer to Question 13

MCL 2.311 governs physical and mental examinations of a party. MCR 2.311(A) states that when the physical condition of a party is in controversy, "the court in which the action is pending may order the party to submit to a physical . . . examination by a physician." This court order "may be entered only on motion for good cause with notice to the person to be examined and to all parties." In addition to the order specifying the time, place, manner, conditions, and scope of the examination, it "may provide that the attorney for the person to be examined may be present at the examination."

Under MCR 2.313(B)(2)(a), a court may order as a sanction for a failure to comply with an order to provide or permit discovery "that the matters regarding which the order was entered or other designated facts may be taken to be established for the purposes of the action in accordance with the claim of the party obtaining the order." While this rule appears to permit the sanction Perry seeks ("establishing" as fact for trial his injury), there is a question as to whether (a) a necessary precondition (violation of an order) has occurred and (b) the physician (who refused to conduct the examination with Yost present) is a "party" or any of the other entities expressly covered by MCR 2.323(B)(2).

Perry's motion for sanctions should be denied by the trial court for at least two reasons. First, in this case, Dwayne never sought a court order directing Perry to submit to a physical exam. Perry agreed to take the physical exam at Dwayne's request and the parties privately arranged the examination. There was no apparent "agreement" whether Perry's lawyer could audit the examination. Under MCR 2.311(A), the court order may provide that the person to be examined *may* have his attorney present at the examination. However, in the absence of a court order allowing his attorney to be present, the rule provides no guidance on whether Perry had a right to demand Yost's presence at the physical examination he volunteered to attend. More important, there is no basis to impose sanctions on Dwayne because, pursuant to MCR 2.313(B)(2), sanctions are appropriate *only if* a party "fails to obey an order to provide or permit discovery, including an order entered under (MCR 2.313(A)) or under MCR 2.311" (emphasis added). Thus, sanctions can be had where there is a failure to comply with a court order compelling discovery entered pursuant to MCR 2.313(A) or MCR 2.311. MCL 2.313(B)(2). However, MCR 2.313 nowhere suggests that violations of informal discovery agreements are sanctionable.

Second, even if there had been a court order under MCR 2.311(A) in place, it is unlikely that the court would sanction *Dwayne* for the *physician's* refusal to cooperate. MCR 2.313(B)(2) refers to "a party, or an officer, director or managing agent of a party, or a person designated under MCR 2.306(B)(5) or 2.307(A)(1) to testify on behalf of a party." Therefore, his failure to obey an order is not sanctionable under MCR 2.313(B)(2).

Going forward, in order to secure Perry's examination, Dwayne should seek a court order requiring Perry to submit to a physical examination. Clearly, since Perry is suing Dwayne for his alleged back injury, Perry's physical condition "is in controversy," so MCR 2.311 is applicable. Moreover, a court order is necessary considering Perry's open refusal to arrange another physical examination with Dwayne. Under these circumstances, Dwayne can likely satisfy the "good cause" requirement of MCR 2.311(A) if information about Perry's back injury is otherwise unavailable. "What may be good cause for one type of examination may not be so for another. The ability of the movant to obtain the desired information by other means is also relevant." *Brewster v Martin Marietta Aluminum Sales, Inc*, 107 Mich App 639, 644 (1981) quoting *Schlagenhauf v Holder*, 379 US 104, 118 (1964). Of course, MCR 2.311 offers protection to Perry. The court can specify in the motion that Perry's attorney, Yost, may be present at the examination.

Student Answer—July 2007

Question 13—Civil Procedure—8 points

When a person's physical condition is relevant to the dispute, the opposing party can require a physical examination by their own expert as part of the discovery process. Here Perry (P) put his back condition at issue and must comply with reasonable discovery requests.

1. P will not be able to get sanctions. P is obligated to comply with reasonable discovery requests. While Dr. Strangelove's actions were not good, they were in no way Dwayne's (D) fault (or his attorney's). D should not be penalized.

Further, D reasonably requested another appointment. D would be helped even further if these attempts were with a different doctor. Sanctions are only awarded when a party acts unreasonably. Dr. Strangelove's acts should not be imputed upon D.

2. As stated above, P put the physical condition in issue. D should be able to compel P to submit to an exam. The fact that the first attempt was unsuccessful should not have a bearing on a second, reasonable request. D should be able to get P's exam.

February 2008—Question 13

Paul Purchaser agreed to exchange a number of autographed photos and other rare sports memorabilia with Danny Dealer. Both parties represented that the items to be exchanged were authentic and provided certificates of authenticity to that end. After the parties completed the deal, Paul discovered that the collectibles he received from Danny were largely forgeries.

You are the lawyer representing Paul Purchaser. In addition to seeking damages for fraud and the return of his authentic collectibles, Paul wants to bring a class action suit against Danny, which would include 21 other people who similarly claim that the items they received in trade with Danny were forgeries. Most of the other collectors exchanged a similar number of items with Danny, but their items involved a wider range of sports and athletes.

Using the Michigan Court Rules, discuss whether: (1) there are any hurdles in pleading a fraud claim, (2) Paul's complaint should be brought as a class action, and (3) any possible actions could be taken in order to protect immediately Paul's memorabilia that is currently in Danny's possession. Explain your answer.

Model Answer to Question 13

1. Fraud: In order to maintain an action for fraud, the circumstances constituting fraud must be stated with particularity under MCR 2.112(B)(1).

2. Class Action: In determining whether Paul has any basis for a class action, an attorney must consider the factors listed in MCR 3.501. Paul has a possible class action *only* if:

(a) The class is so numerous that joinder of all members is impracticable;
(b) There are questions of law or fact common to the members of the class that predominate over questions affected only individual members;
(c) The claims or defense of the representative parties are typical of the claims or defenses of the class;
(d) The representative parties will fairly and adequately assert and protect the interests of the class; and
(e) The maintenance of the action as a class action will be superior to other available methods of adjudication in promoting the convenient administration of justice.

Therefore, numerosity, commonality, typicality, and superiority must be considered.

In determining whether a class action is superior to other methods of adjudication, a court considers the factors listed in MCR 3.501(A)(2):

(a) whether the prosecution of separate actions by or against individual members of the class would create a risk of

(i) inconsistent or varying adjudications with respect to individual members of the class that would confront the party opposing the class with incompatible standards of conduct; or

(ii) adjudication with respect to individual members of the class that would as a practical matter be dispositive of the interests of other members not parties to the adjudications or substantially impair or impede their ability to protect their interests;

(b) whether finally equitable or declaratory relief might be appropriate with respect to the class;

(c) whether the action will be manageable as a class action;

(d) whether in view of the complexity of the issues or the expense of litigation the separate claims of individual class members are insufficient in amount to support separate actions;

(e) whether it is probable that the amount which may be recovered by individual class members will be large enough in relation to the expense and effort of administering the action to justify a class action; and

(f) whether members of the class have a significant interest in controlling the prosecution or defense of separate actions.

When these factors are considered, it is evident that Paul does not have a strong basis for a class action. On the limited facts presented, there is a question regarding whether Paul's claims are representative of the other putative class members. Because Paul's personal claim might predominate over common claims, the "commonality" and "typicality" factors weigh against bringing a class action. Specifically, most of the members of the class will be seeking restoration of their property in addition to any damages for fraud. There is no commonality among these claims as they are for very specific items. Furthermore, each collector would need to show that the item he or she received was not authentic. While Paul may be able to establish a general pattern of fraudulent conduct, it would be difficult for him to establish the counterfeit nature of all of the other traded items. Additionally, such proofs are unnecessary for Paul to prevail on his individual claim. For this reason, the final factor, "superiority," also weighs against a class action lawsuit. There is no reason that all 22 people could not sue Danny, for return of their authentic memorabilia and damages. In short, there is little reason to believe that judicial efficiency will be served if Paul is the lead plaintiff in a class action.

3. Injunctive Relief: In order to protect Paul Purchaser's memorabilia that is currently in Danny Dealer's possession, the lawyer could seek injunctive relief under MCR 3.310, prohibiting Danny Dealer from selling or trading Paul Purchaser's memorabilia.

The object of a preliminary injunction is to preserve the status quo. In order to obtain a preliminary injunction under MCR 3.310(A), the party seeking the injunction bears the burden of establishing that it will suffer irreparable injury if the injunction is not issued. Because a preliminary injunction is a form of equitable relief, it should not be issued where the party seeking it has an adequate remedy at law. *O'Melia v Berghoff Brewing Corp*, 304 Mich 471 (1943). The facts suggest that the items Paul traded were "rare." If the items of memorabilia are, in fact, unique and hard to replace, this might support the argument that mere money damages would be inadequate and that injunctive relief is warranted.

Injunctive relief lies within the discretion of the court. If injunctive relief is granted, the court rules provide that matter must be tried on the merits "within 6 months after the injunction is granted," unless the parties stipulate or good cause is shown. MCR 3.310(A)(5).

Two Student Answers—February 2008

Question 13—State and Federal Procedure—10 points

This is a state civil procedure question.

Issue #1: Under the Michigan court in order to enter a complaint that alleges fraud the plaintiff must plead facts with sufficient particularity that explain the elements of fraud. In this complaint Paul must also plead facts that show that there was an intent to defraud on the part of Danny, and that there was no mutual mistake as to the authenticity of the # of autographed photos and sports memorabilia that was exchanged between the two.

Issue #2: Paul's complaint can be brought as a class action if he can prove 4 things. commonality, adequacy, numerosity, and typicality. There is commonality in the fact that 21 other people allege that the "items they received in trade with Danny are forgeries and that there is an exchange of a similar number of items with Danny. The fact that this is memorabilia is different in sport and athletes is irrelevant. It must show that it is adequate, in that if the court grants relief to the class members all of the class member's grievances and claims will be addressed by one adjudication in the cause of action. This is possibly true here in that the others in the class action will either want many damages or replevin—their jobs back. He must also show numerosity, in that there are so many claimants, it is inefficient and unduly burdensome to adjudicate each issue separately and it is burdensome to join all parties into one suit. 21 plaintiffs probably will satisfy this in that there is a possibility that there will not be jurisdiction for all plaintiffs. And typicality that the representative plaintiff claim is typical of all other claimants that are seeking relief. The facts indicate that the forgeries received by the plaintiff all come from one potential defendant in similar transactions. It is sufficient to say that Paul's complaint should be brought as a class action. However, Paul would have to pay the expenses of modifying the potential class action plaintiffs and giving then the opportunity to opt out of the class action. A class action must be asserted at least 90 days after the complaint is filed.

Issue #3: Paul can seek a preliminary injunction to prevent Danny from selling his items or disposing of them until after the case can be decided on the merits. Here the court may grant a preliminary injunction if it can be shown that there will not be harm to the defendant; irreparable harm may result if one is not issued; and it will cause no burden or harm to the public.

In this case, the court will probably grant the preliminary injunction even though Danny may be temporarily harmed by the inability to sell Paul items to another customer.

Question 13—State and Federal Procedure—9 points

1. Fraud Claim: The claim for fraud must be plead with specificity. Statute of limitations for contracts is 5 years and for tort is 3 years. The person being sued must be given notice by a summons. The summons must be accomplished by the complaint.

2. A class action suit requires numerosity, meaning that there are several people the same claim against the same defendant. Generally a large number of people at 25-100 persons.

Another requirement is commonality. The complaints of each person is similar and against the same defendant. Another requirement is typicality. The complaints are typical of each other. Lastly, the remedy of bringing the complaint as a class is superior to that of the other remedies.

In this case, there are 21 persons who similarly claim that the items they received in trade with Danny were forgeries. Most of the other collectors exchanged a similar number of items with Danny, but their items involved a wider range of sports and athletes. Thus the elements of numerosity, commonality, and typicality have been met. Moreover, it would be in the interest of justice both financially and efficiency to try these cases as a class with Paul being the lead Plaintiff, rather than to have each one of these try their cases separately.

3. Paul could seek an injunction against Danny to either return them or not to sell them, or destroy them or damage them, until the case goes to court.

July 2008—Question 1

The Michigan Department of Correction (DOC) and Downriver Fence Maintenance (DFM) were parties to a contract where DFM had agreed to maintain the razor wire fences at all DOC correctional facilities in exchange for a $500 monthly fee. In January 2007, DOC stopped paying because it could no longer afford the $500 monthly fee due to budget constraints. DFM filed suit against DOC for breach of contract in Wayne Circuit Court. The case went to trial and the jury delivered a verdict in favor of DFM. The next day, DOC brought a motion for summary disposition, arguing that the circuit court lacked subject matter jurisdiction to hear their claim. DFM opposes the motion, arguing that DOC has waived the issue of subject matter jurisdiction by failing to raise it in its first responsive pleading.

Evaluate the merits of both DOC's motion for summary judgment and DFM's waiver agreement.

Model Answer to Question 1

Wayne Circuit Court lacks subject matter jurisdiction to hear the breach of contract claim against DOC. The Court of Claims has exclusive jurisdiction over "claims and demand, liquidated and unliquidated, ex contractu and ex delicto, against the State and any of its departments, commissions, boards, institutions, arms or agencies." MCL 6000.6419(1)(a). DOC is a department of the State of Michigan. MCL 791.201. A breach of contract claim is the type of claim that falls within the purview of MCL 600.6419(1)(a). Thus, this claim belongs in the Court of Claim and not circuit court. See also *Parkwood v State Housing Dev Auth*, 468 Mich 763 (2003).

DOC's motion to dismiss was likely brought under MCR 2.116(C)(4) for lack of subject matter jurisdiction. DFM argues that DOC has waived this issue because it failed to raise it in its first responsive pleading, such as the answer or a dispositive motion. DFM's argument will not prevail. Certain motions for summary disposition must be raised, at latest, in a party's responsive pleading. For instance, if the motion is brought pursuant to MCR 2.116(C)(1). *See also* MCR 2.116(D)(2) (providing time limits to raise defenses brought under MCR 2.116(C)(5), (6), and (7).) However, a motion for summary disposition brought pursuant to MCR 2.116(C)(4) "may be raised at any time." MCR 2.116(D)(3). It cannot be waived and need not be preserved. DOC, therefore, was not required to assert its defense of lack of subject matter jurisdiction in its first responsive pleading.

Accordingly, the circuit court should grant DOC's motion for summary disposition and dismiss the breach of contract claim.

Student Answer—July 2008

Question 1—Civil Procedure—9 points

1. DOC's Motion for Summary Disposition

A Motion for Summary Disposition under 2.116(c) tests the sufficiency of the Plaintiff's claim. All evidence, affidavits, pleadings, etc., are viewed in the light most favorable to the non-moving party. If it is determined that no genuine issue of material fact exists, movant is entitled to judgment as a matter of law.

Here DOC waited until after the jury verdict to bring this motion. This is likely too late. Instead they may have been able to bring a Motion for Judgment Notwithstanding the Verdict. (JNOV)

This motion will most likely not be successful.

2. Wayne County Circuit Court's Jurisdiction.

In MI, Circuit, District, Probate Courts are courts of general jurisdiction. Appellate courts are courts of limited jurisdiction. Circuit Courts have jurisdiction for cases where there is a dispute worth over $25 K.

Courts of general jurisdiction can hear all cases not falling under original jurisdiction and or federal court jurisdiction.

Here, this case was brought in W.C.C. most likely because the aggregate amount of the contract was more than $25K. Also, "Downriver" is likely in the close proximity/ and or headquartered in Detroit which is in Wayne County. DOC may argue that it is a division of State Government and as such would not fall under the jurisdiction of W.C.C. However, this contract dispute would most likely stand in W.C.C.

3. Waiver of Subject Matter Jurisdiction

Subject Matter Jurisdiction can be pled at any time during the proceedings, and as such, is not waived here.

Comment: This is an example of how good writing can really pay off. Although the examinee essentially missed the core issue that the Court of Claims has exclusive jurisdiction over claims against the state, leading at most to a score of 6, this examinee alluded to it in the last paragraph of Issue #2.

February 2009—Question 2

A barefoot Peter Piper picked a peck of pickled peppers, and he subsequently developed rashes on his hands and feet. His nearsighted dermatologist, Doctor Duck, did not have his contact lenses in place that day, and therefore could not see how severe the rashes on Peters' feet were. Instead, he thought all of Peter's rashes were minor and prescribed a cream to heal them. Unfortunately, the rashes on Peter's feet did not heal, but instead quickly turned gangrenous, requiring amputation of his feet.

Peter's attorney, Robert Reedem of Reedem & Weape, filed a notice of intent to file a medical malpractice claim against Duck and complied with all of the procedural requirements of the medical tort reform statute before filing his complaint for medical malpractice in circuit court. Along with service of process and a copy of the complaint, Reedem sent Duck a discovery request including interrogatories and request for production of documents demanding the following information: (a) Duck's medical files pertaining to his diagnosis and treatment of Peter; (b) Duck's medical files pertaining to his diagnosis and treatment of the other patients he saw on the day he treated Peter; (c) any malpractice insurance agreement covering Duck's medical practice; (d) Duck's net worth, assets, and liabilities; and (e) whether Duck has been a defendant in other medical malpractice complaints.

Duck has retained you as his attorney. Which, if any, of the requested materials are discoverable under Michigan law? Explain your answer.

Model Answer to Question 2

Discovery is available in circuit courts after the commencement of an action. MCR 2.302(A)(1). A civil action commences with the filing of a complaint. MCR 2.101(B). Additionally, interrogatories and request for the production of documents may be served on a civil defendant with service of the summons and complaint. MCR 2.309(A)(2) and MCR 2.310(C)(1).

The general rule governing discovery is that a party may obtain discovery on any matter as long as it is (a) not privileged and (b) relevant to the subject matter involved in the pending action. MCR 2.302(B)(1). Materials are discoverable even if they are not themselves admissible in court, as long as the information sought "appears reasonably calculated to lead to the discovery of admissible evidence." MRE 2.302(B)(1).

Peter's own medical records are discoverable. Although medical records are ordinarily privileged under the statutory physician-patient privilege, MCR 600.23157, the privilege belongs to the patient, not the doctor. Accordingly, Peter may intentionally and voluntarily waive his physician-patient privilege. *Kelly v Allegan Circuit Judge*, 382 Mich 425 (1969). As Peter's physician, Duck is a "custodian" of Peter's medical records, as the term is used in MCR 2.314(D)(1). As such, he must "comply with a properly authorized request for the medical information within 28 days after the receipt of the request" for a patient's medical information. *Id.*

Although relevant to whether Duck was unprepared to practice medicine on the day in question, Duck can, however, assert the physician-patient privilege to prevent discovery of the medical records of his other (nonparty) patients. The names and records of nonparty patients are protected by the physician-patient privilege. *Dorris v Detroit Osteopathic Hosp*, 460 Mich 26, 34 (1999).

The existence and terms of Duck's personal medical malpractice insurance policy are discoverable under express provision of MCR 2.302(B)(2). Even though MCL 500.3030 specifically precludes any reference to liability insurance during trial, the amount or extent of insurance coverage is a matter that affects the way a case may be prosecuted or defended, and so is relevant to the cause of action. Accordingly, MCR

2.302(B)(2) specifically allows a party to obtain discovery "of the existence and contents of an insurance agreement under which a person carrying on an insurance business may be liable to satisfy part or all of a judgment."

Duck's personal finances are not discoverable. *Bauroth v Hammoud*, 465 Mich 375 (2001), held that the financial status of a defendant physician (beyond insurance) is not relevant in a medical malpractice action. Moreover, the request is not reasonably calculated to lead to the discovery of admissible evidence.

The existence of previous medical malpractice lawsuits is discoverable. It is relevant because it may show that Duck has a habit of being negligent in certain material ways (such as practicing medicine without his contact lenses in place). Furthermore, it is not covered by any recognized privilege of Michigan law. The physician-patient privilege, MCL 600.2157, applies only to "information that [a] person has acquired in attending a patient in a professional character." Accordingly, it does not apply to the mere existence of other medical malpractice lawsuits.

Three Student Answers—February 2009

Question 2—Civil Procedure—9 points

This is a Michigan Civil Procedure Issue regarding discovery of five different pieces of information. Michigan has a very liberal policy regarding the rules of discovery. The general rule is that if the information is relevant and discoverable then it should be provided per the discovery request.

1) Duck's Medical Files regarding treatment of Peter is highly relevant and are easily discoverable and should be provided to Peter's attorney.
2) Duck's medical files regarding every patient he saw on the day he treated Peter is not relevant in any way to Peter's case, it would be incredibly voluminous to provide, and may be illegal as HIPA violation. Because it is not relevant and would be impractical if not illegal to supply, Peter's attorney probably should be denied this discovery request.
3) Duck's malpractice insurance is relevant and easy to obtain. While it may not be used as evidence later, it is relevant to Peter's attorney in building his case. It would probably be discoverable.
4) Duck's net worth, assets are probably not relevant to Peter's case unless he was a sole practitioner. If he is a sole practioner, then his personal financial information would be relevant and reasonably obtainable.
5) Duck's prior treatment record regarding lawsuits is highly relevant and reasonably obtainable and would probably be a reasonable request by Peter's attorney.

Question 2—Civil Procedure—8 points

Rules of Civil Procedure documents that are within scope of case may be discovered by production of documents or interrogation.

A) Duck's medical files: Discoverable within course of discovery because medical records are directly related to the case, and the doctor patient privilege is waived because it's directly at issue here. It is not work-product and could not be found otherwise. The request is specific and not overbroad, therefore, the records are discoverable.

B) Other patients records: undiscoverable even though evidence of other negligent acts that day is relevant. Doctor-patient privilege still exists as to those records that the privilege has not been waived and that information is not discoverable pursuant to MI Rules of Civ Pro.
C) Medical insurance: undiscoverable to show possibility of negligence or to prove ability to pay. But may be discoverable to show ownership, control, or license.
D) Duck's net worth, assets, and liabilities: undiscoverable-documents do not tend to show any fact in question. Discoverable document must tend to show a element of the issue presented. Here malpractice needs to show negligence of money available. That is a collection issue not an issue that goes to a genuine issue of material fact.
E) Evidence of prior complaints: may be admissible, because it goes to question of whether doctor is reckless or acts within a reasonable person in same profession with good standing in the community. A professional opinion is important to show if a reasonable doctor would have acted this way. If found to show that it goes to show material fact then it's admissible, it may be used to show standard of care.

Question 2—Civil Procedure—8 points

2(a) The Plaintiff can ask the court for a court order to obtain Duck's medical files pertaining to his diagnosis and treatment of Peter, as Duck is being sued for malpractice, his diagnosis of Peter is in controversy. As a result, if Duck refuses to produce the said document, he may be sanctioned.

(b) However, Peter might not be able to obtain Duck's medical files pertaining to his diagnosis are treatment of "the other patients" he saw on the day he treated Peter. In Duck's defense it is a violation of doctor-patient privilege protected by the law. Unless Peter can clearly show the relevancy of other patient's otherwise confidential information is related to his case, the court is unlikely to allow such materials to be discoverable.

(c) Under Michigan Evidence Rule, the insurance agreement is not admissible to prove liability unless it's used for other proper purpose, i.e. ownership, control, agency. Here, it is unlikely to be found discoverable as Peter's purpose of the document is to prove Duck's liability which is prohibited under Michigan law.

(d) Duck's net worth, assets, and liabilities may be deemed irrelevant to Peter's malpractice lawsuit against Duck. It may be not discoverable.

(e) It may be discoverable to find out whether Duck has been a defendant in other medical malpractice complaints. If for a proper purpose and those complaints found to be related to or similar to the instant complaint and the probative value out weighs the prejudicial effect.

July 2009—Question 2

Paul Potine was an avid kayaker. On May 4, 2005, Potine went kayaking along the Red Cedar River in East Lansing, Michigan, in his brand new, state-of-the-art kayak. Drunk Donald, a resident of Kentucky, was operating a small motorboat along the river and enjoying both the unseasonably warm May weather and a few too many Margaritas. Potine noticed Donald motoring erratically toward him. Afraid that

Donald did not see him, Potine began shouting and waving his paddle to make Donald aware of his presence. Despite Potine's warnings, Donald plowed into Potine's kayak from behind at a high rate of speed, flipping it over. Potine did not suffer any physical injuries, but his kayak, valued at $2,000, was destroyed.

On June 15, 2009, Potine filed suit in Ingham Circuit Court alleging that Donald negligently operated his motorboat, causing injury to Potine's property. He sought $2,000 in damages. Process was validly served on Donald at his Kentucky home. With the help of his attorney, Sam Shady, Donald filed an answer to the suit on July 22, 2009. Donald denied being negligent, but did not raise any affirmative defenses.

After dismissing Shady as his counsel, Donald has come to your firm seeking help for his defense. Your boss, a partner at the firm, believes that Donald might be able to have the suit dismissed for lack of personal jurisdiction (MCR 2.116(C)(1)), lack of subject-matter jurisdiction (MCR 2.116(C)(4)), and failure to file the suit within the appropriate statute of limitations (MCR 2.116(C)(7)).

Your boss has asked you to prepare a memorandum for him explaining the likelihood of Donald prevailing on each of these grounds, in advance of a meeting with Donald that will occur later today, July 28, 2009.

Model Answer to Question 2

Donald will not succeed in a motion for summary disposition under MCR 2.116(D)(1). A civil defendant must make a claim that the court lacks personal jurisdiction over him in his first motion for summary disposition or in his first responsive pleading, whichever is first. MCR 2.116(D)(1). Although Donald did not do so in his July 22, 2009 responsive pleading, Donald may amend his pleading once as a matter of course, as long as it is done within 14 days of serving the pleading. MCR 2.118(A)(1). An amended pleading may introduce a defense that otherwise would be waived. *Harris v Lapeer Public School System*, 114 Mich App 107 (1982). Accordingly, he may amend his responsive pleading to question the trial court's personal jurisdiction over him. He has one week remaining to do so as a matter of course, beyond which he must seek either Potine's consent or leave from the court before he can amend his complaint. MCR 2.118(A)(2).

Nevertheless, Donald's personal jurisdiction claim still must fail. It is true that Donald neither lives in Michigan, nor was served with process in Michigan. Accordingly, the courts of Michigan do not have general jurisdiction over Donald. MCR 600.701. However, because the alleged tort occurred in Michigan, Michigan courts have limited personal jurisdiction over Donald to render a personal judgment against Donald arising out of his alleged negligence. MCL 600.705(2). Therefore, this cause of action is appropriately brought in a Michigan court.

Donald's claim that the Ingham circuit court does not have subject-matter jurisdiction is meritorious. A party may raise the issue of a court's lack of subject-matter jurisdiction at any time during the proceedings, MCR 2.116(D)(4), so Donald does not need to amend his responsive pleading to include this ground for relief. The Ingham circuit court does not have subject-matter jurisdiction over Potine's lawsuit. Rather, the district courts have exclusive jurisdiction in civil actions when the amount in controversy does not exceed $25,000. MCL 600.8301(1). Accordingly, this civil action can only be pursued in district court.

Finally, Donald's claim that the statute of limitations has passed is also likely to be meritorious. Donald must raise his statute of limitations defense in his first responsive pleading. He must, therefore, amend his July 22, 2009 pleading to raise this issue. Donald may amend his responsive pleading once as a matter of course, as long as it is done within 14 days of serving the pleading. MCR 2.118(A)(1). He has one week remaining to do so as a matter of course, beyond which he must seek either Potine's consent or leave from the court to amend his complaint. MCR 2.118(A)(2).

In Michigan, the statute of limitations for tort actions involving injury to property is 3 years. MCL 600.5805(10). Because the alleged negligence occurred on May 4, 2005, the statute of limitations bars any action commenced on or after May 5, 2008. Potine's action is untimely, and therefore Donald is entitled to summary disposition on this basis.

Three Student Answers—July 2009

Question 2—Civil Procedure—9 points

This is a civil procedure action. Donald a client of ours wants his suit with the Plaintiff be dismissed for lack of PJ, SMJ, and failure to file a suit within the appropriate statute of limitations.

In order to have a successful suit a court must have both personal jurisdiction and subject matter jurisdiction. SMJ is whether Michigan has power over the type of claim. Michigan circuits courts/trial courts are courts of original and general jurisdiction. Original jurisdiction means that they are courts of first impression (go there first). The courts of general jurisdiction means that Michigan courts have jurisdiction over all types of claims except those where the amount in controversy is $25,000 or less, in which district courts have jurisdiction over the matter or if federal courts have jurisdiction over weird matters like maritime or cases involving ambassadors. The claim amount is a negligence claim for $2,000.00 in property damage. This amount would qualify jurisdiction proper in district court.

In federal court SMJ is proper if claim arises under federal law, statute, etc. and there is complete diversity (plaintiff and defendant are from different places) and the amount in controversy is more than $75, 000.00 But here, district court in Michigan is proper for SMJ. In order to be successful in SMJ motion to defeat it. Donald can raise this motion at anytime but it seems district court in Michigan has proper jurisdiction.

In addition to SMJ, the court must also have PJ that is Michigan courts power over the defendant and his property. In order to have PJ there are three ways. There is consent, presence, and Michigan's Long Arm Statute. There are two types of consent. Express consent is where the defendant agrees to be sued in Michigan, where a contract between the parties exists in Michigan, or where the injury occurred. The second type of consent is implied consent. Implied consent exists where the defendant has failed to object to PJ in his first response, then which it is forever waived. The defendant has 21 days to respond if it's in state service, if not in state he has 28 days. Here, the defendant did not expressly consent to be sued in Michigan, but it seems as though implied consent is present. The defendant was served out of state service in which the defendant had 28 days to respond and he failed to state an affirmative defense of Michigan lacking PJ over him.

Therefore, he has waived this defense forever. He may not come back and raise PJ again. The defendant has impliedly consented to PJ in Michigan. In addition to consent PJ over a person can be established through presence. Presence is available where the defendant is domicile in Michigan, actually present when served, and doing business in Michigan that is regular, systematic, and continuous. Donald's domicile is

Kentucky. His is there and he had intent to return there after being on the river with his motorboat in Michigan. Donald was actually present in continuous business. Therefore, there is no PJ based on presence. Lastly, PJ can be established through Michigan's Long Arm Statute. Under this statute Michigan has PJ where land is involved and located in Michigan, where the injury occurred, a marriage interest is involved, where an insurance contract is, and where a transaction of business occurred. The only factor present here would be that the injury to the boat occurred in Michigan, therefore under the Long Arm Statute Michigan would have PJ. Because the defendant failed to raise PJ as an affirmative defense in his first response he cannot bring it up later, it is forever waived.

In addition to a successful PJ claim the PJ claim must also be constitutional, that is the defendant must have established enough minimum contacts that it would be reasonable to believe that you can be sued in Michigan. Donald purposely availed himself of the protections of Michigan. He was operating a motorboat in the state and was negligent when he hit the plaintiff. There are enough minimum contacts to establish PJ in Michigan against the defendants.

The last claim is the statute of limitations claim on his negligence suit. In Michigan the statute of limitations for a negligence claim is 3 years. It must be filed within 3 years from which it was discovered. The injury to the boat occurred on May 4, 2005 and the plaintiff was clearly aware at the time the injury occurred, however, she did not file suit until June 15, 2009, which was 4 years later. This action would definitely be barred by the statute of limitations, it has exceeded the 3 year limit, but Donald failed to raise this defense in his first response. This claim would also be barred from being brought up later. Donald should have put the statute of limitations affirmative defense in his first responsive pleasing; therefore, it is waived.

Comment: Many examinees did well on this question, but like this answer, missed the 14-day rule that allows you to amend your pleadings. In this question, there still was a week to amend the answer to raise the affirmative defenses. The grader typically only took off 1 point for this error likely because so many missed it.

Question 2—Civil Procedure—9 Points

To: Boss Attorney
From: Attorney
Re: Likelihood of Donald Prevailing on Grounds for Suit

1. Dismissed for Lack of Personal Jurisdiction

In Michigan, personal jurisdiction is the court's jurisdiction over the person. Michigan Courts have jurisdiction over the person's who are domiciled in the District where the claim is brought and or in tort cases where the injury occurred.

Moreover, a motion for Lack of Personal Jurisdiction must be raised in a Motion in response, or it's waived. Here, Potine was injured in East Lansing, Michigan. Potine filed suit in Ingham Circuit Court. If personal jurisdiction is not proper. If Ingham is in East Lansing, then Personal Jurisdiction is proper and Donald would not be able to file a motion to dismiss.

2. Lack of Subject Matter Jurisdiction

In Michigan the DISTRICT Courts have subject matter jurisdiction over claims $25,000 or less. Circuit court has jurisdiction over $25,000 or more. Subject Matter jurisdiction can be filed at any time. Here, the tort claim for damage of the Kayak was $2,000 and district court has jurisdiction. Therefore, Donald will prevail if he filed a motion for lack of subject matter jurisdiction to dismiss a complaint.

3. Failure to file within Statute of Limitation

In Michigan, the statute of limitations for a tort claim is 3 years. Here, the injury occurred on May 4, 2005-Potine didn't file until June 15, 2009-approximately 4 years-well beyond the 3 years statute of limitations. Therefore, Donald can file a motion to dismiss for failure to file within the statutory limits which can be filed with a motion or in the response.

Question 2—Civil Procedure—8 points

To: Boss
From: Associate
Date: 7/29/09
Re: Donald's Potential Defenses

This is a civil procedure question. Donald's best defenses to the negligent operating charges lie in asserting that there has not been proper procedure.

The first issue is that Donald's first attorney, Sam Shady (SS) failed to raise defendant's defenses in their answer. Unfortunately, per the FRCP and the Michigan Rules of Civil Procedure, any defenses not raised in the first pleading are deemed waived. Here, SS failed to assert any of Donald's possible defenses when SS filed an answer to P's complaints these defense may be waived.

It is possible that D may get the suit dismissed for lack of personal jurisdiction. PJ exists when a court asserts jurisdiction over the person (parties) involved. To have a valid claim, the court must be able to assert proper personal jurisdiction, subject matter jurisdiction and venue must be proper. Proper PJ lies with the court who has jurisdiction in the area where the defendant resides (is domiciled). Here, that is Kentucky since the facts state that D is from KY. Also, PJ may be found where the events took place if the defendant purposely availed himself to the area. Possibly D could argue PJ is not proper because this was not an event involving purposeful availment.

Also D may be able to have the suit dismissed for lack of Subject Matter Jurisdiction (SMJ). SMJ is when the court has jurisdiction over the subject of the suit. Here, the suit is based on a negligence claim for about $2,000 in property damages. The property court in Michigan for a suit of $2,000 that involves property damage would be the district court. Therefore, because the suit should have been brought in district court, D may get it dismissed for lack of SMJ.

Additionally, the D may have a statute of imitations defense. The statute of limitations in Michigan for this type of claim is generally 3 years. The suit brought by P here against D was brought in over 3 years. Facts state the accident took place 5/4/05 and the suit wasn't brought until 6/15/09. This is over 4 years from the date of injury to date of claim and may be too remote from the injury date and void the SOL.

Overall, its likely D will be able to get the suit dismissed on one of these grounds.

February 2010—Question 1

You are the new associate in a Michigan law firm and you are taking over the circuit court files of another associate who left due to a long, serious illness.

In reviewing your newly acquired files, you discover an unfiled motion for summary disposition based on lack of subject matter jurisdiction. However, the file also contains a scheduling order issued by the judge that states, among other things, that "all dispositive motions must be filed, served and heard not more than 30 days after the settlement conference." The settlement conference was two months ago and the trial is set for 18 days from now.

You must meet with your supervising attorney to discuss the status of your files. **What will you tell your supervising attorney about whether the summary disposition motion should be filed, whether it will be heard, and what other steps might need to be taken to protect your client's interests? Explain your answer.**

Model Answer to Question 1

MCR 2.166 governs summary disposition motions. A motion for summary disposition based on a lack of subject matter jurisdiction is brought under MCR 2.115(C)(4). MCR 2.166(D) addresses when summary disposition motions must be raised. The grounds for the motion dictate which subrule applies. Subrules(D)(3) and (4) provide:

> (3) The grounds listed in subrule (C)(4) and the ground of governmental immunity may be raised at any time, regardless of whether the motion is filed after the expiration of the period in which to file dispositive motions under a scheduling order entered pursuant to MCR 2.401.
>
> (4) The grounds listed in subrule (C)(8), (9), and (10) may be raised at any time, unless a period in which to file dispositive motions is established under a scheduling order entered pursuant to MCR 2.401. It is within the trial court's discretion to allow a motion filed under this subsection to be considered if the motion is filed after such period.

MCR 2.116 (D)(3) and (4) were amended by the Michigan Supreme Court effective September 1, 2007. Before then, (D)(3) provided "the grounds listed in subrule (C)(4), (8), (9), and (10) may be raised at any time." The Staff Comment of the 2007 amendment states the amendments:

> Clarify that motions for summary disposition based on governmental immunity or lack of subject-matter jurisdiction may be filed even if the time set for dispositive motions is scheduling order has expired. Defects in subject-matter jurisdiction cannot be waived and may be raised at any time.

It is well established that subject matter jurisdiction can be considered at any stage of a proceeding because it calls into question the power of the court to hear a case." *Sumpter v Kosinski*, 165 Mich App 784, 797 (1988). Subject matter jurisdiction "can never be conferred by the actions of the parties." *Hastings v Hastings*, 154 Mich App 96, 99 (1986). Subject matter jurisdiction can also be raised on appeal. *Orloff v Morehead Mfg Co*, 273 Mich 62, 66 (1935).

Therefore, the supervising attorney should be advised that there is a dispositive motion to file but that the filing deadline has been missed. However, because a summary disposition motion regarding a lack of subject matter jurisdiction can be filed "at any time under MCR 2.116(D)(3), this rule will prevail over the trial court's scheduling order that places limits on the filing of motions.

However, the supervising attorney should also be told that the trial is in 18 days and summary disposition motions need at least 21 days notice. MCR 2.116(G)(1)(a)(i). Thus a motion to adjourn the trial to allow filing of the motion for summary disposition would be needed to have the motion heard before trial. One argument could be that the prior attorney's illness prevented him from timely filing the motion and that constitutes good cause for an adjournment. Additionally, it could be argued that a dispositive motion based on lack of subject matter jurisdiction should be heard before a trial is conducted. MCR 2.116(G) also contemplates the trial court setting a different period for the filing of motions and any replies.

Student Answer—February 2010

Question 1—Civil Procedure—8 points

This is a Civil Procedure question. The issue presented is whether a motion for summary disposition(s) can be filed based on lack of subject matter jurisdiction(s) even though the scheduling order issued by the judge states all dispositive motions must be filed, served, and heard not more than 30 days after the settlement conference.

According to the rules of Civil Procedure, a motion challenging SMJ (subject matter jurisdiction) can be challenged and filed at any time while the case is pending, even on first appeal. In this case, the case is still pending and is set for trial in 18 days. So, the rules of civil procedure allow for a motion challenging SMJ or a lack thereof could be filed now and at any time while this case is pending.

Although the motion for SD (summary disposition) is going to come in outside of the scheduling order issued by the judge; the scheduling order does not have to be strictly adhered to if there is good cause that can be shown as to why this motion for SD could not be filed, served and heard not more than 30 days after the settlement conference and it is now 2 months after the settlement conference.

In this case, good cause can be shown that I am now the new associate attorney on the case due to the previous associate leaving the firm due to a long, serious illness. An illness of which he has been suffering from prior to my taking over the case and thus is the reason for the motion for SD being unfiled.

I will tell all of the preceding to my supervising attorney; that the motion for SD should be filed to dispose of the case due to lack of subject matter jurisdiction thereby protecting my client's interest in getting rid of the case; that it will be heard by the judge since lack of SMJ can be challenged at any time while the case is pending, and if the judge does not want to hear the case because it's not within scheduling order, that there is good cause for the delay, and this is not an attempt to delay the trial or create an unfair hardship or disadvantage on opposing party.

Additionally, to protect my client's interests I will review the unfiled motion for SD that I found and make sure it was done with diligence and competence to make sure we give it our best shot to win the motion. Additionally, I will update my client on the status of the case.

July 2010—Question 1

Plaintiff sued defendant in circuit court for injuries from a car accident. Plaintiff contended defendant ran a red light. Defendant did not answer plaintiff's complaint; however, within the time for answering, defendant instead filed a motion for summary disposition under MCR 2.116(C)(10). In his motion, defendant claimed plaintiff had run the red light and that, pursuant to the court rule, "except as to the amount of damages, there is no genuine issue as to any material fact" and, consequently, defendant was entitled to judgment as a matter of law. Attached to defendant's motion were (1) his own affidavit, (2) affidavits of two bystander witnesses, and (3) the deposition testimony of a shopkeeper standing outside at the corner in question. All indicated they had seen plaintiff run the red light, leading defendant to his conclusion that no factual issue existed as to who had run the light.

After service of defendant's motion, plaintiff responded with a motion to enter a default against defendant for failing to answer plaintiff's complaint. Plaintiff also filed a response to defendant's summary disposition motion. Plaintiff contended in his response that there was a genuine issue of material fact, i.e., who had run the red light. Attached to plaintiff's response were (1) a reference to the paragraph in his complaint repeating that defendant had run the red light, (2) a letter from a witness stating he had heard from someone the next day that defendant had run the red light, and (3) an unsworn "opinion letter" from a body shop owner opining that the damage was indicative of defendant running the red light.

What motions should be granted or denied and why?

Model Answer to Question 1

Plaintiff's motion for entry of a default should be denied. When served with a complaint, a defendant "must serve and file an answer or *take other action permitted by law or these rules* within 21 days after being served with the summons and a copy of the complaint." MCR 2.108(A)(1), emphasis added. Because defendant took other action, filing and serving his motion for summary disposition within 21 days, his action precluded a default being entered against him. A defendant may file an answer or take other action. Doing neither could expose him to default. A summary disposition motion under MCR 2.116(C)(10) can be filed at any time. Defendant was on solid ground by responding by filing his motion, so plaintiff's motion must be denied.

Defendant's motion for summary disposition should be granted. Defendant has properly supported his motion for summary disposition where plaintiff has not supported his response. In *Skinner v Square D Co*, 445 Mich 153, 160-161 (1994), the Supreme Court discussed the parties' obligations under MCR 2.116(C)(10):

> The Michigan Court Rules provide a precise description of the respective burdens that litigants must bear when a motion for summary judgment is filed pursuant to MCR 2.116 (C)(10). Specifically, MCR 2.116 (G)(4) mandates that the party seeking summary judgment must specify the issues for which it claims there is no genuine factual dispute. Provided the moving party's motion is properly supported, MCR 2.116(G)(4) dictates that the opposing party must then respond with affidavits or other evidentiary materials that show the existence of a genuine issue for trial. If the opposing party does not so respond, the rule provides that 'judgment, if appropriate, shall be entered against him or her.' MCR 2.116(G)(4). In a similar fashion, this Court has explained the burden of the nonmovant as follows:
>
> Once a party is challenged as to the existence of the facts upon which he purports to build his case, the sum and substance of the summary

judgment proceeding is that general allegations and notice pleading are not enough. Matters upon information and belief and alleged common knowledge are not enough. *That party must come forward with at least some evidentiary proof, some statement of specific fact upon which to base his case. If he fails, the motion for summary judgment is properly granted.* [Durant v *Stahlin*, 375 Mich 628, 640; 135 NW2d 392 (1965) (emphasis added).] (Footnotes omitted.)

Defendant has specifically identified the issue about which he believes there is no genuine issue as to any material fact. Defendant has supported his motion with affidavits, admissions, depositions, or other admissible evidence. Defendant supported his motion with affidavits involving eyewitness observations. Once defendant did this, it was then incumbent on plaintiff to respond in a fashion to substantiate his belief that a material factual issue existed.

Plaintiff's burden was not carried by what he filed. His own restatement of what was in his complaint is insufficient because a responding party may not simply rest on mere allegations in the complaint. Moreover, the letters from the witness and the expert are not in any admissible format. Additionally, the content is of questionable admissibility. The evidence plaintiff has marshaled in support of his response to defendant's motion is insufficient to create the factual dispute necessary to defeat defendant's motion. Plaintiff's motion should be denied and defendant's motion granted.

Two Student Answers—July 2010

Question 1—Civil Procedure—8 points

Motion for Defendant

In Michigan, a complaint filed under MCR 2.116 (C)(11) can be filed at any time. When this complaint is filed the court should consider all affidavits, pleadings, and any other legally relevant evidence. In the light most favorable to the non-moving party, in this case the defendant may be permitted to file the complaint and his affidavit, affidavits of two bystander witnesses and the affidavit of the shopkeeper may be permitted.

Although Evidence may be logically relevant if it is not legally relevant the evidence is not permitted. In this case, the defendant and two bystanders on its face, seem to show first hand knowledge of the event; additionally if the shop keeper, who was standing on the corner, has first hand knowledge and no sensory issues (eyesight failure) then his affidavit will be permitted.

Michigan deems that any answer that is not responded to will be deemed admitted to a complaint. However, although defendant did not respond to the complaint he did file a timely (C)(10) motion. Additionally, the Defendant may also raise the issue of removing the matter to District Court if the damages exceed $25,000.00. The motion to remove this case can be considered of response

Thus, the motions raised by the defendant should be granted.

Plaintiff's motion

The Plaintiff must file a timely response to the (C)(10) motion. In this case, the plaintiff has filed a timely response. Additionally the plaintiff has asked for a default judgment which would allow for the plaintiff to succeed in this law suit. The defendant, in this case, has asserted facts that looked in the light most favorable to him should be weighed by a jury considering the affidavits and pleadings. Additionally, #1 plaintiff has entered an affidavit by one witness stating that he heard someone the next day . . ." This affidavit may not be legally relevant because it contains hearsay. Hearsay is an out of court statement made for the truth of the matter asserted. There are no exceptions or exclusions that would make this statement admissible; therefore, this statement will not be able to come in. #2 An opinion letter by the shop owner may not come in because a lay person is not technically deemed to be allowed to state an opinion on the facts of damages in this case. Therefore this affidavit may not be permitted. #3 Finally, the only other evidence that Plaintiff asserts is referenced back to the affidavits. Therefore on these facts and in the light most favorable to the non-moving party the court should grant the motion for summary disposition and the defendant should be successful.

Question 1—Civil Procedure—8 points

Motion for Summary Disposition under MRC 2.116(C)(10)

Under MI law, generally when a (C)(10) motion and a motion for summary disposition as to a genuine issue of material fact, the court has to look at all of the evidence in the light most favorable to the non moving party to determine if there is an issue that the jury needs to decide.

Here in considering the Defendant's motion, the judge would look to the elements of negligence. Under MI negligence it must be established that there is a duty, breach, causation, and damages. A Plaintiff has to establish that there is a prima facis case for negligence in order to survive the defendant's motion for summary disposition under MCR 2.116 C(10). Here, the Defendant has an abundance of evidence to indicate that he did not run the red light and cause the accident that resulted in the plaintiff's injury. He has provided Swann affidavits from himself, two witness, and deposition testimony of a shopkeeper. All swearing to the fact that the plaintiff was the one who ran the red light this indicates a strong case for the defendant. However, the plaintiff in his response to the defendant's motion would argue or has argued, that he has an opinion letter from the mechanic, albeit unsworn, a letter from a witness stating he had heard from someone the next day, that the defendant had run the red light and a reference to his complaint, indicating his statements to the facts he indicated as to defendant's liability, all of these things should shed some doubt as to whether the defendant is telling the truth and this as to whether there was a breach of his duty.

Here, it is clear from the evidence from the plaintiff that they are all hearsay documents, generally, not admissible when offered for the truth of the matter asserted.

For summary disposition (10). Even in the light most favorable to the Plaintiff (non-moving) the facts support the defendant's motion for summary disposition and the motion for defendant should be granted. Also, there doesn't need to be a prima face case as to damages.

The motion for defendant's failure to respond:

Generally, a defendant can respond to a plaintiff's complaint by filing a motion for summary disposition. These dispositive motions should be filed in defendant's first response to the plaintiff's complaint. So here, when the defendant filed his motion for summary disposition in response to the plaintiff's complaint he was responding.

Even though generally a defendant must file answer within 21 days of receiving service, and in their answer deny or admit the Plaintiff's allegations, this was not needed here since he did so by way of summary disposition. Once the motion for summary disposition has been granted or denied, then the defendant may file an answer. Obviously only if denied. So here the motion to enter a default must be denied as well.

Also hearsay is an out of court statement offered to prove the truth of matter asserted as to the defendant's documents for responding motion.

TORTS/NO FAULT INSURANCE

Questions, Model Answers, and Student Answers

The following section includes prior Michigan Bar Exam questions and model answers for **Torts and No Fault Insurance**. Many of the questions also include actual student answers with the amount of points that were earned to give you a better idea of what the graders expect. The student answers are immediately following the model answer for each question. Please pay close attention to the points received on each question. Although most samples represent "good" answers (i.e., received 8, 9, or 10 points), there are some samples that received 7 points (the minimum "passing" score for an essay), and a few that received very low scores to help you better understand the grading process and what is expected.

February 2001—Question 10

The City of East Grand Mountain, Michigan, approved the construction of a new library in the late 1980s. The city awarded a construction contract to the low bidder, Tooth & Nail Construction Company. Tooth & Nail completed the construction of the new library in February of 1991. The city immediately occupied the building and commenced its library operations. The library was open to the general public, no fees were charged, and the operation was supported solely by tax dollars.

On July 10, 1998, the library closed for the day, and the doors were locked at the usual closing time of 6 p.m. At 6:15 p.m., lights began to flicker in the science fiction section. This had never occurred before. The library maintenance person, Joe Fix, went to a junction box in the basement of the library to investigate. Joe noticed that the junction box was hot. Rubber gloves, rubber boots, and a fire extinguisher were hanging nearby for use in electrical emergencies.

Without using safety equipment, Joe Fix opened the door to the junction box. He did not know that the flickering of lights was caused by a cut in the insulation of an electrical line in the junction box, which was done in 1991 by an employee of Tooth & Nail's subcontractor, Current Events, Inc.

When Joe opened the door to the junction box, sparks began to fly, Joe was electrocuted, and a fire began. The fire spread throughout the building, and the building burned to the ground.

Unknown to Joe, or anyone else, a library patron, Bob Frye, had been in the stacks engrossed in a book when the library was closed. At 6:10 p.m. Bob looked at his watch, realized the library was closed, but decided to finish his reading unless someone asked him to leave. Bob died in the fire.

Bob's family appears in your office on June 10, 2000, and wants to retain you to sue the City of East Grand Mountain, Tooth & Nail Construction Company, Current Events, Inc. and the Estate of Joe Fix.

What legal principles must you consider when evaluating the suggested claims and the limitations and defenses to those claims?

Model Answer to Question 10

The City of East Grand Mountain is a governmental agency, and the operation of a library is a governmental function. As a general proposition, the City is entitled to governmental immunity from tort liability absent a recognized exception (MCL 691.1407).

There is a statutory exception to that immunity involving the ownership and maintenance of public buildings (MCL 691.1406). However, the governmental agency must have actual or constructive knowledge of the defect. No such knowledge is apparent from these facts.

Joe Fix is also the beneficiary of governmental immunity so long as his actions did not amount to gross negligence (MCL 691.1407(2)(c)). Ignoring the hot junction box and failing to utilize safety equipment are arguably gross negligence. However, the use of the safety equipment may not have prevented the fire but only protected Joe Fix so that he would be able to take appropriate action to extinguish the fire. There is, therefore, a proximate cause issue regarding the actions of Joe Fix.

The electrical contractor, Current Events, clearly breached its duty to use reasonable care.

Current Events was acting as an agent (subcontractor) of Tooth & Nail in the execution of its contract. Tooth & Nail is liable for the torts of its subcontractor agent.

However, the claims against a contractor resulting from an improvement to real property is limited by a six-year statute of repose which statutory period begins to run from the time of occupancy, completion, or acceptance of the work. The period of time may be extended to ten years in the case of gross negligence. As a result, a claim against either contractor is time barred unless the actions of Current Events would be found by the jury to constitute gross negligence.

A discussion may be made of the status of Bob Frye. The duty owed by a possessor of land to a person entering upon that land depends on the status of the visitor. A visitor has either been invited and is, therefore, an "invitee", is present with permission and is therefore a "licensee," or is on the premises without permission and is therefore a "trespasser." While the Restatement of Torts would classify Frye as a "public invitee," the Michigan Supreme Court recently ruled that a person is an invitee on a premises only if the premises is "held open for a commercial purpose," *Stitt v Holland Abundant Life Fellowship*, 462 Mich 591 (2000). It seems likely that Bob was a licensee under current Michigan law at the time he entered the library. Once the library closed with his knowledge, his status arguably changed from invitee to licensee or from licensee to trespasser. A land owner owes a licensee a duty only to warn of hidden dangers the owner knows or has reason to know of. The land owner owes an invitee a duty not only to warn of hidden dangers but to make the premises safe. The City, therefore, did not owe and did not breach a duty to Bob as either a licensee or a trespasser.

Student Answer—February 2001

Question 10—No Fault—None Available

> **Comment:** Students did not do well on this question. Therefore, there are no student answers on file. Many missed the governmental immunity issue, or if they identified it, they forgot about the public buildings exception.

February 2001—Question 12

On a snowy day in Grand Rapids, Dennis Finch opened the door to his vintage 1976 AMC Gremlin, which was legally parked northbound on Madison Ave., and sat down in the driver's seat. Dennis kept his door open and his legs outside the vehicle while he knocked the snow from his moonboots. Jack Gallo was speeding southbound on Madison Ave. and lost control on the icy surface. Jack's car crossed the center line and clipped Dennis' open car door, closing the door on Dennis' legs. Jack's car continued further and collided head-on with the car driven northbound by Nina Van Horn. Dennis suffered bruises on both his legs, was treated at the emergency room and was released with no follow-up treatment warranted. Jack suffered multiple fractures, resulting in several hospital visits and two months off work. Nina, who was wearing her seatbelt, was not injured. Her car was damaged, however.

Jack Gallo has come to you for legal advice regarding his rights and liabilities, as well as the rights and liabilities of the other parties to this accident. **Advise Jack on the responsibility for payment of all medical bills, lost wages, pain and suffering damages, and vehicle collision damage for each of the individuals involved and their respective vehicles. Assume that each individual was a Michigan resident, each owned the vehicle they were operating, and each had the appropriate insurance coverage, listing them as the named insured.**

Model Answer to Question 12

Dennis Finch: Dennis will receive his first-party no-fault benefits from his own insurance carrier which would include payment of his medical bills for treatment related to the injuries he sustained in the accident, his lost wages, if any (at 85% of his wages for the first three years), and replacement service benefits, if any (at $20 per day for the first three years). (MCL 500.3107) Under personal protection insurance, an insurer is liable to pay benefits for accidental bodily injury arising out of the ownership, operation, maintenance, or use of a motor vehicle as a motor vehicle. (MCL 500.3105) The priorities section of the no-fault code, MCL 500.3114, states that primary responsibility for payment of first-party no-fault benefits lies with the insurance policy where the injured party is a named insured. In the present case, Dennis is considered an occupant of his vehicle.

Generally, when accidental bodily injury arises out of the ownership, operation, maintenance, or use of a parked motor vehicle as a motor vehicle, the injury is not compensable unless an exception applies. (MCL 500.3106) In the present matter, however, since there was a moving vehicle also involved in causing the injury, finding an exception to the parked vehicle exclusion is irrelevant.

With regard to the collision damage done to Dennis' vehicle, that damage is the responsibility of Jack Gallo's insurer. While the no-fault code generally does not allow a tort claim for property damage, an exception to that rule applies to damage to vehicles that are parked in a manner as not to cause unreasonable risk of the damage which occurred. (MCL 500.3121, .3123) In the present case, Dennis' vehicle was not parked in such a manner and is, therefore, treated as any other "tangible property" under no-fault property protection insurance.

As to any third-party tort claim, Dennis Finch may not maintain an action for non-economic (pain and suffering) damages against Jack Gallo arising out of this accident. Dennis cannot show that his injuries exceed the requisite tort threshold (death, serious impairment of body function, or permanent serious disfigurement) in order to recover from Jack in tort. (MCL 550.3135) Further, Dennis' lost wages and replacement services, if any, do not exceed the daily, monthly, or three-year limitations on first-party benefits. (MCL 550.3107(1)(b)&(c), .3135(3)(c).

Finally, Dennis faces no tort liability from any party for his role in this accident.

Jack Gallo: Jack will receive his first-party no-fault benefits from his own insurance carrier, which would include payment of his medical bills for treatment related to the injuries he sustained in the accident, his lost wages (at 85% of his wages for up to three years), and replacement service benefits, if any (at $20 per day for the first three years). MCL 500.3107. The rationale for the insurer's liability for payment of first-party benefits MCL 500.3105, and the priority for payment of such benefits, MCL 500.3114, is discussed in greater detail above.

With regard to the collision damage to Jack's vehicle, that damage will be the responsibility of Jack or his own insurance carrier. The no-fault code does not allow a tort claim for property damage to a non-parked vehicle. Jack's recovery of any benefits for the damage to his own vehicle will depend on the terms of his insurance policy and the amount of coverage purchased. MCL 500.3121, .3123. As discussed above, Jack Gallo's insurer will be responsible for the property damage to Dennis Finch's vehicle. As to the damage to Nina Van Horn's vehicle, Jack remains liable in "mini-tort" for up to $500.00 to the extent that Nina's damages are not covered by her own insurance. MCL 500.3135(e)(d). The remainder of the property/collision damage suffered by Nina is her own responsibility or that of her own insurance carrier, depending on the terms of her insurance policy and the amount of coverage purchased, MCL 500.3135(e)(b), and is considered the "at fault" party.

Nina VanHorn: With regard to the property damage to her vehicle, Nina must look to her own insurer for payment of any collision damage, depending on the terms of her policy and the amount of coverage purchased. MCL 500.3121, .3123. Nina may, however, sue Jack for a "mini-tort" for up to $500.00 to the extent that her damages are not covered by her own insurance. MCL 500.3135(3)(d).

Finally, Nina faces no tort liability from any party for her role in this accident.

Student Answer—February 2001

Question 12—No Fault—8 points

With respect to Jack's liabilities to Dennis, who was sitting with his car door open when Jack crossed the center line speeding and lost control on the icy surface, thereby clipping Dennis' door and closing it on his legs, it would be appropriate to begin with a short discussion of MI being a no fault jurisdiction. That is to say, Jack has insurance on himself and on his car and Dennis has the same for himself and his car. Michigan law states that no matter what happens, no matter who hits who or who was at fault (so to speak), no one is, per se, to blame. All Michigan drivers are required to possess no fault insurance on the vehicles they drive, as the fact pattern here states the parties do. Dennis will have to pay the deductible on his insurance, which he may be able to later receive from Jack, for damage on his car and medical bills. The facts state that Dennis had to go to the hospital for bruises, but no follow up treatment was required. The only way Jack would be responsible for the same would be if he killed Dennis, if he caused serious disfigurement, or if a bodily function was seriously injured or impaired, none of which appear to be the case where Jack and Dennis are concerned.

With regard to Jack's liabilities to Nina, whom he collided head on with, the same applies. Nina appears to not have any injuries, so Jack bears no responsibility here; however, his car was damaged. Nina, carrying no fault insurance, will have her vehicle repaired at the expense of her insurance and if she is responsible for the deductible, she may sue on all claims to recover that from Jack.

In addition, Jack will be responsible under his own no fault insurance for his own injuries, including multiple fractures, hospital visits, and time off of work.

In conclusion, Jack may have little to no liability for his actions due to no fault insurance, to either Dennis or Nina.

July 2001—Question 12

Samuel Powers, a California resident, operating a semi-tractor/trailer owned and registered to his employer in California, was involved in a motor vehicle accident on I-94 in Wayne County. Ohio resident Zack Morris caused the accident when he lost control of his semi-tractor/trailer, crossed the median and struck the Powers' vehicle. The Morris vehicle was owned by and registered to his Ohio employer, whose insurance carrier filed a certificate of compliance pursuant to MCL 500.3163 stating that any accidental bodily injury occurring in this state arising from the operation or use of motor vehicle by an out-of-state resident who is insured under its automobile policy will be subject to the Michigan no fault system. The insurer of the Powers' vehicle had not filed such a certification. Powers and Morris were both seriously injured in the collision.

Mr. Powers has come to you for legal advice regarding his right and liabilities, as well as the rights and liabilities of the other parties to this accident. **Advise him on the responsibility for payment of all medical bills, lost wages, pain and suffering, damages, and vehicle collision damage for each of the individuals involved and their respective vehicles.**

Model Answer to Question 12

Samuel Powers: Samuel is not entitled to Michigan first-part no-fault benefits since he was not a resident of this state, and was not insured by an insurer which has filed §3163 certification. MCL 500.3113. Samuel must seek recovery of his economic damages (medical bills, wage loss, etc.) from his own insurer or that of his employer pursuant to the terms of those policies and the insurance statutes in California. He may also be entitled to workers' compensation benefits.

The collision damage to Samuel's vehicle is likewise governed by the terms of the California policy and the Michigan No-Fault Act does not apply. Samuel's employer (the owner of the damaged vehicle) is, however, entitled to pursue a "mini-tort" claim against Morris for up to $500 to the extent that the damages to Samuel's vehicle are not covered by its own insurance. MCL 500.3135(3)(d).

Regarding a third-party tort claim, Samuel Powers may maintain an action for non-economic (pain and suffering) damages against Morris arising out of this accident. Samuel should be able to show that his "serious injuries" meet the requisite tort threshold (death, serious impairment of body function, or permanent serious disfigurement) in order to recover from Morris in tort. MCL 500.3134. An out-of-state resident who is not otherwise required to purchase a no-fault policy is not necessarily precluded from seeking third-party tort recover, even though he may not be entitled to first-party benefits.

Finally, Powers faces no tort liability from any party for his role in this accident.

Zack Morris: Since the insurer of Zack Morris' vehicle has filed §3163 certification, Zack is entitled to Michigan first-party no-fault benefits. Under personal protection insurance, an insurer is liable to pay benefits for accidental bodily injury arising out of the ownership, operation, maintenance or use of a motor vehicle as a motor vehicle. MCL 500.3105. The priorities section of the Michigan No-Fault Act states that primary responsibility for payment of first-party no-fault benefits to employees who are injured while occupying a motor vehicle owned or registered by the employer lies with the insurer of the furnished vehicle. MCL 500.3113(3). Therefore, Zack will receive economic damages from his employer's automobile insurer which would include payment of his medical bills for treatment related to the injuries he sustained in the accident, his lost wages, if any (at 85% of his wages up to the statutory maximum for the first three years), and replacement service benefits, if any (at $20 per day for the first three years). MCL 500.3107. It should be noted, however, that to the extent that Zack Morris is entitled to workers' compensation benefits for his injuries, those benefits may be "set-off" from the no-fault benefits otherwise required to be paid by the no-fault insurance carrier. MCL 500.3109 explains that "benefits provided or required to be provided under the laws of any state or the federal government shall be subtracted from the personal protection insurance benefits otherwise payable for the injury." This provision is designed to avoid the duplication of benefits.

With regard to the collision damage done to Zack's vehicle, that damage will be the responsibility of Zack's employer or its insurance carrier. Zack's (employer's) recovery of any benefits for the damage to his employer's vehicle will depend on the terms of the Ohio automobile insurance policy and the amount of coverage purchased. MCL 500.3121, .3123.

Zack may not maintain any third-party tort suit against Samuel for non-economic damages for the reason that Zack was more than 50% at fault for the accident (MCL 500.3135(2)(b)) and is considered the "at fault" party. He does, however, still face tort liability to Samuel as discussed herein.

Student Answer—July 2001

Question 12—No Fault—None Available

Comment: Students did not do well on this question. Therefore, there are no student answers on file.

February 2002—Question 12

Alan Able planned to host a party at his home to celebrate a promotion he had received from his employer. He ordered food for the party from a catering company, including six gallons of ice cream. He invited lots of his friends to attend the party.

Bob Baker, an employee of the catering company, came to Able's house to deliver the food and ice cream. Able told Baker to put the ice cream in an old freezer in Able's garage. Baker followed Able's instructions, but cut his hand badly on the freezer's door handle. Because the freezer was so old, a part of the handle had become rusty and jagged, causing Baker's injury. Baker told Able that he had not noticed the sharp part of the handle when he opened the freezer, but that after he was hurt he looked carefully and did see the problem.

Later that day, Able's friends began arriving for the party. Able told one of them, Claire Carter, that there was ice cream in the freezer in the garage. Carter went to get some, and cut her hand severely on the freezer door handle.

The day after being injured, Baker sought medical attention for his cut. He had an allergic reaction to an anesthetic the doctor used, which caused paralysis in his hand. This allergy is extremely rare, and neither Baker nor the doctor had any reason to know Baker had it, to anticipate it, or to act differently in any way because of it. The paralysis is accompanied by severe pain.

Baker and Carter each seek damages from Able for their injuries. Discuss the strengths and weaknesses of their claims.

Model Answer to Question 12

This question involves issues of duty, proximate cause, and comparative negligence. Baker and Carter each have strong cases against Able, but there is a possibility that their own conduct in failing to notice the danger could reduce or bar recovery.

Baker's claim: Baker would be treated as an invitee for defining the duty owed by Able to Baker, because Baker was on Able's land for a purpose which was mutually beneficial to Baker and to Able. *See Doran v Combs*, 135 Mich App 492, 496 (1984). Able therefore owed Baker a duty to warn Baker of any known dangers, and to make the premises safe. This required Able to inspect the premises and, depending upon the circumstances, make any necessary repairs or warn of any discovered hazards. *See Stitt v Holland Abundant Life Fellowship*, 462 Mich 591, 596-597 (2000).

A jury could reach a number of conclusions that would support imposing liability on Able. It could conclude that Able would have discovered the dangerous freezer handle if he had inspected the premises adequately. It could also conclude that Able had not repaired the handle and that Able did not warn Baker about it.

Assuming that Able had liability for Baker's cut, Able would be liable for Baker's paralysis as well. A tortfeasor takes the victim as the tortfeasor finds the victim. Unusual extent of injury, because of the victim's unusual susceptibility, is not a defense. *See Wilkinson v Lee*, 463 Mich 388 (2000).

With regard to Baker's possible comparative fault, a jury question might be presented by Baker's statement that after the injury Baker did see the hazard. If it was possible to see the hazard after the injury, perhaps a reasonably prudent individual would have seen it before being hurt. If the jury concluded this basis that Baker had been negligent, Baker's recovery of economic damages would be reduced to reflect his percentage of responsibility. With regard to non-economic damages, if the jury concluded that Baker's negligence was greater than Able's, then Baker would not be entitled to any award for non-economic damages, such as damages for the severe pain. See MCL 600.2959 (2001).

Carter's Claim: Carter would be treated as a licensee for the purpose of defining the duty owed by Able to Carter, since Carter was Able's social guest. *See Preston v Sleziak*, 383 Mich 442, 453 (1970). Able therefore owed Carter a duty to warn of any hidden dangers Able knew or had reason to know, if Carter did not know about them or have reason to know about them. *See Stitt v Holland Abundant Life Fellowship, supra*.

Able definitely had knowledge of the hazard by the time Carter was hurt, since Baker had told him how he had suffered his injury. If the hazard was obvious, or if for any other reason Carter would have had reason to know about it, then Able would have been free from any obligation to warn Carter about it. However, if the hazard was not obvious, or if Carter acting reasonably might have been unaware of it, then Able would have had a duty to warn Carter about it. The fact that Baker saw the hazard after being hurt is not likely to be controlling on the issue of how obvious it was or of whether a reasonably acting person would have seen it. A jury would have to decide this question. Clearly, Able failed to provide a warning. This lack of a warning could be basis for liability.

Comparative fault principles would not affect Carter's claim. If failing to see the hazard was unreasonable, Able would have had no duty, and Carter would have no recovery. This lack of recovery would be based on a duty analysis, not a comparative fault analysis. *See Lugo v Ameritech Corp, Inc*, 464 Mich 512 (2001).

Student Answer—February 2002

Question 12—Torts—None Available

> **Comment:** Students did not do well on this question. Therefore, there are no student answers on file.

July 2002—Question 2

Jack Bauer is an employee of Fox Builders, a real estate developer and general contractor. David Palmer is an employee of 24/7 Plumbing Company. On the morning of June 1, 2002, the two men met at the Fox Builders headquarters and Mr. Bauer agreed to give Mr. Palmer a ride to the Fox construction site, where Mr. Palmer was to inspect the construction and provide Fox Builders with a bid for a plumbing subcontract.

Mr. Bauer drove a pick-up truck owned by Fox, with Mr. Palmer as his front seat passenger, on County Road 17 in Swamp County, Michigan. The road is maintained by the Swamp County Road Commission. As they approached a sharp curve, a bright yellow road sign was posted, advising of the approaching curve and with a curve advisory speed of 35 miles per hour. Mr. Bauer was operating the vehicle at approximately 35 m.p.h. as they approached the curve, but he did not see the sign since he was adjusting stations on the radio. Nevertheless, Jack Bauer returned his full attention to the roadway prior to actually entering the curve. As the vehicle rounded the curve, Mr. Bauer was unable to negotiate the curve because of his speed, lost control, and the truck careened off the roadway into a field. Both men suffered significant injuries, requiring hospitalization, prolonged medical treatment and lost time from work. Upon further investigation by law enforcement officials and experts for the road Commission, it was determined that the curve could only be safely negotiated at speeds of 25 m.p.h. or less.

David Palmer, a Michigan resident, has come to you for legal advice regarding his rights arising out of this accident. Provide a discussion of all courses of legal action available to Mr. Palmer for all damages he sustained in this accident.

Model Answer to Question 2

David Palmer will first receive his worker's disability compensation benefits from the workers' compensation insurance carrier for his employer, 24/7 plumbing Company, since his injuries "arose out of and in the course of employment." MCL 418.301. These workers' compensation benefits include payment for all medical, rehabilitation and treatment bills associated with the injuries he sustained as a result of this accident, MCL 418.315, as well as his lost wages, calculated at 80% of the after-tax value ("net") of his weekly wages, which continue indefinitely so long as he is out of work. MCL 418.301

In addition to these workers' compensation benefits, David is entitled to limited benefits under the Michigan No-Fault Automobile Insurance Act, MCL 500.3101, *et seq.*, since the injuries he sustained arose "out of the ownership, operation, maintenance, or use of a motor vehicle as a motor vehicle." MCL 500.3114, states that David Palmer must first seek benefits from his own personal No Fault carrier (where he is the named insured) and then from any policies issued to David's spouse or resident relatives. MCL 500.3114(1). Only if there are still no available policies does David Palmer collect no-fault benefits from the insurer of the owner of the vehicle in which he was a passenger. MCL 500.3114(4). Davis is not required to establish that he suffered a "threshold injury"' MCL 500.313, in order to receive first-party no fault benefits.

All amounts received by David Palmer in workers' compensation benefits may be subtracted or "set off" from the no-fault benefits otherwise payable for his injuries. MCL 500.3109. Since all of his medical bills are paid by the workers' compensation carrier, none are the responsibility of the no-fault insurance carrier. However, under no-fault, David would otherwise be entitled to 85% of his gross wages for the first three years after the accident. MCL 500.3107(1)(b). Accordingly, the no-fault carrier may only set-off the amount of wage loss paid by the worker's compensation between 80% of the net wages (paid by worker's compensation) and 85% of the gross wages (the full amount available under no-fault). MCL 500.3107(1)(b). Finally, the no-fault carrier is still responsible for payment of replacement/household service expenses, at a maximum of $20 per day for the first three years after the accident, reasonably incurred by David in obtaining services he would have performed for himself or his dependents had he not been injured. MCL 500.3107(1)(c).

As to any third-party tort claims, David Palmer may not maintain an action for damages against the Swamp County Road Commission arising out of this accident. According to the Supreme Court ruling in *Nawrocki v Macomb County Road Commission*, 463 Mich 143 (2000), the "highway exception" to governmental immunity does not impose a duty to install, maintain, repair, or improve traffic control devices, which are not considered part of the "highway." With regard to this area of the law, however, there are still arguments which may be made that an individual employee of the road commission may be found liable for an act of gross negligence related to the placement of the improper signage. This is still an unsettled area of the law, however.

One may also argue that David Palmer may have a tort claim against Jack Bauer for the negligent operation of a motor vehicle. In order to do so, David will be required to establish that he has suffered a "threshold injury" meaning that he has suffered a "serious impairment of a body function" or "permanent serious disfigurement." MCL 500.3135. Under the present circumstances, however, there is no indication that Jack Bauer's inattention to the signage had anything to do with the accident. In fact, even if Bauer had been looking at the sign, he was not traveling over the posted advisory speed limit. The facts show no other evidence of negligence on the part of Jack Bauer and David Palmer will have a difficult time making his proofs on proximate cause against Bauer.

The following are additional aspects to this factual scenario which are not essential to the basic understanding of the rights of the parties involved. Should an examinee spot these issues, however, credit should be given as appropriate:

1. Any property damage which occurred to the field where the vehicle came to rest is the responsibility of the no-fault carrier of the Fox Builder's truck. (MCL 500.3121.)
2. Any collision damage to the vehicle itself is the responsibility of Fox Builder's no-fault carrier, to the extent that this coverage was purchased and according to the terms of the no-fault contract. Collision damage coverage is an option which may be purchased for a higher premium, but is not required under the Michigan No-Fault Code.
3. If Palmer was able to somehow sustain a claim against Bauer, he could also make a claim against Fox Builders (the owner for the vehicle involved) under the Michigan Owners Civil Liability Act, MCL 257.401, and under the common law theory of negligent entrustment of a motor vehicle.
4. Nevertheless, should Palmer realize any recovery in tort for his injuries, he is required by the Worker's Compensation Act, MCL 418.827(5) to first reimburse his employer or insurance carrier for any amounts paid to him in worker's compensation benefits out of the proceeds of the tort action.

Student Answer—July 2002

Question 2—No Fault & Worker's Comp—7 points

I would first advise Mr. Palmer that in Michigan, Worker's Compensation is the exclusive remedy for job related injuries. His most likely recovery will come from his employer 24/7 Plumbing Company because Michigan law requires all employers to carry worker's compensation insurance.

However, depending on its independent contractor status, 24/7 may be considered an employee (subcontractor) of Fox Builders, in which case Palmer would be entitled to recover benefits from Fox Builders' insurance carrier. The facts that indicate Mr. Palmer was working for Fox are, 1) Palmer met Fox at F.B.'s headquarters, 2) He was in a vehicle driven by Bauer, a F.B. employee, 3) To a Fox construction site where he was to provide a plumbing bid for possible subcontract.

Under either employer however, Mr. Palmer will be entitled to recover for his work related injuries because he was within the scope of employment (driving from F.B. HQ to construction site). He will be able to recover 80% of his after tax weekly wage and all medical benefits will be covered. He may even choose his own doctor within 10 days.

Secondly, I would advise Mr. Palmer that if he wasn't covered by worker's compensation, he may be covered by Michigan No Fault law. In Michigan, drivers of registered vehicles must carry No Fault Insurance. For First party recovery claims a passenger may recover damages from the driver's insurance company for injuries resulting in a car accident in Michigan regardless of fault. Mr. Palmer will be able to recover for all medical losses and wage loss equaling 85% of his after tax weekly wage and he will be entitled to $20 per day for replacement services for the period of three years.

I would further inform Mr. Palmer that Michigan No Fault does provide for third party claims for negligence causing bodily harm above the No Fault threshold, death, services impairment of bodily function, or permanent serious disfigurement. The facts indicate both men suffered significant injuries. If Mr. Palmer's injuries exceed the No Fault we will also file a third party claim.

Comment: Notice that this question is a combination question of both No Fault and Workers' Compensation. The bar examiners have done this a few times. Realistically, both Workers' Compensation and No Fault are subsections of Torts. Watch out for a combination question that could also have a Torts claim for negligence if the "threshold injury" is met.

July 2002—Question 3

For a party for a children's soccer team, Alan Able set up a small portable barbecue grill in a neighborhood park to cook hot dogs and hamburgers. The players were all nine and ten year olds. One of them was Able's son, Bruce Able.

Because he was having trouble getting the charcoal to ignite in the grill, Alan Able went to a nearby gas station, "FastFuelCo," and bought a small amount of gasoline. He used one of the station's self-service pumps to put the gasoline into a plastic bottle that had originally contained milk. The bottle was not designed for storage or transportation of gasoline. Federal and state statutes prohibit the use of this type of bottle for gasoline.

About ten children were standing near the grill. Alan Able told them to stay away from it, but some of them continued to hang around nearby, talking to each other and kicking soccer balls. Alan Able poured a small amount of gasoline onto the charcoal. Although Alan had believed that the charcoal was cold, some of it was hot enough to ignite the gasoline. The gasoline he poured onto the charcoal and the rest of the gasoline in the plastic bottle, burst into huge flames.

Alan Able was burned. His son, Bruce Able, was burned. Also, another child, Carl Cates, was burned. Bruce and Carl were standing next to the grill when the flames erupted. Daisy Davis, a parent who was attending the party, rushed to the grill to attempt to help the children and sustained a serious burn when she banged into the hot grill. Ed Evans, an assistant coach who was not a parent of any of the children at the party, suffered a heart attack from the upset of seeing Bruce and Carl in the flames.

Bruce Able, Carl Cates, Daisy Davis, and Ed Evans all seek damages from Alan Able, claiming that his violation of the statutes and his use of the gasoline were negligent. Discuss the significant legal issues in these suits.

Model Answer to Question 3

The significant legal issues in the suits against Alan Able are: Alan's possible negligence, Bruce and Carl's possible negligence, Alan's possible defense of parental immunity, duty owed to a rescuer, and duty owed to protect a bystander from emotional distress.

Was Alan Able Negligent? The reasonable person standard applies to Able's conduct. A jury could properly find that it is unreasonable to pour gasoline onto charcoal that a person has been trying to ignite in other ways, since there is some risk that the charcoal may be hot enough to ignite the gasoline. The statutory violation would not support the plaintiffs' claim of negligence, since the purpose of the statute is to insure the safe transportation and storage of gasoline, not to protect against dangerous uses of gasoline. While violation of relevant safety statute is prima facie evidence of negligence, *Zeni v Anderson*, 397 Mich 117 (1976), to be applicable, a statute must have been enacted to protect against the type of harm the plaintiff suffered. *Beals v Walker*, 416 Mich 469 (1982).

Were Bruce and Carl Negligent? A child's standard of care would apply to the conduct of a ten-year old. *Fire Insurance Exchange v Diehl*, 206 Mich App 108, 119-120 (1994). A jury could determine whether the children's disobedience to the adult's instruction to stay away from the grill was negligent. Comparative negligence principles would apply if either child was considered to have acted negligently.

Is the Action by Bruce Barred by Parental Immunity? A parent is immune from tort liability to his or her child: (1) where the alleged negligent act involves an exercise of reasonable parental authority over the child; and (2) where the alleged negligent act involves an exercise of reasonable parental discretion with respect to the provision of food, clothing, housing, medical and dental services and other care. *Plumley v Klein*, 388 Mich 1, 8 (1972). In *Carey v Meijer, Inc.*, 160 Mich App 461 (1987), immunity was withdrawn where the defendant parent's conduct involved "direct commission of a wrongful act, placing the child in close proximity and turning on an electric range burner." The facts of this problem are similar, and could be characterized as involving ordinary negligence, not conduct specifically related to parental authority and supervision.

Alan Able would owe a duty to Daisy Davis under the rescuer doctrine. Danger invites rescue, and one who causes danger, as by starting a dangerous fire, will be treated as one who has caused an injury suffered by a rescuer. *Roberts v Vaughn*, 459 Mich 282 (1998).

Alan Able owed no duty to Ed Evans to protect him from the consequences of emotional distress. There is no duty to protect someone from emotional upset sustained as a result of seeing a non-relative's injury. *See Maldonado v National Acme Co*, 73 F3d 642 (6th Cir 1996), *Toms v McConnell*, 45 Mich App 647 (1973). It is highly unlikely that Michigan courts would recognize the coach-player relationship as equivalent to a familial one.

Two Student Answers—July 2002

Question 3—Torts—8 points

Bruce v Alan

Parental immunity. Bruce is Alan's son, so Alan would raise a defense of parental immunity should Bruce try to sue him in a negligence action. But Bruce may have a claim in a criminal context of parental neglect rather than tort.

Carl v Alan

Alan owes a duty to Carl. Alan should have known that 9-10 year old would possibly want to be near the grill where hotdogs and hamburgers would be cooked. A simple verbal warning was probably not enough to insulate him from liability. Carl would be compared to other 9-10 year olds in a similar situation. Plus, Carl can show that Alan was negligent per se, by virtue of the fact that Alan placed gasoline in the milk container in violation of a statute. Carl needs to show the causal connection-Bruce poured the gas on the coals causing flames to erupt. Foreseeable.

Daisy v Alan

Daisy claim comes is under a "rescuer" action. Alan should reasonably foresee that any injury he caused would invite a rescuer & therefore he also becomes liable to the rescuer for any injuries. Here, If Alan is found to have caused the injuries to the kids, Daisy's attempted rescue was foreseeable & Alan is liable for her injuries as well.—Daisy may also have a claim for negligent infliction of emotional distress as the parent of one of the injured kids.

Ed v Alan

Ed would raise a claim of negligent infliction of emotional distress. But, as a bystander, he was not related to anyone injured. Ed was not the parent of any child injured.

Question 3—Torts—8 points

The Issues

What was Able's duty to the children: as licensees? Was his violation of the statute conclusive proof of Negligence? Can his own child sue him? Can a parent who "rescued" sue him? Was he liable for Ed's heart attack?

Even though this picnic was not at Able's home, he would have certain duties to the children as licensees (social guest). It is not a high duty to inspect or keep safe, but it is a duty to warn of known dangers.

Bruce

Bruce, even though Able's son, is allowed to sue his father. Family immunities used to not allow this, but modern case law allows a child to sue a parent.

Carl

A licensee, Carl, may sue if not warned of known dangers. Carl can argue Able violated the statute, endangering him with the very thing the statute was designed to prevent: improper storage might lead to leakage or explosion. And that Able is liable for "negligence per se." And that Able did not adequately warn him of the danger Able could see before hand.

Daisy

Daisy will argue she should get damages since "danger invites rescue," and her rescue was foreseeable because of Able's negligence.

Ed

Ed will argue he should recover, since he suffered the heart attack as a result of Able's negligence, a form of negligent infliction of emotional distress.

Able's Side

Able will argue he did warn the children but the children were not cooperating, so they themselves were contributory negligent. And this was not his home, so he should not have a duty to licensees. And that the statute was not designed for the purpose of avoiding this kind of danger.

Conclusion

Since Able did violate the statute (which probably was, at least in part, designed to prevent this kind of mishap), that will at least be a piece of evidence that shows negligence. And even though the picnic was not at his home, he will probably have a duty to licensees since he invited them to come to the park. He will likely be found liable to Bruce and Carl and Daisy (as a foreseeable rescuer), but probably not Ed, since Ed was not a family member, and his distress causing the heart attack was not from witnessing a family member's injury. However, the children may have their damages reduced to the extent of their contributory negligence (standing too near the grill after warning).

February 2003—Question 4

Alan Able experienced some severe indigestion and went to his doctor, Bruce Baker, seeking treatment. Dr. Baker is a general practitioner. Dr. Baker referred Able to another doctor, Carol Carter, for some diagnostic x-rays. Dr. Carter is a specialist in radiology.

The x-ray procedure required that the patient drink a quantity of a liquid containing certain chemicals. Dr. Carter asked Able whether he was aware of any allergies. Able told Dr. Carter that he had no history of allergies. Dr. Carter then gave the liquid to Able and Able drank it.

Able suffered a severe allergic reaction to the liquid. He incurred large medical expenses for treatment, and has experienced a great deal of pain and emotional distress due to the allergic reaction.

Although Able told Dr. Carter that he had no history of allergies, in fact Able knew that he had experienced numerous allergic reactions to medicines and foods in the past.

Able believes that Dr. Baker should not have referred him to a radiologist and should have used other less risky diagnostic methods before ordering x-rays.

Able believes that he lied to Dr. Carter about allergies because he has a psychological impairment that makes him want to impress authority figures.

Able believes that Dr. Carter gave him twice as much of the liquid as she should have because she was confused about how many ounces are in a quart, and that consuming the extra amount of the substance intensified the harms he suffered.

Able plans to sue Dr. Baker and Dr. Carter, seeking damages for past medical expenses and past and future pain and suffering.

1. **Assume that a jury would be required to evaluate the conduct of Able, Baker and Carter. What standard of care would apply to each individual, and what requirements, if any, would a court impose for proof of the standard of care?**
2. **Discuss the strengths and weaknesses of any causation defenses that Dr. Baker might reasonably raise.**
3. **Assume that a jury found that Able's damages were $100,000 for medical expenses and $100,000 for past and future pain and suffering. Also assume that in allocating responsibility for Able's injury, a jury assigned responsibility of 55% to Able, 10% to Baker and 35% to Carter. For what damages would Baker be liable? For what damages would Carter be liable?**

Model Answer to Question 3

The standard of care applicable to Able would be the reasonable person standard. Although Able contends that he has a psychological disability, that category of impairment does not preclude application of the usual tort standard of reasonable care. A jury would be permitted to reach a conclusion about Able's conduct based on its own common knowledge.

The standard of care applicable to a general practitioner like Dr. Baker is the "recognized standard of acceptable professional practice of care in the community in which the defendant practices or in a similar community" (MCL 600.2912a). Testimony from an expert with knowledge of that same or similar locality standard would be required to establish whether general practitioners would ordinarily order x-rays as an initial step in treating symptoms like Able's.

The standard of care applicable to a specialist like Dr. Carter is "the recognized standard of practice or care within that specialty: (MCL 600.2912a). Testimony from an expert with knowledge of a national standard for radiology would be required to establish whether the dose administered by Dr. Carter was appropriate. There is a slight possibility that Dr. Carter's alleged negligence would fit within the common knowledge exception to the requirement of expert testimony in medical malpractice cases, as lay jurors could understand the issues associated with weights and measures. *See Dorris v Detroit Osteopathic Hospital*, 460 Mich 26, 44-46 (1999) (while issues of ordinary negligence can be judged by common knowledge and experience of a jury, allegations about hospital staffing decisions require expert testimony). However, expert testimony would likely be required to determine what dosage should have been given, even if jurors could then understand a deviation from that proper dosage without the help of an expert.

Dr. Baker might contend that the conduct of the plaintiff and the conduct of Dr. Carter were both superseding causes of the plaintiff's injury. A proximate cause is one that in a natural and continuous sequence, unbroken by any new, independent cause, produces the injury, without which such injury would not have occurred. *Weissert v Escanaba*, 298 Mich 443, 452 (1941). An intervening cause breaks the chain of causation and constitutes a superseding cause which relieves the original actor of liability, unless it is found that the intervening act was "reasonably foreseeable." *See*, e.g., *Moning v Alfono*, 400 Mich 425, 442 (1977).

A jury would be justified in concluding that negligent conduct by a patient in his interaction with another doctor was foreseeable. Similarly, a jury would be justified in concluding that a foreseeable consequence of conduct that leads a plaintiff to seek medical treatment would be negligent medical treatment. *See Reed v City of Detroit*, 108 Mich 224 (1896) (defendant who negligently injures plaintiff is also liable for further injuries done to plaintiff by the malpractice of a seemingly competent physician engaged to treat the injury); *Stahl v Southern M. R. Co*, 211 Mich 350, 355 (1920). ("If a person receives an injury through the negligent act of another, and the injury is afterwards aggravated, and a recovery retarded through some accident not the result of want of ordinary care on the part of the injured person, he may recover for the entire injury sustained, as the law regards the probability of such aggravation as a consequent and natural result likely to follow from the original injury"); *Gulick v Kentucky Fried Chicken Mfg Corp*, 73 Mich App 746, 750 (1977) ("appellants faced potential liability on the principle that they are liable for all foreseeable consequences including that a doctor may act negligently in treating the plaintiff's original injury").

If a jury assigned the plaintiff 55% of responsibility for his injury, the Comparative Fault statute would allow him to recover 45% of his economic damages (past and future medical expenses), but would preclude him from recovering any part of his noneconomic damages (pain and suffering). (MCL 600.2959). Dr. Baker would be liable for 10% of the economic damages, or $10,000. Dr. Carter would be liable for 35% of the economic damages, or $35,000. Each defendant's liability would be several, and not joint.

Two Student Answers—February 2003

Question 4—Torts—9 points

In every negligence action there are four requirements; duty, breach, causation, and a showing of damages.

Duty of Able

Issue: What standard of care should the jury apply to Able.

Rule: Able would be held to the standard of a reasonable and prudent person in his position. Despite his mental condition he will still be held to the "average person" standard.

Application: Here, we're told (even despite his mental condition) that he (Able) purposely told the doctor that he had no allergies even though he knew this wasn't true. This is not what a reasonable person would do. This is especially true with all the reports of allergic reaction to the chemicals. This will come into play when the jury is making a determination on whether he breached this duty.

The jury may view this failure to disclose at least a proximate cause of the injuries because it is foreseeable that someone with allergies could be allergic to the chemical. Failure to disclose this information means the doctor wasn't aware of this when giving him the chemical.

Thus, the jury may find that Able assumed this risk when going into the procedure and will likely reduce damage for comparative negligence.

Duty of Carter

Issue: What is the standard of care Carter will be held to?

Rule: Carter will be held to the standard of care of a reasonable and prudent doctor in good standing as a radiologist specialist. The standard applied to doctors is a national standards as opposed to the previous standard which was community standard. The reason for this is because modern doctors have more access to information globally (like through the Internet).

Application: Carter will argue that she was reasonable and that it was Able failing to disclose this information that caused the injury. In giving him the medicine, Carter felt assured that he was giving proper information. Thus her choice to give the chemical was based on that information.

However, it could also be argued that if Baker had sent Carter the charts of Able, there was a duty to double check those charts. If Carter didn't have the charts any reasonable and prudent radiologist specialist would check.

Conclusion: I think there's a strong case to show Carter breached her duty if it's found that she should have consulted the charts.

It's foreseeable that failing to check for allergies with such a serious procedure, would directly lead to this damage.

Duty of Baker

Issue: What is the duty of Baker owed to Able?

Rule: As with Carter, Baker owed the duty to act as a reasonable and prudent doctor based on national standards. However, he's only held to standard of a general practitioner.

Application: Baker as a reasonable and prudent general practitioner should have made sure that any records of allergies were reported to Carter.

If he didn't it could be said that he breached his duty and that it was foreseeable that non-disclosure could result.

Causation

Issue: Dr. Baker's causation, however, is the next issue.

Rule: As with Carter and with Able conduct, it must be the factual cause. This means that but for their conduct the accident wouldn't have happened.

It must also be the proximate cause meaning that their conduct was the foreseeable consequence.

Application: Here Baker will argue that he had no way to foresee that Able would lie about his history. This is especially true if Baker had not disclosed it to Baker. Thus, his part is too remote breaking causation.

This is a tough call here and would be a jury question.

Damages

Issue: What damages can Able recover?

Rule: Michigan is a comparative negligence state

Noneconomic: If the defendant is more than 50% at fault no recovery.

Economic: If the defendant is any at fault damages are reduced by that percent.

Application: Here, Baker and Carter would only be liable for economic damages. Baker's liable for 10% and Carter is liable for 35%.

Question 4—Torts—9 points

Able

Able will be held to a standard of an ordinary reasonable person or patient here. An ordinary reasonable person is an objective standard to which the court considers to be the "average" person in the community or "man on the streets". He will be held to this standard despite his psychological impairment. This is not factored into the standard unless such an impairment is infancy (being a child), having a disability (like blindness) or having a profession skill (like being a doctor). The only place this will matter is when damages are considered because under the Egg Shell Doctrine Dr. Baker and Dr. Carter must take the victim as they find him, with his psychological impairment. So if the injury the cause makes Able's impairment worse then they will be held liable for that.

Proof of the standard affecting Able is by clear and convincing evidence that he is an ordinary prudent and reasonable person. Actually this is simply presumed by the court in Tort situations.

Baker & Carter

Because Baker and Carter have the professional skills of being a doctor—general practitioner and a specialist in radiology they will be held to a higher degree of care then Able. They must act as a reasonably prudent person or doctor with like knowledge, skills and experience within that professional community. So Baker must act as any general practitioner would with the same skills and knowledge and Carter must act similarly as a specialist in radiology. Although you could use clear and convincing evidence again here to prove their skill, experience and knowledge, this is also a standard that is presumed in regard to those individuals who hold themselves out as professionals.

Baker—Causation Defenses

Causation refers to some type of linkage between a duty owed and an injury incurred. Causation is of 2 types—factual and legal causation.

Factual Causation general follows the "but for" test i.e. But for Dr. Bakers conduct Able would have haven injured. The defense to this is an "Even if test", here "even if Dr. Baker had not referred Able out, his indigestion could have lead to acid reflux cause, esophagus cancer and created a worse situation i.e. Able would still suffer an injury. There is no guarantee that despite what Dr. Baker did or did not do Able would not be harmed. Was he the proximate cause of Able's injury? No. Because he did not breach the duty he owed to Able, that of a reasonably prudent physicians. As a general practitioner he could not help him further so he referred him to someone—Dr. Carter, who could help him. Legal causation essentially says that we want someone to pay.

There are 2 defendants here, a substantial factor test may be used to determine which defendant is more at fault, if that can not be determined then Baker and Carter will be joint and severally liable for injuries to Able.

Legal Causation is a weak defense for Baker especially if society and the court simply just want someone to pay because it's fair.

Factual Causation is a strong defense for Baker because he acted as he should toward his patient; he was not negligent in his referral (no breach of duty). And he ultimately or proximately did not cause Able's injuries. It may have been a foreseeable injury in Dr. Carter's line of work but not in Dr. Bakers.

Damages

Michigan is a comparative negligence state. There are 2 types of Comparative Negligence—Pure and Partial. Pure Negligence allows the plaintiff to recover regardless of his percentage of fault. If he's 90% at fault he can still recover 10%. Partial Comparative Negligence allows the plaintiff to recover if his percentage of fault is less then 50%. His damage award will be reduced by his percentage of fault. If plaintiff is 50% + at fault he's barred from recovery. Michigan is a pure comparative negligent state as to economic damages (medical, loss wages) but is only a partial comparative negligent state as to non-economic damages (pain and suffering).

Able will not recover for pain and suffering because he is 55% at fault by not telling about his allergies. He will recover 45% worth of $100,000 for economic damages from Baker and Carter. 90% responsible in regards to Baker only being 10% i.e. Able gets 10% recovery from Baker. 75% responsible in regard to Carter i.e. Able can recover 35% economic damages from Carter.

July 2003—Question 5

Alan Able was eating dinner at Fine Foods, an elegant restaurant in a quiet rural town. Two other diners, Bruce Baker and Carl Collins, were seated at a nearby table. Suddenly, Baker and Collins began to argue. Baker picked up a glass vase from the table and began to wave it at Collins. Collins stood up and started to walk away. Baker then stood up holding the vase, and began to follow Collins. The restaurant owner saw Baker get up and rushed towards him to get the vase away from him. As he was doing that, the owner asked another patron to use a cell phone to call the police.

Baker shouted "I'm going to get you, Collins," and threw the vase at Collins. The vase missed Collins and hit Able's shoulder, injuring Able. Able walked quickly out of the restaurant to avoid further trouble, and tripped in a pothole in the restaurant's parking lot, injuring his leg. Able did not notice the pothole because he was looking around the parking lot trying to remember where he had parked his car.

Fine Foods had not been the scene of any serious fights in the past, although police had been called to the restaurant twice in the preceding year to deal with intoxicated patrons who were becoming aggressive.

Able seeks damages from Fine Foods on two negligence theories: (1) failure to protect against criminal conduct by a patron; and (2) failure to maintain its parking lot properly. Able seeks damages from Baker on an intentional tort theory. Discuss the significant issues raised by these claims.

Model Answer to Question 5

Introduction: Able's claim against Fine Foods based on a duty to protect against criminal conduct is likely to be unsuccessful. His claim against Fine Foods with regard to negligent maintenance of the parking lot is also likely to be unsuccessful. His claim against Baker is likely to be decided in his favor, although a jury would be permitted to assign a share of responsibility to Able if it finds that he was negligent in failing to see the pothole.

Third-party criminal conduct: With regard to criminal conduct by a patron, the duty Fine Foods owes to Able is "to respond reasonable to situations occurring on the premises that pose a risk of imminent and foreseeable harm to identifiable invitees." *See MacDonald v PKT, Inc.* 463 Mich 322, 325-326 (2001). The business operator is required to respond by "reasonably expediting the involvement of the police." *MacDonald, supra* at 326. Past events at the location, even if criminal, do not alter or increase this duty.

The situation at the restaurant involved a risk of imminent and foreseeable harm to invitees because Baker was acting in an aggressive manner. Also, the owner of Fine Foods obviously believed the situation involved risk, since he took steps to summon the police. Therefore, the duty recognized in *MacDonald* would apply. The method the owner used to summon the police was to ask a patron to make a phone call. The reasonableness of this effort might be a jury question.

If a jury found that the restaurant owner's effort fell below the standard reasonable response, then issues of causation would need to be addressed. Was the owner's lapse a cause-in-fact of any harm to Able? Able must prove that the defendant's conduct was both a cause in fact and a legal, or proximate, cause of his damages. *See Skinner v Square D Co.*, 445 Mich 153, 162-163 (1994). The defendant's conduct will be considered a cause in fact of damages if the damages, more than likely, would not have occurred but for the at-fault conduct. *See Haliw v City of Sterling Heights*, 464 Mich 297, 310 (2001).

A jury would be required to conclude that the restaurant owner's conduct was not a cause-in-fact of harm, since even if the owner had used another method of summoning the police, Able would have suffered his injuries before police could have been expected to reach the restaurant.

Premises Liability: With regard to premises liability, the duty Fine Foods owes an invitee like Able is to exercise reasonable care to protect the invitee from an unreasonable risk of harm caused by a dangerous condition on the land. However, this duty does not require precautions against open and obvious dangers that the invitee might reasonably be expected to discover. *Lugo v Ameritech Corp*, 464 Mich 512, 516-517 (2001) (invitor had no duty to protect invitee from pothole in parking lot). *See also Riddle v McLouth Steel Products Corp*, 440 Mich 85, 96 (1992). The pothole was likely open and obvious.

Intentional Torts: Baker's conduct could satisfy the definition of assault or of battery, depending on a jury's conclusion as to his intent. As stated in *Espinoza v Thomas*, 189 Mich App 100 (1991):

> An assault is defined as any intentional unlawful offer of corporal injury to another person by force, or force unlawfully directed toward the person of another, under circumstances which create a well-founded apprehension of

imminent contact, coupled with the apparent present ability to accomplish the contact. *Tinkler v Richter*, 295 Mich 396, 401; 295 NW 201 (1940); *Prosser & Keeton*, Torts (5th ed), §9, p 39. A battery is the willful and harmful or offensive touching of another person which results from an act intended to cause such a contact. *Tinkler, supra*; *Prosser & Keeton, supra*.

Liability for either tort would extend to physical harms caused by the defendant's conduct. While Baker's intent was to commit a tort against Collins, Baker will be liable to Able under the intentional tort doctrine of transferred intent. *See Adams v National Bank of Detroit*, 444 Mich 329 (1993), (one who intends to commit the tort of false imprisonment against a particular individual will be liable for that tort even if a different individual suffers the harm).

Comparative Negligence Statute: Able may have been negligent in failing to avoid the pothole. Baker could assert a comparative fault defense based on that negligence. In *Lamp v Reynolds*, 249 Mich App 591 (2002), the court noted that the state's comparative fault statutes define the term "faulty" to include intentional conduct. *See* MCL 600.6304(8). It recognized that a Michigan Supreme Court decision rendered prior to the adoption of the current statute had rejected application of comparative fault doctrines where an actor's conduct was intentionally tortious. *See Hickey v Zezulka* (On Resubmission), 439 Mich 408, 442 (1992). However, the court concluded that "distinguishing types of at-fault conduct is no longer a proper consideration when determining the viability of a comparative fault defense pursuant to the statutes at issue here (MCL 600.2957, 600.2959 and 600.6304)."

Student Answer—July 2003

Question 5—Torts—8 points

Failure to protect against criminal conduct by patron:

This is a negligence question that we must look at (1) duty, (2) breach, (3) causation (4) damages.

Fine Foods had a duty to protect his patrons from other dangerous customers. Here, Able will argue the Fine Foods has had prior knowledge incidents w/intoxicated patrons, and that Fine Foods did not take steps to insure Able's safety.

Fine Foods breached his duty when another patron threw the vase and injured Able. Fine Foods will argue that he took steps for Able's safety by calling police and rushing to stop the vase from getting thrown. But for, Fine Food not supplying a safe restaurant Able was injured and received damage.

Fine Foods will be found negligent for breaching his duty to protect his patron.

Failure to maintain its parking lot properly.

Fine Foods has a duty to an invitee to inspect the premises and warn about any known defects.

Here, the facts do not state if Fine inspected the premises or had any warnings.

Able was not looking where he was going and the pot hole was open and obvious, if he would have paid attention he would have not fell in hole. The Supreme Court of Michigan has stated that an owner does not have warn if the defect is open and obvious.

If the courts find the owner liable, Fine will ask for comparative neg. Able was at fault for not looking where he was going. If court finds Able at fault then Fine will only be liable for his portion of responsibility.

Baker for intentional tort.

Able will have a claim against Baker of battery. Baker intended to hit Collins w/the vase.

In tort, the intent can be transferred to a third-party.

A battery is an offensive touching. Here, Baker offensive touched Able and the intend transferred from Collins to Able.

February 2004—Question 1

Last month Alan Able clipped a "trial visit coupon" from a newspaper advertisement that entitled him to a trial visit at a health club and fitness center called Better Fitness Center (BFC). He went to BFC, presented the coupon, and asked if he had to pay a fee. The person at the desk told Able that there was a $5.00 fee and that he would have to sign a "sign-in" list so that Better Fitness Center could keep track of who used its coupons. The "sign-in" list had a printed paragraph at the top and lines for about twenty signatures below that paragraph. Able asked whether BFC had any treadmills, and then signed on one of the lines.

Able changed into exercise clothes in a locker room, and then went to an area of the facility where there were a large number of exercise machines. A short while later, Able was found dead on the floor against a wall near a treadmill. The cause of death was a head injury.

The back of the treadmill was positioned only about three feet from the wall where Able was found. Most exercise facilities place treadmills further away from walls because a person who uses a treadmill may be propelled backwards off the treadmill if he or she slips or loses balance. A person who is propelled off a treadmill may hit something like a wall or another machine if a wall or another machine is too close to the back of the treadmill.

No witness can be found who saw what happened to Able. The following descriptions are among the possible explanations for how Able suffered his fatal injury. Able might have:

1. slipped while using the treadmill and been propelled backwards off the treadmill and into the wall, or
2. fallen while walking among the exercise machines and hit his head on the floor, or
3. been pushed into a wall or machine by another person.

The treadmill Able was near was not in motion when Able was found, but it is equipped with a timer that turns the machine off after a period of time selected by a user has expired.

The entire text of the sign-in list's printed paragraph reads:

> MEMBER SIGN-IN. I understand that I am not entitled to a refund for membership fees or daily visit fees for any reason. I understand that BFC

endeavors to provide adequate numbers of exercise machines for the number of members expected to be present, but that BFC does not guarantee availability of any specific machine at any time. I agree that BFC is held harmless for damages owed due to discrepancies between its conduct and applicable definitions of legal duty.

Assume that you represent Able's estate. The estate is suing BFC seeking damages for Able's death on the theory that BFC was negligent to place its treadmill so close to a wall and that this negligence caused Able's death.

Discuss the strengths and weaknesses of your case with respect to proof you will need to present, and defenses you anticipate BFC will raise.

Model Answer to Question 1

The significant issues with regard to the strengths and weaknesses of the plaintiff's case involve: (1) proof of the defendant's negligence; (2) cause-in-fact; (3) proximate cause; and (4) effect of the "sign-in" form.

1. Defendant's Negligence: The defendant owed the plaintiff a duty of reasonable care, either as a matter of general negligence law or as a matter of premises liability law. With regard to premises liability, the duty BFC owes an invitee like Able is to exercise reasonable care to protect the invitee from an unreasonable risk of harm caused by a dangerous condition on the land. This duty does not require precautions against open and obvious dangers that the invitee might reasonably be expected to discover. *Lugo v Ameritech Corp*, 464 Mich 512, 516-517 (2001) (invitor had no duty to protect invitee from potholes in parking lot). The relationship between the treadmill and the wall would, of course, be obvious to anyone who saw both the treadmill and the wall, but the fact that close spacing could be dangerous might well be unknown and, therefore, "not discoverable" to people who are not experienced in the layout of exercise facilities.

The plaintiff's strongest proof of unreasonable conduct is BFC's failure to comply with industry custom. This failure is relevant but not conclusive on the question of BFC's negligence. *See Marietta v Cliffs Ridge, Inc.*, 385 Mich 364 (1971):

> The standard by which the negligent or nonnegligent character of the defendant's conduct is to be determined is that of a reasonably prudent man under the same or similar circumstances. *McKinney v Yelavich* (1958), 352 Mich 687. The customary usage and practice of the industry is relevant evidence to be used in determining whether or not this standard has been met. Such usage cannot, however, be determinative of the standard. As stated by Justice Holds:
>
> "What usually is done may be evidence of what ought to be done, but what ought to be done is fixed by a standard of reasonable prudence, whether it usually is complied with or not." *Texas and Pacific R. Co. v Behymer* (1903), 189 US 468, 470 (23 S Ct 622, 47 L Ed 950).

2. Cause-in-Fact: Was BFC's placement of the treadmill, if negligent, a cause-in-fact of any harm to Able? Able must prove that the defendant's conduct was both a cause-in-fact and a legal or proximate cause of his damages. *See Skinner v Square D Co.*, 445 Mich 153, 162-163 (1994). The defendant's conduct will be considered a cause-in-fact of damages if the damages, more than likely, would not have occurred but for the at-fault conduct. *See Haliw v Sterling Heights*, 464 Mich 297, 310 (2001).

This case involves an unwitnessed injury that could have been caused in a variety of ways. A causation theory must have a basis in established fact. Additionally:

> [a] basis in only slight evidence is not enough. Nor is it sufficient to submit a causation theory that, while factually supported, is, at best, just as possible as another theory. Rather, the plaintiff must present substantial evidence from which a jury may conclude that more likely than not, but for the defendant's conduct, the plaintiff's injuries would not have occurred. *Skinner*, at 45 Mich 164-165.

The plaintiff must provide a basis for a jury finding that more likely than not Able would have been free from injury if the treadmill had been located better. In other words, the plaintiff must show that slipping while using the treadmill was more likely than falling while near the treadmill or being pushed by another user of the club. Because Able's injury was fatal, it is likely that it involved force greater than the force of a fall or of being pushed to the ground. That stronger force could likely have been due to the motion of the treadmill.

3. Proximate Cause: If the plaintiff shows that negligent selection of the treadmill's location was a cause-in-fact of the injury, the plaintiff must also establish proximate causation. A proximate cause is one that in a natural and continuous sequence, unbroken by any new, independent cause, produces the injury, without which such injury would not have occurred. *Weissert v Escanaba*, 298 Mich 443, 452 (1941). Falling from the treadmill into the wall would be a direct result of poor placement of the treadmill.

4. "Sign-in" Form: The "sign-in" form purports to release BFC from liability for negligence. A release that is fairly made will be enforced even if it excuses an actor from liability for negligence. *See Xu v Gay*, 257 Mich App 263 (2003). However, if it is obtained by fraudulent or overreaching conduct, it will be void. *See Skotak v Vic Tanny Int'l, Inc.*, 203 Mich App 616 (1994). The language in this release might not have clearly communicated that it was an agreement to release BFC from negligence liability, since it did not include words like *release* or *waiver* and did not state that one who signed it was giving up negligence claims. Additionally, the defendant's employee lied about the effect of the document by saying that its purpose was solely to keep track of coupon usage. For these reasons, the form would likely fail to protect BFC from liability for negligence.

Student Answer—February 2004

Question 1—Torts—None Available

Comment: Students did not do well on this question. As a result there are no examples of "good" student answers. In general most students talked about the duty issue, but failed to discuss causation or the waiver. Remember, in every negligence claim, you want to make sure all four elements are discussed (duty, breach, causation, and damages). Quite often the elements that are not a central issue can be quickly dismissed in a sentence.

July 2004—Question 12

Alan Able was employed as a sales representative for a company that provided tutoring services for junior high and high school students. One day he went to a public high school to meet with some guidance counselors to explain his company's services to them. The guidance counselors had made appointments to see Able. He hoped that the counselors would recommend his company's tutoring services to students at the school.

On his way to the guidance counselors' offices, Able entered a men's bathroom. Because a sink's drain was not working properly, there was a chronic leak causing a puddle of water on the bathroom floor. The bathroom was brightly lit and the puddle was visible. Able slipped on the puddle and fell. He broke his hip and suffered intense pain.

Able sued the public school system that operates the high school in which he was injured. He sought damages for his injury, claiming that the school system was negligent in failing to repair the drain.

Discuss the basis for Able's suit and whether it will be successful.

Model Answer to Question 12

Under the current state of the law, Able is likely to lose. Although Able may be able to invoke the public building exception to governmental immunity, the open and obvious danger limitation on the duty owed to Able would likely preclude recovery.

When a plaintiff brings a negligence claim arising out of an alleged building defect against a governmental entity, a two question analysis is warranted. *Johnson v Detroit*, 457 Mich 695 (1998). The first question involves whether plaintiff's claim invokes the public building exception to governmental immunity. A governmental agency is generally immune from tort liability if it is engaged in the exercise or discharge of a governmental function. MCL 691.1407(1); *Swell v Southfield Public Schools*, 456 Mich 670, 674 (1998). The public building exception to governmental immunity provides:

> Governmental agencies have the obligation to repair and maintain public buildings under their control when open for use by members of the public. Governmental agencies are liable for bodily injury and property damage resulting from a dangerous or defective condition of a public building if the governmental agency had actual or constructive knowledge of the defect and, for a reasonable time after acquiring knowledge, failed to remedy the condition or to take action reasonably necessary to protect the public against the condition. MCL 691.1406.

In order for the public building exception to apply, plaintiff must establish the following: (1) a governmental agency is involved; (2) the public building in question is open for use by members of the public; (3) a dangerous or defective condition of the public building itself exists; (4) the governmental agency had actual or constructive knowledge of the alleged defect, and; (5) the governmental agency failed to remedy the alleged effective condition after a reasonable period. *Sewell, supra*, at 675.

These elements appear to be satisfied in Able's case.

(1) The school is operated by a governmental agency.
(2) The school building and the bathroom in which Able was injured are probably characterized as open to the public. *See Kerberski v Northern Michigan University*, 458 Mich 525 (1998) (the public building exception can apply to buildings to which the building has limited access and to areas within the buildings that are not open for use by the general public).
(3) The defectiveness of the conditions is conceded.
(4) Actual or constructive notice is probable for the leak since it existed long enough for a puddle to accumulate.
(5) Failure to correct each defect is also definite.

However, invoking the public building exception does not negate traditional tort law principles. *Johnson, supra*, at 710; *Kerbinski, supra*, at 525 n 5. A conclusion that the public building exception applies merely establishes that the government defendant undertook a duty to maintain its public building in good repair. This duty is only a general duty owed to the general public. Able must still demonstrate the elements of the negligence claim, including the duty owed to Able under the circumstances.

Application of the open and obvious doctrine would likely bar recovery. The open and obvious doctrine attacks the duty element of negligence. *Lugo v Ameritech Corp, Inc*, 464 Mich 152 (2001). The trial court must determine (1) whether there was an open and obvious condition, and (2) whether there were special aspects of the condition that made it unreasonably dangerous despite being open and obvious. *Lugo, supra*, at 526. The determination of whether a condition is open and obvious is governed by an objective standard: "Would an average user with ordinary intelligence have been able to discover the danger and the risk presented upon casual inspection?" *Novotney v Burger King Corp* (On remand), 198 Mich App 470, 475 (1993).

"Only those special aspects that give rise to a uniquely high likelihood of harm or severity of harm if the risk is not avoided will serve to remove that condition from the open and obvious danger doctrine." *Lugo, supra*, at 519. The puddle in the high school bathroom would not be such a hazard since it did not pose an extraordinarily high risk and since it could be avoided by an individual who encountered it.

Student Answer—July 2004

Question 12—Torts—9 points

Able suit will be brought as a duty owed to invitee and it may challenge that public school system is liable as a government agency tort action if gross negligent or statutory exception.

The public school system owes Able a duty to warn of known dangerous defect and duty to make reasonable inspection to discover the defect and make it safe.

Able is an invitee, as he is in the premise for a commercial purpose - provide tutorial services to the school.

Breach of that duty caused him to suffer a broken hip and its in a lot of pain.

Public school is the cause in fact and the proximate and legal cause of his injury. But for the failure of repairing the drain, Able would not have stepped into the puddle of water and fall and break his hip.

Public school defenses (PS) - it only has to warn if known and not obvious dangerous condition. The defect was not known and even if known the bathroom was brightly lit and the puddle was visible therefore PS need not notify or warn him of obvious and open danger.

PS might also argue that as government unit, it enjoys a broad grant of tort immunity and unless PS was grossly negligent or it falls under the statutory exception to immunity like 1) highway exception 2) public building or private enterprise, Able cannot bring a tort action against PS.

February 2005—Question 6

Computer Skills Center (CSC) opened a computer training business in a store that had formerly housed a fast food restaurant.

Alan Able enrolled in a course of study at CSC that was comprised of twenty (20) two-hour classes scheduled in a four week period. He signed a contract agreeing to pay for the classes. The contract specified stated:

> I understand that Computer Skills Center reserves the right to cancel registration and prohibit me from attending classes if I fail to respect rules and policies of Computer Skills Center. I agree to waive and/or disclaim any right to assert a negligence claim against Computer Skills Center for negligence, gross negligence, or any intentionally tortious conduct that may injure me.

Able attended several classes without any problems. When he arrived at CSC's facility for his fifth class, he was free to sit at any of several available computer tables. He chose a table with a chair that had a sharp split piece of wood protruding from the top of its back. When Able pulled the chair away from the table, the sharp portion of the damaged chair back cut his hand severely.

Able went to a hospital emergency room to have the cut treated. Because he had to wait there for several hours and because treatment took an additional hour, he was unable to keep an appointment for a job interview with ABC Corporation. The ABC job involved the type of computer work for which the CSC training course was preparing Able. Able did not get the ABC job.

Able has discovered that the chairs used at CSC had been used at the store when it was a restaurant. A statute in effect at the time the store was a restaurant and at the time Able was injured provided that in order to facilitate cleanliness and protect patrons from food poisoning, restaurant furnishings were required to be made from materials that could be cleaned thoroughly, such as metal or plastic, or if chairs were made with wood or fabric components, those components were required to meet specified standards relating to their resistance to bacteria. The chair that caused Able's injury did not satisfy the requirements of the statute.

Able has sued CSC claiming it acted unreasonably in providing a dangerous chair for his use. He seeks damages for his medical expenses and for lost future income due to his failure to obtain employment with ABC Corporation. Discuss the strengths and weaknesses of Able's case.

Model Answer to Question 6

Able's case is very weak. The release is probably effective to shield CSC from liability. Even if the release were rejected, Able would fail to establish a breach of duty because the hazard was probably open and obvious and the statute has no effect. Even if the release were rejected and CSC was found to have breached a duty, the future economic losses are too remote to be charged to the defendant.

Release: A release of liability for negligence is valid if it is fairly and knowingly made. *See Wyrembelski v St Clair Shores*, 281 Mich App 125 (1996). The release language in the document Able signed is clear. It uses the words "waive" and "disclaim." While extension of the waiver to liability for gross negligence or intentional torts is problematic, there is no basis on the facts of this case to raise a claim of either gross negligence or intentional tort.

Breach of Duty: CSC as a premises possessor is obligated to exercise reasonable care to protect its invitee (Able) from an unreasonable risk caused by dangerous condition. *Bertrand v Alan Ford, Inc*, 449 Mich 606, 609 (1995). This duty does not require CSC to protect Able from an open and obvious danger unless that danger has "special aspects" that make the risk unreasonable. Special aspects would be characteristics that make the danger extremely difficult to avoid, like a puddle of water located in a position that required an invitee to traverse it to leave a building. *See Lugo v Ameritech Corp, Inc*, 464 Mich 512, 518 (2001). Since many chairs were available, Able could not argue that the dangerous chair he used was a condition with special aspects that prevent the defendant from invoking the open and obvious danger element of the definition of duties owed to an invitee.

The statute does not help Able establish breach of a duty. Violation of a relevant safety statute is prima facie evidence of negligence (subject to a jury's consideration of excuses for violation—an issue not presented in this question). *Zeni v Anderson*, 397 Mich 117 (1976). However, to be applicable, a statute must have been enacted to protect against the type of harm the plaintiff suffered. *Beals v Walker*, 416 Mich 469 (1982). This statute was enacted to promote cleanliness in connection with food service enterprises. Basic doctrines of negligence per se would prevent its application to the operation of a computer training school since cleanliness was not at issue in connection with Able's injury and since the flaw in the chair is different from the type of flaw that the statute was meant to regulate against.

Proximate Cause: The causation portion of Able's case with regard to his physical injury is strong, since if CSC had breached a duty to protect him from physical injury, the medical consequences of that physical injury would be a proximate result of that breach. With regard to Able's claim for economic damages flowing from a missed appointment (assuming again that Able had been able to prove breach of a duty), Able's proximate cause case is weak. Proximate cause is usually a factual issue for the jury to determine. *Schutte v Celotex Corp*, 196 Mich App 135, 138 (1992), but this claimed economic injury is likely too speculative to be a legitimate element of damages. *See also Skinner v Square D Co*, 445 Mich 153 (1994) (cause-in-fact cannot be satisfied by a theory that is a mere possibility or suggests a course of events that is, at most equally as probable as other courses of events).

Two Student Answers—February 2005

Question 6—Torts—9 points

Able is injured and seeks compensation from CSC. The first issue is the exculpatory clause contained in Able's contract with CSC. Generally, these clauses are upheld in Michigan and will release CSC from liability for ordinary negligence. However, in cases of gross negligence, these clauses are void. Therefore if CSC's negligence was ordinary and we presume Able signed the contract, CSC will be released from liability for Able's injury. If Able's injury was due to gross negligence on the part of CSC, then the clause will be void and CSC will be liable.

Able seeks damages for his medical claim. The facts show that although Able could sit at any table, he chose one whereby a sharp piece of wood protruded and that he was aware of this fact. Since Able declined to choose a safer place to sit, he may have been contributory negligent. If the court determines Able was contributory negligent, Able may not prevail in his claim for medical damages, or his recovery may be reduced by the % of fault attributed to him.

On the other hand, CSC is an invitee. An invitee is a classification whereby a facility is open to members of the public. A computer training business is open to the public and therefore, CSC is an invitee. An invitee has a duty to keep the premises safe for its occupants and to reasonably inspect the premises to ensure there are no dangers present. The court may find that upon reasonable inspection, CSC could have become aware of the dangerous chair and thereby avoided Able's injury. If the court finds CSC's failure to inspect was gross negligence, Able will recover medical damages. If the court determines that CSC's negligence was ordinary negligence, Able will have assumed the risk and because of the exculpatory clause will probably not recover for medical expenses.

Additionally, since the restaurant seems to be in violation of the state statute prohibiting use of these chairs, the court will probably determine that this is not negligence per se because it fails the class of persons, class of risk test. This means that the type of injury Able sustained is not the type of injury the statute seeks to prevent. The violation of the statute is irrelevant for Able's purpose.

As to his claim for lost future income, most of the elements of negligence exist here, but not all of them. CSC may have had a duty to keep Able safe, which is breached, and but for the breach, Able would not be injured. However, the cause in fact element is missing because it is not foreseeable to CSC that its negligence in not removing the broken chair would cause Able to lose out on a job opportunity.

Further, the delayed treatment at the hospital may also be deemed as an intervening cause, and therefore Able will probably not prevail on his lost future income claim.

Question 6—Torts—8 points

In order to show a prima facie case for negligence, the plaintiff must prove that the defendant owed him a duty of care, breached that duty and that the defendant's breach was cause in fact and legal cause of their injury/damages (to have a case in tort, the plaintiff must suffer damages).

Duty of care can arise out of a special relationship between the plaintiff and defendant. Here CSC owed Able a duty of care because Able was an invitee on the premises. Able was on the premises for the purposes of CSC's business, which was open to the public. Therefore CSC owed Able a duty of protection against all dangers known to it or that should have been known through reasonable inspection.

An invitor cannot contract away its duty of care through a waiver clause as seen in the facts. Moreover, one cannot agree to waive intentional torts committed upon them. Because of Able's status as an invitee (and because the waiver clause is of no effect) Able can recover because of CSC's breach of duty. CSC breached its duty by failing to discover and protect against the chair on which Able injured his hand. Therefore, Able can sue for the damage to his hand.

In Michigan the theory of pure comparative negligence is applied to economic damages. Under this theory, the plaintiff will recover no matter how much they are at fault. Therefore, under these facts Able will be able to recover his medical expenses. But he will not be able to recover lost wages because he was not an employee of ABC at the time of his injury and there is no guarantee that he would have gotten the job had he not missed the interview.

Lastly, the statute included in the facts is not appropriate to Able's situation because he was injured in a school, not a restaurant and he did not suffer the type of injury (food poisoning) the statute sought to protect against. Moreover, Michigan does not recognize negligence per se violating a statute is only evidence of negligence.

Therefore, Able will likely recover his damages to his hand because CSC's breach of duty to its invitees. But won't recover for lost wages.

July 2005—Question 9

At a baseball game between two high school teams, a player named Alan Able was at bat. He was not playing well that day, and he struck out. He began to walk back to his dugout, as is customary, carrying his bat. He felt frustrated and upset, and he suddenly stopped and hurled the bat behind him in the general direction of the infield where the opposing team's pitcher and other players were waiting for the next batter to approach home plate.

None of the players in the field were looking at Able when he threw the bat. Unfortunately, the bat hit Bruce Baker, a player who was playing first base. The bat hit Baker in the side of the face, making a loud noise. Baker immediately fell to the ground and was unconscious. Baker was taken to a hospital where it was determined that he had sustained a serious brain injury.

Baker's mother, Bonnie Baker, saw this incident and started sobbing hysterically as she became aware that her son had apparently suffered a significant injury. Since that time, she has suffered from anxiety and depression related to the incident, but has had no other symptoms.

Alan Able had a history of difficulty in controlling his emotions. Once he pushed a schoolmate down three steps at the entrance to a building. On another occasion, he slammed a door in the face of a person he thought had insulted him. Able's father, Amos Able, had consulted with a psychiatrist about this conduct. The doctor had examined Alan Able and recommended to Amos Able that his son participate in sports as a way of learning how to handle frustration better.

Bruce Baker has sued Alan Able and Amos Able, seeking damages in tort for the injuries he suffered. Bonnie Baker has sued Alan Able and Amos Able, seeking damages for emotional distress. Discuss the significant issues raised by each of these claims.

Model Answer to Question 9

Introduction: Bruce Baker's claim against Alan Able is governed by a limited duty rule: A participant in a recreational sport such as baseball can be liable to another participant for an injury only if the injury was inflicted recklessly or intentionally. The facts of this case could likely support a finding of reckless conduct by Alan Able.

Bruce Baker's claim against Amos Able seeks damages for negligent parental supervision. The facts fail to support this claim, since Amos Able apparently followed expert advice in allowing Alan Able to play baseball.

Bonnie Baker's claim against Alan Able is based on the theory of negligent infliction of emotional distress. To succeed on this claim, Bonnie Baker would have to show (among other factors) that Alan Able acted tortiously towards her son and that she suffered physical manifestations of emotional distress caused by seeing Alan Able's conduct. While Alan Able may have committed a tort, Bonnie Baker has no physical manifestations of distress.

Bonnie Baker's claim against Amos Able requires a showing that Alan Able breached a duty owed to Bonnie Baker and that Amos Able acted unreasonably as a parent. The facts fail to support each of these showings.

Because they were participating in a recreational sport, Alan Able's only duty towards Bruce Baker was to refrain from injuring him recklessly or intentionally. In *Ritchie-Gamester v City of Berkley*, 461 Mich 73, 89 (1999), the plaintiff was injured while ice skating during an open skating session by another skater skating backwards, who ran into her causing her to fall and allegedly sustain injuries. The Supreme Court affirmed the trial court's dismissal of the plaintiff's negligence claim, holding that "co-participants in a recreational activity owe each other a duty not to act recklessly." *Ritchie-Gamester, supra.*

Alan Able's conduct could be characterized as reckless. The Supreme Court has defined recklessness as follows:

> One who is properly charged with recklessness or wantonness is not simply more careless than one who is only guilty of negligence. His conduct must be such as to put him in the class with the willful doer of wrong. The only respect in which his attitude is less blameworthy than that of the intentional wrongdoer is that, instead of affirmatively wishing to injure another, he is merely willing to do so. The difference is that between him who casts a missile intending that it shall strike another and him who casts it where he has reason to believe it will strike another, being indifferent whether it does so or not.

Gibbard v Cursan, 225 Mich 311, 321 (1923), quoting *Atchison, T & SF R Co v Baker*, 79 Kan 183, 189-190; 98 P 804 (1908). Throwing a bat as Alan Able did cannot be characterized as part of the game of baseball; furthermore there is a high probability of serious injury inherent in the act. If the conduct is found to have been reckless, Bruce Baker would be entitled to recover. If the conduct was found to have been careless or unreasonable, but not reckless, then Bruce Baker's claim would fail.

Bruce Baker might have a claim against Amos Able. In *Amer States Ins Co v Albin*, 118 Mich App 201, 206 (1982), the court explained the liability for a parent under a negligent parental supervision theory:

> The law in Michigan is that a parent is under a duty to exercise reasonable care so to control his minor children as to prevent them from intentionally harming others or from so conducting themselves as to create an unreasonable risk of bodily harm to them if the parent knows or has reason to know that he has the ability to control his children and knows or should know of the necessity and opportunity for exercising such control. *Dortman v Lester*, 380 Mich 80, 84; 155 NW 2d 846 (1968), citing *May v Goulding*, 365 Mich 143; 111 NW 2d 862 (1961); *Muma v Brown*, 378 Mich 637; 148 NW 2d 760 (1967).

Assuming that Alan Able, a high school student, is a minor, Bruce Baker's claim can succeed against Amos Able only if Alan Able committed a tort against Bruce Baker and if Amos Able failed to exercise reasonable care in connection with Alan Able's likely conduct. The facts show that Amos Able consulted a psychiatrist and received advice suggesting that participation in sports would be a good thing for Alan Able. Also, the bad conduct by Alan Able that led to the psychiatric advice was itself bad but not entirely startling for an adolescent. The fact that the misconduct was only moderately severe further supports the conclusion that Amos Able acted reasonably in response to it.

Bonnie Baker's claim against Alan Able would be for negligent infliction of emotional distress, also known as bystander liability. To establish a claim for negligent infliction of emotional distress, a plaintiff must establish:

> (1) "the injury threatened or inflicted on the third person must be a serious one, of a nature to cause severe mental disturbance to the plaintiff"; (2) the shock must result in actual physical harm; (3) the plaintiff must be a member of the immediate family, or at least a parent, child, husband or wife; and (4) the plaintiff must actually be present at the time of the accident or at least suffer shock "fairly contemporaneous" with the accident.

Wargelin v Sisters of Mercy Health Corp, 149 Mich App 75, 81 (1986), quoting *Gustafson v Faris*, 67 Mich App 363, 368-369 (1976).

To recover for negligent infliction of emotional distress, a plaintiff must establish that he or she suffered "a definite and objective physical injury." *Daley v LaCroix*, 384 Mich 4, 12-13 (1970).

Bonnie Baker could show that there was a serious injury inflicted, that it was inflicted on her son, and that she saw it as it happened. She will fail, however, to show that she suffered physical harm as a result of her emotional distress, as the problem's facts state only that the experience led her to suffer anxiety and depression.

It should be noted that Bonnie Baker's claim would also fail if it was determined that Alan Able did not commit a tort against Bruce Baker.

Bonnie Baker's claim against Amos Able would require her to show that Alan Able, Amos Able's son, breached a duty to her and that negligent supervision by Amos Able was a cause of that injury. As shown in the prior section, Alan Able did not breach a duty to Bonnie Baker, since the elements of the tort Bonnie Baker sought to establish include a showing of physical harm that Bonnie Baker did not suffer. Even if Alan Able had breached a duty owed to Bonnie Baker, establishing that Amos Able acted unreasonably as a part would be unlikely, for the reasons given above in the discussion of Bruce Baker's negligent supervision claim against Amos Able.

Student Answer—July 2005

Question 9—Torts—8 points

This is a tort claim involving Bruce Baker.

BAKER

Alan Able struck Baker when Alan threw his baseball bat behind him. This was not a battery. A battery is an intentional, offensive/harmful contact with plaintiff/plaintiff's person. Alan did not intend to strike Baker.

However, there is a potential negligence claim against Alan Able. For a negligence claim, plaintiff must prove: 1) Duty, 2) Breach, 3) Causation—Actual & Proximate, and 4) damages.

The standard of duty of care is a reasonable prudent person under the circumstances. Alan Able, by throwing his bat, did not act like one under the circumstances. He breached his duty when he threw the bat in the direction of the field. Further, there are no causation problems—Alan Able directly caused Bruce Baker's injuries as the bat hit Bruce Baker. As a result, Baker sustained brain injury. Therefore, Baker can recover all his expenses as a result of injury against Alan Able. No defenses—Bruce did not assume the risk of someone throwing a bat the way Alan Able did.

AMOS ABLE

Amos is the father of Alan Able and will not be liable for his son's/Alan's negligence. While a parent is no longer immune from his child's actions/torts, the parent has wide discretion in his/her child's actions. Only if Amos knew Alan was predisposed of violent actions/torts against other individuals could Bruce have a claim. Here, there are no such facts. To the contrary, Amos was told by a psychiatrist that Alan should participate in sports.

BONNIE

The theory that Bonnie is claiming is an Emotion distress theory. Intentional inflection of emotional distress requires that D's/Able's actions be 1) extreme & outrageous (beyond bounds of all decency), 2) that D acted intentionally/recklessly and 3) severe emotional distress. Bonnie was present at the game where she personally witnessed her son's/Bruce Baker's injury. The facts indicate that Bonnie suffered anxiety & depression.

I don't think that Bonnie can recover under IIED, or under the Bystander rule of IIED, as Alan Able did not know that Bonnie/victim's family would be at the game & intend she/Bonnie would get ED.

Bonnie can't recover under negligent infliction of ED—this requires a negligent act; plus, Bonnie must have witnessed the accident & suffered physical harm—none.

Comment: This was a complex tort question with multiple issues. Most students did not do well on this question. This answer is missing the issue related to the limited duty rule when participating in recreational sports (only liable for reckless or intentional conduct), yet it still receives 8 points.

February 2006—Question 13

Alan Able had been feeling sick for several weeks. His general practitioner, Dr. Bruce Baker, suggested that he be examined by Dr. Charles Carter, a specialist in diseases of the blood. Mr. Able called Dr. Carter's office and asked to make an appointment. The office manager told Mr. Able that Dr. Carter would see him, but that Dr. Carter required all of his patients to sign various forms in connection with his medical practice.

Mr. Able made an appointment and went to Dr. Carter's office on January 5, 2004. Before Dr. Carter examined Mr. Able, the office manager asked Mr. Able to sign a series of forms. One of them described Mr. Able's privacy rights. Another form was titled "Exculpatory Agreement," and stated, "I hereby release Dr. Charles Carter from all suits, claims, liability, or demands of any character, which I or my heirs, executors, administrators, or assigns hereafter can, shall, or may have arising out of conduct by Dr. Carter." Mr. Able signed all of the forms.

Dr. Carter examined Mr. Able and ordered a number of blood tests. A week later, Dr. Carter told Mr. Able that he was generally in good health, but that he needed to exercise, eat better, and get more rest. Dr. Carter told Mr. Able that he would like to examine him again in about four months.

On May 4, 2004, Dr. Carter examined Mr. Able again. After the examination, Dr. Carter told Mr. Able that he had a very serious and usually fatal blood disease. Alan Able received treatment for the disease, but died in September 2004.

Mr. Able's estate has brought a wrongful death action against Dr. Carter, alleging that he should have diagnosed the disease in January, and that if treatment had started in January, Mr. Able's chance of survival would have been 60%, but that his chance of survival in May, when Dr. Carter actually made the diagnosis, had decreased to 40%.

To support the allegation that Dr. Carter should have diagnosed Mr. Able's disease in January 2004, the estate plans to introduce testimony from Dr. Baker, a general practitioner. To establish the survival chances, the estate plans to introduce testimony from a physician who is a specialist in blood diseases.

Discuss the strengths and weaknesses of the estate's case.

Model Answer to Question 13

There are three issues with regard to the claim by the estate against Dr. Carter: the effect of the release, the adequacy of the proof that Dr. Carter should have made an earlier diagnosis, and proof of causation (whether loss of a 60% chance of survival is an adequate basis for a finding of proximate cause).

Release: The release will not protect Dr. Carter from the estate's claim. In *Cudnik v William Beaumont Hospital*, 207 Mich App 378 (1994), the court held that, on public policy grounds, a signed release purporting to release a hospital from negligence liability was unenforceable. This position is held by the overwhelming majority of states that have addressed the question. The court noted that medical services are of great public importance, are a practical necessity, and that the release (as is true of the release in this question) was in standardized contract offered by an actor with an advantage in bargaining strength over any member of the public who sought medical services. This issue has not been treated by the Michigan Supreme Court.[1]

1. In *Paul v Lee*, 455 Mich 204 (1997), the court stated that the holding in *Cudnik* suggesting that all covenants not to sue or releases from liability in the context of medical treatment are invalid and unenforceable, even those involving nonessential, non-life threatening medical treatment, as dicta. This suggests that the court would likely apply the factors the *Cudnik* court specified on a case-by-case basis; the facts of this problem involve treatment for a serious health problem, not the kind of "nonessential non-life threatening" medical situation covered by the dicta in *Cudnik*.

Expert Testimony: Since the estate's claim requires proof of the standard of care applicable to a specialist in diseases of the blood,[2] testimony from a general practitioner would be inadequate unless that general practitioner had experience or some other basis that gave him a basis for knowing how specialists in diseases of the blood would normally act in the circumstances presented to the defendant in January 2004.

The estate's proof regarding survival chances does not present this problem, since the question states that the testate would provide testimony by an expert on that precise topic.

Proximate Cause: The estate's proof is not adequate to support a finding in favor of the state on proximate cause. Where a plaintiff seeks recovery for malpractice that caused loss of a chance of survival, MCL 600.2912a(2) provides: "In an action alleging medical malpractice, the plaintiff cannot recover for loss of an opportunity to survive or an opportunity to achieve a better result unless the opportunity was greater than 50%." The opportunity to survive, at the time Dr. Carter allegedly committed malpractice, was 60 percent. Pursuant to *Fulton v Pontiac General Hospital*, 253 Mich App 70 (2002), the estate must show that the opportunity to survive was reduced by greater than 50 percent because of the alleged malpractice. In other words, MCL 600.2912a(2) requires the estate to show the decedent's chances of survival fell more than 50 percentage points between the time of the alleged malpractice in January and the discovery of the blood disease in May.

---

2. MCL 600.2169 provides in part:

(1) In an action alleging medical malpractice, a person shall not give expert testimony on the appropriate standard of practice or care unless the person is licensed as a health professional in this state or another state and meets the following criteria:

(a) If the party against whom or on whose behalf the testimony is offered is a specialist, specializes at the time of the occurrence that is the basis for the action in the same specialty as the party against whom or on whose behalf the testimony is offered. However, if the party against whom or on whose behalf the testimony is offered is a specialist who is board certified, the expert witness must be a specialist who is board certified in that specialty.
(b) Subject to subdivision (c), during the year immediately preceding the date of the occurrence that is the basis for the claim or action, devoted a majority of his or her professional time to either or both of the following:

(i) The active clinical practice of the same health profession in which the party against whom or on whose behalf the testimony is offered is licensed and, if that party is a specialist, the active clinical practice of that specialty.
(ii) The instruction of students in an accredited health professional school or accredited residency or clinical research program in the same health profession in which the party against whom or on whose behalf the testimony is offered is licensed and, if that party is a specialist, an accredited health professional school or accredited residency or clinical research program in the same specialty.

* * *

(2) In determining the qualifications of an expert witness in an action alleging medical malpractice, the court shall, at a minimum, evaluate all of the following:

(a) The educational and professional training of the expert witness.
(b) The area of specialization of the expert witness.
(c) The length of time the expert witness has been engaged in the active clinical practice or instruction of the health profession or the specialty.

Student Answer—February 2006

Question 13—Torts—None Available

July 2006—Question 4

XYZ Corporation operated an indoor ice rink where amateur teams competed in the sport of hockey, and individuals could receive lessons in hockey and ice skating and could practice those skills. XYZ charged fees for the use of its facility. The facility was in a medium-size city where several other ice rinks also were located.

One evening, while taking a skating lesson, a fifteen-year-old boy named Andy Able was injured. Another teenager, named Bruce Baker, was practicing skating. He was a skater of somewhat below-average ability who knew the limits of his skill. Despite this knowledge, Bruce tried to skate very quickly and make a sharp turn near Andy. Bruce fell down, colliding with Andy. Andy suffered a concussion.

On the same evening, a fourteen-year-old boy named Cory Charles was injured. While about thirty people were skating in the rink, an adult named David Drake wrapped a towel around his head covering his eyes and attempted to skate very quickly from one side of the rink to the other. This maneuver required him to skate in the close vicinity of numerous other skaters. He collided with Cory, causing Cory to suffer a broken leg. At the time, Cory was absentmindedly looking up at the ceiling instead of paying attention to other skaters on the ice. Because Cory had an unusual bone disease, treating this injury required medical procedures that were more expensive and painful than would ordinarily be required to treat a broken leg.

David's conduct received widespread publicity in the city where the rink is located. Television and newspaper reports emphasized the danger David created. Following this publicity, XYZ Corporation experienced significant economic losses due to a decrease in the number of skaters choosing to use its facility.

Discuss the significant issues in the following three lawsuits brought in connection with these events:

1. **Andy against Baker, seeking damages for Andy's concussion;**
2. **Cory against David, seeking damages for Cory's broken leg; and**
3. **XYZ Corporation against David, seeking damages for the decrease in revenue linked to publicity about David's conduct.**

Model Answer to Question 4

Introduction: This question involves a number of duty questions: what duty of care do participants in recreational activities owe to each other, what is the child's standard of care, and whether there is a tort duty to protect others from mere economic harm. It also requires application of the "eggshell-skull" rule, basic concepts of recklessness, and comparative fault principles.

Issue 1: Andy Against Baker, Seeking Damages for Andy's Concussion: The standard of care owed by Baker to Andy is to refrain from recklessness, because they were engaged in a recreational activity. *See Ritchie-Gamester v City of Berkley*, 461 Mich 73 (1999), (skating injury case would be governed by recklessness standard).

Bakers conduct may have been unwise, or negligent, but it cannot sensibly be characterized as reckless. The Michigan Supreme Court has stated:

> One who is properly charged with recklessness or wantonness is not simply more careless than one who is guilty of negligence. His conduct must be such as to put him in the class with the willful doer of wrong. The only respect in which his attitude is less blameworthy than that of the intentional wrongdoer is that, instead of affirmatively wishing to injure another, he is merely willing to do so. The difference is that between him who casts a missile intending that it shall strike another and him who casts it where he has reason to believe it will strike another, being indifferent whether it does so or not.

Gibbard v Cursan, 225 Mich 311, 321 (1923), quoting *Atchison, T & SFR Co v Baker*, 79 Kan 183, 189-190 (1908). Baker skated so fast that he was unable to control his motion, but his skill when he did so was only moderately below average. It is common knowledge that people improve their athletic skills by practicing and by testing their limits. Society seeks to encourage that kind of conduct, rather than to discourage it by characterizing it as reckless.

Issue 2: Cory Against David, Seeking Damages for Cory's Broken Leg: David owed Cory duty to refrain from recklessness. Considering the standard of recklessness, David was likely reckless. Everyone knows that it is highly dangerous for an adult man to skate quickly while he is unable to see where he is going. In the language of Michigan State Supreme Court, David was essentially "a missile" and David cast it "where he has reason to believe it will strike another, being indifferent whether it does so or not."

Cory's conduct, if negligent, must be taken into account. The child's standard of care applies to Cory, since he was fourteen years old at the time of his injury. Minors are required to exercise "that degree of care which a reasonably careful minor of the age, mental capacity and experience" of other similarly situated minors would exercise under the circumstances. MCJI2d 10.06 (emphasis added). *See also Fire Ins Exchange v Diehl*, 450 Mich 678, 688 (1996), overruled in part on other grounds *Wilkie v Auto-Owners Ins Co*, 469 Mich 41 (2003); *Stevens v Veenstra*, 226 Mich App 441, 443 (1997). Applying that standard, a jury might well find that Cory was negligent, since being aware of one's surroundings while on a crowded ice rink would seem necessary and reasonable to many teenagers of Cory's age.

If a jury were to find that David had acted recklessly and Cory had acted negligently, the comparative fault statute would require a reduction in damages to which Cory would otherwise have been entitled. MCL 600.2959 requires such a reduction since it covers all fault including even intentional conduct as well as any other breach of legal duty.

Cory's unusual weakness does not preclude recognition of the full effect of David's conduct on Cory. The "eggshell skull" rule requires a defendant to take the plaintiff as he or she finds him or her.

Issue 3: XYZ Corporation Against David, Seeking Damages for the Decrease in Revenue Linked to Publicity About David's Conduct: David owed no duty to XYZ to refrain from tortuous conduct that could be a cause-in-fact of economic harm to XYZ. XYZ may recover for the economic effects of David's conduct only if David's conduct also inflicted physical harm on XYZ's property. *See Henry v Dow Chemical Co*, 473 Mich 63, 75-76 (2005). ("We therefore reaffirm the principle that a plaintiff must demonstrate a present physical injury to person or property in addition to economic losses that result from that injury in order to recover under a negligence theory [for economic losses]").

Student Answer—July 2006
Question 4—Torts—8 points

Andy v Baker

The first issue is whether Andy can prevail in a negligence action against Baker. To prove negligence a plaintiff must establish that Baker had a duty of reasonable care, Baker breached the duty of reasonable care, that there was proximate and cause-in-fact, and that Andy suffered damages. Baker owed a duty of reasonable care to Andy. Baker should have exercised greater care knowing his lack of skating ability. He breached the duty of care when, with knowledge of his limitations, he made a sharp turn and collided with Andy. Baker was the proximate cause and cause in fact of Andy concussion. Andy has clearly suffered damages with a head concussion.

Therefore Andy should prevail in a negligence action against Baker.

Cory v David

The issue is whether Cory will prevail in a negligence action against Davis. Cory must show that David breached a duty to exercise reasonable care, that the injury was the proximate cause and cause in fact, and damages. In this case, David had a duty to exercise reasonable care and he breached the duty by skating while his eyes were covered. This was the proximate cause and cause in fact of Cory's injury. Cory suffered damages by a broken leg.

The next issue is whether Cory was contributory negligent by looking up at the ceiling instead of paying attention. If so, then his damages will be reduced according to his percentage of negligence.

The next issue is whether David should pay damages because Cory has bone disease. The rule is that a defendant the plaintiff as he finds them and accepts their diseases. Therefore, David is liable to the full extent of Cory's injury.

XYZ Corp v David

In order for XYZ Corp to prevail in an action against David for lost revenue they must show that David owed them a duty of reasonable care. In this case David was a paying customer- and invitee. He owed XYZ no duty of care. Therefore, XYZ probably won't prevail in an action against David.

February 2007—Question 5

Paula Passenger, a Michigan resident, was riding in an automobile driven by her boyfriend Mike Van Der Broek. As they were driving, they were discussing their relationship. When Paula broached the subject of marriage, Mike became extremely distracted. He lost control of the car and collided with a telephone pole. Mike escaped relatively unscathed, but Paula sustained severe injuries to her knees as a result of the crash.

The following are the undisputed facts regarding Paula's injury: She was hospitalized for a month and she missed a total of two months of work from her $6,000 per month job as an engineer. After she was released from the hospital, she required six months of physical therapy. Before the accident, she enjoyed attending sporting events, dancing and, occasionally, rock climbing. With physical therapy she has been able to continue participating in some of these activities, but she cannot participate as fully as she had been able to before. Specifically, when attending sporting events, she must leave her seat and walk around every half hour or she will experience pain. She can still dance, but she is no longer able to Samba, which had been her favorite type of dance. Her doctor has opined that she may be able to Samba again after more physical therapy. Finally, she can no longer go rock climbing per her doctor's orders. Paula was able to continue at her job as an engineer with no restrictions and she is able to perform all of her normal household chores. Her medical expenses have been paid.

Paula has asked for your advice. Assume Mike's negligence was a proximate cause of her injuries. Prepare a memorandum discussing what types of damages she can potentially recover in a suit against Mike and what she must show in order to recover. State and explain your conclusion about the merits of her claim for damages.

Model Answer to Question 5

Under the Michigan no-fault system, a person suffering an injury arising out of an automobile accident must look to his or her insurer first for first-party no-fault benefits. MCL 500.3114(1). If Paula does not have no-fault insurance, she would next look to the policy of an insured relative with whom she shares a domicile. *Id.* If she had no such relative, then she would look to the insurer of the owner or registrant of Mike's vehicle, then to Mike, the operator's, insurer. MCL 500.3114(4). If none of those parties is insured, then Paula would look to the assigned claims plan. MCL 500.3172(1).

Under MCL 500.3135(3)(c), Mike remains liable for economic damages in excess of those reimbursed as first-party benefits. The facts state Paula's medical expenses have been paid and the question only asks about a suit against Mike so there is no issue about those expenses. The facts state Paula lost two months from her $6,000 per month job. The current wage-loss benefit is approximately $4,400 per month, which is less than 80% of her monthly salary. In other words, wage-loss benefits she received from her insurer would not have covered her total wage loss. She may recover those economic damages in an action against Mike.

Paula may recover non-economic damages from Mike if she has suffered death, serious impairment of body function, or permanent serious disfigurement. MCL 500.3135(1). Because Paula did not die and there is no indication of disfigurement, she must show a serious impairment of body function. The statute defines "serious impairment of body function" as "an objectively manifested impairment of an important body function that affects the person's general ability to lead his or her normal life." MCL 300.3135(7).

The Michigan Supreme Court has articulated a multi-step process for determining whether a plaintiff has reached the threshold for non-economic damages. *Kreiner v Fischer*, 471 Michigan 109, 131-134 (2004). The court must first determine if there is material factual dispute concerning the nature and extent of the plaintiff's injuries. *Id.* at 131-132. The question clearly states that the facts surrounding the nature of the injury are undisputed. Thus, the court may determine whether Paula has suffered a serious impairment of bodily function as a matter of law, MCL 500.3135(2)(a)(i), and the court can move on to the next step. Second, the court must determine if an important body function has been impaired and if that impairment is objectively manifested. *Id.* at 132. In this case, Paula's use of her legs has been impaired by the accident, allowing the court to proceed to the next step. The final step is "a multi-faceted inquiry" to determine "whether the course of the plaintiff's normal life has been affected." *Id.* The court provided the following non-exhaustive list of factors to evaluate the affect on a person's ability to lead his or her life: "(a) the nature and extent of the impairment, (b) the type and length of treatment required, (c) the duration of impairment, (d) the extent of any residual impairment, and (e) the prognosis for eventual recovery." *Id.* at 133.

Applying the factors to this case, it is arguable that Paula does not have a serious impairment of body function for purposes of the no-fault act. The examinees should discuss the facts supporting and contravening this conclusion. Her hospital stay was severe. She is able to work and participate in most of the activities she enjoyed before the accident, with the exception of rock climbing. As there is no indication that rock climbing was a major part of the course of her life, her loss of the ability to participate in that activity does not entitle her to non-economic damages.

Comment: In July 2010, the Michigan Supreme Court overruled the original Kreiner test for determining whether the threshold for "Serious Impairment of a Bodily Function" based on Kreiner v Fischer, 471 Mich 109, 683 NW 2d 611 (2004), and replaced it with a different test in McCormick v Carrier, 2010 WL 3063150 (Mich). The former Kreiner test has been repeatedly tested on the Michigan Bar Exam. Please note that when going through old essays from February 2010 and before, such as the one above, the model answers will be based on Kreiner and are no longer correct. You can still use the essays for practice, though; simply replace the "Rule" from the Kreiner test with the new McCormick test to determine if the threshold is met. The model answer above has been updated with the McCormick test on page 49 of this book. Please use the updated model answer in place of the one above for the current law.

Student Answer—February 2007

Question 5—No Fault—8 points

Paula's recovery is governed by the rules of no-fault.

The issue is whether she can potentially recover for hospitalization, lost wages, physical therapy and loss of quality of life in a third party claim from Mike because his negligence was a proximate cause of Paula's injuries.

Michigan's no-fault insurance provides for the cost of medical expenses, lost wages and personal injury as a result of injury arising out of the occupation or operation of a motor vehicle. An individual who sustains an injury has a first party claim against his/her own insurance claim. Michigan provides for a third party claim against the person responsible for the accident in the instances when a threshold is met that includes a death or the serious impairment of a bodily function.

Here, Paula would not be able to assert a 3rd party claim against Mike for his negligence because Paula's resulting injuries do not meet the threshold requirement. Paula is alive and reasonably well. She is able to work and her injuries do not impede her bodily functions. Not being able to dance the Samba will not allow for additional recovery. Paula may be able to assert and recover the mini-tort of $500 allowed under the law—as this typically provides for deductibles—if she was required to pay them.

Therefore, Paula's recovery will be limited to the maximum amount allowed under the mini-tort. Her claim for damages will be provided for by her own insurance carrier unless she was uninsured. If she was uninsured, then Mike would have to pay for all of her lost wages and hospital costs and therapies.

July 2007—Question 14

Peter Plaintiff purchased an electric bagel slicer from The Department Store. Mega Manufacturer produced the electric bagel slicer. The only warning label on the bagel slicer referenced the risk of electric shock. Neither the Department Store nor Mega made any express warranties regarding the bagel slicer, and the package had the following statement in bold, conspicuous letters: **"The seller and manufacturer disclaim all warranties of merchantability."**

Peter used the slicer successfully to slice many bagels. He also used the slicer on produce, such as apples and carrots. Eventually, he decided to see how durable the slicer was by slicing nonfood items. He was able to cut through a magazine and a pen, but when he attempted to slice a wooden cutting board, the slicer's blade broke off and severed two of Peter's fingers.

Peter has approached you to discuss the possibility of a lawsuit. Advise Peter as to whom he may sue, the possible cause(s) of action, and the likelihood of success. Explain your answer.

Model Answer to Question 14

Products liability is governed by statute in Michigan. MCL 600.2945, *et seq.* There are two possible causes of action under the statute. A plaintiff can sue for harm caused by a defective product, MCL 600.2946(2), or harm caused by the manufacturer or seller's failure to warn of a material risk, MCL 600.2948. Either cause of action may apply because here there was no warning that the product posed a risk of severing fingers and the broken blade may be the result of a defect. There are two entities that could be liable under the statute—the seller and the manufacturer.

Under the statute, a seller other than a manufacturer is only liable if one of the following conditions is met: (1) "The seller failed to exercise reasonable care, including breach of any implied warranty, with respect to the product and that failure was a proximate cause of the person's injuries," or (2) "[t]he seller made an express warranty as to the product, the product failed to conform to the warranty, and the failure to conform to the warranty was a proximate cause of the person's harm." MCL 600.2947(6). Neither of these conditions applies. The facts make clear that seller made no express warranties. The seller effectively disclaimed the warranty of merchantability, MCL 440.2316(2). And no facts support an implied warranty for fitness for a particular purpose under MCL 440.2315, because the seller must have known the particular purpose for which the goods are required and the buyer must have relied on the seller's skill or judgment to select or furnish suitable goods. As neither condition is met here, the seller is not a proper party. The only remaining party is the manufacturer.

However, plaintiff's likelihood of success against the manufacturer is remote. The primary obstacle to plaintiff's lawsuit is MCL 600.2947(2), which provides that "[a] manufacturer or seller is not liable in a product liability action for harm caused by misuse of a product unless the misuse was reasonably foreseeable. Whether there was a misuse of a product and whether misuse was reasonably foreseeable are legal issues to be resolved by the court." This standard makes such claims more amenable to dismissal on motions as the Legislature has defined the foreseeability issue as a legal one.

A "misuse" is statutorily defined as "use of a product in a materially different manner than the product's intended use. Misuse includes uses inconsistent with the specifications and standards applicable to the product, uses contrary to a warning or instructions provided by the manufacturer, seller, or another person possessing knowledge or training regarding the use or maintenance of the product, and uses other than those for which the product would be considered suitable by a reasonably prudent person in the same or similar circumstances." MCL 600.2945(e).

Using the bagel slicer as a general chopping blade for non-food items is unlikely to "be considered suitable by a reasonably prudent person in the same or similar circumstances." Further, there is no indication that such a misuse was foreseeable. Because MCL 600.2947(2) is an absolute bar to liability, if it applies it would preclude both a failure to warn and a defective product claim.

The failure to warn claim would face an additional hurdle. Under MCL 600.2948(2), "[a] defendant is not liable for failure to warn of a material risk that is or should be obvious to a reasonably prudent product user or a material risk that is or should be a matter of common knowledge to persons in the same or similar position as the person upon whose injury or death the claim is based in a product liability action." The statute employs an objective standard and does not require manufacturers to warn of obvious material risks. *Greene v AP Products*, 475 Mich 502, 509-510 (2006). In this case, the material risk of breaking the bagel slicer cutting blade while cutting hard non-food items and injuring oneself in the process "should be obvious to a reasonably prudent product user." Thus, there is no duty to warn of that risk.

The likelihood of success is minimal.

Student Answer—July 2007

Question 14—Torts—9 points

The issue is who can Peter sue & for what causes of action.

First, Peter can sue Mega on a strict (products) liability theory. To prevail, Peter must establish that 1) the seller was a merchant, 2) the product suffered from a defect, 3) the product was in this condition when it left hands of the manufacturer, 4) foreseeable user doing a foreseeable use. In this case, Mega was a merchant who produces electric bagel slicers. The product suffered from a defect because the blade broke off. The product was in the same condition as when it left the hands of the manufacturer because it was sold at the dept. store & the court will presume it moved through the ordinary channels to get there. Lastly, Peter was the one who bought it, thus he was a foreseeable user but it is foreseeable that Peter would use a bagel in the bagel slicer or maybe bread or any other food product but it is not foreseeable to mega that a person would put a magazine or a wooden cutting board in a bagel slicer. Thus, this element is not met & would preclude Peter from any recovery on a products liability cause of action.

The 2nd suit which Peter could bring would be a suit against mega for an implied warranty. A manufacturer may not be disclaimed by an express warranty but they may disclaim both implied warranties if done correctly. To disclaim an implied warranty of merchantability the manufacturer must put it in conspicuous writing & mention the word merchantability. In this case, mega did both, thus that warranty was disclaimed. The warranty of fitness for a particular purpose just has to be written that you disclaim all warranties. The facts indicate mega did this. Thus, Peter would have no success bringing this action.

February 2008—Question 15

Sergeant Mike McHanus of the Michigan State Police was pursuing Danny Defendant on a busy Michigan highway. Danny had stolen the car he was driving, and both Danny and Sergeant McHanus were traveling at excessive speeds. During the chase, Sergeant McHanus did not come into contact with Danny's vehicle, but Danny rammed the car of Patty Plaintiff, causing Patty to suffer a serious impairment of body function. After the collision with Patty's car, the chase continued. In an attempt to end the chase, Sergeant McHanus raced ahead of Danny and tried to position his car perpendicular to the highway. As Sergeant McHanus turned his car into position, he lost control and the car spun into a pedestrian, Valerie Victim, causing her a permanent serious disfigurement.

Ignoring Danny's percentage of fault, discuss Patty Plaintiff's and Valerie Victim's respective chances for success in a lawsuit filed against the Michigan State Police and Sergeant McHanus. Explain your answer.

Model Answer to Question 15

Because the plaintiffs seek tort recovery for injuries arising from use of an automobile and they are suing governmental entities, both the No Fault Act, MCL 500.3135, and the Government Tort Liability Act, MCL 691.1401, *et seq.* (GTLA) must be addressed. As to the No Fault Act, tort remedies are barred unless a plaintiff pleads and proves that they have met statutory threshold for noneconomic damages. In this case, the facts clearly establish that the two plaintiffs have met the statutory threshold as they have both suffered either a "permanent and serious disfigurement" or a "serious impairment of body function." MCL 500.3135(1).

Because both plaintiffs are suing a government agency, they must plead in avoidance of governmental immunity. The exception to government immunity that applies to these facts is the "motor vehicle exception." MCL 691.1405.

Patty Plaintiff's claim is similar to those presented in *Robinson v City of Detroit*, 462 Mich 439 (2000). In *Robinson*, the Michigan Supreme Court held that an innocent passenger of a fleeing vehicle could not maintain a claim against the government where "the pursuing police vehicle did not hit the fleeing car or otherwise physically force it off the road or into another vehicle or object." *Id.* at 457. The Court also held "that the decision to pursue a fleeing motorist, which is separate from the operation of the vehicle itself, is not encompassed within a narrow construction of the phrase 'operation of a motor vehicle.'" *Id.* The facts presented involve a third-party, but the analysis is the same as in *Robinson*. Because the sergeant's vehicle never came into contact with either Patty or Danny's vehicle, the accident between Danny and Patty could not have "resulted from" the negligent operation of Sergeant McHanus' vehicle.

Robinson also discussed the requirements for avoiding governmental immunity when suing an individual government employee. MCL 691.1407(2) enumerates the three requirements for a government employee to avoid liability. First, the employee must be acting or reasonably believe that he is acting within the scope of his authority. Second, the agency must be engaged in the exercise of a governmental function. Third, the employee's conduct cannot "amount to gross negligence that is the proximate cause of the injury or damage." The only element that could be disputed in this factual scenario is the third. In *Robinson*, the Court held that immunity applies "unless the employee's conduct amounts to gross negligence that is the one most immediate, efficient, and direct cause of the injury or damage". *Robinson* at 462. With regard to Patty Plaintiff's claims, the sergeant's conduct, like the officers' conduct in *Robinson*, cannot be the most immediate cause because it was Danny's reckless conduct that caused Patty's injuries. Therefore, Patty will not likely have success suing either the State Police or Sergeant McHanus.

Valerie Victim's claims should be analyzed under the same GTLA tests. However, because Sergeant McHanus hit her, her suit has a higher likelihood of success. There would most likely be a question of fact whether the sergeant was negligent for purposes of the agency's liability and grossly negligent of purposes for his liability. MCL 691.1405 and 1407(2)(c).

Student Answer—February 2008

Question 15—Torts No Fault—8 points

This is a no fault/torts question/threshold injury

Patty's chance of success against Michigan State police (MSP) and Sgt. McHanus.

Under Michigan law, Patty cannot go after Sgt. McHanus individually. Usually government is immune unless there is an exception. The exception here is government vehicle (police car) and gross negligence.

Also Patty suffered a threshold injury, allowing her to pursue a negligence claim against MSP. If no threshold injury then she would solely go through her own no fault. Here she can get benefits from no fault. → 85 percent loss wages, for 3 years and $20 per day for 3 years for household service expenses.

Danny is the one that hit Patty but if he can show that Sgt acted in gross negligence during the high speed pursuit she may be able to recover against MSP.

Patty may want to show gross negligence by pointing out excessive speed, officer should have known that a chase like this is likely to put innocent people in danger.

Valerie's Claim:

Valerie will have a harder time showing that officer acted in gross negligence conduct?

Here the officer raced ahead of Danny and tried to position himself perpendicularly but he lost control. He wanted to stop the excessive speed chase that safest way possible.

Valerie may be able to show gross negligence. Courts usually rule that an innocent bystander should be allowed to bring a claim. Valerie also suffered a threshold injury. In tort you take victim as is. Usually for motor vehicle claims you would have to exhaust all no fault remedies.

No fault

Set off if win negligence claim for Patty's claim may apply.

Ran out of time . . .

July 2008—Question 3

Big Manufacturer, Inc. holds a monthly muskrat dinner for its employees. Danny Defendant and Carolyn Carowner, two employees of Big Manufacturer, attended last month's dinner. Because Carolyn enjoyed one too many beers at the muskrat dinner, she asked Danny to drive her home. However, Danny did not drive to work that day, so he drove Carolyn home in Carolyn's car. On the way to Carolyn's, Danny negligently crashed into Paula Plaintiff, causing a severe injury to her shoulder.

The following are the undisputed facts regarding Paula's injury: She was hospitalized for four months and she is physically unable to return to her job as a martial arts instructor. She will require physical therapy for many years. Before the accident, she enjoyed skeet shooting, playing soft ball, and playing tuba in her community orchestra. With physical therapy she has been able to continue playing the tuba, however, she had to quit the orchestra, and her doctor has forbid her from skeet shooting or playing softball. Her ability to do household chores has been severely limited.

Paula wants to know if she has a viable claim for non-economic damages against Danny, Carolyn, or both. She also wants to know what portion of her damages, if any, each party will be responsible for. **Draft a memo to Paula explaining your answers to her questions.**

Model Answer to Question 3

Under Michigan law, both the owner and operator of a motor vehicle are liable for "an injury caused by the negligent operation of [a] motor vehicle" if the owner expressly or impliedly consents or knows about the use of the vehicle. MCL 257.401(1). The facts of the case make clear that Danny negligently drove the vehicle and Carolyn consented to his use of the vehicle. Therefore, both Carolyn and Danny may be held liable.

However, Paula may only recover non-economic damages from Danny and Carolyn if she has suffered death, serious impairment of body function, or permanent serious disfigurement. MCL 500.3135(1). Because Paula did not die and there is no indication of disfigurement, she must show a serious impairment of body function. The statute defines "serious impairment of body function" as "an objectively manifested impairment of an important body function that affects the person's general ability to lead his or her normal life." MCL 500.3135(7).

The Michigan Supreme Court has articulated a multi-step process for determining whether a plaintiff has reached the threshold for non-economic damages. *Kreiner v Fischer*, 471 Mich 109, 131-134 (2004). The court must first determine if there is a material factual dispute concerning the nature and extent of the plaintiff's injuries. *Id.* at 131-132. The question clearly states that the facts surrounding the nature of the injury are undisputed. Thus, the court may determine whether Paula has suffered a serious impairment of bodily function as a matter of law, MCL 500.3135(2)(a)(i), and the court can move on to the next step. Second, the court must determine if an important body function has been impaired and if that impairment is objectively manifested. *Id.* at 132. In this case, Paula's use of her shoulder has been impaired by the accident, allowing the court to proceed to the next step. The final step is a "multifaceted inquiry" to determine "whether the course of the plaintiff's normal life has been affected." *Id.* The Court provided the following non-exhaustive list of factors to evaluate the affect on a person's ability to lead his or her life: "(a) the nature and extent of the impairment, (b) the type and length of the treatment required, (c) the duration of impairment, (d) the extent of any residual impairment, and (e) the prognosis for eventual recovery." *Id.* at 133.

Applying the factors to this case, it is arguable that Paula does have a serious impairment of body function for purposes of the No-Fault Act. The examinee should discuss the facts supporting and contravening this conclusion. Her hospital stay was long, and the residual effects of the impairment have been somewhat severe. She is no longer able to work or participate in most of the activities she enjoyed before the accident, with the exception of tuba playing. Therefore, it appears that Paula has suffered a serious impairment of body function for purposes of the statute.

With regard to the liability of Carolyn and Danny, both would be responsible for the entirety of Paula's non-economic damages. Michigan has abolished joint and several liability for most torts; however, the recent case of *Kaiser v Allen*, 480 Mich 31 (2008), held that the statute abolishing joint and several liability foes does not apply to MCL 257.401(1). While Carolyn or Danny may be able to seek contribution from the other, Paula can collect all of her damages from either Carolyn or Danny. However, Paula is entitled to only one recovery for her injuries.

Comment: In July 2010, the Michigan Supreme Court overruled the original Kreiner test for determining whether the threshold for "Serious Impairment of a Bodily Function" based on Kreiner v Fischer, 471 Mich 109, 683 NW 2d 611 (2004), and replaced it with a different test in McCormick v Carrier, 2010 WL 3063150 (Mich). The former Kreiner test has been repeatedly tested on the Michigan Bar Exam. Please note that when going through old essays from February 2010 and before, such as the one above, the model answers will be based on Kreiner and are no longer correct. You can still use the essays for practice, though; simply replace the "Rule" from the Kreiner test with the new McCormick test to determine if the threshold is met. A "canned answer" with the new McCormick test is on page 49 of this book for a different question. Simply replace it with the overruled Kreiner test above.

Two Student Answers—July 2008

Question 3—Torts/No-Fault—8 points

Paula has a viable claim for non-economic damages against Danny and perhaps Carolyn as well if Carolyn acted negligently in allowing Danny to drive her car.

At issue is whether Paula's injury was significant enough to meet the threshold requirement to allow her claim to proceed as an ordinary tort claim based upon negligence affording her recovery for her injuries.

Under the law of no-fault, in order to move beyond the statutory guidelines of everyone sues their own insurance company in the event of an automobile accident a party must meet a threshold requirement of having suffered as a result of the accident either death or a permanent disability or problem with bodily function or physical disfigurement. The threshold is met when the driver was negligent in their driving causing the accident that resulted in the injury. Once the injury is established, the claim moves on an ordinary tort claim.

Here, Paula was in the hospital for four months. During that time she was unable to work. Because they anticipate her needing therapy for many years, it can be inferred that she has serious bodily impairment or disability. Her continued inability to perform some the tasks she enjoyed for leisure may also prevent her from the same type movements and physical requirements in her professional life.

Danny may be responsible for her wage loss, medical expenses, as well as replacement services. Paula may also be able to assert a claim for pain and suffering. If Carolyn acted negligently in allowing Danny to drive, Paula may be able to hold them jointly and severally liable as well.

Therefore Paul has a viable claim for non-economic damages.

Question 3—Torts/No-Fault—8 points

This is a No-Fault Insurance Question.

The issue is "whether Paula has suffered non-economical damages to meet the no-fault tort threshold to recover for her injuries?

Under Michigan no-fault insurance law, each insurer collects from their own insurance medical expenses, lost wages up to 85%, and $20 per day replacement costs.

In order to recover non-economical damages, there must be a 1) death; which Paula is CLEARLY NOT dead, 2) permanent disfigurement; she was hospitalized for shoulder injury which may be severe BUT not permanently disabled. Also, she was physically unable to return to her job as a martial art instructor, but is able to do physical therapy in order to gain her strength back, or 3) serious impairment of a bodily function; facts state with therapy she is able to continue playing her tuba, even though she had to quit the orchestra.

Paula will ARGUE that because she had to quit the ORCHESTRA and is unable to return to work as a "martial arts" instructor she has satisfied a "serious BODILY FUNCTION."

Also, the fact she is no longer able to enjoy skeet shooting or playing softball.

Danny and Carolyn will ARGUE, Paula has NOT suffered ANY permanent disfigurement or serious bodily function, because with PHYSICAL THERAPY she will one day be able to enjoy such activities again.

Further, the facts do not discuss the type of injury to meet the "threshold tort" required for non-economic loss of pain and suffering. A shoulder injury is NOT serious bodily function; even though Paula will argue playing tuba and martial arts is all arm.

If, they are NOT, insured under the "Owner Liability Act" for negligent driving. Carolyn as the owner of the car, liability can be imputed to her for the NEGLIGENCE of Donald's driving if Plaintiff were to meet "No-Fault" threshold tort requirement.

Under "Michigan Owner Liability Act" owner is responsible for the negligent driving of their vehicle, with NO CONSENT, but consent is USUALLY PRESUMED and w/ Carolyn being in the vehicle, consent was given.

Paula would be able to collect replacement services of $20 per day for the inability to do household chores, reasonable medical expenses and 85% wages loss for the 4 months she was in the hospital and off work.

As to Big Manufacturers being imputed for vicarious respondent superior liability, would be highly unlikely because this was not in course of employment. Since it was after work, it was not in the course of employment.

Lastly, Paula will argue severe injury to her shoulder MEETS THE THRESHOLD torts requirement as serious impairment of bodily function. Since she is a tuba player and martial arts instructor, use of arm and shoulder this argument should fail.

Paula does not meet serious bodily function, no missing finger, or arm chopped off with physical therapy she will regain movement.

No-threshold requirement for Paula against neither Danny nor Carolyn, her insurance under NO-FAULT will cover her claim.

February 2009—Question 3

Diligent Developments, Inc. (D & D) is a non-profit organization that builds and donates public parks. D & D purchased a piece of property, Blackacre, in the City of York, Michigan for the purpose of constructing a park complete with a playground and athletic fields. D & D posted "No Trespassing" signs along the border of Blackacre and mailed a notice to abutting landowners informing them that Blackacre was not open to the public. Occasionally, neighborhood children would enter the property to play in the fields, but each time they were discovered, a D & D employee escorted them off the property.

In order to develop the site, D & D had to install a drainage system which required a significant amount of digging and produced several large piles of dirt. Due to financing delays, D & D did not work on or visit the site for a four-day period beginning on a Thursday. On the Friday that D & D was not at the site, Curious Chris, a 12-year-old boy living in a house abutting Blackacre, noticed the large dirt piles and went out to play on them with two other boys from the neighborhood. Chris and the other boys decided to dig holes in the dirt piles large enough for them to sit inside. Chris' mother, Absent Amber, saw the boys playing on the dirt piles, but did not stop them because she did not believe that their digging was dangerous. The next day, Chris and the other boys continued playing on the dirt piles. Unfortunately, one of the holes collapsed while Chris was inside it. The other boys ran for help, and Amber called 911. Chris suffered several serious injuries due to the weight of the dirt collapsing on him.

Amber, next friend of Chris, has filed a lawsuit against D & D seeking recovery of damages on two theories: (1) premises liability and (2) creating and maintaining an attractive nuisance.

You are an associate at the law firm of Downs, Rivers & Diamond, which has been retained to defend D & D. Assess the merits of Amber's case. Explain your answer.

Model Answer to Question 3

Premises Liability: A landowner's duty to a visitor depends on that visitor's status. Michigan recognizes three common-law categories of persons who enter upon the land or premises of another: invitee, licensee and trespasser. *Stit v Holland Abundant Life*, 462 Mich 591, 596 (2000). An invitee is a person who enters upon the land of another upon an invitation. *Id.* A licensee is a person who is privileged to enter the land of another by virtue of the possessor's consent. *Id.* And a trespasser is a person who enters upon another's land without the landowner's consent. *Id.*

Blackacre was not open to the public. D & D posted "No Trespassing" signs and notified abutting landowners through the mail that Blackacre was private property. D & D neither expressly nor implicitly invited Chris onto its property, nor consented to his entry onto its land. Therefore, Chris was a trespasser.

A landowner owes no duty of care to an undiscovered trespasser except to refrain from injuring him by willful and wanton misconduct. *Id.* Willful and wanton misconduct requires an intent to harm or such indifference to whether harm will result as to be the equivalent of a willingness that it does. *Burnett v City of Adrian*, 414 Mich 448,

455-456 (1982); *James v Leco Corp*, 170 Mich App 184, 193 (1988). Nothing in the facts provided suggests that D & D intended that the dirt piles would cause harm or exhibited such indifference as to be equivalent to a willingness that harm would occur to anyone. The dirt piles alone were not inherently dangerous and even Amber did not believe that they or her child's activity on them was dangerous. Moreover, D & D did not have any notice that the children were digging holes in the dirt piles prior to the accident. It does not appear that Amber's premises liability claim is very strong.

Attractive Nuisance: The doctrine of attractive nuisance imposes liability on landowners for injuries suffered by trespassing children. Michigan has adopted the five-part test from 2 Restatement Torts, 2d, 5339, p 197:

> A possessor of land is subject to liability for physical harm to children trespassing thereon caused by an artificial condition upon the land if
>
> (a) the place where the condition exists is one upon which the possessor knows or has reason to know that children are likely to trespass, and
>
> (b) the condition is one of which the possessor knows or has reason to know and which he realizes or should realize will involve an unreasonable risk of death or serious bodily harm to such children, and
>
> (c) the children because of their youth do not discover the condition or realize the risk involved in intermeddling with it or in coming within the area made dangerous by it, and
>
> (d) the utility to the possessor of maintaining the condition and the burden of eliminating the danger are slight as compared with the risk to children involved and
>
> (e) the possessor fails to exercise reasonable care to eliminate the danger or otherwise to protect the children." *Murday v Bales Trucking, Inc*, 165 Mich App 747, 751-752 (1988).

In order for a possessor of land to be held liable for injury to a trespassing child, all five conditions must be met. *Id.* at 752. "The term 'attractive nuisance' is a misnomer (or historical leftover) because it is not necessary, in order to maintain such an action, that the hazardous condition be the reason that the children came onto the property." *Pippin v Atallah*, 245 Mich App 136, 146 fn 3 (2001). Elements (a) and (c) appear to favor Amber, while elements (d) and (e) may require development before they can be resolved in favor of either party. However, it appears unlikely that plaintiff will be able to establish element (b). The dirt piles alone did not involve an unreasonable risk of death or serious bodily harm. The dirt piles were only made dangerous by Chris' digging. Moreover, it is certainly arguable that Chris' digging did not create an unreasonable risk of death or serious bodily harm; even his mother, Amber, saw Chris digging and did not believe that he was in any danger. Element (b) also poses a problem for Amber because D & D did not and had no reason to know about the danger created by Chris' digging. This is a critical point because whether the danger was created by Chris or D & D is irrelevant. *Id.* p 143. D & D is responsible for a condition only if it knows or has reason to know that it existed. *Id.* Because D & D was not at the property after Chris dug the holes, it did not know or have any reason to know about the dangerous condition that Chris created. *Id.* Accordingly, it is unlikely that Amber can establish element (b).

Amber, therefore, is unlikely to recover in tort under either of her theories of recovery.

Student Answer—February 2009

Question 3—No-Fault—None Available

July 2009—Question 3

Tipsy Tammy attended "Girls Night Out" at her favorite bar, Carolyn's Cavern. Although it was apparent that she was thoroughly enjoying the evening, Tipsy Tammy did not slur her speech, show a lack of balance or deviate from her normally jovial mood. After having several drinks within two hours, Tipsy Tammy decided to drive home. While driving, Tipsy Tammy crossed into Polly Plaintiff's lane. In order to avoid Tipsy Tammy's car, Polly intentionally drove off the road and onto Holly Homeowner's lawn, destroying several valuable lawn ornaments in the process. Tammy was stopped nearby, and a test revealed that her blood alcohol content was .226 grams per 100 milliliters of blood (nearly three times the legal limit).

Polly broke her arm in the accident. The break was extremely painful and required surgery and the insertion of a medical pin to stabilize the break. Polly was not able to do her job as a court reporter transcribing hearings or participate in her bowling league for three months. She was able to return to her prior activities in full after she recovered. Polly sued Carolyn's Cavern and Tipsy Tammy, seeking non-economic damages (pain and suffering).

You are the law clerk for the judge presiding over both actions. Each defendant has moved for summary disposition. Carolyn's Cavern has argued that Polly's claim against it is prohibited by the Dramshop Act. Tipsy Tammy has argued that Polly's claim is prohibited by the No-Fault Act.

Assess each party's argument and make a recommendation whether to grant or deny each party's motion.

Model Answer to Question 3

The Dramshop Act provides a cause of action for plaintiffs injured by a visibly intoxicated person against a retail establishment that unlawfully sells alcohol to the visibly intoxicated person, if the unlawful sale is a proximate cause of the injury. MCL 436.1801(3); *Reed v Breton*, 475 Mich 531, 537-538 (2006). Proof of "visible intoxication" requires objective manifestations of intoxication. *Reed, supra* at 542; *Miller v Ochampaugh*, 191 Mich App 48, 59-60 (1991). Circumstantial evidence such as Tipsy Tammy's blood alcohol content taken after the accident cannot alone demonstrate that Tipsy Tammy was visibly intoxicated. *Reed, supra* at 542-543. Polly cannot demonstrate that Tipsy Tammy was visibly intoxicated because Tipsy Tammy did not show any objective manifestations of intoxication—she did not slur her speech, show a lack of balance or change her mood. Accordingly, Carolyn's Cavern is entitled to summary disposition under the Dramshop Act.

The No-Fault Act generally bars actions for non-economic damages, unless the injured person suffered an objectively manifested impairment of an important body function that affects the person's general ability to lead his or her normal life. MCL 500.3135(1), (7). Whether a plaintiff meets that standard involves a multi-step process in which the court determines: (1) whether there is a material factual dispute concerning the nature and extent of the person's injury; (2) whether an important body function has been impaired; and (3) whether the impairment affects the person's general ability to lead her normal life by comparing her life before and after the accident and the significance of impact on the course of her life. *Kreiner v Fischer*, 471 Mich 109, 131-133 (2004). There is no dispute that Polly broke her arm and it took three months to heal. A broken arm is a serious impairment of an important body function. Polly's injury, however, did not affect her general ability to lead her life or alter the course of her life. Polly's injury was not extensive or pervasive and her recovery was relatively short. Polly's life before and after the accident is indistinguishable. Thus, her general ability to lead her life and the course of her life were unaffected and Tammy is entitled to summary disposition. *See Kreiner, supra* at 135-136.

Student Answer—July 2009

Question 3—No Fault/Torts—10 points

This is a torts question dealing with the No Fault and Dram Shop Acts.

No Fault is the exclusive remedy in Michigan where you are in a car accident. The act covers only motor vehicles—which are vehicles that have more than 2 wheels that are made to be used on a public highway. The act requires drivers to get No-Fault Insurance. When in an accident the first person you would look to would be your own insurance coverage; if uninsured, look to insurance of relative in house; if they don't have insurance you then look to the insurance of the driver. Under the No-Fault Act where you are injured you can recover economic damages. These damages include wage loss for 85% of total earnings for up to 3 years, medical care for reasonable medical services, funeral expenses, $20.00/day to do things like laundry & grocery shopping that you no longer can do, and this is capped at 3 years, rehabilitation for changing the house to make more accessible for in-home care. This is capped at 3 years. There are also survivor benefits, if you die your decedents get this. If you can prove death, serious, permanent disfigurement or serious bodily injury you can also recover non-economic damages which include pain and suffering, loss of consortium, etc. To prove serious bodily injury you must show your injury prevents you from being able to carry on your normal life, it's an objective manifestation. In determining this court will look to see if any factual dispute that there is a serious bodily injury or impairment or even if a factual dispute, that the dispute is not important in determining whether a serious and important bodily function. The court will look at what the injured parties' life was like before and after the injury. In this case Polly would be able to receive her economic damages and first party claim that would be paid from her insurance company. She will probably be able to get her noneconomic damages. After the accident Polly had a broken arm and was required to have surgery and had to have a medical pin inserted into her arm. She was no longer able to do her job as a court reporter transcribing hearings or participate in her bowling league for 3 months. During this time she could recover non-economic damages, but in Michigan there is a cap on non-economic damages so the recovery would be limited. Non-economic damages are based on partial comparative negligence which states that if the plaintiff were more than 50% at fault she would be barred from this recovery, but if less than 50% at fault she would recover damages minus her percentage fault. It doesn't seem Polly was more than 50% at fault because Tammy was driving drunk and in order to avoid Tammy's car she had to swerve and enter Homeowner's lawn. In emergency situations like this Polly would be permitted to do so, but she will have to pay for the lawn ornaments she destroyed. After Polly recovered (3 months) she will be no longer be able to recover non-economic damages.

Under the Dram Shop Act the owner of a business who sells alcohol to a clearly intoxicated person can be liable if that person goes out and causes an injury. However, this claim will not work because Tammy did not appear drunk, her speech was not slurred, and she did not show lack of balance, she was in her normal jovial mood. Carolyn's bar would not be liable to Polly because there was no clear indication that Tammy was drunk and to them she seemed fine. Tammy will therefore be primarily liable to Polly.

Comment: Many examinees did well on the No Fault issue, but did not know the Michigan Dram Shop Act as this is the first time it was ever tested. This is a good example of why you must know the Michigan distinctions on the MBE subjects (here, Torts), and not gamble in your preparation.

February 2010—Question 2

Two best friends, Parker and Daisy, were leaving the movie theater after seeing the latest vampire movie. The two teenagers were standing in the lobby when they began arguing over the ending of the movie. Frustrated by the conversation, Daisy took the lid of her drink and threw it in Parker's face. As she stomped off, Daisy threw her cup and remaining ice on the floor near the entrance of the movie theater. Johnny, a movie theater employee, witnessed the whole scene and was laughing so hard he could barely stand up. He finally managed to grab a wet floor sign and position it next to where Parker had been standing. Unfortunately, he got sidetracked when he was explaining the drama to his buddy and forgot to pick up Daisy's cup or put a wet floor sign near the entrance.

A few minutes later, another crazed vampire fan, Sara, came barreling through the entrance. She slipped on the wet floor and fell hard on her elbow. As she struggled to get up, she noticed she was sitting in a sticky puddle of cola and melted ice. Johnny came over to help her and noticed that her arm looked broken. Sara later went to the hospital for her broken arm. Other than having to wear a cast for six weeks and missing the opening of her favorite move, Sara recovered fully and is back to normal.

After the argument with Daisy, Parker was so upset at having cola spilled all over her Team Werewolf t-shirt, that she ran out the opposite entrance door and into the parking lot. Just then, Fred, who was only paying attention to finding a parking spot closest to the entrance, didn't see Parker until he hit her with his car. Parker suffered from a deep laceration on her left forearm, which ultimately left an ugly scare.

Utilizing Michigan law, discuss all claims that Parker and Sara could raise from the events as described above. Explain your answer.

Model Answer to Question 2

Parker v Daisy—Battery: In order to establish a claim of battery, a plaintiff must demonstrate that the defendant had the intent to cause a harmful or offensive contact with another person, or knowing, with substantial certainty, that such contact would result. *Boumelhem v BIC Corp*, 211 Mich App 175, 184 (1995). Here, the facts indicate that Daisy took the lid off her drink and intentionally threw it in Parker's face. She knew with substantial certainty that the contents of her cup would come into contact with Parker's face. Thus, Parker could sue Daisy for battery.

Sara v Movie Theater—Premises Liability: A prima facie case of negligence requires a party to establish: (1) a duty, (2) breach of that duty, (3) proximate cause, and (4) damages. *Jones v Enertel, Inc*, 254 Mich App 432, 437 (2002). In general, a premises possessor owes a duty to an invitee to exercise reasonable care to protect the invitee from an unreasonable risk of harm caused by a dangerous condition on the land. *Lugo v Ameritech Corp, Inc*, 464 Mich 512, 516 (2001). However, the duty generally does not encompass warning about or removing open and obvious dangers unless the premises owner should anticipate that special aspects of the condition make even an open and obvious risk unreasonably dangerous. *Id.*, pp 516-517. Whether a hazardous condition is open and obvious depends on whether it is reasonable to expect that an average person with ordinary intelligence would have discovered the danger and risk presented upon casual inspection. *Novontney v Burger King Corp* (On Remand), 198 Mich App 470, 474-475 (1993).

Here, Sara is clearly an invitee and the movie theater owes a duty to protect her from unreasonable risks of harm caused by a dangerous condition, like a slippery floor. As such, the movie theater probably had a duty to clean up the wet floor when the danger became obvious. The facts indicate that Johnny knew of the danger. The movie theater can be held vicariously liable for the negligence of an employee if it was committed while the employee was acting within the scope of his employment. *Rogers v JB Hunt Transport, Inc*, 466 Mich 645, 649 (2002). But the facts indicate that only a few minutes had lapsed from when Daisy spilled her drink and when Sara slipped. Additionally, the facts as presented allow for discussion on whether the danger was open and obvious, i.e., Sara came barreling through the entrance—was she paying attention? Was the danger hidden? Did it have any special aspects?

Parker v Fred—No-Fault: Under Michigan law, the operator of a motor vehicle is liable for an injury caused by the negligent operation of a motor vehicle. MCL 257.401(1). However, Parker can only recover non-economic damages if she suffered death, serious impairment of a body function, or permanent serious disfigurement. MCL 500.3135(1).

Here, the facts indicate that Fred was not paying attention to the roadway when he hit Parker with his car. Therefore, this claim would clearly fall under the No-Fault Act. Therefore, Parker could only recover non-economic damages for pain and suffering if she can prove a permanent serious disfigurement based on the ugly scar left on her forearm. Whether a scar is a permanent serious disfigurement depends on the scar's physical characteristics rather than its effect on the person's ability to lead a normal life. *Kosack v Moore*, 144 Mich App 485, 491 (1985). Whether a scar is serious must be answered by resorting to common knowledge and experience. *Nelson v Myers*, 146 Mich App 444, 446 (1985). The scar must be readily noticeable; a hardly discernable scar is not a permanent serious disfigurement. *Petaja v Guck*, 178 Mich App 577, 579-580 (1989). The facts as presented could support an argument for a permanent serous disfigurement. As such, Parker could recover in an action against Fred.

Two Student Answers—February 2010

Question 2—Torts/No-Fault—10 points

Parker

Utilizing Michigan Law, Parker ("P") may have a claim against Daisy for battery and Fred for negligence under the Michigan No-Fault Insurance Act. However, "P" would not have a valid claim against the movie theatre for the acts of Daisy and Fred.

Sara

Utilizing Michigan Law, Sara may assert a premises liability claim against the movie theatre if she can prove that the theatre failed to warn or protect her from an unknown danger that was not open and obvious because she was an invitee.

Parker v Daisy

Parker ("P") may assert a claim of battery against Daisy ("D"). Under Michigan tort law, battery is defined as an intentional obtrusive touching of another without legal consent. Here D frustrated over a conversation took off the lid of her drink and threw it at "P." Although she did not physically touch P's person she compelled an object with the intent to harm or commit bodily injury to P. As a result, she may face battery charges in a criminal or civil court.

Parker v Fred

Under Michigan Law, a person who negligently drives, operates or uses a motor vehicle that causes an accident may be liable for personal injuries that result to another party. In order to recover non-economic damages, however, the non-fault party must show that a serious injury or disfigurement to a body part occurred.

Here, Fred ("F") was not paying attention to "P" or other pedestrians in the parking lot. As a result, he hit P with his car. Fred's action could be seen as negligent if he owed P a duty as a reasonable driver in the same situation and he failed to act on the duty. A reasonable driver must pay attention to the road and not let distractions such as finding a parking space distract him. Because F acted negligently and was the proximate cause of P's injuries, P can sue Fred to pay for his medical bills, if P does not have auto insurance. Because Michigan is a no-fault state when it comes to motor vehicle accidents P will have to look to his or his family members insurance first before collecting money for his medical bills. P is not seriously injured in this case, therefore, he has not met a threshold for non-economic injury or damage recovery. Parker has not lost use of any of his bodily functions. Therefore, he may only be able to recover for the cost of his medical bills.

Sara v Movie Theatre

Under Michigan's Premise Liability Statute an owner who opens his doors to the public and invite guest in order to confer a business profit has a duty to inspect his premises and prevent invitees from being harmed while on the property.

Here, Sara ("S") would be considered an invitee of the movie theatre. She was on the premises because it was open to the public and she conferred a benefit to the owners by paying for movie tickets. Sara may assert that the owner of the Movie Theatre owed her a duty to inspect the premises and prevent her fall by cleaning up the pop immediately. S may suggest that because Johnny failed to wipe up the pop immediately and that as an agent of the Movie Theatre a duty was breached to her as an invitee which was the proximate cause of her injuries.

The Movie Theatre may assert that under Michigan Law a premises owner is not liable for dangers that are open and obvious or visible. Here, S should have seen the sticky puddle of cola and melted ice and could have avoided her fall by walking around what was open and obvious. Past case law in Michigan has held slippery glossy floors are "open and obvious" dangers and premises owner cannot be held liable if an invitee does not avoid such dangers. This may be a close call for S she must show she did not reasonably see the pop.

Question 2—Torts/No-Fault—10 points

Parker (P) v Daisy (D)—Battery

This claim of action is an intentional tort claim. P will be able to claim that D committed a battery on her. A battery is the intentional harmful or offense contact of another. Here, in this fact pattern, after a heated argument, D intentionally threw her drink in P's face. This is also harmful or offensive contact because it did in fact hit her in the face. It does not matter that D didn't physically touch P with a body part of her own. All that matters is that the drink came from D. D will be liable of battery to P, it doesn't matter that she was not actually harmed by the drink hitting her face.

Sara (S) v Johnny (J)/Movie Theater- Negligence

S will be able to recover in a negligence if she can prove negligence on the part of the Movie Theater. In order to prove negligence S must prove that the theater had a duty, breaches that duty, there was causation, and that she suffered damages. Here, S's status at the theater was that of an invitee. She was there as a paying customer at a place that was open to the public. The theater owed her a duty of reasonable care and to keep the premises safe from any conditions that they knew of or should have known of. In this situation, J was an employee working in the scope of his employment. The facts say that he saw the mess because he put the wet floor sign up, but then he did not clean it up before S slipped and fell, hurting herself. By not cleaning this up, the theater breached its duty of care. They may be able to argue that the condition was open and obvious, but that does not excuse their duty to clean up the mess because they were on notice of its existence.

The theater was also the cause of S's injury because if they would have cleaned up, S never would have slipped in it and she would not have been hurt like the facts say she was. The theater could argue that they are not at fault because the mess wouldn't have been there if it wasn't for D spilling the drink to begin with, but this argument won't work because spills at a theater are common and the theater has a duty to clean them up regardless of the situation.

Lastly, the facts tell us the S broke her arm, so she suffered damages. She was in a cast for 6 weeks. All elements of negligence were met; therefore the theater is liable to S under the theory of negligence.

P v Fred- No Fault

Under No-fault a P can recover for economic damages for accidental bodily injury arising from ownership, operation, use, and maintenance of a motor vehicle as a motor vehicle regardless of fault.

A Plaintiff can sue in tort for negligence if she can show that the injury she received resulted in death, permanent and serious disfigurement, or serious impairment of a important bodily function. Here, if the ugly scar were to qualify as a permanent and serious disfigurement or an impartial bodily injury, we would go to the Kreiner test to determine if a negligence action can be brought. For Kreiner: 1) There has to be a material factual dispute as to the nature and intent of the injury, 2) The impaired has to show that the impairment was objectively manifested, and 3) the injury was a serious impairment that affected the Plaintiff normal life. For the third factor you look to the nature and extent of the injury, type and length of the injury, duration, recovery, and system of recovery. If the test is met, you can sue for negligence.

July 2010—Question 2

Officer Stokes worked proudly for a municipal police department in the state of Michigan. On the evening of July 4, 2010, Officer Stokes initiated a traffic stop after he witnessed a vehicle fail to stop at a stop sign. Although the lights and siren on Officer Stokes's police vehicle were activated, the driver failed to stop. Officer Stokes was able to force him off the road and the driver eventually came to a complete stop. Officer Stokes immediately ordered the driver out of the vehicle. Once out of the vehicle, Officer Stokes pushed the driver up against the vehicle, slammed his face onto the hood, and proceeded to frisk him. The driver struggled and was momentarily able to break free from the officer's grasp. In an attempt to subdue him, Officer Stokes sprayed the driver in the face with pepper spray and again slammed him down on the hood of the vehicle. Every time the driver attempted to resist Officer Stokes's grasp, he was again slammed into the hood of the vehicle. Officer Stokes then handcuffed the driver and for good measure, pushed him face-first into the patrol car. On the way to the station, the driver kept complaining that the handcuffs were too tight. At this comment, Officer Stokes just laughed at him. By the time they got to the station, the driver's face was swollen and discolored but he did not require medical treatment. Additionally, there were purple bruises beginning to form around his wrists where the handcuffs were cutting into the skin.

The driver has threatened suit against Officer Stokes and the police department. Discuss any potential claims that could be made by the driver as well as the likelihood of their success, including any potential defenses.

Model Answer to Question 2

The driver could possibly file suit alleging an assault and battery by Officer Stokes. The police department would be vicariously liable for the tort of its employee, Officer Stokes. However, a police officer, as a governmental employee, is immune from tort liability unless his conduct rises to the level of gross negligence. The facts presented probably do not support a case of excessive force. As such, Officer Stokes and the police department will be immune from any liability for the injuries sustained by the driver.

Assault & Battery: In order to establish claims of assault or battery, a plaintiff must demonstrate that the defendant had the intent to cause a harmful or offensive contact with another person, or knowing, with substantial certainty, that such contact would result. *Boumelhem v BIC Corp*, 211 Mich App 175, 184 (1995). Here, Officer Stokes slammed the driver's face on the hood of the vehicle, sprayed him in the face with pepper spray, and put his handcuffs on too tight. As such, all three actions by Officer Stokes would constitute assault and battery.

Vicarious Liability: The vicarious liability of a municipality for the torts of its employees is based on the doctrine of respondeat superior. Such liability generally can be imposed only where the individual tortfeasor acted during the course of his or her employment and within the scope of his or her authority. *Meadows v City of Detroit*, 164 Mich App 418, 431 (1987), citing *Ross v Consumers Power Co* (on rehearing), 420 Mich 567, 624 (1984). Accordingly, to the extent that Officer Stokes is liable for an assault and battery, his employer would be liable as well.

Governmental Immunity: However, under the governmental immunity act, a governmental employee is not liable in tort for personal injuries as long as the employee's "conduct does not amount to gross negligence that is the proximate cause of the injury or damage." MCL 691.1407(2)(c). "Gross negligence" is defined as "conduct so reckless as to demonstrate a substantial lack of concern for whether an injury results." MCL 691.1407(7)(a). For example, an officer is grossly negligent if the force used is excessive. If Officer Stokes (the governmental employee) is immune, so then will be his employer.

Excessive Force: In subduing a suspect, a police officer may use a substantial level of force that may even result in injury to the suspect if the use of that force was necessary. *See Sudul v Hamtramck*, 221 Mich App 485-486 (1997) citing *Burns v Malak*, 897 F Supp 985 (ED Mich 1995). To determine whether the amount of force used by a police officer was justified, the Court must determine whether the force was "objectively reasonable under the circumstances." *VanVorous v Burmeister*, 262 Mich App 467, 482 (2004) citing *Brewer v Perrin*, 132 Mich App 520, 528 (1984). "Police officers . . . must be given a wide degree of discretion in determining what type of action will best ensure the safety of the individuals involved . . . the general public and the apprehension of wrongdoers." *Brown v Shavers*, 210 Mich App 272, 276 (1995) quoting *Ross v Consumers Power* Co *(on rehearing)*, 420 Mich 567, 659 (1984). As such, if the force is determined to be excessive, then the governmental employee is liable in tort for the plaintiff's injuries.

Conclusion: A claim against the officer and therefore the police department will likely fail. Absent a showing of gross negligence, Officer Stokes and the police department are governmentally immune from the driver's lawsuit for assault and battery. The officer's actions—slamming the driver's face into the hood of the vehicle while attempting to subdue and frisk him, spraying him with pepper spray, and handcuffing him tightly—must be measured by "what was objectively reasonable under the circumstances." The driver here did not immediately stop, had to be forced off the road, and resisted more than one time Officer Stokes' efforts. While the handcuffing too tightly may constitute excessive force, the claimed injuries are nonexistent or minimal (no medical treatment required) and, therefore, not sufficient to support a claim of excessive force. *Oliver v Smith;* 269 Mich App 560 (2006). Because the driver cannot make out a claim of excessive force, he cannot establish the gross negligence exception to governmental immunity and his claim must fail.

Three Student Answers—July 2010

Question 2—Torts—10 points

There could be torts claim in this case. The driver could sue Officer Stokes for battery. Battery is defined as a harmful or offensive touching with intent to cause this harmful and offensive touching.

In this case, a battery occurred when Stokes pushed the driver against the vehicle and slammed his face onto the hood. Stokes also sprayed the driver in the face with pepper spray, which could also constitute a battery because he intentionally caused something to hit the driver. The facts state that Stokes repeatedly slammed the driver into the hood of the vehicle. The handcuffs were also too tight. This could also be a battery because Stokes may have intentionally placed them on the driver in a manner that would cause the handcuffs to be too tight. The facts also state that there were purple bruises framing around the driver's wrists. The driver's face was also swollen and discolored all of these facts indicate that a battery occurred.

The driver may also sue Stokes for assault, which is the intentional creation of an apprehension of fear of physical harm. In this case, Stokes was physically imposing. He immediately slammed the driver's face onto the hood of the car as soon as the driver stepped out of the car. Stokes placed the driver in an apprehension of fear that was reasonable. Stokes repeatedly slammed the driver's head into the vehicle and pushed him face first into the patrol car. Stokes behavior created a reasonable apprehension of fear in the driver because he repeatedly slammed his face into the car. This could be seen as police brutality.

The police department could claim governmental immunity, which can be claimed in tort cases only. To claim governmental immunity there must be a state actor and action by the state actor. In this case, Stokes is a state actor because he is a police officer. The police department may be able to claim governmental immunity because this case doesn't fall under any exceptions.

Furthermore, the driver may sue the police department under respondent superior. The police may be held vicariously liable for the torts of Stokes because he works for them and his conduct arose out of and during the course of his employment for the police department. Therefore, the department may be held liable for Stokes' conduct.

Question 2—Torts—9 points

This question regarding the subject of government immunity as well as torts. The driver has potential claims of Battery and Assault, and Intentional Infliction of Emotional Distress. A battery claim can be brought but the plaintiff or the driver in this case must establish that there was intent causation and damages. Here, clearly the P.O. Officer intentionally caused the contact to substantially occur, by purposefully slamming the driver up against the hood, spraying him with pepper spray and just pushing him up against the car. Which resulted in bruising on his face, swollen and discolored bruising. Thus battery is established.

Assault, is also a possible claim for driver, since the P.O. placed the driver in imminent apprehension of an offensive contact. The driver was sure to be intimidated by the police, opening him out of car and immediately slamming him against the hood, thus assault is easily established here as well.

Thirdly there is a claim of intention inflection of emotional distress. (IIED)
To establish this you must show that there was intentional and reckless disregard when outrageous and extreme conduct caused the plaintiff emotional distress. Damages are not required as to physical damages. The driver can show that maybe since he was tightly handcuffed to where he received purple bruising on his wrist, that he suffered distress. Moreover, the other elements are easier to show, because the P. Officer placed the cuffs on his hands, slammed him against the hood repeatedly

without any regard for his life and emotional well being. Moreover, under IIED, his intent to cause him (driver) emotional distress when he laughed after the driver said the handcuffs were too tight. Showing he knew that they were tight and didn't care. Generally all of the roughing up of the driver was extreme and outrageous conduct by the police officer.

However, the police and the police department have some defenses possibly. The police department will claim Governmental immunity. Here a government agency would be able to excuse itself form liability when it involves an intentional tort. So municipal departments such as the police department will not be liable for police officer Stokes intentional claims.

However, there may be an issue if Officer Stokes was acting within the scope of his employment when the action occurred. Here, clearly officer Stokes was making a routine stop, when he stopped the driver, for not stopping at a stop sign. Furthermore, the driver was resisting arrest, when he was roughed up by officer. Officer Stokes was probably following department procedure that has been okayed by the department. So possibly the department can be sued here by driver despite governmental immunity.

As to the driver, he would again argue that he was acting in compliance with the police department procedure. Generally when a party is resisting arrest, the police have discretion in how the subdue the person. Officer Stokes would argue that he was resisting arrest and so he had to make sure he got him under control, by pepper spraying him, slamming him to the ground and handcuffing him. Thus he should have a privilege as a police officer as necessity to effectuate the arrest. Therefore he can probably charge Officer Stockes with battery & assault, & less likely with Intentional Infliction of Emotional Distress.

Question 2—Torts—8 points

This is a criminal/tort with governmental immunity.

The drive could make several claims that his rights were violated. After a traffic stop where driver was forced off of the road he was immediately ordered out of the vehicle, hw was not arrested or put into custody or read his Miranda rights but was frisked in violation of Michigan law. The officer had probable suspicion to search car and containers and to do a plain feel. When the officer sprayed driver in the face it could amount to a battery offensive touching with intent to do harm. Where harm actually occurred. Before the spray was assault—the officer put driver in an apprehension of death or great bodily harm with intent. I do not feel that driver would be very successful on his accounts because he was fleeing and attempting to resist arrest and in Michigan an officer has a right to apprehend a fleeing felon with what ever force necessary.

Another defense is governmental immunity. Generally a government agent acting with the scope of their employment is exempt from liability unless an exception applies or they were grossly negligent or the government acknowledges and accepts actions. Here there doesn't seem to be gross negligence, the officer was acting with in scope of employment and no exceptions highway, buildings, motor vehicle etc.

CLUSTER FIVE

SALES

Questions, Model Answers, and Student Answers

The following section includes prior Michigan Bar Exam questions and model answers for **Sales**. Many of the questions also include actual student answers with the amount of points that were earned to give you a better idea of what the graders expect. The student answers are immediately following the model answer for each question. Please pay close attention to the points received on each question. Although most samples represent "good" answers (i.e., received 8, 9, or 10 points), there are some samples that received 7 points (the minimum "passing" score for an essay), and a few that received very low scores to help you better understand the grading process and what is expected.

February 2001—Question 11

On May 13, 2000, Baker Manufacturing Co. sent a written purchase order to Ajax Supplies Inc. to buy 50 electronic switches from Ajax's catalog for $7,350.00. Ajax shipped promptly, with an accompanying invoice, and Baker accepted and paid for the goods. There was no single document signed by both Ajax and Baker evidencing any contract between them.

One of the switches was defective, causing a machine to overheat in Baker's factory. A fire resulted, destroying some of Baker's inventory in an adjacent area.

Attorneys for Ajax and Baker are discussing Ajax's potential liability. One contentious issue that has come up in these negotiations arises from the fact that, shortly after the fire, Baker received a desperate inquiry from Zcorp seeking to purchase certain items that were unexpectedly and temporarily in short supply. Unfortunately, Baker's inventory of these items was damaged in the fire, and Baker had to reject the offer. Baker says that Zcorp offered to pay twice the standard price for the items, and it claims that Ajax should compensate it for this lost profit.

Answer the following two questions:

1. **Will the lack of a signed written agreement between Ajax and Baker limit Baker's ability to pursue a breach of contract claim?**
2. **What is the best defense Ajax could raise to Baker's lost profits claim? (Assume that Baker has adequate evidence of Zcorp's offer.)**

Model Answer to Question 11

1. No. The course of performance between the parties establishes a contract even in the absence of a writing, so there is no statute of frauds defense. In addition, it is likely that the invoice sent by Ajax is a writing that makes the contract enforceable against it.
2. The best defense would be that this particular economic injury was unforeseeable. The UCC provides that consequential damages such as those Baker seeks are recoverable only to the extent that the loss was of the kind that the seller could fairly anticipate. The loss here was too remote.

Discussion: (1) Under UCC §2-201 (MCL 440.2201), the most straightforward answer to this question is provided in subsection (3)(c): no defense based on lack of a writing is available "with respect to goods for which payment has been made and accepted or which have been received and accepted." Here, the course of dealings between the parties amply established the existence of a contract, and no written agreement is needed. *See, e.g., R G Moeller Co v Van Kampen Const Co*, 57 Mich App 308 (1971).

As a separate matter, it is also quite likely that Ajax's invoice, which no doubt contains some form of corporate "signature," is a sufficient writing on which Baker could assert a claim. In this sense, there are two reasonable explanations for the answer that should be given credit.

(2) UCC §2-715 (MCL 440.2715) incorporates the principal holding of the famous case of *Hadley v Baxendale*, which limits consequential damages to those risks that are known and/or foreseeable at the time of contracting to the party charged with the breach. The statute says that consequential damages include "any loss resulting from general or particular requirements and needs of which the seller at the time of contracting had reason to know and which could not be prevented by cover or otherwise." The foreseeability problem seems clear here. It is also possible that Ajax could have prevented the loss by reasonable precautionary efforts (a mitigation-type defense), but the facts here do not clearly indicate that this is viable. Thus, it is not as good a defense as lack of foreseeability.

Student Answer—February 2001

Question 11—Sales—8 points

This question involves UCC Article II for the sale of goods. The G/R is that between merchants, there doesn't need to be a signed written agreement, as is often the case in an ordinary common law contract action. On our facts, we have BMC sending a purchase order (offer), and Ajax accepting by shipping the requirements promptly. Baker accepted and paid for the goods. So, even if no documents on evidencing a K [contract], we still have a K given the transactions noted, given the sale of goods between merchants.

Therefore, Baker will still be able to pursue a breach of K (BOC) claim against Ajax.

The best defense Ajax could raise against Baker's lost profit claim is that the loss to Baker is unforeseeable (as to Ajax foreseeing Baker losing money to Zcorp). On our facts, Baker received a "desperate inquiry" from Zcorp seeking to purchase certain items that were unexpectedly and temporarily in short supply. It is doubtful Ajax would have known of this potential loss to Baker, or should have known of it.

In the event that the CT did find Zcorp's request for switches were foreseeable, Baker should only get reasonable, foreseeable lost profits. On our facts, Baker should get no more than what it would have received from Zcorp, which is twice the standard price for the items—these are the reasonable consequential damages. These are damages that are reasonably foreseeable.

July 2001—Question 11

You are counsel to a food services company, Apex, and are negotiating a contract to purchase a large, customized computer system from Benson Computers Inc. for use in managing inventory more efficiently. The existing system being used by Apex is badly outmoded and has been crashing more and more frequently. Benson has promised initial installation by March 1, with a 60-day period for working out any problems. Conformity with all specifications is promised by May 1. Apex's management is very nervous—they like the Benson proposal best on the merits, but are worried about the lengthy time for compliance with the specifications. Other vendors have offered to do the work faster. Apex wants you to make sure that any contract contains language that would make Benson "suffer mightily" in terms of what it would have to pay Apex in the event of failure to perform on time.

To what extent can you accommodate your client's wishes by drafting the contract in such a way that (assuming it agrees to the deal) Benson will be penalized severely if it breaches?

Model Answer to Question 11

Penalty clauses are not enforceable under the UCC. However, a liquidated damage clause may be fixed in such an amount that is reasonable in light of the anticipated harm to be caused by a breach, assuming (as here) that actual damages would be difficult to measure. The client is entitled to ask for a liquidated damages clause that fairly reflects the significant risk of harm to the business that would come from a delay in delivery and installation. This sum may be large enough that it operates to deter Benson from breaching.

Discussion: The UCC, as adopted in Michigan, provides that "damages for breach by either party may be liquidated in the agreement but only at an amount which is reasonable in light of the anticipated or actual harm caused by the breach, the difficulties of proof of loss, and the inconvenience or non-feasibility of otherwise obtaining an adequate remedy. A term fixing unreasonably large liquidated damages is void as a penalty." MCL 440.2718. This by and large reflects the common-law rule barring "penalty clauses" in contracts.

The key here is good faith. Damages would be hard to measure in the event of a delay in delivery, given the quality differences between the old system and the one Benson has promised. So long as the amount Apex proposes bears a reasonable resemblance to what actual damages might be, the liquidated damages clause would be appropriate—even if it has the effect of making Benson "suffer mightily" if it breaches.

Two Student Answers—July 2001

Question 11—Sales—8 points

Article 9 sales provisions of the UCC govern the contract since the transaction is between merchants. Good faith governs all transactions in article 9 so the statement of the client wanting to make Benson (B) pay mightily if it breaches would concern me.

I would draft a liquidated damages provision in the contract. These provisions must be a reasonable estimate of the damages by both parties at the time the contract was made. The damages provisions must not act as a penalty to B.

There should also be a time is of the essence provision built into the contract since there are inherent problems with the computer system.

It may be beneficial for both parties to build an incentive for early completion into the K. It would work similar to the penalty provision except it would reward B for early completion by paying them more if the K was done ahead of schedule.

If B does not conform to the initial deadline on March 1, Apex (A) could demand assurances from B. If the assurances are not given, A could consider the contract breached.

Also, if there were smaller deadlines in the K, A can make sure B meets the requirements of the K. If the deadlines were met, A could consider that B has anticipatory breach of the K if the breach of the K substantially impairs the value of the contract to A.

Question 11—Sales—8 points

The issue is whether Apex can draft a penalty clause against BCI (Benson) where the later will be *severely* penalized for its breach of K in providing timely computer services. The G/R is that a penalty clause is not enforceable if the damages to be suffered by the defendant are too extensive and the damages are reasonably calculable. On our facts, Apex is concerned about getting the new computer up to compliance with specification. However, there is no mention of how much $ it will lose and over how long if the new system is not compliant. It would be advisable for Apex to determine the actual costs it would suffer in the event BCI's new computer system is non-functional for any length of time. Our facts do not indicate that Apex is a Ford service company (which likely supplies many different and diverse retailers) and wants a "large, customized computer systems" for personal inventory needs. Given this important info, Apex should determine its actual losses and if fair, an approximate of expected damages, draft this amount into the contract if BCI doesn't install the computer system in an efficient, reasonable manner.

Given our situation and my advice to my client, Apex, I would suggest apprising potential defendant, BCI of the "time of the essence" to get the computer operational within the 60-day period from March 1 to May 1. I would list the reasonable calculated damages, sufferable for loss, divisible by the amount of days over March 1. This is, in effect, a reasonable liquidated damages clause (this is where a breacher must pay damages for breach of K terms reasonable in light of anticipated & foreseeable breach). Damages may include consequential or incidental expenses or other costs as acquired because of the breach.

In court practice, a liquidated damages clause is allowed to be drafted into a contract where a penalty clause would not. A penalty clause is viewed or construed as taking, or synonymous with it.

February 2002—Question 11

Malcor, Inc. is a manufacturer of electronic auto parts. While it produces most of its products internally from basic materials, a few of the components that it uses are purchased from suppliers with which it has longstanding close relationships. One of those suppliers is National Electronics, a diversified company that, among other things, produces microchips customized for Malcor's needs. Malcor has a detailed long-term requirements contract with National for these goods.

National has recently encountered cash flow problems, and is seeking funding by selling off some of its assets. It recently entered into a deal to sell all the assets associated with its microchip division to Omega Corp. This deal provides for the assignment of all profitable executory contracts from National to Omega, including that with Malcor.

Malcor is surprised by this news and not sure whether they want to deal with Omega. They have been told that Omega plans to assign far fewer employees to the production task that Malcor had. In any event, they also think they might be able to strike a more favorable supply contract with someone else. Malcor executives seek your advice on the following questions:

1. **Under what circumstances can a sales contract like this be assigned without the buyer's consent?**
2. **If the contract can be assigned and Omega breaches, does Malcor have any recourse against National?**
3. **Assuming that the contract is assignable, would Malcor be justified in terminating the contract immediately because of Omega's plans with respect to staffing the job? Is there anything short of termination that Malcor might do to protect itself?**

Model Answer to Question 11

1. Sales contracts such as this can be assigned without the consent of the other party unless the assignment would materially change Malcor's burden, risk or chance of obtaining return performance or Malcor has a substantial interest in having National perform. The question here would be whether Omega's undertaking to perform materially prejudices Malcor's expectation of adequate performance.
2. Yes. The effect of an assignment of the contract is an assignment of the rights and a delegation of the obligations. A delegation does not discharge the obligations of the original party to the contract.
3. Omega has not repudiated the contract by either words or conduct, and hence cancellation by Malcor because of the staffing concerns would be premature (and likely a breach by Malcor). The assignment does create reasonable grounds for uncertainty about performance by Omega. Failure to receive such assurances could be grounds for termination later on.

Analysis: MCL 440.2210, as adopted in Michigan, sets forth the basic rules in this area, including those set forth in the model answer. An assignment of an executory "contract" is construed as an assignment of the rights and a delegation of the obligations under the contract. The delegation of duties is permissible unless the other party has a substantial interest in performance by the original party. Especially when the original party is a business entity, courts today tend to allow delegation to another business entity (which, after all, could change ownership or staffing on its own in the normal course of business). The one thing that the UCC does do for a party to a contract in Malcor's position, is give it rights to demand reasonable assurances of performance in light of the assignment.

Student Answer—February 2002

Question 11—Sales—None Available

July 2002—Question 1

Mercury Photographics Inc. ("MPI") was planning an expansion of its business into a new line of digital copiers. It entered into a contract with Nalkiel Technology Co. ("NTC") for NTC to supply it with a specified number of switching devices that were necessary in order to convert some existing machinery into machinery capable of producing the new copiers. MPI made clear to NTC the intended use of these devices and their essential role in the production process and the need for delivery within 45 days of the contract date.

On the final date for delivery specified in the sales contract, NTC sent word that "production difficulties" made it impossible to deliver on time, and estimated that delay would be for at least another month or two. At this point in time, MPI could have arranged with another supplier to produce the switches at a higher cost, but all other suppliers gave an estimate of six to eight weeks for delivery. MPI informed NTC that, "without waiving any rights to sue for breach as a result of the delay," it would await NTC's tardy delivery.

NTC finally delivered the switches three months later. By the time the new copiers were ready for sale, one of MPI's main competitors had also launched a new copier with much fanfare, and MPI's new line was not as profitable as anticipated. MPI is now preparing its estimate of damages caused by the breach, which will focus on profits lost during the three-month delay.

What difficulties might MPI face in establishing its claim for consequential damages?

Model Answer to Question 1

There are two main difficulties that might be encountered. First, NTC may argue that MPI failed to mitigate damages by not covering in a timely fashion with another manufacturer, choosing instead to await delivery from NTC notwithstanding its inability to give a firm estimate of delivery. The question here would be whether MPI acted unreasonably in not taking alternative action.

The second difficulty is in demonstrating lost profits with reasonable certainty. New lines of business are hard to evaluate with any precision, and what MPI would have gained by launching its new product three months earlier might be too speculative to support an award of damages here. While courts do not demand absolute precision, they do insist on some evidentiary basis beyond guesswork.

Discussion: This is a classic problem of consequential damages to the buyer in a case of seller's breach, addressed by UCC 27-715; MCL 440.2715. There are three main limits on recovery. First is the duty to mitigate: the victim may not sit back and let losses pile up, but must take reasonable steps necessary to keep the harm to a minimum. *Valley Die Cast Corp v ACW Inc*, 25 Mich App 321 (1970). Here, failure to find an alternative source of supply could be unreasonable, especially if its last minute explanation for why it was breaching and when it would be able to perform was evasive. This is a fact question, but would surely be raised in litigation. The mere fact that the other vendors would charge a higher price would not necessarily be determinative.

The rule of reasonable certainty is also well recognized. Lost profits must be based on a reasonable evidentiary base (e.g. comparable product launches). But new lines of business pose difficult problems, although here there may be a comparable product launch from which to extrapolate—MPI's main competitor's launch of a new copier. While courts are not unduly rigorous in demanding determinative proof, *see Temp, Inc v Rapid Electric Sales & Service Inc.*, 132 Mich App 93 (1984), they insist on something more than speculation.

The third main limitation—foreseeability of the consequential damages, as articulated in the famous case of *Hadley v Baxendale*—does not seem to apply here. NTC was on notice of the special needs of MPI and the likely consequences of delay, and thus would presumably be held responsible if the other two conditions for recovery are satisfied.

Student Answer—July 2002

Question 1—Sales—None Available

July 2002—Question 4

Alice Able owned an antique vase and pocket watch which she wished to have appraised. She found the name of a downtown antiques dealer in the yellow pages and drove into the city to have the dealer appraise the items.

Able parked her car in a garage owned and operated by a downtown hotel. Entry to the garage was controlled by a mechanical gate. Upon entering the garage, the driver of a car presses a button on a machine that then dispenses a ticket and lifts the gate. The ticket notes the time and date. When a driver leaves the garage, he or she hands the ticket to an employee of the hotel who works at the exit booth. The employee charges the driver the appropriate fee based on the hours the driver's car was parked at the garage. From time to time, a security officer employed by the hotel patrols the garage. For the most part, however, the attendant at the exit booth is the only hotel employee working in the parking garage. A notice stating, "Remember to Lock your Car" appears on the tickets dispensed by the machine at the entrance of the garage and on several signs located throughout the interior of the garage.

Able received the ticket dispensed by the machine located at the garage entrance. She parked her car in the garage and locked her vehicle. She then carried the vase and pocket watch to the antiques dealer whose shop was located about two blocks from the parking garage. The dealer was impressed with both the vase and the watch. He told Able he wanted to do some more research on both items and asked her to return in a few hours at which time he promised to have written appraisals ready for her. Able left to do some other shopping. She did not know the dealer was in financial straits.

About twenty minutes after Able left the antique store, the dealer sold her pocket watch to Bob Byer. Byer paid a fair price for the watch and knew nothing of how the dealer had acquired the item. Shortly thereafter, Carla Crash entered the antique shop. Fingering Able's vase, she dropped it and broke it to pieces. Crash apologized profusely and offered to pay damages for the vase. The dealer accepted $250 from her which the dealer used to pay a bankruptcy lawyer who filed a bankruptcy petition for the dealer that afternoon.

When Able returned to the shop for her appraisals, the antiques dealer was closed. Worse, her car was missing from the parking garage. The car has not been recovered although no one recalled seeing the vehicle leave the garage.

Able has retained you. She asks your advice on whether she can successfully sue the hotel for the value of her car and Crash for the value of the vase she left with the antiques dealer. Able also wants to know if she can recover the watch from Byer. What advice will you give Able? Explain.

Model Answer to Question 4

This question raises issues from the common law of the bailments and the Uniform Commercial Code. First, the hotel that owned the parking garage will contest whether it had possession of Able's car and hence the duty of a bailee. Second, the woman that broke Able's vase, Crash, will raise her settlement with the antiques dealer as a defense in Able's action as bailor. Generally, a tortfeasor's settlement with a bailee bars a subsequent recovery by the bailor. Finally, the Uniform Commercial Code will make it difficult for Able to recover the watch from Byer. The antique dealer seems to have been a merchant who dealt in antique goods, like the watch. As such, he could transfer Able's title to a buyer in the ordinary course of business.

Liability of the Garage: A bailment is a relationship whereby one person, known as the bailor, gives to another, called the bailee, the temporary use and possession of property. The bailor retains title to the goods but the bailee has possession or temporary custody of them. *See, e.g., Goldman v Phantom Freight, Inc.*, 162 Mich App 472 (1987). 5 Mich L & Practice 2d, Bailments, 1 (2000). A bailment does not arise unless the bailee has control over the goods. In parking garage cases, liability often turns on the owner of the garage. Generally, if a car and its keys are left with a parking lot attendant, the courts will find a bailment. On the other hand, if the car is parked and locked on a wholly unattended lot, the courts rarely find a bailment. *See generally*, Annotation, *Liability for Loss of Automobile Left at Parking Lot or Garage*, 13 ALR 4th, 362, 366-368 (1982). If a bailment has occurred, the owner of the parking lot or garage has undertaken the duties of a bailee and is generally held to be liable for a stolen car without a need for proving specific acts of negligence. *Id.* at 366-367. A Michigan statute largely codifies the foregoing principles of the common law. The statute presumes a garage owner for hire is liable for loss or damage to a car if "possession . . . care, custody or control" of the vehicle has been delivered to the garage owner or the owner's agent. MCL 256.541 (2001).

The hotel stands in something of a middle ground if one considers the bailment cases involving parking lots. Militating against a finding that the hotel has undertaken the duties of a bailee are the facts that Able parked her car herself and retained her keys. It's unlikely any employee of the hotel ever touched her car and the hotel gave her ample warning to lock her vehicle. On the other hand, the hotel garage was not wholly unattended. The hotel employee at the exit booth apparently let the car exit the garage, perhaps without a ticket. The hotel did provide some security in the garage and access to the facility was controlled. Under similar circumstances, courts in other jurisdictions have found bailments and hence liability on the part of the garage owner. *See, e.g., Allen v Hyatt Regency Nashville Hotel*, 668 SW 2d 286 (Tenn Sup Ct 1984). There is, however, ample authority for a contrary view. Annotation, *Liability for Loss of Automobile Left at Parking Lot or Garage, supra*, 13 ALR 4th at 404-416 (collecting cases reaching both results). In short, Able should be advised she has a sound legal basis for suit but the hotel will undoubtedly challenge whether it had sufficient custody of her car so as to constitute a bailment.

Settlement with the Bailee: In contrast, to the ample legal authority on bailments and parking lots, relatively few cases have addressed the preclusive effect of a tortfeasor's settlement with the bailee on any suit by the bailor for damage to bailed goods. The common law rule, first announced in a leading English case, compensated the bailee for such losses. *The Winkfield*, 1902 P42 (Ct App 1901). To the extent the tortfeasor has settled with the bailee in good faith for the value of the goods, the tortfeasor has a defense in any action by the bailor. *See generally*, C. E. Becraft, Annotation, *Bailment-Effect of Settlement by Bailee as a Bar in Action by Bailor*, 47 Mich L Rev 109 (1948). Thus, under the common law, Crash's settlement with the antique dealer would likely bar Able's suit against Crash for the value of the vase. Able should be advised that absent a showing that the settlement was inadequate or in bad faith, she will be unlikely to recover against Crash. She should file a proof or claim in the antique dealer's bankruptcy proceeding.

Sale of the Watch: At common law, a bailee was not considered to have any title to the bailed good and thus could not sell the goods to anyone. Under the Uniform Commercial Code, however, a person who entrusts goods to a merchant who deals in goods of the kind, empowers the merchant to sell the entruster's title to a buyer in the ordinary course of business. MCL 440.2403(2). A buyer in the ordinary course of business is a person who buys the goods in good faith without notice that the sale contravenes the rights of others. MCL 440.1201(9). The sale of Able's watch to Byer appears to have been an ordinary course sale. The antiques dealer sells old watches. Byer paid a fair price in good faith. Able therefore is unlikely to be successful in a suit to recover the watch from Byer. Again, her remedy, if any, would be through a claim in the antique dealer's bankruptcy proceeding.

Two Student Answers—July 2002

Question 4—Personal Property (with sales issue)—10 points

This is a personal property question. Alice will mostly recover the value of her car from the hotel. Since the garage where her car was stolen was owned and operated by a downtown hotel, Alice was owned a higher duty of protection and the hotel will be liable for the loss of her vehicle because of the Innkeeper's heightened duty of care.

Here, they charged Alice for parking their structure, had a security officer patrolling the garage and had a parking attendant to take the ticket exit booth. Alice even remembered to "lock her car." The hotel will be liable for the value of her car.

This is also a bailor-bailee situation where the hotel will be liable for lost, stolen, or damaged property left in its care.

Second, can Alice recover for the vase? Possibly, however, Crash did pay value for the broken vase to Antique dealer who fraudulently gave the $250 to his bankruptcy attorney. An owner of personal property that has been misappropriated will be able to collect the item's fair market value from the individual who misappropriated or converted the property to his own use. Able will have to go after Antique dealer, not Crash.

Finally, can A recover the watch from Byer? Probably. Antique dealer did not have title to the watch and sold it to Byer. Although, as an antiques dealer in the business of selling watches, Byer had no knowledge of the misappropriation and believed he was purchasing the watch from a legitimate seller, which may give Byer a defense.

Question 4—Personal Property—8 points

The Issues

What recovery can Able get from the hotel? What from the Antiques dealer? The hotel was not a merchant but a bailee of Able's car: As a bailee, it has a duty that was limited to protect the car.

The Car

Able will argue the hotel was a secured creditor since it possessed the car; but probably this will not be found, as the hotel was not in the business of selling cars, but merely a bailee holding the car for the bailor, and as such, not liable for its theft. Able can seek damages for negligent caring for his property perhaps, but not for conversion.

The Vase and Watch

Since Able delivered his 2 other items to a dealer in the course of his normal business he can argue this was a secured transaction, since the dealer had possession of the property to recover the value of the property, but since dealer is bankrupt, the recovery won't be too much. He will get pennies on the dollar in value.

The Buyer

Buyer will be protected in his purchase, since he paid value for the watch without notice of any problem, and from a merchant in the ordinary course of business. He is, such a "good faith purchaser," and will have priority over even Able. The dealer had voidable title to the watch, but can convey good title to a good faith purchaser.

July 2002—Question 12

Bill Jones owned a large tract of land that had more white birch on it than any other property in the Western United States. Exclusive Furniture Company specialized in white birch furniture and entered into a written five-year contract with Bill who was to furnish 50,000 linear feet of white birch each year, for a total of 250,000 linear feet for the five-year term of contract. For the first two years of the contract, Bill was to be paid $7 per linear foot and for the last three years he was to be paid $8.50 per foot. The contract also provided that in the event Bill could not, or did not, supply the required quantity in any one year, Exclusive could terminate the contract and seek other suppliers. Bill would be responsible for any extra cost that Exclusive would have to pay to fulfill the contract.

In the first year of the contract, Bill was a little slow in getting started and was only able to supply Exclusive with 35,000 linear feet of wood. Exclusive did not terminate the contract or purchase the difference from another supplier. In the second year, Bill supplied Exclusive with 45,000 linear feet. Exclusive was about to declare the contract terminated and seek another supplier but knew that the price of white birch was now $10 a linear foot and rising. Bill and Exclusive agreed in writing that Bill would provide 40,000 linear feet for the remaining three-year period at $9 per linear foot. Bill only supplied 25,000 linear feet for the third full year and Exclusive notified Bill that the contract was terminated. Exclusive then found a new supplier at the then best available price of $12 a linear foot. Exclusive sued Bill claiming damages for the difference between $12 a linear foot and $7 a linear foot for the shortages for the first three years and for the balance of the 100,000 linear feet for the remaining two years.

Discuss the issues presented and the arguments of each party.

Model Answer to Question 12

The principal issue presented deals with the effect of a modification of a contract. While under the facts of this case there exists consideration for the modification, that is not a necessary element for the modification to be enforceable under Michigan law when the modification is in writing. MCL 566.1. The modification did not address the contingency present in the original contract of Bill not being able to perform or how damages were to be calculated. Furthermore, the modification did not address the shortages that occurred in the first two years of the contract.

Generally speaking, absent an intent to the contrary, a modification agreement will normally supersede prior agreements covering the same subject matter. When the subsequent agreement only covers a portion of the subject matter covered by the earlier agreement, Michigan courts have held that there has been no merger and that portion of the earlier agreement that has not been modified remains in effect. *Joseph v Rottschafer*, 2348 Mich 606 (1929).

The contract itself was for a total of 250,000 linear feet. It did not anticipate being completed until the end of five years. It did, however, anticipate the possibility of shortages each year and provided for a method of calculating damages for this nonperformance.

Since the modification did not release Bill from the shortages occurring in the first two years, he could be held responsible for the increase in the cost of the lumber as per the agreement. The facts of this case do not state if there was an increase in the cost of the birch during the first two years of the existence of the contract and if there was an increase, how much it was.

Exclusive has a duty to mitigate its damages and could not sit back and do nothing as the price rose. Bill would argue that he should not be held responsible for the difference between the $12 and $7 a foot since the shortages could have been made up at the end of the second year at the $10 per linear foot cost and perhaps less.

Bill would also claim that the modification raised the price to $9 a linear foot and that this expressly changes the linear foot price and therefore changed the difference that he could be charged for a shortage from $7 to $9. According to the contract terms, Bill was to be responsible for any extra that Exclusive would have to pay to fulfill the contract, so beginning the third year, the difference would be between the $9 and $12 a linear foot figure, not the $8.50 a linear foot and not the $7 per linear foot.

Exclusive would contend that Bill could not take advantage of the $9 linear foot price since he never fully performed under the modification at that price. Exclusive would contend that, at best, Bill would be responsible for the difference between the $8.50 linear foot price and the $12 price. The court would have to determine if Bill substantially performed under the modified agreement before Bill would be allowed to obtain the benefit of this agreement. Based on the facts presented, it would appear unlikely that a court would determine that Bill substantially performed under the modified agreement where the price would be $9 per linear foot. *See Pulpwood Co v Perry*, 158 Mich 272 (1909).

Student Answer—July 2002

Question 12—Contracts—7 points

The contract between Bill Jones (Jones) & Exclusive Furniture Company (EFC) is within the statute of frauds and appears to be valid. Within the contract is a termination clause and a clause regarding remedy for any breach—liquidated damages.

A modification of a contract must be written if the original (& modification) are subject to the statute of frauds. Here the parties put the modification in writing as required. The modified contract allows for Jones to get $9 per linear foot, not $7.

Jones will argue he should only have to pay the difference between 12/9 not 12/7 & that EFC waived its right to recover the first 3 years because they continued to do business even after Jones' breach. To impose liability for the first 3 years is a penalty—not liquidated damages.

EFC will argue to hold Jones to the original contract & the modification only applied to the quantity and price—not the damages clause.

Comment: This is another example of an answer that is not very good, but earns a minimum passing score of 7 points because it correctly identifies the issues and gives a basic definition in a conclusory fashion. Be sure to do a thorough application of the facts to the rules to earn additional points.

February 2003—Question 5

Everfreeze Manufacturing Corp. sells freezers and other sorts of refrigeration equipment. It sold a large industrial freezing unit to Stansbury Foods Inc. pursuant to a written form contract that conspicuously did three things of significance: it created a limited warranty with respect to the freezing unit's performance and disclaimed any other warranties; it provided that the only remedy for any defects was that Everfreeze would repair or replace the unit; and it excluded any form of consequential damages. Everfreeze was aware of the freezing unit's crucial role in Stansbury's production line.

Upon delivery, the freezing unit was installed and became part of Stansbury's production process. There were small problems at first, but nothing unusual. Over time, however, the problems became more serious, apparently due to a latent defect that gradually affected more and more of the unit. Some six months after delivery, the unit was failing with considerable frequency. Everfreeze has tried to make repairs, but has now concluded that it cannot do so without taking out the unit and installing another one. This will take considerable time, during which—because there is no alternative freezer—a large portion of Stansbury's production line would be shut down. Stansbury estimates that lost profits due to the defects and this replacement procedure would exceed $100,000.

If you were representing Stansbury, what legal claims might you make in order to protect your client's economic interests and seek recovery for its losses? (You may assume that Everfreeze was in breach of the limited warranty.) Evaluate your chances of success.

Model Answer to Question 5

The question is what remedy Stansbury can pursue, given that the contract limits the available remedy to "repair or replace." That could be struck down on one of two possible grounds. One is unconscionability, if the court thought that the inequality of bargaining power and "take it or leave it" form of negotiation resulted in the imposition of a commercially unreasonable term. Given that both parties are businesses and the limitations package was conspicuous, it is not likely that this would succeed. The better argument would be that the limited remedy "failed of its essential purpose." Under the UCC, such a limited remedy can be disregarded under such circumstances, and if so, Stansbury could resort to other remedies made available to it by the law. Courts have often found such failure when a defect is undetectable until such time when repair or replacement is not an effective cure.

If there is "failure of essential purpose," Stansbury should argue that the exclusion of consequential damages was part of the package of terms that fail, and thus can also be disregarded. Its success here is uncertain. Many courts have struck down exclusions of consequential damages on this basis, making it an argument worth pursuing. It should be recognized, however, others have treated such exclusions as separate and distinct limitations to be upheld unless they are unconscionable. And, as noted above, the unconscionability argument would not be easy to win.

Student Answer—February 2003

Question 5—Sales—None Available

July 2003—Question 6

Saraworks, Inc. of Grand Rapids, Michigan has long been in business as a regional distributor of beauty care products manufactured by other companies. More recently, it has also developed its own product lines that it sells to retailers. In 2002, it entered into a ritten contract with High Fashion, Inc. whereby Saraworks agreed to be High Fashion's exclusive wholesale distributor in the region for its entire product line. No duration term was stated in the contract, which was structured as a requirements contract whereby Saraworks would specify the quantity of goods it would purchase from High Fashion based on the volume of its sales of those items to retailers. The parties at the time indicated that they anticipated a "long-term, mutually beneficial relationship."

In January of this year, after lengthy internal deliberations, Saraworks determined that it would be more profitable if it focused its attention solely on its own product lines. Over the course of a few weeks, it redeployed its sales personnel to concentrate on its own products, leading to a 70% drop-off in its purchases and resales of all other products, including High Fashion. In May 2003, Saraworks sent a letter to High Fashion describing its "strategic redirection" and indicating its willingness to "work with High Fashion, if necessary, to find a more suitable distribution arrangement."

Evaluate the likelihood that High Fashion could maintain a successful breach of contract action against Saraworks. (You may assume that no other express terms of the contract address these issues and that the contract includes a standard integration clause.)

Model Answer to Question 6

The UCC provides that in an exclusive dealing sales contract such as this, the distributor is obligated to use its "best efforts" to sell—a more demanding standard than just good faith. By easing any substantial efforts to promote the High Fashion line, Saraworks seems to have violated this implied obligation. The 70% drop certainly suggested that Saraworks was making no serious effort to market High Fashion's products.

Saraworks' likely defense is that because the contract was indefinite in duration, it had no continuing obligation to act on High Fashion's behalf. The UCC, however, provides a sales contract of indefinite duration—though terminable at will by either party—requires reasonable notification prior to termination. Saraworks' notification came substantially after the cessation of best efforts and might well not be considered effective until High Fashion has a reasonable opportunity to make alternative arrangements.

Analysis: Note—this problem is written to avoid the scope question of whether a distributorship agreement that does not contain some qualify specification is outside of Article 2 of the UCC. *See Lorenz Supply Co v American Standard Inc*, 419 Mich 610 (1984).

This problem requires knowledge of two important UCC provisions. Section 2306(2) (MCL 440.2306) states that "[a] lawful agreement by either the seller or the buyer for exclusive dealing in the kind of goods concerned imposes unless otherwise agreed an obligation by the seller to use best efforts to supply the goods and by the buyer to use best efforts to promote their sale." Note that if this were not an exclusive dealing arrangement, the standard would be whether Saraworks' reduced quantity demands were in good faith and not unreasonably disproportionate to stated estimates or comparable prior demands. Saraworks might still be in breach under that lower standard, but the case is made much easier by the element of exclusivity.

The other relevant provision is §2-309 (MCL 440.2309), which says that in the absence of a specified duration in a sales contract the contract lasts for a reasonable time but "may be terminated at any time by either party." The key here, however, is that this termination requires—"[t]ermination of a contract by one party . . . requires that reasonable notification be received by the other party." An Official Comment says that normal practice and good faith mean that notification should be effective so as to "give the other party reasonable time to seek a substitute arrangement" (comment 8).

Student Answer—July 2003

Question 6—Sales—None Available

February 2004—Question 3

Color Products Corp is a manufacturer of specialized paper and plastic goods used in advertising and marketing. It entered into a written contract with Distributor Inc.

whereby it agreed to supply 5,000 cartons of preprinted color display panels beginning in January 2004. The delivery schedule called for 1,000 cartons to be delivered in January, with the remaining installments in March, June, August and October. These panels will be used for a marketing campaign at franchises supplied by Distributor.

When the first delivery came in January, the buyers at Distributor discovered that the colors did not conform to the specifications in the purchase order. What was delivered was quite usable, but not an exact match to other items to be used in the campaign. Color has apologized, saying that the error was due to an inventory glitch. They could have correct colors in a couple of weeks, and expect that all future deliveries will be conforming.

An executive at Distributor asks you what its options are. She says that they have been having second thoughts about whether they may have over-spent on the planned campaign, and would like to be able to reject this installment, cancel the contract with color and come up with some less costly alternative. She hopes that the flaws can be the basis for cancellation and non-payment.

What would you advise? Why?

Model Answer to Question 3

Article 2 of the Uniform Commercial Code creates a special rule for installment contracts such as this. In contrast to the perfect tender rule that exists for single lot sales, the buyer's ability to reject a nonconforming delivery arises only when the nonconformity substantially impairs the value of that installment and cannot be cured. Because the nonconformity seems to be fairly minor and Color is willing to cure, the ability to reject even this first installment is doubtful. As to the contact as a whole, the Code is even more demanding. The defects in one installment must substantially impair the value of the whole contract for there to be grounds to cancel. Given the circumstances, rejection and cancellation might well operate as a breach by Distributor. The fact that Distributor's real reason for wanting out of the contract has nothing to do with the defects, only bolsters this risk because that might be seen as bad faith.

Discussion: Section 2-162 of the UCC (MCL 440.2612) and its official commentary make clear that, whatever the standards are for rejection in sales contracts generally (and the "perfect tender" rule normally does apply), installment contracts are treated differently. A leading recent case demonstrating this is *Midwest Mobile Diagnostics v Dynamics Corp of America*, 965 F Supp 1003 (W.D. Mich 1997). "The buyer may reject any installment which is non-conforming if the non-conformity substantially impairs the value of that installment and cannot be cured . . . but if the non-conformity does not fall within subsection (2) and the seller give adequate assurances of its cure the buyer must accept that installment." In turn, subsection (3) says that cancellation of the contract in its entirety is justifiable only if the nonconformity "substantially impairs the value of the whole contract." The case law has been relatively strict in applying the substantial performance standards when goods are to be delivered in installments.

Even apart from all this, there is a question of Distributor's good faith. Using a minor defect as an excuse for escaping a bad bargain may itself operate as a violation of the UCC's good faith requirement.

Student Answer—February 2004

Question 3—Sales—9 points

Under Article 2 of the UCC, the sale of goods are governed under the Perfect Tender Rule—if goods are not exactly conforming to what was ordered then it is reason to breach the contract under an installment contract. The goods are delivered in installments and the UCC states that a buyer of goods can reject an installment if it substantially impairs the value of the installment and if the nonconforming goods in the installment substantially impair the value of the entire contract then you can reject the entire contract.

Here, we have the sale of goods which are the 5000 cartons of preprinted color display panels. The contract between Colors Products and Distributors calls for delivery in 5 installments therefore creating an installment contract governed under Article II of the UCC. Under the UCC a buyer has a reasonable time to inspect the goods and under the Perfect Tender Rule if goods are nonconforming then it does not satisfy the Perfect Tender Rule; therefore it is grounds for breach. However, installment contacts are treated a little differently if one installment is not perfect and *does not* substantially impair the value of the entire contract then you cannot reject entire contract. You can reject the installment but according to the facts, it does not look like the nonconforming goods in the 1st installment substantially impaired the value of the entire contract, therefore, if this is an installment contract—Distributor cannot revoke the entire contract. However, Distributor can argue that this was not an installment contract therefore the general rule applies where goods are nonconforming; the seller is in breach as long as Distributor had a good faith basis for denying the goods. According to the facts, it appears that contract is installment therefore Distributor can use the nonconforming goods to sue for damages.

Distributor cannot cancel entire contract because courts will find that this is an installment contract and since according to the facts delivery of nonconforming goods did not cause a substantial impairment of the value of entire contract. Distributor cannot terminate because it would lie in breach.

Question 3—Sales—8 points

As the rejection of the current installment, it will depend upon whether the color difference is a material breach. Because it is for a specific campaign and doesn't exactly match other items to be used, I would argue that the breach is material and they can reject this shipment as non-conforming goods. Under the UCC, they have to allow Color Products the opportunity to cure the defective shipment, which the facts indicate that Color plans to do. It will depend on whether "a couple of weeks" is reasonable as to the launch of the ad campaign and whether Color knew of it, facts that are not indicated here, whether the cure is reasonable or if Distributor can refuse to pay for the first installment.

As to future shipments under the contract, Distributor will probably have to accept them. The contract appears to be valid. It is in writing (over $500 must be in writing—sales of goods) and states the quantity. The contract also is one contract rather than a divisible contract. Color has stated that the future shipments will conform so Distributor has no belief to assert anticipatory repudiation. Also, Color is a specialty manufacturer and this appears it is specialty goods with no general market so Distributor would pay damages on the contract if it breaches. I would also advise Color that over-spending is not a defense.

I would advise Distributor that they will not be liable for the current shipment if color is a material breach and cure time is not appropriate but that it will be responsible for future shipments and can't cancel the contract.

February 2004—Question 10

Acme Stereo and Television Company ("Acme") went out of business last week. Before its business failed, Acme sold audio and video equipment at retail. Acme offered home delivery for most of the items sold.

On its last day in business, Acme's delivery truck attempted to deliver a boxed stereo to Betty Baxter in unit 4B of a multi-unit apartment building. Baxter did not answer her door bell, so the driver left the box in the building's rental office. No one was in the office at the time, but the door was open and the driver placed the box inside the open door. Now, no one who works in the office claims to have seen the stereo. It was never delivered to Baxter.

Later that same day, the driver attempted to deliver a television set to Cathy Carswell. When he arrived at her door, he saw a note Carswell had left there that requested the set be delivered to her neighbor, Deanna Davis. Carswell had asked Davis to accept delivery of the set earlier that morning. Davis had agreed to do so and she took delivery of the television from Acme's driver. Before Carswell picked up the television from her neighbor, however, a small fire in Davis' living room destroyed it. The fire was caused by a frayed electrical cord leading to an old table lamp Davis had meant to throw away long ago.

Finally, the driver attempted to deliver a radio to Ed Evergreen who had purchased the item the week before for use in his living room. Evergreen was not home so the driver returned the radio to Acme's warehouse where it is now claimed by Acme's creditors.

Assess the strengths and weaknesses of each of the following claims and explain who should prevail on each claim:

1. **A suit for the value of Baxter's lost stereo filed by Baxter against the owner of her building who runs the rental office;**
2. **A suit by Carswell against Davis for the damage to the television set; and**
3. **An action filed by Evergreen to recover the radio he ordered.**

Model Answer to Question 10

This question raises personal property issues from the law of bailments and sales. Generally, a bailee has a duty to use a proper degree of care in exercising custody over bailed goods. The duty does not arise, however, if there is no bailment. Ordinarily, a bailee must consent to a bailment. The owner of Baxter's apartment building did not. Baxter, therefore, has a weak claim for the lost stereo. Davis, on the other hand, did undertake the duties of a bailee by accepting custody of the television for Carswell. She appears, however, to be a gratuitous bailee and is only liable under traditional principles of law for gross negligence. Her carelessness in using the lamp with the frayed cord probably does not rise to that level. Finally, under

the Uniform Commercial Code, a buyer of goods acquires a specifically enforceable right to the goods once they have been identified to the contract of sale.
In Evergreen's case, that was done when the goods were marked for delivery to him and he should be able to recover his radio.

Baxter's Claim for the Stereo: In the problem, Baxter is suing the owner of her apartment building for the value of the stereo that Acme's delivery driver left in the rental office. It does not seem, however, that the owner of the building owed Baxter a duty to care for the stereo. The facts do not warrant a finding that the owner undertook the duties of a bailee. Ordinarily, a bailment cannot arise without the bailee's consent. The bailee generally must accept care and custody of the bailed goods. *See generally*, 5 Mich L & Prac 2d, Bailment §4 (2000). No one in the rental office undertook that duty for the owner of the building. Thus, absent some agreement or practice of accepting deliveries for the tenants, the owner of the apartment building should not be liable to Baxter for the value of the lost stereo.

Carswell's Claim for the Damage to the Television: Davis, by contrast, did undertake the duties of a bailee. Carswell did ask Davis to accept delivery of the television set and Davis agreed to do so. Davis took physical possession of the set with an obligation to turn it over to Carswell, thus creating a bailment. *See, e.g., National Ben Franklin Ins Co v Bakhaus Contractors, Inc*, 124 Mich App 510, 512, n2 (1983) ("The term bailment imports the delivery of personal property by one person to another . . . for a specific purpose, with a contract, express or implied, that . . . the property [be] returned or duly accounted for when the special purpose is accomplished or the bailor claims it.")

Bailments are generally classified as to whether the relationship benefits the bailor, the bailee or both. *See generally*, 5 Mich L & Prac 2d, Bailment §3 (2000). Traditionally, these classifications have been used to define the bailee's duty of care in exercising custody over the bailed goods. Thus, if a bailment was for the sole benefit of the bailee, the law required the bailee to use the highest degree of care in the custody of the goods. A benefit that was mutually beneficial, on the other hand, called for the exercise of ordinary care. A bailment for the sole benefit of the bailor, often called a "gratuitous bailment," entailed an even lower standard of care. *See generally*, 5 Mich L & Prac 2d, Bailment §6 (2000). Under traditional principles, a gratuitous bailee was only liable for gross neglect if the bailed goods were damaged while in the bailee's possession. *Cadwell v Peninsular State Bank*, 1995 Mich 407 (1917). Recent commentators, however, have criticized the traditional classification scheme. They generally have proposed a single standard of care for all bailments, often stated as a duty of reasonable care under the circumstances. *See, e.g., Kurt Phillip Autor, Bailment Liability: Toward a Standard of Reasonable Care*, 61 So Cal L Rev 2117 (1988).

Under either the traditional or modern approach, Carswell will have difficulty recovering from Davis. Davis accepted the duties of a bailee as a favor, without consideration. She did not treat the television any less carefully than she did her own things. Under the common law standard applied in Michigan for gratuitous bailees, she would not likely be found grossly negligent.

Evergreen's Claim to Recover the Radio: The Uniform Commercial Code expanded the right to a buyer of goods to specific performance of the contract of sale. Under §2-716(3) of the Code a buyer of consumer goods has a specifically enforceable right to the goods as soon as they have been identified to the contract. UCC §2-716(2), official comment 3 (2003). Goods are identified to a contract when they have been marked for shipment. UCC §2-501(1)(b) (2003).

In the problem, Evergreen purchased the radio for his personal, household use. He would thus have a superficially enforceable right to the radio once it had been boxed for delivery to his house. He should therefore be able to recover the radio from Acme's creditors. It should be noted that even if one of those creditors had a security interest in Acme's inventory, Evergreen would take free of the interest as a buyer in the ordinary course of business. *See* UCC §9-320(a) (2003).

Student Answer—February 2004

Question 10—Sales—None Available

July 2004—Question 10

On April 1, Magna Manufacturing Company entered into a written contract with Breakstone Products, Inc. whereby Magna agreed to build and deliver twelve customized machines for use in Breakstone's production facility. The total contract price was $200,000, and the delivery date for the machines was August 15. Magna promptly began work assembling the materials for and designing the required machines. Three weeks later, however, Breakstone notified Magna that it was "canceling" the contract because one of its major customers had suddenly revised its requirements from Breakstone such that production facility would have to be redesigned completely. Breakstone offered to compensate Magna for any out-of-pocket expenses it had incurred.

Magna has asked for your advice. **First, how likely is it that Breakstone could escape responsibility under the contract because of its customer's unexpected change of requirements? Second, should Magna nonetheless complete the work on the machines and tender them to Breakstone as called for under the contract? Assume that Magna has spent $20,000 performing the contract thus far, and that it would cost Magna an additional $140,000 to complete performance. If Magna does not complete performance, will it lose any effective remedy?**

Model Answer to Question 10

Breakstone is unlikely to have any excuse. Defenses like impracticability and frustration rarely give a buyer the right to avoid responsibility under a sales contract simply because of a change in a third party's plans, especially if the buyer made no effort to protect itself from that risk. Hence, Breakstone's premature cancellation most likely operated as an anticipatory repudiation, giving Magna the right to cancel and seek an appropriate remedy.

As to remedies, Magna should probably "stop work and salvage." The UCC gives the seller the option of completing production when this would be a reasonable means of mitigating damages. Here, however, that would be wasteful unless the goods are readily marketable to someone else, which is unlikely because the goods are customized for Breakstone's needs. If stopping work is the more reasonable course of action, then Magna will be made whole by being awarded the "sunk" costs associated with its performance plus its lost profit.

Discussion: UCC §2-615 (MCL 440.2615) creates only a defense of impracticability for sellers; however, courts in jurisdictions other than Michigan acknowledge that the same concept can be read to protect buyers as well, but only if a stringent test is satisfied; performance must be rendered prohibitively expensive by an unforeseen occurrence for which the party seeking avoidance bears no blame. It is highly likely that Breakstone bears the risk of its customer's changed requirements, especially if there was no contract protecting Breakstone from misplaced reliance. Hence, Breakstone's cancellation was a present breach of contract, even though time for performance had not yet come, under the law of anticipatory repudiation (UCC §2-610; MCL 440.26610). That gives the seller, Magna, the right to cancel its own performance and seek a remedy (UCC 2-703; MCL 440.2703).

Like the common law of contracts, the UCC effectively imposes a duty to mitigate damages. UCC 2-704(2); MCL 440.2704(2) states that, as to goods that are uncompleted at the time of breach, seller may continue production, only if doing so is a "reasonable commercial judgment"—which could be the case, for example, if the goods would have substantial value to other potential buyers in the marketplace. But that seems unlikely here because of the customized quality of the goods. If stopping work is the more reasonable course of action, then the UCC affords an acceptable remedy in §2-708(2), MCL 440.2708(2); essentially, the sum of the sunk costs plus (net) lost profit, which includes reasonable overhead. Another way of expressing this is the contract price less costs saved by not having to complete performance and less any residual value to what remains.

Two Student Answers—July 2004

Question 10—Sales—7 points

Whether Breakstone could escape liability under the contract because the unexpected changes?

UCC applies to this contract, it is for the sale of goods of more than $500. There are no issues of validation here, there was an offer, acceptance and consideration is properly met.

Performance of the contract as to Breakstone under the contract Magna agreed to build and deliver by August 15, 12 customized machine. This contract called for an express promise to pay 200K on delivery by Breakstone.

Can Breakstone's promise be excused?

Courts generally abhors condition and enforce promises to avoid forfeitures. Here, if Breakstone can argue that there is commercially impracticable or impossibility to perform under the contract because of an unanticipated and unforeseen situation will render performance under the contract impracticable. An unexpected change of requirement however, thus rendering the contract impractical to perform. As noted, Breakstone's able to perform the contract. When notification of the cancellation, the reason for canceling was that one of its customer changed its requirement. There is no facts indicating that Breakstone's entire clientele has changed its requirements thus rendering the contract impractical. If anything, Breakstone is going to incur a loss if the contract is enforced. Losses are always anticipated. Breakstone cannot minimize its loss by claiming that the contract is now impractical.

Magna's remedy under the contract and duties: Magna is under an obligation to build 12 customized machines and deliver by August 15.

However, since Breakstone has irrefutable told Magna to cancel the contract he may rely on that and suspend performance since there has been a complete repudiation. Magna has a duty to mitigate damages and cannot continue working on the machine.

Remedy under the contract as a non-breaching party he is entitled to the expected profits he was going to receive that would be the $200K under the contract. Since however, he did not fully perform but incurred $20K, he should receive back or deduct back from the contract.

Question 10—Sales—7 points

The characterization of the contract will make or break Breakstone's ability to escape responsibility due to the unexpected change of requirements.

The contract, from the facts has been reduced to a writing and contains material terms, such as price, delivery date and subject matter.

This contract calls for Magna to build 12 customized machines—this is key. This contract is also between "merchants" and therefore the Uniform Commercial Code would apply to guide in a dispute. When a contract calls for the production of specialized goods and prior to deliver date, the buyer indicates its desire to "cancel" the contract we look to the rights and obligations of each party at the time of breach to determine damages.

Here Breakstone in good faith negotiated a contract with Magna. Through no fault of Breakstone, the purpose of their need for the specialized machines became obsolete when one of its major customers revised their need.

Breakstone is now in a position to have to pay for 12 special machines it has no need for. The contract purpose has become frustrated. Breakstone's options are to take the machines and try and re-sell them or cover and go after its major customer for the difference in price. But that's not the question—can Breakstone breach without liability is the question.

The UCC would allow a party in this circumstance to repudiate the contract and calculate damages up to that point. The contract was only 3 weeks old. The facts tell us that Magna had started performance but no machines have yet been built.

If a substantial portion of the contract had been completed by Magna, then Breakstone would not be so lucky and a breach at that time would be much more costly.

Again, only because the change was unforeseeable by Breakstone and not through any direct fault does the Uniform Commercial Code show some compassion to allow it to end the contract at the time it became pointless for Magna to perform.

Breakstone will still be responsible for the $20,000 already spent and the unrealized profit of $40,000 for a total of $60,000 in damages for its breach.

Magna would not under the Uniform Commercial Code be permitted to continue to build the machines and then force them down Breakstone's throat.

Magna will not lose any remedy for not completing performance but will be entitled to all its remedies as stated earlier—profit plus costs.

February 2005—Question 5

Manufacturing Corp. and User, Inc. entered into a written contract that called for Manufacturing to produce and deliver monthly installments of switching devices as per User's requirements over a two-year period, at a fixed priced. The contract included detailed specifications for the devices. On page 6 of the agreement, buried in a lengthy list of terms and conditions, there was a clause that stated that "this agreement may not be modified or rescinded except by a writing signed by both parties." The agreement was a form contract prepared by User.

Shortly after performance began, Manufacturing discovered that it could customize the devices more easily if some minor modifications were made to the specifications. It contacted the principal purchasing agent at User who consulted with some people in the group using the devices, who agreed that the modification would pose no problem. Over the telephone, the principal purchasing agent informed Manufacturing that the change was acceptable to User. Thereupon, User made some modifications in its production process to cut out a number of steps.

Upon delivery, it turned out that the modified devices did not work as expected and caused breakdowns and delays for User. User has demanded compensation for breach with respect to the already-delivered goods and insisted on immediate restoration to the original specifications for all deliveries forthcoming, including one scheduled for two weeks from now.

Is Manufacturing liable for breach for deviating from the original specifications, and can User now properly insist that all future deliveries conform to the original specifications?

Model Answer to Question 5

No oral modification clauses are valid and enforceable, and nothing suggests any unconscionability here. However, the UCC clearly provides that an attempt at modification may operate as a waiver. Manufacturing can properly claim waiver here, which protects it from liability for breach. The UCC goes on to say that a party that has made a waiver may retract it by reasonable notification, unless the retraction would be unjust in light of detrimental reliance on the waiver. Manufacturing would thus at least be given a reasonable amount of time to reconfigure its process before being required to deliver fully conforming goods. Were the reliance on the waiver severe enough, there might even be an argument that the waiver is unretractable.

Discussion: UCC §2-209 (MCL 440.2209) provides the governing rules. Subsection (2) states that a "signed agreement that excludes modification or rescission except by a signed writing cannot be otherwise modified or rescinded." That changed the older common-law approach. *See West Central Pack Corp v A F Murch Co*, 109 Mich App 493 (1981). Subsection (4) then says that "although an attempt at modification or rescission does not satisfy (subsection [2]) it can operate as a waiver." And subsection (5) says that a "party who has made a waiver affecting an executory portion of the contract may retract the waiver by reasonable notification received by the other party that strict performance will be required of any term waived, unless retraction would be unjust in view of a material change of position in reliance on the waiver."

Waiver is an equitable doctrine, and hence not subject to rule-like application. But here, all the standard conditions seem satisfied. The Users agent seemingly had the authority to act on the company's behalf, and did so deliberately and with internal consultation. Manufacturing presumably relied to its detriment by incurring costs in making the changes. Fairness dictates that they should be excused from liability for the already-delivered items: User was in a superior position to assess its needs upon Manufacturing's request. (This problem avoids the more controversial issue under 2-209[4] of what happens when there is waiver without reliance—the so-called election waiver. Compare *Wisconsin Knife Works v National Metal Crafters*, 781 F2d 1280 (7th Cir 1986) (reliance required) with *BMC Indus v Barth Indus*, 160 F3d 1322 (11th Cir 1998) (waiver is more broadly construed)).

Similarly, it is impossible to say with certainty whether the waiver is retractable. We would have to know more about the extent of the detrimental reliance. But at the very least, Manufacturing has a reasonable time to adjust to the retraction.

Student Answer—February 2005

Question 5—Sales—7 points

Is manufacturer liable to User for the deviation in the devices sent to User as modified?

Pursuant to the UCC in a sale of goods between two merchants a contract to be valid need only state the quantity; whereas price and other terms can be provided by the market or customs in the trade.

Here, manufacturer entered into an installment contract with User. The facts do not clearly indicate "all" of User's requirements but its "requirements" over two years, so one will conclude there is a valid contract because the quantity is of the requirements User will require for that two year period.

The terms of the contract further stated that any modifications should be made in writing. Pursuant to UCC any modification as long as done in good faith between two merchants will satisfy the Statute of Frauds requirement, unless otherwise stated. Here there was a written modification clause which was not clearly visible to the manufacturer.

Manufacturer contacted Users principal purchasing agent who agreed (orally) to the modification of the device as sought out by Manufacturer. At no point in time did the principal purchasing agent seek to have manufacturer put it in writing, and so manufacturer will argue User waived the written modification clause and should be estopped from raising it as a defense because manufacturer relied on User's principal agents authorization to make the change on the device.

The modification devices did not suit User's use but before demanding compensation, it is User's duty to first notify manufacturer that the modified devices are not conforming to its necessary use.

Since no date was specified by the parties it appears Manufacturer would have a reasonable time to cure the defects of the devices.

As a result of User's principal purchasing agent's authorization of the use and deliver of the modified device by Manufacturer no breach shall result from Manufacturer's performance.

If User wishes to have all future deliveries conform to original specifications, it (User) must timely notify Manufacturer of its intention so that Manufacturer can reasonably make arrangements to proceed to satisfy and perform the contract.

Comment: Most students did very poorly on this sales question. This is the best answer out of all I received, and it only rated 7 points. Please take the time to compare the model answers to these student answers to see where they went wrong.

Question 5—Sales—3 points (Bad Answer)

UCC Article 2 governs the sale of goods by merchants. The first issue is whether Manufacturing is liable for breach for deviating from the specifications in the contract. Article 2 has abandoned the mirror image rule that states that the acceptance must mirror the offer. The exceptions are if the writing specifically states that the parties must agree upon any deviation or the party objects within a reasonable time. Here, this is a requirements contract that specifically states that the agreement can't be modified without a writing signed by both parties. Therefore, Manufacturer has breached the contact by getting oral consideration.

The next issue is whether the breach is material. In an installment contract Article 2 states that as an installment contract the breach is not material unless it affects the whole contract. Here there is no material breach. The breach didn't affect the whole contract only that particular installment.

The next issue is whether User can insist all future installments conform to the contract. When seller sells non-conforming goods, buyer can rescind the contract or insist seller cure the breach by selling conforming goods. Within time for performance User can insist that Manufacturer cure the breach by sending the original devices that were agreed to in the contract.

> **Comment:** This examinee knew his or her stuff, but missed issues and defined different principles than ones asked. For example, the examinee missed the waiver issue and oral modification. Please compare this answer to the model answer to see the errors.

February 2006—Question 14

Arcadia Marina & Supply sells, among other things, fishing boats and yachts. On May 15, Jon Myers entered into a written contract to purchase a particular boat from Arcadia's inventory for $79,500. Because of unexpected difficulties in obtaining credit from various lenders he approached, Myers was unable to make the purchase and thus defaulted on the contract. A few days after Myers failed to complete the purchase, Arcadia sold the same boat to another purchaser for the same price, $79,500.

1. **What is the likelihood that Myers' inability to obtain credit would excuse him from performance? Explain your answer.**
2. **Assuming that Myers breached the contract and has no other defenses available to him, would Arcadia be able to recover damages against him notwithstanding the resale? Explain your answer.**

Model Answer to Question 14

1. In the absence of a term in the contract making the purchase contingent on obtaining satisfactory financing, Myers bears the risk of not obtaining the needed financing. Here there is no evidence of such an agreement. Because the risk of not obtaining financing was perfectly foreseeable, Myers had little grounds for arguing "frustration of purpose" or impracticability, and is bound to the contract.

2. Although it sold the boat for the same price, Arcadia could reasonably argue that it was a "lost volume" seller. This would require Arcadia to show that even had Myers purchased the boat as per the contract, it would have been able to make the second sale as well—selling a substantially similar boat to that same customer a few days later. If so, it is entitled to its lost profit on the contract with Myers; it is not made whole just because of the resale.

Discussion: Part 1 is a fairly straightforward result: absent evidence of an agreement to the contrary, there is no implied condition that the buyer find satisfactory financing before being obligated to perform a contract for the sale of goods. Part 2 is harder: normally, reselling the goods at the same price would mean that there are no damages (putting aside the possibility of incidental costs associated with the resale). However, courts have constructed UCC §2-708 (Mich Code Ann 440.2708) to allow recovery by the lost volume seller who can show that it was selling essentially "fungible" goods so that had there been no breach the subsequent sale would have occurred anyway—giving the seller profits on two transactions, not just one, *e.g.*, Calamari & Perillo, Contracts sec. 14.23. Whether Arcadia could make that showing here is not entirely clear; it applies most clearly where the seller has an essentially unlimited supply of goods. But at least one famous case has recognized the possibility with respect to pleasure boats (*Neri v Retail Marine Corp*, 285 NE2d 311 [NY 1972]).

Two Student Answers—February 2006

Question 14—Sales—10 points

This is a sales contract question. Myers would defend on impossibility due to his inability to gain financing. However, to obtain relief under impossibility usually requires that the parties can't foresee the event creating impossibility. Here, Myers would have known that he would require financing and could have negotiated the purchase in such a way as to make obtaining financing a condition of sale. Under the facts given, Myers would likely be held to the contract.

If Arcadia keeps boats such as this in stock and has a ready market for them, Arcadia will be able to recover the lost profit from Myers. Under contract law, if a business has a ready market and is able to sell all the inventory it stocks readily, it is entitled to recover the lost profit from a breaching party. Here the facts state that Arcadia was able to sell the boat within a few days which would establish the existence of a readily available market.

> **Comment:** Notice that the examinee still got full-credit even without stating the buzzword "lost volume" seller. This is because the concept was defined.

Question 14—Sales—10 points

Issue 1

Myers' inability to obtain credit will probably not excuse him from performance unless it was explicitly stated in the written contract that the effect of the contract was subject to Myers obtaining credit. Another way that inability to obtain financing would excuse performance would be if Myers and Arcadia had orally agreed that obtaining financing was a condition precedent to the contract taking effect. Neither of these seems to be the case in this situation, so Myers' inability to obtain financing will not excuse his performance.

Issue 2

Arcadia will be able to recover damages against Myers not withstanding the resale. Under the UCC, Arcadia can recover from Myers his lost profit from the sale of the boats. Because Arcadia keeps these boats in inventory the lost profits he would have made on the sale of two boats instead of one. If Myers had completed the contract, Arcadia would have made a profit on the sale as well as the subsequent sale to the next purchaser. So, Arcadia can recover damages from Myers for the amount of profit that Arcadia would have made on the sale to Myers.

July 2006—Question 5

Majestic Paperboard Co., in early April 2006, entered into a written contract by which it agreed to supply Boatwright Corp. with a substantial quantity of customized paperboard at an agreed price. Delivery was to be made in three equal installments, with the first by October 1, the second by November 15, and the third by December 31, 2006.

In recent months, there has been talk of financial trouble and significant layoffs at Majestic. Boatwright very much needs the paperboard in a timely fashion, but has been unable to get anyone at Majestic to confirm or deny that production will occur as specified. The person at Majestic with whom the contract was negotiated "is no longer with the company." Boatwright's management now (i.e., July 2006) fears that Majestic will not perform as promised, and will be insolvent before the end of the year, so that a lawsuit for breach would be futile. It believes that Majestic's failure to communicate is an expression of bad faith, and would like to cancel the contract immediately and seek other vendors.

Draft a memorandum to Boatwright regarding its legal options.

Model Answer to Question 5

Canceling immediately would be risky—it is not likely that Majestic has committed a bad faith anticipatory breach of contract simply because of its equivocation. Courts tend to hold that a party repudiates only by words or actions that demonstrates an unequivocal unwillingness or inability to perform. Were Boatwright to cancel immediately, it might be considered the party in breach.

However, the UCC does provide a mechanism for a situation such as this. When one party has reasonable grounds for insecurity as to whether it will receive the promised performance, it can in writing demand adequate assurances of due performance. If the other party fails to provide adequate assurances within a reasonable time not exceeding thirty days, then it is deemed to have repudiated the contract—and the demanding party is free to cancel. Boatwright should make such a demand, insisting on adequate assurance that Majestic is willing and able to produce and deliver the paperboard as promised.

Discussion: One of the hardest issues in the law of sales (and contracts generally) is knowing how to respond when the other party appears unable or unwilling to perform the contract, but does not say so explicitly. Section 2-609 of the UCC (MCL 440.2609) provides a useful tool in this situation. As under the common law, a party does not commit anticipatory repudiation except by unequivocal words or actions. Indeed, a premature termination can make the terminating party the first material breacher. *See Harlow & Jones v Advance Steel Co*, 424 F Supp 770 (ED Mich 1976). However, the code says that when there are reasonable grounds for insecurity, the insecure party may demand adequate assurances of due performance, and failure to so respond to such a demand constitutes grounds for termination. Full credit should be given for recognizing this course of action. As commentators have pointed out, even under this process, the insecure party faces considerable uncertainty—what kinds of assurances can be demanded, for example? *See* JJ White, *Eight Cases and Section 251*, 67 Cornell L Rev 841 (1982). A good answer need not go so far as to indicate precisely what should be demanded. At the very least, a clear answer as to intention and some demonstration of ability would be appropriate.

Student Answer—July 2006

Question 5—Sales—8 points

To: Boatwright Co.
From: Law Associate

This is a sales question regarding adequate assurances. Under Michigan law governing the sale of goods, when there is a doubt regarding the performance of another party, before performance is due—the party in doubt must ask for adequate assurances. This is done by sending a letter to the party & requesting a response regarding the contract. The party has 30 days to respond. If a response is not received then the other party can consider it a breach and cover—find another vendor. If the party does respond stating there will be performance the party who sent the letter must wait for the delivery date.

Here, MPC & BC have a contract for paperboard. BC is concerned about MPC performing. The delivery date is 3 months away. BC must immediately send an adequate assurances letter. MPC will have 30 days to respond. BC cannot use rumors as a reason to cancel the contract, because then BC will be in breach. BC must follow the procedure set forth under the UCC. Therefore, BC cannot just cancel the contract.

Under the UCC, there is a good faith requirement in dealings. The presumption is that both parties want to contract. Here, it would be bad faith for BC to accuse MPC of bad faith without first sending an adequate assurance letter.

February 2007—Question 11

Lane Products, Inc. was interested in purchasing 10,000 action figures, customized with certain colors and accessories, to use in promoting a new product that it was about to roll out. The buyer for Lane called a sales representative of Terrific Toy Co. to ask whether Terrific wanted to do the production work and, if so, to offer a price for delivery on or before March 1. A few days later, Terrific faxed a bid to Lane of $30,000. According to Terrific's sales representative, Lane's buyer called a few days later to accept. Terrific then proceeded to customize the figures (which it had in its inventory) by painting them and adding the accessories. Terrific then prepared the shipment.

In a telephone call made by Terrific in mid-February to obtain delivery information, Lane's buyer said Lane was no longer interested in the action figures—the new product roll out had been put off indefinitely—and denied ever accepting Terrific's bid, claiming that all he had ever done was "express interest." Terrific's people are furious; they say they clearly remember a firm order.

You are counsel to Terrific. Assuming that you could persuade a court that Lane had indeed accepted Terrific's offer, what major obstacle to recovery for breach of contract do you still face? What are your best arguments for recovery?

Model Answer to Question 11

This is a classic "statute of frauds" problem. Although Terrific may have sent a writing, Lane's purported acceptance was oral. Because the contract is for the sale of goods valued at more than $1000, it is prima facie unenforceable unless a sufficient written memorandum exists.

However, the UCC has one exception that may well apply here. If the goods are to be specially manufactured for the buyer and not suitable for sale to others, and the seller has at least made a substantial beginning to their manufacture, then the contract is enforceable even though oral. Painting and adding accessories to the action figures may meet this test, because other buyers would be uninterested in the customized version of the toys. Under the UCC, this is the best argument. (Apart from the UCC, Terrific might try to argue promissory estoppel against Lane, but it is not clear that this argument is either easier or better.)

Discussion: Besides the statute of frauds issue, there are no other obvious impediments to recovery. But the UCC insists on a writing signed by the party to be charged. MCL 440.2201. There is no such writing or signature here. Note, by the way, that the "old" UCC statute of frauds used $500 as the cut off for what has to be in writing; Michigan and some other states have revised that figure—in Michigan's case, in 2002, to $1000.

MCL 440.2201 does provide for a number of exceptions. If a merchant sends a confirmation of the contract sufficient against the sender and the recipient doesn't object within ten days, the sender can enforce (subsection 2). But that doesn't apply here. Nor have the goods been accepted and paid for, which is another exception (subsection 3[c]). Lane seems prepared to deny the contract, so it does not look as if the "admissions" exception (subsection 3[b]) will work—though there might be some pretrial effort to try to force an admission.

The best argument then, is the "specially manufactured goods" exception (subsection 3[a], permitting enforcement "if the goods are to be specially manufactured for the buyer and are not suitable for sale to others in the ordinary course of the seller's business and the seller, before notice of repudiation is received and under circumstances which reasonably indicate that the goods are for the buyer, had made either a substantial beginning to their manufacture or commitments for their procurement"). *See Webcor Packaging Corp v Autozone Inc*, 158 F3d 354 (CA 6, 1998); *SC Gray Inc v Ford Motor Co*, 92 Mich App 789 (1979). Although more facts would be required to be certain (e.g., how easily could the customized toys be resold?), that standard seems to be met here.

There has been much litigation over whether, assuming the UCC denies enforceability of a particular contract, the aggrieved party can sue in equity—invoking the doctrine of promissory estoppel—to nonetheless recover. Michigan appears to fall into the category of jurisdictions that allow this. *See Fairway Mach Sales v Continental Motors*, 40 Mich App 270 (1972). But it is unclear how or why Terrific would be better off invoking this. If a court denied the "specially manufactured goods" exception (e.g., on grounds that the goods could readily enough be resold to others), then it would be unlikely to find grounds for an estoppel either. Still, an examinee who recognizes this possibility, but not the specially manufactured goods provision, should receive reasonable credit.

Three Student Answers—February 2007

Question 11—Sales—10 points

Issue

Whether a contract that violates the statute of frauds can still be enforced under the UCC.

Rule

The UCC requires that all contracts for goods in excess of value $500 be in writing and have some definiteness. In order to get around or recover from the statute of frauds we have to apply the exception to the UCC. The UCC will allow oral-indefinite contracts when the item being *bargained for is unique* and performance has begun and under a *theory of promissory estoppel*—Terrific (TER) will have to show the elements of promissory estoppel which are:

1. There was a promise,
2. That there was reliance upon the promise,
3. That the reliance was foreseeable and justifiable—

TER had a promise with Lane because of the phone conversations between the two organizations. TER offered to customize and Lane accepted. These phone conversations are definite enough under the UCC to allow a contract formed.

Next we see if there was *Reliance*—Reliance can be shown by TER proceeding to customize the figures which it had in its inventory and prepay them for shipment, thereby relying on the promise.

Foreseeability

Was it foreseeable that TER would rely on this promise and start to perform? Yes because Lane gave a delivery date of March 1. This date shows that TER had to start production in order to get the products ready for March first delivery. Also, 10,000 Action figures is a lot of figures, therefore, TER had to make sure it could handle the inventory. All of the other normal Statute of Fraud issues don't really apply.

TER has met the elements of promissory estoppel; therefore, TER can be excused from a formal writing due to promissory estoppel and because of the uniqueness of the production product. If TER begins producing the unique product they can get around the Statute of Frauds by beginning to perform on the contract. In essence, TER will be able to enforce the contract and avoid the Statute of Frauds because of an exception under the UCC.

Question 11—Sales—8 points

This is a sales issue between two merchants and thus the UCC will apply.

Based on the facts, if this is a valid contract if Lane accepted Terrific's offer, we would then have offer, acceptance, and consideration and this agreement would be examined under the Uniform Commercial Code (UCC), since it is the sale of goods between two merchants.

The first obstacle to recovery would be the statute of frauds. The statute of frauds is a doctrine that mandates forms of agreement that must be in writing such as real property transactions and sales of goods and services over $500 and $5,000 respectively.

Here, we have an agreement. The offer was for sale of 10,000 action figures for $30,000, thus we have consideration which is a bargained-for purpose to enter into the contract. Since the court believes there is acceptance, we have a valid contract. However, there is no writing to prove that this agreement occurred. Lane Products could raise the defense of statute of frauds since this was a sale of goods over $500, and since there is no writing to prove this, this agreement would be unenforceable.

Terrific Toy can counter that the statute of frauds doctrine under the UCC is inapplicable when there is part performance. Here, Terrific received confirmation when a sales representative of Terrific received a phone call from Buyer, after faxing the bid to Lane Products, accepting the offer. They had already performed on the agreement by painting the action figures that they already had and provided their accessories. According to the facts, Terrific Toys customized the action figures to Lane Products' specifications and thus we have part performance, and all was missing was the delivery information. Thus this element has been met.

Another argument is that Terrific Toys created action figures customized to Lane Products' needs and thus it would be special manufactured goods not possible for resale in their ordinary course of business. The general rule is the statute of fraud will come into play if the goods are specially manufactured goods and the seller cannot sell them in the course of ordinary business.

Here, 10,000 action figures were designed customized for Lane Products and thus would meet the requirement that the statute of fraud is inapplicable here.

As for the obstacle of a firm offer, if it is held to be true, then the acceptance would be imputed as any acceptance to any offer is.

Another argument for recovery would be promissory estoppel. Promissory estoppel operates however there is an offer and the offeree relies on it for consideration or forbearance and it would cause a substantial harm and hardship to the offeree if the contract is not enforced. Based on the facts, they relied on Lane's acceptance and to not enforce this contract under promissory estoppel would cause Terrific to suffer a serious harm of having 10,000 action figures to remain in their possession.

Terrific may mitigate damages and sell the toys and collect the difference from Lane or demand specific performance and make Lane accept the toys and pay for them or sue them for breach of contract.

Question 11—Contracts/Sales—8 points

Breach of contract

Under the UCC, goods over $500 involving merchants must be in writing. Here, the facts state that Lane wants to purchase 10,000 action figures (goods) and Terrific faxed a bid to Lane of $30,000, which puts it well over the $500 requirement. Therefore, a major obstacle is that there was no writing based on statute of frauds.

However, the statute can be overcome, if there are specially manufactured goods. Here, Lane is interested in customized Action Figures with certain colors and accessories. Certainly this would qualify as a specially manufactured goods. Therefore, the writing of a contract would be excused; and Terrific can now sue for breach.

July 2007—Question 2

Sigma Corp. is a chemical manufacturer that has long supplied certain synthetic chemicals to Beta, Inc. for use in Beta's manufacturing plant. Beta makes parts that are sold to a large automobile company under a multi-year contract.

On May 1, Sigma wrote to Beta stating that all future orders would be subject to a 7% price increase because of increased energy and other costs. On May 10, Beta responded in writing that this was acceptable so long as the price increase was approved by the auto company. Beta immediately contacted the auto company but for a variety of reasons, never received approval. On May 30, Beta ordered 100 containers of a particular chemical; the purchase order contained the older, unadjusted price. On June 5, Sigma shipped the chemicals and attached an invoice with the adjusted, higher price. Beta promptly used the chemicals in its plant, and has now tendered payment to Sigma at the price contained in the original purchase order.

Was the contract formed between the two parties? If so, what is the price? If not, what is a court likely to do? Explain your answer.

Model Answer to Question 2

Beta and Sigma were aware that they had not come to a clear understanding about price prior to Beta's purchase order, and the two writings—the purchase order and the acknowledgment—are inconsistent on price. Thus, there was no contract formed by the writings; this does not appear to be a case where Beta's response or Sigma's invoice could be construed as a definite and seasonable expression of acceptance.

There could, however, be a contract by *performance*: Sigma's shipment and Beta's use. This is how many courts decide cases such as these under the more liberalized test for contracting in the face of a "battle of the forms." If a court were to find such a contract, then the price would be set by the UCC's "gap-filler," which is a reasonable price at the time of delivery.

On the other hand, a court might decide, in light of the unresolved disagreement about price, that the conduct simply did not manifest any intent to contract. Because the goods cannot be returned to the seller, however, the result would probably still be the same: Beta has to pay the reasonable value at the time of delivery.

Discussion: This question is based on a recent Sixth Circuit Court of Appeals decision applying Michigan law, *Gage Products Co v Henkel Co*, 393 F3d 629 (CA 6, 2004). See also Boettcher & Gerish, *Enforceable Contracts Without Agreement on Price*, 84 Mich B J 34 (June 2005).

There are three UCC provisions potentially at issue here: MCL 440.2204, .2207 and .2305. Each reflects the liberalized view of the UCC that offer and acceptance should not be determined by formalities or who had the "last shot." Thus, most courts applying §2207 reject the idea that acceptance of delivered goods operates as acceptance of whatever writing was last put on the table (i.e., the invoice) because that is unlikely to reflect intent. Given that the writings do not seem to establish a contract but that the parties seem to be acting as if there is one, §2207(3) states that the implied contract is to be enforced using the Code's gap-fillers. The relevant gap-filler, §2305, says that where the parties intend to contract but have not agreed to a price, the price is a reasonable price at the time and place of delivery.

As *Gage* indicates, it is possible in a case like this to say that no contract was intended because the parties had two inconsistent views about the price, and neither was unreasonable in its beliefs. But then §2305(4) says that a buyer unable to return the goods must pay the reasonable value at the time of delivery. Although a price and value are different words, they probably mean the same thing in this instance.

Wrong answers here are that sales contracts are not enforced absent agreement on price, or that there is still a "last shot" approach under the Code, i.e., that buyer is bound to the invoice price simply because it accepted the goods.

Student Answer—July 2007

Question 2—Sales—8 points

The first issue is whether a valid contract has been formed between Sigma (S) and Beta Inc. (B). In order to have a valid contract the parties must have mutual assent, a meeting of the minds as to what they are agreeing to, and an offer, an acceptance, and a bargained for exchange, (consideration).

Here, S and B both seem to be merchants entering into a contract for chemicals—which are assumed to be goods and Art. 2 of the UCC would apply. The contract is for more than 1 year so then the Statute of Frauds would apply. Contracts like these would need to be in writing, signed, describing the item, and the price. Here, there was an exchange of writings between S and B. The writings did not seem to actually come to an agreement as of the price of the chemicals. Both of the writings stated different terms as to the price, however when S shipped the chemicals (which had a different term than B indicated) B promptly used the chemicals. Under the UCC 2-207 battle of the forms if the K b/t merchants acted like they formed a K by their conduct then a K is formed as to the terms which their writings agree. Thus a k can be implied.

Price

As for the price of the contract, the UCC will as mentioned above have the contract terms apply as to the matching, agreed ones. For terms in which the K is missing the UCC adds or fills with Gap fillers. As to price, the UCC would apply a reasonable price K or look to a price that is reasonable in the trade or industry.

February 2008—Question 9

Last year, Wolverine Manufacturing Co. entered into a three-year supply contract with Spartan Products Inc., pursuant to which Wolverine agreed to deliver to Spartan certain goods that Spartan uses in its production facility. The contract is in writing and meets all the requirements for enforceability under the UCC.

Last month, Wolverine's owner announced that the portion of its business that supplies the goods to Spartan was being sold to a company based in Texas, Lone Star Inc. All the assets and liabilities relating to this line of business will be transferred to Lone Star, and all of Wolverine's existing contract rights and obligations relating to this business will be assigned to Lone Star. Some of Wolverine's employees will join Lone Star. Wolverine will continue to operate its other lines of business. Wolverine has notified Spartan of this sale, thanking Spartan for its business and expressing regret that their mutually beneficial relationship would soon be over.

Although Spartan has been satisfied with Wolverine's performance thus far under the contract, it no longer considers the contract's terms particularly favorable, and would like to be free to negotiate a new contract with other suppliers.

As counsel to Spartan, answer the following:

1. **Can Wolverine assign or delegate its obligations to Lone Star regardless of Spartan's consent to the transfer, or would such a transfer over Spartan's objection instead operate as a breach by Wolverine, thereby freeing Spartan to negotiate with other suppliers? Explain your answer.**
2. **If Spartan consents to the delegation to Lone Star and thereafter Lone Star fails to perform as specified, who is liable to Spartan for damages? Explain your answer.**

Model Answer to Question 9

(1) The obligations under a contract for the sale of good can be delegated to a third party without the consent of the other party unless the other party has a "substantial interest" in having the original party perform. Under the facts here, there is nothing to suggest that Woverine's performance is so unique or special that it could not also be done by Lone Star, and so the assignment and delegation will likely be permitted regardless of Spartan's consent.

(2) A delegation does not relieve the delegating party of its obligations under the contract unless the other party to the contract agrees to release that party and substitute a new one (a novation). Merely consenting to a delegation does not create a novation, and thus Spartan could sue Wolverine if Lone Star fails to perform. Most likely, Spartan could also sue Lone Star directly, because the acceptance by Lone Star of the assignment and delegation by Wolverine operates as promise to perform that Spartan can enforce.

Discussion: The status of contract rights and obligations in the sale of a business (or a part thereof) is an important business law issue. Section 2-210 of the UCC (MCL 440.2210) sets forth the basic rules here. First, under subsection (1), obligations are presumptively delegable "unless the other party has a substantial interest in having his original promisor perform or control the acts required by the contract." While there may be circumstances where such a substantial interest exists, e.g., where special skills are called for—the facts in this problem give no indication that this is anything but a standard commercial relationship. Absent such special facts, courts are usually willing to facilitate the sale of a business by allowing the contractual obligations to be transferred to the buyer without the need for the other party's consent.

Subsection (1) then goes on to say that "[n]o delegation of performance relieves the party delegating of any duty to perform to any liability for breach."
See *Plastech Eng Prod v Grand Haven Plastics*, 2005 WL 736519 (Mich Ct App 2005). A party can seek the consent of the original party to a release and substitution—called a novation—but this requires express assent to the novation. Consenting to the delegation is not enough. There is no evidence here of any assent by Spartan to a novation, and hence Wolverine remains liable for any breach by Lone Star.

The UCC also makes Lone Star liable. Subsection (5) states that a contractual assignment is typically treated as both an assignment of rights and a delegation of duties, "and its acceptance by the assignee constitutes a promise by him to perform those duties. This promise is enforceable by either the assignor or the other party to the original contract." In essence, the Code treats the other party (here, Spartan) as a third party beneficiary of the assignment and delegation.

Student Answer—February 2008

Question 9—Sales—None Available

July 2009—Question 7

Dribble, Inc. has a long-standing contractual relationship with Waffle, Inc. to purchase red and white striped basketballs for sale in Dribble's sporting goods stores. For many years, Dribble purchased 500 basketballs per month from Waffle pursuant to a written contract. Dribble paid $10 for each basketball. A certain number of basketballs were delivered by Waffle to each of Dribble's retail stores based on Dribble's standing instructions. Dribble and Waffle's written contract expired on December 15, 2008 and was not renewed.

On December 16, 2008, the Presidents of Dribble and Waffle agreed to continue their arrangement for the purchase of basketballs without the formality of a written agreement. The agreement provided that Waffle would continue to sell Dribble 500 red and white striped basketballs each month at a cost of $10 each.

Waffle's President forwarded to Dribble's President a letter dated December 17, 2008, confirming their agreement. The letter stated that Waffle agreed to sell Dribble the same number of basketballs each month that were previously sold at a cost of $10 each. The letter was signed by Waffle's President. Dribble's President did not open the envelope that contained the letter from Waffle's President because he believed it was just another Waffle promotional brochure. Dribble's President did not sign the letter and did not respond in any way to the contents of the letter.

On December 21, 2008, Waffle sold its basketball business to Premier, including all commitments to sell basketballs to third parties, including Dribble.

In January 2009, Premier delivered 500 brown basketballs to Dribble's headquarters location. Dribble informed Premier that it did not want the basketballs because it did not have a contract with Premier for the purchase of basketballs and, in any event, Premier's performance did not conform with its long-standing arrangement with Waffle.

Premier left the basketballs with Dribble and sued for the total sale value of the basketballs, i.e., $5,000.

Analyze Dribble's rights and responsibilities. Analyze Premier's rights and responsibilities. Explain your answer.

Model Answer to Question 7

The likely result is that a court will find an enforceable oral contract between Dribble and Premier.

The general rule under the Uniform Commercial Code in Michigan is that an oral contract for the sale of goods of $1,000 or more is not enforceable unless there is a writing sufficient to indicate that a contract for sale has been made between the parties and signed by the party against whom enforcement is sought. In this case there is no writing signed by Dribble. MCL 440.2201(1).

An exception to the general rule requiring a writing signed by the party to be charged applies to oral contracts between merchants (Dribble and Waffle are merchants), commonly referred to as the merchant confirmation.

A merchant confirmation sent by one party to the other party within a reasonable time is sufficient for enforcement of an oral contract, if the party receiving the writing has reason to know its contents and does not object within a reasonable time. *See* MCL 440.2201(2).

The confirming letter from Waffle's President to Dribble's President is a merchant confirmation delivered within a reasonable time. Even though Dribble's President did not review the contents of the letter, Waffle could argue that Dribble's President had reason to know its contents, because the confirming letter was sent only one day after the oral agreement. Dribble's President did not object to the writing.

In addition, it could be argued that the oral contract is enforceable because the red and white striped basketballs have been specially manufactured for Dribble. MCL 440.2201(3)(a).

Waffle can delegate its performance under the oral contract to Premier, since there is no agreement precluding a delegation and the facts do not indicate that Dribble had a substantial interest in having Waffle perform the contract, i.e., the manufacture of basketballs. MCL 440.2210(1).

The likely result is that Premier and Waffle breached the contract.

Although the merchant confirmation did not expressly state the number of basketballs covered by the oral agreement or that the basketballs should be red and white striped, the letter from Waffle's President states that the oral agreement is for the same number of basketballs each month that were previously sold. The course of performance between Dribble and Waffle can be used to establish these terms as part of the oral agreement. MCL 440.2208(1). Similarly, the course of performance between Dribble and Waffle was that basketballs were delivered to Dribble's retail stores as directed by Dribble. MCL 440.2208(1).

Premier's performance of the contract was nonconforming, i.e., not a perfect tender, because it did not deliver red and white striped basketballs and did not deliver the basketballs to Dribble's retail stores.

Because Premier's performance is nonconforming, Premier cannot recover $5,000 it requested as relief in the lawsuit against Dribble.

Even though Dribble can reject the nonconforming goods delivered by Premier, it has an obligation to store the goods for a reasonable period of time for instructions from and/or retrieval by Premier.

Student Answer—July 2009

Question 7—Sales—8 points

Dribble's Right: The issue as between the Dribble-Waffle oral argument on December 16 violates the statute of frauds.

The S of F's requires that a sale of goods governed by the UCC which is $500 or over must be in writing. Here, the facts state that the agreement between the two presidents was oral, violating statute.

However, there is an exception to this rule. If writing is not present but one of the parities by a memorandum issues notice to the other party that a contract has been consummated but the other party does not respond within a reasonable time, the Statute of Frauds will be satisfied. Here, the facts state that Dribble's president did not open the letter which contained the confirmation. If he would have opened it he would have realized that the parties to the contract were identified, the price was clearly stated and the time of performance was included. A confirmation letter not responded to satisfies the S of F's. Here the contract will be valid.

Next is the assignment from the Seller (Waffle) to Premier (the assignee). Under the common law all assignments (other than personal services contract and long term "requirements" contracts are assignable. So the assignment will be valid and Dribble will need to honor the performance from Premier.

Therefore, Dribble cannot argue that they do not have a contract with Premier.

Next is the issue of delivery of nonconforming "brown" basketballs. Under the UCC when a Seller delivers nonconforming goods the Buyer has one of three options: a) he can accept them as they are, b) he can accept any commercially complaint materials and reject the rest, or c) he can outright reject the entire shipment.

Here, the fact that the contract was for red and white basketballs and what was delivered was "brown" basketballs does not constitute a material breach. Dribble has the right to reject the entire shipment. There, the suit will not be successful because the goods are not conforming under the UCC and Dribble has the right to reject them.

Although not stated in the facts, had Premier delivered the goods earlier than the contract date, he would have an opportunity to cure the defects (i.e. deliver red and white basketballs).

July 2010—Question 12

Chip is a long-time Michigan resident who has always dreamed of purchasing a boat large enough to take extended tours of the Great Lakes. After years of saving, Chip managed to put aside a considerable amount of money to purchase a large boat. In June 2008, Chip met with Grumby, a salesman for Minnow Boat Sales. After discussion and negotiation, Chip decided to purchase a new 40-foot Jolly-Craft cabin cruiser for $120,000.00. Chip made a $40,000.00 down payment and financed the remaining $80,000.00.

After his first trip with the boat, Chip noticed that soot collected throughout the boat. Chip contacted Grumby and was told this was usually caused by bad fuel but sometimes occurred during the engine's normal break-in period. Chip continued to use the boat. At the end of the boating season in September, Chip contacted Grumby and told him the soot problem had not gone away. Chip complained that the soot dirtied the boat, soiled clothes, and generally adversely affected his enjoyment of the boat. Grumby sent a mechanic to assess the boat. The mechanic acknowledged an abnormal amount of soot and believed the problem was a low quality air filter. The mechanic replaced the filter while the boat was in winter storage.

The next year during several short trips in May and June, Chip again noticed soot collecting in the boat. He notified Grumby that the problem had not been resolved. Grumby sent a more experienced mechanic this time to address the problem. This mechanic also acknowledged an abnormal amount of soot but believed that one of the boat's engines was producing excessive smoke that was being drawn back into the boat, resulting in the buildup of soot. The mechanic altered the fuel mixture, which visibly reduced the smoke and buildup of soot. Chip agreed that the alteration visibly reduced the smoke to some extent, but on longer trips the engine still produced smoke that would collect into soot. The mechanic opined that the smoke could not be entirely eliminated on longer trips.

In August 2009, Chip wrote to Grumby saying that he did not want the boat because of the soot problem and wanted a full refund. Grumby refused, explaining that the soot was trivial and did not affect the value of the boat.

Can Chip recover the purchase price of the boat? Explain your answer.

Model Answer to Question 12

The transaction is governed by Article 2 of the Uniform Commercial Code, which governs contracts, whether oral or written, that involve the sale of goods. See MCL 440.2102. Chip entered into an agreement with Minnow Boat Sales, MCL 440.2204(1), to purchase the boat, MCL 440.2106(1), an item movable at the time identified in the contract for sale. MCL 440.2105(1).

Chip can revoke his acceptance of the boat. To prove a revocation claim, a plaintiff must show: (1) the buyer accepted a lot or commercial unit whose nonconformity substantially impairs its value to him; (2) he accepted based on a reasonable assumption that the nonconformity would be cured or without discovering the nonconformity if his acceptance was reasonably induced either by the difficulty of discovery before acceptance or the seller's assurances; (3) he revoked acceptance within a reasonable time after discovering (or should have discovered) the grounds for the revocation; and (4) he revoked before any substantial change in the condition of the goods. MCL 440.2608(1), (2).

In regard to (1), Chip accepted the boat and must establish that the soot problem substantially impairs the boat's value to him. In interpreting this requirement the Michigan Supreme Court has held that "a buyer must show the nonconformity has a *special devaluing effect on him* and that the buyer's assessment of it is factually correct." *Colonial Dodge, Inc v Miller*, 420 Mich 452, 458 (1984) (emphasis added).

Chip can persuasively argue that buildup of soot on longer trips devalues the boat's value to him. Chip would maintain he specifically purchased the boat for longer trips. He can also claim that the buildup of soot on these trips is more than a nuisance, requiring him to clean the boat and damaging his clothes. A buyer in Chip's position could reasonably find that the soot devalues the boat. Although Minnow Boat Sales may contend that the soot is trivial and does not substantially reduce the value of the boat, the Michigan Supreme Court has upheld the revocation of acceptance for goods where the nonconformity does not substantially impair the good's monetary value. In *Colonial Dodge*, 420 Mich at 458-459, the Court upheld a finding of revocation of acceptance of a car because the dealer failed to include a spare tire. Dismissing arguments that "a missing spare tire is a trivial defect" that is "easy to replace," the Court focused on the value of the spare tire to the purchaser. *Colonial Dodge*, 420

Mich at 458-459. The purchaser had expressed the spare tire's value by purchasing special tires and indicating he had to travel extensively, often in the city. The Court found these concerns sufficient to establish that the car had a substantial impairment. Likewise, while the presence of soot may not affect the monetary value of the boat, the presence of soot substantially impairs the value of the boat to Chip.

In regard to (2), the question does not suggest that Chip could have discovered the soot problem before actually operating the boat. Further, after being aware of the defect, Chip only used the boat after receiving assurances from Grumby that the soot would eventually abate.

In regard to (3), Chip can persuasively argue that he revoked acceptance within a reasonable time after discovering the grounds for the revocation. Here, Chip initially informed Grumby of the soot and was assured that the problem would eventually go away. Chip waited and notified Grumby that the problem had not gone away. Grumby then attempted to repair the problem, but Chip could not have learned that the defect had not been corrected until the next boating season. Thus, for much of the time between Chip's acceptance of the boat and his attempt to revoke his acceptance, Grumby was attempting to fix the boat. "The seller's attempts to repair are likewise a factor in determining whether the buyer notified the seller of revocation within a 'reasonable time' after discovering the defect." *Head v Phillips Camper Sales*, 234 Mich App 94, 106 (1999) (buyer properly revoked acceptance of pop-up camper nearly one year after purchase and three attempted repairs). Here, considering the continuing efforts to correct the soot problem, and the inability to discover whether the first repair worked, Chip can persuasively argue that he revoked his acceptance within a reasonable time.

In regard to (4), there is no evidence of a substantial change to the boat. The facts only indicate the boat was subjected to normal wear and tear, which cannot amount to a "substantial" change in the goods.

Therefore, Chip should be advised that he has a credible claim to revoke his acceptance of the boat. Under the UCC remedy of revocation, the buyer is treated as if the goods were rejected at the outset and the buyer is entitled to a refund of the purchase price paid. MCL 440.2711(1).

Chip can also be advised that even without an express warranty, he may pursue implied warranty claims under the UCC, MCL 440.2314 and MCL 440.2315.

The stronger of the implied warranty claims is that the boat was not merchantable or fit for an ordinary purpose under MCL 440.2314. The warranty of merchantability requires that the goods sold be of average quality within the industry. *Computer Network, Inc v AM Gen Corp*, 265 Mich App 309, 316-317 (2005). Merchantable is not a synonym for perfect. *Id.* Chip will stress that the boat produces an "abnormal" amount of soot and cannot be wholly repaired. Grumby will maintain that the boat produces an acceptable amount of soot. The conflicting evidence will likely produce a question of fact in regard to whether the boat was of "average quality" or fit for an "ordinary purpose" of pleasure riding under MCL 440.2314. Notably, this resolution will focus on an objective "usage of trade," and not whether the soot problem substantially impairs the boat's value to Chip. Also, damages under a UCC warranty claim are generally limited to the difference between the value of the boat at the time of acceptance and the value of a boat that produces average soot. MCL 440.2714. Accordingly, even a successful claim for breach of a warranty of merchantability may not entitle Chip to a "full refund."

Chip is less likely to prevail in a claim under the implied warranty of fitness for a particular purpose under MCL 440.2315. A warranty of fitness for a particular purpose requires that the goods sold be fit for the purpose for which they are intended; to take advantage of this type of warranty, the seller must know, at the time of sale, the particular purpose for which the goods are required and also that the buyer is relying on the seller to select or furnish suitable goods. *Computer Network, Inc v AM Gen Corp*, 265 Mich App at 316-317. Here, Chip expressed to Grumby his purpose to tour the Great Lakes with a boat. While the boat he purchased may produce excessive soot, there is no evidence that the boat cannot nonetheless tour the Great Lakes. Accordingly, Chip would not likely prevail in action for breach of the implied warranty of fitness for a particular purpose under MCL 440.2315.

Student Answer—July 2010
Question 12—Sales—None Available

SECURED TRANSACTIONS

Questions, Model Answers, and Student Answers

The following section includes prior Michigan Bar Exam questions and model answers for **Secured Transactions.** Many of the questions also include actual student answers with the amount of points that were earned to give you a better idea of what the graders expect. The student answers are immediately following the model answer for each question. Please pay close attention to the points received on each question. Although most samples represent "good" answers (i.e., received 8, 9, or 10 points), there are some samples that received 7 points (the minimum "passing" score for an essay), and a few that received very low scores to help you better understand the grading process and what is expected.

July 2008—Question 13

Grand Construction Company required additional operating capital to finance various ongoing projects. To acquire this additional capital, Grand Construction Company inquired about a loan from Okay Bank. As part of the approval of the loan, Okay Bank required a security interest in Grand Construction Company's existing assets as well as any property later acquired by Grand Construction Company. Both parties agreed to the terms of the loan and executed a security agreement. Okay Bank filed a financing statement pertaining to the security agreement on January 15, 2008.

On March 21, 2008, Grand Construction Company purchased new cement mixing equipment from Quick Set Cement. Grand Construction Company took possession of the cement mixing equipment on March 21, 2008. Two days later, Grand Construction Company also agreed to purchase cement molding equipment from Quick Set Cement. To finance the purchase of both pieces of equipment, Grand Construction Company executed a security agreement granting Liberty Bank a security interest in the two pieces of equipment purchased from Quick Set Cement.

On March 23, 2008, Liberty Bank paid Quick Set Cement for both pieces of equipment. On April 7, 2008, Liberty Bank filed a financing statement describing the two pieces of equipment covered by the security agreement.

Grand Construction Company defaulted on the loan to Okay Bank. As a result of the default, Okay Bank filed a claim against Grand Construction Company to take possession of the cement mixing equipment as well as other property. Liberty Bank disputed the right of Okay Bank to take possession of the cement mixing equipment claiming that its security interest had priority.

1. **Did Okay Bank have a security interest in the cement mixing equipment and, if so, was its security interest perfected? Explain your answer.**
2. **Did Liberty Bank have a security interest in the cement mixing equipment and, if so, was its security interest perfected? Explain the answer.**
3. **As between Okay Bank and Liberty Bank, who has a superior claim to the cement mixing equipment? Explain your answer.**

Model Answer to Question 13

This question involves an interpretation of the Uniform Commercial Code (UCC).

1. A security agreement can cover after acquired property. 9-204(1). Since Okay Bank's security agreement covers after acquired property, Okay Bank's security interest covers the cement mixing equipment.

   The filing of a financing statement perfects a security interest. 9-310(1). Okay Bank perfected its security interest when it filed its financing statement on January 15, 2008.
2. A purchase money security interest arises when a person incurs a financial obligation to acquire all or part of designated collateral. 9-103(b). In this case, Liberty Bank acquired a purchase money security interest when it loaned money to Grand Construction Company to purchase the cement mixing equipment from Quick Set Cement.

   Perfection of a purchase money security interest in non-inventory equipment is a two-step process. 9-203 and 9-310. First, it must attach, and second, a financing statement must be filed. Attachment in this case occurred based on the following: Liberty Bank entered into a security agreement with Grand Construction Company, the security agreement was in writing signed by Grand Construction Company, Liberty Bank gave value, and Grand Construction Company had rights in the cement mixing equipment. 9-203. As a result, Liberty Bank's security interest attached.

   The security interest was perfected by the filing of the finance statement by Liberty Bank on April 7, 2008, since the purchase money security interest had previously attached.
3. The UCC generally provides a preference for a purchase money security interest. A purchase money security interest in goods other than inventory has priority over a conflicting security interest in the same collateral if the purchase money security interest is perfected at the time the debtor possesses the collateral or within twenty days. 9-324(1).

The preference provided to a purchase money security interest supersedes the general rule in 9-322(1)(a) that priority is given to the first party to file a financing statement covering the collateral or to perfect its security interest.

Further, the perfected purchase money security interest has priority even if the secured party knows that a conflicting security interest has been created and/or that the holder of the conflicting security interest has filed a prior financing statement covering the same collateral.

Based on the facts in the question, Liberty Bank has priority over Okay Bank because it holds a perfected purchase money security interest. Liberty Bank perfected its purchase money security interest when it filed its financing statement on April 7, which was within twenty days of Grand Construction Company's possession of the cement mixing equipment.

Student Answers—July 2008

Question 13—Secured Transactions—9 points

1. Okay Bank does have a security interest in the cement mixing equipment. The Bank's agreement with Grand Construction (GC) included all existing assets and property later acquired. This is an after acquired clause. A security interest is perfected when the creditor gives value, the debtor has rights in the collateral, and the financing statement is filed.

   Here, the cement mixing equipment was acquired within the time limit imposed by Article 9 therefore it is included in the after acquired clause. The Bank gave value, GC has rights in the collateral and the financing statement was filed.
2. Liberty Bank also has a security interest in the cement mixing equipment. A purchase money security interest (PMSI) arises when the creditor loans money to buy personal property, here the mixer, and immediately takes a security interest in the property.

   The loan from Liberty was used to purchase the equipment. The creditor gave value. GC had rights in the collateral, and the financing statement was filed. Liberty Bank has a PMSI in the mixing equipment.
3. Between two perfected security interests the first to file wins. However, there are exceptions, one of which involves a PMSI. A PMSI in property wins over a perfected security interest as long as it is perfected within 20 days. Here, the cement missing equipment was purchased on March 23 and the financing statement was filed April 1. Liberty Banking has the superior interest in the equipment.

February 2009—Question 8

Big Bobs has been in the business of selling big screen televisions for many years. In 2008, Big Bobs undertook an expansion of the business by obtaining a loan from Bounty Bank. As a condition to providing the loan, Bounty Bank insisted on a security interest against Big Bobs' inventory, including other collateral. Big Bobs and Bounty Bank agreed to the loan and a security interest with Big Bobs' inventory as collateral. Bounty Bank timely filed an appropriate financing statement on September 20, 2008 regarding its security interest in Big Bobs' inventory.

After obtaining the loan, Big Bobs expanded its inventory by purchasing big screen televisions which were delivered by the manufacturer on November 8, 2008. Joe Spartan, an avid college football fan, was interested in purchasing a big screen television for his family from Big Bobs, but was strapped for cash. Therefore, he obtained a loan from City Bank. City Bank paid the loan proceeds directly to Big Bobs on November 22, 2008 so Joe Spartan could purchase a big screen television. The television was delivered on November 26, 2008. As collateral for the loan, Joe Spartan granted City Bank a security interest in the big screen television. City Bank never filed a financing statement pertaining to its security interest.

On December 5, 2008, Joe Spartan obtained a loan from National Bank to purchase presents for the holiday season. As collateral for the loan, Joe Spartan used the big screen television purchased from Big Bobs on November 22, 2008. An appropriate security agreement was executed in connection with the loan. National Bank timely filed an appropriate financing statement on December 6, 2008 regarding its security interest in the big screen television.

Joe Spartan defaulted on the loans with City Bank and National Bank on January 22, 2009 after he lost his job at the end of December 2008.

Even though Big Bobs had high expectations regarding the sale of big screen televisions, on January 5, 2009, Big Bobs discovered it did not have enough money to pay its employees and, as a result, immediately closed its business and defaulted on its loan with Bounty Bank.

After the defaults, the various parties attempted to gain possession of the big screen television purchased by Joe Spartan from Big Bobs.

Answer the following: What are the respective legal rights (if any) of Bounty Bank, Joe Spartan, City Bank, National Bank and Big Bobs to the big screen television? List the order of priority (from highest to lowest) to Joe Spartan's big screen television with your reasoning.

Model Answer to Question 8

Bounty Bank: Bounty Bank's security interest in Big Bobs' inventory, including the big screen television purchased by Joe Spartan, was perfected by timely filing an appropriate finance statement. MCL 440.9310(1).

Joe Spartan: A buyer in the ordinary course of business takes free of a security interest created by the buyer's seller, even if the security interest is perfected and the buyer knows of its existence. MCL 440.9320(1). A buyer in the ordinary course of business is a buyer from a person in the business of selling goods of that kind. MCL 440.1201(9). Since Big Bobs is in the retail business of selling televisions, Joe Spartan took free of Bounty Bank's perfected security interest.

City Bank: City Bank has a purchase money security interest in the big screen television, since it loaned the money to Joe Spartan to purchase the television. MCL 4450.9103(1).

A purchase money security interest in a consumer good is perfected when it attaches. MCL 440.9309(a). A consumer good is defined as a good that is used or bought for use primarily for personal, family, or household purposes. MCL 440.9102(1)(w). Joe Spartan purchased the big screen television for family use, so it is a consumer good.

A security interest attaches when value is provided, the debtor has rights in the collateral, and a security agreement exists that includes the collateral. MCL 440.9203(2).

Since City Bank's purchase money security interest in the big screen television attached, the security interest is perfected, even though City Bank did not file a finance statement.

City Bank has priority over Bounty Bank to the television, even though Bounty Bank's security interest was perfected first. The general priority rule of first to perfect does not apply because Joe Spartan purchased the big screen television free of Bounty Bank's perfected security interest because he purchased the television from Big Bobs in the ordinary course of business. MCL 440.9320(1). As a result, City Bank's security interest has priority over Bounty Bank's security interest, even if City Bank does not have a perfected security interest.

National Bank: National Bank's security interest was perfected when it timely filed an appropriate finance statement. MCL 9310(1). National Bank does not have a purchase money security interest.

City Bank's purchase money security interest has priority over National Bank's security interest since it was the first to perfect its security interest.

Order of Priority: The order of priority from highest to lowest to the big screen television is as follows: City Bank, National Bank, and Joe Spartan. Bounty Bank and Big Bobs have no legal right in the big screen television, and, therefore, no priority, because Big Bobs sold the big screen television in the ordinary course of business.

Student Answer—February 2009

Question 8—Secured Transactions—None Available

NEGOTIABLE INSTRUMENTS

Questions, Model Answers, and Student Answers

The following section includes prior Michigan Bar Exam questions and model answers for **Negotiable Instruments**. Many of the questions also include actual student answers with the amount of points that were earned to give you a better idea of what the graders expect. The student answers are immediately following the model answer for each question. Please pay close attention to the points received on each question. Although most samples represent "good" answers (i.e., received 8, 9, or 10 points), there are some samples that received 7 points (the minimum "passing" score for an essay), and a few that received very low scores to help you better understand the grading process and what is expected.

February 2010—Question 9

Battery Corporation is developing a new battery for use in the growing electric automobile market. Battery searched for a talented engineer to assist in the final development of such a battery. Bill Buck applied for the position, but had little engineering ability. Bill Buck impersonated Tom Lion, an experienced engineer with extensive knowledge regarding battery technology. Bill Buck presented to Battery a fake identification that he was Tom Lion and used Tom Lion's social security number. Battery offered Bill Buck a job (believing he was Tom Lion).

Bill Buck demanded a $50,000 hiring bonus, since he believed he would be immediately fired after Battery discovered that he was not Tom Lion and had little engineering ability. Battery agreed to pay a hiring bonus; however, it did not have adequate liquid assets to pay Bill Buck a $50,000 hiring bonus at the time he commenced employment. Therefore, it offered to pay Bill Buck a hiring bonus on the condition that he remained employed for six months. Bill Buck agreed to this condition, although he had no intention of waiting six months to negotiate the instrument. As a result, Battery hired Bill Buck. Battery paid the hiring bonus of $50,000 by executing an instrument in which it agreed to pay on demand $50,000 on the order of Tom Lion. However, the condition that the hiring bonus would be paid only if Bill Buck completed six months of employment was not included on the face of the instrument.

One day after receiving the instrument from Battery, Bill Buck presented the instrument to Cashrich Company, a check cashing company. Cashrich charges a ten percent fee for its service. Bill Buck again used Tom Lion's social security number and face identification and endorsed the instrument to Cashrich for payment. Cashrich paid Bill Buck $45,000 in cash ($50,000 less its ten percent service fee). Cashrich did not know that Bill Buck had represented to Battery that he would not demand payment of the $50,000 until he had been employed by Battery for six months.

On the same day it purchased the instrument, Cashrich demanded payment of $50,000 from Battery. Battery denied payment on the instrument on the basis that Bill Buck had not been employed by Battery for six months. Cashrich filed suit to recover the face value of the instrument, i.e., $50,000.

Analyze the rights of Cashrich Company to collect on the $50,000 instrument from Battery Corporation. Explain your answer.

Model Answer to Question 9

Cashrich Company will likely recover the $50,000 from Battery Corporation if it is a holder in due course and exercised ordinary care in taking the instrument.

To acquire holder in due course status, the instrument must satisfy the requirements of a negotiable instrument under the Uniform Commercial Code. Pursuant to MCL 440.3104 (1), a negotiable instrument is an unconditional promise or order to pay a fixed amount of money if the following apply:

1. Must be payable to bearer or to order at the time it is issued or first comes into possession of a holder.
2. Must be payable on demand or at a definite time.
3. Must not state other undertaking by the person promising payment to do any act in addition to the payment of money.

Based on the facts, the instrument is a negotiable instrument because it is payable on demand on the order of Tom Lion and does not state any other condition to payment. Bill Buck's statement that he would not present the instrument for payment until after he was employed by Battery for six months does not change this result because the condition was not contained on the face of the instrument.

If Cashrich is a holder in due course, it takes the negotiable instrument free of any defenses by the maker, Battery Corporation. MCL 440.3305(2). To establish status as a holder in due course, the holder must have taken the instrument for value, in good faith, and without notice that the instrument contains an unauthorized signature or that any party has a defense to payment on the instrument. MCL 440.3302(1)(b). Also, when the instrument was negotiated to the holder, it does not bear apparent evidence of forgery to call into question its authenticity. MCL 440.3302(1)(a).

Based on the facts, Cashrich likely is a holder in due course because it (a) gave value ($45,000), (b) took the instrument in good faith and (c) did not have notice of Battery's defenses that Bill Buck (Tom Lion) would not demand payment until he had been employed by Battery for six months or that Bill Buck impersonated Tom Lion in acquiring the negotiable instrument (Cashrich was presented with Tom Lion's social security number and fake identification).

Cashrich must exercise ordinary care in paying and taking the instrument from an imposter, such as Bill Buck, so that it does not substantially contribute to the loss. MCL 440.3404(4). Cashrich likely exercised ordinary care in accepting the instrument from Bill Buck, since in purchasing the instrument it was presented with Tom Lion's social security number and fake identification and only charged its usual service fee.

Student Answer—February 2010

Question 9—Negotiable Instruments—None Available

DOMESTIC RELATIONS

Questions, Model Answers, and Student Answers

The following section includes prior Michigan Bar Exam questions and model answers for **Domestic Relations**. Many of the questions also include actual student answers with the amount of points that were earned to give you a better idea of what the graders expect. The student answers are immediately following the model answer for each question. Please pay close attention to the points received on each question. Although most samples represent "good" answers (i.e., received 8, 9, or 10 points), there are some samples that received 7 points (the minimum "passing" score for an essay), and a few that received very low scores to help you better understand the grading process and what is expected.

February 2002—Question 10

A client comes into your office and explains that she and her husband have been married for twenty-five years, but have been separated for the last eighteen months. At the time of the separation, the two of them prepared a document entitled "Parenting Agreement" which basically provided for the parents to have joint custody, but for the three children, all girls (ages 5, 10, 15) to live with the mother and visit the father on alternate weekends. The parties have orally modified the agreement several times, but the amount of parenting time for each parent has remained consistent. Your client wants to return to the original agreement although she is sure her husband will want custody, or at least, to keep the most recent visitation arrangement in place. The current arrangements have been in place for approximately eight months. Your client hopes the judge will talk to the children because then the judge will see how much she has invested in the children and how little her husband has been in the girls' lives.

Your client informs you that she is proceeding with the divorce since it is clear that her husband is involved with another woman. Apparently his involvement with the other woman began after the separation.

Your client informs you that her husband comes from a wealthy family. Your client is currently living in the house worth $200,000. The house is owned free and clear. The house was purchased six years ago for $150,000, with the down payment of $100,000 coming from his parents and the balance being paid off from her husband's earnings. In addition, he has a retirement plan, a 401(k) worth approximately $400,000. He has been employed with his employer for thirty years. Your client informs you that she just wants to be fair and does not think it would be right to take her husband's retirement since he earned it. In addition, there is a money market account worth $300,000 which was started by a gift of $175,000 fifteen years ago, from the husband's father. This account was simply left to grow, no monies were deposited or withdrawn since the initial deposit. Your client's family is fairly poor but they have helped in finishing the basement and building a deck on the house. They have also been generous in providing childcare for the parties' numerous social and business vacations and meetings.

What issues are involved in the case, and how would you expect a court to rule if the case goes to trial?

Model Answer to Question 10

The following issues exist:

Children: If the husband proceeds with his request for custody, the court will have to determine if there is an established custodial environment. If there is an established custodial environment it will be the father's burden to show, by clear and convincing evidence, that it is in the best interest to change the current arrangement. The judge will need to determine whether the arrangement for the last eighteen months establishes a custodial environment. Presumably the judge will decide a custodial environment has been established, since despite the verbal changes, the amount of parenting time has been consistent. It would then be necessary for the court to review the eleven factors of the Child Custody Act to determine whether the father has met his burden. The judge is required to talk to the children to determine their preference. This conference can take place in chambers, but it must be for the sole purpose of determining the children's preference. It cannot be used as a fact-finding mission for the gathering of other information. In addition, the court will have to make a determination as to whether the five-year old is of a sufficient age to express a reasonable preference. In all likelihood, the judge will want to talk to all the children.

Spousal Support: Given the length of this marriage and the disparity in the earning capacity of the parties, spousal support would, in all probability, be an issue. Probably some spousal support would be awarded, as rehabilitative alimony. The duration would probably be dependent on how long it would take for the wife to finish her education and become established. The amount would depend, to a large degree, on the husband's ability to pay and the wife's needs.

Fault: The fact that the husband is apparently involved with another woman could enter into the issue of custody, spousal support, or property settlement. For spousal support and property settlement the court would have to determine whether his actions were a cause of the breakup of the marriage. It would also be doubtful that the judge would find that his girlfriend caused a breakup of the marriage, given the fact that the parties were already separated. Since there is no evidence that his involvement with another woman was in the presence of the children, this fact should not be considered as one of the factors in the Child Custody Act, even as to the moral fitness of the parties.

Property Settlement:

a. **House:** The house would be a marital asset. Perhaps the husband would obtain a lien on the house for one-half of the equity. The fact that the down payment came from his parents is irrelevant since that payment has clearly been commingled in the asset.
b. **Money Market:** The judge would probably determine that the $300,000 money market was not a marital asset since it came directly from his parents and it was maintained as a separate asset, i.e., there was no commingling.
c. **Retirement:** The 401(k) should be considered to be a marital asset. However, perhaps the marital asset portion would not be the full $400,000 since the husband was employed at the company prior to the marriage. It would depend upon the facts of the case as to what, if any, reduction from the $400,000 would be made to recognize the husband's premarital share.

Dart v Dart, 460 Mich 573 (1999); *Molloy v Molloy*, 247 Mich App 348 (2001); and *Fosket v Fosket*, 247 Mich App 1 (2001).

Student Answer—February 2002

Question 10—Domestic Relations—7 points

Child Custody

When dealing w/child custody, a parent will either have sole physical custody or joint physical custody. Here, the agreement made b/w (between) the husband & wife (H & W) is that wife would have sole physical custody of the 3 girls. And there is a presumption that both parents have joint legal custody that is that both parents help to make the important decisions in the children's lives. Even the wife may have sole physical custody, the husband is allowing to have parenting time. Here, the father would have the children every other week. And if the husband & wife (H & W) get along then the court will allow the two parties to modify & decide what the parenting time will be. This is the case here, we have the H & W deciding when the parenting time will be. Since the wife wants to return to the original agreement, she will now have to use the court system & get it modified & set in stone. In determining whether we should grant the wife's wishes, we will look at the "Established Custodial Environment" and the preference of the children. Here, the Established Custodial Environment has been w/the mother for the past eight months, and furthermore she has invested so much into their lives that they will probably grant my client's wish to return to the original agreement.

Divorce & Property Settlement

A divorce completely ends the marriage. In MI, we are a no-fault state for divorce. Therefore all the parties need to state is that there has been a breakdown of the marriage (i.e. irreconcilable differences). this seems to be the cause here and the wife is now seeking to have her separation become a permanent-divorce. The real issue here is about the property settlement. Fault in MI only comes into play when we are determining the property settlement. Things to look at is the length of the marriage (here 25 years), past conduct or prior acts (here the husband was unfaithful/ infidelity even though it may have started after the separation). What each party has contributed to the marriage, etc. When property is brought into the marriage we have to look and see whether it is active or passive. The current home was purchased 6 yrs ago for $150,000, w/the down payment coming from the husband's parents & the husband paying the rest off. However, wife's parents helped finish, the basement & build a deck. Therefore, the home will probably be classified as active property & split amongst the two. 401K here is not an issue. Lastly, the money market account worth $300,000, which was started by a gift from the husband's father & no monies were deposited or w/drawn from it. Therefore, this will be passive property & the husband will keep it. Over all though, MI considered the property community property & each party gets half unless there is some fault (here infidelity) & the wife may only get an extra 5% to 10%.

The wife may also ask for alimony b/c she is used to living in a better life style, she has been married for 25 years and these are two things looked at in giving alimony.

February 2003—Question 6

Gail Douglas contacts you and explains that she has been married for ten years but has been separated from her husband for the last four months and would like to proceed with a divorce. Gail has discovered her husband has been involved in another relationship for the past three years. Prior to the separation, Gail and her husband lived in Chicago, but Gail moved to Michigan 3½ months ago. Gail and her husband, both 32 years old, have two children (ages 2 and 5). Over Gail's objection, Gail's husband left his employment and has worked from his home in Chicago for the past year and taken care of the children while Gail worked as a legal assistant in a large law firm. Her husband's real estate practice has not been profitable since his decision to leave his former employer. His income has been reduced from $250,000 to $26,000 per year. Gail continues to make $40,000. Since the separation, the children have lived with Gail and been placed in daycare and visit their father on the weekends. Gail fears her husband will seek full custody and child support.

Gail informs you that her husband comes from a wealthy family and, she discovered on her honeymoon, that his parents set up a trust for him when he was eighteen years old which is now worth approximately 1 million dollars. Their home in Chicago, which her husband continues to live in, is worth $250,000. The home was purchased one year after the marriage. The down payment was withdrawn from the trust ($50,000). Gail paid off the mortgage last year. Both Gail and her husband have retirement accounts which were opened after the marriage. Gail's retirement account is worth approximately $200,000 while her husband's account is worth $350,000. Gail would like a portion of his retirement account as she feels she has been paying most of the household expenses since her husband began working from home. She also would like half of her husband's trust to compensate her for the emotional trauma she feels she has suffered because of her husband's infidelity.

Finally, Gail informs you that two hours before their wedding, her husband's family asked her to sign a prenuptial agreement. She didn't read it, but did sign it because she feared the wedding would be called off if she refused.

Identify and discuss the issues applying Michigan law.

Model Answer to Question 6

The following issues exist:

Jurisdiction: In order to file a complaint for divorce in Michigan, Gail must reside in Michigan for 180 days and in county for 10 days. Gail will either have to file in Illinois or wait 2½ months to meet the Michigan residency requirement.

Child Custody and Support: When addressing child custody, the court's controlling guide is the "best interests of the child." The court may take into account the child's preference if the child is old enough to express a preference. Parental fitness and fault may be an issue, even though Michigan is a no-fault divorce state, but must be considered along with all other factors. The court must also address whether an "established custodial environment" exists. If an "established custodial environment" exists, the court cannot enter an order to change the custodial environment unless clear and convincing evidence exists that the change would be in the best interests of the child. Four months is most likely insufficient to establish a custodial environment, especially since the children stayed at home with the husband for the past year. The court's decision will focus on the best interest of the child.

To determine whether Gail or Gail's husband will be required to pay child support, the court (through the Friend of the Court) will apply the Michigan Child Support Formula. The formula is based upon the needs of the child and the actual resources of the parent. The court may deviate from the formula if it determines that application would be unjust or inappropriate. In this case, child support most likely will be awarded depending on which party is granted custody. Income may be imputed to husband because of the voluntary reduction in income.

Spousal Support: Permanent or rehabilitative spousal support can be awarded in Michigan. The court must consider a number of factors including the length of the marriage, the respective incomes of the parties, past relations and conduct, ability to work, and need. Spousal support may be an issue in this case because of the length of the marriage and the husband's significant "voluntary" reduction in income. Spousal support may also hinge on the property awarded to the parties in this matter and whether any of husband's separate property (trust) is invaded and awarded to Gail.

Property Settlement:

(a) **Trust**—Husband's trust is most likely separate property and will be awarded to husband since it was set up by his parents and was, for the most part, maintained as a separate asset. The money that was withdrawn from the trust and applied towards the purchase of the marital home will probably not be considered a separate asset as it was commingled with a marital asset.

(b) **Marital Home**—Marital asset that will be divided between the parties. The fact that Gail paid off the mortgage last year will probably have little or no effect on the court's award as husband's trust made the down payment.

(c) **Retirement Accounts**—The retirement accounts will be marital assets. Division will depend on whether the accounts were established prior to the marriage. If most of the funds were accumulated during the marriage, the entire account will most likely be a marital asset. If the court awards one party's retirement account, or a portion thereof, to the other party, a Qualified Domestic Relations Order must be executed by the court as a part of the divorce judgment.

(d) **Fault** may play a role in the court's division and award of marital assets. If the court finds that husband's affair was a cause of the breakdown in the marriage, the court may even invade his separate asset (trust) to compensate Gail and/or may award her a significant portion of the marital assets (more than 50%-50%), although the standard in Michigan is an "equitable division" of the marital assets.

Prenuptial Agreements: The above property division may be affected by the prenuptial agreement Gail signed prior to the marriage. A prenuptial agreement is a valid contract under Michigan law. This agreement may affect the trust, retirement accounts, and spousal support. If the court finds the agreement was obtained through frauds, duress or mistake, or misrepresentation or nondisclosure of material fact, the court may find the prenuptial agreement void and unenforceable. Marriage is considered a sufficient consideration for the contract. Gail may argue that the agreement is invalid because husband did not disclose the existence of the trust or balance of the retirement account. Gail may also argue that the agreement was executed under duress in that it was presented to her on the day of the wedding.

Student Answer—February 2003

Question 6—Domestic Relations—10 points

Issue

Does Michigan have jurisdiction (JDX) for the divorce?

Rule

JDX would be in Michigan for a divorce if there is property division and children if the plaintiff has resided in the state for 180 days and in the county for 10 days. A way to get around this may be that the court can look to where the children reside to establish JDX. Here, the children are with Gail in Michigan therefore, the court will probably find JDX.

Issue

Is divorce proper?

Rule

Michigan is no fault state for divorce and all that needs to be shown is a breakdown of the marriage. Fault can be an issue when one party has been unfaithful, but this will only allocate a 5% to 10% increase in the judgment. Furthermore, an amount for spousal support may be issued if set in the divorce decree. Spousal support is given when there is a long duration of the marriage. Here, the couple was married for ten years and Gail may be entitled to spousal support and in addition there was infidelity. If spousal support is granted it is income to the recipient and deductible to the payer. In conclusion, if JDX is found to be proper Gail will receive a divorce and probably get spousal support if it is placed in the divorce judgment.

Issue

Who will have custody of the children and what is their duty?

Rule

When there is a dispute as to child custody, we look at many factors to see what to do. For example, we look at the "established custodial environment" of the child. Where they currently reside, go to school, etc. We look at the best interest of the child, love, affection, etc. given to child. We look at the fault of either parent (i.e., infidelity). We look at the mental state and health of each parent, etc.

Here, since Gail has the children, Gail has the established custodial environment. Furthermore, when looking at the best interest of the children, Gail will argue that because Gail's husband has been involved in another relationship for 3 years it would not be in the best interest of the children to move them in a home with another woman. Furthermore, she is making more money right now than him and they are in preschool in Michigan therefore she will probably have the established custodial environment and it would be in the children's best interest to live with her. Because of the age of the children, a judge may take them into his chambers, but not say what they said, but being age 2 and 5 there will be little preference as to what they want. Therefore, Gail will probably retain sole physical custody and both parents will have joint legal custody—important decision made by both of them.

Issue

Are the children entitled child support and additional support?

Rule

Child support in Michigan is determined by guidelines based off the income of the parents. In addition, a child is entitled to medical insurance, day care, and any other agreement by both parents. This is based off their income. You must pay child support until the child turns 18 years old, marries or dies, unless child is full time in high school—then 19½ years old.

Here, the children will be given child support by their father set by the Michigan guidelines and Gail will receive in addition, shared by both to them, money for day care and insurance.

Issue

What will occur with the Property Division of the marriage?

Rule

Normally, property is divided 50/50. However, if a marital asset is brought into the marriage, we must determine if it is active or passive. Active means the property is used during the marriage. Passive means it is stagnant during the marriage.

Here, husband will argue trust was stagnant; it was passive marital property and only to the extent of the $50,000 can be shared. Gail will argue that since any amount of money was used for the $1 million trust, then it made the property active and therefore she is entitled to it. In conclusion, the court will probably find that only to the extent of the $50,000 was active and not the whole $1 million. Since the $50,000 was put into the $250,000 home which the husband continues to live in and which Gail paid off—this is active property and this will be shared. To the retirement account—this was active, they opened it after the marriage and they will share the total of $550,000 between the two of them. Gail will only succeed on the emotional trauma 5% to 10% in what she will receive because of husband's infidelity. This 5 to 50% max or may not come out of the trust.

Issue

Was there a valid prenuptial agreement?

Rule

A prenuptial agreement is valid if there is full disclosure of the parties finances and each party is afforded a separate attorney. A prenup acts in face of a divorce to tell each party was they are entitled to.

Here, Gail may have a valid defense of duress because she signed the prenup without her own attorney, it was given to her only 2 hours before her wedding, and she truly feared the wedding would be called off. However, husband will argue that she did in fact sign it and therefore is not entitled to the $1 million trust. In conclusion, the court will probably find in this situation the prenup to be invalid due to duress and therefore Gail may be entitled to the property stated above.

July 2003—Question 4

Your grandmother, Mary D. Foryears contacts you for some legal advice. Your grandparents have been married for 52 years. Your grandfather, Ben L. Foryears, is exhibiting signs of dementia and Mary wants to file for divorce. She asks you for some advice regarding the consequences of seeking a divorce from Ben.

In 1951, Ben enlisted in the Army and was sent off to fight in the Korean War. Ben and Mary eloped the night before Ben's ship sailed. Neither Ben nor Mary remembers much of the ceremony as they had a few too many Old Fashions, which led to the decision to elope. They were married by what they believe was a licensed magistrate and Ben went off to war the next day.

Mary's parents were less than thrilled when they found out about the marriage and feared Ben's only reason for marrying Mary was to get at the family fortune. At the time of the marriage, Ben had no idea as to the enormous amount of wealth held by Mary's family.

After Ben returned from the war, he and Mary started a family and had six children. Ben and Mary invested the money she received from the family fortune and built a home in Louisiana. Ben also used a portion of the family fortune to start a furniture business. Ben ran the business for 40 years. Mary never stepped foot in the store, nor did she ever draw a paycheck from any other employer. The business continues to operate under the management of one of their children, with Ben as the sole shareholder. At Mary's insistence, her name was never placed on the stock certificates because she thought the business was "a harebrained idea" from day one, and she was convinced Ben would go bankrupt. Mary told Ben she never wanted anything to do with the business. The business owns a number of assets including the vehicles driven by both Ben and Mary.

As a result of her expensive taste in clothes, jewelry, and afternoon teas at the club, Mary has admitted to you that she had long ago spent most of the remaining money she received from the family fortune.

What issues are involved and what principles will guide your advice?

Model Answer to Question 4

The following issues exist:

Validity of Marriage: The consent of the parties capable in law of contracting is essential to a valid marriage. The law of contracts dictates whether a person has the ability to enter into a marriage contract. A marriage can be deemed invalid and annulled for fraud, duress, mistake, lunacy, inability to contract due to age, and intoxication. It must be shown that one of the parties did not have the ability to enter into a contract. In this case, Mary will have a difficult, if not impossible, time seeking an annulment. The passage of 52 years along with six children will most likely convince a court that the parties were not intoxicated to such a degree as to establish lack of consent. Whether the magistrate who conducted the ceremony was duly licensed may also be an issue as to the validity of the marriage, but again it would be highly unlikely the court would determine the marriage invalid under the facts of this case. MCL 551.2; 551.4; *Chudnow v Chudnow*, 2001 WL 672571 (April 27, 2001): *Castle ex rel Gulliver v Deising*, 2001 WL 633702 (May 25, 2001).

Property Settlement:

(a) **Family Fortune:** Mary may successfully argue that the remainder of the family fortune is a separate asset if it has been maintained as a separate asset. While separate estates may be invaded if necessary to provide suitable support and maintenance of the other party, Ben is financially secure as the result of his successful business. *Reeves v Reeves*, 226 Mich App 490 (1997); MCL 552.19, 552.23, 552.1101.

(b) **Marital Home:** Marital asset that will be divided between the parties. While Mary's family fortune was used to purchase the home, it was considered "commingled" when used to buy the marital home. (Same authority.)

(c) **Business:** The business and assets held by the business will most likely be marital assets and divided "equitably" between the parties. While a portion of the family fortune was used to buy the business, the fortune was commingled to purchase a marital asset. Although Mary never became involved in the business, she will most likely also receive a portion of the business as a marital asset. The courts usually award "stay at home" mothers an equitable division of a husband's business when declaring the business a marital asset. *Reeves v Reeves*, 226 Mich App 490 (1997); *Hanaway v Hanaway*, 208 Mich App 278 (1995) (see same authority cited above).

Two Student Answers—July 2003

Question 4—Domestic Relations—9 points

To file for divorce the plaintiff must be a resident of Michigan for 180 days, and live in county 10 days.

There only needs to be basis of a breakdown in marriage, as Michigan is a no-fault state.

— An annulment for lack of capacity—intoxication would not be available, as they would have had to cure the defect w/in a reasonable time from date of marriage, and in this case it has been 52 years.

— Grandma should check on the status of the marriage license, if the license is not real then they are not married, because Michigan does not recognize common law marriage.

If found to be married Michigan is a 50/50 state. Each party will receive 50% of the assets.

There is a question of the inheritance, and the rule generally states that the other spouse cannot receive that part in divorce. The exception is if the spouse co-mingles the funds.

In this case the wife used the money to build their home. The home will be split 50/50. Even though the business was invested by her money, he ran the business. The funds of the business were used to support both parties and therefore should be split 50/50.

The vehicles are not personal property but business property and will have to be included in the assets.

All personal property each party should be able to keep.

Comment: This is a brief answer, but it hits all the issues. The one-point deduction is likely because the student said "Michigan is a 50/50 state." This is not correct. Michigan has "equitable distribution," which does not always mean a 50/50 split.

Question 4—Domestic Relations—8 points

The first issue to address in this domestic relations question is that Michigan is a no-fault divorce state and the party seeking the divorce must only plead a breakdown in the martial relationship. On these facts, the facts, the fact that Ben is exhibiting signs of dementia is sufficient grounds for Mary to file for a divorce in Michigan.

The next issue is whether both Ben and Mary's intoxication is grounds for having the marriage annulled as being void. An annulment can result when the marriage was never legal in the first place. Here, I might advise Mary that she could seek an annulment based on she and Ben's lack of consent due to intoxication. A marriage is a legally enforceable agreement in which both parties must consent to before entering. However, the downfall to Mary seeking an annulment is that she could not collect alimony from Ben because the court will treat Ben and Mary as having never been married. This could be damaging to Mary because the facts state that she never worked, so therefore, there is a substantial disparity in income and she and Ben have been married 52 years, a long-term marriage. Based on these two factors, I might advise Mary to seek a divorce instead so that she could collect permanent alimony.

The next issue is if Mary does seek an annulment or divorce, is the parties home, vehicles and assets of the business marital property, that acquired after the marriage. Because Mary co-mingled her family fortune with the marital estate by investing it in a home, the home would be marital property and plus, the home was acquired after the marriage. Secondly, because the family fortune was used to start the couple's business after the marriage, the assets derived there from would also be considered marital property. The fact that Mary doesn't work there is irrelevant. Finally, the fact that both parties' vehicles are considered assets owned by the business started after the marriage, they are also marital property.

Finally, if Mary seeks a divorce and can establish a custodial environment based on the "best interests of the child" standard used by the courts, she could obtain custody over her children and child support. The burden is by clear and convincing evidence. However, it is very likely her children are over 18 considering the length of marriage, so that may not be an issue.

February 2004—Question 2

In 1979, Ed married Susan. Two weeks prior to the marriage, Ed insisted Susan sign an agreement that provided that if they were to ever file for divorce, Susan would have custody of any minor children born during the marriage and Ed would pay Susan $275 per month per child for support. No other terms were addressed in the agreement.

In 2002, Susan filed for divorce and sought custody of the parties' minor children, Seth (10 years old) and Gavin (16 years old). The courts awarded Susan full custody of the children and granted Ed liberal visitation. The court also ordered that Ed pay $100 per month per child for child support. Ed left Michigan and has never paid a dime to Susan or the children. Ed moved back to Michigan in 2003.

Seth is now 11, and Gavin 17 in his senior year of high school. He will graduate on June 5, 2004 and turn 18 on July 1, 2004. Susan wants Ed to pay support for Gavin until he is 19½ and to contribute to future college expenses, but Ed refuses to do so stating, "The boy can pay for his own college!" Ed wants the child support award reduced on July 1, 2004, because Gavin will be 18. Susan argues that her expenses will not change and that her needs are the same.

In addition, Susan's parents have not spoken to Ed or Susan in 10 years, but are now interested in visitation rights in connection with their grandchildren. Since 1994, Ed and Susan have refused to allow the grandparents to see the children because of a family dispute.

Susan seeks your advice regarding the following issues:

A. Is the 1979 agreement between the parties addressing child custody and support a valid agreement?
B. Can Susan force Ed to pay support until Gavin is 19½?
C. Can Susan recover from Ed for back child support?
D. Is Ed entitled to a reduction in his child support obligation if Gavin turns 18, graduates and moves out of Susan's house?
E. What rights do the grandparents have as far as visitation is concerned?

How will you advise Susan? Why?

Model Answer to Question 2

A. No. Parents may enter into a prenuptial agreement to address marital property and spousal support, but parents may not bargain away a child's right to adequate support. Provisions that attempt to put a ceiling on support available in the future are unenforceable. Although a court may consider an agreement between the parties, the court is not bound by it. *Bowman v Coleman*, 35 Michigan 390 (1959); *Carlston v Carlston*, 182 Mich App 501 (1990); *Ballard v Ballard*, 40 Mich App 37 (1972). A court is also not bound to a parties' agreement regarding custody. A court may take the parties' stipulation into consideration, but the court must find that the arrangement is in the best interests of the child. *Koron v Melendy*, 207 Mich App 188 (1994).

B. No. Michigan's child support laws allow courts to order post-majority support for the benefit of a child between the ages of 18 and 19½ if the child: (1) is regularly attending high school full time; (2) has a reasonable expectation of completing sufficient credits to graduate from high school, and (3) is living full time with the payee of support or at an institution. *Rowley v Garvin*, 221 Michigan App 699 (1997). When Gavin turns 18, he will no longer be a high school student and thus would not be eligible for post-majority support.

C. Yes. Although Susan has waited for a year to collect on the child support arrearage, she can collect at any time. An income withholding order or a contempt order may be issued to enforce this obligation. MCL 552.151; MCL 552.607.

D. Yes. Parents are jointly obligated to support a minor until a minor is emancipated by operation of law. Emancipation occurs when a minor is validly married, reaches 18 (or 19½ if the child meets the criteria above), or is on active military duty. MCL 722.4. If Gavin graduates or moves out of Susan's house, Ed is not required to pay child support for his benefit regardless of Susan's needs or expenses.

E. As of July 31, 2003, the right of grandparents to ask the court for visitation with their grandchildren no longer exists. *DeRose v DeRose*, 469 Michigan 320 (2003). Michigan's Grandparenting Time statute was declared unconstitutional because it removed all deference from the parents.

Two Student Answers—February 2004

Question 2—Domestic Relations—9 points

Issue A—1979 agreement:

The 1979 agreement between Ed and Susan is probably invalid. Usually, people can't contract issues regarding child support, since technically (legally) the child support is for the child (and the parents can't waive the child's right to support.) Also, given that the agreement was signed just two weeks before the marriage, either of the parties could argue that they were under duress when they signed, afraid of the other calling off the wedding at the last minute.

Issue B—CS to 19½:

Susan probably cannot force Ed to pay child support until Gavin is 19½. Child support generally ends at age 18. There may be other circumstances not given that would warrant the extension, but otherwise, Gavin's child support will probably end on July 1, 2004, when he turns 18. If he had still been in high school, to the age of 19½, the support could be extended to 19½, but Gavin graduates on June 5, almost a month before his 18th birthday. Ed's support for Gavin will likely end on July 1, 2004.

Issue C—Back support:

Susan can definitely recover the back child support Ed has not paid. She is entitled to $100 per month, per child, beginning with the month the child support order was issued in 2002. Ed left the state, and may not have seen the children, but that doesn't remove or excuse his liability to pay child support.

Issue D—Reduction:

The child support order says Ed must pay $100 per child, per month. If Gavin turns 18, graduates and moves out of Susan's house, Ed's child support with respect to Gavin will end. The $100 per month would not be reduced; Ed would just pay it for one child and not two.

Issue E—Grandparent's rights

Grandparents do not have rights when it comes to visitation of grandchildren. This issue was decided by the US Supreme Court within the last couple years. Even without the Supreme Court ruling, courts look to why the parents are denying the visitation to begin with. Since Susan is alive, and they are her parents, the court would assume Susan has a good reason to deny the visitation, and the court would not question her role as the parent to make that decision.

Question 2—Domestic Relations—9 points

Ed and Susan signed a prenuptial agreement regarding child custody and child support. These were established before any children were born.

Susan filed for divorce 23 years later, with 2 minor children. The Court established child custody and child support payments in light of the conditions and family structure at the *time of the divorce*, and would not hold the 23-year-old agreement valid for support payments. Too many issues could change over 23 years to consider those contractual agreements binding.

Ed was instructed by the Court to pay 200/month in child support—and he failed to pay anything. He is now responsible for *all* back child support and this could be garnished from his wages. Susan should seek help from the court to obtain all past due support.

Susan could seek payment for Gavin to age 19½ if he needs that much time to graduate from high school. Ed need only pay to age 18 or 19½ to complete high school—whichever the child needs—the facts do not specify if Gavin may be a bit "behind" in stand education schedule.

Ed will be entitled to a reduction in child support payments after Gavin graduates from high school and is 18 years old, or if he moves out of Susan's house and is emancipated. If Gavin isn't living with his mother—she does not need financial support for the child.

As far as the grandparent's visitation rights—some states allow court ordered grandparent visitation rights. Michigan does not follow this idea of constitutionally encouraged family rights—Michigan believes this infringes on the family privacy rights of *parents* to decide how to raise their children and that the *parents* should decide who visits, how often, and when. The courts recognized the value of extended family relationships, but did not believe the risk to parental control was outweighed by grandparents' need for contact with their grandchildren.

Susan should seek child support and back payments, and get it for Gavin if he qualifies as needing it to finish high school. She does not need to tolerate the grandparents' demands for visitation and should pursue all back payments due through "friend of the court" sanctions.

July 2004—Question 11

Abbie and Bill were married in early 2001. Bill was 58 years of age and Abbie 22 years of age. Abbie had a one-year-old child, Danny, from a prior relationship with Bob. One year after Abbie and Bill married, Bill adopted Danny. Bill and Danny became very attached to each other. Bill had inherited a substantial amount of money on his uncle's death three years before Bill and Abbie were married. Bill used a good portion of it to pay cash for a new home for himself and Abbie. Bill continued to work at his regular job as a forest ranger, from which he earned a reasonable, if modest, income. Abbie continued working part-time as a bank teller, but her principle job was as their homemaker. Bill always treated Abbie kindly throughout their marriage. He used his inheritance to supplement his income so that the two of them could live comfortably and take expensive vacations. He bought Abbie a new Audi and Saab convertible. Bill was a model spouse. After two years of marriage to Bill, Abbie began to see Bob again, and they reactivated their sexual relationship. Abbie and Bill's marriage subsequently deteriorated, and in 2004, Abbie brought a divorce action against Bill pleading that there had been a breakdown of the marriage relationship to the extent that the objects of matrimony had been destroyed and there remained no reasonable likelihood that the marriage could be preserved. Abbie got a temporary order giving her exclusive possession of the house during the pendency of the action, and parental rights and responsibilities over Danny. Two days after Bill left the house pursuant to the temporary order, Bob moved into the house and lived there with Abbie and Danny. Bill was anxious to get the divorce over with and he tried to negotiate a reasonable property settlement and make suitable child support arrangements with Abbie. Unable to reach a settlement, they tried the case as a contested divorce. Abbie asked the court to grant her title to the house and its contents, the Audi and the Saab convertible, spousal support, and child support.

1. **What arguments will Abbie make to support her demands for property, maintenance and child support?**
2. **What arguments may Bill make in opposition to her demands?**

Model Answer to Question 11

1. The first consideration when dividing property in divorce proceedings is determining marital and separate assets. *Reeves v Reeves*, 226 Michigan 490 (1997). Separate assets are typically those owned by one party prior to the marriage or acquired by one spouse through gift or inheritance during the marriage. *Reeves.* A court may only award one party's separate property to the other if the claimant meets one of two tests: (1) that he or she contributed to the acquisition, improvement or accumulation of the property, or (2) that the award to him or her out of the marital assets is insufficient for the suitable support and maintenance of the claimant and any children in his or her care. MCL 552.401 and MCL 552.23. All marital property is subject to equitable division by the family court. *Sparks v Sparks*, 440 Mich 141 (1992). The court must consider many factors in deciding what is equitable including: (1) the duration of the marriage; (2) contributions of the parties to the marital estate; (3) the age of the parties; (4) the health of the parties; (5) life status of the parties; (6) necessities and circumstances of the parties; (7) earning ability of the parties; (8) past relations and conduct of the parties, and (9) general principles of equity. *Sparks.* Some criteria favor Abbie, while others favor Bill. Abbie will emphasize the following: Bill's vocational skills and therefore his earning ability are superior to hers; she will have custody of Danny and therefore the court should award her the home or the right to live there for a reasonable time; and her contribution as homemaker to the family.

In deciding whether to award spousal support to Abbie, the court must make findings on each of the following relevant factors: (1) the parties' past relations and conduct; (2) the length of the marriage; (3) the parties' ability to work; (4) the source and amount of property awarded to the parties; (5) the parties' ages; (6) the ability to pay spousal support; (7) the parties' present situation; (8) the parties' needs; (9) the parties' health; (10) the prior standard of living of the parties and whether the parties support others; and (11) general principles of equity. *Sparks*. Abbie will emphasize that she and Bill enjoyed a high standard of living during the marriage and that she needs the support to allow her to continue to enjoy that high standard of living and to provide for Danny.

When Bill adopted Danny, he became Danny's father. Bill owes an unavoidable duty to support his son. Tactically, Bill would be well advised not to weaken his arguments against a property settlement and spousal support by attempting to avoid his clear obligation for Danny's support under the child support guidelines.

2. Bill's strong points for property division are the short duration of the marriage; neither made any contribution to the education, training, or increased earning power of the other; each has more or less equal opportunity for future acquisition of capital assets and income; essentially all of their substantial property was acquired through Bill's prenuptial wealth; Abbie will not be saddled with any debts; and that the "respective merits of the parties" weighs very heavily in Bills' favor concerning past conduct and relations of the parties. Regarding spousal support, Bill will point out that Abbie has made a new household with Bob, which weighs against or diminishes her demand for maintenance because of Bob's presumed earning capacity which is a financial resource available to Abbie. Although Abbie and Bill did establish a fairly high standard of living during the marriage, Bill will argue that the marriage was very short in duration and the standard was artificially high because it was based on Bill's inheritance, not on his earnings.

Two Student Answers—July 2004

Question 11—Domestic Relations—9 points

Michigan is a no-fault divorce state. Abbie has complied with pleading requirement by filing for a divorce and including the language about the breakdown in the marriage relationship.

Fault can be taken into account when determining the property settlement. The facts tell us Bill was a model spouse and Abbie is the one at fault for engaging in an extra-marital affair. So, she is at fault and this is going to affect how much property she receives in the distribution.

To decide what is marital property or not, we look to how and when the property was acquired.

Bill received his inheritance before the marriage but he commingled the funds into the marital estate when he used a good portion of it to buy the marital home. So, the home is part of the marital estate. Bill also used the rest of the inheritance for support of the family—so even though Bill will try and argue he should get a credit for the inheritance amount, he will lose.

The cars will also be included in the marital estate even though Abbie will try and argue he bought them solely for her use.

Abbie can ask for the house, its contents and the cars but the court is going to pretty much split the assets down the middle—with more assets, maybe 5% to Bill in the distribution. If Abbie wants to physically keep the items she will have to pay Bill the difference in cash.

As for alimony, the courts will look to the characteristics of the parties to determine if alimony maintenance is necessary. Here Bill is substantially older at 58, while Abbie is young at 22. Her young age will mean that she is most likely able to re-bound after the divorce financially. Plus, she already has a job as a bank-teller. This is also a short term marriage of close to 3 years. Most likely the courts will not find Abbie is in need of spousal support. Nothing indicates that her age, health, job skills, etc. are so low that she cannot start working full time if she needs to. The court will take into account the lifestyle the parties were accustomed to during the marriage, so perhaps Bill may have to pay for a few years a mediocre sum.

As for child support—when Bill adopted Danny be became the father with all rights and privileges.

Since he is not the primary caretaker, they will share joint legal custody with physical to the mother. Bill will have to pay child support in the amount calculated according to the child support formula. Taken into consideration will be the number of children Bill has to currently support. We only know of one child. He'll be responsible for child support until Danny reaches the age of 18 or 19½ if still in high school.

The fact that Bob moved in with Abbie before the divorce was final would be important if custody were in issue as to the moral fitness of Abbie but not conclusive. Nothing in the facts tell us Bill was contesting custody though.

Question 11—Domestic Relations—8 points

I. Property—Home

In a Domestic Relations setting all that is required to marry is a license and a ceremony. At the time of divorce, if filed in Michigan, there are different requirements. As this case involves a minor child, they will have a 6 month period to wait before the divorce is finalized.

In Michigan, marital property is divided by a fair and equitable manner, no formula is involved. However, considerations are made for fault of the parties when it comes to the child support and spousal support. Also, considerations of separately owned and titled property may remain in the owners' possession after the marriage. The home was paid for with money from Bill's inheritance and this is marital property, therefore, they are both entitled to a fair and equitable division and if they cannot agree it may have to be sold and if one does not buy out the other, whoever is granted custody may dictate how the home is handled.

The contents will also be divided in a fair and equitable manner and again if the parties cannot agree then the court will decide the matter. Bill may make an argument that he used his inheritance to buy the house and therefore he is entitled however, by using the inheritance for the marriage it lost it's identity and the home and contents became subject to marital property division. The same argument is to be made for both cars in that they will be deemed marital property as well.

II. Spousal Support

In Michigan a spouse is entitled to obtain two types of spousal support either rehabilitative or permanent which can be paid in either a lump sum or installments. Permanent support is just that permanent support and rehabilitative support is meant to help a spouse regain financial independence after the marriage. There are factors a court looks to in deciding support like age of the parties, their dependency, their status, their health, their earning capacity, etc. Here Abbie will argue she relied on Bill for income while she only worked part-time. Bill will argue that due to the difference in age she has a superior earning capacity and that should not have to pay. Also, here a court will consider the fault of the one party in determining the award and Abbie's infidelity will go against her.

III. Child Support

Here, these monies are owed to the child and after a Friend of the Court recommendation and order is made, income is imputed the parties if necessary and an award is fashioned. Here also the courts look to such factors as the status, age, health, etc. of the parties. Bill will argue as Danny is not his child he should not have to pay. That argument will fail because of his adoption of the child.

IV. Custody

Custody is determined by the best interest of the child and due to an established custodial environment will likely go to Abbie as Bill left home for a period of time. In Michigan, one can get sole physical or joint custody. Here as the established custodial environment, the mother will likely get custody and the father reasonable parenting time.

February 2005—Question 4

In 1990, Beth and Bob graduated from high school and decided to get married. After struggling for three years, they purchased their first home. Bob had saved up some money from his job at the local grocery store and his income permitted the couple to qualify for a mortgage loan. Beth had yet to find employment after graduation and had never contributed financially to the couple's expenses. Bob did not have Beth's name placed on the deed for their new home.

Beth had three children over the next five years. In 2000, Beth met Joe, the local mechanic, and left Bob and the children. After moving in with Joe, he hired Beth to fill a bookkeeping position at the shop. Six months later, Bob filed for divorce seeking full custody of the children and child support. Two months after filing for divorce, Bob Jr., their youngest child, was diagnosed with cancer. Both Beth and Bob had bone marrow drawn to determine whether they were compatible donors, and it was discovered that Bob was also not the biological father of Susie, their middle child, although she could not identify the father. Bob had his eldest child tested, and it was confirmed that she was his biological child. Bob comes to you seeking advice on the following issues:

A. If you were the judge, would you award Bob custody of his three children even though it has been determined that he is not the biological father of Bob Jr. and Susie? Explain the reasons for your decision.

B. If Bob is awarded full custody, will the court order Beth to pay child support to Bob? Discuss the analysis which will be used by the court to decide this issue.

C. Does Beth have any interest in the home that Bob purchased during the marriage? Explain your answer.

Model Answer to Question 4

A. Yes. Michigan does recognize the "equitable parent" doctrine when a child is born and conceived during the marriage and the parent and child acknowledge a relationship as parent and child, although the husband is not the biological father. The husband must desire the rights of paternity and must be willing to pay child support. *Atkinson v Atkinson*, 160 Mich App 601 (1987). This doctrine essentially allows a third party to exercise parental rights, including custody and parenting time. The court has refused to extend this doctrine when the parties are not married and the child was born out of wedlock. The decision as to who gets custody of the minor children will be based on what is in the best interests of the children.

B. A child has an inherent right to support, but whether or not Beth is ordered to pay child support will depend upon the Michigan Child Support Formula. The court is mandated to apply the Michigan Child Support Formula when establishing child support. Formula is based on the actual resources of the parent and the needs of the child. Numerous factors are considered such as parental income, family size, the ages of the children, child care, dependent health care coverage costs, and other criteria. The Michigan Child Support Formula also takes into consideration the amount of time spent with the non-custodial parent and credit is allowed for consecutive time spent with the non-custodial parent.

C. Yes. Although Bob somehow managed to have the deed executed without Beth named as a grantee, Beth would still have an interest in the property. Marital property is defined as property accumulated during the marriage as a result of one or both parties' contributions or efforts during the marriage. This is generally interpreted to mean property acquired during the marriage, excluding gifted or inherited property or passive appreciation of premarital property. *Reeves v Reeves*, 226 Mich App 490 (1997). Furthermore, MCL 552.101 requires the court make a provision in lieu of dower of the wife in the property of the husband. Finally, property division in Michigan follows the rule of equitable distribution. The court will apply a number of considerations including the source of the property, contribution towards the acquisition, the number of years of the marriage, the needs of the parties and the causes of the divorce. It is not clear whether Beth would be entitled to half of the equity in the property, but she does have an interest, if only her dower interest.

Student Answer—February 2005

Question 4—Domestic Relations—9 points

In deciding an issue of custody, the court looks to the best interests of the child. In considering the best interests of the child, the court considers factors such as, the ability of each parent to nurture, support (emotionally and economically) the child, raise the child in terms of things such as religious beliefs, and basically be there both physically and emotionally to meet all of the child's needs. Although who the child is currently living with does not necessarily determine custody, the longer the child has been living with one parent, the greater weight the court may give to that parent. Courts do not like to upset the stability of the child's environment if possible.

It has been determined that two of the three children are not Bob's biological children. However, if Bob has treated each child as if he were the father, in terms of emotional and monetary support, and if willing to continue in this role, I do not think the court would automatically preclude Bob from receiving custody of the children if it were convinced that Bob really wanted custody and it was in the children's best interest to live with Bob.

The court may also consider that Beth abandoned the children for six months in order to live with Joe. The court may consider whether Beth even wants custody, or more importantly, if her decision to abandon the children was one influenced by Joe.

If Bob is awarded custody, the child support paid will be determined by the Michigan Child and Family guidelines. This is a pre-determined formula based on income of each party and considers factors such as how many children are in the family, including children being supported by either party as a result of a prior marriage. Therefore, based on these guidelines, the court will determine if and how much one or both parties will pay for child support. While the guidelines do consider the income of each party, it is not sympathetic to a parent who is without employment. In this case, the determination will be made on the party's potential income that could be earned.

Beth does have an interest in the marital home. The home was purchased with money earned by Bob during the marriage. Therefore, the home was purchased with marital assets, and Beth is entitled to ½ interest in the home. The fact that Beth's name is not on the deed is irrelevant because the law does not require her name to be on the deed to acquire an interest in the property.

Lastly, Michigan is a no-fault divorce state. This means that the fact that Beth left Bob for another man will not, in all likelihood weigh in Bob's favor in terms of custody or any other dispositive matter concerning the marriage. While the court may acknowledge the abandonment, it will not assign either party any degree of fault per se.

July 2005—Question 8

Evan and Jill met each other in 1989 during their senior year of college at Wolvertan University. Shortly after graduation, Evan purchased a home with money his grandmother left him and the two of them moved in together. For the next ten years, Evan and Jill lived together and held themselves out as husband and wife, although they were never officially married. They accumulated assets worth approximately two million dollars during the ten-year period. At no time did Evan and Jill execute a written agreement regarding their cohabitation. Evan supported their arrangement as a stockbroker. Jill enjoyed painting, but has yet to sell a print.

On July 4, 1999, Evan and Jill celebrated the holiday at Evan's family home on Lake Toxicated. Both Evan and Jill overindulged on Fourth of July Fizzlers and at 3:00 a.m., convinced a college buddy, now an ordained minister, to marry them on the beach surrounded by a few other college friends. Neither Evan nor Jill had applied for a marriage license prior to the impromptu ceremony.

Evan and Jill awoke the next day at 1:30 p.m. and drove two hours to their home in the city. Neither had any recollection of the previous night's events. Two weeks later, while unpacking their suitcases from the holiday vacation, Jill discovered a piece of notebook paper that appeared to recite the same statements found on an official marriage certificate. She presented the piece of paper to Evan and both decided that one of their college friends was playing a joke, as it was common among their circle of friends to discuss their ten-year "unofficial" marriage. Evan and Jill did not mention the paper again until two weeks later, when Jill received a call from Bill, a friend, claiming to have been best man at the ceremony. Jill subsequently moved out and called you to seek advice on the following issues:

1. **Will the court treat Evan and Jill as husband and wife due to the fact that they held themselves out as husband and wife for ten years and accumulated significant property together? Explain your answer.**
2. **What, if any, interest does Jill have in the property accumulated by herself and Evan over the ten-year period they lived together and held themselves out as husband and wife? Explain your answer.**
3. **Can Jill force Evan to support her now that they no longer cohabitate? Explain your answer.**
4. **Are Jill and Evan legally married? Explain your answer.**

Model Answer to Question 8

1. No. Prior to 1957, Michigan law might have recognized Evan and Jill's cohabitation relationship as a common law marriage. Common law marriages were abolished in Michigan in 1957. Common law marriages are only recognized in Michigan (1) if the couple had a valid common law marriage prior to January 1, 1957, or (2) if the couple legally entered into such a marriage in a state permitting it. MCL 551.2; MCL 750.335. At present, an unmarried male and female cohabitating by agreement who do not fall into one of the categories for a valid common law marriage violate MCL 750.335, which prohibits male and female "lewd and lascivious" cohabitation.
2. Jill will most likely have no interest in the real property purchased by Evan unless, since the "marriage," the deed has been placed in both of their names. Jill will have a right to the assets purchased by her during the relationship. Michigan courts will recognize a contract implied in fact if the parties have an express agreement based upon independent consideration regarding their cohabitation. In *re Lewis Estate*, 168 Michigan App 70 (1988). The court will enforce an agreement made during the relationship on proof of additional independent consideration. The agreement must be express or implied in fact because the court will not recognize a contract implied at law since this would, in effect, recognize common law marriages. *Featherstone v Steinhoff*, 226 Michigan App 584 (1997); *Whitson v Kaltz* (Unpublished opinion per curiam of the Court of Appeals, issued Sept 20, 2002 [Docket No. 229289]).
3. No. Michigan courts have yet to recognize "palimony" as a legitimate award in cohabitation cases. Palimony is defined as "meaning similar to alimony except that the award, settlement or agreement arises out of a nonmarital relationship

of the parties. Black's Law Dictionary. Although recognized by other states, Michigan courts have yet to recognize an award of support payments on the termination of a cohabitation relationship.

4. No. For a marriage to be valid in Michigan, the following must be true: (1) the parties must not already be married, (2) the parties must not be of the same sex, (3) the parties must not be related within a prohibited degree of consanguinity, (4) the parties must be of marriageable age, (5) the parties must be mentally competent, and (6) the parties must be entering into the marriage without fraud or duress. For a marriage to be valid, a license must be obtained at least three days before the ceremony, unless the waiting period is waived by the clerk. MCL 551.103a. Evan and Jill failed to obtain a marriage license and, thus, they are not legally married. Furthermore, if solemnized in Michigan, a marriage that is prohibited by law because either party was not capable in law of contracting at the time of the solemnization is absolutely void. MCL 552.1. It could be argued that due to their severe intoxication, neither Evan nor Jill was mentally capable of contracting at the time of the ceremony.

Two Student Answers—July 2005

Question 8—Domestic Relations—10 points

The issue is whether Evan and Jill will be treated as husband and wife due to the fact that they held themselves out as such for 10 years. The facts in this case seem to reflect a common law marriage. They lived together, they held themselves out as husband and wife to the public and their friends, and they accumulated assets together. However, Michigan does not recognize common law marriages unless they were entered into prior to 1957. Since this relationship was entered into in 1989, Michigan would not recognize it as a common law marriage. Based on the facts, Evan and Jill will not be treated as husband and wife simply because they held themselves out as such.

The next issue is what interest if any does Jill have in the property accumulated over the 10 years. Jill has *no interest* in the property. Evan purchased the home with his own money and the two million dollars that was accumulated was because of Evans job as a stockbroker. Jill painted but never sold a painting. Jill and Evan could simply be regarded as roommates where Jill took advantage of Evans work. She lived rent free and had advantage of the two million dollars. In conclusion, Jill has no interest in the property accumulated over the 10 years.

The next issue is whether Jill can force Evan to support her now that they no longer cohabitate. The answer is no. They will be treated as simply roommates. The only time one may have to support the other is if they were legally married and one was seeking alimony and support from the other. In that case, the court would use the Michigan Support formula to determine the amount. But here, since they were never legally married, Evan has no duty to support Jill just because they are no longer living together.

The next issue is whether Jill and Evan are legally married if they consider the ceremony at the lake a valid marriage, they would be incorrect. To be a valid marriage both parties must have capacity to enter into the marriage and there must be a legal marriage license. Here the parties were so intoxicated that they do not remember what they had done the previous night. Therefore, they did not have the capacity to enter into the marriage, and the "marriage" would be voidable. Also there was never a marriage license that was applied for. There was only a piece of notebook paper that recited the same statement that was on a marriage license. This would not be viewed as a legal document.

Because both parties were so visibly intoxicated, neither had the capacity to enter into a marriage and therefore it would be voidable and not legally binding.

Question 8—Domestic Relations—10 points

1. The court will not treat them as husband and wife. The state of Michigan has not recognized common law marriage since the 50's or 60's. The court will not treat them as husband and wife even though they have lived together 10 years and accumulated significant assets.
2. Jill has an interest mostly in just the property she accumulated. Mostly just her personal property and any "gifts" she can say were given by Evan. They had no agreement in writing therefore each takes what they personally own.
   If she and Evan ran a business together an argument could be made for a partnership or joint enterprise, however, the facts state that Evan worked and made the $$ while she stayed home and painted and never sold a painting.
3. Jill can't force Evan to support her. They are not married and never were therefore Evan owes her no duty to support her. In Michigan you must have been married to receive alimony/payments. They were never married = no support.
4. They are not legally married for 2 reasons.
   A. Michigan requires a marriage license and has a mandatory waiting period until the marriage takes place. This "cooling down" period is so that people have time to think before making such a big decision. Jill and Evan got married on spur of the moment with no license. Exactly what waiting period is for.
   B. They were intoxicated when they "got married on the beach." So intoxicated that they never even remembered the "ceremony." If they were drunk both of them would have had to acknowledge the marriage for it to be valid, notwithstanding the license. If they are broke up Evan just has to say marriage is invalid cause he was drunk and court will find it never happened.

February 2006—Question 15

Nicholas was a penniless teenager who came to Wolverine, Michigan, from a village in Europe at the end of the Second World War. He was befriended by Stan and Kathy and their daughter, Sophia, who had come from the same village before the war. They gave Nicholas a room in their home and a job in the bakery that they owned.

Nicholas and Sophia became enamored with each other. Soon, Sophia was cleaning his clothes and preparing his meals when he came home late from night school. One day in 1955, Nicholas gave her a ring, and the two solemnly pledged fidelity and told each other that this was more than being married in a church.

While Stan and Kathy chided the couple to get married, many people thought that Nicholas and Sophia were married, having seen the two living in the same house for nearly a decade. Sophia introduced new friends and customers in the bakery to "My Nick." Nicholas sometimes referred to Sophia as "The Mrs."

Nicholas bought a house and moved out of Stan and Kathy's home, but continued working at their bakery. Stan told Nicholas that one day the business would be his.

On June 1, 1962, Sophia announced that she was pregnant. Stan and Kathy were furious and confronted Nicholas. Nicholas was told in no uncertain terms that he was fired and no longer welcome in Wolverine unless he married Sophia immediately. Nicholas agreed.

The next day, Stan took Sophia and Nicholas to the clerk of the county for a marriage license and stood by as it was completed. Later, Stan called the church and reserved July 6 for the wedding. Sophia bought a dress. Nicholas moved some of her effects from her parents' home and put her name on his bank accounts.

On the appointed day, Stan and Kathy drove with Sophia to get Nicholas. The two went into the church where Father Tiramisu performed a hasty ceremony with only the parish cat looking on.

Sophia had a child, Nicholas, Jr., on March 1, 1963. Within a few months, however, she returned to her parents' home with Nicholas, Jr. because of Nicholas' constant harangues that he was not the father.

Sophia has called you to seek advice on the following issues:

1. **Were Nicholas and Sophia legally married? Explain your answer.**
2. **What, if any, interest does Sophia have in the property accumulated by herself and Nicholas over the period they lived together and held themselves out as husband and wife? Explain your answer.**
3. **What support can Sophia claim for Nicholas, Jr.? Explain your answer.**

Model Answer to Question 15

1. No. The relationship before January 1, 1957, did not meet the standard of a common-law marriage, which requires a present agreement to live together as husband and wife by people who are free to marry and the subsequent cohabitation as husband and wife. *In re Estate of Leonard*, 45 Mich App 679 (1973). Nicholas and Sophia are both free to marry because they are not already married and over the age of consent in 1955. However, a pledge of fidelity and a ring do not constitute present intent to be husband and wife. Also, neither declared in 1962 that a marriage already existed. The two did not cohabit together as there was no immediate change in living arrangements in the house.

   The relationship after the July 6, 1962, ceremony is not a common-law marriage because common-law marriage was abolished on January 1, 1957. The relationship after July 6, 1962, is not a statutory marriage. There were not two witnesses as required by MCL 551.9 and the license was void on July 6, because that was more than 30 days after application, which was June 2, "the next day" after June 1, 1962, when the pregnancy was announced. MCL 551.103a, last sentence (as effective in 1962).

2. Sophia can claim and keep the ring that Nicholas gave her, the effects moved from her parents' home, and the joint bank accounts. She cannot keep or claim any part of the house that Nicholas bought; he had it before any marriage and did not include her on the title.
3. Sophia can claim support from Nicholas upon proving paternity of Nicholas, Jr. MCL 722.712(1).

Student Answer—February 2006

Question 15—Domestic Relations—None Available

July 2006—Question 6

The class of 2002 at Michigan State University included Desmond Jones from England and Molly Smith, the valedictorian of her high school in Chicago. The two met in class and fell in love. At the end of the school year, Desmond gave Molly a bracelet before returning home for the summer.

Desmond and Molly returned to school and shared a two bedroom apartment with their roommates from the dorm. The romance continued. The two exchanged expensive pens to write each other after the end of their sophomore year.

As juniors, Desmond and Molly shared a one bedroom apartment and made no secret about living together. Rent, utilities and the cable were paid by Molly from a joint checking account that Desmond had opened and funded with his student loan. Molly bought groceries and household supplies with her money from a part-time job. Each kept a personal laptop and cell phone. The two exchanged watches at the end of the school year.

During the summer, Desmond inherited a large sum of money and the affects from an uncle who died. He used this to buy and richly furnish a condo in East Lansing, Michigan. He told Molly that she could quit her job. She did.

The two lived in the condo for their senior year. Molly told the condo association that she was married in order to qualify as a resident there. After spring break, Molly discovered that she was pregnant, but said nothing about it.

Just before graduation, Desmond proposed to Molly in order to gain citizenship and remain in the U.S. to attend graduate school. When Molly accepted, he gave her a ring and planned a wedding and honeymoon on northern Michigan's Mackinac Island.

A marriage license was obtained from the Ingham County Clerk in Lansing and the two went to Mackinac Island that day. During a sunset cruise the next evening, Desmond gave the ship's captain the license and $50 to marry them. The captain performed the ceremony with the happy couple standing on the stern while the first mate steered.

Three weeks later, Desmond and Molly separated after a fight when Desmond learned of the pregnancy, and Molly of the application for citizenship.

1. **Are Desmond and Molly married, and why?**
2. **What property belongs to Molly, and why?**
3. **What is the responsibility of Desmond to the child when Molly gives birth, and why?**

Model Answer to Question 6

1. No. The marriage was not solemnized by a qualified person. The captain of the cruise ship is not among those people enumerated in MCL 557.1(1)(a)-(i). Also, at best, there was only one witness to the ceremony, the first mate, and not two as required by MCL 551.9.

   A complete answer could include:
   - The legal capacity to marry by recognizing that Desmond and Molly are of opposite sex, over the age of consent, and not already married to another. Citizenship is not relevant.
   - Consent was freely given to marry even though each had a motive that was secreted from the other.
   - The license was defective because it was used in a county other than the one in which it was issued as required when the parties are both residents of another state as here. MCL 551.101, last sentence. Also, the license was used within three days without good cause as required by MCL 551.103a.
     Also, a complete answer could include:
   - No common law marriage by cohabitation in the junior and senior years of school because common law marriage was abolished after January 1, 1957. MCL 551.2.
2. The personal laptop and cell phone which Molly had are hers. The bracelet, expensive pen and wrist watch that Desmond gave to her as gifts are hers because these were gifts intended for her. So is the engagement ring for the same reason.

   Molly has one-half interest in the checking account as it was jointly held.

   Molly has no interest in the condo or its furnishings as these were an inheritance before any "marriage" and there is no indication of joint tenancy in any title.
3. A complete answer should point out that the responsibility for a child depends on the status as a parent, not marriage. Desmond is responsible if he admits paternity or it is established by evidence of a DNA test if he denies it. MCL 712.12. Desmond might contest, arguing he is not the father.

Student Answer—July 2006

Question 6—Domestic Relations—8 points

The issues here are regarding marital interests under Domestic Relations.

1. Desmond and Molly are in fact married. However, the issue here is whether a Ship Captain can perform the ceremony & sign the appropriate license. To be considered married in Michigan, various elements need to be met such as adults beyond the age of minority, consensual agreement made w/o duress, competence of the parties, between male/female, witnessed, licensed by the state and executed w/all the formalities required, this includes the person performing the ceremony for the couple. Here, a ship's captain is performing the ceremony which is valid as long as he has the applicable permit to do so, which the facts don't state. Typically, to be effective a ship's captain & the vessel he commanded had to be out to sea. Since the facts state that they

were on a sunset cruise during the ceremony, their marriage ought to be viewed as valid.

2. Since Michigan is not a community property state, the property brought into the union while as single people would be delegated back and any property acquired during their short marriage would be evenly distributed. The question alludes to a common law marriage which is precluded in Michigan; therefore Molly will acquire the property interests she had previously. For example, she can keep her cell phone & laptop, her interest in the checking account that an accounting would have to be performed on and she can keep her pen & watch. Since Desmond acquired the condo before they got married, he gets to keep that.
3. Desmond's responsibility to the child can be only two things.
   A. First, he can petition a court for custody. To prove he is custodial capable, he will have to show an ability to care for the child, financial capability, time, love, & support, as well as moral fortitude. Still, however, courts typically will be extremely reluctant to separate the traditional caregiver from her baby. Therefore, it is unlikely he would prevail on this point. Desmond would however, most likely have to contribute towards the child's expenses in monthly payments or other as the court required.
   B. Lastly, defendant could petition a court for a paternity test to ensure that the child is in fact his. If the child isn't then he wouldn't have to deliver support payments. Further, if the wedding was based on the pretense that she was carrying his baby, this might disqualify the marriage thereby making it void.

February 2007—Question 10

Gabe and Julie married and raised their two boys, Vinnie and Arnold, in Kalamazoo, Michigan, while continuing as teachers at James Buchanan High in Kalamazoo. But after eight years, Julie quit teaching and left Gabe and the boys to live with Sam on the other side of town. Gabe asked for a divorce. Julie agreed provided that she could visit Vinnie and Arnold often. And so, the circuit court granted the divorce, granted custody to Gabe, and allowed Julie to share in deciding the proper care and upbringing of the boys and to visit often.

Although Julie did visit and had gifts on all birthdays and holidays, she abruptly canceled many visits and cut short others to spend time alone or with Sam. The boys refused to stay with Julie after Sam broke the arm of Arnold in a rage about a lamp that was broken while Arnold was playing with Vinnie.

A year later, Gabe accepted an offer to teach more than 100 miles away at Warren G. Harding High in Mt. Pleasant, Michigan, at a ten percent increase in pay. Gabe sold the house and relocated with Vinnie and Arnold. Julie learned of the relocation six weeks later after calling the house to cancel a visit.

1. **Discuss whether a motion by Julie opposing the relocation of the children by Gabe will be successful. Explain your answer.**
2. **Discuss the arguments that would be made in a proceeding to terminate Julie's parental rights.**

Model Answer to Question 10

1. A complete answer should recognize that MCL 722.31 applies. This statute applies because the custody of Vinnie and Arnold is governed by a court order and has been changed by the relocation of more than one hundred miles. MCL 722.31(1), second sentence.

   A complete answer should also recognize and explain that the exceptions do not apply. The exception for consent established by MCL 722.31(2) does not apply because Gabe did not have the consent of Julie as she only discovered the change weeks after the move. Gabe did not have the consent of the court as he took the job, sold the house and moved.

   - **Compliance with and use of parenting time.** Julie has not used the visiting time allowed by the circuit court. Gabe was not inspired to move to defeat visits by Julie. See MCL 722.31(4)(b).
   - **Modifying parenting time.** It will be difficult to preserve the relationship between Julie and the boys. She will have a long trip and have to stay overnight in a hotel to visit. The boys refuse to visit her.
   - **Financial advantage.** The motive for gaining financial advantage from opposing the change, MCL 722.31(4)(d), is not present. Julie will have no financial advantage if the change is rescinded or allowed.
   - **Domestic violence.** This is a factor to consider MCL 722.31(4)(e), but the only domestic violence was in Julie's home with Sam.

   The exception for the distance before the move described by MCL 722.31(3) does not apply. The distance between Julie and the boys before the move was less than 100 miles as she lived with Sam "on the other side of town." And, relocation does not bring the boys closer to Julie.

   The exception allowed for changing the residence of children by the terms of the order establishing custody, MCL 722.31(5), does not apply because the circuit court order did not describe how to change the residence of the boys.

   Finally, a complete answer should discuss the likelihood of success if Julie does actually oppose the relocation in view of the criteria for approving a change of residence of more than 100 miles, which are described by MCL 722.31(4)(a)-(e). The quality of life for the children and Gabe should be the same or better as the city of Mt. Pleasant is about the same size as Kalamazoo and is also a "university town." Gabe will earn more, which should improve the life of all three.

2. A complete answer should recognize that the termination of parental rights is governed by MCL 712A.19b, which provides for termination when there is clear and convincing evidence that:

   (3)(b) The child or a sibling of the child has suffered physical injury or physical or sexual abuse under 1 or more of the following circumstances:

   (iii) A nonparent adult's act caused the physical injury or physical or sexual abuse and the court finds that there is a reasonable likelihood that the child will suffer from injury or abuse by the nonparent adult in the foreseeable future if placed in the parent's home.

Under MCL 712A.19b(5), if the court finds there are grounds for termination, "the court shall order termination of parental rights and order that additional efforts for reunification of the child with the parent not be made, unless the court finds that termination of parental rights to the child is clearly not in the child's best interests."

One of the boys, Arnold, had physical injury, a broken arm. It was caused by Sam who was "a nonparent adult." Finally, a court could conclude that injury was likely were the boys placed in the home of Julie and Sam because of the refusal by the boys to ever return there for even a visit which evinces their opinion of the likelihood of injury in the future and from the personality of Sam who was so enraged over minor property damage from the routine play of young boys.

A complete answer could also explain that other grounds such as desertion, abuse, conviction for certain crimes by Julie are not present. MCL 712A.19b(a)(ii), (k) and (l).

Student Answer—February 2007

Question 10—Domestic Relations—8 points

A motion by Julie opposing the relocation of the children by Gabe will not be successful.

The issue regarding the children's relocation is what is in the best interest of Vinnie and Arnold and whether Julie has the right to insist that the children continue to live in Kalamazoo.

Under MI domestic relations law, in determining what living arrangement would be in the best interest of the children of divorce, the court considers a number of factors such as the present living situation, the hardship relocation would present to the established relationship with the non-custodial parent, the custodial parent's ability to obtain comparable employment and the established relationships with the community, i.e. school, sport teams, etc. and the extended family. The court is also likely to speak with the children regarding their living situations and take into account their wishes provided the children are old enough to participate or capable to participate in the conversation. The judge has tremendous discretion to weigh his or her decision based upon the finding so the listed factors—which may include additional consideration and the wishes of the children.

Here Julie opposes the relocation however her parenting thus far demonstrates to the judge a lack of commitment to her children. Julie initiated the separation from her children. Although Michigan is a no-fault divorce state, [Julie] did not seek custody of the boys and was comfortable with frequent visits. Since the divorce, Julie has been inconsistent and unreliable with her visits, frequently canceling visits without notice. Additionally, there is a concern for the safety of her children when in her care as one of her children has sustained a broken arm at the hands of her live-in Sam. Gabe's decision to relocate and eventually move was six weeks past when Julie even became aware that her children were not where she saw them last.

Therefore, Julie would be unsuccessful in opposing the relocation because her involvement has been limited. Once the court considers the previously mentioned factors balanced with what the children want, Julie will be unsuccessful.

In proceeding to terminate Julie's parental rights, the arguments that will be made are that she is an unfit parent because the children's safety and well-being are at risk and that she in effect has abandoned them.

An unfit parent is on who either unable or chooses not care or provide for the children whether or not the children are in the parent's custodial presence. The judge will review the parent's history with the child, the established relationship, ability and actual means that the parent affords the children.

Here Julie has been inattentive to her children. She goes weeks without talking with them so much that they were able to relocate without her knowledge. When Julie does have her children, based upon her associations, the children were victims of potential abuse that resulted in physical injury.

Therefore strong arguments could be made in proceeding to terminate Julie's parental rights.

July 2007—Question 1

Ward proposed to June on Christmas Eve 1974, she accepted and the two planned a wedding after Ward graduated from law school the following May. In April, the two signed an agreement that each would have "complete control of his or her property and any property that either acquired in an individual capacity" with one exception. The exception was that Ward "shall be awarded the residence at 485 Mapleton, Mayville, Michigan in the event of divorce." Ward said that this was needed because June did not have much money. The couple was married the next month.

Initially Ward practiced law from the home, but had success and soon was able to buy a small office building. The earnings from his practice and the rents from tenants in the building went into Ward's own checking account from which he paid his business expenses and funded his pension. June worked while raising their two children, Walter and Theodore. Her pay was deposited into her own checking and savings account at a bank and was used to pay the mortgage on the home and all of the other expenses of the family.

In celebration of their tenth anniversary, the couple bought a condo in Florida to use for vacations and retirement. The deed said that the two were "tenants by the entirety" as required by the rules of the condo association. Sometime later, June signed a quitclaim deed to Theodore.

Ten years later, June was fired from her job and the two began arguing about money. June hired a lawyer, no one who Ward knew, and sued her employer for wrongful termination. She received $750,000.00 in a settlement. She used some to pay the remaining mortgage on the home, college tuition for Walter, and fully fund her 401(k). But the arguing continued, so June bought a house, moved there with Theodore, and filed for divorce.

While the divorce was pending, Mayville condemned the office building to expand a road and paid Ward $250,000.00.

Discuss and answer the following issues presented by these facts:

1. **Is the prenuptial agreement between Ward and June valid?**
2. **Is the home at 485 Mapleton a marital asset?**
3. **Is the condo in Florida a marital asset?**
4. **Is the $250,000.00 for the office building a marital asset?**

Model Answer to Question 1

1. **Yes.** The agreement between Ward and June is valid. A complete answer should include that a prenuptial agreement about the division of property in the event of divorce is valid in Michigan and can be voided when obtained through fraud, duress, misrepresentation or withholding a material fact, unconscionable when reached, or the circumstances are so changed that enforcement would be unfair. The prenuptial agreement is not void *ab initio* simply because it was reached before 1991, when it was first expressly held that prenuptial agreements governing the division of property upon divorce could be enforced. *Reed v Reed*, 265 Mich App 131, 141-142 (2005), *Rinvelt v Rinvelt*, 190 Mich App 372 (1991). *Reed* held there was no clear authority supporting the conclusion that the parties' 1975 prenuptial agreement was void merely because it was entered into before *Rinvelt* was decided.

   There is no circumstance allowing a court to void the agreement. There was no fraud, duress, mistake, misrepresentation, or withheld fact. That Ward was a recent graduate of law school is not important to this.

   The agreement was not unconscionable when reached. The exception that Ward would get the home at 485 Mapleton was to guarantee that he would get his investment in it.

   There was no unforeseen change in circumstances. The duration of the marriage, children, and accumulation of wealth are all changes, but are all changes that are anticipated when the agreement was reached. *Reed*, pp 144-147.

   A complete answer may also include that June has the responsibility or "burden" to void the prenuptial agreement as the one who might challenge the claim by Ward under it. *Reed*, pp 147-148.
2. The home at 485 Mapleton is a marital asset. A complete answer should recognize that the prenuptial agreement does not actually exclude the home at 485 Mapleton from other marital assets. It only awards it to Ward in the event of divorce. *Reed*, p 153.

   A complete answer should recognize that the law allows separate assets to be invaded when one or another of two statutory exceptions occurs. One is when a party to divorce demonstrates added need. The other is for contribution to the acquisition, improvement, or accumulation of the property. MCL 552.23(1), MCL 552.401.

   Here, June probably cannot demonstrate additional need as she has her own home, a fully funded 401(k), and money left from the settlement of her lawsuit. She also has professional job skills. However, June did contribute to the acquisition of the home at 485 Mapleton by using both her pay while employed and the proceeds from the lawsuit to pay the mortgage. Ward will receive the home because of the prenuptial agreement, but he must repay June the money that she paid toward the mortgage.

3. **Yes.** The condo in Florida is a marital asset. A complete answer should recognize that this property is not subject to the prenuptial agreement having not been acquired by Ward or June in an individual capacity. It was acquired as tenants by the entireties, *Reed*, p 154, and the later quitclaim deed by June was invalid because a quitclaim deed to a third party cannot terminate a tenancy by the entireties. *French v Foster*, 307 Mich 361, 364 (1943), *Reed*, p 154.
4. The $250,000.00 is not a marital asset. The proceeds are from the condemnation of the office building that was titled to Ward and which he acquired with only his money earned from the practice of law and the rents that were paid by tenants. June was not a payee of the proceeds of the condemnation. June did not pay anything towards the acquisition of the office building. *Reed*, p 156.

Two Student Answers—July 2007

Question 1—Domestic Relations—8 points

The first issue to discuss is whether the prenuptial agreement signed in April by Ward & June is valid. In Michigan, a prenuptial agreement is valid as long as it is in writing, signed by both parties & is a full & fair disclosure of all the parties' property. A prenup is not valid if it is limiting parental or child care rights, which is not the case here. In this case it looks like the parties gave full disclosure of their property, the 485 residence, & both were in agreement about each keeping the property that they acquired in their individual capacities. Therefore, b/c the agreement was voluntarily signed with full disclosure, the prenuptial agreement between June & Ward will be valid in Michigan.

The next issue to look at is whether the home at 485 Mapleton is considered a marital asset. The prenup. agreement states that Ward shall be given the house in the case of a divorce. While this may be a valid agreement, however there are facts to indicate the home was a marital asset. Each party kept separate banking accounts. Ward spent his earnings on his business & his pension. June, however, spent part of her income to pay the mortgage on the 485 Mapleton home. June also used money she received in a wrongful termination settlement to pay the remaining mortgage on the home.

Although the prenup gives the home to Ward, June has a very valid claim that because she paid the mortgage & upkeep on the home it is a marital asset and should be divided as such in the divorce judgment.

The next issue is whether the condo is a marital asset. The couple bought the condo together for their anniversary & is considered property acquired during the marriage. However, since June assigned her portion of the property to her son by a quitclaim deed, Ward & Theodore now own the property by tenancy in common & it is no longer considered part of the marital assets. (Or the assignment was not valid because both parties of a tenancy by entireties need to agree to the division. Therefore property would still be part of marital asset & divided equally.)

The final issue to discuss is whether the $250,000 acquired by Ward for the office building is considered a marital asset. Ward opened the office by himself but was supported by June while she took care of the kids & pd the mortgage so he could concentrate on opening his business. The proceeds from the condemnation of the office building would be a marital asset b/c it was acquired during the course of their marriage.

Comment: This is a well-written answer, but the answer to the last issue is incorrect, which is why 2 points were deducted.

Question 1—Domestic Relations—9 points

Issue 1: Prenuptial Agreement

Both parties agreed to enter into a prenuptial agreement without any duress, fraud, etc. The contract was put into writing, satisfying the statute of frauds for contracts, and signed by both parties.

Each party agreed to retain their respective property separate, including any acquired property, with the exception of the house. The writing itself appears valid and it does not include any stipulations as to child support or custody (which would make that portion invalid), so the prenuptial agreement appears valid on its face.

Issue 2: Home at 458 Mapleton

The issue here is whether the prenuptial agreement, which states the marital home belongs to Ward, in the "event of divorce" has an effect on the marital asset.

Now it is not clear, when one home was purchased or by who, but even if it was purchased by Ward, funds have been commingled. June was paying the mortgage. Also, even if one spouse's name is on the title, it is considered a marital asset held by both. However, the prenuptial has specified that Ward will keep the home in the event of divorce.

Therefore, Ward will keep the home and it will be considered a marital asset. So Ward may have to pay June her portion of the house (buy her out). There is no agreement about the child staying in his home either because he is in college and the other moved into June's new house she bought with her individual money.

Issue 3: The Condo in Florida Marital Asset

It does not seem clear who put the down payment and/or paid for the condo in Florida. However, they bought it as a 10th anniversary celebration & were planning on using it as a vacation and retirement home.

Regardless if only one name is on the deed, it is considered marital property. Also, they held as tenants by the entirety. So at this point they both own the home & it is definitely a marital asset.

Does the effect of the condo association's rules that it be owned as "tenants in entirety" and the quit claim deed have an effect on this being a marital asset & distributed evenly as Michigan is a no fault state and property & assets is close to equally being given to each spouse?

The requirement by the condo association that it be held as "tenants by entirety" may be invalid as putting a restraint on transfer of property. So it is likely the quit claim deed will be effective and Ward and Theodore will own as tenants in common. So this will no longer be a marital asset divided among Ward and June equally.

Issue 4: $250,000 for Office Building

Issue is whether this is a marital asset because of the pre-nup and the "own property" clause. Ward did use his own money to pay for the building and it appears none of that money was commingled so as to give June access to half.

There may be an argument that she raised the kids and used her own money towards family expenses, including tuition. So maybe she should receive some of this money as a marital asset. However, this money was kept separate & she chose to use her own money for the family.

June also kept some of her money separate, had her own settlement, due to no loss of consortium claim in tort, makes it all hers. She also has her own home paid with her own money and her own 401K, so no need to touch Ward's pension, probably offset one another & personal money contributed.

Only other way to touch personal property is if there is not enough money to make fair in distribution, for support, etc. Here, there seems to be enough so Ward keeps house (prenup valid), condo, and $250,000.

February 2008—Question 8

Karen and James, who live in Michigan, are the parents of two children, Nicholas and Noah. Nicholas is 10 years old, and Noah is 7. Karen and James were divorced three years ago through a Consent Judgment of Divorce, which gives Karen primary physical custody of the children and James parenting time two evenings per week (4:30 p.m.–7:30 p.m.) and alternating weekends. The judgment also specifies that Karen and James shall have equal decision-making rights regarding important decisions regarding the children and that they shall inform and consult each other regarding those decisions.

This parenting time schedule was followed for one year, until James remarried. At that time, he moved ninety miles away to a busy urban area to live in his new wife's home. James now lives with his new wife and her two children from her first marriage. Due to the travel time, James exercises only his alternating weekend parenting time. The Judgment was not modified. James continues his job as a professional with an automotive supplier and he has always been current with his child support, and he provides health insurance for the children.

Noah has severe autism, the severity of which did not reveal itself until about six months after the divorce. He requires constant supervision at home, as well as special education services at his school, which Karen has vigorously pursued.

Like James' current wife, Karen was a stay-at-home mother during their marriage. Karen lacks any education past high school or formal job training. After the divorce, Karen found that the best employment she could obtain was working as an exotic dancer during the lunch shift. She explains that allows her to see her children off to school and to be home when school ends, which is important as there are few caregivers willing or qualified to care for Noah. She can provide her analysis which shows that this employment pays more for significantly fewer hours, than any other job for which she is qualified.

Nicholas has recently received several school detentions for angry interactions with classmates. The school called Karen and James in for a meeting. During this meeting, James learned of Karen's employment. James determined that Nicholas was acting out because he felt neglected by Karen, who is required to provide the majority of her attention and parenting to meeting Noah's special needs. James also learned that Karen had started Noah on a controversial and very restrictive nutritional therapy thought to help autistic children (although the effectiveness of this therapy is controversial, no one has ever alleged it is harmful).

Karen explained that she had stopped consulting James regarding educational or medical decisions for the children because he was not around during the week.

James filed a motion for a change in physical custody of the children. In his motion, he argued that he was better able to provide a suitable home for the children based on his employment and his current wife's availability as a full-time mother. James also asserts that during a recent parenting time weekend at his home, Nicholas cried when he had to return to Karen's home and he begged to stay with his father.

Discuss:

1. **The procedural process the court will follow, including any specific burdens of proof; and**
2. **The law which should be applied and an application of that law to the facts of this case.**

Model Answer to Question 8

Preface: This is a post-judgment, change of custody question. The actual outcome (whether the motion is granted) is irrelevant as the family law judge is given great discretion over its application of the facts to the best interests of the children. How the candidate applies the facts is much less important than their knowledge of the threshold issue (significant change in circumstances or proper cause), the burden of proof (differs depending on whether there is an established custodial environment), and knowledge of the best interests of the children factors

* *

In matters regarding children (i.e., child support, parenting time, physical and legal custody), the divorce court has continuing jurisdiction to modify the judgment when there is a significant change in the circumstance. A court has no authority to reconsider in the best interests of a child or the existence of an established custodial environment. *Vodvarka v Grasmeyer*, 259 Mich App 499 (2003), *Dehring v Dehring*, 220 Mich App 163 (1996). The alleged improper cause/change in circumstance *may not be a normal life change*, but must be something generally not anticipated or predictable at the time of the consent judgment. *Vodvarka*. The proper cause/change in circumstances that James may allege here are:

a. Nicholas is getting into trouble at school—may not be sufficient as it has just begun and is not significant but it is new since the Judgment—a court could go either way on this and that could go either way on this and that conclusion is irrelevant;
b. Noah has begun a new medical therapy without his consultation, so Karen has violated the Judgment (this is properly cured by a show cause motion, not a change in custody—a change in custody is based on the best interest of the children—custody is not a reward and its loss is not a punishment for bad acts by either parent);

c. The severity of Noah's autism was not known until after the Consent Judgment (a change in circumstance but only if James can establish that he is better able to respond to the autism than Karen is); and
d. James has remarried, has a stay-at-home wife, two stepchildren living in his home, and he can now provide a better home environment for the children (*Vodvarka* specifically states that remarriage is a normal life event, therefore foreseeable, and therefore not a proper change in circumstances to reconsider child custody).

The court cannot change custody absent an evidentiary hearing; *Mann v Mann*, 190 Mich App 526 (1991), which should not be scheduled unless the moving party can provide an offer of proof sufficient that, if proved, it would comprise a significant change of circumstances or proper cause. At the evidentiary hearing, the first threshold is whether an established custodial environment exists. This is important because where an established custodial environment exists is a necessary determination before the standard of proof can be determined. MCL 722.27. An established custodial environment is defined as follows: "the custodial environment of a child is established if over an applicable time, the child naturally looks to the custodian in that environment for guidance, discipline, the necessities of life, and parental comfort. The age of the child, the physical environment, and the inclination of the custodian and the child as to permanency of the relationship shall also be considered." MCL 722.21(1)(a)(c).

If an established custodial environment exists, a change may be made only on clear and convincing evidence that it is in the child's best interest; if there is no established custodial environment or both parents have an established custodial environment, a preponderance of the evidence standard is sufficient to change custody. MCL 722.27.

There is an established custodial environment with Karen in this case, as the children have lived with her for an appreciable amount of time and naturally look to her for comfort, guidance, and the necessities of life; therefore, James must prove by clear and convincing evidence that it is in the best interests of the children to exchange custody. (*Stringer v Vincent*, 161 Mich App 429 [1987]).

The court will then turn to the substantive law. Before making a child custody determination, the court is required to make a finding on each of the child custody factors. *Overall v Overall*, 203 Mich App 450 (1994). The child custody factors are the following (MCL 722.21):

A. The love, affection, and other emotional ties existing between the parties involved and the child;
B. The capacity and disposition of the parties involved to give the child love, affection, and guidance and to continue the education and raising of the child in his or her religion or creed, if any;
C. The capacity and disposition of the parties involved to provide the child with food, clothing, medical care, or other remedial care recognized and permitted under the laws of this state in place of medical care, and other material needs;
D. The length of time the child has lived in the stable, satisfactory environment, and the desirability of maintaining continuity;
E. The permanence, as a family unit, of the existing or proposed custodial home or homes;

F. The moral fitness of the parties involved;
G. The mental and physical health of the parties involved;
H. The home, school, and community record of the child;
I. The recognizable preference of the child, if the court considers the child to be of a sufficient age to express preference;
J. The willingness and ability of each of the parties to facilitate and encourage a close and continuing parent-child relationship between the child and the other parent or the child and the parents;
K. Domestic violence, regardless of whether the violence was directed against or witnessed by the child;
L. Any other factor considered by the court to be relevant to a particular child custody dispute.

Not every factor is relevant to every case, but a court must make a finding on each factor (even if only to say it is irrelevant). *Overall, supra*. The judge makes their finding based on the best interest factors overall; there is no numerical "scoring." The important factors given the case presented are:

A. The length of time the child has lived in a stable, satisfactory environment, and the desirability of maintaining continuity. Karen will argue that the children have lived in a stable, satisfactory environment. They have always lived with her and she has always taken care of them their basic needs have always been met reliably, and Noah has received all of the medical and special needs care he needs. Karen would also argue that because Noah has special needs, he is less likely than other children to respond well to change and it is especially important that he remain in a consistent environment. Karen would argue that it is James that made their environment less stable, when he moved away and limited his involvement in their lives. Karen will also argue that as a single parent with the two children, her family unit has been very stable, whereas James' has changed quite a bit with a new marriage and the introduction of two new children. Karen will argue that James has contributed to the children's difficulties by not using the parenting time he had—he should not now receive primary physical custody.

   James will respond by arguing that the environment that Karen provides may be stable, but that it is not satisfactory. He will argue that there is no desirability to maintain continuity.
B. The permanence, as a family unit, of the existing or proposed custodial home or homes: Karen will argue that her family unit is very stable and has not changed since the divorce, while James' family unit is relatively new and untested. James will argue that his new family is permanent as he has committed to his new wife through marriage.
C. The moral fitness of the parties involved: James will argue that he is more morally fit than Karen, as evidenced by his traditional job and family life. He will argue that Karen's profession is immoral and she is a poor role model for the children.

   Karen will argue that the custody factors are limited to how they impact the children, immoral behavior to which the children are not exposed and which do not affect the parenting is irrelevant to this determination. If the children are unaware of her job as an exotic dancer and are not exposed to it, it is legally irrelevant to this factor. This factor—and the entire analysis—seeks to evaluate parents solely as to how it relates to how they will function as a parent; it does not seek to determine which parent is morally superior as a human being. *Fletcher v Fletcher*, 447 Mich 871 (1994). Karen will also likely argue that her employment is perfectly legal and it is the responsible way for her to support her children.

D. The home, school and community record of the child: James will argue that Nicholas' community record indicates that he is failing and is at risk and that a change is necessary.

   Karen will argue that Noah's record shows that she has been committed to his well being. Karen will respond that Nicholas may be having trouble because of his father moving away, or that this may be normal difficulties experienced during childhood, not rising to the level of a significant change in circumstances or proper cause.

E. The recognizable preference of the child, if the court considers the child to be of sufficient age to express preference: The court is required, upon request of either parent, to interview the minor children. This interview is done privately by the court and the statements of the children are not revealed to either party or the attorneys. *Fletcher v Fletcher*, 200 Mich 505 (1993). The judge has the discretion to attach whatever importance he or she decides to the statements of the child. The court must limit its discussions with the child to a determination of the child's preference. *Molloy v Molloy*. At no age is the preference of the child determinative of the custodial situation. *Fletcher v Fletcher*, 200 Mich 505 (1993).

   An answer should not indicate any gender bias. That there is no longer any "tender years" doctrine or gender bias regarding custody of children (i.e., moms are not given a preference solely because they are moms) (established by MCL 722.5, repealed by 1970 PA 91, replaced by MCL 722.21).

For extra credit, a great answer could add that: the evidentiary hearing could be heard in front of a referee or the family court judge; if done in front of a referee, either party is entitled to a *de novo* review prior to a change being made. The court rules specifically define a *de novo* hearing as including a review by a Family Court judge based on a review of the transcript and exhibits from the referee hearing and does not require a live hearing (MCR 3.215[F][2]); and that the court rules require that the post-judgment cases go back in front of the same judge throughout the minority of the child, so that the judge remains familiar with the circumstances of the family (MCR 8.111[D]).

Student Answer—February 2008

Question 8—Domestic Relations—None Available

July 2008—Question 14

Sanjeev and Greta met while in college at the University of Michigan, were married in 2000 in Ann Arbor, and divorced in 2007. They have two children, Annika, age 6, and James, age 3. When they divorced, they agreed to joint legal custody of the children. Although they both spend lots of time with the children, Sanjeev is noted as their primary physical custodian in the Judgment. They live near one another and share parenting time with the children with Sanjeev having responsibility for the children approximately 60% of the time and Greta having responsibility for the children approximately 40% of the time. The parents equally share holidays and equally share important decision making for their children. Neither party has remarried. The children are very involved in school, Scouts, their child care community and community sports teams. The children are flourishing, happy, healthy children and they enjoy their time with both parents. Both parents are very involved with their schools and activities.

Greta is a physician and professor at the University of Michigan. She works at its hospitals, and she is also on the tenure track for a faculty position there. She has long sought the faculty position and will be considered for that position in two years. She has studied and worked for over ten years after her undergraduate graduation for consideration for the position. Sanjeev is a research chemist, who was employed doing pharmaceutical research for a national pharmaceutical company, whose research facilities are headquartered in Ann Arbor.

A few months ago, Sanjeev received shocking news that the research facility where he is employed will be closed in its entirety. Sanjeev was offered the opportunity to move to Connecticut to continue his employment, or his employment would be terminated. He earnestly looked for work in Ann Arbor and surrounding areas, but has been genuinely unable to find suitable work which makes use of his skills and education. Greta earnestly investigated employment in Connecticut, but it is impossible to join the tenure track at any university at this stage in her career.

Sanjeev has petitioned the court to move the children to Connecticut with him, where he would be the primary parent, although he has offered Greta nearly all of the school breaks, holidays, and summers with the children. Greta has countered by requesting the children remain in Michigan and spend the same schedule with Sanjeev.

Please discuss:

A. The procedural process the court will follow, including any specific burdens of proof; and

B. The substantive law that should be applied and an application of that law to the facts of this case.

Model Answer to Question 14

A. Sanjeev's Petition:

1. Because MCL 722.31 prohibits moving a child's domicile greater than 100 miles without court permission, an evidentiary hearing will be held in which the court will address the factors listed in MCL 722.31(4). These factors are:
   - (a) Whether the legal residence change has the capacity to improve the quality of life for both the child and the relocating parent;
   - (b) The degree to which each parent has complied with, and utilized his or her time under a court order governing parenting time with the child, and whether the parent's plan to change the child's legal residence is inspired by that parent's desire to defeat or frustrate the parenting time schedule;

(c) The degree to which the court is satisfied that, if the court permits the legal residence change, it is possible to order a modification of the parenting time schedule and other arrangements governing the child's schedule in a manner that can provide an adequate basis for preserving and fostering the parental relationship between the child and each parent; and whether each parent is likely to comply with the modification;

(d) The extent to which the parent opposing the legal residence change is motivated by a desire to secure a financial advantage with respect to a support obligation;

(e) Domestic violence, regardless of whether the violence was directed against or witnessed by the child.

2. Regardless of whose motion prevails, the court will be required to modify parenting time because the current schedule will no longer work. MCL 722.27a lists several factors to consider and states that parenting time shall be granted to a parent in a frequency, duration, and type reasonably calculated to promote a strong relationship between the child and the parent granted parenting time. Among the factors are the inconvenience to, and burdensome impact or effect on, the child of traveling for the purpose of parenting time and whether a parent can reasonably be expected to exercise parenting time in accordance with the court order and any other relevant factors.

B. Greta's Petition: In deciding Greta's case, Greta has asked for a change of custody. There must be an evidentiary hearing. *Mann v Mann*, 190 Mich App 526 (1991). At the evidentiary hearing, the first threshold is whether an established custodial environment exists. If an established custodial environment exists, the burden of proof to allow a change is clear and convincing evidence that it is in the child's best interest; if there is no established custodial environment, a preponderance of the evidence standard is sufficient to change custody. MCL 722.27. Here there is an established custodial environment with both parties in this case, as the parties share substantial parenting time, they use that time, and the children are flourishing. The children have lived with both parties for an appreciable amount of time and naturally look to both for comfort, guidance, and the necessities of life; therefore, a party requesting a modification must prove by clear and convincing evidence that it is in the best interests of the children to change custody. An established custodial environment is not determined by having 51% of the children's time.

The court is required to make a finding on each of the child custody factors, even if only to say it is irrelevant. *Overall v Overall*, 203 Mich App 450 (1994). The Child Custody factors (also known as the "best interests" factors) are listed in MCL 722.21. The important factors given the case presented (the rest do not apply) are:

1. The length of time the child has lived in a stable, satisfactory environment, and the desirability of maintaining continuity. Obviously, continuity is impossible. The children are going to be separated from one parent.
2. The permanence, as a family unit, of the existing or proposed custodial home or homes. Neither has changed—this factor illustrated "family" or "social" permanence more than physical permanence unless frequent changes are likely, not the fact scenario here.
3. The moral fitness of the parties involved. Not an issue here. An applicant may note, for extra points, that this factor—and the entire analysis—seeks to

evaluate parents solely as to how it relates to how they will function as a parent; it does not seek to determine which parent is morally superior as a human being. *Fletcher v Fletcher*, 447 Mich 871 (1994).

4. The home, school, and community record of the child. The children are flourishing. This may help support Greta's case.
5. The recognizable preference of the child, if the court considers the child to be of sufficient age to express preference. The court is required, upon request of either parent, to interview the minor children. This interview is done privately by the court and the statements of the child are not revealed to either party or the attorneys. *Fletcher v Fletcher*, 200 Mich App 505 (1994). The judge has the discretion to attach whatever importance he or she decides to the statements of the child. The court must limit its discussions with the child to a determination of the child's preference. *Molly v Molly*, 243 Mich App 595 (2000). At no age is the preference of a child determinative of the custodial situation. *Fletcher v Fletcher*, 200 Mich App 505 (1994). And, there is no longer any "tender years" doctrine or gender bias regarding custody of children, i.e., moms are not given a preference solely because they are moms.

Student Answers—July 2008

Question 14—Domestic Relations—8 points

The court will look at the circumstances in light of the best interest of the children.

Under the law, the state will review the petition reviewing the current arrangement, and will not make a change in custody unless there has been a substantive change in circumstance or it is otherwise proper.

Here Sanjeev (S) and Greta (G) have joint legal custody and share in raising the kids fairly equally. S has primary physical custody. Under Michigan law, the sex of the primary care giver is not an issue. Here S the father has physical custody.

Under the law, the review will look at which parent has an established custodial environment, meaning they provide love, affection, disciple and material support for the children, and the children have a relationship that depends on the party. The burden of proof if one party has not established that they have this is clear and convincing evidence that the party is not providing for custodial environment. Here both parents according to the facts have this environment, so the burden is only reasonable. S will not therefore likely have to prove he has established it; he is asking to maintain custody and more. The children are flourishing, involved in sports and enjoy time with both parents. The substantive law to be applied here is the child custody and support law. Under these circumstances S wants to show that he needs to move to make money and support the kids. G has also tried to find work in the Connecticut area, but must complete medical studies in Ann Arbor.

Under the law, the best interest of the children includes both support and a relationship with both parents. The analysis must go through each factor and the judge must make a determination, even if it is irrelevant in the case at bar. The judge must balance these factors and look at the best interest of the child as paramount. Here the balance is between financial well-being and a relationship with mom (G) becoming long-distance. Each factor will need to be scrutinized. Here it is clearly a substantial change in circumstance to have no job available locally.

February 2009—Question 7

George and Jane dated while attending the University of Michigan and married just after graduation. The two decided that Jane would go on to the U of M Dental School where she had been admitted, while George would work to pay the tuition and costs, the living expenses, and save to attend the U of M Business School after Jane graduated. George worked full-time and all of the overtime offered at Spacely Sprockets, a factory job that he took because he could find no other work with his B.A. in Music History.

After they had their first child, Judy, George quit work so Jane could finish Dental School. George also remained home after Jane graduated and began practicing at an established dental office following the birth of their son, Elroy.

Over the next fifteen years, the family lived in a 3,500 square foot home in a "gated" community, went on vacations to foreign countries, and the children attended private schools as Jane's practice expanded to where she was earning $325,000 annually. Then, Jane decided to divorce George to marry an orthodontist with whom she had been having an affair.

George agreed to the divorce, agreed to accept half of the existing marital property, and agreed to have physical custody of the two children. After child support payments under the Michigan Child Support Formula, Jane was left with $175,000 annually and George had $40,000 annual income from some investments.

George wants spousal support from Jane. Can George receive spousal support? What are the factors that favor a claim for spousal support? What arguments can Jane present to deny a claim for spousal support by George? Explain your answer.

Model Answer to Question 7

Spousal support would most likely be awarded on the basis of the factors outlined below. The particular amount of spousal support, if quoted by the examinee, is not important. The examinee's familiarity with the factors pertinent to making the determination is what is being tested.

A divorce court has the discretion to award alimony as it considers just and reasonable. MCL 552.23, *Ianitelli v Ianitelli*, 199 Mich App 641, 642-643 (1993). Relevant factors for the court to consider include the length of the marriage, the parties' ability to pay, their past relations and conduct, their ages, needs, ability to work, health and fault, if any, and all other circumstances of the case. *Id.* at 643; *Demman v Demman*, 195 Mich App 109, 110-111 (1992). The main objective of alimony is to balance the incomes and needs of the parties in a way that will not impoverish either party. *Hanaway v Hanaway*, 208 Mich App 278, 295 (1995).

A full analysis of the pertinent factors would include the following:

(a) Length of the marriage. This is a 19-year, long-term marriage. This weighs in favor of supposal support.

(b) Parties' ability to pay. Jane has ample ability to pay. Disparity in income and lifestyle is relevant, but there is no legal right for the parties to live in the same lifestyle. This factor weighs in favor of spousal support.

(c) Past relations and conduct. Both parties worked hard and contributed equally—although differently—to the family unit. (A good answer should not weigh a contribution within the home as less valuable than one outside the home—*Hanaway*). This is a neutral factor in this matter.

(d) Their ages. The inference is George and Jane are middle-aged. That is young enough for George to retrain and re-enter the work force. Jane has already "arrived" in her career and enjoys a higher earning potential for that reason. This factor is more neutral.

(e) Needs. George will need more support than Jane because the children remain at home and that will impact his ability to earn. Also, George will need financial assistance because he has not supported himself and the family financially. This factor favors George.

(f) Ability to work. Jane can obviously work. George can work, but he has no relevant and timely training and has been out of the workforce for 19 years. This factor weighs in favor of George. On Jane's behalf, the examinee might note that George is expected to work and courts can assign income if they wish as if he was working.

(g) Health. There is no reason to think that either party has health issues.

(h) Fault. Jane is at fault for the breakdown of the marriage due to her extramarital affair. This will weigh in George's favor. Jane would emphasize, however, that the court should not use spousal support to punish her, nor may the court weigh this factor more heavily than the others.

Finally, an examinee may discuss George's contribution to Jane's acquisition of her degree as a property issue—this is a claim under *Postema v Postema*, 189 Mich App 89 (1991). The exam question is not a *Postema* question. A *Postema* claim is separate and distinct from spousal support; it is not a factor in a spousal support determination. Nevertheless, an astute examinee may note the issue. A grader should not penalize the examinee for such recognition, but reward it, particularly because Jane's advance degree can be considered a result of a "concerted family effort" under *Postema*.

Two Student Answers—February 2009

Question 7—Domestic Relations—9 points

Can George get spousal support? The court will look at several factors to determine if a spouse should receive child support. Some of these factors are:

1. how long marriage lasted
2. age of parties
3. ability of spouse to pay
4. relationships in past and conduct
5. what property spouse will get as result of divorce
6. earning capacity of spouse requesting support
7. other factors that court may consider in determining equity
8. standard of living of parties.

If spouse can establish that spousal support is needed then court can grant it.

George can establish that he needs spousal support. There is a great disparity between George's and Jane's income. His is $90,000 and Jane's is $175,000. George stayed home with the kids and worked while Jane went to dental school so it is only fair that spousal support be provided. George will also have custody of children. George and Jane had a high standard of living and this is something George had grown accustomed to. They traveled to foreign countries and lived in a 3,500 square foot home. Jane also was having an affair during the marriage and is now going to marry an orthodontist which means her high standard of living will continue even though due to her bad conduct (marital affair) that marriage has dissolved.

Jane will argue that George does not need spousal support. He's getting half the marital property, he's still young and educated so he can get a well-paying job.

Question 7—Domestic Relations—8 points

This is a family relations issue regarding spousal support.

Spousal support may be awarded when one spouse is predominately the "bread winner" and one spouse makes substantially less in income. The court may use any number of factors in determining an appropriate amount of spousal support. Spousal support is not limited to women. Men may claim spousal support.

Here, George and Jane agreed after marriage that George would work to put Jane through Dental school. This is something the court will look at in determining the necessity and amount of support. It will be assessed based on the value of his contribution to her education, not the value of her degree.

The court will also look at the living arrangements whereby George stayed home and raised Elroy establishing a living environment where George was completely dependant on Jane's income. Also, George became accustomed to a lifestyle of living in a large house, many vacations, private schools. The court will use established lifestyle in awarding support. Also, the court will factor in Jane's extramarital affair as a consideration of a spousal support award.

Jane will probably argue that George does have an income from Investments and that she is paying half of her income in child support. Because the family court is a court of equity. The court can use these factors as well if it chooses to. But generally spousal support is based on husband/wife economic positioning, lifestyle, education, and extramarital affairs.

George will probably be able to establish a need for spousal support and will probably be successful in obtaining it from Jane.

July 2009—Question 9

Pat the lawyer's client, Gertrude Guard, explained to Pat that she was thinking of divorcing her husband, Gary Guard, but she needed some advice. She and Gary, both prison guards in Ionia, Michigan, earning approximately the same salary, had lived together for nearly 10 years before they decided to marry. They lived in an apartment to save money because they planned to build a home on 5 acres of land that Gary's father deeded to him during the eighth year they lived together. The land was given free of any encumbrances. For tax purposes, Gary quit claimed the property to himself and Gertrude after they were married. After 10 years of cohabitating and 5 years of marriage (without having children), the couple's joint bank account, which they had agreed to use for the construction of the home, was worth approximately $60,000. However, explained Gertrude, she was sure that Gary was having an affair. In addition, she was worried about her future because she had slipped on a grape at the local supermarket and injured her leg, making it difficult for her to effectively perform her guard duties. In fact, she had settled the case and received a $5,000 settlement check from the supermarket that was specifically designated for her pain and suffering, although she had not yet cashed the check. Three questions are raised:

1. The market value of the 5 acres is less now then it was when the property was transferred to Gary. Will Gertrude receive anything in a divorce for the 5 acres of land?
2. Will Gertrude be awarded spousal support?
3. Should Gertrude cash the settlement check from the supermarket now or should she wait until she files for divorce, or even wait until the divorce is final?

How should Pat respond to Gertrude's questions? Identify the issue(s) presented and explain your answers.

Model Answer to Question 9

1. Land: The first question here is whether the property is separate or marital. A court would almost certainly find it was separate because: (1) it was given as a gift to Gary before the parties' marriage, and Michigan law does not recognize the acquisition of "marital" rights with respect to a couple living together but not married, *Korth v Korth*, 256 Mich App 286 (2003); *Reeves v Reeves*, 226 Mich App 490 (1997); and (2) the property was given as a gift to Gary, and gifts are generally considered to be separate property. *Dart v Dart*, 460 Mich 573 (1999). Note that putting a spouse's name on property does not render it marital property as opposed to separate property, although it can weigh in favor of such a finding. *Reeves, supra; Korth, supra*. Gertrude might have had an argument that she ought to receive a share of any appreciation in the value of the land, but there was no increase in the land value. Even if the property is deemed to be separate, it can be divided if (1) the claimant spouse contributed to the acquisition, improvement or accumulation of the property, MCL 552.401; or (2) the award to the claimant spouse out of the parties' marital assets is insufficient for the suitable support and maintenance of the claimant, MCL 552.23. See *Reeves, supra*. It is very unlikely that the court would invade separate property in this short-term childless marriage where the spouses' incomes are similar.

2. Spousal Support: This was a short-term childless marriage and the parties have the same income. The object in awarding spousal support is to balance the incomes and needs of the parties so that neither will be impoverished, and the factors that the trial court would consider would be: (1) the past relations and conduct of the parties, (2) the length of the marriage (note that the parties' 10-year cohabitation does not count towards this factor—*Korth, supra*), (3) the abilities of the parties to work, (4) the source and amount of property awarded to the parties, (5) the parties' ages, (6) the abilities of the parties to pay alimony, (7) the present situation of the parties, (8) the needs of the parties, (9) the parties' health, (10) the prior standard of living of the parties and whether either is responsible for the support of others, (11) contributions of the parties to the joint estate, (12) a party's fault in causing the divorce, (13) the effect of cohabitation on a party's financial status , and (14) general principles of equity. *Olson v Olson*, 256 Mich App 619, 631 (2003). *Note, however, that this is a comprehensive list that applicants should not be expected to replicate, and many cases* *contain other, shorter lists of factors. See*, for instance, *Magee v Magee*, 218 Mich App 158, 162 (1996), stating that the trial court should consider "the length of the marriage, the parties' ability to pay, their past relations and conduct, their ages, needs, ability to work, health and fault, if any, and all other circumstances of the case."

In this case, Gertrude's attorney might argue that Gary's affair, i.e., his fault in causing the divorce, his ability to move in with his dad, and Gertrude's injury and potential inability to work in the future, justifies some sort of spousal support. However, because of the parties' income parity, the short-term nature of the marriage, and the fact that Gertrude will receive the settlement money and a share of the joint account, a spousal support award of any significance would be unlikely.

3. Settlement Check: The award for pain and suffering is separate property and the check can be cashed before the divorce is final without consequence. Although causes of action are generally marital property, *Heilman v Heilman*, 95 Mich App 728 (1980), and assets acquired right up until the divorce judgment is entered are considered to be acquired "during the marriage," *Byington v Byington*, 224 Mich App 103 (1997), awards for pain and suffering are personal to the injured party. *Bywater v Bywater*, 128 Mich App 396 (1983). Note that the check should not be deposited into the joint account because Gary could argue that it was a contribution to the marital estate. In addition, it would be all right for Gertrude to take the money for the attorney fees from the joint account, although it would be counted against her in the final property settlement.

Two Student Answers—July 2009

Question 9—Domestic Relations—9 points

1. 5 acres. While this property was a gift to Gary from his father before the parties married, if the parties made improvements to the land such as erecting a home or building a pond on the land, Gertrude would be entitled to one-half the increase in value accrued during the marriage. The value should be determined by the value at the time it was given to Gary minus the current value. Here the value is less now so Gertrude would receive ½ of value at time received it minus value now. It should also be considered that a joint bank account of $60,000 is what was used to build the home.

2. Spousal support is based on a number of factors:

Length of marriage
Age of parties
Needs of parties
Health of parties
Income of parties
Ability of parties to work
Current situation of parties
Past relations and conduct of parties
General principles of equity including fault

And is at the Court's discretion. The parties were married 5 years. The ages of the parties are unknown but it is assumed they are middle age since they were together 10 years before they married and now married 5 years. The parties had no children. Both parties are employed and earning about the same. While Michigan is a no-fault sate, fault is a factor considered by the Court in determining alimony.

If Gary is having an affair and responsible for the breakdown of the marriage, that would certainly be a factor in deciding that Gert should receive alimony. Usually the predominating factors in awarding alimony are long term marriage and disparity in income on the parties. This is a relatively short term marriage and both parties earn about the same. However, Gert may be unable to work due to her leg injury and as such may need alimony in order to support herself. The purpose of alimony is to balance the incomes of the parties without creating undue hardship on one party.

Gertrude should hold the settlement check. While it was paid to her for *her* pain and suffering, it was paid during the marriage and as such is a marital asset. All marital assets must be disclosed to the other party and it will be the judge's decision whether this check in its entirety should be awarded to Gertrude.

Question 9—Domestic Relations—8 points

1. Yes, Gertrude will receive something in the divorce for the 5 acres of land. Here, Gary's father deeded to Gary 5 acres—this was before the two were married. At this point the land is Gary's. However, Gary quit claimed the property himself and Gertrude after they had married. This is now marital property. As such, Gertrude is entitled to the property if they divorce, and Gary is also entitled. Marital property and it will be considered by the courts division of marital property—which in Michigan is an equitable division of the parties' property.
2. Yes, Gertrude will be awarded spousal support. This involves the *Sparks* factors. Married parties are entitled to spousal support. The court looks at the length of the marriage—here the parties lived together for 10 years—but married 5 years—the longer the marriage, the more likely to get support. Court also looks at ages of parties, ability to pay support, need, fault, health of parties, kids, etc. Here ability to work, take care of itself Pat may have to pay her because of her injury. Yes, should get spousal support.
3. As for settlement check, she should wait to cash it until after divorce is final. It was for her pain and suffering. As long as she doesn't comingle it with marital property, then its hers. If she cashes it and comingles with hers and Gary's accounts, or spends it on marital stuff—then it's marital asset and he'd be entitled to it.

As for spousal support—Gary was having an affair—this goes to fault and will be considered.

February 2010—Question 8

Lisa and her husband Larry were married in 2002 and they have two children, ages 4 and 6. During the early years of their marriage they lived with Lisa's parents in Lansing, Michigan to save money. In January 2008, Larry abandoned looking for work in Michigan and, over Lisa's objection, moved by himself to Ohio and began working as a waiter there. Larry convinced Lisa to come and stay with him in Ohio for the summer of 2008, during which time the couple attempted to reconcile. Larry's explosive temper often got the best of him, however, and after a few serious outbursts, Lisa and the children moved back to Michigan and resumed living with Lisa's parents in September 2008. Lisa began working at a daycare. She earns about the same income there as Larry earns at his job, although Lisa does not need to pay rent or utilities while she lives with her parents.

In December 2009, Lisa received a telephone call from Larry, who, with Lisa's consent, has the children in Ohio to celebrate his birthday. During their conversation, Lisa asked Larry to begin paying child support. Larry became angry and threatened to file for divorce in Ohio and seek custody of the children.

Lisa visits your law office seeking advice on the following three questions:

1. Since Lisa lives with her parents and since Lisa's and Larry's incomes are roughly the same, Larry says Michigan's child support guidelines are not applicable and the parties can decide themselves how much (if any) support is paid. Assuming a divorce action has been filed, is Larry correct?
2. If Lisa files for divorce in Michigan before Larry voluntarily returns the children, does Michigan have jurisdiction over the children's custody, even though the last time the family lived together was in Ohio in the summer of 2008 and the children are not now in Michigan?
3. If a Michigan court were to determine custody, what would be the likely results?

How do you respond to Lisa's questions? Explain your answers.

Model Answers to Question 8

1. **No.** A court must order support in the amount determined by applying the child support formula unless it determines from the facts of the case that application of the formula would be unjust or inappropriate. MCL 552.605(2). If the court deviates from the formula, it must set forth on the record: (1) the amount determined by the formula; (2) how the ordered support deviates from the formula; (3) the value of property or other support ordered in lieu of child support, if applicable; and (4) the reasons the application of the formula would be unjust or inappropriate. MCL 552.605(2); *Ghidotti v Barber*, 459 Mich 189, 191 (1998). There is no reason to deviate from the guidelines in this case. The parties' incomes will be factored directly into the calculation of the guidelines, and the support Lisa receives from her parents can be attributed to her income. See Michigan Child Support Formula Manual, §2.05.
2. **Yes.** A Michigan court would have authority to take jurisdiction over the custody of the children. Interstate custody disputes are governed by the Uniform Child-Custody Jurisdiction and Enforcement Act (UCCJEA). The UCCJEA sets forth several grounds for finding of jurisdiction over a custody dispute, the most important of which is that "[Michigan] is the home state of the child on the date of the commencement of the proceedings, or was the home state of the child within 6 months before the commencement of the proceeding and the child is absent from this state but a parent or person acting as a parent continues to live in this state." MCL 722.1201(1)(a).

   The "home state" is defined as "the state in which a child lived with a parent or a person acting as a parent for at least 6 consecutive months immediately before the commencement of a child-custody proceeding." MCL 722.1102(g).

   Since Lisa has lived with the children in Michigan since the fall of 2008, i.e., more than six months, Michigan is the home state, arguably because the children lived in Michigan for six consecutive months before the filing of the proceeding. Even if the children are in Ohio, Lisa is still in Michigan, so Michigan was the home state "within six months before the commencement of the proceeding."

3. In Michigan, every custody determination must be based on the "best interest of the child." MCL 722.25(1). The first step is to determine whether an "established custodial environment" has been established by either party, because a judge may not issue an order changing an established custodial environment absent clear and convincing evidence that such a change is in the best interests of the child. MCL 722.27(1)(c). This is an essential first step in any custody dispute. *Stringer v Vincent*, 161 Mich App 429, 434 (1987). The custodial environment is established if, over an appreciable time, the child naturally looks to the custodian in that environment for guidance, discipline, the necessities of life, and parental comfort. MCL 722.27(1)(c). Here, given the fact that the children have lived with their mother in Michigan all of their lives, except for one summer in Ohio, the court would definitely find that an established custodial environment existed with Lisa in Michigan. Larry would thus have a very high burden on establishing that it would be in the best interest of the children to move to Ohio.

The list of factors a court must consider in determining the best interest of the child set forth at MCL 722.23:

(a) The love, affection, and other emotional ties existing between the parties involved and the child.

(b) The capacity and disposition of the parties involved to give the child love, affection, and guidance and to continue the education and raising of the child in his or her religion or creed if any.

(c) The capacity disposition of the parties involved to provide the child with food, clothing, medical care or other remedial care recognized and permitted under the laws of this state in place of medical care, and other material needs.

(d) The length of time the child has lived in a stable, satisfactory environment, and the desirability of maintaining continuity.

(e) The permanence, as a family unit, of the existing or proposed custodial home or homes.

(f) The moral fitness of the parties involved.

(g) The mental and physical health of the parties involved.

(h) The home, school, and community record of the child.

(i) The reasonable preference of the child, if the court considers the child to be of sufficient age to express preference.

(j) The willingness and ability of each of the parties to facilitate and encourage a close and continuing parent-child relationship between the child and the other parent or the child and the parents.

(k) Domestic violence, regardless of whether the violence was directed against or witnessed by the child.

(l) Any other factor considered by the court to be relevant to a particular child custody dispute.

Specifically, the following factors should be noted: (a) Lisa is likely to have more significant emotional ties with the children since she has been raising them without Larry; (b) Larry's explosive temper would arguably impact his ability to provide love, affection and guidance, (c) the parties' income are equal, so neither is in a better position to provide for the children's physical needs, and in fact Lisa might be better positioned because of the support from her parents; (d) stability and continuity favor Lisa; and (f) Larry's "moral fitness" could be a question because he left his wife and children, and he threatened a custody fight after Lisa requested child support.

Given that the known factors tend to weigh in Lisa's favor, and the established custodial environment is with Lisa in Michigan, she would very likely be awarded physical custody of the children.

Student Answer—February 2010

Question 8—Domestic Relations—8 points

This is a domestic relations question.

1. No, Larry is not correct. Every state has guidelines on how child support is calculated. It is not decided amongst the parties. If the divorce is filed in Ohio, I believe child support would not be part of the decree. More than likely Michigan's child support guidelines are applicable and along with the guidelines, some factors are looked at such as needs of the children, ability of parties to pay, income of both parents, etc.
2. Yes, Michigan does have jurisdiction over the children's custody because Michigan is the children's home-state. It is where they have lived for the preceding 6 months with a parent. Although they are in Ohio now, temporary stays away from Michigan are okay because children are coming back after their visit from Ohio to celebrate Larry's birthday.
3. The likely result for custody would be that Lisa would be the custodial parent, they would live with her in Michigan. There are factors that are looked at when determining the custody of children. Primarily what is in the best interest of the child is what is looked at; who do the children look to for their care and custody; chances of domestic violence, ability to support children.

Here Larry abandoned his family 2 years ago and moved to another state. He had an explosive temper so there is risk of child abuse and domestic violence and his ability to support and provide for the children is less than Lisa's ability.

Lisa on the other hand has had the children with her at most times so I'm sure they look to her for care, support and custody. She is living with parents and can provide a more stable home in Michigan. Based on the totality of the circumstances and what is in the best interest of these children, Lisa should have custody. Larry's abandonment and explosive temper may qualify him for rights as a parent to be involuntary terminated and that is a big strike against him.

July 2010—Question 11

Abe and Betsy were married in 2004, and lived in Ypsilanti, Michigan. At the time, Betsy was studying education at Eastern Michigan University. Abe worked as a bartender at a local restaurant. In 2006, Abe and Betsy had a son, Sam. Both parents provided care for Sam after he was born, with Abe watching him during the day and

Betsy watching him most evenings. Abe's parents in Detroit helped out quite a bit and Betsy's parents in Columbus, Ohio, made occasional visits.

Betsy obtained her Master's Degree in Education in the spring of 2008 and began looking for work in Michigan. By that time, she and Abe were frequently arguing over everything from money to Betsy's career plans. Betsy decided that she could no longer stay with Abe and filed for divorce in Michigan.

After Betsy filed for divorce in late 2008, she moved into a separate apartment. Sam stayed with Abe during the day and with Betsy in the evenings and most nights. In January 2009, on Betsy's motion, the family court entered a temporary order granting the parties joint legal and physical custody. The order provided for parenting time to be divided "as agreed" by the parties. After the order was entered, Betsy frequently asked Abe to take Sam for longer hours so she could interview for jobs in Michigan and elsewhere.

Before a final judgment was entered, Betsy called Abe and told him that she was taking Sam and moving to Columbus, Ohio because she had been offered a teaching position there. She informed Abe that she intended to move in with her parents until she could find her own home and suitable daycare. The new job would provide her and Sam with better health care benefits and a higher standard of living than they had in Ypsilanti.

Abe complained that Columbus was a three hour drive, and nearly 200 miles from Ypsilanti, but Betsy would not relent. She stated that if Abe did not consent to the move, she would hire an attorney and file a motion with the family court to change the custody order.

Betsy filed a motion to change domicile. Abe filed an answer opposing any change in Sam's domicile, asserting that such a change would be tantamount to granting Betsy physical custody.

Discuss the arguments for and against each party's position. Explain your answer.

Model Answer to Question 11

This is a change of domicile question that raises issues under MCL 722.31, often called the "100-mile rule." The statute applies in cases where the parents share joint legal custody and live within 100 miles of each other at the time the case is commenced. The statute provides that the child's residence is with each parent, and it prohibits the parents from moving more than 100 miles from the legal residence at the time the case was commenced. The statute applies to interstate changes of domicile. *Brown v Loveman*, 260 Mich App 576 (2004), lv den 470 Mich 881 (2004). In order for Betsy to take Sam to Columbus, she will need to either obtain Abe's consent, or obtain the court's permission by filing a motion to change Sam's legal residence. The court would look at the following five factors to make the decision (MCL 722.31):

1. Whether the legal residence change has the capacity to improve the quality of life for both the child and the relocating parent. Here, it does appear that the change of legal residence would improve the quality of life for Betsy.
   In Columbus she would earn a stable income, with a good job, with health care benefits, and be near her parents. Betsy would likely argue that the change of residence would benefit Sam because of her increased income, better health

care, and the stability of a more permanent home (after she found a place of her own). A single home would be better than moving Sam from apartment to apartment on an almost daily basis—an arrangement that is not sustainable in the long run. In Columbus, Betsy would also be close to her parents, who could aid in caring for Sam. The court might also want to know about the quality of the schools and neighborhoods in both Columbus and Ypsilanti.

2. The degree to which each parent has complied with, and utilized his or her time under, a court order governing parenting time with the child, and whether the parent's plan to change the child's legal residence is inspired by that parent's desire to defeat or frustrate the parenting time schedule. Although the facts suggest that Betsy increasingly relied on Abe to take care of Sam, there is no indication that she did not exercise parenting time she was given by court order. This factor should not favor either party.
3. The degree to which the court is satisfied that, if the court permits the legal residence change, it is possible to order a modification of the parenting time schedule and other arrangements governing the child's schedule in a manner that can provide an adequate basis for preserving and fostering the parental relationship between the child and each parent; and whether each parent is likely to comply with the modification. Betsy may need to offer generous parenting time to Abe because this factor works against her. She will assert that it is possible to provide sufficient parenting time for Abe such that he and Sam will continue to have a significant relationship with each other. Distance does not mean no contact—Sam would be able to maintain contact through e-mails, telephone, perhaps a webcam, and other electronic means of communication. Abe should argue that Columbus is too far away for him to maintain the type of contact with Sam that both he and Sam are accustomed to having, and electronic communication is no substitute for face-to-face interaction. He would likely be limited to long weekends, holidays and time in the summer (although Betsy may have summers off, in which case she will want to be with Sam too). At least one Court of Appeals decision has found the disruption of the father's time with his child to be important, holding that §722.31(4)(c) required the denial of the motion to relocate, in part because of the negative impact to the minor child of not having the father involved in his life on an almost daily basis. *Grew v Knox*, 265 Mich App 333 (2005).

4-5. The extent to which the parent opposing legal residence change is motivated by a desire to secure a final advantage with respect to a support obligation, and domestic violence. These are not factors here.

Betsy would have the burden of proving the beneficial nature of the move by a preponderance of the evidence. *Brown, supra* at 600. Good arguments can be made on both sides of this issue, but it does not seem likely that the trial court would approve the move to Columbus if it included both Betsy and Sam, *i.e.*, the trial court might say that Betsy can change her residence, but not Sam's residence.

It is important to recognize that a move such as the one contemplated by Betsy involves a two-step process. If the family court were to determine that Betsy had met her burden with respect to the five factors under MCL 722.31(4), it would next have to determine if the new arrangement amounted to a change in Sam's custodial environment. Abe's response to Betsy's motion should argue that Betsy does not meet the five-part 100-mile test, but that even if she does, the move would alter Sam's established custodial environment and Betsy cannot establish by clear and convincing evidence that the change would be in Sam's best interest. A custodial environment is established if "over an appreciable time the child naturally looks to the custodian in that environment for guidance, discipline, the necessities of life, and parental comfort. The age of the child, the physical environment, and the inclination of the custodian and the child as to permanency of the relationship shall also be considered." *Brown, supra* at 595, quoting MCL 722.27(1)(c). In this situation, a custodial environment is very likely established in Ypsilanti, with both parents. The argument *against* an established custodial environment is that when Betsy moved to a new apartment, the environment became "unestablished" and it has not settled into a new established environment because of the uncertainty surrounding the divorce. Here, Betsy would argue that Sam did not have a custodial environment with Abe, or if he did, Sam would be able to maintain that environment when he was with Abe during his parenting time. Abe would argue that he could not maintain the custodial environment in the event of Sam's move to Columbus.

If a custodial environment has been established, and the move would alter that established environment, changing custody would require a hearing wherein Betsy would have to establish, by clear and convincing evidence, that the proposed change was in Sam's best interest. MCL §722.27(1)(c); *Brown, supra; Rittershaus v Rittershaus*, 273 Mich App 462 (2007).

The list of factors a court must consider in determining the best interest of the child are set forth at MCL 722.23. Note that the test-taker should not be expected to provide the whole list, but should focus on a few of the factors that are relevant here.

Specifically, the following factors should be noted: (a) love and affection between parents and child—both parents have strong ties to Sam, and Abe's ties are likely to be disrupted by a long distance move; (b) capacity to provide love, affection and guidance—the question does not state which parent Sam primarily looks to for the provision of his physical and emotional needs, but if there was a clear winner here, it could be important in determining Sam's best interests; (c) capacity to provide food, clothing, medical care, and other physical needs—Betsy would be better able to provide for Sam's care because she will have more money, have better benefits, work a more normal schedule, and have her parents around to assist in childcare—Sam also has his parents close by, though his work at night would make finding care difficult during his work hours; (d) length of time in a stable environment—this factor would tend to favor Abe because Sam has lived in a more or less stable environment with both parents his entire life, although that life was arguably disrupted when Abe and Betsy separated; (e) permanence of family unit—the permanence of the Ypsilanti environment is questionable because the parties live in apartments and it is clear that the divorce will cause a disruption in the custodial homes; (f) and (g)—moral, mental and physical fitness are not issues here; (h) home and school records are not at issue; (i) child's preference—Sam is likely too young (4 years old) for the court to give his preference, if any, much weight. Note that there is no "tender years" doctrine in Michigan that would favor Betsy because she is the mother; and (j), (k), and (l)—there is no evidence that either party would be unwilling to encourage the parental relationship of the other, no evidence of domestic violence, and the question does not suggest other factors that are not accounted for in the prior list.

There is no clear answer to the question of what the judge would do. The key here is the test-taker's ability to recognize the issues, articulate the standards, and apply the standards to the facts.

Two Student Answers—July 2010

Question 11—Domestic Relations—10 points

In this domestic relations case many issues come into play. First, whether a judge procedurally can change the order and whether substantively the order would be in the best interest of the child.

1. 100 mile rule: A spouse cannot move a child over 100 miles with the consent of the other parent or an order form the court. Here, Betsy is not getting consent form Abe so the process is proper since she is trying to move Sam over 100 miles.

2. A judge of friend of the court may upon determining all facts state a recommendation before going to the merits. If the FOC gives a recommendation the parties may either agree or request that the judge review. In this instance a judge will review the facts and evidence de novo. Here, there would need to be both procedurally issues raised as well as substantive.

a. Whether an established custodial environment exists: An ECE exists where over an appreciable period of time the child naturally looks to that parent for the parental love an guidance. If there is an ECE the adverse party must show by clear and convincing evidence that a change in circumstances exists to warrant a modification. But Betsy will need more than this. The judge will have to determine if the move is best for all parties.

In order for a move to exist for a modification, the judge will have to determine 1. whether the or not the move would provide a better quality of life for both parent and child. 2. Whether the parties have complied with pervious order and the likelihood the parties will comply with the new order or if the purpose is to frustrate the current order. 3. Whether there are any financial motives. 4. In and if the event the court changes the order will it protect the interest of maintaining family unity and keep the relationship between both parents and the child the same. 5. Any domestic violence issues.

Here, B will state that the move is for a better quality of life than the Ypsilanti standard of living would offer if the move was permitted and since the order is as agreed her purpose is not to frustrate the order, but provide better for her son. There are no financial motives because she is going to be working alone and since the facts don't say anything to the child support issue, it is purely for the better well-being of her and Sam. It will only harm the parties' ability to remain close to their son if not allowed. A will argue the opposite that the move is only to get Sam away from his father. Further, that the domicile would be 3 hours away from his father. This is insufficient for a court to use and him to use as the argument for not consenting. Although, it may alter the physical custody Betsy would state that a change in time could be determined where Sam sees A more lengths of time rather than daily. (i.e. for weeks or during the summer) the difference between physical custody and legal custody is physical is day-to-day decisions where as legal custody goes to the life-changing decisions. Thus, B has shown enough.

3. The judge will then determine whether the move would be in the best interest of the child. In MI, the Best Interest factors that determine a child custody issue are all

applicable and have a decision, however, only those relevant to each case are weighed and determined. Some of those factors include, the parties abilities to provide for lone and affection of the child, provide food and shelter, the ages of the parties and whether their abilities are to provide, the amount the child has been in the custodial environment, the school record and community history of the child, health of the parties, ability to maintain relationships between parents and child as well as with each other to keep the idea of family relations healthy, and whether domestic violence are problematic. Although, this list is not all inclusive the 12 factors are weighed according to which is relevant. Here, B will argue that the child is only 2 years old and she is ready and willing to provide for him everything a good single mother can while working, and that she is able to maintain the environment. She is trying to provide better health care benefits and not take away Sam's opportunity to a better life. A will argue that the best interest of the child is with him, however, a quick rebut is that the evidence is not sufficient to determine which the best interest is for the child, but the judge will decide and that will be the order.

Question 11—Domestic Relations—8 points

Under MI law, child custody is determined by the courts. Before a parent can change domicile, the court may consider certain factors if the other party objects to the move. The factors that the court will use to determine if custody should be modified to allow a parent to move more than 100 miles away w/a child are the following: 1) Will the move improve financial conditions for the parent and child? 2) Will the move better the lives of the parent and child? 3) Is the move an effort by the custodial parent to frustrate the visitation rights of the non-custodial parent? 4) Will the other parent have a realistic chance of seeing the child if the move is granted? 5) also the custodial parents move motivated by financial gain?

In this case, Betsy filed a motion to change domicile before the court entered a final judgment regarding custody. Based on the factors Betsy will argue that the move will help her financial situation so that she can provide for Sam. The facts indicate that she and Sam would have health care benefits and a higher standard of living if they move to Columbus.

Betsy will also argue that the move is not an attempt to frustrate Abe's visitation rights. The facts do not indicate that Betsy doesn't want Abe to see Sam. Betsy could also argue that a three hour drive is not that far & that Abe will be able to see Sam.

Abe can argue that Columbus is too far & that he would not be able to see Sam. Abe will further argue that the move is unnecessary b/c Betsy could find a teaching position in Michigan. Abe can further argue that this is pre-mature b/c a final judgment has not been ordered yet. Furthermore, Abe could argue that Sam would be placed in daycare is she moved to Columbus. If Betsy stays in MI, Abe could watch Sam while Betsy worked, as they had done while Betsy was getting her education.

Although the move would be good financially for Betsy and Sam, Abe would not be able to see Sam. The court should first determine which parent will have custody of the child, which it does by determine the best interest of the child. There are several factors that are used to determine that. The court also decides where the child's established custodial environment is; which is where over an appreciable time, the child looks to the guarding in that environment for discipline, love, guidance, affection, parental comfort, and the necessities of life. In this case, it seems both parents provide these things equally for Sam. Therefore, the court should rule on this issue first before allowing Betsy to move to Columbus w/Sam.

WORKER'S COMPENSATION

Questions, Model Answers, and Student Answers

The following section includes prior Michigan Bar Exam questions and model answers for **Worker's Compensation**. Many of the questions also include actual student answers with the amount of points that were earned to give you a better idea of what the graders expect. The student answers are immediately following the model answer for each question. Please pay close attention to the points received on each question. Although most samples represent "good" answers (i.e., received 8, 9, or 10 points), there are some samples that received 7 points (the minimum "passing" score for an essay), and a few that received very low scores to help you better understand the grading process and what is expected.

July 2001—Question 10

Suede Schuman decided to build an Elvis Presley museum in Nashville, Michigan. After procuring a satisfactory design from his architect, Delight Design Professionals, P.C., he retained Fair and Square Construction Company to build the museum. The several subcontractors hired by Fair and Square included Over the Top Roofing Company. Harold Hightower was a roofer employed by Over the Top. He had 25 years of experience as a roofer, 20 of those years with his current employer.

Over the Top had safety belts and safety lines in all of their trucks for use by their employees while working at heights as prescribed by the Michigan Occupational Safety and Health Act (MIOSHA) rules. Harold Hightower, because of his extensive experience, chose not to utilize that safety equipment.

On one or two occasions during the installation of the roof on the museum, the job site was visited by Gary Gadget, an inspector for the Department of Labor. Hightower was working on the roof on each occasion. Inspector Gadget issued no citation to any contractor on the job site during his visits.

On September 21, 2000, Hightower lost his footing, fell, and landed on Gary Fallwell, an electrician.

The accident was reported to the Department of Labor, which sent Inspector Gadget back to the site. He issued a citation against Over the Top for failing to provide its employees with a safe place to work—specifically, the failure to provide safety equipment and training to employees regarding the use thereof.

Mr. Hightower and Mr. Fallwell, unknown to each other, each make an appointment to see you on February 28, 2001. Each inquires of you regarding possible causes of action against Fair and Square, Over the Top, the Department of Labor, and Gary Gadget.

What advice do you give to Hightower, and why? What differences are there, if any, in your advice to Fallwell?

Model Answer to Question 10

The general contractor has the obligation to take reasonable steps within its supervisory and coordinating authority to guard against readily observable, avoidable dangers in common work areas which create a high degree of risk to a significant number of workers. *Fund v General Motors Corp*, 392 Mich 91 (1974). Since the failure to utilize fall protection and the risk of falling is arguably readily observable and the roof, and certainly the ground below, are likely common work areas, Hightower has a logical argument that Fair and Square would have liability for the failure to exercise its responsibility for job site safety. MCL 418.827(8).

Over the Top has an obligation under MIOSHA regulations to provide its employees with a safe place to work. However, workers' compensation is the exclusive remedy against an employer for injuries sustained in the course and scope of one's employment. (The singular exception: Intentional torts.)

The Department of Labor, as the employer, is responsible for the negligence of Gary Gadget when he is acting in the course and scope of his employment enforcing MIOSHA. However, as a governmental agency, the Department of Labor is immune from tort liability resulting from the exercise of a governmental function. Inspector Gadget is entitled to a similar immunity as long as he is acting in the course and scope of his governmental authority and function. There is an exception to the immunity of Inspector Gadget, but not for the Department of Labor as an institution, for gross negligence. Gross negligence is defined as "conduct or a failure to act that is so reckless that it demonstrates a substantial lack of concern for whether an injury will result." Michigan SJI2d 14.10. It is arguable that the failure to enforce a MIOSHA regulation which puts workers in danger constitutes gross negligence.

The answers are the same with regard to Gary Fallwell's inquiry, except that Gary Fallwell may sue Over the Top, because he was not one of its employees.

Hightower's refusal to utilize available safety devices likely constitutes comparative negligence on his part. Any recovery of Hightower against any defendant will be reduced by the percentage of total fault attributed to him. That same negligence provides the basis of liability of Hightower and, on the basis of *respondeat superior*, Over the Top to Fallwell for his injuries.

Extra Credit: A conflict of interest exists if you are retained to represent both Hightower and Fallwell and Fallwell wishes to pursue a claim against Hightower or claims negligence against Over the Top for Hightower's negligence on the basis of *respondeat superior.*

Student Answer—July 2001

Question 10—Torts/Workers' Compensation—8 points

Hightower v Over the Top

Since Hightower (H) was injured on the job during the course of his employment, the Michigan workers compensation rules would govern his recovery against his employer Over the Top.

Hightower (H) v Fair & Square (F/S)

F/S is a general contractor who has the duty to protect licensee against known open and obvious dangers—a duty of reasonable care. F/S used reasonable care in employment of the subcontractors. The safety equipment was available for use by H and it was reasonable for him to use them.

H v Dept Labor

The department of labor would have governmental immunity from any cause of action against them. Labor would be liable under vicarious liability respondeat superior theory. Employers liable for the torts of their employees.

H v Gadget (G)

Gadget would only be liable for gross negligence a willful or deliberate act which would be outside of the scope of his employment. Failure by G to issue a citation would not be a willful or deliberate act.

Fallwell (F)

The injuries to Fallwell occurred arising out of the course of employment and the Michigan workers compensation statute would govern his recovery. The only way for F to take the claim out of the workers compensation statute would be an intentional tort by the employee—gross negligence.

H could claim negligence per se in violation of the MIOSHA statute since the type of injury (H) falling is consistent with the type of harm.

F could not claim negligence per se since his injuries are not consistent with the type of harm in violation of the statute.

H and F are the same as regarding the department of labor and Gadget.

July 2001—Question 12

Samuel Powers, a California resident, operating a semi-tractor/trailer owned and registered to his employer in California, was involved in a motor vehicle accident on I-94 in Wayne County. Ohio resident Zack Morris caused the accident when he lost control of his semi-tractor/trailer, crossed the median and struck the Powers' vehicle. The Morris vehicle was owned by and registered to his Ohio employer, whose insurance carrier filed a certificate of compliance pursuant to MCL 500.3163 stating that any accidental bodily injury occurring in this state arising from the operation or use of motor vehicle by an out-of-state resident who is insured under its automobile policy will be subject to the Michigan no fault system. The insurer of the Powers' vehicle had not filed such a certification. Powers and Morris were both seriously injured in the collision.

Mr. Powers has come to you for legal advice regarding his right and liabilities, as well as the rights and liabilities of the other parties to this accident. **Advise him on the responsibility for payment of all medical bills, lost wages, pain and suffering, damages and vehicle collision damage for each of the individuals involved and their respective vehicles.**

Model Answer to Question 12

Samuel Powers: Samuel is not entitled to Michigan first-part no-fault benefits since he was not a resident of this state, and was not insured by an insurer which has filed §3163 certification. MCL 500.3113. Samuel must seek recovery of his economic damages (medical bills, wage loss, etc.) from his own insurer or that of his employer pursuant to the terms of those policies and the insurance statutes in California. He may also be entitled to workers' compensation benefits.

The collision damage to Samuel's vehicle is likewise governed by the terms of the California policy and the Michigan No-Fault Act does not apply. Samuel's employer (the owner of the damaged vehicle) is, however, entitled to pursue a "mini-tort" claim against Morris for up to $500 to the extent that the damages to Samuel's vehicle are not covered by its own insurance. MCL 500.3135(3)(d).

Regarding a third-party tort claim. Samuel Powers may maintain an action for non-economic (pain and suffering) damages against Morris arising out of this accident. Samuel should be able to show that his "serious injuries" meet the requisite tort threshold (death, serious impairment of body function, or permanent serious disfigurement) in order to recover from Morris in tort. MCL 500.3134. An out-of-state resident who is not otherwise required to purchase a no-fault policy is not necessarily precluded from seeking third-party tort recovery, even though he may not be entitled to first-party benefits.

Finally, Powers faces no tort liability from any party for his role in this accident.

Zack Morris: Since the insurer of Zack Morris' vehicle has filed §3163 certification, Zack is entitled to Michigan first-party no-fault benefits. Under personal protection insurance, an insurer is liable to pay benefits for accidental bodily injury arising out of the ownership, operation, maintenance or use of a motor vehicle as a motor vehicle. MCL 500.3105. The priorities section of the Michigan No-Fault Act states that primary responsibility for payment of first-party no-fault benefits to employees who are injured while occupying a motor vehicle owned or registered by the employer lies with the insurer of the furnished vehicle. MCL 500.3113(3). Therefore, Zack will receive economic damages from his employer's automobile insurer which would include payment of his medical bills for treatment related to the injuries he sustained in the accident, his lost wages, if any (at 85% of his wages up to the statutory maximum for the first three years), and replacement service benefits, if any (at $20 per day for the first three years). MCL 500.3107. It should be noted, however, that to the extent that Zack Morris is entitled to workers' compensation benefits for his injuries, those benefits may be "set-off" from the no-fault benefits otherwise required to be paid by the no-fault insurance carrier. MCL 500.3109 explains that "benefits provided or required to be provided under the laws of any state or the federal government shall be subtracted from the personal protection insurance benefits otherwise payable for the injury." This provision is designed to avoid the duplication of benefits.

With regard to the collision damage done to Zack's vehicle, that damage will be the responsibility of Zack's employer or its insurance carrier. Zack's (employer's) recovery of any benefits for the damage to his employer's vehicle will depend on the terms of the Ohio automobile insurance policy and the amount of coverage purchased. MCL 500.3121, .3123.

Zack may not maintain any third-party tort suit against Samuel for non-economic damages for the reason that Zack was more than 50% at fault for the accident (MCL 500.3135[2][b]) and is considered the "at fault" party. He does, however, still face tort liability to Samuel as discussed herein.

Student Answer—February 2001

Question 12—Workers' Compensation—None Available

July 2001—Question 15

Philip Thump worked as a laborer for Dilbert Candy, a sole proprietor. On May 15, 2001, after having worked through the morning at a Lansing construction site, Philip, Dilbert, and another employee, Mack Sacks, adjourned to a local tavern for lunch. Two pitchers of beer were consumed during lunch. The three men returned to the job site. A few hours later, the men returned to Dilbert's pickup truck to go to another construction site. Mack sat in the front passenger seat and Philip sat in the back open bed of the truck. Dilbert was driving erratically, hitting the brakes and swerving in and out of the lanes. Philip was eventually thrown from the bed of the truck to the pavement. The impact caused Philip to suffer a skull fracture and closed head injuries. Philip also suffers from post-traumatic stress syndrome. Every time he comes into close proximity of a pickup truck, he has convulsions.

Philip had previously ridden in the back of Dilbert's truck between seven to nine times. According to Philip, on most of those occasions, Dilbert engaged in very "erratic" driving and "enjoyed pranks, particularly watching us roll around in the back of the truck." Philip had also advised Dilbert that he did not like being thrown around in the back of the truck. Except for the injuries sustained on May 15, Philip concedes that he has never suffered any injuries while sitting in the bed of Dilbert's' truck.

You are an attorney for the law firm of Awl, Thatt & Moore, LLP. Advise Philip on his available remedies, if any, for the injuries he sustained in the accident.

Model Answer to Question 15

The injuries occurred during Philip's course of employment. An employee's claim for benefits under the Worker's Disability Compensation Act (WDCA) is his exclusive remedy against his employer for on-the-job injuries. The only exception to the exclusive remedy provision is an intentional tort by the employer. Pursuant to MCL 418.131(1), in order to establish an intentional tort by the employer, the worker must (1) prove that the employer specifically intended an injury; (2) sufficiently prove that the employer had actual knowledge that injury was certain to occur. See *Gay v Morley*, 460 Mich 738; 596 NW2d 922 (1999).

Philip should be advised that it is unlikely that he will be able to recover under the intentional tort exception to worker's compensation. Philip did not present any direct evidence that Dilbert had "specifically intended" to injure Philip nor has he demonstrated that Dilbert had "actual knowledge that an injury was certain to occur." Although Philip's allegations suggest conduct by Dilbert that was reckless or even deliberately indifferent, such allegations sound in gross negligence and are therefore insufficient to constitute an intentional tort within the meaning of the WDCA. *Gray, supra* at 744. Thus, the evidence that Dilbert drove in an erratic manner at the time of the accident, and in previous instances, is insufficient to establish an intentional tort.

Thus, Philip's recovery is limited to benefits available under the WDCA, including wage loss benefits and medical benefits covering physical and psychiatric injuries. Pursuant to MCL 418.301(2), in order to establish mental disability, a plaintiff must prove: (1) that he suffered mental disability; (2) that it arose out of actual events of employment, not unfounded perceptions thereof; and (3) that the event contributed to, aggravated, or accelerated the mental disability in a significant manner. See *Gardner v VanBuren Public Schools*, 445 Mich 23; 517 NW2d 1 (1993). Provided Philip can show that his post-traumatic stress syndrome arose out of the automobile accident, and the accident significantly contributed to, aggravated, or accelerated the syndrome, then he will recover compensation for mental disability.

Student Answer—July 2001

Question 15—Workers' Compensation—None Available

February 2002—Question 13

Pooch Pasquale, an internationally renowned expert in canine psychology and the author of a recently published book titled *Bad Dog Is as Bad Dog Does*, was asked by Yippy Skippy Chow'n'More, Inc. (YSC), a large pet supplies corporation subject to Michigan Worker's Compensation Act, to judge its annual Li'l Dogs Competition. Pooch, anxious to promote his book and happy to serve in such a prestigious capacity, agreed to judge the event in exchange for a one-year pass to the Lhasa Apso Wax Museum, a lifetime supply of Cat-Be-Gone spray, and all the beef-flavored coffee and donuts he could consume during the event.

On the day of the competition, Pooch was munching on YSC-provided beef-flavored donuts and scoring contestants in the Most Fashionable Sweater category when he was viciously attacked by a French poodle named Fang, rendering him totally and permanently disabled. An investigation revealed that, the day before the event, YSC's chief operating officer had circulated an internal memo stating that, although Fang had seriously injured the judge in last year's Li'l Dogs Competition and was "certain to attack again", he was nevertheless going to be permitted to compete in this year's event because he was "so darn cute." The memo recommended that YSC personnel attending the event carry with them YSC-brand Poodle Stop-'n'-Spray as a precautionary measure.

Pooch filed a tort claim against YSC in Oakland circuit court seeking damages for medical expenses, pain and suffering, and mental distress stemming from his injuries. Pooch alleges that YSC knew that Fang was trained to kill and that YSC should have warned him that Fang had a particular propensity for attacking people in possession of meat-filled pastry.

You are an attorney at Belvedere, Beaurigard, and Champ, LLP, the firm hired to represent Pooch in this litigation. YSC has filed a motion for summary disposition, contending that the Worker's Disability Compensation Act provides Pooch's sole remedy for his injuries. How will you oppose YSC's motion?

Model Answer to Question 13

Michigan's Worker's Disability Compensation Act (WDCA), MCL 418.101 *et seq.*, requires that employers provide compensation to employees for injuries suffered in the course of an employee's employment, regardless of fault. MCL 418.301; *Hoste v Shanty Creeek Mgt, Inc*, 459 Mich 561, 570 (1999). In return for this almost automatic liability, an employee's claim for benefits under the WDCA is his exclusive remedy against his employer for on-the-job duties. MCL 418.131; *Hoste, supra* at 570. The only exception to the exclusive remedy provision is an intentional tort, which exists only when an employee is injured as a result of a deliberate act of the employer and the employer specifically intended an injury. MCL 418.131(1); *Gray v Morley*, 460 Mich 738, 741-742 (1999).

A threshold question is whether Pooch was YSC's "employee" at the time of his injury and thus subject to the WDCA's exclusive remedy provision. Under §161(1) of the Act, "employee" is defined, in pertinent part, as including "[e]very person in the service of another, under any contract of hire, express or implied" and "[e]very person performing service in the course of the trade, business, profession, or occupation of an employer at the time of the injury." In determining whether an individual is an employee under §161(1), courts generally apply an "economic reality" test, which includes such factors as whether the individual may be terminated at will; whether the individual furnishes his own equipment and supplies; whether the individual primarily depends upon the job for payment of his living expenses; and whether the employer has control over the individual.

In order to receive benefits under the WDCA, it is not enough for an individual to be employed pursuant to a "contract"; rather, he must be employed pursuant to a contract "of hire," under which he receives payment intended as wages. This does not include "payment" in the form of gratuities or privileges that serve merely as accommodations. *Hoste, supra* at 573-575.

Applying these principles, Pooch was not YSC's "employee" for purposes of the WDCA. The "job" was a one-time event upon which Pooch was not dependent for payment of his living expenses and YSC apparently exerted little control over him. Furthermore, Pooch was not operating under a "contract of hire" at all, but instead was merely a volunteer. The privileges he received in exchange for his services as judge were not payment intended as wages, but only as accommodations or gratuities. Because Pooch was not YSC's "employee," but rather an individual assisting another with a view toward furthering his own interests, he would not be entitled to benefits under the WDCA, and is thus not subject to the exclusive remedy provision.

Moreover, Pooch's attorney should argue that, even if Pooch were YSC's employee, his injury falls within the "intentional tort" exception to the WDCA's exclusive remedy provision. An employer is deemed to have intended to injure if the employer had actual knowledge that an injury was certain to occur and willfully disregarded that knowledge. MCL 418.131(1). Thus, under §1313(1), a plaintiff must show that the employer deliberately acted or failed to act while possessing either of the following states of mind: (1) the employer acted with the purpose of inflicting injury upon the employee, or (2) the employer had actual knowledge that injury was certain to occur and willfully disregarded that knowledge. See *Travis, supra; Palazzola v Karmazin Products Corp*, 223 Mich App 141 (1997). When the employer is a corporation, a plaintiff must establish that a supervisor or managerial employee has the requisite intent. *Travis, supra* at 171-174.

Although the threshold for establishing an intentional tort is very rigorous, and although Pooch may not be able to overcome this burden, there is at least some evidence in this case that arguably tends to show that an intentional tort occurred. There is evidence that YSC employees knew that Fang had seriously injured someone at last year's event. The internal memo is arguably evidence that YSC's chief operating officer had actual knowledge that injury was certain to occur and willfully disregarded that knowledge. Thus, Pooch's attorney should make this alternative argument.

Student Answer—February 2002

Question 13—Workers' Compensation—7 points

The issue is whether Pooch only has a claim arising under the workers disability compensation act.

In Michigan workers compensation is provided to an employee who sustained an injury or disease while performing his job.

Although workers compensation is available to most employees there are some exceptions to people that are covered under workers compensation. One of those exceptions is an independent contractor. In this case Pooch is analogous to an independent contractor because he was approached by YSC to provide them a service of hosting a dog show. He was not regularly employed by YSC.

Since Pooch is an independent contractor & independent contractors are excluded by the workers compensation act, Pooch can sue YSC in tort. Pooch is allowed to sue in tort but he must prove the elements of his case. Pooch would not sue in tort & make a claim against the workers compensation plan of YSC. So even if Pooch is not an independent contractor he can still choose to sue in tort but not under both theories.

Comment: This is not a very good answer, but it is a good example of what constitutes a passing score of 7 points. This individual correctly identified the issues and provided very skimpy basic definitions, but did very little in terms of analysis (application of the rules to the facts). Hence, only 7 points were awarded.

July 2002—Question 2

Jack Bauer is an employee of Fox Builders, a real estate developer and general contractor. David Palmer is an employee of 24/7 Plumbing Company. On the morning of June 1, 2002, the two men met at the Fox Builders headquarters and Mr. Bauer agreed to give Mr. Palmer a ride to the Fox construction site, where Mr. Palmer was to inspect the construction and provide Fox Builders with a bid for a plumbing subcontract.

Mr. Bauer drove a pick-up truck owned by Fox, with Mr. Palmer as his front seat passenger, on County Road 17 in Swamp County, Michigan. The road is maintained by the Swamp County Road Commission. As they approached a sharp curve, a bright yellow road sign was posted, advising of the approaching curve and with a curve advisory speed of 35 miles per hour. Mr. Bauer was operating the vehicle at approximately 35 m.p.h. as they approached the curve, but he did not see the sign since he was adjusting stations on the radio. Nevertheless, Jack Bauer returned his full attention to the roadway prior to actually entering the curve. As the vehicle rounded the curve, Mr. Bauer was unable to negotiate the curve because of his speed, lost control, and the truck careened off the roadway into a field. Both men suffered significant injuries, requiring hospitalization, prolonged medical treatment and lost time from work. Upon further investigation by law enforcement officials and experts for the road Commission, it was determined that the curve could only be safely negotiated at speeds of 25 m.p.h. or less.

David Palmer, a Michigan resident, has come to you for legal advice regarding his rights arising out of this accident. Provide a discussion of all courses of legal action available to Mr. Palmer for all damages he sustained in this accident.

Model Answer to Question 2

David Palmer will first receive his worker's disability compensation benefits from the workers' compensation insurance carrier for his employer, 24/7 plumbing Company, since his injuries "arose out of and in the course of employment." MCL 418.301. These workers' compensation benefits include payment for all medical, rehabilitation and treatment bills associated with the injuries he sustained as a result of this accident, MCL 418.315, as well as his lost wages, calculated at 80% of the after-tax value ("net") of his weekly wages, which continue indefinitely so long as he is out of work. MCL 418.301.

In addition to these workers' compensation benefits, David is entitled to limited benefits under the Michigan No-Fault Automobile Insurance Act, MCL 500.3101, *et seq.*, since the injuries he sustained arose "out of the ownership, operation, maintenance, or use of a motor vehicle as a motor vehicle." MCL 500.3114, states that David Palmer must first seek benefits from his own personal No Fault carrier (where he is the named insured) and then from any policies issued to David's spouse or resident relatives. MCL 500.3114(1). Only if there are still no available policies does David Palmer collect no-fault benefits from the insurer of the owner of the vehicle in which he was a passenger. MCL 500.3114(4). Davis is not required to establish that he suffered a "threshold injury"' MCL 500.313, in order to receive first-party no fault benefits.

All amounts received by David Palmer in workers' compensation benefits may be subtracted or "set off" from the no-fault benefits otherwise payable for his injuries. MCL 500.3109. Since all of his medical bills are paid by the workers' compensation carrier, none are the responsibility of the no-fault insurance carrier. However, under no-fault, David would otherwise be entitled to 85% of his gross wages for the first three years after the accident. MCL 500.3107(1)(b). Accordingly, the no-fault carrier may only set-off the amount of wage loss paid by the worker's compensation between 80% of the net wages (paid by worker's compensation) and 85% of the gross wages (the full amount available under no-fault). MCL 500.3107(1)(b). Finally, the no-fault carrier is still responsible for payment of replacement/household service expenses, at a maximum of $20 per day for the first three years after the accident, reasonably incurred by David in obtaining services he would have performed for himself or his dependents had he not been injured. MCL 500.3107(1)(c).

As to any third-party tort claims, David Palmer may not maintain an action for damages against the Swamp County Road Commission arising out of this accident. According to the Supreme Court ruling in *Nawrocki v Macomb County Road Commission*, 463 Mich 143 (200), the "highway exception" to governmental immunity does not impose a duty to install, maintain, repair, or improve traffic control devices, which are not considered part of the "highway." With regard to this area of the law, however, there are still arguments which may be made that an individual employee of the road commission may be found liable for an act of gross negligence related to the placement of the improper signage. This is still an unsettled area of the law, however.

One may also argue that David Palmer may have a tort claim against Jack Bauer for the negligent operation of a motor vehicle. In order to do so, David will be required to establish that he has suffered a "threshold injury" meaning that he has suffered a "serious impairment of a body function" or "permanent serious disfigurement." MCL 500.3135. Under the present circumstances, however, there is no indication that Jack Bauer's inattention to the signage had anything to do with the accident. In fact, even if Bauer had been looking at the sign, he was not traveling over the posted advisory speed limit. The facts show no other evidence of negligence on the part of Jack Bauer and David Palmer will have a difficult time making his proofs on proximate cause against Bauer.

The following are additional aspects to this factual scenario which are not essential to the basic understanding of the rights of the parties involved. Should an examinee spot these issues, however, credit should be given as appropriate:

1. Any property damage which occurred to the field where the vehicle came to rest is the responsibility of the no-fault carrier of the Fox Builder's truck. (MCL 500.3121.)
2. Any collision damage to the vehicle itself is the responsibility of Fox Builder's no-fault carrier, to the extent that this coverage was purchased and according to the terms of the no-fault contract. Collision damage coverage is an option which may be purchased for a higher premium, but is not required under the Michigan No-Fault Code.
3. If Palmer was able to somehow sustain a claim against Bauer, he could also make a claim against Fox Builders (the owner for the vehicle involved) under the Michigan Owners Civil Liability Act, MCL 257.401, and under the common law theory of negligent entrustment of a motor vehicle.
4. Nevertheless, should Palmer realize any recovery in tort for his injuries, he is required by the Worker's Compensation Act, MCL 418.827(5) to first reimburse his employer or insurance carrier for any amounts paid to him in workers' compensation benefits out of the proceeds of the tort action.

Student Answer—February 2003

Question 2—Workers' Compensation—None Available

July 2003—Question 2

Wally Washington was a door-to-door salesman for the Emperor Entryway Emporium, a large door manufacturer in the Detroit area. His work often required him to travel out of the local area to make client calls.

On April 11, 2003, Wally was in Traverse City, Michigan on assignment. On the first day of his assignment, he made his normal client contacts when an unexpected storm passed through town. Wally went into the Lucky Loon Tavern to wait for the storm to pass. The storm lasted about ninety minutes. However, Wally spent the remainder of the day in the Lucky Loon, where he played darts, shot pool and drank beer.

Around 8:30 p.m., Wally tripped over a parking beam while walking back to his motel. He suffered a concussion as well as a badly fractured ankle. A test administered at the hospital revealed that Wally's blood alcohol level was 0.18%.

As a result of the fractured ankle, Wally is unable to perform his duties as a door-to-door salesman. He contacts your law firm, Harry, Schmoe & Shurly, LLP, inquiring about possible worker's compensation disability benefits.

Advise Wally Washington on his available worker's compensation remedies, if any, for the injuries he sustained in the incident. Please limit your discussion to worker's compensation only.

Model Answer to Question 2

Wally Washington will be unable to collect worker's compensation benefits. Under the Worker's Disability Compensation Act, an employee is entitled to receive compensation benefits if he "receives a personal injury arising out of and in the course of employment" by an employer who is subject to the act. MCL 418.301(1).

An employee who suffers an injury arising out of and in the course of employment is eligible for compensation benefits regardless whether the employer was at fault for the injury. In return, the employer is immunized from tort liability, except in narrow circumstances. MCL 418.131.

As a traveling employee, Wally was within the scope of his employment on the trip to Traverse City. Workers are presumed to be in the course of employment in many circumstances, including traveling to and from work (MCL 418.301[3]). However, where the injury occurs "in the pursuit of an activity the major purpose of which is social or recreational," the injury is not covered under the act.

In considering whether §301(3) is applicable, the focus is on the major purpose of the activity the injured worker was engaged in at the time of the injury. If the major purpose was social or recreational, benefits are precluded.

At the time of the accident, Wally had concluded a several hour span of playing darts, shooting pool, and drinking beer. While Wally was unable to work during the storm, he chose not to resume working after the storm passed. Because the major purpose of Wally's activities was social or recreational, Wally will be unable to collect benefits under the Worker's Compensation Act. See *Eversman v Concrete Cutting & Breaking*, 463 Mich 86 (2000).

Three Student Answers—July 2003

Question 2—Workers' Compensation—9 points

Worker's Compensation and Disability Act applies to all injuries sustained while in the course of employment. The employee must be an employee and not an independent contractor. Injuries incurred while in the scope of employment are covered. Injuries must be reported within the statutory period or shortly after injury was discovered. The remedies to worker's comp are only remedies available to employee who incurred injury while within scope of work unless the cause of injury is outside the scope of employment.

In this case, Wally Washington (Wally) suffered an injury that renders him unable to perform his duties as a door to door salesman, this injury is the type of injury covered but there must be a causal relationship between injury and employment.

Wally will have a hard time arguing that injury arose out of employment. Why? Because he abandoned work that day. He started out the day within the scope of employment thus he was covered from the point of travel to client's sales calls. He would have even been covered through storm if he continued to work past storm. He would have been covered but he abandoned his work purpose when he deviated greatly and abandoned work. He would not be able to recover.

He would also have to prove that he was an employee and not a contractor. Crt. would look at whether he was hired on to work permanently, whether company dictated how business was performed or whether he decided, if there was a contract for specific work. If he was a contractor act doesn't apply.

Question 2—Workers' Compensation—9 points

In order to obtain workers compensation benefits we must be able to show that Mr. Washington was working while he suffered his injury. The facts tell us that Mr. Washington spent a good part of his day in the Lucky Loon tavern. While he did conduct some business activity the morning of the incident, he spent the remainder of the day drinking beer—probably not something that is considered one of his job duties. While there may be times that having a drink with a client will be within the scope of employment that is probably not the case here. The facts do not tell us that Mr. Washington was conducting any business while at the bar and while he was sent to Traverse City on a business trip—activities. His conduct can fall outside the scope of employment. Under the idea of detour and folic an employee is be making a quick stop to do some banking. This is something that is foreseeable so this type of behavior falls under the scope of employment as a detour. However, under the facts we are given here Mr. Washington is likely to be considered to be on a frolic. These incidents fall outside the scope of employment. Here the employee does that is unforeseeable and well outside his employment duties. If Mr. Washington would have simply waited out the rain then went back to work this would have been a much closer case. But because he remained at the bar after the rain had stopped and continued to drink beer he was outside the scope of employment therefore workers compensation benefits will not be available to him.

Question 2—Workers' Compensation—8 points

Under the Workers Disability Compensation Act (WDCA), WDCA benefits are the employee's exclusive remedy if the employee suffers an injury or disease while acting within the course and scope of his employment. The employee is entitled to 80% of his after-tax wage loss as long as he remains out of work, vocational/rehabilitation services and physical and psychiatric care.

The first issue in this workers compensation question is whether Wally was still considered to be acting within the course and scope of his employment when he entered the tavern or whether he was on a frolic. A frolic is a substantial deviation from the employee's job such that he is considered as acting outside the scope of his employment. On these facts, Wally would argue that he was merely on a detour, which is a slight deviation from one's job and thus he entered the tavern and sustained his injuries afterwards while still acting within the course and scope of his employment. The defense, Emperor, Wally's employer would argue that Wall was either on a frolic because one does not go to a bar to drink and play pool while acting as a door-to-door salesman or that his job had already ended for the day because after Wally left the bar he was injured while walking back to his motel. The defense has a good argument here because it was 8:30 at night when he was injured and even though there was a storm that held him up from working, most salesmen would not continue going door-to-door at this time of night.

Therefore, based on the reasons above, I would advise Wally that he probably does not have a good case for WDCA benefits and that his sole remedy, if any, might be with the Lucky Loon Tavern.

February 2004—Question 7

Prentiss Pennick, disillusioned by the practice of law, decided instead to work as a crane operator for the Dempster Demolition Company. On October 20, 2003, Pennick injured his right wrist while operating the main hoist of the crane. After the required surgery was performed and rehabilitation was completed, Pennick was left with limited mobility in his wrist. He was unable to resume his work as a crane operator.

Dempster Demolition Company voluntarily paid worker's compensation benefits during the period of surgery and rehabilitation, but refused to continue to pay wage loss benefits when Pennick was unable to return to work as a crane operator. Pennick filed a timely claim with the Worker's Compensation Bureau, seeking weekly wage loss benefits.

At the compensation hearing, plaintiff asserted that he was entitled to compensation benefits because he was disabled, as evidenced by his inability to return to work as a crane operator.

You are the attorney representing the Dempster Demolition Company. **What is the strongest counter-argument you can make to the magistrate regarding Pennick's entitlement to weekly wage loss benefits?**

Model Answer to Question 7

The strongest argument Dempster Demolition can make is that Prentiss Pennick is not "disabled" for the purposes of the Worker's Disability Compensation Act (WDCA) because he has suffered no limitation in his wage earning capacity. Because Pennick is not disabled, he is not entitled to weekly wage loss benefits.

Disability is statutorily defined, MCL 418.301(4):

> "[D]isability" means a limitation of an employee's wage earning capacity in work suitable to his or her qualifications and training resulting from personal injury or work related disease. The establishment of disability does not create a presumption of wage loss.

Therefore, Pennick is disabled only if he has suffered a limitation in his wage earning capacity in work suitable to his qualifications and training. In *Sington v Chrysler Corporation*, 467 Michigan 144 (2002), the Court held that "capacity" meant "maximum output or producing ability." Therefore, Pennick would suffer a compensable disability if his wrist injury resulted in a reduction of his maximum wage earning ability in work suitable to his qualifications and training.

In order to determine whether Pennick has suffered a diminished maximum wage earning ability, it must be ascertained what types of jobs are within Pennick's qualifications and training, and whether those jobs pay as much as he earned working as a crane operator. Even if Pennick was determined to be completely disabled as a crane operator, he would not be considered disabled for the purposes of the WDCA if he were able to perform an equally well-paying job suitable to his qualifications and training.

In this case, at least one of the jobs within Pennick's qualifications and training is that of a lawyer. If Pennick's wrist injury does not prevent him from working as a lawyer, and if his wages as a lawyer would be at least as much as he would earn working as a crane operator, he would not be considered disabled and would not be entitled to weekly wage loss benefits.

Student Answer—July 2004

Question 7—Workers' Compensation—9 points

The strongest argument for Dempster Demolition Company is that Pennick's training as a lawyer gives him skills to seek employment making higher wages, generally, than a crane operator.

The purpose of weekly wage loss benefits is to compensate an employee who is unable to return to work in another capacity. This is designed to make up for the difference between the wages in the new position versus the wages in the previous position.

Pennick's wrist injury prevents him from operating a crane but won't prevent him from practicing law. He can return to work as a lawyer and should not suffer a wage loss thereby defeating his claim for wage loss benefits.

Comment: Although this student response is brief, it answers the call of the question, provides an appropriate application of the facts to the law, and reaches the right conclusion. This response would have received 10 points if it provided the definition of "disability" under the WDCA.

July 2004—Question 3

Skippy Sloth has worked as an accountant for Ace Accounting Company for the past eight years. Skippy weighs 320 pounds, smokes two packs of cigarettes per day and subsists on fast food, pizza and beer. On April 12, 2004, Skippy had a heart attack while preparing tax returns. The heart attack left Skippy unable to return to work as an accountant.

Skippy retained a local attorney and filed a claim for worker's compensation wage loss benefits, claiming that the heart attack left him totally disabled.

You are a first-year associate working at Lee & Yee, the law firm representing Ace Accounting Company. A partner has asked you to prepare a memo outlining the correct legal principles applicable to this case as well as Skippy's chances of prevailing on the merits.

Model Answer to Question 3

In order to establish entitlement to worker's compensation benefits, Skippy Sloth must prove that he has suffered "a personal injury arising out of and in the course of employment." MCL 418.301(1).

However, under MCL 418.301(2), mental disabilities and conditions of the aging process, including "heart and cardiovascular conditions," are compensable if the employment contributes to, aggravates, or accelerates the condition "in a significant manner."

Certainly, Skippy Sloth's weight, smoking and dietary habits are factors that contributed to his heart attack. However, if his work as an accountant aggravated or contributed to his heart attack "in a significant manner," then he can collect benefits, his lifestyle choices notwithstanding.

It is certainly possible that the stress of preparing tax returns during tax season maybe aggravated or accelerated Skippy Sloth's heart attack. It is unclear, however, that his employment contributed to his heart attack "in a significant manner." This will be a question of fact for the magistrate to decide.

Student Answer—July 2004

Question 3—Workers' Compensation—8 points

Workers compensation allows covered employees of covered employers to receive benefits if the employee has an injury or disease that disables the employee and the injury or disease must be work related.

Injuries that are work related are usually easy issues, e.g. broken arm, pulled muscle, etc. A work related disease is more difficult, but they may include things like black lung, or asbestos.

If the employee is disabled for more than a week he is qualified for workman's compensation benefits.

However, there is a trade off. The employee receives benefits but cannot sue the employer for the injury. The employer does have the right to retain the employee or give them a job that they can do. Workman Compensation benefits do have limits. The employee's pay caps at 85% but not higher than $4,000 a week for a high income earner.

In this case we are told Skippy worked as an account for Ace accounting company for 8 years. Skippy had a heart attack while preparing tax returns and has filed for workman's compensation.

A heart attack is not a typical injury or disease found in a work place. However, it does not rule out workman's compensation but Skippy will have to prove that the work he performed is the cause of his heart attack. He will have to significant stress to cause a heart attack.

Although in Skippy's case it will be more difficult because he weighs 320 pounds, he is a heavy smoker—2 pack a day, he eats fast food, pizza and drank beer.

However, if Skippy can show the heart attack was work related, he will be entitled to workman's compensation.

Comment: The last three paragraphs were the key to getting the 8 points. Please note that this response incorrectly states the wage loss benefit under Workers Compensation at 85%. It is 80%.

February 2005—Question 13

Patty Pompadour was a renowned hair stylist at Dapper Dan's Salon. Patty was a temperamental artist, and became upset whenever a client did not share Patty's artistic vision. One day, Patty gave a new customer, Betty Beyer, an elaborate hairstyle for an upcoming holiday event. The hairstyle, entitled "Christmas Enchantment," included a working string of twinkling lights, a dozen candy canes, and a large illuminated star. When Betty saw the finished hairdo, she became irate, threw the star across the salon, and left the salon without paying. Crestfallen, Pompadour ran out of the salon weeping uncontrollably.

Patty Pompadour never returned to the salon. Pompadour retained a local attorney and filed a claim for worker's compensation wage loss benefits, claiming to be totally disabled. Pompadour's treating physician believes that Patty's debilitating depression was caused by the extreme humiliation and stress suffered that day. The salon retained its own expert, who opined that Patty's depression stemmed from her longstanding narcissistic personality disorder.

You are a first-year associate working at Vangel & Tomché, the law firm hired by Dapper Dan's insurance carrier to represent the salon. A partner has asked you to prepare a memo outlining the correct legal principles applicable to this case as well as Pompadour's chances of prevailing on the merits.

Model Answer to Question 13

In order to establish entitlement to worker's compensation benefits, Patty Pompadour must prove that she has suffered "a personal injury arising out of and in the course of employment." MCL 418.301(1). However, under MCL 418.301(2), mental disabilities are compensable only if the employment contributes to, aggravates, or accelerates the condition "in a significant manner." In addition, mental disabilities are compensable only when they arise "out of actual events of employment, not unfounded perceptions thereof."

In *Robertson v Daimler Chrysler*, 465 Mich 732 (2002), the Court held that, to satisfy the mental disability requirements of 301(2), a claimant must demonstrate that (a) an actual employment event led to the claimed mental disability and (b) the claimant's perception of the employment event was grounded in fact or reality, not delusion. In analyzing the claimant's perception, the magistrate must apply an *objective* standard to the employment event and determine how a reasonable person would have perceived the event under like circumstances.

The first prong of the *Robertson* test has been met because the claimed disabling employment event—the scene that erupted after the elaborate coiffure was revealed to Betty Beyer—*actually* occurred. Moreover, in evaluating Pompadour's perception, the magistrate will have to determine whether a reasonable person would have perceived the altercation as stressful and humiliating. In this instance, it is certainly plausible that a reasonable person would have found the event to be humiliating and stressful.

Assuming that Patty successfully meets the two prongs of the *Robertson* test, the statute also requires that Patty prove her employment contributed to her debilitating depression "in a significant manner." Given the opposing testimony of the expert witnesses, this will be a question of fact for the magistrate to decide.

Student Answer—February 2005

Question 13—Workers' Compensation—8 points

To: Supervising Partner
From: 1st Year Associate
Re: Dapper Dan; Patty Pompadour

Workers' Compensation; Psychiatric Disorder; Total Disability

PP's claim must be denied on the merits.

The applicable law as it related to this case is the Michigan Workers Disability and Compensation Act (MWDCA) as it specifically applies to psychiatric disorders and total disabilities.

The MWDCA is the *exclusive remedy* for an employee injured within the course and scope of their employment. In order to receive MWDCA benefits, the employee must prove (1) they are an employee; (2) of an employer subject to the MWDCA; (3) that they suffer from a personal injury or occupational disease; (4) that both arise out of and occurred within the course and scope of their employment; (5) that they have a disability under MWDCA; and (6) that they have suffered a related wage loss.

According to the facts of record, Patty Pompadour (PP) was a stylist (therefore an employee of) Dapper Dan's (DD) salon and that DD carries worker's compensation insurance (proof that he is subject to the MWDCA).

However, there is some dispute as to whether PP suffered from a personal injury or occupational disease. An occupational disease arises out of the conditions *"particular"* to the employer's work while a personal injury arises out of an event. However, in order for a psychiatric disorder (debilitating depression) to be covered under the MWDCA PP must prove (1) that she suffers from the psychiatric disorder; (2) that it stems from an event that occurred in connection with their employment and that the event actually happened; (2) that the employee's perception of the event is grounded in fact or reality instead of imagination or delusion; (3) and the event aggravated or accelerated the disorder in a *significant manner.*

According to the facts of record, there is a conflict as to the existence of PP's debilitating depression. While PP's own treating physician believes her depression was caused by extreme humiliation suffered at work; our own expert believes that her depression derives from other, non-work related services. PP is claiming that the cause of her depression *did* occur during working hours, while she was performing her required duties; therefore the connection between work and the disability may be established. The MWDCA also requires that PP's perception of the event be grounded in fact.

According to the facts of record, after Betty Beyer expressed her disapproval of the hairdo, PP ran out of the shop weeping uncontrollably and has not returned to work. Frankly, it is not that serious. PP's perception of the event is overblown and based on her own delusions of grandeur (or the lack thereof).

Lastly, the act of requires that the event contribute to the disability in a *significant manner.* Betty Beyer's rejection of PP's hair do was heated but did not rise to the level of so extreme or outrageous as to cause or aggravate a pre-existing mental disorder in any significant manner. Inherent in PP's profession is the possibility of rejection and the current rejection does not rise to any notable significance as to cause a mental break.

Therefore, in accordance with the foregoing analysis, PP lacks the requirement of a personal injury or occupation disease as required to receive benefits under the MWDCA. Therefore she has no disability or related wage loss because she has not been working because she has not wanted to, not because of a disability or injury under the MWDCA. The MWDCA does not award benefits for bruised ego or hurt feeling and PP's claim must be denied on the merits.

> **Comment:** This is a good answer. The main missing component that prevented a perfect score was the failure to discuss the "objective" standard in viewing the event. Also, this student reached a definitive conclusion. If you are unsure how a court will conclude, state that and don't commit. Instead, you could say, "the court will likely decide . . ."

July 2005—Question 14

Waldo Wiggams was employed by the Motley Maintenance Corporation, a large corporation with offices located all across the state. One day Waldo was assigned to a crew cleaning up a factory prior to renovation. Ben Boss, the maintenance crew leader, instructed Waldo to clean a chemical holding tank. Boss did not provide Waldo with any further instructions or provide a protective jumpsuit. After working inside the tank for approximately 30 minutes, Waldo passed out. The supervisor immediately called 911. Within a few minutes, EMS arrived, pulled Waldo from the tank, and transported him to the hospital. The physician's examination revealed that Waldo had been exposed to chloramines gas. The gas was created after Waldo's cleaning solvent (bleach) was mixed with ammonia left inside the chemical holding tank. The investigation after the incident indicated that Ben Boss knew that some of the tanks at the factory contained ammonia, but forgot to pass this information along to Waldo or the rest of the work crew. Boss was also aware that the crew was given bleach to use as a cleaning solvent, but was unaware that bleach and ammonia could not be combined.

As a result of the exposure to the chloramines gas, Waldo Wiggams suffered extensive damage to his nasal passages, trachea and lungs. As a result, Waldo is completely unable to work. He requires a ventilator, oxygen, home health care and extensive therapy several times per week.

Waldo has consulted with your law firm, Huey & Plow, to determine Waldo's recourse against the Motley Maintenance Company. **Based on the preliminary information given to you by Waldo, please draft a substantive memo identifying possible bases of recovery for Waldo and his likelihood of success.**

Model Answer to Question 14

Workers' Compensation Benefits: Waldo will be able to collect workers' compensation benefits. Under MCL 418.301(1), an employee who receives a personal injury arising out of and in the course of employment can collect benefits as provided under the act. Under MCL 418.301(4), an employee is "disabled" if he suffers a limitation in his wage-earning capacity in work suitable to his qualifications and training resulting from a work-related injury. In this case, because Waldo is completely unable to return to work, he would be considered "disabled" under the act.

Tort Claim: Waldo will be unable to prevail against the Motley Maintenance Corporation. The Workers' Disability Compensation Act provides that the right to the recovery of benefits shall be the employee's exclusive remedy for a personal injury. The only exception to this exclusive remedy is an intentional tort. An intentional tort exists only when an employee is injured as a result of a deliberate act of the employer and the employer specifically intended an injury. An employer is deemed to have intended the injury if the employer had actual knowledge that an injury was certain to occur and willfully disregarded that knowledge. MCL 418.131(1).

Thus, under §131(1), a plaintiff must show that the employer deliberately acted or failed to act while possessing either of the following states of mind: (1) the employer acted with the purpose of inflicting injury upon the employee, or (2) the employer had actual knowledge that injury was certain to occur and willfully disregarded that knowledge. *See Gray v Morley*, 460 Mich 738 (1999); *Palazzola v Karmazin Products Corp*, 223 Mich App 141 (1997).

In this case, there is no evidence that Ben Boss acted with the purpose of inflicting injury on Waldo. Moreover, the facts of this case do not indicate that Ben Boss had actual knowledge that injury was certain to occur. While Ben Boss knew that some of the tanks contained ammonia, he simply forgot to convey that information. While his actions were arguably negligent, they are insufficient to establish an intentional tort. Similarly, Ben Boss may have been negligent in failing to provide Waldo with protective clothing. However, there is no evidence that a protective jumpsuit would have protected Waldo from the debilitating respiratory injuries. Moreover, there is no evidence that Ben Boss was aware of the effects of mixing the bleach and ammonia together; therefore Ben cannot be said to have had knowledge that injury to Waldo was certain to occur.

Absent evidence of an intentional tort, Waldo Wiggams' recovery is limited to those benefits provided under the Workers' Disability Compensation Act. Therefore, Waldo should be advised to pursue compensation benefits, but should be advised that a tort claim is unlikely to succeed.

Student Answer—July 2005

Question 14—Workers Compensation—10 points

In Michigan, when an employee is injured while working, he may bring a claim against his employer under the Workers Disability Compensation Act which is an insurance scheme designed to provide relief to the injured employee. To bring a claim under the WDCA, the injured person must claim they are an employee of a covered employer who was injured because of an incident that arose out of or in the commission of his employment, there must be a disability and because of the disability there must be a related wage loss. Generally, this is the exclusive remedy against the employer. However, this exclusive remedy provision does not apply if the employer committed an intentional tort against the employee. Under the WDCA, the injured person is entitled to wage loss benefits up to 85% if applicable, replacement services, if applicable up to $20/day, medical bill reimbursement, vocational rehabilitation. Here Waldo meets all of the requirements of the WDCA and therefore, he will at least be able to get WDCA benefits.

The issue becomes whether Waldo can claim that Motley Maintenance committed an intentional tort against him. Waldo will argue that since Ben Boss did not provide a protective jumpsuit or any instructions and because Boss knew some of the tanks contained ammonia and did not warn him, they intentionally caused his injury.

Boss will argue that it was not intentional, he simply forgot to warn. Boss will argue that he was unaware of the effects of mixing bleach and ammonia. Since he was not aware of the consequence, he was not intentionally harming Waldo. Boss will also argue that if he intentionally wanted Waldo to be injured, he would not have called 911.

Since the facts do not indicate that Boss acted intentionally, Waldo will not be able to bring an intentional torts claim against Motley. In conclusion, Waldo would be limited to his remedies under the WDCA.

> **Comment:** This is an excellent answer, but there is an error the grader didn't catch. WDCA only provides 80% of net wage loss, not 85%.

February 2006—Question 3

Wilma Warrington, a former Olympic medalist, had, upon retirement from competitive figure skating, become a professional skater and worked in various Ice Capades. Slick Skating Supply, a Michigan manufacturer of ice skates and skating supplies, lured Wilma away from the Ice Capades and hired her to become its spokesperson. Wilma's job required her to promote the company's products and to entertain large-chain retail buyers in the hopes that the buyers would sell Slick's merchandise in their stores.

On January 3, 2004, Slick Skating Supply sponsored a dinner for several retail buyers at the Acme Athletic Club. The event, which was widely publicized, featured Wilma as its celebrity host. The dinner included wine with every course as well as an open bar. Wilma consumed a great deal of wine during dinner while entertaining clients. After dinner concluded several hours later, Wilma took the buyers to the athletic club's ice skating rink to demonstrate the company's newest line of figure skates. While attempting to perform a Triple Lutz, Wilma fell on the ice, injuring her back and head. A blood test administered at the hospital revealed that Wilma's blood alcohol level was 0.15% at the time of the incident.

Wilma's injuries required surgery as well as a lengthy period of rehabilitation. Slick Skating Supply voluntarily paid workers' compensation medical benefits during the period of Wilma's surgery and rehabilitation, but refused to pay wage-loss benefits after rehabilitation. As a result of her injuries, Wilma is completely unable to ice skate and is no longer able to perform her duties as a spokesperson for Slick Skating Supply. She has contacted your law firm, Ginger, Mook & Dwain, LLP, inquiring about possible workers' compensation wage-loss benefits.

Discuss whether Wilma Warrington will be able to recover wage-loss benefits for the injuries she sustained at the Athletic Club.

Model Answer to Question 3

Wilma Warrington may be able to collect workers' compensation wage-loss benefits. Under the Workers' Disability Compensation Act, an employee is entitled to receive compensation benefits if he or she receives a personal injury arising out of and in the course of employment by an employer who is subject to the act. MCL 418.301(1). However, where an employee's injury occurs in the pursuit of an activity the major purpose of which is social or recreational, the injury is not covered under the Act. MCL

418.301 (3). In considering whether 301 (3) precludes benefits, the focus is on the major purpose of the activity the injured worker was engaged in at the time of the injury. If the major purpose was social or recreation, benefits are not permitted.

The major purpose of the dinner was to promote Slick Skating Supply's line of merchandise. At the time of the incident, Wilma was entertaining corporate buyers at a dinner sponsored by Slick Skating Supply. Wilma was required to attend the event, and was injured while demonstrating the company's new line of figure skates. Although the event was in some respects social, because the *major purpose* of Wilma's activities was work related rather than social or recreational, Wilma is not precluded from collecting benefits under the Workers' Disability Compensation Act. See *Eversman v Auto-Owners Ins Co*, 463 Mich 86 (2000).

In order to be entitled to weekly wage-loss benefits, Wilma must establish a "disability," which is statutorily defined by MCL 418.301(4):

> "[D]isability" means a limitation of an employee's wage-earning capacity in work suitable to his or her qualifications and training resulting from a personal injury or work-related disease. The establishment of disability does not create a presumption of wage loss.

Therefore, Wilma is disabled only if she has suffered a limitation in her wage-earning capacity in work suitable to her qualifications and training. In *Sington v Chrysler Corporation*, 467 Mich 144 (2002), the court held that "capacity" meant "maximum output or producing ability." Therefore, Wilma suffered a compensable disability if she can no longer earn her maximum wages in work suitable to her qualifications and training as a result of her back and head injuries.

In order to determine whether Wilma has suffered a diminished maximum wage-earning ability, it must be ascertained what types of jobs are within her qualifications and training, and whether those jobs pay as much as she earned working as a spokesperson for Slick Skating Supply. Even if Wilma was determined to be completely disabled as a spokesperson, she would not be considered disabled for the purposes of the WDCA if she were able to perform an equally well-paying job suitable to her qualifications and training.

The facts do not indicate whether Wilma has training or qualifications in employments other than as a skater or a spokesperson. Presuming there are no other jobs within Wilma's qualifications and training that pay as much as her spokesperson position with Slick Skating Supply, she would be "disabled" under MCL 418.301(4) and would be entitled to wage-loss benefits under the WDCA.

Two Student Answers—February 2006

Question 3—Worker's Compensation—10 Points

This is a Worker's Compensation question.

Slick Skating should provide Wilma with wage-loss benefits for her back and head injuries.

The issue is whether Wilma will be able to recover wage-loss benefits under her employer's worker's compensation.

Worker's compensation benefits are an employee's sole remedy against an employer when they are injured on the job during the course of employment. There is an exception which may allow the employee to recover under a tort theory, and that deals with the employer being liable for intentional acts that they were involved in that led to the employee's injury.

Typically, when an employee is injured the employee can recover lost wages and medical benefits. In this case both of these were paid.

In addition, wage-loss benefits are also paid if it is proven that the employee can no longer perform the duties of her job. Wages are generally paid for an extended period of time. Or if it is deemed that the employee can take another position that is still within the range of compensation formerly received, the employee will take that position.

In this case, Wilma fell on the ice injuring her back and head. The facts indicate Wilma is unable to skate and is no longer able to perform her duties as a spokesperson.

The facts don't specify the extent of Wilma's injuries so based on the assumption that she is unable to perform her duties, even after rehabilitation, Slick Skating will be responsible for wage-loss benefits.

It should be noted that even though Wilma was drinking (a great deal), her negligence in skating will not be a defense for her employer. Entertaining and skating were the basis of her employment.

Question 3—Workers' Compensation—8 points

Issue #1: Whether Wilma can recover wage-loss benefits from Slick Skating supply?

Under Michigan's Workers Compensation Act, any person who is injured while working has an exclusive remedy of Workers Compensation Benefits. These benefits includes payment of all related medical bills, all rehabilitation expenses, wage-loss at 85% of current wages for up to three years and home service care at $20 a day for three years.

Here, since Wilma was injured at work. During her spokesperson duties which included figure skating and promoting products she is entitled to wage-loss benefits at 85% of her wages for up to three years.

Skate supply would argue that after rehabilitation of her injuries, that Wilma was not hurt anymore and that their liability was extinguished.

Wilma would counter that she has the right to perform the same or substantially similar job doing the same duties as before. Since Wilma could not skate anymore (which was part of her job) she is still due wage-loss until her three year period is finished.

> **Comment:** This is an excellent answer and would be a 10 if it weren't so brief and if it didn't incorrectly state the wage loss benefit (it's 80% of net wages, not 85%). This examinee identified the issues and gave the correct rules, but did very little application of the facts. Hence only an 8 was assigned instead of a 10.

July 2006—Question 8

After working many years as a commodities broker, Peter Pious decided to pursue his lifelong dream of becoming a rodeo clown. He took a job with the Downsville Dandy Rodeo, a local Michigan rodeo with four dozen employees. Peter became Clappy the Cowboy Clown, replete with spurs, holster and a water pistol. After several months on the job, Peter was injured when an angry two-ton bull annihilated Peter's clown barrel and trampled him, resulting in a concussion, three broken ribs, a broken hand and a dislocated jaw. It is uncontested that, as a result of his injuries, Peter can no longer work as a rodeo clown.

Downsville Dandy Rodeo paid Peter worker's compensation benefits while Peter was recuperating from his injuries, but ceased paying benefits after he fully recovered. Peter filed a timely claim with the Worker's Compensation Bureau, seeking weekly wage loss benefits. At the compensation hearing, Peter asserted that he was entitled to compensation benefits because he was disabled, as evidenced by his inability to return to work as a rodeo clown.

You are an associate at Melton, Ryan and Jeffrey, the law firm representing the Downsville Dandy Rodeo. What is the strongest argument you can make to the magistrate that Peter Pious is not entitled to weekly wage loss benefits?

Model Answer to Question 8

The strongest argument Downsville Dandy Rodeo can make is that Peter Pious is not disabled for the purposes of the Workers Disability Compensation Act (WDCA), because he has suffered no limitation in his maximum wage-earning capacity. Because Peter Pious is not disabled for the purposes of the statute, he is not entitled to weekly wage loss benefits.

Disability is statutorily defined, MCL 418.301(4):

> "Disability" means a limitation of an employee's wage earning capacity in work suitable to his or her qualifications and training resulting from personal injury or work-related disease. The establishment of disability does not create the presumption of wage loss.

Peter Pious is disabled only if he has suffered a limitation in his wage-earning capacity in work suitable to his qualifications and training. In *Sington v Chrysler Corporation*, 467 Mich 144 (2002), the Court held that "capacity" meant "maximum output or producing ability." Therefore, Peter suffers a compensable disability only if his injuries result in a reduction of his maximum wage-earning ability in work suitable to his qualifications and training.

In order to determine whether Peter has suffered a diminished maximum wage-earning ability, it must be ascertained what types of jobs are within Peter's qualifications and training, and whether those jobs pay as much as he earned as a rodeo clown. Even if Peter was determined to be completely disabled as a rodeo clown, he would not be considered disabled for the purposes of the WDCA if he were able to perform an equally well-paying job that was suitable to his qualifications and training.

In this case, at least one of the jobs within Peter's qualifications and training is that of a commodities broker. If Peter's injuries do not prevent him from working as a commodities broker, and if his wages as a commodities broker would at least be as much as he would earn working as a rodeo clown, he would not be considered disabled and would not be entitled to weekly wage-loss benefits.

Two Student Answers—July 2006

Question 8—Worker's Compensation—10 points

This is a worker's compensation question.

Worker's compensation is an exclusive remedy, when available, for Peter Pious (P) to recover against his employer.

The strongest argument that P not be entitled to weekly wage loss benefits is that P is not totally prohibited from seeking employment but only that as a rodeo clown. He has the prerequisite skill to perform as a commodities broker as he did for many years prior to becoming a clown. Therefore as a denial of his weekly wage loss benefits he will not be precluded from earning a living.

The purpose of weekly wage loss benefit would be to sustain if no longer could obtain gainful employment in any capacity. Or, he could obtain the benefit while he was being trained to seek gainful employment. However, since he has the training and has worked for many years as a commodities broker, he should not qualify for the weekly wage loss benefit based on his ability to earn a wage in another employment.

Question 8—Worker's Comp—8 points

Under WDCA, an employee injured in the scope of and during course of employment is entitled to WDCA as an exclusive remedy. The only exception is the intentional tort.

Here, Peter was working as a rodeo clown & was injured by a bull.

On the other hand the DDR could argue that Peter is really a commodities broker, because he worked many years as one. They could say that he only worked for several months, not years, as he did in his other job.

However, WDCA covers employees if disabled from the job they were doing. A person is disabled if they can no longer work doing what they were doing. It has nothing to do with the fact that he could do something else. So, Peter was a clown—he was injured. He can no longer be a clown, because he is disabled.

On the other hand DDR can say that Peter is fully recovered, so where he can be a clown, there are other duties at the rodeo he can perform. Where Peter would have to take the other job. Peter can argue that because it was his dream that's all he can or will do. Therefore, he will not be entitled to wage loss benefits if there is suitable work for him by the employer.

February 2007—Question 12

George M. Dallas, vice president of Polk Enterprises, made reservations for an evening seminar on developments in the law concerning employee relations presented by the law firm of Mason, Clifford & Toucey, P.C. Dallas urged two supervisors in one of his plants—Nathan Clifford and George Bancroft—to attend the seminar. Both agreed.

The day of the seminar, the two left work a bit early, went home and changed and met to drive together in Clifford's car. However, they never arrived at the seminar because, while driving there, Clifford crashed into a tree after hitting a pothole. Clifford died from a head injury at the scene. Bancroft was physically unharmed, but sought mental health care due to watching Clifford die.

Bancroft eventually obtained a job elsewhere as a supervisor for less pay rather than return to Polk, because returning to Polk only reminded him of Clifford's death.

Can Bancroft receive any workers' disability compensation benefits? Explain your answer.

Model Answer to Question 12

Concerning the relationship between the automobile accident and the employment, a complete answer should recognize that the standard is one established by a statute—the first sentence of MCL 418.301(1)—and requires an injury "arising out of and in the course of" employment. Although driving in a non-company car and although the accident occurred after regular work hours, this injury should be deemed to arise out of and in the course of employment largely because the owner definitely urged the supervisors to attend and because attendance would benefit the employer. Contrast, *James v Auto Lab Diagnostics*, 474 Michigan 1061 (2006); *Camburn v Northwest School Dist*, 459 Michigan 471 (1999).

Concerning the occurrence or non-occurrence of a personal injury, Bancroft may have a mental injury or psychological injury from seeing Clifford die. A complete answer should recognize that Bancroft may have this kind of psychiatric injury, even though he suffered no physical injury.

Concerning disability and possible entitlement to weekly wage-loss benefits, a complete answer should recognize that disability is not the physical or psychological impairment itself, but, by statute, is a limitation of one's maximum wage-earning capacity in work suitable to one's qualifications and training. And, the limitation of the ability to work is not the inability to resume the same job for the same employer when injured. So, the fact Bancroft will not or cannot work for Polk does not, in itself, demonstrate disability. If he can perform such equally well-paying work elsewhere, then he is not disabled. *Sington v DaimlerChrysler Corp*, 467 Michigan 144 (2002). If he is only able to earn less post-injury (as he presently is), then he is disabled but only partially disabled. His weekly rate of compensation would be a partial rate considering the difference in pay.

Besides weekly compensation benefits, the workers' compensation statute provides for payment of reasonable and necessary medical treatment for work-related injuries. MCL 418.315. Bancroft's mental health care costs would be recoverable.

Student Answer—February 2007

Question 12—Workers' Compensation—8 points

In Michigan to recover for *workers disability* compensation the following must have been met. The injury must have taken place *within the scope of employment*, there *must be wage loss, injury or disease*.

Here, this did take place within the scope of employment because the seminar that George and Clifford were attending was work related. The injury does not have to be in the employer's premises, but it can be in furtherance of work goals.

Further recovery under workers comp 80% recovery is the following: reasonable medical expenses, lost wages, physical ailment/disfigurement, pain and suffering and certain economic damages. Here, Bancroft was not physically harmed, but sought mental healthcare due to watching Clifford die. Therefore, he may be able to collect for mental pain and anguish. Also, an employee can take *another position* and it does not have to be for the same pay. Here, Bancroft took a job as a supervisor somewhere else but for less pay, however, worker's comp generally will pay the remainder of lost wages if the person does not return to the same position, but here, Bancroft went to another employer, so there is a chance he may or may not obtain recovery under worker's compensation.

Bancroft may also have an opportunity to recover under No-fault insurance if either worker's compensation does not pay or it will supplement worker's cop. In MI no fault insurance is applicable when you are in an auto accident and it does not access fault. The insured can recover up to 85% under First party or third party benefits. However, the facts don't indicate that the accident definitely happened in Michigan and only in Mason. But if it did, he may be able to recover for reasonable medical expenses, lost wages, pain and suffering under no fault as well.

July 2007—Question 3

ABC is a small but comprehensive construction company. ABC was in the process of constructing a three-floor office building, the largest project ABC ever handled. One task at this project required some of ABC's construction workers to walk on elevated beams. Within the first few weeks of the project, three of the ABC workers fell from the beams and suffered serious injuries. After the injuries, ABC found it difficult to persuade its other construction workers to work on the elevated beams. The workers believed the beams were inherently unsafe. ABC then sought to hire additional construction workers willing to do all aspects of construction work, including work on elevated beams.

Joe Brown responded to an ABC advertisement for such construction workers. Joe had been working for many years as a self-employed subcontractor in the construction industry. However, he liked the idea of leaving that behind to obtain a steady job for ABC with its fringe benefits, hourly pay, and union membership.

Joe was hired by ABC. Two weeks after his hire, Joe fell from an elevated beam. He slightly injured his knee in the fall. Following medical treatment, all doctors agreed that, with the bad knee, Joe is now permanently unable to work on elevated beams, but that is Joe's only medical restriction. Unfortunately, ABC cannot return Joe to work because its present needs require the ability to work on the elevated beams.

Unemployed, Joe now seeks legal advice on what legal remedies, if any, he may have against ABC. You are an associate in the law firm Joe engages.

The managing partner of the law firm directs you to prepare a legal memorandum identifying potential avenues of relief and the strengths and the weaknesses of any case Joe may have. Without discussing any potential issues involving the Americans with Disabilities Act or the Persons with Disabilities Civil Rights Act, please prepare such a memorandum for the managing partner.

Model Answer to Question 3

The question is designed primarily to test if the examinee can identify the following three issues:

1. Does Joe have a viable cause of action for an intentional tort because ABC assigned him work that is arguably inherently dangerous?
2. Was Joe an "employee" of ABC and, therefore, able to pursue a workers' compensation action or was he a self-employed subcontractor and, as such, not covered by the workers' compensation statute?

3. Assuming a workers' compensation remedy, is it likely Joe will collect disability wage loss benefits on the basis of his permanent physical limitation and the inability of ABC to return him to work?

With respect to the question of whether Joe has a remedy for an intentional tort, the correct answer is that he does not have such a remedy. The Worker's Disability Compensation Act is an employee's "exclusive remedy against the employer" for a work-related injury. MCL 418.131(1). There is an exception for an intentional tort. However, this exception is exceedingly narrow because the statute defines an intentional tort as follows:

> An intentional tort shall exist only when an employee is injured as a result of a deliberate act of the employer and the employer specifically intended an injury. An employer shall be deemed to have intended to injure if the employer had actual knowledge that an injury was certain to occur and willfully disregarded that knowledge. *Id.*

Here, while ABC knew of the dangerous condition, there is nothing to suggest ABC specifically intended an injury. Nor is there any suggestion ABC had actual knowledge an injury was certain to occur and willfully disregarded that knowledge. An inherently dangerous condition and "substantial certainty" of injury are not enough to bring the case within the exception. *Gray v Morley* (after remand), 460 Mich 738 (1999); *Travis v Dreis & Krump Manufacturing Co*, 453 Mich 149 (1996).

With respect to the question of whether or not Joe was an "employee" so as to be covered by the workers' compensation act, he is covered. He is a person engaged under a "contract of hire" with ABC. MCL 418.161(1)(a). And he is not excluded from the "employee" category by MCL 418.161(1)(n), which provides: "Every person performing service in the course of the trade, business, profession, or occupation of an employer at the time of the injury, if the person in relation to this service does not maintain a separate business, does not hold himself or herself out to and render service to the public, and is not an employer subject to this act." While Joe had previously held himself out to render service to the public as an independent subcontractor (and perhaps maintained a separate business as well), he abandoned that line of work and by "the time of the injury" had become an employee of ABC. Such things as hourly pay, fringe benefits, and union membership are hallmarks differentiating employees from independent contractors.

With respect to Joe's remedies under the Worker's Disability Compensation Act, Joe will have difficulty obtaining weekly disability benefits. While he can no longer do the elevated work necessitated at times by construction workers, that inability does not necessarily render him disabled under MCL 418.301(4) and *Sington v Chrysler Corporation*, 467 Mich 144 (2002). Joe would need to demonstrate that "all" equally well-paying jobs suitable to his qualifications and training are precluded by his work injury. Since he could perform work other than tasks on elevated beams, his chances of prevailing on the disability question are not good. He can recover medical expenses under the workers' compensation act regardless of whether he obtains wage loss benefits. MCL 418.315(a).

In sum, Joe has no intentional tort remedy. He is an "employee." As such, his remedies are confined to those provided by the workers' compensation statute.

Under that statute, he could receive medical benefits related to his knee injury, but a successful claim for weekly workers' compensation benefits is unlikely.

Student Answer—July 2007

Question 3—Workers' Compensation—8 points

The issue is what relief may Joe seek against ABC. In MI, Workers Compensation is an *exclusive remedy* for on-the-job injuries. To recover under workers comp, Joe must show: (1) *that he was an employee*, (2) he *received an injury* or disease, (3) *arising from the ordinary course of business*, (4) he actually *sustained an injury or disease*, and (5) he had *lost wages*. In this case, Joe was hired by ABC, which means he was an employee. The facts also state that he fell from an elevated beam & injured his knee. Joe fell from this beam while he was in the course of his employment. The facts also state that he would be unable to work on elevated beams in the future & that is why ABC hired him & that now they have no use for him. Because Joe was injured at work while working he would be able to collect from ABC. I would advise Joe that he would collect from his employer all medical expenses which are *reasonable & necessary*. He would also be able to collect *80%* of his wages for up to 3 yrs as well as replacement services of up to $20 per day.

If Joe wanted to sue his employer civilly, I would advise him that because of workers comp, that the only way Joe can do this is if his employer acted intentionally which means that his employer had the purpose of inflicting injury on Joe or had knowledge that the injury was certain to occur. In the facts, it states that 3 of ABC's employees had fallen from the beam & had suffered serious injury, but he could not persuade his other workers to go up on the beam after this. Because only 3 of his workers were injured & he was not sure that everyone who went up there would be injured, I believe this would not rise to the level of purpose or knowledge on the part of ABC. In conclusion, I believe that Joe's best avenue would be to collect under Workers Compensation because ABC's behavior did not rise to the level of an intentional tort & that if Joe decided to go that route he would not recover.

Comment: This is a good answer, but the examinee did not address the "disability" issue relating to wage loss. Also, there is a mistake in law resulting in the 2-point reduction. The $20 per day replacement services is a benefit under No Fault Insurance Act. It is *not* a benefit of Workers' Comp.

February 2008—Question 7

John worked for an automobile supply company. He had a longstanding sports-related right knee problem, dating back years before he began working for the company.

The company where John worked afforded its employees a one hour lunch each day, from noon to 1:00 p.m. Employees were not paid for the hour lunch. Employees were free to eat at the company's cafeteria, in the lunchroom, or they could leave the premises and go to lunch off-site. John and a couple of his fellow employees typically went to lunch off-site at a local tavern and drank a few beers with their lunch.

One day John and his fellow employees went to lunch at their usual tavern during the noon lunch hour. Along with his hamburger, John drank three beers. John and his fellow workers returned to work by 1:00 p.m. and resumed their work duties. Shortly thereafter, John—feeling in a playful mood—tossed his work glove at a fellow employee. The fellow employee responded by pushing John. John felt immediate pain in his right knee and went to the plant medical department.

The plant medical department treated John's minimal symptoms with an ice pack and pain medication and suggested he return to work. John refused to return to work, said he suffered a work-related injury, and went home.

You are the attorney for the company. The company calls you and asks whether John's knee complaint is compensable under Michigan workers' compensation law. What would you advise them? Explain your answer.

Model Answer to Question 7

Two primary issues need to be addressed, in no particular order.

First, the workers' compensation statute only covers incidents that constitute a "personal injury arising out of a course of employment." MCL 418.301(1). The fact that John had a pre-existing sports related knee injury would not preclude a claim that his most recent problem is compensable under the workers' compensation system because employers take their employees as they are with their pre-existing problems, *e.g., Sheppard v Michigan National Bank*, 348 Mich 577 (1957). Therefore, the mere fact that John had a pre-existing problem would not bar a workers' compensation claim.

However, where an employee brings to the workplace a pre-existing problem and alleges work aggravated that problem, the employee must demonstrate the work event caused a problem "medically distinguishable" from the pre-existing problem. *Rakestraw v General Dynamics Land Systems, Inc*, 469 Mich 220 (2003). If the work event merely aggravates the symptoms of the pre-existing problem, no "medically distinguishable" personal injury has occurred. *Rakeshaw, supra* at 226-230; *Fahr v General Motors Corp*, 478 Mich 922 (2007). John would need to demonstrate a change in the underlying pathology of his pre-existing condition in order to meet the "personal injury" requirement. *Fahr, supra.* Here, there is no indication the push at work caused anything more than symptomatic expression of his pre-existing problem. Therefore, without further proof that something medically distinguishable occurred, the company could legitimately reject John's claim that he suffered a work-related injury. It may be that John can later demonstrate by medical proof that something medically distinguishable did occur. But, on these facts, the company can say "no medically distinguishable" injury occurred. More important than the final answer to this question is the examinee's ability to recognize this issue and display knowledge of the pertinent case laws, most especially *Rakestraw*.

Second, there is a question whether John's alleged injury is due to his "intentional and wilful misconduct" MCL 418.305. This provision of the workers' compensation statute says: "If the employee is injured by reason of his intentional and willful misconduct, he shall not receive compensation under the provisions of this act." John's playful tossing of a glove is not likely to be determined "intentional and wilful misconduct," as opposed to mere "horseplay" at work. Injuries resulting from "horseplay" at work can be compensable because "horseplay" is viewed as a natural consequence of employees working together, *e.g. Crilly v Ballou*, 353 Mich 303 (1958).

However, John's drinking at lunch may have prompted his playfulness and that drinking might be considered "intentional and willful misconduct." Whether it is or is not might depend on the company's rules regarding drinking at lunch, the enforcement of such rule, and the like. The crucial point for the examinee is to recognize that the company might have a MCL 418.305 defense. If the company views John's drinking as "intentional and willful misconduct" and the cause for his playfulness, then his injury might be considered to have occurred "by reason of" his misconduct. It is not necessary that the injury arise contemporaneously with the misconduct. If the injury flowed directly and predictably from misconduct, then the injury is deemed to have occurred "by reason of" the misconduct. *Daniel v Department of Corrections*, 468 Mich 34 (2003).

Again, the answer as to whether or not the drinking is "intentional and willful misconduct" and the answer as to whether the alleged injury occurred "by reason" of that misconduct is not crucial. The crucial point is that the examinee recognizes the company may have a defense under MCL 418.305 and discuss that statute's criteria for operation.

Student Answer—February 2008

Question 7—Workers' Compensation—None Available

July 2008—Question 15

Darrell Smith is 22 years old and a Michigan resident. There is a history of mental illness in Darrell's family; and, Darrell had a difficult childhood with substance abuse by his father and protracted financial difficulties at home. While still living at home, Darrell procured his first full-time job as a computer programmer for a large Michigan bank that has significant real estate holdings. Darrell enjoyed his position at the bank and performed his job well for the first year.

Shortly thereafter, however, the decline in Michigan's real estate market led the bank to downsize by releasing a number of its employees. The downsizing caused an increased workload for those employees remaining. Darrell escaped the downsizing, but now found his job too demanding. After working for a couple weeks following the downsizing, Darrell told the bank he could no longer continue because the work was now too stressful.

Darrell did not report to work for the following three weeks upon advice of his family doctor. The bank accepted Darrell's inability to continue working in the more demanding environment and could not offer him a less stressful position in Michigan. The bank did, however, send Darrell a letter offering him a special position at the bank's North Carolina branch. The letter explained that there Darrell could provide financial advice to customers in a casual, relaxed atmosphere. The letter explained Darrell's salary there would only be slightly less than what he had earned in Michigan. The letter told Darrell to report there in a month.

Darrell does not want to relocate to North Carolina and he cannot return to work for the bank in Michigan. **He seeks your legal advice on whether he has a viable claim for weekly wage loss benefits for a mental disability under the Michigan workers' compensation statute and his chance of success with any such claim. What would you advise Darrell? Explain your answer.**

Model Answer to Question 15

The question seeks to determine whether the examinee can identify and discuss two issues: (1) Can Darrell arguably obtain workers' compensation benefits for a mental disability and what are the elements of such a claim; and, (2) What is the effect, if any, of the bank's offer of North Carolina employment?

With respect to the first issue, Darrell can claim mental disability benefits under Michigan's Worker's Disability Compensation Act, specifically under MCL 418.301(2)—MCL 418.401(2)(b). These provisions—both of which read the same—say:

> Mental disabilities and conditions of the aging process, including but not limited to heart and cardiovascular conditions, shall be compensable if contributed to or aggravated or accelerated by the employment in a significant manner. Mental disabilities shall be compensable when arising out of actual events of employment, not unfounded perceptions thereof.

Darrell should be counseled that he would need to demonstrate that the "stress" he encountered at work was not an "unfounded perception" of the workplace but one grounded in reality. *Robertson v Daimler Chrysler Corporation*, 465 Mich 732 (2002). And, he would need to demonstrate that such work stress contributed "in a significant manner" toward his psychological problems. The determination of whether work's contribution is "significant" or not is made by comparing the potential non-work-related explanations for the problem (family history, childhood difficulties, etc., here) to work's contribution. *See Holden v Ford Motor Co (After Remand, On Second Remand)*, 226 Mich App 138 (1997); *Lombardi v William Beaumont Hospital (On Remand)*, 199 Mich App 428 (1993); compare also, *Farrington v Total Petroleum, Inc.*, 422 Mich 201 (1993).

It does not appear from the facts that Darrell's perception of overwork was "an unfounded perception," given the reality of the downsizing and the bank's apparent acceptance of Darrell's perception of stress. And, although Darrell has a family history of mental illness and other non-work-related stressors, he has a good argument, the work stress did not contribute "in a significant manner" toward his mental difficulties. Therefore, Darrell has a viable mental disability claim worth pursuing.

With respect to the issue of the bank's North Carolina job offer, the examinee is expected to display some familiarity with Michigan's workers' compensation rules relating to job offers to disabled employees. The job offer described in the question appears in most respects to be "a bona fide offer of reasonable employment from the previous employer" under MCL 418.301(5)(a). "Reasonable employment" is a statutory term of art that includes work tailored to accommodate restrictions resulting from a work injury. MCL 418.301(9); *McJunkin v Cellasto Plastic Corp*, 461 Mich 590 (2000). An employee is not entitled to weekly benefits if he or she refuses a bona fide offer of reasonable employment "without good and reasonable cause." MCL 418.301(5)(a). But, to be "bona fide," the offer of reasonable employment must be an offer of work "within a reasonable distance from that employee's residence." MCL 418.301(9). An offer of work in North Carolina would not be considered "within a reasonable distance" of Darrell's residence. Therefore, the offer would not be bona fide and Darrell can refuse it without any legal repercussions.

Examinees in answering the question might also discuss whether Darrell meets the definition of "disability" in MCL 418.301(4) as explained in *Sington v Chrysler Corp*,

467 Mich 144 (2002). There is no harm in such a discussion, but the question is not designed to elicit comment on that subject.

In sum, Darrell has a viable workers' compensation claim for a work-related mental disability. And, the employer's offer of work in North Carolina is not an offer he must accept at the risk of forfeiting weekly workers' compensation benefits.

Two Student Answers—July 2008

Question 15—Workers' Compensation—9 points

An employee can file a claim for any injury that arises out of and in the course of employment. Worker's compensation is the sole remedy for an employee injured while they are working unless the employee committed an intentional tort. An employee may be able to file a worker's compensation claim for a mental disability if the employee's condition was aggravated or accelerated because of work.

To establish a claim of disability for a mental illness the employee must be able to demonstrate that the disability was work related, based upon or attributed to a work event and not just a belief or delusion that is the consequence of their disease. Disability means you are unable to perform at all. To have to perform a different job function does not render on disabled. If work is available within one's work restrictions or abilities within the company, an employee is expected to accept the other role provided it is a reasonable work assignment.

Here, Darrell may have a viable claim for weekly wage loss if the increased workload was the work event that agitated or aggravated his pre-existing medical condition/mental illness. For the period in time he was unable to work, he would receive benefits after satisfying the seven day waiting/qualification period. Moving to North Carolina for a less stressful position may not be reasonable and although an accommodation he may not be required to accept it.

Therefore Darrell would probably be successful for weekly wage loss benefits for a mental disability if he can demonstrate that the increased workload for the remaining employees after the downsizing is what aggravated his condition. If he were not permanently disabled, then he would have to accept a position within his abilities.

Question 15—Workers' Compensation—8 points

(Q) Can Darrell receive Workers Compensation for a mental disability?

Under the workers compensation disability act and employee can turn to his employer for compensation for work related injuries that are the result of employment. A mental disability is compensable where the disability actually exists and is based on actual events and not grounded on merely perceived events. This is true even if the employee had the mental illness prior to employment as long as it was aggravated by employment.

Workers compensation benefits pay for lost wages until the employee is able to come back to work or can find comparable work in his field.

Employer has offered less stressful employment but requires travel to North Carolina. Darrell may successfully argue that this is unreasonable substitution of employment and he is not required to accept.

The bank may argue that Darrell's job is not one with specialized degree and therefore he can find a comparable job that is less stressful.

February 2009—Question 9

John is 55 years old and is a high school graduate. He worked for an automobile company for 15 years on the assembly line. Prior to that time, he held other manual jobs.

John found that the bending necessary to perform his tasks on the assembly line at the automobile company aggravated his arthritic back condition, a condition that pre-existed his tenure at the automobile company. John stopped working saying he could no longer perform any of the assembly line tasks due to his back pain.

John seeks your legal advice on the merits of a workers' compensation claim for weekly wage loss benefits.

Identify and discuss the issue(s) presented in John's case under Michigan law. Address what type of information you, as his attorney, will need to elicit and develop in order to properly evaluate John's chances of prevailing on a claim for weekly wage loss benefits.

Model Answer to Question 9

There are two issues that should be identified and discussed, in no particular order. First, there is the issue of whether John's back condition is work related for worker's compensation purposes. The second issue is whether John can prove that he is "disabled" and thus entitled to weekly wage loss benefits under 418.301(4), as recently informed by the Michigan Supreme Court's decision in *Stokes v Chrysler LLC*, 481 Mich 266 (2008).

With respect to the work relatedness issue, the fact that John brought to the workplace a pre-existing condition does not preclude a finding that his back condition is work related. Where work aggravates a pre-existing condition in a compensable manner, the resultant problem is deemed wholly work related for workers' compensation purposes. E.g., *Smith v Lawrence Banking Company*, 370 Mich 169 (1963). Aggravation of a pre-existing condition in a compensable manner requires the claimant to demonstrate more than just aggravation of the symptoms of the preexisting condition. The claimant must demonstrate that work aggravation produced a problem "medically distinguishable" from the pre-existing problem. *Rakestraw v General Dynamics Land Systems*, 469 Mich 220 (2003). A medically distinguishable problem occurs where there has been a "change in the pathology" of the condition. *Fahr v General Motors*, 478 Mich 922 (2007). Furthermore, if the pre-existing condition is a "condition of the aging process," i.e., a condition that naturally progresses with the passage of time, the claimant must demonstrate that work contributed toward the pre-existing problem "in a significant manner," rather than only insignificantly. MCL 418.301(2); MCL 418.401(2)(b).

Therefore, in addressing the work relatedness issue in John's case, the examinee must demonstrate that he or she is aware of the need to prove a "medically distinguishable" problem, a "change in pathology." And, a thorough analysis would also include consideration of the possibility that John's arthritis might be deemed a "condition of the aging process" requiring "significant" work contribution. The type of information an attorney will need to elicit in order to properly evaluate John's claim will include prior medical records to determine whether John's problem is a condition of the aging process and current medical information designed to answer the question of whether John has a problem "medically distinguishable" from his pre-existing condition. The attorney would also want to know the frequency of John's bending at work to determine the significance of work's contribution and whether John suffered any specific traumatic events at work.

With respect to the second "disability" issue, the *Stokes* decision requires the claimant to present proofs on four different elements in order to make a prima facie case of disability and thereby successfully pursue weekly wage loss benefits. First, the claimant is required to fully disclose all of his qualifications and training, including education, skills, experience, and training "whether or not they are relevant to the job the claimant was performing at the time of injury." Second, the claimant needs to provide a reasonable means to assess employment opportunities at all such suitable jobs within the same salary range, including the jobs to which his or her qualifications and training might "translate." The claimant must not limit consideration to just the jobs that he has actually performed in his work life. Third, the claimant must demonstrate the work injury prevents him from performing some or all of such jobs. And, fourth, if there are any jobs suitable to his qualifications and training he is capable of performing post-injury, he must show that he has made a "good faith attempt to procure post-injury employment if there are jobs at the same salary or higher."

Therefore, with respect to the second issue, the examinee should display familiarity with this legal standard of disability articulated in *Stokes* which built on *Sington v Chrysler Corp*, 467 Mich 144 (2002). John's attorney will need to elicit from John information regarding his skills, experience, training, hobbies and the like, in addition to all the specific jobs he had previously performed. *Stokes* mentions, though it does not mandate, that claimants like John consider producing vocational testimony and a "transferable skills analysis" in order to establish how his qualifications and training might translate to other jobs beyond those he had previously performed. Finally, John's efforts to procure suitable post-injury work within his physical restrictions are important.

In sum, to prevail with a workers' compensation claim for weekly wage loss benefits, John needs to demonstrate his condition is work related and he must satisfy the Stokes "disability" criteria. John ostensibly has a claim, but whether it is meritorious and warrants pursuit will depend on the results of the inquiries identified above. The examinee must demonstrate he or she recognizes these two issues, knows the crucial legal criteria, and knows what information will need to be collected in order to properly evaluate the case.

Student Answer—February 2009

Question 9—Workers' Compensation—None Available

July 2009—Question 8

Jack works for an automobile supply company where business has recently declined. Jack had suffered a serious work-related back injury last year. Believing Jack would not be able to procure work elsewhere because of the severe restrictions resulting from that back injury, Jack's employer created a job tailored to meet Jack's restrictions. The job was not a meaningful one, but the employer felt obliged to help Jack.

Within a year of Jack's injury, it became evident that the automobile supply company was destined to close due to adverse economic conditions. Jack and the other employees were so advised. Jack told his employer he wanted workers' compensation benefits once the plant closed, given the work injury he sustained 11 months earlier. The employer told Jack it would continue to pay for any medical care associated with his injury, but it would not pay him weekly wage-loss benefits. The employer's reason was Jack will be out of work due to adverse economic conditions, not due to his work injury. The employer assured Jack that he would receive unemployment compensation benefits upon the plant closing.

Does Jack have a basis to make a successful claim for weekly workers' compensation benefits under Michigan law? Why or why not? Does Jack's anticipated receipt of unemployment compensation benefits have any impact on a claim for weekly workers' compensation benefits under Michigan law? Why or why not?

Model Answer to Question 8

Jack should be advised to file a claim for weekly workers' compensation benefits because he has an excellent chance of receiving weekly benefits. Michigan's workers' compensation statute offers generous protections to employees disabled by work injuries who return to work postinjury at what is characterized under the statute as "reasonable employment." MCL 418.301(5)-(9); *McJunkin v Cellasto Plastic Corp*, 461 Mich 590 (2000). "Reasonable employment," formerly called "favored work," is post-injury work that can be performed by an employee deemed "disabled" under MCL 418.301(4) and *Stokes v Chrysler, LLC*, 481 Mich 266 (2008). The exam question is structured such that Jack is to be considered "disabled," given his severe restrictions and the employer's tacit concession Jack is unable to work elsewhere. The "make work" nature of Jack's work virtually confirms that Jack is laboring at the heavily favored work clearly fitting within the rubric of "reasonable employment."

A person, such as Jack, who labors at post-injury "reasonable employment . . . for less than 100 weeks" and who "loses his or her job for *whatever* reason . . . shall receive compensation based upon his or her wage at the original date of injury." MCL 418.301(5)(e) (emphasis added); *Russell v Whirlpool Financial Corporation*, 461 Mich 579 (2000). Therefore, even though Jack's cessation of work will be due to the plant closing, §301(5)(e) protects his right to weekly compensation because he will have lost his job after having performed less than 100 weeks of "reasonable employment."

Jack's receipt of unemployment compensation benefits does not preclude receipt of weekly workers' compensation benefits. Jack can receive both. MCL 418.358; *Paschke v Retool Industries*, 445 Mich 502 (1994). If Jack receives both benefits, his weekly workers' compensation benefits will be reduced dollar-for-dollar by the unemployment compensation benefits. MCL 418.358. Unemployment compensation benefits are usually much less than weekly workers' compensation benefits. And, in any event, unemployment compensation benefits are limited in duration, whereas weekly workers' compensation benefits can continue for Jack's lifetime.

In discussing whether Jack can receive weekly workers' compensation payments, examinees might address the question of whether Jack is "disabled" under §301(4)/*Stokes* and/or whether his wage loss relates to his disability under the second sentence of §301(4). The question is structured to avoid delving into those issues. If an examinee delved into those issues nevertheless and discussed §301(5)-(9) and the unemployment compensation provision of §358, they are entitled to additional (not less) consideration for awareness of deeper latent issues. Finally, an examinee might discuss the time lag between Jack's injury and his claim for weekly benefits. As long as the "reasonable employment" and unemployment issues are correctly addressed, discussion of the timeliness of Jack's claim should also not be held against an examinee. Jack's claim is clearly timely. MCL 418.381.

Student Answer—July 2009

Question 8—Workers' Compensation—8 points

This is a workers compensation question. In Michigan, workers compensation is an employees exclusive remedy for an on the job disability. The only exception is for an intentional tort. In order for an employee to qualify for workers' compensation benefits, there are five criteria he must meet:

1. He must be an employee of an employer covered by the Workers Disability Comp. Act;
2. He must have either sustained an injury or suffered an occupational disease;
3. Which arose out of and was in the scope and course of employment;
4. He must establish a disability; and
5. He must have incurred wage loss.

There is no question here as to whether Jack is employed covered by workers comp. medical benefits will be paid for so long as are "reasonable and necessary." Wage loss is calculated by the highest paid 39 weeks of the last 52 added together and divided by 39. Wage loss. This amount is 80% of after tax. Last year it was capped at $65,000. Wage loss will continue "so long as the employee is disabled."

If an employee returns to work but leaves before 120 weeks, there is a presumption the benefits continue. Any person or retirement will be deducted from workers comp. An employer may reduce liability by offering the disabled employee a job that complies with their disability that is reasonable and not too far away. Here, the employer is no longer able to offer Jack this job. Therefore, his workers' comp benefits will continue for so long as he is disabled. The employer may provide vocational rehabilitation for up to two years. However, Jack still may not be able to receive both workers compensation and unemployment. This is because his workers comp benefits are because he is unable to find another job based on his skill, qualifications, and training. He is not entitled to have both.

He must disclose to his employer any other skills he has (i.e. his resume), any other jobs he could do and why he can't get one of them. It would also have to go to a mediator first.

Comment: Many examinees did not do well on this question because they were unaware of the very specific 100-week rule that is part of "reasonable employment" and/or they were unaware of the impact unemployment benefits would have on a Workers' Comp claim.

February 2010—Question 7

Joan has had various allergies since childhood. With appropriate treatment through the years, she managed them well and they did not adversely affect her in any significant way. Joan graduated from high school and then obtained an Associate's Degree in medical record keeping from a community college.

After graduation, Joan did not look for work in the medical field, but rather decided to work with a friend she had met in college at a company named 3C's. This company develops and sells granite countertops. At 3C's, Joan worked a portion of the day in the small plant helping mix chemicals used to clean the granite. She spent the majority of her time in the office. There, she took orders, communicated with customers, and prepared invoices.

Shortly after beginning work for 3C's, Joan began to notice rash-like irritations on her hands. She visited a doctor who did patch testing and determined Joan was highly allergic to one of the chemicals used at 3C's to clean granite. The doctor advised Joan that she had most likely always been allergic to this chemical, along with her other allergic sensitivities. But, since she had not encountered the substance until she worked at 3C's, the allergic reaction had never manifested itself. The doctor advised Joan not to return to work at 3C's because this type of chemical permeates the atmosphere and would be present even in the office area.

Joan seeks your legal advice as to whether she has any workers' compensation remedies against 3C's. Will she be successful in seeking payment from 3C's of medical expenses related to her chemical exposure? Will she be successful in seeking disability (weekly wage loss benefits) from 3C's based upon her inability to return to work for it? Explain your answer utilizing Michigan law.

Model Answer to Question 7

The attorney should advise Joan it is very likely she has a workers' compensation remedy for the medical treatment related to her exposure at the workplace. But, her claim for weekly wage loss benefits is much more tenuous. The disability claim will be unsuccessful if all Joan can demonstrate is an inability to return to work at 3C's.

Employees are entitled under the workers' compensation statute to have the employer pay for medical treatment resulting from a "personal injury arising out of and in the course of employment." MCL 418.301(1); MCL 418.315(1). Joan's skin irritations would almost certainly be deemed a personal injury arising out of and in the course of employment. The fact that Joan brought to the work place a latent sensitivity to the chemicals does not preclude benefits because the employer takes the employee as it finds him or her. *See Deziel v Difco Laboratories, Inc*, 394 Mich 466, 475-76 (1975). Where the employee brings to the workplace a pre-existing problem, however, the employee must demonstrate that work caused a condition "medically distinguishable" from the pre-existing condition itself; that is, the employee must prove work caused a change in the pathology of the pre-existing problem. *Rakestaw v General Dynamics Land Systems*, 469 Mich 220, 234 (2003); *Fahr v General Motors Corp*, 478 Mich 922 (2007). Here, Joan would argue that work exposure caused a change in pathology and produced a problem "medically distinguishable" from her previously quiescent problem.

An examinee may argue that here work merely elicited the symptoms of a pre-existing latent condition and symptomatic aggravation does not satisfy *Rakestraw/ Fahr*. While that point might be debated, the previously dormant nature of Joan's condition and the lack of indication that the skin irritations are just temporary should yield the conclusion that she has suffered a work-related personal injury. The ultimate answer is less important than recognition of the "personal injury" *Rakestraw/Fahr* rule and recognition that a pre-existing problem does not necessarily preclude a claim the employer is responsible for aggravating it.

Disability (Wage-Loss) Benefits: To prove entitlement to weekly wage loss benefits, the employee must demonstrate that he or she is "disabled." The workers' compensation statute defines "disability" as follows: "disability" means a limitation of an employee's wage earning capacity in work suitable to his or her qualifications and training resulting from a personal injury or work related disease." MCL 418.301(4) (first sentence); MCL 418.401(1). The Supreme Court has emphasized that an employee's inability to return to his or her last job or the inability to return to just one type of employment that he or she had performed in the past does not, standing alone, suffice to demonstrate "disability." *Stokes v Chrysler LLC*, 481 Mich 266, 278-79 (2008); *Sington v Chrysler Corp*, 467 Mich 144, 155 (2002). The one exception can be where the employee is only qualified and trained to do one type of job and has no skills that might transfer to other job fields. Joan's community college degree, as well as the skills she used in working at 3C's, qualify her to perform other suitable work. Consequently, Joan's inability to return to 3C's will not, standing alone, suffice to prove "disability." Joan's only chance of prevailing on this issue would be to demonstrate that all other work suitable to her qualifications and training, e.g., working in the medical field, performing customer relations and clerical type of work elsewhere, etc., is either not currently available in the labor marketplace or pays less than her maximum earning capacity. *Stokes*, 481 Mich at 280-81. And, in this regard, Joan would need to show she is making a good faith job search for all work suitable to her qualifications and training and/or that all available work pays less than she earned at 3C's. *Id.* at 283.

Two Student Answers—February 2010

Question 7—Workers' Compensation—8 points

The question is whether Joan can recover medical expenses and lost wages from 3C's a company she is working for. For an allergic reaction.

The first question is whether Joan can get worker's comp. for medical expenses.

In order to get worker's comp. an employee must suffer an injury that arises out of and is in the course of their employment. Here Joan works for a brief period of time during the day in a chemical part of 3C's corp. the rest of the day she is working books. During the course of her time in the chemical part of the plant she has an allergic reaction. This injury would arise out of and be in the course of her employment. The Dr. said this much. The Dr. also said that Joan probably already had this allergy. In workers comp. it is not important whether you already had the condition but only that you accelerate, aggravate or make worse the injury. Here the Dr. said the injury was worse due to work and she should not go back, So, Joan should get her medical expenses paid. However, it will be tougher for disability.

2) Joan would like disability or weekly wage loss benefits.

To get disability it must be shown that a person's wage loss earning potential has been limited. You look at Joan from before and after the injury.

Here Joan left 3C's by her doctor's order even though she only spent a short time every day in the chemical area. It is possible she could have continued employment without going into the chemical plant. She also spends most of her day at the office and has a degree in medical record keeping. It seems unlikely she has lost her ability to make the same wage. She must mitigate and try to get a similar job. If she cannot and 3C's only needs her if she can work in chemicals the first part of the day then they must pay some wage loss.

Question 7—Workers' Compensation—8 points

For a worker to make a successful worker's comp claim, she must prove 4 elements: (i) she is a worker covered by MI worker's comp; (ii) she has suffered an injury or disease (iii) She suffered the injury or disease during the course of her employment; and (iv) she has suffered damages.

As to the first element, MI workers comp covers all MI employees and employers in MI except for: federal government employees, marine merchants & workers interstate railroads. Here Joan works at 3C's a Michigan Co in Michigan, thus she is covered employee.

As for the second element, Joan must prove she suffered an injury or disease. Here she suffered a rash-like irritation on her hands. Clearly she has been injured.

Thirdly, Joan must also show she suffered her injury directly through course of her employment. Joan has a bit of a problem here b/c she has a pre-existing allergies condition and her injury is an allergic reaction. Joan most likely has always been allergic to the chemicals, & therefore she must show her injury was a medically distinguishable from her normal allergies. Here, Joan did not suffer this reaction until she began working at 3C's. Thus, her injury here is medically distinguishable from her preexisting allergies.

Having satisfied the 1st 3 elements, Joan must now prove damages. She is entitled, if she can prove them to both medical expenses and lost wages. She can recover the medical expenses for her injury b/c she is a covered employee, who was injured during the course of her employment, and has had to paid for diagnosis and treatment.

To recover lost wages, she must show she cannot work any job based on her training and experience qualify her to work, at the same rate of compensation. Here, Joan's training qualifies her to work in the medical records field & is not limited her job at 3C's. Thus it is unlikely that she will qualify for lost wages. However, if she obtains suitable employment based on her training and experience and is paid less than she made at 3C's, she may be entitled to some lost wages to make up the difference in pay.

Therefore Joan will be successfully in seeking payment for medical expenses and is unlikely to get lost wages.

July 2010—Question 10

ABC is a company that markets athletic footwear. It owns a two-story building from which it operates its business. In an effort to maintain good employee relations and foster a healthy work environment, ABC provides a lounge and exercise area for employees to use, if they wish, on the first floor of the building. The area has high definition television and exercise equipment, including a treadmill. ABC strictly insists that the area is to be used only when the employee is on his or her scheduled lunch time.

Craig and Jessica are employees of ABC. They each have different scheduled lunch times. Because Craig is romantically interested in Jessica, he would occasionally leave his work area during Jessica's lunch time to join her in the lounge and exercise area. While joining Jessica there during her lunch time one day, Craig tried to impress Jessica with how fast he could run on the treadmill. While running on the treadmill, he unfortunately fell and injured his knee.

Craig believes his injury should be considered an injury covered by Michigan's Worker's Disability Compensation Act.

What are Craig's best arguments that the injury is covered by workers' compensation? What are the employer's best arguments that the injury is not covered? What is the likely outcome if the issue is litigated? Explain your answer.

Model Answer to Question 10

Craig would argue that his injury is one "arising out of and in the course of employment." MCL 418.301(1). The injury occurred on the employer's premises during regular work hours. And, the employer created the risk of such injury by providing a treadmill for employees. While Craig was not actually working at the time of his injury, workers' compensation coverage can extend to include "horseplay" activities incidental to the workplace. *E.g., Crilly v Ballou*, 353 Mich 303 (1958); *Petrie v General Motors Corp*, 187 Mich App 198 (1991). Craig would also emphasize that the overall purpose of the area was to maintain and promote employee health and morale. In that sense, ABC was encouraging employee use of the equipment. Since he was engaging in employee camaraderie and in a fitness activity, he was fulfilling an objective the employer at least subtly encouraged. *Thomason v Contour Fabricators Inc*, 255 Mich App 121 (modified in part and remanded), 469 Mich 960 (2003). Craig would also argue that, while he knew of the employer's lunch time policy, he had been leaving his work post to visit Jessica during her lunch time previously, and he had not been reprimanded by ABC for doing so. *See Backett v Focus Hope, Inc*, 482 Mich 269 (2008).

ABC would argue that, although the injury occurred on employer premises and Craig was arguably engaged in a risk ABC created, the activity was elective, not required. Moreover, ABC would argue there should be no coverage under either one of two exclusionary provisions in the Worker's Disability Compensation Act. MCL 418.301(3) provides in pertinent part:

> An employee going to or from his or her work, while on the premises where the employee's work is to be performed, and within a reasonable time before and after his or her working hours, is presumed to be in the course of his or her employment. Notwithstanding this presumption, an injury incurred in the pursuit of an activity the major purpose of which is social or recreational is not covered under this act.

The Michigan Supreme Court has explained that the social and recreational exclusion in the second sentence above has general application and is not limited to injuries sustained while going to and coming from work. *Eversman v Concrete Cutting & Breaking*, 463 Mich 86 (2000). Relying on this defense, ABC would argue the "major" purpose of Craig's activity at the time of Craig's injury was "social or recreational." That is, even if there is deemed to be some work-related purpose to his activity, the "major" reason why he was running fast on the treadmill was for the social reason of impressing Jessica and/or the recreational use of the treadmill itself.

The employer would also urge the following exclusion in MCL 418.305, "If the employee is injured by reason of his intentional and willful misconduct, he shall not receive compensation under the provisions of this act." ABC would emphasize its strict policy against using the area except during one's lunch time and that Craig was not on his lunch time when using the area. *Brackett, supra.* Craig's conduct should therefore constitute "misconduct." And, Craig's actions were "intentional and willful," not negligent. Finally, the employer would argue his injury was "by reason of" his misconduct, i.e., by reason of his breaking the rule. *Daniel v Department of Corrections*, 468 Mich 34 (2003). ABC might argue it was unaware of Craig's prior breaches of the rule and that is why it had not been previously reprimanded.

The examinee's projection of the outcome of the issue if litigated is less important than the examinee's ability to make cogent arguments for each side. In terms of the result, Craig would likely be able to rebuff the §305 willful misconduct claim on the basis that the misconduct (breaking the rule) was not the immediate cause of injury, as opposed to his using the treadmill. That is, using the treadmill, per se, is not misconduct; it is simply when the treadmill is used that is arguably "misconduct." Craig will have a more difficult time with the §301(3) social and recreational exclusion, however. It is more likely than not that the injury would be deemed not covered because Craig was injured in pursuit of an activity whose "major purpose" was "social or recreational."

Student Answer—July 2010

Question 10—Workers' Compensation—None Available

PART III ACTUAL MICHIGAN BAR EXAMS

Recent Michigan Bar Exams are provided for you to complete under timed conditions for practice. This exercise should be done one or two weeks before the bar exam (after studying the material and completing Part II of this book). These should be considered your "dress rehearsals" for the real deal and you should do them as if they were the real deal.

FEBRUARY 2011 MICHIGAN BAR EXAMINATION

ESSAY PORTION

MORNING SESSION

QUESTION 1 **THE ANSWER TO THIS QUESTION SHOULD GO IN BLUEBOOK I**

Meredith and her boyfriend, McDreamy, were out on a date. Because his mother, Abby, wanted him to make a good impression, McDreamy was allowed to drive his mother's brand new Camaro. Although he was driving, he was texting his friend to give him the details of his date with Meredith. He looked up at the last moment, just in time to notice that he was driving into oncoming traffic. He swerved to avoid an oncoming car, but clipped the fender anyway. His car spun out of control and smashed into a tree. Meredith was taken to the hospital for her injuries.

It is undisputed that Meredith suffered the following injuries: a fractured bone in her leg that required a surgical procedure to install a metal rod; she wore a cast for two months and was on crutches temporarily; she underwent several months of physical therapy; she was off from work for approximately two months; per her doctor's instructions, she was not allowed to lift anything over five pounds or do household chores for approximately three months, but now has no restrictions; she also loved to bicycle before the accident but cannot anymore because it causes her too much pain; she still has difficulty standing or sitting for prolonged periods of time.

Assuming McDreamy will completely admit liability as to the cause of the accident, assess under Michigan law whether Meredith is entitled to any non-economic damages for her injuries. Additionally, who are the potential defendants? Explain your answers.

*******THE ANSWER TO THIS QUESTION SHOULD GO IN BLUEBOOK I*******

-1-

QUESTION 2 **THE ANSWER TO THIS QUESTION SHOULD GO IN BLUEBOOK I**

Deliriously Delightful Depot (DDD) is a Michigan corporation whose stated corporate purpose is to bake and deliver unique baked goods throughout the mid-Michigan area. The company was founded in 1985 by Dan York and several of his family members. The articles of incorporation permit only 100 shares, all of equal class and series. Dan owns 30%, while his brother Greg owns 52% of the corporation. Dan's Uncle Bob and his cousin Chris each own 9%.

Thirty days prior to the annual shareholder's meeting, notice was personally given to all shareholders that a proposal to amend the articles of incorporation to expand its stated corporate mission was to be presented at the upcoming meeting. The following resolution was presented:

> To buy, sell, hold and otherwise deal in, acquire, and dispose of vintage and/or antique automobiles, vintage and/or antique automobile parts, and related automobile memorabilia.

The proposed amendment was adopted by a vote of 52 shares to 48 shares. Subsequently, a certificate amending the articles of incorporation was filed with the State of Michigan.

Dan, the Director of Creative Development of DDD, voted against the adoption of the resolution. He claimed that the amendment to the articles of incorporation was invalid and interfered with the company's purpose of creating distinctive confectionary delights. When Dan sought to transfer his shares of the company to his friend Faye as a belated birthday gift, Greg reminded Dan that a shareholder agreement was unanimously executed in 1999, requiring shareholders to sell their shares to the other shareholders of DDD.

Infuriated, Dan filed a lawsuit. First, Dan claims that because he is the creative genius behind DDD's success, his shares should have twice the voting weight of the other shares. Second, Dan seeks to have the amended articles of incorporation declared invalid. In the alternative, Dan seeks to have the shareholder agreement prohibiting the transfer of shares declared void.

Discuss the merits of Dan's claims regarding (1) the voting weight of his 30 shares; (2) the validity of the amended articles of incorporation; and (3) the likelihood that Dan will be able to transfer his shares to his friend Faye. Explain your answers.

*******THE ANSWER TO THIS QUESTION SHOULD GO IN BLUEBOOK I*******

-2-

QUESTION 3 **THE ANSWER TO THIS QUESTION SHOULD GO IN BLUEBOOK I**

The Chips, Chips, and More Chips Cookie Company (Chips) has been baking and selling cookies for 40 years. One of its best customers, Warbucks Coffee, refused to pay for a purchase of 2400 dozen cookies for its many stores because Warbucks said Chips had changed its decades-old, beloved recipe without notice. After Chips could not persuade Warbucks that the recipe was the same as ever, Chips sued Warbucks for the purchase price, $28,800 or $1 per cookie. Warbucks filed an answer to Chips' complaint, disputing it owed Chips the money.

The case was assigned to a Michigan circuit court judge who, in accordance with the court rules, referred the case for case evaluation. Chips was happy with the referral because, as its president complained, "I don't want to spend $25,000 on lawyers and all of their nonsense to get my $28,800." After both sides attended the case evaluation, the panel made a unanimous award of $24,700 to Chips. Chips accepted the award but Warbucks rejected, all the while contending the recipe had changed and the cookies were not right.

Wanting to bring the lawsuit to an end, Chips' attorneys then prepared and filed a motion for summary disposition. Warbucks responded and the court heard oral arguments from counsel. During oral argument, Warbucks' lawyer was pressed on the validity of his client's defense: *i.e.*, that Warbucks did not owe the money because of the changed cookie recipe. Warbucks' lawyer responded that indeed the cookies had been delivered and the number of cookies was correct. The problem, counsel argued, was that the recipe had changed. When pressed again, counsel responded (1) he did not know how it had changed; (2) he had made no inquiry into the subject; (3) that he had relied on Warbucks because they knew more about cookies than he did; and (4) Warbucks was a good, long-time client and he would not doubt the word of its employees. Counsel conceded he had signed the answer to the complaint and the response to the motion.

The trial judge granted the motion for summary disposition by Chips and entered judgment for the $28,800 requested. The trial judge ruled that Warbucks had failed to show there was a genuine issue of material fact under MCR 2.116(C)(10).

Happy about winning, but irritated about the money Chips had to "spend on lawyers," Chips' president wants Warbucks, or someone to pay for "all the lawyers' fees" Chips paid.

-3-

What motion(s) should Chips' lawyers make under any applicable Michigan statutes and the Michigan Court Rules to be reimbursed for money Chips spent on legal fees? What is the possibility of success of each motion? Explain your answers.

*****THE ANSWER TO THIS QUESTION SHOULD GO IN BLUEBOOK I*****

-4-

<u>**GO TO BLUEBOOK II**</u>

QUESTION 4 **THE ANSWER TO THIS QUESTION SHOULD GO IN BLUEBOOK II**

Dan Defendant was playing poker at a local casino with Victor Victim. During the course of the game, a dispute broke out when Victor accused Dan of unethical conduct. The two men exchanged words and tensions escalated until the poker room manager intervened. After hearing a recount of what occurred, the manager concluded that Dan acted improperly and asked Dan to leave. Dan became so infuriated that two security guards had to restrain him and escort him to his car. As he was exiting the poker room, Dan pointed at Victor and proclaimed, "You will not make it home alive!" Dan got in his car, drove to the rear of the casino and retrieved a .38 caliber loaded handgun that he had in the trunk of his car. Dan then drove back to the front of the casino and parked across the street from the valet entrance, where he sat with gun in hand and waited for Victor to leave the casino.

When Victor exited from the casino three hours later, Dan rolled down his window and fired six shots in the direction of Victor, emptying his gun. Dan immediately left the scene. Victor died at the scene from a gunshot wound to the head. Dan was arrested and charged with first-degree premeditated murder. During the jury trial, it was undisputed that five bullets were found in the wall over the door from which Victor exited, 25 feet above the ground. It was also undisputed that the fatal bullet ricocheted off the carport overhang 30 feet above the ground, before it struck and killed Victor. Dan testified and admitted to all of the facts stated above. Nonetheless, Dan testified that he did not intend to kill Victor. Dan testified that he intended "only to scare Victor by shooting over his head into the wall of the casino."

At the close of the evidence, the trial judge indicated her intent to instruct the jury on first-degree premeditated murder and asked the litigants if other instructions should be given. Dan Defendant's lawyer asked that the jury also be instructed on involuntary manslaughter. The prosecution objected to the involuntary manslaughter instruction, and asked for an instruction on second-degree murder. Defense counsel objected to the second-degree murder instruction.

Should the trial court give the jury an instruction on second-degree murder? Explain your answer.

Should the trial court give the jury an instruction on involuntary manslaughter? Explain your answer.

*******THE ANSWER TO THIS QUESTION SHOULD GO IN BLUEBOOK II*******

-5-

<u>QUESTION 5</u> **THE ANSWER TO THIS QUESTION SHOULD GO IN BLUEBOOK II**

In the late 1990's, Cherry Hill was a sparsely populated town located in northern Michigan. However, many Michigan real estate developers recognized that Cherry Hill's proximity to the Great Lakes offered a unique opportunity to turn this small community into a tourist hotspot. Over the next decade, developers constructed luxury resorts, golf courses, fishing lodges and ski resorts in and around Cherry Hill. Residents from neighboring states began purchasing vacation homes in the Cherry Hill area. Though still charming, the once sleepy town now bustled with restaurants, clubs, art studios, and an array of retail shops.

With the development came jobs, although most of the positions were seasonal and did not pay a high wage. Several low-income subdivisions and apartment complexes emerged in and around Cherry Hill in which most of the seasonal employees lived with their families. This population influx caused a strain on local public schools. All the local public schools were overcrowded and lacked sufficient infrastructure to effectively educate students.

The local school board realized that the only way to ensure school operations was to raise revenue. The board considered the use of a recently enacted statute that authorized the board of a school district to levy property taxes for school operating purposes. The statute specifically and expressly exempted "homesteads" and "recreational property" from the tax. "Homestead" was defined as that portion of a dwelling or unit in a multiple-unit dwelling owned and occupied as a principal residence by an owner of the dwelling or unit. "Recreational property" was defined as luxury resorts, golf courses, fishing lodges and ski resorts. At a public hearing, many Cherry Hill property owners whose principal residence was outside of Michigan, objected to paying the majority of the school operating tax and receiving no benefit. The school board nonetheless passed a resolution levying the highest tax possible under the statute.

A large group of non-exempt property owners who resided outside of Michigan, formed a taxpayer organization and filed a declaratory action in the state circuit court against the school board alleging that both the "homestead" and "recreational property" exemptions were discriminatory.

Assess the potential merits of the plaintiff's claims under Article IV of the United States Constitution and the 14th Amendment of the United States Constitution, as well as any corresponding provision(s) under the Michigan constitution. Explain your answer.

*******THE ANSWER TO THIS QUESTION SHOULD GO IN BLUEBOOK II*******

-6-

QUESTION 6 **THE ANSWER TO THIS QUESTION SHOULD GO IN BLUEBOOK II**

On December 1, 2008, Peter Perpetrator and Oscar Occupant were enjoying a few beers with Wendy Witness at a local pub. The three left the pub together, with Peter and Oscar leaving in Peter's car and Wendy leaving in her car. The two cars departed the pub in opposite directions. Shortly after leaving the pub, Peter's car ran a red light and struck a car traveling through the intersection, instantly killing the occupant. Peter and Oscar were ejected from their car, with Oscar sustaining fatal injuries and Peter sustaining only minor injuries. Peter was treated and released from a local hospital, when he was immediately arrested and orally given his *Miranda* rights. Upon arriving at the police station, Peter signed a form acknowledging his *Miranda* rights. The oral and written statements fully complied with the requirements of law and it is undisputed that Peter understood his *Miranda* rights.

For four hours, Officer Jones questioned Peter in an interrogation room about the events of the evening. Peter ignored the officer's questions. Finally, Peter stated, "I am tired, I want to go to bed." Jones placed Peter in a holding cell with a bed and Peter went to sleep. The next morning, while preparing Peter to be transported to court, Jones again asked Peter about what had transpired the prior evening. Peter said, "I was not drunk. I only had two beers. I was distracted by my cell phone and that is why I ran the red light. I am so sorry."

Peter was charged with two counts of involuntary manslaughter and released on personal bond. The court found Peter to be indigent and appointed counsel to represent him. Defense counsel filed a witness list, which identified Peter and Wendy Witness as the only defense witnesses. Wendy was never interviewed by police and never gave a statement to any party regarding her testimony. On March 1, 2009, Peter's appointed counsel died unexpectedly. The trial court instructed the court clerk to appoint new counsel and set the matter for a pretrial conference. The court clerk did not appoint counsel and failed to set the matter for a conference.

On June 1, 2010, the court clerk discovered that no action was taken on Peter's case. The trial court immediately appointed Lisa Lawyer to represent Peter. Peter informed Lisa that Wendy will testify that Oscar was driving Peter's car on the night of the accident. Lisa tried to locate Wendy, but Wendy had moved out of Michigan and nobody knew where she could be found. The trial court set a September 1, 2010 trial date. Lisa filed two motions with the court: a motion to suppress Peter's statement to Officer Jones; and a motion to dismiss with prejudice all charges against Peter.

-7-

How should the court rule on the motion to suppress Peter's statement? Explain your answer.

How should the court rule on the motion to dismiss with prejudice the charges against Peter? Explain your answer.

*****THE ANSWER TO THIS QUESTION SHOULD GO IN BLUEBOOK II*****

-8-

GO TO BLUEBOOK III

QUESTION 7 **THE ANSWER TO THIS QUESTION SHOULD GO IN BLUEBOOK III**

At the height of the real estate bubble in 1998, Jamie, an up-and-coming medical professional, purchased a beautiful vacation home in northern Michigan for $200,000. Her initial purchase was financed by Local Bank, to whom she granted a mortgage. On the same day the sale closed, Local Bank properly recorded its mortgage.

Five years after the initial purchase, Jamie decided to construct an addition to the home. Jamie financed the $100,000 addition by executing a second mortgage on the home, which was granted to National Bank. National Bank properly recorded its mortgage, which contained a power of sale clause. The home's addition was subsequently completed.

In November 2009, Jamie fell upon hard economic times and could no longer afford to pay the mortgages on her vacation home. Realizing that the value of the home was now substantially less than the remaining principal on her mortgage, she ceased paying both mortgages that month but continued to use the property. National Bank decided to foreclose on its mortgage, so it posted notice of the impending foreclosure by sale in the county newspaper for each of the four weeks in February 2010, and nailed a copy of the foreclosure to the front door of the vacation home. On March 15, 2010, a public foreclosure sale was held wherein National Bank, the highest bidder, purchased the home for the outstanding balance ($80,000) of the mortgage, and a sheriff's deed was executed in National Bank's name the same day.

In April 2010, the ABC Corporation announced that it wished to purchase property in the area in order to develop a large, government-subsidized wind farm in northern Michigan. Jamie, realizing that the property suddenly became very valuable once again, now wishes to keep the home.

Assess: (1) whether National Bank's foreclosure was valid; (2) assuming the foreclosure was valid, what options, if any, exist for Jamie to reassert her interest in the foreclosed vacation home; and (3) the status of Local Bank's mortgage. Explain your answers.

*******THE ANSWER TO THIS QUESTION SHOULD GO IN BLUEBOOK III*******

-9-

QUESTION 8 **THE ANSWER TO THIS QUESTION SHOULD GO IN BLUEBOOK III**

After Dwayne's wife died in 2001, Dwayne created a valid trust for the benefit of his son Paul. The language of the trust requires the trustee, Big Bank, to pay, $25,000 per year to Paul for 20 years. After the expiration of the 20-year period, the remainder of the trust is to be evenly distributed between Ed and Scott, Dwayne's best friends. The trust contains the following language:

> No interest of any beneficiary in the income or principal of this trust shall be transferable by the beneficiary, nor shall such interest be subject to the claims of the beneficiary's creditors by garnishment, attachment, or other legal process.

When Dwayne died in September 2004, the trust's assets were worth nearly $3,000,000. In accordance with the directives of the trust, Big Bank paid Paul $25,000 every January 1st for several years. In June 2010, Paul filed a petition to set aside the trust. Paul claimed that Dwayne lacked capacity to form the trust, that the trust did not reflect Dwayne's true intent, that the trust was the result of the undue influence of Ed and Scott.

In July 2010, Paul's ex-wife Sara filed a claim seeking an interest in Paul's annual trust distribution. Sara sought to enforce a valid child support judgment which was currently approximately $39,000 in arrears. Sara demanded that the entire amount of the child support arrearage be paid in full.

Assume that this is otherwise a valid testamentary trust under Michigan law. Discuss the likelihood of success of: (1) Paul's challenge to the validity of the trust; and (2) Sara's claim against Paul's annual trust distribution. (3) Would the analysis regarding Sara's claim be different if the trust contained the following distribution provision in addition to the above-quoted provision: "The trustee is hereby given the power to pay the beneficiary in such amounts as the trustee in its sole judgment shall determine."

Explain your answers.

*******THE ANSWER TO THIS QUESTION SHOULD GO IN BLUEBOOK III*******

-10-

QUESTION 9 THE ANSWER TO THIS QUESTION SHOULD GO IN BLUEBOOK III

Gina Giftgiver is the aunt of Nancy Niece. Two months before Nancy's 21st birthday, Gina told Nancy she would give Nancy her pearl necklace and $20,000 on Nancy's 21st birthday, no strings attached. The next week, Gina was critically injured in an automobile accident and was hospitalized in the Intensive Care Unit. When Nancy visited Gina in the ICU, Gina was about to undergo serious surgery. When she was wheeled into the operating room, Gina handed Nancy her diamond bracelet and said, "I want you to have this if I don't make it."

Remarkably, Gina recovered from her injuries and returned home. On Nancy's 21st birthday, Gina invited Nancy over to her house and presented her with the pearl necklace. The next morning Nancy called Gina to thank her for the necklace and casually inquired about the $20,000. Gina erupted in anger, told Nancy that she wasn't getting any money, and demanded that Nancy return both the pearl necklace and the diamond bracelet at the next family gathering. In the meantime, Nancy has visited your office for some legal advice.

Assess: (a) whether Nancy is required to return the pearl necklace to Gina; (b) whether Nancy is required to return the diamond bracelet to Gina; and (c) whether Gina is legally obligated to give Nancy the $20,000 gift she promised. Explain your answers.

*******THE ANSWER TO THIS QUESTION SHOULD GO IN BLUEBOOK III*******

-11-

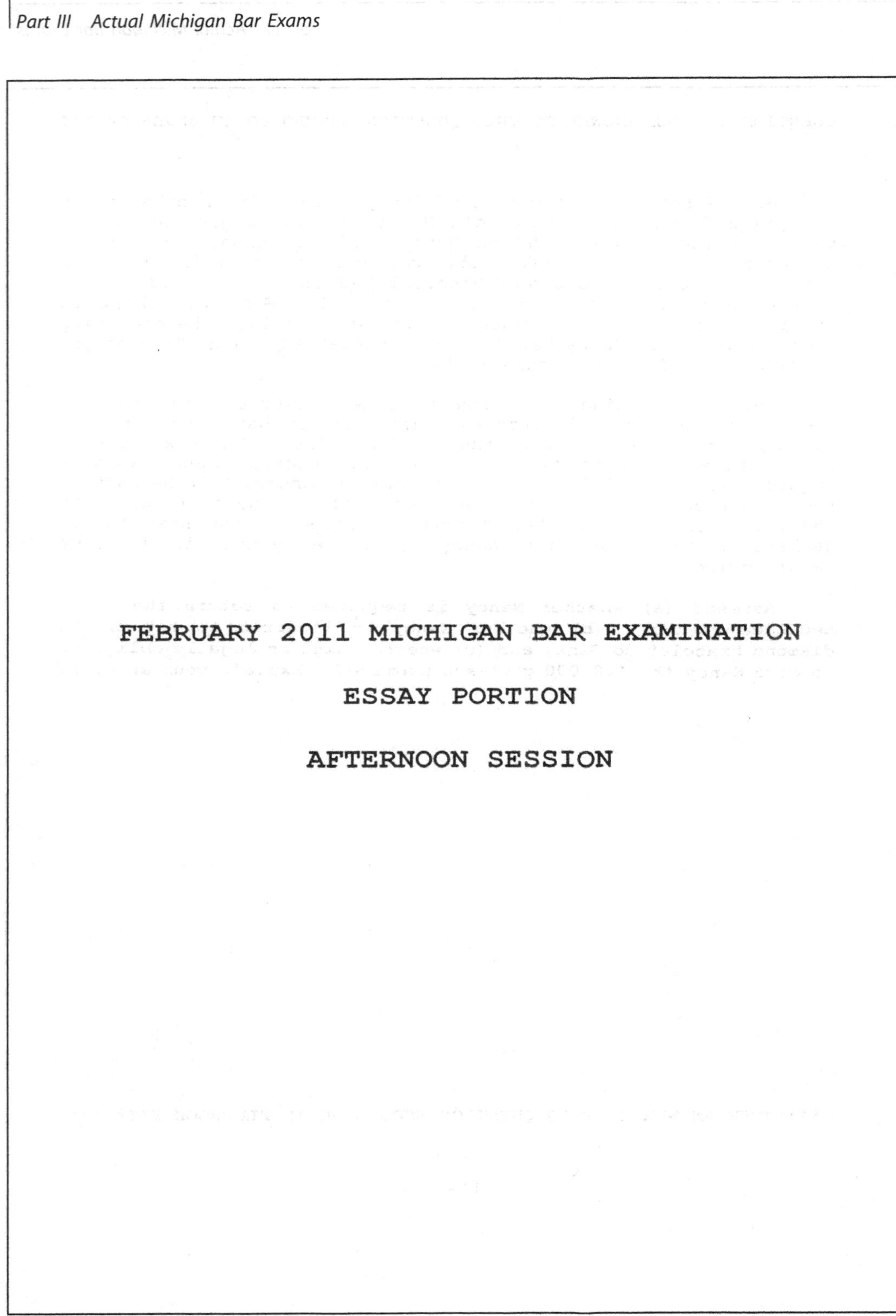

FEBRUARY 2011 MICHIGAN BAR EXAMINATION

ESSAY PORTION

AFTERNOON SESSION

QUESTION 10 **THE ANSWER TO THIS QUESTION SHOULD GO IN BLUEBOOK IV**

Claire is 20 years old and employed in the billing department of XYZ Corporation (XYZ), a medium-sized medical supply company. Recently XYZ's employees asked XYZ to provide a parking lot for the employees, something they felt they needed due to the scarcity of nearby public parking. XYZ begrudgingly agreed and did provide the employees a parking lot.

One morning Claire drove her car to work, arriving approximately 20 minutes prior to her usual 9:00 a.m. starting time. She parked her car in the employer-provided parking lot. After exiting her car and while walking toward the employee entrance, she stumbled on a few random pebbles on the ground in the parking lot and twisted her right knee. She reported to work and told her employer of her knee problem. Because Claire's job did not require her to be on her feet much, she did not miss any time from work that day or thereafter.

Over the next few days, Claire's knee continued to bother her. She initially dismissed the problem as not serious because she had suffered a strained ligament in the same knee while playing soccer as a high school senior, 1½ years earlier. When the knee pain worsened over the ensuing days, however, Claire decided to see a doctor. After a thorough examination, including appropriate diagnostic films and tests, the doctor told Claire she had aggravated the previously strained ligament and the ligament was now torn and required surgery.

Claire asked XYZ to pay for her surgery and related medical treatment via its workers' compensation insurance. XYZ refused telling Claire this was primarily a soccer-related injury and, in any event, workers' compensation coverage does not encompass injuries occurring in the parking lot while on the way to work.

Answer the following two questions presented by the above facts in accord with Michigan workers' compensation law:

(1) Given Claire's preexisting soccer-related ligament injury, can XYZ be held liable for a subsequent tear of the same ligament? Explain your answer.

(2) Is Claire's alleged injury in the parking lot within the scope of the Workers' Disability Compensation Act? Explain your answer. Explain which workers' compensation rules are engaged in reaching your conclusion.

*******THE ANSWER TO THIS QUESTION SHOULD GO IN BLUEBOOK IV*******

-12-

QUESTION 11 **THE ANSWER TO THIS QUESTION SHOULD GO IN BLUEBOOK IV**

Sticker, Inc. is a Michigan company that designs and manufactures adhesive labels for a variety of purposes. Organics, LLC, is a Michigan company that produces organic fruit for distribution to independent local produce markets throughout the state of Michigan. Organics sought to expand its distribution by selling its produce to chain grocery stores. Organics learned that to sell produce in grocery stores, its fruit had to be identified by type, size and how it was grown.

A representative of Organics inquired into whether Sticker could provide labels that Organics could attach to its fruit and/or its fruit containers. The representative phoned Sticker and spoke to a salesman, who indicated that Sticker had previously provided such labels to other companies. The two generally discussed the number of labels required, price, and shipping arrangements. The representative of Organics said that he would discuss the conversation with his superiors, and if they agreed to the terms discussed, he would provide Sticker a written offer memorializing those terms for a yearly contract. Sticker received the offer, reviewed it, and filled in the agreed terms on a Sticker's purchase order form. The reverse side of the purchase form included a conspicuous statement expressly disclaiming any warranty of merchantability and further indicating that the product was sold "as is" and that there are no warranties which extend beyond the description on the face of the document. Organics received the purchase order form, read the handwritten terms on the front page, and simply filed it.

In May, Organics informed Sticker that it required labels for the upcoming blackberry and raspberry season. Sticker produced the labels and shipped the required amount to Organics. The labels were attached to the plastic berry containers, the produce was successfully shipped, and Organics received no complaints from the grocery stores about its product. In late August, Organics informed Sticker that it required labels for the upcoming plum and apple season. Sticker again produced the labels and shipped the required amount to Organics. Organics' employees attached the labels directly to the plums but soon discovered that many of the labels they attached had fallen off. Organics called Sticker and complained about the problem and a Sticker's representative indicated that sometimes the adhesive did not bond directly to some fruits. He also told Organics that it had purchased the labels "as is" and that there would be no refund or any replacement labels. Organics expressed concern that the labels would not be suitable for other large orders, including apples, its largest crop, which soon needed to be distributed. Organics cancelled payment to Sticker for

-13-

the shipment of plum and apple labels and refused to order any more of their labels from Sticker.

Can Sticker recover the payment for the plum and apple labels that Organics cancelled? Explain your answer.

Can Organics refuse to order any further labels from Sticker within the one-year contract period? Explain your answer.

*******THE ANSWER TO THIS QUESTION SHOULD GO IN BLUEBOOK IV*******

-14-

QUESTION 12 THE ANSWER TO THIS QUESTION SHOULD GO IN BLUEBOOK IV

Mia and Ronaldo began dating in 2000. At the time, Mia had sole custody of her 5-year-old son from another relationship. Ronaldo, who was the accountant for his family's soccer apparel business, proposed to Mia after they had dated for a little over a year. Upon learning that his son had proposed, Ronaldo's father became very concerned. He explained to Ronaldo that the family's soccer apparel store was doing very well. He was planning to open in new locations across the state, but he wanted to keep the business in the family. He also wanted Ronaldo to eventually take over the business, but he did not want Mia or her son to have any interest in the business should Ronaldo die or divorce Mia. He encouraged Ronaldo to get a written agreement from Mia waiving any interest in the business.

Ronaldo took his father's advice, but he only told Mia that his father was concerned about making sure that she would never be liable for any business debts. He did not mention any plans for opening new stores and keeping the business in the family because he did not want Mia to think poorly of his father. Mia agreed to sign a prenuptial agreement, and in 2002, she and Ronaldo signed a written agreement stating that each party waived any interest in the other party's previously owned property, as well as property acquired in their individual names during the marriage. The agreement also provided that, in the event of divorce, Mia would not have any claim or interest in Ronaldo's family business, and neither party would seek or be entitled to spousal support. At the time the agreement was signed, neither Mia nor Ronaldo had any substantial assets, and each was generally aware of what the other owned. Neither Mia nor Ronaldo had the agreement reviewed by an attorney.

Mia and Ronaldo were married in 2002 shortly after they signed the prenuptial agreement. Living in Michigan, Mia worked as a nurse and Ronaldo soon became the manager of his family's business. The business grew substantially and new stores were opened throughout the state.

In 2010, Mia discovered that Ronaldo was exchanging sexually explicit e-mails with other women and it appeared that he had engaged in one or more affairs. She immediately filed for divorce. Ronaldo's income at the time was approximately $100,000 per year, and Mia's was $65,000. Ronaldo expected to take over the family business within the next two or three years, at which point his income would substantially increase.

Mia filed a motion for declaratory relief with the family court. In her motion, she indicated that she had no desire to claim

-15-

any ownership in the soccer apparel business, but she wanted the prenuptial agreement to be declared void and she wanted substantial spousal support.

Discuss: (1) whether the prenuptial agreement between Mia and Ronaldo is valid; and (2) whether, if the court were to find that the prenuptial agreement was not valid, Mia can receive spousal support. Explain your answers.

*****THE ANSWER TO THIS QUESTION SHOULD GO IN BLUEBOOK IV*****

-16-

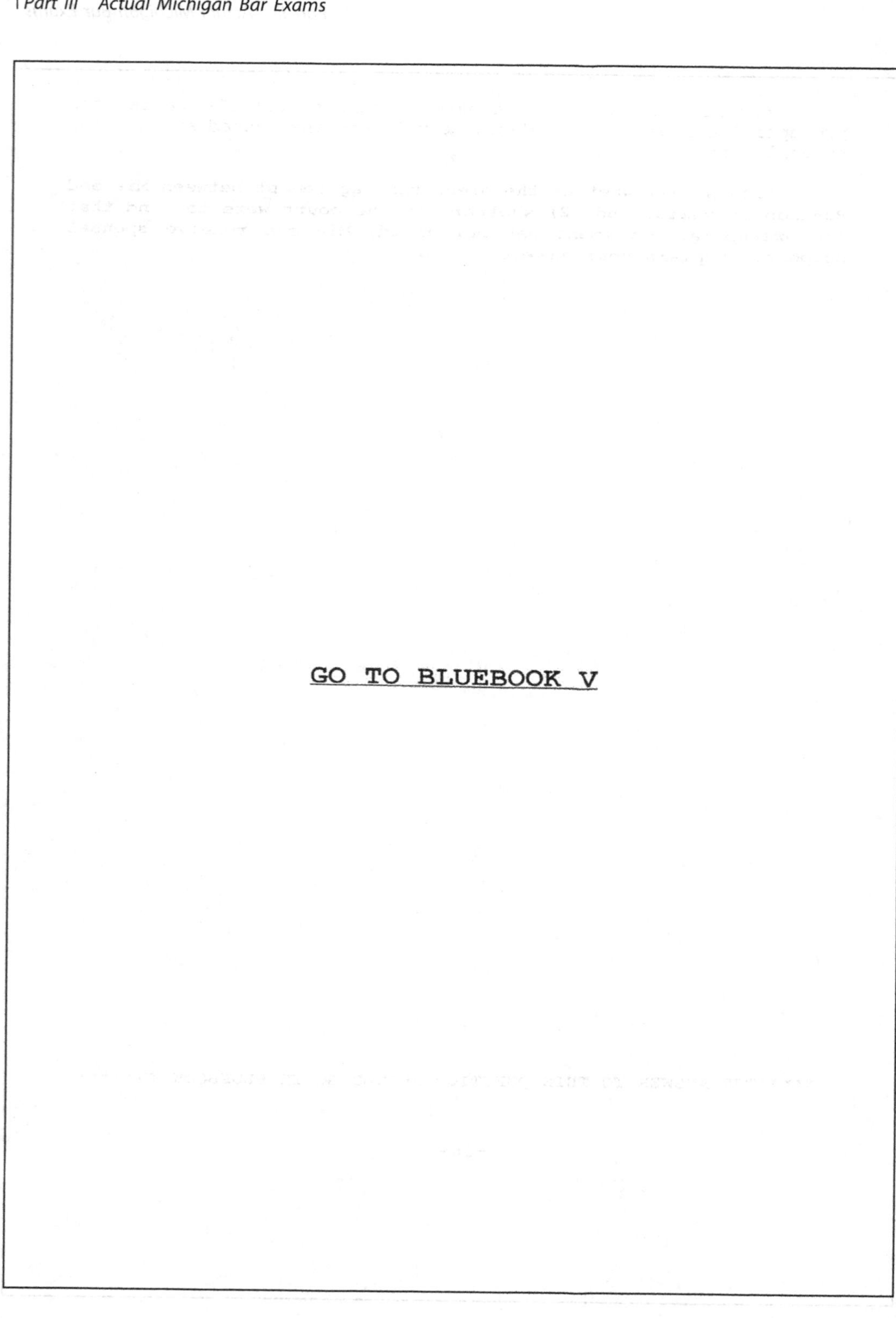

GO TO BLUEBOOK V

<u>QUESTION 13</u> **THE ANSWER TO THIS QUESTION SHOULD GO IN BLUEBOOK V**

After initially retaining attorney Amy Adams to represent him in a personal injury case, and after Adams had done substantial work on the case, Bob Barnes fired Adams and hired you because of your reputation as an outstanding plaintiff's personal injury lawyer. You, too, did a considerable amount of work on the case, and eventually you obtained a settlement of $90,000.00. (For purposes of this question, there are no costs associated with the litigation.)

Upon hearing of the settlement, Adams writes to you demanding a fee of $40,000.00 based on her claim of a verbal fee agreement with Barnes. According to Adams, that fee agreement provided that if Barnes terminated her services and was later successful in obtaining a recovery, her fee would be 1/3 of the present value of the case as of the time her services were terminated. Several days before Barnes fired her, defense counsel had offered in writing to settle the case for $120,000.00. When you ask Barnes if Adams' claim as to a verbal agreement and its terms is accurate, he agrees that it is.

1. Is Adams entitled to the $40,000.00 fee she is demanding? Explain your answer.

2. If Adams is not entitled to $40,000.00, how much is she entitled? Explain your answer.

*******THE ANSWER TO THIS QUESTION SHOULD GO IN BLUEBOOK V*******

-17-

QUESTION 14 **THE ANSWER TO THIS QUESTION SHOULD GO IN BLUEBOOK V**

Brawny Corporation ("Brawny") manufactures industrial machinery in Michigan using complex, largely robotic assembly lines. When a line breaks down, Brawny sometimes calls Speedy Service Corporation ("Speedy Service"), a nearby business that provides repair services for specialized factory equipment. After a line breakdown disrupted production about two months ago, Brawny's production manager phoned Speedy Service and asked that its representatives assess the problem and quote a price for fixing it. While Speedy Service's crew was at the plant as requested assessing the situation, a crew member was injured when he slipped on a patch of ice in Brawny's parking lot.

On January 3, Speedy Service delivered to Brawny a signed price quotation on its standard quotation form. The front of the form had a large area for a description of the job and the quoted price, which Speedy Service filled in as follows:

> Complete labor and materials for troubleshooting, repair and testing of assembly line: $15,000 (no overtime work, no guaranteed completion date)
> OR, to guarantee completion of repairs within 3 business days: $25,000 total labor and materials.

The back of the printed Speedy Service quotation form contained a number of terms, including these:

> Customer [*i.e.*, Brawny] shall indemnify and, if requested, defend Speedy Service against all claims, injuries and losses arising out of or related to the performance of the work covered by this quotation.
>
> Customer's acceptance includes agreement to all terms appearing on the back of this quotation. To accept, return this form with your purchase order number or communicate acceptance in another reasonable manner.

On January 4, Brawny delivered one of its own purchase order forms to Speedy Service. The space on the front of the form labeled "Terms of Purchase" read:

> Begin quoted assembly line repairs as soon as possible for the price stated in your Jan. 3 quotation, subject to all terms on both sides of this purchase order.

-18-

One of the several terms on the back of Brawny's purchase order that differed from Speedy Service's proposed terms read:

> Seller is solely responsible for, and shall defend Brawny against, any injuries or claims asserted against Brawny arising out of or related to Seller's furnishing the services covered by this Purchase Order.

Speedy Service sent a crew to Brawny to begin the repair job that afternoon. The crew worked well into the night and, using lots of overtime, completed the repairs within 48 hours. Brawny's on-site production manager was told by the Speedy Service crew leader when the team arrived that they planned on working overtime and on finishing the job as soon as they could. The production manager complimented the crew leader on the speed with which the project was finished.

Speedy Service subsequently invoiced Brawny for $25,000. When Brawny sent Speedy Service a check for $15,000 marked "payment in full," Speedy Service returned the check and wrote Brawny that it owed $25,000 "in accordance with the terms of our accepted quotation."

Meanwhile, Speedy Service's injured employee has threatened to sue Brawny, claiming that Brawny's negligence caused his slip-and-fall injury. Brawny has demanded that Speedy Service acknowledge its responsibility for providing Brawny's defense to that claim, but Speedy Service has refused to do so.

Answer the following questions and fully explain your reasoning: (1) How much does Brawny owe Speedy Service for the repair job, and on what legal theory? (2) Is Speedy Service responsible for providing Brawny's defense against the negligence claim made by Speedy Service's employee?

*******THE ANSWER TO THIS QUESTION SHOULD GO IN BLUEBOOK V*******

-19-

QUESTION 15 THE ANSWER TO THIS QUESTION SHOULD GO IN BLUEBOOK V

The Smiths' divorce trial is starting next week, and the main focus will be whether Mr. Smith was having an extra-marital affair. To prove that he was, Mrs. Smith will be calling her private investigator, Mr. Clark, to testify about a conversation he overheard between Mr. Smith and the alleged paramour, Diane. Specifically, while walking along a sidewalk, Clark saw Mr. Smith and Diane in a neighborhood park. After getting within earshot, Clark listened to the end of the conversation where Diane said, "You told me you loved me and that you would marry me as soon as you could leave your wife." In response, Mr. Smith nodded his head affirmatively, simultaneously hugged her, and then said, "I know about all that, but if you show up at trial and testify to that, I promise you that the world as you know it will be over and there will be hell to pay." Furious and frightened by this threat, Diane responded, "I can't believe you are doing this to me; I have been like a second wife to you all of these years." She then left the country and is not expected to return until after the trial.

Clark went to Mrs. Smith's attorney, and related what he overheard. Mrs. Smith's attorney was thrilled with this evidence, realizing that he could use it to prove that an affair was taking place and obtain a better property division. He sent a process server out to serve Diane with a subpoena, but she could not be located for trial. Mrs. Smith's attorney also contacted Mr. Smith's attorney hoping this damaging evidence would gain Mrs. Smith a last-minute settlement. Instead, it resulted in a motion *in limine* from Mr. Smith's attorney, seeking to preclude Clark from testifying about Diane's statement.

Assess under the Michigan Rules of Evidence (1) whether Diane's first statement ("you told me you loved me") can be attributed to Mr. Smith as a party admission and admitted through Clark; and (2) whether Diane's second statement ("I can't believe you are doing this to me") is admissible through Clark. Explain your answer.

*******THE ANSWER TO THIS QUESTION SHOULD GO IN BLUEBOOK V*******

-20-

FEBRUARY 2011 MICHIGAN BAR EXAMINATION MODEL ANSWERS

ANSWER TO QUESTION NO. 1

The No-Fault Act generally bars actions for noneconomic damages, unless the injured person suffered an objectively manifested impairment of an important body function that affects the person's general ability to lead his or her normal life. MCL 500.3135(7).

Although there is no factual dispute regarding the nature and extent of Meredith's injuries, she will still need to meet the serious impairment threshold test in order to be able to collect non-economic damages.

The court uses a three-prong test in order to determine whether a plaintiff meets the threshold for recovery of non-economic damages under the No-Fault Act. The court determines whether there has been: (1) an objectively manifested impairment, that is, observable or perceivable from actual symptoms or conditions; (2) of an important body function, that is, a body function of great value, significance, or consequence to the injured person; that (3) affects the person's general ability to lead his or her normal life, that is, influences some of the plaintiff's capacity to live in his or her normal manner of living; *McCormick v Carrier*, 487 Mich 180 (2010) overruling *Kreiner v Fischer*, 471 Mich 109 (2004), and *Netter v Bowman*, 272 Mich App 289 (2006). MCL 500.3135(7).

For purposes of determining whether a plaintiff has sustained an "objectively manifested impairment" under the No-Fault Act, the focus is not on the injuries themselves, but how the injuries affected a particular body function. *Id.*

Under the "serious impairment of body function" threshold, the requirement that the impairment "affects the person's general ability to lead his or her normal life" requires that a person's general ability to lead his or her normal life has been affected, not destroyed; thus, courts should consider not only whether the impairment has led the person to completely cease a pre-incident activity or lifestyle element, but also whether, although a person is able to lead his or her pre-incident normal life, the person's general ability to do so was nonetheless affected. *Id.* There is no temporal requirement as to how long an impairment must last in order to have an effect on the person's general ability to live her normal life. *Id.*

There is no dispute that Meredith fractured her leg, was in a cast, had a metal rod surgically inserted, and was off work for approximately two months. A broken leg is observable. Meredith went to the hospital, there were presumably x-rays taken, a metal rod was surgically inserted into her leg, and she wore a cast for approximately two months. Her injury affected the use of her leg which is a body function that is of significance to her. She was on crutches temporarily and still has difficulty sitting or standing for prolonged periods of time.

The main issue is whether Meredith's injury affected her ability to lead her normal life. The facts suggest that Meredith was in a cast, then on crutches and unable to have unrestricted use of her leg for approximately two months. Additionally, she was unable to lift anything or do household chores for approximately three months. And lastly, she is unable to bicycle post-accident because of the pain. Although her injury was not extensive and her recovery period was relatively short, her ability to lead her normal life is nonetheless affected. As such, it appears that Meredith may have suffered a serious impairment of a body function for purposes of the statute and will be able to request non-economic damages.

Meredith will be able to sue both McDreamy and his mother, Abby, for her damages. Under Michigan law, both the owner and operator of a motor vehicle are liable for "an injury caused by the negligent operation of [a] motor vehicle" if the owner expressly or impliedly consents or knows about the use of the vehicle. MCL 257.401(1). Here, the facts indicate that McDreamy's mother, Abby, consented to the use of her car. As such, Meredith could sue both

-2-

McDreamy and Abby, as both could be held liable for her damages.

-3-

ANSWER TO QUESTION NO. 2

Voting weight: Pursuant to MCL 450.1301, a corporation may issue the number of shares authorized in its articles of incorporation. Here, DDD's articles of incorporation permit only 100 shares. Furthermore, MCL 450.1301 specifically indicates that "[t]he shares may be all of 1 class or may be divided into 2 or more classes." Thus, having only one class of shares is explicitly permissible under Michigan law. Additionally, in the absence of any limitation or designation applicable to separate series contained within a class of shares, "each share shall be equal to every other share of the same class." Thus, despite Dan's claim that his creative genius should be afforded some additional quantum of voting weight, nothing in DDD's articles of incorporation or Michigan law supports this claim.

Amendment of the Articles of Incorporation: A corporation may amend its articles of incorporation if "the amendment contains only provisions that might lawfully be contained in the original articles of incorporation filed at the time of making the amendment." MCL 450.1601. Specifically, a corporation may amend its articles of incorporation in order to "[e]nlarge, limit, or otherwise change its corporate purposes or powers." MCL 450.1602(b). Thus, DDD's articles of incorporation may be permissibly amended to include dealing in vintage automobiles, so long as that purpose would have been proper originally. See also *Detroit & Canada Tunnel Corp v Martin*, 353 Mich 219 (1958). Although unrelated to its confectionary business, dealing in vintage automobiles is a legal enterprise and could have been included in the original articles of incorporation.

As far as the procedure regarding shareholder amendment of the articles of incorporation is concerned, MCL 450.1611(4) requires that notice be given to each shareholder entitled to vote "within the time and in the manner" provided in the Corporation Act for giving notice of shareholder meetings. MCL 450.1404(1) permits notice "not less than 10 nor more than 60 days" before the date of the shareholder meeting, and allows notice to be given "personally, by mail, or by electronic transmission." Thus, the 30-day personal notice provided by DDD to Dan and the other voting shareholders is sufficient.

The articles of incorporation are amended "upon receiving the affirmative vote of a majority of the outstanding shares entitled to vote on the proposed amendment and, in addition, if any class or

-4-

series of shares is entitled to vote on the proposed amendment as a class, the affirmative vote of a majority of the outstanding shares of that class or series." MCL 450.1611(5). It is noteworthy that the voting requirements for amending the articles of incorporation "are subject to any higher voting requirements" provided in the Corporation Act for specific amendments or in DDD's articles of incorporation. Once the amendment is approved by a majority of the shares entitled to vote, a certificate of amendment must be filed with the state. MCL 450.1611(7); MCL 450.1631.

A shareholder who does not vote for (or consent in writing to) a proposed amendment of a corporation's articles may dissent and is entitled to receive payment for his shares, if amending the articles of incorporation either: (a) "[m]aterially alters or abolishes a preferential right of the shares having preferences;" or (b) "[c]reates, alters, or abolishes a material provision or right in respect of the redemption of the shares or a sinking fund for the redemption or purchase of the shares." MCL 450.1621(1). Nothing in the fact pattern indicates that amending DDD's articles of incorporation to include dealing in vintage cars has any impact on Dan's shares or affects Dan's redemption of his shares. Thus, he is not entitled to receive payment for his shares pursuant to MCL 450.1621 and 450.1762.

Shareholder agreement restricting share transfer: Pursuant to MCL 450.1472(1) a restriction on the transfer of corporate shares may be imposed by "the articles of incorporation, the bylaws, or an agreement among any number of holders or among the holders and the corporation." A transfer restriction is not binding with respect to shares issued before the restriction was adopted "unless the holders are parties to an agreement or voted in favor of the restriction." Thus, while the shares issued in 1985 would not ordinarily be bound by the 1999 shareholder agreement, Dan's shares are affected by the agreement because he was party to the unanimous agreement.

MCL 450.1473(a) explicitly permits restrictions on the transfer of shares of a corporation if the restriction"[o]bligates the holders of the restricted instruments to offer to the corporation or to any other holders of bonds or shares of the corporation or to any other person or to any combination thereof, a prior opportunity to acquire the restricted instruments." Thus, Dan may properly be precluded from transferring his 30% interest in DDD to his friend Faye, and may be required to sell his shares to the other shareholders of DDD.

-5-

ANSWER TO QUESTION NO. 3

The general rule is that a party normally bears the cost of their own attorney. However, a court may order a party or counsel to pay for the other party's attorney fees if a statute or court rule allows, or if provided by the common law. *Smith v Khouri*, 481 Mich 519, 526 (2008).

Statutory authority exists for the award of attorney fees. MCL 600.2591. To come within the ambit of the statute, a claim or defense must be deemed frivolous. Not every losing claim or defense is automatically deemed frivolous. Rather, "frivolous" is defined in the statute as meaning that at least one of the following conditions is met: (1) the primary purpose of the party's action or defense was to harass, embarrass or injure the prevailing party; (2) the party had no reasonable basis to believe that the facts underlying the party's legal position were in fact true; or (3) the party's position was devoid of legal merit. Sanctions under the statute can be imposed against the party and the attorney.

The Michigan Court Rules also allow for the imposition of an attorney fee award. MCR 2.114(D), (E) and (F) allow an award against a party or their counsel for violation of MCR 2.114(D). Subsections (D)(2) and (3) provide that the attorney's signature constitutes a certification that to the best of the attorney's knowledge, information and belief, formed after reasonable inquiry, that the document is well grounded in fact, and is not interposed for any improper purpose. For a violation of these requirements, sanctions, including reasonable attorney fees, may be awarded under subsection (E). Additionally, under subsection (F), sanctions may be awarded for a frivolous claim or defense as provided under MCR 2.625(A)(2), which allows for the imposition of costs as provided by MCL 600.2591.

Applying the foregoing principles to the facts at hand, Chips could seek an attorney fee award against both Warbucks and its counsel. To prevail, however, Chips would have to establish that the Warbucks defense was frivolous and/or that Warbucks' lawyer signed the answer and response to the motion in violation of the court rule. This should not be too difficult to establish because Warbucks' counsel all but conceded at oral argument on the summary disposition motion that he did virtually nothing in the way of reasonable inquiry into his client's only defense, *i.e.*, the recipe change. Accordingly, Warbucks' answer and response to the motion

-6-

could not be the product of a "belief well-grounded in fact," as MCR 2.114(D)(2) requires, for signature. Likewise, it appears the defense was frivolous as defined by statute.

Additionally, and irrespective of a finding of frivolousness, because the case went to case evaluation, MCR 2.403(O) applies. Chips accepted the case evaluation of $24,700. Warbucks rejected. Chips was awarded $28,800 by the trial court's granting its summary disposition motion. Because Warbucks did not better the case evaluation award by more than 10% and the evaluation was unanimous, Chips is entitled to attorney fees necessitated by Warbucks' rejection of the case evaluation. Under the facts provided, this would include the fees involved in preparing and arguing the motion for summary disposition. Under MCR 2.403, case evaluation sanctions are awarded only against the party, not the attorney. Lastly, MCR 2.403(O)(11) provides that where the "verdict" is the result of a motion as provided in MCR 2.403(O)(2)(c), the court may, "in the interest of justice" refuse to award actual costs. The facts presented, however, do not indicate that such a declination is called for. *Haliw v Sterling Heights, 266 Mich App 444 (2005)*.

In sum, Chips has a very good chance to prevail in its efforts for reimbursement of attorney fees by arguing that Warbucks' defense should be deemed frivolous and because Warbucks defense was advance without adherence to 2.114. Chips also has an excellent chance of recovering a portion of the total attorneys' fee as case evaluation sanctions.

-7-

ANSWER TO QUESTION NO. 4

Defendant was charged with first-degree premeditated murder. Second-degree murder and involuntary manslaughter are necessarily included lesser offenses to first-degree premeditated murder. A trial court must instruct on the primary charge plus any lesser included offenses that are supported by a rational view of the evidence. *People v Mendoza*, 468 Mich 527, 541 (2003).

Should the trial court give the jury an instruction on second-degree murder?

As stated above, the trial court must instruct on second-degree murder if that instruction is supported by a rational view of the evidence. The elements of second-degree murder are:

1. Defendant caused the death of the decedent.
2. Defendant had one of the following three states of mind:
   a. defendant intended to kill the decedent;
   b. defendant intended to do great bodily harm to the decedent; or
   c. defendant knowingly created a very high risk of death or great bodily harm knowing that death or such harm would be a likely result of his actions.
3. The killing was not justified, excused or done under circumstances that reduce it to a lesser crime. CJI2d 16.5; See *People v Roper*, 286 Mich App 77, 84 (2009).

Here a rational view of the evidence would support giving a second-degree murder instruction. The evidence presented at trial establishes that Dan Defendant shot the bullet that killed Victor Victim. Therefore, the first element of second-degree murder is satisfied. The evidence may also support the second element of second-degree murder--that Dan had the state of mind required for a second-degree murder conviction. Specifically, the evidence established that Dan threatened that Victor "will not make it home alive." Dan waited in his car with a loaded handgun for three hours, until Victor exited the casino. Upon seeing Victor, Dan fired his gun repeatedly in the direction of Victor, ultimately killing him with a bullet to the head. The final element of second-degree murder is one of exclusion by factual finding. That is, the fact finder must conclude as a matter of fact that the killing was not justified, excused or done under circumstances that reduce it to a lesser crime. There is no evidence that would suggest the killing was justified or excused. As discussed below,

-8-

Dan's testimony that he did not intend to harm Victor may support an involuntary manslaughter conviction. The mere possibility of a lesser conviction, however, is not enough to keep the trial court from instructing on second-degree murder. If the jury rejects Dan's testimony, there is ample evidence to support a second-degree murder conviction.

For these reasons, the trial court should give an instruction on second-degree murder.

Should the trial court give the jury an instruction on involuntary manslaughter?

Pertinent to the facts presented here, the elements of involuntary manslaughter are:

1. Defendant caused the death of the decedent.
2. Defendant acted in a grossly negligent manner in doing the act that caused the death.
3. Defendant caused the death without lawful excuse or justification. CJI2d 16.10; See *People v Herron*, 464 Mich 593, 604 (2001).

Elements one and three are not at issue. Dan Defendant shot the bullet that resulted in the death of Victor Victim and nothing presented at trial suggests that Dan Defendant had a legal justification or excuse for killing Victor. Thus, whether the trial court should instruct the jury on involuntary manslaughter will turn on whether a rational view of the evidence supports the conclusion that Dan Defendant acted in a grossly negligent manner when causing the death of Victor.

Gross negligence, by its terms, means something more than carelessness. "It means willfully disregarding the results to others that might flow from an act or failure to act." CJI2d 16.18; see *People v Orr*, 243 Mich 300, 307 (1928). In order to establish gross negligence in criminal law, a prosecutor must establish the following elements beyond a reasonable doubt:

1. Defendant knew of the danger to another.
2. Defendant could have avoided injuring another by using ordinary care.
3. A reasonable person would conclude that a likely result of defendant's conduct was serious injury. *Id.*

Here, based on the proofs admitted by Dan Defendant at trial, a fact finder could reasonably conclude that firing a gun in a public area results in danger to those in the area. A reasonable

-9-

person exercising ordinary care and good judgment would not fire a gun in a public area under the circumstances presented in this case. Finally, a reasonable person would recognize the substantial risk of serious injury that likely would result from Dan's actions. Dan Defendant testified that he intended "only to scare Victor by shooting over his head, into the wall of the casino." If the fact finder accepts this testimony, there would be sufficient evidence to support the conclusion that Dan did not act with the intent to kill. Nonetheless, Dan's conduct could be deemed grossly negligent and sufficient to support a conviction of involuntary manslaughter.

For this reason, the trial court should also give an instruction on involuntary manslaughter.

-10-

ANSWER TO QUESTION NO. 5

I. Article IV of the United States Constitution.

A group of people who own property within Michigan but reside outside of Michigan allege they are being discriminated against because of their non-residence status. This argument implicates the Privileges and Immunities Clause of the United States Constitution, which provides that "[t]he Citizens of each State shall be entitled to all Privileges and Immunities of Citizens in the several States." US Const, art IV, §2. The object of the clause is said to place "the citizens of each State upon the same footing with the citizens of other States, so far as the advantages resulting from citizenship in those States are concerned." *Lunding v New York Tax Appeals Tribunal*, 522 US 287, 296 (1998), quoting *Paul v Virginia*, 75 US 168, 179 (1869). Plaintiffs will argue that they are being "subjected in property or person to taxes more onerous than the citizens of the latter State are subjected to." *Lunding*, 522 US at 296, quoting *Shaffer v Carter*, 252 US 37, 56 (1920).

The school board will argue that the statutory terms under attack do not distinguish between residents and nonresidents of Michigan. Rather, the statute awards a homestead exemption to persons who utilize their property as their principal residence. Thus, Michigan residents who do not utilize their Cherry Hill property as their principal residence are treated the same as the non-resident plaintiffs. *Citizens for Uniform Taxation v Northport Public School Dist*, 239 Mich App 284 (2000). Likewise, persons who utilize their property as "recreational" as that term is defined under the statute would also be entitled to the recreational exemption, regardless of whether they reside within Michigan. The school board's argument has legal merit. Because nonresidents and residents are not treated differently, the Privileges and Immunities Clause is not violated.

Even though plaintiff, under the facts of this question, may correctly assert that the statute "impose[s] substantially the entire tax burden on nonresident property owners," the actual amount of the tax paid by nonresidents is not relevant under the Privileges and Immunities Clause. The relevant question is whether nonresidents do not pay taxes that are "more onerous in effect than those imposed *under like circumstances* upon citizens of [Michigan]" *Lunding*, 522 US at 297 (emphasis added). Here, the statute imposes the very same amount of tax upon Michigan citizens that choose to

-11-

purchase a vacation (non-homestead) home within the school district as those residents from other states. Simply because more nonresidents happen to live within the school district does not render the statute violative of the Privileges and Immunities Clause.

II. 14th Amendment of the United States Constitution and Michigan Const 1963, art 1, §2.

Equal protection of the law is guaranteed by both the federal and Michigan constitutions, US Const, AM XIV; Const 1963, art 1, §2. Both guarantees afford similar protection. *Shepherd Montessori Ctr Milan v Ann Arbor Twp*, 486 Mich 311, 318 (2010). The purpose of the equal protection guarantee is to secure every person against intentional and arbitrary discrimination, whether occasioned by express terms of a statute or by its improper execution. *Village of Willowbrook v Olech*, 528 US 562, 564 (2000). The equal protection guarantee requires that persons under similar circumstances be treated alike; it does not require that persons under different circumstances be treated the same. *Shepherd Montessori, supra*, 486 Mich at 318.

When a legislative classification is challenged as violative of equal protection, the validity of the classification is measured by one of three tests. *Crego v Coleman*, 463 Mich 248, 259 (2000). Crucial to the analysis under the Equal Protection Clause is the applicable standard of review to be applied to the challenged statute. *Dep't of Civil Rights ex rel Forton v Waterford Twp*, 425 Mich 173, 190 (1986).

An inherently suspect classification is one encompassing a discrete and insular minority that has been saddled with such disabilities, or subjected to such a history of purposeful unequal treatment, or relegated to such a position of political powerlessness, as to command extraordinary protection. *San Antonio Independent School Dist v Rodriguez*, 411 US 1, 28 (1973). Here, the statute does not implicate any of the suspect classifications, which include race, ethnicity, national origin, or alienage.

Neither does the statute implicate other classifications, which are suspect but not inherently suspect, including gender, mental capacity or illegitimacy, which are subject to the middle-level substantial relationship test. *Shepherd Montessori, supra*, 486 Mich at 319.

Accordingly, the statute should be examined under the traditional rational basis test. *Phillips v Mirac, Inc*, 470 Mich

-12-

415, 434 (2004). Under the rational basis test, legislation is examined for whether it creates a classification scheme rationally related to a legitimate governmental purpose, and the legislation is presumed to be constitutional. *Shepherd Montessori Ctr Milan v Ann Arbor Twp*, 486 Mich at 318-319. The burden of proof is on the person attacking the legislation to show that the classification is arbitrary. *Shepherd Montessori, supra*, 486 Mich 319; *Idziak, supra*, 484 Mich 570; *Clark, supra*, 243 Mich App 427. A rational basis for legislation exists when any set of facts is known or can be reasonably assumed to justify the discrimination.

Under the rational basis test, plaintiff would be hard pressed to show that the exemption for homestead properties is arbitrary. Ownership of a primary residence is an indeed compelling state interest which is promoted by decreasing the burden of property taxes on homesteads. Thus, the exemption from the property tax authorized by the statute is rationally related to a legitimate state interest.

Under the rational basis test, plaintiff would be unable to show that the exemption for the listed recreational properties is arbitrary. Although the promotion of the listed "recreational properties" is certainly not as compelling as government's interest in police power or home ownership, the exemption of those properties from the tax cannot be said to be illegitimate. These facilities are all open to the general public and, widely speaking, can be said to have some benefit, whether educational, physical or social. On the other hand, non-homestead properties can have uses other than recreation and need not be open to the public. Unlike the listed types of property, non-homestead properties can readily be imagined as used for purposes unrelated to social welfare, such as a convenient second home, a private guesthouse, storage area, etc.

Notably, the above analysis does not preclude legitimate argument noting potential weaknesses of a rational basis finding, including that the "recreational purposes" exemption is under inclusive. In other words, the statute does not regulate all those that own property and use it strictly for recreational purposes similarly. Further, there may be argument suggesting that the statute may unfairly exempt those with political clout, despite a real factual basis for this conclusion. However, these arguments have routinely been rejected. For example, in *Railway Express Agency, Inc v New York*, 336 US 106 (1949), the United States Supreme Court upheld an ordinance that banned all advertising from the side of trucks except to advertise the truck owner's business. The Court stated that "[i]t is no requirement of equal protection that all evils of the same genus be eradicated or none at all."

-13-

Id., at 110. Given this steady trend toward deference to government regularity, and the strong presumption of constitutionality given to tax legislation under these circumstances, *Citizens for Uniform Taxation*, 239 Mich App at 290, plaintiff's claims have little chance of success.

-14-

ANSWER TO QUESTION NO. 6

How should the court rule on the motion to suppress Peter's statement?

The trial court should deny the motion to suppress Peter's statement to Officer Jones.

The right against self-incrimination is guaranteed by both the United States and Michigan Constitutions. US Const, Am V; Const 1963, art 1, §17; *Dickerson v US*, 530 US 428, 433 (2000); *People v Cheatham*, 453 Mich 1, 9 (Boyle, J.), 44 (Weaver, J.) (1996); *People v Bassage*, 274 Mich App 321, 324 (2007).

Where a defendant decides to speak and waive his *Miranda* rights, anything he says, or does not say, is admissible until he invokes his right to silence. *People v McReavy*, 436 Mich 197, 217-218 (1990). Here, the facts inform us that defendant was informed of his *Miranda* rights and that "Peter understood his *Miranda* rights." Further, there is insufficient evidence indicating that Peter invoked his *Miranda* right to remain silent. Although Peter did not say anything for a significant amount of time while in custody, he did not unambiguously or unequivocally invoke the *Miranda* right to remain silent. *Berghuis v Thompkins*, ___ US ___; 130 S Ct 2250, 2260; 176 L Ed 2d 1098, 1112-1113 (2010). At most, Peter only indicated that he was tired and that he wanted to go to bed. At no point did Peter state that he wanted to remain silent or that he did not want to talk to police. *Id.* Thus, Peter did not invoke his "right to cut off questioning." *Id.* citing *Michigan v Mosley*, 423 US 96, 103 (1975).

Notwithstanding a defendant's failure to invoke his *Miranda* right to remain silent, statements of an accused made during custodial interrogation are inadmissible unless the accused voluntarily, knowingly and intelligently waives his Fifth Amendment rights. *Miranda v Arizona*, 384 US 436, 444 (1966); *People v Gipson*, 287 Mich App 261, 264 (2010). Waiver can be implied when a defendant who has been advised of his *Miranda* rights and has understood them makes an uncoerced statement. *Berghuis*, 130 S Ct 16 2261. The prosecutor must establish a valid waiver by a preponderance of the evidence. *People v Harris*, 261 Mich App 44, 55 (2004).

Again, the facts inform us that Peter was informed of his

-15-

Miranda rights and that "Peter understood his *Miranda* rights." From this, it follows that "he knew what he gave up when he spoke." *Berghuis,* 130 S Ct at 2262. Further, Peter's answer to Jones revealed his intent to mitigate his own culpability in the crime. Peter could have simply ignored Jones but he instead attempted to lessen his culpability, stating, "I was not drunk. I only had two beers. I was distracted by my cell phone and that is why I ran the red light. I am so sorry." Further, there is no evidence at all that Peter's statement was coerced. Although he had been interrogated the night before, Peter had only been asked the one question the next morning and was clearly rested when he made the statement.

For these reasons, the trial court should deny the motion to suppress Peter's statement to Officer Jones.

How should the court rule on the motion to dismiss with prejudice the charges against Peter?

The trial court should deny the motion to dismiss.

The right to a speedy trial is guaranteed to criminal defendants by the federal and Michigan constitutions as well as by statute and court rule. US Const, Am VI; Const 1963, art 1, §20; MCL 768.1; MCR 6.004(A); *People v Williams,* 475 Mich 245, 261 (2006). A formal charge or restraint of the defendant is necessary to invoke speedy trial guarantees, *People v Rosengren,* 159 Mich App 492, 506 n 16 (1987). The delay period commences at the arrest of the defendant. *Williams,* 475 Mich at 261.

The defendant must prove prejudice when the delay is less than 18 months. *People v Collins,* 388 Mich 680, 695 (1972); *People v Waclawski,* 286 Mich App 634, 665 (2009). A delay of more than 18 months is presumptively prejudicial to the defendant, and shifts the burden of proving lack of prejudice to the prosecutor. *Williams,* 475 Mich at 262. In determining whether a defendant has been denied a speedy trial, a court must weigh the conduct of the parties. Relevant factors include: (1) the length of the delay; (2) the reasons for the delay; (3) whether the defendant asserted his right to a speedy trial; and (4) prejudice to the defendant from the delay. *Vermont v Brillon,*_____ US _____; 129 S Ct 1283, 1290; 173 L Ed 2d 231, 239-240 (2009); *Williams,* 475 Mich at 261. Prejudice to the defense occurs when there is a substantial chance that the defense to the charge is substantially impaired by the delay. *Williams,* 475 Mich at 264; *People v Gilmore,* 222 Mich App 442, 461-462 (1997); *People v Ovegian,* 106 Mich App 279, 285 (1981).

-16-

Here, the length of the delay is significant and weighs in favor of granting defendant's motion. If the court sticks to its most recent schedule, the trial will not commence until 21 months after the accident date. The reason for the delay is neglect by the court system. This type of delay cannot in any way be attributed to the defendant. To the contrary, scheduling delays and delays caused by the court system are attributed to the prosecution. However, such delay weighs only slightly in favor of granting the motion, as delays caused by the court system are generally given minimal weight. *Williams*, 475 Mich at 263. Moreover, defendant cannot be blamed for failing to assert his speedy trial rights in a more timely fashion. The trial court found that defendant was indigent and entitled to appointed counsel. The trial court also knew that the counsel originally appointed to represent defendant had died and that defendant was in need of new counsel. Once appointed, Lisa Lawyer acted with due diligence in bringing a motion to dismiss. Thus, this factor weighs in favor of granting defendant's motion. The final factor, however, weighs strongly in favor of denying defendant's motion. Because the delay exceeds 18 months, the burden rests on the prosecution to establish a lack of prejudice to defendant's case. Defendant will argue that his case is crippled without Wendy, who would have testified that he was not driving the car. However, this assertion flies in the face of defendant's statement that he ran the red light because he was distracted by his cell phone. Further, Wendy has no first-hand knowledge of who was driving Peter's car at the time of the accident. The prosecution will point out that nobody knows what Wendy would have testified to, since she never gave a statement to the police or the defense. However, reviewing the facts in a light most favorable to defendant, all Wendy could testify to was that Oscar drove the car when leaving the pub. Wendy did not witness the accident. Any inference drawn from Wendy's putative testimony would be defeated by Peter's statement to Officer Jones.

For these reasons, the court should deny Peter's motion to dismiss.

-17-

ANSWER TO QUESTION NO. 7

(1) National Bank properly foreclosed on Jamie's mortgage.

Michigan law allows for a mortgagee to *foreclose by advertisement*, which thereby allows mortgagees to forego judicial proceedings where there has been a default in the mortgage, such as failure to pay. MCL 600.3201; MCL 600.3204. However, in order to do so, certain conditions must be met. First, because non-judicial foreclosure is contract-based, there must be a power of sale clause in the mortgage; also, the mortgage must have been properly recorded, and it must not otherwise be in foreclosure at the time the mortgagee seeks to foreclose. MCL 600.3201; MCL 600.3204(1)(c); MCL 600.3204(1)(b). Second, the mortgagee must *publish notice* that the mortgage will be foreclosed by sale "by publishing the same for 4 successive weeks at least once in each week, in a newspaper published in the county where the premises included in the mortgage and intended to be sold, or some part of them, are situated." MCL 600.3208, see also MCL 600.3212. Third, within 15 days after the first publication of the notice, the mortgagee must post a *copy of the notice* in a conspicuous place upon a part of the premises. MCL 600.3208. A *public foreclosure sale* must be held on the set date, and within 20 days of the sale, the purchaser must record the deed with an accompanying affidavit setting forth the information regarding redemption, MCL 600.3216; MCL 600.3232.

In this case, National Bank properly foreclosed by advertisement on Jamie's property after Jamie defaulted on her mortgage. The facts specifically note that the mortgage document contained a power of sale clause and was properly recorded by National Bank. National Bank properly published for four consecutive weeks in the local newspaper notice of the sale, and properly posted notice of the sale prominently on the property within 15 days of the first publication. (Note: it is irrelevant if Jamie received actual notice of the sale either through publication or as located on the property.) Finally, National Bank purchased the property on the set date at the sheriff's sale and properly recorded its new deed. A mortgagee may, in good faith, purchase the property at the sale. MCL 600.3228.

Note also: because this property is not Jamie's principal residence, separate notice by mail and other services are not required to be given pursuant to MCL 600.3205a in order to foreclose by advertisement. MCL 600.3205a has otherwise been

-18-

repealed by the Legislature, which will become effective on July 5, 2011.

(2) Even though the property has been properly foreclosed, Jamie may exercise her right to redeem the property.

The statutory right of redemption provides the homeowner of a foreclosed property the right to recover the property from the purchaser by paying the amount the purchaser paid for the property, taxes, insurance, fees, and interest that has accumulated. MCL 600.3240(1)-(2); *Gerasimos v Continental Bank*, 237 Mich 513, 518-519 (1927). In order to exercise the right of redemption, however, a homeowner must act within the time period set by statute. See MCL 600.3240(7)-(12). Subject to exceptions not applicable here (*e.g.*, abandonment), for a residential home subject to a mortgage excused after January 1, 1965, where the outstanding balance is more than 66-2/3% of the original indebtedness secured by the mortgage, the redemption period is 6 months from the date of the sale. MCL 600.3240(8).

Even though the property has been validly foreclosed, Jamie may redeem the property by paying National Bank the purchase price, as well as taxes, insurance, and other fees and interest accumulated within the statutory period. Because Jamie's mortgage was executed after January 1, 1965, and because the outstanding balance ($80,000) is more than 66-2/3% of the original mortgage ($100,000), and because none of the other statutory exceptions regarding the redemption period apply here, the redemption period applicable here is 6 months from the date of the sale. Jamie must thus actually tender the redemption amount to a proper person within 6 months, and by doing so she can recover the property and enjoy full privileges and liabilities of ownership. See *Flynn v Korneffel*, 451 Mich 186 (1996);l *Schulthies v Barron*, 16 Mich App 246 (1969). Jamie thus has until September 15, 2011 to redeem.

(3) Local Bank's preexisting mortgage remains as a valid encumbrance on the property.

Generally, foreclosures wipe out junior interests (those that come later in time), but do not displace senior interests (those that came earlier), and thus the purchaser of a property at a foreclosure sale takes the property subject to senior interests. Michigan statutory law explicitly provides that "no person having any valid subsisting lien upon the mortgaged premises, or any part thereof, created before the lien of such mortgage took effect, shall be prejudiced by any such [foreclosure] sale, nor shall his rights or interests be in any way affected thereby." MCL 600.3236.

-19-

Here, Local Bank's mortgage was executed and validly recorded prior to the mortgage of National Bank. Therefore, even though National Bank has foreclosed on its mortgage, Local Bank's mortgage (a senior interest) remains as a valid encumbrance on the property, to which National Bank (as the purchaser at the foreclosure sale) or Jamie (if she redeems within the redemption period) will be subject.

-20-

ANSWER TO QUESTION 8

Paul's Capacity to Challenge the Trust:

Under the doctrine of election (also termed estoppel by acceptance) a beneficiary who elects to accept the benefits of a trust is thereafter barred from challenging the validity of the trust, including claims of insufficient capacity or undue influence. *In re Beglinger Trust*, 221 Mich App 273 (1997); *Holzbaugh v Detroit Bank & Trust Co*, 371 Mich 432 (1963). Thus, under the doctrine of election, Paul would be precluded from challenging the validity of the trust because he elected to accept benefits under the trust.

However, a recent amendment to the Michigan Trust Code may permit Paul to challenge the trust based on undue influence. Public Act 2009, No. 46, applies to "all trusts created before, on, or after" the statutory effective date of April 1, 2010. MCL 700.8206(1)(a). MCL 700.7406 was amended to simply state that a "trust is void to the extent its creation was induced by fraud, duress, or undue influence." The statutory provision contains no exception or exclusion for those who have accepted trust benefits. Therefore, a plausible argument could be made that Paul retains the ability to challenge the trust based on a claim of undue influence under the new statutory amendment, despite accepting the $25,000 annual benefit.

Spendthrift Clause:

The clause described in the fact pattern is a "spendthrift provision," a trust provision that "restrains either the voluntary or involuntary transfer of a trust beneficiary's interest." MCL 700.7103(j). Spendthrift provisions are valid and enforceable in Michigan. MCL 700.7502(1). Spendthrift provisions generally preclude the beneficiary's creditors from satisfying the beneficiary's debt with the beneficiary's trust interest.

However, there are several exceptions to this rule. MCL 7007504(1)(a)-(c) states that a trust beneficiary's interest may be reached to satisfy an enforceable claim where the claims involve:

(a) A trust beneficiary's child or former spouse who has a judgment or court order against the trust beneficiary for support or maintenance.
(b) A judgment creditor who has provided services that

enhance, preserve, or protect a trust beneficiary's interest in the trust.

(c) This state or the United States.

Because Sara has a "judgment or court order against the trust beneficiary for support or maintenance," Sara may reach Paul's trust interest despite the spendthrift provision in order to satisfy the child support obligation.

However, Sara will not be able to recoup the entire amount of the arrearage all at once. MCL 700.7504(2) states that the court shall order all or part of a judgment satisfied "only out of all or part of distributions of income or principal as they become due." Because Paul's annual trust distribution is only $25,000 per year, the most Sara could receive is $25,000 when the distribution is due on January 1. However, the remainder of the arrearage can be paid in subsequent years.

Discretionary Trust Provision:

The alternate clause described in the fact pattern is a "discretionary trust provision." Such a provision exists where the trustee is given the discretion to determine whether, or in what amount, to distribute trust assets to beneficiaries. MCL 700.7103(d)(i-v).

If the trust contained a discretionary trust provision, Sara could not file a claim against Paul's trust distribution. MCL 700.7504, the statutory provision permitting certain types of claims to be enforced against a beneficiary's trust interests, specifically does not apply to a trust containing a discretionary trust provision. MCL 700.7504(3). Rather, where a discretionary trust provision exists, a trust beneficiary's creditor does not have a right to any amount of trust assets, and trust property cannot be reached until the assets are "distributed directly to the trust beneficiary." MCL 700.7505. Thus, Sara would be required to attempt to collect the past due child support from Paul after he receives the trust distribution.

-22-

ANSWER TO QUESTION NO. 9

The Pearl Necklace: Whether Nancy is required to return the pearl necklace to Gina turns on whether a valid *inter vivos* gift occurred. A valid *inter vivos* gift transfer title to the donee and requires three elements: (1) the donor must have the present intent to transfer title gratuitously to the donee; (2) actual or constructive delivery of the subject matter to the donee must occur, unless it is already in the donee's possession; and (3) the donee must accept the gift. *Detroit Bank v Bradfield*, 324 Mich 124, 130-131 (1949). It appears that Nancy will be entitled to keep the pearl necklace. The facts indicate that Gina intended to give Nancy the necklace, that it was actually delivered to Nancy, and that Nancy accepted the necklace. Because the necklace is a valid *inter vivos* gift, Nancy will not be required to return the necklace to Gina.

The Diamond Bracelet: Whether Nancy is required to return the diamond bracelet turns on whether the bracelet was an *inter vivos* gift or a gift *causa mortis*. A gift *causa mortis* does not transfer title to the donee until the death of the donor because it is "revocable during the lifetime of the donor." *In re Reh's Estate*, 196 Mich 210, 218 (1917). A gift *causa mortis* requires three elements: (1) the gift must be made with a view of the donor's death from a present sickness or peril; (2) such actual or constructive delivery of the subject matter must occur as the circumstances permit; and (3) the donor's intent must be conditioned to become absolute only upon the donor's death. *Id.* Here, the facts indicate that each of the three elements of a gift *causa mortis* is met. First, Gina made the gift in view of her death. Second, she actually delivered the bracelet to Nancy. Finally, Gina's donative intent was expressly conditional on her death. Accordingly, the bracelet was the subject of a gift *causa mortis* and not an *inter vivos* gift. Gina can revoke the gift at any time before her death, and her demand that Nancy return the bracelet shows her intent to do so. Therefore, Nancy will not be entitled to keep the bracelet.

The $20,000: Whether Nancy is entitled to receive the money turns on whether a valid *inter vivos* gift occurred merely by Gina's intent to give the gift in the future. As stated, the elements of an *inter vivos* gift are: (1) the donor must have the present intent to transfer title gratuitously to the donee; (2) actual or constructive delivery of the subject matter to the donee must

-23-

occur, unless it is already in the donee's possession; and (3) the donee must accept the gift. Even if Gina intended to give Nancy the money at some point in the future, Gina did not have the *present* intent to transfer the money. Furthermore, no actual or constructive delivery occurred to effect the transfer of title in the money. Mere expressions of the intention to give a gift do not legally transfer title without actual or constructive delivery of the subject matter. *Loop v DesAutell*, 294 Mich 527, 532 (1940). This is true even when the intent is accompanied by a promise. See *Sanilac Co v Aplin*, 68 Mich 659 (1888). Moreover, the promise to make a future gift is not itself enforceable. *White v Grismore*, 333 Mich 568, 574 (1952).

-24-

ANSWER TO QUESTION NO. 10

With respect to the first question, Claire's preexisting soccer related injury does not act as a bar to workers' compensation benefits because employers take their employees as they are. *E.g., Deziel v Difco Laboratories*, 394 Mich 466, 476 (1975). This is true even if the soccer injury is the primary cause of the problem. Employers can be held responsible for aggravation of preexisting non-work related conditions. *Id.* However, an employer is not liable for a work event that aggravates just the symptoms of a preexisting problem. *Rakestraw v General Dynamics Land Systems, Inc*, 469 Mich 220, 228 (2003). The employer is only responsible if the event aggravates the preexisting condition so as to create a distinct problem "that is medically distinguishable from the preexisting non-work related condition." *Rakestraw*, 469 Mich at 234. "[T]o demonstrate a medically distinguishable change in an underlying condition, a claimant must show that the pathology of that condition has changed." *Fahr v General Motors Corp*, 478 Mich 922 (2007).

Applying these rules, Claire's preexisting soccer injury is not a bar to recovery. And, her torn ligament would constitute a pathological change, a problem medically distinguishable from her preexisting soccer injury, so as to qualify as a compensable injury for workers' compensation purposes as required by *Rakestraw/Fahr*.

With respect to the second question, the injury must be one "arising out of and in the course of employment" to be covered by the Workers' Disability Compensation Act. MCL 418.301(1). This is a bifurcated requirement. The "arising out of" component is an inquiry into the risk created by the employment. *Pierce v Michigan Home and Training School*, 231 Mich 536, 537-538 (1925); *Hopkins v Michigan Sugar Company*, 184 Mich 87, 90-91 (1915). The "in the course of" component is an inquiry into the time and place of injury. *Id.* Both requirements must be met for there to be workers' compensation coverage. *Ruthruff v Tower Holding Corp (On Reconsideration)* 261 Mich App 613, 618-623 (2004); *Thomason v Contour Fabricators, Inc*, 255 Mich App 121 (2003), *as modified* 469 Mich 960 (2003).

Generally speaking, injuries sustained while going to or coming from work are not compensable. *E.g., Burchett v Delton-Kellogg School*, 378 Mich 231, 235 (1966). But, there is a statutory presumption relating to the "in the course of" component.

-25-

The statutory presumption says:

> An employee going to or from his or her work, while on the premises where the employee's work is to be performed, and within a reasonable time before and after his or her working hours, is presumed to be in the course of his or her employment. MCL 418.301(3) (first sentence).

Case law has extended the meaning of "premises" for purposes of this provision to include parking lots owned, leased or maintained by the employer. *Simkins v General Motors Corp (after remand)*, 453 Mich 703, 727 (1996); *Ruthruff, supra*.

Applying these rules, Claire was in the parking lot (on the premises) within a reasonable time before her work hours (20 minutes). Therefore, the statutory presumption applies and the injury occurred "in the course of" her employment. The "arising out of" requirement is also satisfied because it is a risk of employment that employees may stumble on debris on employer premises. Compare, *Dulyea v Shaw Worker Co*, 292 Mich 570 (1940).

The employer should, therefore, pay for the surgery and related medical treatment because Claire has sustained a compensable work related injury that is one "arising out of and in the course of employment." MCL 418.301 (1). Employers are responsible for reasonable and necessary medical care related to work injuries. MCL 414.315(1).

-26-

ANSWER TO QUESTION NO. 11

The transaction falls under Article 2 of the Uniform Commercial Code, which governs contracts, whether oral or written, that involve the sale of goods. See MCL 440.2102. The contract involved the purchase of labels, an item movable at the time identified in the contract for sale. MCL 440.2105(1).

Here, Organics made a written offer that memorialized terms of a contract and Sticker attempted to accept the offer through a purchase order form that added a term not in the offer. Although not the focus of the call of the question, an answer may initially question whether the purchase order form operated as an acceptance, given its additional disclaimer. In this regard, MCL 440.2207(1) controls the issues and provides:

> (1) A definite and seasonable expression of acceptance or a written confirmation which is sent within a reasonable time operates as an acceptance even though it states terms additional to or different from those offered or agreed upon, unless acceptance is expressly made conditional on assent to the additional or different terms.

Here, there is no indication that the purchase order form states that "acceptance is expressly made conditional on assent to the additional or different terms," and thus there is no real reason to dispute that the purchase order form operated as an acceptance.

The more relevant question is whether the disclaimer became part of the contract. The remainder of MCL 440.2207 provides that:

> (2) The additional terms are to be construed as proposals for addition to the contract. Between merchants such terms become part of the contract unless:
>
> (a) the offer expressly limits acceptance to the terms of the offer;
>
> (b) they materially alter it; or
>
> (c) notification of objection to them has already been given or is given within a reasonable time after notice of them is received.
>
> (3) Conduct by both parties which recognizes the existence of

-27-

> a contract is sufficient to establish a contract for sale although the writings of the parties do not otherwise establish a contract. In such case, the terms of the particular contract consist of those terms on which the writing of the parties agree, together with any supplementary terms incorporated under any other provisions of this act.

The question reflects that both parties are merchants under the UCC. MCL 440.2104. Further, there is no indication that the offer expressly limits acceptance to its terms and there was no timely objection. MCL 440.2207(2)(a) and (c).

Thus, the only remaining question whether the disclaimer was part of the contract is whether it "materially altered" the contract. "[M]aterial additional terms do not become part of the contract unless expressly agreed to by the other party." *Power Press Sales Co v MSI Battle Creek Stamping*, 238 Mich App 173, 182 (1999), quoting *American Parts Co v American Arbitration Ass'n*, 8 Mich App 156, 173-174 (1967) (internal quotation and citation omitted). Although there is no case law on point, Michigan courts have recognized that "clauses such as those listed in Code comment four, like warranty disclaimers, are routinely deemed material as a matter of law." *Id.*, at 180. Further, given the discussion between the Organics' representative and the Sticker representative in which the Sticker representative indicated that Sticker had provided such labels to other companies, Organics could reasonably be surprised that Sticker would not ensure that the labels would adhere to its product, and suffer hardship as a result of this reliance. Accordingly, a correct answer should simply conclude that the disclaimer clause materially alters the contract and will not be enforced as a matter of law.

In regard to the second question, an answer should conclude that Organics has a strong argument to refuse to order any further labels from Sticker within the one-year contract period.

MCL 440.2612 provides that:

> An "installment contract" is one which requires or authorizes the delivery of goods in separate lots to be separately accepted, even though the contract contains a clause "each delivery is a separate contract" or its equivalent.
>
> (2) The buyer may reject any installment which is nonconforming if the nonconformity substantially impairs the value of that installment and cannot be cured or if the nonconformity is a defect in the required documents; but if the nonconformity does not fall within subsection (3) and the

-28-

seller gives adequate assurance of its cure the buyer must accept that installment.

(3) Whenever nonconformity or default with respect to one or more installments substantially impairs the value of the whole contract there is a breach of the whole. But the aggrieved party reinstates the contract if he accepts a nonconforming installment without seasonably notifying of cancellation or if he brings an action with respect only to past installments or demands performance as to future installments.

Here, the contract clearly authorizes the delivery of goods in separate lots to be separately accepted. The call of the question does not relate to Organics' decision to reject the plum and apple labels, but asks whether Organics can refuse to order "further labels from Sticker within the one-year contract period." The relevant question is whether the "nonconformity . . . with respect to one or more installments substantially impairs *the value of the whole contract*" and "there is a breach of the whole." MCL 440.2612(3). Here, a strong argument can be made that the failure of the labels to adhere directly to fruit impairs the value of the entire contract. As indicated, Organics entered into the contract because "to sell produce in grocery stores its fruit had to be identified by type, size and how it was grown." Thus, the defect is not a minor nonconformity and is not insignificant to the entire contract. Also, the damages could be considered substantial, as Organics expressed concern that the labels could not be used for other "larger orders." Also very important is that Organics has a reasonable apprehension that the defect will not be cured and that the labels would not adhere to other fruits. When Organics called Sticker and complained about the problem, Sticker's representative simply indicated that sometimes the adhesive did not bond direct to "some fruits," leaving Organics to wonder which fruits could then be distributed. The representative also clearly indicated there would be no refund or any replacement labels. Organics has a strong position to cancel the entire contract under MCL 440.2612(3).

-29-

ANSWER TO QUESTION NO. 12

1. MCL 557.28 states "[a] contract relating to property made between persons in contemplation of marriage shall remain in full force after marriage takes place." Michigan courts have held that prenuptial agreements are enforceable in the context of divorce. *Rinvelt v Rinvelt*, 190 Mich App 372 (1991). To be enforceable, prenuptial agreements must be "fair, equitable, and reasonable under the circumstances, and must be entered into voluntarily, with full disclosure, and with the rights of each party and the extent of the waiver of such rights understood." *Id.* at 378-379. The agreement "should be free from fraud, lack of consent, mental incapacity, or undue influence." *Id.* at 379. Because of the relationship of extreme mutual confidence between the parties, a prenuptial agreement creates a special duty of disclosure that is not present in an ordinary contract. *In re Estate of Benker*, 416 Mich 681, 689 (1982).

Prenuptial agreements may be voided if certain standards of "fairness" are not satisfied. *Reed v Reed*, 265 Mich App 131, 142-143 (2005). The *Reed* court stated that, "[a] prenuptial agreement may be voided (1) when obtained through fraud, duress, mistake, or misrepresentation or nondisclosure of material fact, (2) if it was unconscionable when executed, or (3) when the facts and circumstances are so changed since the agreement was executed that its enforcement would be unfair and unreasonable." *Id.* The party challenging the agreement bears the burden of proof and persuasion. *Rinvelt, supra* at 382.

Here, Ronaldo was not honest with Mia about the reason for the prenuptial agreement. He consciously chose not to inform Mia of the fact that his father wanted to limit her ability to claim an interest in the business, and the fact that there were plans for rapid expansion. Assuming that she discovers Ronaldo's prior knowledge, Mia will argue that the agreement was obtained through nondisclosure of a material fact. The issue will be whether the unrevealed motives were "material" facts, given that Mia has no desire to obtain an interest in the business anyway. However, she would argue that Ronaldo did not make a full and frank disclosure of his true interest in the family business, which, in the end, made his potential income substantially more than hers. *In re Estate of Benker*, 416 Mich 681, 692-693 (1982) (discussing presumption of non-disclosure). Note that the fact that Mia was not advised by an attorney works in her favor, as does the fact that the agreement made no provision for her after the divorce, and

-30-

she was potentially waiving far more than he was. *Id.*

Mia might also argue that the substantial growth in the business constituted a change in circumstances rendering the enforcement of the agreement unfair or unreasonable. To determine if a prenuptial agreement is unenforceable because of a change in circumstances, the focus is on whether the changed circumstances were reasonably foreseeable either before or during the signing of the prenuptial agreement. *Reed,* 265 Mich App at 144. However, if the clear language of a prenuptial agreement envisions that the parties will obtain separate assets during the marriage, the fact that one party's assets grew significantly more than the other party's assets is not unforeseeable, and thus not a change in circumstances requiring the court to void the agreement. *Reed,* 265 Mich App at 146-147. The expansion of a business is unlikely to be considered unforeseeable by a court.

There is no clear answer to the question of what the judge would do. The key here is the test-taker's ability to recognize the issues, articulate the standards, and apply the standards to the facts.

2. MCL 552.23(1) provides:

> Upon entry of a judgment of divorce or separate maintenance, if the estate and effects awarded to either party are insufficient for the suitable support and maintenance of either party and any children of the marriage as are committed to the care and custody of either party, the court may further award to either party the part of the real and personal estate of either party and spousal support out of the real and personal estate, to be paid to either party in gross or otherwise as the court considers just and reasonable, after considering the ability of either party to pay and the character and situation of the parties, and all the other circumstances of the case.

The factors that a court examines to determine if spousal support is warranted are: (1) the past relations and conduct of the parties, (2) the length of the marriage, (3) the abilities of the parties to work, (4) the source and amount of property awarded to the parties, (5) the parties' ages, (6) the abilities of the parties to pay alimony, (7) the present situation of the parties, (8) the needs of the parties, (9) the parties' health, (10) the prior standard of living of the parties and whether either is responsible for the support of others, (11) contributions of the parties to the joint estate, (12) a party's fault in causing the divorce, (13) the effect of cohabitation on a party's financial

-31-

status, and (14) general principles of equity. *Berger v Berger*, 277 Mich App 700, 726-727 (2008).

The applicant should not be expected to list every one of these factors, but should focus on those that are relevant to the facts presented in the question. Specifically: (1) Ronaldo's conduct--engaging in sexually explicit e-mails and having affairs--obviously works against him because it is his "past conduct" and he is at fault for causing the divorce; (2) the length of the marriage (8 years) might tend to favor Ronaldo, as this was arguably more than a short-term marriage but it would not classify as a long-term marriage; (3) the fact that Mia will not receive an interest in Ronaldo's family's business suggests that she is giving up a potentially significant asset and taking little in the property settlement, and that Ronald will continue to earn substantially more than her, so the economic disparity favors Mia and Ronaldo certainly has an ability to pay; (4) Mia is also responsible for her son, which is a factor in her favor, but (5) she is earning enough to arguably make a comfortable living, even without help from Ronaldo, and there is nothing indicating that she could not continue to work and live comfortable. General principles of equity might also tend to favor Mia, in that Ronaldo failed to reveal to Mia that by signing a prenuptial agreement she was giving up any interest in a rapidly expanding business. Under the circumstances, some amount of spousal support for a limited period of time might be expected.

Again, there is no clear answer to the question of what the judge would do, and the key is the test-taker's ability to apply the spousal support factors to the facts presented in the question.

-32-

ANSWER TO QUESTION NO. 13

1. **Adams is not entitled to a $40,000.00 fee**. Her fee agreement with Barnes was unethical in that:

(1) it potentially allowed her to receive a fee of greater than 1/3 of the actual net recovery in a personal injury case (as she, in fact, sought to obtain), in violation of MCR 8.121, the maximum share permissible in such cases. The fee agreement and her attempt actually to obtain a fee greater than 1/3 each constituted a violation of MRPC 1.5(a), which prohibits a lawyer from entering into an agreement for, charging or collecting an illegal or clearly excessive fee;

(2) it purported to create a "present value" when the notion of a "present value" as to a pending action is illusory. *Cf., e.g., Walton v Hoover, Bax & Slovacek, LLP,* 149 SW3d 834 (Tex App 204) aff'd in part, rev'd in part, remanded by 206 SW3d 557 (2006), judgment vacated 2007 Tex App Lexis 929. Even where, as here, a specific settlement offer had been made shortly before Barnes terminated Adams' services, a client is entitled to consider factors other than money in determining whether to accept or reject an offer, each of which is an aspect of the "value" of the case. Also, a lawyer is obligated to abide by the client's decision as to accepting a settlement offer. MRPC 1.2(a). (In a personal injury action, for example, a client may wish to accept a lower offer than the lawyer thinks is appropriate in order to minimize stress and risk; in a suit between two businesses, the client may wish to settle for less than might be available in order to preserve the opportunity for future business with the opponent);

(3) it significantly interfered with the client's right to counsel of choice, since the fee-sharing formula of the fee agreement penalized Barnes for terminating the attorney-client relationship by potentially depriving successor counsel of an opportunity to receive any fee, let alone a meaningful fee based on *quantum meruit.* With exceptions not applicable here, a client has the right to terminate the services of their attorney at any time and for any reason, *cf.* Restatement The Law Governing Lawyers 3d, §32(1), and a fee agreement that penalizes the client for exercising that right is unethical, *cf.* Restatement, §40(2)(c); and,

(4) it was not in writing, in violation of MRPC 1.5(c), which requires contingent fee agreements to be in writing.

-33-

2. **Adams is not entitled to any fee**. Where an attorney has engaged in misconduct in the course of a representation and the attorney's services are severable, the attorney may not collect (or must refund) the portion of the attorney's fee generated by the misconduct. *Cf. e.g., Polen v Melonakos*, 222 Mich App 20 (1997). Where, however, the conduct is not severable, the attorney is not entitled to any fee. *Evans & Luptak v Lizza*, 251 Mich App 187 (2002); *Idalski v Crouse Cartage*, 229 F Supp 2d 730 (ED Mich 2002). In this case, the fee agreement itself violated the rules of professional conduct in multiple respects, and the agreement was void as a matter of public policy and unenforceable. *Id.* In these circumstances, Adams' misconduct would not be deemed to be severable, and she would not be entitled to any fee.

-34-

ANSWER TO QUESTION 14

1. <u>UCC v Common Law</u>. The primary purpose of the contract between Brawny and Speedy Service was the provision of repair services, not the sale of goods. Therefore, the dispute must be resolved under Michigan's common law of contracts rather than Article 2 of the Uniform Commercial Code.

2. <u>Is there a contract and what are its terms</u>? Speedy Service's quotation is an offer to Brawny to have Speedy Service perform the repair work on the terms stated in Speedy's quotation form. The quotation offers Brawny a choice of two price/urgency options; in either case the offer also includes the terms on the back of the quotation form. To create a contract, an offeree's acceptance must be unambiguous and in strict conformance with the offer. *Kloian v Domino's Pizza, LLC*, 273 Mich App 449, 452 (2006). A contract requires mutual assent (sometimes called a "meeting of the minds") on all essential terms. *Id.* at 453.

Brawny's January 4 communication to Speedy Service was not sufficient to create a contract. It did not specify which of the two price/urgency alternatives Brawny was choosing, and those alternatives differed on terms so important that there can be no contract without them: the contract price and timetable for completing the work. In addition, Speedy Service's quotation form made clear that Speedy insisted on acceptance of all terms on the back of the form in order for there to be an effective acceptance. Brawny rejected this when it stated that the parties' agreement would be subject to all terms of its own form. We know from the facts that the indemnity terms (and other provisions) of the Speedy Service and Brawny forms were quite different. This is an additional reason why Brawny's request that Speedy begin work was not effective in creating a contract. In fact, because Brawny proposed different terms, it was a counteroffer. A counteroffer operates as a rejection of the original offer unless the counterofferor indicates a different intention (for example, is simply asking whether the offeror will modify the original offer.)

Although Brawny's January 4 communication did not plainly tell Speedy Service which of the two price/urgency alternatives that Speedy had originally proposed Brawny desired, it certainly does not suggest that Brawny regarded the expedited timetable as unacceptable. The best reading is that Brawny's counteroffer allowed Speedy to choose the timetable for completion. An offeree is entitled to accept an offer either by promising to perform or by

-35-

ANSWER TO QUESTION 15

Hearsay "is a statement, other than one made by the declarant while testifying at the trial or hearing, offered in evidence to prove the truth of the matter asserted." MRE 801(c). A "statement" can be a written or oral assertion or nonverbal conduct of a person, if it is intended by the person as an assertion. The "declarant" is a person who makes a statement. MRE 801(b). Hearsay is not admissible unless it comes within an exception. MRE 802.

Not all out-of-court statements offered to prove the truth of the matter asserted are hearsay. In particular, a statement is not hearsay if it is offered against a party and is one of which the party has manifested an adoption or belief in its truth. MRE 801(d)(2)(B).

A prior statement is excepted from the hearsay rule if the declarant is unavailable to testify at trial, and the statement is "offered against a party that has engaged in or encouraged wrongdoing that was intended to, and did, procure the unavailability of the declarant as a witness." MRE 804(b)(6). One way that a declarant may be "unavailable" is if the declarant is absent from the hearing and the proponent of the testimony has been unable to procure the declarant's attendance by process or other reasonable means. MRE 804(a)(5).

Additionally, all admissible evidence must be relevant. MRE 402. Relevant evidence is "evidence having any tendency to make the existence of any fact that is of consequence to the determination of the action more probable or less probable than it would be without the evidence." MRE 401. And, finally, relevant evidence can always be excluded if its probative value is substantially outweighed by the danger of unfair prejudice, or because it would confuse the issues, waste time, etc. MRE 403.

The initial question is whether the content of Diane's first statement can be attributed to Mr. Smith, *i.e.*, whether Mr. Smith manifested an adoption or belief in its truth. MRE 801(d)(2)(B). "An adoptive admission is the express adoption of another's statement as one's own. It is conduct on the part of a party which manifests circumstantially that party's assent in the truth of a statement made by another. . . . In order to find adoptive approval of the other's statement the circumstances surrounding the other's declaration must be examined." *Shemman v American Steamship Co*, 89

-38-

Mich App 656, 673 (1979), quoting *Durbin v K-K-M Corp*, 54 Mich App 38, 50 (1974). Here, Mr. Smith's conduct in nodding his head affirmatively, coupled with his simultaneously hugging her and commencing his statement with "I know about all that," is sufficient to manifest his belief in the truth of Diane's statement. Mr. Smith's gestures and statement are all affirmative acts or statements reflecting his agreement to what Diane just stated, especially considering the context of the conversation. Thus, the better conclusion is that this is an adoptive admission by Smith and can be admitted through Clark, who witnessed it. However, an applicant could also correctly recognize that Mr. Smith's conduct was somewhat ambiguous, because nodding of the head and hugging do not tell us much about what he was thinking, and it is not necessarily clear what part of Diane's statement his "I know about all that" was directed to. An applicant with that perspective could legitimately argue that the circumstances were not sufficiently clear to establish an adoptive admission.

Diane's second statement to Mr. Smith ("I can't believe you are doing this to me") would also be admissible. Although this second statement meets the definition of hearsay as it is an out-of-court statement offered to prove the truth of the matter asserted, *i.e.*, that Diane was in love with Mr. Smith and they had been having an affair, it arguably falls within two hearsay exceptions.

The first is the exception stated in MRE 804(b)(6). To gain admission under MRE 804(b)(6), the proponent must show that (1) defendant engaged in or encouraged wrongdoing, (2) that the wrongdoing was intended to procure the declarant's unavailability, and (3) that the wrongdoing did procure the unavailability. *People v Jones*, 270 Mich App 208, 217 (2006). Clearly, the statement is being offered against Mr. Smith, and evidence suggests that Mr. Smith engaged in wrongdoing to prevent Diane from testifying. The facts suggest that Mr. Smith's threat to Diane about testifying to the truth at trial is what led to her leaving the country. The threat also led to Mrs. Smith not being able to subpoena Diane for trial, *i.e.*, to Diane being unavailable under the rules of evidence. MRE 804(a)(5). Thus, the statement would be admissible.

Another exception under which Diane's second statement likely could be admitted is MRE 803(2), the so-called "excited utterance" exception. MRE 803(2) allows admission of a "statement relating to a startling event or condition made while the declarant was under the stress of excitement caused by the event or condition." According to the facts, Diane was "furious and frightened" at the time because she had just been threatened by Mr. Smith. This arguably qualifies as a "startling event or condition" (though much

-39-

of the case law involves statements made in the wake of crimes and accidents) and Diane's statement related to that startling event.

The applicant should also briefly discuss the relevancy of the evidence, and whether it is otherwise excluded because of the criteria within MRE 403. As already noted, it is relevant and not excluded under MRE 403 as Diane's statement goes to the heart of the issue at trial.

-40-

JULY 2011 MICHIGAN BAR EXAMINATION

ESSAY PORTION

MORNING SESSION

QUESTION 1 THE ANSWER TO THIS QUESTION SHOULD GO IN BLUEBOOK I

Betty's Best Burgers, a national fast food chain, has had a location just off the high-traffic expressway on a busy Michigan street. The business has been there ten years and has been run by the owner of the property, Sam Seller. Betty's and Sam's ten-year contract is coming to an end and both parties have some interest in a ten-year renewal of their agreement. During negotiations, Betty's continued to demand more and more from Sam such as better signage, improved lighting, and repaired parking areas -- all of which are expensive. Sam balked at these demands and returned the new contract to Betty's unsigned, one day before the ten-year agreement ended.

Unbeknownst to Sam, Betty's learned that Sam was negotiating with Handy's Hamburger Haven to enter into a contract for use of Sam's property for one of Handy's stores. Infuriated, Betty's filed a one-count complaint in the local circuit court for injunctive relief. Specifically, Betty's requested an order prohibiting Sam from allowing Handy's to take over the location and operating a fast food business there.

At the hastily scheduled hearing on Betty's request, the court learned the following: (1) the prior ten-year contract has expired; (2) the renewal contract was never signed; (3) Handy is one of Betty's chief competitors; (4) Sam, in compliance with the old contract, has taken down all signage relating to Betty's and offered its return to Betty's; (5) despite the excellent location, Sam's profits are the worst of the 200 restaurants operated under Betty's name and, accordingly, Betty's share of those profits is equally dismal; and (6) as Betty's suspected, Sam has been talking to Handy's.

Discuss the factors the court must consider in passing on Betty's request for an injunction and indicate, after an analysis of the salient facts, whether the court will grant or deny the injunction.

*****THE ANSWER TO THIS QUESTION SHOULD GO IN BLUEBOOK I*****

-1-

QUESTION 2 THE ANSWER TO THIS QUESTION SHOULD GO IN BLUEBOOK I

The Rippy Company, a properly formed Michigan corporation, designs and manufactures men's bow ties. The corporation's articles of incorporation indicate that the Rippy Company "elects to have shareholder preemptive rights," but provides no further elaboration. Dan Dion and his sister Carolyn Cail each own 100 shares of Rippy stock.

In July 2010, the company sustained heavy financial losses after its new product line, Gouda cheese bow ties, did not sell as well as anticipated.

In order to raise badly needed capital, the board of directors voted to call a special meeting of the shareholders, proposing to issue an additional 100,000 shares of Rippy corporate stock. The board provided 15 days notice to all shareholders of record by e-mail, describing the purpose of the meeting. Because Dan was going on an extended vacation and was unsure whether he would return in time for the shareholder meeting, Dan forwarded the e-mail to his sister Carolyn from his personal e-mail account. The message sent along with the forwarded e-mail authorized Carolyn to vote for the resolution on Dan's behalf by proxy. At the August 14, 2010 meeting, Carolyn took a copy of the e-mail Dan sent to her as proof of her proxy authorization and voted both her shares and Dan's shares in favor of the stock issuance. The stock issuance was approved by 58% of the shares entitled to vote. A certificate amending the articles of incorporation was filed with the state, and the proper authorizations were obtained from the Michigan Corporation and Securities Commission.

Two weeks later, the board of directors sent out notice to all shareholders of record, indicating that the 100,000 shares would be offered to the shareholders for $10 per share, and that each shareholder would be entitled to purchase 5 shares for every share of Rippy stock currently held. The notice also provided that if any shareholder failed to claim all or part of the shares before November 1, 2010, that the board of directors would sell the shares to other interested Rippy shareholders on a lottery basis for the same price. When Dan Dion returned from his vacation on November 21, 2010, he discovered that all 100,000 shares of the newly offered Rippy stock had been purchased. All but 4 shareholders (including Dan) had opted to purchase their share of the new stock. Dan's share was sold to Greg Greedy, a fellow Rippy shareholder. Dan demanded to purchase 500 shares of stock for $5,000, but Greg refused.

-2-

Using Michigan law, assess the validity of Dan's claims challenging (1) the validity of the proxy Dan gave to his sister Carolyn; (2) the vote of the shareholders authorizing the additional issuance of stock; and (3) the terms prescribed by the board of directors for the acquisition of Rippy stock.

*****THE ANSWER TO THIS QUESTION SHOULD GO IN BLUEBOOK I*****

-3-

<u>QUESTION 3</u> **THE ANSWER TO THIS QUESTION SHOULD GO IN BLUEBOOK I**

Police were dispatched to the scene of a reported felonious assault. The report received was that a male had attacked a young woman in a parking lot and left on foot heading northbound on First Avenue. An officer and his canine partner arrived at the scene and witnessed a young man, later identified as Peter, running along a nearby sidewalk. The officer released his dog but also yelled at the man to stop. Peter immediately stopped and placed his hands in the air. Before the officer could command the dog to stop, the dog jumped up on Peter and bit him in the shoulder.

It was later determined by the officer that Peter had just been out jogging and was not the man involved in the attack on the young woman. Nonetheless, Peter suffered serious injuries to his shoulder, which required multiple surgeries, time off work, and exceptional pain and suffering.

In Michigan, the following statute applies to dog bites making it a strict liability tort:

"(1) If a dog bites a person, without provocation while the person is on public property, or lawfully on private property, including the property of the owner of the dog, the owner of the dog shall be liable for any damages suffered by the person bitten, regardless of the former viciousness of the dog or the owner's knowledge of such viciousness. MCL 287.351."

Peter is suing the police officer and his employer, the city, based on a strict liability theory for the damages he suffered as a result of the dog bite. Evaluate the likelihood of success of Peter's lawsuit. Explain your answer.

*******THE ANSWER TO THIS QUESTION SHOULD GO IN BLUEBOOK I*******

-4-

GO TO BLUEBOOK II

QUESTION 4 **THE ANSWER TO THIS QUESTION SHOULD GO IN BLUEBOOK II**

Paul Plaintiff owns a retail fur shop located in the National Bank Building in Gaylord, Michigan. His business is the selling and repairing of fur coats as well as storage of furs in the off season. Paul is one of several tenants in the building, which is owned by Larry Landlord. Paul has a written lease and leases three rooms. One room is a show room for the display and sale of furs. Another is a work room for repairs, which is adjacent to the show room. The third is a climate controlled storage room located in the back of the building off a common area shared by all tenants.

Larry Landlord entered into a contract with Quick Repair Company to repair the common portion of the building used by the tenants, including Paul. Their agreement required Quick Repair to furnish labor and material to repair the common area according to the specifications prepared by Larry Landlord's architect. In addition, the contract provides:

"All work to be performed pursuant to the plans provided by the architect and specifications provided therein and in such a way and manner as to cause a minimum of disruption to the building tenants."

Neither Paul nor any other tenant was a party to the contract.

Victor Vendor came to see Paul at the fur shop. Victor brought a box of twenty-two sable hats which he wanted Paul to buy for resale. Paul was reluctant, but agreed to discuss it over lunch with Victor. Victor asked Paul if he could store his sable hats in Paul's climate controlled storage room while they ate. Paul agreed. Paul and Victor went to lunch and were gone for two hours.

Quick Repair entered the building just after Paul left. Seeing that his shop was closed, they immediately undertook to perform demolition work in the common area in Paul's absence. When Paul returned from lunch with Victor, he walked into his storage room and saw his furs covered with dirt, wet plaster and dust. Victor discovered that his sable hats were covered with the same debris. All of the damaged inventory had to be professionally cleaned and repaired before either Paul or Victor could display their items in a showroom for potential sale. The delay caused both Paul and Victor to miss an entire fall/winter season when sales of their respective inventory are typically at peak levels.

Paul intends to sue Quick Repair for damage done to the furs and his loss of sales that are attributable to that damage. Victor

-5-

QUESTION 6 THE ANSWER TO THIS QUESTION SHOULD GO IN BLUEBOOK II

Dan Defendant's house caught fire and suffered smoke damage. Dan was not present at the time of the fire, but was the last person home before it started. When Dan returned home, the fire department was putting out the fire. Dan told a fireman the fire was an accident. He claimed that he mistakenly left food on his stove and forgot to turn the stove off. The state has charged Dan with arson on account of the fire even though the report from the state's arson expert was inconclusive.

In a pre-trial motion, the prosecutor seeks to introduce evidence at trial of three other fires involving Dan which occurred over the last five years. In 2010, Dan's sailboat caught fire after he and a group of friends had been drinking and smoking cigarettes in the boat's cabin; when Dan stayed behind to lock up, he neglected to ensure that no lit cigarettes were left behind. In 2008, the engine of Dan's car erupted in fire immediately after he exited the vehicle. The car was completely destroyed, and Dan had to pay the balance owed on the car. In 2007, Dan's house was severely damaged by fire when Dan put his roommate's sweater on a propane heater to dry out. The fire started right after Dan and his roommate left the house. Dan claimed all three fires were accidents and was never charged with a crime relating to any of the previous fires. He filed for, and collected, insurance proceeds on the sailboat and house fires. He did not have comprehensive automobile insurance coverage and, therefore, did not file an insurance claim for the car engine fire.

The prosecutor argues that the evidence concerning the three prior fires is admissible to prove Dan's scheme, plan or system in doing a bad act, and absence of mistake or accident.

Dan's attorney has objected to the introduction of this proposed evidence on the grounds that: (1) Dan was not charged with a crime for any of the other fires; (2) Dan received little money as a result of the fires; (3) the events are not similar to each other or the fire now charged; and (4) there is no proof that Dan set any of the other fires.

Discuss the analysis the trial court should engage in when ruling on the prosecutor's motion, and address the grounds favoring, as well as weighing against, the admission of the evidence.

*****THE ANSWER TO THIS QUESTION SHOULD GO IN BLUEBOOK II*****

-8-

GO TO BLUEBOOK III

QUESTION 7 THE ANSWER TO THIS QUESTION SHOULD GO IN BLUEBOOK III

Vienna Victim owns two pieces of heirloom jewelry with immeasurable sentimental value: a diamond watch that has been appraised for $3,000 and a gold bracelet that has been appraised for $2,000. Earlier this month, she brought both items into Oliver's Jewelry Boutique for repair and cleaning, and paid for the services in advance. Believing the bracelet to have been beyond repair as a piece of jewelry, the store's sole proprietor, Oliver Owner, pocketed the bracelet, melted it, combined it with other gold he had in his possession, and placed the resulting pure gold ingot in his vault to be sold to an investor.

Oliver repaired the watch as instructed, but he neglected to place the watch in his state-of-the-art vault, instead leaving it on the store's counter night after night. A burglar broke into the store one night and stole Vienna's watch from the store. All the items in the vault, including the gold ingot, were untouched. The burglar advertised the watch on the Internet and sold the watch to Dan Defendant, who (after some intense negotiations) paid $500 for it.

Vienna attempted to pick up her jewelry from Oliver's store and learned what had occurred. She was able to trace the watch to Dan. Dan refused to return the watch to Vienna. The burglar's identity is unknown.

Assess the viability of potential remedies available to Vienna against Dan Defendant and/or Oliver Owner. Explain your answers.

*******THE ANSWER TO THIS QUESTION SHOULD GO IN BLUEBOOK III*******

-9-

<u>QUESTION 8</u> THE ANSWER TO THIS QUESTION SHOULD GO IN BLUEBOOK III

Dennis Davis was out in the woods hunting when he was accidentally shot by a fellow hunter. After spending several days on life support, Dennis died. Dennis was divorced, and had an estate worth approximately $1,000,000 after his debts and expenses were paid. No testamentary documents were found among his personal effects.

Surviving Dennis are his two siblings--his half brother Paul and his brother Scott. Dennis is also survived by Timmy Taylor, a 15-year old developmentally disabled foster child who has lived with Dennis since the age of two. Lastly, after reading Dennis' obituary, Ed Ermine appeared, claiming to be Dennis' biological father.

DNA testing ordered by the probate judge administering the Estate of Dennis verified that Ed Ermine is Dennis and Scott's biological father. Paternity had not previously been established. Scott claims that neither he nor Dennis ever knew Ed or knew that he was their biological father. Rather, the boys were raised by their stepfather, who was Paul's father. Both Paul and Scott claim that Ed neither visited nor supported Dennis and Scott during their childhood. Scott also claims that Paul is entitled to a lesser share of the estate because Paul and Dennis have only one parent in common.

Using Michigan law, discuss what claims the following parties would have to the estate of Dennis: (1) Timmy, (2) Ed, (3) Paul and Scott.

*******THE ANSWER TO THIS QUESTION SHOULD GO IN BLUEBOOK III*******

-10-

<u>QUESTION 9</u> **THE ANSWER TO THIS QUESTION SHOULD GO IN BLUEBOOK III**

Julie and Nick both moved to Michigan in September 2010 in order to attend college. They entered into separate one-year lease agreements with the Caravaggio Apartment Complex (commonly known as the CAC) to rent adjoining apartments; the owner-manager of this complex is Michael.

Although neither tenant had problems moving into the complex and was generally satisfied with their apartments early in the leases, both started to notice that the CAC was not as great as it was held out to be. The breaking point came, however, in late December when each tenant noticed a serious mold infestation developing from within the walls of their apartments. Julie, who had allergies, became sick despite her best efforts to clean and clear the apartment of the presence of mold. Nick's efforts at clearing the problem also failed and he was forced to stay at a friend's house several days each week.

Both Julie and Nick reported these developments to Michael immediately, to no avail. Michael informed them that the presence of mold was not his fault, and because correction of the problem was not required by their lease contract, he would have to wait until spring in order for work crews to complete the structural work needed to rectify the problem. Julie informed Michael that this was unacceptable and that she was terminating her lease immediately. Julie vacated her apartment by the end of the month, paying no further rent. Nick instead refused to pay rent during the pendency of the problem and contacted the city's housing authority. The housing authority forced Michael to rectify the mold problem, which was completed by the end of January.

Although Michael was forced to correct the mold issue, he decided that Nick was a problematic tenant and decided to seek Nick's eviction. Michael served eviction papers on Nick on February 15, citing Nick's failure to pay rent for one month and new allegations that Nick hosted loud parties that had resulted in "many" complaints from "anonymous" sources; Nick retorted that Michael was just being "spiteful." Michael also decided to sue Julie for breach of contract, seeking to collect rent for the balance of the term of the lease agreement. Both Julie and Nick defended the actions asserting their rights to the fullest extent under Michigan law.

Discuss the rights and duties of the parties under Michigan law, and in particular address whether Michael may lawfully evict Nick and whether Julie is liable for breaking her lease.

*******THE ANSWER TO THIS QUESTION SHOULD GO IN BLUEBOOK III*******

-11-

JULY 2011 MICHIGAN BAR EXAMINATION

ESSAY PORTION

AFTERNOON SESSION

QUESTION 10 **THE ANSWER TO THIS QUESTION SHOULD GO IN BLUEBOOK IV**

On December 22, 2010, Dan Defendant made a withdrawal from an ATM machine from his own bank account. He put the money in his pocket and turned around. Ronald Graham was standing in line behind him, and was a much bigger man (in both height and weight) than Dan. Lynn Tracy was in line behind Ronald and was in an obvious hurry, so Ronald let Lynn use the machine ahead of him. Dan continued to count his money as Lynn made her withdrawal. After withdrawing her money, Lynn hurriedly walked away and unknowingly dropped two twenty dollar bills. Ronald quickly picked up the dropped money. After Ronald picked it up, Dan said, "I'll give it to her." Ronald said, "No, I'll give it." Dan then put his hand in his coat pocket and said, "I said I'll give it to her. I have a gun," and took the two twenty dollar bills from Ronald. Dan ran in the direction of Lynn, and once he caught up with her, handed her five dollars and said, "You dropped this." Dan then walked away quickly. In the meantime, Ronald called the police and walked toward Lynn. When he reached Lynn he said, "You dropped forty dollars. How much did he give you?" Lynn said, "Five dollars." Ronald then ran after Dan. Dan, seeing that Ronald was running at him, picked up a large tree branch and swung it at Ronald, stating "Get away from me." Ronald stepped back just quickly enough for Dan to miss him. Dan ran. The police arrived and arrested Dan.

The prosecution charged Dan Defendant with armed robbery and felonious assault. **Discuss whether the above facts introduced at trial support a conviction of the crimes charged beyond a reasonable doubt.**

*******THE ANSWER TO THIS QUESTION SHOULD GO IN BLUEBOOK IV*******

-12-

QUESTION 11 THE ANSWER TO THIS QUESTION SHOULD GO IN BLUEBOOK IV

"Neighbor-watchers," a local "crime-stoppers" organization in Bigville, Michigan, received an anonymous tip identifying four students at the Bigville public high school as drug dealers. The tipster claimed she had observed all four students selling drugs while on school grounds and was able to provide identifying information about each of these "big sellers" in varying detail.

The tipster identified one of the "big sellers" as her former friend, Buddy Weeden. According to the tipster, Weeden was a senior from whom the tipster and her boyfriend used to purchase the illegal drug Ecstasy in the school parking lot after school. Additionally, the tipster suspected Weeden of selling marijuana to a freshman and believed that Weeden kept a machete in the glove box of his blue Chevy Tahoe. The tipster identified the second "big seller" as John McCracken, a senior that the tipster had seen selling cocaine in the school parking lot out of his black Ford F-150. The third "big seller" was Mark Highland, a student the tipster described as a junior whom she had observed selling Ecstasy at school. The tipster never saw Highland with his own vehicle, however. The fourth "big seller" was Sean Grassmeyer. The tipster described Grassmeyer as a male Caucasian in the junior class. The tipster claimed to have seen Grassmeyer selling marijuana "from the school, his truck and the Bigville City Park."

"Neighbor-watchers" forwarded the tip to the school liaison-police officer, who verified that Weeden, McCracken, and Grassmeyer drove the vehicles described in the tip and also discovered that Highland did not have a vehicle registered with the school. The officer then forwarded this information to the high school principal. The principal was disturbed, but not surprised, since he had previously heard from a counselor at the local junior high school that Grassmeyer was associated with drug activity there. Also, the principal already knew that Grassmeyer drove a truck. Deciding to take action, the principal first searched Weeden's Tahoe, but much to his chagrin, no drugs were found. Undeterred, the principal decided to search Grassmeyer's truck and invited Grassmeyer and the liaison officer to accompany him during the search. Through the truck's passenger window, the principal noticed a plastic bag behind a seat, although he could not determine what was inside the bag. Without Grassmeyer's consent, and with the officer looking on, the principal proceeded to search the truck where he found marijuana and drug-trafficking supplies inside the plastic bag. Grassmeyer was promptly arrested and charged with possession with intent to deliver marijuana.

-13-

Grassmeyer's attorney has filed a motion to suppress the marijuana and drug trafficking supplies as "fruit of an unconstitutional search" under the United States and Michigan Constitutions.

How should the circuit court rule on the motion? Explain your answer. (For purposes of this question, you should assume the Bigville public schools do not have a contractual "implied consent" policy permitting school officials to search a student's property while that student's belongings are on school property.)

*******THE ANSWER TO THIS QUESTION SHOULD GO IN BLUEBOOK IV*******

-14-

<u>QUESTION 12</u> THE ANSWER TO THIS QUESTION SHOULD GO IN BLUEBOOK IV

Northern High School's football team was in the state finals against their rival, Southern High School. Southern was led by their all-state fullback, Sammy McGuire, who it was rumored used illegal anabolic steroids to enhance his performance. The game was being played at Northern's field.

One Northern student in attendance at the game, John Smith, was upset that McGuire would cheat by using illegal drugs, so he brought a sign to the game protesting McGuire's alleged use of steroids. The large 4' x 5' picket sign stated the following in bright blue wording: "Sammy McGuire says: Steroids, breakfast of champions." Smith, worried that the sign might run afoul of the school policy prohibiting advocacy of drug use, decided to wait until McGuire ran for a touchdown before revealing the picket.

McGuire scored in the first quarter, and Smith quickly ran to the front of the stands and marched back and forth, showing the sign to the entire crowd. In that crowd was McGuire's father, who was greatly offended by the sign. He raced down to Smith and took the picket sign away. Smith reacted quickly, taking the sign back from Mr. McGuire and running away (while still showing the sign to the fans). Seeing this commotion, Northern's principal, Mrs. Lady, stopped Smith and snatched the picket sign away from him. In doing so, Lady informed Smith that he was a poor example for the student body, was acting in violation of school policy, and would be suspended for 5 days.

Smith subsequently sued both Mrs. Lady and Mr. McGuire for declaratory relief, alleging pursuant to the appropriate federal statute, that his First Amendment right to the freedom of speech had been violated when the picket sign was taken away and he was subsequently suspended. Both Mrs. Lady and Mr. McGuire have filed motions for summary disposition. Mr. McGuire asserts that the First Amendment claim fails to state a claim against him upon which relief can be granted. Mrs. Lady argues that there was no genuine issue of material fact that Smith cannot establish a violation of the First Amendment.

Should the motions be granted? Explain your answer.

*******THE ANSWER TO THIS QUESTION SHOULD GO IN BLUEBOOK IV*******

-15-

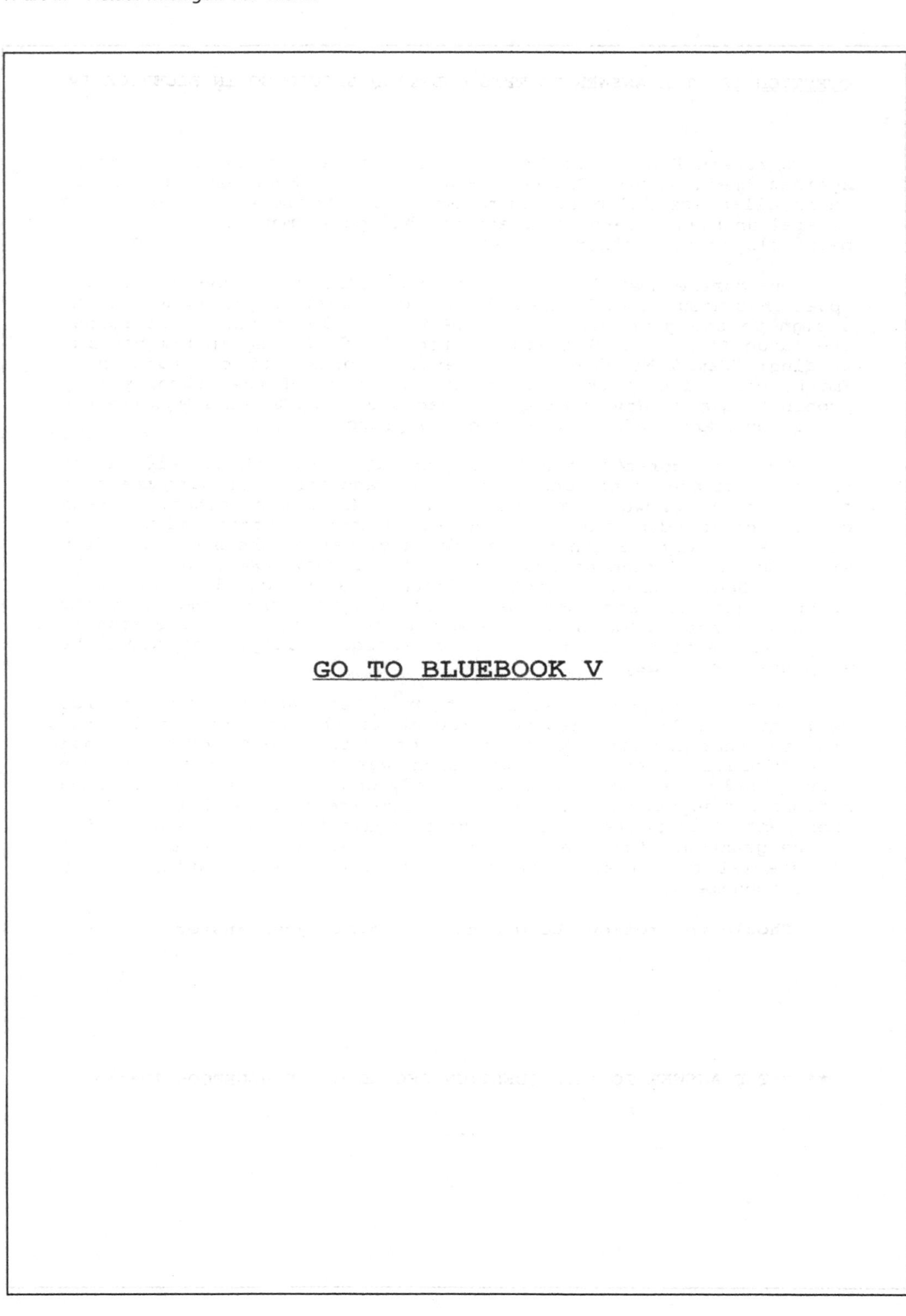

GO TO BLUEBOOK V

<u>QUESTION 13</u> **THE ANSWER TO THIS QUESTION SHOULD GO IN BLUEBOOK V**

Stella Seller recently retired from a successful career as a business executive and moved to a lakeside cottage in Anytown, Michigan. To supplement her income, she used a small workshop to create decorative stone statues. She began selling her statues at art fairs, bazaars and popular roadside stands. Stella also took photos of her statues to offer them for sale through a website she created.

Brenda Buyer had recently graduated from college, purchased a home, and wanted to decorate her garden with a statue. Brenda saw the cement statues on Stella's website and saw a gargoyle she really liked. Brenda called the number to ask about availability and price of the statue. Stella answered and confirmed that she had two gargoyles available, and the price was $1,400 each. Stella added that customers typically pick up the statues and that she would hold onto it for Brenda. She also mentioned that since Brenda lived in a nearby town, Stella could ask people that stopped by if anyone would kindly drop it off at Brenda's home. Brenda replied, "that sounds great--I sure would appreciate it, if you could do that," and "I can't wait to see that statue in my garden." Stella filled out an invoice on her business' letterhead, noting the price as $1,400, and mailed it to Brenda.

A week later, Stella's younger brother and his friend stopped at her house. Since her younger brother had arrived in his pickup truck, Stella suggested that it shouldn't be a problem for him and his friend to deliver the statue. She mentioned that Brenda had just graduated from college and may tip them for their trouble. The statue was easily loaded into the bed of the pickup. Unfortunately, the statue was destroyed when the pickup truck swerved to avoid a deer that leapt in the truck's path causing the truck to strike a guardrail. Police determined that Stella's younger brother had acted properly under the circumstances. Two weeks later, Brenda called Stella demanding her gargoyle statue. Stella refused, and demanded $1,400.

Analyze and discuss whether there is an enforceable contract between Stella and Brenda. Assuming there is an enforceable contract, are Stella and Brenda in breach of contract? Explain your answer.

*******THE ANSWER TO THIS QUESTION SHOULD GO IN BLUEBOOK V*******

-16-

QUESTION 14 THE ANSWER TO THIS QUESTION SHOULD GO IN BLUEBOOK V

Mary and Tom were married in 2000, after graduating from college together. Using money from their wedding, they put $10,000 down on a house. Tom began his career as a grade school teacher and Mary found an entry level management position in a renewable energy company. They did not have children.

In 2002, Tom's father died, leaving him a $75,000 inheritance. Tom used $5,000 to pay off the loan on his car and put the rest of the money into a certificate of deposit (CD) titled in both his and Mary's names. Mary quickly moved up the corporate ladder as her employer's business grew.

In June 2010, Mary and Tom decided to separate. Unbeknownst to Tom, Mary was having an affair with a business associate. She wrote out a short agreement providing that she would stay in the marital home and be solely responsible for the mortgage payments. At that time, the fair market value of the home had decreased to the point that it was roughly equal to the remaining amount owed on the mortgage. Mary noted in the agreement that Tom was willing to give up any interest he had in the home if his name could be removed from the mortgage. Both Mary and Tom signed the agreement and Tom moved into an apartment. Mary refinanced the mortgage on the home with a loan in her name alone.

Mary confessed her infidelity to Tom in January 2011, and filed for divorce. The significant assets of the parties were their retirement accounts, the CD, the home, the home furnishings, and joint savings and checking accounts to which both had contributed. By that time, Mary earned significantly more than Tom.

When the parties met to discuss the division of their assets, Tom claimed that the agreement he signed was invalid and that he was entitled to at least $5,000 from Mary for his half of the down payment on the home. He also argued that Mary's affair was the reason their marriage failed, and because of her fault in causing the divorce and the fact that she earned far more than him, he would receive more than half of the parties' marital assets should the case go to trial. Mary claimed that the CD was marital property, or that at a minimum, the interest earned on the CD during the marriage was marital property.

Analyze: (1) Tom's claims regarding the parties' written agreement and his alleged entitlement to more than half of the parties' marital assets; and (2) Mary's claims regarding the CD.

*******THE ANSWER TO THIS QUESTION SHOULD GO IN BLUEBOOK V*******

-17-

QUESTION 15 **THE ANSWER TO THIS QUESTION SHOULD GO IN BLUEBOOK V**

ABC is a small but growing company that sells "green" carpet cleaning products. It anticipates an upsurge in business and plans to clear debris from a section of its warehouse to increase the warehouse's capacity to store products.

Joe, a college graduate, is one of ABC's ten employees. His job is to negotiate with sales agents and oversee the condition and operation of the warehouse. His job requires him to be on his feet eight hours per day. After learning that ABC will be clearing debris from the warehouse, Joe suggests to ABC that his son, Brandon, help in the debris clearing job in exchange for pizza, soft drinks, and the company's tickets to a Detroit Tiger's baseball game. The owner likes this cost-saving idea and agrees to this arrangement with Brandon.

The day arrived to clear the debris. Brandon and Joe during the normal workday were clearing the debris in the warehouse when an accident occurred. While lifting a heavy beam with Joe's help, Brandon hurt his back and dropped the beam on Joe's foot, crushing it. Brandon required medical attention for his back injury, but it was otherwise a minor problem. Joe's injury was more serious. His doctor told him he would never be able to work again at a job requiring him to be on his feet eight hours per day.

Joe and Brandon approach ABC seeking workers' compensation benefits. ABC says it has no liability to Brandon. ABC says it will pay for the medical treatment of Joe's injury, but not for any time lost from work.

Apply Michigan law to answer the following questions posed by the above facts:

1. Does ABC have any workers' compensation liability to Brandon? Explain your analysis.

2. Does ABC have any workers' compensation liability for weekly wage loss benefits to Joe? Explain your analysis.

*******THE ANSWER TO THIS QUESTION SHOULD GO IN BLUEBOOK V*******

-18-

JULY 2011 MICHIGAN BAR EXAMINATION MODEL ANSWERS

ANSWER TO QUESTION NO. 1

Injunctive relief is largely an equitable remedy, although governed by MCR 3.310. There are four main factors a court must consider: Whether (1) the moving party has made the required demonstration of irreparable harm, (2) the harm to the moving party absent the injunction outweighs the harm it would cause the adverse party, (3) the moving party showed that it is likely to prevail on the merits, and (4) there will be harm to the public interest if an injunction is issued. *Detroit Firefighters Association v Detroit*, 482 Mich 18, 34 (2008).

(1) Whether there has been a demonstration of irreparable harm.

This is the most significant factor. The harm must be particularized and must be real and imminent, not speculative. The harm must typically not be compensable by monetary damages.

No facts presented demonstrate irreparable harm to Betty's if the injunction does not issue. Betty's profits are low, the lowest of 200 stores. Even if those profits are lost, Betty's loss is determinable and compensable in money. Moreover, this low profit level has occurred even though the location might be considered desirable. If Betty's loses that location, locations may nevertheless be open. That Betty's cannot operate out of that location is not irreparable harm.

(2) Whether the harm to the moving party absent the injunction outweighs the harm it would cause the adverse party.

While some harm could come to Betty's by loss of the location, the greater harm is to Sam who will be forced to operate a Betty's when Sam does not want to do so. Sam may get a better deal from Handy's, a deal they would lose if the injunction were issued.

(3) Whether the moving party showed that it is likely to prevail on the merits.

At the crux of this matter, Betty's would have to show it has a legally enforceable contract to operate its location at Sam's property. However, the prior contract has expired. The new contract was never signed. Absent some other non-contractual theory, which the facts do not support, Betty's has nothing to enforce. Therefore, it is likely Betty's would lose, not win.

(4) Whether there will be harm to the public interest if an injunction is issued.

This is not a case directly affecting the public's interest. The public has been aware of the Betty's location for some time. That location would be replaced by a Handy's. The switch in business does not have a significant (or maybe even any) impact on the public interest.

Conclusion: Consideration of the factors for injunctive relief warrants the conclusion the injunction should not be issued. Betty's does not prevail on the most salient factor, demonstration of irreparable harm; and does not prevail on the weighing of the harm and likelihood of success on the merits factors. Lastly, the public interest is not affected and is thus a non-issue.

-2-

ANSWER TO QUESTION NO. 2

1. **Validity of the proxy from Dan to Carolyn**: Michigan law expressly permits shareholders to authorize other persons to act for them by proxy. MCL 450.1421(1). A proxy is generally only valid for 3 years, unless otherwise provided in the proxy. §1421(2). A proxy may be granted by means of "telegram, cablegram, or other means of electronic transmission." §1421(3)(b). If a proxy is granted in such a manner, it must "either set forth or be submitted with information from which it can be determined that the telegram, cablegram, or other electronic transmission was authorized by the shareholder." Additionally, if the electronic transmission is determined to be valid, the inspectors or persons making the validity determination must specify the information upon which they relied. The facts indicate that the e-mail was sent from Dan's personal e-mail, included the notice sent from the corporation to Dan, and specifically authorized Carolyn to vote for the resolution for Dan by proxy. Because the e-mail contains information from which it can be determined that the e-mail was authorized by Dan, his challenge to the validity of the proxy will most likely be unsuccessful.

2. **Validity of the shareholder vote**: Increasing the aggregate number of shares in a corporation is specifically contemplated as a basis upon which to amend the articles of incorporation under Michigan law. MCL 450.1602(d). The only issue to be determined is whether the proper procedures were followed regarding the amendment of the articles of incorporation.

MCL 450.1611(4) requires that notice be given to each shareholder of record entitled to vote "within the time and in the manner" provided for giving notice of shareholder meetings. MCL 450.1404(1) permits notice "not less than 10 nor more than 60 days" before the date of the shareholder meeting, and specifically permits notice to be given by electronic transmission. The 15-day notice provided to Dan by electronic transmission is sufficient under the statute. However, even if the notice given to shareholders was insufficient, Dan waived any deficiencies in the notice because he was present at the meeting by his authorized representative, holding his proxy. MCL 450.1404(4); *Foote v Greilick*, 166 Mich 636, 642 (1911).

The articles of incorporation are amended if supported by a majority of the outstanding shares entitled to vote. MCL 450.1611(5). This is higher than the general requirement for

-3-

shareholder approval, which is a majority of votes cast. MCL 450.1441(2). The voting requirements for amending the articles of incorporation may be subject to even greater requirements as prescribed by law or in the articles of incorporation. MCL 450.1611(5). Once the amendment is approved, a certificate of amendment must be filed with the state. MCL 450.1611(7); MCL 450.1631. Because the facts indicate that the amendment to the articles of incorporation was approved by 58% of the shares entitled to vote, and the appropriate certificate was filed with the state, the amendment to the articles of incorporation is valid.

3. **Preemptive Rights:** Shareholders in Michigan do not have *any* preemptive rights to acquire a corporation's unissued shares unless such a right is created by (1) the articles of incorporation or (2) an agreement between the corporation and 1 or more shareholders. MCL 450.1343(1). Here, the facts indicate that the articles of incorporation provide for preemptive rights.

If preemptive rights are created by a statement in the articles (or agreement) that the corporation "elects to have preemptive rights," or words of similar import, Michigan law lists several "principles" that apply to the preemptive rights unless otherwise provided. Included among the listed principles is that the shareholders' preemptive rights are "granted on uniform terms and conditions prescribed by the board to provide a fair and reasonable opportunity to exercise the right to acquire proportional amounts of the corporation's unissued shares upon the decision of the board to issue them." MCL 450.1343(2)(a). Here, because the facts indicate that the preemptive rights are mentioned in the articles of incorporation without additional provisions, the principles listed in the statute would be applicable. Thus, in order to challenged the terms established by the board, Dan would have to show that the terms and conditions were not uniform, or that Dan was not provided "a fair and reasonable opportunity" to exercise his right to acquire his share of Rippy stock.

The facts indicate that notice was sent to all shareholders, describing the terms and conditions for shareholders to exercise their preemptive rights. The terms and conditions described appear to be uniform -- all shareholders were offered the opportunity to purchase 5 shares for every share of Rippy stock currently held, for the price of $10 per share. Any unclaimed shares could be purchased by interested stockholders on a lottery basis for the same price. The only remaining question is whether the November 1, 2010 deadline denied Dan "a fair and reasonable opportunity" to purchase his share of Rippy stock. The facts indicate that the board of directors' notice to all stockholders of record was sent out on August 28, 2010, approximately two months prior to the

-4-

November 1, 2010 deadline. Without additional facts, it is unlikely that Dan will be able to show that giving him two months time to claim his preemptive rights denied him "a fair and reasonable opportunity."

-5-

ANSWER TO QUESTION NO. 3

Michigan recognizes a strict liability cause of action against dog owners for damages resulting from dog bites. If a dog bites a person, without provocation while the person is on public property, or lawfully on private property, including the property of the owner of the dog, the owner of the dog shall be liable for any damages suffered by the person bitten, regardless of the former viciousness of the dog or the owner's knowledge of such viciousness. MCL 287.351.

Here, the facts indicate that Peter was out jogging on a sidewalk, presumably on public property. The facts do not indicate that Peter did anything to provoke the dog. In fact, Peter followed the officer's commands precisely and immediately stopped and put his hands up when ordered to do so. Peter was nonetheless bitten by the dog and suffered numerous injuries.

In a strict liability tort action, liability is not fault-based. It is not dependent, for example, on whether negligent, intentional, or accidental conduct caused the harm; rather, civil liability is imposed for the wrongful conduct irrespective of fault. *Tate v City of Grand Rapids*, 256 Mich App 656, 660 (2003). As such, in this case it would not matter that the officer was mistaken in his belief that Peter was the assailant.

Pursuant to this statute alone, the Police Department would be liable for Peter's injuries. However, Michigan's Governmental Tort Liability Act (GTLA), MCL 691.1407(1) provides in pertinent part:

"Except as otherwise provided in this act, a governmental agency is immune from tort liability if the governmental agency is engaged in the exercise or discharge of a governmental function."

The statute grants broad immunity to governmental agencies, extending immunity "to all governmental agencies for *all* tort liability whenever they are engaged in the exercise or discharge of a governmental function." *Nawrocki v Macomb Co Rd Comm*, 463 Mich 143, 156 (2000) (emphasis in original). The police activity of investigating a felony certainly constitutes the exercise or discharge of a governmental function. None of the exceptions to immunity apply. Thus the city would be immune from suit. *Tate, supra*.

With respect to the liability of the police officer, an

-6-

officer or employee of a governmental agency is immune from tort liability for an injury to a person or damage to property caused by the officer or employee if all of the following are met:

(a) The officer, employee, member, or volunteer is acting or reasonably believes he or she is acting within the score of his or her authority.

(b) The governmental agency is engaged in the exercise or discharge of a governmental function.

(c) The officer's, employee's, member's, or volunteer's conduct does not amount to gross negligence that is the proximate cause of the injury or damage. MCL 691.1407(2).

Here, the facts are clear that the officer was responding to a dispatch call in an attempt to apprehend a suspect of a felonious assault. The officer reasonably believed he was acting within the scope of his employment when he released his dog on the subject. "Police officers, especially when faced with a potentially dangerous situation, must be given a wide degree of discretion in determining what type of action will best ensure the safety of the individuals involved and the general public, the cessation of unlawful conduct, and the apprehension of wrongdoers. *The determination of what type of action to take, e.g., make an immediate arrest, pursue a suspect, issue a warning, await backup assistance, etc., is a discretionary-decisional act entitled to immunity."* *Brown v Shavers*, 210 Mich App 272, 277 (1995) (emphasis in original).

The officer was clearly engaged in the exercise of a government function when he was attempting to apprehend the suspected criminal. Gross negligence is defined in MCL 691.1407(7) as "conduct so reckless as to demonstrate a substantial lack of concern for whether an injury results." There is nothing in the facts that suggest that the police officer's actions rose to the level of gross negligence. Thus, there is no likelihood that Peter would be successful in his suit against the police officer.

-7-

ANSWER TO QUESTION NO. 4

This question implicates the ability of third-party beneficiaries to enforce a contract. The governing Michigan statute, MCL 600.1405, provides:

"Any person for whose benefit a promise is made by way of contract, as hereinafter defined, has the same right to enforce said promise that he would have had if the said promise had been made directly to him as the promisee.

"(1) A promise shall be construed to have been made for the benefit of a person whenever the promisor of said promise had undertaken to give or to do or refrain from doing something directly to or for said person.

* * *

"(2)(b) If such person is not in being or ascertainable at the time the promise becomes legally binding on the promisor then his rights shall become vested the moment he comes into being or becomes ascertainable if the promise has not been discharged by agreement between the promisor and the promisee in the meantime."

An intended beneficiary acquires a right under a contract by virtue of a promise. Restatement 2d, Contracts, §302(1).

The statute creates the status of third-party beneficiary to a contract. The statute provides protection to only those persons as to which the promisor undertakes an obligation directly or for that person or class or persons. *See Koenig v South Haven*, 460 Mich 667 (1999). The operative word in the statute to determine who holds the status of a beneficiary is "directly." The purpose of this statutory language is to assure that parties to a contract are clearly aware of the scope of their contractual undertaking in regard to third parties.

The statute creates rights only in third parties who are directly referred to in the contract. A third-party beneficiary may be specifically named in the contract or may be a member of a class, provided the class is sufficiently described to be reasonably identifiable. Such a class must be less than the world at large and cannot be designated by reference to the public at large. *Koenig, supra.*

The court will use an objective standard to determine from the contract itself whether the promisor undertook to give, to do, or refrain from doing something directly to, or for, the third-party

-8-

beneficiary. *See Koenig, supra*, at 680; *Guardian Depositors Corp v Brown*, 290 Mich 433, 437 (1939).

An incidental beneficiary is one who may be indirectly and only incidentally benefitted by the contract. Incidental beneficiaries are not covered by the statute and acquire no rights by virtue of a promise. Restatement 2d, Contracts §302(2). Therefore, a third person cannot maintain an action on a contract merely because he would receive a benefit from its performance or because he was injured by the promisor's breach of that contract. *See Greenlees v Owen Ames Kimball Co*, 340 Mich 670 (1974).

(a) Paul

In this instance, Paul was not identified in the contract by name nor was he a party to the contract. However, a class of persons, the tenants of the building, was specifically designated in the contract. Therefore, Quick Repair knowingly and expressly undertook an obligation directly for the benefit of the specific class of persons who were reasonably identified in the contract, the tenants. The language of the contract provides that Quick Repair will minimize any disruption to the tenants, including Paul. Quick Repair's promise in the contract comes within the third-party beneficiary statute, for it directly benefits the tenants who carry on operations in the building. Therefore, Paul was a member of the class that had been sufficiently described or designated in the contract, to wit, a tenant of the building. Paul therefore may proceed to maintain a breach of contract action under a third-party beneficiary theory to recover damages for the harm done to his furs and his loss of sales due to the business disruption.

(b) Victor

Victor vendor, however, is not a tenant of the building. Thus, as opposed to being a specifically designated person or a member of a reasonably identified class of persons who directly benefit from the contract, Victor is an indirect and incidental beneficiary of the contract. An incidental beneficiary has no rights under the contract. Victor cannot maintain an action against Quick Repair based on the contract between Larry Landlord and Quick Repair even though he suffered damages from Quick Repair's breach of the contract.

-9-

ANSWER TO QUESTION NO. 5

Several Michigan Rules of Professional Conduct (MRPC) come into play under this scenario.

Various rules prohibit the lawyers from altering the document. MRPC 3.4(a) provides that a lawyer shall not "unlawfully obstruct another party's access to evidence; unlawfully alter, destroy, or conceal a document or other material having potential evidentiary value; or counsel or assist another person to do any such act." The electronic information at issue here (the electronic version of the document including metadata) clearly has evidentiary value.[1] Also, the court has resolved the question as to whether it is a "document" which must be turned over within the meaning of the plaintiff's discovery request. If a LawFirm lawyer alters the electronic version or responds to the discovery request without producing it, or assists in such activity, the question of MRPC 3.4(a)'s applicability depends upon whether this activity is unlawful. As the comment to MRPC 3.4 notes:

"Other law makes it an offense to destroy material for purpose of impairing its availability in a pending proceeding or one whose commencement can be foreseen. Falsifying evidence is also generally a criminal offense. Paragraph (a) applies to evidentiary material generally, including computerized information."

Violation of discovery rules or orders may also establish unlawfulness for purposes of MRPC 3.4(a).[2]

In additional to violating MRPC 3.4(a), the conduct proposed here could also constitute a violation of other sections of MRPC 3.4, such as MRPC 3.4(b), prohibiting the falsification of

---

[1]See *DC Ethics Op* 341 (2007) ("Because it is impermissible to alter electronic documents that constitute tangible evidence, the removal of metadata [from a document requested in discovery] may, at least in some instances, be prohibited . . . [by DC Rule 3.4(a)].")

[2]See 2 G. Hazard, W. Hodes & P. Jarvis, *The Law of Lawyering,* §30--4 at 30--7-9 (3d ed). See also *Restatement (Third) of the Law Governing Lawyers* §118(2).

-10-

evidence.[3]

The withholding, destruction, or alteration of the electronic document by Partner or Associate would also constitute a violation of MRPC 3.4(c), which provides that a lawyer shall not knowingly disobey an obligation under the rules of a tribunal except for an open refusal based on an assertion that no valid obligation exists." Failure to produce discoverable evidence constitutes a violation of the Michigan Court Rules on discovery. It is clear from the facts that any such withholding of the document would be a knowing violation of the rule. Finally, it cannot be argued that this would be an open refusal based on an argument that there is no valid obligation to produce the document; the proposed action is surreptitious, not above-board. Also, although MRPC 3.4(c) does not specifically reference the violation of court orders, courts and discipline agencies consistently hold that knowing violation of an order constitutes a violation of this rule.[4]

Yet another provision of MRPC 3.4 would be violated if the CEO's plan were to be carried out. A Michigan lawyer shall not "fail to make reasonably diligent efforts to comply with a legally proper discovery request by an opposing party." MRPC 3.4(d).[5]

Finally, the plan would run afoul of various provisions of MRPC 8.4, which provides that it is misconduct for a lawyer to:

"(b) engage in conduct involving dishonesty, fraud, deceit, misrepresentation, or violation of the criminal law, where such

---

[3]Alteration of physician's reports was held to violate Louisiana MRPC 3.4(b) (prohibiting lawyers from falsifying evidence in *In re Watkins*, 656 So 2d 984 (la 1995).

[4]See ABA/BNA Lawyers Manual on Professional Conduct; 61:721 ("Courts uniformly apply Rule 3.4(c) to require compliance with court orders even though the text speaks of obeying 'rules.'"). See also, *Grievance Administrator v Stefani*, ADB 09-47-GA (March 2, 2010 Hearing Panel Report of Misconduct), at pp 23-25 (subpoenaing documents from non-party witness in violation of MCR 2.305(A)(5) and court's order constitutes violation of MRPC 3.4[c]). The panel's report is available at: http://www.adbmich.org/statuts/STEFANI_09-47-GA.PDF

[5]See *Meier v Meier*, 835 So 2d 379 (Fla Dist Ct App 2003) (appellate court cited Florida Bar Rules 3.4(a), (c) and (d) in requiring lawyer to produce documents requested in discovery despite client's instruction to withhold them).

-11-

conduct reflects adversely on the lawyer's honesty, trustworthiness, or fitness as a lawyer;

"(c) engage in conduct that is prejudicial to the administration of justice".

As has been discussed above, falsifying evidence is generally a criminal offense.[6] The conduct here is also clearly dishonest.[7] Additionally, the proposed conduct would be prejudicial to the administration of justice.[8]

Thus, Associate may not alter the electronic document by removing the metadata from it.

It is also not permissible for Associate to return the document to the CEO so that he may alter it if the CEO's alteration would violate other law (such as a criminal statute or a discovery rule, which may be applicable to parties). MRPC 1.2(c) provides that: "A lawyer shall not counsel a client to engage, or assist a client, in conduct that the lawyer knows is illegal or fraudulent, but a lawyer may discuss the legal consequences of any proposed course of conduct with a client." Return of the document to the CEO might be deemed assistance in light of the fact that Partner and Associate are aware that the original in their possession will be altered if returned to the CEO.[9] Accordingly, Partner and

---

[6]Compare, *In re Watkins*, 656 CO 2d 984 (LA 1995) (lawyer who altered physician reports regarding social security claimant violated not only 3.4(a) and (c) but also 8.4(b) (criminal conduct reflecting adversely on fitness) (c) (conduct that is dishonest, etc.) and (d) (conduct prejudicial to the administration of justice).

[7]See, e.g., *Florida Bar v Burkich-Burrell*, 659 SO 2d 1082 (FL 1995) (submission of false interrogatory answers violated Florida Rule 8.4(c), which prohibits a lawyer from engaging in conduct involving dishonesty, fraud, deceit or misrepresentation). Compare *In Re Sealed Appellant*, 194 F2d 666 (CA 5, 1999) (backdating stock certificate to avoid it being considered a fraudulent conveyance violated Louisiana Rule of Professional Conduct 8.4(c) ("It is professional misconduct for a lawyer to . . . engage in conduct involving dishonesty, fraud, deceit or misrepresentation".)

[8]*In re Watkins, supra*, n 6.

[9]See Michigan Ethics Opinion RI-345 (October 24, 2008), available at http://michbar.org/opinions/ethics/numbered_opinions/RI-345.htm

-12-

Associate must determine whether alteration of the electronic document would constitute a violation of law whether conducted by themselves or their client.

LawFirm must withdraw form representing GeneriCorp if the representation will result in violation of the Rules of Professional Conduct or other law. MCR 1.16(a)(1). Thus, if the client insists on alteration of the document by LawFirm (or Partner or Associate, it (they) must withdraw pursuant to MCR 1.16(a)(1) because carrying out this objective of the representation would violate at least the Rules of Professional Conduct discussed about (MRPC 3.4 and 8.4) and possibly criminal law. Also, if GeneriCorp insists on the return of the document and then provides LawFirm with a "corrected" document which does not contain the relevant metadata, LawFirm will have to withdraw under those circumstances as well if such alteration/spoliation is prohibited by criminal law in Michigan (as the comment to MRPC 3.4 suggests). MRPC 1.2(c); MRPC 1.16(a)(1). Continued representation after facilitating the alteration of evidence would not be allowed under MRPC 1.16.

If the plan is carried out, both Partner and Associate will have committed misconduct. Because Partner has direct supervisory authority over Associate, Partner is required to make reasonable efforts to ensure that Associate conforms to the Rules of Professional Conduct. MRPC 5.1(b). That obligation would not be met if the plan is carried out. In fact, because Partner ordered Associate to alter or facilitate the alteration of the document, Partner would be responsible for Associate's violation of the rules. MRPC 5.1(c)(1). The Rules of Professional Conduct bind a lawyer even when he is following orders. MRPC 5.2(a). Associate, as a subordinate lawyer, would escape responsibility for violating the rules of professional conduct only if Associate acts in accordance with his supervisory lawyer's (Partner's) reasonable resolution of an arguable question of professional duty. MRPC 5.2(b). On these facts, including Associate's familiarity with sanctions decisions, the question does not appear arguable and the resolution does not seem reasonable.

-13-

ANSWER TO QUESTION NO. 6

"Other Acts" evidence is admissible per MRE 404(b)(1):

MRE 404(b)(1) provides:

"Evidence of other crimes, wrongs or acts is not admissible to prove the character of a person in order to show action and conformity therewith. It may, however, be admissible for other purposes, such as proof of motive, opportunity, intent, preparation, scheme, plan, or assisting in doing an act, knowledge, identity or absence of a mistake or accident when the same was material, whether such other crimes, wrongs or acts are contemporaneous with, or prior or subsequent to the conduct at issue in the case."

As the Michigan Supreme Court explained in *People v Sabin (After Remand)*, 463 Mich 43, 56 (2000):

"404(b)(1) does not require the exclusion of otherwise admissible evidence. Rather, the first sentence of MRE 404(b)(1) reiterates the general rule, embodied in MRE 404(a) and MRE 405, prohibiting the *use* of evidence of specific acts to prove a person's character to show that the person acted in conformity with character on a particular occasion. The second sentence of MRE 404(b)(1) then emphasizes that this prohibition does not preclude using the evidence for other relevant purposes. MRE 404(b)(1) lists some of the permissible uses. This list is not, however, exhaustive." (Emphasis in original).

Evidentiary safeguards employed when admitting "Other Acts" evidence:

The state has the burden to establish that the evidence it seeks to introduce is relevant to a proper purpose in the non-exclusive list contained in MRE 404(b)(1) or is probative of a fact other than the character or criminal propensity of the defendant. *People v Crawford*, 458 Mich 376 (1998). The fact that the evidence may reflect on a defendant's character or propensity to commit a crime does not render it inadmissible if it is also relevant to a non-character purpose. "Evidence relevant to a non-character purpose is *admissible* under MRE 404(b) *even if* it also reflects on a defendant's character. Evidence is *inadmissible* under this rule *only* if it is relevant *solely* to the defendant's character or

-14-

criminal propensity." *People v Mardlin*, 487 Mich 609, 615-616 (2010). (Emphasis in original).

For "other acts" evidence to be admissible, the state has the burden of establishing that the evidence: (1) is offered for a proper purpose (not propensity) within MRE 401; (2) is relevant under MRE 402 to an issue or fact of consequence at trial under MRE 401; and (3) the danger of unfair (undue) prejudice does not substantially outweigh the probative value of the evidence under MRE 403 in view of the availability of other means of proof and other facts. A limiting instruction by the court can be given upon request under MRE 105.

The state must establish a proper purpose for the admission of the evidence within MRE 401:

The state argues that the "other acts" evidence is admissible to show Dan's scheme, plan or system in doing an act and absence of mistake or accident. Since the grounds articulated by the prosecution establish a permissible purpose for admission, the state's initial burden is satisfied and the next inquiry is whether the evidence is relevant to the theories identified by the prosecution.

The state must establish that the evidence is admissible under MRE 402:

The fact that the prosecution has identified a permissible theory of admissibility does not automatically render the "other acts" evidence relevant in a particular case. *Sabin* at 60. The trial court must determine "whether the evidence, under a proper theory, has a tendency to make the existence of a fact of consequence in the case more or less probable then it would be without the evidence." *Id.*

Under the facts presented here, an examinee could appropriately conclude that the prior acts evidence will be deemed relevant under a theory that Dan had devised a plan which he used repeatedly to carry out separate but very similar crimes, wrongs or acts. Such acts of similar misconduct have been held by the Michigan Supreme Court to be logically relevant and admissible if the charged and uncharged acts are "sufficiently similar to support an inference that they are manifestations of a common plan, scheme or system." *Sabin* at 63. With respect to the sailboat and house fires, the following facts support the prosecution's theory: (1) the first erupted immediately after Dan left the premises; (2) Dan's personal property was damaged and Dan sought and collected insurance proceeds; (3) the fires were started by a seemingly

-15-

careless act which any adult would recognize as a fire hazard; and (4) Dan was responsible for the act that caused the fire. The car engine fire, on the other hand, is sufficiently different from the other fires that it likely would not be deemed admissible under the theory of a common plan, scheme or system.

The evidence of all three prior fires could be found admissible to prove the absence of mistake under the theory known as the "doctrine of chances." "Under this theory, as the number of incidents of an out-of-the-ordinary event increases in relation to a particular defendant, the objective probability increases that the charged act *and/or* the prior occurrences were not the result of natural causes." *People v Mardlin*, 487 Mich 609, 616 (2010) (emphasis in original). "If a type of event linked to the defendant occurs with unusual frequency, evidence of the occurrences may be probative, for example, of his criminal intent or of the absence of mistake or accident because it is objectively improbable that such events occur so often in relation to the same person due to mere happenstance." *Id* at 617. See also *Crawford*, 458 Mich 367, 392-393. Here, an examinee could appropriately argue that the past fires are logically relevant to the objective probability that the fire now at issue was intentionally set since three prior fires involving Dan's property in the past five years is out-of-the-ordinary. Additionally, Dan benefitted from two of the three prior fires and was responsible for the acts, which Dan chalks up to carelessness, that started the fires. An examinee could also argue that the prior uncharged acts should not be admitted under the doctrine of chances because they are not similar to the charged act and Dan has not been involved in such incidents more frequently than the typical person.

<u>The state must establish that the evidence is admissible under MRE 403:</u>

Unfair prejudice is defined as the "danger that marginally probative evidence will be given undue or pre-emptive weight by a jury." *Crawford*, 458 Mich at 398. The court must determine whether the danger of unfair prejudice substantially outweighs the probative value of the proposed evidence in view of other means of proof and other facts. Here, there is a potential for prejudice but the evidence of the prior fires (with the possible exception of the car engine fire) is probative in rebutting Dan's defense that the fire for which he is now being charged was an accident. It is also the only means of proof for the prosecution since the expert's report was inconclusive. Additionally, if the occurrence of the other fires is admitted, the jury can consider Dan's explanation for those events and give each incident whatever weight it deems appropriate. The defense can also require that the trial court

-16-

issue a limiting instruction to mitigate the potential for prejudice. While the prosecution likely has the stronger argument under MRE 403 for admission of the evidence at issue, an examinee could also argue--and deserve credit for--the opposite result.

-17-

ANSWER TO QUESTION NO. 7

A bailment is created when the owner of personal property (the bailor) delivers his or her property to the possession of another (the bailee) in trust for a specific lawful purpose. *In re George L. Nadell & Co*, 294 Mich 150, 154 (1940). Here, Vienna Victim and Oliver Owner entered into a bailment agreement whereby Vienna delivered her jewelry (bracelet and watch) to the possession of Oliver for repair and cleaning. Although the bailment temporarily transferred physical possession of the jewelry from Vienna to Oliver, a bailment does not alter the title of personalty. See *Dunlap v Gleason*, 16 Mich 158 (1867).

Vienna can recover her watch from Dan: MCL 600.2920 codifies the common law action for *replevin* and allows someone to recover specific personal property that has been "unlawfully taken or unlawfully detained," as long as the plaintiff has a right to possess the personalty taken or detained. MCL 600.2920(1)(c). Vienna remains the title owner of her watch because, as stated, a bailment does not change the title of personalty. Accordingly, even a good faith recipient of property (*i.e.*, Dan) lacks title to that property as against the rightful owner (Vienna). *Ward v Carey*, 200 Mich 217, 223 (1918).

An action for conversion against Dan, as someone buying stolen property, will not be successful, unless there is evidence that Dan knew that the bracelet was stolen. MCL 600.2919a(1)(b). No such evidence is present here, as the facts indicate an arms length business transaction between Dan and the burglar.

Vienna can recover monetary damages from Oliver for conversion of her bracelet: Under the common law, a bailee converted a bailor's property by using it in an unauthorized way and in defiance of the bailor's title in the property, for instance, by using the property himself, *Bates v Stansell*, 19 Mich 91 (1869). Michigan has codified the tort action of conversion at MCL 600.2919a, which allows the owner of personal property to recover "3 times the amount of actual damages sustained, plus costs and reasonable attorney fees" when another person "convert[s] property to the other person's own use." In this case, Oliver converted Vienna's bracelet to his own use, *i.e.* creating a gold ingot for sale to investors, and not for the intended purpose of the bailment. Vienna's actual damages from Oliver's conversion are $2,000, the appraised value of the bracelet. Accordingly, she will be able to collect $6,000 in monetary damages from Oliver, the statutory award for treble damages, in addition to costs and attorney fees.

The availability of this remedy "in addition to any other right or remedy the person may have at law or otherwise," MCL 600.2919a(2), does not necessarily preclude an action to recover the property (*i.e.*, what was known under the common law as a replevin action), MCL 600.2920. However, where property sought to be recovered has been destroyed, a common law replevin action will not lie. *Gildas v Crosby*, 61 Mich 413 (1886). Oliver's destruction of the bracelet left Vienna with the sole remedy of a conversion action for monetary damages.

Vienna can likely recover monetary damages from Oliver in connection with her stolen watch: The obligations of a bailee depend on the nature of a particular bailment: whether the bailment is for the benefit of the bailee, for the benefit of the bailor, or for the mutual benefit of both parties. The nature of the bailment here was for the mutual benefit of both parties, because Oliver agreed to repair and clean Vienna's jewelry, and Vienna paid Oliver for this service. See *Godfrey v City of Flint*, 284 Mich 291 (1938). As the bailee in a bailment for the mutual benefit of both parties, Oliver is bound to exercise ordinary care of the subject matter of the bailment and is liable to Vienna if he fails to do so. *Id.* at 297-298.

The failure of a bailee to return the property subject to a bailment is prima facie evidence of negligence, and it becomes the bailee's burden to establish that his negligence was not the proximate cause of the bailor's damages. *Columbus Jack Corp v Swedish Crucible Steel Corp*, 393 Mich 478 (1975). "This may require a defendant-bailee to produce evidence of the actual circumstances surrounding the origins of the fire or the theft, including the precautions taken to prevent the loss." *Id.* at 486. The facts here provide strong evidence that Oliver was negligent in protecting Vienna's watch from the burglar: although Oliver had a state-of-the-art vault readily available to him, he failed to place Vienna's watch inside the vault for several nights in a row. Placing the watch inside the vault would likely have prevented the theft of the watch, since the items inside the vault were untouched. Such circumstances are likely to create a fact question for a jury to decide whether Oliver is liable to Dan for the loss. See *id.* at 486 n 3.

Although Vienna has the right to proceed to recover monetary damages for the theft of her watch, the extent of monetary damages that Oliver owes Vienna is affected by whether Vienna pursues an

-19-

action to recover the watch from Dan. By law, damages confined to the detention of personal property cannot be recovered twice. *Briggs v Milburn*, 40 Mich 512 (1879). Thus, if she elects to recover the watch from Dan, whatever monetary damages that Oliver owes Vienna are mitigated by the recovery of the watch. Nevertheless, Vienna may also be entitled to other damages reasonably foreseeable from Oliver's negligence. See *Solecki v Courtesy Ford, Inc*, 16 Mich App 691 (1969).

-20-

ANSWER TO QUESTION 8

Because the facts indicate that Dennis died without a testamentary document, Dennis's estate will be distributed according to the laws governing intestate succession, MCL 700.2101 *et seq.*

(1) Timmy Taylor: Where a decedent dies without a surviving spouse, as is the case here, the decedent's estate passes first to the decedent's descendants by representation. MCL 700.2103(a). Thus, if Timmy is Dennis's descendant, he will take the entire estate. However, the statutory definition of descendant contemplates "the relationship of parent and child," MCL 700.1103(k), and the statutory definition of "child" specifically excludes "a foster child." MCL 700.1103(f). Under the statutory scheme, Timmy cannot take Dennis's estate.

Michigan recognizes the doctrine of adoption by estoppel. See *Perry v Boyce*, 323 Mich 95 (1948). Under this equitable doctrine, a child is entitled to inherit as if he were adopted where a parent promises to adopt the child but does not. Because the facts do not indicate that Dennis ever promised to adopt Timmy, adoption by estoppel cannot be used as a basis to award Dennis's estate to Timmy.

(2) Ed Ermine: If the decedent has no surviving descendants, his estate next goes to "the decedent's parents equally if both survive or to the surviving parent." MCL 700.2103(b). As Dennis's mother did not survive him, Ed would take Dennis's entire estate if Ed were determined to be Dennis's parent.

Under Michigan law, where a child is born out of wedlock, a man may be considered a child's natural father for the purposes of intestate succession under one of the several circumstances listed in MCL 700.2114(1)(b)(i)-(v). Under subsection (v), a probate judge may determine that a man is a child's father "regardless of the child's age or whether or not the alleged father has died," using the standards contained in the Paternity Act, MCL 722.711 *et seq*, including DNA testing. MCL 722.716. Because the DNA results were conclusive, Ed Ermine is Dennis's "natural father" under the law.

This does not mean, however, that Ed is entitled to inherit from Dennis. MCL 700.2114(4) states that a natural parent is "precluded" from inheriting from a child "unless that natural

-21-

parent has openly treated the child as his or hers, and has not refused to support the child." Both prongs of the statute must be satisfied in order for Ed to take as Dennis's heir. *In re Turpening Estate*, 258 Mich App 464 (2003). If Scott's and Paul's testimony is credited, and the judge finds as fact that Ed neither visited nor supported Dennis during his childhood, there would be a sufficient basis to preclude Ed from inheriting Dennis's estate.

3. **Paul and Scott**: If the decedent has no surviving descendant or parent, then the decedent's estate passes to "the descendants of the decedent's parents or of either of them by representation." MCL 700.2103(c). Because Timmy does not qualify as a descendant, and Ed is precluded from taking as a natural parent, Paul and Scott would each take 50% of Dennis's $1,000,000 estate.

While Scott claims that Paul should take a smaller share of the estate because Paul and Dennis have only one parent in common, Michigan law specifically provides that "relative of the half blood inherits the same share he or she would inherit if he or she were of the whole blood." MCL 700.2107. Thus, Scott's claim would fail, and the brothers would share equally in Dennis's estate.

-22-

ANSWER TO QUESTION NO. 9

In Michigan, landlords have a general duty to keep residential premises in a habitable condition. This is commonly known as the implied warranty of habitability, and represents a duty imposed on all residential leases. In every lease, the lessor covenants that "the premises and all common areas are fit for the use intended by the parties" and that he will "keep the premises in reasonable repair during the term of the lease or license, and [will] comply with the applicable health and safety laws of the state and of the local unit of government where the premises are located." MCL 554.139. These provisions generally require that the lessor provide premises that are reasonably suited for residential use, and is a change from the common law in which no general duty to provide habitable property existed. See generally, *Allison v AEW Capital Management LLP*, 481 Mich 419, 440-442 (2008) (Corrigan, J., concurring). Generally speaking, where the lessor breaches the warranty, a tenant may move out and terminate the lease, or may stay and sue for damages.

In the face of Michael's failure to take corrective action, the presence of substantial mold in a leased estate represents a serious health hazard that likely renders the estate untenantable or unfit for occupancy. Michael's outright refusal to correct this problem caused him to be in breach of the implied warranty of habitability. Indeed, the facts specifically note that the mold caused Julie to become sick and forced Nick to seek residence elsewhere during at least part of the relevant time period.

Michael v Julie: Where premises are rendered untenantable, Michigan statutory law provides that a lessee or occupant may "quit and surrender possession of the building, and of the land so injured, destroyed, or rendered untenantable or unfit for occupancy." MCL 554.201. A lessee who does so is "not liable to pay to the lessor or owner rent for the time subsequent to the surrender." MCL 554.201.

In this case, the presence of mold represented a serious health hazard in violation of local housing law and thus likely rendered Julie's apartment untenantable, particularly in light of Michael's refusal to rectify the problem. Because Michael breached the warranty of habitability, Julie therefore had the right to leave her apartment and surrender possession back to Michael. Furthermore, she is not liable for rent that would have been due after the time of surrender. Thus, Michael's action against Julie

-23-

alleging breach of their housing contract and claiming damages for unpaid rent should likely fail.

Michael v Nick: Nick's situation is slightly different from Julie's because, although he also had the right to terminate his lease and leave the premises, he decided to stay, withhold rent until Michael made the premises habitable, and notified health officials who could force Michael to take the necessary corrective measures.

The enactment of the comprehensive statutory scheme governing landlord-tenant law has been held to impose mutuality between the tenant's duty to pay rent and the landlord's duty to maintain the premises in habitable condition. A tenant is therefore allowed under this scheme to withhold rent payments when a landlord fails in this duty. *Rome v Walker*, 38 Mich App 458 (1972). Nick's withholding of rent for the time period in which it took Michael to return his apartment to a habitable condition thus does not provide legal grounds for eviction.

More important to this question, however, is the recognition that this fact pattern raises an issue of retaliatory eviction. In an action by a landlord to recover possession of realty, Michigan law provides to the tenant the defense of retaliatory eviction. MCL 600.5720. Statutory law specifically provides the situations in which the defense may be raised, including where the termination is intended as a penalty for a tenant's attempt to secure or enforce rights under the lease or the law, or where the termination is intended as a penalty for the tenant's "complaint to a governmental authority with a report of [the landlord's] violation of a health or safety code or ordinance." MCL 600.5720(1)(a), (b); see also *Frenchtown Villa v Meadors*, 117 Mich App 683 (1982).

Moreover, there exists a rebuttable presumption in favor of the defense of retaliatory eviction if the tenant shows that, within 90 days before the commencement of summary proceedings seeking eviction, he attempted to secure or enforce rights against the landlord or to complain against the landlord by action in a court or through a governmental agency. A landlord may rebut the presumption if he establishes by a preponderance of the evidence that the termination was not in retaliation for such acts. MCL 600.5720(2).

Since Nick wishes to remain in possession of his apartment during the fixed period of his remaining tenancy, he can raise the defense of retaliatory eviction in the eviction proceedings. Nick successfully complained to a local health authority regarding Michael's refusal to correct a serious health condition on the

-24-

premises, thereby enforcing his rights under state law and local housing code. Moreover, the fact that Nick did so within 90 days prior to the eviction proceeding will allow him to take advantage of the presumption that the attempted termination of the tenancy was a penalty, retribution, or otherwise in retaliation for Nick's decision to exercise his rights. As noted above, Nick's refusal to pay rent during the time in which Michael was in breach of his duty of habitability was a lawful action. And although Michael also alleges that several other residents have complained that Nick throws loud parties, Michael will have to establish by a preponderance of the evidence that this is the actual, good faith reason that Michael is seeking to terminate Nick's tenancy. Because those claims appear from the facts to be largely unsubstantiated, it is likely that Nick will prevail.

-25-

ANSWER TO QUESTION NO. 10

1. **Reasonable Doubt**: Reasonable doubt is defined in CJI2d 3.2(3) as:

"A reasonable doubt is a fair, honest doubt growing out of the evidence or lack of evidence. It is not merely an imaginary or possible doubt, but a doubt based on reason and common sense. A reasonable doubt is just that--a doubt that is reasonable, after a careful and considered examination of the facts and circumstances of this case."

II. **Armed Robbery**:

A. Elements: To prove the charge of armed robbery (MCL 750.529 and 750.530) the prosecutor must establish each of the following four elements beyond a reasonable doubt.

1. The defendant used force or violence or assaulted or put the complainant in fear.

2. The defendant did so while he was in the course of committing a larceny. A "larceny" is the taking and moving of someone else's property or money with the intent to take it away from that person permanently.

"In the course of committing a larceny" includes acts that occur in an attempt to commit the larceny, or during the commission of the larceny, or in flight or attempted flight after the commission of the larceny, or in an attempt to retain possession of the property or money.

3. The complainant was present while defendant was in the course of committing the larceny.

4. That while in the course of committing the larceny the defendant:

a. Possessed a weapon designed to be dangerous and capable of causing death or serious injury; or

b. Possessed any other object capable of causing death or serious injury that the defendant used as a weapon; or

c. Possessed any object used or fashioned in a manner to

lead the person who was present to reasonably believe it was a dangerous weapon or,

d. Represented orally or otherwise that he was in possession of a weapon.

B. **Discussion**: The first element was fulfilled because Dan put Ronald Graham in fear when he announced he had a gun. The second element is fulfilled because Ronald was put in fear during the commission of a larceny. The larceny occurred when Dan took and moved Lynn Tracy's money from Ronald with the intent to keep it. Dan knowingly gave Lynn a lesser amount of money and kept the greater amount of money. Alternatively, Ronald was put in fear in Dan's flight after the larceny when he swung the stick at Ronald. The third element is satisfied because Ronald was present during the course of the larceny, and even though Ronald was not required to be either the owner or rightful possessor of the money, he had a superior interest in it because he possessed the money when it was taken by Dan. *People v Cabassa*, 249 Mich 543, 546-547 (1930); *People v Needham*, 8 Mich App 679, 684-685 (1967). The fourth element is also satisfied because Dan defendant orally represented to Ronald that he possessed a gun. It is alternately satisfied as Dan swung the stick at Ronald to effectuate his escape (flight) or to keep the stolen money.

III. **Felonious Assault**:

A. Elements: CJI 2d 17.9 (MCL 750.82) provides the state has the duty to prove each of the following elements beyond a reasonable doubt:

1. The defendant either attempted to commit a battery on the complainant or did an act that would cause a reasonable person to feel or apprehend an immediate battery. A battery is the forceful or violent touching of the person or something closely connected with the person.

2. The defendant intended to either injure the complainant or make the complainant reasonably fear an immediate battery.

3. At the time, the defendant had the ability to commit a battery, appeared to have the ability or thought he had the ability.

4. That the defendant committed the assault with a dangerous weapon. See *People v Jones*, 443 Mich 88, 100 (1993); *People v Avant*, 235 Mich App 499, 505 (1999).

-27-

In CJI 2d 17.10, a dangerous weapon is defined as:

1. A dangerous weapon is any object that is used in a way that is likely to cause serious physical injury or death.

2. The way an object is used or intended to be used in an assault determines whether or not it is a dangerous weapon. If an object is used in a way that it is likely to cause serious physical injury or death, it is a dangerous weapon.

The prosecutor has the burden of proving that the weapon was dangerous or an object was used or intended for use as a weapon. See *People v Goolsby*, 284 Mich 375 (1938); *People v Brown*, 406 Mich 215 (1979). Whether an object is a dangerous weapon under the circumstances of the case is a question for the fact finder. *People v Barkley*, 151 Mich App 234 (1986), *People v Jolly*, 442 Mich 458 (1993).

B. Discussion: Dan can be convicted of felonious assault for attempting to strike Ronald with a large tree branch.

The first element is fulfilled because the defendant attempted to commit a battery by swinging the tree branch at Ronald. It could also be established because Ronald was in immediate fear of a battery as the tree branch was swung at him, causing him to quickly step back. The second element is fulfilled because Dan specifically intended to swing the branch at Ronald, *i.e.* "Get away from me." The third element is fulfilled because Dan had the ability to commit the battery because he possessed and swung the tree branch. Fourth, the defendant committed the assault with a large tree branch. Although an argument can be made that a tree branch does not constitute a dangerous weapon within the statute, the better argument is that because it can cause serious physical injury or death, it qualifies as a dangerous weapon. See *People v McCadney*, 111 Mich App 545, 549-550 (1981) (holding that a stick can be a dangerous weapon).

-28-

ANSWER TO QUESTION NO. 11

This question seeks to have the applicant identify the law governing searches by school officials and reliance on anonymous tips, and then to discuss whether there existed a "reasonable suspicion" sufficient to justify the search of Grassmeyer's truck and the admission of the evidence discovered during the search.

Both the federal and state constitutions guarantee the right to be secure from unreasonable searches and seizures. *People v Smith*, 420 Mich 1, 18-19 (1984), quoting Const 1963, art 1, §11 and US Const, Am IV. The applicant should recognize that the Michigan Constitution in this regard is generally construed to provide the same protection as the Fourth Amendment to the United States Constitution, which is incorporated against the states under the due process clause of the Fourteenth Amendment. *People v Levine*, 461 Mich 172, 178 (1999). See also *Mapp v Ohio*, 367 US 643 (1961). Evidence obtained in violation of the Fourth Amendment is subject to suppression in state court. *People v Cartwright*, 454 Mich 550, 557-558 (1997).

As a preliminary matter, the applicant should address the presence of the liaison officer during the search. Although the Fourth Amendment generally requires police to obtain a warrant before conducting a search, police may search a vehicle without a warrant if there is probable cause to believe the vehicle contains evidence of a crime or contraband. *Pennsylvania v Labron*, 528 US 938, 940 (1996); *People v Garvin*, 235 Mich App 90, 102 (1999). Here, although there is no evidence of probable cause, the fact that the officer was present (and even forwarded the tip to the principal) had no effect on the search's validity as the officer did not initiate or even participate in the search. *People v Perreault*, 486 Mich 914 (2010); see, also, *Shade v City of Farmington*, 309 F3d 1054, 1060 (CA 8, 20902) (search constitutional "where school officials, not law enforcement officers, initiated the investigation and the search").

Unlike police officers, school officials need only a "reasonable suspicion" of an infraction of school disciplinary rules or a violation of the law when searching a student or his property (including a vehicle) on school grounds. *Perreault*, 486 Mich at 915 (Markman, J., concurring), quoting *New Jersey v TLO*, 469 US 325, 341-342 (1985); *People v Kazmierczak*, 461 Mich 411, 418-419 (2000). A "reasonable suspicion entails something more than an inchoate or unparticularized suspicion or 'hunch,' but less

-29-

than the level of suspicion required for probable cause." *People v Champion,* 452 Mich 92, 98 (1996), citing *United States v Sokolow,* 490 US 1 (1989).

The impetus behind the principal's search was an anonymous tip. Whether this tip was sufficient to constitute a reasonable suspicion depends on "the *totality of the circumstances* with a view to the question whether the tip carries with it *sufficient indicia of reliability* to support a *reasonable suspicion* of criminal activity." *People v Faucett,* 442 Mich 153, 169 (1993) (emphasis in original). A sufficiently detailed anonymous tip may provide a reasonable suspicion, especially where corroborating circumstances outside the tip are present. *Id.* at 170-172.

Arguably, the tip here was sufficiently reliable to support a reasonable suspicion. It identified four students whom the tipster had personally seen selling drugs on school grounds. The tipster was personally involved in the drug activity with one of these students (Weeden). Although greater detail was provided about Weeden and the search of his vehicle yielded no contraband, the tipster had also provided identifying details about the other students, including their names, grades at school, the vehicles they drove, and the types of drugs they sold. As for Grassmeyer, the tip additionally specified Grassmeyer's race and where he would sell drugs. Moreover, the corroborating circumstances concerning Grassmeyer pointed to the tipster's reliability. Specifically, the liaison-officer verified the students' vehicles, and additionally, the principal was aware before receiving the tip that Grassmeyer drove a truck and that he had been previously associated with drug activity. *People v Perreault,* 287 Mich App 168, 180-181 (2010) (O'Connell, J., dissenting), rev'd for reasons stated in Court of Appeals dissenting opinion, 486 Mich 914 (2010).

This information, taken as a whole, was sufficient to create a reasonable and particularized suspicion that Grassmeyer was selling drugs from the school parking lot. It was not based on a hunch and corroborating circumstances existed. Therefore, the search was reasonable under the Fourth Amendment and the circuit court should deny Grassmeyer's motion.

-30-

ANSWER TO QUESTION NO. 12

Mr. McGuire's Motion: It is well-settled that the Constitution only restricts the government, not private actors. *Rendell-Baler v Kohn*, 457 US 8340, 837 (1982); *Public Utilities Comm v Pollak*, 343 US 451, 461 (1972); *Behagen v Amateur Basketball Assoc*, 885 F2d 524, 530 (CA 10, 1989). Consequently, Smith cannot maintain a claim against Mr. McGuire because he was not a government employee or volunteer. There is also no evidence that he was acting on behalf of the school or Mrs. Lady, or that there was any nexus or joint action between the two actors, *Behagen, supra.* Instead, the facts show only that he acted in reaction to a negative statement being made about his son. Since the Constitution does not restrict a private individual's actions, Smith cannot state a First Amendment claim against Mr. McGuire.

Mrs. Lady's Motion: The second question pertains to Mrs. Lady and whether school officials can prevent a student at a school sponsored event from displaying a message that could be interpreted as support for drug use. The First Amendment to the U.S. Constitution prohibits the government from infringing on the freedom of speech. However, in the school context, an initial principle to recognize is that although students do not shed their constitutional rights at the schoolhouse gate, *Tinker v Des Moines Ind Comm Schools*, 393 US 503, 506 (1969), students do not have constitutional rights consistent with adults in other settings. *Bethel School Dist No 403 v Fraser*, 478 US 675, 682 (1986). School officials retain the right to exercise authority consistent with constitutional safeguards to prescribe and control conduct in the schools. *Tinker*, 393 US at 507. Thus, the "rights of students 'must be applied in light of the special characteristics of the school environment.'" *Morse v Frederick*, 551 US 393, 397 (2007), quoting *Hazelwood School District v Kuhlmeiner*, 484 US 260, 266 (1988).

Here, under the foregoing case law, and particularly *Morse*, the best argument is that Mrs. Lady did not violate Smith's free speech rights under the First Amendment, so the court should grant her motion. First, there is no dispute under the facts that there was a school policy against advocating drug use, and the school is empowered to enforce such rules. Although the statement on the picket sign is somewhat ambiguous, it can reasonably be considered a statement advocating drug use, for it states that steroids are "the breakfast of champions." See *Morse*, 551 US at 401-402 ("Bong

-31-

Hits 4 Jesus" sign found to be advocacy for drug use). Mrs. Lady immediately considered it a violation of school policy, and Smith was concerned that it might be. Hence, the best conclusion is that the sign violated school policy.

Second, the school policy did not violate Smith's limited right to free speech. The school had the authority to enforce its rules at a school function, which this home football game surely was. The school also had an interest in stopping student drug use, a compelling interest of the school. Furthermore, the message made a serious allegation against a student from another high school, which in fact caused the initial disruption in the stands. *Defoe v Spiva,* 625 F3d 324, 340 (CA 6, 2010) (Rogers J., concurring) (noting that disruption is not required, but even threat of disruption goes beyond the abstract desires in *Tinker*). Those interests, coupled with the student's limited free speech rights, suffice to preclude Smith from establishing a First Amendment violation against Mrs. Lady. Additionally, it did not involve political speech which is at the core of First Amendment protections, as it was not displayed or being utilized in a debate on the use of drugs in sports, or other such political debate.

-32-

ANSWER TO QUESTION NO. 13

The transaction falls under Article 2 of the Uniform Commercial Code (UCC), which governs contracts, whether oral or written, that involve the sale of goods. See MCL 440.2102. The contract involved the purchase of a stone statue, an item movable at the time identified in the contract for sale. MCL 440.2105(1). Here, there was a contract. The parties' discussion in regard to the subject matter, the quantity and the price showed sufficient agreement to establish a contract. MCL 440.2204. The contract was also recognized through Stella's execution of an invoice even though the price did not match the agreement. A contract for sale "does not fail for indefiniteness if the parties have intended to make a contract and there is a reasonably certain basis for giving an appropriate remedy." MCL 440.2204(3).

The next question is whether the contract is enforceable. The refusal to recognize the contract implicates the statute of frauds. MCL 440.2201, entitled "[f]ormal requirements; statute of frauds" provides in relevant part that:

"(1) Except as otherwise provided in this section, a contract for the sale of goods for the price of $1,000.00 or more is not enforceable by way of action or defense unless there is a writing sufficient to indicate that a contract for sale has been made between the parties and signed by the party against whom enforcement is sought or by his or her authorized agent or broker. A writing is not insufficient because it omits or incorrectly states a term agreed upon but the contract is not enforceable under this subsection beyond the quantity of goods shown in the writing."

As mentioned, the invoice is a writing sufficient to indicate that a contract for sale has been made between the parties. From the invoice and its envelope receipt we can identify the parties, Stella and Brenda, and that the contract involved one statue priced at $1,400.

The significant question is whether there is sufficient evidence that the writing was "signed by the party against whom enforcement is sought," or Stella. MCL 440.1201(39) provides that "signed" includes any symbol executed or adopted by a party with present intention to authenticate a writing, including a carbon copy of his or her signature. Here, there is at least a question of fact in regard to whether Stella signed the invoice. There is some authority suggesting that letterhead alone in some

-33-

circumstances meets the "signed" criteria. Here, the invoice was on letterhead and Stella's hand printed notations specify that the essential terms of the contract, and it was sent to Brenda's address. There is persuasive evidence that the invoice reflected an overall intention to authenticate the contract. Thus, the contract is enforceable.

Some test takers may note that there was no objection within ten days as required by the statute of frauds. However, this requirement applies "[b]etween merchants," and there is no indication that Brenda is a merchant.

Last is the question whether either Stella is in breach of contract for failing to deliver the statue, or Brenda is in breach for failing to remit payment. The parties' contract did not address which party bore the risk of loss during transit. Accordingly, a gap filler provision of the UCC is applicable, MCL 440.2509, which provides in part:

"(1) Where the contract requires or authorizes the seller to ship the goods by carrier

"(a) if it does not require him to deliver them at a particular destination, the risk of loss passes to the buyer when the goods are duly delivered to the carrier even though the shipment is under reservation (section 2505); but

"(b) if it does require him to deliver them at a particular destination and the goods are there duly tendered while in the possession of the carrier, the risk of loss passes to the buyer when the goods are there duly so tendered as to enable the buyer to take delivery."

Here, the contract "authorizes" Stella to ship the statue, MCL 440.2509(1), but she was not "required" to deliver the statue to a particular location. MCL 440.2509(1)(a). Stella informed Brenda that customers typically pick up the statues but that she would hold onto the statue. Stella also mentioned that she would ask people that stopped by if anyone would kindly drop off the statue at Brenda's home. This statement did not oblige Stella to deliver the goods to Brenda or bear the risk of loss for the goods while in transit.

Moreover, under Article 2 of the UCC, "the 'shipment' contract is regarded as the normal one and the 'destination' contract as the variant type." *Eberhard Mfg Co v Brown*, 61 Mich App 268, 271 (1975). Further, "[t]he seller is not obligated to deliver at a named destination and bear the concurrent risk of loss until arrival, unless he has specifically agreed so to deliver or the commercial understanding of the terms used by the parties

-34-

contemplates such delivery. *Id.* citing MCL 440.2503 (Official UCC Comment 5). Under Michigan law, "a contract which contains neither an F.O.B. term nor any other term explicitly allocating loss is a shipment contract." Here, the risk of loss passed to Brenda when the goods were duly delivered to Stella's brother. Accordingly, Brenda is in breach of contract and liable for $1,400.

Some test takers may alternately conclude that the risk of loss had not passed to Brenda because Stella is a merchant and Stella's brother was not a "carrier," *i.e.*, professional transportation service, under the Code. Though not supported by legal authority, this conclusion is arguable and may reflect positively on a test taker's application and reasoning in regard to this issue.

ANSWER TO QUESTION 14

1. **Tom's claim regarding the parties' postnuptial agreement**: Tom is wrong. Postnuptial agreements between the parties who intend to live together as man and wife are unenforceable in the event of divorce. *Wright v Wright* 279 Mich App 291 (2008). But agreements signed in contemplation of separation or divorce are enforceable, and in fact are favored because they further the public policy of settlement over litigation. *In re Berner*, 217 Mich 612 (1922); *Lentz v Lentz*, 271 Mich App 465 (2006). Postnuptial agreements are subject to the traditional standards for contracting under which they are enforceable absent fraud, duress, or mistake. *Id.* at 473-474, 478.

There is no indication of fraud, duress or mistake in the facts presented by the question. At most, Tom might argue that Mary's concealment of her affair constituted some type of fraud. Note, however, that at the time Tom released his interest in the home, its value was equal to the amount owed on the mortgage, so he would not be entitled to the return of his $5,000 investment even if the postnuptial agreement was invalid (both he and Mary essentially lost the value of their investment.)

2. **Tom's claim regarding Mary's fault for the divorce and the disparity in income**: The distribution of property in a divorce is controlled by statute. MCL 552.1 *et seq.* The goal in distributing marital assets in a divorce proceeding is to reach an equitable distribution of property in light of all the circumstances. The trial court need not divide the marital estate into mathematically equal portions, but any significant departure from congruence must be clearly explained. *Berger v Berger*, 277 Mich App 700, 716-717 (2008). In dividing the marital property, the trial court must review the relevant property-division factors set forth in *Sparks v Sparks*, 440 Mich 141, 159-160 (1992): (1) duration of the marriage, (2) contributions of the parties to the marital estate, (3) age of the parties, (4) health of the parties, (5) life status of the parties, (6) necessities and circumstances of the parties, (7) earning abilities of the parties, (8) past relations and conduct of the parties, and (9) general principles of equity. There may even be additional factors that are relevant to a particular case, and the determination of relevant factors will vary depending on the facts and circumstances of the case. *Id.*

A circumstance "to be considered in the determination of

-36-

property division is the fault or misconduct of a party." *Davey v Davey*, 106 Mich App 579, 581-582 (1981). However, "the trial court must consider all the relevant factors and not assign disproportionate weight to any one circumstance." *Sparks*, 440 Mich at 158. In dividing the marital estate, the goal is to achieve equity, not to punish one of the parties. *Sands v Sands*, 442 Mich 30, 36-37 (1993).

Tom is therefore correct that Mary's affair and the disparity in income might make a difference in the distribution of the parties' marital assets, but in this case, any deviation from the standard 50/50 split would likely be minimal. The parties are relatively young and their marriage was not long term, there is not a great disparity in the value of their separate property, and even if their earning abilities differ, Tom can support himself without help from Mary. There is no clear answer to the question of the degree to which any deviation from the presumptive equal division of marital assets would be warranted, but the test taker should be able to apply the applicable property division factors to the facts presented in the question.

Note that this question *does not* call for an analysis of when *separate* assets (as opposed to *marital* assets) may be invaded. Examinees may note that a spouse's separate assets can be subject to division under two statutorily created exceptions: (1) when the property awarded to one party is not sufficient for the suitable support of one party or the party's children (MCL 552.23), or when one party contributed to the acquisition, improvement or accumulation of the property (MCL 552.401). Since Tom has not asked for a share of Mary's separate property, these statutes are not applicable.

3. **Mary's claim regarding the inheritance**: When a trial court divides property in a divorce proceeding, it must first determine what property is marital and what property is separate. *Reeves v Reeves*, 226 Mich App 490, 493-494 (1997). Generally, marital assets are subject to being divided between the parties, but separate assets may not be invaded. *McNamara v Horner*, 249 Mich App 177, 183 (2002). The first question here is whether the property is separate or marital. A court would almost certainly find it was separate because it was an inheritance. "[P]roperty received by a married party as an inheritance, but kept separate from marital property, is deemed to be separate property not subject to distribution." *Dart v Dart*, 460 Mich 573, 584-585 (1999). Note that putting a spouse's name on property does not render it marital property as opposed to separate property. *Reeves, supra*.

-37-

Separate assets, however, may become marital property when they are commingled with marital assets and the parties treated such assets as marital property. *Pickering v Pickering*, 268 Mich App 1, 12-13 (2005). Here, the funds were not intermingled with the parties' marital funds. The money was not put into the family checking account to pay general bills, but instead was segregated in a separate investment account that remained segregated throughout the marriage. The only use of the inheritance was to pay for Tom's car, which could arguably be considered a marital obligation, but the fact that only Tom's car was paid off suggests that Tom intended to keep the inheritance separate.

With respect to the interest earned on the CD during the parties' marriage, "[T]he appreciation of an actively managed account during the parties' marriage is marital property." *Maher v Maher*, 488 Mich 874 (2010); *Dart v Dart*, 460 Mich 573 (1999). Here the account was not actively managed, so the interest did not become marital property. Mary does not have a good claim for the CD or the interest earned on the CD during the marriage.

-38-

ANSWER TO QUESTION 15

The injury itself is unquestionably one "arising out of and in the course of" work. MCL 418.301(1). It arose from a risk at the workplace and on employer premises. *E.g. Ruthruff v Tower Holding Corp (On Reconsideration)*, 261 Mich App 613 (2004). While this might be noted by the examinee, resolution of the questions turns on the following analysis.

(1) ABC does not have any workers' compensation liability to Brandon. The reason is that Brandon would not be considered an "employee" as defined under the Workers' Disability Compensation Act (Act). Only "employees" are entitled to collect workers' compensation benefits. *Hoste v Shanty Creek Management, Inc*, 459 Mich 561, 564 (1999). The Act defines "an "employee" as every person in the service of another "under any contract of hire, expressed or implied." MCL 418.161(1). The Supreme Court has explained that the "of hire" aspect of this phrase means the worker must be receiving "payment intended as wages, *i.e.*, real palpable, and substantial consideration." *Hoste*, 459 Mich at 576. *Hoste's* rational is that Michigan's workers' compensation system "provide[s] benefits to those who have lost a source of income. It does not provide benefits to those who can no longer take advantage of a gratuity or privilege that serves merely as an accommodation." *Id.* at 575. In the *Hoste* case itself, a ski patroller for Shanty Creek was injured. He had received from Shanty Creek "privileges of free skiing, complementary hot beverages, and meal discounts" in exchange for his patrol services. *Id.* at 577. That consideration was not deemed substantial enough to be considered "payment intended as wages." *Id.* at 575. Therefore, benefits were denied because he was not deemed an employee.

Here ABC's pizza, soft drinks, and Detroit Tigers baseball game tickets would similarly be viewed as a gratuity rather than "payment intended as wages." And, Brandon did not "los[e] a source of income. He would not be considered an "employee" of ABC and, therefore, he is ineligible for workers' compensation. The examinee might note this leaves Brandon free to consider a civil action against ABC, since the Act's "exclusive remedy" provision would be inapplicable. The exclusive remedy provision only shields employers from civil actions brought by an "employee." MCL 418.131(1).

(2) ABC's position on weekly wage loss benefits to Joe is less certain. In order to prove an entitlement to weekly wage loss

-39-

benefits, Joe needs to demonstrate that his injury constitutes a "disability, as that term is defined in MCL 418.301(4) of the Act. The Supreme Court has explained that the inability to return to one's last job is, generally speaking, not enough to prove disability. *Stokes v Chrysler, LLC*, 481 Mich 266, 281-283 (2008); *Sington v Chrysler Corp*, 467 Mich 144, 161 and 156-157 (2002). Instead, the employee must demonstrate an inability to perform "all jobs within his qualifications and training" at his maximum earning capacity; that requires employee to offer proofs on "the proper array of alternative available jobs" suitable to their qualifications and training. *Stokes*, 481 Mich at 283. These requirements contemplate proofs speaking to the employee's "full range of available employment options," not just the inability to perform prior jobs. *Id.* at 282.

Here Joe's inability to perform his ABC job due to his inability to stand for eight hours would not necessarily preclude him from doing other work, such as sedentary work. Given that he is a college graduate and has experience negotiating with sales agents, there is arguably other work suitable to his qualifications and training that would not demand standing for eight hours per day. Therefore, depending on what other available work might be suitable to Joe's qualifications and training, he may or may not be eligible for weekly benefits. The examinee should demonstrate recognition of the need to prove more than just the inability to return to one's last job.

-40-